That's the Joint!

This newly expanded and revised second edition of *That's the Joint!* brings together the most important and up-to-date hip-hop scholarship in one comprehensive volume. Presented thematically, the selections address the history of hip-hop, identity politics of the "hip-hop nation," debates of "street authenticity," social movements and activism, aesthetics, technologies of production, hip-hop as a cultural industry, and much more. Further, this new edition also includes greater coverage of gender, racial diversity in hip-hop, hip-hop's global influences, and examines hip hop's role in contemporary politics.

With pedagogical features including author biographies, headnotes summarizing key points of articles, and discussion questions, *That's the Joint!* is essential reading for anyone seeking deeper understanding of the profound impact of hip-hop as an intellectual, aesthetic, and cultural movement.

Murray Forman is Associate Professor of Communication Studies at Northeastern University. He is the author of *The 'Hood Comes First: Race, Space, and Place in Rap and Hip-Hop* (Wesleyan University Press, 2002) and *One Night on TV is Worth Weeks at the Paramount: Popular Music on Early Television* (Duke University Press, 2012). He is also a past recipient of a National Endowment for the Humanities Research Fellowship.

Mark Anthony Neal is Professor of Black Popular Culture in the Department of African and African American Studies at Duke University. He is the author of four books: *What the Music Said: Black Popular Music and Black Public Culture* (1998), *Soul Babies: Black Popular Culture and the Post-Soul Aesthetic* (2002), *Songs in the Keys of Black Life: A Rhythm and Blues Nation* (2003), and *New Black Man: Rethinking Black Masculinity* (2005), all published by Routledge. Neal hosts the weekly webcast *Left of Black* in collaboration with the John Hope Franklin Center at Duke University. A frequent commentator for National Public Radio, Neal maintains a blog at NewBlackMan (http://newblackman.blogspot.com/). You can follow him on Twitter @NewBlackMan.

That's the Joint!
The Hip-Hop Studies Reader
Second edition

Edited by
Murray Forman and Mark Anthony Neal

Routledge
Taylor & Francis Group

NEW YORK AND LONDON

Second edition published 2012
by Routledge
711 Third Avenue, New York, NY 10017

Simultaneously published in the UK
by Routledge
2 Park Square, Milton Park, Abingdon, Oxon OX14 4RN

Routledge is an imprint of the Taylor & Francis Group, an informa business

© 2004, 2012 Taylor & Francis

First edition published 2004 by Routledge

Library of Congress Cataloging in Publication Data
That's the joint! : the hip-hop studies reader / edited by Murray Forman
and Mark Anthony Neal.—2nd ed.
    p. cm.
    Includes bibliographical references and index.
    1. Rap (Music)—History and criticism. 2. Rap (Music)—Social aspects. 3. Hip-hop.
    I. Forman, Murray, 1959- II. Neal, Mark Anthony.
    ML3531.T43 2011
    782.42164909—dc22
    2011017033

ISBN13: 978-0-415-87325-3 (hbk)
ISBN13: 978-0-415-87326-0 (pbk)
ISBN13: 978-0-203-86527-9 (ebk)

Typeset in Minion by Swales & Willis Ltd, Exeter, Devon

Dedicated to the memory of
Guru (Keith Elam).
R.I.P.

Contents

Acknowledgments

We are grateful to the numerous individuals who offered their sustained support for *That's the Joint!* including the teachers and students that incorporated it into their courses and their personal libraries. We were also assisted by an array of anonymous reviewers and by friends and colleagues who provided carefully considered comments and suggestions.

With this revised edition we necessarily surrendered some very fine essays in order to accommodate current perspectives and contemporary issues. Thanks to all of the authors who participated in this project – past and present – for their brilliance and eloquence. Carolann Madden, Stan Spring, and especially Matt Byrnie at Taylor and Francis were patient and consistently conscientious throughout the production process; our sincere thanks to each of you.

Finally, a huge resonant shout out is due to all the hip-hop heads, artists, entrepreneurs, media folks, and activists and community organizers who create, promote and generally amplify the culture on a daily basis.

Murray Forman
Mark Anthony Neal

General Introduction

Murray Forman

I think hip-hop artists will have no choice but to talk about different things and more positive things, and try to bring a brighter side to that because, even before Barack, I think people had been tired of hearing the same thing.

(Common, 2008)[1]

As the first decade of the twenty-first century came to a close, a lament was frequently heard about the sorry state of hip-hop. Nas's well-calibrated declaration that "hip-hop is dead" (Nas, 2007) is still often evoked, although many seem to overlook the statement's deliberate provocation and its multivalent meanings that castigate the corporate dilution of hip-hop, the meandering quality and aesthetics of hip-hop's artistic practices, and the failure to inscribe a sustainable social critique or establish a sound political cadre in and through hip-hop. Tricia Rose offers a nuanced reading of Nas's polemic, suggesting "hip hop is not dead, but it is gravely ill. The beauty and life force of hip hop have been squeezed out, wrung nearly dry by the compounding factors of commercialism, distorted racial and sexual fantasy, oppression, and alienation. It has been a sad thing to witness" (Rose, 2008: ix).

The notion of bearing witness is highly appropriate here as scholars, too, closely scrutinize hip-hop's evolution even as they participate fully as producers and creative agents or as audience members and fans; the stances are not antithetical. The academic enterprise employs various methodologies and theoretical approaches in the exploration of hip-hop's cultural expressions, illuminating emergent phenomena and explaining the latent potentials among hip-hop's various cultural forms. Facilitating this enterprise and enriching the scholarly focus on hip-hop in the U.S. and around the world are the primary objectives of *That's the Joint!*

Although hip-hop artists have long demonstrated a capacity for articulating complex issues and amplifying critical perspectives about constraining socio-political conditions—especially those that most directly impact African-American individuals and communities—this aspect is often deemed unsuitable to commercial interests. The commercial status of hip-hop emerges in numerous essays throughout *That's the Joint!*, with specific attention in Part VII. Yet, as Yvonne Bynoe (2004) and other scholars assert, there is no necessary contradiction in politically "conscious" MCs making recordings for a commercial market, nor is it impossible for cultural progressives to find satisfaction or even overt pleasure in hip-hop's more sexualized or aggressive "gangsta" productions, as Mark Anthony Neal (2005) notes. As the essays in this book indicate, hip-hop scholars interrogate the industrial composition of contemporary hip-hop while simultaneously probing the affective and intellectual dispositions that are infused in both hip-hop production and hip-hop reception.

For those who insist on equating all of hip-hop's creative output with its most obvious element—rap music—hip-hop's faltering status is measured in basic industrial terms, as if the commercial industry is the primary arbiter of taste, quality, or cultural virtue. This perspective is fueled by the fact that, while the entire music industry has experienced a steep decline over the past decade due to digital disintermediation, data generated by the Recording Industry Association of America (RIAA) or the Nielsen organization indicate that rap music sales were particularly grim, plummeting by roughly 21 percent between 2008 and 2009. Internet reintermediation and online music purchases, however, have increased drastically in this same period, and rap remains among the preferred choices in this digitized configuration; rap's status is even more assured in the arguably less significant category of ring-tone sales. Taking such data into account, this book seeks to establish a balance between industrial analysis and social critique, acknowledging that rap music and other commercial forms are undeniably relevant to contemporary hip-hop. Part VI also explores the aesthetics and artistic techniques involved in hip-hop and rap, analyzing the creative funk and flow while reminding us that cultural production also relies on the idiosyncratic abilities associated with raw talent *and* the mechanics of the professional milieu within which creative labor is situated.

Still, in the context of industrial production and commodity value, it is worth quoting the brilliantly talented and politically engaged artists Dead Prez (stic.man and M-1), who remind us with their track "Bigger Than Hip-Hop" that the inherent cultural attributes that inform rap are deep and multifaceted and hip-hop should not, therefore, be reduced to any single object or medium:

> Hip hop means sayin' what I want never bite my tongue
> Hip hop means teaching the young
> If you feelin' what I'm feelin' then you hearin' what I'm sayin'
> cause these fake fake records just keep on playin'
> ("Bigger Than Hip Hop," Dead Prez, 2000)

Taking this same Dead Prez song as the title of his book, M.K. Asante, Jr. reinforces the notion that hip-hop emerges from a state of cultural convergence. As he asserts, hip-hop is forged within particular circumstances encompassing contradictory and contestational interests as well as circulating across varied media platforms, yet it is oriented toward a decidedly alternative set of values that are frequently at odds with the cultural mainstream: "When we consider hip hop's origins and purpose, we understand it is a revolutionary cultural force that was intended to challenge the status quo and the greater American culture" (Asante, Jr., 2008: 8).

With the first edition of *That's the Joint!* in 2004 we audaciously introduced the term "hip-hop studies" with full awareness that no such designation or discipline actually existed within the academy. We were not merely intent on provocation; what else could we call the focused study of hip-hop? What term of reference could realistically encompass the array of theoretical and analytical approaches characterizing research on hip-hop's vast and unwieldy practices? Faculty and students were already doing "hip-hop studies," yet even after roughly a decade of serious attention hip-hop remained a marginal force, jostling for intellectual space and scholarly props. Paraphrasing Asante, hip-hop studies presented a pointed "challenge" to the academic "status quo."

We noted then that hip-hop was central to many courses across the disciplines and its themes were regularly accommodated in academic conferences and seminar proceedings throughout the country, but there was no core and certainly nothing resembling a consensus on what hip-hop studies might be and how it could progress. Over the intervening years, however, the trajectory has turned toward a more consistently meticulous area of study accompanied by a proliferation of research and teaching focused on hip-hop as an expressive form and as a vibrant social force. The struggle remains as to how to properly position the study of hip-hop culture—in all of its wild, unruly, and complicated forms—within the academy without sacrificing scholarly rigor or imposing an elitist and unrealistic academic canon, for, as Preston (2008) notes, academic texts of this nature are unavoidably implicated in the production of particular kinds of knowledge.

As the essays in *That's the Joint!* indicate, hip-hop studies adopts many of the core analytical concepts of "intersectionality," which, according to Patricia Hill Collins, provides

> an interpretive framework for thinking through how intersections of race and class, or race and gender, or sexuality and class, for example, shape any group's experience across specific social contexts. The existence of multiple axes within intersectionality (race, class, gender, sexuality, nation, ethnicity, age) means neither that these factors are equally salient in all groups' experiences nor that they form uniform principles of social organization in defining groups.
>
> (Collins, 1998: 108)

In *That's the Joint!* we accept that the diverse cultural forms affiliated with hip-hop are inextricably interwoven with social and political praxis and that the emergent research necessarily delves into the details of what can be termed "a hip-hop way of life." In Part II the grounded realities of diverse racial and ethnic groups are explored within an array of socio-cultural and intersecting contexts. The essays in this part assess hip-hop's undeniable African-American origins, querying the formation of distinct identities within hip-hop while simultaneously interrogating the definitions of authenticity that often dominate discussions pertaining to cultural hybridity and the risk of appropriation as hip-hop circulates ever further afield and is more deeply embraced in the social mainstream. The essays in *That's the Joint!* celebrate the many cultural achievements that have evolved under the hip-hop banner while challenging hip-hop's practitioners and citizens of the amorphous "hip-hop nation" to build infrastructure and create the conditions for positive change. In this regard, hip-hop studies, at its best, constitutes engaged and progressive research.

Much has been made of hip-hop's endless capacity for reinvention. Faced with shifting technologies, new aesthetic values and cultural tastes, or revised industrial standards, hip-hop's creative workers demonstrate boundless innovation and flexibility, affirming that hip-hop is not solely beholden to commercial mandates. Hip-hop's most committed advocates reinforce the reality that hip-hop is anything but static. Since its inception, hip-hop has inflected conditions at multiple scales, and it remains a vital force in the articulation and expression of culture, politics, and identity for literally millions of people around the world. This is to say that hip-hop is an essential facet of everyday life and of experiential *being*, a cornerstone of individual and communal existence.

This innovation and flexibility is also evident in hip-hop studies as scholars revisit previously examined phenomena, employing new or more refined theoretical tools in their analyses, or identify altogether new, emergent phenomena. Academic research has introduced several important intellectual adjustments over the past several years that warrant mention. For instance, despite orthodox beliefs to the contrary, it has been a rather long time since hip-hop has been wholly coupled with the social construct "youth" even though such associations are continually reinforced in the media as well as in casual discourse. Hip-hop's origins in the mid- to late 1970s may seem like deep history to many younger heads, yet for those who were there it may seem like just yesterday. Early memorabilia and archival artifacts (carefully collected and displayed with varying effectiveness at multiple sites including the Smithsonian National Museum of American History, the Rock and Roll Hall of Fame, and the Experience Music Project as well as in many smaller archival settings) help to elucidate hip-hop's historical legacies and serve as interpretive tools for younger folks, hinting at an antidote to Nas's reflective comment, "we've forgotten our past. We've forgotten our genesis. And we suffer for this loss. . . . No movement can thrive if it doesn't recall its birth. We need to be able to learn from our history if we are going to take control of our future" (Nas, 2007: 155).

Contemporary hip-hop encompasses an expansive social demographic, including pre-teens, tweens, teenagers, and twenty-somethings as well as individuals who are well past the designation "youth." Among this wider group, some hip-hop veterans are now, in fact, eligible for membership in the American Association of Retired Persons (AARP), and we live in an era when many of hip-hop's pioneers and early aficionados are themselves parents and, in some cases, grandparents. For hip-hop studies this means that high school students, college undergraduates, and graduate researchers, as well as junior and senior faculty members, form hip-hop's scholarly cohort; we are all in this together whether we recognize it or not.

While Bakari Kitwana popularized the term "hip-hop generation" to describe those born between 1965 and 1984 (Kitwana, 2002), countless hip-hop scholars are reframing the analyses and debates around hip-hop in explicitly generational terms. Asante (2008) introduces the term "post-hip-hop generation" to identify a younger group whose politics, social practices, and aesthetic preferences bear a different allegiance to hip-hop than that of their predecessors. Marc Lamont Hill (2009) explores the themes of memory, nostalgia, aesthetics, and generational identity with the observation that different age-based experiences inflect one's vantage on the world, inevitably producing different understandings of what hip-hop is and what its texts mean.

The age factor has produced an interesting set of shared allegiances and a powerful affective alignment across divergent age groups, yet it is also often a source of tension and disagreement as generational dissonance emerges in relation to taste distinctions and other facets of social experience (including ideological orientations or relationships with institutional authorities, including the harsh realities of an unforgiving criminal justice and penal system or the uncertainties related to dire economic conditions and a grim employment environment). Hip-hop's art forms present powerful and sophisticated means for defining social malaise but they also offer options for articulating the spirit of hope and love—terms that hip-hop's *haters* often fail to link with the culture and its proponents. In this new edition of *That's the Joint!*, especially in Part I, it is our objective to conjoin essays from hip-hop's earlier phases with more recent scholarly interventions, facilitating a productive historical dialogue ("old school" voices emanating from "back in the day" converging with contemporary "new school" ideas and progressive imaginings) while acknowledging hip-hop's transitional characteristics.

Many compelling projects have produced impressively potent analyses over the past several years that demand explicit attention in this revised edition of *That's the Joint!* For example, in its earlier phase the strong tendency in hip-hop studies was to directly challenge the prevalence of sexism and misogyny (in rap lyrics and video mainly) and to deconstruct patriarchal patterns of authority and forms of hyper-masculinity that informed these prejudices. As the essays in Part IV illustrate, hip-hop scholars have not remotely abandoned such concerns, although they have also expanded the frame of critical analysis, refining their feminist and gender critique, embarking on intensified interrogations of multiple masculine identity positions and a more extensive analysis of women's agency. Of further relevance in this regard, scholars have also embraced queer theory as a means of further explaining the ways that social identities are constructed and social relations are navigated in and through hip-hop's sensibilities and practices. Summoning the notion of intersectional analysis, we can see that the intensification of hip-hop's gender studies produces an elaborated understanding of the alignments between gender and sexuality and other factors including race, class, age, and locale.

In yet another context, outlined in Part III, whereas hip-hop's socio-spatial concerns remain paramount, these have shifted substantially as artists, fans, and industrial entities around the world take up hip-hop and redefine it within their own specific localities and cultural contexts. This is not a new phenomenon, as we noted in the book's first edition, but it is an area that has expanded in scope and consequently grown in this volume. Scholars from around the world introduce their own penetrating analyses of global cultural practices, explaining the processes through which individuals take up hip-hop's expressive forms in order to challenge structural authority, articulate their own agency, and define their identities in locally meaningful ways. It is essential that we not lose sight of hip-hop's distant reach, for, as Paul Gilroy cautions in his essay here, the risk associated with what he calls "Americocentrism" in hip-hop—and in hip-hop studies—is that it will obscure the global activity of cultural producers and audiences alike while eliding the actual extent of hip-hop's influences in different national, regional, and local environments and in places where diverse racial and ethnic identities prevail (Gilroy, 1992).

The current international research also explores multiple contexts within which hip-hop has collided with established authorities and social conventions, a research development that is most clearly addressed in Part V. In some instances artists and hip-hop activists place themselves at great risk, especially where repressive military regimes or malicious ideological foes rule with relentless cruelty and violence—a shout out here to Hamé and Ekoué of the Paris-based group La Rumeur (Brown, 2004). The stakes always vary and it is in the differences and distinctions across the cultural spectrum that we can learn exactly how flexible hip-hop is and how it functions as a crucial factor in the articulation of cultural resistance and the expression of multiple emotional and psychological orientations that are always implicated in one's political activities.

At this juncture, some of the most impressive developments in hip-hop studies specifically address political ideology and street-level activism. The terms "conscious rap" and less frequently "rapitivism" have subsequently emerged to describe a particular form of artistic or aesthetic cultural work. "Conscious hip-hop" suggests reflection on, and intellectual engagement with, pressing social issues (most often involving themes of race, gender, and class struggle). As Michael Eric Dyson explains, conscious rap consists of "rap that is socially aware and consciously connected to historic patterns of political protest and aligned with progressive forces of social critique" (Dyson, 2007: 64).

Dyson's explicit reference to historical patterns is pertinent, since the conscious rap subgenre owes a clear debt to established forms of African-American political-artistic expression of the 1960s and 1970s (including the work of the Black Arts Movement and music by artists such as Gil Scott-Heron, the Last Poets, or the Watts Prophets) and other concurrent social movements. Indeed, most so-called conscious hip-hop artists are extremely aware of the legacy they uphold and of their responsibilities and connections to previous periods in African-American political struggle and aesthetic innovation. Yet conscious hip-hop also functions in ways that are highly responsive to contemporary socio-political contexts and conditions, aligning it with various community interests *and* artistic strategies today . . . *now*. Thus, while hip-hop's elements and expressive forms serve as powerful means of articulating complex social issues, each must also be understood as just one facet within a much wider system of cultural practices through which political ideologies are processed and proposed in immediate and urgent contexts.

No cultural text is released into a vacuum and so it would be remiss here not to acknowledge two of the most important events that have occurred over the past five years, especially since they form an indisputable backdrop to this revised edition of *That's the Joint!* The first involves one of the most galvanizing events for many hip-hop-identified youth in the U.S.: the inability of the government (under President George W. Bush) to protect the citizens of New Orleans following Hurricane Katrina and to alleviate the suffering and destruction in other areas along the Gulf of Mexico coastline in August 2005. The government's ineffectiveness was shocking, and the nation—and, indeed, the world—watched in abject horror as the victims of the tragedy were largely left to fend for themselves in the storm's immediate aftermath. New Orleans is renowned as a vital cultural center, and its contributions to American music are many and varied. It is the cradle of jazz music and the source of zydeco as well as other hybrid musical forms. Throughout the late 1990s New Orleans also emerged as a major center of hip-hop production, with artists affiliated with the powerhouse record labels No Limit and Cash Money spurring the Southern hip-hop scene while drawing attention to the intricacies of existence in the city's wards through their rap lyrics and music videos that placed the city front and center.

New Orleans is also a city with a predominantly African-American population; the 2000 census placed the city's black citizenry at just over 67 percent (though more recent post-Katrina estimates indicate a decrease in this figure due to sustained displacement). As the devastation of Katrina became clear, the media images reinforced the fact that the flooding inordinately impacted black families, especially those who lived in the hard-hit Lower Ninth Ward.[2] The first and perhaps most incendiary hip-hop statement on the tragedy emerged quickly, during NBC-TV's live September 2, 2005 telethon broadcast of the *Concert for Hurricane Relief*, when hip-hop MC and producer Kanye West abruptly veered off script, uttering his now-famous line "George Bush doesn't care about black people." Though his statement is unsubstantiated (severe ineptitude and incredibly poor delegation skills do not necessarily amount to indifference or a lack of care), West absolutely cut to the core of the issue by declaring that black citizens are routinely exposed to unfair and imbalanced treatment within the white-dominated institutional power structures. As many of the essays in *That's the Joint!* show, this perspective has been a consistent theme in hip-hop almost since its inception, and it remains of central relevance to contemporary hip-hop studies.

Subsequent expressions of outrage emerged from the hip-hop community;[3] Mos Def released "Katrina Klap (Dollar Day)" in 2005, a song based on the rhythmic structure of the 2004 track "Nolia Clap" (a tribute to the central city's Magnolia Projects by New Orleans MCs Juvenile, Wacko and Skip). The track and accompanying video constitute a homage to New Orleans and articulate a derisive rebuke of the government's bungling of the tragedy, cleanup, and subsequent attempts at community revitalization. Juvenile himself also conveyed the imagery of Katrina's aftermath via his 2006 video "Get Ya Hustle On" featuring footage shot in the lingering wreckage of the Lower Ninth Ward. The critical theme was amplified among black youth and others aligned with hip-hop as acknowledged in the text accompanying the video *Katrina Knows* (produced by Harvard University's Hip-Hop Archive):

> Katrina was a wake-up call to the hip-hop generation. And we didn't even know we were asleep! But Katrina knew. We knew about injustice, racism, class elitism and regional arrogance. We knew we had a president, congress and a country that seemed to be clinging to old school notions of the American dream, where the perfect America was one without cities, diversity and hip-hop. Katrina came with a vengeance and with all the lessons from the past and lessons for the future. It's like the storm knew we were asleep at the wheel!
> (http://www.hiphoparchive.org/prepare-yourself/katrina-knows)

While Katrina is described as a "wake-up call" it also serves as a catalyst, motivating hip-hop-identified individuals of all ages to more directly engage in political activism and social change.

On another front, leading up to John Kerry's failed electoral bid in 2004, campaign workers and new voters were called to action and there was an unprecedented outpouring of energy from the hip-hop nation. Hip-hop artists had occasionally rallied around prior voter registration campaigns in the attempt to mobilize young first-time voters to participate in electoral politics, but this was different. While many hip-hop-oriented political initiatives[4] were lauded by long-time activists and by established political operatives, they were also criticized for lacking a solid and sustainable agenda.[5] According to hip-hop organizer Jeff Johnson, "there was very little substance underneath that movement. Vote or Die, but I'm not going to tell you how. Vote or Die, but I'm not going to help you organize" (in Jones, 2008: E2). Though many of these organizations were dormant between national elections, by 2008 there was a renewed groundswell of energy and support for the campaign of Senator Barack Obama from within the extended hip-hop community and among the nation's college students.

As Obama gained momentum during the 2008 campaign, hip-hop artists and scholars alike emerged in droves as persuasive commentators on national politics and the social landscape, offering pithy analyses and expressing an urgent need for change. While Obama's multiracial identity was often a factor in their engagement (with misplaced utterances about the dawn of a "post-racial society"[6]), so too was his age. He is generally accepted as a member of the hip-hop community, having grown and matured in a world with hip-hop; in 1979 when the first major rap recording, "Rapper's Delight" (by the Sugarhill Gang), was released, Obama was 18 years old. By the time MTV began airing rap music videos on the program *Yo! MTV Raps* in 1988, he was 27, and during his campaign he openly admitted to enjoying rap music and listening to music by Jay-Z, Ludacris and others on his iPod (Wenner, 2008). On several occasions different rap artists along with hip-hop impresario Russell Simmons accompanied him at campaign appearances.

Obama's musical tastes and his hip-hop endorsements impressed some members of the hip-hop generation, but, as Jay-Z notes on the track "Streets Is Watching," detractors were also "waiting for you to break, make your first mistake" as the discussions and scrutiny shifted away from the lighter aspects of music and leisure preferences toward policy issues and leadership. Obama's candidacy received widespread acceptance among African-American voters and other young people who had been marginalized or vilified within American social institutions, yet on the track "Black President" (released before Obama's election) Nas raises pertinent questions about accountability, putting Obama on notice that, while his presidency was a point of pride and celebration, he must continue to earn the trust and support of his hip-hop constituents:

> I think Obama provides hope and challenges minds
> Of all races and colors to erase the hate
> And try and love one another, so many political snakes
> We in need of a break
> I'm thinkin' I can trust this brotha
> But will he keep it way real?
> Every innocent nigga in jail gets out on appeal
> When he wins—will he really care still?

As Obama has made clear time and again (drawing in part from his experience as a community organizer in Chicago's South Side neighborhoods[7]), he clearly comprehends many of the vital issues and conditions that influence those who are most deeply immersed in hip-hop's discourses and cultural practices. Phonte Coleman of the group Little Brother confirms this relationship, summing up the feelings of many when he exclaims, "I just think we're excited about the possibility of a president who really understands what it's like to be us" (Hale, 2008).

Changing socio-political landscapes always produce new and adaptable research tools, as the essays in this second edition demonstrate, and the growing number of scholars mining the deep veins of hip-hop culture contributes to a proliferation of interests, approaches, and outcomes. Many hip-hop heads within the academy and those working in community-based agencies and organizations are honing their skills, preparing for their future roles as leaders, policy makers, or politicians. At this juncture we adamantly repeat our claim from the first edition of *That's the Joint!* that "research and writing, whether in journalistic or academic contexts, are absolutely part of the wider hip-hop culture. Analyzing, theorizing, and writing about hip-hop are also forms of cultural labor and should accordingly be regarded as consequential facets of hip-hop." With this reminder, we anticipate that the conceptual gulf between the 'hood or the streets and the academy will continue to narrow and that continued attention to what hip-hop is, what it does, and what it can be might foster future coalitions and progressive solutions to a host of social ills. This is where we stand.

Notes

1 In McLaughlin (2008).
2 For an illuminating documentary of the Katrina crisis and its devastating impact in the Ninth Ward, the 2008 film *Trouble the Waters* (directed by Tia Lessin and Carl Deal) follows the travails of New Orleans

MC Black Kold Madina (Kimberly Rivers Roberts) before, during, and after the hurricane's onslaught.

3 Hip-hop tracks about Katrina proliferated after the tragedy. The Harvard Hip-Hop Archive offers a very partial list, including B. Down and Big Rags, "Katrina"; Jay Electronica, "When the Levees Broke"; Jay-Z, "Minority Report"; Lil Wayne, "Georgia Bush"; Lil Wayne with Robin Thicke, "Tie My Needs"; and Papoose and Razah, "Mother Nature." See http://www.hiphoparchive.org/prepare-yourself/katrina-knows/the-music.

4 Hip-hop impresario Diddy initiated Citizen Change with great fanfare in 2004 with the slogan "Vote or Die," and various organizers, such as the Boston Hip-Hop Summit Youth Voter Registration Event that was launched at the 2004 Democratic National Convention in Boston, also took up the cause at the local grassroots level (Jones, 2008). The Hip-Hop National Convention also emerged as an important source of focused political discourse, endeavoring to introduce a series of priorities and action items that might filter up to policy architects and lawmakers.

5 For a critical report on the ideological and practical discrepancies between different hip-hop constituencies at the 2004 Los Angeles conference hosted by the Hip-Hop Summit Action Network, see Baker (2004).

6 For a valuable analysis of the 2008 Obama campaign and presidential election and the concept of a "post-racial" America, see the journal *Souls: A Critical Journal of Black Politics, Culture, and Society*, vol. 11, no. 1, January–March, 2009.

7 Obama addresses his community organizing experience in detail in his first memoir, describing the decision in 1983 to "organize black folks. At the grass roots. For change" (Obama, 1995: 133).

References

Asante, Jr., M.K. (2008). *It's Bigger Than Hip Hop: The Rise of the Post-Hip-Hop Generation*. New York: St. Martin's Press.

Baker, Rob "biko." (2004). "'Take Me to Your Leader': A Critical Analysis of the Hip-Hop Summit Action Network," *Socialism and Democracy*, 18:2, July–December, pp. 215–219.

Brown, Daniel. (2004). "Rap and Censorship in France," in *Shoot the Singer!: Music Censorship Today*, edited by Marie Korpe. New York: Zed Books, pp. 197–208.

Bynoe, Yvonne. (2004). *Stand and Deliver: Political Activism, Leadership, and Hip Hop Culture*. New York: Soft Skull Press.

Collins, Patricia Hill. (1998). *Fighting Words: Black Women and the Search for Justice*. Minneapolis: University of Minnesota Press.

Dyson, Michael Eric. (2007). *Know What I Mean?: Reflections on Hip-Hop*. New York: Basic Civitas.

Gilroy, Paul. (1992). "It's a Family Affair," in *Black Popular Culture*, edited by Gina Dent. Seattle, WA: Bay Press, pp. 303–316.

Hale, Andreas. (2008). "Strength in Numbers," *The Source*, August, pp. 62–66.

Hill, Marc Lamont. (2009). *Beats, Rhymes, and Classroom Life: Hip-Hop Pedagogy and the Politics of Identity*. New York: Teachers College Press.

Jones, Vanessa. (2008). "Getting out the Vote Isn't Enough so Hip-Hop Grows into a New Role," *The Boston Globe*, May 13, pp. E1–2.

Kitwana, Bakari. (2002). *The Hip Hop Generation: Young Blacks and the Crisis in African American Culture*. New York: Basic Civitas.

McLaughlin, Eliott C. (2008). "Rapper Common: Obama Will Change Hip-Hop's Attitude," *CNN.com Entertainment*, December 9.

Nas. (2007). "Outro," in *Know What I Mean?: Reflections on Hip Hop*, by Michael Eric Dyson, pp. 153–156.

Neal, Mark Anthony. (2005). *New Black Man*. New York: Routledge.

Obama, Barack. (1995). *Dreams From My Father: A Story of Race and Inheritance*. New York: Three Rivers Press.

Preston, Graham Chia-Hui. (2008). "Intellectuals Will Only Half Listen: The Needs and Futures of Hip-Hop Studies," in *Knowledge as Value: Illumination Through Critical Prisms*, edited by Ian Morley and Mira Crouch. New York: Rodopi, pp. 109–124.

Rose, Tricia. (2008). *The Hip Hop Wars: What We Talk About When We Talk About Hip Hop—and Why It Matters*. New York: Basic Civitas.

Souls: A Critical Journal of Black Politics, Culture, and Society. (2009). 11:1, January–March.

Wenner, Jann. (2008). "A Conversation With Barack Obama: The Candidate Talks About the Youth Vote, What's on His iPod and His Top Three Priorities as President," *Rolling Stone*, July 10.

Part I

"Hip-Hop Ya Don't Stop"
Hip-Hop History and Historiography
Murray Forman

"Back in the day" remains a common expression within hip-hop. It is most frequently employed to describe the past and to mark moments in the evolution of the hip-hop culture. The phrase is often imbued with a certain nostalgia, acknowledging benchmarks, transitional phases, or influential aesthetic innovations realized within general historical contexts. Yet for all of its rhetorical potency and casual utility it remains an inexact expression, like a form of shorthand that communicates information but lacks precision or accuracy. Over the years the phrase has been applied widely and wildly, and it is not rare to hear discussions about 1970s Bronx block parties, the 1982 release of Grandmaster Flash and the Furious Five's "The Message" (Sugar Hill), the 1988 rise of N.W.A., or the 1993 launch of Bad Boy Entertainment all framed as occurrences from "back in the day," depending on one's generational vantage. The contributions in this part address hip-hop's nascent phase, tracing some of the attitudes, trends, and policies that influenced and informed hip-hop in moments described as "back in the day."

Hip-hop's development and expansion are the topic of considerable scholarly analysis (Hager, 1984; Toop, 1984; Hebdige, 1987; Rose, 1994; Chang, 2005), and there is much value in revisiting its history and historiography, including articles published in an industry trade magazine such as *Billboard* or in the popular press. Essays and social commentary on the New York City hip-hop scene written in the late 1970s and early 1980s offer a real time feel, evoking the crackling energies and broader sensibilities of an emergent cultural sector. Testimonials by hip-hop's pioneers and groundbreaking artists from this formative era serve a similar purpose, reminding us about the key people and places that influenced hip-hop culture at the beginning. While they may opt for a temporal perspective—positioning the erupting hip-hop phenomena within a historical context— these writings benefit from an immediacy and proximity to events, detailing transitional forces at the instant they occur. They isolate key elements of innovation and socio-cultural change, providing insights on the undulating composition of the cultural terrain and identifying the ruptures from which hip-hop's alternative practices emanated.

The evolution of hip-hop corresponds with cultural theorist Raymond Williams's observation that the process of "formal innovation" is gradual, and, while "residual" cultural practices from prior eras continue, new "emergent" cultural forms and practices may arise that challenge or disrupt the cultural dominant. Hip-hop constitutes an emergent cultural form, but so, too, does early writing about hip-hop, for as Williams explains in reference to innovation and emergent cultural forms

> there are always important works which belong to these very early stages of particular forms,
> and it is easy to miss their formal significance by comparison with preceding or succeeding

mature examples. ... It is then easy to miss one of the key elements in cultural production: innovation as it is happening; innovation in process.

(Williams, 1981: 200)

Though they were written well before hip-hop's influence and authority were guaranteed—when the shouted declaration "hip-hop, ya don't stop" expressed a combination of defensiveness and willful optimism—several of the articles featured here reflect an awareness that change *was* stirring. They offer a chronicle of an era when hip-hop still constituted an unknown "emergent" force that was being processed and aligned with prevailing cultural experiences and meanings. These articles and essays are, thus, also crucial facets of hip-hop's emergent cultural practices.

Robert Ford, Jr. and Nelson George are among hip-hop's earliest commentators who observed *and* participated in its cultural manifestation, attending events and writing about them for a wider audience; both went on to establish careers in the music, film, and video industries primarily catering to a hip-hop audience. Jorge "Popmaster Fabel" Pabon, too, was more than a casual spectator of the changes occurring in his midst, acquiring a visceral and cognitive relationship with hip-hop's unique rhythm and flow at a young age. These writers provide documentation of hip-hop's formative moments from a first-hand point of view while presenting visual descriptions of hip-hop in its earliest stages. Theirs are not abstract narratives culled from inconsequential sources but a series of accounts framed by individuals whose immediate environments were under radical revision when hip-hop's style, vernacular, and sensibilities spread, gradually informing the lingua franca of an entire generation.

Participatory engagement is significant in hip-hop, and one's documented presence lends an important element of authenticity to accounts from the past. We obviously were not all in attendance at DJ Kool Herc's 1973 Bronx parties at 1520 Sedgwick Avenue or at the subsequent park, schoolyard, or street jams, but the ongoing circulation of participant testimonials (and, similarly, the establishment of photographic archives, collections, and books: Shabazz, 2001; Paniccioli, 2002; Cooper, 2004) help to forge links between the past and the present, facilitating our contemporary understanding of the landscapes within which hip-hop's pioneers lived, loved, and labored. Though it may have fallen out of favor and, thus, out of use in recent years the expression "keepin' it real" still resonates, enunciating a pledge of fidelity and a commitment to accuracy that are evident in the explanation and discussions about localized contexts and conditions at hip-hop's inception.

There are many ways of relaying hip-hop history, but the essays and articles included in this part also emphasize the relational aspects engendered within the various practices of DJing, MCing, B-boying and graffiti or aerosol art. By delineating the points of competition and conflict as well as the connective lines of artistic collaboration the authors remind us about where hip-hop's cultural forms were spawned and how they evolved together. The streets figure prominently here, as they were—and remain—a crucial signifier of hip-hop identity and authenticity. Having long been portrayed as an undisciplined space that is prone to its own codes and standards, the streets also often constitute the unruly Other to proper, mainstream, or cultured society. In a more antagonistic dynamic, the streets harbor threat and chaos, the source of revolutionary unrest and disturbance; these values have, for better or worse, been grafted onto hip-hop throughout its evolution.

This perspective surfaces in Craig Castleman's account of the clashes between urban teens and New York City's civic authorities through the 1970s. Relying on reports in *The New York Times*, Castleman describes events from hip-hop's gestational phase, capturing the contexts and conditions within which early graffiti was defined in the media for the public at large. Here, we see how the force of authority came to bear on youths in particular ways, including direct repression by police and the criminal justice system as well as via discursive violence that is extended through the vilification and dehumanization of youths armed with nothing more than magic markers and aerosol paint cans. In this account it is obvious that the media, too, are implicated in the tensions of the moment, amplifying the crisis and promoting an image of urban youth as part of what

Stanley Cohen terms a "moral panic" perpetrated by teenage "folk devils" (Cohen, 1972). As graffiti was politicized, its young perpetrators were concurrently demonized, criminalized, and racialized, leading conservative critic Nathan Glazer to claim "while I do not find myself consciously making the connection between graffiti-makers and the criminals who occasionally rob, rape, assault, and murder [subway] passengers, the sense that all are part of one world of uncontrollable predators seems inescapable" (1979: 4).

These early accounts and historical retrospectives illustrate that hip-hop's continued vitality should not be taken for granted. Antagonisms between the social mainstream and hip-hop have flourished at virtually every stage of hip-hop's evolution, and it is only through the resilience and capacity for innovation among its proponents—artists, audiences, and street-level supporters—that it has survived. These various points of conflict have an undeniably ideological character as well, especially when we consider the different values and perspectives that emerge around issues of race and class as well as such factors as age, gender, or locale. Indeed, it is sheer folly to conceive of hip-hop outside of an ideological analytical mindset, since the genre of rap music and the practices associated with B-boying and graffiti are each capable of articulating counter-hegemonic intentions and have done so throughout hip-hop's three decades of existence.

While the appropriative apparatuses of late capitalism have exerted considerable influence on hip-hop culture at various moments, as the "founding fathers" Kool Herc, Afrika Bambaataa, and Grandmaster Flash indicate, hip-hop's commercial character is nothing new. There were always territorial battles and competition for audiences within a loosely commercialized setting, albeit one that was highly localized and independent. The encroachment of commercialism has in many instances actually enabled hip-hop's survival, at the very least introducing the means for young creative artists to receive remuneration for their efforts. Greg Tate's critique is instructive, however, for while he cites the many problems associated with large-scale corporate incursions within hip-hop he is even more concerned about what has been lost or left behind, identifying the erosion of political values among the hip-hop generation as a particular point of crisis. In his view, commercial interests have eroded much of hip hop's radical potential for social change and collective activism. Moreover, contemporary hip-hop artists are increasingly losing a connection with the values of a previous generation in which cultural practices and the arts were much more closely aligned with political objectives and socially responsive commitments. Hip-hop does, in fact, play an important role in many street-level youth advocacy agencies and grassroots political organizations, but these initiatives often stand alone and are almost nowhere to be seen in the commercial realm.

There exists a sharply defined set of generational differences that form a gulf between younger hip-hop heads and adults. Yet while this phenomenon is common across society (DJ Jazzy Jeff and the Fresh Prince summed it up adequately in 1988 with their recording "Parents Just Don't Understand") generational dissonance is now also clearly evident within hip-hop itself. Such dissonance is the outcome of distinctly separate experiences and attitudes toward hip-hop and its socio-cultural values, the product of often radically different understandings of hip-hop's cultural history. The essays in this part bring some of the old school themes, issues, and sentiments forward for reflection and analytical discussion as hip-hop culture evolves toward its fourth decade of existence and impact.

REFERENCES

Chang, Jeff. (2005). *Can't Stop, Won't Stop: A History of the Hip-Hop Generation*. New York: St. Martin's Press.
Cohen, Stanley. (1972). *Folk Devils and Moral Panics*. London: MacGibbon & Kee.
Cooper, Martha. (2004). *Hip Hop Files: Photographs, 1979–1984*. Berlin: From Here to Fame.
Glazer, Nathan. (1979). "On Subway Graffiti in New York," *Public Interest*, 54, Winter, pp. 3–11.
Hager, Stephen. (1984). *Hip-Hop: The Illustrated History of Break Dancing, Rap Music, and Graffiti*. New York: St. Martin's Press.
Hebdige, Dick. (1987). *Cut 'n' Mix: Culture, Identity and Caribbean Music*. New York: Routledge.

Paniccioli, Ernie. (2002). *Who Shot Ya? Three Decades of Hip Hop Photography*. New York: Amistad.

Rose, Tricia. (1994). *Black Noise: Rap Music and Black Culture in Contemporary America*. Middletown, CT: Wesleyan University Press.

Shabazz, Jamel. (2001). *Back in the Days*. New York: powerHouse Books.

Toop, David. (1984). *The Rap Attack: African Jive to New York Hip Hop*. Boston, MA: South End Press.

Williams, Raymond. (1981). *Culture*. London: Fontana Press.

1

The Politics of Graffiti

Craig Castleman provides an impressively explicit synopsis of graffiti's rise and evolution in New York City, commencing with the obscure but ubiquitous tags by "TAKI 183" in 1971. As he explains, graffiti rapidly expanded from a casual urban youth practice to a fully evolved cultural pastime, simultaneously acquiring the status as a point of crisis and moral panic among civic authorities. This chapter offers a convincing explanation of the processes by which young black, white and Puerto Rican youths were defensively positioned against State power and, as graffiti evolved, its youth practitioners were increasingly placed under police surveillance and constraint.

Castleman's perceptive analysis also links the anti-graffiti crusade to a narrow, genteel urban aesthetic and internal administrative agendas involving, among other things, budgetary battles pertaining to New York's Metropolitan Transit Authority expenditures. The harsh punitive measures targeting mainly blacks and Latinos through much of the 1970s and early 1980s, along with the implementation of subway "buffing" and cleaning technologies, altered the cultural climate and eventually ended the "golden age" of subway graffiti in New York.

The Politics of Graffiti

Craig Castleman

In 1972 subway graffiti became a political issue in New York City. In that year and the two following, a variety of elected and appointed city officials, particularly Mayor John V. Lindsay, devised and debated graffiti-related policies and programs and issued numerous public statements on the subject.

In examining the progress of subway graffiti as a political issue, New York's newspapers and magazines serve as a revealing and important resource, for not only did they report the graffiti policies of public officials but seemingly played a role in motivating and shaping them as well.

By summer 1971 the appearance of the mysterious message "Taki 183" had sufficiently aroused the curiosity of New Yorkers to lead the *New York Times* to send one of its reporters to determine its meaning. The results of his search, published on July 21, 1971, revealed that Taki was an unemployed seventeen year old with nothing better to do than pass the summer days spraying his name wherever he happened to be. He explained, "I just did it everywhere I went. I still do, though not as much. You don't do it for girls; they don't seem to care. You do it for yourself. You don't go after it to be elected president."[1] The reporter interviewed other neighborhood youths, including Julio 204 and Ray A.O. (for "all over"), who were following in the footsteps of Taki, to whom they referred as the king, and he spoke with an official of the MTA who stated that more than $300,000 was being spent annually to erase graffiti. Patrolman Floyd Holoway, a vice-president of the Transit Patrolmen's Benevolent Association questioned by the reporter as to the legal machinery relating to graffiti writing, explained that graffiti was barred only by MTA rules, not by law. Thus writers under the age of sixteen could only be given a lecture, not a summons, even if they were caught in the act of writing on the walls. Adult writers could be charged with malicious mischief and sentenced to up to a year's imprisonment.

Taki confessed that as he grew older, he worried more about facing adult penalties for writing graffiti but admitted, "I could never retire ... besides ... it doesn't harm anybody. I work. I pay taxes too. Why do they go after the little guy? Why not the campaign organizations that put stickers all over the subways at election time?"[2]

The *Times* article presented Taki as an engaging character with a unique and fascinating hobby, and this seemed to have a profound effect on the city's youth. Taki became something of a folk hero, and the ranks of the graffiti writers increased enormously. However, though each day brought numerous new writers to the walls and the subways were marked with names from top to bottom, 1971 brought no further press coverage of graffiti.

In spring 1972 another article on graffiti appeared in the press. It was intended not to help familiarize New Yorkers with the writers but to declare war on them. On May 21 city council president Sanford Garelik told reporters, "Graffiti pollutes the eye and mind and may be one of the worst forms of pollution we have to combat." He called upon the citizens of New York to band together and wage "an all-out war on graffiti" and recommended the establishment of a monthly "antigraffiti day" on which New Yorkers, under the auspices of the Environmental Protection Agency, would scrub walls, fences, public buildings, subway stations, and subway cars.[3]

The *Times*'s management followed up on Garelik's statement by printing an editorial denouncing the "wanton use of spray paint to deface subways." They praised Garelik's "noble concept" of an antigraffiti day but questioned its lasting appeal. Rather than burden the populace with the responsibility for cleaning up graffiti, the *Times* called upon the city administration to ban the sale of spray paint to minors and thus stop graffiti at its source.[4]

Taking his cue from both the *Times*'s and Garelik's suggestions, Mayor Lindsay announced his own antigraffiti program in late June. The mayor's proposal called for the fining and jailing of anyone caught with an open spray can in any municipal building or facility. Lindsay was highly agitated at the time of the announcement, and Robert Laird, his assistant press secretary, admitted to a *Times* reporter that "the unsightly appearance of the subways and other public places created by the so-called graffiti artists has disturbed the Mayor greatly."[5]

Lindsay again addressed the graffiti problem in extemporaneous comments before a large crowd at the rededication ceremonies for Brooklyn's Prospect Park boathouse in late August. Standing before the white ceramic exterior of the newly renovated structure, Lindsay noted that he had asked for tighter legislation against graffiti vandalism but said that police action alone would not cure the problem. Pleading for greater public interest in the problem, the mayor exclaimed, "For heaven's sake. New Yorkers, come to the aid of your great city—defend it, support it and protect it!"[6]

Lindsay's graffiti legislation had been referred to the city council's General Welfare Committee in early August, but the members had shown little inclination to deal with it at that time. (The council meets only twice during the summer months, and committee activity is virtually suspended from July to September.) Impatient with the committee's foot dragging, Lindsay insisted that they hold a special meeting on graffiti on August 31. The mayor asked a number of top administration officials, including the deputy mayor, the parks commissioner, and the MTA chief administrator, to testify in favor of the legislation. But only four members of the fifteen-member committee were present at the session, and no action was immediately forthcoming.[7]

Meanwhile MTA chairman Ronan publicly gave his support to Mayor Lindsay's graffiti campaign. On October 28 he told reporters that he had instructed the transit police to charge "such miscreants with 'malicious mischief,'" and he urged the mayor to stress the seriousness of "this blighting epidemic" to the courts.[8] Later that same day Mayor Lindsay held a ceremony in his office at which he officially commended one of Dr. Ronan's transit policemen, patrolman Steven Schwartz, for his "personal crusade" against graffiti. Schwartz alone had apprehended thirteen writers in the previous six months, a record for graffiti arrests unmatched in the department. The mayor followed up the ceremony with a statement that it was the "Lindsay theory" that graffiti writing "is related to mental health problems." He described the writers as "insecure cowards" seeking recognition.[9]

The General Welfare Committee submitted a graffiti bill to the city council in mid-September stating that the use of markers and spray paint to write graffiti has "reached proportions requiring serious punishment for the perpetrators" and that such defacement and the use of "foul language" in many of the writings is "harmful to the general public and violative of the good and welfare of the people of the city of New York."[10] The bill proposed to eliminate graffiti by making it illegal to carry an aerosol can of paint into a public facility "unless it is completely enclosed in a sealed container." It specified that "no person shall write, paint or draw any inscription, figure or mark of any type" on any public property. Judges were given wide latitude in dealing with such offenses, but the law stated that it was the council's intent that any person guilty of writing graffiti "should be punished so that the punishment shall fit the crime." In this spirit the bill recommended that judges sentence writers "to remove graffiti under the supervision of an employee of the public works office, New York City transit authority or other officer or employee designated by the court."[11] The bill also recommended that merchants selling spray paint or markers be required to register with the Police Department and to keep a record of the names and addresses of all persons who purchase such merchandise.[12]

The day after the General Welfare Committee approved the bill, the *Times* published an editorial stating that graffiti "are day-glo bright and multicolored, sometimes obscene, always offensive." The editorial praised the committee for getting tough with "youthful vandals" and announced that "graffiti are no longer amusing; they have become a public menace."[13]

Perhaps intending to spur the full council on to faster action on the graffiti law, Mayor Lindsay on October 5 announced the formation of a graffiti task force under the direction of his chief of staff, Steven Isenberg. The task force, which included among its members the heads of a number of city agencies, was designed to coordinate "tough new programs" for the enforcement of the expected graffiti legislation.[14] The mayor further stated that

> the ugliness of graffiti and the ugly message—often obscene or racist—has generated widespread support for the City's campaign to end this epidemic of thoughtless behavior. Even those who once possessed mild amusement about graffiti are becoming increasingly indignant at the damage being done.... I know the problem is complex, but we have to roll up our sleeves and solve it. The assault on our senses and on our pocketbooks as we pay the clean-up costs must be stopped.[15]

The graffiti bill was approved unanimously by the full city council on October 11, minus the section on control of the sale of spray paint, which had aroused opposition from merchants and was considered by the council to be "too controversial."[16] Mayor Lindsay, who signed it into law on October 27, was pleased with the bill but warned merchants to "self-regulate" their sales or he would impose further legislation that would make it illegal to sell spray paint to anyone under eighteen years of age.[17]

There was also antigraffiti action on other fronts. Science came to the aid of graffiti fighters with the invention, by E. Dragza of the Samson Chemical Corporation, of an "artproof acrylic polymer hydron" which he named Dirty Word Remover (DWR).[18] On July 31 Mayor Lindsay announced that Dragza's formula, renamed Hydron 300, was to be sprayed on a library in Queens, another in Brooklyn, and a firehouse in the Bronx, to facilitate the removal of graffiti from their walls. The mayor expressed hopes that use of the "Teflon-like coating" would help to make graffiti removal "easier and less costly." The cost of the experiment was set at $5,000.[19] Results of the test were never made public.

Inspired by the growing campaign against graffiti, private citizens also got involved in the "graffiti war" of 1972. In November the Kings County Council of Jewish War Veterans invited "citizens of good will" to join their bucket brigade to clean graffiti off the monument to President John F. Kennedy in Brooklyn's Grand Army Plaza.[20] The Boy Scouts and Girl Scouts staged their own graffiti cleanup day when more than 400 scouts spent a day partially cleaning six IND trains. Each participating scout received a citizenship medallion in honor of his or her achievement from the Avon Products Corporation.[21]

Other New Yorkers devised ingenious solutions to the problem. E.A. Sachs, for example, in a letter to the *New York Times* suggested that the MTA paint subway vehicles with a "multicolored spray" that would "camouflage any attempts at graffiting."[22] M.W. Covington, also in a letter, made the more drastic suggestion that a "massive police assault" be launched against graffitists who deface Central Park monuments.[23] R.H. Robinson of Brooklyn showed great ingenuity in his suggestion that large fines levied on convicted graffitists be divided between the city and persons turning in the graffitists. He noted that he had already assembled a lengthy list of offenders in his own neighborhood.[24] Of more than a dozen letters concerning graffiti that appeared in the *Times* that winter, only one was sympathetic to the writers. The letter writer, P.R. Patterson, hailed youths who paint graffiti for "cheering up the depressing environment in the poorer areas of the city" and accused most people of being "guilty of subduing the desire to mark up subways as a protest against the indignities of the city bureaucracy."[25]

Early in 1973 Steven Isenberg announced that over the year the police had arrested 1,562 youths for defacing subways and other public places with graffiti. Of those arrested, 426 eventually went to court and were sentenced to spend a day in the train yards scrubbing graffiti.[26]

Two weeks after Isenberg's announcement Frank Berry, the executive officer of the transit authority, announced that conventional "quick treatment" graffiti writing had reached the "saturation level" and was being supplanted by "large . . . multi-colored inscriptions that may cover one-half or more of a subway car's outer surface." The alarming proliferation of such "grand design" graffiti constituted, according to Berry, distinct danger to riders because "they can block the vision of riders preparing to enter or leave through the door." In light of these new developments Berry called for an increase in the number of graffiti arrests to eliminate the possibility of a "grand design" epidemic.[27]

On February 26 the New York City Bureau of the Budget completed a detailed work plan for Mayor Lindsay's graffiti task force. The report began by stating that antigraffiti efforts in 1972 had cost the city $10 million, yet they had not been sufficient to reduce "the city-wide level of graffiti defacement" below "fifty percent surface coverage," a level that it declared "unacceptable."[28] It thus proposed that the city engage in a graffiti prevention project that would seek to reduce the level of defacement to an acceptable 10 to 20 percent. The cost of such a project was estimated to be $24 million.[29]

Under the control of a project management staff team appointed by the mayor, the proposed project would coordinate efforts by various city agencies and private corporations toward four major project elements:

- Technological improvements: Testing and implementing the use of high-performance paints, coatings, and solvents for graffiti-defaced surfaces.
- Security measures: Testing and implementing increased security measures in those areas of the city where security may deter graffiti vandalism.
- Motivation of graffiti vandals: Testing and implementing psychological measures aimed at either inhibiting vandalism or diverting vandals elsewhere.
- Control of graffiti instruments: Testing and implementing the feasibility of manufacturer and retailer restrictions on packaging and display of graffiti instruments.[30]

Under these categories the report listed nearly one hundred specific tasks, the completion of which would lead to the achievement of the overall objectives. The tasks included "implementing and monitoring psychological field-testing for graffiti vandalism prevention and developing procedures for monitoring of procedures involved in implementation of restrictions." Mayor Lindsay devoted a month to study of the report before releasing it or commenting on it publicly.

Meanwhile on March 26 *New York Magazine* published a long article by Richard Goldstein, "This Thing Has Gotten Completely Out of Hand." His reference was not to the growing graffiti fad but to the city's fight against it. Goldstein, giving the pro-graffiti forces their first published support, stated that "it just may be that the kids who write graffiti are the healthiest and most assertive people in their neighborhoods." He further declared graffiti to be "the first genuine teenage street culture since the fifties. In that sense, it's a lot like rock 'n' roll."[31]

In the same issue the *New York Magazine* management presented a "Graffiti 'Hit' Parade" in which it gave "Taki awards" to a number of graffitists in categories labeled "Grand Design" and "Station Saturation." Award-winning works were reproduced in full color in the magazine. They declared the emergence of grand design pieces a "grand graffiti conquest of the subways" and ridiculed chairman Ronan, Mayor Lindsay, and the *Times* for their attitude toward the new art form. The Taki Awards article also contained a statement in praise of graffiti from pop artist Claes Oldenberg that was reprinted in the catalog for two subsequent UGA exhibitions and was quoted in a number of magazine and newspaper articles about graffiti, as well as Norman Mailer's book, *The Faith of Graffiti.* Said Oldenberg:

> I've always wanted to put a steel band with dancing girls in the subways and send it all over the city. It would slide into a station without your expecting it. It's almost like that now. You're standing there in the station, everything is gray and gloomy and all of a sudden one of those graffiti trains slides in and brightens the place like a big bouquet from Latin America. At first it seems anarchical—makes you wonder if the subways are working properly. Then you get used to it. The city is like a newspaper anyway, so it's natural to see writing all over the place.[32]

The day after the *New York* articles appeared, Mayor Lindsay called a press conference at which he discussed the findings and proposals contained in the graffiti prevention project report. He stated that copies of the work plan would be sent to the heads of the MTA, the Environmental Protection Agency, the board of education, and all other agencies and authorities concerned with graffiti prevention. He ridiculed "those who call graffiti vandalism 'art'" and asked the citizens of New York to join him in denouncing the graffiti vandals. "It's a dirty shame," said the mayor, "that we must spend money for this purpose in a time of austerity. The cost of cleaning up graffiti, even to a partial extent, is sad testimony to the impact of the thoughtless behavior which lies behind ... the demoralizing visual impact of graffiti."[33]

As graffiti continued to appear on subways and other city property, Mayor Lindsay became increasingly angry, not only at supporters of graffiti and the writers themselves but at his own staff for their inability to control the problem. In an interview with a *Sunday News* reporter, Steven Isenberg "smiled when he recalled two times when Mayor Lindsay burst into his office and—with four-letter fervor—ordered him to 'clean up the mess.' One time the Mayor had snipped a ceremonial ribbon at the opening of a Brooklyn swimming pool that was already covered with graffiti and the other time he had spotted a graffiti-laden bus in midtown. 'I certainly got reamed out,' Isenberg recalled."[34]

The mayor's anger over the continued appearance of graffiti on the subways exploded publicly on June 30, 1973. Steven Isenberg explained, "When the Mayor went to mid-town to publicize the parking ticket step-up, he took the subway back to City Hall and what he saw made him madder than hell."[35] Immediately upon his return to his office the mayor called a hurried press conference at which he snapped, "I just came back from 42nd Street in one of [MTA chairman] Dr. Ronan's graffiti-scarred subway cars, one of the worst I've seen yet."[36] The mayor stated that the extent of name marking in the trains and stations was "shocking" and pointed out that the antigraffiti force he had organized the year before had come up with a plan to prevent the writing through increased police surveillance of lay-ups, train yards, and stations. "Since the time the plan was sent to the MTA I haven't heard a word," he said. "I don't think they even bothered to look at it. They don't give a damn and couldn't care less about being responsive to elected officials."[37]

A few months later in an interview with Norman Mailer, Lindsay explained that his aggravation with graffiti was due to the fact that it tended to nullify many of his efforts to provide the city's subway passengers with "a cleaner and more pleasant environment" in which to travel. At that time the mayor was also attempting to justify the city's massive expenditures for new subway cars, which, once covered with graffiti, "did not seem much more pleasant" than the old cars.[38]

The graffiti policies that were established during the Lindsay administration are still being pursued. The MTA continues to scrub trains only to find them immediately redecorated. The police continue to apprehend writers only to see them released, unpunished, by the courts. It would seem that the failure of the city's expensive antigraffiti policies should be a matter of great concern to the press and elected officials; however, the management, expense, and overall wisdom of New York City's antigraffiti policies have not been criticized publicly by either politicians or the press and thus continue unchanged.

Norman Mailer attributed Lindsay's attitude toward graffiti to the fact that the mayor had earlier sought the Democratic presidential nomination in 1972 and that graffiti had been

an upset to his fortunes, ... a vermin of catastrophe that these writings had sprouted like weeds over the misery of Fun City, a new monkey of unmanageables to sit on Lindsay's overloaded political back. He must have sensed the Presidency draining away from him as the months went by, the graffiti grew, and the millions of tourists who passed through the city brought the word out to the rest of the nation: "Filth is sprouting on the walls."[39]

It is doubtful that graffiti played as important a role in Lindsay's declining political fortunes as Mailer speculates. Evidently, however, Lindsay believed that graffiti was a problem significant enough to rate a substantial amount of his attention, and thus it became a political issue during his administration.

The fact that there has been very little reduction in the amount of graffiti that has covered the city's subways since 1971 can be seen as proof that the city's antigraffiti policies have failed. John deRoos, former senior executive director of the MTA, has placed the burden of blame for this failure on the city's judicial system: "Almost all graffiti can be traced to people who have been arrested at least once. But the courts let them off. Six, seven, eight, or nine times."[40] In an interview former transit police chief Sanford Garelik also laid the blame for the failure of the MTA's graffiti arrest policies on the courts: "The transit police are doing their job but what's the use of making arrests if the courts refuse to prosecute? Graffiti is a form of behavior that leads to other forms of criminality. The courts have to realize this ... anything else is an injustice to the public."

Chief Judge Reginald Matthews of the Bronx Family Court has replied to such criticism of the courts' handling of graffiti: "Graffiti is an expression of social maladjustment, but the courts cannot cure all of society's ills. We have neither the time nor the facilities to handle graffiti cases; in fact, we cannot always give adequate treatment to far more serious crimes. Graffiti simply cannot be treated by the juvenile justice system as a serious thing, not in New York."

Not everyone in the MTA and the transit police blames the courts. Reginal Lewis, a car maintenance foreman at the MTA, puts the blame on the transit police for "not keeping the kids out of the (train) yards." Detective sergeant Morris Bitchachi, commander of the MTA's ten-member graffiti squad, blamed the city's Department of Social Services for not providing special rehabilitation programs for "known graffiti offenders."

City University professor George Jochnowitz had another idea: "The *New York Times* is … responsible for the prevalence of graffiti. On July 21, 1971, an interview with Taki 183, a previously unknown graffiti dauber, appeared.… The glorification of this vandal by the nation's most prestigious newspaper was not without effect. Within months a minor problem became a major one."[41]

After 1975 there was little press coverage of graffiti, a reflection of the city government's reluctance to publicize the city's continuing failure to control the graffiti phenomenon. This, combined with the seeming unwillingness of the press to bring criticism upon itself through the publication of other Taki-style reports, led to a near press blackout on the subject of graffiti.

In 1980 the blackout ended when the *New York Times Magazine* published a long article about three graffiti writers: NE, T-Kid, and Seen. Other newspapers followed suit, featuring articles on other writers and on the current state of the graffiti phenomenon.

In September 1981 the mayor's office broke its silence when Mayor Koch declared that "New Yorkers are fed up with graffiti," and announced a 1.5 million dollar program to provide fences and German Shepherd watchdogs for the Corona trainyard. MTA chairman Richard Ravitch had at first rejected the idea, stating that, "fences are not going to work. It is likely that they would be cut and the dogs would get out and perhaps injure someone in the neighboring community."[42] Ravitch quickly gave in to pressure from the mayor, however, and a double set of razor wire-topped fences were quickly installed, between which six dogs patrolled the perimeter of the yard. Mayor Koch and the press were present on the day the dogs were released and the mayor declared, "We call them dogs, but they are really wolves. Our hope is that the vandals will ultimately get the message."[43]

To test the effectiveness of the fences and dogs, all of the trains stored at the yard were painted white and the mayor asked the MTA to inform him immediately if any graffiti was painted on them. For the following three months the trains were watched closely and no graffiti appeared on the outsides of the trains. Declaring the Corona experiment a success, the mayor announced on December 14 that the city would increase its contribution to the MTA by $22.4 million to fund the installation of similar fences at the other eighteen train yards operated by the authority. The mayor stated that the new security installations would not feature attack dogs because, at $3,000 per year apiece, their maintenance had proved too expensive. Instead, coils of razor wire would be placed between the fences. Said Koch, "I prefer to think of these as steel dogs with razor teeth. And you don't have to feed steel dogs."[44] Ravitch said that he was pleased by the mayor's decision to increase transit financing and that the MTA would attempt to complete construction of the new fences within six months.

Privately, MTA officials expressed doubts that the fences would, ultimately, be effective. Graffiti writers did so as well. Said Ali, "We haven't gone over the fences at Corona because it's on a lousy subway line. If they fence a popular yard like Pelham or Coney Island, the writers won't be stopped by razor wire, dogs, or laser towers. We'll get past the fences. Wait and see." Daze said, "All the fences will do is keep most of us out of the yards. We'll still be able to hit the trains in the lay-ups, and we'll bomb the insides and the outsides of in-service trains with tags—big spray-paint tags like nobody's ever seen. The MTA can't stop us from doing that unless they put a cop on every car." Bloodtea continued, "All they're doing is moving graffiti from the outsides of the trains to the insides. It's the inside graffiti—the tags—that the public hates. All the mayor is doing is getting rid of the outside pieces that the public likes, the big colorful pieces."

According to mayoral aide Jack Lusk, the yard-fencing program is the first step in a long-range antigraffiti program. Said Lusk;

"The public hates graffiti and it's up to us to do something about it. Fencing the yards will take care of some of it. Beyond that we're planning a series of antigraffiti television, radio, and print advertisements featuring the slogan. 'Make your mark in society, not on it.' We're also considering sponsoring antigraffiti citizens' groups; legislation banning the sale of spray paint and markers to minors; and possibly the establishment of a special transit court that will handle crimes like graffiti and other forms of vandalism. Even though the mayor does not have direct authority over the MTA, the public holds him responsible for the state of the subways. The public is frightened and disgusted by graffiti and they want us to do something about it. We're going to do whatever is necessary to wipe it out."

Study Questions

1. What different sets of values are used to describe graffiti as "art" or as "pollution?"
2. Apart from the legal issues, what ethical concerns arise when graffiti is placed on private or public property?
3. Should "quick treatment" tags and larger, more sophisticated and elaborate "grand design" pieces be subject to the same kinds of official condemnation?

Notes

1. "'Taki 183' Spawns Pen Pals," *New York Times*, July 21, 1971, p. 37.
2. Ibid.
3. "Garelik Calls for War on Graffiti," *New York Times*, May 21, 1972, p. 66.
4. "Nuisance in Technicolor," *New York Times*, May 26, 1972, p. 34.
5. "Fines and Jail for Graffiti Will Be Asked by Lindsay," *New York Times*, June 26, 1972, p. 66.
6. "Lindsay Assails Graffiti Vandals," *New York Times*, August 25, 1972, p. 30.
7. Edward Ranzal, "Officials Testify in Favor of Mayor's Graffiti Bill," *New York Times*, September 1, 1972, p. 25.
8. Edward Ranzal, "Ronan Backs Lindsay Antigraffiti Plan," *New York Times*, August 29, 1972, p. 66.
9. Ibid.
10. "Stiff Antigraffiti Measure Passes Council Committee," *New York Times*, September 15, 1972, p. 41.
11. New York Administrative Code, Section 435–13.2 (1972).
12. "Stiff Administrative Measure Passes Council Committee," *New York Times*, September 15, 1972, p. 41.
13. "Scratch the Graffiti," *New York Times*, September 16, 1972, p. 28.
14. "Lindsay Forms 'Graffiti Task Force,'" *New York Times*, October 5, 1972, p. 51.
15. Office of Mayor John V. Lindsay, press release, October 4, 1972.
16. "Antigraffiti Bill One of Four Gaining Council Approval," *New York Times*, October 11, 1972, p. 47.
17. "Lindsay Signs Graffiti Bill," *New York Times*, October 28, 1972, p. 15.
18. "New Chemical May Curb Graffiti," *New York Times*, April 22, 1972, p. 35.
19. Office of Mayor John V. Lindsay, press release, July 31, 1972.
20. "Antigraffiti 'Bucket Brigade' Planned," *New York Times*, November 13, 1972, p. 41.
21. "Boy Scouts Scrub Graffiti Off Walls of Subway Cars," *New York Times*, February 25, 1973, p. 35.
22. E. H. Sachs, Jr., letter, *New York Times*, December 24, 1972, Sec. 8, p. 2.
23. M. W. Covington, letter, *New York Times*, December 26, 1972, p. 32.
24. R. H. Robinson, letter, *New York Times*, June 5, 1972, p. 32.
25. P. R. Patterson, letter, *New York Times*, December 14, 1972, p. 46.
26. *New York Times*, January 14, 1973, p. 14.

27. "Fight against Subway Graffiti Progresses from Frying Pan to Fire," *New York Times*, January 26, 1973, p. 39.
28. Bureau of the Budget of the City of New York, *Work Plan—Graffiti Prevention Project* (February 26, 1973), p. 2.
29. Ibid., p. 3.
30. Ibid., p. 2.
31. Richard Goldstein, "This Thing Has Gotten Completely Out of Hand," *New York Magazine*, March 26, 1973, pp. 35–39.
32. "The Graffiti 'Hit' Parade," *New York Magazine*, March 26, 1973, pp. 40–43.
33. Murray Schumach, "At $10 Million, City Calls It a Losing Graffiti Fight," *New York Times*, March 28, 1973, p. 46.
34. James Ryan, "The Great Graffiti Plague," *New York Daily News Sunday Magazine*, May 6, 1973, p. 33.
35. James Ryan, "The Mayor Charges MTA Is Soft on Graffiti," *New York Daily News*, July 1, 1973, p. 2.
36. Alfred E. Clark, "Persistent Graffiti Anger Lindsay on Subway Tour," *New York Times*, July 1, 1979, p. 47.
37. Ibid.
38. Norman Mailer, *The Faith of Graffiti* (New York: Praeger/Alskog Publishers, 1974).
39. Ibid.
40. Owen Moritz, "The New Subway," *New York Daily News*, December 5, 1978, p. 37.
41. George Jochnowitz, "Thousands of Child-hours Wasted on Ugly Daubings," *New York Post*, October 20, 1978, p. 43.
42. Ari L. Goldman, "Dogs to Patrol Subway Yards," *New York Times*, September 15, 1981, p. 1.
43. Ibid.
44. Ari L. Goldman, "City to Use Pits of Barbed Wire in Graffiti War," *New York Times*, December 15, 1981, p. B-1.

2
Zulus on a Time Bomb
Hip-Hop Meets the Rockers Downtown

Jeff Chang is one of hip-hop's most eloquent and thorough historians and here he documents the period in which the nascent hip-hop scene really became a *SCENE*. Chang identifies points of cohesion across different communities, interests, and practices and the formation of an early sustaining infrastructure that reinforced the burgeoning hip-hop culture. He also explains the convergence of two distinct scenes as the uptown hip-hop crews encountered downtown artists and gallery mavens in New York, resulting in a vibrant syncretic environment. Of crucial importance in Chang's historical narrative is the detail with which he identifies cross-racial cooperation and the collaborations of older and younger individuals who found a mutual bond in hip-hop.

Chang also introduces us to some of the most renowned graffiti artists of all time—Fab Five Freddy, Futura 2000, Lady Pink, Lee Quinones, and Zephyr recounting how early aerosol artists gradually conceived of themselves as professionals, merging their work on brick walls and New York subways with canvases destined for more genteel gallery sites. With this particular account, Chang provides convincing evidence that refutes the views of haters and critics that have, since the early days, denied hip-hop a place in the annals of art culture.

Zulus on a Time Bomb: Hip-Hop Meets the Rockers Downtown

Jeff Chang

Pop artists made art out of pop culture. These tough kids are reversing the process, making pop culture out of art.

—Kim Levin

It wasn't about your little local neighborhood. It was always you were going all-city, that's what you were supposed to do. So why shouldn't art be all-city?

—Charlie Ahearn

To uptown kids like Crazy Legs and DOZE, their culture was simply what it was. It didn't need external validation. It even thrived with opposition. It needed nothing but its own codes, its own authority. But downtown, other people were beginning to see something big in it. "It was a high school youth culture," says Charlie Ahearn, an East Village filmmaker who was venturing to the Bronx to soak up the new energy. "And to me, it was a radical avant-garde culture."

The youth movements seemed to look like a single culture, just as Afrika Bambaataa had envisioned years before with Zulu Nation, an expression of a new generation of outcast youths whose worldview felt authentic, original, and liberating. This first wave of downtowners—white baby boomer outsiders, young white bohemian dropouts, white art rebels, Block post-jazzsters—were enthralled. They were the earliest adopters, the ones who placed themselves closest to the fire, and they would be central in bringing hip-hop to the world.

Boomer Outsiders

Soft-spoken sculptor named Henry Chalfant had come of age during the stifling fifties in Sewickley, Pennsylvania, a tiny white-picket fence town north of rusting Pittsburgh. His father ran the family's steel-pipe manufacturing firm. His mother had helped found a private-care institution for handicapped children. In the Allegheny Valley, Chalfant's very name evoked aristocracy and connection. His great-great grandfather, the area's pioneering Henry, was an innkeeper and proprietor so beloved that a town east of Pittsburgh had been named for him in 1914. But the younger Henry felt alienated in the land of his ancestors.

"We used to argue over whose family was poorer while being driven to school by the chauffeur," he says. "I was definitely unhappy where I grew up, which was very privileged, very white, very hide-bound, rule-bound, and rather empty.

"So you know," he chuckles, "I drove fast—hot rods, motorcycles. Generally I was a menace in that way." When he graduated, he sped toward the California sunset, where he enrolled at Stanford in 1958. He majored in classical Greek, immersed himself in art and became a sculptor, and when Berkeley students closed the McCarthy era with their Free Speech Movement and anti-war demonstrations, he was drawn into that as well.

In 1967, he left the Bay Area for Europe with his wife, the actress Kathleen Chalfant, to soak up art and sculpture in Barcelona and Rome. But on frequent visits back to New York City, he became intoxicated by the colorful, intricate graffiti on the sides of the subway cars. These weren't Pompeii scrawls in the dustbins of history. They were alive, mysterious, alluring, dangerous. In 1973, he and Kathleen moved to New York permanently, and he began to photograph the tags. "What immediately peaked my interest was seeing what seemed to be all these rebellious kids. What I ended up doing was living it to the hilt the second time through—not my own adolescence, but vicariously through these writers," he says.

From the summer of 1976 to 1979, Chalfant went out on weekends to document the train art. Writers began to notice the balding white man, standing for hours on subway platforms with an expensive camera, snapping furiously and sometimes futilely when the trains screeched into the stops, and figured he was either a cop or one of them, a die-hard junkie for aerosol art. One day he found himself staring at a writer named NAC, who was also taking pictures. They got to talking. When Chalfant let him know what he was doing, NAC told him to drop by the Writer's Bench at 149th Street after school one day. The writers befriended him and brought him into the fold, passing him through their crews, calling him to brag about their latest victories, which he then went out to capture on film. Chalfant's hobby became a daily obsession. In turn, he opened up his Greenwich Village studio to them.

Uptown, ZEPHYR and FUTURA were gathering writers at Sam Esses's studio to begin translating graffiti for the art gallery world. Chalfant's Grand Street studio, by contrast, was a library of subway style. The photos were the best the writers had ever seen. After 1978, Chalfant had begun using a motor-drive on his camera. While standing in one spot, he could shoot entire cars on a flat angle. The photos presented the cars as if they had just pulled up to the station in their full glory. Younger writers especially flocked to Chalfant's studio to study the photos and learn the styles.

Like the ambivalent anthropologist, Chalfant realized he had altered the scene. "In the old days before photography, you would get style from a king. He would grant you this style and then you could copy the outline if you were part of his crew," he says. "But when people from other parts of the city start rocking your style, you weren't happy. Someone like SKEME, he was getting a lot of fame and for about a year, he was taking over everything. And a lot of his style came from my photos of DONDI." But Chalfant's interest had never been merely academic. He wanted to be taken, he says, "by the daily surprise of it all."

In September 1980, Chalfant displayed his photos publicly for the first time in an exhibition at the O. K. Harris Gallery in Soho. He was astonished at the reception he got. The few print reviews he got were brief and lukewarm, but the streets spoke loudly. "They came to the gallery as if on a pilgrimmage," Chalfant says.[1]

From across the city, hundreds of graffiti writers arrived dressed in their flyest customized denims and sneakers, all color and swagger and joy. The writers took over the gallery, gazing at the twenty shots of whole-car murals in a rush of recognition and future shock. They spilled out of the tiny gallery back onto the street, tagging each other's books and the storefront walls. They formed new crews, secured affiliations and made plans. Chalfant, the quiet student of the youth culture, and all of his less worldly art-world peers were awestruck anew at how big the thing really ly was.

Dondi White brought Martha Cooper, a newsphotographer for the *New York Post* and an urban folklorist to meet Chalfant. Cooper and Chalfant were aware of each others' work and had privately nursed a professional jealousy, but in person the vibes melted away and they greeted each other as long-lost colleagues. Both understood that the writers' eye-zapping virtuosity and the art's butterfly ephemerality demanded documentation and advocacy.

Chalfant shot the trains as if they were already in the museums. Cooper contextualized them as they rushed through the grimy backdrop of the dying city—"Art vs. Transit," as her famous shot of a 1982 train by DURO, SHY 147 and KOS from CIA illustrated, a metaphor for bottom-up urban renewal. Together they began making a case for graffiti. Glazed to boredom by abstraction, "the art-world was ready for it," Chalfant says.

Events snowballed. Once the Esses Studio closed, the energy ZEPHYR and FUTURA had gathered moved into spaces like ALI's Soul Artists workshop, the center of "Zoo York," and the Fashion Moda storefront gallery in the South Bronx. In October, Fashion Moda's "Graffiti Art Success for America," put together by CRASH, opened in the South Bronx. In December, the New Museum brought many of the pieces down for an exhibition at its location in Greenwich Village. All of a sudden, there no longer seemed to be an expiration date on a graffiti lifestyle. Writers considered making a living at it. Major museum curators and gallery owners, eagerly sniffing out the new, began to venture out of their safe Manhattan turfs with their checkbooks.

The week after Christmas, *The Village Voice* announced the art-world's new alignment with street culture in a cover story by graf's public defender Richard Goldstein called "The Fire Down Below." There were fashionable black-and-white portraits of PINK, ZEPHYR, FAB 5 FREDDY and FUTURA 2000 and a full-color pullout section featuring Chalfant's iconic photos of classic trains by Lee Quiñones, BLADE, SEEN, DONDI, KELL and FUTURA. The sense of anticipation was palpable. Goldstein quoted FAB 5 FREDDY, on his way to a gallery opening of his works in Milan: "With a little time and paint, anything is possible."[2]

Young Bohemians

The walls of northern segregation could come down, for one thing.

As New York City staggered out of the 1970s—bloodied and broke—it was more separate and less equal than ever, the culmination of three decades of top-down urban renewal, Third World dislocation and white flight. During the decade, more than 1.2 million whites, fully a quarter of the white population—including almost a third of whites in Brooklyn and half of whites in the Bronx—had abandoned the city. Poverty rates soared, especially in those two boroughs.[3]

Pop culture mirrored the segregation. Movies like *Badge* 373 and *Fort Apache: The Bronx* looked, especially to Blacks and Latinos, like exploitative tales that reinforced race and class hatred more often than they raised empathy. At the end of the '70s, Puerto Rican and Black activists, led by the former Young Lord Richie Perez and other veterans of the Black and Brown Power movements, organized to boycott such films and demand more faithful and truthful media representations. At one protest, two brown Bronx girls carried a picket saying, "Fort Apache—Indians are not savages. Neither are we."[4] Even pop music, with its long history of crossover and miscegenation, offered little hope. After disco, radio cleaved into ever more rigid rock (white) and urban (Black) formats.

Yet graffiti had infected the young post-hippies gathering in Central Park. Through the decades, the locus of the city's young bohemia had shifted northward, from Greenwich Village to Central Park's Bethesda Fountain, and then into the heart of the Park at the field behind the Naumberg Bandshell. The "parkie" scene embraced native and immigrant sons and daughters of philosophers and kings, hard-hat workers and maids.

To ZEPHYR, a Jewish kid from the Upper East Side who cut classes to hang out, the scene behind the bandshell was an opening into a different world. "You get out of school, fuckin' get your little bag of reefer, going to the park, meeting up with your homeboys, kids from Brooklyn, the Bronx," he says. "It was extremely mixed, like a freak scene of young kids. Some of the kids were really from wealthy families and then some were like more down and out, some were home-less. But it was really cool because that scene went on for, I'd say, the better half of a decade."

There, the "parkies" found a safe space to experiment with drugs (especially marijuana and psychedelics), sex and style. "The cops had a total hands-off policy. There was fucking clouds of pot smoke. It looked like the parking lot of a Grateful Dead concert. Imagine that every day, seven days a week." When he met writers like BILL ROCK, MIN ONE, REVOLT and others there, ZEPHYR's secret obsession with graffiti flowered. Through graffiti, the parkies' scene began to mix with the punk-era art-activists of the East Village.

Art Rebels

As soon as they were able—1973, to be precise—Charlie Ahearn and his twin brother, John, had moved from their upstate middle-class collegiate suburb of Binghamton to New York City to become contemporary artists. Charlie enrolled in the Whitney Museum's program and found an apartment in the middle of the heroin-bingeing East Village. He and John became part of an artists' movement there called Co-Lab—a collective determined to, he says, "get the hell out of the art world, get the hell out of art galleries and find a way to be creative in a larger sense."

"Coming from a middle-class background, I always wanted to be as adventurous as possible, to see a larger picture," Ahearn says. "The idea was people that are involved in any kind of struggle are interesting. It's not about going into a studio and making work and selling it in an art gallery. You go right out there. You're an activist. You're changing things by creating stuff."

Charlie went down to the Alfred E. Smith projects in the Lower East Side, at the Manhattan end of the Brooklyn Bridge, with a Super 8 camera. He filmed the kids practicing martial arts and then played the film back for them. He was as taken as they were with the all-day kung-fu festi-vals in Times Square, then a pre-redevelopment *Taxi Driver* carnival of red-bulb burlesque and Five Percenter ciphers. And so he collaborated with the kids to do their own kind of homage, which he called "The Deadly Art of Survival."

While filming, he had become captivated by Lee Quiñones's handball court murals—animals and spacemen floating and roaring off the walls in bright comic-book colors. "I would ask kids in the neighborhood, who painted these murals? And they'd go, 'Lee!' Like it was the most obvi-ous thing cause he's so famous, one of the most up graffiti artists in New York City. And I'd say, 'Okay, where can I find him?' And everyone would go, 'I don't know, he's around but he's kinda secretive. He's hard to find.'"

When Lee ventured by the set one day, Ahearn cornered him. "He had this big afro and he was this skinny kid with a motorbike. And I'd say, 'I want to work with you on this movie.' And he said, 'Bet.' And I said, 'Well, how can I get to you? Do you have a phone number?' 'Nah, I'll just be around.' And then he'd never be around," laughs Ahearn. "He was mythical."

In June 1980, the Co-Lab collective took over an abandoned massage parlor in Times Square at 41st Street and Seventh Avenue for a massive exhibition. "Everyone just sort of rushed in, bum-rushing the place and throwing artwork up," Ahearn says. "There was a lot of street art at the time, and there was a lot of homeless people making sort of weird things on the street, that all became part of the show. So graffiti slipped in there, it seemed like a very natural thing to include in the show."

The show would be widely reviewed, remembered as historic. A new crop of graffiti-inspired "street artists" were introduced in the show—Jean-Michel Basquiat, Kenny Scharf and Keith Haring. And Ahearn finally got to work with Lee Quiñones and his partner, FAB 5 FREDDY.

In Search of a Post-Jazz Cool

Frederick Brathwaite was a tall slim African American raised in the do-or-die Bed-Stuy. He looked out at the world from behind his ever-present Ray-Bans, as if he had just stepped out of Minton's Playhouse.

He had spent his childhood in casual proximity to Black genius. The bebop elite frequented his family's house, people like Bud Powell, Thelonious Monk, Clifford Brown, and Freddy's god-father Max Roach. His grandfather had been an associate of Marcus Garvey. His father, an accountant, was in the audience at the Audubon Ballroom when Malcolm X was shot. Freddy was born with an awareness of walking proudly through history.

Brathwaite wanted to become a serious artist. But he was also searching for an artform he could organize his own worldview around—the same way his father saw his world through jazz. He found fresh energy in the Brooklyn mobile DJ scene, at shows thrown by Grandmaster Flowers, Maboya, and Pete DJ Jones. On hooky trips he went to the Metropolitan Museum of Art to study its collections of art and armor. He immersed himself in Caravaggio, Duchamp, Boccioni and Warhol. And he tagged BULL 99 and SHOWDOWN 177.

Graffiti brought it all together. "I had looked at all the movements that were kind of radical, like Futurism, the Dadaists, the Impressionists, the Abstract Expressionists into the Pop Artists. To me, it was like, wait a minute, this shit is a lot like what graffiti is," he says. "So I was thinking about how to make moves into the art world, but still keep the integrity of what graffiti was."

He too was inspired by Lee Quiñones's work, and decided he needed to meet the artist. Sometime in 1978, he boldly strode into Lee's high-school classroom. Before being told to leave, Freddy whispered to Lee to meet him outside after school. Lee was suspicious, but when they spoke, they realized they had found the perfect foil in each other. Lee was shy and elusive, Freddy radiated confidence and cool. Lee kept his thoughts to himself, Freddy talked to anyone. Through Lee, Freddy met the rest of the Fabulous Five—all in various stages of retiring from the lines— and was brought into the crew. As FAB 5 FREDDY, he painted trains and walls and publicized graffiti in the downtown art scene. In early 1979, he appeared in a *Village Voice* article about graf-fiti, smoking a cigarette under Lee's GRAFFITI 1990 mural, and offering his contact info. By the end of the year, the two had landed the first graffiti art show in Italy, at the Galleria La Medusa.

FAB floated right into the burgeoning downtown scene. He hung out at *Interview* magazine editor Glen O'Brien's cable access show, a central hub of the New Wave/No Wave movement. He partied at the Mudd Club with Deborah Harry and Blondie, Jean-Michel Basquiat, Keith Haring and Andy Warhol. At the same time, he was checking out Grandmaster Flash and the Furious Four at the Smith Houses with Lee, and collecting bootleg cassettes of all the rap crews. The nine-teen-year-old found himself moving through two very different worlds, and he had both the charisma and the desire to bring them together.

Four Movements to One Culture

Bambaataa's vision of a revolutionary youth culture was unfolding before FAB's eyes and he began to see what his role could be. "As a painter at the time, and having read a lot about art, I wanted to make sure that we weren't perceived as folk artists," he says.

"Not everybody doing graffiti had aesthetic intentions, but many did. Those that did were the ones that drove the development from just simple tags to elaborate window-down wildstyle. Those heads were on some creative shit. I wanted to make sure that the scene that I was coming from was actually seen in that light, basically that we were smart enough to understand that game as well," he says.

"I once read somewhere that for a culture to really be a complete culture, it should have a music, a dance and a visual art. And then I realized, wow, all these things are going on. You got the graffiti happening over here, you got the breakdancing, and you got the DJ and MCing thing. In my head, they were all one thing," he says. FAB understood the history of artistic movements, and he realized that he was right at the beginning of a big one. He had an idea to set it off.

At the Times Square Show, Mudd Club and Co-Lab co-conspirator Diego Cortez introduced Charlie Ahearn and FAB 5 FREDDY. FAB had seen "The Deadly Art of Survival" and knew Ahearn could be just the person to speak to. Ahearn recalls, "Fred told me that he wanted to make a movie with me. He said, 'We should make a movie about this graffiti thing', and he said he knew Lee Quiñones. So I said if you can bring Lee to me, come by tomorrow and I'll give you guys fifty dollars 'cause I wanted them to do a mural outside the building. They came by the next day. And I said, 'Okay, here we are, the three of us.' That became the beginnings of the idea of *Wild Style*."

Ahearn and FAB began a year of immersion in the culture, finding themselves one night in a far corner of the north Bronx, at a party presided over by Chief Rocker Busy Bee and DJ Breakout. "It was in a place called The Valley. It's in a large park and it was dark. I remember there was a dub reggae band playing and the other side was hip-hop music. And we wandered to the hip-hop music," Ahearn says. "I often wonder what would have happened had we ended up going toward the dub band.

"Fred and I were standing by the side of this little tiny stage," he recalls. "This guy next to me later told me he was sweating bullets because he thought I was a cop. Everyone *always* thought I was a cop. I don't blame them. For a year that I was hanging out there, I never saw anyone that was from downtown or that was white hanging out in any place I went to.

"So Busy Bee was there and he says, 'What are you doing here?' and I said, 'I'm Charlie Ahearn and I'm here to make a movie about the rap scene.' And he takes me by the hand and he leads me out on the stage where there's a microphone and there's an audience."

Ahearn's twin, John, had moved to the Bronx two years before, and was becoming something of an art-world star for his cast sculptures of his neighbors on Walton Avenue, an area where the Savage Skulls had once roamed. Another close associate, Co-Lab member Stefan Eins, had opened a gallery he called Fashion Moda on East 147th Street at Third Avenue in the heart of the South Bronx. "The Bronx was a hip place to go if you were an artist, everybody was going up there," Charlie says. "But *this* was not the same. It was a totally different scene—high school kids—and it was wild.

"It was dark and Busy Bee leads me out onto stage, to the microphone—and you gotta understand, everybody who is anybody in hip-hop is right *there*. The Funky 4 were there, Mercedes Ladies, all these people were all in the audience right there. So Busy Bee puts his arm around me and he says, 'This here is Charlie Ahearn and he's my movie producer. We're making a movie about the rap scene.' Boom! That's all it took."

Ahearn and FAB became regular guests of the biggest rap crews in the scene, frequenting clubs like the Ecstasy Garage, the T-Connection and the Disco Fever. As he had done at Smith Houses, Ahearn took pictures, made slides, and brought them back to project them on the walls of the clubs. He was practicing his activist art.

When he met graf writers CRASH and DAZE, he walked them the short distance from their residences to meet Eins at the Fashion Moda. "No graffiti artist had ever heard of Fashion Moda," Ahearn says, despite the fact that the gallery was only two blocks from the Writer's Bench. "CRASH organized the 'Graffiti Art Success for America' show. Fashion Moda became one of the capitals of graffiti in a month."

FAB 5 FREDDY was thrilled to be meeting all of his Bronx heroes, and he began opening doors for them downtown. Grandmaster Flash says, "FAB was like one of the town criers. He would come into the hood where whites wouldn't come and then go downtown to where whites would, and say, 'Listen there's some music these cats is playing, man, it's hot shit. You gotta book these guys.' So I got my first taste of playing for an audience that wasn't typically Black."

FAB invited Bambaataa down to play at Keith Haring's black-light art exhibition in a tiny church basement on St. Mark's Place called Club 57. It was exactly the kind of opportunity Bambaataa had been waiting for. The crowd loved it, and FAB brought Bam and his Zulu Nation DJs, Jazzy Jay and Afrika Islam, back to play at venues like the Jefferson Hotel and the Mudd Club.

In April 1981, FAB curated an art show at Mudd Club called "Beyond Words: Graffiti-Based, -Rooted and -Inspired Work." The line-up read like a who's-who of the punk, subway graf, and street art scenes. Photos by Cooper and Chalfant hung next to canvases and installations by Lee, PHASE 2, LADY PINK, ZEPHYR DONDI, John Sex, Jean-Michel Basquiat, Keith Haring, Alan Vega, Iggy Pop and FAB's notorious running partner, RAMMELLZEE, an eccentric painter and freestyler obsessed with military codes and alphabet armaments.

At the opening, FAB brought in the Cold Crush Brothers, the Fantastic Freaks, and Bambaataa's Jazzy Five MCs to perform. "That was the first official time when hip-hop really hit downtown," FAB says. "It was wildly received. All these cool new wave heads came down and loved it. I knew nobody had a sense or clue about anything because barely any real rap records had hit the market commercially, maybe 'Rapper's Delight,' but nobody really understood it as like a scene."

When the hip-hoppers met the rockers, parkies, and freaks downtown, a weird new nightclub elite emerged. "We used to go to Bowl-Mor and we would bowl," ZEPHYR laughs. The high-flying, Studio 54, velvet-rope, VIP-exclusive club era was over. People were going downtown where gutter-familiar scenesters mixed freely, the picture of a wild and fabulous new pluralism.

"We had this team called the Pinheads," ZEPHYR says. "It was a big mix of people from the Mudd Club. FAB 5 FREDDY was down with us, and Grace Jones used to come down and go bowling.[5] These very new-wave/punk type people from downtown, less eccentric folks, some of the old hippie dudes like me and my boys. And then of course, from the Bronx, you had a little more macho folks. Everything overlapped. It was really surreal."

On the season's shortlist, race and class segregation was out, cultural crossover was in. "There was this shifting and mixing that was very exciting to people," says Ahearn. "The racial thing was a big deal. Mixing a lot of Black, Puerto Rican and white people downtown all together is very combustible, because people are coming from very different types of areas and they are getting used to the idea that they can hang out with each other."

Graffiti Success in America

Before long, the elite of the art-world came calling. Once cloaked in secrecy and code and executed under the constant threat of violence, graffiti suddenly became a very public performance, for the consumption of high society. The temporary and fleeting tried to fix itself as permanent.

Graffiti had flirted with the big-time in 1973, when Hugo Martinez secured for his elite graffiti union, the United Graffiti Artists, a Twyla Tharp commission and a downtown exhibition at the Razor Gallery. UGA got an avalanche of publicity, including a *Newsweek* article, and even sold some canvases for as much as $2,500. But by 1975, UGA had fizzled amidst slacking patronage and internal discord. Other similar community-based efforts to bridge graf and the art world, like Jack Pelzinger's NOGA and ALI's Soul Artists, also eventually faded.

As the 1980s arrived, Modernism was dead. Minimalism and Conceptualism had become increasingly cold, detached, cerebral, feeble. The art world thought it was ready for something authentic and passionate, something innocent and incandescent. It wanted to feel deeply again. After an era of self-referentiality and white-room obscurantism, the art world wanted a door-opening gust of the sights, smells and tastes of the real world.

Upper Manhattanites and Europeans who had supported the explosion of Pop Art during the 1960s rushed in to buy anything marketed as graffiti. In a year, Jean-Michel Basquiat—who had never painted on a train—went from homelessness to international art stardom, commanding as much as $10,000 a canvas. Teenage bombers found they could cut school and pocket $200 for a quick canvas on the way to the lay-up.

Many of the paintings were little more than tags, albeit with a buff-proof, overglowing impertinence that came with the "for sale" sign. And although collectors oohed and awed at the novelty of it all, dealers pushed the writers to give them more complex work, to make statements. Some of them did. As journalists and the media gathered to watch, ZEPHYR painted an unfurling American flag. Then he slammed a big, wildstyle "Z" across it, daring critics to embrace a new idea of "American graffiti."

PINK, the youngest of the gallery writers, displayed a feminist take on war, psychological repression and sex work. CRASH fostered the link between Pop and graffiti, sampling Lichtenstein, Warhol and Rauschenberg. Lee Quiñones moved toward an intense social realism, abandoning words and cartoons for harrowing scenes, such as the lonely, desparing junkie shooting up between the Statue of Liberty and an American flag in "Society's Child."

The most influential—DONDI, PHASE 2, RAMMELLZEE and FUTURA—developed new visual languages. PHASE 2, whose 1973 canvases had been widely recognized as defining the early genre, continued deconstructing the letter into hard lines, third eyes, horns, drills, spikes, arches, Egyptian pharaohs and dogs, pure geometrics. RAMMELLZEE's canvases swirled with forces locked in struggle, a visual analogue of his insurgent theories about the letterand word as armored vehicle in a militarized world. DONDI, the high priest of wildstyle, played with letters, arrows, often faceless head and bodies, constantly commenting on the various representations of himself in the world—names, diagrams, checking account numbers, currency.

The most visually accessible of the artists, FUTURA, provided critics with a target they could interpret. Some called him the Watteau or Kandinsky of graffiti; others used him to deride the entire movement as empty and directionless. He combined a militant, almost architecturally precise line and an understanding of industrial design and fonts with a nonpareil spatial sense of the abstract and the fantastic. He became the most famous in-house performance graffiti writer of the "Wheels of Steel" night at Negril and the Roxy, and his best work perfectly captured the atom-crashing, buzzsaw energy of the time, the rapture of the cipher, the cut, the light, the truss and the arc.

The graffitiists' work was remarkable for their outsiderness, the way in which they completely collided with the big-money gallery sensibility. Art critic Elizabeth Hess called the moment "a genuine disruption of form in the history of art."[6] In a *People Magazine* feature, Claudio Bruni, the man who had set off the frenzy by bringing FAB 5 FREDDY and Lee Quiñones to Italy in 1979, said, "To me, it was not just vandalism. It was the new expression of art, unsophisticated but very real. An art so strong it hurt people."[7]

Cynics thought the art world's embrace of graffiti represented the worst kind of white liberal guilt, a bizarre flirtation with the repressed Other. But the artists remained hopeful. ZEPHYR said, "People might say graffiti looks really out of place in a gallery. But I think it's good if graffiti is out of place. Sneaking into these places is just what graffiti is supposed to do."[8]

A Riot of Their Own

As the Reagan era commenced, hip-hop was a force that had begun reintegrating the downtown clubs, and vaulted society's outcasts into the rarified art world. But these places still represented the fringes of the avant-garde. On the streets, reality was still as color-coded and divided as ever.

FAB FIVE FREDDY says, "Things were relatively polarized. There was a term called 'bridge-and-tunnel,' which was the people that came from the outer boroughs that were really just dumb, ignorant white kids that were really racist. And they would cause problems for everybody. They would want to fight, you know what I mean? Like tough, kinda street white kids that was really not on some creative shit."

At the same time, across the Atlantic, punk's great idealists, The Clash, were so enchanted with rap that they recorded one in early 1980 called "The Magnificent Seven" for their epic *Sandinista!* album. When they arrived in New York the following summer, they were thrilled to find it had become an unlikely hit on the Black radio station, WBLS. With Don Letts, their partner and documentarian, they took a video camera to Times Square to film graf writers, b-boys, rappers and boombox renegades.

The Clash had come a long way, ideologically and musically, since they had issued "White Riot," a naive, revolutionary statement of solidarity with the West Indian immigrant rebels of the 1976 Nottinghill Carnival riots. That record had paradoxically left many wondering whether the record wasn't expressing neo-Nazi sentiments. "White riot!" they had shouted, "I wanna riot, a riot of my own!" In fact, they were searching for audiences who, as Strummer rapped on "This Is Radio Clash," recognized Sugar Minott's ghettology as Afrika Bambaataa's Lil' Vietnam.

They were set to play eight nights in June 1981 at an aging Times Square disco, the Bonds International, and they announced their stand with a dramatic unfurling of a magnificent banner painted by FUTURA. But on the eve of their opening, the fire department threatened to shut down the club for overselling the shows, and their fans finally had their white riot when mounted police stormed down Broadway to meet the punks in the streets.

The Clash compromised by agreeing to perform eleven additional gigs, and hurried to find opening acts. In yet another naive act of solidarity, they booked Grandmaster Flash and the Furious Five. But, as Michael Hill wrote in *The Village Voice*, "Rather than achieve a cultural crossover, it threatened to widen the gap."[9]

When Flash and the Furious Five stepped onstage on The Clash's opening night, the white punks stood bewildered as Flash began his "Adventures on the Wheels of Steel" routine on three turntables. Then the Furious Five, dressed in fly leather suits, jumped onstage and started rapping and dancing. Some in the crowd began shouting their disgust. They hadn't come to see no disco. When Flash paused so that the Five could try to regain the crowd, the crew found themselves ducking a hail of beer cups and spit. The next night, dressed down this time in street clothes, they suffered the same reception. They left the stage angrily, with Melle Mel admonishing, "Some of you—not all of you, but some of you—are *stupid*," never to return.[10]

The Clash responded by excoriating their own fans in interviews, and future Bronx-bred openers, The Treacherous Three and ESG, received marginally better treatment. But in 1981, the American punks clearly wanted the riot to remain exclusively their own.

Rocking and Fighting

While the British punks learned something about American racism, the downtowners found their own liberal assumptions being tested.

Henry Chalfant was managing the Rock Steady Crew. It had begun in an innocent, fortuitous way. A couple of months after the O. K. Harris show, Martha Cooper and he were in his studio and she showed him pictures of her next project. Cooper explained that a year before, she was called on assignment to a "riot-in-progress" at a Washington Heights subway station. When she got there, she encountered a group of kids in Pro-Keds and transit cops who were still scratching their heads. Whatever had happened was apparently over, so the cops told the kids to show her what they were doing. A kid stepped up, went down and spun on his head. Cooper was stunned. She said, "I called *The Post* and said, 'Well, this is more interesting than a riot—they were dancing!"

For the better part of the following year she and NYU dance professor Sally Banes had tried to track down b-boys and b-girls, frequenting high school dances and rap shows to see if they could find anyone who did it. "Everybody said, 'Ah, we don't do that anymore. It's finished, over,' " Cooper recalled. When they caught back up with the High Times Crew, the members said they were now into roller-skating.

With Cooper's story in mind, Chalfant later asked some graffiti writers at his studio if they had ever heard of folks who did a dance called "rocking." TAKE ONE said he knew the best in the city. He happened to be in a crew called Rock Steady. The next day, TAKE brought Crazy Legs and Frosty Freeze to Chalfant's studio. Chalfant saw them dance, and asked them if they would like to perform at a graffiti slide show he was doing at a Soho loft performance space near his studio called The Common Ground, a name which would later prove rich in irony.

Chalfant had been at FAB's "Beyond Words" show the month before, and he invited FAB FIVE FREDDY and RAMMELLZEE to come and rap. He, too, wanted to present graffiti, DJing, rapping, and b-boying together. The term "hip-hop" was not yet being popularly used to describe the youth movements, so Chalfant called the show "Graffiti Rock." On the Common Ground's promotional postcard, which also advertised a performance-painting event and a Chekhov reading, the event was described this way: "Using music, rapping, and dance, graffiti artists transform the static image into a unique performance dynamic. Scupltor/photographer Henry Chalfant coordinates graffiti artists in a multifaceted performance event."

Rock Steady decided to stage a battle. They split their crew into two, and he, Banes and Cooper bought them t-shirts customized with iron-on letters. They began energetic rehearsals. DOZE recalls being stunned by RAMMELLZEE's bizarre freestyling. "I was like, 'Who the fuck is this?' This fucking guy was like, 'Werrnnnnnt werrnnnnnt! Rock rock! Plop plop fizz fizz oh what a relief it is! Bob! Jellybeans! Spam! Ham!' " he laughs. "I figured, this guy is off his wig."

More important, Banes and Cooper landed a cover story in *The Village* Voice. Titled "To the Beat Y'all: Breaking Is Hard to Do," it was the first major story on b-boying. Cooper's photos from the Graffiti Rock practices were evocative: Frosty Freeze in a leftward feint, Ty Fly suspended in a back-flip. Banes, for the first time in print, speculated on b-boying's origins:

> For the current generation of B Boys, it doesn't really matter that the Breakdown is an old name in Afro-American dance for both rapid, complex footwork and a competitive format. Or that a break in jazz means a soloist's improvised bridge between melodies. For the B Boys, the history of breaking started six or seven years ago, maybe in the Bronx, maybe in Harlem. It started with the Zulus. Or with Charlie Rock. Or with Joe from the Casanovas, from the Bronx, who taught it to Charlie Rock. "Breaking means going crazy on the floor. It means making a style for yourself."[11]

The article was also perhaps the first to link graffiti, rapping and b-boying—which Banes called "forms of ghetto street culture" that were all "public arena(s) for the flamboyant triumph of virility, wit, and skill. In short, of style."[12]

The line that most captured the liberal imagination was this one:

> [B]reaking isn't just an urgent response to pulsating music. It is also a ritual combat that transmutes aggression into art. "In the summer of '78," Tee [of the High Times Crew] remembers, "when you got mad at someone, instead of saying, 'Hey man, you want to fight?' you'd say, 'Hey man, you want to rock?' "

Rocking instead of fighting—the idea would become one of the most enduring myths of hip-hop—but history would once again belie it.

Many around town seemed to be talking about the "Graffiti Rock" event, including Rock Steady's envious rivals. The afternoon before the show, Chalfant had gathered everyone for a dress rehearsal at the Common Ground. They were interrupted by a Dominican crew from Washington Heights. "We had a war with this crew called the Ball Busters back then 'cause we were Zulus," says DOZE. Afrika Bambaataa remembered the beef as one "between Puerto Ricans and Dominicans." Chalfant says that he later pieced together that the beef had begun in a violent dispute over graffiti turf between affiliates of the Rock Steady Crew and the Ball Busters, and that it had likely spilled over along ethnic lines. Whatever the case, this wasn't something that would be settled with a rhythm and a dance.

The Ball Busters walked into the Common Ground loft, and while a number of white downtowners looked on, the words began to fly. Someone shouted that there was a gun, RAMMELLZEE and his DJ crew pulled out machetes, Chalfant called the police, and the Ballbusters chased a Rock Steady-affiliated graffiti writer out of the loft toward the subway station.

The next day, one of Chalfant's graf-writing friends called him and said, "We've got it all worked out. We've got a lot of back. We've got shotguns in the car. We've got a nine millimeter for you. The Salsoul Brothers are gonna come and police it." But when large crowds, including many of the East Village art and nightclub elite, gathered to see the show that afternoon, Chalfant stood at the door to send them away. The violence had caused the Common Ground's owner to pull the plug.

The Folkies

Hip-hop's future was still unclear. It might be a folk art, a cultural expression whose authenticity needed to be preserved. Or it might be a youth uprising, a scream against invisibility that wanted nothing more than to be heard by the world.

One future offered a nicely trimmed path to folk art museums and cultural institutions that might nurture hip-hop in a small safe world. The other was a bumpy, twisting road, which might lead to cultural, economic and social significance, but also to co-optation, backlash and censure. Hip-hop's downtown advocates, especially the older ones, understood the tensions. They favored authenticity over exploitation, and they vacillated between being protective of the culture and championing it.

Cooper and Banes made presentations at folk-culture and academic conferences, met with corporate event planners and civic arts programmers, and pitched stories to magazines like *The Smithsonian* and *National Geographic World*. Cooper recalls that her folklorist peers were "genuinely excited and enthusiastic." But they also had their limits. Cooper and Banes attended one mind-numbing meeting with a city-funded arts group interested in doing a film series on forms of New York City street dance. After much struggle, the group accomplished nothing other than arrive at this yawner of a definition: "Street dance is nontheatrical participatory dance in environments available to the public."[13] Predictably, the project fizzled. Meanwhile, the file of rejection letters from magazine and book editors got fatter.

Cooper arranged for the Rock Steady to perform at the High Bridge Library. The librarians produced a crude stick-figured flyer for "BREAKING, RAPPING & GRAFFITI, an original blend of dancing, acrobatics and martial arts," and appended a special note at the bottom: "Young adults especially invited." Then Chalfant landed a summer show for the Rock Steady Crew in the plaza of the Lincoln Center. This time, DOZE drew a graf-style flyer depicting a ski-goggled, big afroed b-boy smirking and saying, "Breaking or otherwise known as (B-Boy) is a competitive warlike dance, making the opponent look bad." The news media, including ABC's 20/20 news-magazine show, came out in droves.

Chalfant had coordinated and filmed a battle between Rock Steady and the Dynamic Breakers at the United States of America roller rink in Queens earlier in the year.[14] He wanted to restage that battle. "I thought that would really be authentic," he says. "What I hadn't banked on was that the crews would bring all their neighborhood."

The Rock Steady Crew rolled out thick, their people from all the boroughs representing fresh and bold in light grey jumpsuits. Their Queens rivals, the Dynamic Rockers, came out just as deep in beige and maroon athletic suits. The plaza was transformed into a massive cipher. A small raised stage was placed at the center and covered with kitchen floor linoleum. Hundreds of seats were set up around it. As the battle intensified, the circle enclosed and most of the audience could no longer see the action. The crowd drifted away.

But as the temperatures rose, so did a few tempers, and the battle deteriorated into small fights. Just as the USA battle had ended, so did this one—with a lot of riffing and posturing about who actually won. "And it ended in a kind of mini-wilding spree," Chalfant adds. "A few hot-dog stands were kicked over, and on the train that I got onto, the Broadway local, somebody punched out a window."

To say that Rock Steady's biggest shows had been a little rough around the edges was an understatement. But Chalfant possessed a sense of humor and no small feeling of responsibility for them. Despite his misgivings about his abilities, he gallantly labored on as their manager. "I was the only one who was kind of like an adult with connections," he says.

"I was a terrible manager in terms of finding gigs," he says, smiling and shaking his head. "I got things like the Clearwater Festival, a Pete Seeger thing on the Hudson River in Croton-on-Hudson, which was complete culture clash for everyone. I had a Volkswagen van and we all piled in and we went up. There were all these nice little people. There was somebody trying to do sign language for RAMMELLZEE's rap, Rock Steady looking at the vegetarian food and going, 'Eccccccch!' It was a big, big culture clash!"

He adds, "I know we tried to get something done with commercials—McDonald's and others. We'd put together a package, like, 'Here's this amazing dance group!' And—nothing."

Chalfant's business relationship with Rock Steady would not last much longer. Perhaps the artist in him objected to wringing commerce from the culture, or perhaps he was too old and settled to have the hunger for it. "Crazy Legs and I have often talked about it. 'Henry, you should have been our manager,'" Chalfant says with a twinge of sadness, "but I wasn't good enough, or really aggressive."

When hip-hop finally broke through two years later, its global demand blindsided Chalfant, Banes and Cooper. "Graffiti became huge internationally and I wasn't prepared for that. I never thought that would happen," Chalfant says. Within a year and a half, Banes and Cooper had to retool their pitches to discuss how b-boying "had drastically changed from a folk art form to the hottest entertainment of New York's nightlife ... sparking world-wide interest in hip-hop style."[15] In their book proposal, they promised to discuss why graffiti, rapping, and b-boying is "not taken seriously because it diverges drastically from the 'proper' Euro-American high culture our educational system imposes."[16] So the rejection letters continued to pile up. The three were still struggling to try to present the youth movements as purely as they had first encountered them.

Separately, Chalfant and Cooper had been shopping graffiti books to no avail. They teamed together and suffered two more years of rejections from New York publishing houses. They were told that Norman Mailer's 1974 book *The Faith* of *Graffiti* was the last word on the subject. Chalfant says, "The other reason, truly, was that they were scared, and they were afraid that they'd get hell."

Their book, *Subway Art*, was finally accepted and published in 1984 by a London-based house, Thames and Hudson. The book brought the energy of the Writer's Bench and Chalfant's studio into the world, and became a style canon and study-guide for the third, now global generation of aerosolists. Subway *Art* went on to sell more than 200,000 copies.

With American and British public television, foundation and government arts grants and even support from Nathan Glazer, though not a penny from the William Bennett-run National Endowment for the Humanities, Chalfant and documentary filmmaker Tony Silver put together the classic hip-hop movie *Style Wars*. Shot between 1981 and 1983, it captured the youth movements in a moment of high flux as they stood on the brink of becoming a generation's global culture.

The movie had begun as a short on b-boying, but when Chalfant and Silver ran out of money,

Rock Steady blew up on the downtown scene and were no longer available. So after hearing Kathy Chalfant describe the drama Henry was living through with his graffiti-writing friends—it was an aria, he later said—Silver shifted the focus to graffiti. He was convinced that they had a Wagnerian opera on their hands: Here was a street art poised on becoming a legitimate art-form; but first it would have to get through Mayor Koch, MTA chief Richard Ravitch and a snarling graf writer named CAP ONE. *Style Wars* stands as a landmark achievement for hip-hop film, the seminal documentary of graffiti and b-boying.

All these works now evoke an era of Apollonian innocence. But at the time, the downtowners felt they had backed into an ideological wasp's nest. The movie had a successful run on PBS stations across the country, proving especially popular in West Coast markets like Seattle and the San Francisco Bay Area. But after a single showing on the PBS outlet in New York, it never returned. The documentary's sympathetic portrayal of graf artists was deemed irresponsible.

When Silver and Chalfant began screening *Style Wars* for audiences around the country, many people their age thought the two should have known better. Even some liberals who had survived the '60s with their long-hair values intact were upset. Chalfant wrote, "The audience at any showing of *Style Wars* attended by Tony or me always raises the same questions: in one, angry citizens berate us for encouraging vandalism everywhere, and in the other, the purists ask if we regret being part of a process that has destroyed urban folk culture."[17]

World's Famous

For Malcolm McLaren, all these earnest folkies were only worthy of being pranked. Authenticity was a bad word, exploitation was not.

McLaren was a carrot-topped London art student energized by the Parisian spirit of '68, who then embarked on a career of anarchic fun-making. By 1977, with an eye on the Big Idea and a gift for self-promotion, he had succeeded like no other Situationist before him, dropping the Sex Pistols on quaint old England like a blitz bomb. After the spectacular collapse of the Sex Pistols and the post-colonial pop candy of Bow Wow Wow, McLaren's first "serious" project was a sendup of global folk dances called *Duck Rock*.

For the project, McLaren positioned himself as a sort of arch-browed, postmodern Alan Lomax. He would go around the world collecting ethnic dance music on a little tape recorder and brand it all with his general dadaist nonsense. "I think it's gonna be the biggest thing that ever happened. I think it's gonna be the most truthful," he boasted to one journalist. "And I think it's gonna create an awareness that will bring together whatever they're doing in El Salvador or Peru with whatever they're doing in Zululand or Appalachia."[18]

McLaren had realized the future was in global rhythms, what marketers would later call "world beat." He owed this new worldview to Afrika Bambaataa. Arriving in New York City the same summer as The Clash, McLaren met Michael Holman, a downtown club promoter and one of Rock Steady Crew's new managers, who took him up to Bronx River Community Center for a Zulu Nation throwdown. Hip-hop was pastiche, bricolage. It was worldly wise and you could dance to it. Best of all, it was dangerous.

McLaren later admitted he was scared out of his wits. At the end of the night, when a fight broke out and the entourage was hustled to a back wall as the fists and knives flew, all of his stereotypes were confirmed, and, typically, he had come up with a plan for how to exploit them. He began by asking Bambaataa, the Soul Sonic Force and the Rock Steady Crew to open Bow Wow Wow's downtown show at the Ritz. Then, he made plans to visit the Zulu townships of South Africa.

Back in London, his partner, Vivienne Westwood, matched McLaren's musical ambition with a line of "ethnic hobo" clothing, a style that made its models look like raccoons wearing shopping bags. McLaren's young associate in New York, Ruza Blue, opened a nightclub called

Negril in the East Village where she booked the Zulu Nation DJs and the Rock Steady Crew. McLaren returned to recruit a DJ crew to front the project, and after lots of heads turned him down, the World's Famous Supreme Team, a two-man crew of Five Percenters named Just Allah the Superstar and Cee Divine the Mastermind who had a rowdy, popular late-night show at WHBI, finally agreed.

In the fall of 1982, he unleashed a stunning little single called "Buffalo Gals." McLaren's collaborator Trevor Horn tried to replicate the feel of Bam's funky breaks, using brand-new sampling technology to add on Supreme Team show call-ins, township jive groans, Just Allah's rap, and McLaren's interpretation of the old "hilltopper" song. The video, shot in the middle of the freaky Greenwich Village Halloween parade, featured the Rock Steady Crew popping and breaking, Dondi White painting a graf piece and Westwood's models going round the outside and looking like hobos. With a video, a radio show, a nightclub, and a clothing line all ready for consumption, McLaren and his team had come up with hip-hop culture's first corporate synergy plan.

The album that followed, *Duck Rock*, was backwards brilliant. Using hip-hop's global vacuum signifier intake as their method, McLaren and Horn brought together popular and religious regional dance music—*merengue, mbaqanga*, mambo, sacred Lukumi drumming, the odd square dance and, of course, hip-hop. The Supreme Team's raucous, hilarious radio call-ins held the whole thing all together. In a sense, a hip-hop worldview allowed McLaren to sum up the "world music" genre a decade before its fixture in the First World pop marketplace, and deconstructed it at the same time. In the United States, the record was released by the pioneering "world music" label, Chris Blackwell's Island Records.

The *Duck Rock* video captured scintillating double dutch and township dance performances and gave many outside of New York their first glimpse of graffiti, b-boying, popping, and DJing. In an inspired signifier mashup, McLaren played a British redcoat mock-shocked, upside down, and bleeding to death on a battlefield—the opening scene of *Zulu* redux. As a *shebeen*-styled guitar beat unfurled, the scene cut to township dancers kicking up dust while wearing Rock Steady-style cotton tees emblazoned with iron-on letters that read, ZULUS ON A TIME BOMB.

McLaren told journalists that in darkest South Africa he had regaled the Zulus with tales of the Sex Pistols, which inspired them to pen some of *Duck Rock*'s songs. But this was just his crude imperialist fantasy. In fact, far from being "folk" songs he'd discovered in a distant village, the township jive and merengue songs had been local pop hits in the '70s, replayed note-for-note by pick-up bands in Johannesburg and New York City. Their inspirations—such as the "Indestructible Beat" of South African guitarist and composer Marks Mankwane, his legendary Makgona Tsohle Band, and the groaner, Mahlathini, and vocal group, the Mahotella Queens—went unacknowledged and uncredited. A flood of lawsuits would follow. Perhaps it was perfectly hip-hop.

On the other hand, McLaren's self-serving pomo-imperialist-as-new-rock-star mythology was annoying. The longform video shredded context, running b-roll of Brazilian carnival over Dominican merengue, even as McLaren gave goofy, lyrical shouts to rock-n-roll, calypso, "m-m-m-mambo" and "discago"—*descarga*, that is. Brain-curdling bushman stereotypical images accompanied the sacred batá rhythms. In the same year *Duck Rock* was released, Robert Farris Thompson's book on the diasporic links between African and African-American art and philosophy, *Flash of the Spirit*, came out. Bambaataa had inducted McLaren into the same world of rhythm and soul that Thompson was describing, but McLaren had returned from his journey with less than half the story, and that portion was scrambled.

Duck Rock's liner notes mocked folkie earnestness and anthropological "discovery." Moreover, they seemed to anticipate an academic petrifaction of the hip-hop subject. But the liner notes also revealed McLaren's crassly exploitative desire, the dark underside of his ironic distancing:

The performance by the Supreme Team may require some explaining but suffice it to say, they are d.j.'s from New York City, who have developed a technique using record players like instruments, replacing the power chord of the guitar by the needle of the gramophone, moving it manually backwards and forwards across the surface of the record. We call it 'scratching.'

Despite McLaren's ambitions, *Duck Rock* never became "The Great Hip-Hop Swindle." Instead of McLaren swallowing hip-hop, hip-hop devoured him. He would not fully comprehend the lessons Bambaataa and his followers had taught him until long afterward. By then, he had become a parody of himself, remaking *Duck Rock* in myriad failed ways before finally giving up on a recording career. Years later Bambaataa himself would chuckle at the mention of McLaren's name and dismiss him with two words: "culture vulture."

Now that they were no longer invisible, the young rebels made it clear that they wanted more. FAB 5 FREDDY told a journalist, "I didn't want to be a folk artist, I wanted to be a fine artist. I wanted to be a *famous* artist."[19]

Study Questions

1. What similarities linked the burgeoning uptown hip-hop scene and the downtown art scene in New York in the early 1980s?
2. How were galleries and other art spaces important for early hip-hop artists?
3. What were the commercial implications of putting graffiti/aerosol art on canvases?

Notes

1. "Henry Chalfant: Photographer to the Cars," *East Village Eye* (August 1982), 24.
2. Goldstein, "The Fire Down Below," 58.
3. Michael A. Steargman, *The Dynamics of Rental Housing in New York City* (Piscataway, N.J.: Rutgers University Center for Urban Policy Research, 1982), 51, 54, 147.
4. Richie Perez, "Committee Against Fort Apache: The Bronx Mobilizes Against Multinational Media," in *Cultures in Contention*, ed. Douglas Kahn and Diane Neumaier (Seattle: Real Comet Press, 1985), 195. Photo by Jerry Kearns.
5. See the cover of her 1985 *Island Life* compilation for an idea of what her bowling form might have looked like!
6. Elizabeth Hess, "Graffiti R.I.P.: How The Art World Loved 'Em and Left 'Em," *Village Voice* (December 22, 1987), 41.
7. Michael Small, "When Graffiti Paintings Sell for Thousands, the Art World Sees the Writing on the Wall," *People* (August 22, 1983), 50.
8. Ibid., 52.
9. Michael Hill, "The Clash at the Clampdown," *Village Voice* (June 10–16, 1981), 74.
10. Robert Christgau, "Magnificent Seven," *Village Voice* (November 2, 1982), 59.
11. Sally Banes, "To the Beat Y'all: Breaking Is Hard to Do," *Village Voice* (April 22–28, 1981), 31.
12. Ibid.
13. From the notes of Martha Cooper.
14. This is the battle scene featured in *Style Wars*.
15. From an article proposal by Sally Banes and Martha Cooper, "Breaking: From the Bronx to Shinjuku" (undated, probably 1983); from the files of Martha Cooper. (Note: They eventually did get a piece in *Folklife Annual* [1986], 8–21.)
16. From a book proposal by Sally Banes and Martha Cooper, "Rapping, Writing and Rocking: Street Style in New York" (undated, probably 1983); from the files of Martha Cooper.
17. Henry Chalfant, "Making Style Wars," *SVA Newsletter* (Spring 1987), 16.
18. Lloyd Sachs. "A Hard Sell; Malcolm McLaren's Square Dancing Music," *Playboy* (October 1983).
19. Susan Orlean, "Profiles: Living Large," *New Yorker* (June 17, 1991), 44.

Appendix

Word

Banes, Sally. "To the Beat Y'all: Breaking Is Hard to Do." In *The Village* Voice. April 22–28, 1981. Also available in *And It Don't Stop: The Best American Hip-Hop Journalism of the Last 25 Years*, edited by Raquel Cepeda. New York: Faber & Faber, 2004.
———. "Breakdancing: A Reporter's Story." In *Folklife Annual*. 1986. Includes photos by Martha Cooper.
Bromberg, Craig. *The Wicked Ways of Malcolm McLaren*. New York: HarperCollins, 1989.
Coming from the Subway: New York Graffiti Art. France: VBI, 1992.
Cooper, Martha, with interviews by Akim Walta. *The Hip-Hop Files: Photographs 1979–1984*. Germany: From Here to Fame, 2004.
Goldstein, Richard. "The Fire Down Below." In *The Village Voice*. December 24–28, 1980.
Hess, Elizabeth. "Graffiti R.I.P.: How The Art World Loved 'Em and Left 'Em." In *The Village Voice*. December 22, 1987.
New York Graffiti @ 149 St. website http://www.@149st.com
Witten, Andrew ZEPHYR, and Michael White. *Dondi White Style Master General*. New York: Regan Books, 2001.
Zephyr Graffiti website, http://www.zephyrgraffiti.com

Image

Downtown 81. DVD. Edo Bertoglio, director. Patrick Montgomery and Glen O'Brien, co-producers. Originally released 1981.
Duck Rock. VHS. Malcolm McLaren, producer and director, 1983.
Style Wars. Tony Silver, director. Tony Silver and Henry Chalfant, producers, 1983.
Westway to the World. DVD. Don Lefts, director, 2001. Includes "Clash on Broadway" filmed in 1981.

Sound

The Clash. *The Clash*. LP. U.S. Version. Epic, 1979.
———. *Sandinista!* 3-LP. Epic, 1981.
ESG. *A South Bronx Story*. 2-LP. Soul Jazz, 2000.
"Live Convention '81." 12-inch single. Disco Wax, 1981.
"Live Convention '82." 12-inch single. Disco Wax, 1982.
Malcolm McLaren. *Duck Rock*. LP. Island, 1983.
Soweto Never Sleeps. LP. Shanachie, 1986.

3

B-Beats Bombarding Bronx: Mobile DJ Starts Something With Older R&B Disks *and* Jive Talking N.Y. DJs Rapping Away in Black Discos

In two brief articles that were among the first reports on hip-hop in the music industry's primary trade magazine *Billboard*, Robert "Rocky" Ford, Jr. provides first-person accounts of the nascent DJ scene in the Bronx. The location and character of DJ and MC parties, as well as record stores selling the recorded material underlying the DJ's work, are locally situated and Ford's reports reinforce the fact that, in 1978–79, there already existed a vibrant cultural infrastructure encompassing nightclubs, independent record retail outlets, and audiences.

Ford's articles served notice to the music industry that DJ and MC practices were thriving in New York's upper boroughs and although it took almost another five years for the major entertainment conglomerates to acknowledge hip-hop's cultural legitimacy and importance, black entrepreneurs in the Bronx, Harlem, Queens, and elsewhere nurtured an active scene. Ford's observations reflect the extent to which hip-hop was already part of an entertainment and leisure economy and was, thus, a commercially-oriented phenomenon almost from the start. It is also interesting to note how the early MCs did not yet envision rapping as an end in itself but as a bridge to future endeavors in the broadcasting industry.

B-Beats Bombarding Bronx: Mobile DJ Starts Something With Older R&B Disks* *and* Jive Talking N.Y. DJs Rapping Away in Black Discos**

Robert Ford, Jr.

NEW YORK—A funny thing has been happening at Downstairs Records here.

The store, which is the city's leading disco product retailer, has been getting calls for obscure r&b cutouts such as Dennis Coffy's "Son of Scorpio," on Sussex, Jeannie Reynolds' "Fruit Song" on Casablanca, and the Incredible Bongo Band's "Bongo Rock" on Pride.

The requests, for the most part, come from young black disco DJs from the Bronx who are buying the records just to play the 30 seconds or so of rhythm breaks that each disk contains.

The demand for these records, which the kids call B-beats, has gotten so great that Downstairs has had to hire a young Bronxite, Elroy Meighan, to handle it.

According to Meighan the man responsible for this strange phenomenon is a 26-year old mobile DJ who is known in the Bronx as Kool Herc. It seems Herc rose to popularity by playing long sets of assorted rhythm breaks strung together.

Other Bronx DJs have picked up the practice and now B-beats are the rage all over the borough, and the practice is spreading rapidly.

Herc, who has been spinning for five years, says that his unique playing style grew from his fascination with one record, "Bongo Rock." "The tune has a really great rhythm break but it was too short so I had to look for other things to put with it," Herc relates.

Since Herc was not completely satisfied with the new disco product coming out at the time, he started looking in cutout bins for tunes with good rhythm breaks.

Herc's intensive searching for tunes has now even come up with a new remake of "Bongo Rock." The '73 tune has been covered by a group called the Arawak All-Stars on an apparently Jamaican-based label, Arswal Records.

Herc has also found that some of the rhythm breaks get better response when they are played at a faster speed. Herc plays tunes such as the Jeannie Reynolds record at 45 rather than the $33^1/_3$ at which it was recorded.

Herc thinks the popularity of B-beats stems from the kids' dissatisfaction with much of today's disco product. "On most records, people have to wait through a lot of strings and singing to get to the good part of the record," Herc believes. "But I give it to them all up front."

Herc hopes that some day he will be able to produce an entire B-beat album featuring "Bongo Rock" and other obscure numbers. Till then he plans to keep packing them in at the clubs and dances he works in the Bronx.

*From *Billboard*, July 1, 1978, p. 65.
**From *Billboard*, May 5, 1979, p. 3.

NEW YORK—Rapping DJs reminiscent of early r&b radio jocks such as Jocko and Dr. Jive are making an impressive comeback here—not in radio but in black discos where a jivey rap commands as much attention as the hottest new disk.

Young DJs like Eddie Cheeba, DJ Hollywood, DJ Starski, and Kurtis Blow are attracting followings with their slick raps. All promote themselves with these snappy show business names.

Many black disco promoters now use the rapping DJs to attract young fans to one-shot promotions, and a combination of the more popular names have filled this city's largest hotel ballrooms.

The young man credited with reviving the rapping habit in this area is DJ Hollywood, who started gabbing along with records a few years ago while working his way through school as a disco DJ.

Hollywood is now so popular that he has played the Apollo with billing as a support act. It is not uncommon to hear Hollywood's voice coming from one of the countless portable tape players carried through the city's streets. Tapes of Hollywood's raps are considered valuable commodities by young blacks here.

A close friend and disciple of Hollywood's, Eddie Cheeba, has been working as a mobile jock for five years and talking over the records for the last two. He now travels with an entire show, which includes seven female dancers and another DJ, Easy Gee, who does most of the actual spinning. Cheeba and his Cheeba Crew are now booked two months in advance.

Cheeba says the rapping craze grew out of a need for something more than records.

"These people go to discos every week and they need more than music to motivate them," Cheeba observes. "I not only play records, but I rap to them and they answer me."

Though they often work before crowds in the thousands, Cheeba and most of the popular rapping DJs do not get records from labels or from pools. Most of them buy their own product and do so without complaining.

As DJ Starski puts it, "Most of the records the labels send us won't go up there anyway, so I'd rather buy what I want."

Starski is one of the most popular DJs with high school and college age blacks in the Bronx and Manhattan. He has played almost every major black club and ballroom in the area. He generally works with Cool DJ AJ, who does not rap but is a master of B-beats. B-Beats are series of short rhythm breaks strung together to sound like one song.

Starski is proud of his ability to excite a crowd with his rapping. "It's a beautiful thing to see a dance floor full of people dancing to your music and answering your rap," Starski says.

Kurtis Blow, the most popular rapping DJ in Queens, hopes disco will be a springboard into broadcasting for him. Blow, a student at CCNY, has been working about a year and got his first break at the now defunct Small's Paradise. Blow built a following at Small's and is now booked solid for weeks.

Cheeba already had a shot at radio during a fill-in run last summer at Fordham's WFUV-FM.

Study Questions

1. What is the relationship between early hip-hip and disco?
2. What role did local record retail outlets play in early hip-hop?
3. In what particular ways was rap commercialized in its emergent phase?

4

Hip-Hop's Founding Fathers
Speak the Truth

The Nelson George interview with three of rap music's originators—Afrika Bambaataa, Kool DJ Herc, and Grandmaster Flash—presents a reflective look at the atmosphere within which hip-hop evolved while detailing the competitive nature of their relations within localized commercial market conditions. George, who for over twenty-five years has provided astute journalistic and cultural analysis of hip-hop, elicits descriptions of urban social change, technological issues, and aesthetic innovation from hip-hop's "founding fathers" and, through their words, it is evident that the early hip-hop scene was a fragmented amalgamation of practices, interests, and objectives.

Rap is a highly appropriative music, borrowing inventively from myriad sources in the creation of new sonic forms. Moreover, rap music relies on the appropriation and rechanneling of music technologies, especially the turntable, mixer, and vinyl record which, in the hands of DJ trailblazers, were invested with new meanings and applications. Describing the merging of electronic technologies with new lyrical styles and stage craft, George offers a valuable profile of early hip-hop performance and the formation of what are today acknowledged as established hip-hop conventions. In this interview, one of the more resonant features is the emphasis on family and community as nurturing forces that provide an essential foundation for the work and play among hip-hop's first professional DJs.

Hip-Hop's Founding Fathers Speak the Truth

Nelson George

Kool DJ Herc. Afrika Bambaataa. Grandmaster Flash. Old School, you say? Hell, these three are the founding fathers of hip-hop music—the progenitors of the world's dominant youth culture. For them, hip-hop is not a record, a concert, a style of dress or a slang phrase. It is the constancy of their lives. It defines their past and affects their view of the future. As DJs in the '70s, these three brothers were the nucleus of hip-hop—finding the records, defining the trends, and rocking massive crowds at outdoor and indoor jams in parts of the Bronx and Harlem.

What hip-hop was and has become is the subject of the first collective interview involving Herc, Bambaataa and Flash—the first time, in fact, that Herc has spoken on record in over ten years. One late summer evening they sat together, first in a Broadway photography studio and later at The Source's offices, telling stories, laughing at old rivalries and setting history straight.

Kool DJ Herc (aka Clive Campbell) used the sound systems of the Caribbean as the model for his mammoth speaker setup. But the sensibility that led him to scout for obscure records and mesh beats from blaxploitation soundtracks with Caribbean dance hits, soul grooves and novelty records was born of the hectic world that was the Bronx during the Carter administration. Hip-hop's sonic montage was conceived by him in city parks and school yards, where crowds flocked to hear him play, grooving to the beats he unearthed. Fact is, there were no B-boys until Herc labeled them so.

If Kool Herc is the base, then Bambaataa and Flash are twin pillars who complemented and extended the original vision. Bam came through New York's early '70s gang banging era unharmed but wiser. Seized by an enormous musical curiosity and a communal vision of African-American empowerment, he founded the Zulu Nation, the single most enduring institution in hip-hop. While labels and clubs have come and gone, the Zulu Nation emerged from the Bronx River Community Center into a collective with adherents around the world. At its center all these years is Bambaataa, who found musical inspiration in rock, Third World music and, most crucially, the electronic instrumentation that would support his breakthrough group, the Soul Sonic Force.

Grandmaster Flash (Joseph Saddler) was a teenager fascinated by records and audio circuitry. Aside from having a wide musical interest, Flash became intrigued with the possibilities the technology surrounding music suggested for innovation. The concept of scratching—now the backbone of hip-hop DJing—came out of his laboratory (with an assist from his friend Grand Wizard Theodore). Flash's introduction of the "beat box" turned DJs from beat mixers to beat makers. And the building blocks of rapping as we know it were laid by the crew that gathered around Flash—initially, Kid Creole, his brother Melle Mel and the late Cowboy.

The conversation that evening was wide ranging, including issues of historical detail and philosophy. Who was the first to scratch a record? Was DJ Hollywood the first hip-hop rapper? What was the relationship between break dancing and rapping? Who first played "Apache"? These and other often-debated questions are addressed by the people who were in the eye of the cultural hurricane.

In a broader sense, Herc, Bambaataa and Flash talk at length about the all-embracing musical curiosity that inspired hip-hop's creation and how debates about "hardcore" and "sell-out" records run contrary to the scene's roots. The wholesale dissing of women, the increasing violence between rival rap posses and the control of rap's manufacture by major corporations troubles them. The camaraderie of these rivals-turned-griots, the good humor in their remembrances and the vivid descriptions of epic park parties are a powerful contrast to the Black-on-Black crime that scars much contemporary hip-hop.

Because of their shared affection and respect, this conversation is not mere nostalgia—it is a testament to why mutual respect is integral to hip-hop's future.

AFRIKA BAMBAATAA: Most people today, they can't even define in words, hip-hop. They don't know the whole culture behind it.

GRANDMASTER FLASH: You know what bugs me, they put hip-hop with graffiti. How do they intertwine? Graffiti is one thing that is art, and music is another.

KOOL DJ HERC: I was into graffiti. That's where Kool Herc came from.

THE SOURCE: Were people doing tags and shit when you were playin'?

BAM: No, they did tags on the wall. See before the whole word hip-hop, graffiti was there before that. But really when the Zulu Nation pulled the whole thing together and we laid down the whole picture. You know, the graffiti and the breakdancers.

HERC: That's where the graffiti artists were congregating at. Going to the Factory West, or going to the Sand Pad, or going down to the Nell Guen on 42nd Street, or going to the Puzzle up there on 167th street, or to the Tunnel. That's where the graffiti guys used to hang out. That's how hip-hop came a long way.

BAM: It was there with the street gang movement. The gangs would've started dying down, but you still had the graffiti crews coming up into the hip-hop culture. Once everything started coming into place, we started doing shows and traveling into different boroughs. Then we started traveling to different states and that's when we threw everything together.

HERC: And the thing about graffiti was, I was the guy with the art. I liked graffiti flyers. My graffiti friend used to do my flyers.

BAM: Sometimes we didn't need flyers, we just say where we gonna be and that's where we at.

HERC: Block party, we gonna be over there, be there! That was it.

FLASH: Or what might happen is, if I'm playin', I'll say "Herc's givin' a party tomorrow in the street," or if Bam's playin', Bam will say, "Flash will be here."

THE SOURCE: Ok, how does breakdancing, or breaking fit into all that?

FLASH: It was basically a way of expressing how the music sounds. Early breakdancing you hardly ever touched the floor. I would say, maybe this is a bad comparison, but it was more like a Fred Astairish type of thing—stylin', the hat, you know, touchin', white laces, finesse, that's where the two intertwined. It was like just one particular couple would draw a crazy crowd in the street. Stylin', nothing sweaty, they wouldn't break a sweat. Just fly. Like Eldorado, like Mike, Sasa, Nigger Twins, Sister Boo.

BAM: You had Mr. Rock, the Zulu Queens, the Zulu Kings.

THE SOURCE: So when did it get involved with guys getting' on the floor?

BAM: Well the first form of breakdancing started with the street gangs with a dance called "Get on the Good Foot" by James Brown. There were a lot of women who was really into the breakdancing too that would tear the guys up in the early stages. But then it all came together.

HERC: They started to bet money.

BAM: The first era lasted for a while then it died down. And then the second generation came.

HERC: The Puerto Ricans carried breakdancing.

FLASH: They took it to the next level for sure.

HERC: They carried all forms of hip-hop music with dancing.

FLASH: It died for a while then it came back and it was this new acrobatic, gymnastic type of style.

BAM: And really with some of them, they had been doing this since '77 and it never really died with them. Especially with the Rock Steady Crew, the New York City Breakers, and a couple of those crews.

THE SOURCE: OK, the phrase B-boy. What does that mean to you?

HERC: The boys that break. When somebody go off in the neighborhood, "Yo, I'm ready to break on somebody," so we just say B-boys, you know, breakers.

THE SOURCE: So it doesn't necessarily mean, he's a dancer? It's an attitude or somebody who does something?

FLASH: You don't have to be a dancer!

HERC: B-boys, these are the boys, these are the boys that break. So we call 'em B-boys.

THE SOURCE: Let me ask you, is there a time where you remember the whole style of the hat sideways attitude coming in? Where you said this is a new style as opposed to what had gone before? Is there a point where you said, "Oh he's a B-boy. This is new."

FLASH: I think when actually dancers started making contact, like doing jump kicks and kicking people on the floor, that's when the hat started going like this [Flash turns his hat sideways]. It was like, "I ain't dancing with you, I'm gonna try to hurt you." That's when the hat went to the side.

BAM: With some of them, they did hurt some. Some people got hurt. When they danced against each other, or especially if they had different crews. All through the time there was a struggle. You had your peaceful moments and you had your straight-up battles.

HERC: After a while guys would start to say, "Well you gonna have to pay to see me dance." Or, "If you want to take me out or discredit me you have to put some money up."

THE SOURCE: Like Basketball. What were the records that made them do that?

ALL: James Brown, "Give It Up, Turn It Loose."

BAM: "Apache" was the national anthem.

HERC: "Just Begun."

FLASH: "Black Heat," remember that one?

BAM: "Family . . . " by Sly and the Family Stone.

THE SOURCE: To find these beats, you would go to Downstairs Records and just find a ton of records?

ALL: No we didn't just go to Downstairs!

FLASH: That was one of Herc's spots.

HERC: That spot to me was where I find shit that wouldn't be nowhere else, or I found something that I could say, "Hey this is good." I'd go to somebody's house and they'd say, "Herc, I know you like records, run through my records. I got a whole lot of stuff there."

FLASH: Or girls' houses for sure. Dope.

HERC: Or going to one of Bam's parties and I hear something and I say, "I could use this with this."

BAM: I took music from around the whole world. I was playin' so much crazy shit, they called me the master of records.

FLASH: He was the man. He was the king of the records.

HERC: When I go to his party, I'm guaranteed to be entertained by some shit I don't hear other people play. Then I step to Mr. Bam, "What's that one?"

THE SOURCE: Tell me five records you might play in a row back in the day?

BAM: Well you would hear something from the Philippines by a group named Please which did a remix for "Sing a Simple Song."

FLASH: You might hear "Fernando" by Bob James, I might play that with a …

HERC: You might hear "Fat Sap from Africa" or "Seven Minutes of Funk." "Babe Ruth."

FLASH: Or how about on the back side of the Incredible Bongo Band, the other one, "Bongolia."

BAM: You could hear "The Return of Planet Rock" by the Incredible Bongo Band. "Sing, Sing, Sing," "Sex" by Bobby Knight.

THE SOURCE: Who was the first person to take the record in the bathtub and wipe the labels off?

FLASH: That was me. People were getting too close, you know. I will give all due respect to my boys right here, but you know, other people.

HERC: He put us on a wild goose chase [everyone laughs].

BAM: I had a way of telling things from the color of the album. I could know if it was Mercury or Polygram. Then I would try to see who it sounded like.

FLASH: Hey Bam, I followed you on a Saturday with glasses on. I seen one bin you went to, pulled the same shit you pulled, took that shit home—and the break wasn't on the mutha-fucka [everyone is hysterical].

BAM: I used to tell people, "Do not follow me and buy what I buy," and I went into a record store and everyone was waitin' around to see what I pulled. So I pulled some Hare Krishna records [everyone laughs]. It had beats but …

FLASH: You couldn't play that bullshit. I got a crate full of bullshit.

HERC: If I go somewhere and I hear something, I give the DJ respect. I don't try to say, "I played it." 'Cause the first time I heard "Seven Minutes of Funk," I was with this girl I used to talk to, and we were at this place called The Point, and it was like a movie. The minute we hit the door, people knew who we were, and we didn't know people knew who we were. All we heard was … [Herc hums the "Seven Minutes of Funk" bassline which was used on EPMD's "It's My Thing"] The further we walk in the party the record was still going. I was like, "That shit is ruff."

THE SOURCE: Who discovered "The Mexican"?

BAM: Herc got "The Mexican."

THE SOURCE: What kind of equipment did you have in the late '70s, early '80s?

FLASH: I had six columns and maybe two bullshit bass bottoms. I didn't have much of a system. I was going to school and I had a messenger job. I also had electronic experience though, so a lot of the stuff I make-shifted. I didn't really hear a real heavy, heavy, heavy system until I heard this man [Herc] out in the park. It was incredible.

THE SOURCE: Where did you get your equipment?

HERC: My old man bought a Sure P.A. system for his band he used to be with. The band fell off and the speakers wound up in my room. My pops was a little strict and told me to not touch 'em. I never did play 'em but another kid in the neighborhood had the same system and played his. So I asked him how to hook up the Sure P.A. to the system. They wouldn't tell me. So I borrowed one of my father's friend's systems 'cause I wouldn't touch the Sure stuff in the house. What they was doing was using one of the channels from the turntables and using the brain itself to power the whole thing. My shit was, I used the pre-amp, used the speakers wires put into a channel, and used the two knobs to mix. I got more sound than they ever got.

THE SOURCE: What kind of turntables were you using?

HERC: At first I started with Gerards [laughs]. Then from there I went downtown and I seen two Technics 1100As and I went and got 'em.

FLASH: They're still the best turntables in the world right now, the 1100A, but you can't find 'em. Because of the tork and the pick-up. You could have the hand the size of a monkey and that thing would still turn. The actual design of that turntable was incredible. I was never able to afford 'em so I had to adjust my touch to cheaper turntables.

THE SOURCE: But the questions is, who started it?

FLASH: There was this family called the Livingstons, OK. There was Gene, Claudio, and this little kid named Theodore. Now, before we actually became Grandmaster Flash and the Furious Five, I kept my equipment at Gene Livingston's house. What he would tell me is because his little brother was so interested was, "Don't let Theodore in the room, don't let Theodore on the turntables!" Now when he went to work, I would tell Theodore to come on in and let me see what you can do. Now, he had an ability to take the needle and drop it and just keep it going. He had such a rhythm that was incredible. I begged Gene for like a year and a half to take this little kid out in the park with us as the team to get larger notoriety. He didn't like the idea of it. After a while this little kid kinda outshined his big brother. So what Theodore did for scratchin' is this—where I had expertise on the back-spin or fakin' the faze, what Theodore would do with a scratch was make it more rhythmical. He had a way of rhythmically taking a scratch and making that shit sound musical. He just took it to another level.

THE SOURCE: People don't appreciate how much technical knowledge went into the creation of music. You had to really study turntables and speakers and the entire thing.

FLASH: Break-up plenty of equipment to get what it was.

THE SOURCE: So you had to custom-make everything.

FLASH: I had to custom-make my cue system also. I couldn't afford a mixer with a built-in cue system where you could hear turntable one or two in advance. I had to actually get a single pole–double throw switch, crazy glue it to the top of my mixer, build an external mix on the outside just strong enough to drive a headphone, so when you clicked it over you would hear the other turntable in advance. But this whole idea of hearing the cut ahead of time took three years to come into being.

THE SOURCE: How did you create the beat box?

FLASH: For some reason the world seems to think the beat box is something you do with your mouth. The beat box was an attempt to come up with something other than the techniques I created on the turntables to please the crowd. There was this drummer who lived in the Jackson projects who had this manually operated drum box he used to practice his fingering. I begged him to sell it to me. Then I found a way to wire it into my system and called it the beat box. The drummer taught me how to use it. When my partner Disco Bee would shut the music off, I would segue into it, so you couldn't tell where the music stopped and I started.

THE SOURCE: Bam, where do you trace your interest in music to?

BAM: I'll give credit to my mother. When I was growing up in the '60s, I used to hear a lot of the Motown sounds, James Brown sounds, the Stax sounds, Isaac Hayes and all of them. As well as Edith Piaf, Barbra Streisand, the Beatles, the Who, Led Zeppelin. From there I started knowing about a lot of different music and that's when I first heard African music from Miriam Makeeba. I was listening to this sister talk about things about South Africa which I didn't really understand at the time. One movie that grabbed my attention was this movie called Zulu. At the time when you were seeing Black people on TV, you would see us in degrading roles. So to see this movie with Black people fighting for their land was a big inspiration for me. Then here comes this guy that I used to not like at first, I though he was weird and crazy, which was Sly Stone. But once I heard "Sing a Simple Song," "People," and "Stand," I switched totally to this sound of funk. Then I seen the whole Motown start changing. The Temptations started getting psychedelic. I was a gang member by that time. From '69 to about '75 I was in the Black Spades but, like a lot of these young great Black musicians, I was a visionary. I said to myself, "When I get older, I'ma have me a Zulu Nation." I just waited for the right time.

THE SOURCE: You went from gangs to doing parties—how did you make that transition to being a DJ?

BAM: Well before Flash, Herc, all of us, there was Disco DJs happening in the areas. Flowers, Kool DJ Jones, Lovebug Starski, and Kool DJ Dee. Those were who I follow at one time. Then you started hearing the sound that was coming from my brother Kool DJ Herc. Then when I came out with my system, Herc was like an angel looking over me. Then when I changed over to giving my big party, I didn't have to worry about having it packed 'cause I was in control of all the gangs out there anyway. So when I changed over and brought everybody from the street gangs into the Zulu Nation, when I gave the first big function, everyone knew who I was and backed me up.

THE SOURCE: People have always speculated that the rise of hip-hop caused the gangs to disappear in New York or changed them over. What would you say the relationship was to the rise of hip-hop parties to the gangs of New York?

BAM: Well, I would say the women were more important. The women got tired of the gang shit. So brothers eventually started sliding slowly out of that 'cause they had people that got killed. Cops were breakin' down on people. The cops actually had a secret organization called the "purple mothers" that were ex-Vietnam veterans that would roll on gang members. There was a lot of crazy shit going on in the struggle of the gangs and the transition from the gangs dying down and the women putting their foot down. Drugs helped destroy the gangs too. Now one thing people must know, that when we say Black we mean all our Puerto Rican or Dominican brothers. Wherever the hip-hop was and the Blacks was, the Latinos and the Puerto Ricans was, too.

THE SOURCE: What do you think now when people say that there's a certain style of music that's considered hip-hop, and a certain style that's not considered hip-hop? Claims that some records are fake hip-hop records and some are real?

BAM: They're ignorant. They don't know the true forms of hip-hop. Just like I tell 'em, you got all styles of hip-hop, you gotta take hip-hop for what it is. You got your hard beats, you got your gangsta rap, you got your electro-funk sound which came from the party rock sound, you got your Miami bass, you got the go-go from DC. We was playin' go-go years ago. If you really with Teddy Riley, he came to Bronx River parties and heard go-go music and just flipped it up and now you got new jack swing. All of this was all part of hip-hop.

FLASH: It's all about different tastes. It could be hard drums like a Billy Squire record. It could be the bass hitting and drums soft like "Seven Minutes of Funk." It could have the hallway echo effect of "Apache."

HERC: We can't let the media define this for us. Someone says it's got hardcore beats and talkin' about bitches sucking dick, that's hardcore. That same person says that Jazzy Jeff & the Fresh Prince are soft, it's not hip-hop. It is hip-hop. It's just another form. It's about experimenting and being open.

BAM: Different generations have lost the true meaning. We were teaching the public when we did parties in the park.

THE SOURCE: Tell me about doing parties in the park.

HERC: See, the park playin' is like playin' for your people. You give them something free. Sometimes it's hot and a lot of the clubs didn't have no air conditioner. So I gave parties out in the park to cool out while summer's there. To play in the park is to give the fans and the people something.

BAM: We'd play for everybody. You'd play certain records that grabbed the old, you played the straight up hip-hop records . . .

FLASH: You can actually experiment 'cause now you have a wider audience coming. You have like mothers and fathers and a wide spread of people. You can actually test your new-found jams to see how they work on the public right then and there. You'll know right then and there if you got something, as soon as you play it.

BAM: We were selling cassettes of our mixes that were really our first albums. We had luxury cabs like OJ and the Godfathers and Touch of Class that would buy our tapes.

FLASH: How it worked was people would call for a car, and if they had a dope Herc tape, or a dope Bam tape, or a dope Flash tape, that particular customer might stay in the cab all day long. So these cab drivers were making extra money and at the same time they were advertising us. Like Bam said, it was like cuttin' an album, but it was on tape.

THE SOURCE: The first hip-hop I ever heard was on a tape that was sold in Brooklyn. I saw it on Fulton Street, and that's first time I realized it was being passed around the city.

BAM: Circulating. If you look at it, everything's repeating itself now. Look at all the DJ tapes now. You have Ron G, Kid Capri, Doo Wop. All these kids are doing the same things we did twenty something years ago. It's like life is returning back to the surface. Just like your hearing a new rebirth of funk. All of the stuff is coming back, like Pumas . . .

FLASH: Bell bottoms, teardrops, the big high-heel shoes.

THE SOURCE: Talking about style, your two groups were both stylistically influenced by funk groups.

BAM: I could tell you about that. A lot of the rappers used to dress regular and then we got more into presenting people with something. You know, when you're payin' five, ten dollars to come in, you want to see people dressed up.

FLASH: You know what, we was like businessmen. In a very simplistic sort of fashion. It was like three corporations and we carefully did things without realizing it.

BAM: We was businessmen at like thirteen, fourteen. Making our own parties. We had payrolls. Picking the venues or the streets or the centers. Dealing with the politics, or deciding whether you needed police. We dealt with so much business at such a young age.

THE SOURCE: One of the things you hear is that battling the essence of hip-hop. But you're saying that that was something that came afterwards. At the root of it was some kind of fellowship.

FLASH: Yeah. Experimental musically, but it was a fellowship.

THE SOURCE: Would guys roll up who were tryin' to make a rep and challenge you one-on-one?

FLASH: You can't take away three or four years of establishment in one night. You can't do that. You'll just be a statistic. Bam, Herc and myself already had a science on how to control our crowd. At that time you definitely had to earn it. Not in days, weeks, months—it took years to get a little bit of respect. Then you had to pass through one of the three of us.

BAM: You couldn't even come in our areas to play or else you dealt with us with respect. We would make sure you couldn't play one of the clubs or even come into the community.

THE SOURCE: I remember a club called 371. This was DJ Hollywood's club. What did you guys think about that whole scene?

BAM: Hollywood, himself, was more like disco oriented.

THE SOURCE: I've heard Hollywood was the first hip-hop rapper.

FLASH: No, the first people I heard talk on the microphone and do it extremely well and entertain the crowd and wasn't talkin' to the beat of the music, was Herc's people. Coke La Rock. He would just talk while Herc was cuttin'.

HERC: Little phrases and words from the neighborhood that we used on the corner is what we would use on the mic. Like we talkin' to a friend of ours out there in the crowd.

BAM: And when they got rhymin' it came from the Furious when they added Melle Mel.

FLASH: It was Cowboy, then it was Kid Creole, and Melle Mel. There were these dancers Debbi and Terri who used to go through the crowds shouting "Ho!" and people picked up on that. Cowboy came up with a lot of phrases and had a powerful voice that just commanded attention. "Throw your hands in the air!" "Clap to the beat!" "Somebody scream!" all came from Cowboy. Kid Creole and his brother Melle Mel were the first to really flow and have a poetic feel to their rhymes. They were the first rhyme technicians. They were the first to toss a sentence back and forth. Kid would say, "I," Mel would say, "was," Kid would say, "walking," Mel would say, "down." They just tossed sentences like that all day. It was incredible to watch, it was incredible to hear. Along with Coke La Rock with Herc, they were the root. It was Cowboy, Kid Creole and Melle Mel for quite a while before it became the five of us. Like syncopating to the beat of music was incredible. You just didn't get it overnight. You had to play with it, develop it, break things, make mistakes, embarrass yourself. You had to earn it.

THE SOURCE: Is it a real important distinction between Hollywood and what you were doing?

FLASH: He did come in around the same era. He was there and made a mark. It was just he was a softer side of music. Something we might not play, he would jam and kill it. He was a disco rapper. He'd rap over things like "Love is the Message" which I would never play. Things that were on the radio he'd do for the crowds at after-hours clubs.

THE SOURCE: For a lot of people, Disco Fever was the first place where they heard hip-hop.

ALL: No.

THE SOURCE: OK, then what was that place's significance.

FLASH: There was a lot of clubs between Flash, Bam, and Herc. But the clubs started diminishing slowly but surely. Fatalities were happening there, there, and there. Things got a little bad for everybody. This guy Sal at the Fever resisted at first, but then decided to take a chance on it. What happened was the Fever became a later meeting point for a lot of mobile jocks and new stars at the time. At any given time Camacho would walk in there, Herc would walk in there, Kurtis Blow, Sugarhill Gang, a member of the Commodores. I mean it was like this place was quite well known.

HERC: What the Fever did was give hip-hop a place with disco lights, fly, you could come nice. It had a prime location next to the Concourse. It had a downtown atmosphere uptown.

THE SOURCE: When the Sugar Hill Gang made "Rapper's Delight," hip-hop was now on record. You guys were the founders of this style, yet it was a while before you guys got involved with making records. Did you discuss recording in the mid-'70s?

FLASH: I was approached in '77. A gentleman walked up to me and said, "We can put what you're doing on record." I would have to admit that I was blind. I didn't think that somebody else would want to hear a record re-recorded onto another record with talking on it. I didn't think it would reach the masses like that. I didn't see it. I knew of all the crews that had any sort of juice and power, or that was drawing crowds. So here it is two years later, and I hear "To the hip-hop, to the bang to the boogie," and it's not Bam, Herc, Breakout, AJ. Who is this?

HERC: And when I heard [Big Bank] Hank [of the Sugar Hill Gang], I was like, what? I knew Hank. I didn't really appreciate that Hank knew me personally, had been to my house, was from the neighborhood, and never once said, "Herc, I'm doing something." Never, until this day.

BAM: 'Cause he never gave credit to Grandmaster Casanova Fly, who is called Grandmaster Caz these days from the Cold Crush Brothers, for the rhymes.

THE SOURCE: Now did he literally write them and Hank took them?

HERC: Caz used to come to the Sparkle where Hank was a doorman. He used to get on the mic and Hank heard him. That's when Hank saw the scene growing. I went to New Jersey—my girlfriend knew him—and he was working in a pizza shop down there. I just said, "When Sylvia [Robinson, of Sugar Hill Records] hear the real deal, she gonna know." And I was happy to be in the Fever when she seen the truth. And it was hell with them after that. To see Melle Mel and them on stage.

FLASH: 'Cause the cream of the crop like Caz, The Fantastic Five was in there.

THE SOURCE: Again, you guys did eventually make records. You got with Bobby Robinson who had Enjoy Records in Harlem for years.

FLASH: Yeah we got with Bobby. We was playin' at a club on 125th street. All I know was he made me very nervous 'cause I knew what my age bracket was, and here was this old man who came in at about 11:00, and he stayed to the end of the party. So I said to myself, "Either he's the cops, he's somebody's father looking for his daughter, or something's gonna go down here." So then when we were breaking down the equipment at the end of the night, he stepped me and said, "Flash, do you think it's possible that we can get together and possibly put together a record." You know, I went back to the folks, talked about it, and we did it.

THE SOURCE: How much did he pay you?

FLASH: Maybe a thousand a man. Not bad.

THE SOURCE: Almost all the people who came at this point were still Black though, am I right?

BAM: Record companies, yeah they were still Black.

THE SOURCE: It was still a Black thing in the sense that to find out about it you had to be near the grass roots.

FLASH: These were little record companies that were selling records out the trunk of their car. They were only looking for cream of the crop rappers to do this. At that time, all they wanted was what Sylvia was doing.

THE SOURCE: A lot is going on right now. We're talking about '80, '81. We have the first rap records. The music is starting to spread in terms of your appearances outside of the Bronx. Did you get the sense that it was getting out of control?

FLASH: I wanted to push it.

HERC: I was mad when Sugar Hill came first and did their thing.

BAM: I was the one who was always more independent. I would just sit back and watch to see where things were going before I stepped into it. 'Cause I was watching Flash be successful moving his stuff, I was happy. Then this white guy came down and checked us out named Malcolm MacLaren. And Tom Silverman came down and checked me out in Bronx River with Arthur Baker. First Malcolm MacLaren came, 'cause he said, "There's this Black kid playin' all this rock and other type of music to a Black and Spanish audience." When he seen this, he invited me to come play at the Ritz with Bow Wow Wow. So when I came and did that show, I brought everybody together like Rock Steady and all the groups. That's where I first met them and we all came under the Zulu Nation. There was this guy Michael Holman who used to invite me down to DJ at the Mudd Club, then to Negril with my son Afrika Islam, D.St., Whiz Kid.

Then we used to get too big for that so we went to Danceteria and got too big for that until finally the Roxy became our home. Then Flash and them came and played the Ritz on the Sugar Hill tour with Sequence and the West Street Mob. With the Roxy it became like an international world club. Everyone was coming to the Roxy. Then you had the clubs that didn't want hip-hop nowhere down there like the Limelight. They would make a dress code 'cause there were too many Blacks and Puerto Ricans coming into the neighborhood. That's when I started fighting racism down in the club scene. I would say, "If you don't let my Blacks or Puerto Ricans in, I'm gonna leave." That's when we started gettin' power in the clubs.

THE SOURCE: How did you feel about the whole process of going from having parties to doing records?

FLASH: I'd have to say, I wasn't ready. I was content with what I was doing. I think what happened was when Herc stopped playing eight hours a night. Flash stopped playing, Bam stopped playing, the street thing flipped. Like one DJ would play eight different clubs in one night and not really have an audience anymore. You lost your home champion because there was nobody there. I would have personally like to stay away from records a little longer. Not to say that I wouldn't want to make records 'cause records was the next plateau for spreading the musical word.

BAM: Everyone was nervous. It took the excitement away. We didn't have the parties. Everyone would go out and buy the record.

FLASH: It was a thing to me coming into the place at six and taking two-and-a-half hours to set up the sound system and make sure the EQs were right and the crates were right. It was fun.

BAM: Plus a lot of people in the early records were gettin' robbed. That's something a lot of people don't want to talk about it. A lot of people now who know they can make money have to know what the Old School went through.

FLASH: You know what's really sad to know and see, is that these people have never really seen a block party—like a block party that goes ten or twelve hours. Starting at noon and ending at midnight. I mean you have to really be in a party for hours to watch a DJ expand on what he would play. That would separate the men from the boys as far as the DJ is concerned. The way I see it, the less times he repeats something in a ten hour period, the more qualified he is. That's why we would come up with ten-fifteen crates of records. So we wouldn't have to play anything twice.

THE SOURCE: You all seem to feel there's a sense of community about the hip-hop scene during the party cra that's never really been recaptured.

BAM: Today it gets sickening with the disrespecting of self. To me a lot of brothers and sisters lost knowledge of self. They're losing respect of the "us syndrome" and getting into the "I syndrome." You can't build a nation with an "I" you got to build a nation with a "us." The disrespecting of the Black women—you got some sisters that go into the category "bitches," although you got a lot of the Black women that don't deserve that.

THE SOURCE: I want to get into the whole area of the media and rap's evolution. How do you feel the history rap has been told? Do you think it has been distorted in any way?

FLASH: There are those out there that made a great attempt to accuracy. Then there are those who are just doing it to make a dollar. I think to this point it hasn't been really told. I'm not going to try to toot my own horn, but I think the only ones that can really tell you the story are Herc, Bam, Breakout and myself. Either you can hear his-story or history, and the only way you gonna hear the real historical views on it is by the people who were actually there—who actually took it from nothing and built into whatever it became to be. Some people don't dig deep enough to find out what happened back then. They just fix it so it's comfortable for the reader, which is really dangerous.

BAM: My thing from studying history and listening to great leaders like Elijah, Malcolm, and Minister Farrakhan, I see that everything is planned by design. Even in the industry, nobody talked to the Black and Latino and said, "Do y'all want to get rid of vinyl?" They never had no survey. But the next thing you know vinyl is out the door and CDs are in. I always told people that there was people in the industry that was tryin' to destroy hip-hop. They couldn't do it. That's why Zulu Nation, TC Islam and all of us are pushing a united hip-hop front. Cause you got a lot of people from the Old School who are really mad. Melle Mel, Kurtis Blow, Kevi Kev, a lot of old timers who didn't get their due respect or even the money that they should have made. You got people who are opening the door that are out of there now who ain't paying no mind where the history come from.

THE SOURCE: When you say Old School guys are mad, who owes them? Where did the point come where they were left behind?

BAM: A lot of the companies, a lot of friction happened between the companies. You had companies that was robbing people by not telling them about publishing. Some artists' albums went gold but they didn't give them no money. You know, here's a leased car instead of royalties.

THE SOURCE: Well let me ask you something—who owns hip-hop now?

BAM: White industry.

HERC: Whites.

BAM: The white industry owns it now because they control all the record companies. And all our people that make money worry about Benz's and big houses and fly girls instead of being Black entrepreneurs. You need to take the business back.

THE SOURCE: Herc, you're one of the people that there's a great mystique or mystery about. Tell us about the decisions you made during the period when rap came out on records.

HERC: I was maintained as far as running the sound system and giving parties. The mic was always open for the MCs. My thing was just playin' music and giving parties. I wasn't interested in making no records.

THE SOURCE: What do you most like about hip-hop culture today?

FLASH: Contrary to the media and to the powers that be, hip-hop has a vibe. Under all the crush and blows, being called a fad, it now has its own category and is stronger than ever. I thank God that I'm here to see it. It's quite a compliment to walk down the street and be told, "Flash do you realize you're a legend?" But a lot of times legends die young and don't get to see what they seeded. I'm glad to see it.

THE SOURCE: What about hip-hop culture at this point do you dislike the most?

FLASH: I think that somebody went around and said that in order to cut a hit record, we have to disrespect our brothers, sisters, mothers and children. What people don't realize here is that hip-hop has a large influence on people. What you say maybe just frivolously, somebody can seriously go out and go do. I'm not sayin' that what we're doing is not right, but it shouldn't be the only way that a record is made. Like if you listen to ten records, seven of them is either disrespecting our sisters, or hurting people.

THE SOURCE: Bam, what do you like most about what's going on now?

BAM: I love that hip-hop has become international. I love when I go to France and hear French hip-hop groups. I love when I go to England and hear British hip-hop groups. I love to see hip-hop groups all through Africa. Hip-hop has taken a lot of brothers and sisters who might be doing negative things and have gotten into the rap world to see other people's way of life. Hip-hop has also had a force to unite people together. You have all people of color trying to understand what's happening with the Black problem. Some are getting educated about negative and positive things.

Nelson: Herc, what aspect of hip-hop culture do you like the most?

HERC: That it's still here. It's giving youth a chance to pay for education if they want to. Giving 'em a chance to go overseas. It's here, it ain't going nowhere. Music was always our way of information—it was the drums. They took it away from us in Africa, now we found it again. The music is our fuckin' drums man. All I could say right now as far as rappers out here today is: be true to the game.

Study Questions

1. How was competition a factor among hip-hop's first DJs?
2. What factors or logic guided the selection of records among hip-hop's pioneering DJs?
3. Why was territory an issue for Kool Herc, Afrika Bambaataa, and Grandmaster Flash?

5

Physical Graffiti
The History of Hip-Hop Dance

Jorge "Popmaster Fabel" Pabon writes with the utmost authority on the subject of b-boying. As an early innovator of what he terms "hip-hop dance," Pabon perfected many of what are today standard dance moves and he was ideally situated as a youth in Spanish Harlem to observe hip-hop's explosion. His emphasis on facticity seeks to reposition theory as a valid but secondary factor in the narrativization of hip-hop's formative phase. This is not to undermine the viability of theoretical analysis but, as he argues, theory is reinforced when it is grounded in real-world experience.

Pabon calls attention to the evolution of both b-boying practices and the distinct terminology that facilitated communication of an emergent art form, reminding us about the important local and regional distinctions that influenced hip-hop dance in various enclaves. Here, too, he identifies specific dance moves and their creators, details that are often lost in the retelling of b-boy history. Even as he cautions against the inherent risks that accompany commercial appropriation of the b-boy stance, Pabon celebrates the fact that b-boys and b-girls have, through their commitments to the form, influenced the modern dance world in multiple ways, reconfiguring the physical motion of bodies throughout the world.

Physical Graffiti: The History of Hip-Hop Dance*

Jorge "Popmaster Fabel" Pabon

Preface

As we complete the third decade of what has been termed *hip-hop culture*, much has yet to be explored regarding its roots, history, terminology, and essence. Deciphering theories from facts is a gradual, seeming endless process since many resources are scattered, leaving missing links in the chains of history. Nevertheless, it is safe to say that there are authentic facts, proven by sound testimony and evidence, regarding hip-hop history. These truths, unanimously agreed upon by the pioneers of the culture, should constitute the "hip-hop gospel," whereas the questionable theories should remain as footnotes until proven to be fact.

In order to properly report the history of hip-hop dance forms, one must journey both inside and outside of New York City. Although dance forms associated with hip-hop did develop in New York City, half of them (that is, popping and locking) originated and developed on the West Coast as part of a different cultural movement. Much of the media coverage in the 1980s grouped these dance forms together with New York's native dance forms (b-boying/b-girling and uprocking), labeling them all "breakdancing." As a result, the West Coast "funk" culture and movement were overlooked and underrated as the public ignorantly credited hip-hop as the father of the funk dance forms. This is just one example of misinformation that undermines the intricacies of each dance form, as well as their origins and structure. The intent behind the following piece is to explore the past, present, and future of these dance forms and their contributions to the performing arts worldwide.

Note: The facts in this piece were obtained through conversations with and/or public appearances by Boogaloo Sam, Poppin' Pete, Skeeter Rabbit, Sugar Pop, Don Campbellock, Trac 2, Joe-Joe, King Uprock, DJ Kool Herc, Afrika Bambaataa, and other pioneers. Information was also obtained from various interviews in magazines.

In the early 1970s, the unnamed culture known today as hip-hop was forming in New York City's ghettos. Each element in this culture had its own history and terminology contributing to the development of a cultural movement. The common pulse that gave life to all these elements is rhythm, clearly demonstrated by the beats the DJ selected, the dancers' movements, the MCs' rhyme patterns, and the writer's name or message painted in a flowing, stylized fashion. The culture was identified in the early 1980s when DJ Afrika Bambaataa named the dynamic urban movement "hip-hop." The words *hip-hop* were originally used by MCs as part of a scat style of rhyming; for example: "Hip Hop y'all, and ya don't stop, rock on, till the break of dawn."

*"Physical Graffiti" is dedicated to the legendary Skeeter Rabbit of the Electric Boogaloos. Rest In Peace.

At about the same time, certain slang words also became titles of the dance forms, such as *rockin'* and *breakin'* used generally to describe actions with great intensity. Just as one could rock the mic and rock the dance floor, one could rock a basketball game or rock some fly gear. The term *break* also had more than one use in the '70s. It was often used as a response to an insult or reprimand; for example, "Why are you breakin' on me?" Break was also the section on a musical recording where the percussive rhythms were most aggressive and hard driving. The dancers anticipated and reacted to these breaks with their most impressive steps and moves.

DJ Kool Herc, originally from Jamaica, is credited with extending these breaks by using two turntables, a mixer, and two of the same records. As DJs could recue these beats from one turntable to the other, finally, the dancers were able to enjoy more than just a few seconds of a break! Kool Herc also coined the terms *b-boy* and *b-girl*, which stood for "break boys" and "break girls." At one of Kool Herc's jams, he might have addressed the dancers just before playing the break beats by saying, "B-boys, are you ready? B-girls, are you ready? The tension started to mount, and the air was thick with anticipation. The b-boys and b-girls knew this was their time to go off!

Some of the earliest dancing by b-boy pioneers was done upright, a form that became known as "top rockin'." Toprockin's structure and form fuse dance forms and influences from uprocking, tap, lindy hop, James Brown's "good foot", salsa, Afro-Cuban, and various African and Native American dances. There's even a top-rock Charleston step called the "Charlie Rock"! Early influences on b-boying and b-girling also included martial arts films from the 1970s. Certain moves and styles developed from this inspiration.

African slaves introduced *Capoeira*, a form of self-defense disguised as a dance, to Brazil. This form has some movements that are very similar to certain b-boy and b-girl steps and moves. Unlike the popularity of the martial arts films, *Capoeira* was not seen in the Bronx jams until the 1990s. Top rockin' seems to have developed gradually and unintentionally, leaving space for growth and new additions, until it evolved into a codified form.

Although top rockin' has developed an identifiable structure, there is always space for individual creativity, often expressed through the competitive nature of the dance. The same is true of all dance forms associated with hip-hop and West Coast funk: as long as dancers represent the root forms of the dances, the rest can be colored in with his or her own flavors.

As a result of the highly competitive nature of these dances, it wasn't long before top rockers extended their repertoire to the ground with "footwork" and "freezes." For instance, one dancer might start top rocking, then drop to the ground suddenly, going into leg shuffles, then a freeze, before coming to his feet. His opponent might have to do twice as much floorwork or a better freeze to win the battle. The fancy leg movements done on the ground, supported by the arms, were eventually defined as "footwork" or "floor rocking." In time, an impressive vocabulary of footwork, ground moves, and freezes developed, including the dancers' most dynamic steps and moves.

Top rockin' was not replaced with floor rocking; it was added to the dance, and both were key points in the dance's execution. Many times one could tell who had flavor and finesse just by their top rockin' before the drop and floor rock. The transition between top and floor rockin' was also important and became known as the "drop." Some of these drops were called front swipes, back swipes, dips, and corkscrews. The smoother the drop, the better.

Equally significant was the way dancers moved in and out of a freeze, demonstrating control, power, precision, and, at times, humor. Freezes were usually used to end a series of combinations or to mock and humiliate the opponent. Certain freezes were also named, the two most popular being the "chair freeze" and the "baby freeze." The chair freeze became the foundation for various moves because of the potential range of motion a dancer had in this position. The dancer's hand, forearm, and elbow support the body while allowing free range of movement with the legs and hips. From the chair freeze came the floor trac, back spin with the use of arms, continuous back spin (also known as the windmill), and other moves. These moves pushed the dance in a new direction in the early 1980s, the era of so-called power moves.

The first spins done in b-boying were one-shot head spins originally known as pencils, hand spins originally known as floats, knee spins, and butt spins. The first back spin came from a butt spin. Once a dancer gained momentum on his butt he could lie back and spin into a freeze. The next phase of back spin came from a squatted position, tucking the arm and shoulder under the body onto the floor, then rolling onto the back and spinning. This spin developed from the neck move (a move in which the dancer rolls from one shoulder to the other). Finally, the backspin, from the foundation of a chair freeze, was developed.

Power moves is a debatable term since it is questionable which movement requires more power: footwork and freezes or spins and gymnastics. One notable point introduced by B-Boy Ken Swift is that spins are fueled by momentum and balance, which require less muscular strength than footwork and freezes. The laws of physics prove this to be true: spins require speed, and speed creates momentum. The advent of power moves brought about a series of spins that became the main focus of the media and the younger generations of dancers. The true essence of the dance was slowly overshadowed by an overabundance of spins and acrobatics that didn't necessarily follow a beat or rhythm. The pioneers didn't separate the "power moves" from the rest of the dance form. They were b-boys who simply accented their performance with incredible moves to the beat of the music.

In the late 1960s and early '70s, dancers from Brooklyn played a major role in the creation and development of another dance form in hip-hop culture known as rocking. Eventually, this dance became known as uprocking. Inspired by similar or the same break beats used by b-boys and b-girls, this dance was more confrontational. Typically, two opponents faced each other and engaged in a "war dance" consisting of a series of steps, jerks, and the miming of weapons drawn against each other. There were also the "Apache Lines" where one crew stood in a line facing an opposing crew and challenged each other simultaneously. This structure was different from b-boying/b-girling since dancers in b-boy/b-girl battles took turns dancing, while uprocking was done with partners. Uprocking was also done to records played from beginning to end. In Brooklyn, DJs played the whole song and not cut break beats. This allowed the uprockers to react to the song in its entirety, responding to the lyrics, musical changes, and breaks.

Just as power moves became the focus of b-boying/b-girling, one particular movement known as "jerking" became the highlight of uprocking. Jerking is a movement that is used in direct battles, typically repeated throughout the break of the record. Today, uprocking consists almost entirely of jerking; the original form has been all but forgotten by the younger generation.

Uprocking also depended on quick wit, humor, and finesse as opponents attempted to humiliate each other. Winning meant displaying the swiftest steps, being receptive to the rhythms and counterrhythms of the music and the opponent, and catching the opponent off guard with mimed assaults, humor, and endurance. Uprocking consisted of quick arm and leg movements, turns, jumps, drops, and freezes. This dance was similar in spirit to b-boying/b-girling, yet different in form. Some practitioners believe top rockin's first inspiration came from uprocking. The two forms developed simultaneously from similar inspirations yet kept their own identities.

The West Coast was also engaged in a cultural movement throughout the 1970s. This scene was nourished by soul, R&B, and funk music at outdoor functions and discotheques.

In Los Angeles, California, Don Campbell, also known as Don Campbellock, originated the dance form "locking". Trying to imitate a local dance called the "funky chicken," Campbell added an effect of locking of the joints of his arms and body that became known as his signature dance. He then formed a group named "The Lockers," who all eventually shared in the development of this dance. The steps and moves created by these pioneers were named and cataloged. Some of them include the lock, points, skeeters, scooby doos, stop 'n go, which-away, and the fancies. Certain members of The Lockers incorporated flips, tucks, dives, and other aerial moves reminiscent of the legendary Nicholas Brothers. The main structure of the dance combined sharp, linear limb extensions and elastic-like movement.

The "lock" is a specific movement that glues together combinations of steps and moves similar to a freeze or a sudden pause. Combinations can consist of a series of points done by extending the arms and pointing in different directions. Dancers combined fancy step patterns with the legs and moves done in various sequences. The Lockers also jumped into half splits, knee drops, and butt drops and used patterns that would take them down to the ground and back up to their feet. This dance gained much of its popularity through The Lockers' various televised performances, which included *The Tonight Show, The Dick Van Dyke Show, The Carol Burnett Show,* and *Saturday Night Live.*

In 1976, the Electronic Boogaloo Lockers was formed in Fresno, California, by Sam "Boogaloo Sam" Solomon, Nate "Slide" Johnson, and Joe "Slim" Thomas. Since the group's inception, Sam has continued to recruit and help each member master his individual form. Some of Sam's early inspirations were Chubby Checker's "Twist," a James Brown dance called "The Popcorn," "The Jerk," cartoon animation, and the idiosyncrasies of everyday people. From these many influences, Sam combined incredible steps and moves, conceiving a dance form that he named "Boogaloo." This form includes isolated sharp angles, hip rotations, and the use of every part of the body. Sam's brother, Timothy "Poppin' Pete" Solomon, described Boogaloo as a dance that was done by moving the body continuously in different directions.

He also compared the body to a musical instrument in which the movement was as varied as the notes. Originally, "popping" was a term used to describe a sudden muscle contraction executed with the triceps, forearms, neck, chest, and legs. These contractions accented the dancer's movements, causing a quick, jolting effect. Sam's creation, popping, also became known as the unauthorized umbrella title to various forms within the dance, past and present. Some of these forms include Boogaloo, strut, dime stop, wave, tick, twisto-flex, and slides. The transitions between steps, forms, and moves were fluid, unpredictable, and precise, and delivered with character and finesse. Various forms were clearly showcased throughout the dancer's solos and group routines. Eventually, popping was also misrepresented and lost its purity, as younger generations strayed from its original forms.

The titles "Electric Boogie" and "Boogie" were given, in ignorance, to the dance, in New York, after the Lockers and Electric Boogaloos performed on the television program *Soul Train.* Unaware of the dance's history, New Yorkers attempted to name the dance after The Electric Boogaloos (derived from The Electronic Boogaloo Lockers).

Dancers in Los Angeles also distorted the name by calling it "pop-locking," while in France it was called "The Smurf." Elements of pantomime were merged with the dance, diluting its original essence. Miming creates illusions of the body without a rhythmic structure, whereas popping and Boogaloo create movement synchronized to rhythmic patterns. Most of the time, this fusion was done unsuccessfully since one would stray from the beat of the music.

Other townships in central California are credited with creating original forms of dance as well. Each region was identified by its style: San Jose was known for "flying tuts" and "dime stopping"; San Francisco had the "Chinese strut"; "Fillmore strutting" originated, obviously, in the Fillmore neighborhood. Oakland became known for "Frankenstein hitting" and "snake hitting." East Palo Alto was also known for "snake hitting." "Roboting" and "bopping" were popularized in Richmond. Sacramento had its own dances called "oak parking," "bustin'," and "sac"-ing (pronounced "sacking"). Dime stopping, strutting, and hitting all predate popping and have their own histories within the West Coast funk movement. In summary, all of these dance styles have contributed to the evolution of phenomenal forms of expression.

A connection between the East and West Coast movements is certain records that are danced to by b-boys/b-girls, uprockers, and lockers. One example is "Scorpio" by Dennis Coffey and the Detroit Guitar Band. For the most part, each dance form had a different musical influence, dress code, and terminology (all of which were mismatched and misrepresented during the 1980s media coverage of these dance forms).

As relatively new dance forms, b-boying/b-girling, uprocking, locking, and popping are rarely seen in a theatrical setting. They are usually performed in music videos, commercials, or films for just a few seconds, revealing very little of their full potential. In many cases, the filming of these dances has been poor, capturing only part of the body, taking away from the full impact of the steps, moves, and illusions. The film editing of these dances also deprives the audience of transitions and composition, since the editors are usually unfamiliar with the structures of the dance forms. Proper consultation with the dancers concerning filming and editing can remedy this recurring problem.

Another challenge related to the commercialization of the dance forms is the loss of spontaneous performance. In a cipher, the circular dance space that forms naturally once the dancing begins, the dancers can direct their performance in various directions, uninhibited and free from all counts and cues. This freedom is the key to creativity since the dancer is constantly challenged with variations in music, an undefined dance space, and potential opponents among the audience. The transition from cipher to stage has had its effects on the dancers and their craft.

What were once improvisational forms of expression with spontaneous vocabulary became choreography in a staged setting. A stage performance creates boundaries and can restrict the free-flowing process of improvisation. The dancers are challenged in a different way. Nailing cues and choreography become the objectives.

Another major difference between the original dance forms and staged versions is the positioning of the audience, since most traditional theatres have the audience facing the stage in one direction. Having to entertain an audience in one general location requires the dancer or choreographer to consciously space the performance, allowing the best viewing of the dance. In order to preserve the true essence and dynamics of these dance forms, they should exist as a social and cultural reality celebrated in their natural environments, that is, at jams, events, clubs, and so on. Theatrical film and video productions can be used as vehicles for their preservation as long as the essence of the form isn't compromised and diluted in the process.

The same concern applies to the story lines and scripts pertaining to the dances' forms and history. The mixing and blending of popping, locking, b-boying/b-girling, and uprocking into one form destroy their individual structures. Unfortunately, the younger generations of dancers either haven't made enough effort to learn each dance form properly or lack the resources to do so. However, the outcome is the same: hybrid dances with unclear form and structure.

In addition, each of the dance forms is performed best with its appropriate musical influences. Intermixing dance forms and their musical forms dissolves their structures and ultimately destroys their identities. Dancing on beat is most important. Riding the rhythm makes the difference between dance and unstructured movement. The formula is simple: submission to the music, allowing it to guide and direct, equals dancing.

Finally, the best way to preserve the dances is by learning from the earliest available sources or a devoted practitioner of the forms. The pioneers of these dance forms hold the key to the history and intentions of the movement. They remain the highest authorities, regardless of other opinions or assumptions.

Unraveling the history of locking, popping, b-boying/b-girling, and uprocking takes us toward a true understanding of their essence and significance in the world today. Many other genres of dance have borrowed without giving credit to their rightful owners. We hope we will see the day when these dances are clearly distinguished and given their due respect. Every so often, the dance world is introduced to innovations that revolutionize the arts. The hip-hop and West Coast funk movements have succeeded in replenishing the world with new, exciting dance forms that entertain and change the lives of many people worldwide.

Study Questions

1. How are competition or battling important to the art and practice of "hip-hop dance?"
2. How might the concept of "power moves" in hip-hop dance be applied to other aspects of hip-hop?
3. What cultural characteristics and conditions provide linkages between hip-hop dance and hip-hop music?

6
Hip-Hop Turns 30
Whatcha Celebratin' For?

In his essay, esteemed culture critic and musician Greg Tate adopts a familiar role of a hip-hop curmudgeon, but he does not do so simply to be curmudgeonly. Rather, he advances a serious critique of late hip-hop from the perspective of someone who watched it grow and bloom over the previous three decades. Written at the dawn of hip-hop's fourth decade and framed within the reelection of President George W. Bush, Tate addresses a series of shortcomings that remain unresolved both within and external to the hip-hop culture.

On the surface his analysis displays a basic art vs. commerce dilemma whereby the corrosive institutional powers of corporate appropriation are pitched against hip-hop's creative potentials. Yet in typical Tate fashion, there is much more than that at stake. Here, he explores generational dissonance, the disconnection between contemporary hip-hop and older sustaining forms of black cultural and political expression, and the apparent failure to clearly articulate a workable agenda that might, within contemporary conditions, facilitate real improvement in the lives of impoverished and struggling citizens. Society's tribulations demand strong responses and Tate seeks to realign hip-hop with the grand tradition of engaged cultural activism that has proven to be essential in virtually every prior instance of black political progress in America.

Hiphop Turns 30: Whatcha Celebratin' For?

Greg Tate

We are now winding down the anniversary of hiphop's 30th year of existence as a populist art form. Testimonials and televised tributes have been airing almost daily, thanks to Viacom and the like. As those digitized hiphop shout-outs get packed back into their binary folders, however, some among us have been so gauche as to ask, What the heck are we celebrating exactly? A right and proper question, that one is, mate. One to which my best answer has been: Nothing less, my man, than the marriage of heaven and hell, of New World African ingenuity and that trick of the devil known as global hyper-capitalism. Hooray.

Given that what we call hiphop is now inseparable from what we call the hiphop industry, in which the nouveau riche and the super-rich employers get richer, some say there's really nothing to celebrate about hiphop right now but the moneyshakers and the moneymakers—who got bank and who got more.

Hard to argue with that line of thinking since, hell, globally speaking, hiphop is money at this point, a valued form of currency where brothers are offered stock options in exchange for letting some corporate entity stand next to their fire.

True hiphop headz tend to get mad when you don't separate so-called hiphop culture from the commercial rap industry, but at this stage of the game that's like trying to separate the culture of urban basketball from the NBA, the pro game from the players it puts on the floor.

Hiphop may have begun as a folk culture, defined by its isolation from mainstream society, but being that it was formed within the America that gave us the coon show, its folksiness was born to be bled once it began entertaining the same mainstream that had once excluded its originators. And have no doubt, before hiphop had a name it was a folk culture—literally visible in the way you see folk in Brooklyn and the South Bronx of the '80s, styling, wilding, and profiling in Jamel Shabazz's photograph book Back in the Days. But from the moment "Rapper's Delight" went platinum, hiphop the folk culture became hiphop the American entertainment-industry sideshow.

No doubt it transformed the entertainment industry, and all kinds of people's notions of entertainment, style, and politics in the process. So let's be real. If hiphop were only some static and rigid folk tradition preserved in amber, it would never have been such a site for radical change or corporate exploitation in the first place. This being America, where as my man A.J.'s basketball coach dad likes to say, "They don't pay niggas to sit on the bench," hiphop was never going to not go for the gold as more gold got laid out on the table for the goods that hiphop brought to the market. Problem today is that where hiphop was once a buyer's market in which we, the elite hiphop audience, decided what was street legit, it has now become a seller's market, in which what does or does not get sold as hiphop to the masses is whatever the boardroom approves.

The bitter trick is that hiphop, which may or may not include the NBA, is the face of Black America in the world today. It also still represents Black culture and Black creative license in unique ways to the global marketplace, no matter how commodified it becomes. No doubt, there's still more creative autonomy for Black artists and audiences in hiphop than in almost any other electronic mass-cultural medium we have. You for damn sure can't say that about radio, movies, or television. The fact that hiphop does connect so many Black folk worldwide, whatever one might think of the product, is what makes it invaluable to anyone coming from a Pan-African state of mind. Hiphop's ubiquity has created a common ground and a common vernacular for Black folk from 18 to 50 worldwide. This is why mainstream hiphop as a capitalist tool, as a market force isn't easily discounted: The dialogue it has already set in motion between Long Beach and Cape Town is a crucial one, whether Long Beach acknowledges it or not. What do we do with that information, that communication, that transatlantic mass-Black telepathic link? From the looks of things, we ain't about to do a goddamn thing other than send more CDs and T-shirts across the water.

But the Negro art form we call hiphop wouldn't even exist if African Americans of whatever socioeconomic caste weren't still niggers and not just the more benign, congenial "niggas." By which I mean if we weren't all understood by the people who run this purple-mountain loony bin as both subhuman and superhuman, as sexy beasts on the order of King Kong. Or as George Clinton once observed, without the humps there ain't no getting over. Meaning that only Africans could have survived slavery in America, been branded lazy bums, and decided to overcompensate by turning every sporting contest that matters into a glorified battle royal.

Like King Kong had his island, we had the Bronx in the '70s, out of which came the only significant artistic movement of the 20th century produced by born-and-bred New Yorkers, rather than Southwestern transients or Jersey transplants. It's equally significant that hiphop came out of New York at the time it did, because hiphop is Black America's Ellis Island. It's our Delancey Street and our Fulton Fish Market and garment district and Hollywoodian ethnic enclave/empowerment zone that has served as a foothold for the poorest among us to get a grip on the land of the prosperous.

Only because this convergence of ex-slaves and ch-ching finally happened in the '80s because hey, African Americans weren't allowed to function in the real economic and educational system of these United States like first-generation immigrants until the 1980s—roughly four centuries after they first got here, 'case you forgot. Hiphoppers weren't the first generation who ever thought of just doing the damn thang entreprenurially speaking, they were the first ones with legal remedies on the books when it came to getting a cut of the action. And the first generation for whom acquiring those legal remedies so they could just do the damn thang wasn't a priority requiring the energies of the race's best and brightest.

If we woke up tomorrow and there was no hiphop on the radio or on television, if there was no money in hiphop, then we could see what kind of culture it was, because my bet is that hiphop as we know it would cease to exist, except as nostalgia. It might resurrect itself as a people's protest music if we were lucky, might actually once again reflect a disenchantment with, rather than a reinforcement of, the have and have-not status quo we cherish like breast milk here in the land of the status-fiending. But I won't be holding my breath waiting to see.

Because the moment hiphop disappeared from the air and marketplace might be the moment when we'd discover whether hiphop truly was a cultural force or a manufacturing plant, a way of being or a way of selling porn DVDs, Crunk juice, and S. Carter signature sneakers, blessed be the retired.

That might also be the moment at which poor Black communities began contesting the reality of their surroundings, their life opportunities. An interesting question arises: If enough folk from the 'hood get rich, does that suffice for all the rest who will die tryin'? And where does hiphop wealth leave the question of race politics? And racial identity?

Picking up where Amiri Baraka and the Black Arts Movement left off, George Clinton realized that anything Black folk do could be abstracted and repackaged for capital gain. This has of late led to one mediocre comedy after another about Negroes frolicking at hair shows, funerals, family reunions, and backyard barbecues, but it has also given us Biz Markie and OutKast.

Oh, the selling power of the Black Vernacular. Ralph Ellison only hoped we'd translate it in such a way as to gain entry into the hallowed house of art. How could he know that Ralph Lauren and the House of Polo would one day pray to broker that vernacular's cool marketing prowess into a worldwide licensing deal for bedsheets writ large with Jay-Z's John Hancock? Or that the vernacular's seductive powers would drive Estée Lauder to propose a union with the House of P. Diddy? Or send Hewlett-Packard to come knocking under record exec Steve Stoute's shingle in search of a hiphop-legit cool marketer?

Hiphop's effervescent and novel place in the global economy is further proof of that good old Marxian axiom that under the abstracting powers of capitalism, "All that is solid melts into air" (or the Ethernet, as the case might be). So that hiphop floats through the virtual marketplace of branded icons as another consumable ghost, parasitically feeding off the host of the real world's people—urbanized and institutionalized—whom it will claim till its dying day to "represent." And since those people just might need nothing more from hiphop in their geopolitically circumscribed lives than the escapism, glamour, and voyeurism of hiphop, why would they ever chasten hiphop for not steady ringing the alarm about the African American community's AIDS crisis, or for romanticizing incarceration more than attacking the prison–industrial complex, or for throwing a lyrical bone at issues of intimacy or literacy or, heaven forbid, debt relief in Africa and the evils perpetuated by the World Bank and the IMF on the motherland?

All of which is not to say "Vote or Die" wasn't a wonderful attempt to at least bring the phantasm of Black politics into the 24-hour nonstop booty, blunts, and bling frame that now has the hiphop industry on lock. Or to devalue by any degree Russell Simmons's valiant efforts to educate, agitate, and organize around the Rockefeller drug-sentencing laws. Because at heart, hiphop remains a radical, revolutionary enterprise for no other reason than its rendering people of African descent anything but invisible, forgettable, and dismissible in the consensual hallucination-simulacrum twilight zone of digitized mass distractions we call our lives in the matrixized, conservative-Christianized, Goebbelsized-by-Fox 21st century. And because, for the first time in our lives, race was nowhere to be found as a campaign issue in presidential politics and because hiphop is the only place we can see large numbers of Black people being anything other than sitcom window dressing, it maintains the potential to break out of the box at the flip of the next lyrical genius who can articulate her people's suffering with the right doses of rhythm and noise to reach the bourgeois and still rock the boulevard.

Call me an unreconstructed Pan-African cultural nationalist, African-fer-the-Africans-at-home-and-abroad-type rock and roll nigga and I won't be mad at ya: I remember the Afrocentric dream of hiphop's becoming an agent of social change rather than elevating a few ex-drug dealers' bank accounts. Against my better judgment, I still count myself among that faithful. To the extent that hiphop was a part of the great Black cultural nationalist reawakening of the 1980s and early '90s, it was because there was also an anti-apartheid struggle and anti-crack struggle, and Minister Louis Farrakhan and Reverend Jesse Jackson were at the height of their rhetorical powers, recruitment ambitions, and media access, and a generation of Ivy League Black Public Intellectuals on both sides of the Atlantic had come to the fore to raise the philosophical stakes in African American debate, and speaking locally, there were protests organized around the police/White Citizens Council lynchings of Bumpurs, Griffiths, Hawkins, Diallo, Dorismond, etc. etc. etc. Point being that hiphop wasn't born in a vacuum but as part of a political dynamo that seems to have been largely dissipated by the time we arrived at the Million Man March, best described by one friend as the largest gathering in history of a people come to protest themselves, given its bizarre theme of atonement in the face of the goddamn White House.

The problem with a politics that theoretically stops thinking at the limit of civil rights reform and appeals to white guilt and Black consciousness was utterly revealed at that moment—a point underscored by the fact that the two most charged and memorable Black political events of the 1990s were the MMM and the hollow victory of the O.J. trial. Meaning, OK, a page had been turned in the book of African American economic and political life—clearly because we showed up in Washington en masse demanding absolutely nothing but atonement for our sins—and we did victory dances when a doofus ex-athlete turned Hertz spokesmodel bought his way out of lethal injection. Put another way, hiphop sucks because modern Black populist politics sucks. Ishmael Reed has a poem that goes: "I am outside of history ... it looks hungry ... I am inside of history it's hungrier than I thot." The problem with progressive Black political organizing isn't hiphop but that the No. 1 issue on the table needs to be poverty, and nobody knows how to make poverty sexy. Real poverty, that is, as opposed to studio-gangsta poverty, newly-inked-MC-with-a-story-to-sell poverty.

You could argue that we're past the days of needing a Black agenda. But only if you could argue that we're past the days of there being poor Black people and Driving While Black and structural, institutionalized poverty. And those who argue that we don't need leaders must mean Bush is their leader too, since there are no people on the face of this earth who aren't being led by some of their own to hell or high water. People who say that mean this: Who needs leadership when you've got 24-hour cable and PlayStations. And perhaps they're partly right, since what people can name and claim their own leaders when they don't have their own nation-state? And maybe in a virtual America like the one we inhabit today, the only Black culture that matters is the one that can be downloaded and perhaps needs only business leaders at that. Certainly it's easier to speak of hiphop hoop dreams than of structural racism and poverty, because for hiphop America to not just desire wealth but demand power with a capital P would require thinking way outside the idiot box.

Consider, if you will, this "as above, so below" doomsday scenario: Twenty years from now we'll be able to tell our grandchildren and great-grandchildren how we witnessed cultural geno-cide: the systematic destruction of a people's folkways.

We'll tell them how fools thought they were celebrating the 30th anniversary of hiphop the year Bush came back with a gangbang, when they were really presiding over a funeral. We'll tell them how once upon a time there was this marvelous art form where the Negro could finally say in public whatever was on his or her mind in rhyme and how the Negro hiphop artist, staring down minimum wage slavery, Iraq, or the freedom of the incarcerated chose to take his emanci-pated motor mouth and stuck it up a stripper's ass because it turned out there really was gold in them thar hills.

Study Questions

1. What values underlie Tate's critique of hip-hop's corporate/commercial tendencies?
2. How are Black cultural politics of the past relevant to contemporary hip-hop?
3. What dominant images and ideals are distributed worldwide through U.S.-based hip-hop?

Part II

"No Time for Fake Niggas"
Hip-Hop Culture and the Authenticity Debates

Mark Anthony Neal

In an essay published in *The New York Times* (August 22, 1999), hip-hop journalist Touré made a principled effort to outline the contours of the "Hip-Hop Nation." At the time *The New York Times* seemed like an odd place to work out the attributes of cultural formation, long attributed to the mythologies of black and brown urban life. Touré's motivations, though, are informed by the very reason that *The New York Times* would sanction the piece in the first place: hop-hop had exploded into one of the most powerful cultural phenomena of the post-civil rights era, and it was an open secret that hip-hop's most visible consumers were the kids and grandkids of the *Times*'s readership.

More than a decade later, questions about authenticity in hip-hop seem quaint—the genre seemingly long past the threshold of what anybody would deem as an authentic sub-culture. Too much money has been made, too many icons exposed, too many martyrs buried (literally and rhetorically), too much branding of the hip-hop lifestyle carried out, and too many nostalgic cries uttered for a return to a time when things were supposedly purer. If there is something authentic about contemporary hip-hop it's likely being done by some kid on her computer in her room, who ain't ever heard of anything called the "old school."

And yet it is this lack of authenticity in what has come to be called hip-hop that makes its role in American society so fascinating. When the founding generation of hip-hop came into public view, there was no way to see them but as some authentic distillation of a black and brown under-class. Many folk have wanted to hold on to that narrative, despite the fact that the literal face of contemporary hip-hop would be a Romare Bearden-inspired collage of several multimillionaires, all long removed from whatever 'hood still claims their names. What made hip-hop authentic wasn't its symbols, its trinkets, or even the people. What made hip-hop authentic was its process—a good ole American DIY ethic, grounded in the "make-a-way-out-of-no-way" ethos that has been the fuel for Black American progress for more than two centuries and perfectly pitched for those of the post-civil rights generation who are stuck on the "not-ready-for-integration" subway. The process that is hip-hop is not proprietary to the Bronx, New York City, the East Coast, or the United States and the Caribbean for that matter, which is why in every place in the world where hip-hop is relevant there's an accompanying narrative about authentic beginnings in that part of the world. The point is that hip-hop has never been as "real" as we've been led to believe.

The chapter "No Time for Fake Niggas: Hip-Hop Culture and the Authenticity Debates" takes its title from Lil' Kim's "No Time," a mid-1990s mantra of authentic hip-hop expressed in the midst of a bi-coastal war of words and deeds that ultimately led to the deaths of two of hip-hop's most celebrated wordsmith-warriors. The acrimony between Bad Boy Entertainment and Death Row Records was the by-product of a long-simmering feud that pitted East Coast hip-hop sensibilities against those expressed by West Coast artists. Because of the significance of New York City in the lore of hip-hop, the East Coast had always been seen as the symbolic center of the hip-hop world. This "coast supremacy" was challenged in the early 1990s as artists such as N.W.A., Ice Cube, Snoop Dogg, Warren G, Digital Underground, Tupac, and even Hammer emerged as some of the genre's most bankable performers. For most of the twenty-first century, both coasts have been worshipping at the feet of the Dirty South. Times have changed.

At the crux of the East Coast versus West Coast feud was a fundamental belief that the experiences of those on one coast marked them as more authentic—more gangsta, more ghetto, more hard-core—than those on the other. In other words, one 'hood was more authentically hip-hop, and by extension black, than the other. In his essay "It's a Family Affair" Paul Gilroy openly asks:

> if the 'hood is the essence of where blackness can be found, which 'hood are we talking about? How do we weigh the achievements of one 'hood against the achievements of another? How is black life in one 'hood connected to life in others? Can there be a blackness that connects, articulates, synchronizes experiences and histories across the diaspora space?
>
> (Gilroy, 1992: 308)

Gilroy's comments speak to not only the difficulties of assessing authenticity—as if there is some assessment tool that can be used that is akin to "No Child Left Behind" or rather "No Hood Left Behind"—but the futility of it all, as if there's some intrinsic value in living in the *most* insidious crucible of urban disaffection. But valuable it is, when it's your claim to fame, which translates into unit sales and a regular rotation on the video channel of your choice.

Robin Kelley easily links bi-coastal authenticity debates to the fascination among social scientists and urban ethnographers about ghetto life. According to Kelley, some of these scholars "treat culture as if it were a set of behaviors. They assume that there is one identifiable ghetto culture, and what they observe was it" (Kelley, 1997: 22). He adds that, "although these social scientists came to mine what they believed was *the* 'authentic Negro culture,' there was real gold in them thar ghettos since white America's fascination with the pathological urban poor translated into massive books sales" (ibid.: 20). Thus both hip-hop artists (regardless of whether they are actually from the ghetto) and the scholars who write about the environment that produced them (and write about them also) have a clear commercial stake in representing the "ghetto real" in their work. Ultimately Kelley suggests that the real question that these ethnographers pose (and hard-core rappers readily answer) is "what kind of 'niggers' populate the inner city?" (ibid.: 16).

In a challenging and provocative essay "On the Question of Nigga Authenticity," Ronald A.T. Judy would have us believe that even the notion that there is an "authentic" nigger is rife with essentialists' views of black life and culture that have not fully taken into account the significant impact of hip-hop. According to Judy, "understanding the possibilities of nigga authenticity in the emerging realities of transnational capital is a humbling undertaking . . . the general consensus is 'this nigga is deadly dangerous,'" an "assumption that this nigga of the present age is somehow related to the 'bad nigger' of slavery and the postbellum South" (Judy, 1994: 213). Beyond the perhaps simplistic generational distinctions made between the words "nigger" and "nigga," Judy argues that "nigga defines authenticity as adaptation to the force of commodification. . . . Authenticity is hype, a hypercommodified affect whose circulation has made hip-hop global" (ibid.: 229). In Judy's view hip-hop is an "utterance of a habit of thought toward an increasingly rationalized and fragmented world of global commodification. It is thinking about being in a hypercommodified world" (ibid.: 214) where "nigga designates the scene, par excellence, of commodification, where one is among commodities" (ibid.: 228).

Outside the theoretical observations made by Judy with relation to the authenticity debates within hip-hop there have always been concrete queries as to *who* belongs to the Hip-Hop Nation. In the early days of hip-hop, when it fermented in so many of New York's black and brown (and working-class ethnic) communities, it might have been an African-American form, but there was no denying it's Nuyorican flavor. Those communities were tangibly visible then, just as the organic influences of Puerto Ricans are within most contemporary understandings of hip-hop's developing years. Juan Flores asserts that, as the "commercialization process involves the extraction of popular cultural expression from its original social context and function," it seems that the "Latinization" of hip-hop has meant its distancing from the specific national and ethnic traditions to which it had most directly pertained (Flores, 2000: 116). Even the notion of an essentialized Spanish-speaking presence in hip-hop can be challenged if one considers the very different formations of Puerto Rican and Chicano hip-hop. For example, the Nuyorican experience—the navigation between distinct Puerto Rican sensibilities derived from life in New York City—that marked so many of the first generation of Puerto Rican hip-hop artists is very different than those of "La Raza" rappers like Kid Frost and the Aztlan Underground. According to Raegan Kelly, "To call yourself Chicano is to claim La Raza, to locate your origin within the struggle of a people for land and for cultural, political and economic self-determination" (Kelly, 1993: 72). The idea of an authentic Latino/a or Chicano/a voice in hip-hop is as bankrupt as the notion of an authentic Latino/a or Chicano/a voter.

Oliver Wang and Usama Kahf further complicate the neat lines of difference and authenticity erected around hip-hop by reimagining the spaces and places where hip-hop took root. In the essay "Arabic Hip-Hop: Claims of Authenticity and Identity of a New Genre," Kahf writes, "Hip-Hop is appropriated and transformed by local artists in different parts of the world who are searching for emancipatory and empowering avenues of expression in the midst of a reality that continues to shut doors in their faces" (Kahf, 2007: 359). But, as Kahf notes, even artists in the Middle East are "faced with the challenge of making hip-hop an authentic new channel of Arab culture and not an affront to its heritage or an imitation of the west" (ibid.: 360–361). Authenticity presents a wholly different challenge for rap artists of Asian descent, as Oliver Wang details in his essay "Rapping and Repping Asian: Race, Authenticity and the Asian American." Explaining the absence of Asian rappers in mainstream rap music, Wang writes: "it comes down to the issue of marketability and, intimately related to that, how racially inauthentic Asian Americans are in a social world of fans, artists, media and industry, where blackness is normative" (Wang, 2007: 36). Wang adds that for Asian American rappers—in a genre that privileges "realness" and where "takeness can discredit an artist beyond redemption"—"their racial difference creates a crisis of racial inauthenticity that supersedes other factors" (ibid.: 36).

Ultimately all concerns about authenticity in hip-hop begin and end with the fear of the proverbial white rapper. Given the historical examples of white artists who trafficked in black expressive culture, often to greater acclaim and financial success than their black counterparts, fears and anxieties about white rappers have some basis. The career and legacy of the late Elvis Presley loom large in this equation, as Gilbert B. Rodman makes (facetiously) clear in his essay "Race ... and Other Four Letter Words: Eminem and the Cultural Politics of Authenticity." Rodman ask rhetorically, "Is Eminem the Elvis of rap: a White man who makes Black music credibly, creatively and compellingly? Or—alternately—is Eminem ... the Elvis of rap: a White man who's unfairly achieved fame and fortune by making Black music, while Black artists with equal (if not greater) talent languish in poverty and obscurity?" (Rodman, 2006: 106). The significance of Eminem is palpable enough that the answer to Rodman's query is not really an either/or response, but rather a both/and reality. This both/and equation is a useful response for general inquiries about authenticity within hip-hop. As Rodman writes, "questions about Eminem's racial authenticity mask a more subtle, but no less disturbing agenda—one that's about maintaining rigid lines between the races when it comes to behaviors, attitudes, and politics" (ibid.: 108–109). When Rodman says that Eminem violates those lines "deliberately, forcefully, repeatedly, and threateningly," he could be talking about hip-hop itself (ibid.: 109).

REFERENCES

Flores, Juan. (2000). "Puerto Rocks: Rap, Roots, and America," *From Bomba to Hip-Hop: Puerto Rican Culture and Latino Identity.* New York: Columbia University Press.

Gilroy, Paul. (1992). "It's a Family Affair," in *Black Popular Culture*, edited by Gina Dent. Seattle, WA: Bay Press.

Judy, R.A.T. (1994). "On the Question of Nigga Authenticity," *Boundary*, 2, Fall.

Kahf, Usama. (2007). "Arabic Hip-Hop: Claims of Authenticity and Identity of a New Genre," *Journal of Popular Music Studies*, 19:4.

Kelley, Robin D.G. (1997). *Yo' Mama's Disfunktional: Fighting the Culture Wars in Urban America*. Boston, MA: Beacon Press.

Kelly, Raegan. (1993). "Hip-Hop Chicano: A Separate but Parallel Story," in *It's Not About a Salary: Rap, Race and Resistance in Los Angeles*, by Brian Cross. New York: Verso.

Rodman, Gilbert. (2006). "Race ... and Other Four Letter Words: Eminem and the Cultural Politics of Authenticity," *Popular Communication*, 4:2.

Wang, Oliver. (2007). "Rapping and Repping Asian: Race, Authenticity and the Asian American," in *Alien Encounters: Popular Culture in Asian America*, edited by Mimi Thi Nguyen and Thuy Linh Nguyen Tu. Durham, NC: Duke University Press.

7

Puerto Rocks
Rap, Roots, and Amnesia

As a scholar Juan Flores's work provides a critical link between organic forms of popular and folk culture that have long circulated in Puerto Rico and emerging forms of popular culture that have taken root in the United States, New York in particular, with continuous migration patterns of Puerto Ricans.

While the Nuyorican formations—the rich exchanges between native Puerto Rican experience and those within the city of New York—that Flores highlights have been critical to the development of hip-hop culture in the United States, Flores isolates concerns that, with the transition from folk culture to popular commodities, valuable national and ethnic traditions are eroded. Flores's essay raises important questions about the role that commercial popular culture plays in the diminishment of ethnic practices and what role contemporary artists and critics should play in strengthening those connections.

Puerto Rocks: Rap, Roots, and Amnesia

Juan Flores

By the early 1990s, hip-hop had finally broken the language barrier. Though young Puerto Ricans from the South Bronx and El Barrio have been involved in breakdancing, graffiti writing, and rap music since the beginnings of hip-hop back in the 1970s, it was only belatedly that the Spanish language and Latin musical styles came into their own as integral features of the rap vocabulary. By the mid-nineties, acts like Mellow Man Ace, Kid Frost, Gerardo, and El General became household words among pop music fans nationwide and internationally, as young audiences of all nationalities came to delight in the catchy Spanglish inflections and the *guaguancó* and merengue rhythms lacing the familiar rap formats. Mellow Man Ace's "Mentirosa" was the first Latino rap record to go gold in the summer of 1990; Kid Frost's debut album *Hispanic Causing Panic* instantly became the rap anthem of La Raza in the same year; Gerardo as "Rico Suave" has his place as the inevitable Latin lover sex symbol; and El General has established the immense popularity of Spanish-language reggae-rap in the Caribbean and Latin America.

Who are these first Latin rap superstars and where are they from? Mellow Man Ace was born in Cuba and raised in Los Angeles, Kid Frost is a Chicano from East L.A., Gerardo is from Ecuador, and El General is Panamanian. But what about the Puerto Ricans, who with their African American homeboys created hip-hop styles in the first place? They are, as usual, conspicuous for their absence, and the story is no less startling for all its familiarity. Latin Empire, for example, the only Nuyorican act to gain some exposure among wider audiences, is still struggling for its first major record deal. Individual emcees and deejays have been scattered in well-known groups like the Fearless Four and the Fat Boys, their Puerto Rican backgrounds all but invisible. Even rap performers from Puerto Rico like Vico C, Lisa M, and Rubén DJ, who grew up far from the streets where hip-hop originated, enjoy greater commercial success and media recognition than any of the Puerto Rican b-boys from the New York scene.

This omission, of course, is anything but fortuitous and has as much to do with the selective vagaries of the music industry as with the social placement of the Puerto Rican community in the prevailing racial-cultural hierarchy. As the commercialization process involves the extraction of popular cultural expression from its original social context and function, it seems that the "Latinization" of hip-hop has meant its distancing from the specific national and ethnic traditions to which it had most directly pertained. But instead of simply bemoaning this evident injustice, or groping for elaborate explanations, it is perhaps more worthwhile to trace the history of this experience from the perspectives of some of the rappers themselves. For if New York Puerto Ricans have had scant play within the "Hispanic rap market," they have one thing that other Latino rappers do not, which is a history in hip-hop since its foundation as an emergent cultural practice among urban youth.

Such an emphasis is not meant to imply any inherent aesthetic judgment, nor does it necessarily involve a privileging of origins or presumed authenticity. Yet it is easy to understand and sympathize with the annoyance of a veteran Puerto Rican deejay like Charlie Chase when faced with the haughty attitudes he encountered among some of the rap superstars from the Island. "The thing about working with these Puerto Rican rappers," he commented, reflecting on his work producing records for the likes of Lisa M and Vico C, "they are very arrogant! You know, because they are from Puerto Rico, and I'm not, right? I feel kind of offended, but my comeback is like, well, yeah, if you want to be arrogant about that, then what are you doing in rap? You're not a rapper. You learned rap from listening to me and other people from New York!"[1] Actually this apprenticeship was probably less direct than Charlie Chase claims, since they more likely got to know rap through the recordings, videos, and concert appearances of Run DMC, LL Cool J, and Big Daddy Kane than through any familiarity with the New York hip-hop scene of the early years.

Where did those first platinum-selling rappers themselves go to learn the basics of rap performance? Again, Charlie Chase can fill us in, by remembering the shows he deejayed with the Cold Crush Brothers back in the early 1980s.

> When we were doing shows, you know who was in the audience? The Fat Boys. Whodini. Run DMC, L.L. Cool J, Big Daddy Kane. Big Daddy Kane told me a story one time, he said, "You don't know how much I loved you guys." He said, "I wanted to see you guys so bad, and my mother told me not to go to Harlem World to see you guys perform because if she found out I did she'd kick my ass!" And he said, "I didn't care, I went. And I went every week. And I wouldn't miss any of your shows." That's how popular we were with the people who are the rappers today.

To speak of Puerto Ricans in rap means to defy the sense of instant amnesia that engulfs popular cultural expression once it is caught up in the logic of commercial representation. It involves sketching in historical contexts and sequences, tracing traditions and antecedents, and recognizing hip-hop to be more and different than the simulated images, poses, and formulas the public discourse of media entertainment tends to reduce it to. The decade and more of hindsight provided by the Puerto Rican involvement shows that, rather than a new musical genre and its accompanying stylistic trappings, rap constitutes a space for the articulation of social experience. From this perspective, what has emerged as "Latin rap" first took shape as an expression of the cultural turf shared, and contended for, by African Americans and Puerto Ricans over their decades as neighbors, coworkers, and "homies" in the inner-city communities. As vernacular cultural production prior to its commercial and technological mediation, hip-hop formed part of a more extensive and intricate field of social practice, a significant dimension of which comprises the long-standing and ongoing interaction between Puerto Rican and Black youth in the shared New York settings. Not only is the contextual field wider, but the historical reach is deeper and richer as well: the Black and Puerto Rican conjunction in the formation of rap is prefigured in important ways in doo-wop, Latin boogaloo, Nuyorican poetry, and a range of other testimonies to intensely overlapping and intermingling expressive repertoires. Thus when Latin Empire comes out with "I'm Puerto Rican and Proud, Boyee!" they are actually marking off a decisive moment in a tradition of cultural and political identification that goes back several generations.

I have gained access to this largely uncharted terrain by way of conversations and interviews with some of the protagonists of Puerto Rican rap. Early hip-hop movies like *Wild Style* and *Style Wars*, which documented and dramatized the prominent participation of Puerto

Ricans, sparked my initial interest and led to a burst of research (which hardly anyone took seriously at the time) and a short article published in various English and Spanish versions in the mid-1980s. At that time, the only adequate written consideration of Puerto Ricans had to do with their role in the New York graffiti movement, as in the excellent book *Getting Up* by Craig Castleman and an important article by Herbert Kohl. Steven Hager's *Hip-Hop* includes a valuable social history of youth culture in the South Bronx and Harlem at the dawn of hip-hop, with some attention to the part played by Puerto Ricans in graffiti, breakdance, and rap music.[2] Otherwise, and since those earlier accounts, coverage of Puerto Rican rap has been limited to an occasional article in the *Village Voice* or *Spin* magazine, generally as a sideline concern in discussions of wider style rubrics like "Hispanic," "Spanish," or "bilingual" rap. Primary evidence of a historical kind is even harder to come by, since Puerto Rican rhymes were never recorded for public distribution and many have been forgotten even by their authors.

Chasin' the Flash

Charlie Chase calls himself "New York's Number One Puerto Rican DJ," and that's how he's been known since back in the seventies when he was blasting the hottest dance music on the waves of WBLS and in the early eighties when he was deejay for the legendary Cold Crush Brothers. When he says "Number One," he means not only the best but also the first: "When I started doing rap, there were no Hispanics doing it. If there were I didn't know about it. Anyway, I was the first Hispanic to become popular doing what I did. I was a deejay."

Charlie was born in El Barrio in the 1950s, and though his family moved a lot it was always from one Puerto Rican and Black neighborhood to another.

I grew up in Williamsburg from the age of two to nine. I moved to the Bronx, on Brook Avenue and 141st, ¡que eso por allí es candela! I grew up there from ten to about thirteen, then I moved back to Brooklyn, over in Williamsburg, Montrose Avenue, por allá on Broadway. Then we moved back to the Bronx again, 161st and Yankee Stadium. From there we went to 180th and Arthur, and from there it was Grand Concourse and 183rd, then Valentine and 183rd, then back to 180th. I mean, we moved, man! I've been all over the place, and it's like I've had the worst of both worlds, you know what I mean?

Charlie's parents came from Mayagüez, Puerto Rico. Though family visits to the Island were rare, that Puerto Rican background remained an active influence throughout his upbringing. At home he was raised on Puerto Rican music. "You see I always listened to my mother's records. She was the one who bought all the Latin records. She bought them all. She bought Tito Puente, she was into trios, el Trio Los Condes." Even his career in music seems to have been handed down to him as part of that ancestry.

I come from a family of musicians. My grandfather was a writer and a musician; he played in bands. So did my father; he played in trios. So I kind of followed in their footsteps. My father left me when I was ten and I never learned music from him; he didn't teach me how to play instruments. For some reason or other, it must have been in the blood, I just picked up the guitar and wanted to learn.

Charlie makes clear that he didn't start off in rap or as a deejay. "I'm a bass player. I played in a Spanish ballad band, merengue band, salsa band, rock band, funk band, Latin rock band. I produced my first album at the age of sixteen and it was a Spanish ballad album. We played with the best, Johnny Ventura, Johnny Pacheco, Los Hijos del Rey, Tito Puente. The name of the group was Los Giramundos." So it turns out that Charlie Chase, famed deejay for the Cold

Crush Brothers, started off gigging in a Latin band when he was fifteen years old and could have had a whole career in salsa. "Yeah," he recalls, "but there was no money in it. There were a lot of people being ripped off.... I said, man, I want to do something else." Fortunately, he did have somewhere to turn, for alongside his inherited Latin tradition there was his dance music and R&B. Talking about his transition to deejaying he remembers:

> I was a music lover. I grew up listening to WABC, Cousin Brucie, Chuck Leonard, all of these guys, and I was always into music. In school I would always have the radio on. It was always a big influence in my life and then I turned into a musician. I started playing with the band, and then a few years later I got into deejaying, and then the deejaying was making more money for me than the band.

It all seems to make sense, I thought, but what about that name? What's a Puerto Rican doing with a name like Charlie Chase? "My name was Carlos," he said. "Charlie is a nickname for Carlos." Fine, I said, but what about Chase? "Chase?" he repeated, hesitantly. "There is a story behind that which I never told anybody, and I don't know if I want to say it. Because when this person reads this, he is going to be so souped." (Little was I to know how much this little story has to say about the situation of young Puerto Ricans in the early days of rap.)

> I made up my name because of Grandmaster Flash. Flash is a friend of mine. I first saw Flash doing this, cutting and all of this, and I saw that and I said, aw, man, I can do this. I was deejaying at the time, but I wasn't doing the scratching and shit and I said, I can do this, man. I'll rock this, you know. And I practiced, I broke turntables, needles, everything. Now "Chase" came because I'm like, damn, you need a good name, man. And Flash was on top and I was down here. So I was chasing that niggah. I wanted to be up where he was. So I said, let's go with Charlie Chase.

There's no telling how "souped" Grandmaster Flash will get when he finds out, but his friend and main rival (along with Grandmaster Theo) back in the days, grew up as Carlos Mandes. "It's Mandes," Charlie emphasized, "m-a-n-d-e-s. Not Méndez." Whatever the origin of his Puerto Rican name, ever since he started chasing the Flash Carlos Mandes has been known, by everyone, as Charlie Chase. He doesn't even like it when "Mandes" appears on the records he wrote. "Nobody knows my name was Carlos Mandes. They'd laugh. They'd snap on me."

Charlie might think that Mandes sounds corny now, but at the time the problem was that it didn't fit. He never tires of telling about how difficult it was to be accepted as a Puerto Rican in rap, especially as a deejay, and because he was so good. "A lot of Blacks would not accept that I was Spanish. You know, a lot of times because of the way I played they thought I was Black, because I rocked it so well." As a deejay he was usually seated in back, behind the emcees and out of sight. In the beginning, in fact, his invisibility was a key to success. "I became popular because of the tapes, and also because nobody could see me. Since they thought I was Black, you know, because I was in the background." Even when they saw him, he says that "they still wouldn't believe it. They are like, 'no, that's not him! That's bullshit! That's not him!' A few years went by and they accepted it, you know. I was faced with a lot of that. You know, being Hispanic you're not accepted in rap. Because to them it's a Black thing and something that's from their roots and shit."

"What the fuck are you doing here, Puerto Rican?" Charlie remembers being faced with that challenge time and again when he went behind the ropes, among the rappers, at the early jams. He had to prove himself constantly, and he recalls vividly the times when it took his homeboy Tony Tone from DJ Breakout and Baron to step in and save his skin. "I turn around and see him breaking on them and I hear what he's saying and I'm like, oh shit!" As tough as it got, though, Charlie knew very well that he wasn't out of place. "I was the type of kid that, you know, I always grew up with Black people.... My daughter's godfather is Black. He's like my brother, that guy."

But the best proof was that Charlie was with the Cold Crush Brothers, who were all Black. "We all grew up in the streets, man. It's like a street thing. Once you see that the guy is cool, then you're accepted, everything flows correctly." And it's not that Charlie just did everything like the other brothers, to fit in. Aside from his "mancha de plátano," those indelible earmarks of the Puerto Rican, he had his own personal style about him that he wasn't about to give up just to be one of the boys. He remembers about Cold Crush that "the only thing was, it was a trip when it came to the dressing bit. You see, I don't dress like the average hip-hopper and never did. They wanted to wear Kangols, Martin X, and these British walkers and all that stuff at the time, and I was like, that's not me, fellas. That's not me, man. At that time, I combed my hair back in a DA." Not only did he refuse to fit the mold, but Charlie's insistence helped the group arrive at the look that helped to establish their immense popularity in those years. "We came up with a look that everybody copied afterwards, which we all felt comfortable with. It was the leather and stud look, which we popularized in rap and through that look we became hard."

Besides, as alone as he was sometimes made to feel, Charlie knew that he wasn't the only Puerto Rican who was into rap. "Hispanics always liked rap, young Puerto Ricans were into it since the beginning. I wasn't the only one who felt the same way about music like that. There were plenty of them, but they didn't have the talent, they just enjoyed it. Me, I wanted to do it, you know. Forget it, there were plenty of people. I mean, when you grow up in the streets, it's a street thing, man." In its street beginnings, Puerto Ricans were an integral part of the rap scene, and not only as appreciative fans. Though their participation in production and performance was submerged (far more so than in breaking and graffiti), they were an essential and preponderant presence in the security crews that, in the gang environment, made the whole show possible. "It was rough, man," Charlie recalls.

> All of my crew, the whole crew, were Spanish, maybe two or three Black guys. They were all Spanish, and when we jammed we had bats. If you crossed the line or got stupid, you were going to get batted down, alright? And that was that. That was my crew, they would help me with records, they were security. The guys in my group were Black, but the rest of the guys, security, were Hispanic.... People'd be like, yo, those are some wild Spanish motherfuckers. Don't mess with them, man.

But with a little coaxing Charlie will even call to mind some other Puerto Rican rappers from those days. There was Prince Whipper Whip and Ruby D (Rubén García) from the Fantastic Five, OC from the Fearless Four with Tito Cepeda, Johnny who was down with Master Don and the Def Committee. "Then there was this one group," Charlie recalls, "that wanted to do Latin rap songs, way back. And they had good ideas and they had great songs, but they just didn't have enough drive, you know? They had a great idea, they had a routine. They had these crazy nice songs, but they just weren't ambitious enough.... Robski and June Bug, those were the guys." Years before anybody started talking about "Latin rap," Robski and June Bug were busy working out Spanglish routines and even rendering some of the best rhymes of the time into Spanish. "They took our songs and translated them into Spanish. They blew our heads, man! It was weird, because they actually took everything we said and turned it into Spanish and made it rhyme. And they did a good job of it."

But in those days using Spanish in rap was still a rarity, especially in rhymes that were distributed on tapes and records. It wasn't only lack of ambition that prevented Robski and

June Bug from making it, "'cause at that time," Charlie says, "a lot of people were doing it underground, but they couldn't come off doing it, they couldn't make money doing it. The people that did it, did it in parties, home stuff, the block, they were the stars in their ghetto." But Charlie himself, "chasing the Flash," was with the first rap group to be signed by CBS Records, the first rap group to tour Japan, the group that played in the first hip-hop movie, *Wild Style*. At that level, rapping in Spanish was still out of the question. Charlie explains what it was like for him to face this constraint, and gives a clear sense of the delicate generational process involved in the entry of bilingualism into commercially circumscribed rap discourse.

> I always stressed the point that I was Hispanic doing rap music, but I couldn't do it in Spanish, you understand? But that was my way of opening the doors for everybody else to do what they're doing now. You see, there are certain degrees, certain levels and steps that you have to follow. And being that I was there at the very beginning, that was the I way I had to do it, That was my contribution. I feel sorry that I couldn't do it then, but I want to do it now and I'm making up for it, because now I can.... I wanted everybody to know that I was Spanish, rocking, ripping shit up. In a Black market.

At that early stage in negotiating Puerto Rican identity in rap, the key issue was not language but what Charlie calls "the Latin point of view"; pushing rhymes in Spanish was not yet part of the precarious juggling act.

> For me it's the Latin point of view. You see, what I emphasize is that I'm Hispanic in a Black world. Not just surviving but making a name for myself and leaving a big impression. Everything that happened to me was always within the Black music business, and I always was juggling stuff all of the time, because I had to be hip, I had to be a homeboy. But I also had to know how far to go without seeming like I was trying to kiss up or something, or "he's just trying to be Black." When you deal with the people I deal with, especially at a time when rap was just hard core and raw, you're talking about guys who were *títeres*, you know, tough guys. I had to juggle that. I had to play my cards correct.

If Spanish wasn't yet part of the "Latin point of view," the music was, especially the rhythmic texture of the songs, which is where as the deejay Charlie was in control. He remembers sneaking in the beat from the number "Tú Coqueta," right "in the middle of a jam. I'm jamming. I throw that sucker in, just the beat alone, and they'd go off. They never knew it was a Spanish record. And if I told them that they'd get off the floor." Even the other rappers couldn't tell because the salsa cuts seemed to fit in so perfectly. "It was great! I would sneak in Spanish records. Beats only, and if the bass line was funky enough, I would do that too. Bobby Valentín stuff. He played bass with the Fania All-Stars, and he would do some funky stuff." As a bassist in Latin bands, Charlie knew the repertoire to choose from.

But he also knew that he had to walk a fine line and that he was ahead of his time, not only for the R&B-savvy rappers but for Latin musical tastes as well. In fact it was because of the resistance he faced from the Latin musicians, and not only the better pay, that Charlie decided to leave Los Giramundos and go into rap full time.

> Sometimes I'd go to gigs and in between songs I'd start playing stuff from rap music and the drummer would like it too, and he'd start doing some stuff. And sometimes people would get up to dance to it and the rest of the guys in the band would get furious at us, and they would say, "What are you doing? If you're not going to play a song, don't do it." They would break on me. They didn't want that stuff.

Not that Charlie didn't try to interest Latin musicians in mixing some elements of rap into their sound. He especially remembers working on a record concept with Willie Colón.

> He could have had the first Latin hip-hop record out and it would have been a hit. It was a singing rap. He was singing, right, there was a little bit of rap, and I was scratching. I did the arrangements. What happened was, the project was being held and held and held. What happened? He put out the record, an instrumental! He took out all the raps, then he overdubbed. Killed the whole project. He slept on it.

But as Charlie learned early on, when it comes to the emergence of new styles in popular music it's all a matter of timing. He himself had trouble relating to the use of Spanish in rap when he first heard it on record. Back in 1981 the group Mean Machine came out with the first recorded Spanish rhymes in their "Disco Dream," a side that deeply impressed some of the present-day Latino rappers like Mellow Man Ace and Latin Empire when they first heard it, though that was some years after it was released. But Charlie knew Mean Machine when they started and recalls his reaction when "Disco Dream" first came out. "It was strange, and it was new. At first I didn't jive with it because I was so used to it and I myself got so caught up in that whole R&B thing that when I heard that, it didn't click with me. And I was like, 'Naw, this is bullshit!' " But with time tastes changed, as did Charlie's understanding of himself and his own role. "And then," he goes on, "something made me realize one day that, wait a minute, man, look at you, what are you? You don't rap like they do, but you're Hispanic just like them, trying to get a break in the business. And I said, if anything, this is something cool and new."

Seen in retrospect, Mean Machine was only a faint hint of what was to become Latino rap in the years ahead. The Spanish they introduced amounted to a few party exhortations rather than an extended Spanish or bilingual text. Charlie draws this distinction, and again points up the changing generations of Latino presence in rap.

"The way that they did it was not like today. Today it's kind of political, opinionated, and commercial, and storytelling. What they did was that they took a lot of Spanish phrases, like 'uepa' and 'dale fuego a la lata, fuego a la lata,' stuff like that, and turned them into a record." However perfunctory their bilingualism and fleeting their acclaim, Mean Machine's early dabbling with Spanglish rhymes did plant a seed. Puerto Rock of Latin Empire attests to the impact "Disco Dream" had on them:

> They didn't continue. After one record, that was it. I know them all, we keep in contact. Mr. Schick came out with, "Tire su mano al aire / Yes, means throw your hands in the air / y siguen con el baile means / dance your body till you just don't care." And then it ended up with, "Fuego a la lata, fuego a la lata / agua que va caer." So we were like bugging! We were more or less doing it but in English and got crazy inspired when we heard that record. We was like, Oh, snap! He wrote the first Spanish rhyme! We was skeptical if it was going to work, and when we heard the record we were like, it's going to work.[3]

The disbelief and strategic invisibility that surrounded Latino participation in rap performance in the early years gave way to a fascination with something new and different. Charlie sees this process reflected in the changing fate of his own popularity among hip-hop audiences. "It was kind of complicated," he recalls. If at first he became popular because "nobody could see me," he later became even more popular because "everyone found out I was Hispanic. And it was like, 'yo, this kid is Spanish!' and 'What? Yo, we've got to see this!' " Once he began to feel this sense of curiosity and openness, a new stage appeared in rap history, and Charlie was quick to recognize its potential, commercially and politically. He tells of how his enthusiasm caught the attention among some of the Latin musicians, especially his friend Tito Puente, who seemed to be fondly reminded of their own breakthrough a generation before.

> These guys, they love it. Because for one, it's for them getting back out into the limelight again, you know, in a different market.... The musicians are very impressed to see that somebody like me wants to work with them in my style of music. And when I tell them about my history they are very impressed because in their day, when they came out, they were the same way. When Tito Puente came out, he was doing the mambo and it was all something new. It was all new to him, too. So he can relate to what I'm doing. And for him it's almost like a second coming.

After the decade it has taken for Puerto Rican rap to come into its own, Charlie now feels that the time is right for the two sides of his musical life to come together, and for full-fledged "salsa-rap" to make its appearance.

> For this next record I want to do a project, where I want to get all the East Coast rappers together, I want to get POW, I want to get Latin Empire, I want to get a few other guys that are unknown but that are good. I want to join them, I want to bring in Luis "Perico" Ortíz, I want to bring Tito, I want to bring Ray Barretto, you know. Bring them to handle all the percussion stuff and then my touch would be to bring in the rap loops, the beats, the bass lines, the programming. I'll program and also arrange it. And they will come in, Luis "Perico" would do the whole horn section, Tito would come in and handle all the percussion section, and Ray Barretto would handle the congas. And I would get my friend Sergio who is a tremendous piano player, a young kid, he's about twenty-four, twenty-five now, he works for David Maldonado. I just want to kick this door wide open, once and for all, and that's the way I'm going to do it.

As ambitious as such a project may sound, bringing together Puerto Rican musicians across musical traditions is only half of Charlie's strategy for promoting Latino unity. For "if any Hispanics want to make it in this business," he claims, "they've got to learn to pull together, no matter where you're coming from, or it's not going to work. It's not going to work, man. Kid Frost on the West Coast right now, he's got a little thing going. He and I are working around a few things. He's got his Latin Alliance on the West Coast. I've got a lot of Latin people who work with me on this. I'm trying to form something here where we can merge, cover the whole United States. That's the best way we can do it, if we unify."

Yet with his repeated emphasis on Latino unity, Charlie has more than commercial success in mind. His own experience, he now feels, leads him to set his sights on the political and educational potential of his musical efforts.

> Because what I did, I had to unite with Black people to get my success and become Charlie Chase, "New York's Number One Puerto Rican DJ." Ironically, I did it with Black people. Which proves, man, that anybody can get together and do it. If I did it with Black people, then Hispanics can do it with Hispanics and do a much better job. That's my whole purpose right now. I mean, I have made my accomplishments, I have become famous doing my thing in rap, I have respect. Everybody knows me in the business. I have all of that already, man. I've tasted the good life, I've toured the world, I've done all of that. Now I want to do something meaningful and helpful. Hopefully, because a lot of kids are being steered the wrong way.

Puerto Rocks

Moving into the 1990s, then, the prospects and context have changed for Latino rap. Hugely popular albums like *Latin Alliance, Dancehall Reggaespañol* and *Cypress Hill* have been called a "polyphonic outburst" marking the emergence of "the 'real' Latin hip-hop." Kid Frost's assembly of Latin Alliance is referred to as "a defining moment in the creation of a nation-wide Latino/Americano hip-hop aesthetic." Unity of Chicanos and Puerto Ricans, which has long eluded politicos and admen, is becoming a reality in rap, and its potential impact on the culture wars seems boundless: "Where once the folks on opposite coasts were strangers, they've become one nation 'kicking Latin lingo on top of a scratch', samplin' substrate.... There is no question that we are entering an era when the multicultural essence of Latino culture will allow for a kind of shaking-out process that will help define the Next Big Thing."[4] Not only is the use of Spanish and bilingual rhyming accepted, but it has even become a theme in some of the best-known rap lyrics, like Kid Frost's "Ya Estuvo," Cypress Hill's "Funky Bi-lingo," and Latin Empire's "Palabras." Latino rappers are cropping up everywhere, from the tongue-twisting, "trabalengua" Spanglish of one Chicago-Rican group to the lively current of Tex-Mex rap in New Mexico and Arizona.[5] And it's not only the rappers themselves who have been building these bicultural bridges: Latin musical groups as varied as El Gran Combo, Wilfredo Vargas, Manny Oquendo's Libre, and Los Pleneros de la 21 have all incorporated rap segments and numbers into their repertoires.

But while he shares these high hopes, a seasoned veteran of "the business" like Charlie Chase remains acutely aware of the pitfalls and distortions involved. After all, he had witnessed firsthand what was probably the first and biggest scam in rap history, when Big Bank Hank and Sylvia Robinson of Sugar Hill Records used a rhyme by his close friend and fellow Cold Crush brother Grandmaster Caz on "Rapper's Delight" and never gave him credit. The story has been told elsewhere, as by Steven Hager in his book, but Charlie's is a lively version.

This is how it happened. Hank was working in a pizzeria in New Jersey, flipping pizza. And he's playing Cas' tape, right? Sylvia Robinson walks in, the president of Sugar Hill. She's listening to this, it's all new to her. Mind you, there were never any rap records. She says, "Hey, man, who's this?" He says, "I manage this guy. He's a rapper." She says, "Can you do this? Would you do this on a record for me?" And he said, "Yeah, sure. No problem." And she says, "Okay, fine." So he calls Cas up and says, "Cas, can I use your rhymes on a record? Some lady wants to make a record." You see what happened? Cas didn't have foresight. He couldn't see down the road. He never imagined in a million years what was going to come out of that. He didn't know, so he said, "Sure, fine, go ahead." With no papers, no nothing. And it went double platinum! Double platinum! "Rapper's Delight." A single. A double platinum single, which is a hard thing to do.

Charlie doesn't even have to go that far back to reflect on how commercial interests tend to glamorize and, in his word, "civilize" rap sources. He tells of his own efforts to land a job as an A&R (artist and repertoire) person with a record label. "All of this knowledge, all of this experience. I have the ear, I'm producing for all of these people. I mean, I know. You cannot get a more genuine person than me. I can't get a job." The gatekeepers of the industry could hardly be farther removed from the vitality of hip-hop. "I go to record labels to play demos for A&R guys that don't know a thing about rap. They talk to me and they don't even know who I am. White guys that live in L.A. Forty years old, thirty-five years old, making seventy, a hundred thousand a year, and they don't know a thing! And they're picking records to sell, and half of what they're picking is bullshit. And I'm trying to get somewhere and I can't do it."

As for promoting bilingual rap, the obstacles are of course compounded, all the talk of "pan-Latin unity" notwithstanding. "Not that long ago," Charlie mentions, "Latin Empire was having trouble with a Hispanic promoter at Atlantic Records who wouldn't promote their records. You know what he told them? (And he's a Latino.) He told them, 'Stick to one language.' And that's negative, man. You're up there, man, pull the brother up." And of course it's not only the limits on possible expressive idioms that signal a distortion but the media's ignorance of rap's origins. *Elle* magazine, for example, announced that Mellow Man Ace "has been crowned the initiator of Latin rap," their only evident source being Mellow Man himself: "I never thought it could be done. Then in 1985 I heard Mean Machine do a 20-second Spanish bit on their 'Disco Dream.' I bugged out." And the Spanish-language *Más* magazine then perpetuated the myth by proclaiming that it was Mellow Man Ace "quien concibió la idea de hacer rap en español" ("whose idea it was to do rap in Spanish").[6]

The problem is that in moving "from the barrio to *Billboard*," as Kid Frost puts it, Latino rappers have faced an abrupt redefinition of function and practice. The ten-year delay in the acceptance of Spanish rhymes was due in no small part to the marketing of rap, through the eighties, as a strictly African American musical style with a characteristically Afrocentric message. Charlie Chase confronted this even among some of his fellow rappers at the New Music Seminar in 1990 and appealed to his own historical authority to help set the record straight.

> I broke on a big panel. Red Alert, Serch from Third Base, Chuck D, the guys from the West Coast, these are all my boys, mind you, these are all of my friends. So I went off on these guys because they were like "Black this, and Black music," and I said "Hold it!" I jumped up and I said, "Hold up, man. What are you talking about, a Black thing, man? I was part of the Cold Crush Brothers, man. We opened doors for all you guys." And the crowd went berserk, man. And I grabbed the mike and I just started going off. I'm like, "Not for nothing, man, but don't knock it. It's a street thing. I liked it because it came from the street and I'm from the street. I'm a product of the environment." I said that to Serch, I pointed to Serch, 'cause that's his record from his album. And I said, "Yo, man, rap is us. You're from the street, that's you man, that's rap. It ain't no Black, White or nothing thing, man. To me, rap is colorblind, that's that!" The niggahs were applauding me and stuff. I got a lot of respect for that.

Latin Empire has had to put forth the same argument in explaining their own project. As Rick Rodríguez aka "Puerto Rock" puts it, "When it comes to hip-hop I never pictured it with a color." They too are a "product of the environment" and see no need to relinquish any of their Puerto Rican background. "Our influence," Puerto Rock says, "is the stuff you see around you. Things you always keep seeing in the ghetto. But they don't put it in art. It's streetwise. The styles, the fashions, the music is not just for one group. Everybody can do it. But too many Puerto Ricans don't understand. There's a big group of Latinos that's into hip-hop, but most of them imitate Black style or fall into a trance. They stop hanging out with Latin people and talking Spanish. I'm proving you can rap in Spanish and still be dope." Puerto Rock's cousin and partner in Latin Empire, Anthony Boston aka MC KT, has had to deal even more directly with this stereotype of rap, as he is often mistaken for a young African American and was raised speaking more English than Spanish. KT's rhymes in "We're Puerto Rican and Proud!" serve to clarify the issue:

> I rarely talk Spanish and a little trigueño
> People be swearin' I'm a moreno
> Pero guess what? I'm Puertorriqueño.
> Word'em up.

All jokes aside, I ain't tryin' to dis any race
And

Puerto Rock
He'll announce everyplace . . .

M.C. KT
That I'll perform at, so chill, don't panic
It is just me, Antonio, another deso Hispanic.

To drive the point home, the initials KT stand for "Krazy Taino": "It's fly," Puerto rock comments. "With a 'K,' and the 'r' backwards like in Toys-"R"-Us. In our next video he's going to wear all the chief feathers and that. Nice image. With all the medallions and all that we've got. Like in Kid Frost in his video, he wears the Mexican things. That's dope, I like that. Tainos have a lot to do with Puerto Ricans and all that, so we're going to boost it up too. Throw it in the lyrics."

But KT didn't always signal the Puerto Rican cultural heritage, and in fact the derivation of their names shows that their struggle for identity has been a response against the stereotyped symbolism of rap culture. "MC KT is his name because before Latin Empire we were called the Solid Gold MCs. KT stood for karat, like in gold." The group gave up the faddish cliché Solid Gold because they had no jewelry and didn't like what it stood for anyway. When they started, in the early eighties, "We worked with a few different trend names. We started off with our name, our real names, our nicknames. Like Tony Tone, Ricky D, Ricky Rock, all of that. Everything that came out, Rick-ski, every fashion. Double T, Silver T, all of these wild Ts." After trying on all the conformist labels, Rick finally assumed the identity that was given him, as a Puerto Rican, in the African American hip-hop nomenclature itself; he came to affirm what marked him off. "And then I wound up coming up with Puerto Rock," he explains, "and I like that one. That's the one that clicked the most. The Puerto Ricans that are into the trend of hip-hop and all that, they call them Puerto Rocks. They used to see the Hispanics dressing up with the hat to the side and all hip-hop down and some assumed that we're supposed to just stick to our own style of music and friends. They thought rap music was only a Black thing, and it wasn't. Puerto Ricans used to be all crazy with their hats to the side and everything. So that's why they used to call the Puerto Ricans when they would see them with the hats to the side, 'Yo, look at that Puerto Rock, like he's trying to be down.' They used to call us Puerto Rocks, so that was a nickname, and I said, 'I'm going to stick with that. Shut everybody up.'"

The name the group's members chose to replace Solid Gold was arrived at somewhat more fortuitously, but equally reflects their effort to situate themselves in an increasingly multicultural hip-hop landscape.

Riding around in the car with our manager, DJ Corchado, we were trying to think of a Latin name. We was like, the Three Amigos, the Latin Employees, for real, we came up with some crazy names. We kept on, 'cause we didn't want to limit ourselves, with Puerto Rican something, yeah, the Puerto Rican MCs. We wanted Latin something, to represent all Latinos. So we was the Two Amigos, the Three Amigos, then we came up with many other names, Latin Imperials, Latin Alliance. And then when we were driving along the Grand Concourse my manager's car happened to hit a bump when I came out with the Latin Employees. Joking around, we were just making fun and when the car hit the bump my manager thought I said "Empire." I was like, what? Latin Empire! I was like, yo, that's it! As soon as they said it, it clicked. It's like a strong title, like the Zulu Nation.

Groping for names that click, of course, is part of the larger process of positioning themselves in the changing cultural setting of the later eighties. The decision to start rhyming in Spanish was crucial and came more as an accommodation to their families and neighbors than from hearing Mean Machine or any other trends emerging in hip-hop. "In the beginning it was all in English and our families, all they do is play salsa and merengue, they thought you were American. They considered it noise. "'Ay, deja ese alboroto,' 'cut out that racket,' you know. We said, 'Let's try to do it in Spanish, so that they can understand it, instead of complaining to us so much.' They liked it. They was like, 'Oh, mi hijo.'" And when they tried out their Spanish with the mostly Black hip-hop audiences, they were encouraged further. "We used to walk around with the tapes and the big radios and the Black people behind us, 'Yo, man, that sounds dope, that's fly!' They be like, 'yo, I don't understand it, man, but I know it's rhyming and I hear the last word, man, that's bad' they be telling us. We was like, oh, snap! Then I used to try to do it in the street jams and the crowd went crazy."

Acceptance and encouragement from the record industry was a different story, especially in those times before Mellow Man Ace broke the commercial ice. Atlantic did wind up issuing "We're Puerto Rican and Proud," but not until after "Mentirosa" went gold, and then they dragged their feet in promoting it. Since then, aside from their tours and the video "Así Es la Vida" which made the charts on MTV Internacional, Latin Empire has been back in the parks and community events. They believe strongly in the strong positive messages of some rap and have participated actively in both the Stop the Violence and Back to School campaigns. They pride themselves on practicing what they preach in their antidrug and antialcohol rhymes. They continue to be greeted with enthusiastic approval by audiences of all nationalities throughout New York City, and on their tours to Puerto Rico, the Dominican Republic, and, most recently, Cuba.

Their main shortcoming, in the parlance of the business, is that they don't have an "act," a packaged product. As the author of "The Packaging of a Recording Artist" in the July 1992 issue of *Hispanic Business* suggests, "To 'make it' as a professional recording act, you must have all the right things in place. Every element of what a recording act is must be considered and exploited to that act's benefit. The sound, the image, the look—all these factors must be integrated into a single package and then properly marketed to the public." In the packaging and marketing process, the artists and the quality of their work are of course secondary; it's the managers, and the other gatekeepers, who make the act. The article ends, "So while quality singing and a good song are the product in this business, they don't count for much without strong management."[7]

The pages of *Hispanic Business* make no mention of Latin Empire, concentrating as they do on the major Hispanic "products" like Gerardo, Exposé, and Angelica. What they say about Kid Frost is most interesting because here they are dealing with a Latino rapper who is "on his way to stardom in the West Coast Hispanic community" and cannot be expected to "lighten up on who he is just to get that cross-over audience." Clearly the main danger of the artist crossing over is not, from this perspective, that he might thereby sacrifice his focus and cultural context, but that he could lose out on his segment of the market. "It's so tempting for an artist to do that once they've gained acceptance. But you risk losing your base when you do that and you never want to be without your core audience. That's why we work as a team and always include our artists and their managers in the packaging and marketing process."[8]

Latin Empire's members can't seem to get their "act" together because they remain too tied to their base to endure "strong management." Their mission, especially since rap "went Latin," is to reinstate the history and geography of the New York Puerto Rican contribution to hip-hop and counteract the sensationalist version perpetrated by the media. In some of their best-known numbers like "El Barrio," "Mi Viejo South Bronx" and "The Big Manzana," they take us deep into the Puerto Rican neighborhoods and back, "way back, to the days of *West Side Story*," when the New York style originated. Tracing the transition from the gang era to the emergence of the "style wars" of hip-hop, they tell their own stories and dramatize their constant juggling act between Black and Latino and between Island and New York cultures. In another rhyme, "Not Listed," they "take hip-hop to another *tamaño* [level]" by emphasizing the particular Puerto Rican role in rap history and countering the false currency given new arrivals. They end by affirming these ignored roots and rescuing the many early Puerto Rican rappers from oblivion:

> Y'all need to see a médico
> but we don't accept Medicaid
> we don't give no crédito
> we only give credit where credit is due
> we got to give it to the Mean Machine
> and the other brothers who were out there
> lookin' out for Latinos
> some kept it up, some chose other caminos
> but we can't pretend that they never existed
> cause yo, they were out there, just not listed.

In another of their rhymes Latin Empire's members address the music business itself, lashing out at the counterfeits and subterfuges facing them in their "hungry" battle for a fair record deal. Some of "Kinda Hungry" sounds like this:

> Yeah that's right I'm hungry,
> in other words, yo tengo hambre.
> Those who overslept caught a calambre.
> Fake mc's hogging up the posiciones,
> but all we keep hearing is bullshit canciones.
> Don't be feeding mis sueños.
> You might be the head of A&R but I want to meet the dueños.
> So I can let 'em know como yo me siento
> and update 'em on the Latino movimiento
> 'cause I'm getting tired of imitadores
> that shit is muerto, that's why I'm sending you flores,
> En diferentes colores.
> I'm like an undertaker ...
> I still don't understand how they allowed you to make a
> rap record que no sirve para nada.
> I'll eat 'em up like an ensalada.
> Speakin' about food you want comida?
> Na, that's not what I meant,
> what I want is a record deal en seguida
> so we can get this on a 24 track
> put it out on the market and bug out on the feedback.
> Huh, tú no te debas cuenta,
> a nigga like me is in effect en los noventas.
> Straight outta Vega Baja
> the other candidates?
> I knock 'em out the caja, knock 'em out the box
> because I'm not relajando I truly feel it's time

> I started eliminando mc's givin' us a bad nombre.
> I can't see TNT nor my righthand hombre
> the Krazy Taino sellin' out,
> there's no way, there's no how,
> that's not what we're about.
> We're all about looking out for my gente,
> here's some food for thought, comida para la mente.

With all their "hunger" for recognition, members of Latin Empire also feel the burden of responsibility for being the only Nuyorican rap group given any public play at all. They realize that, being synonymous with Puerto Rican rap, they are forced to stand in for a whole historical experience and for the rich variety of street rappers condemned to omission by the very filtering process that they are confronting. A prime example for them of the "not listed" is the "righthand hombre" mentioned here, MC TNT. Virtually unknown outside the immediate hip-hop community in the South Bronx, TNT is living proof that hardcore, streetwise rhyming continues and develops in spite of the diluting effects and choices of the managers and A&R departments. Frequently, Puerto Rock and KT have incorporated TNT into many of their routines, and his rhymes and delivery have added a strong sense of history and poetic language to their presentations.

Like Puerto Rock, TNT (Tomás Robles) was born in Puerto Rico and came to New York at an early age. But in his case, childhood in the rough neighborhoods on the Island figures prominently in his raps, as in this autobiographical section interlaced with samples from Rubén Blades's salsa hit "La Vida Te Da Sorpresas":

> Este ritmo es un invento
> Cuando empiezo a rimar le doy el roo por ciento
> No me llamo Chico, o Federico
> Dónde naciste? Santurce, Puerto Rico
> Cuando era niño no salía'fuera
> porque mataban diario en la cantera
> Esto es verdad, realidad, no un engaño
> mi pae murió cuando yo tenía seis años
> La muerte me afectó con mucho dolor
> pues mi mae empaquetó y nos mudamos pa' Nueva York
> cuando llegué era un ambiente diferente
> pero no me arrepentí, seguí para frente
> y por las noches recé a Dios y a la santa
> porque en mi corazón el coquí siempre canta.

[This rhyme is an invention / When I start to rhyme I give it 100 percent / My name isn't Chico or Federico / Where were you born? / Santurce, Puerto Rico / When I was a boy I didn't go out / 'cause there were killings / in the quarry every day / This is true, reality, not a hoax / my father died when I was six / his death caused me a lot of pain / well my mother packed up and we moved to New York / when I arrived it was a very different atmosphere / but I didn't regret it, I moved ahead / and at night I prayed to God and the holy mother / because in my heart the *coquí* frog always sings.]

By the late 1970s, as an adolescent, TNT was already involved in the gang scene in the South Bronx and took part in the formation of Tough Bronx Action and the Puerto Rican chapters of Zulu Nation. By that time he was already playing congas in the streets and schoolyards and improvising rhymes. When he first heard Mean Machine in 1981, he recalls, he already had note-books of raps in Spanish, though mostly he preserved them in his memory.

TNT also goes by the epithet "un rap siquiatra" ("a rap psychiatrist"): in his lively, story-telling rhymes he prides himself on his biting analysis of events and attitudes in the community. He responds to the charges of gangsterism by pointing to the ghetto conditions that force survival remedies on his people. "Livin' in a ghetto can turn you 'to a gangster" is one of his powerful social raps, and in "Get Some Money" he addresses the rich and powerful directly: "he threw us in the ghetto to see how long we lasted / then he calls us a little ghetto bastard." His "Ven acá tiguerito tiguerito," which compares with anything by Kid Frost and Latin Alliance in sheer verbal ingenuity, captures the intensity of a combative street scene in El Barrio and is laced with phrases from Dominican slang. His programmatic braggadocio is playful and ragamuffin in its effect, yet with a defiance that extends in the last line to the very accentuation of the language:

> Soy un rap siquiatra un rap mecánico
> óyeme la radio y causo un pánico
> te rompo el sistema y te dejo inválido
> con un shock nervioso te ves bien pálido
> no puedes con mi rap
> aléjate aléjate
> tómate una Contact y acuéstate
> o llame a los bomberos que te rescaten.

[I'm a rap psychiatrist, a rap mechanic hear me on the radio and I cause a panic / I break your system and I leave you an invalid / with a nervous shock you look pretty pale / you can't deal with my rap / go away, go away / take a Contac and go to bed / or call the firefighters to come rescue you.]

By the mid-1990s, at twenty-five, MC TNT was already a veteran of Spanish rap battles, still "unlisted" and awaiting his break, yet constantly working on his rhymes and beats every moment he can shake off some of the pressure. He is the closest I have run across to a rapper in the tradition of Puerto Rican plena music, since like that of the master *pleneros* his work is taking shape as a newspaper of the barrios, a running, ironic commentary on the untold events of everyday Puerto Rican life. When all the talk was of referendums and plebiscites to determine the political status of Puerto Rico, TNT had some advice for his people to contemplate:

> Puerto Rico, una isla hermosa,
> donde nacen bonitas rosas,
> plátanos, guineos y yautía,
> Sasón Goya le da sabor a la comida.
> Y ¿quién cocina más que la tía mía?
> Pero el gobierno es bien armado,
> tratando de convertirla en un estado.
> Es mejor la dejen libre (asociado?).
> Cristóbal Colón no fue nadie,
> cruzó el mar con un bonche de salvajes.
> Entraron a Puerto Rico rompiendo palmas,
> asustando a los caciques con armas.
> Chequéate los libros, esto es cierto.

pregúntale a un cacique pero ya está muerto.
¿Cómo él descubrió algo que ya está descubierto?
Boricua, ¡no te vendas!

[Puerto Rico, a beautiful island / where there are pretty roses, / plantains, bananas, and root vegetables, / Goya seasoning gives the food flavor / And who cooks better than my own aunt? / But the government is well armed, / trying to convert it into a state / It's better to leave it free (associated?) / Christopher Columbus was nobody, / he crossed the sea with a bunch of savages, / they entered Puerto Rico destroying the palm trees, / terrifying the Indian chiefs with their weapons. / Check out the books, this is true, / ask one of the Indian chiefs but they're already dead. / How could he discover something already discovered? / Puerto Rico, don't sell yourself!]

Like other Latino groups, Puerto Ricans are using rap as a vehicle for affirming their history, language, and culture under conditions of rampant discrimination and exclusion. The explosion of Spanish-language and bilingual rap onto the pop music scene in recent years bears special significance in the face of the stubbornly monolingual tenor in today's public discourse, most evident in the crippling of bilingual programs and services and in the ominous gains of the "English Only" crusade. And of course along with the Spanish and Spanglish rhymes, Latino rap carries an ensemble of alternative perspectives and an often divergent cultural ethos into the mainstream of U.S. social life. The mass diffusion, even if only for commercial purposes, of cultural expression in the "other" language, and above all its broad and warm reception by fans of all nationalities, may help to muffle the shrieks of alarm emanating from the official culture whenever mention is made of "America's fastest-growing minority." Latin rap lends volatile fuel to the cause of "multiculturalism" in our society, at least in the challenging, inclusionary sense of that embattled term.

For Puerto Ricans, though, rap is more than a newly opened window on their history; rap *is* their history, and Puerto Ricans are an integral part in the history of hip-hop. As the "Puerto rocks" themselves testify in conversation and rhyme, rapping is one of many domains within a larger field of social and creative practices expressive of their collective historical position in the prevailing relations of power and privilege. Puerto Rican participation in the emergence of hip-hop music needs to be understood in direct, interactive relation to their experience in gangs and other forms of association among inner-city youth through the devastating blight of the seventies. "Puerto rocks" are the children of impoverished colonial immigrants facing even tougher times than in earlier decades. They helped make rap what it was to become, as they played a constitutive role in the stylistic definition of graffiti writing and breakdancing.

In addition to these more obvious associations, the formative years of rap follow closely the development of both salsa and Nuyorican poetry, expressive modes which, especially for the young Puerto Ricans themselves, occupy the same creative constellation as the musical and lyrical project of bilingual and bicultural rap. Musically, rap practice among Puerto Ricans is also informed by the strong antecedent tradition of street drumming and, at only a slight remove, their parallel earlier role in styles like doo-wop, boogaloo, and Latin jazz. In terms of poetic language, Spanglish rap is embedded in the everyday speech practices of the larger community over the course of several generations, and even echoes in more than faint ways the tones and cadences of lyrics typical of plena, bomba, and other forms of popular Puerto Rican song.

Like these other contemporaneous and prefiguring cultural practices, the active presence of Puerto Ricans in the creation of rap bears further emphatic testimony to their long history of cultural interaction with African Americans. Hip-hop emerged as a cultural space shared by Puerto Ricans and Blacks, a sharing that once again articulates their congruent and inter-mingling placement in the impinging political and economic geography. It is also a sharing in which, as the story of rap reveals, the dissonances are as telling as the harmonies, and the distances as heartfelt as the intimacy. The Puerto Ricans' nagging intimation that they are treading on Black turf and working in a tradition of performative expression most directly traceable to James Brown and Jimmy Castor, the dozens and the blues, makes rap into a terrain that is as much contested as it is coinhabited on equal terms. Jamaican dubbing, with its strong Caribbean resonance, serves as a bridge in this respect, just as reggae in more recent years is helping to link rap to otherwise disparate musical trends, especially in its reggaespañol dance-hall versions. In the historical perspective of Black and Puerto Rican interaction, rap is thus a lesson in cultural negotiation and transaction as much as in fusions and crossovers, especially as those terms are bandied about in mainstream parlance. If multiculturalism is to amount to anything more than a wishful fancy of a pluralist mosaic, the stories of the "Puerto rocks" show that adequate account must be taken of the intricate jostling and juggling involved along the seams of contemporary cultural life.

What is to become of Latino rap, and how we appreciate and understand its particular messages, will depend significantly on the continuities it forges to its roots among the "Puerto rocks." Recuperating this history, explicitly or by example, and "inventing" a tradition diver-gent from the workings of the commercial culture, makes for the only hope of reversing the instant amnesia that engulfs rap and all forms of emergent cultural discourse as they migrate into the world of pop hegemony. Charlie Chase, TNT, and the other "Puerto rocks" were not only pioneers in some nostalgic sense but helped set the social meaning of rap practice prior to and relatively independent of its mediated commercial meaning. That formative partici-pation of Latinos in rap in its infancy is a healthy reminder that the "rap attack," as Peter Toop argued some years ago now, is but the latest outburst of "African jive," and that the age-old journey of jive has always been a motley and inclusive procession. And as in Cuban-based salsa, the Puerto Rican conspiracy in the present volley shows how creatively a people can adopt and adapt what would seem a "foreign" tradition and make it, at least in part, its own. To return to the first "Puerto rock" I talked with in the early 1980s, I close with a little rhyme by MC Rubie Dee (Rubén García) from the South Bronx:

> Now all you Puerto Ricans you're in for a treat,
> 'cause this Puerto Rican can rock a funky beat.
> If you fall on your butt and you start to bleed,
> Rubie Dee is what all the Puerto Ricans need.
> I'm a homeboy to them 'cause I know what to do,
> 'cause Rubie Dee is down with the black people too.[9]

Study Questions

1. How has hip-hop transitioned from a folk art in its early days into its more commercial form today?
2. In what ways did the ethnic and national traditions of Puerto Rico inform hip-hop culture?
3. What are examples of Puerto Rican expressive culture that can be found in contempo-rary hip-hop?

Notes

1. Quotes of Charlie Chase are from my interview with him, "It's a Street Thing!" published in *Calalloo* 15.4 (Fall 1992): 999–1021.
2. See my article, written in 1984, "Rappin', Writin' and Breakin': Black and Puerto Rican Street Culture in New York City," *Dissent* (Fall 1987): 580–84 (also published in *Centro Journal* 2.3 [Spring 1988]: 34–41). A shortened version of the present chapter appeared as "'Puerto Rican and Proud, Boy-ee!': Rap, Roots, and Amnesia," in Tricia Rose and Andrew Ross, eds., *Microphone Fiends: Youth Music and Youth Culture*, pp. 89–98 (New York: Routledge, 1994). Other references are Craig Castleman, *Getting Up: Subway Graffiti in New York* (Cambridge: MIT Press, 1982); Herbert Kohl, *Golden Boy as Anthony Cool: A Photo Essay on Naming and Graffiti* (New York: Dial, 1972); Steven Hager, *Hip-Hop: The Illustrated History of Break Dancing, Tap Music, and Graffiti* (New York: St. Martin's, 1984). See also David Toop, *The Rap Attack: African Jive to New York Hip-Hop* (Boston: South End, 1984).
3. Quotes from Latin Empire are from my interview with them, "Puerto Raps," published in *Centro Journal* 3.2 (Spring 1991): 77–85.
4. Ed Morales, "How Ya Like Nosotros Now?" *Village Voice*, November 26, 1991, 91.
5. For an overview of Latino rap, see Mandolit del Barco, "Rap's Latino Sabor," in William Eric Perkins, ed., *Droppin' Science: Critical Essays on Rap Music and Hip-Hop Culture* (Philadelphia: Temple University Press, 1996), 63–84.
6. Elizabeth Hanley, "Latin Raps: Nuevo ritmo, A New Nation of Rap Emerges," *Elle*, March 1991, 196–98; C.A., "El rap latino tiene tumbao," *Más* 2.2 (Winter 1990): 81.
7. Joseph Roland Reynolds, "The Packaging of a Recording Artist," *Hispanic Business* 14.7 (July 1992): 28–30.
8. Ibid.
9. Cited in Flores, "Rappin', Writin', and Breakin.'"

8
It's a Family Affair

With the publication of his book *The Black Atlantic* (1993), Paul Gilroy has long been positioned to provide alternative understandings to our notions of black nationalism and diaspora. Gilroy's fixation with the cultural exchanges that occurred amongst the black diaspora via the circuits of the Atlantic ocean, challenged models that argued for the hegemony of Africa in diasporic formations. "It's a Family Affair" extends those arguments within the realm of black popular culture.

In his essay, Gilroy challenges the idea that essential black identities are tied to specific locations. Furthermore, Gilroy challenges the notion that any one black community is representative of the most authentic black community or experience. Thus Gilroy's essay is perfectly pitched to debates within hip-hop about which "'hood," in the parlance of an earlier era, was "keeping it (more) real."

It's a Family Affair

Paul Gilroy

The complicated phenomena we struggle to name as black nationalism, cultural nationalism, and neonationalism have now been so reconfigured that our essentially nineteenth-century, or maybe even eighteenth-century, understanding of them has to be abandoned. Everywhere, as a result of both internal and external pressures, the integrity of the nation-state as the primary focus of economic, political, and cultural action, has been compromised. The impact of this on nationalist ideologies (black and otherwise) is particularly important and needs to be taken into account. I am not satisfied with just pinning the prefix "neo" onto nationalism and feeling that we've done the job of analyzing it. If we are to distinguish the contemporary discourses of black nationalism from the black nationalisms of the past, we have to examine the novel modes of information and cultural production in which they circulate.

Perhaps the easiest place to begin is to think about the changes in information and communication technologies that have taken all nationalisms away from their historic association with the technology of print culture. This is one way of conceptualizing the changed notions of space and time we associate with the impact of the postmodern and the postindustrial on black cultures. If we are to think of ourselves as diaspora people, how do we then understand the notion of space? How do we adjust our understanding of the relationship between spatialization and identity formation in order to deal with these techno-cultural changes? One thing we might do is take a cue from Manuel Castells,[1] who describes the shift from an understanding of space based on notions of place and fixity to an understanding of place based on flows. Or, what another exiled Englishman, Iain Chambers, introduces in his very suggestive distinction between roots and routes.[2] (I don't think this pun has quite the same force in American versions of English.) If we're going to pick up the vernacular ball and run with it, then maybe the notion of the crossroads—as a special location where unforeseen, magical things happen—might be an appropriate conceptual vehicle for rethinking this dialectical tension between cultural roots and cultural routes, between the space marked out by places and the space constituted by flows. The crossroads has a nicely Africalogical sound to it too: a point at which the flows of black popular cultures productively intersect.

These issues point to the way we will have to refine the theorizing of the African diaspora if it is to fit our changed transnational and intercultural circumstances. Though the current popularity of Afrocentrism points to other possibilities, we might consider experimenting, at least, with giving up the idea that our culture needs to be centered anywhere except where we are when we launch our inquiries into it. Certainly, we will have to find a better way to deal with the obvious differences between and within black cultures—differences that live on under the signs of their disappearances, constituting boundaries that stubbornly refuse to be erased.

I wish I had five bucks for every time I've heard the trope of the family wheeled out to do the job of recentering things when the debates of the last few days promised to question the spurious integrity of ideal racial culture. The trope of the family is especially significant right now when the idea of belonging to a nation is only infrequently invoked to legitimate the essence of today's black political discourses. Certainly in England, and probably in the United States, as well, there are a number of other legitimization strategies, but the invocation of "race" as family is everywhere. Its dominance troubles me because, at the moment, in the black English constituency out of which I speak, the trope of the family is not at the center of our discussion of what a black politics could or should be. And I'll return to that point later.

Afrocentricity names itself "systematic nationalism" (that's what Molefi Kete Asante calls it),[3] but it is stubbornly focused around the reconstitution of individual consciousness rather than around the reconstruction of the black nation in exile or elsewhere. The civic, nation-building activity that defined the Spartan-style aspirations of black nationalism in the nineteenth century has been displaced in favor of the almost aesthetic cultivation of a stable, pure, racial self. The "ism" in that nationalism is often lacking, too; it is no longer constructed as a coherent political ideology. It appears more usually as a set of therapies—tactics in the never-ending struggle for psychological and cultural survival. In some nonspecific way, then, a new idea of Africanness, conveniently disassociated from the politics of contemporary Africa, operates transnationally and interculturally through the symbolic projection of "race" as kinship. It is now more often a matter of style, perspective, or survivalist technique than a question of citizenship, rights, or fixed contractual obligations (the things that defined nationality in earlier periods).

Indeed, though contemporary nationalism draws creatively on the traces of romantic theories of national belonging and national identity, derived from the ethnic metaphysics of eighteenth-century Europe, Afrocentric thinking attempts to construct a sense of black particularity *outside* of a notion of a national identity. Its founding problem lies in the effort to figure sameness across national boundaries and between nation-states. The first sentence of Asante's "Nia—The Way" can be used to illustrate this: "This is the way that came to Molefe in America."[4] But the text's elisions of African-American particulars into African universals belie this modesty. Look also at the moment in the same text where the author struggles with the fact that only thirty-seven percent of the blacks who live in the Western hemisphere live in the United States. Forty percent, he muses to himself, live in Brazil. What do we do about that? Where are their inputs into Africalogical theory?

The understanding of blackness that emerges routinely these days gets projected, then, onto a very different symbolic landscape than it did in either nineteenth-century black nationalism, in Garveyism, or in the nationalism of the Black Power period. The new popular pantheon of black heroes is apparently a diasporic one—Marcus, Malcolm, Martin, Marley, Mandela, and *Me*! The narcissistic momentum of that masculine list is another symptom of a cultural implosion that must work against the logic of national identity. The flow is always inward, never outward; the truth of racialized being is sought, not in the world, but in the psyche. I know that the moment of epistemological narcissism is necessary in building movements that actually move, but doesn't it abandon the world of public politics, leaving us with a form of therapy that has little to offer beleaguered communities?

Some of the rhetoric of nationalism, however, does remain. It's there in the service of groups like the Five Percent Nation and the Nation of Islam. But for them it legitimates an ideology of separation that applies as viciously within the race as it does between blacks and whites. If there is still a coherent nationalism in play though—and I say this from my own perch in London—I want to suggest that it is the nationalism of black Americans. This nationalism is a powerful subtext in the discourse of Afrocentricity, but it has evolved from an earlier period in black U.S. history. It is a very particular way of looking at the world that, far more than it expresses any exilic consciousness of Africa, betrays a distinctively American understanding of ethnicity and cultural difference. The family is the approved, natural site where ethnicity and racial culture are reproduced. In this authoritarian pastoral patriarchy, women are identified as the agents and means of this reproductive process.

This is where the question of the family begins to bite: representations of the family in contemporary black nationalism, transcoded—maybe wrongly—from London, appear to mark the site of what can, at the least, be called an ambivalent relationship to America. So, recognizing this, I don't want to call it Afrocentrism any more. I want to call it Americocentrism. And I want to suggest that it has evolved in a very uneasy mode of coexistence with the pan-African political discourses that gave birth to it. Of course, the identification with Africa, on which that Americocentrism is premised, is necessarily partial and highly selective. Contemporary Africa, as I have said, appears nowhere. The newly invented criteria for judging racial authenticity are supplied instead by restored access to original African forms and codes. It is significant, however—and this is where the trope of the family begins to look like a disaster for black feminism—that those definitions of authenticity are disproportionately defined by ideas about nurturance, about family, about fixed gender roles, and generational responsibilities. What is authentic is also frequently defined by ideas about sexuality and patterns of interaction between men and women that are taken to be expressive of essential, that is, racial, difference. This authenticity is inseparable from talk about the conduct and management of bitter gender-based conflicts, which is now recognized as essential to familial, racial, and communal health. Each of these—the familial, the racial, the communal—leads seamlessly into the next. Where was that heavy chain of signifiers forged? Whose shackles will it make? How does that conjunction reveal the impact, not just of an unchanged Africa, but of a contemporary America?

Now, the changed status of nationality in black political discourse can also be felt in the way the opposition between the local and the global has been reinscribed in our culture and in our consciousness. Today, we are told that the boys, and the girls, are from the 'hood—not from the race, and certainly not from the nation. It's important that the 'hood stands in opposition to foreign things—if you remember John Singleton's film—in opposition to the destructive encroachments of Seoul-to-Seoul Realty or the idea of turning the ghetto into black Korea. (Does Singleton's choice of that proper name for the Korean menace signal a rebuke to Soul II Soul?)

From London, the untranslatability of the term "hood" troubled me. I thought it marked a significant shift away from the notion of the ghetto, which is eminently exportable, and which carries its own very interesting intercultural history that we should be able to play with. But, if the 'hood is the essence of where blackness can now be found, which 'hood are we talking about? How do we weigh the achievements of one 'hood against the achievements of another? How is black life in one 'hood connected to life in others? Can there be a blackness that connects, articulates, synchronizes experiences and histories across the diaspora space? Or is it only the sign of Larry Fishburne's patriarchal power that holds these different local forms of blackness together?

This matters not just because images of black sociality not derived from the family seem to have disappeared from our political cultures, but also because, if Tim Dog is to be believed, Compton is as foreign to some blacks in New York as Kingston, London, Havana, Lagos, Aswan, or Capetown—possibly even more so. His popular outrage against West Coast Jheri curls and whack lyrics registers (as does his claim that all that gang shit is for dumb mother-fuckers) disappointment and frustration that the idea of a homogeneous national community has become impossible and unthinkable. Maybe this is what happens when one 'hood speaks to another.

> Ah, shit. Motherfucker step to the ring and cheer.
> The Tim Dog is here.
> Let's get right down to the nitty gritty.
> And talk about a bullshit city.
> Talking about niggers from Compton.
> They're no comp and they truly ain't stompin'.
> Tim Dog, a black man's task,
> I'm so bad, I wear Superman's mask.
> All you suckers that rip from the West Coast,
> I'll dis' and spray your ass like a roach.
> You think you're cool with your curls and your shades,
> ... and you'll be yelling outrage.
> A hard brother that lives in New York.
> We suckas are hard, and we don't have to score.
> Shut your mouth, or we come out stompin'.
> And yo Easy, fuck Compton.[5]

Now, I don't pretend to understand everything Tim Dog's performance means here in the United States, but in London it has a very particular meaning. This has to do with a bewilderment about some of the self-destructive and sibling-cidal patterns of sociality that have been a feature of black U.S. inner-urban life. The same tension between the local and the global—implosion at one end, dissemination at the other—is, again, part of the story. Of course, when these things come down the transnational wire to us in Europe and to black folks in other parts of the world, they become metaphysical statements about what blackness is. And we have to deal with them on that basis.

Obviously, there are other voices, and there are other subject positions. In fact, one of the things I find troubling in debates about rap is that I don't think anyone actually knows what the totality of its hypercreativity looks like. I am a compulsive consumer (user, actually) of that culture, but I can't keep up with the volume of hip-hop product anymore. I don't know if anyone can. There is simply too much of it to be assimilated, and the kinds of judgments we make have to take that volume into account. It's a flood—it's not a flow, it's a flood, actually—and just bobbing up and down in the water is not enough.

But when we come back to the family, the idea of hip-hop as a dissident, critical space looks more questionable. Ironically, it is precisely where the motivation is constructive that the pastoral patriarchy of race as family gets reproduced. Another voice I want to present answers, in a sense, the calculated nihilism of Tim Dog. It's an attempt, by KRS 1 (Chris Parker), to locate the politics of race in what he describes as the opposition between civilization and technology—an interesting opposition because of its desire to hold onto the narrative of civilization and make it part of a grand narrative of black development. But this attempt is notable not just for its humanism—humanity versus technology—but for the extraordinary emphasis that falls on the family. I wonder how much the trope of the family allows him to hold the very diverse forces of this new racialized humanism together.

> Be a Man, not a sucker.
> And don't disrespect your baby's mother.
> When the pressure's on, don't run for cover.
> We gotta move on and be strong for one another.

You can't just be a lover, build the nation.
We gotta start with better relations.
'Cause the family is the foundation.
We're here to heal, and we're here for the duration.
Multi-educating.

Definitely develop your African mind because we are all family. And once we see that we are all brothers and sisters no matter what, we go far beyond the nuclear family—from an Afrocentric point of view.[6]

I don't want to be forced into the position of having to point out that it may not help to collapse our intraracial differences into the image of ourselves as brothers and sisters any more than I want to be forced into the position of saying that we don't all recognize our own images in the faces of Clarence Thomas and Anita Hill (which adorn the posters for this event) but that is some of what this Americocentric obsession with family brings to mind. I recognize that the discourse of racial siblinghood is a democratic one. I know it emerged from the communitarian radicalism of the church and that, as W.E.B. Du Bois pointed out long ago in *The Souls of Black Folk*, this happened in a period before the slaves enjoyed the benefits of nuclear family life. The political language of brotherhood and sisterhood can be used in ways that accentuate an image of community composed of those with whom we disagree. From this perspective, the differences we still experience, in spite of white supremacy's centripetal effects, might be seen as a precious and potentially productive resource. However, at the moment, the wind is blowing in another direction.

Obviously, not all of this popular culture wants to bury its differences in images of an organic, natural, racial family. And I have been especially engaged by the voices within hip-hop culture that have sought other strategies for living with difference and building on the hybrid qualities of the form itself to affirm the value of mixing and what might be called creolization. There are some absorbing poetic attempts to explore the consequences of a new political ontology and a new historicity. I am excited, for example, by Rakim's repeated suggestion that "it ain't where you're from, it's where you're at." It grants a priority to the present, emphasizing a view of identity as an ongoing process of self-making at a time when myths of origins hold so much appeal. Sometimes that kind of idea is strongest where the Caribbean styles and forms, very often dominated by pan-African motifs, are most developed. Caribbean popular cultures have their own rather more mediated and syncretized relationships to Africa. But it's also important to remember that reggae has constructed its own romance of racial nihilism in gun culture, misogyny, and machismo.

Rebel MC's "Wickedest Sound" comes from London and points to a different notion of authenticity.[7] Its racial witness is produced out of semiotic play rather than ethnic fixity, and a different understanding of tradition emerges out of the capacity to combine the different voices, styles, and motifs drawn from all kinds of sources in a montage of blackness(es). This version of the idea of authenticity, premised on a notion of flows, is also alive in diaspora culture. It's dear to me because it appeared within the version of hip-hop culture that we have produced in London. There are, of course, African-American traces here struggling to be heard among the Caribbean samples, but, happily, the trope of race as family is nowhere in sight.

Against this playful, vibrant, postracial utopia—which argues that there is no betrayal in the acknowledgment of a white listening public—an Americocentric, postnationalist essence of blackness has been constructed through the dubious appeal to family.

There have been other periods in black political history where the image of race as family has been prominent. The nineteenth-century ideas of a nationality exclusively concerned with male soldier-citizens were produced in a period when an anti-imperialist or an anti-racist political project among diaspora blacks was unthinkable. We would do well to reconsider them now because they haunt us. In *Africa or America*, Alexander Crummell drew his theory of nationality and racial personality from the work of Lord Beaconsfield (Benjamin Disraeli):

> Races, like families, are organisms and the ordinance of God. And race feeling, like family feeling, is of divine origin. The extinction of race feeling is just as possible as the extinction of family feeling. Indeed, race is family. The principle of continuity is as masterful in races as it is in families, as it is in nations.[8]

This discourse of race as community, as family, has been born again in contemporary attempts to interpret the crisis of black politics and social life as a crisis solely of black masculinity. The family is not just the site of cultural reproduction; it is also identified as the mechanism for reproducing the cultural dysfunction that disables the race as a whole. And since the race is nothing more than an accumulation of families, the crisis of black masculinity can be fixed. It is to be repaired by instituting appropriate forms of masculinity and male authority, intervening in the family to rebuild the race.

Even hip-hop culture—the dissonant soundtrack of racial dissidence—has become complicit with this analysis. It's interesting, in thinking about the changing resonance of the word "nation" in black culture, that reports say Michael Jackson wants to call his new record company Nation Records. (One of the extraordinary things about the Jacksons is that they have turned their dysfunctionality as a black family into such an interesting marketing strategy.) Images of the black family complement the family tropes of the cultural forms themselves. These images are all around us in the selling of black popular culture. They are so visible in the marketing of Spike Lee and his projects that they point to the value of reading his oeuvre as a succession of Oedipal crises.

On the strange kind of cultural loop I live, I saw Marlon Riggs's powerful film *Tongues United* for the second time on the same night I first saw *Boys N the Hood*. (We get these things in a different sequence than in the States.) Listening to that authoritative voice saying that black men loving black men was *the* revolutionary act—not *a* revolutionary act but *the* revolutionary act—the force of that definite article set me to thinking about *Boyz N the Hood*. I know there are differences between these two projects. I have an idea of where some of them dwell. But aren't there also similarities and convergences in the way that love between men is the common focus of these "texts"?[9]

Let me say why I think the prominence of the family is a problem. Spreading the Oedipal narrative around a bit can probably produce some interesting effects, but this bears repeating: the trope of the family is central to the means whereby the crisis we are living—of black social and political life—gets represented as the crisis of black masculinity. That trope of the family is there, also, in the way conflict, within and between our communities, gets resolved through the mystic reconstruction of the ideal heterosexual family. This is the oldest conservative device in the book of modern culture. Once again, *Boyz N the Hood* is the most obvious illustration of an authentically black and supposedly radical product that is complacently comfortable working within those deeply conservative codes. In Isaac Julien's recent film *Young Soul Rebels*, the fragile image of nonfamilial community that appears has been much criticized. It's the point at which the film ends and a kind of surrogate, joyfully disorganic, and synthetic kin group constitutes itself slowly and tentatively—in and around desire, through music, affirmation, celebration, and play.

Lest this look like a binary split between conservative, familial Americana and the truly transgressive counterculture of black Britons, I want to amplify what I take to be a similar note of disorganicity in the way that kinship can be represented. It is drawn from an American hip-hop record popular on both sides of the Atlantic right now—a tune called "Be a Father to Your Child" by Ed O.G. and Da Bulldogs.[10] It's been very popular in London, partly because of the sample it uses—a seventies black nationalist love song called "Searching" from Roy Ayers—which gets transposed into a different conceptual key by this contemporary appropriation. Two things interest me about this cut. First of all, the object of desire in the original version of the tune was gendered female; it is about searching for the love of a black woman. In the Ed O.G. version, the object of desire is ungendered. I found the opening up of that signifier suggestive. It means that when Ed O.G. talks about familial obligation, he's not saying be a father to your son—he's saying be a father to your child.

Second, and more important, Ed O.G. makes the pragmatic *functionality* of family the decisive issue, not the biological payback involved in family life. If you are responsible for producing a child with someone, he says, and that child is being supported by somebody else who is prepared to father it effectively when you fail, then back off and let him get on with it—even if that person is not the biological parent. That small gesture is something I want to celebrate. I think it shows—though I don't want to sound prescriptive about this—that the struggle over the meaning of family is alive within the culture, that a critical perspective on these complex questions isn't something that needs to be imported into that vernacular from outside by people like us. We don't play that role.

> Hey yo, be a father.
> It's not, Why bother?, son.
> A boy can make 'em, but a man can raise 'em.
> And if you did it, admit it. Then stick with it.
> Don't say it ain't yours, 'cause all women are not whores.
> Ninety percent represent a woman that is faithful.
> Ladies can I hear it?
> *Thank you.*
> When a girl gets pregnant, her man is gonna run around,
> dissin' her for now, but when it's born he wants to come around
> talkin' that I'm sorry for what I did.
> And all of a sudden, he now wants to see his kid.
> She had to bear it by herself and take care of it by herself.
> And givin' her some money for milk don't really help.
> Half of the fathers and sons and daughters don't even want to take 'em.
> But it's so easy for them to make 'em.
> It's true, if it weren't for you, the child wouldn't exist.
> Afterwards, he's your responsibility, so don't resist.
> Be a father to your child …
> See, I hate when a brother makes a child and then denies it.
> Thinkin' that money is the answer, so he buys it
> a whole bunch of gifts and a lot of presents.
> It's not the presents, it's your presence and the essence
> of bein' there and showin' the baby that you care.
> Stop sittin' like a chair and havin' your baby wondering
> where you are or who you are.
> Who you are is daddy.
> Don't act like you ain't 'cause that really makes me mad, G,
>   to see a mother and a baby suffer.
> I had enough o' brothers who don't love the
> fact that a baby brings joy into your life.
> You can still be called daddy if the mother's not your wife.

> Don't be scared, be prepared.
> 'Cause love is gonna getcha.
> It'll always be your child, even if she ain't witcha.
> So, don't front on your child when it's your own,
> 'cause if you front now then you'll regret it when it's grown.
> Be a father to your child ...
> Put yourself in his position and see what you've done.
> But just keep in mind that you're somebody's son.
> How would you like it if your father was a stranger,
> and then tried to come into your life and tried to change the
> way that your mother raised ya.
> Now wouldn't that amaze ya?
> To be or not to be.
> That is the question.
> When you're wrong, you're wrong.
> It's time to make a correction.
> Harrassin' the mother for bein' with another man.
> But if the brother man can do it better than you can, *let 'im.*
> Don't sweat 'im, dude.
> Let him do the job that you couldn't do ... [11]

I'll end by saying that even the best of this familialization of politics is still a problem. I don't want to lose sight of that. I want to have it both ways: I want to be able to valorize what we can recover; and I want to be able to cite the disastrous consequences that follow when the family supplies not just the only symbols of political agency we can find in the culture, but the only object upon which that agency can be seen to operate as well. Let's remind ourselves that there are other possibilities. Historically, black political culture's most powerful notions of agency have been figured through the sacred. They can also get figured through the profane, and there, a different idea of worldly redemption can be observed. Both of these possibilities come together for me in the traditions of musical performance that culminate in hip-hop. In them, we find what I call the ethics of antiphony—a kind of ideal communicative moment in the relationship between the performer and the crowd that surpasses anything the structures of the family can provide.

Study Questions

1. Does any community formation have a monopoly on the black experience?
2. How do questions about realness and authenticity limit our understanding of black communities and practices that don't adhere to popular presentations of black pathology?
3. How might we think about diaspora as a concept within hip-hop practices?

Notes

1. Manuel Castells, *The Informational City* (Oxford: Basil Blackwell, 1991).
2. This distinction has also been employed in similar ways by Dick Hebdige and James Clifford. See Iain Chambers, *Border Dialogues* (New York: Routledge, 1990).
3. Molefi Kete Asante, *Afrocentricity* (Trenton, N.J.: Africa World Press, 1988).
4. Ibid.
5. Tim Dog, *Fuck Compton* [EP], Columbia Records, 1991. CD/Cassette.

6. H.E.A.L. [Human Education Against Lies], KRS 1, "Family Got to Get Busy," *Civilization Against Technology*, Elektra/Asylum Records, 1991. CD/Cassette.

7. Rebel MC, "Wickedest Sound," *Black Meaning Good*, Desire Records LUVCD12.

8. Alexander Crummell, *Africa or America* (Springfield, Mass.: Willey and Co., 1891), 46.

9. I use the word "texts" in quotation marks because I don't think any analysis that appropriates these cultural forms exclusively as texts will ever be adequate.

10. Ed O.G. & Da Bulldogs, *Life of a Kid in the Ghetto*, Mercury Records, 1991. CD/Cassette.

11. Ibid.

9

On the Question of Nigga Authenticity

In his essay "On the Question of Nigga Authenticity" philosopher and critical theorist Ronald A.T. Judy examines one of the most recognizable tropes of hip-hop culture. Judy makes clear distinctions between the uses and meanings of the pejoratives nigger/nigga to make a collateral point about the circulation of black bodies within exploitive labor systems.

At the crux of Judy's highly theoretical argument is a redefinition of authenticity as that which adapts to the pressures of capitalist consumption. Given the history of blacks as exploited laborers, Judy argues that hip-hop's relationship to the marketplace was a logical development. Rather than read hip-hop's crass commercialism as some form of "sell out," Judy argues that hip-hop's adaptability to the forces of commodification is evidence of its authenticity.

On the Question of Nigga Authenticity

R.A.T. Judy

Almost every law and method ingenuity could devise was employed by the legislatures to reduce the Negroes to serfdom,—to make them slaves of the state, if not of individuals.... [T]he Negro is coming more and more to look upon law and justice, not as protecting safeguards, but as sources of humiliation and oppression.

W.E.B. Du Bois, The Souls of Black Folk

Real Niggaz don't die.

Dr. Dre

The straight up nigga.—There is the story of the hard-core OG, down with the One Percent Nation, who kicked the pure fact in 1991 and declared this the era of the nigga.

"It is the end of black folk, and the beginning of global niggadom," he proclaimed.

The brother got props from a serious transnational corporation that gave his record global distribution in two media formats: audio and video. It was picked up and echoed in all formats of the news media, becoming a great event. Folks started buggin', and a panic set in. In other words, there was considerable acrimony. How has this brother gotten so lost? some asked. Why would a serious transnational corporation be associated with a nigger? asked others who had considerable capital investment but little understanding of the communicability of affect. Those concerned with the OG's soul wondered out loud where we have come to as a people. They wanted to know if this was the beginning of the end of black folk. Have our children come to achieve what four hundred years of slavery and oppression could not, the death of black folk?

The OG stepped to these believers and busted 'em out.

"This is not the beginning of the end of black folk," he said.

"They are always already dead wherever you find them. The nurturing haven of black culture which assured memory and provided a home beyond the ravishing growth of capitalism is no longer. There cannot be any cultural authenticity in resistance to capitalism. The illusion of immaterial purity is no longer possible. It is no longer possible to be black against the system. Black folk are dead, killed by their own faith in willfully being beyond, and in spite of, power. Will beyond power has no passion, only affect. Black folk have killed themselves by striving to conserve themselves in a willful affect—the productive labor of modern subjects, a.k.a. work. Black folk, who have always been defined in relation to work, went the way of work.

"There is a motto circulating these days: Real Black Folks Work. And where else can you find real black folk except in the killing fields, which is, by definition, the place for nonproductive consumption—the end of work? The killing fields, then, are the place of non-work for complete consumption of needless workers. Real black folk are already dead, walking around consuming themselves in search of that which is no longer possible, that which defines them. Understand that the killing fields are everywhere; and whoever is born after us in the killing fields will belong to a higher history, the history of the nigga. You all are upset by this because you don't know what it is to be a nigga. A nigga is that which emerges from the demise of human capital, what gets articulated when the field nigger loses value as labor. The nigga is unemployed, null and void, walking around like ... a nigga who understands that all possibility converts from capital, and capital does not derive from work."

After this, the OG's record sales grew rapidly; so did the acrimony, and increasing pressure was put on the transnational corporation to be responsive to community standards of decency. No Niggaz Allowed was the sentiment, and the OG was censured. Ending his contractual relation with the transnational, he dropped more science.

"You all ain't ready yet. You cannot even hear what is being spoken by your own children, let alone understand, because you got your heads up your asses and are on capitalism's dick. You may think I'm too early, but I'm just in time. Some straight up niggaz with attitude done already busted some serious nigga moves."

At the same time he ended his contractual relation with the transnational, he incorporated his own independent label and hooked up with another transnational network of distribution. When called to account for his own blatant embrace of capitalism, his only reply was: "It's a home invasion."

Understanding the possibilities of nigga authenticity in the emerging realities of transnational capital is a humbling undertaking. From the pulpit to the lectern, from the television news desk to the op-ed pages of the leading papers, the general consensus is "this nigga is deadly dangerous." It is this nigga who gang-bangs, this nigga who is destroying the fabric of society, who has spread across the country like an infestation, bringing an epidemic of death and despair to black America. All this, on the assumption that this nigga of the present age is somehow related to the "bad nigger" of slavery and the postbellum South, an assumption that remains to be tested.

Citing Leon R. Harris's 1925 essay, "The Steel-Drivin' Man," as its principal literary quotation, the *Oxford English Dictionary* defines *nigga* as a southern pronunciation of *nigger*, whose variant forms are *niggah, nigguh*, and *niggur*: "Howdy niggahs, ... how's you all dis mawnin'."[1] The next quotation is from Chester Himes's *Black on Black*: "Niggah, ef'n yo is talkin' tuh me, Ah ain' liss'nin'."[2] The *h* gets dropped in Paulette Cross's recording of a joke told to her by Ronald Taylor, of Milwaukee, Wisconsin, in 1968: "There's this uh—black cat from the north, ya know, he's a bad nigga.... There's this nigga who went to the 'Sip, you know, uh—Mississippi.... They end up losing all of their money to that big nigga who is supposed to be the epitome of 'nigga-ness'."[3] The irregular spelling of the term persisted, however, well into the mid-seventies, which is when the OED's citations end. *Nigga* became the dominant form with the emergence of hard-core gangster rap, as a particular expression of hip-hop around 1987. Since then, real niggaz have been associated with hip-hop and hard-core rap, and the latter identified as an index of social malaise. As Joe Wood discovered in his search for "the real thing" in Mississippi, the domain of "real niggaz" is global:

Down here, traditional blues has lost stagger lee's [*sic*] spirit to hip-hop's real niggaz.... Folks do listen to other music, but the essential music—the "real" thing—is the nihilistic capitalistic hard-core hip-hop rap shit.... [W]e want the real niggaz even when they're fronting all that bitch shit because of this: in America, violence and making dollars make for respect and those motherfuckers are getting it.[4]

Employing *nigga* in this way leads to consideration of the seemingly unavoidable question of authenticity in relation to commodification: Can a commodified identity be authentic? Understanding the movement from nigger to nigga means recalling the historical systematic employment of nigger as an exchange value, as well as giving some consideration to a set of problems specific to the issue of human capital at the end of political economy. The objective is to determine whether or not hard-core gangster rap's employment of the category nigga is an attempt to think an African American identity at the end of political economy, when work no longer defines human being.

Nigga to Nigger

What is hard-core rap? We know it is an expression of something called hip-hop. What is hip-hop? It is a kind of utterance: "Hip-hop hooray ho hey ho," an utterance of a habit of thought toward an increasingly rationalized and fragmented world of global commodification. It is thinking about being in a hypercommodified world. Rap is a way of this thinking that cannot itself be rigorously thought about without thinking hip-hop. To think about rap is to think about hip-hop, although not necessarily in the way of hip-hop. Thinking about rap in the way of hip-hop is to think it hard core, to think it like a nigga.

Thinking about the nigga, to put it schematically, lies at the crux of two genealogical procedures.[5] One, which traces the origins of rap to recognized African American rhetorical forms (toasts, shouts, and various forms of signifying or verbal games) and tropes, leads to a kind of utopian historicism that is grounded in the concept of the morally legitimate tradition of African American resistance to dehumanizing commodification. This account allows for a morally legitimate form of rap that is stylistically hard core, while still belonging to the tradition of the African American liberation struggle dating back to spirituals, a struggle characterized by the deification of "knowledge as possessing an inherent power that emancipates."[6] The other genealogy traces the development of gangster rap as a rupture in this morally legitimate tradition of resistance, whose origin is not in the form of rap itself but in a moral malaise engendered by the conditions of capitalism's hegemony over all aspects of life.

We are not yet accustomed, however, to thinking at the crux, to thinking hard core. Instead, the predominant thinking about rap is obsessed with the question of its historical and ideological significance for African American society. In turning to the question of significance we are concerned with rap's significance *for*. Rap is *for* African American society. It is an expression of this society's utterance. It serves this society's purpose: the constitution of subjects of knowledge. This is also a conservative purpose; it aims at keeping the African American experience through its conversion into knowledge. Knowledge gives significance to experience; in so doing it liberates significance from experience. What is this significance, and how is it liberated in knowledge? Of significance is the difference between having experience and knowing it, between being a slave and knowing oneself in slavery. This is the difference of the knowing that adheres to an ancient oracular utterance: "Know your self." The slave who knows him- or herself to be other than the experience of slavery, knows him- or herself to be in that knowing. Whatever the nature of the experience, however cruel the task at hand, however abject the economy of phenomenal bodies as commodities, the slave knows him- or herself as being heterogeneous from the it that is used up in slave labor. Knowledge liberates in announcing the heterogeneity of the instance of self-knowing, of apperception, from experience. Such self-knowing is what is called human nature. The human is that creature which knows itself knowing. The human can be enslaved but never *is* a slave. The human can be designated a phenomenal thing of the slave experience, *nigger*, but never *is* a nigger. This is a liberal knowledge that presumes the universality of apperception without knowing it and makes the human the significance of experience. The purpose of African American society, then, is the liberation of humans as subjects of knowledge from the subject of experience, from the commodified nigger of slavery.

Thinking about hard-core rap in terms of its significance for African American society is a way of disposing of it, unless we are willing to think it *with* the commodified nigga. Thinking with the nigga is to become concerned with it as an expression of an emergent utterance—hip-hop—which does not work according to the purpose of liberal knowledge. Yet, because we have failed to think about rap at the crux, *nigga* is misread as *nigger*. Once this association is made, the departure of hard core from the purpose of African American society can only be thought of as regressive. In this regressive thought, the hard-core nigga is an expression of angry, self-destructive violence, the armed and insatiable beast of capitalism that knows only exchange-value and the endless pursuit of greater pleasure: "You know that the jungle creed says that the strongest must feed on any prey at hand." The nigga of hard core blurs with the gang-banger, mackdaddy, new-jack, and drug-dealer, becoming an index of the moral despair engendered by a thoroughly dehumanizing oppression, and hence inevitably bearing a trace of that dehumanization: "And I was branded a beast at every feast before I ever became a man." In regressive thought, the hard-core nigga is the *bad nigger* become *gangster*.[7] In this way, we are prevented from truly thinking about the significance of hard-core rap.

Truly thinking about the significance of hard-core gangster rap requires that we disengage the question of its significance from that of its significance for African American society. The place to begin this disengagement is the identification of nigga with bad nigger. In order to establish hard-core rap's connection to the African American tradition, it has become convenient to differentiate between morally legitimate hard-core rappers and those who are amoral or nihilistic.[8] The former, the heroic *badmen* hard-core rappers, are considered to be a continuation of the *badman* figure of African American folklore—a Railroad Bill, who may be either radically secular or religious. This differentiation is of some use here, because it goes directly to the problematic relationship between nigger and nigga that frames this discussion. It is particularly so in its identification of the hard-core nigga with the *bad nigger*, who, like the *badman*, is a figure of folklore.

Someone who has elaborated this differentiation and identification to a considerable extent is Jon Michael Spencer. But what does Spencer mean by bad nigger and badman; what definition does he give of these terms? He doesn't give a definition of the bad nigger as such, but provides negative example and explanation: "The attitude of the 'bad nigger' is not negritude, it is narcissism and hedonism, and it is genocidal. The 'bad nigger' is not viewed as a hero by the masses of the black community, whose safety and moral stability he threatens." He has considerably more to offer, by way of definition, on the badman.

> The hard-core rappers, who engage in the insurrection of subjugated knowledges are "badmen" practicing self-determinative politico-moral leadership. They are ... political rappers ... who speak "attitudinally" but with knowledge about the conditions that the establishment has effected in their communities: social jingoism (such as black stereotyping) and civil terrorism (such as police-on-black crime). In response, the political rappers, alongside a new group of Christian rappers, advocate the formation of community; unity over disunity, economic self-determination over black-on-black crime and "gang banging."

For them it is knowledge, and only knowledge, that can lead to the overcoming of the fear, deception, and hatred that cause division and disrupt community.[9]

The difference is attitudinal, then; it is a difference in order and type of knowledge. The badman possesses a knowledge of self, which the bad nigger lacks. This knowledge is of political significance, in that it is the basis for a type of morality, or self-government, which then forms the basis for community self-determination, which belongs to economy.

Leaving aside the question of the bad nigger for the moment in order to focus on the badman as the source of hard core's legitimate genealogy, attention is drawn to the fact that Spencer defines politics in terms of how self-government relates to the art of properly governing the community and identifies the latter with economy. This is no small point. In Spencer's definition of the badman, we hear an echo of the liberal concept of political economy, the notion that the upward continuity of government defines community: effective good government of the community derives upward from good government of family, which derives from individual morality, or self-government. Spencer has drawn a very tight circle, whose epicenter is reason, or the epistemological project of modernity. The badman who has self-knowledge is, by definition, the subject of knowledge. In this sense, the function of the badman is pedagogical, providing a model of the formation of the leader; hence Spencer's definition of him as "practicing self-determinative politico-moral leadership." There is a downward continuity involved in this model of leadership in the implication that when the community is well run, then the head of the family will know how to properly govern his family (this is the idea of role-modeling that has become the sine qua non of grass-roots community work among urban African Americans today), which means that individuals will behave as they should. They will *police* themselves.

It is extremely significant that the positive force of Spencer's badman is his strong sense of social propriety, his understanding that strict obedience to social codes is essential for collective survival. The badman is the self-consciously representative black, he is an instantiation of morality above the law. Keep in mind that for Spencer, the question of morality in rap is a question of authenticity; the heroic badman is a figure of legitimate moral resistance to white oppression. It is a figure that recurs in various expressions of black folklore and popular culture, from the stories of High John the Conqueror to the blues. As the present-day avatar of this figure, the *badman* hard-core political rapper lets rap belong to a continuous tradition of community conservation as the moral response to a singular form of oppression. According to Spencer, that tradition is rooted in the African American spiritual-blues impulse, which is a kind of oppositional knowledge, a joyous science that is dropped by hard-core gospel rappers, such as PID (Preachers in Disguise), ETW (End Time Warriors), D-Boy Rodriguez, and MC Hammer—badman as *homo Africanus Americanus moralis*.

The problem is that the most vital and resilient form of rap is the hard-core nigga gangster rap (so much so that even pop rap icon LL Cool J moved into the ranks of rhetorical bangers with his single "Here's How I'm Comin' "). This popularity of the nigga is what prompted Spencer to differentiate between the badman and the bad nigger in the first place. To understand this, we must take up again the question of the bad nigger that was set aside earlier. The objective of the argument for the heterogeneity of the badman and bad nigger is to establish rap's authenticity as an African American form by rescuing it from the "genocidal" tendencies of the bad nigger.

Its centrality to Spencer's argument notwithstanding, the sharp distinction between these two figures is a radical departure from how their relationship has been understood by those who know about such things. Since Brearely's 1939 essay, "Ba-ad Nigger," folklorists and historians of African American slave culture have understood the postbellum folklore figure of the badman to derive from the antebellum bad nigger.[10] The folklorist John W. Roberts has recently disputed this association.[11] The basis of that critique is Roberts's analysis of the sociopolitical circumstance under which late-nineteenth-century African American folklore developed. Given that both the badman and the bad nigger are characterized in terms of their resistance to the law, the most significant aspect of postbellum sociopolitical circumstances relative to these figures is the law. As W.E.B. Du Bois remarked in *The Souls of Black Folk* (1902), and subsequently analyzed in *Black Reconstruction* (1935), the systematic use of the law by white authorities to disenfranchise blacks after the resumption of home rule in the South caused blacks to make avoidance of the law a virtue.[12] Roberts elaborates this into the argument that maintaining internal harmony and solidarity within one's own community was a form of protection against the law of the state. In this understanding, the black community becomes the police in order to not give the police any reason or cause to violate it.

In other words, Roberts anticipates Spencer and claims that the postbellum black community was, in fact, self-policing in order to preempt any intrusion from the external law of the state. Concurring with the generally accepted interpretation of the bad nigger as anticommunitarian, flaunting the morality of the community as well as the law, Roberts argues the illogic of a newly emancipated people, striving to establish and defend their right to participate in the general community of America, celebrating a figure that challenged the very virtue of morality on which community survival depended. The bad nigger was not only uncelebrated in the black community but despised as a threat to civil society. By contrast, according to Roberts, the badman of black folklore challenges the unjustness of the law of the state, while preserving the moral law of the community.

The disassociation of the badman and bad nigger as two distinct tropes addresses Spencer's essential concern with hard-core political rap, which is how it can be employed to reconstitute a community in crisis. The badman political hard-core rapper will regain the morality that Roberts claims preserved the postbellum community from both the law and bad niggers. But what category of individual did this community consist of? Apparently, they were neither badmen nor bad niggers, but something else. What both Spencer and Roberts forget is that there were niggers other than bad ones. This is a vexing issue, precisely because *nigger* was for quite some time the term used to designate African American slaves as commodity. Understandably, Spencer may have elided this issue for fear that it would distract too much from the paramount question of hard-core rap's amorality. In fact, it goes right to the heart of the matter. For understanding nigga as the analog of bad nigger, and the latter as the index of devastating amorality, first requires an examination of the presupposed community of niggers. Can there even be a "community" of niggers, as opposed to a "bunch" or a "collection"? This involves determining the basis for differentiating between the bad nigger and that which is simply a nigger. Doing that means a philological digression.

Niggerdom

According to the *Oxford English Dictionary*, *nigger* belongs to the French *negre*, which, like its Spanish cognate, *negro*, was used in early modern time to designate black people. It appears to have come into English through the Dutch, sometime in the sixteenth century, and by the seventeenth century, it appeared in variant forms: *neeger, neager, negar, negre*. In its earliest known literary reference of 1587, it is already associated with slavery: "There were also in her 400 neegers, whome they had taken to make slaves."[13] By the time it reaches the Virginia colony, it simply designates black people as slave-labor, as in Captain John Smith's 1624 observation: "A Dutch man of warre that sold us twenty Negars."[14] The Latinate, *niger*, was used by Hellowes in 1574: "The Massgets bordering upon the Indians, and the Nigers of Aethiop, bearing witnes"; and by Reginald Scot in 1584 in the precise sense of black-of-color: "A skin like a Niger."[15] By the time Samuel Sewall began writing his *Diary*, the appellation also referred to slave-labor as property: "Jethro, his Niger, was then taken" (1 July 1676); "Met a Niger Funeral" (20 October 1712).[16] In 1760, G. Wallace argued "Set the Nigers free, and, in a few generations, this vast and fertile continent would be crouded with inhabitants."[17] Robert Burns added the second *g* to the Latinate in 1786: "How graceless Ham leugh at his Dad, Which made Canaan a nigger."[18] Hence, *niggerdom* as the designation of black people in general, whose despised status Henry Fearon (1818) thought was deserved—"The bad conduct and inferior nature of niggars (negroes),"[19]—and William Faux (1823) lamented—"Contempt of the poor black or nigger, as they are called, seems the national sin of America."[20]

Of particular importance in this regard is the belonging-togetherness of the categories *nigger* and *work*, an association articulated in the American English expression "to work like a nigger," as in George Eliot's incidental remarking in 1861: "Charles . . . will . . . work like a nigger at his music";[21] or Twain's more renowned "He laid into his work like a nigger."[22] *Nigger* could mean exceptionally hard work, because niggers, by definition, are labor commodities (i.e., nigger is an index of productive labor that is somebody else's property). A nigger is both productive labor and value, a quantitative abstraction of exchange: the equivalent of three-fifths of a single unit of representational value. The value of the nigger is not in the physical body itself but in the energy, the potential force, that the body contains. That force is there in the nigger body, standing-in-reserve, as it were, for its owner to consume as he/she likes. That force is the thing that the planter owns. It is the property of the planter that is the nigger. The nigger is that thing.

Understanding the thingness of the nigger in the context of knowing a bad nigger from that which is simply a nigger leads to consideration of the relationship between things and humans, which is a question of commodification. Fearon's identification of *nigger* and *negro* leads to such a consideration. In spite of the casualness of his identification, such has not always been obvious. Whereas *neger* comes into English through Dutch already associated with the commodification of black peoples' labor, and hence is far more a substantive, *negro*, and its variant, *negroe*, first occur in the literary record as anglicizations of the Spanish and Portuguese descriptive adjective, *negro*. In 1555, Richard Eden, translating Pedro Martir de Angleria's *Decadas del Nuevo Mundo*, writes, "They are not accustomed to eate such meates as doo the Ethiopians or Negros."[23] And, in 1580, Frampton states that in "all Ginea the blacke people called Negros doe use for money . . . certayne little snayles." The confusion of *negro* with *niger* is already noticeable, however, in Sewall's *Diary*, when after regularly referring to "Nigers," he claims to have "essay'd . . . to prevent Indians and Negros being Rated with Horses and Hogs" (22 June 1716). Given Sewall's effort to disabuse the colonists of the notion that black-labor was their property, his employment of "Negro" as a substantive synonymous with "Niger" can be understood as his attempt to define "Negros" as humans, hence his capitalization of the terms. Be that as it may, *negro* was generally employed in the lower-case as a descriptive adjective of color until the twentieth century, when Booker T. Washington, among others, began to agitate for its capitalization as a positive racial designation, preferred over *colored*. Accordingly, *negro* or *Negro* was utilized to designate a human identity, in opposition to *nigger*, which designated a commodity-thing. The widespread use of the appellation *nigger* among antebellum slaves as an approbatory term of affiliation can be taken as an ironic "misnaming." It is a paralipsis that reveals the historical order of appellation, turning the nigger-thing back into the black (negro) human who forms community bonds.

Now, if a negro is a black human, and a nigger is a thing or a human-become-thing, what is a bad nigger? John Little, a fugitive slave living in Canada, wrote in 1856 that "a 'bad nigger' is the negro who is put in the stocks or put in irons. . . . 'Boy, what have you got that on you for? That shows a damned bad nigger . . . if you weren't a bad nigger you wouldn't have them on.' "[24] Little draws attention to the double entendre of *bad nigger* in the antebellum South. In the view of the white planters, *bad nigger* designated an obstreperous, dangerous nigger, who threatened the order of the plantation by refusing to submit to its laws. For the slaves, *bad nigger* indicated an individual who, in challenging the laws of slavery, refused to be a nigger-thing.

A bad nigger, then, is an oxymoron: rebellious property. In rebellion, the bad nigger exhibits an autonomous will, which a nigger as commodity-thing is not allowed to exhibit. There is little more dangerous than a willful thing; through the exhibition of autonomous will, the bad nigger marks the limits of the law of allowance by transgressing it. The bad nigger frightens both white planter and other slaves because he/she reveals the impossibility of completely subjugating will; it can only be eliminated in death, and the bad nigger, by definition, does not fear death. The bad nigger embraces death, and in that embrace steps beyond standing-in-reserve, beyond thingness. This frightens the planter, not only because the force that he understood to be his property is being withheld but because it is withheld through an unknowable agency, through the will of another, an unbridled, lawless force. The bad nigger indicates individual sovereignty, which is to say he is self-possessed.

What is at stake here is not the obvious problem of the bad nigger embodying the Enlightenment subject (i.e., exhibiting the characteristics of the autonomous subject who is the cornerstone of both civil society and the state). The real threat of the bad nigger is in exhibiting the groundlessness of the sovereign individual. Being a nigger appearing as a human, the bad nigger indicates the identification of human with thing, that the human can only be among things, cannot be beyond or abstracted from things. The bad nigger is the human-cum-thing. Little noted this when he remarked that "the man who was a 'bad nigger' in the South is here [in Canada] a respected, independent farmer."[25] Another instance of paralipsis, Little's conversion of bad nigger into respected independent farmer reveals the contrariness of liberal civil society. The bad nigger indexes a radical incommensurability, on the one hand exhibiting the individual sovereignty that forms the basis of moral order in liberal theories of political economy; on the other, embodying the lawlessness that morality is supposed to contain. We should not fail to note that Little's bad nigger starts out "the negro who is put in the stocks or put in irons," marking once again the ironic movement from nigger to negro. That which is called simply nigger is essentially the black human. The difference between the bad nigger and the simple nigger, then, is that the former indexes the open-ended possibilities of being among things—lawlessness; and the latter, converted into the negro, is the basis for community identity and collective resistance against continued dehumanization under capitalism—a community of moral beings. The bad nigger, by definition, is that human-cum-thing that is not subject to work. This thingness of the human puts into jeopardy community, when the latter is understood as being based on the communicability of sentiments or feelings.

Das Nigga Affekt

Although we have a keener sense of what a bad nigger is in relation to a simple nigger, that understanding has only enabled a beginning or preliminary exploration of the possibilities of nigga authenticity. Very schematically, we can say that in regressive thought, the nigga is conflated with the bad nigger as *homo criminalis*, constituting a threat to the survival of the community by giving the police cause to attack. But what is the relationship between the police and this community? To summarize what we have discovered thus far about the latter, it is a community of moral beings, grounded in values that transcend the domain of things. In community, through moral-based knowledge, the nigger-thing becomes the negro-subject. The police, as agents of the state, work to maintain the order of things, to enforce the laws of property. In other words, the function of the police, as officers of the courts, is to turn the negro back into a nigger. In the legal system, one is a nigger-thing; only in the community is one a human-subject. Because the moral order enables this negro-subject—*homo Africanus Americanus moralis*—it must be preserved at all times and cost. The state-authorized armed regulatory force of the police must be kept out. This is achieved through the community's governing itself. In this perspective, it is society, not just police in the narrow sense of the authorized armed regulatory force, but police in the broader sense of governmentality, that the nigga threatens to undermine.

In terms of governmentality, hard-core nigga gangster rap is an index of a general crisis of morality in the black community. Spencer recognizes this moral crisis as issuing from a collapse in the overall social fabric, resulting in the dissolution of the family. The broader social crisis results, in turn, from an inability to distinguish any longer the domain of economy from those of culture and politics. The result is the end of morality as the basis for identity beyond commodification. Another way of putting things is that the identification of society as economy has led to the displacement of the negro-subject with the nigger-thing from *within* the community. Although the crisis Spencer refers to as the emergency of black initially resulted from the emergence of an unbridled transnational capitalism, he understands its principal agent to be hard-core rap itself. More precisely, Spencer understands the hyper-commodification of the hard-core nigga to be a chief component in the demise of black people.

In response, the badman hard-core political rapper is called for in social defense, which we should not forget was the slogan of the penal theory put forward by Franz von Liszt ("Die Aufgaben und die Method der Strafrechtswissenschaft") and the social school of law. In that theory, social defense involves intimidation, in the instance of occasional delinquents, and neutralization, in the case of hardened criminals. Between these two extremes are the various modes of preventive intervention collectively called "social hygiene" in the International Union of Penal Law. The aim of social hygiene is to eradicate the social conditions that breed the criminal, or, as it were, the nigga. The police, then, is the order of governmentality called community—that is, the disciplinary practices that construct society as an economy of well-managed individuals. What does it mean, though, when community is identified with moral police? Here, it means that any nigger who doesn't obey the law and take moral responsibility for his actions is a bad nigger.

It is a grave error, however, to identify the bad nigger with the hard-core gangster rapper, because regressive thought cannot comprehend the hard-core nigga. When the Original Gangster, Ice-T, exclaims, "I'm a straight up nigga," he is reiterating the difference between a nigga being and being a nigga.[26] Knowing that difference requires an understanding of what is the nature of experience in a global economy. When the OG further points out how the process of consuming rap is tantamount to the "niggafication" of white suburban youth, he is doing more than remarking on the inevitability of popular culture's dissemination; he is also remarking on the equally inevitable loss of experience to commodified affect.[27] This is the age of hypercommodification, in which experience has not become commodified, it is commodification, and *nigga* designates the scene, par excellence, of commodification, where one is among commodities. Nigga is a commodity affect. The OG offers exhibition of this, on the one hand, reminding us that his rhymes come from "experience," and, on the other hand, claiming that virtually everyone involved in the commodified affect of his experience is a nigga:

> I'm a nigga, not a colored man,
> or a black, or a Negro.
> or an Afro American, I'm all that.
> Yes! I was born in America true,
> does South Central
> look like America to you?

> I'm a nigga, a straight up nigga
> from a hard school. . . .
> I'm a nigga in America,
> and that much I flaunt,
> cause when I see what I like,
> yo I take what I want.
> I'm not the only one,
> That's why I'm not bitter,
> cause everybody is a nigga to a nigga.[28]

The nigga is constituted in the exchange of experience for affect. This is not identical with the bad nigger who jeopardized community by insisting on having unmediated free experience. Such an insistence requires an essential innocence of identity, a way of understanding experience that is simply impossible right now. A nigga forgets feelings, recognizing, instead, that affects are communicable, particularly the hard-core ones of anger, rage, intense pleasure. One can belong with millions of others in an asynchronic moment of consumption of the same affect, the same passion. This is not empathy. The possibility of the nigga rests on the twofold of experience and affect, and the fact that experience is essentially unfungible; it cannot be sold as is but must be abstracted and processed by the formulaic functions of transnational capitalism. Knowing this, the hard-core gangster rapper traffics in affect and not values. In this sense, hard-core rap is the residual of the nonproductive work of translating experience into affect—it is pulp fiction, drawing into its web all the real nigga experiences it can represent in the affective constitution of niggaz.

The status as being at once both rooted in experience and available for appropriation marks nigga as the function by which diverse quotidian experiences and expressions are "authenticated" as viable resistance to the dominant forms of power. Nigga realizes that the end of political economy involves a shift in the technologies of government, and not a general problem of government. A crucial aspect of hard-core rap is how it strives to expose and problematize the technologies of government by constantly becoming an expression of overflowing energy that is pregnant with future. This is why, at those moments in which rap's appropriation by the transnational economy appears to signal its comprehension and diluting, hard core is reclaimed as the source (i.e., KRS-1, Run-DMC, Naughty by Nature). When Public Enemy released "Don't Believe the Hype" in 1989, they were marking how popular culture is itself a technology of government. That is to say, designating the contradiction (other/appropriate) that is constitutive of popular culture, *nigga* defines *authenticity* as adaptation to the force of commodification. Rap becomes an authentic African American cultural form against its appropriation as transnational popular culture.

Authenticity, then, is produced as the value everybody wants precisely because of the displacement of political economy with economy; it is not engendered by virtue of its relation to that which has to be protected from commodification so that African Americans might know themselves as a collective identity against a particular social, political, and historical threatening reality. Authenticity is hype, a hypercommodified affect, whose circulation has made hip-hop global—which is why the immanent critique of rap fails. This is not to suggest that rap is no longer African American but rather that one condition of being African American is participating in the consumption of rap. Put differently, hard-core rap, in its formal and rhetorical strategies, is akin to the blues as understood by Ralph Ellison: an oppositional cultural movement that is thoroughly symbolic in the face of political domination. But, whereas the blues is a collective response to political domination, the hegemony rap contends with is of another order, the global hypercommodification of cultural production, in which the relation of cultural object to group being no longer matters politically. Nigga is not an essential identity, strategic or otherwise, but rather indicates the historicity of indeterminate identity.

With regard to understanding nigga authenticity, then, the question is not what is nigga authenticity but whether or not nigga can be either authentically or inauthentically. Understanding whether nigga can be either authentically or inauthentically is an existential task. In other words, nigga poses an existential problem that concerns what it means (or how it is possible) to-be-human. In contrast, the badman and bad nigger pose a moral problem that concerns the structures and relations of humans—their governability. There is a familiar cast to this formulation of authenticity. Hard-core's nigga returns us to the existentialist preoccupation with the difference between the subject of knowledge and the subject of experience. In these terms, the question of nigga authenticity is an ontological question about the a priori features of human being, and the structures it is concerned with have to do with the habits of thought by which certain *types* of consciousness are possible. The moral-political question is concerned with particular acts, decisions, or modes of behavior—it is an ontical question.

In the reading of nigga as an index of black emergency, it is presupposed that authentic being derives from morality. That is, the nigger becomes the negro through moral behavior, or good works, founded on morality as a governmental habit of thought (police as internalized control). At the root of the despair about the demise of black morality is the recognition that ontical matters are made possible by the habits of thought of human being. With this recognition, we understand that it is an error to think that being negro existentially (i.e., being a black human) results from a particular set of morally determined social decisions and acts. To think in this way is to turn away from the question of what it means to-be-human, precisely because it refuses to take care of the question of how a person really is. Moral behavior, by definition, is an ontologically inauthentic way to be. Still, in understanding the hard-core nigga to be amoral, even this way of thinking recognizes in the nigga an emergent habit of thought at the end of black morality. As such, the question of nigga authenticity is not a moral question but is about the very possibility of being human: it is a strictly existential matter. In wanting to understand what it is to be a real nigga, it is crucial to remember that humans are the entities to be analyzed. To be nigga is ontologically authentic, because it takes care of the question of how a human really is among things. Niggadom, then, is a new dogmatics—that is, an attempt to formulate an ontology of the higher thinking called "hip-hop science."[29]

Study Questions

1. How have the forces of commodification changed the content and impact of contemporary hip-hop culture?
2. What is the distinction to be made between the labor of black bodies and the labor of black culture?
3. How has hip-hop deployed the pejoratives nigger/nigga in distinctive and even progressive ways?

Notes

1. Leon R. Harris, "The Steel-Drivin' Man," *The Messenger 7* (1925): 386–87, 402.
2. Chester Himes, "Black on Black," in *Black on Black, Baby Sister, and Selected Writings of Chester Himes* (Garden City, N.Y.: Doubleday, 1973), 139.
3. Paulette Cross, *The Folklore Forum* 2, no. 6 (Nov. 1969): 140–61.
4. Joe Wood, "Niggers, Negroes, Blacks, Niggaz, and Africans," *Village Voice* (17 Sept. 1991), 28–29.
5. With three notable exceptions, by and large, the thirteen significant books on rap published in the past ten years have focused on its genealogy. There is a preoccupation with pointing out rap's "authentic

origins" in antecedent African American forms of expression. David Topp's *Rap Attack: African Jive to New York Hip Hop* (Boston: South End, 1984) leads the way as an example of popular ethnography. In this same category is Havelock Nelson and Michael A. Gonzales's *Bring the Noise: A Guide to Rap Music and Hip-Hop Culture* (New York: Harmony, 1991). Six of the books are journalistic, and more than a little impressionistic, exposés: see Nelson George et al., *Fresh Hip-Hop Don't Stop* (New York: Random House, 1985), Nelson George, *Buppies, B-Boys, Baps and Bohos* (New York: HarperCollins, 1992), Steven Hager, *Hip Hop: The Illustrated History of Break Dancing, Rap Music, and Graffiti* (New York: St. Martin's Press, 1984), Keith Elliot, *Rap* (Minneapolis: Lerner Publications, 1987), Mark Costello and David Wallace, *Signifying Rappers: Rap and Race in the Urban Present* (New York: Ecco Press, 1990), and William Hauck Watkins, *All You Need to Know about Rappin'* (Chicago: Contemporary Books, 1984). Houston Baker's *Black Studies, Rap, and Academy* (Chicago: University of Chicago Press, 1993) is a meditation on rap's significance for academics, and Bill Adler's *Tougher than Leather: The Authorized Biography of Run-DMC* (New York: New Amsterdam Library, 1987) is a group biography. Of the exceptions mentioned earlier, two of them—Tricia Rose's *Black Noise: Rap Music and Black Cultural Resistance in Contemporary American Popular Culture* (Middletown, Conn.: Wesleyan University Press, 1994), and Joseph D. Eure and James G. Spady's *Nation Conscious Rap* (New York: PC International, 1991)—are attempts to elaborate on rap in the context of what might be termed the political economy of hip-hop. The third exception— Greg Tate's *Flyboy in the Buttermilk* (New York: Simon and Schuster, 1992)—is an exhibition of hip-hop aesthetic critique. As for journal and newspaper articles, the contributions of Greg Tate to *Village Voice*, and of Jon Pareles to the *New York Times* have been prodigious. Finally, Jon Michael Spencer's academic journal, *Black Sacred Music: A Journal of Theomusicology*, became a forum for scholarship on rap, in vol. 5, no. 1 (Spring 1991), a special issue, entitled *The Emergency of Black and the Emergence of Rap*.

The dominant tendency is to categorize rap into periods of development, with each successive period characterized by rap's greater, more diversified circulation. The model for this periodization has been David Topp's *Rap Attack: African Jive to New York Hip Hop*, whose paramount concern was with establishing rap's "rootedness" in African American forms of cultural expression. Following Topp's model, Ronald Jemal Stephens delineates three definitive periods of rap. The first period, dating from roughly 1973 to 1985, Stephens calls the "boogie woogie hip-hop wave," the hallmark of which are the Sugarhill Gang's 1979 "Rapper's Delight," and the 1982 release of Grandmaster Flash and the Furious Five's "The Message" ("Nation of Islam Ideology in the Rap of Public Enemy," in *Black Sacred Music*). Michael Eric Dyson calls this same period "message rap" ("The Three Waves of Contemporary Rap Music," in *Black Sacred Music*). The second period, the rock 'n' roll hip-hop wave (which Dyson calls "pop rap") is marked by the success of Run-DMC's "King of Rock," Tone Loc's "Wild Thing," as well as that of LL Cool J. The third period Stephens calls the "hard-core hip-hop wave." In spite of some differences of the defining moments of rap's development—for example, Dyson identifies periods solely on the basis of lyrical themes, while Stephens follows changing economies of circulation as well as lyrical content—the tertiary periodization of rap appears to be the dominant analytical model.

6. Spencer, *The Emergency of Black*, 2.
7. Writing for the *New York Times* in 1990, Jon Pareles identifies hard-core "gangster rap" as a style initiated by KRS-1 but commonly associated with the Los Angeles rappers Ice-T, Ice Cube, and NWA, and the Houston-based Geto Boys. He delineates its definitive features as rapid-fire style of delivery and "terrifying" lyrical thematics. Among the latter are: "scenes of inner-city violence, sometimes as cautionary tales, sometimes as fantasies and sometimes as chronicles without comment; detailed put-downs (with threats of violence) of anyone the rappers dislike; at least a song or two per album about sexual exploits; belligerent foul-mouthed personas ... the bad guys from innumerable police shows [who,] armed and desperate, [tell] the story the way they see it; the denouncing of ghetto violence as genocidal and aimed at black youth [Pareles calls this the political theme]; the connection of crime and drugs to poverty or [poverty-induced] insanity; machismo, or the translation from boyhood to manhood through combat or sexual exploits; and a reflexive, unquestioning homophobia and a sexism that easily slides into misogyny, as general sensation turns back onto the closest targets" (Jon Pareles, "Gangster Rap: Life and Music in the Combat Zone," *New York Times*, 7 Oct. 1990). Pareles further characterizes gangster rap as being formally hybrid, a jumble of "brilliance and stupidity, of vivid story telling and unexamined consciousness ... mock-documentaries, political lessons, irony, and self promotion." The focus of Pareles's article is on the Geto Boys, whose first major release of 1989 was released by the Rap-a-Lot label but rejected by the record pressing plant and withdrawn from circulation by its distributor, Geffen Records. Pareles reviews the remix re-release of the tracts of this album. These remixes appeared on a second release by the Geto Boys, entitled *The Geto Boys*, without a distributor's name and with a disclaimer by Def American Recordings, stating that its manufacturer and distributor "do not condone or endorse the content of this recording, which they find violent, sexist, racist, and indecent." *The Geto Boys* is most definitely all of this, graphically describing murder, rape, and mutilation. However, the leap in Pareles's logic is that of

example: in other words, holding that a definite and specific instantiation of a discourse is generalized by analogy. The Geto Boys becomes the synecdoche of a loosely knit collection of rappers: Ice Cube, NWA, CPO, Kool G Rap, DJ Polo, and Audio Two, all of whom become categorized as gangster rappers.

8. Spencer, *The Emergency of Black*, 1–13.

9. Spencer, *The Emergency of Black*, 8.

10. Eugene Genovese draws heavily from Brearely's elaborations, emphasizing the nihilistic aspect of the "baad nigger" and associates him with the badman of folklore. See *Roll Jordan Roll: The World the Slaves Made* (New York: Vintage, 1972), 436–37, 625–29.

11. John W. Roberts, *From Trickster to Badman: The Black Folk Hero in Slavery and Freedom* (Philadelphia: University of Pennsylvania Press, 1989), 171–219.

12. W.E.B. Du Bois, *The Souls of Black Folk* (1902; reprint, New York: Fawcett, 1961), 31, 131; *Black Reconstruction in America, 1860–1880* (1935; reprint, New York: Atheneum, 1962).

13. *Oxford English Dictionary*, compact ed., 1982.

14. Captain John Smith, *A True Relation of Virginia* (1608; reprint, Boston: Wiggin and Lunt, 1866).

15. Reginald Scot, *Discoverie of Witchcraft* (1584; reprint, Totowa, N.J.: Rowman and Littlefield, 1973), 122.

16. Samuel Sewall, *Diary of Samuel Sewall*, 1674–1729, ed. M. Halsey Thomas (New York: Farrar, Straus and Giroux, 1973).

17. *Oxford English Dictionary*, compact ed., 1982.

18. Robert Burns, "Ordination," in *The Complete Works of Robert Burns* (New York: Houghton, Mifflin and Company, 1987).

19. Henry Bradshaw Fearon, *Sketches of America; a Narrative of a Journey of Five Thousand Miles Through the Eastern and Western States of America; Contained in Eight Reports Addressed to the Thirty-nine English Families by Whom the Author Was Deputed, in June 1817, to Ascertain Whether Any and What Parts of the United States Would be Suitable for Their Residence. With Remarks on Mr. Birkbeck's "Notes" and "Letters"* (London: Longman, Hurst, Rees, Orme, and Brown, 1818), 46.

20. William Faux, *Memorable Days in America: Being a Journal of a Tour to the United States, Principally Undertaken to Ascèrtain, by Positive Evidence, the Condition and Prospects of British Emigrants; Including Account of Mr. Birkbridge's Settlement in Illinois* (London: W. Simpkin and R. Marshall, 1823), 9.

21. George Eliot, Letter dated 13 Apr. 1861, in *The Yale Edition of the George Eliot Letters*, 9 vols. (New Haven: Yale University Press, 1975), 3:404.

22. Mark Twain, *A Tramp Aboard* (Hartford, Conn.: American Publishing Company, 1879), 40.

23. Pedro Martir de Angleria, *Decades of the Newe Worlde or West India*, trans. Richard Eden (Londini: In aedibus Guilhelmi Powell, 1555), 239.

24. Benjamin Drew, *A North-Side View of Slavery. The Refugee: or the Narratives of Fugitive Slaves in Canada. Related by Themselves, with An Account of the History and Condition of the Colored Population of Upper Canada* (1856; reprint, New York: Negro Universities Press, 1968), 203, 219–20.

25. Drew, *A North-Side View of Slavery*, 219–20.

26. Ice-T, "Straight up Nigga," *Original Gangster* (New York: Sire Records), 1991.

27. Ice-T, *The Ice-Opinion: Who Gives a Fuck*, ed. Hedi Siegmund (New York: St. Martin's Press, 1994), 144–45.

28. Ice-T, "Straight up Nigga," *Original Gangster*.

29. Of course, in pursuing such a science, we are well advised to recall Dilthey's qualification: "All dogmas need to be translated so as to bring out their universal validity for all human life. They are cramped by their connection with the situation of the past in which they arose" (Graf Paul Yorck to W. Dilthey, in Rudolph Bultmann, "New Testament Mythology" in *Kerygma and Myth*, ed. Hans-Werner Bartsch, trans. Reginald H. Fuller [London: SPCK, 1960], 23).

10

Arabic Hip-Hop
Claims of Authenticity and Identity of a New Genre

The stark reality of hip-hop's immense popularity and global appeal is that it now reaches audiences and locales far removed from the insular, yet cosmopolitan, spaces that initially nurtured it. In every place on the globe where hip-hop has taken hold, there are local histories about its origins that are as important as the narratives that circulate in the United States. Such is the case with hip-hop in the Middle East, as Usama Kahf argues.

According to Kahf, hip-hop appeals to youth in the Middle East who value its emancipatory energy. Kahf notes, though, that hip-hop's politicized appeal must also adhere to the specific and local cultural histories and practices that are organic to political struggle in the Middle East.

Arabic Hip-Hop: Claims of Authenticity and Identity of a New Genre

Usama Kahf

Hip hop is a unique form of expression that has crossed social, cultural, and national boundaries in the last couple of decades, from Europe and South America to Africa and the Middle East. "Disseminated widely through Americanized mass media (such as MTV), today hip hop is a common global genre of western culture. Some indigenous peoples employ it for their own needs, while others see it as a threat to local musical tradition" (Korat 2007: 7). While it was brought to life by the African-American community in the United States, hip hop's ruptures into different cultures around the world were not driven by any of the homogenizing and imperialist forces of western culture that usually seek to take over local and indigenous heritages in the name of democracy and capitalism. Instead, hip hop continues to locate its narrative space in the margins of each society, as it faces a constant dilemma of being assimilated and commodified toward the center (Caglar 1998: 243).

Hip hop is appropriated and transformed by local artists in different parts of the world who are searching for emancipatory and empowering avenues of expression in the midst of a reality that continues to shut doors in their faces. These artists, whether in France (Orlando 2003), Germany (Caglar 1998; Bennett 1999), Colombia (Forero 2004), or Israel/Palestine (Vens 2004), are voicing their frustration with everything about the status quo, including the traditional forms of expression that are propagated and maintained by that status quo as official and authentic. Many have found that hip hop gives them the space as well as the freedom to participate in the public discourse of their society, and to provide a critical perspective on both their ethnic community and the larger community into which they are threatened with assimilation (McLeod 1999: 136). These indigenous hip hop artists recognize the origins of hip hop in African-American culture,[1] but the common experience of being oppressed that they share with blacks in the west inspires them to break the musical norms of their societies and give birth to a new hybrid genre of music.[2] This new genre takes on the beats and rhythms of western hip hop as well as unique flavors of the local culture, including its language, dialect, musical instruments, and local issues, and transforms itself beyond imitation to invention and cultural creativity.

Palestinian hip hop emerged for the first time in 2001,[3] making it the first crossover of hip hop in the third millennium (Carney 2005), though Israeli hip hop rappers like Subliminal sprang up in the late 1990s (Vens 2004: 36). Palestinian hip hop groups and individual artists surfaced one after the other inside the borders of Israel or what they call "Palestine '48." This new subgenre quickly gained popularity in a country with half its population under the age of 18 (Nissenbaum 2005: 2). For example, despite not having a formal recording contract, DAM's 2001 single, "Meen

Erhabi? [Who's the terrorist?],"[4] was downloaded more than a million times from an Arabic hip hop Web site (Winder 2004: 1).[5] It is difficult to estimate how widespread Palestinian hip hop has become because all the news reports simply say it is becoming more popular every day. The number of Palestinian hip hop groups and artists has exponentially grown since 2001.[6]

As Israelis and Palestinians fail to resolve their differences through continuing peace talks, and as the latest Palestinian Intifada destroyed the lives of thousands of Palestinians and hundreds of Israelis, these hip hop artists "could not take it anymore." They incorporated western and eastern music with powerful and politically charged lyrics that "tell it how it is,"[7] attempt to reflect their reality of suffering and offer solutions to the status quo. They also broke with traditional Arabic music by rapping in Palestinian urban dialect as well as in Hebrew and English.

The Arabic hip hop genre has faced strong resistance from various cultural forces. Abbas, who traces the development of this genre across the Arab world, argues that this resistance was not necessarily the result of musical evaluation, but rather a natural reaction to anything that sounds western as well as the response of people who feel directly implicated and threatened by hip hop's criticism of their way of life (2007: 11). Resistance to the existence and legitimacy of this genre necessarily invites some sort of response from Arabic hip hop artists. Thus, the establishment of a solid footing for the new subgenre of Palestinian hip hop requires these artists to focus on claims of authenticity and self-definition.

Arabic hip hop is a new phenomenon to the Middle East, and has since spread to countries like Egypt, United Arab Emirates, Morocco, Bahrain, Lebanon, Kuwait, and even Iran (Carney 2005). Since hip hop is generally known to have originated in the west,[8] these artists are faced with the challenge of making hip hop an authentic new channel of Arab culture and not an affront to its heritage or an imitation of the west. They mention this imitation critique and their response in various songs.[9] In a culture that is, to speak in general terms, enshrined in traditionalism and conformity, any revolutionary step requires an active focus on linking that step with the goals and interests of the local culture and its values. How the torch bearers of different Arabic hip hop subgenres define and carve this genre into existence will make a difference in their success and acceptance by their local communities. Authenticity and credibility are crucial starting points for any analysis of this new genre, because in the Arab cultural context credibility is more than a prerequisite to getting heard.[10] It makes the difference between being labeled a traitor or imitator of the west and getting respect as a voice of legitimate resistance.

It is important to note here that Arabic hip hop is not one amorphous being.[11] London-based Arabic rapper Eslam Jawad defines Arabic hip hop, in its "purest form," as hip hop in the Arabic language from the Arab world "speaking about local issues that are specific to the Arab world" (Abbas 2007: 9). But this definition is indeed too broad. Arabic hip hop encompasses many subgenres that have developed in various parts of the Arab world as well as among Arab communities in western countries. Analyzing the development of the entire genre is perhaps a topic for a dissertation or book because each subgenre is different and arises out of different cultural and political conditions. Often the only thing these subgenres may have in common is their use of the Arabic language and some Arabian musical instrument like the "*duf*" or the Arabian wooden flute.[12]

In this article, I focus on Palestinian hip hop primarily because Palestinian youth are at a unique crossroad of oppressive cultural and political forces. Frankenberg argues that "the oppressed can see with the greatest clarity, not only their own position but ... indeed the shape of social systems as a whole" (1993: 8). Orbe adds "that research that focuses on nondominant group communicative experiences seeks to inform the development of communication theory, explore the dynamics of power, culture and communication, and celebrate the spirit of human ingenuity" (1998: 3). Oppressive cultural forces intensify for Arab-Israelis or Palestinians living inside Israel and carrying Israeli identification cards. One in five Israelis are Arabs, but the Arab minority is marginalized and distrusted by both the Israelis and their Palestinian counterparts on the other side of the wall. Arab-Israelis are faced with the challenge of fighting for equal rights and representation without becoming so mainstream as to jeopardize their "Palestinian-ness" in the eyes of their brethren (Abbas 2007: 34). Tamer Naffar sheds light on this crossroad in an interview with *The Guardian*. He states, "We're strangers here. When I go on a bus I'm also scared—bombs cannot separate between Jews and Muslims and Christians. I feel that fear with them but I cannot feel happiness with them. If you go to a mall and you speak Arabic on the phone, people look at you. You feel like a monster. It's a land for the Jewish, so I have no place here" ("The Great Divide," 2005: 4).

The Palestinian hip hop subgenre represents resistance to the norms of both Palestinian and Israeli society. In that sense, the entire subgenre may be analogized to "conscious" or political American hip hop popularized by Public Enemy in the late 1980s. However, the analogy may be misleading because "conscious" rap is not just an element of Palestinian hip hop like it is an element of hip hop in the United States. Instead, the entire subgenre is a "conscious" reaction to the realities of life in Israel and the Palestinian territories. But this subgenre is not necessarily more "conscious" or political than Egyptian, Kuwaiti, or Moroccan hip hop. Thus, identifying the subgenre as solely "Palestinian" does not risk essentializing it to a nationalist identity. The descriptive word "Palestinian" conjures up the general set of conditions that gave rise to Palestinian hip hop.

In this article, I will analyze authenticity claims in Palestinian hip hop to answer the research question: How do Palestinian hip hop artists establish legitimacy in relation to hip hop and in relation to their own cultural and political realities? The artifact of my analysis is a collection of 45 tracks from ten Palestinian hip hop artists and bands.[13] For the purpose of this article, I translated some of the Arabic lyrics into English.

In examining these new artifacts of Arabic hip hop, I argue that Palestinian hip hop claims its authenticity by (1) addressing real social problems that the artists claim are unspoken about in their community, (2) focusing on people's shared experiences of suffering, and (3) distinguishing the uniqueness of hip hop as a form of expression and resistance. Ultimately, I believe that a detailed look at authenticity claims in Palestinian hip hop will reveal that hip hop only maintains its empowering potential and "authentic" voice of the oppressed margins when it positions itself in opposition to the mainstream without the goal of becoming mainstream, or in other words, when it has a reference point in the status quo to which it is responding and against which it is revolting.

This article will be divided into four sections. First, I will lay out the significance and importance of studying the authenticity claims of Arabic hip hop. Second, I will explore relevant research and methodological approaches to the study of hip hop. Third, I will apply those methodological approaches to Arabic hip hop and analyze its claims of authenticity. Finally, I will discuss some conclusions that emerge from this analysis.

Justification

An analysis of the shaping of the new Palestinian hip hop subgenre is justified for two reasons. First, this analysis contributes to our understanding of how authenticity works as the initial goal of new and insurgent genres of music. Authenticity claims in hip hop have been studied as a response to the mainstreaming of American hip hop (McLeod 1999: 136). In other words, McLeod's study examined authenticity as it functions to maintain the purity and identity of "real" vs. commercialized and fake hip hop. However, in this article, I will examine how authenticity functions to establish the identity of the genre in the first place, and to shape it within its different overlayered contexts. The research question or focus of this article is: what sort of linguistic, performative, musical, and argumentative strategies do Palestinian hip hop artists use to establish their credibility and the cultural authenticity of their new genre of choice? There are certainly other aspects of Palestinian hip hop besides authenticity claims that I do not explore in this analysis, such as issues of public discourse, public sphere, publics and counterpublics, news media agenda setting, the politics of representation of nation and history, popular narrative and its means of production, circulation and engagement, hegemony and counter-hegemony. While these issues are relevant and significant, an analysis of authenticity claims is a foundational step, perhaps even a prerequisite, for a comprehensive discussion of Palestinian hip hop. I invite the readers of this chapter to take this conversation to the next step.

Second, since Palestinian hip hop is a new subgenre within the context of Arabic music and culture, and since no other paper has analyzed it before, the first and most important question to ask is how do the artists shape the identity of this subgenre, claim its authenticity and present it to the world? In other words, what is Palestinian hip hop? Is it a unique invention, a fad that is fed by a following of western popular culture, both or neither? Palestinian hip hop is still in its early stages, in a phase of development upon which its future success will depend. It is those entrepreneurs of the genre that are attempting to push it in particular directions by defining its goals, its free style, and its location in society. Their efforts are constantly in jeopardy of cooptation and commodification by ideological forces like capitalism or by radical and powerful groups like Hamas. The artists, though often responsive to their audiences, are trying to be the agenda setters. They grab the microphones and express their intentions to speak their mind no matter what the critics say. For instance, Tamer Naffar refers to Palestinian hip hop as "the CNN of Palestine," or a way to broadcast the news (Nissenbaum 2005: 1). In "The Microphone is in Control," DAM rap:

> You can hear us, ignore us
> Try to stop us, you only get us closer
> To our mother, we stand, we never soften
> We never forge, we never weaken.
> The microphone is in control
> The mic is one of the fingers of your hand.
> MC. The mic is in control
> His lyrics are sharp, they cut our hands.
> Here who gave it strength?
> Me, me, me me.

The question then becomes, how much control can these artists really exert over the Palestinian hip hop agenda, over what it stands for and what perspectives are disseminated or circulated?

Hip Hop: Authenticity and Performance

Since its inception in the urban 'hoods of the United States in the mid-1970s, many scholars in different fields, including cultural studies, have studied hip hop's capacity to empower marginalized people to circumvent the constraints on expression that are imposed upon them by various social structures and regimes of communication. Many of those involved in the study of hip hop attribute much of the consolidation of theories and research about hip hop to Tricia Rose and her influential 1994 book, *Black Noise*. According to Rose, hip hop music is "a form of rhymed storytelling accompanied by highly rhythmic, electronically based music" (*Black Noise* 1994: 2). Hip hop continually displays a clever transformative creativity that is able to use technology in different ways to carve out new spaces for the expression of identity and experiences (Forman 2000: 65). Hip hop has the potential to empower marginalized members of society by speaking to their experiences and frustrations at the system as well as uniting them around a common banner and identity, such as nationalism (Watkins 2001: 374). As an example of a uniting force for oppressed groups, "the language of nation is appropriated by the hip hop community as a vehicle for contesting the changing discursive and institutional structures of racism" (Decker 1994: 100).

Hip hop's power to inspire activism and community involvement can also be very political (Stapleton 1998: 220). This means that, as Russell A. Potter notes in his book, *Spectacular Vernaculars,* hip hop culture creates a "new vernacular" of "insurrectionary knowledges" that are juxtaposed to traditional "historical societal forces" allowing the oppressed to at last "fight the powers that be" (1995: 23). Hip hop has the potential to empower people by creating a resistance vernacular that breaks form from the established vernaculars of discourse. A resistance vernacular is not necessarily empowering, but it could be, given the right ingredients, which vary with the circumstances. "The cultural significance of hip hop cannot be reduced to singular or essentialist explanations but must be understood rather as a series of strategies which are worked out and staged in response to particular issues encountered in local situations" (Bennett 1999: 80–81). In discussing these strategies, Alim contends that many "hip hop artists vary their speech consciously to construct a street-conscious identity, allowing them to stay connected to the streets" (2002: 288). This connection with the street inspires hip hop artists to participate in the reconstruction of their past, the reevaluation of their present, and the inspiration to change and affect the future.

Ironically, as hip hop becomes more and more mainstream, artists face the dilemma of being "inside a mainstream culture they had, in part, defined themselves as being against" (McLeod 1999: 136). Thus, to preserve their "pure" and "real" identities, hip hop artists engage in a rhetoric of authenticity by reasserting their credibility and drawing clear lines around their identities. According to Boyd, one of the most overt demonstrations of this drive for authenticity was "white rapper Vanilla Ice's claim that [though he's white] he could identify with blackness because he himself had experienced its poverty-stricken lifestyle" (1994: 292). This is because one of the ways in which authenticity has been constructed in the discourse of American hip hop is around race and economic class. However, authenticity is not a construct unique to hip hop, but rather it characterizes the discourse of subcultures that are threatened with assimilation by and into a larger culture.[14] This means that authenticity is also the goal of artists who start up new genres of music or make a revolutionary innovation in their society. As Rose argues, "a style that has the reflexivity to create counter-dominant narratives against a mobile and shifting enemy may be one of the most effective ways to fortify communities of resistance and simultaneously reserve the right to communal pleasure" ("A Style Nobody Can Deal With," 1994: 85).

In this article, I examine the lyrical and musical choices made by Palestinian hip hop artists to give authenticity to their new genre. McLeod's study of the reoccurring invocations of authenticity in American hip hop provides an appropriate method for analyzing the lyrics of Arabic hip hop. McLeod used the conceptual apparatus of semantic dimensions to analyze how authenticity, as a linguistic construction, is used by the hip hop community in the United States. He inductively derived six dimensions of authenticity by which hip hop artists try to distinguish between "real" and "fake" hip hop. Since these dimensions were inductively derived from American hip hop culture, they do not all necessarily apply or exist as significant dimensions of authenticity in Arabic hip hop. Therefore, I will follow the same format of McLeod's analysis and derive the dimensions I can identify in Arabic hip hop, and then analyze what symbols are used to support the authenticity of the Palestinian subgenre.

However, a linguistic/textual analysis of hip hop is incomplete and potentially takes the lyrics out of the context of their performance and rids them of their narrative and performative effects. A performance approach to the study of hip hop, such as the approach posited by Dimitriadis (1990: 361), is necessary in order to locate the narrative construction of authenticity within its context. Focusing excessively on the micro-textual level might lead the critic to overlook the effect that all kinds of contexts have on the artifact. It might also lead the critic to ignore the overall narrative and story of the artifact if that narrative cannot be reduced to particular texts.

This is even more true when analyzing Arabic hip hop because particular narratives and contextual meanings might be lost in translation. Thus, to balance this study between a textual analysis of the dimensions of authenticity and a contextual/narrative analysis of the hip hop as a performance, I will interject my own understanding and interpretation of the contexts and narratives of the Arabic hip hop that I analyzed and understood in Arabic, whenever the textual analysis takes me in directions that I think contradict the context or narrative of the lyrics. I have been involved with an Arabic *nasheed* band for nine years, and have worked as an interpreter/translator in the past. From these experiences, I learned that the Arabic language is frequently elusive, making translation a constant balancing act between the textual, contextual and performative meanings of words.[15] This is precisely why the critic must be personally involved with Arabic hip hop lyrics because they can have dramatically different meanings on paper, on CD, and in live performance.[16] The reader may choose to not trust my "own understanding" of the context, but it is more dangerous to create a false pretense of objectivity and to separate myself from the lyrics by some artificially deduced method of interpretation.[17]

Analysis: Three Dimensions of Authenticity

Authenticity in Palestinian hip hop is constructed around three basic dimensions: social-political, emotional-experiential, and rhetorical dimension. These dimensions operate as sites of identification in which the artists delineate between the authentic voice of Palestinian hip hop and other genres of music, including Arabic pop and the resistance-oriented and distinctly religious *nasheed* genre. Each dimension highlights particular symbols and strategies that are used to claim authenticity. They are also not mutually exclusive as there are stories and forms that transform and combine these dimensions. For example, some lyrics define Palestinian hip hop as a sociopolitical critique and in doing so create identification with various audiences who share common conscience-invoking experiences with the artists.

In the social-political dimension, hip hop artists claim authenticity by addressing the "reality" on the Palestinian street, a "reality" which the current forces of their society as well as popular culture and other musical genres do not sufficiently acknowledge. In the emotional-experiential dimension, hip hop artists use the symbols of "victim" and "terrorist" as the focal points of authenticity between the real "victim" and the real "terrorist." Finally, in the rhetorical dimension, hip hop artists discuss the form of hip hop and the audiences they choose to address in order to distinguish Palestinian hip hop as legitimate. In "Hip Hop Arabi," Khalifa E. raps:

> We used to dream of western rap,
> and now I'm singing, Hip hop Arabi
> They say that Arabic rap is just a fad
> and that it will go away soon,
> But they don't live here and
> don't know what's going on,
> So if you want, come see how awesome
> the war we're going through is.

Social/Political Dimension

The first way in which Palestinian hip hop artists claim authenticity is by addressing specific social problems that they claim are ignored in Arabic music and popular culture. The Social/

Political dimension refers to how these artists claim authenticity by focusing on certain social or political challenges facing their communities, or in other words, authenticity based on content, not form or style. Simply addressing these issues is not what creates authenticity, but rather the way in which the lyrics and the performance of these lyrics corner their audiences or make them face the reality of these social problems. Palestinian hip hop artists creatively carve their space as community workers in a way that leaves their audiences unable to deny the existence or the significance of these problems. For most of these artists, music is a tool for social commentary. As rapper Tamer Naffar states, "[a]rtists can be the best politicians. It's our duty to reach out into the world with a message" (Thomas 2005: 11). Authenticity for this new form of expression is achieved by putting society and individuals on the defensive, by being critical of how individuals are participating in and perpetuating the destruction of their society.

The social problems that many Palestinian hip hop songs address include the abundance of drug use among Palestinians, obsession with the material world (the Mercedes, the cash, etc.), economic injustice and classism among the Palestinians, and people getting blinded and distracted from their political and economic realities by such irrational forces as love and romance. Arab-Israeli rapper Tamer Naffar describes his hip hop protest as levied against Zionism as well as "against the Arab male dictatorship in the Middle East, against the drug deals and criminals who destroy our neighbourhoods and our youth, and against the way many musicians produce shallow material just to fill big bank accounts" (Thomas 2005: 11).

For example, in their song titled "Taste of Pain," the group strategically named Taste of Pain (TOP) discusses the economic imbalance they see between those isolated in the academic world and the students. "If you're asleep, I still can feel what's wrong ... The students can't afford their books; their accounts are frozen. And yet the teachers are wearing expensive Versace suits, and you only have a problem with what the students are wearing." A denunciation of the elitism of the academic world and of people's obsession with school uniforms and conformity is an act that is unique to Palestinian hip hop. Few Arabic musicians and artists dare to put things so bluntly and expose a reality that has been ignored and underrepresented. Later in the same song, TOP raps: "So here comes this guy, saying his love, his girlfriend is upset at him, and he's balling his eyes out like this is his number one concern! Then the next day he came to talk to me about his second love!"

Here and in similar verses in other songs, TOP is bringing to the surface a problem they see in their own people's system of priorities. Arabic music, for the most part, encourages this prioritization of romance and love over the daily socio-political problems that are ravaging the land. In their song, "50 Years," TOP say: "I'm an original/indigenous Arab, who's going on rapping, regardless of what they say about him, and whoever doesn't like it, they should go listen to Abdul Haleem or Amro Diab."[18] These two Egyptian singers are depicted as symbols of popular music's focus on love and romance. There is also a clear implication that TOP are only going to talk about "serious" issues and those who feel uncomfortable with such "real" discussions should go pretend like everything is fine and dandy and take refuge in love music. And as Mahmood from the group MWR raps in their song, "Introduce Yourself":

> I'm the M., and I'm rapping poison, and I won't stop,
> and I won't shut up until my mission is accomplished,
> That's important, cuz I have a lot of stuff to say, new stuff,
> Not like all these romantic love songs that keep repeating the same stuff.

In these lines, Mahmood is distinguishing between mainstream Arabic music and Arabic hip hop along the lines of what social issues and "reality" they address. This is Mahmood's way of saying that Palestinian rappers have their priorities in order more so than popular Arabic music.

This attack on the legitimacy of romantic love songs may be just a hollow tactic for establishing the political identity of Palestinian hip hop. While romantic love songs are often criticized by the clergy (and here by hip hoppers) as morally destructive, they do play an important role in the Arab psyche, providing an idealistic escape from the difficulties of the Arab "situation." These artists are perhaps simply responding to those who might lump them together with other genres of Arabic music. Palestinian hip hop artists need to define themselves in relation to other genres and that definition must itself be critical of whatever it is that other genres stand for.

Moreover, the music that is most commonly associated with the Palestinian resistance, the *nasheed* genre, focuses on messages of inspiration as well as a mourning of the suffering imposed by others (namely, Israelis and Americans) on the Palestinian people. Palestinian hip hop artists must also distinguish themselves from other local resistance vernaculars like *nasheed*. Here, instead of calling out the *nasheed* genre by name, they make that distinction by offering a different perspective on the social/political problems they see within their communities. An example of this kind of attitude toward traditional Arabic *nasheed* is DAM's song, "Whatever Happens to the Times":

> The disease starts on the outside and penetrates the Arabs
> We listen to traditional music, while we're being beaten up,
> "Here's another Arab running away, giving up on his land,
> Till when shall the cemeteries of my people keep getting overcrowded
> The number of corpses is multiplying, more and more"
> But we are the guys of DAM coming here,
> To stop the addicts, to stop the spilling of Arab blood,
> Because death is spreading amongst us like a disease.

The internal quote in this excerpt is satirical in nature, depicting the contrast between the types of message typically advanced in *nasheed* and the messages of Palestinian hip hop. According to the artist, the hip hop voice is less about poetic drama and more about finding solutions. Thus, Palestinian hip hop artists claim authenticity by contending to be more in tune than other genres with the social and political reality of Palestinian youth.

Drug use is also another social problem that plagues Palestinian youth, at least according to many of the Arabic hip hop artists. If there is any widespread use of narcotics in the Palestinian community, the Palestinian authorities and leaders as well as the driving forces of Arabic popular culture do not want to admit it, in the same way that many African governments denied for years how widespread the AIDS epidemic is in their countries. This is because in a community with rigid walls between the public and private domains, admitting the widespread existence of such problems could bring shame to the entire community. Once you lost your "face," you lost your dignity, and it is near impossible to gain it back. Despite this cultural context, several Palestinian hip hop artists point, in their songs, to the destruction that drugs have wreaked on Palestinian youth. This confirmation and depiction of reality on the Palestinian street is based on knowledge that exists outside of the realm of social institutions and authorities. Thus, hip hop artists claim authenticity by being their own sources of information. They depend on their experiences and observation as authentic sources of validation of the existence and significance of the social problems that Palestinians face on a daily basis. For example, hip hop artist Khalifa E. raps in his song, "Hip Hop Arabi":

> From what's going on around us, we turned out this way.
> From what we've seen with our eyes, our minds turned out this way.
> And the people we interact with all the time,
> Some of them love us, some can't stand us, and others keep bothering us.

Instead of relying on institutional, authority-privileging evidence, they rely on their own experiences. This is significant because it denies the opportunity for critics to argue with the artists in an institutional/legalistic framework that requires authority-based and scientifically validated evidence and statistics to prove accusations and claims about reality. Relying on individual experiences constitutes a rejection of such inductive framework for the evaluation and authentication of knowledge. To borrow a phrase from Social Judgment Theory, I argue that relying on individual experience as the source of validation of reality narrows the latitude of rejection to only those critics who are willing to deny and to dismiss the personal experiences of the hip hop artists themselves as well as the people they depict.

Emotional/Experiential Dimension

The Emotional/Experiential dimension revolves around how the artists establish their credibility by narrating their unique experiences of being oppressed and creating empathy and identification with their various audiences. Here, Palestinian hip hop artists claim authenticity for their genre by pointing to the common experiences of suffering that they share with Israelis and other Palestinians as human beings. This focus on victimhood produces two kinds of authenticity claims: credible victim and compassionate peacemaker. First, Palestinian hip hop artists establish their credibility to talk about issues surrounding the Israeli/Palestinian conflict, as well as about human suffering, by positioning themselves as victims of Israeli military aggression and occupation. This happens on both the individual and community level.

On an individual level, several Palestinian hip hop artists such as TOP, DAM, Rami, and Wlad El Hara (Boys of the 'Hood) claim that they have been personally affected by Israeli military aggression, such as having friends, classmates, cousins and close relatives who were killed by Israeli missile strikes or sniper bullets. For example, DAM raps: "You murdered the dearest people to me, you see, I by myself, my family has been kicked out into homelessness." Having that personal touch creates identification with other Palestinians and brings hip hop down to the streets and positions it as the voice of the common people, not the voice of privileged ivory tower kids.

On the community level, victimhood is claimed for all Palestinians. This involves a reweaving of history and reliving of experiences from a point of view different from that of mainstream media. For these artists, rapping in itself identifies them as an oppressed group. In their song "Why Do They Say That About You, Rap?" the group Wlad El Hara raps: "Even though rap was born to the blacks whose roads were blocked in their faces, we are black too, because we share those experiences, and we are the newest soldiers of rap." In their song "50 Years," TOP state: "Rap was for the black folks, but I'm gonna start a revolution. We came today to wake people up, and start working from the foundations up. All the time and in all places, so that we don't forget what has happened to us."

Interestingly, Palestinian hip hop artists seem to somewhat mimic American mainstream hip hop's styles of clothing, wearing baggy clothes and some bling-bling around their necks. This leads to local criticism and resistance by radical groups. For example, a rally in September, 2005, to celebrate the end of Israeli military rule in the Gaza Strip, held amid the rubble of Israel's largest settlement, came to an abrupt end when supporters of Hamas stoned the new rap group, Palestinian Rapperz or PR, as they performed on stage (Nissenbaum 2005: 3). Mohammed al Fara, a member of PR, told the Jewish World Review, "They didn't like the music. Hamas guys were mostly upset because a lot of girls were excited about us and they were waving their hands as we sang" (Nissenbaum 2005: 3). Despite this kind of local resistance to their music, these artists consider and refer to themselves as the "blacks" of Israel. They do not adopt the terminology of American "black" hip hop, but instead they analogize their struggle to that of African Americans.

Moreover, the lyrics of all these hip hop groups constantly attempt to dispel the stereotype of Palestinians in the resistance as all being terrorists. Many of the artists try to turn the label of terrorist toward the Israeli military and government. The group DAM,[19] in their most famous song, "Who's the Terrorist?" provide a perfect example of this rewriting of history in lyrics about the real "terrorist":

> Who's the terrorist? Am I the terrorist?
> How am I the terrorist and I'm living in my country?
> Who's the terrorist? You're the terrorist!
> You're eating me alive, while I'm living in my country!
> You're murdering me, like you murdered my grandparents
> Do I turn to the Law (courts)? That would be a waste,
> Cuz you, the enemy, play the roles of witness, attorney and judge!
> And you judge against me, trying to bring an end to me!
> Your dream is that our numbers go down, yet we're the minority already!
> Your dream is that the minority becomes the majority at the cemetery!
> You call this a Democracy? I swear you're like Nazis
> Cuz you keep raping the Arab Identity,
> And got her pregnant, but she gave birth to a boy,
> and named him: "suicide bombing mission"!
> And then you call us terrorist!
> It's like you hit me, and then pretended like you're crying,
> You beat me and complained,
> And when I reminded you that you started it,
> You jumped and opened your mouth and said:
> "You force your little children to throw rocks,
> their families should contain them at home."
> What? Huh? It's like you forgot that your bombs has
> contained those families under the rubble of their homes!
> And now when my pains are revolting, you call me terrorist!

Despite the obvious anger and frustration at Israeli aggression against the Palestinians, the same artists also claim authenticity by identifying with the suffering of innocent Israelis, in an attempt to put out their hands in a gesture for peace and reconciliation. Tamer Naffar, in one of his solos in which he inter-splices Hebrew with Arabic lyrics, raps:

> Believe me his blood is like my blood and the tear is in his eye just like it's in mine,
> There's no difference between him and me, both of us are flesh and bones of humanity.
> So why all the hatred and the racism and excessive cursing that fuels the murder,
> And human life is wasted this easy over nothing, over where I'm from and who I am,
> You take my rights away. What happened to this world? People of the world,
> Wake up, get up and answer me back. What happened to forgiveness and love?

Thus, authenticity is claimed by establishing a credible position of both victim and compassionate human being who wants peace. The "real" victim is distinguished from the fake victim who is actually the victimizer. Within the lyrics of most of the songs I listened to and translated, I noticed this strategy of defining and delineating between those who are "really" after "peace" and those who are not, and between those who are "real terrorists" and those who are "real victims."

Rhetorical Dimension

The Rhetorical dimension involves authenticity claims based on the form and style the artists adopt to identify this new genre. Palestinian hip hop artists claim authenticity by distinguishing and explaining what hip hop is to them, why they chose it as a form, and what their goals are in using it. Many of the Palestinian hip hop songs I examined involve a discussion of the communicative choices that the artists made and the implications of those choices. This kind of explicit discussion is quite telling of how new this genre is to Arab culture and how its entrepreneurs explain and justify their choices to themselves and others. These artists discuss their choices of form and audience in order to locate and identify Palestinian hip hop as an authentic new voice of expression and resistance.

The form of Palestinian hip hop undertakes a self-definition in nearly every song. Specifically, some artists define hip hop as a form that gave them a voice, something that other genres of music and other avenues of expression in their society denied them. Instead of having other people speak for them and attempt to capture their experiences in an elitist snapshot from above, these artists decided to take up the free form of rap. As SAY point out in their song, "Who Are We?," Arabic rap is "the language of the street." It does not follow the rules of grammar and metric rhyme that traditional poetry-driven music follows. Thus, its form constitutes a vernacular of resistance against the traditional avenues of expression, avenues that many of these artists say have been closed in their faces. Authenticity claims for this new genre lie at the juncture of this kind of delineation between the form of Palestinian hip hop as uniquely that of a resistance vernacular for the marginalized and the inaccessible form of other kinds of music. In the following passage from the song, "Why Do They Say That About You, Rap?" by the rap group Wlad El Hara, authenticity claims are centered around a discussion of what critics say about the emerging genre of Arabic rap.

> Why do they talk smack about Arabic rap?
> Is it because you're ready to express everything that's in your heart?
> Everything was wrapped up in fear before Arabic rap started,
> So we're always gonna be grateful to rap, cuz it gave us the voice
> To be the advocates of freedom, to put an end to hatred,
> And to represent the voices of the marginalized minority.
> Rap allowed us to express our pains, to voice our criticism
> It's from the heart, and that's why there's a lot of people
> who criticize the legitimacy of Arabic rap and dismiss it as noisy!
> We find truth and reality in rap, the truth and reality that you are trying to avoid and escape
>   from.
> So stop trying to run away from reality,
> cuz its gonna eventually catch up to you. But what reality?
> It's the reality of our world that's closing every door in our face,
> but we're slowly opening those doors one by one, and rap is our key
> And we're gonna break down those doors, and destroy those barriers,
> With words, words that turn the mirage in the desert into real water!
> They laugh at Arabic rap, and say it's dumb and that those who tried it weren't successful
> But not every one that hears it will understand it and believe in it.
> They reacted against it and said it was wrong, and that it doesn't belong to us and
>   shouldn't be among us.
> They said that rap is harming us,
> But we said that rap has crossed the border just to reach us,
> even though it didn't come to life or start on our soil and under our sky.

With rap, we express our thoughts.
With rap, we improve and transform ourselves.
We're crying about our situation, and there's nobody to complain to,
So in order to even start talking, we chose rap, and only rap.
Because the map is full of thick lines, and when rap saw that even the word "Arabic" is sick
      and wounded, with fire in its heart,
it was rap that came to try and heal those wounds, and to recollect
the letters of the Arabic identity.

There are numerous other verses and passages that express similar ideas about the form of hip hop and its empowerment of the margins of society, but this passage contains all the common claims of authenticity that identify Palestinian hip hop as resistance.

The form of Palestinian hip hop is also unique in that it combines western beats with eastern musical instruments and sounds. This is talked about as authentic in several of the songs because it constitutes cultural progress and innovation, not imitation. Thus, the older genres of music are marked as old and stagnant, while the new Arabic hip hop genre claims its authenticity by providing creative change and aesthetic contributions to popular culture. Arabian instruments that can be heard throughout Palestinian hip hop music include the *"duf"* and Arabian wooden flute. *Duf* is a hand-held drum made with different animal skins and has a distinctly Arab sound. It mixes well with western drums and digital beats because it usually has a lot of bass and reverberation in its sound. The wooden flute is a simple instrument often associated with nomadic Bedouin farmers and shepherds. For many Arabs, its unique emotionally charged sound conjures images of the shepherd sitting on a rock in the desert and playing the flute for his herd of sheep or camels.

Furthermore, authenticity in the rhetorical dimension is also constructed around the scope and reach of Palestinian hip hop to different audiences. In essence, Palestinian hip hop claims an edge over traditional forms of music by addressing and speaking to a multitude of audiences. Palestinian hip hop artists crossover linguistically between Arabic, English and Hebrew, though the majority of their lyrics are in Arabic. This inter-splicing of languages is not prominent or prevalent in mainstream or even underground (*nasheed* genre) resistance music. The *nasheed* genre is often associated with the religious sector of the population. This genre is characterized by its use of primarily drum and percussion instruments, proper Arabic language and rural dialects, and strict meter and rhyme in its poetic lyrics (no freestyle or prose-like poetry). *Nasheed* is also the music of choice for many in the Palestinian resistance movement, especially militant groups. Palestinian rappers are basically sharing the resistance stage with a genre that had traditionally dominated and monopolized that stage. Their linguistic and poetic choices are also breaking form with how the *nasheed* genre has defined the resistance vernacular.

Additionally, the grammatical and second-person construction of Palestinian hip hop lyrics make them specifically addressed to particular audiences as well as to general audiences at the same time. As Forman points out, in hip hop, "there are different messages being communicated to listeners who occupy different spaces and places and who identify with space or place according to different values of scale" (2000: 88). Palestinian hip hop addresses several audiences at the same time, and the artists indicate the importance of addressing all their audiences in the lyrics. Authenticity is claimed through this ability to transform culture and language. There are three overlapping layers of audiences that are addressed in Palestinian hip hop: Palestinians and Arabs, Israelis, and the rest of the world.

For the Palestinian and Arab audience, hip hop artists claim the genre and their lyrics as expressions of their frustrations, anger and solidarity. This audience is addressed using the Palestinian urban dialect, a dialect that is not represented in *nasheed* music. Instead, Palestinian *nasheed* groups rely either on proper Arabic or on rural Palestinian dialects, which represent nostalgic elements of the simplicity of nomadic or tribal life. In some of the self-critical hip hop songs that talk about the social reality of Palestinians, the Palestinian/Arab audience is addressed by the pronoun "you" or "we."

For the Israeli audience, Palestinian hip hop artists often direct and address their lyrics toward either the Israeli government or Israeli civilians. They do this by inter-splicing lyrics between Hebrew, English and Arabic. Hip hop is very popular among Israeli youth, with such groups as Subliminal rallying thousands of youths at concerts to listen to nationalistic messages of solidarity (Vens 2004: 37). The Palestinian artists rap in Hebrew in a form that is popular among Israeli youth in order to identify with them and communicate frustrations about their government's policies. Several songs reach out to their Israeli neighbors to say: "We're all human, same blood, same flesh, so let's stop killing each other, and tell your government that" (SAY, "Traitors"). Another example of a passage that is linguistically and contextually addressed to Israeli civilians is the chorus of Tamer Naffar's song "O People":

> O people, this is getting out of hand, this is wrong,
> Eyes that can't go to sleep, fear of and retaliation against
> and by innocent humans. Tears are in the eyes, and in the
> sad and sorrowful heart. It's a strange world,
> but to whom do we address our grievances and complain?

Within this address and reaching out to Israeli civilians, hip hop artists make a clear distinction between Israeli civilians and Israeli military and government. This distinction is significant for two reasons. First, it gives authenticity to the subgenre of Palestinian hip hop through the diversity and specificity of its audiences. Second, it also participates in the delineation between real and fake "victims" in the emotional/experiential dimension of authenticity.

Finally, the third overlapping audience is the rest of the world. Several songs contain the calling phrase "O people." This may not be the most accurate translation, because these words in the linguistic context of the lyrics are an address to the world, to the people who are watching from the sidelines, and to the people who are blinded with propaganda. In their song, "Propaganda," Wlad El Hara talk about the distortions of reality in western and Israeli media. The chorus of the song contains the phrase: "Enough is enough O people of the world, our lives have been devalued." This marks a calling out to the rest of the world to stop and look at the "reality" on the Palestinian "street." The inclusion of this broad audience is not unique to Palestinian hip hop, but it is the combination of the different audiences that authenticate the voices of Palestinian hip hop. All of these audiences are inter-related; the depiction of human suffering and the severity of the status quo are common stories that are told to each audience in different ways. No other genre of Arabic music is as accessible to and as inclusive of all these different audiences at the same time.

These three audiences are more than theoretically inter-related. The artists envision and address these audiences in their lyrics, music and performance. Whether all of these audiences actually listen to what the artists are trying to say is not the issue, though it is the goal. Palestinian hip hop is unique and innovative because it addresses these audiences, especially Israeli Jews, in a language they understand and in a musical form they can identify with. Critics of hip hop often point to the risk that hip hop artists may end up preaching to the choir; their political messages are difficult to circulate outside of that choir. For example, Michael Warner talks about how the messages circulated in gay and lesbian magazines can only go so far because homophobic conservatives never read them anyway (2002: 424). If that is the case here, then no matter what audience is addressed or how persuasive the lyrics are, hip hop artists and their immediate audiences might get a false sense of empowerment when in fact they have no impact at all on the power structures they critique.

This is why authenticity is where this struggle to be heard begins. Palestinian hip hop artists are focusing on claims of authenticity by defining themselves as either better than or different from other musical genres in the ways they reach out to different audiences. They do not expect the whole world to listen, but they are certainly trying their best to make it more likely that people outside of the "choir" would listen. Essentially, audience is a significant juncture of authenticity for Palestinian hip hop because artists reflect and "report" on the reality of their brothers and sisters on the "street." As Morgan also argues, "it is a person's ties to the audience/generation and urban youth that bring him or her into existence. An artist is a composite of his or her audience—representing his and her own experiences that are shared—and the audience determines whether the artist can assume that role" (2002: 117).

Implications and Discussion

Arabic hip hop is an expanding genre that rocked the Palestinian street just a few years ago with a never-before heard combination of beats and free-form lyrics. Just like most dramatic innovations in popular culture, Palestinian hip hop struggles to define itself and weed off critics who deny its legitimacy and empowering potential as a new genre of Arabic music. The way in which the Palestinian pioneers of Arabic hip hop give shape to this genre is intriguing and significant, as it highlights the need for the artists' active involvement in self-definition. This means that without direction and a focus on establishing authenticity for the hip hop voice of resistance, hip-hip does not automatically and naturally align itself with the margins and with resistance. I remember when the first professional Palestinian hip hop song, "Who's the Terrorist?" was released to the world from Israel on the internet in 2001. Most of my friends, as well as members of the Arabic *nasheed* band that I am involved with, thought it was "cool." But they still laughed it off as a fad that would come and go because there was no serious direction behind it and because it relied on imitation. However, six years after those initial reactions, it seems that the emerging hip hop community of Palestinians has risen up to the challenge of defining and giving direction to Palestinian hip hop.

In examining how authenticity is invoked by these artists in a variety of contexts and dimensions, I came to this conclusion. Authenticity claims in Palestinian hip hop are made around three dimensions: social-political, emotional-experiential, and rhetorical. What distinguishes hip hop from other genres of Arabic music along those dimensions is (1) the extent to which it exposes and depicts the true "reality" of Palestinian daily life, (2) its demarcation between the real "victim" and the real "terrorist," and (3) the locating of its form in the margins of society as well as its transformation and breaking of linguistic barriers in addressing a multitude of audiences. Thus, Palestinian hip hop artists position themselves against other genres in all these ways, and they establish their credibility to speak about Palestinian suffering from the position of "victims." The demarcation of authenticity depends on how much they identify themselves as victims and how much they are self-critical of their community.

Ultimately, there are two implications of this active focus on providing a bright line for what is an authentic voice and what is not. First, the voices of marginalized victims become prioritized in hierarchy over other voices. Just because people live in the center and not the margins does not mean that they do not experience systemic oppression, only that theirs is less obvious, and that they have more resources to counter such forces. Instead of constructing boundaries around their identities, Palestinian hip hop artists should recognize the inherent value of every person's voice and experiences. For example, romantic love songs do serve a role in the survival of Arab culture, and that role should not be taken out of context and scapegoated for the problems of Palestinian youth. While experiences of oppression and marginalization can and should be exposed, doing so should not be at the expense of de-authenticating everybody else's experiences, voices and preferred avenues of expression.

Second, this focus on constructing the authenticity of Palestinian hip hop at the margins of victimhood replaces "might makes right" with "victim makes right," which is the same logic of victimhood that the Israeli government and army speak with. While this might be slightly balanced with the artists' criticism of the preoccupations of Palestinian youth and society, it still constitutes a mere 180 degrees reversal of the same rhetoric that these artists are "revolting" against. Thus, authenticity claims give identity and shape to the new genre of Arabic hip hop and establish its footing in the Palestinian "street," but that comes at the expense of the uncritical perpetuation of a hierarchy that allows certain voices to oppress others just because of the social location that these voices carve for themselves.

Study Questions

1. How are the messages of hip-hop, political or otherwise, altered when they circulate globally?
2. What is it about hip-hop culture that marks it as possessing emancipatory powers?
3. Why is hip-hop politicized globally in ways that it is no longer politicized in the United States?

Notes

1. Their audiences, on the other hand, might be less knowledgeable about the origins of hip hop.
2. In the trailer to Jackie Salloum's documentary on Palestinian hip hop named "Sling-shot Hip hop," Tamer Naffar, the first Palestinian to rap in Arabic, states "We are the black people of the Middle East." See www.slingshothiphop.com, last accessed June 24, 2007.
3. Though, Tamer Naffar started rapping in Palestine in 1998. He is a member of the influential group DAM (See Abbas 2005: 34).
4. DAM stands for "da Arab emcees." It also means blood in both Hebrew and Arabic. DAM consists of three MCs, including Tamer Naffar, the first Palestinian MC to rap in Arabic (See Abbas 2007: 34).
5. Winder is probably referring to www.arabrap.net.
6. In 2005, I counted about 20 groups with downloadable songs. There may be more that have not gone online yet.
7. This, of course, assumes that whoever was doing the "telling" did not tell "it" how it "is."
8. While hip hop is generally associated with the west, how it originated is not common knowledge outside the United States and outside the circles of indigenous hip hop groups.
9. This is discussed in more detail in the analysis section.
10. Well, perhaps I should establish my own credibility for making such a general statement about "Arab culture." Here is my authenticity claim. I am a member of the club; I carry my Arab identity in my face, name, memories, and heart. I do not claim to be an expert on "Arab culture," but my statements based on personal experience are probably a better educated guess or description of general cultural values than what social scientific or quantitative research can offer. Besides, I do not hold these general statements out as "truths," and I do not imply that every "Arab" puts a lot of emphasis on credibility. I am simply sketching a not-to-scale picture of "Arab culture," and then trying to figure out where on that canvas Arabic hip hop belongs.
11. The same is true of "Arabic culture." It is not one amorphous being; it is a mosaic of different dialects, cultures, nationalities, and religions.
12. Even those instruments vary throughout the Arab world, as different countries often have their own indigenously developed and flavored musical instruments. "Duf" and wooden flute are commonly used in Palestine, but they are only examples of some of the "Arabic" instruments that can be observed on Palestinian hip hop tracks. The significance and description of how "duf" and wooden flute sound are discussed on pp. 378–79.
13. All of these tracks were available for free online at www.arabrap.net. This web site has shut down sometime since I last accessed it in April, 2007, but it was an entrepreneurial web site put together by some Palestinian hip hop artists and dedicated to featuring news about as well as samples from all the Arabic hip hop albums that have already been distributed. Now, some of these tracks are available at web sites like www.arabrappers.net, www.dampalestine.com, and www.bornhere.net.

14. See, for example, Sarah Thornton's 1996 book, *Club Cultures: Music, Media and Subcultural Capital*, in which she analyzes authenticity claims in the British "rave" subcultures.

15. To test this translation dilemma, I read some Palestinian hip hop lyrics online before listening to their corresponding tracks. I also compared my own translations of the lyrics to the translations provided by the artists or their fans online. In the end, it seemed clear to me that some meanings of words, phrases and verses may significantly vary between the written and the spoken, and between different people's translations. This is why I avoided citing other translations but my own. When I sat down to translate the lyrics I cite throughout this article, I retranslated several times in order to get as close as I could to the message that could be understood from listening to the songs as opposed to reading them.

16. Unfortunately, I have not had the pleasure of attending an Arabic hip hop concert. I am waiting until the world gets so glocalized that Palestinian hip hoppers start playing shows in Los Angeles, California!

17. The ethical translator/interpreter does not rely just on the dictionary, but also on her/his auditory and visual perceptions of words.

18. Abdul Haleem is an old school favorite of Arabic music enthusiasts; he died in 1977. Amro Diab, on the other hand, is a popular star in contemporary Arabic music, with such top hits as "Habibi Ya Noor el Ain."

19. DAM was started by Tamer Naffar, the first Arabian MC and the person credited with pioneering and venturing into Arabic hip hop.

Works Cited

Abbas, Basel. "An Analysis of Arabic Hip Hop." Diss. SAE Institute, London, 2005. 7 July 2007 <http://www.saeuk.com/downloads/research/basel_abbas. pdf>.

Alim, H. Samy. "Street-Conscious Copula Variation in the Hip Hop Nation." *American Speech* 77 (2002): 288–304.

Bennett, Andy. "Hip Hop am Main: The Localization of Rap Music and Hip Hop Culture." *Media, Culture & Society* 21 (1999): 77–91.

Boyd, Todd. "Check Yo Self Before You Wreck Yo Self: Variations on a Political Theme in Rap Music and Popular Culture." *Public Culture* 7 (1994): 289–312.

Caglar, Ayse S. "Popular Culture, Marginality and Institutional Incorporation: German-Turkish Rap and Turkish Pop in Berlin." *Cultural Dynamics* 10 (1998): 243–60.

Carney, Natalie. "South Central? South Bronx? No, It's the Middle East." *Egypt Today* 26 (Oct. 2005). 7 July 2007 <http://www.egypttoday.com/ article.aspx?ArticleID=5884>.

Decker, Jeffrey Louis. "The State of Rap: Time and Place in Hip Hop Nationalism." In *Microphone Fiends: Youth Music & Youth Culture*. Ed. Andrew Ross and Tricia Rose. London: Routledge, 1994, 99–121.

Dimitriadis, Greg. "Hip Hop to Rap: Some Implications of an Historically Situated Approach to Performance." *Text and Performance Quarterly* 19(1990): 355–69.

Forero, Juan. "For Colombia's Angry Youth, Hip Hop Helps Keep It Real." *The New York Times* 16 Apr. 2004.

Forman, Murray. "'Represent': Race, Space and Place in Rap Music." *Popular Music* 19 (2000): 65–90.

Frankenberg, Ruth. *White Women, Race Matters: The Social Construction of Whiteness*. Minneapolis: U of Minnesota P, 1993.

Korat, Yael. "Indigenization of Modernity and Inventiveness of Tradition: The Case of Israeli Hip-Hop." 24 April 24 2006. New York University, Anthropology Dept. 7 July 2007 <http://homepages.nyu. edu/?k682/FinalAnth3.doc>.

McLeod, Kembrew. "Authenticity Within Hip Hop and Other Cultures Threatened with Assimilation." *Journal of Communication* 49 (1999): 134–50.

Morgan, Marcyliena. *Language, Discourse and Power in African American Culture*. Cambridge: Cambridge UP, 2002.

Nissenbaum, Dion. "Palestinians Embracing Hip-Hop to Push Perspective of the Victims." *Jewish World Review* 29 Sept. 2005/25 Elul 5765. 7 July 2007 <http://www.jewishworldreview.com/0905/arab_bip-hop.php3>.

Orbe, Mark P. *Constructing Co-Cultural Theory: An Explication of Culture, Power, and Communication*. Thousand Oaks, CA: Sage Publications, 1998.

Orlando, Valerie. "From Rap to Rai in the Mixing Bowl: Beur Hip Hop Culture and Banlieue Cinema in Urban France." *Journal of Popular Culture* 36 (2003): 395–15.

Potter, Russell A. *Spectacular Vernaculars: Hip Hop and the Politics of Postmodernism*. Albany: State U of NY P, 1995.

Rose, Tricia. "A Style Nobody Can Deal With: Politics, Style and the Postindustrial City in Hip Hop." In

Microphone Fiends: Youth Music & Youth Culture. Ed. Andrew Ross and Tricia Rose. London: Routledge, 1994, 71–88.

Rose, Tricia. *Black Noise: Rap Music and Black Culture in Contemporary America.* Hanover, NH: Wesleyan UP, 1994.

Stapleton, Katina R. "From the Margins to Mainstream: The Political Power of Hip Hop." *Media, Culture & Society* 20 (1998): 219–34.

"The Great Divide." *The Guardian* 11 March 2005. 7 July 2007 <http://arts. guardian.co.uk/features/story/0,11710,1434554,00.html>.

Thomas, Amelia. "Israeli-Arab Rap: An Outlet for Youth Protest." *Christian Science Monitor* 21 July, 2005, 11.

Vens, Hartwig. "Hip Hop Speaks to the Reality of Israel." *World Press Review* 51 (2004): 36–38.

Warner, Michael. "Publics and Counterpublics (abbreviated version)." *Quarterly Journal of Speech* 88 (2002): 413–25.

Watkins, S. Craig. "A Nation of Millions: Hip Hop Culture and the Legacy of Black Nationalism." *The Communication Review A* (2001): 373–98.

Winder, Rob. "Rival Rappers Reflect Mid-East Conflict." *BBC News* 26 Nov. 2004. 7 July 2007 <http://news.bbc.co.Uk/2/hi/middle_east/4039399.stm>.

11

Lookin' for the "Real" Nigga
Social Scientists Construct the Ghetto

In this seminal essay from the field of Black Cultural Studies, historian Robin D.G. Kelley challenges social science renderings of black cultural practices as pathological. Employing his own insight as a figure who is a product of the very pathological environments that social scientists write about, Kelley highlights the experiential logic of black urban communities.

Kelley's observations are important in understanding the ways that some hip-hop artists are not simply tethered to the pathologies that we assign to them and their culture, but employ such pathological narratives for an audience ready and willing to consume black pathology as something authentic.

Lookin' for the "Real" Nigga: Social Scientists Construct the Ghetto

Robin D.G. Kelley

Perhaps the supreme irony of black American existence is how broadly black people debate the question of cultural identity among themselves while getting branded as a cultural monolith by those who would deny us the complexity and complexion of a community, let alone a nation. If Afro-Americans have never settled for the racist reductions imposed upon them—from chattel slaves to cinematic stereotype to sociological myth—it's because the black collective conscious not only knew better but also knew more than enough ethnic diversity to subsume these fictions.

Greg Tate, *Flyboy in the Buttermilk*

The biggest difference between us and white folks is that we know when we are playing.

Alberta Roberts, quoted in John Langston Gwaltney, *Drylongso*

"I think this anthropology is just another way to call me a nigger." So observed Othman Sullivan, one of many informants in John Langston Gwaltney's classic study of black culture, *Drylongso*.[1] Perhaps a kinder, gentler way to put it is that anthropology, not unlike most urban social science, has played a key role in marking "blackness" and defining black culture to the "outside" world. Beginning with Robert Park and his protégés to the War on Poverty inspired ethnographers, a battery of social scientists have significantly shaped the current dialogue on black urban culture. Today sociologists, anthropologists, political scientists, and economists compete for huge grants from Ford, Rockefeller, Sage, and other foundations to measure everything measurable in order to get a handle on the newest internal threat to civilization. With the discovery of the so-called underclass, terms like *nihilistic, dysfunctional,* and *pathological* have become the most common adjectives to describe contemporary black urban culture. The question they often pose, to use Mr. Othman Sullivan's words, is what kind of "niggers" populate the inner cities?

Unfortunately, too much of this rapidly expanding literature on the underclass provides less an understanding of the complexity of people's lives and cultures than a bad blaxploitation film or an Ernie Barnes painting. Many social scientists are not only quick to generalize about the black urban poor on the basis of a few "representative" examples, but more often than not, they do not let the natives speak. A major part of the problem is the way in which many mainstream social scientists studying the underclass define *culture*. Relying on a narrowly conceived definition of culture, most of the underclass literature uses *behavior* and *culture* interchangeably.

My purpose, then, is to offer some reflections on how the culture concept employed by social scientists has severely impoverished contemporary debates over the plight of urban African Americans and contributed to the construction of the ghetto as a reservoir of pathologies and bad cultural values. Much of this literature not only conflates behavior with culture, but when social scientists explore "expressive" cultural forms or what has been called "popular culture" (such as language, music, and style), most reduce it to expressions of pathology, compensatory behavior, or creative "coping mechanisms" to deal with racism and poverty. While some aspects of black expressive cultures certainly help inner city residents deal with and even resist ghetto conditions, most of the literature ignores what these cultural forms mean for the practitioners. Few scholars acknowledge that what might also be at stake here are aesthetics, style, and pleasure. Nor do they recognize black urban culture's hybridity and internal differences. Given the common belief that inner city communities are more isolated than ever before and have completely alien values, the notion that there is one discrete, identifiable black urban culture carries a great deal of weight. By conceiving black urban culture in the singular, interpreters unwittingly reduce their subjects to cardboard typologies who fit neatly into their own definition of the "underclass" and render invisible a wide array of complex cultural forms and practices.

"It's Just a Ghetto Thang": The Problem of Authenticity and the Ethnographic Imagination

A few years ago Mercer Sullivan decried the disappearance of "culture" from the study of urban poverty, attributing its demise to the fact that "overly vague notions of the culture of poverty brought disrepute to the culture concept as a tool for understanding the effects of the concentration of poverty among cultural minorities."[2] In some respects, Sullivan is right: the conservatives who maintain that persistent poverty in the inner city is the result of the behavior of the poor, the product of some cultural deficiency, have garnered so much opposition from many liberals and radicals that few scholars are willing even to discuss culture. Instead, opponents of the "culture of poverty" idea tend to focus on structural transformations in the U.S. economy, labor force composition, and resultant changes in marriage patterns to explain the underclass.[3]

However, when viewed from another perspective, culture never really disappeared from the underclass debate.[4] On the contrary, it has been as central to the work of liberal structuralists and radical Marxists as it has been to that of the conservative culturalists. While culturalists insist that the behavior of the urban poor explains their poverty, the structuralists argue that the economy explains their behavior as well as their poverty.[5] For all their differences, there is general agreement that a common, debased culture is what defines the "underclass," what makes it a threat to the future of America. Most interpreters of the "underclass" treat behavior as not only a synonym for culture but also as the determinant for class. In simple terms, what makes the "underclass" a class is members' common behavior—not their income, their poverty level, or the kind of work they do. It is a definition of class driven more by moral panic than by systematic analysis. A cursory look at the literature reveals that there is no consensus as to precisely what behaviors define the underclass. Some scholars, like William Julius Wilson, have offered a more spatial definition of the underclass by focusing on areas of "concentrated poverty," but obvious problems result when observers discover the wide range of behavior and attitudes in, say, a single city block. What happens to the concept when we find people with jobs engaging in illicit activities and some jobless people depending on church charity? Or married employed fathers who spend virtually no time with their kids and jobless unwed fathers participating and sharing in child care responsibilities? How does the concept of underclass behavior hold up to Kathryn Edin's findings that many so-called welfare-dependent women must also work for wages in order to make ends meet?[6] More importantly, how do we fit criminals (many first-time offenders), welfare recipients, single mothers, absent fathers, alcohol and drug abusers, and gun toting youth all into one "class"?

When we try to apply the same principles to people with higher incomes, who are presumed to be "functional" and "normative," we ultimately expose the absurdity of it all. Political scientist Charles Henry offers the following description of pathological behavior for the very folks the underclass is supposed to emulate. This tangle of deviant behavior, which he calls the "culture of wealth," is characterized by a "rejection or denial of physical attributes" leading to "hazardous sessions in tanning parlors" and frequent trips to weight-loss salons; rootlessness; antisocial behavior; and "an inability to make practical decisions" evidenced by their tendency to own several homes, frequent private social and dining clubs, and by their vast amount of unnecessary and socially useless possessions. "Finally," Henry adds, "the culture of the rich is engulfed in a web of crime, sexism, and poor health. Drug use and white collar crime are rampant, according to every available index. . . . In sum, this group is engaged in a permanent cycle of divorce, forced child separations through boarding schools, and rampant materialism that leads to the dreaded Monte Carlo syndrome. Before they can be helped they must close tax loopholes, end subsidies, and stop buying influence."[7]

As absurd as Henry's satirical reformulation of the culture of poverty might appear, this very instrumentalist way of understanding culture is deeply rooted even in the more liberal social science approaches to urban poverty. In the mid- to late 1960s, a group of progressive social scientists, mostly ethnographers, challenged the more conservative culture-of-poverty arguments and insisted that black culture was itself a necessary adaptation to racism and poverty, a set of coping mechanisms that grew out of the struggle for material and psychic survival.[8] Ironically, while this work consciously sought to recast ghetto dwellers as active agents rather than passive victims, it has nonetheless reinforced monolithic interpretations of black urban culture and significantly shaped current articulations of the culture concept in social science approaches to poverty.

With the zeal of colonial missionaries, these liberal and often radical ethnographers (mostly white men) set out to explore the newly discovered concrete jungles. Inspired by the politics of the 1960s and mandated by Lyndon Johnson's War on Poverty, a veritable army of anthropologists, sociologists, linguists, and social psychologists set up camp in America's ghettos. In the Harlem and Washington Heights communities where I grew up in the mid- to late 1960s, even our liberal white teachers who were committed to making us into functional members of society turned out to be foot soldiers in the new ethnographic army. With the overnight success of published collections of inner city children's writings like *The Me Nobody Knows* and Caroline Mirthes's *Can't You Hear Me Talking to You?*, writing about the intimate details of our home life seemed like our most important assignment.[9] (And we made the most of it by enriching our mundane narratives with stories from *Mod Squad, Hawaii Five-O*, and *Speed Racer*.)

Of course, I do not believe for a minute that most of our teachers gave us these kinds of exercises hoping to one day appear on the *Merv Griffin Show*. But, in retrospect at least, the explosion of interest in the inner city cannot be easily divorced from the marketplace. Although these social scientists came to mine what they believed was the "authentic Negro culture," there was real gold in them thar ghettos since white America's fascination with the pathological urban poor translated into massive book sales.

Unfortunately, most social scientists believed they knew what "authentic Negro culture" was before they entered the field. The "real Negroes" were the young jobless men hanging out on the corner passing the bottle, the brothers with the nastiest verbal repertoire, the pimps and hustlers, and the single mothers who raised streetwise kids who began cursing before they could walk. Of course, there were other characters, like the men and women who went to work every day in foundries, hospitals, nursing homes, private homes, police stations, sanitation departments, banks, garment factories, assembly plants, pawn shops, construction sites, loading docks, storefront churches, telephone companies, grocery and department stores, public transit, restaurants, welfare offices, recreation centers; or the street vendors, the cab drivers, the bus drivers, the ice cream truck drivers, the seamstresses, the numerologists and fortune tellers, the folks who protected or cleaned downtown buildings all night long. These are the kinds of people who lived in my neighborhood in West Harlem during the early 1970s, but they rarely found their way into the ethnographic text. And when they did show up, social scientists tended to reduce them to typologies—"lames," "strivers," "mainstreamers," "achievers," or "revolutionaries."[10]

Perhaps these urban dwellers were not as interesting, as the hard-core ghetto poor, or more likely, they stood at the margins of a perceived or invented "authentic" Negro society. A noteworthy exception is John Langston Gwaltney's remarkable book, *Drylongso: A Self-Portrait of Black America* (1981). Based on interviews conducted during the 1970s with black working-class residents in several Northeastern cities, *Drylongso* is one of the few works on urban African Americans by an African American anthropologist that appeared during the height of ghetto ethnography. Because Gwaltney is blind, he could not rely on the traditional methods of observation and interepretation. Instead—and this is the book's strength—he allowed his informants to speak for themselves about what *they* see and do. They interpret their own communities, African American culture, white society, racism, politics and the state, and the very discipline in which Gwaltney was trained—anthropology. What the book reveals is that the natives are aware that anthropologists are constructing them, and they saw in Gwaltney—who relied primarily on family and friends as informants—an opportunity to speak back. One, a woman he calls Elva Noble, said to him: "I'm not trying to tell you your job, but if you ever do write a book about us, then I hope you really do write about things the way they really are. I guess that depends on you to some extent but you know that there are more of us who are going to work every day than there are like the people who are git'n over."[11] While his definition of a "core black culture" may strike some as essentialist, it emphasizes diversity and tolerance for diversity. Gwaltney acknowledges the stylistic uniqueness of African American culture, yet he shows that the central facet of this core culture is the deep-rooted sense of community, common history, and collective recognition that there is indeed an African American culture and a "black" way of doing things. Regardless of the origins of a particular recipe, or the roots of a particular religion or Christian denomination, the cook and the congregation have no problem identifying these distinct practices and institutions as "black."

Few ghetto ethnographers have understood or developed Gwaltney's insights into African American urban culture. Whereas Gwaltney's notion of a core culture incorporates a diverse and contradictory range of practices, attitudes, and relationships that are dynamic, historically situated, and ethnically hybrid, social scientists of his generation and after—especially those at the forefront of poverty studies—treat culture as if it were a set of behaviors. They assume that there is one identifiable ghetto culture, and what they observed was it. These assumptions, which continue to shape much current social science and most mass media representations of the "inner city," can be partly attributed to the way ethnographers are trained in the West. As James Clifford observed, anthropologists studying non-Western societies are not only compelled to describe the communities under interrogation as completely foreign to their own society, but if a community is to be worthy of study as a group it must possess an identifiable, homogeneous culture. I think, in principle at least, the same holds true for interpretations of black urban America. Ethnographers can argue that inner city residents, as a "foreign" culture, do not share "mainstream" values. Social scientists do not treat behavior as situational, an individual response to a specific set of circumstances; rather, inner city residents act according to their own unique cultural "norms."[12]

For many of these ethnographers, the defining characteristic of African American urban culture was relations between men and women. Even Charles Keil, whose *Urban Blues* is one of the few ethnographic texts from that period to not only examine aesthetics and form in black culture but take "strong exception to the view that lower-class Negro life style and its characteristic rituals and expressive roles are the products of overcompensation for masculine self-doubt," nonetheless concludes that "the battle of the sexes" is precisely what characterizes African American urban culture.[13] Expressive cultures, then, were not only constructed as adaptive, functioning primarily to cope with the horrible conditions of ghetto life, but were conceived largely as expressions of masculinity. In fact, the linking of men with expressive cultures was so pervasive that the pioneering ethnographies focusing on African American women and girls—notably the work of Joyce Ladner and Carol Stack—do not explore this realm, whether in mixed-gender groupings or all-female groups. They concentrated more on sex roles, relationships, and family survival rather than expressive cultures.[14]

Two illuminating examples are the debate over the concept of "soul" and the verbal art form known to most academics as "the dozens." In the ethnographic imagination, "soul" and "the dozens" were both examples par excellence of authentic black urban culture as well as vehicles for expressing black masculinity. The bias toward expressive male culture must be understood within a particular historical and political context. In the midst of urban rebellions, the masculinist rhetoric of black nationalism, the controversy over the Moynihan report, and the uncritical linking of "agency" and resistance with men, black men took center stage in poverty research.[15]

Soul was so critical to the social science discourse on the adaptive culture of the black urban poor that Lee Rainwater edited an entire book about it, and Ulf Hannerz structured his study of Washington, D.C., on it.[16] According to these authors, *soul* is the expressive lifestyle of black men adapting to economic and political marginality. This one word supposedly embraces the entire range of "Negro lower class culture"; it constitutes "essential Negroness." Only authentic Negroes had soul. In defining *soul*, Hannerz reduces aesthetics, style, and the dynamic struggle over identity to a set of coping mechanisms. Among his many attempts to define *soul*, he insists that it is tied to the instability of black male-female relationships. He deduced evidence for this from his findings that "success with the opposite sex is a focal concern in lower-class Negro life," and the fact that a good deal of popular black music—soul music—was preoccupied with courting or losing a lover.[17]

Being "cool" is an indispensable component of soul; it is also regarded by these ethnographers as a peculiarly black expression of masculinity. Indeed, the entire discussion of cool centers entirely on black men. Cool as an aesthetic, as a style, as an art form expressed through language and the body, is simply not dealt with. Cool, not surprisingly, is merely another mechanism to cope with racism and poverty. According to Lee Rainwater and David Schulz, it is nothing more than a survival technique intended to "make yourself interesting and attractive to others so that you are better able to manipulate their behavior along lines that will provide some immediate gratification." To achieve cool simply entails learning to lie and putting up a front of competence and success. But like a lot of adaptive strategies, cool is self-limiting. While it helps young black males maintain an image of being "in control," according to David Schulz, it can also make "intimate relationships" more difficult to achieve.[18]

Hannerz reluctantly admits that no matter how hard he tried, none of the "authentic ghetto inhabitants" he had come across could define *soul*. He was certain that soul was "essentially

Negro," but concluded that it really could not be defined, for to do that would be to undermine its meaning: it is something one possesses, a ticket into the "in crowd." If you need a definition you do not know what it means. It's a black (male) thang; you'll never understand. But Hannerz obviously felt confident enough to venture his own definition, based on his understanding of African American culture, that *soul* was little more than a survival strategy to cope with the harsh realities of the ghetto. Moreover, he felt empowered to determine which black people had the right to claim the mantle of authenticity: when LeRoi Jones and Lerone Bennett offered their interpretation of soul, Hannerz rejected their definitions, in part because they were not, in his words, "authentic Negroes."[19]

By constructing the black urban world as a single culture whose function is merely to survive the ghetto, Rainwater, Hannerz, and most of their colleagues at the time ultimately collapsed a wide range of historically specific cultural practices and forms and searched for a (*the*) concept that could bring them all together. Such an interpretation of culture makes it impossible for Hannerz and others to see soul not as a thing but as a discourse through which African Americans, at a particular historical moment, claimed ownership of the symbols and practices of their own imagined community. This is why, even at the height of the Black Power movement, African American urban culture could be so fluid, hybrid, and multinational. In Harlem in the 1970s, Nehru suits were as popular and as "black" as dashikis, and martial arts films placed Bruce Lee among a pantheon of black heroes that included Walt Frazier and John Shaft. As debates over the black aesthetic raged, the concept of soul was an assertion that there are "black ways" of doing things, even if those ways are contested and the boundaries around what is "black" are fluid. How it manifests itself and how it shifts is less important than the fact that the boundaries exist in the first place. At the very least, *soul* was a euphemism or a creative way of identifying what many believed was a black aesthetic or black style, and it was a synonym for black itself or a way to talk about being black without reference to color, which is why people of other ethnic groups could have soul.

Soul in the 1960s and early 1970s was also about transformation. It was almost never conceived by African Americans as an innate, genetically derived feature of black life, for it represented a shedding of the old "Negro" ways and an embrace of "Black" power and pride. The most visible signifier of soul was undoubtedly the Afro. More than any other element of style, the Afro put the issue of hair squarely on the black political agenda, where it has been ever since. The current debates over hair and its relationship to political consciousness really have their roots in the Afro. Not surprisingly, social scientists at the time viewed the Afro through the limited lens of Black Power politics, urban uprising, and an overarching discourse of authenticity. And given their almost exclusive interest in young men, their perspective on the Afro was strongly influenced by the rhetoric and iconography of a movement that flouted black masculinity. Yet, once we look beyond the presumably male-occupied ghetto streets that dominated the ethnographic imagination at the time, the story of the Afro's origins and meaning complicated the link to soul culture.

First, the Afro powerfully demonstrates the degree to which soul was deeply implicated in the marketplace. What passed as "authentic" ghetto culture was as much a product of market forces and the commercial appropriation of urban styles as experience and individual creativity. And very few black urban residents/consumers viewed their own participation in the marketplace as undermining their own authenticity as bearers of black culture. Even before the Afro reached its height of popularity, the hair care industry stepped in and began producing a vast array of chemicals to make one's "natural" more natural. One could pick up Raveen Hair Sheen, Afro Sheen, Ultra Sheen, Head Start vitamin and mineral capsules, to name a few. The Clairol Corporation (whose CEO supported the Philadelphia Black Power Conference in 1967) did not hesitate to enter the "natural" business.[20] Listen to this Clairol ad published in *Essence Magazine* (November 1970):

No matter what they say ... Nature Can't Do It Alone! Nothing pretties up a face like a beautiful head of hair, but even hair that's born this beautiful needs a little help along the way.... A little brightening, a little heightening of color, a little extra sheen to liven up the look. And because that wonderful natural look is still the most wanted look ... the most fashionable, the most satisfying look you can have at any age ... anything you do must look natural, natural, natural. And this indeed is the art of Miss Clairol.

Depending on the particular style, the Afro could require almost as much maintenance as chemically straightened hair. And for those women (and some men) whose hair simply would not cooperate or who wanted the flexibility to shift from straight to nappy, there was always the Afro wig. For nine or ten dollars, one could purchase a variety of different wig styles, ranging from the "Soul-Light Freedom" wigs to the "Honey Bee Afro Shag," made from cleverly labeled synthetic materials such as "Afrylic" or "Afrilon."[21]

Second, the Afro's roots really go back to the bourgeois high fashion circles in the late 1950s. The Afro was seen by the black and white elite as a kind of new female exotica. Even though its intention, among some circles at least, was to achieve healthier hair and express solidarity with newly independent African nations, the Afro entered public consciousness as a mod fashion statement that was not only palatable to bourgeois whites but, in some circles, celebrated. There were people like Lois Liberty Jones, a consultant, beauty culturist, and lecturer, who claimed to have pioneered the natural as early as 1952! She originated "Coiffures Aframericana" concepts of hair styling which she practiced in Harlem for several years from the early 1960s.[22] More importantly, it was the early, not the late, 1960s, when performers like Odetta, Miriam Makeba, Abby Lincoln, Nina Simone, and the artist Margaret Burroughs began wearing the "au naturelle" style—medium to short Afros. Writer Andrea Benton Rushing has vivid memories of seeing Odetta at the Village Gate long before Black Power entered the national lexicon. "I was mesmerized by her stunning frame," she recalled, "in its short kinky halo. She had a regal poise and power that I had never seen in a 'Negro' (as we called ourselves back then) woman before—no matter how naturally 'good' or diligently straightened her hair was." Many other black women in New York, particularly those who ran in the interracial world of Manhattan sophisticates, were first introduced to the natural through high fashion models in au naturelle shows, which were the rage at the time.[23]

Helen Hayes King, associate editor of *Jet*, came in contact with the au naturelle style at an art show in New York, in the late 1950s. A couple of years later, she heard Abby Lincoln speak about her own decision to go natural at one of these shows and, with prompting from her husband, decided to go forth to adopt the 'fro. Ironically, one of the few salons in Chicago specializing in the au naturelle look was run by a white male hairdresser in the exclusive Northside community. He actually lectured King on the virtues of natural hair: "I don't know why Negro women with delicate hair like yours burn and process all the life out of it.... If you'd just wash it, oil it and take care of it, it would be so much healthier.... I don't know how all this straightening foolishness started anyhow." When she returned home to the Southside, however, instead of compliments she received strange looks from her neighbors. Despite criticism and ridicule by her co-workers and friends, she stuck with her au naturelle, not because she was trying to make a political statement or demonstrate her solidarity with African independence movements. "I'm not so involved in the neo-African aspects of the 'au naturelle' look," she wrote, "nor in the get-back-to-your-heritage bit." Her explanation was simple: the style was chic and elegant and in the end she was pleased with the feel of her hair. It is fitting to note that most of the compliments came from whites.[24]

What is also interesting about King's narrative is that it appeared in the context of a debate with Nigerian writer Theresa Ogunbiyi over whether black women should straighten their hair or not, which appeared in a 1963 issue of *Negro Digest*. In particular, Ogunbiyi defended the right of a Lagos firm to forbid employees to plait their hair; women were required to wear straight hair. She rejected the idea that straightening hair destroys national custom and heritage: "I think we carry this national pride a bit too far at times, even to the detriment of our country's progress." Her point was that breaking with tradition is progress, especially since Western dress and hairstyles are more comfortable and easier to work in. "When I wear the Yoruba costume, I find that I spend more time than I can afford, re-tying the headtie and the bulky wrapper round my waist. And have you tried typing in an 'Agbada'? I am all for nationalisation but give it to me with some comfort and improvement."[25]

Andrea Benton Rushing's story is a slight variation on King's experience. She, too, was a premature natural hair advocate. When she stepped out of the house sporting her first Afro, perhaps inspired by Odetta or prompted by plain curiosity, her "relatives though I'd lost my mind and, of course, my teachers at Juilliard stole sideways looks at me and talked about the importance of appearance in auditions and concerts." Yet, while the white Juilliard faculty and her closest family members found the new style strange and inappropriate, brothers on the block in her New York City neighborhood greeted her with praise: " 'Looking good, sister,' 'Watch out, African queen!' " She, too, found it ironic that middle-class African woman on the continent chose to straighten their hair. During a trip to Ghana years later, she recalled the irony of having her Afro braided in an Accra beauty parlor while "three Ghanaians (two Akan-speaking government workers and one Ewe microbiologist) . . . were having their chemically-straightened hair washed, set, combed out, and sprayed in place."[26]

No matter what spurred on the style or who adopted it, however, the political implications of the au naturelle could not be avoided. After all, the biggest early proponents of the style tended to be women artists whose work identified with the black freedom movement and African liberation. In some respects, women such as Abby Lincoln, Odetta, and Nina Simone were part of what might be called black bohemia. They participated in a larger community—based mostly in New York—of poets, writers, musicians of the 1950s, for whom the emancipation of their own artistic form coincided with the African freedom movement. *Ebony, Jet,* and *Sepia* magazines were covering Africa, and African publications such as *Drum* were being read by those ex-Negroes in the States who could get their hands on it. The Civil Rights movement, the struggle against apartheid in South Africa, and the emergence of newly independent African nations found a voice in recordings by various jazz artists, including Randy Weston's *Uhuru Afrika,* Max Roach's *We Insist: Freedom Now Suite* (featuring Abby Lincoln, Roach's wife), Art Blakey's "Message from Kenya" and "Ritual," and John Coltrane's "Liberia," "Dahomey Dance," and "Africa." Revolutionary political movements, combined with revolutionary experiments in artistic creation—the simultaneous embrace and rejection of tradition—forged the strongest physical and imaginary links between Africa and the diaspora.[27] Thus, it is not surprising that Harold Cruse, in one of his seminal essays on the coming of the new black nationalism, anticipated the importance of the style revolution and the place of the au naturelle in it. As early as 1962, Cruse predicted that in the coming years "Afro-Americans . . . will undoubtedly make a lot of noise in militant demonstrations, cultivate beards and sport their hair in various degrees of la mode au natural, and tend to be cultish with African- and Arab-style dress."[28]

Of course, he was right. By the mid-1960s, however, the Afro was no longer associated with downtown chic but with uptown rebellion. It was sported by rock-throwing black males and black-leathered militants armed to the teeth. Thus, once associated with feminine chic, the Afro suddenly became the symbol of black manhood, the death of the "Negro" and birth of the militant, virulent Black man.[29] The new politics, combined with media representations of Afro-coifed black militants, profoundly shaped the ethnographic imagination. As new narratives were created to explain the symbolic significance of the natural style, women were rendered invisible. The erasure of women, I would argue, was not limited to histories of style politics but to ghetto ethnography in general.

The masculinism of soul in contemporary ghetto ethnography has survived to this day, despite the last quarter-century of incisive black feminist scholarship. The ethnographic and sociological search for soul has made a comeback recently under a new name: the "cool pose." In a recent book, Richard Majors and Janet Mancini Bilson have recycled the arguments of Lee Rainwater, Ulf Hannerz, Elliot Liebow, and David Schulz, and have suggested that the "cool pose" captures the essence of young black male expressive culture. Like earlier constructors of soul, they too believe that the "cool pose" is an adaptive strategy to cope with the particular forms of racism and oppression black males face in America. "Cool pose is a ritualized form of masculinity that entails behaviors, scripts, physical posturing, impression management, and carefully crafted performances that deliver a single, critical message: pride, strength, and control." Echoing earlier works, the cool pose is also a double-edged sword since it allegedly undermines potential intimacy with females.[30] By playing down the aesthetics of cool and reducing the cool pose to a response by heterosexual black males to racism, intraracial violence, and poverty, the authors not only reinforce the idea that there is an essential black urban culture created by the oppressive conditions of the ghetto but ignore manifestations of the cool pose in the public "performances" of black women, gay black men, and the African American middle class.

A more tangible example of black urban expressive culture that seemed to captivate social scientists in the 1960s is "the dozens." Yet, in spite of the amount of ink devoted to the subject, it has also been perhaps the most misinterpreted cultural form coming out of African American communities. Called at various times in various places "capping," "sounding," "ranking," "bagging," or "dissing," virtually all leading anthropologists, sociologists, and linguists agree that it is a black male form of "ritual insult," a verbal contest involving any number of young black men who compete by talking about each other's mama. There is less agreement, however, about how to interpret the sociological and psychological significance of the dozens. In keeping with the dominant social science interpretations of the culture concept, so-called ritual insults among urban black youth were either another adaptive strategy or an example of social pathology.

The amazing thing about the sociological and ethnographic scholarship on the dozens, from John Dollard's ruminations in 1939 to the more recent misreadings by Roger Lane and Carl Nightingale, is the consistency with which it repeats the same errors. For one, the almost universal assertion that the dozens is a "ritual" empowers the ethnographer to select what appears to be more formalized verbal exchanges (e.g., rhyming couplets) and ascribe to them greater "authenticity" than other forms of playful conversation. In fact, by framing the dozens as ritual, most scholars have come to believe that it is first and foremost a "contest" with rules, players, and mental scorecard rather than the daily banter of many (not all) young African Americans. Anyone who has lived and survived the dozens (or whatever name you want to call it) cannot imagine turning to one's friends and announcing, "Hey, let's go outside and play the dozens." Furthermore, the very use of the term *ritual* to describe everyday speech reinforces the exoticization of black urban populations constructing them as Others whose investment in this cultural tradition is much deeper than trying to get a laugh.[31]

These problems, however, are tied to larger ones. For example, white ethnographers seemed oblivious to the fact that their very presence shaped what they observed. Asking their subjects to "play the dozens" while an interloper records the "session" with a tape recorder and notepad has the effect of creating a ritual performance for the sake of an audience, of turning spontaneous, improvised verbal exchanges into a formal practice. More significantly, ethnographers have tailor-made their own interpretation of the dozens by selecting what they believe were the most authentic sites for such verbal duels—street corners, pool halls, bars, and parks. In other words, they sought out male spaces rather than predominantly female and mixed-gender spaces to record the dozens. It is no wonder that practically all commentators on the dozens have concluded that it is a boy thing. The fact is, evidence suggests that young women engaged in these kinds of verbal exchanges as much as their male counterparts, both with men and between women. And they were no less profane. By not searching out other mixed-gender and female spaces such as school buses, cafeterias, kitchen tables, beauty salons, and house parties, ethnographers have overstated the extent to which the dozens were the sole property of men.[32]

Folklorist Roger Abrahams, who pioneered the study of the dozens in his book on black vernacular folklore "from the streets of Philadelphia," is one of the few scholars to appreciate the pleasure and aesthetics of such verbal play. Nevertheless, he argues that one of the primary functions of the dozens is to compensate for a lack of masculinity caused by too many absent fathers and domineering mothers, which is why the main target of insults is an "opponent's" mother. "By exhibiting his wit, by creating new and vital folkloric expression, [the dozens player] is able to effect a temporary release from anxiety for both himself and his audience. By creating playgrounds for playing out aggressions, he achieves a kind of masculine identity for himself and his group in a basically hostile environment."[33] David Schulz offers an even more specific interpretation of the dozens as a form of masculine expression in an environment dominated by dysfunctional families. He writes: "Playing the dozens occurs at the point when the boy is about to enter puberty and suffer his greatest rejection from his mother as a result of his becoming a man. The dozens enables him to develop a defense against this rejection and provides a vehicle for his transition into the manipulative world of the street dominated by masculine values expressed in gang life." It then serves as a "ritualized exorcism" that allows men to break from maternal dominance and "establish their own image of male superiority celebrated in street life."[34]

Allow me to propose an alternative reading of the dozens. The goal of the dozens and related verbal games is deceptively simple: to get a laugh. The pleasure of the dozens is not the viciousness of the insult but the humor, the creative pun, the outrageous metaphor. Contrary to popular belief, mothers are not the sole target; the subjects include fathers, grandparents, brothers, sisters, cousins, friends, food, skin color, smell, and hairstyles. I am not suggesting that "your mama" is unimportant in the whole structure of these verbal exchanges. Nor am I suggesting that the emphasis on "your mama" has absolutely nothing to do with the ways in which patriarchy is discursively reproduced. However, we need to understand that "your mama" in this context is almost never living, literal, or even metaphoric. "Your mama" is a generic reference, a code signaling that the dozens have begun—it signifies a shift in speech. "Your mama" is also a mutable, nameless body of a shared imagination that can be constructed and reconstructed in a thousand different shapes, sizes, colors, and circumstances. The emphasis on "your mama" in most interpretations of the dozens has more to do with the peculiar preoccupation of social science with Negro family structure than anything else. Besides, in many cases the target is immaterial; your mama, your daddy, your greasy-headed granny are merely vehicles through which the speaker tries to elicit a laugh and display her skills. In retrospect, this seems obvious, but amid the complicated readings of masculine overcompensation and ritual performance, only a handful of writers of the period—most of whom were African Americans with no affiliation with the academy—recognized the centrality of humor. One was Howard Seals, who self-published a pamphlet on the dozens in 1969 titled *You Ain't Thuh Man Yuh Mamma Wuz*. In an effort to put to rest all the sociological overinterpretation, Seals explains: "The emotional tone to be maintained is that of hilariously, outrageously funny bantering."[35] Compare Seals's comment with linguist William Labov, who, while recognizing the humor, ultimately turns laughter into part of the ritual and thus reinforces the process of Othering:

The primary mark of positive evaluation is laughter. We can rate the effectiveness of a sound in a group session by the number of members of the audience who laugh.

A really successful sound will be evaluated by overt comments ... the most common forms are: "Oh!," "Oh shit!" "God damn!," or "Oh lord!" By far the most common is "Oh shit!" The intonation is important; when approval is to be signalled the vowel of each word is quite long, with a high sustained initial pitch, and a slow-falling pitch contour.[36]

Without a concept of, or even an interest in, aesthetics, style, and the visceral pleasures of cultural forms, it should not be surprising that most social scientists explained black urban culture in terms of coping mechanisms, rituals, or oppositional responses to racism. And trapped by an essentialist interpretation of culture, they continue to look for that elusive "authentic" ghetto sensibility, the true, honest, unbridled, pure cultural practices that capture the raw, ruffneck "reality" of urban life. Today, that reality is rap. While studies of rap and Hip Hop culture have been useful in terms of nudging contemporary poverty studies to pay attention to expressive cultures, they have not done much to advance the culture concept in social science. Like its progenitor, the dozens, rap or Hip Hop has been subject to incredible misconception and overinterpretation. Despite the brilliant writing of cultural critics like Tricia Rose, Greg Tate, George Lipsitz, Brian Cross, James Spady, dream hampton, Seth Fernando, Jonathan Scott, Juan Flores, Touré, and others, a number of scholars have returned to or revised the interpretive frameworks developed by the previous generation of ethnographers.[37]

For example, in a very recent book on poor black youth in postwar Philadelphia, Carl Nightingale suggests that the presumed loss of oral traditions like toasting (long, often profane vernacular narrative poetry performed orally) and the dozens, and the rise of rap music and similar commercialized expressive cultures partly explains the increase in violence among young black males. The former, he argues, has played a positive role in curbing violence while the latter is responsible for heightening aggression. He thus calls on young black men to return to these earlier, presumably precommercial cultural forms to vent emotions. Nightingale advocates resurrecting the ring shout, drumming, singing the blues, even toasting, to express black male pain and vulnerability.

The suggestion that rap music has undermined black cultural integrity is made even more forcefully in a recent article by Andre Craddock-Willis. He criticizes nearly all rap artists—especially hard-core gangsta rappers—for not knowing the "majesty" of the blues. The Left, he insists, "must work to gently push these artists to understand the tradition whose shoulders they stand on, and encourage them to comprehend struggle, sacrifice, vision and dedication— the cornerstones for the Black musical tradition."[38] (A tradition, by the way, that includes the great Jelly Roll Morton, whose 1938 recording of "Make Me a Pallet on the Floor" included lines like: "Come here you sweet bitch, give me that pussy, let me get in your drawers / I'm gonna make you think you fuckin' with Santa Claus.")[39]

On the flip side are authors who insist that rap music is fundamentally the authentic, unmediated voice of ghetto youth. Tommy Lott's recent essay, "Marooned in America: Black Urban Youth Culture and Social Pathology," offers a powerful critique of neoconservative culture-of-poverty theories and challenges assumptions that the culture of the so-called underclass is pathological, but he nevertheless reduces expressive culture to a coping strategy to deal with the terror of street life. For Lott, the Hip Hop nation is the true voice of the black lumpen-proletariat whose descriptions of street life are the real thing. "As inhabitants of extreme-poverty neighborhoods," he writes, "many rap artists and their audiences are entrenched in a street life filled with crime, drugs, and violence. Being criminal-minded and having street values are much more suitable for living in their environment." Of course, most rap music is not about a nihilistic street life but about rocking the mike, and the vast majority of rap artists (like most inner city youth) were not entrenched in the tangled web of crime and violence. Yet, he is convinced that Hip Hop narratives of ghetto life "can only come from one's experiences on the streets. Although, at its worst, this knowledge is manifested through egotistical sexual boasting, the core meaning of the rapper's use of the term 'knowledge' is to be *politically* astute, that is, to have a full understanding of the conditions under which black urban youth must survive."[40]

By not acknowledging the deep visceral pleasures black youth derive from making and consuming culture, the stylistic and aesthetic conventions that render the form and performance more attractive than the message, these authors reduce expressive culture to a political text to be read like a less sophisticated version of *The Nation* or *Radical America*. But what counts more than the story is the "storytelling"—an emcee's verbal facility on the mic, the creative and often hilarious use of puns, metaphors, similes, not to mention the ability to kick some serious slang (or what we might call linguistic inventiveness). As microphone fiend Rakim might put it, the function of Hip Hop is to "move the crowd." For all the implicit and explicit politics of rap lyrics, Hip Hop must be understood as a sonic force more than anything else.

Despite their good intentions, ignoring aesthetics enables these authors not only to dismiss "egotistical sexual boasting" as simply a weakness in political ideology but also to mistakenly interpret narratives of everyday life as descriptions of personal experience rather than a revision of older traditions of black vernacular poetry and/or appropriations from mainstream popular culture. To begin with rap music as a mirror image of daily life ignores the influences of urban toasts and published "pimp narratives," which became popular during the late 1960s and early 1970s. In many instances the characters are almost identical, and on occasion rap artists pay tribute to toasting by lyrically "sampling" these early pimp narratives.[41]

Moreover, the assumption that rappers are merely street journalists does not allow for the playfulness and storytelling that is so central to Hip Hop specifically, and black vernacular culture generally. For example, violent lyrics in rap music are rarely meant to be literal. Rather, they are more often than not metaphors to challenge competitors on the microphone. The mic becomes a Tech-9 or AK-47, imagined drive-bys occur from the stage, flowing lyrics become hollow-point shells. Classic examples are Ice Cube's "Jackin' for Beats," a humorous song that describes sampling other artists and producers as outright armed robbery, and Ice T's "Pulse of the Rhyme" or "Grand Larceny" (which brags about stealing a show).[42] Moreover, exaggerated and invented boasts of criminal acts should sometimes be regarded as part of a larger set of signifying practices. Growing out of a much older set of cultural practices, these masculinist narratives are essentially verbal duels over who is the "baddest." They are not meant as literal descriptions of violence and aggression, but connote the playful use of language itself.[43]

Of course, the line between rap music's gritty realism, storytelling, and straight-up signifyin(g) is not always clear to listeners nor is it supposed to be. Hip Hop, particularly gangsta rap, also attracts listeners for whom the "ghetto" is a place of adventure, unbridled violence, erotic fantasy, and/or an imaginary alternative to suburban boredom. White music critic John Leland, who claimed that Ice Cube's turn toward social criticism "killed rap music," praised the group NWA because they "dealt in evil as fantasy: killing cops, smoking hos, filling quiet nights with a flurry of senseless buckshot." This kind of voyeurism partly explains NWA's huge white following and why their album *Efil4zaggin* shot to the top of the charts as soon as it was released. As one critic put it, "In reality, NWA have more in common with a Charles Bronson movie than a PBS documentary on the plight of the inner-cities." NWA members have even admitted that some of their recent songs were not representations of reality "in the hood" but inspired by popular films like *Innocent Man* starring Tom Selleck, and *Tango and Cash*.[44]

Claims to have located the authentic voice of black ghetto youth are certainly not unique. Several scholars insist that Hip Hop is the pure, unadulterated voice of a ghetto that has grown increasingly isolated from "mainstream" society. Missing from this formulation is rap music's incredible hybridity. From the outset, rap music embraced a variety of styles and cultural forms, from reggae and salsa to heavy metal and jazz. Hip Hop's hybridity reflected, in part, the increasingly international character of America's inner cities resulting from immigration, demographic change, and new forms of information, as well as the inventive employment of technology in creating rap music. By using two turntables, and later digital samplers, deejays played different records, isolated the "break beats" or what they identified as the funkiest part of a song, and boldly mixed a wide range of different music and musical genres to create new music. And despite the fact that many of the pioneering deejays, rappers, and break dancers were African American, West Indian, and Puerto Rican and strongly identified with the African diaspora, rap artists wrecked all the boundaries between "black" and "white" music. Deejay Afrika Islam remembers vividly the time when Hip Hop and punk united for a moment and got busy at the New Wave clubs in New York during the early 1980s. Even before the punk rockers sought a relationship with uptown Hip Hop deejays, Afrika Islam recalls, in the Bronx they were already playing "everything from Aerosmith's 'Walk This Way' to Dunk and the Blazers." Grand Master Caz, whose lyrics were stolen by the Sugarhill Gang and ended up in *Rapper's Delight* (the first successful rap record in history), grew up in the Bronx listening to soft rock and mainstream pop music. As he explained in an interview, "Yo, I'd bug you out if I told you who I used to listen to. I used to listen to Barry Manilow, Neil Diamond, and Simon and Garfunkel. I grew up listening to that WABC. That's why a lot of the stuff that my group did, a lot of routines that we're famous for all come from all white boy songs."[45]

If you saw a picture of Caz, this statement would seem incongruous. He looks the part of an authentic black male, a real ruffneck, hoodie, "G," nigga, criminal, menace. And yet, he is a product of a hybrid existence, willing to openly talk about Simon and Garfunkel in a book that I could only purchase from a Nation of Islam booth on 125th Street in Harlem. He is also the first to call what he does "black music," structured noise for which the beat, no matter where it is taken from, is everything. Moreover, like the breakers who danced to his rhymes, the kids who built his speakers, the deejay who spun the records, Caz takes credit for his creativity, his artistry, his "work." This is the "black urban culture" which has remained so elusive to social science; it is the thing, or rather the process, that defies concepts like "coping strategy," "adaptive," "authentic," "nihilistic," and "pathological."

Revising the Culture Concept: Hybridity, Style, and Aesthetics in Black Urban Culture

Aside from the tendency to ignore expressive/popular cultural forms, and limit the category of culture to (so-called dysfunctional) behavior, the biggest problem with the way social scientists employ the culture concept in their studies of the black urban poor is their inability to see what it all means *to the participants and practitioners*. In other words, they do not consider what Clinton (George, that is) calls the "pleasure principle." If I may use a metaphor here, rather than hear the singer they analyze the lyrics; rather than hear the drum they study the song title. Black music, creativity and experimentation in language, that walk, that talk, that style, must also be understood as sources of visceral and psychic pleasure. Though they may also reflect and speak to the political and social world of inner city communities, expressive cultures are not simply mirrors of social life or expressions of conflicts, pathos, and anxieties.

Paul Willis's concept of "symbolic creativity" provides one way out of the impasse created by such a limited concept of culture. As Willis argues, constructing an identity, communicating with others, and achieving pleasure are all part of symbolic creativity—it is literally the labor of creating art in everyday life. Despite his distrust of and vehement opposition to "aesthetics," he realizes that, in most cases, the explicit meaning or intention of a particular cultural form is not the thing that makes it attractive. The appeal of popular music, for example, is more than lyrical: "Songs bear meaning and allow symbolic work not just as speech acts, but also as structures of sound with unique rhythms, textures and forms. Thus, it is not always what is sung, but the *way* it is sung, within particular conventions or musical genres which gives a piece of music its communicative power and meaning."[46] Indeed, words like *soul* and *funk* were efforts to come up with a language to talk about that visceral element in music, even if they did ultimately evolve into market categories. Over two decades ago, black novelist Cecil Brown brilliantly captured this "thing," this symbolic creativity, the pleasure principle, soul, or whatever you want to call it. Writing about the godfather of soul, James Brown, he argued that his lyrics are less important than how they are uttered, where they are placed rhythmically, and "how he makes it sound." "What, for instance, does 'Mother Popcorn' mean? But what difference does it make when you're dancing to it, when you are feeling it, when you are it and it you (possession). It's nothing and everything at once; it is what black (hoodoo) people who never studied art in school mean by art."[47]

Yet to say it is a "black" thing doesn't mean it is made up entirely of black things. As Greg Tate makes clear in his recent collection of essays, *Flyboy in the Buttermilk*, and in the epigraph to this chapter, interpreters of the African American experience—in our case social scientists—must bear a large share of the responsibility for turning ghetto residents into an undifferentiated mass. We can no longer ignore the fact that information technology, new forms of mass communication, and immigration have made the rest of the world more accessible to inner city residents than ever before.[48] Contemporary black urban culture is a hybrid that draws on Afrodiasporic traditions, popular culture, the vernacular of previous generations of Southern and Northern black folk, new and old technologies, and a whole lot of imagination. Once again, James Clifford's ruminations on the "predicament of culture" are useful for exposing the predicament of social science. He writes: "To tell … local histories of cultural survival and emergence, we need to resist deep-seated habits of mind and systems of authenticity. We need to be suspicious of an almost-automatic tendency to relegate non-Western (read: black) peoples and objects to the pasts of an increasingly homogeneous humanity."[49]

Study Questions

1. Do rap artists have a responsibility to present the most authentic view of their lives and cultures?
2. In what ways have hip-hop journalists and scholars been just as misguided as Kelley suggests that social scientists have been?
3. How culpable are hip-hop artists in the reproduction of racial stereotypes?

Notes

1. John Langston Gwaltney, *Drylongso: A Self-Portrait of Black America* (New York: Random House, 1980), xix.
2. Mercer L. Sullivan, "Absent Fathers in the Inner City," *The Annals* 501 (January 1989): 49–50.
3. Recent proponents of a new "culture of poverty" thesis include Ken Auletta, *The Underclass* (New York: Random House, 1982); Nicholas Lemann, "The Origins of the Underclass: Part I," *Atlantic Monthly* 257 (June 1986): 31–61, and "The Origins of the Underclass: Part II," *Atlantic Monthly* 258 (July 1986): 54–68; Nicholas Lemann, *The Promised Land: The Great Black Migration and How It Changed America* (New York: Knopf, 1991); Charles Murray, *Losing Ground: American Social Policy, 1950–1980* (New York: Basic Books, 1984); and Lawrence Mead, *The New Dependency Politics: Non-Working Poverty in the U.S.* (New York: Basic Books, 1992). These works are quite distinct in scope, methods, and ideology from the pioneering studies of Oscar Lewis, who introduced the "culture of poverty" idea to American social science. Unlike the more recent works, he did not argue that poor people's behavior is the *cause* of their poverty. Rather, he insisted that capitalism impoverished segments of the working class, who were denied access

to mainstream institutions. The culture they created to cope with poverty and disfranchisement was passed down through generations and thus led to passivity and undermined social organization. Lewis had no intention of using the culture-of-poverty thesis to distinguish the "deserving" from the "undeserving poor." See Oscar Lewis, *The Children of Sanchez* (New York: Random House, 1961) and *La Vida: A Puerto Rican Family in the Culture of Poverty, San Juan and New York* (New York: Random House, 1966).

Critics of the culture-of-poverty thesis are many, and they do not all agree with each other as to the relative importance of culture or the causes of poverty. See especially Charles Valentine, *Culture and Poverty: Critique and Counter-Proposals* (Chicago: University of Chicago Press, 1968); Herbert J. Gans, "Culture and Class in the Study of Poverty: An Approach to Antipoverty Research," in *On Understanding Poverty: Perspectives from the Social Sciences*, ed. Daniel Patrick Moynihan (New York: Basic Books, 1968); Sheldon Danzinger and Peter Gottschalk, "The Poverty of *Losing Ground*," *Challenge* 28 (May–June 1985): 32–38; William Darity and Samuel L. Meyers, "Does Welfare Dependency Cause Female Headship? The Case of the Black Family," *Journal of Marriage and the Family* 46, no. 4 (1984): 765–79; and Mary Corcoran, Greg J. Duncan, Gerald Gurin, and Patricia Gurin, "Myth and Reality: The Causes and Persistence of Poverty," *Journal of Policy Analysis and Management* 4, no. 4 (1985): 516–36.

4. Michael Katz, "The Urban 'Underclass' as a Metaphor of Social Transformation," in *The Underclass Debate: Views from History*, ed. Michael Katz (Princeton, N.J.: Princeton University Press, 1993), 3–23.

5. The most prominent of the structuralists adopt some cultural explanation for urban poverty, suggesting that bad behavior is the outcome of a bad environment. William Julius Wilson's most recent work argues that the lack of employment has eroded the work ethic and discipline of the underclass, leading to behaviors that allow employers to justify not hiring them. See especially William Julius Wilson, *When Work Disappears: The World of the New Urban Poor* (New York: Knopf, 1996); William J. Wilson, *The Truly Disadvantaged: The Inner City, the Underclass, and Public Policy* (Chicago: University of Chicago Press, 1987); David T. Ellwood, *Poor Support: Poverty in the American Family* (New York: Basic Books, 1988); Elijah Anderson, *Streetwise: Race, Class, and Change in an Urban Community* (Chicago: University of Chicago Press, 1990); Elijah Anderson, "Sex Codes and Family Life among Poor Inner City Youth," *The Annals* 501 (January 1989): 59–78; Troy Duster, "Social Implications of the 'New' Black Underclass," *Black Scholar* 19 (May–June 1988): 2–9; Christopher Jencks, *Rethinking Social Policy: Race, Poverty, and the Underclass* (Cambridge: Harvard University Press, 1992); Mark S. Littman, "Poverty Areas and the Underclass: Untangling the Web," *Monthly Labor Review* 114 (March 1991): 19–32; Jacqueline Jones, *The Dispossessed: America's Underclasses from the Civil War to the Present* (New York: Basic Books, 1992); Douglas G. Glasgow, *The Black Underclass: Unemployment and Entrapment of Ghetto Youth* (New York: Random House, 1981); William Julius Wilson and Loic J. D. Wacquant, "The Cost of Racial and Class Exclusion in the Inner City," *The Annals* 501 (January 1989): 8–25; John D. Kasarda, "Caught in a Web of Change," *Society* 21 (November/December 1983): 41–47; John D. Kasarda, "Urban Industrial Transition and the Underclass," *The Annals* 501 (January 1989): 26–47; Maxine Baca Zinn, "Family, Race, and Poverty in the Eighties," *Signs* 14, no. 4 (1989): 856–74; Mary Corcoran, Greg J. Duncan, and Martha S. Hill, "The Economic Fortunes of Women and Children: Lessons from the Panel Study of Income Dynamics," *Signs* 10, no. 2 (1984): 232–48; Mary Jo Bane, "Household Composition and Poverty," in *Fighting Poverty: What Works and What Doesn't*, eds. Sheldon Danzinger and Daniel Weinberg (Cambridge: Harvard University Press, 1986); David Ellwood, *Poor Support* (New York: Basic Books, 1988); Barry Bluestone and Bennett Harrison, *The Deindustrialization of America* (New York: Basic Books, 1982); Richard Child Hill and Cynthia Negrey, "Deindustrialization and Racial Minorities in the Great Lakes Region, USA," in *The Reshaping of America: Social Consequences of the Changing Economy*, eds. D. Stanley Eitzen and Maxine Baca Zinn (Englewood Cliffs, N.J.: Prentice-Hall, 1989); Elliot Currie and Jerome H. Skolnick, *America's Problems: Social Issues and Public Policy* (Boston: Little, Brown and Co., 1984); Carl Nightingale, *On the Edge: A History of Poor Black Children and Their American Dreams* (New York: Basic Books, 1993); and Staff of *Chicago Tribune*, *The American Millstone: An Examination of the Nation's Permanent Underclass* (Chicago: Contemporary Books, 1986). While most of these authors focus on deindustrialization and the effects of concentrated poverty, Douglas S. Massey and Nancy A. Denton have argued that racial segregation is the key to explaining the persistence of black urban poverty. See their *American Apartheid: Segregation and the Making of the Underclass* (Cambridge: Harvard University Press, 1993).

6. Kathryn Edin, "Surviving the Welfare System: How AFDC Recipients Make Ends Meet in Chicago," *Social Problems* 38 (November 1991): 462–74.

7. Charles P. Henry, *Culture and African-American Politics* (Bloomington, Ind.: Indiana University Press, 1990), 12–13. Likewise, social philosopher Leonard Harris asks us to imagine what would happen if we used the same indices to study the "urban rich": "Suppose that their behavior was unduly helpful to themselves; say they rarely married, had more one-child families, were more likely than previous rich to be sexual libertines practicing safe sex, were health conscious, and were shrewd investors in corporate and ghetto property without moral reflection." Leonard Harris," Agency and the Concept of the Underclass," in *The Underclass Question*, ed. Bill E. Lawson (Philadelphia: Temple University Press, 1992), 37.

8. Lee Rainwater, *Behind Ghetto Walls: Black Families in a Federal Slum* (Chicago: Aldine Publishing Co., 1970); Elliot Liebow, *Tally's Corner: A Study of Negro Streetcorner Men* (Boston: Little, Brown and Co., 1967); Ulf Hannerz, *Soulside: Inquiries into Ghetto Culture and Community* (New York: Columbia University Press, 1969); Carol B. Stack, *All Our Kin: Strategies for Survival in a Black Community* (New York: Harper and Row, 1974); Betty Lou Valentine, *Hustling and Other Hard Work: Life Styles in the Ghetto* (New York: Free Press, 1978); Joyce Ladner, *Tommorrow's Tommorrow: The Black Woman* (Garden City, N.Y.: Anchor, 1971); David Schulz, *Coming Up Black: Patterns of Ghetto Socialization* (Englewood Cliffs, N.J.: Prentice-Hall, 1969).

9. Stephen M. Joseph, ed., *The Me Nobody Knows: Children's Voices from the Ghetto* (New York: Avon Books, 1969); Caroline Mirthes and the Children of P.S. 15, *Can't You Hear Me Talking to You?* (New York: Bantam Books, 1971).

10. These typologies are drawn from Hannerz, *Soulside*; William McCord, John Howard, Bernard Friedberg, Edwin Harwood, *Life Styles in the Black Ghetto* (New York: W. W. Norton, 1969).

11. Gwaltney, *Drylongso*, xxiv, xxxii.

12. James Clifford, "On Collecting Art and Culture," in *The Predicament of Culture: Twentieth-Century Ethnography, Literature, and Art* (Cambridge: Harvard University Press, 1988), 246. Don't get me wrong. The vast and rich ethnographic documentation collected by these scholars is extremely valuable because it captures the responses and survival strategies hidden from economic indices and illuminates the human aspects of poverty. Of course, these materials must be used with caution since most ethnographies do not pay much attention to historical and structural transformations. Instead, they describe and interpret a particular community during a brief moment in time. The practice of giving many of these communities fictitious names only compounds the problem and presumes that region, political economy, and history have no bearing on opportunity structures, oppositional strategies, or culture. For an extended critique, see Andrew H. Maxwell, "The Anthropology of Poverty in Black Communities: A Critique and Systems Alternative," *Urban Anthropology* 17, nos. 2 and 3 (1988): 171–92.

13. Charles Keil, *Urban Blues* (Chicago: University of Chicago Press, 1966), 1–12, 23.

14. Stack, *All Our Kin*; Ladner, *Tommorrow's Tommorrow*. This dichotomy also prevails in Anderson's more recent *Streetwise*.

15. Lee Rainwater, ed., *Soul* (Trans-Action Books, 1970), 9.

16. Rainwater, *Soul* (especially essays by John Horton, Thomas Kochman, and David Wellman); Ulf Hannerz, "The Significance of Soul" in *ibid.*, 15–30; Hannerz, *Soulside*, 144–58. For other interpretations of soul, see Keil, *Urban Blues*, 164–90; William L. Van Deburg, *New Day in Babylon: The Black Power Movement and American Culture, 1965–1975* (Chicago: University of Chicago Press, 1992), 194–97; Claude Brown, "The Language of Soul," in *Mother Wit from the Laughing Barrel: Readings in the Interpretation of Afro-American Folklore*, ed. Alan Dundes (New York: Garland Publishing Co., 1981), 232–43; and Roger D. Abrahams, *Positively Black* (Englewood Cliffs, N.J.: Prentice-Hall, 1970), 136–50.

17. Hannerz, "The Significance of Soul," 21.

18. Schulz, *Coming Up Black*, 78, 103; Rainwater, *Behind Ghetto Walls*, 372. See also John Horton, "Time and Cool People," in Rainwater, *Soul*, 31–50.

19. Hannerz, "The Significance of Soul," 22–23.

20. Robert L. Allen, *Black Awakening in Capitalist America: An Analytic History* (Garden City, N.Y.: Doubleday, 1969), 163; Van Deburg, *New Day in Babylon*, 201–2.

21. Van Deburg, *New Day in Babylon*, 201–2.

22. Lois Liberty Jones and John Henry Jones, *All about the Natural* (New York: Clairol, 1971).

23. Andrea Benton Rushing, "Hair-Raising," *Feminist Studies* 14, no. 2 (1988): 334; Jones and Jones, *All about the Natural*; Helen Hayes King and Theresa Ogunbiyi, "Should Negro Women Straighten Their Hair?" *Negro Digest* (August 1963): 68.

24. King and Ogunbiyi, "Should Negro Women Straighten Their Hair?" 69–70, 71.

25. King and Ogunbiyi, "Should Negro Women Straighten Their Hair?" 67–68.

26. Rushing, "Hair-Raising," 334, 326.

27. Harold Cruse, *Rebellion or Revolution?* (New York: Morrow, 1968); Norman C. Weinstein, *A Night in Tunisia: Imaginings of Africa in Jazz* (New York: Limelight Editions, 1993); Penny von Eschen, *Democracy or Empire: African Americans, Anti-Colonialism, and the Cold War* (Ithaca, N.Y.: Cornell University Press, 1997); Immanuel Geiss, *The Pan-African Movement* (London: Methuen and Co., 1974); Robert Weisbord, *Ebony Kinship: Africa, Africans, and the Afro-American* (Westport, Conn.: Greenwood Press, 1973); P. Olisanwuch Esedebe, *Pan-Africanism: The Idea and Movement, 1776–1963* (Washington, D.C.: Howard University Press, 1982).

28. Cruse, *Rebellion or Revolution?*, 73.

29. As Linda Roemere Wright's research reveals, ads and other images of Afrocoifed women in *Ebony* magazine declined around 1970, just as the number of images of black men with Afros was steadily rising. See

Linda Roemere Wright, "Changes in Black American Hairstyles from 1964 through 1977, As Related to Themes in Feature Articles and Advertisements" (M.A. thesis, Michigan State University, 1982), 24–25.

30. Richard Majors and Janet Mancini Billson, *Cool Pose: The Dilemmas of Manhood in America* (New York: Lexington Books, 1992), 4.

31. Historian Roger Lane treats the dozens as a manifestation of a larger pathological culture: "Afro-American culture was marked by an aggressively competitive strain compounded of bold display, semiritualistic insult, and an admiration of violence in verbal form at least. 'Playing the dozens,' a contest involving the exchange of often sexual insults directed not only at the participants but at their families, especially their mothers, was one example of this strain." Lane, *Roots of Violence in Black Philadelphia, 1860–1900* (Cambridge: Harvard University Press, 1986), 146–47. See also Roger D. Abrahams, *Deep Down in the Jungle: Negro Narrative Folklore from the Streets of Philadelphia*, new ed. (Chicago: Aldine, 1970), 52–56; Herbert Foster, *Ribin', Jivin', and Playin' the Dozens* (Cambridge, Mass.: Ballinger, 1986); Thomas Kochman, *Black and White Styles in Conflict* (Chicago: University of Chicago Press, 1981), 51–58; Majors and Billson, *Cool Pose*, 91–101; and Nightingale, *On the Edge*, 26–28. There are some remarkable exceptions, such as the work of linguists, historians, literary scholars, and first-person practitioners, who treat the dozens as a larger set of signifying practices found in black vernacular culture or focus on the art and pleasures of verbal play. For these authors, the dozens is not merely a mirror of social relations. See Claudia Mitchell-Kernan, "Signifying, Loud-talking, and Marking," in *Rappin and Stylin' Out: Communication in Urban Black America*, ed. Thomas Kochman (Urbana, Ill.: University of Illinois Press, 1972); H. Rap Brown, *Die, Nigger, Die* (New York: Dial, 1969); Geneva Smitherman, *Talkin' and Testifyin': The Language of Black America* (Boston: Houghton Mifflin Co., 1977), 128–33; Henry Louis Gates, Jr., *The Signifying Monkey: A Theory of African-American Literary Criticism* (New York: Oxford University Press, 1988), especially 64–88; and Houston Baker, *Long Black Song: Essays in Black American Literature and Culture* (Charlottesville, Va.: University Press of Virginia, 1972), 115. Despite disagreements between Baker and Gates, both try to make sense of black vernacular culture—including the dozens—as art rather than sociology. Although Lawrence Levine took issue with the functionalist approach to the dozens over fifteen years ago, he did not reject it altogether. He suggests that the dozens helped young black children develop verbal facility and learn self-discipline. See Lawrence Levine, *Black Culture and Black Consciousness: Afro-American Folk Thought from Slavery to Freedom* (New York: Oxford University Press, 1977), 345–58.

32. Levine, *Black Culture and Black Consciousness*, 357. A beginning is Marjorie Harness Goodwin, *He-Said-She-Said: Talk as Social Organization among Black Children* (Bloomington, Ind.: Indiana University Press, 1990), especially 222–23. However, Goodwin emphasizes "ritual insult" as a means of dealing with disputes rather than as an art form and thus is still squarely situated within social scientists' emphasis on function over style and pleasure.

33. Roger D. Abrahams, *Deep Down in the Jungle*, 60, 88–96; see also Roger D. Abrahams, *Talking Black* (Rowley, Mass.: Newbury House Publishers, 1976).

34. Schulz, *Coming Up Black*, 68. In McCord, et al. *Life Styles in the Ghetto*, Edwin Harwood argues further that the lack of a father leads to violent uprisings and low self-esteem among black male youth: "Negro males who are brought up primarily by mothers and other female relatives pick up from them their hostility toward the males who are not there, or if they are, are not doing worth-while work in society. In such an environment it must be difficult to develop a constructive masculine self-image and the ambivalent self-image that does emerge can only be resolved in ways destructive both to the self and the society, through bold and violent activities that are only superficially masculine. If this analysis is correct, then the Negro youth who hurls a brick or an insult at the white cop is not just reacting in anger to white society, but on another level is discharging aggression toward the father who 'let him down' and females whose hostility toward inadequate men raised doubts about his own sense of masculinity" (32–33).

35. Eugene Perkins, *Home Is a Dirty Street: The Social Oppression of Black Children* (Chicago: Third World Press, 1975), 32.

36. William Labov, *Language in the Inner City: Studies in the Black English Vernacular* (Philadelphia: University of Pennsylvania Press, 1972), 325. David Schulz, however, does not even trust the laughter of his subjects. He writes, "With careful listening one becomes suspicious of the laughter of the ghetto. So much apparent gaiety has a purpose all too often in the zero-sum contest system of interpersonal manipulation for personal satisfaction and gain" (Schulz, *Coming Up Black*, 5).

37. See, for example, Venise T. Berry, "Rap Music, Self-Concept and Low Income Black Adolescents," *Popular Music and Society* 14, no. 3 (Fall 1990); Nightingale, *On the Edge*, 132–33, 162–63, 182–84; Wheeler Winston Dixon, "Urban Black American Music in the Late 1980s: The 'Word' as Cultural Signifier," *Midwest Quarterly* 30 (Winter 1989): 229–41; Mark Costello and David Foster Wallace, *Signifying Rappers: Rap and Race in the Urban Present* (New York: Ecco, 1990); and Andre Craddock-Willis, "Rap Music and the Black Musical Tradition: A Critical Assessment," *Radical America* 23, no. 4 (June 1991): 29–38. The case of Hip Hop might be unusual since social scientists working on the black urban poor have been con-

spicuously silent, leaving most of the discussion to music critics and cultural studies scholars. The result has been a fairly sophisticated body of work that takes into account both aesthetics and social and political contexts. See, for example, Tricia Rose, *Black Noise: Rap Music and Black Culture in Contemporary America* (Hanover, N.H.: Wesleyan University Press, 1994); Tricia Rose, "Black Texts/Black Contexts," in *Black Popular Culture*, ed. Gina Dent (Seattle: Bay Press, 1992), 223–27; Tate, *Flyboy in the Buttermilk*; Juan Flores, "Puerto Rican and Proud, Boy-ee!: Rap, Roots, and Amnesia," in *Microphone Fiends: Youth Music and Youth Culture*, ed. Tricia Rose and Andrew Ross (New York: Routledge, 1994), 89–98; William Eric Perkins, ed., *Droppin' Science: Critical Essays on Rap Music and Hip Hop Culture* (Philadelphia: Temple University Press, 1996); Joseph G. Eure and James G. Spady, *Nation Conscious Rap* (Brooklyn: P. C. International Press, 1991); James G. Spady, Stefan Dupree, and Charles G. Lee, *Twisted Tales in the Hip Hop Streets of Philadelphia* (Philadelphia: UMUM LOH Publishers, 1995); Brian Cross, *It's Not About a Salary … Rap, Race and Resistance in Los Angeles* (London: Verso, 1993); Michael Eric Dyson, *Reflecting Black: African-American Cultural Criticism* (Minneapolis: University of Minnesota Press, 1993); George Lipsitz, *Dangerous Crossroads: Popular Music, Postmodernism, and the Poetics of Place* (London: Verso, 1994); Jeffrey Louis Decker, "The State of Rap: Time and Place in Hip Hop Nationalism," *Social Text* 34 (1989): 53–84; Jonathan Scott, "'Act Like You Know': A Theory of Hip Hop Aesthetics" (unpublished paper in author's possession, 1994); and S. H. Fernando, *The New Beats: Exploring the Music, Culture and Attitudes of Hip Hop* (New York: Anchor Books, 1994). Two good general histories are Steve Hager, *Hip Hop: The Illustrated History of Breakdancing, Rap Music, and Graffiti* (New York: St. Martin's Press, 1984); and David Toop, *Rap Attack 2* (London: Pluto Press, 1991).

38. Craddock-Willis, "Rap Music and the Black Musical Tradition," 37.

39. "Rockbeat," *Village Voice* 39, no. 4 (January 25, 1994): 76.

40. Tommy Lott, "Marooned in America: Black Urban Youth Culture and Social Pathology," in *The Underclass Question*, ed. Bill E. Lawson (Philadelphia: Temple University Press, 1992), 71, 72, 80–81.

41. Digital Underground's song "Good Thing We're Rappin'," *Sons of the P* (Tommy Boy Records, 1991) is nothing if not a tribute to the pimp narratives. One hears elements of classic toasts, including "The Pimp," "Dogass Pimp," "Pimping Sam," "Wicked Nell," "The Lame and the Whore," and perhaps others. Even the meter is very much in the toasting tradition. (For transcriptions of these toasts, see Bruce Jackson, *"Get Your Ass in the Water and Swim Like Me": Narrative Poetry from Black Oral Tradition* [Cambridge: Harvard University Press, 1974], 106–30.) Similar examples which resemble the more comical pimp narratives include Ice Cube, "I'm Only Out for One Thing," *AmeriKKKa's Most Wanted* (Priority Records, 1990) and Son of Bazerk, "Sex, Sex, and More Sex," *Son of Bazerk* (MCA Records, 1991).

42. Other examples include Capital Punishment Organization's aptly titled warning to other perpetrating rappers, "Homicide," *To Hell and Black* (Capitol Records, 1990); NWA's "Real Niggaz," *Efil4zaggin* (Priority Records, 1991); Dr. Dre's "Lyrical Gangbang," *The Chronic* (Deathrow/Interscope Records, 1992); Ice Cube's, "Now I Gotta Wet'cha," *The Predator* (Priority Records, 1992); Compton's Most Wanted's, "Wanted" and "Straight Check N' Em," *Straight Check N' Em* (Orpheus Records, 1991); as well as many of the songs on Ice Cube, *Kill at Will* (Priority Records, 1992); Ice T, *OG: Original Gangster* (Sire Records, 1991); Ice T, *Power* (Warner Bros., 1988); NWA, *100 Miles and Runnin'* (Ruthless Records, 1990). See also chapter 8 of my book *Race Rebels: Culture, Politics, and the Black Working Class* (New York: The Free Press, 1994).

43. Ice T [and the Rhyme Syndicate], "My Word Is Bond," *The Iceberg/Freedom of Speech … Just Watch What You Say* (Sire Records, 1989); Ice Cube, "J. D.'s Gafflin'," *AmeriKKKa's Most Wanted* (Priority Records, 1990). West Coast rappers also create humorous countercritiques of gangsterism, the most penetrating is perhaps Del tha Funkee Homosapien's hilarious, "Hoodz Come in Dozens," *I Wish My Brother George Was Here* (Priority Records, 1991).

44. See John Leland, "Rap: Can It Survive Self-Importance?" *Details* (July 1991): 108; Frank Owen, "Hanging Tough," *Spin* 6, no. 1 (April 1990): 34; and James Bernard, "NWA [Interview]," *The Source* (December 1990): 34.

45. Quoted in Spady and Eure, *Nation Conscious Rap*, xiii, xxviii. On the early history of Hip Hop in New York, see Rose, *Black Noise*; Hager, *Hip Hop*; and Toop, *Rap Attack 2*.

46. Paul Willis, *Common Culture: Symbolic Work at Play in the Everyday Cultures of the Young* (Boulder, Colo.: Westview Press, 1990), 1–5, 65.

47. Cecil Brown, "James Brown, Hoodoo and Black Culture," *Black Review* 1 (1971): 184.

48. For insightful discussions of the way information technology in the late twentieth century opened up new spaces for building cultural links between black urban America and the African diaspora, see Lipsitz, *Dangerous Crossroads*; and Paul Gilroy, *The Black Atlantic: Modernity and Double-Consciousness* (Cambridge: Harvard University Press, 1993).

49. James Clifford, *The Predicament of Culture: Twentieth-Century Ethnography, Literature, and Art* (Cambridge: Harvard University Press, 1988), 246.

12

Hip-Hop Chicano
A Separate but Parallel Story

Though the presence of Puerto Ricans and Dominicans is critical to understanding hip-hop in its organic stages in New York City in the 1970s, as hip-hop has expanded nationally and internationally, so has its relationship with Spanish speaking artist and audiences. With the popularity of West Coast hip-hop in the late 1980s and early 1990, Chicano/a, Mexican and Mexican, American rappers also became part of the musical landscape.

Raegan Kelly examines the generation of La Raza rappers whose appearance on the hip-hop scene also signaled the heightened visibility of historical debates about land and national boundaries related to US expansions. The appearance of Chicano/a rappers also challenges narratives that suggest that there is a single Latino/a voice in hip-hop, or American political discourse for that matter.

Hip-Hop Chicano: A Separate but Parallel Story

Raegan Kelly

What's up Homie? Don't you know me?
Si mon.
Ain't you the brother of the mas chingon?
Straight up, and I'm down with the Raza
Kid Frost got my back
Boo Yaa's en la casa
Cause every day things get a little crazier
As I step to the microphone area
First I call my city
Puro Los Angeles
[lights up & cops a hit] Yeah homes
That's what the ganga says ...

                                        Cypress Hill, "Latin Lingo"

Laying claim to the gangsta persona is a favorite theme in hiphop. Reading the wax, Toddy Tee, Schooly D, and NWA get major props ... but for the concepts of *carnelismo, calo* terminology (homeboy, OG, etc.), the pachuco/cholo/gangsta style of dress, and the lowered ride, proper respect is due the *varrio*.

Chicano gangs, or "street syndicates," have been a fact of life in LA since the early 1930s (some claim earlier); accordingly their history, memory, and culture are long and strong. Defined by Martin Sanchez Jankowski as (roughly) adaptational organizations whose primary goal is survival through self-reliance,[1] "gang youth," while always a target of the media and law enforcement, have become, in LA at least, social pariahs without peer. To take pride visibly in this position is one way of inverting it, but the presence of colors, oversized Dickies, pendeltons, street lingo and fire power within the language and style of hiphop is only in small part fantasy-fulfillment—many of those who talk the talk have walked the walk.

Paralleling the development of gang culture were the rise of the lowrider and the zoot suiter in LA. In the *varrio*, self-reliance and brown pride go hand in hand, and a large percentage of brown hiphop integrates commentary on race and cultural difference into straightforward narratives of life on the streets. Sen Dogg of Cypress Hill exemplifies the West Coast B-boy in "Latin Lingo"—he declares his homies, his Raza, his hood, LA hiphop (and, of course, a phat blunt) in a particularly West Coast combination of English, *pachuquismo*, and hiphop slang. Both linguistically and stylistically, aspects of the West Coast gangsta, whether it be Kid Frost,

Ganxsta Ridd (of the Boo Yaa Tribe) or Ice Cube in a pendelton, Dickies and a lowered '63 S.S., originated with *pachucos* and Zoot Suiters of 1940s *varrios* of east Los Angeles.

Like the "Teddy Boy" of Harlem, the *pachuco* was the ultimate expression of cultural resistance, anarchy, and (in)difference in the North American south west of the 1940s. Generally identified as Chicano gang members (although most were not)[2] *pachucos* sported pompadours, wide-shouldered extra-long fingertip coats, high-waisted "drape" pants with pegged ankles and reat pleats, wide-brimmed hats, long watch chains, and *fileros*. Much has been written in detail about the "Zoot Suit Riots" that took place in Los Angeles in 1943, but what matters is precisely what caused civilians and sailors to roam the streets in mobs looking for young Chicanos to beat down. In *The Zoot-Suit Riots*, Mauricio Mazon describes their hatred as being comprised of a mixture of patriotic fervour and fear (mixed with envy) of difference, and of themselves.

To the good citizens of LA, "[Zoot Suiters] seemed to be simply marking time while the rest of the country intensified the war effort."[3] *Pachucos* openly smoked marijuana, spoke their own tongue, had their own style of music, dance and dress. Most infuriating, however, was that *pachucos* and zoot suiters spent so much time developing their own insular culture while good "patriotic" Americans built bombers 9-to-5 and went off to war. *Pachucos* didn't have a good "work ethic." They didn't seem to care, had their own set of priorities, and this pissed people off. (The attacks weren't completely symbolic, of course—it was around this time that the California Youth Authority camps were established, and an increasingly militant approach to law enforcement in Los Angeles was adopted.[4]

The Lowered Ride

Although the east side of Los Angeles was generally regarded as being overrun by gangs, violence, and an undocumented workforce,[5] what was to become one of the largest *varrios* in the south west had its own fast developing political, musical and street culture. In the early fifties a "basic car plan" was initiated by the First Street Merchants and the sheriff's department, and the tradition of car clubs began among east Los Angeles youth.[6] Originally designed to provide an alternative to gangs, car clubs became a focal point for social life in the *varrio*, providing a place to work, hang out, listen to music, gain knowledge of self-expression and cultural identity through the art of car customizing.

Chicanos have been customizing cars since the forties. The concept of a fully customized car, top to bottom, front to back, inside and out, took years to develop, but from the very beginning it was treated as an art form. Generally starting with a used American standard, a clay model, and much ingenuity and love, customizers take bits and pieces off different automobiles out of scrap yards, alter them and put them together to create a totally new and unique car. Bill Hines is one of *Lowrider* magazine's "Legends of Lowriding"; his first custom was a '41 Buick convertible with "chopped top" and a Cadillac front end. Known to some as the "King of Lead" for his ability totally to rework a body with a lead paddle and a spray gun, he was also one of the first to design a hydraulic lift system for raising and lowering custom cars (using modified aircraft landing gear parts), California-style, in 1964. (The first lifted custom was purportedly done by the Aguirres of San Bernardino, California, on a 1956 Corvette).[7] Hydraulics served a dual function—to raise a lowered vehicle for driving long distances (protect the underside), and to keep the cops away (riding too slow was a ticketable offense). "I remember a guy with this candy turquoise '63 Ford ... that wanted to fool the cops. So, he had me juice it in front and back. He'd cruise with it laid until the cops spotted him. They couldn't figure it out. They didn't know what a lift was."[8]

To drive a beautifully customized ride low and slow down one of LA's main thoroughfares is an expression of pride, pride in being different, taking one's time, being Chicano. Jesse

Valdez, another of the original lowriders and former leader of one of LA's best-known car clubs, The Imperials, remembers the heyday of lowriding: "In '66, '67, '68—we'd cruise Downey, Paramount, Whittier. That's when everybody was lowriding; Chicanos, black guys, white guys."[9] Whittier Boulevard, a unifying site for east LA through to the mid-seventies, was the site of the Eastside Blowouts, the Chicano political protests of '71–72; it provided a focal point for the *muralista* movement of the same time and Luis Valdez's 1979 movie *Boulevard Nights*. (Valdez's film, a classic Hollywood document of *varrio* street life in LA, opened ironically just after the boulevard was permanently closed to cruisers.) Favorites of the car culture tended to be instrumentals with sparse lyrics and heavy basslines—"Whittier Boulevard" by Thee Midniters, "Lowrider" by WAR (previously Señor Soul), "More Bounce" by Zapp.

Latin Lingo

> Calo is the privileged language of the Mexican-American barrio ... (It) was neither a *pachuco* nor a new world contribution. Calo has its ancient roots buried deeply in the fertile gypsy tongue (Calé, Romano, Zincalo and Calogitano ...) ... fractured in spelling, crippled in meaning; mutilated French, English, Italian, and the dead languages of Latin, Greek, and Hebrew, plus medieval Moorish, Calo, originally *Zincalo*, was the idiom of the Spanish Gypsies—one of the many minorities in Spain. The *conquistadores* brought Calo to the New World. Already identified by the upper classes as the argot of the criminal, the poor, and the uneducated, Calo and its variants became well known to the conquered Indian ...
>
> Mauricio Mazon, *The Zoot-Suit Riots*, p. 3

To followers of scat and the spoken-word traditions of jazz and bebop, Calo probably sounds little different than the jive scat of Cab Calloway or the inverted *Vout* language of Slim Gaillard. In some ways today it operates much like early hepster phraseology—hip Calo terms like homeboy and loc have completely penetrated hiphop and gang culture. But for the *pachucos* of the forties and in the *varrios*, of today, Calo is also an important way to mark cultural difference/peripherality through language. Frequently referred to as "Spanglish" (half English, half Spanish) Calo is in fact a tongue all its own, a "living language" whose words and meanings change from location to location and person to person.

> Muy Loco, Crazy
> Ever since I come from Mexico
> I don't want to do the Mambono
> All I want to do is go go go
> When the crazy band she starts to blow
> All the *señoritas* say to me
> Come on Pancho dance with me
> Pancho Pancho don't go to the Rancho
> Til you do the Pancho Rock with me
> Lalo Guerrero and His Orchestra, "Pancho Rock"

The great Latin bandleader Lalo Guerrero was one of the first to incorporate Calo into the Los Angeles club scene in the forties. *Pachuco* and zoot cultures gravitated towards the big band sound, which Guerrero fused with the structures of swing and rumba in songs like "Chuco Suave," "Marijuana Boogie," and "Vamos a bailar."[10] Another Calo favorite was the Don Tosti band's "Pachuco Boogie," characterized by Johnny Otis as Chicano Jump Blues, "which consisted of a jump type shuffle with either Raul [Diaz] or Don [Tosti] rapping in Calo about getting ready to go out on a date. Very funny stuff and another candidate for the title of the first rap record."[11]

Through the fifties and sixties East Los Angeles developed an active recording and club scene, which, as Steven Loza explains in *Barrio Rhythm*, "was integrally related to the black music experience, for musical as well as economic reasons."[12] The influence went both ways, and in 1952 African American saxophonist Chuck Higgins released the hit single "Pachuco Hop." Loza quotes Ruben Guevara's description of the east LA music scene in the late fifties and early sixties at El Monte Legion Stadium, which reads like an early description of Go-Go:

> A lot of Anglo kids copied not only the styles (hair, dress) but the dances, the most popular of which were the Pachuco Hop, Hully Gully, and the Corrido Rock ... the Corrido was the wildest, sort of an early form of slam dancing. Two or three lines would form, people arm in arm, each line consisting of 150 to 250 people. With the band blasting away at breakneck rocking tempo, the lines took four steps forward and four steps back, eventually slamming into each other (but making sure that no one got hurt).... After the dance, it was out to the parking lot for the grand finale. Where's the party? *Quien tiene pisto? Mota?* Who's got the booze? Weed? Rumors would fly as to which gangs were going to throw *chingasos*—come to blows. The Jesters Car Club from Boyle Heights, which dominated the Eastside, would parade around the parking lot in their lavender, maroon or gray primered cars, wearing T-Timer shades (blue or green colored glasses in square wire frames).[13]

Latin and Afro-Cuban rhythms seem to have penetrated the early hiphop scene at least a decade before we hear any bilingual or Calo phraseology. In the early seventies, at the same time as lowriders in Califas were bumpin' the sounds of Tierra, Señor Soul, and Rulie Garcia and the East LA Congregation, Jimmy Castor was creating hiphop beats in New York using a fusion of "one-chord riffing, a Sly Stone pop bridge, fuzz guitar, timbales breaks, and an idealistic lyric applicable to any emergent movement."[14] David Toop credits Jimmy Castor with being a hiphop innovator, at the center of the Latin soul movement in the sixties and highly influenced by Latin masters like Cal Tjader, Chano Pozo, and Tito Puente.[15] Seven years later Afrika Bambaataa would redefine "influence," straight cutting Slim Gaillard's unique *Vout* lyrics into the mix.

In *Hip-Hop: The Illustrated History*, Steven Hager describes the early tagging and writing scene in 1970s New York as being racially integrated: the first tagger on record, Taki 183, was Greek; the second, Julio 204, was Chicano; and Tracy 168, a young white kid living in Black Spades territory, founded one of the scene's largest crews, "Wanted," in 1972.[16] The internationally known Lee Quinones and Lady Pink (stars of *Wild Style*)[17] were both Puerto Rican, as were the members of the all-time great breaking group, the Rock Steady Crew.

In the Bronx, funk and early hiphop entered the already hot Puerto Rican street and dance scene around 1977–78, with members of the Zulu Nation schooling Puerto Ricans in the ways of breakdancing and Puerto Rican DJs like Charlie Chase spinning funk and sporting early B-boy styles at their then disco-dominated block parties.[18] Rammelzee ('Ramm-elevation-Z—Z being a symbol of energy which flows in two directions)[19] and RubyD, recently dubbed the Puerto Rican Old School by West Coast Puerto Rican funkster Son Doobie of Funkdoobiest, rocked the mike all over NYC. The 1983 hit "Beat Bop" (Rammelzee vs. K-Rob) showcases what Rammelzee is known best for—what he dubbed "slanguage,"[20] an ingenious combination of freestyle metaphor and over-the-top hiphop drops delivered in the Shake Up King's particular nasal drawl:

> Just groovin' like a sage y'all
> Break it up, yeah, yeah, stage y'all
> Like a roller coaster ride that can make ya bump
> Groovin with the rhythm as you shake yer rump—rock rock ya don't stop
> You got it now baby—ya don't stop
> Just hiphop the day, yeah doobie doo
> Yeah scoobie doo, whatcha wanna do crew?
> Just freak it, ya baby, just freak up, ya ya baby
> Drink it up here, I know my dear
> I can rock you out this atmosphere
> Like a gangster prankster, number one bankster
> Got much cash to make you thank ya
> Rock on to the break a dawn—Keep it on now keep it on
> I know Zee Zee that can rock quick
> Like a high kind a class
> Hand yer rhythm to the stick ...
>
> Rammelzee vs. K-Rob, "Beat Bop"

In 1980 a young Samoan dancer named Sugar Pop would move west from the streets of New York to bring breaking to the poplockers of south central, Venice and Hollywood in Los Angeles. One of the groups Sugar Pop encountered was the Blue City Crew, a group of Samoan poplockers coming out of Carson in south LA. In Topper Carew's movie *Breakin and Entering* about the early eighties breaking scene in LA, the crew talks about how the advent of street dancing correlated with a drop in gangbanging in the hoods and *varrios* of LA—homies were taking their battles to the dance floor. "In LA it ain't like that.... If you got the moves, you can hold down. That's all it is."

It was also around this time that hiphop started to penetrate the LA Chicano dance scene. In the mid- to late seventies Chicanos were throwing giant dance parties at Will Rogers State Beach, Devonshire Downs and in parks and roller rinks in the San Fernando Valley, complete with battling mobile DJs, hundreds of Curwen Vegas, MCs to keep the crowd hyped and, of course, circling helicopters. Precursors of today's massive rave scene (which are approximately 75 percent Chicano in Los Angeles), the music of choice at these parties was alternative/new wave, disco, and early techno-based hiphop (Egyptian Lover, Magic Mike, Melle Mel, Grandmaster Flash). Due to popular demand, in 1983–1984 Uncle Jam's Army set up special Valley-side gigs at the Sherman Square roller rink in Sherman Oaks. Young Chicano, Latino, and Samoan MCs, many of them former dancers, were working their way through the LA house party scene at this time, but one of the earliest to make it to wax was Arthur Molina, Jr. (aka Kid Frost) in 1984 with the single "Rough Cut." The music, written by David Storrs of Electrobeat Records (the same Storrs who wrote the music for Ice T's "Body Rock"),[21] has a decidedly early West Coast flavor, but lyrically the song bears a strong resemblance to Run DMC's "It's Like That," also released in 1984.

> Sometimes you wait around
> Rockin' cold hard streets
> People strugglin' hard
> Just tryin' to make ends meet
> I just stand tough
> hold down my feet

Never understand the meaning
of the word Defeat
So you see it's like that
And that's the way it is
But when I'm on the microphone, it goes something like this:
Body breakin' Booty shakin'
Good money for the makin'
You just put it in my pocket
Cause you know I got talent
It's Rough, it's Tough
Let me see if you can handle my stuff
It's Rough Rough Rough Rough Rough ...

Kid Frost, "Rough Cut"

The earliest bilingual hiphop song that I've heard on record is out of New York—Carlos T (aka Spanish Fly) and the Terrible Two's hit "Spanglish."[22] Rapping over a classic Grandmaster Flash beat the Terrible Two dominate the song in English, with Carlos T coming in short and fast. "This is the way we harmonize, everybody, everybody, I said Danse funky danse, y que danse, todo mundo, todo mundo."

In 1989 the Cuban-born Mellow Man Ace kicked bilingual lyrics throughout his album *Escape from Havana*, generally alternating line for line between English and Spanish, as in "Mentirosa," or verse for verse, as he does in "Rap Guanco," over the Kool and the Gang bassline from Lightnin' Rod's[23] cut "Sport" on the *Hustlers' Convention* album of 1973:

... I'm the lyrical, miracle founder of the talk style
Put together intelligently wild
And what I came up with is called Rap Guanco
Different than house, nothing like GoGo
And if you're wonderin' damn how'd he start this
Well, last year I opened my own market
Cause it was time for somethin' new to come along and I thought
A bilingual single, that can't go wrong ...
...
Ahora si que vengo [And now yes I'm coming]
Sabroso si caliente ... [Flavor very hot] ...

Mellow Man Ace, "Rap Guanco"

A year later, Kid Frost hit the streets with his classic adaptation of the Gerald Wilson/El Chicano tune "Viva La Tirado," "La Raza," matching in syntax and lingo the Pachuco street slang (Calo) of East LA.

Quevo
Aqui'stoy MC Kid Frost
Yo estoy jefe [I am in charge]
My *cabron* is the big boss
My *cuete* is loaded [pistol/rod]
It's full of *balas* [bullets]
I'll put it in your face
And you won't say *nada*. [nothing]
Vatos, cholos, call us what you will [Chicano homeboys, lowriders]

You say we are assassins,
Train ourselves to kill
It's in our blood to be an Aztec warrior
Go to any extreme
And hold to no barriers
Chicano and I'm brown and proud
Want this *chingaso*? [smack, wack, as in "beat down"]
Si mon I said let's get down
...
The foreign tongue I'm speaking is known as Calo
Y sabes que, loco? [And you know what, loc?]
Yo estoy malo [I am mean/bad]
Tu no sabes que I think your brain is hollow? [Don't you know that ...]
...
And so I look and I laugh and say *Que pasa?* [What's happening?]
Yeah, this is for La Raza.

Kid Frost, "La Raza," *Hispanic Causing Panic*

"La Raza" is important for several reasons. It marks a radical change in Kid Frost's work—the distance between the non-committal "So rough, so tough" of "Rough Cut" and "It's in our blood to be an Aztec warrior / Go to any extreme" marks a change in consciousness, at least of his perception of hiphop as a language of consciousness. Frost's use of Calo is an appeal to the authenticity of the streets and the *pachuco* lifestyle, but within the context of the song it is also a nod to Chicano pride, as is the claim "Chicano and I'm brown and proud." The term Chicano, derived from *mechicano* and once considered derogatory and indicative of lower-class standing, applies to all people of Mexican descent/all people of indigenous descent. To call yourself Chicano is to claim La Raza, to locate your origin within the struggle of a people for land and for cultural, political and economic self-determination. Also, Frost's use of an El Chicano hit, as opposed to the less culturally specific beat of "Rough Cut," is a nod to the *veteranos* (who to this day remain partial to Oldies over hiphop).

The early nineties have been watershed years for Chicano hiphoppers—a peak moment being the 1991 release of Cypress Hill's first album. Showcasing the combined talents of Mellow Man Ace's brother Sen Dogg, B-Real, DJ Muggs, *Cypress Hill* integrates the best of Rammelzee's hiphop tricknology, the Calo rap of Don Tosti and Raul Diaz, bad-ass West Coast gangsta mythology, humor, and trademark beats.

Gangsta Rid, What's up Y'all?
"It's a tribe thing ... "
...
"Hey where you from homies?"
It's on
He sees 'em reach for his gun
Buckshot to the dome
He jumps in the bomb
Homies in tha back but she just wants to go home
But he trips to the store
Homeboy needs a 40
White boy's at the counter
Thinkin' "O Lordy Lordy"
Pushin' on the button

Panickin' for nuttin'
Pigs on the way
Hey yo he smells bacon ...
   ...
Scooby doo y'all, scooby doo y'all
A scooby doo y'all
A doobie doobie doo y'all ...

Cypress Hill, "Hole in the Head," 1991

It's a Tribe Thing

I am a revolutionary ... because creating life amid death is a revolutionary act. Just as building nationalism in an era of imperialism is a life-
giving act.... We are an awakening people, an emerging nation, a new
breed.

Carlos Muñoz, Jr., *Youth Identity, Power*, p. 76

Corky Gonzales's Crusade for Justice in 1969 brought people from every corner of the *varrio*
together in the name of self-determination and La Raza. One of the concepts put forth during
the course of the conference was that Chicano students, needing "revolutionary role models,
would do well to emulate their brothers and sisters in the streets, the *vatos locos* of the *varrio*,
Carnelismo, or the code of absolute love in Chicano gangs, was to be adopted by radical
student nationalists as the locus of their developing ideology.[24]

The Chicano hiphop that has made it to wax in the last two years frequently assimilates
some combination of street mentality and nationalist politics, whether it be as simple as giving
the nod to brown pride, or as complex as the cultural nationalism of Aztlan Underground.
The gangsta presently dominates brown hiphop, good examples being Proper Dos (west LA),
RPM (Valley), Street Mentality (Pico/Union), The Mexicanz (Long Beach) and Brown Town
(east LA), to name a few. The music: generally simple beats, frequently scary, down with
ganga, *rucas* and *cuetes*, sometimes intentionally educational, and occasionally hilarious.
Groups like Of Mexican Descent represent a new generation of lyrical wizards, working in
two tongues, with breath control, and kicking knowledge of self.

Cypress Hill are at the center of one of LA's finer hiphop posses, the Soul Assassins. The more
recent group Funkdoobiest (consisting of Puerto Rican and Sioux MCs and a Mexican DJ)
are down, as well as the Irish American group House of Pain, and allied are the Samoan
brothers of the Boo Yaa Tribe, Mellow Man Ace, and Kid Frost. For me, the Soul Assassins
represent some of the most radical (and difficult) aspects of living in Los Angeles. On one
hand they describe the celebration of difference through hiphop (and the fierce potential in
collaboration and in the music), on the other, their lyrics frequently demarcate territorial and
personal boundaries (BOOM-in-your-face). But at its most elemental, the beats of hiphop
are about walking all over those boundaries with no apologies.

Out of the east we've heard from groups like the Puerto Rican Powerrule (New York), and
Fat Joe the Gangsta (Bronx), there's a Brewley MC in Puerto Rico, and reggae español posses
in Panama and Mexico, but brown hiphop seems to be coming to fruition on the West Coast.
Although the Latin Alliance project didn't hold, hopefully the concept was not outmoded but
a little ahead of its time. In a city where 10 per cent of the world's population of El Salvado-
rans lives around MacArthur Park (downtown), the possibilities for cross-cultural collaboration and unity seem, well, massive. And with cats like Kid Frost, Cypress, AUG, Proper Dos,
and OMD sharpening their skills in every corner of LA, hiphop is where to make it happen.

After all, it still remains true that (referring back to the Samoan brother from Carson City) in LA hiphop if you are down, you can hold down.

Special Thanks to Bulldog and Tate.

Study Questions

1. In what ways have Chicano/a rappers represented the historical political tension of their region?
2. How do Spanish speaking rappers on the West Coast challenge popular representations of a Latino/a voice?
3. How do the differences between Chicano/a rappers on the West Coast and Puerto Rican/Dominican rappers on the East Coast, mirror those of Black Americans on both coasts?

Notes

1. Martin Sanchez Jankowski, *Islands in the Street,* Berkeley, Los Angeles and Oxford, 1991, pp. 25–7.
2. Mauricio Mazon, *The Zoot-Suit Riots; The Psychology of Symbolic Annihilation,* Austin, 1984, p. 5.
3. Ibid, p. 9.
4. Ibid, p. 108.
5. Steven Loza, *Barrio Rhythm; Mexican American Music in Los Angeles,* Urbana and Chicago, 1993, p. 42.
6. Ibid.
7. Dick DeLoach, "Bill Hines: The King of Lead," *Lowrider Magazine,* April 1992, p. 52.
8. Ibid, p. 53.
9. Dick DeLoach, "Jesse Valdez and Gypsy Rose," *Lowrider Magazine,* October 1992, p. 56.
10. *Barrio Rhythm,* p. 71.
11. Ibid, p. 81.
12. Ibid.
13. Ibid, p. 83.
14. David Toop, *Rap Attack 2: African Rap to Global Hip Hop,* London and New York, 1991, p. 22.
15. Ibid, p. 24.
16. Steven Hager, *Hip-Hop: The Illustrated History,* p. 21.
17. *Wild Style,* Charlie Ahearn, 1981. A 35mm rap-umentary about the early integration of the different elements of hiphop culture in New York. Also starring Fred Braithwaite and Patty Astor.
18. *An Illustrated History of Hip Hop,* p. 81.
19. *Rap Attack 2,* p. 122.
20. Ibid.
21. Billy Jam, liner notes on *West Coast Rap, The First Dynasty,* Vol. 2, 1992, Rhino Records.
22. On *Greatest Hits of the Zulu Nation,* circa 1982.
23. AKA Jalal of the Last Poets.
24. Carlos Muñoz, Jr., *Youth, Identity, Power: The Chicano,* Verso, 1989, p. 76.

Further Reading

Rodolfo F. Acuna, *A Community Under Siege: A Chronicle of Chicanos East of the Los Angeles River;* 1945–1975. Monograph no. 11/Chicano Studies Research Center Publications, Los Angeles: University of California 1984.

Rodolfo F. Acuna, *Occupied America; A History of Chicanos,* New York: HarperCollins 1988.

Dick DeLoach, "Bill Hines: The King of Lead," *Lowrider Magazine* 14, 1992, pp. 52–3.

Dick DeLoach, "Jesse Valdez and Gypsy Rose," *Lowrider Magazine* 14, 1992, pp. 56–8.

Willard Gingerich, "Aspects of Prose Style in Three Chicano Novels: *Pocho, Bless Me, Ultima* and *The Road to Tamazunchale* in ed. Jacob Ornstein-Galicia, *Form and Function in Chicano English,* Rowley, Massachusetts: Newbury House 1994.

Steven Hager, *Hip-Hop: The Illustrated History, Rap Music and Graffiti*, New York: St. Martin's Press, 1984.

Martin Sanchez Jankowski, *Islands in the Street*, Berkeley, Los Angeles and Oxford: University of California Press 1991.

George Lipsitz, *Time Passages; Collective Memory and American Popular Culture*, Minneapolis: University of Minnesota Press 1990.

Steven Loza, *Barrio Rhythm: Mexican American Music in Los Angeles*, Urbana and Chicago: University of Illinois Press 1993.

Mauricio Mazon, *The Zoot-Suit Riots; The Psychology of Symbolic Annihilation*, Austin: University of Texas Press 1984.

Carlos Muñoz Jr, *Youth, Identity, Power; The Chicano Movement*, London and New York: Verso 1989.

Harry Polkinhorn, Alfredo Velasco and Mal Lambert, *El Libro De Calo; Pachuco Slang Dictionary*, San Diego: Atticus Press 1983.

Stan Steiner, *La Raza: The Mexican Americans*, New York, Evanston, and London: Harper & Row 1970.

David Toop, *Rap Attack 2: African Rap to Global Hip Hop*, London and New York: Serpent's Tail 1991.

13

Authenticity Within Hip-Hop and Other Cultures Threatened With Assimilation

Kembrew McLeod's chapter represents one of the earliest attempts to historicize the authenticity debates within hip-hop culture. McLeod achieves this by indexing a range of meanings and practices within hip-hop that have been used to assign authenticity. At the center of McLeod's essay is the phrase "keeping it real" which served as a mantra for perceptions of realness within hip-hop throughout the 1990s.

At the time that McLeod's chapter was published, hip-hop was still very much tethered to black cultural production and thought to circulate solely within spaces where such production was valued. Thus artists who reached beyond those confines, both in content and audience, were often read as inauthentic. But as McLeod suggests, even given those realities, authenticity claims were regularly challenged.

Authenticity Within Hip-Hop and Other Cultures Threatened With Assimilation

Kembrew McLeod

In this chapter, I examine claims of authenticity and the contexts under which these claims are made within a form of African American culture: hip-hop. Hip-hop music—popularly known as rap music—grounds, reflects, and is at the center of an African American, youth-oriented culture that originated in the Bronx, New York, during the mid-1970s (Neal, 1999). Rose (1994) described hip-hop music as "a form of rhymed storytelling accompanied by highly rhythmic, electronically based music" (p. 2). By using a method of understanding authenticity claims as structured, meaningful discourse, I seek to demonstrate how the concept of authenticity lies at the nexus of key cultural symbols in hip-hop.

These reoccurring invocations of authenticity are not isolated to hip-hop culture. They also take place in other cultures that, like hip-hop, are threatened with assimilation by a larger, mainstream culture. By mapping the range of meanings associated with authenticity as the meanings are invoked discursively, we can gain a better understanding of how a culture in danger of assimilation actively attempts to preserve its identity. Further, using the conceptual apparatus of semantic dimensions used by Seitel (1974), Katriel and Philipsen (1981), and Carbaugh (1989, 1996), I highlight how that culture's most central and powerful symbols are organized and given meaning vis-à-vis authenticity within a discursive system. Whereas I employ semantic dimensions to understand the significance of authenticity discourse in hip-hop culture, Seitel (1974) employed semantic dimensions to understand the use of metaphors in Haya culture. Seitel stated, "Studying metaphors can uncover basic underlying principles that people use to conceive of and evaluate their own speech interactions" (p. 66). Although the specific symbols referenced in authenticity discourse cannot be generalized beyond hip-hop culture, the interpretive framework I use can be applied to other cultures in danger of assimilation in order to understand how authenticity is at the intersection of powerful cultural symbols, and how those symbols are invoked to maintain pure identity.

Although Lull (1985, 1987), Garofalo (1997), Thornton (1996), Duncombe (1997), and others examined the assimilation and commodification of subcultural expression, they did not engage in a systematic examination of how a politics of authenticity functions to maintain a culture's identity. In his study of authenticity discourse in country music, Peterson (1997) paraphrased the observations of Maurice Halbwachs by stating that "authenticity is not inherent in the object or event that is designated authentic but is a socially agreed-upon construct" (p. 5). This "socially agreed-upon construct" is a sign, a discursive formation with multiple meanings. It is at the center of not just hip-hop, but many cultures and subcultures threatened with assimilation, such as insurgent forms of rock music, "rave" communities, underground gay discos, jazz scenes, country music, zine-making communities, and African-American culture, generally

(Duncombe, 1997; Ennis, 1992; Frith, 1981; Garofalo, 1997; hooks, 1992; Lubiano, 1996; Lull, 1987; Neal, 1999; Peterson, 1997; Thornton, 1996). For instance, Lull (1987) argued that authenticity was valued in punk rock communities because of the "commodification of the punk ethic" (p. 227). I will return to a broader discussion of the ways in which authenticity is signified in cultures threatened with assimilation in the final section.

A Brief History of Hip-Hop Music's Commercial Ascendancy

As a culture that is distinct from the larger African-American culture from which it emerged, hip-hop contains the key elements of Carbaugh's (1988) definition of a culture; there are "patterns of symbolic action and meaning" that are deeply felt, commonly intelligible, and widely accessible to members of the hip-hop community (p. 38). Hip-hop culture, broadly speaking, incorporates four prominent elements: breaking (i.e., break dancing); tagging or bombing (i.e., marking the walls of buildings and subways with graffiti); DJ-ing (i.e., collaging the best fragments of records by using two turntables); and MC-ing (i.e., rapping; Hager, 1984). In the late 1990s, hip-hop music is extremely popular. Despite the fact that hip-hop musical, clothing, and linguistic styles vary from one locale to another, one concept that is commonly invoked is authenticity. In fact, authenticity has been invoked by hip-hop fans and artists throughout the 1990s, spoken in terms of being "true," "real," or "keepin' it real."

After a decade of existing on the margins of mainstream popular culture, hip-hop music began to sell more than before. In 1988, the annual record sales of hip-hop music reached $100 million. This accounted for 2% of the music industry's sales. The next year, *Billboard* added rap charts to its magazine, and music video outlet MTV debuted *Yo! MTV Raps*, which quickly became the network's highest rated show (Samuels, 1995; Silverman, 1989). By 1992, rap generated $400 million annually, roughly 5% of the music industry's annual income (Vaughn, 1992). These estimates climbed to $700 million in annual revenues for rap in 1993 (Rose, 1994). Within only a few years, hip-hop music was transformed from a being an aspect of a small subculture identified with young, city-dwelling African Americans to a genre that had been absorbed into mainstream U.S. popular culture. Everything from soft-drink commercials to "White" pop music appropriated hip-hop music's musical and visual style.

By 1999, exactly 20 years after the first hip-hop record was released, hip-hop music and the culture from which it emerged were firmly entrenched within mainstream U.S. culture. In the course of one month in 1999, *Time* magazine devoted its cover story to hip-hop, Fugees member Lauryn Hill took home the first Album-of-the-Year Grammy awarded to a hip-hop artist, and MTV (which, a dozen years before, had been reluctant to air hip-hop music videos) devoted 7 days of its programming to the music during its much-hyped "Hip-Hop Week" (Farley, 1999). In 1998, hip-hop music sales continued to outpace music industry gains in general (a 31% increase over the previous year, compared to the music industry's 9% increase), and hip-hop outsold the previous top-selling format, country music (Farley, 1999).

During hip-hop music's dramatic ascendancy in the 1990s, hip-hop artists and fans found themselves in a contradictory situation that other subcultural groups confronted with widespread acceptance previously faced: being "inside" a mainstream culture they had, in part, defined themselves as being against. By selling millions of albums to White teens and appearing on MTV, hip-hop artists (and their fans) have had to struggle to maintain a "pure" identity. They preserved this identity by invoking the concept of authenticity in attempting to draw clearly demarcated boundaries around their culture.

With this in mind, I aim to answer the following questions in my analysis of hip-hop. First, what do authenticity claims mean to people within the hip-hop community, and how does the invocation of authenticity function? Second, does the invocation of authenticity make appeals to solidarity across racial, gender, class, or cultural identity formations? Third, what are the contexts in which authenticity is invoked? Fourth, how and why are authenticity claims—specifically, the term, "keepin' it real"—contested by some members of the hip-hop community? Finally, how do the community members that use these terms resolve the apparent contradiction between being both outside mainstream U.S. culture and very much inside it as well?

Method

As a listener of hip-hop music for many years, a reader of hip-hop magazines, and, later, a music journalist who primarily writes about hip-hop, I noticed that claims of authenticity had become a significant part of the vernacular of hip-hop artists and fans. After hearing "keepin' it real" (or some variation of that phrase) hundreds or thousands of times in the past decade, I began to question why it was used so often.

Because authenticity exists as a discursive construction, a linguistic-oriented method was an appropriate way to analyze how it is used in communities threatened with assimilation. Starting from the concept of authenticity, I employed the conceptual apparatus of semantic dimensions used by Seitel (1974), Katriel and Philipsen (1981), and Carbaugh (1989, 1996). This allowed me to deduce meaning from the data I collected. I drew heavily from the method of analysis and phrasing used by the above-mentioned authors.

Seitel (1974) defined a semantic dimension as "a two-valued set that is used to conceive of and evaluate aspects of language use" (p. 51). He stated that it is described and analyzed through indigenous literal statements. Unlike quantitative research, this qualitative study did not bring an a priori coding scheme to the analysis of data. Rather, like Seitel (1974), Katriel and Philipsen (1981), and Carbaugh (1989, 1996), I derived an indigenous coding scheme from the data. The unit of analysis was not the hip-hop community, broadly, but was any discursive context in which the following two symbols co-occurred: "authenticity" and "hip-hop." Therefore, my data for this study were potentially any place where a discourse of authenticity and hip-hop co-occurred. However, to be systematic, I limited what I examined to discourse primarily intended to be received within the hip-hop community. This included, for the purpose of this study, hip-hop magazines (a 6-month period), Internet discussion groups that focus on hip-hop (a 3-month period), hip-hop song lyrics (a 6-year period), and press releases sent to hip-hop music critics (a 6-month period). Significantly, my corpus of authenticity discourse in hip-hop included more than 800 authenticity claims.

The above-mentioned data were analyzed in the following way. First, I set the criteria for what constituted a symbol of authenticity discourse as being any appearance of the terms "true," "real" (and any derivation of that word, such as "realness"), and "authentic" (or any derivation of that word, such as "authenticity"). The semantic dimensions of authenticity discourse were inductively derived from the data by questioning what the listener needed to know in order to process the term "keepin' it real," or other such invocations of authenticity. This was done by looking at key cultural symbols of authenticity. For instance, when Meen Green stated, "I try to keep it real for the street," he was associating authenticity with "the street," or the urban neighborhoods from which he and many hip-hop artists came (Meen Green, personal communication, November 13, 1997). This constituted a type of distinctive features analysis that Seitel (1974), Katriel and Philipsen (1981), and Carbaugh (1989) employed. After carefully scrutinizing themes that were most prominent in my data, and noting the number of times these themes appeared, I formulated six tentative dimensions (although I was careful to recognize that frequency does not necessarily constitute saliency). I returned to ray data several times to check the validity and to obtain speakers' terminology for those dimensions.

Next, to confirm the validity of the semantic dimensions I selected, I conducted 23 individual, tape-recorded, phone interviews with a wide range of hip-hop artists, from multimillion selling artists to underground, cult artists (MC Eiht, Meen Green, DJ Muggs of Cypress Hill, DJ Spooky,

Frankie Cutlass, Cee-lo and Big Gipp of Goodie Mob, Killah Priest, Cappadonna and Method Man of Wu-Tang Clan, Rass Kass, Hell Razah of Sunz of Man, Voodoo, Wyclef and Pras of the Fugees, MC Lyte, Kool Keith, Lou Nutt and Flaggs of Land of Da Lost, Guru and DJ Premier of Gang Starr, and Mixmaster Mike and Q-bert of the Beastie Boys and Invisibl Skratch Piklz). I asked five open-ended questions that were followed up with more specific queries that probed the answers given to those questions: What does the phrase "keepin' it real" mean to you? Who, in hip-hop, isn't keepin' it real? What makes someone real in hip-hop? What makes someone fake in hip-hop? How do you feel about the way the phrase "keepin' it real" is used in hip-hop?

The following list specifies the volume of collected data where symbols of authenticity and hip-hop co-occurred at least once: 45 hip-hop magazine articles, totaling 93 pages (from *Rap Pages, Rap Sheet*, and *The Source*[1]); 11 letters to the editor printed in two hip-hop magazines; 187 individual postings to Internet discussion groups that focus on hip-hop (heretofore called "hip-hop newsgroups"), which ranged from 20 words to 500 (averaging around 100 words); 23 interviews that, when transcribed, totaled 47 pages of single-spaced text; 2 interviews with hip-hop fans that, transcribed, totaled 5 typed, single-spaced pages of text; an interview with Dave Paul, president of a hip-hop record company, which totals 3 typed, single-spaced pages; 2 interviews with 2 hip-hop record company executives, totaling 5 pages collectively; 1 interview with Haze, a hip-hop clothing designer and graffiti artist, totaling 2 single-spaced pages; 241 hip-hop songs; and 33 hip-hop record company press releases that announced the release of 33 different hip-hop albums.

Authenticity Claims Within Hip-Hop Discourse

Invocations of authenticity are performed often, resonate deeply, and are widely shared by members of the hip-hop community. By understanding the discourse that centers around authenticity within distinct, but interrelated, semantic dimensions, we can see how the key symbols of a culture threatened with assimilation are drawn upon and organized to maintain that culture's identity. Authenticity is invoked around a range of topics that include hip-hop music, racial identification, the music industry, social location, individualism, and gender and sexual roles. Profanity and slang are used in discourse often to emphasize the claims about authenticity that the speaker or writer is trying to support.

When I interviewed DJ Muggs, a member of the multiplatinum group Cypress Hill, he dismissed the use of the phrase "keepin' it real" in what to me seemed an irritated manner, claiming it was a trendy, "flavor of the month" term. Nevertheless, Muggs acknowledged that the term was widely used within hip-hop, sighing, "Trust me, I did about 200 interviews last year and in every one was that question, 'What's keepin' it real to you?' " (DJ Muggs, personal communication, October 31, 1997).[2] In a similar illustration of the ubiquity of the term, hip-hop journalist Angela N. (1997) stated in a hip-hop newsgroup posting, "You haven't lived until you've edited a 2-hour interview and heard 'keepin it real' after every other sentence, tried to cut most of them out of the finished product, then have your boss ask you 'could you do *something* about all of these 'keeping it real's?" The fact that claims of authenticity are such a pervasive part of hip-hop discourse is an explicit indication that something is going on. That something can be rendered intelligible by examining the data I collected using the conceptual apparatus of semantic dimensions.

Keepin' it real and various other claims of authenticity do not appear to have a fixed or rigid meaning throughout the hip-hop community. Keepin' it real is a floating signifier in that its meaning changes depending on the context in which it is invoked. I demonstrate here how the identities of hip-hop community members are constituted vis-à-vis authenticity, in both a conscious and unconscious manner. The conceptual framework of semantic dimensions allows me to interpret the range of meanings that are associated with claims of authenticity, meanings that are deeply bound up with this culture's key symbols of identity.

Table 13.1 Support Claims of Authenticity

Semantic Dimensions	Real	Fake
Social-psychological	staying true to yourself	following mass trends
Racial	Black	White
Political-economic	the underground	commercial
Gender-sexual	hard	soft
Social locational	the street	the suburbs
Cultural	the old school	the mainstream

Table 13.1 outlines six major semantic dimensions of meaning inductively derived from the data that may be active when hip-hop community members (i.e., hip-hop fans, artists, and critics) invoke authenticity. Although each dimension of meaning deploys different and distinct cultural terms, these semantic dimensions are deeply interrelated and can provide a way of comprehending authenticity claims as rich, meaningful discourse that draws upon important cultural symbols. The six semantic dimensions are labeled social-psychological, racial, political-economic, gender-sexual, social-locational, and cultural. Within each dimension, I have identified two exemplars of oppositionally defined symbols drawn from the speakers' language.

Social-Psychological Dimension (Staying True to Yourself vs. Following Mass Trends)

The discourse placed 'within the social-psychological dimension highlights the valorization of individualism and the demonization of conformity in the discourse of hip-hop community members. For many, keepin' it real refers to—employing a phrase that is often used—staying true to yourself. Moreover, by "representing who you are in actuality to the best of your ability," as hip-hop newsgroup user Christina Hsu (1997) stated, one is not conforming to the media-generated representations of youth-culture movements. In another example of staying true to yourself, Spice 1 told hip-hop magazine, *The Source*, "Basically, I'mma try to make my art the same thing as my life. In the past, my life was going where my art was going because I try to keep it as real as I can" (Burke, 1997, p. 71). Essentially, he was stating that he wants his music to be an accurate representation of his own life world. That, according to many people within the hip-hop community, is a fundamental component of portraying oneself as authentic.

Wu-Tang Clan member and multiplatinum solo artist, Method Man (personal communication, January 30, 1998), told me, "Basically, I make music that represents me. Who I am. I'm not gonna calculate my music to entertain the masses. I gotta keep it real for me." MC Eiht is a self-identified "underground" hip-hop artist, although, like Method Man, he records for a major record label, and his recordings have gone platinum. Eiht (personal communication, November 20, 1997) told me, "Basically, my format doesn't change. If I sell 2–3 million records on this record it's because of me. It's not because of an image change or because of the record company." Individualism is a key component of the discourse that surrounds claims of authenticity that, within the social-psychological dimension, is played against the negative symbols of "the masses" or "mass trends" and aligned with "staying true to yourself " and "representing who you are."

I believe that one reason DJ Muggs had such a seemingly negative reaction when I brought up the term keepin' it real was because his group, Cypress Hill, had been criticized for selling a large number of records to White suburban kids. When I asked him if he associated this type of criticism with the term keepin' it real, DJ Muggs (personal communication, October 31, 1997) said, "Yeah. Keepin' it real. I hate that fuckin', um, yeah. *I just try to be who I am.* People be too worried about how many records I sold and that I was on fuckin' MTV [emphasis added]."

Racial Dimension (Black vs. White)

To its core community members, hip-hop remains strongly tied to Black cultural expression. For instance, one person stated in a hip-hop newsgroup, "White boys shouldn't rap because rap is black!" (Black36865, 1997). Robert Mashlin (1997) wrote to the White readers of a hip-hop newsgroup, "F@#$ all this sh@# that's happenin' to hip-hop. It's cuz all these crab-ass pecker-wood execs and all these other mainstream, bullsh#@ views are gettin into hip-hop—man, F@#$ that! This music wasn't made fo ya'll—stay da F@$# away from it—listen to house of pain, snow and vanilla" (Mashlin, 1997). House of Pain, Snow, and Vanilla Ice were three successful White artists during the early 1990s who appropriated hip-hop musical styles, and the three were used as symbols of identity to represent an inauthentic whiteness.

It should be noted that explicit anti-White sentiments are rarely made in hip-hop. Instead, pro-Black statements are more typical. For instance, the lyrics of Common's (1994) song, "In My Own World," include: "I love Black thighs, you sisters better realize/The real hair and real eyes get real guys." Here, authenticity is clearly identified with having Black traits (i.e., "real hair and real eyes"), and the "real guys" Common talks about are implicitly Black like him. Ice Cube has occasionally said that, when he speaks, he is not talking to White America. During an interview, Ice Cube explained this statement by saying that he has no problem with White people, but his messages are directed toward a Black audience (hooks, 1994). By disassociating oneself from "blackness," a hip-hop artist opens himself or herself to charges of selling out.

Political-Economic Dimension (Underground vs. Commercial)

There are many different methods of selling out. One significant way falls within the political-economic dimension, which addresses the topic of commercial success versus underground or street credibility. One significant kind of sell-out is going "commercial," that is, the distancing of an artist's music and persona from an independently owned network of distribution (the underground) and repositioning oneself within a music business culture dominated by the big five multinational corporations that control the U.S. music industry. There are other distinctions, such as the radio and MTV (which represent the commercial) versus 12-inch singles and hip-hop clubs (which represent the underground). The latter, 12-inch singles and hip-hop clubs, are media that can be used to disseminate hip-hop music locally by avoiding mainstream mass media channels such as the radio and MTV. In an interview with the Hieroglyphics in *Urb*, group member Casual said a previous group he was in was "never about making hits." Casual continued, "We were about making real underground hip-hop" (Tai, 1997, p. 58). Another hip-hop newsgroup writer drew an overt link between authenticity and independence when he stated, "Newsgroups aren't corporate owned, thus, it's 'keepin' it real' " (Carlton, 1997).

Popular award shows are another mainstream genre that is despised by hip-hop community members. For instance, Tupac (1994) raps in his song, "I Don't Give a Fuck," "The Grammy's and the American Music shows pimp us like hoes/ They got dough but they hate us though/ You better keep your mind on the real shit/And fuck trying to get with these crooked ass hypocrites."

Being "true" is another common word used in authenticity claims. The following excerpt from the letters to the editor section of the hip-hop magazine, *The Source*, is an example of this. In one letter, Cronic Jhonez (1997) is angry that *The Source* did a cover story on the commercially successful hip-hop artist Puff Daddy. Chronic Jhonez (1997) wrote, "I can't believe [Puff Daddy] said he loved Hammer. ... What true hip-hop fan had any love for Hammer? I guess he should love Hammer, he paved Puffy's way for exploiting hip-hop" (p. 18). My corpus of authenticity discourse is loaded with broadsides against mainstream or commercialized artists whose music is played on television or the radio—those who make "hits." Real, underground hip-hop is defined in opposition to these symbols of identity that represent inauthenticity.

Gender-Sexual Dimension (Hard vs. Soft)

Selling out is also associated with being soft, as opposed to hard. Within the context of hip-hop, these oppositional terms are very clearly gender-specific, with soft representing feminine attributes and hard representing masculine attributes. This type of discourse, which falls within the gender-sexual dimension, directly comments on either one's gender or sexual orientation. An artist who has been repeatedly criticized for selling out is LL Cool J because he has made many love songs that attracted a large female audience, he sells millions of records, and he has incorporated pop styles into his hip-hop music. In the opinion of a hip-hop newsgroup writer, LL Cool J's "soft ass song sucks big time. How 'bout keeping it real?!?" (Driss, 1997). In Canibus's (1997) song, "2nd Round Knockout," he disrespected LL Cool J by claiming, "99% of your fans wear high heels." The group 40 Thevz (1997) began their song, "Mad Doggin" by saying, "I got my real niggaz in the house/Some real motherfuckin' men."

Within hip-hop, being a real man doesn't merely entail having the proper sex organ; it means acting in a masculine manner. Many hip-hop community members have observed that, for various reasons, hip-hop is a male-dominated arena, and it can be overtly homophobic, as a couple writers for *The Source* openly acknowledged (Byers, 1997; Hardy, 1997). To claim one is a real man, one is defining himself not just in terms of gender, but also sexuality, that is, not being a "pussy" or a "faggot." For instance, Tupac (1994) raps in "Heartz of Men," "Now me and Quik gonna show you niggas what it's like on this side/The real side/Now, on this ride there's gonna be some real motherfuckers/and there's gonna be some pussies." In Tupac's lyrics, the Canibus song, and the hip-hop newsgroup writer Driss (1997), there is a clear demarcation between masculinity and femininity, as well as between heterosexuality and homosexuality. Tupac explicitly contrasts being real against those who are "pussies," that is, those whom he labels as feminine.

Social-Locational Dimension (the Street vs. the Suburbs)

Social location refers to the community with which a hip-hop artist and fan identifies himself or herself. Often artists and fans play with the symbols associated with White-dominated U.S. suburbia. They contrast them with a very specific and idealized community that is located in African American-dominated inner cities, a social location that is often referred to within hip-hop as "the street." For many, keepin' it real means not disassociating oneself from the community from which one came—the street. Moreover, it means emphasizing one's ties to the community (which partially explains why so many hip-hop artists mention the name of their neighborhood in their songs). A hip-hop newsgroup posting stated that hip-hop artist Master P is "keepin' it real and not forgetting where he's coming from" (BTP300, 1997). Rass Kass (personal communication, December 11, 1997) told me, "For me, the most important thing is the street. That's what I make my shit for and to do anything else would be fake." The Wu-Tang Clan, another newsgroup member asserted, "keep it real just like in da streets" (QueenB2986, 1997). The Black Moon (1993) song, "Shit Iz Real," contains multiple invocations of authenticity. In this song, the MCs (i.e., rappers) rail against those "who fake real," that is, feign authenticity when they do not have the right to make that claim. The group claims that "Bucktown," where they come from, "is real."

If hip-hop artists are perceived as distancing themselves from their roots, they are considered a sell-out. Consequently, many successful artists are defensive when the sell-out charge is leveled against them. The charge is tightly wrapped up in claims of authenticity. This partially explains why DJ Muggs became so agitated when I brought up the phrase keepin' it real. In the song, "H.I.P.H.O.P.," KRS-ONE (1997) raps, "Dead, two in the head before some A&R can tell me/I must give up the street so that the record company can sell me." Here, KRS-ONE is saying, essentially, that he wouldn't be caught dead allowing a record label employee telling him to disassociate himself from the urban, largely African American communities that KRS-ONE identifies with so that a company can sell his music.

In the song,, "I Ain't Mad at Cha," Tupac (1996) answered charges that his change in social location diluted his authenticity. "So many questions, and they ask me if I'm still down/I moved up out of the ghetto, so I ain't real now?" (Tupac, 1996). In these lyrics, there is a direct link that Tupac drew between moving away from his community and being real (though, in his case, he denied it is true).

Hip-hop artists are often considered sellouts when they distance themselves from their community and sell records primarily to suburban kids, or "teenie boppers [sic]," as one hip-hop newsgroup writer called them (Wright, 1997). "I don't make music for the teeny-boppers [sic]/the coppers, and proper bourge[oisie]," Del the Funky Homosapien (1997) raps in "Help Me Out." In this song, Del aligns himself against the inauthentic, bourgeois teenyboppers who purchase hip-hop music in the suburbs and, in the next verse, he positions himself within the authentic underground. In the discourse that falls within the semantic dimension of social location, claims of authenticity are often negatively defined against the symbols of identity that represent suburbia. Further, authenticity is positively defined by affiliating oneself with the street.

Cultural Dimension (the Old School vs. the Mainstream)

The cultural dimension encompasses the discourse that addresses hip-hop's status as a culture that has deep and resonating traditions, rather than as a commodity. Often this discourse revolves around discussions of what is pure and polluted culture or, respectively, authentic and inauthentic culture. Busta Rhymes (1996) stated in *The Coming* that hip-hop is "a way to live/It's a culture." The discourse of hip-hop fans, critics, and artists contains multiple references to the early days of hip-hop culture—what is commonly referred to as "the old school" or, occasionally, "back in the day." Back in the day is a somewhat romantic reference to a time before hip-hop music became popular. The old school refers to a more close-knit community of break dancers, DJs, MCs, and graffiti artists who helped nurture and develop hip-hop as a culture, and who were not necessarily concerned with making money.

Mixmaster Mike, of the Beastie Boys and the Invisibl Skratch Piklz, told me that people do not have the right to make claims about what is real hip-hop "unless they were brought up into hip-hop like way back in the day. If they know their history between watching *Wild Style* and all that then they'll know what real hip-hop is. … If they just base it upon hip-hop today, what's being played on the radio, then they won't know what real hip-hop is" (Mixmaster Mike, personal communication, November 10, 1997). Invisibl Skratch Piklz member Q-bert made a similar reference to "back in the day," when he blamed the decline of the "experimentalism" that was associated with the old school on commercialism during an interview with me (Q-Bert, personal communication, November 14, 1997). Guru, of the hip-hop group Gang Starr, similarly told me that "you've got to understand hip-hop's past and understand it as a cultural tradition rather than treat it as merely a product. And you have a lot of that happening nowadays, treating hip-hop as a product" (Guru, personal communication, December 1, 1997). On a hip-hop newsgroup post, someone voiced a similar concern: "Young people nowadays think that the REAL hip-hop is what they hear in the radios or what they see on MTV. What they don't know is that it is a culture" (DJ Brian G, 1997). Another newsgroup writer asked, "Who in rap is sticking closest to the roots of hip-hop???" (DJ AMF, 1997). In a discussion about the old school, a newsgroup writer stated that "we just want to keep it real, like it was in the dopest hip-hop movies of back in the day … i.e., *Wild Style*" (NeonEPee, 1997).

For one to be able to make a claim of authenticity, one has to know the culture from which hip-hop comes. Thus, by identifying the old school and back in the day as a period when a pure hip-hop culture existed, hip-hop community members invoke an authentic past that stabilizes the present.

Contesting the Notion of Authenticity Within Hip-Hop Culture

Invocations of authenticity are not used by all members of the hip-hop community. Further, the use of keepin' it real and other such authenticity claims are openly contested by some. By looking at who contests or resists the use of authenticity claims, we can get a better understanding of what is at stake in hip-hop culture. DJ Muggs hates the phrase, keepin' it real, at least partially because his multiplatinum group, Cypress Hill, has been criticized for selling out by becoming popular with a largely White suburban audience. Another person accused of selling out is Will Smith, known earlier in his career as "The Fresh Prince." Smith began as a popular rapper. He then became a well-known actor-comedian with his own television show who, by 1997, had become a bonafide movie star (Rodriguez, 1997). He has been lambasted by hip-hop community members because of his success among White audiences, and is, according to one letter writer in *The Source*, a "fake MC" (Zinc-NE, 1997, p. 18).

In 1997, Smith released *Big Willie Style*, his first album since becoming a movie star. It was obvious Smith was conscious of the criticisms that have been leveled against him, because *Big Willie Style* contained satirical skits that involved a fictional reporter named Keith B. Real (from the fictional magazine, *Keepin' It Real*) who follows Smith around, asking him accusatory questions and calling him a "big-time bourge[oisie] Hollywood sell out." In *Big Willie Style*, Keith B. Real is made to sound like a fool because he asks silly questions that are parodies of types of authenticity claims made within the hip-hop community. In other words, the skits on Smith's album are used to undermine the value of making authenticity claims within hip-hop.

Similarly, a self-identified Black, middle-class, hip-hop newsgroup writer pointed out that many artists are dismissed by people in the hip-hop community because "they're not 'street' enough" (Maverick, 1997). This writer continued, "Why is everyone always defining what elements of culture, particularly Black Culture, are? It seems that we all subconsciously subscribe to the 'keep it real' mentality—some things are Black enough, and others don't seem to measure up to some definition of Blackness" (Maverick, 1997). Those who question or resist the use of authenticity claims tend to be located in opposition to what is deemed authentic by the most vocal hip-hop community members. They are characterized as mainstream, commercial, White suburbs.

Six Semantic Dimensions Summarized

These six dimensions of meaning revolve around different, and relatively specific, cultural terms. However, they are also deeply intertwined. When the identity talk is organized within the six semantic dimensions inductively derived from the discourse studied, it can provide a way of understanding claims of authenticity as drawing upon this culture's most important symbols in ways that attempt to preserve its identity.

Using the native terms I selected to represent the contrastive symbols I identified, a more explicit definition of authenticity in hip-hop can be formed. Being authentic, or keepin' it real, means staying true to yourself (by identifying oneself as both hard and Black), representing the underground and the street, and remembering hip-hop's cultural legacy, which is the old school. To be inauthentic, or fake, means being soft, following mass trends by listening to commercial rap music, and identifying oneself with White, mainstream culture that is geographically located in the suburbs. During a discussion with me about "real" hip-hop, MC Eiht used many of the native terms used within the semantic dimensions I identified.

> *Real, underground* hip-hop is *staying true to what you have always done* and not trying to go *mainstream* or *Top-40* or *Top-20* on *the radio* just to sell records or get your face on *MTV* or be on the Lollapalooza tour. I think being *underground* is just making records that the people on *the street* appeal to. Not to win an award on the *American Music Awards* or a *Grammy* or a *Billboard Music Award*. It's just a fact that you make the music that people on *the street* want to listen to.
>
> (Eiht, personal communication, November 20, 1997, emphasis added)

Now I will return to my questions surrounding the nature of authenticity claims I asked earlier in this chapter. Authenticity may be invoked (in everyday talk, song lyrics, and during my interviews) consciously and strategically, or it may be incorporated in a seemingly random fashion. Regardless, this does not reduce keepin' it real to "just a saying." Even when authenticity is invoked without context, it works as a continuous reminder that hip-hop culture *is* threatened with assimilation. Just as varying styles of personal address are not always consciously used in conversations to solidify group identity formations, they function to do the same thing nonetheless (Carbaugh, 1996). By invoking authenticity, one implicitly or explicitly makes appeals that highlight the importance of particular conceptions of individualism, race, economic activity, gender and sexuality, politics of place, and cultural heritage. These are key symbols in hip-hop cultural discourse. As I discussed in the method section, these semantic dimensions emerged by looking at what key cultural symbols authenticity claims are played off.

Drawing from my discussions of Will Smith and DJ Muggs, invocations of authenticity are often contested by those whose identities are primarily constituted of elements that authenticity is defined against: suburban Blacks, White fans or artists, feminine women, artists who sold millions of records, and the like. The last question I asked—how do they resolve the contradiction of being both outside the mainstream U.S. and very much inside it?—provides an entry point into the last section, in which I more broadly discuss hip-hop as one of many cultures and subcultures threatened with assimilation.

Hip-Hop Culture and Other Cultures Threatened With Assimilation

The multiple invocations of authenticity made by hip-hop community members are a direct and conscious reaction to the threat of the assimilation and the colonization of this self-identified, resistive subculture. Authenticity claims are a way of establishing in-group/out-group distinctions. Therefore, by invoking authenticity, one is affirming that, even though hip-hop music was the top-selling music format in 1998, hip-hop culture's core remains pure and relatively untouched by mainstream U.S. culture. Hip-hop can balance large sales and mainstream success with a carefully constructed authentic self. By organizing the expressions used in hip-hop authenticity discourse into semantic dimensions, identity talk can be understood as structured, meaningful, and a way of comprehending central elements of hip-hop culture from a native's point of view. When hip-hop community members disparage inauthentic symbols of identity and valorize authentic symbols of identity, they implicate themselves in a larger cultural logic shared by other cultures and subcultures threatened with assimilation.

In a study of another self-consciously rebellious subculture that centers around zine-making, Duncombe (1997) observed that authenticity was invoked by community members to distinguish themselves from the mainstream culture that threatened to absorb them. Duncombe (1997) stated, "the authentic self that zinesters labor to assemble is often reliant upon the inauthentic culture from which they are trying to flee" (p. 42). That inauthentic culture included suburban life, conformity, and corporate capitalism. The British "rave" subcultures that Thornton (1996) studied used authenticity in a similar way. Thornton stated, "The social logic of subcultural capital reveals itself most clearly by what it dislikes and by what it emphatically isn't" (p. 105). A vast majority of rave community members, Thornton claimed, used the notion of authenticity to distinguish themselves against what they consider the "mainstream." Thornton demonstrated that participants in rave scenes defined themselves against an inauthentic, feminized, and classed-down mainstream. These are concepts that were used to police the scene's boundaries.

Country, like hip-hop, was transformed from a relatively unprofitable genre that arose from a subculture that was largely dismissed and derided by the mainstream to become a hugely profitable industry. In both cases, this change brought antagonism between those who had previously been inside and the outsiders who came into the musical genre once it became popular and profitable.

As is the case in this study of hip-hop, authenticity is invoked within country music as a referent to a past that is constructed to fit the needs of the present community. Constructions of authenticity center around, among other things, an acknowledgment of a rich cultural heritage, a close connection to its audience, and a genuine expression of one's inner feelings. Peterson (1997) argued that the construction of "authenticity is not random, but is renegotiated in a continual political struggle in which the goal of each contending interest is to naturalize a particular construction of authenticity" (p. 220). Authenticity claims and their contestations are a part of a highly charged dialogic conversation that struggles to renegotiate what it means to be a participant in a culture threatened with assimilation.

Quite a lot has been written on the commodification of rock music. Lull (1985) stated that the commodification of punk and new wave music caused its subcultural status to be "subtly removed" (p. 370). Lull (1987) found, in the punk community he studied, that authenticity was valued in the face of punk's commodification. Garofalo (1997) discussed how the counterculture became commodified through the major record labels' appropriation of 1960s antiestablishment rock. Ennis (1992) similarly wrote about corporate control and rock and roll more generally. Frith (1981) identified three components of an "ideology of rock," all of which implicitly centered around the concept of authenticity: First, a musician's career should evolve organically, not in a prefabricated way; second, rock is an expression of a subcultural identity; third, there must be a real connection between the musician and audience. The ideology of rock emerged during a time when rock was contradictorily both big business and at the epicenter of 1960s rebellion. This ideology further distinguished rock from, and legitimized it against, other forms of popular music.

In a study that focuses on hip-hop, the most obvious place to look for another culture threatened with assimilation is African American culture, more generally. Because hip-hop culture is firmly rooted in African American culture, it comes as no surprise that hip-hop's emphasis on authenticity is similarly emphasized by certain members of the African American community. hooks (1992) emphasized the fact that some of the separatism that occurred in African American communities was not necessarily a "knee-jerk essentialism" (p. 270), and the search for an authentic yet essentialized Black culture was a "concrete response to the fear of erasure" (p. 272). Similarly, Lubiano (1996) stated, "Against the constant distortions of Euro-American ethnocentric dismissal and burial of the African American presence, we respond with an insistence on 'setting the record straight,' 'telling the truth,' 'saying it like it is'" (p. 183). Because these distortions have not ceased, Lubiano (1996) argued, there continues to be a preoccupation among African-Americans with how the dominant culture constructs African American-identified cultural forms.

Conclusion

When faced with the very real threat of erasure via misrepresentation by outsiders like Vanilla Ice, major label executives, and out-of-touch advertising agencies, hip-hop community members attempt to protect their culture by distinguishing authentic and inauthentic expression. The sense that hip-hop culture faces the threat of being erased and transformed into something that is undesirable has led to an increasing number of authenticity claims throughout the 1990s, the period directly connected with hip-hop's commercial ascendancy. Semantic dimensions are used to demonstrate how authenticity claims and their meaningfully structured place within a play of discourse can highlight a culture's key symbols as they are employed to maintain a "pure" identity.

In the final section, I identified similar key cultural symbols that were discussed by Duncombe (1997), Thornton (1996), Peterson (1997), and Frith (1981). These symbols include identifying oneself against suburbia and corporate culture, and a connection to a community and rich cultural heritage. The specific semantic dimensions developed in this paper cannot be generalized beyond hip-hop. However, the method used to derive this information can be used to study other cultures and subcultures threatened with erasure, assimilation, or both, to understand how these cultures similarly employ authenticity to maintain their identity.

Study Questions

1. How did the discourse of "keepin' it real" help further the commercial reach of hip-hop in the 1990s?
2. How is the mantra of "keepin' it real" articulated in contemporary hip-hop culture?
3. How has race changed with regard to marking notions of authenticity?

Notes

1. *The Source* claims in its masthead that it is "Dedicated to True Hip-Hop."
2. It is significant that Muggs had such a negative reaction when I asked him about "keepin' it real." The contestations over claims of authenticity among hip-hop community members such as Muggs are something I will return to later in this chapter because these struggles over authenticity reveal what is at stake within hip-hop culture.

References

Angela N. (1997, November 3). Re: Hey, Hip-Hop, Some Advice [Online]. Available Usenet: rec.music. hip-hop.

Black Moon. (1993). Slave. On *Enta da stage* [CD]. New York: Nervous Records.

Black36865. (1997, November 1). Re: White boyz DO belong in rap [Online]. Available Usenet: rec.music.hip-hop (1997, November 5)

BTP300. (1997, October 20). Re: Master P is wack!!! [Online]. Available Usenet: rec.music.hip-hop (1997, November 6)

Burke, M. (1997, September). Spice 1: Evolution of a g. *The Source*, p. 71.

Busta Rhymes. (1996). The coming. On *The coming* [CD]. New York: Elektra.

Byers, R. K. (1997, December). Other side of the game: A b-boy adventure into hip-hop's gay underground. *The Source*, pp. 106–110.

Canibus. (1998). 2nd round knockout. On *can-I-bus* [CD]. New York: Universal.

Carbaugh, D. (1988). Comment on "culture" in communication inquiry. *Communication Reports 1*(1), 38–41.

Carbaugh, D. (1989). *Talking American: Cultural discourses on Donahue.* Norwood, NJ: Ablex.

Carbaugh, D. (1996). *Situating Selves: The communication of social identities in American scenes.* Albany: State University of New York Press.

Carlton, A. (1997, October 2). Re: Hip-hop books [Online]. Available Usenet: rec.music.hip-hop (1997, November 5)

Common. (1994). In my own world. On *Resurrection* [CD]. New York: Relativity.

Cronic Jhonez. (1997, November). Letter to the editor. *The Source, 97,* p. 18.

Del the Funky Homosapien. (1997). Help me out. On *Beats & lyrics* [CD]. New York: Industry.

DJ AMF. (1997, October 27). Truest in HIP-HOP [Online]. Available Usenet: rec.music.hip-hop (1997, November 6)

DJ Brian G. (1997, October 12). The "REAL" Hip-hop—IMPORTANT MESSAGE [Online] Available Usenet: rec.music.hip-hop (1997, November 6)

Driss. (1997, October 6). Re: Who is the da most skilled lyricist in hip hop [Online]. Available Usenet: rec.music.hip-hop (1997, November 6)

Duncombe, S. (1997). *Notes from the underground: Zines and the politics of alternative culture.* New York: Verso.

Ennis, P. H. (1992). *The emergence of rocknroll in American popular music.* Hanover, NH: Wesleyan University Press.

Farley, J. (1999, February 8). Hip-hop nation. *Time,* pp. 54–64.

40 Thevz. (1997). Mad doggin. On *Honor amongst thevz* [CD]. New York: Mercury.

Frith, S. (1981). *Sound effects. Youth, leisure and the politics of rock 'n' roll.* New York: Pantheon.

Garofalo, R. (1997). *Rockin' out: Popular music in the USA.* Boston: Allyn &. Bacon.

Hager, S. (1984). *Hip-Hop: The illustrated history of break dancing, rap music, and graffiti.* New York: St. Martin's Press.

Hardy, J. E. (1997, December). Boys will b-boys: An open letter to all my homie-sexuals in hip-hop. *The Source,* p. 109.

hooks, b. (1992). Discussion. In G. Dent (Ed.), *Black popular culture: A project by Michele Wallace* (pp. 264–275). Seattle: Bay Press.

hooks, b. (1994). *Outlaw culture: Resisting representations.* New York: Routledge.

Hsu, C. (1997, November 5). Re: What does keep it real mean? [Online]. Available Usenet: rec.music. hip-hop (1997, November 5)

Katriel, T., & Philipsen, G. (1981). "What we need is communication": "Communication" as a cultural category in some American speech. *Communication Monographs, 48,* 301–317.

KRS-ONE. (1997). H.I.P.H.O.P. On *I got next* [CD]. New York: Jive.

Lubiano, W. (1996). But compared to what?: Reading realism, representation, and essentialism in *school daze, do the right thing,* and the Spike Lee discourse. In M. Blount & G. P. Cunningham (Eds.), *Representing black men* (pp. 173–204). New York: Routledge.

Lull, J. (1985). On the communicative properties of music. *Communication Research, 12,* 363–372.

Lull, J. (1987). Thrashing in the pit: An ethnography of San Francisco punk subculture. In T. R. Lindlof (Ed.). *Natural audiences: Qualitative research of media uses and effects* (pp. 225–252). Norwood. NJ: Ablex.

Mashlan, R. (1997, September 30). Re: I'm pissed, so hear me out: F@=% all white influence and all dis "new" hip-hop sh@=! [Online]. Available Usenet: rec.music.hip-hop (1997, November 6)

Maverick. (1997, October 16). Mark Morrison [Online]. Available Usenet: rec.music.hip-hop (1997, November 6)

Neal, A. (1999). *What the music said: Black popular music and black public culture.* New York: Routledge.

NeonEPee. (1997, November 4). The TRUE School Way? [Online]. Available Usenet: rec.music.hip-hop (1997, November 6)

Peterson, R. A. (1997). *Creating country music: Fabricating authenticity.* Chicago: University of Chicago Press.

QueenB2986, (1997, October 4). wu tang [Online]. Available Usenet: rec.music.hip-hop (1997, November 6)

Rodriguez, C. (1997, September). Big Will. *The Source,* pp. 142–150.

Rose, T. (1994). *Black noise: Rap music and black culture in contemporary America.* Hanover, NH: Wesleyan University Press.

Samuels, D. (1995). The rap on rap: The 'black music' that isn't either. In A. Sexton (Ed.), *Rap on rap: Straight-up talk on hip-hop culture* (pp. 39–42). New York: Delta.

Seitel, P. (1974). Haya metaphors for speech. *Language in Society, 3,* 51–67.

Silverman, E. R. (1989, May 29). Rap goes the way of rock 'n roll: Record moguls snap up labels. *Crain's New York Business,* p. 3.

Smith, W. (1997). *Big Willie style* [CD]. New York: Sony.

Tai, J. (1997, October/November). Souls of independence don't speak jive. *Urb,* pp. 58–59.

Thornton, S. (1996). *Club cultures: Music, media and subcultural capital.* Hanover, NH: Wesleyan University Press.

Tupac. (1994). I don't give a fuck. On *2Pacalypse now* [CD]. New York: Interscope.

Tupac. (1996). Heartz of men. On *All eyez on me* [CD]. New York: Interscope.

Vaughn, C. (1992, December). Simmons' rush for profits. *Black Enterprise*, p. 67.

Wright, J. (1997, October 25). Re: Does Puffy know he's WACK? [Online]. Available Usenet: rec.music.hip-hop (1997, November 5)

Zinc-NE. (1997, November). Letter to the editor. *The Source*, p. 18.

14

Race ... and Other Four-Letter Words
Eminem and the Cultural Politics of Authenticity

With the release of *The Slim Shady LP* in 1999, rapper Eminem emerged as one of the most popular and best-selling artists. But it was his whiteness that altered the trajectory of mainstream hip-hop and in particular the discourses about race and whiteness. Unlike Vanilla Ice, Eminem was deemed authentic in ways that few white artists had been and was accepted within black cultural practices. Accordingly discussions about race and authenticity shifted in the aftermath of Eminem's success.

In his essay "Race ... and Other Four-Letter Words: Eminem and the Cultural Politics of Authenticity," Gilbert Rodman examines the "crisis" brought on in hip-hop because of the skill-set and popularity of white rapper Eminem. Rodman thoughtfully marks how Eminem's presence is quite different from that of Elvis Presley—another white performer who excelled within so-called black musical idioms—while also mirroring Presley's success. Rodman notes not only the shifts in American race relations, but important shifts in cultural production.

Race ... and Other Four Letter Words: Eminem and the Cultural Politics of Authenticity

Gilbert B. Rodman

End of the world: best rapper's white, best golfer's black.

—comedian Chris Rock

Gaps

Describing the work on race and racism done at the Centre for Contemporary Cultural Studies at the University of Birmingham in the 1970s, Hall (1992) wrote

> We had to develop a methodology that taught us to attend, not only to what people said about race but ... to what people could not say about race. It was the silences that told us something; it was what wasn't there. It was what was invisible, what couldn't be put into frame, what was apparently unsayable that we needed to attend to.
>
> (p. 15)

As Hall (1992) explained it, those at the Birmingham School took this particular turn because they came to recognize that analyzing media texts to identify and critique the ways that people of color were routinely misrepresented, stereotyped, and demonized was simply not an effective way to struggle against racism. The problem here was *not* that media representations didn't matter in the United Kingdom then—or that they don't matter in the United States today. On the contrary, people of color continue to be regularly depicted as dangerous criminals who threaten to destroy the existing social order; as exotic primitives to be feared, despised, and controlled; as helpless children dependent on charity from the technologically superior West; and as fetishized objects readily available for White appropriation—and as long as images like these remain in heavy circulation, it's vital that cultural critics continue to identify and critique them.

But it's also not enough. Implicit in the focus on "bad" representations, after all, is the notion that enough "good" representations will solve the problem. Perhaps the clearest example of the fundamental flaw in this philosophy can be found in *The Cosby Show*. Although *Cosby* presented a far more uplifting public image of Black people than had previously been the norm on U.S. television, those "kinder, gentler" fictions didn't translate very well into better living conditions for *real* Black people. In fact, the widespread popularity of *Cosby* may actually have made it easier for large segments of White America to believe that the Huxtables' upscale lifestyle was more representative of Black America than was really the case, which, in turn, suggested that there was no longer a socioeconomic gap of any real significance between White and Black America—or, more perniciously, that if such disparities *did* exist, it was because poor Blacks had "failed" to live up to the impossibly picturesque example of Cliff and Claire and their designer-sweater-wearing children. What's ultimately at issue here is not the (in)accuracy of *Cosby's* representations of Black America—after all, it's not as if sitcoms about White families provide us with consistently faithful reflections of White America either—but rather what is *not* represented. In the absence of a range of images of Black people at least as broad and varied as the standard prime-time depictions of Whites, *any* single program, no matter how positive or enlightened or uplifting, carries a representational burden that it can't possibly bear in full.[1]

Following Hall, then, I want to suggest that racism, as it currently lives and breathes in the United States, depends at least as much on the gaps in contemporary public discourse on race as it does on flawed media representations of people of color. There are, of course, more of these silences than I can do justice to in this chapter, and so I won't say as much here as I might about how the "national conversation" on race (such as it is) frequently uses racially coded language (*crime, welfare, the inner city*, etc.) that studiously avoids explicit references to *race*; or how diligently that discourse steers clear of addressing the actual question of *racism*; or how, when racism *is* actually acknowledged, it's too often reduced to a matter of individual prejudice and bigotry, rather than recognized as a set of systematic and institutional discriminatory practices.[2] As important as these silences are, my concern here is a different sort of gap in mainstream U.S. discourses on race: the one that transforms the common, pervasive, and age-old phenomenon of racial blending (in its multiple and various forms) into something invisible, aberrant, and novel.

For instance, the notion that race is a historical invention (rather than a biological fact)—and the corollary notion that racial categories are fluid and variable—is neither recent news nor an especially controversial idea among scientists and scholars who study race.[3] Nonetheless, even in reputable mainstream media discourse, this well-established fact can be treated as if it were a still untested theory—or, at best, an unresolved question.[4] Similarly, men and women from "different" racial groups have come together (even if such unions have not always been characterized by mutual consent) to produce "mixed race" babies for centuries. Yet it wasn't until the 2000 census that the U.S. government officially recognized that "check one box only" is an awkward instruction for many people to follow when asked to identify their race.

The phenomenon of cultural exchange between "different" racial populations also has a long and tangled history, but such exchanges are still often treated as if they were a dangerous new phenomenon. This is especially true in cases where the borrowing that takes place is recognizably more about love than theft[5]: where Whites take up Black styles, forms, and/or genres, not to claim them as their own nor to transform them into something "universal" (and thus something dehistoricized, decontextualized, and deracinated), but in ways that suggest genuine respect for—and even deference toward—Black culture. Jafa (2003) mapped out a historical trajectory of such reverent borrowing that encompasses the influence of African sculpture and photography on Pablo Picasso's invention of cubism, improvisational jazz on Jackson Pollock's abstract painting, and rhythm and blues (R&B) on Elvis Presley's early brand of rockabilly:

> In each of these instances, and despite the seemingly inevitable denial that occurred once influence became an issue, the breakthrough nature of the work achieved was made possible by an initially humble, and thus by definition nonsupremacist, relationship to the catalytic artifact at hand. Just as Beethoven was humble in the face of the body of work that had preceded him, these artists were each students of the work under whose influence they had fallen, students in a fashion which white supremacy would typically make unlikely.
>
> (p. 250)

The "seemingly inevitable denial" that Jafa mentioned is the discursive move that tries to reclaim the art in question as a fundamentally White phenomenon that can be embraced by the dominant culture without any acknowledgment of the aesthetic and cultural miscegenation that originally gave rise to it.[6]

This article focuses on a contemporary example of reverential cultural borrowing: hip-hop superstar Eminem and the public controversies that swirl around him. As a White man working in a musical idiom dominated by Black aesthetic sensibilities—and who does so without trying to evade or denigrate the Black gatekeepers who are the genre's primary critical arbitrators—Eminem poses a significant threat to the culture's broader fiction that this *thing* we call "race" is a fixed set of natural, discrete, and nonoverlapping categories. And it's *this* facet of Eminem's stardom—his public performances of cultural miscegenation—that is the unacknowledged issue hidden at the core of the various moral panics around him.

Norm

Why is it that the only forms of popular culture that apparently have some sort of direct effect on audiences are the *dangerous* ones? No one seems to believe that more Meg Ryan movies will transform the United States into a land of sweetly perky romantics, yet the sort of virtual violence depicted in *The Matrix* could be cited as an "obvious" inspiration for the very real violence that took place at Columbine in 1999. Few people seem willing to claim that popular computer games like *The Sims* will produce a world of brilliant and creative social planners, but it's almost a given that graphically violent games like *Mortal Kombat* will generate armies of murderous superpredator teens bent on terror and mayhem. *The Cosby Show* (as noted earlier) was unable to usher in an era of racial harmony and tolerance, but edgy cartoons such as *South Park* will supposedly turn otherwise angelic, well-adjusted children into foul-mouthed, misbehaving delinquents. And in spite of several decades of pop songs extolling the virtues of peace, love, and understanding, we're not a visibly kinder, gentler, more tolerant people ... but we can safely blame Eminem's brutal, homophobic, misogynist raps for corrupting our youth, poisoning our culture, and unraveling the moral fabric of the nation.

Or so the story goes. I make these comparisons not to argue that we should be unconcerned with the content of our mass media fare nor to suggest that Eminem's music plays an entirely benign role in contemporary U.S. culture. It would be going too far, after all, to claim that popular music has no recognizable impact on social values, or to suggest that, behind his foul-mouthed, criminally psychotic facade, Eminem is really just a misunderstood, lovable little ragamuffin. Rather, I raise the question of Eminem's allegedly harmful influence precisely because the broader discourse around him is far too saturated with overtones of controversy for me to safely ignore the issue. In this climate, any public statement about Eminem is implicitly obligated to focus on his multiple offenses against good taste, common decency, and fundamental moral values.[7] Commentators who "fail" to emphasize such issues—especially those that dare to suggest that Eminem might actually have talent worthy of praise—are themselves subject to stringent critique for ignoring the "real" (and, apparently, the only) story.[8] I don't want to dismiss the moral concerns of Eminem's detractors out of hand, but I also think that, too often, they manage to ignore what's genuinely novel (and important) about Eminem. In the midst of the moral panic that surrounds Eminem, however, it's rhetorically difficult to get to those other questions without first addressing the agendas set by the dominant discourse.

Most of the public debate about Eminem over the past several years has focused on the offensive, antisocial, irresponsible, dangerous, violent, misogynistic, and/or homophobic nature of his lyrics—and there's plenty of grist to be found for this particular mill. Listen to Eminem's first three major label releases and—among other things—you'll hear him insult his fans, drive with a fifth of vodka in his belly, assault his high school English teacher, encourage children to mutilate themselves, kidnap and kill his producer, shoot cashiers during armed robberies, rape his mother, and (at least twice) murder his wife with sadistic brutality. In the hyper-masculine world of Eminem's music, women are invariably "sluts" and "bitches" and "hos," and men he disapproves of are routinely derided as "pussies" and "faggots." It's not surprising, then, that Eminem has been roundly condemned from the right as a despoiler of common decency and morality, and from the left as an obnoxious promoter of a culture of violence that terrorizes women and gays.[9]

Nonetheless, I want to suggest that what matters about the controversy surrounding Eminem is not what it reveals, but what it conceals. To be sure, there are real and important issues at stake in the public furor over Eminem, especially around the questions of misogyny and homophobia. Cultural criticism, however, is not—or at least shouldn't be—an all-or-nothing game, where *any* aesthetic or political flaw necessarily renders a particular work wholly irredeemable, in spite of what laudable qualities it might possess (and, of course, the reverse is equally true). Eminem's music contains more than its fair share of misogynistic and homophobic lyrics, but simply to reduce it to these (as many critics do) doesn't help to explain Eminem. It merely invokes a platitude or a soundbite to explain him *away*.

Much of the moral panic here involves a disturbing sort of scapegoating, where Eminem is made into a bogeyman for social ills that are far larger and far older than any damage that he might have been able to do in a mere 5 years or so of musical stardom. Reading Eminem's critics (from both the left and the right), one gets the impression that he has single-handedly opened up a previously untapped well of bigotry and violence, and that the very novelty and uniqueness of his brand of poison has somehow overwhelmed the aura of peace-loving tolerance that otherwise characterizes the day-to-day life of U.S. culture.

The major complaints lodged against Eminem are the latest in a long history of complaints about the excesses of the mass media. And it would be easy to respond to this very traditional sort of condemnation of the dangers of popular culture with the very traditional litany of rebuttals: that is, to note that mass media effects are rarely as direct or powerful as the "violent lyrics produce violent crime" equation implies, or that the social ills in question arise from an impossibly tangled knot of multiple causes, or that audiences may be using all this "dangerous" media fare to channel their *pre*-existing antisocial attitudes into relatively harmless fantasies. Whatever merits there might be in such rhetorical strategies (all of which can be found in popular defenses of Eminem's music),[10] they ultimately don't do much to change the basic question at hand ("Does Eminem's music pose a threat to public health and safety?"). They merely answer that question in the negative, while leaving the original "moral panic" frame intact.

And that frame desperately needs to be broken. Part of the nature of a moral panic, after all, is that it presents an exaggerated threat to the social order as a way to draw attention away from genuine cracks and flaws in that order.[11] In the case at hand, it's worth noting that mainstream U.S. culture is already rife with misogyny and homophobia, and was so long before Eminem was born: enough so that his hyper-masculine lyrical excesses may actually be the *least* transgressive, *most* normative thing about him. This doesn't gel Eminem off the hook when it comes to his particular renditions of these problematic cultural norms—not at all—but it does suggest that the real stakes in this particular discursive struggle are not those visible on the surface: that Eminem is being taken to task for transgressions that are too disturbing, too unsettling, and too threatening to mainstream U.S. culture to be openly acknowledged. And so what I want to do for the rest of this chapter is to tease out some of *those* silences in the public debates about Eminem: silences that, to my ears anyway, scream out for attention quite loudly.

Role

A significant portion of the case against Eminem revolves around the question of his status as a role model for his (supposedly) youthful audience.[12] He doesn't just depict antisocial violence in his music, the argument goes, he personifies it in compelling fashion through the use of first-person narratives. News stories about domestic violence, for instance, are safe (in part) because they're presented with a sufficiently distanced tone so as not to glorify the brutality involved. Eminem, on the other hand, gives us the story from the batterer's point of view—and does so with a wildly manic glee—that sends the message that it's perfectly okay for men to beat, torture, and kill their wives. Such, at least, is the major rap against Eminem: that his music is simply far too real in its violence and hatred to actually work as safe entertainment.

Buried not very far beneath the surface of this critique, however, is a dicey set of assumptions about the relationship between art and reality. When it comes to the aesthetics and politics of popular music, one of the trickiest words that a songwriter/vocalist can utter is "I". In some cases, the use of first-person address is a straightforward form of autobiographical witnessing, where-as in other cases, it's clearly a temporary adoption and performance of a fictional persona. Taken as an abstract question of form and style, it's relatively easy to recognize that the lines between the autobiographical and the fictional "I" are often hopelessly blurred. True stories, after all, must still be dramatized and performed in their telling, and purely fictional tales often involve honest expressions of their interpreters' experiences and personalities.

When one gets down to specific cases, however, many of those nuances wither away. Tellingly, they often do so in ways that afford already-valorized forms of musical expression more artistic license than other, "lesser" musical genres enjoy. In this respect, mainstream rock, folk, and coun-try musicians have much more liberty to use the first person to utter violently aggressive, sexual-ly provocative, and/or politically strident words than do artists working in genres like dance or rap. Which means—not coincidentally—that the artists most frequently denied the right to use the fictional "I" tend to be women and/or people of color.

For example, John Lennon—while still a lovable mop-top, no less—could sing "I'd rather see you dead, little girl, than to be with another man" ("Run for Your Life").[13] Johnny Cash could boast that he'd "shot a man in Reno just to watch him die" ("Folsom Prison Blues"). Bob Shane (of the Kingston Trio) could stab a woman to death for unspecified reasons and regret nothing other than that he was caught before he could escape to Tennessee ("Tom Dooley"). Eric Clapton could gun down a sheriff in the street without audible remorse or regret ("I Shot the Sheriff"). And Bruce Springsteen could undertake a murderous rampage across Nebraska in which he killed "ten innocent people" with a sawed-off shotgun ("Nebraska").

All of these musical crimes were generally understood to be acceptable forms of dramatic musical fiction—or, at least, none of them sparked any significant wave of moral outrage from the public at large—and all demonstrate quite clearly what Foucault (1969/1999) called "the author function":

> Everyone knows that, in a novel offered as a narrator's account, neither the first-person pronoun nor the present indicative refers exactly to the writer or to the moment in which he [sic] writes but, rather, to an alter ego whose distance from the author varies, often changing in the course of the work. It would be just as wrong to equate the author with the real writer as to equate him [sic] with the fictitious speaker; the author function is carried out and operates in the scission itself, in this division and this distance.
>
> (p. 215)

The musicians cited above are all understood to be "authors" in Foucault's sense of the term (even when, as in Clapton's case, they're singing other people's songs), and so their most violent musical narratives are readily interpreted as artistic fictions.

Musicians who "fail" to be White, straight, economically privileged, and/or male, however, are frequently and forcefully denied comparable artistic license, even when (or perhaps *especially* when) they're working within artistically valorized musical genres such as rock. For instance, when Madonna or Prince sing about sexual escapades in the first person, they're made into poster children for why compact discs (CDs) need parental warning labels—with "critics" such as

Tipper Gore leading the charge to police the musical soundscape.[14] When Alanis Morissette hurls bitter musical invective at a duplicitous ex-lover ("You Oughta Know"), rock critics are quick to accuse her of being an "angry woman" and a "man hater"—whereas male rock stars who offer venomous musical kiss-offs to former girlfriends (e.g., Bob Dylan, Elvis Costello) are lauded as visionary poets. When Ice-T or NWA use music to narrate revenge fantasies about firing back at criminally violent police officers, they're met with public outrage forceful enough to cancel national concert tours and expunge the offending songs from already released albums—and in Ice-T's case, the backlash's racism is underscored by the public framing of his offending song ("Cop Killer") as an example of (everything that's wrong with) gangsta rap, even though it came from an album released by his speed metal band, Body Count. In cases like these, the possibility that these musicians are invoking the fictional "I" is one that the dominant public discourse largely refuses to recognize or accept. "Common sense," it seems, tells us that John Lennon didn't *really* want to kill his first wife when he wrote "Run For Your Life," but that "Cop Killer" *must* be taken as a literal expression of the truth about Ice-T's felonious desires.

Part of Eminem's musical brilliance, then, is his ability to recognize this double standard and to use the tension between the fictional and the autobiographical "I" to fuel his art. His first three nationally released albums—1999's *The Slim Shady LP*, 2000's *The Marshall Mathers LP*, and 2002's *The Eminem Show*—find him self-consciously sliding back and forth between (a) his "real life" identity as Marshall Mathers (who describes as "just a regular guy"); (b) his professional alter ego, Eminem (the self-assured, swaggering rap star); and (c) the fictional character, Slim Shady (the evil trickster persona that *Eminem* [rather than Marshall] sometimes adopts). For example, in "Role Model" (from *Slim*), Eminem complains that his critics can't see through the fictions he's constructed and that the villainous demon they're railing against (Shady) doesn't really exist. In "Stan" (from *Marshall*), Shady explains—with great sensitivity, no less—to an overzealous fan that the violence and venom found in Eminem's music is "just clowning." And in "Without Me" (from *Eminem*), Marshall notes that his fans (and perhaps even his critics) clearly prefer Shady to him. As Carson (2002) described it

> so obsessed with identity that he's got three of them, he uses his alter egos' turf fights to create an arresting conundrum: perspective without distance. Juggling scenarios to flash on not only his reactions but his perceptions about his reaction, even as he baits you about *your* reactions, he analyzes himself by dramatizing himself, and the effect is prismatic because nothing is ever resolved. At one level, a line like "How the fuck can I be white? I don't even exist" ["Role Model"] ... is just another deft reminder that "Eminem" is a persona. But when it comes sideswiping out of the racket, it can sound downright, um, existential—an inversion of the central conceit of Ralph Ellison's *Invisible Man*.
>
> (p. 88)

Given the frequency with which Eminem's music involves first-person narratives, cynical observers have wondered whether Eminem is simply too egotistical to rap about anything other than himself. But this fairly common reading of Eminem's art—and of rap in general—points to a fundamental failure to recognize the historical connection between the deliberately over-the-top lyrical posturing of hip-hop and the longstanding oral traditions of boasting, toasting, and playing the dozens found in African American culture: oral traditions that themselves weave together authentic self-expression and performative hyperbole in ways sophisticated enough to make the "I" being invoked by the speaker impossible to parse neatly.

When push comes to shove, then, whether Eminem really means what he says in his songs is, quite literally, an example of the canonical loaded question: "Have you stopped beating your wife yet?" Without wanting to dismiss Eminem's real-life outbursts of physical violence (which are a separate issue altogether), I think that a better question to ask is this: Why do so many people find it so extraordinarily difficult to envision Eminem (and other rappers) as someone who might have enough creativity, intelligence, and artistry to fashion and perform a convincing fictional persona? To be sure, such a rethinking of Eminem's art doesn't have to result in either respect or approval: One can, after all, still be disturbed and offended by fiction. For that matter, many critics are simply unable to recognize what Eminem does as *art* in the first place, apparently assuming that *art* and *abrasiveness* are mutually exclusive categories.[15]

Nonetheless, at the root of the widespread, collective inability to see Eminem as an *author*, as an *artist*, as a *performer*, we find a cultural bias at least as disturbing as the goriest of his musical fantasies: a bias that rests on the prejudicial notion that "some people" are wholly incapable of higher thinking and artistic creativity—and that their ability to create "fiction" is limited to making minor modifications to their otherwise unvarnished personal experiences. In this case, those "some people" are rappers—which is, in turn, a thinly disguised code for "African Americans" in general. Here, then, is another one of those problematic discursive silences, where criticizing rap or hip-hop becomes a way to utter sweeping condemnations of Black people and Black culture without ever having to explicitly frame such commentary in racial terms.

To be sure, this particular slippage is partially enabled by the discourses of authenticity that play a crucial role in rap aesthetics and hip-hop culture. Critically successful rappers, after all, typically have to establish that they have an "authentic" connection to "street life" and/or "the hood," and they will often justify the violent themes, drug references, and profane language in their music as honest reflections of the real-life environments from whence they came. At the same time, however, the dominant aesthetics of rock, folk, and country *also* depend heavily on questions of "authenticity," but they manage to do so without any serious expectations that the "authenticity" of the musicians in question must be read as "autobiography."

Quite the contrary, as a rock star like Bruce Springsteen can use his small-town, working-class upbringing as a license to compose authentic *fictions* about that culture. The authenticity of a song like "The River" (to take but one example) clearly doesn't depend on the lyrics' faithfulness to Springsteen's personal experience. We know full well that the rock star who we hear on the radio and see on MTV didn't get his high school girlfriend pregnant and wind up trapped in a life of chronic unemployment, melancholic depression, and shattered dreams. In cases like Springsteen's—that is, those typically found in rock, folk, and country contexts—even when one's authenticity is unmistakably connected to biographical facts, that connection actually authorizes musicians to adopt dramatic personae and invent *fictional* scenarios, and the "truth" of those fictions is rarely measured by their proximity to real events.

Perhaps more crucially, we need to remember that authenticity must always be *performed* to be recognized and accepted as such. It's not enough for Springsteen's fans and critics simply to know that he comes from a working-class background. In order to maintain his status as an "authentic" working-class icon, he must continue to dress and talk and perform in ways consistent with mythical standards of "working-class-ness" long after his own daily life has ceased to resemble the lives he sings about. There's a pernicious double standard at work here that affords White musicians the freedom to separate their authenticity from their real lives, a freedom that Black artists rarely enjoy. Of course, as a White man, Eminem seems an odd person to fall victim to such a bias ... but that actually leads directly into the next part of my argument.

Race

Is Eminem the Elvis of rap: a White man who makes Black music credibly, creatively, and compellingly? Or—alternately—is Eminem ... the Elvis of rap: a White man who's unfairly achieved fame and fortune by making Black music, while Black artists with equal (if not greater) talent languish in poverty and obscurity?[16]

Obviously, I've rigged the question so that the answer is inescapable—Eminem *is* the Elvis of rap—but then the question of racial identity as it relates to Eminem's music (which has dogged his career from the start) has been a rigged one all along. After all, no matter what answer one decides upon, to take the question's basic premise at face value is to start from an essentialist (and highly problematic) assumption: namely, that the musical terrain can be neatly divided up into nonoverlapping territories that match up perfectly with the "natural" racial and ethnic categories used to identify people. Black people make Black music, White people make White music—and one dare not cross these lines lightly.

Lest there be any confusion, let me make it clear that my critique of these assumptions is not simply an argument for music as some sort of "color-blind" sphere of cultural activity. On the contrary, questions of race and racial politics are absolutely crucial to understanding *any and every* major form of U.S. popular music since the rise of minstrelsy. Where essentialist models of musical culture run aground is in failing to recognize that the history of U.S. popular music involves an extended series of intermingled and creolized styles that have nonetheless been mythologized as if they were racially pure forms. Jazz, for instance, commonly gets pegged as "Black music" despite the fact that early jazz drew heavily on the instrumental structures of European military marching bands. Similarly, rock has come to be widely understood as "White music" despite the central roles that the blues, R&B, and Black gospel all played in its birth.

Insofar as they help to shape the musical terrain in significant fashion, these racialized ways of categorizing music are very real—and very powerful—but they are not simply natural facts. Rather, they are culturally constructed *articulations*: processes by which otherwise unrelated cultural phenomena—practices, beliefs, texts, social groups, and so on—come to be linked together in a meaningful and *seemingly* natural way.[17] Although it may still make sense to talk about rap as "Black music," it does so only if we acknowledge that such a label bespeaks not some sort of essential blackness at the music's core, but broad and tangled patterns of musical performance, distribution, and consumption that *historically* have been *associated with* African Americans.

Given this, there's no inherent reason why a White man like Eminem can't still be a critically acclaimed rapper, but we can still ask meaningful questions about the relationship of Eminem's music to the broader terrain of U.S. racial politics. In the end, however, the actual questions that critics have asked about Eminem's racial authenticity tell us more about the racism of the culture in which Eminem operates than they do about Eminem himself. As was the case with Elvis before him, questions about Eminem's racial authenticity perpetuate the larger culture's tendency to reduce all racial politics to the level of the (stable, coherent, essentialized) individual. Framing the issue as one of "what's a White man doing making Black music?" helps to deflect attention away from the racism of the culture industry and allows us to duck difficult—yet significant—questions about institutionalized racism and popular music that deserve to be addressed more openly and directly. For instance:

- Why *does Billboard* still segregate its charts along racial and ethnic lines, carving out separate categories for "R&B/Hip-Hop" and "Latin" music in ways that implicitly proclaim the "Hot 100/200" charts to be the province of White America?
- Why *do* rap acts have to pay higher insurance premiums for their concert tours—often high enough to prevent many rappers from touring at all—even when actual incidents of violence and property damage at hip-hop shows are no more common or severe than those at rock or country concerts?[18]
- Why *can't* a genre with as large a fan base as rap—according to the Recording Industry Association of America (RIAA), it's been the second best-selling music in the United States (behind rock) every year since 1999[19]—manage to get radio airplay in proportion to its popularity, even in major urban markets?

If we're going to treat racism in the music industry with the seriousness that we should, *these* structural and institutional issues are the sorts of questions we should focus on first. After all, if the musical terrain is racially segregated to such an extent that a White rapper (or a Black rocker) constitutes a noteworthy transgression—and it is—it's only because the larger institutional forces in play actively work to maintain the tight articulations between specific racial communities and musical genres.

Questions about Eminem's racial authenticity also make it easier for critics to simply ignore *what* he says entirely—from his most violent and disturbing narratives to his most trenchant and insightful sociopolitical commentaries—by simply denying him the moral right to speak at all (at least in his chosen genre/idiom). Focusing on whether Eminem should make "Black music" does little to address questions of racial politics and racism meaningfully. Instead, depending on how one answers the "should he or shouldn't he?" question, such a focus underscores one of two problematic ideas: (a) the essentialist/segregationist notion that Black and White music, Black and White culture, Black and White people should each keep to their own kind, or (b) the naive, "color-blind" myth that race is simply irrelevant to popular music and is thus something that we can ignore completely. Either way, such arguments amount to a form of magical thinking: that is, they attempt to deal with very real—and very complicated—questions of the relationship between race and culture by reducing them to pithy soundbites that transform race into a nonissue.[20]

Perhaps most crucially, though, questions about Eminem's racial authenticity mask a more subtle, but no less disturbing, agenda—one that's about maintaining rigid lines between the races when it comes to behaviors, attitudes, and politics: lines that Eminem violates deliberately, forcefully, repeatedly, and threateningly. And *these* are forceful threats that Eminem *should* follow through on more fully.

Bête

Race *is* at the heart of the Eminem uproar—but not in the way that it's typically framed. The problem with Eminem isn't that he's just another White man ripping off Black culture—he's not the new Vanilla Ice—it's that he manages to perform "Blackness" and "Whiteness" *simultaneously*, blending the two in ways that erase precisely the same racial boundaries that White America has worked the hardest to maintain over the past several centuries.

Perhaps the easiest road into this piece of my argument goes through Miami and draws on another controversial rap act: 2 Live Crew. When their 1989 album, *As Nasty As They Wanna Be*, first went gold (i.e., sold 500,000 copies), there was no public outcry, no lawsuits, no obscenity trials, no moralistic hand-wringing over what havoc this "dangerous" music was wreaking upon its audiences, because the bulk of those sales were in predominantly Black and Latin inner city markets. Where 2 Live Crew ran into a buzzsaw of controversy was when they started to "cross over" to White audiences in significant ways. It's no coincidence that their infamous obscenity trial took place not in Dade County (i.e., Miami, the urban market that the band called home and the site of their strongest fan base), but in Broward County (i.e., the much Whiter, much richer, much more suburban county just north of Miami). As has long been the case, White America has only really cared about the allegedly dangerous effects of popular culture when its own children were the ones purportedly in harm's way. "Hip hop," as Eminem sagely reminds us, "was never a problem in Harlem, only in Boston, after it bothered the fathers of daughters starting to blossom" ("White America").

The moral panic over Eminem and his music is much the same phenomenon, only on a larger and more threatening scale. Eminem, after all, has reached a loftier level of stardom than 2 Live Crew ever dreamed of, and so his cultural and political impact (real or imagined) is of a much higher magnitude. 2 Live Crew faded back into the woodwork pretty quickly after the flap over *Nasty* died down. Eminem, on the other hand, is already one of the top-100-selling artists of all time, with more than 27 million units sold as of March 2006.[21] More important than sheer sales figures, however, is the perceived source of Eminem's threat. His music hasn't "crossed over" from Black to White: It's come *from within* White America, publicly giving the lie to the conceit that there's a neat and immutable line that separates White from Black—with all the dark, dirty, dangerous stuff allegedly living on the "other" side of that line.

Put another way, the vision of itself that mainstream White America works overtime to perpetuate is a vision largely devoid of hate, violence, and prejudice.[22] White America generally ignores or dismisses such attitudes, behaviors, and practices when they manifest themselves in its own ranks, while actively projecting them onto a broad range of marginalized Others: Black bodies, brown bodies, lower class bodies, foreign bodies, and so on. At best (if you can call it that), when White America has to face its own warts and blemishes, it tries to find ways to explain them away as exceptions, as aberrations, as deviations ... *anything* but as a common and pervasive aspect of White America's normal condition.

And Eminem clearly knows all this. For instance, he begins "The Real Slim Shady" with a sneering line—"Y'all act like you never seen a white person before"—that calls his race-baiting critics to task for their inability to understand that someone could walk and talk and rap and act the way that he does and still be White. Even more bluntly, on "The Way I Am," he rails against White folks intent on trying to fix his racial identity in ways that allow *them* to maintain *their* illusions about the stability of race:

> I'm so sick and tired/ of being admired/ that I wish that I/ would just die or get fired/ and dropped from my label/ let's stop with the fables/ I'm not gonna be able/ to top on "My Name Is"/ and pigeonholed into some poppy sensation/ to cop me rotation/ at rock and roll stations/ and I just do not got the patience/ to deal with these cocky Caucasians/ who think I'm some wigger who just tries to be black/ 'cause I talk with an ac/ cent and grab on my balls/ so they al/ ways keep asking the same fuckin' questions./ What school did I go to?/ What 'hood I grew up in?/ The why, the who what, when, the where and the how/ till I'm grabbing my hair and I'm tearing it out.

To be sure, Eminem is not the first artist to blur these lines—not by a long shot—but the manner in which he does so is rare for someone at his level of public visibility. Unlike Vanilla Ice, for instance, Eminem's investment in hip-hop comes across as the sort of genuine passion of a lifelong fan, rather than as a temporary mask that can be (and, in Ice's case, was) removed at the end of the show. Unlike the Beastie Boys, Eminem comes across as someone who cares as much (if not more) about maintaining the overall integrity of hip-hop culture as he does about his commercial success. As Rux (2003) put it, "Eminem may have been born *white* but he was socialized as *black,* in the proverbial hood—and the music of the proverbial hood in America for the last twenty-five years has been hip-hop music" (p. 21).[23]

Historically speaking, this sort of deviance from the heart of Whiteness has been met in three different ways. The race traitor in question has been reassimilated, rendered invisible, and/or excommunicated. And so Eminem's *real* crime may simply be that he's too popular to be ignored, too brash to be pulled back into the bosom of unthreatening Whiteness, and so he must be branded as a demon, a deviant, a monster, a *bête noire*—who's all the more *bête* for "failing" to be *noire*—and then the demon must be cast out, lest his racially blurred performance come to be accepted as a viable option for other members of the White club.

A crucial aspect of this threat to hegemonic Whiteness is the way that Eminem's unwavering self-presentation as "White trash" works to unsettle the dominant cultural mythology that equates Whiteness with middle-class prosperity. If Rux (2003) was right to claim that Eminem was "socialized as Black," to a large extent, it's because of the strong correlation between race and class in U.S. culture. The Blackness in Eminem's background that Rux pointed to is rooted in the fact that Eminem's childhood poverty placed him in the disproportionately Black "'hood" of inner city Detroit. And so it's significant that a number of Eminem's detractors play "the race card" to steer the broader conversation away from the sort of cross-racial, *class-based* alliances that Eminem's popularity suggests might be possible.

This practice was especially pronounced with respect to *8 Mile* (Grazer, Hanson, & Iovine, 2002), Eminem's first foray into Hollywood acting, where a number of critics complained that the film took unfair swipes at the Black bourgeoisie. For example, writing about the film in *The New Republic*, Driver (2002) complained that

> far from untethering hip-hop from race, Eminem's class bait-and-switch simply replaces the fact of blackness—i.e., skin color—with an idea of blackness that equates being black with being poor, angry, and uneducated. Eminem is perpetuating precisely the idea that animated Norman Mailer's 1957 essay "The White Negro." ... Eminem would likely object to Mailer's racist posturing, particularly in light of his steadfast refusal to utter the word "nigger" in any context. "That word," he says, "is not even in my vocabulary." Unfortunately, judging from the evidence, neither is the term "black middle class."
>
> (p. 42)

Somewhat more gracefully—at least insofar as he doesn't repeat Driver's curious error of implicitly treating Eminem as the film's author—but still problematically, Grundmann (2003) wrote that

> despite its honorable intentions, the film ends up exploiting the social reality of the inner city black people it portrays. It turns them into profitable spectacle, while remaining silent on the causes of their oppression. At the same time, the film is openly hostile toward the *Ebony* magazine set, which it juxtaposes with Rabbit's white working-class identity.
>
> (p. 35)

Insofar as (a) the film's principal villains *are* Black and middle class, (b) their class position *is* the pivotal distinction that marks them as threats to the community, and (c) the *real* Black middle class is hardly the principal force working to keep the *real* working class down, there's some merit to these critiques ... and yet it's a perversely narrow-minded and—to be blunt about it—suburban way to read a film that (a) defies Hollywood convention by centering its story on working-class people, (b) refuses to cater to the still far too common stereotypes that portray poor people as thugs and criminals, (c) avoids the trap of representing the middle class as primarily White and/or idyllically benign, and (d) depicts strong examples of working-class solidarity across racial lines. In the eyes of critics worried about the film's open hostility "towards the *Ebony* magazine set," cross-racial alliances are apparently a laudable and welcome goal when it comes to the middle class, but undesirable, disturbing, and threatening when it happens amongst the lumpen proletariat. The sort of critiques that Driver (2003) and Grundmann (2003) offered might be more compelling if the film's narrative presented an unambiguous vision of class mobility for Whites at the expense of cross-racial friendships. Tellingly, however, *8 Mile* ends on a much more subtle note. Rabbit (Eminem) wins the big rap battle against the middle-class Black poser, but he doesn't ride off into the sunset with a new recording contract in his pocket and guaranteed stardom before him while his Black posse remains stuck in the ghetto. Instead, he leaves the club where he's just scored his big triumph so that he can go back to *finish his shift* at the factory where he makes his living. This isn't the triumph of White exceptionalism over the Black bourgeoisie: it's a surprisingly honest (for Hollywood, anyway) acknowledgment that having aesthetic talent doesn't guarantee that one will have financial success. More important, it's an ending that leaves Eminem's character firmly embedded in the same community where he grew up.

Rage

Part of what makes *8 Mile* such an interesting film is the way it negotiates a relatively nuanced understanding of the intersections of race and class in U.S. culture. In moving toward my conclusion, though, I want to focus on a slightly different class-related question—one that turns the harsh glare of the spotlight (or is that a *search*light?) back on *us* as cultural critics: namely, the perceived impropriety of what are popularly (if not entirely properly) understood to be lower class forms of expression, and the concurrent inability of much of the professional managerial class (including us academics) to accept that smart, insightful, and valuable thoughts can come out of "coarse," "inarticulate," and "obscenity-laced mouths.

And Eminem's is an unabashedly coarse mouth. *Fuck, shit, piss, cum, tits, cock, dick, balls, asshole, cunt, pussy, ho, bitch, slut, faggot, jack-off, cocksucker, motherfucker.* All these—and much, much more—are mainstays in Eminem's lyrical lexicon. Significantly, the one time-honored example of linguistic crudity that Eminem emphatically and self-consciously *won't* use is "nigger," but that isolated gesture of political sensitivity, no matter how sincere it is, doesn't manage to save Eminem from being roundly castigated—and dismissed out of hand—for the unrepentant crudeness with which he expresses himself otherwise.

I'm not the first critic (by any means) to point to the role that class prejudices play with respect to whose speech we value and whose we don't, hooks has written on multiple occasions (1994, 2000) about her undergraduate years at Stanford, and how her "failure" to conform to bourgeois standards of classroom decorum—standards that she'd never encountered growing up in rural Kentucky—marked her as a "bad" student, in spite of her articulateness and intelligence. Kipnis's (1992, 1999) work on *Hustler* pointed to the ways in which politically progressive critics who would otherwise applaud the magazine's stinging jabs at big business and big government nonetheless manage to dismiss *Hustler*'s political commentary because of the "low class" nature of the magazine's satire. And Berlant (1996) argued that dominant U.S. media representations of political protest promote a nefarious double standard in which "political emotions like anxiety, rage, and aggression turn out to be feelings only privileged people are justified in having" (p. 408). Poor folks and women and people of color, she argued, must play the role of "the well-behaved oppressed" (p. 408) if they have any hopes of having their political voices heard (much less taken seriously).

Eminem, of course, may never have read hooks or Kipnis or Berlant (or the like)—but that's actually part of my point. His intelligence and wit and keen sense of the political terrain may not derive from the sort of "book learning" that we tend to value in academic settings, but his intellect is no less real for that. Nor is it less insightful simply because it comes in a package that includes four-letter words and unchecked rage. I don't think it's a coincidence, though, that so many critiques of Eminem's music focus on the foulness of his language—and I suspect that at least some of the controversy around him would go away if only he could make his points in more polite and genteel fashion.

But why should he? Especially when many of his sociopolitical critiques *are* angry ones—and often justifiably so. I don't want to simply romanticize Eminem as some sort of organic intellectual or working-class hero—that would be precisely the sort of patronizing elitism that I'm trying to guard against here—but I *do* want to suggest that, as cultural critics, *we* could stand to be more self-reflective about our own class position and biases, and about how readily we dismiss potentially valuable cultural criticism simply because it comes from someone who says "motherfucker" in public without flinching.

And there *is* thoughtful—and even progressive—cultural commentary to be found in

Eminem's music: from pointed quips about a litigation-happy culture[24] to extended rants against President Bush's war on terror,[25] from biting critiques of racism in the music industry[26] to scathing indictments of the classism that made Columbine a "national tragedy" when daily violence in inner city schools can't make the news at all.[27] Although no one's likely to confuse Eminem with Public Enemy anytime soon—political statements remain a sidebar for him, rather than his primary agenda—he's also a more multifaceted and politically engaged artist than his detractors seem able or willing to recognize.

None of this is meant to draw some sort of magical shield around Eminem and his music, nor do I want to suggest that he's not fair game for criticism himself. He clearly understands that language is a powerful tool—and a powerful weapon: "I guess words are a motherfucker./ They can be great./ Or they can degrade./ Or, even worse,/ they can teach hate" ("Sing for the Moment"). And so the sensitivity that he shows when it comes to avoiding "the N-word" is something he could conceivably apply to his unabashed use of the word "faggot" as a general term of insult. And one might hope that someone who displays the sort of intelligence that Eminem does in his rhymes could also recognize that if he *really* wants to provide a better life for his daughter, as he so frequently claims, he might want to reconsider his tendency to portray women as bitches and sluts who (at best) are nothing more than "good fucks."[28]

That being said, I don't want to argue for some sort of simple trade-off here, where we'll agree to forgive Eminem for the violent misogyny of, say, "Kill You" or "'97 Bonnie and Clyde" because the penetrating and insightful sociopolitical critique found in, say, "What I Am" or "Square Dance" makes up for his more disturbing narratives. But I'm even more leery of the reverse trade-off that it seems we may be too eager to make: the one where we let our distaste for Eminem's most disturbing messages simply trump the valuable contributions he *does* have to make to a broader set of conversations about race, class, media, and politics.

Arguably, a large part of what scares many people about Eminem is that they look at him and see bits of themselves that they'd prefer not to acknowledge. After all, it's not as if he single-handedly invented misogyny or homophobia or violent fantasies out of thin air. Those were all present in U.S. culture in significant ways long before Eminem was born, and it's the rare person raised in such a culture who can legitimately claim to be completely free of all such failings. But part of what I think that we—as cultural critics—should value about Eminem is precisely that we can look at him and see bits of ourselves that we *should* acknowledge. And if we happen *not* to be particularly proud of some of those facets of ourselves, that's fine. But, in such a scenario, we should go about the difficult task of working to change those unsavory aspects of our personalities and lifestyles, rather than simply pretending they're not there and/or projecting them onto Other, more marginalized people.

Put another way, when it comes to current public discourses around both race (in general) and Eminem (more specifically), too many scholars and critics (i.e., people like us) fail to adequately acknowledge their own roles—however passive or implicit those might be—in shaping and maintaining some of the more disturbing forms of racial hierarchy and disenfranchisement. I think it's perfectly fine for cultural critics to hold Eminem's feet to the fire for his more egregious lyrical excesses but only if they—*we*—are also self-reflexive enough to do so in ways that aren't ultimately about trying to protect *our* positions of privilege at the expense of others.

A good example of what this sort of nuanced criticism looks like comes from *Ms.*, in which Morgan (1999) carefully registered her concerns with the misogynist aspects of Eminem's music, but then, in terms that resonate strongly with Hall's (1992) admonition to attend to "the silences" in the discourse, she deliberately refused to join the chorus of voices demanding Eminem's censure. "At best," she wrote, "hip-hop is a mirror that unflinchingly reflects truths we would all much rather ignore. ... A knee-jerk reaction to violent hip-hop is often a case of kill the messenger. In the end, it's silence—not lyrics—that poses the most danger" (p. 96). When it comes to Eminem, there are many such silences that deserve to be filled with productive noise, but let me point to three of the biggest.

With respect to gender and sexuality, the silence we most need to shatter is the one that pretends that Eminem's degradation of gays and women is abnormal. After all, the "clean" versions of Eminem's albums that Kmart and Wal-mart (those stalwart retail institutions of middle America) were willing to sell didn't delete the misogyny and homophobia: just the drug references and profanities. Mainstream U.S. culture has a *long* way to go before it can hold Eminem's feet to the fire on this front without hypocrisy.

With respect to class, the silence that Eminem's highly visible "White trash" pride should help dispel is the one around White poverty. Although people of color still remain far more likely to be poor than Whites are, the vast majority (68%) of the people living below the poverty line are White. That's certainly not the face of poverty one is typically shown by the mainstream media, however, which prefers to pretend that Whiteness and affluence go hand in hand.

With respect to race, the silence that Eminem is best positioned to help us break is the powerful taboo against miscegenation: cultural, metaphorical, or otherwise. Given the ongoing apoplexy and fear that have dominated the mainstream discourse on "the browning of America," there's a lot of value to be learned from a figure who manages to blur the lines between Black and White music, Black and White culture, Black and White performance with ease, with talent, and—perhaps most important—with a large dose of humility about his Whiteness.

And if, as a culture, we can't break those silences, then we're in very deep trouble indeed.

Coda

In an earlier draft of this chapter, that last sentence served as my closing thought. But then, suddenly, the ground on which I was working shifted beneath me: not quite so dramatically that I needed to start over from scratch, but enough so that I couldn't just pretend that the changes in the terrain hadn't happened. This is one of the occupational hazards of studying contemporary culture (popular or otherwise). It's a constantly moving target, which makes it difficult (if not impossible) to pin one's objects of study down with any descriptive or critical finality. In the case at hand, the shift in the terrain resulted from the fall 2004 release of Eminem's fourth major-label album, *Encore*, and the unprecedented lack of controversy that it inspired.[29] In the face of apparent public indifference to Eminem's latest efforts to push middle America's moral panic buttons, I had to wonder what had happened to hip-hop's most controversial superstar. Was the moral panic over? Had Eminem finally won over his former detractors? Or had he simply lost his edge?

Encore was clearly a commercial success—it sold more than 4 million copies and, even though it wasn't officially released until November, it was still one of the 100 best-selling albums of 2004—but as both an aesthetic endeavor and a public provocation, it failed. Badly. The most generous critics routinely described the album using adjectives like "spotty," "uneven," and "inconsistent," and the only public controversy involving Eminem since its release—the presence of his phone number in Paris Hilton's hacked cell-phone address book—found him playing an incidental and supporting role in someone else's drama, rather than his more accustomed role as an instigator and gadfly.

In many ways, though, *Encore*'s failure is potentially more interesting than any of Eminem's previous successes, as it helps to demonstrate the extent to which his career actually *is* fueled by a considerable artistic talent. Although his detractors often prefer to understand Eminem as completely talentless—or, perhaps more generously, as someone who wastes his talent on unworthy, amoral endeavors—the double-edged failure of *Encore* underscores how tightly his skills as an auteur and a provocateur are intertwined with one another. Horror stories such as "'97 Bonnie and Clyde" and "Kim" bothered people as viscerally as they did not simply because of the violent misogyny visible on their surfaces, but because they are compelling and powerful works of art.[30]

Encore, on the other hand, fails as art largely because it doesn't try very hard to get under its listeners' skin—and where it does make an effort to provoke, it largely fails because Eminem sounds like he's just going through the motions.

More crucially for my purposes, though, *Encore*'s shortcomings demonstrate how much his artistry depends on the race-blurring aspects of his musical performance. Explaining what distinguishes Eminem from most other White rappers, Carson (2002) wrote that those other artists "deracinate" the music by

> keeping the beats but redefining the attitude as frat-boy acting out. What makes Eminem more challenging is that he's audibly assimilated hip-hop as *culture*. His nasal pugnacity is unmistakably the sound of a White kid for whom this music was so formative that he never heard it as someone else's property.
>
> (p. 88)

Encore ultimately falls apart because Eminem seems to have drifted away from his culturally miscegenated roots and toward a sort of frat-boy prankster aesthetic that was largely absent in his earlier work. Where once he had used music to feud with worthy public targets like censorious politicians and corporate bigwigs (or even compellingly dramatic private targets lik his mother and his ex-wife), now he's picking on the likes of Michael Jackson and Triumph the Insult Comic Dog. And where once he wielded his profanity-filled pen like a keenly honed sword, now he's building entire tracks around the slap-happy adolescent joys of farts, belches, and retching.

The major exception to this downslide—and the song that critics commonly cited as one of the few tracks that helped to elevate the album from "muddled" to "uneven"—is "Mosh." Released as the album's second single, just prior to Election Day in the United States, the song is interesting enough musically, even if it doesn't quite live up to the best of Eminem's previous efforts. It lacks the playfulness and catchy beats of "The Real Slim Shady"; it doesn't flow as smoothly or effortlessly as "The Way I Am"; it doesn't have the same thrilling, in-your-face edginess that characterizes "White America," but it's also something Eminem has never given us before: a full-fledged protest song. "Fuck Bush," Eminem proclaims, "until they bring our troops home," with the rest of the song—and the video that accompanies it—explicitly beckoning the nation to come together and vote "this monster, this coward that we have empowered" out of office. As noted earlier, Eminem's music has never been completely apolitical, but it has also never made politics its central theme as directly or insistently as "Mosh" does.

"Mosh" doesn't manage to save *Encore* (any more than it managed to help defeat Bush), but as a rhetorical gambit, it's pointed enough to suggest that Eminem might, in his own way, be the Madonna of his generation: a controversial—and seemingly dismissible—pop star who turns out to be a much more outspoken figure when it comes to political issues than most observers (fans included) would have imagined possible. One early believer in Eminem's potential for politically progressive musical agitation was Carson (2002):

> Right now, dissing his would-be censors aside, our hero's political acumen is roughly on a par with Daffy Duck's. But with his flair for topicality, a few more skids in the Dow ould turn him as belligerent as Public Enemy's Chuck D, and wouldn't *that* be interesting?
>
> (p. 90)

And though most of *Encore* sounds more like "Daffy Duck" than anything Eminem had ever released before, the forceful pugnacity of "Mosh" provides reason to believe—or at least hope—that Eminem might someday really turn out to be "our hero" after all.

Acknowledgments

Many friends and colleagues—far too many to list here, though they all have my thanks—offered helpful comments on previous versions of this essay. My special thanks, however, go out to Charles Acland, Marcy Chvasta, Stacy Holman Jones, Michael LeVan, and Margaret Werry.

Study Questions

1. Are depictions of Eminem as the "Elvis Presley" of rap music fair?
2. What has changed in American race relations to allow for Eminem to attain his status within hip-hop?
3. What has Eminem's success meant for his black peers within hip-hop?

Notes

1. For more on the racial politics of *The Cosby Show*, see Dyson (1993, pp. 78–87), Gray (1995, pp. 79–84), Jhally and Lewis (1992).
2. There are many sources for more detailed arguments about these particular discursive silences and evasions, but some of the best are hooks (2000), McIntosh (1988/1998), Tatum (1999), and Williams (1997).
3. A small portion of this literature includes Berger (1999), Dyer (1997), Frankenberg (1993), Gilroy (2000), Ignatiev (1995), Ignatiev and Garvey (1996), Lipsitz (1998), Omi and Winant (1986), Roediger (1994), Tatum (1999), and Williams (1997).
4. For example, see Begley (1995), Henig (2004), and Wade (2004).
5. And, of course, here I'm borrowing (with love) the phrase *Love and Theft* that Eric Lott (1995) used as the title of his groundbreaking book on blackface minstrelsy.
6. Also see Boyd (2003, pp. 122–127) for a nuanced discussion of the differences between *imitation* and *influence* with respect to White artists working in Black idioms.
7. As Smith (2002) sardonically noted, "Every article ever published on Eminem can be paraphrased thus: Mother, Libel, Guns, Homosexuals, Drugs, Own Daughter, Wife, Rape, Trunk of Car, Youth of America, Tattoos, Prison, Gangsta, White Trash" (p. 96).
8. For instance, both Boehlert (2000/2001) and Hoyt (2000) complained that critics simply have routinely dismissed and/or glossed over Eminem's most offensive lyrics, even as the public controversy raging around Eminem remains the perennial focus of much of what's been written about him in the mainstream press over the past several years.
9. For example, see Boehlert (2000/2001), Brown (2000), DeCurtis (2000), Farley (2000), Frere-Jones (2001/2002), and Hoyt (2000).
10. For example, see Carson (2002), Croal (2000), Doherty (2000), Kim (2001), Morgan (1999), Rux (2003), Smith (2002), and Tyrangiel (2002).
11. Sociologist Stan Cohen described a moral panic as a condition, episode, person or group of persons emerges to become defined as a threat to societal values and interests; its nature is presented in a stylized and stereo-typical fashion by the mass media; the moral barricades are manned [sic] by editors, bishops, politicians and other right-thinking people; socially accredited experts pronounce their diagnoses and solutions; ways of coping are evolved or (more often) resorted to; the condition then disappears, submerges or deteriorates and becomes more visible. Sometimes the object of the panic is quite novel and at other times it is something which has been in existence long enough, but suddenly appears in the limelight. Sometimes the panic is passed over and is forgotten, except in folklore and collective memory; at other times it has more serious and long-lasting repercussions and might produce such changes as those in legal and social policy or even in the way society conceives itself, (quoted in Hall, Crichter, Jefferson, Clarke, & Roberts, 1978, pp. 16–17).
    In extending and updating the notion of the "moral panic" as a category of social analysis, McRobbie (1994) noted that at root the moral panic is about instilling fear in people and, in so doing, encouraging them to try and turn away from the complexity and the visible social problems of everyday life and either to retreat into a 'fortress mentality'—a feeling of hopelessness, political powerlessness and

paralysis—or to adopt a gung-ho 'something must be done about it' attitude. The moral panic is also frequently a means of attempting to discipline the young through terrifying their parents. This remains a powerful emotional strategy. (p. 199)

12. As far as I can tell, Eminem's detractors have simply assumed that his primary audience consists of minors, but I've yet to see any hard data offered in support of this claim. This is a time-honored, if not exactly honest, rhetorical device when it comes to moralistic condemnations of popular culture. Framing the issue as one of "protecting children" not only carries more affective weight than "protecting young adults," but it also implicitly absolves the critics invoking such rhetoric from the need to actually pay attention to what real audiences have to say about their media choices. I don't doubt that Eminem's fan base includes a significant number of minors, but the claim that Eminem's audience is mostly children needs to be backed up with something more than the knee-jerk assumption that popular culture (or, more narrowly, hip-hop) is "just for kids."

13. Lennon quite possibly borrowed this line from Elvis Presley's version of "Baby, Let's Play House."

14. Gore's self-proclaimed fandom for artists such as the Rolling Stones—who didn't exactly make sexually prim music in their heyday—only serves to underscore the fact that there was something more than just sexually provocative lyrics at stake in her attacks on what she called "porn rock."

15. Novelist Zadie Smith (2002) rebutted this attitude by noting that
    Salvador Dali was an asshole. So was John Milton. Eminem's life and opinions are not his art. His art is his art. Sometimes people with bad problems make good art. The interesting question is this: When the problems go, does the art go, too? Oh, and if that word "art" is still bothering you in the context of a white-trash rapper from Detroit, here's a quick useful definition of an artist: someone with an expressive talent most of us do not have. (p. 98)

16. For a more extended discussion of the racial politics of Elvis's stardom, see Rodman (1994).

17. For an extended definition of *articulation* as the term is most commonly used in cultural studies, see Hall (1986).

18. For a more extended discussion of this practice, see Rose (1991).

19. See RIAA (2003b).

20. See Garon (1996) for an especially cogent version of this argument with respect to the blues.

21. See RIAA (2006).

22. For more extended versions of this argument, see Goad (1997), hooks (1994, 2000), Lott (1995), and Williams (1997).

23. Also see Boyd (2003, pp. 127–129).

24. "They say music can alter moods and talk to you/ but can it load a gun up for you and cock it too?/ Well, if it can, then the next time you assault a dude/ just tell the judge that it was my fault/ and I'll get sued." ("Sing for the Moment")

25. "The bogey monster of rap,/ yeah, the man's back/ with a plan to am/ bush this Bush administration,/ mush the Senate's face in,/ push this generation/ of kids to stand and fight/ for the right to say something you might not like/ ... All this terror—America demands action./ Next thing you know you got Uncle Sam's ass askin'/ to join their army or what you'll do for their navy./ You're just a baby gettin' recruited at eighteen./ You're on a plane now eatin' their food and their baked beans./ I'm twenty-eight—they gonna take you 'fore they take me." ("Square Dance")

26. "Look at these eyes, baby blue, baby just like yourself,/ if they were brown, Shady lose, Shady sits on the shelf./ But Shady's cute, Shady knew Shady's dimples would help/ make ladies swoon baby, ooh baby! Look at my sales./ Let's do the math; if I was black I would've sold half./ I ain't have to graduate from Lincoln High School to know that." ("White America")

27. "And all of this controversy circles me/ and it seems like the media immediately/ points a finger at me./ So I point one back at 'em/ but not the index or pinky/ or the ring or the thumb/ it's the one you put up/ when you don't give a fuck/ when you won't just put up/ with the bullshit they pull/ 'cause they full of shit too./ When a dude's gettin' bullied/ and shoots up his school/ and they blame it on Marilyn/ and the heroin./ Where were the parents at?/ And look where it's at:/ middle America./ *Now* it's a tragedy. *Now* it's so sad to see./ An upper class city/ havin' this happen./ Then attack Eminem 'cause I rap this way." ("The Way I Am")

28. For example, one of the anonymous reviewers of this essay seemed willing to accept my general argument concerning the racial politics underlying the moral panic around Eminem but still expressed discomfort at the lack of an unequivocal condemnation of Eminem's sexism and homophobia. Given that the version of this essay read by reviewers already refused to whitewash (pun fully intended) Eminem's more unsavory lyrics, it's hard not to read such a critique as an example of what Williams (1997) called "battling biases": a form of analytical paralysis in which progressive outrage at one form of political injustice is blindly used to reinforce the less-than-progressive status quo along a different axis. "Upon occasion," Williams noted, "the ploughshare of feminism can be beaten into a sword of class prejudice"

(p. 32). The recognition that Eminem's music is more complicated than a straightforward expression of patriarchal privilege doesn't require us to erase Eminem's sexism and homophobia from critical discussions of his public personae. At most, it might require us to inject a bit of productive nuance to our understanding of Eminem's sexual politics. Kipnis's (1999) commentary on the tangled class-gender politics of *Hustler*, for instance, could just as easily be used to describe the misogynistic aspects of Eminem's music: "Doesn't this reek of disenfranchisement rather than any certainty of male power over women? The fantasy life here is animated by a cultural disempowerment in relation to a sexual caste system and a social class system" (p. 151). Such an analysis doesn't let Eminem's violent sexism off the hook—any more than Kipnis simply ignored *Hustler*'s objectification of women—but it also refuses to pretend that our analysis of Eminem's music and stardom can safely be reduced to a single strand of identity politics.

29. Michael Jackson complained that the video for the album's first single, "Just Lose It," was defamatory insofar as it included a satirical swipe at Jackson with respect to the still-pending child molestation charges against him. This "controversy," however, died down almost as quickly as it surfaced.

30. Tori Amos's cover of "'97 Bonnie and Clyde" may be the clearest illustration of the artistry inherent in Eminem's song. In the context of an album (*Strange Little Girls*) where she covers a dozen songs written by men that explicitly construct powerful visions of masculinity, Amos's performance of Eminem's musical fantasy is simultaneously a critical (feminist?) appropriation of the narrative and an absolutely eery embodiment of it.

References

Begley, S. (1995, February 13). Three is not enough: Surprising new lessons from the controversial science of race. *Newsweek, 125,* 67–69.

Berger, M. (1999). *White lies: Race and the myths of whiteness.* New York: Farrar, Strauss & Giroux.

Berlant, L. (1996). The face of America and the state of emergency. In C. Nelson and D. P. Gaonkar (Eds.), *Disciplinarity and dissent in cultural studies* (pp. 397–439). New York: Routledge.

Boehlert, E. (2001). Invisible man: Eminem. In N. Hornby & B. Schafer (Eds.), *Da Capo best music writing 2001: The year's finest writing on rock, pop, jazz, country, & more* (pp. 119–127). Cambridge, MA: Da Capo Press. (Reprinted from Salon.com, June 7, 2000, http://salon.com)

Boyd, T. (2003). *The new H.N.I.C: The death of civil rights and the reign of hip hop.* New York: New York University Press.

Brown, E. (2000, June 26/July 3). Classless clown. *New York, 33,* 153.

Carson, T. (2002, December). This land is his land. *Esquire, 138,* 86, 88, 90, 94.

Croal, N. (2000, May 29). Slim Shady sounds off. *Newsweek, 135,* 62–64.

DeCurtis, A. (2000, August 3). Eminem's hate rhymes. *Rolling Stone, 846,* 17–18, 21.

Doherty, B. (2000, December). Bum rap: Lynne Cheney vs. Slim Shady. *Reason, 32,* 56–57.

Driver, J. (2002, November 25). Class act. *The New Republic, 227,* 42.

Dyer, R. (1997). *White.* New York: Routledge.

Dyson, M. E. (1993). *Reflecting black: African-American cultural criticism.* Minneapolis: University of Minnesota Press.

Farley, C. J. (2000, May 29). A whiter shade of pale. *Time, 155,* 73.

Foucault, M. (1999). What is an author? (J. V. Harari, Trans.). In J. D. Faubion (Ed.), *Aesthetics, method, and epistemology: Essential works of Foucault, 1954–1984* (Vol. II, pp. 205–222). New York: The New Press. (Original work published 1969)

Frankenberg, R. (1993). *White women, race matters: The social construction of whiteness.* Minneapolis: University of Minnesota Press.

Frere-Jones, S. (2002). Haiku for Eminem. In J. Lethem & P. Bresnick (Eds.), *Da Capo best music writing 2002: The year's finest writing on rock, pop, jazz, country, & more* (pp. 138–140). Cambridge, MA: Da Capo Press. (Reprinted from *The Chicago Reader,* May 24, 2001)

Garon, P. (1996). White blues. In N. Ignatiev & J. Garvey (Eds.), *Race traitor* (pp. 167–175). New York: Routledge.

Gilroy, P. (2000). *Against race: Imagining political culture beyond the color line.* Cambridge, MA: Harvard University Press.

Goad, J. (1997). *The redneck manifesto: How hillbillies, hicks, and white trash became America's scapegoats.* New York: Touchstone.

Gray, H. (1995). *Watching race: Television and the struggle for "blackness."* Minneapolis: University of Minnesota Press.

Grazer, B. (Producer), Hanson, C. (Producer/Director), & Iovine, J. (Producer). (2002). *8 Mile* [Motion picture]. United States: Universal Studios.

Grundmann, R. (2003, Spring). White man's burden: Eminem's movie debut in *8 Mile*. *Cineaste, 28*, 30–35.

Hall, S. (1986). On postmodernism and articulation: An interview with Stuart Hall. *Journal of Communication Inquiry, 10*(2), 45–60.

Hall, S. (1992). Race, culture, and communications: Looking backward and forward at cultural studies. *Rethinking Marxism, 5*(1), 10–18.

Hall, S., Crichter, C, Jefferson, X, Clarke, J., & Roberts, B. (1978). *Policing the crisis: Mugging, the state, and law and order*. New York: Holmes & Meier.

Henig, R. M. (2004, October 10). The genome in black and white (and gray). *The New York Times Magazine*, 46–51.

hooks, b. (1994). *Teaching to transgress: Education as the practice of freedom*. New York: Routledge.

hooks, b. (2000). *Where we stand: Class matters*. New York: Routledge.

Hoyt, M. (2000, September/October). An Eminem exposé: Where are the critics? *Columbia Journalism Review, 39,* 67.

Ignatiev, N. (1995). *How the Irish became white*. New York: Routledge.

Ignatiev, N., & Garvey, J. (Eds.). (1996). *Race traitor*. New York: Routledge.

Jafa, A. (2003). My black death. In G. Tate (Ed.), *Everything but the burden: What white people are taking from black culture* (pp. 244–257). New York: Harlem Moon.

Jhally, S., & Lewis, J. (1992). *Enlightened racism:* The Cosby Show, *audiences, and the myth of the American Dream*. Boulder, CO: Westview.

Kim, R. (2001, March 5). Eminem—bad rap? *The Nation, 272,* 4–5.

Kipnis, L. (1992). (Male) desire and (female) disgust: Reading *Hustler*. In L. Grossberg, C. Nelson, P. Treichler, L. Baughman, & J. M. Wise (Eds.), *Cultural studies* (pp. 373–391). New York: Routledge.

Kipnis, L. (1999). *Bound and gagged: Pornography and the politics of fantasy in America*. Durham, NC: Duke University Press.

Lipsitz, G. (1998). *The possessive investment in whiteness: How white people profit from identity politics*. Philadelphia: Temple University Press.

Lott, E. (1995). *Love and theft: Blackface minstrelsy and the American working class*. New York: Oxford University Press.

McIntosh, P. (1998). White privilege: Unpacking the invisible knapsack. In P. S. Rothenberg (Ed.), *Race, class, and gender in the United States: An integrated study* (4th ed., pp. 163–169). New York: St. Martin's.

McRobbie, A. (1994). The moral panic in the age of the postmodern mass media. In *Postmodernism and popular culture* (pp. 198–219). New York: Routledge.

Morgan, J. (1999, August/September). White noise. *Ms., 9,* 96.

Omi, M., & Winant, H. (1986). *Racial formation in the United States: From the 1960s to the 1980s*. New York: Routledge.

Recording Industry Association of America. (2003). *2003 consumer profile*. Retrieved April 10, 2006, from http://www.riaa.com/news/marketingdata/pdf/2003consumerprofile.pdf

Recording Industry Association of America. (2006). *Gold & platinum top artists*. Retrieved April 10, 2006, from http://www.riaa.com/gp/bestsellers/topartists.asp

Rodman, G. B. (1994). A hero to most?: Elvis, myth, and the politics of race. *Cultural Studies, 8,* 457–483.

Roediger, D. R. (1994). *Towards the abolition of whiteness*. New York: Verso.

Rose, T. (1991). "Fear of a black planet": Rap music and black cultural politics in the 1990s. *Journal of Negro Education, 60,* 276–290.

Rux, C. H. (2003). Eminem: The new white Negro. In G. Tate (Ed.), *Everything but the burden: What white people are taking from black culture* (pp. 15–38). New York: Harlem Moon.

Smith, Z. (2002, November). The Zen of Eminem. *Vibe, 10,* 90–98.

Tatum, B. D. (1999). *"Why are all the black kids sitting together in the cafeteria?" and other conversations about race*. New York: Basic Books.

Tyrangiel, J. (2002, June 3). The three faces of Eminem. *Time, 159,* 66–67.

Wade, N. (2004, November 14). Race-based medicine continued. ... *The New York Times*, section 4, p. 12.

Williams, P. J. (1997). *Seeing a color-blind future: The paradox of race*. New York: Noonday.

15

Rapping and Repping Asian
Race, Authenticity, and the Asian American MC

Looking at a broad spectrum of rap performers, Asian American rappers have easily been assigned the position of the most inauthentic. This is the point that Oliver Wang makes in his chapter, "Rapping and Repping Asian" where he argues that within a form of cultural expression where "blackness" is viewed as normative, Asian American identity becomes the very antithesis of blackness.

Wang examines how various Asian American rappers navigate this particular cultural terrain, noting that their very presence within hip-hop culture signals a crisis of racial authenticity. Notions of a specific Asian American experience within hip-hop are also complicated by the same issues of diversity that exist within other racial and ethnic groups.

Rapping and Repping Asian: Race, Authenticity, and the Asian American MC

Oliver Wang

The first song recorded by a rapper of Asian American descent was the 1979 single "Rap-O, Clap-O" by the Latin soul singer Joe Bataan. Born to a Filipino father and African American mother, Bataan was a veritable giant in New York's Latin scene, having been at the forefront of Latin soul in the late 1960s and then scoring a crossover hit with his 1975 cover of Gil Scott-Heron's "The Bottle." That single appeared on an album (also in 1975) entitled *Afro-Filipino*, thereby settling any ambiguity as to how Bataan self-identified. The album's version of Bataan's best-known composition, "Ordinary Guy," changed the lyrics to reflect his ethnic state of mind: "I'm an ordinary guy ... Afro Filipino ... ordinary guy."

Produced by Arthur Baker—a seminal hip hop figure who later produced Afrika Bambataa's "Planet Rock" and other old-school rap hits—"Rap-O, Clap-O" was Bataan's first foray into hip hop, recorded at the very beginning of the music's recorded history. In fact, Bataan himself has claimed that the song was recorded prior to the release of both the Fatback Band's "King Tim III (Personality Jock)"—recognized as the first rap record—and the Sugarhill Gang's "Rapper's Delight," the first breakout rap hit. However, Bataan was unable to release the song first, and in the end, "Rap-O, Clap-O" failed to make much of an impact in the United States, although it did become a high-charting hit in Europe.[1] For the next twenty-five years, Bataan would be one of the first and last Asian American rappers to find such a popular welcome. Although Asian Americans have taken leading roles throughout the rest of the hip hop industry—as disc jockeys, producers, journalists, designers, and so on—within the ranks of recorded rappers they remain a scant presence.[2]

Becoming a rapper, like any professional musician or entertainer, is a highly competitive process. Out of thousands of aspirants, only a handful will see a recording contract, let alone a commercially produced and distributed album. However, Asian American rappers face more than the challenge of climbing up through a corporate meritocracy—race is also a force that can hamper their efforts. Throughout the 1980s and 1990s, almost no rappers of Asian American descent were signed to any of the recording industry's major labels despite numerous success stories by Latino (Cypress Hill, Big Pun) and white (Beastie Boys, Eminem) rappers.[3]

The common excuse given is that "it's a matter of talent," meaning that there are no Asian Americans of recording caliber. "Talent" is an ill-defined and ambiguous concept most often deployed after the fact (i.e., success supposedly confirms the existence of talent, yet not every talented artist is successful). In the past, this red herring of talent has been used to explain the relatively poor sales of female rappers rather than to acknowledge that sexism may play a role.[4] As with women, in the case of Asian American rappers it is unlikely that their relative invisibility is a result of a lack of talent. Rather, it comes down to the issues of marketability and, intimately related to that, how racially inauthentic Asian Americans are in a social world of fans, artists, media, and industry, where blackness is normative.

Although the concept of authenticity girds most Western music cultures, from classical to pop, the idea finds its apotheosis within hip hop.[5] "Realness," even more than lyrical acumen or musical talent, is often praised and rewarded, whereas "fakeness" can discredit an artist beyond redemption.[6] There are various kinds of authenticity based around social identities such as class, gender, and race. For Asian American rappers, their racial difference creates a crisis of racial inauthenticity that supersedes other factors. As noted, this reflects the ways in which blackness is a normative reality in hip hop, though not one that goes uncontested.

In Imani Perry's *Prophets of the Hood: Politics and Poetics in Hip Hop*, she writes about hip hop's indelible relationship to blackness.

> The assertion that hip hop is a form of black American music is in some ways radical (and unpopular) given current trends in hip hop scholarship that emphasize the multiracial origins of the music, in particular the significant contributions of Caribbean, white, and Latino communities and artists. Many critics have resisted the description of hip hop as black American music because they quite appropriately contest any suggestion that it is "100 percent black" given the active participation of other groups in the world of hip hop since the nascent days of the music. Critiques of the description of hip hop as black music also often stand as critiques of racial essentialism, or critiques of the way in which culture is marketed through race at the same time that it is fundamentally hybrid.[7]

However, Perry argues that despite hip hop's syncretism the music and culture must still be understood within the context of American blackness: "Even with its hybridity, the consistent contributions from nonblack artists, and the borrowings from cultural forms of other communities, it is nevertheless black American music."[8] Like others, Perry cites the roots of hip hop in cultural practices created by disenfranchised black and Puerto Rican youth within the postindustrial urban ghettos of 1970s New York.[9] Few dispute this history or the power of its narrative. The idea of black and brown youth crafting a vibrant subculture from the burned-out streets of urban America has helped hip hop fuel the imaginations of marginalized youth across the world as they come to identify hip hop with their own alterity.[10] However, this origin myth can lead to an authenticity paradigm in which African Americans are normative while other ethnic groups find their presence marginalized if not entirely missing.[11]

The absence of hip hop's hybrid histories is not a deliberate act of erasure—though some have argued otherwise[12]—but it is certainly a by-product of how powerfully hip hop's Afro-diasporic roots dominate conversations around rap and race. Scholars have raised concerns over this phenomenon, notably those writing on the Latino contribution to hip hop.[13] Others challenge the centrism that posits the United States as the sole country with a legitimate hip hop narrative.[14] Despite these attempts to diversify hip hop within scholarly discourse,[15] consumption habits by mainstream rap consumers,[16] which are often cited as the rationale behind industry decisions,[17] are still vastly tilted toward African American artists.[18] Nonblack rappers, especially Asian Americans, face a dilemma since their racial difference does not meet the standard of black authenticity held by rap fans and music executives alike.

This challenge poses a paradox to Asian American artists. There are few Asian American rappers in the mainstream because most record labels are wary of signing them out of concern for their commercial viability. However, Asian American artists are unlikely to attain commercial viability until more record labels are willing to put their marketing and promotions resources behind them. In the meantime, the continued absence of Asian American rappers within mainstream media contributes to the perception of their inauthenticity, which further hinders their chances of finding commercial support. In this instance, the marginalization of Asian Americans within the hip hop recording industry becomes a self-perpetuating cycle that is difficult to break.

The following pages explore how select rappers of Asian American descent have dealt with their racial difference through self-conscious deployments of racial and ethnic signifiers in their lyrics, videos, and press material.[19] On one level, I am engaging what I perceive to be these artists' identity politics, that is, the kind of ethnic and racial identities they take on themselves and what their motives are for doing so. At the same time, I am also interested in looking at the wider issue of hip hop and its politics of identity and how racialized bodies fit into a matrix of power within the hip hop industry and fan community.

While I cover a span of approximately fifteen years, my intent is not to present a traditional, narrative history of Asian American rappers. Instead, I historicize one particular aspect—how they position a politics of racial identity within their music. The essay examines if, how, why, and to what ends Asian American rappers deploy ethnic and racial identities in their songs. The choice to express these identities is an individual one, but I argue that there have also been larger trends in the way Asian American rappers choose to deal with race in their marketing and music.

In quick summary, I chart how Asian American rappers in the early 1990s made race a central part of their image production and songwriting. In the mid-1990s, race and ethnicity became much more muted and were replaced with a rhetoric of universalism. In the early 2000s, race was deployed publicly again but as a strategic, "preemptive strike" against potential critics rather than an explicit, politicized embrace of racial identity. I suggest that these changes are reflective of both individual perceptions of race and identity and a general consciousness of racial difference within American hip hop culture at large.

"The Afrocentric Asian": Negotiating Blackness and Asianness

In *New York Ricans from the Hip Hop Zone*, Raquel Z. Rivera's exceptional history and analysis of Puerto Ricans and hip hop, she posits that, "Puerto Ricans who have taken part in New York's hip hop culture have constructed their identities, participated and created art through a process of negotiation with the dominant notions of Blackness and *latinidad*."[20] The term *latinidad* represents "Latino-ness" in the same way that *blackness* functions in African American public culture. It is meant to represent the core essence of what it is to be a Latino. Rivera writes that "caught between *latinidad* and Blackness, Puerto Ricans may fit in both categories and yet also in neither," an explicit acknowledgment that the struggle to define oneself is difficult in the face of dueling politics of identity that force people to choose between identities rather than finding a syncretic middle ground.[21] Rivera's basic argument is that this tension between the two identity poles— blackness and latinidad—has dominated the ways in which Puerto Ricans have to negotiate their position within hip hop. Neither completely black or brown—in the simplified discourse of hip hop's racial politics—Puerto Ricans have had to fight against a racial binary that rarely offers a middle ground. In her words, "Puerto Ricans who participate in hip hop culture have sought to acknowledge their Afro-diasporic Caribbeanness without wholly submerging themselves under the reigning Hispanocentric definition of *latinidad* as nonblack, or under a Blackness that takes only African Americans into account."[22] In other words, forced to choose between worlds, some Puerto Ricans have instead sought to reject the binary logic of declaring one's allegiance to either blackness or *latinidad* at the expense of the other.

In *New York Ricans from the Hip Hop Zone*, Rivera traces the complex paths this tension has followed. She convincingly documents, for example, how Puerto Ricans were assimilated into the pan-*latinidad* category of "Latin rap" that was in vogue in the early 1990s—an attempt at creating a subcategory of hip hop that was meant to acknowledge Latino contributions but also had the effect of erasing differences.[23] Under this pan-*latinidad* rubric, Puerto Ricans were lumped in with Dominican, Cuban, and especially Chicano rappers, despite the significant social differences that exist between these ethnic communities. Most important, Rivera notes that pan-*latinidad*'s "Hispanocentric bent" distanced Latinos from the African diaspora even though many Latinos, especially those from the West Indies (including Puerto Ricans and Dominicans) trace their roots directly back to the slave trade, which brought African slaves to both North America and the Caribbean. Rivera argues that the pan-*latinidad* label, quickly seized on in the media, flourished through people's popular imaginations and as a result effectively remarginalized Puerto Rican identities by denying a unique social history that could embrace both blackness and *latinidad* without contradiction.[24]

Rivera's analysis offers much to this essay's engagement with how Asian American rappers have had to deal with the question of race and identity in their own careers. In her work, Rivera traces the fluid ethnic identities that Puerto Ricans have had to negotiate over time, contextualizing how these change with shifting understandings of race, ethnicity, sexuality, and so on. In similar ways, Asian American rappers have changed their subject positions in relation to race over the last fifteen years.

Of course, this does not suggest that an analysis of Asian Americans in hip hop will reveal similar issues and challenges facing the Puerto Rican community. To begin with, there is no equivalent to *latinida*, let alone blackness, within Asian American cultural discourse. While the very ideas of blackness, *latinidad*, and Asianness are reflective of imagined communities, with Asianness in particular the ties that bind different Asian communities together are far more tenuous.

As many scholars have expressed, most notably the sociologist Yen Le Espiritu in *Asian American Panethnicity*,[25] the possibility of forging a uniform Asian American identity is rent by any number of contrasting, sometimes hostile differences in history, language, culture, class, and so on. While all panethnic identities involve a certain amount of glossing over of difference—this is one of Rivera's key points of criticism as well in the case of pan-*latinidad*—Asian American panethnicity especially is held together by a very fragile thread of political necessity rather than cultural, historical, or social similarity. To put it another way, the concept of blackness is being increasingly problematized,[26] but the concept of Asianness has been problematic from its inception.

However, Asianness is real enough insofar as Asian Americans have to contend with a racialized identity placed on them by external forces. Groups as diverse as Taiwanese, Hmong, and Filipinos have effectively been lumped together and fixed as unchanging others—positioning them in opposition to, or at least separate from, the rest of American society, including both whiteness and blackness. The historian Gary Okihiro rhetorically poses the question, "Is Yellow Black or White?" to acknowledge that Asian Americans are expected to cast their allegiance with one of the two dominant American racial poles while erasing their own subjectivity as Asian Americans.[27] Yet the contradiction is that Asian Americans are always already othered; even if they are racialized in white or black tones, the presumption of their Asianness/otherness makes it difficult for them to be accepted as either.

As such, one of the fundamental tensions with which Asian American rappers have to contend is the distance between Asianness and blackness. Within hip hop, as Rivera notes, there is considerable distance between blackness and *latinidad*, and it goes without saying that whiteness and blackness have had a long, complex, and convoluted history.[28] The perception of difference between Asianness and blackness is no less pronounced, if not greater, especially given the historical forces dividing the two communities, to say nothing of highly publicized, contemporary tensions.[29] Moreover, if contemporary Black masculinity is associated with stereotypes of hypermasculinity and sexuality, physical aggression, and the underclasses, these stand in almost diametric opposition to so-called model-minority stereotypes of Asian masculinity: effete or asexual, passive, and middle class.[30] In other words, one could argue that what largely defines Asian masculinity is the absence of traits associated with black masculinity. These cultural stereotypes only serve to further polarize blackness and Asianness. Thus, Asian American rappers walk into hip hop with an authenticity crisis on their hands before they even open their mouths to rhyme. The remainder of this essay explores how Asian American rappers have dealt with their racial distance through shifting strategies of self-representation.

Rap, Race, and Asian Representation in the Early 1990s

In June of 1992, *SF Weekly*, an alternative paper, put a public face on Asian American rappers. The cover story that week featured Davis Yee, also known as D-Yee and Nunchuck C, sporting a bald head, a throwback baseball jersey and a medallion with Chinese lettering on it. Behind him stood his partner, Rich Francisco, wearing a heavy jacket and beanie hat. Both men wore sunglasses. In the bottom left corner of the cover, a blurb explains who these two were and what they were about: "Breaking It Down: The Asiatic Apostles Are Attacking Stereotypes and Encouraging Dialogue with Their Own Style of Hip Hop—Darow Han Talks to Bay Area Asian American Rappers about the Street Credibility of the 'Model Minority'."[31]

The Asiatic Apostles, who hailed from Davis, California, were far from the only Asian American rappers of the time.[32] While there has yet to be a full accounting of early Asian American rap artists, anecdotally there are stories of Asian Americans, both men and women, rapping at parties and in battles (i.e., competitions) dating back to the late 1970s and throughout the 1980s.[33] What set the Asiatic Apostles apart from their predecessors were their perspectives on art, politics, and hip hop. In the *SF Weekly* article, Yee and Francisco expounded on their mission as rappers: "We need to be very vocal, because Asian Americans are still an 'invisible' minority. Rap is becoming more and more popular among Asians. ... I want our group to stir up controversy and talk about important issues."[34] Yee saw a connection between his work and that of the popular African American rap group Public Enemy, later recalling that he and his partner "thought it was pretty cool what Public Enemy [was] doing, using music as a medium to educate and elevate consciousness. So conveying what we learned in the classes through hip hop was nothing new. But we didn't know too many Asian Americans doing the Public Enemy thing."[35] Public Enemy's front man, Chuck D., was known for calling rap music the "Black CNN," linking the music with access to mass media for African Americans. In similar fashion, Yee recalls that the Apostles wanted to use hip hop as a way to reach a larger Asian American audience and create a dialogue about social issues such as interracial tensions and anti-Asian discrimination.

These were familiar sentiments being expounded by other Asian American rappers at the time. Darow Han, the author of the *SF Weekly* article, was in a rap duo himself, San Francisco's Fists of Fury. In Seattle, there were the Seoul Brothers, in Los Angeles there was Art Hirahara, and in New Jersey there was Yellow Peril.[36] While these groups formed independently, together they established a cohort of early 1990s Asian American rappers who shared many key similarities in their political and artistic approaches to hip hop.

It is important to note that all of these artists came up with the idea to become rappers while in college. The Apostles were attending the University of California, Davis; Fists of Fury's members originally met at Columbia University; the Seoul Brothers (who are brothers in real life) attended the University of Washington; Art Hirahara was at Oberlin College, then UCLA; and the members of Yellow Peril were students at Rutgers University. The collegiate experience weighs heavily here because all of these artists convey social and political knowledge gained through university classes, especially Asian American studies courses. Moreover, in the late 1980s and early 1990s, when these artists were attending school, hip hop had just begun to cross into the mainstream, finding a welcome audience among politically charged college students, just as folk music had among collegians in the 1960s.

Practically every one of these groups was inspired by Public Enemy, a Long Island group that by 1990 had captured the imaginations of listeners worldwide through their assaulting, forceful soundplay, outspoken politicized lyricism, and controversy-plagued celebrity.[37] In various interviews and publications, members of Yellow Peril, Fists of Fury, and the Seoul Brothers all mentioned the importance of Public Enemy to the formation of their groups.[38] For example, Darow Han's rap partner in Fists of Fury, Han-na Che (now known as Hana Choi and formerly known as MC R.A.W., Radical Asian Woman) echoed Davis Yee in her desire to use hip hop as a tool for political agitation: "I was influenced by Public Enemy and it was a perfect form for expressing anger. I wanted to stir shit up."[39]

In its press biography, Fists of Fury is described as "an innovative political rap group ... [whose members] rap about their experience of being Asian Americans"[40] and seek through their music to engage a range of political issues deemed pertinent to Asian Americans. Their output included songs that dealt with interracial dating ("Sleeping with the Enemy"), black-Korean tensions in the inner city ("Black Korea II"), and misogyny and sexism ("Dissed by a Femme"). For one song, "After School," recorded for a three-song demo tape, Han, also known as C.Y.A.T. (Cute Young Asian Terrorist), wrote the following lyrics and chorus.

> First grade to college
> You're pushed to work hard,
> Get all A's on every report card;
> Your teachers will say,
> "Isn't he a bright child,
> Not like the Blacks,
> Who always act wild."
> Everyone expects you to be a genius,
> Valedictorian when you're a senior
> But, hey, brother, sister, haven't you heard?
> Behind your back, they're calling you a nerd!
>
> (Chorus)
> American schools create whitewashed fools
> Cause the man from the caves wants mental slaves[41]
> American schools create whitewashed fools
> Cause the man from the caves wants mental slaves[42]

"After School" offers two threads of social critique. First, the chorus attacks the American educational system, suggesting that schools only serve to indoctrinate youth into accepting hegemonic racial hierarchies that privilege whites. However, the song is directed not at whites but at Asian Americans in an attempt to deconstruct the myth of the overachieving Asian American student[43] and show how it is used to drive a wedge between Asian Americans and African Americans. Han's intent was to challenge the idea *within* the Asian American community that educational achievement should be emphasized at all costs, arguing that by buying into this mentality Asian Americans are "enslaving" themselves to a white supremacy. It is a provocative argument but one in line with Choi's desire to "stir shit up" and agitate as a way to educate.

This kind of approach was popular throughout the cohort of early 1990s Asian American rappers. Yellow Peril's Bert Wang, also known as Shaolin, expressed many of the same sentiments as the Apostles and Fists of Fury, explaining that "Rap, to us, is really about political expression. It's about rebellion. We see it as a medium for disseminating information."[44] In 1995, Yellow Peril released its own sampler tape with a song called "Asian for the Man," which critiqued Asian stereotypes in the mass media.

> House Asian, happy slave, sell out, Hop Sing
> They say it's just movies, just TV, just acting
> But it serves a higher purpose in American society
> Administering self-hate for a racist ideology
> Hop Sings and impostors, ya get the back of my hand
> You sold out our culture, Asian for the Man![45]

Like Fists of Fury's "After School," "Asian for the Man" is a dual critique. Yellow Peril attacked the "racist ideology" of American society and media, but it also took Asian American actors to task for accepting roles that the group deemed demeaning to the image of Asian American men. In effect, Yellow Peril was dialoguing with the larger American society but also calling on members of the Asian American community to take responsibility for their potentially detrimental actions.

What we can see in these examples is that groups such as Fists of Fury, Yellow Peril, and others explicitly expounded racial and ethnic identities through the hip hop they made. In an adaptation of W. E. B. Du Bois's famous perspective on African American culture, this was music *made for, by*, and *about* Asian Americans. While all of these groups also expressed the desire to reach audiences beyond Asian Americans,[46] their foremost commitment was to consciously write songs that dealt with Asian American social issues they deemed important, whether that meant racism in the media, anti-Asian violence, or interracial dating.

These examples show how Asian American rap groups of the early 1990s took a deliberate stand to make their racial identity the foremost part of their image and artistic message. What is also strikingly similar about these groups is how they perceived hip hop as a vehicle for political expression. Bert Wang called it "a medium for disseminating information," Davis Yee saw it as a way to "stir up controversy and talk about important issues," and the members of Fists of Fury wanted to "rap about their experience of being Asian American." Hip hop's perceived power to reach a youthful audience with political or politicized messages was a common thread in the formation and mission of all these groups. As stated by Darow Han in a personal interview, "We just felt that [rap] had a lot of strengths as far as being a cutting-edge medium. Probably politically, it had the most potential. It was the music that most young people who were politically attuned would be listening to."[47]

What is conspicuously absent, in both comments by members of the group and their songs, is an engagement with hip hop as a form of cultural activity or an artistic mode of expression. These artists may be quick to list inspiring artists such as Public Enemy, Boogie Down Productions, and Queen Latifah—the so-called conscious artists of the late 1980s and early 1990s known for their outspoken social agenda. However, very few of them talk about being inspired by the music of hip hop or by the aesthetics of its language and delivery. In other words, this cadre of artists tended to treat hip hop as a means to tap media access. In the process, they often favored the rhetoric of the medium over its aesthetics. As will be seen later, this stood in marked contrast to later Asian American rappers, who pursued hip hop as an end unto itself.

This prioritization of hip hop's politics over its aesthetics came at a cost. With time, all these groups could have balanced the power of their message with an equal competence in their production, but much of their material, both recorded or played live, reflected their limited experience with hip hop's musical craft. For example, for Fists of Fury's "After School," the group recycled a track made popular by New York's Stetsasonic a few years earlier on their hit "Talkin' All That Jazz." Moreover, with the group's limited access to studio equipment, "After School" sounds thin and tinny, lacking the sonic impact that characterized other hip hop productions of that era. The same limitations can be found in many of the songs by the Fists' cohort of peers, a reflection of these groups' desire to focus on the message over the music.

I suggest that this, in no small way, explains why none of these early 1990s groups were able to sustain a viable musical career.[48] In most cases, one or more of the group members lost interest. The Apostles' Davis Yee observed, "The industry is really difficult to break into. I can't speak for the other group members, but I wanted a little more financial stability, which I could not get doing hip hop as a career."[49] Likewise, Choi admitted in her 1998 interview with Judy Tseng, "We were more interested in spreading our political message. We produced our own music and sold our tapes. We knew that our material was not commercially viable."[50]

It is also worth noting that, according to the Fists of Fury's press biography, the group toured almost exclusively at Asian American student and community events rather than playing for more diverse audiences, a trend shared with other Asian American rappers at the time.[51] For example, Davis Yee tellingly recalled that "April was often hectic because it was Asian American month"[52] while Bert Wang noted that "our audiences were predominantly Asian American."[53] While there is some practical logic to this—often rappers will try to establish a core audience before branching out to others—given the topical specificity of their music, it seems more likely that their audience was always intended to be select. Although hip hop has subgenres that appeal to more discerning listeners, as a whole, the music has always been geared toward a populist agenda. Ever since "Rapper's Delight" became a worldwide hit, most aspiring hip hop artists have sought to tap into as wide an audience as they can. The fact that these early 1990s Asian American rappers sought to dialogue specifically (though not necessarily solely) with Asian American listeners limited their appeal and potential to succeed in a competitive industry and environment.

The next generation of Asian American rappers would take a notably different route.[54] While they recognized the importance of maintaining ties to Asian American listeners, they also wanted to fashion viable careers that courted larger, more diverse audiences, and this influenced how they identified themselves to that public. It is not that they lacked an Asian American consciousness but that they saw touting an explicit racialized identity as detrimental to their prospects as recording artists. Instead, they sought to appeal to an idealized hip hop community in which race and ethnicity are downplayed in favor of more seemingly race-neutral values such as "talent," "skills," and "personal expression." While these values are an important part of hip hop's heritage and belief system, they are also the ones most easily deracinated and therefore an attractive alternative for artists seeking to avoid the authenticity dilemma based on race or ethnicity.

"Where You're At": Abilities versus Origins in the Mid-1990s

The Mountain Brothers has the odd distinction of being one of Asian America's most prominent rap groups commercially speaking. Literally, it does commercials. In 1996, it won a national contest to record an ad for Sprite soda. In 1999, the voices of the group's three rappers, Scott Jung (known as Chops), Steve Wei (Styles) and Chris Wang (Peril), were used in a television commercial for Nike sneakers. In both cases, though, the Mountain Brothers cameoed as disembodied voices—the Sprite ad ran on radio only, and in the Nike commercial they provided the voices for three cartoon basketball players: Tim Duncan, Kevin Garnett, and Jason Williams. Until their video "Galaxies" debuted on MTV in 1999, the Mountain Brothers was the most famous Asian American rap group no one had ever seen.

Early in their career, these three Chinese American rappers composed a song entitled "Invisible Man," which speaks to how they, as Asian Americans, do not exist within a black-white racial spectrum. Chops offers the following observations:[55]

> I sit in the aisle in the back of class silent
> 'cause I can't relate
> debate is about race, today that makes me out of place
> only a two-sided coin so me I'm thru tryin to join …
> I'm disagreein with steven believin even the blind could see
> that ebony and ivory could never be applied to me[56]

In these six lines, Chops lays out a succinct summary of American racial awareness and how it marginalizes those who fall out of the black-white binary. In a play on Stevie Wonder's "Ebony and Ivory," Chops argues that Wonder's ode to racial harmony still offers no space for himself, as an Asian American, since he is neither ebony (African American) nor ivory (white). One of the first songs the group recorded, in the mid-1990s, "Invisible Man," would be one of the last times the Mountain Brothers tackled identity politics in its songs. By the time of its first album release, in 1999, the group, like other Asian American rappers from the mid-1990s onward, had turned away from making explicit statements on race and ethnicity and instead focused on a different kind of identity allegiance: as hip hop artists.

Joined by rappers from the mid-1990s onward, such as Los Angeles's Kikou Nishi (Key Kool), Chicago's duo Pacifies, and Orlando's Southstar (real name unknown), the Mountain Brothers has been markedly different from the previous generation. These are artists with ambitions to succeed in the record industry, which necessitates a wider, multiethnic audience than their predecessors, with their focus on Asian American audiences, could attract. Groups such as Yellow Peril, the Asiatic Apostles, and Fists of Fury wanted to make their identities as Asian Americans explicit as a way of directly targeting Asian American listeners. For the Mountain Brothers, Key Kool, and others that followed, the quest for a more diverse audience has meant that many try to downplay their ethnic identities. Although they do not reject their identities as Asian Americans, they choose not to highlight it. Put succinctly by one of hip hop's more lauded lyricists, Rakim, in the song, "I Know You Got Soul": "It ain't where you're from, it's where you're at," which could very well be the mantra for this generation of Asian American rappers.[57]

This difference in attitude is reflected in Chris Wang's comment about who the members of the Mountain Brothers were trying to appeal to: "Our core audience is basically hip hop heads. People who truly appreciate the essence of hip hop music—fat rhymes and fat beats period. People who can understand, comprehend, and enjoy the level of complexity and creativity involved in our lyrics and music."[58] In this short response, Wang introduces a series of shorthand terms and ideas and then explains them succinctly. His group is trying to appeal to "heads," who are "people who truly appreciate the essence of hip hop music," defined by "fat rhymes and fat beats," that is, quality lyrics and music.

Wang does not mention ethnicity or race at all—to him, his core audience has little to do with ethnic heritage. Instead, he wants his music to appeal to the listeners he feels are best able to appreciate the kind of aesthetic that he and his group members work in, that is, "hip hop heads." Jung elaborates further, saying, "Hopefully we have a sound and feel that can appeal to more than just straight heads because that's not too many, and we're hoping to move some units."[59] While Jung concurs with Wang that heads are part of their core audience, he also expresses the hope that more mainstream audiences can appreciate their work since he wants the group to be able to sell more records ("move some units"), and he realizes that straight (meaning dedicated) hip hop heads are not numerous enough to provide the group with the success he desires.

This stands in contrast to the attitudes of older artists, such as the members of the Fists of Fury, who admitted that they knew their "material was not commercially viable." Contemporary Asian American rappers intent on establishing careers in the recording industry need to strategize their commercial viability. Out of this ambition has come the belief that promoting themselves on basis of race or ethnicity hinders them in the marketplace. For example, Nishi, a

Japanese American rapper who released an album, *Kozmonautz* (1995), with a partner, DJ Rhettmatic (who is Filipino American), says, "In hip hop, it's a whole different culture ... and you have to have a certain tact about things. Sometimes if you're too out there, then you lose people."[60] Although he does not use the words *race* or *ethnicity*, Nishi addresses the concern that being too prominent as an "Asian American artist" runs the risk of losing listeners who may not identify with the artist simply on this basis.[61]

Early in his career, Jung made the same observation, noting that, with audiences, "If they don't know what race we are, usually people just dig us because they just listen to the music. And that's what we're mainly about, the music. If they know we're Asian beforehand, there's ... a certain amount of bias and they actually like the music less."[62] Jung's point suggests that the issue of racial authenticity in hip hop has the power to influence how listeners actually *hear* the music. When the group is deracinated, people are more open to the Mountain Brothers' material, but when the group's ethnicity is made explicit, those same listeners become more skeptical. Operating under this logic, Jung talks about the Mountain Brothers being mainly about the music, which, by extension, means that the group is not about its race and ethnicity.[63]

This is a key commonality shared by many Asian American rappers who emerged during or after the mid-1990s. Very few of them make explicit overtures to ethnic-specific audiences, preferring instead to appeal to larger audiences whose presumed interest in the music is based on the quality of their work rather than their ethnicity.[64] Nishi recalls how in the early 1990s he paired up with a rapper of Latino heritage but had to deal with a record label seeking to pigeonhole the two of them: "They were saying 'we want to market you as a Latino group more' and I said 'I'm Asian, why can't we just focus on all realms and be universal?' "[65] Nishi's employment of the term *universal* has less to do with him seeking unanimous approval than with the fact that he does not want to be pigeonholed as solely an Asian American artist.

In contrast, hip hop has a long history of outspoken expressions of racial pride made by African American artists. Yet even the most nationalistic rappers, such as X-Clan, Paris, and (most telling) Public Enemy, have been popular with multiracial audiences. Few are critiqued for being too focused on the black community. This reflects hip hop's racial history and politics; it is nearly impossible to be "too black" in a musical culture so intimately tied to African American cultural history, modes of expression, and personal affirmation. Compounding this is the enduring legacy of blackface and minstrelsy in shaping popular American culture. Much of contemporary popular culture is derived from representations of blackness, however accurate or perverse, and hip hop's syncretic melding of multiple cultural traditions only accentuates the enduring power of blackness within contemporary culture.[66]

These forces emerged from a racialized authenticity that Asian Americans cannot claim. Instead, in an effort to deracinate both themselves and their ideal of hip hop culture, they apply the utopian concept of the "universal," ostensibly a community freed of racial or other social boundaries. It is important to note, however, that the idea of the universal does not stand for the inclusion of *all* colors but instead is meant to represent the absence of color altogether. This desire to appeal to a universal hip hop audience, to target "hip hop heads," is a coded way of acknowledging that being seen as too Asian (versus too black) is a liability. Appealing to the universal is an attempt to alter the terms of authenticity—making it less about race and more about skills and talent.

Related to the ideal of the universal, Asian American rappers have also expressed the belief that hip hop should not be about race or color but about personal expression. This is not a sentiment held just by Asian Americans. Especially in a time when hip hop's appeal is undeniably multiracial and transnational, many have acknowledged that the music and culture have fostered the ability of many kinds of people to express themselves in meaningful and powerful ways. Focusing on personal expression however, also has the same effect as valorizing the universal: it becomes a coded way to avoid the issue of race.

For example, the following exchange between an interviewer, Futuredood, and Southstar, a Chinese Filipino American (real names both unknown), demonstrates some of the contradictions involved in trying to negotiate racial difference as an Asian American rapper.

Q: *(Futuredood)* How does it feel to be working in an industry where you're looked upon as "different" because of your skin color?

A: *(Southstar)* I don't even notice it most of the time because it's all hip hop. I just do what I do and not worry about what anyone else has to say.

Q: Growing up rapping, have you ever had any criticism because of your race? If so, how did you deal with this?

A: Being Asian, it definitely meant I had a lot more to prove. I didn't get respect until I earned it. That's how I approached it. The most important thing was that I believed in myself and never gave up.

Q: After listening to your album, you didn't mention once your nationality. Is this a personal reason, or were you advised not to by your management?

A: I just write music. Whether you're white, black, Asian, or whatever, I feel hip hop is for all, so it never really crossed my mind to blatantly say I'm Chinese and Filipino in a song. My management definitely supports everything I do, and they allow me to say what I want.

Q: Didn't you once mention that you were the "rap Ichiro"?

A: I did mention I'm the rap Ichiro, because I do want to make an impact on hip hop as an Asian MC as Ichiro did in baseball as an Asian player. First Asian to win MVP [most valuable player]. I just feel no matter what nationality you are, if you make good music, it doesn't matter.[67]

These sets of responses reveal a complex, contrasting set of views. On the one hand, Southstar posits that he does not pay attention to how his race is perceived as different in the hip hop industry, but in the very next answer he admits that being Asian is also a liability. Likewise, while he shares that he once called himself the "rap Ichiro" as a way of expressing his ambition to become the "first Asian to win MVP" honors in hip hop, he also says, "I just write music. Whether you're black, Asian, or whatever, I feel hip hop is for all," and "I just feel no matter what nationality you are, if you make good music, it doesn't matter." While not entirely contradictory, Southstar's comments display an awareness of how his ethnicity plays out in complex ways.[68] He strives to maintain a standard based on the ideal that "it's all hip hop" and "hip hop is for all," both of which are alternative ways expressing the desire to be universal.

In these cases, rappers argue that hip hop should ultimately be more concerned with the quality of personal expression than the politics of racial group identity. Nishi explains, "Our whole concept is that we're not trying to exploit the fact that we're Asian. What hip hop culture is all about is it's a way for any person to express themselves. ... What's most important is that you have to have your own flavor."[69] By "we're not trying to exploit the fact that we're Asian" Nishi means they are not attempting to sell his music to audiences solely on the basis of ethnicity. Likewise, the Filipino American Marwin Taba ("KP" of the Pacifics) says, "Our ethnicity really doesn't have to do with skills. You either got 'em or you don't. ... Having skills and perfecting your craft goes beyond one's race."[70] The sentiments expressed by both Taba and Nishi are hardly unique in hip hop. Nishi's statement about personal expression reflects hip hop's validation of the individual's right to self-expression while Taba's valorization of skills relates to hip hop's competitive environment and the rappers' constant drive to distinguish themselves from their peers.

However, Taba's emphasis that his Filipino heritage "really doesn't have to do with skills" means he recognizes that his ethnicity could be treated as a liability and seeks to refocus people's attention on his abilities instead. In a sense, his point is correct—his talents as a rapper have little or nothing to do with his ethnicity. Yet how he is perceived as a rapper is very much subject to racialized scrutiny. The focus on skills is one way for Taba to avoid that problem.

In contrast, African Americans do not face the same standard. For a black artist to express sentiments about his or her blackness is a form of "personal expression" that, more than being accepted, is firmly validated and encouraged within the hip hop community. Especially as rappers of the late 1980s began to revisit the politics of the Black Power movement of the 1960s and 1970s, there emerged a series of overt appeals to blackness. Examples include Run DMC's "Proud to Be Black" (1986), Public Enemy's "Fight the Power" (1989), and X-Clan's "Raise the Flag" (1990), which were commercially successful as well as critically lauded.[71] However, as Nishi pointed out, if Asian American rappers speak out about their experiences as racialized (but not black) beings, this form of "personal expression" runs the risk of casting the artist as "too out there." The irony is that if expressing yourself is one way to gain audience favor, Asian American artists have to be conscious of not expressing those parts of themselves, such as their ethnic or racial identity, that could cause audience alienation. As noted in the beginning of this essay, the canonical narrative of hip hop's roots in African American history and culture dominates the popular imagination of hip hop worldwide. Anything that runs counter to that perception runs the risk of being dismissed as inauthentic or at least held in less regard. In this sense, Nishi's comment about not wanting to exploit his ethnicity is moot since drawing attention to their racial difference would be considered a liability for many of these artists in their own estimation.

On the rare occasions when race or ethnicity is spoken about, it is often made incidental rather than central. One illuminating example comes from the Mountain Brothers' debut album (1999) and their song, "Days of Being Dumb." Jung (Chops) opens the track with these verses:

> flippin' the page / back in the days
> when this little, fat Asian kid would sit makin' beats in the basement
> on a basic roll and drum box / stolen from Scott's
> sneakin' and listenin' to Dr. Rock-N'-Dallas in the PM on weekends[72]

In this example, ethnic identity is mentioned but only as one of many signifiers Chops lays out. Chops not only identifies himself as a "little, fat Asian kid," but he also crafts a narrative of his own hip hop upbringing, inclusive of retail stores where he stole his production equipment and radio stations where he listened to music—dimensions that helped shape who he is an artist. Ethnicity is part of it, but it is not necessarily the most important part. Chops clearly did not write these lines as a way to connect only with other Asian Americans. His appeals are far more than ethnic; they are also geographic and generational. Even musically speaking the lush, organic production of "Days of Being Dumb" recalls the so-called Philadelphia sound pioneered by soul artists such as Gamble and Huff, Dexter Wanzel, the O'Jays, and MSFB. In this way, as an artist Chops identifies himself more with Philadelphia than with his Asian descent.

Elsewhere, in the video for the Mountain Brothers' song "Galaxies," directors Richard Kim and Chris Chan Lee surround the group with a variety of images—some ethnic, many not.[73] For example, members of the group are shown playing mah-jong and eating ramen noodles, ostensibly signifiers of Asianness, but this is staged against a larger backdrop that includes scenes of Styles brushing his teeth, Chops's production equipment, and an extended dance sequence shot in downtown Philadelphia in which the Mountain Brothers is surrounded by a conspicuously multiracial crowd of friends and fans. As Chops puts it in the song itself, the rappers are "Illadelphy Asiatic / representin' from the West End section," a complicated mix of signifiers that says as much about where they're from (West Philadelphia) as about who/what they are (Asiatic / Asian).

Another telling example is the 1999 hip hop compilation *Elephant Tracks* assembled by San

Francisco's Asian American music label, Asian Improv Records.[74] Two-thirds of the album's featured artists are of Asian American descent, including the Mountain Brothers, the Filipino American rap group KNT (Knuckle Neck Tribe), and the multiethnic, Los Angeles group The Visionaries, whose members include Filipino, Japanese, and Chinese Americans. Despite this diverse collection—and the album includes many non-Asian artists as well—the compilation conspicuously avoids billing itself as an Asian American hip hop anthology. There is no explicit mention of ethnicity in any of the liner notes, and save for the pictures of the groups inside the CD packaging there is little to indicate the race or ethnicity of the artists. Ethnicity is clearly a common thread that ties these artists together in concept, but in execution the need to express or reflect on ethnicity is anything but required (that said, it is worth noting that the Mountain Brothers' cut on this anthology is "Community," a song with an explicit antidiscrimination, pro-Asian American solidarity bent).

Elephant Tracks is less concerned with the need to proclaim that Asian American rappers exist than it is with showing what those artists are capable of. This compilation, like the song "Days of Being Dumb" or the video "Galaxies," suggests that contemporary Asian American rappers seek to define their community beyond ethnic or racial ties; instead they try to appeal to larger ties of alliance, allegiance, and experience. They offer the possibility that hip hop, not just as music but as a source of cultural identity, is a potential point of affiliation that can be shared across racial and ethnic lines. This is not to say that hip hop supersedes such powerfully resonant social categories as race, gender, and class, but it acknowledges that hip hop has become a prominent cultural force that many youth, Asian American and otherwise, have experienced over the last two decades. In the words of performance artist and cultural theorist Coco Fusco, "Rap music ... is perhaps today's most resonant cross-cultural American language for defiant self-affirmation."[75] The scenes of the Mountain Brothers in downtown Philadelphia surrounded by a multiethnic crowd of well-wishers are just one example of how Asian American rappers have tried to express Fusco's argument in their own way.

In this social world, hip hop becomes the common thread that ties people together across race, geography, and age. Asian Americans have strategic reasons to champion a more utopian, inclusive ideal of hip hop since it helps deflect attention away from their own racial difference. Yet it also conforms to the philosophy about hip hop's egalitarian embrace of performers of all backgrounds. By seeking to form relationships with other artists and audience members from across the social spectrum, Asian American rappers are putting into practice their own ideas about hip hop's politics of inclusion while simultaneously crafting a space where they can fit into that matrix. By focusing on individual abilities rather than origins, contemporary Asian American rappers have found one way to cope with the expectations of the hip hop audience. But this is not the only strategy they have pursued.

Jin and Juice: Wielding Racial Consciousness at the Millennium

For his stage name, Jin Au-Yeung simply uses his own name: Jin. After spending most of his childhood in Miami, his family relocated to Queens, New York, and on a chance opportunity Jin appeared on the cable network BET's *106 and Park*, a daily television show highlighting rap videos and artists. Every week, *106 and Park* hosts a freestyle battle between opposing rappers, and Jin entered the rotation. Seven weeks later, he emerged undefeated, one of only two rappers to have entered the show's Hall of Fame at the time. With a national television audience viewing his exploits during this two-month run, Jin became what one magazine described as "the Golden Child."[76] With the release of his debut album in the fall of 2004, *The Rest Is History,* a long string of articles followed, many of them drawing attention to the fact that Jin was the first Asian American rapper with a legitimate chance to find mainstream success.[77]

What set Jin apart from his predecessors is that he was invited to join the Ruff Ryders "family," which at the time included top-selling rappers such Eve, Styles P, DMX, and Jadakiss. Whether Jin was more or less skilled than other Asian American rappers was a matter of subjective speculation, but objectively speaking he had far more resources than were available to previous rappers of Asian descent. However, in gaining the attention of the mainstream media and rap pundits, Jin's racial difference became all the more obvious. Yet, rather than downplaying these differences as previous rappers had, Jin strategically embraced them, drawing attention to his race in an attempt to minimize it.

For example, when Jin was on *106 and Park* almost all of his opponents were African American and many of them tried to attack him by ridiculing his racial difference. Examples of their race-baiting rhymes include: "I'm a star / you're just a rookie / leave rap alone / and go back to making fortune cookies" (week 2 versus Sterling);[78] "C'mon man / you ain't tough as me / what you wanna do? / battle me / or sell me dollar batteries" (week 3 versus Skitzoe);[79] and "Who you supposed to be? / Bruce Lee with your pants all sagging / I'll murder you dog / there'll be no return of the dragon" (week 7 versus Sean Nicholas)."[80] Whenever he was baited—and sometimes when he was not—Jin would often flip the race card back on his opponents by embracing his racial difference and then using it to ridicule his rivals. For example, against Sterling, he responded, "You want to say I'm Chinese / son, here's a reminder / check your Timberlands / they probably say 'made in China.' "[81] Against Sean Nicholas, Jin pursued a similar strategy, rhyming "My pants are new / my sweater is new / don't be mad a Chinese kid / dress better than you."[82] Especially in the latter example, Jin drew attention to his perceived outsider status by ridiculing Nicholas for having worse clothes than "a Chinese kid," as if this was something to be doubly ashamed of.

However, when it came time for Jin to release his album, he willingly racialized himself without being prompted. The first single from *The Rest Is History*, "Learn Chinese," opens with a simple statement by Jin: "Yeah, I'm Chinese ... and what?"[83] This was both an affirmation and a challenge. Jin recognized that his audience could not ignore his racial difference, and he was effectively daring potential critics to make an issue of it.

Although Jin prodded listeners to confront the specter of race, the topic was addressed on his terms. He issued a critique against stereotypes in the song, rapping, "This ain't Bruce Lee / ya'll watch too much TV," and proclaimed at the beginning that "The days of the pork fried rice coming to your door are over," symbolically "killing" the archetype of the Chinese delivery boy in favor of a hypermasculine Chinatown gangsta.[84] It must be said that while Jin problematized some stereotypes, he left others in his wake. For example, both the video imagery and the song lyrics for "Learn Chinese" portrayed Chinatown as a dangerous, violent neighborhood—an ironic gesture given how long Chinatown residents have tried to rid themselves of that stigma. In this respect, Jin failed to create an alternative to the problematic constructions of black masculinity; he was merely changing the face of it.

Elsewhere Jin displayed a keener awareness of race. In an early song that did not end up on his album, "I Don't Know," he responded to critics who compared him to the white rapper Eminem.

> I'm no Eminem / but I'm not wack either /
> The only reason you compare me to him /
> Is because I'm not black either[85]

These lines demonstrated how Jin was intimately aware of how race played into perceptions of him. He responded to accusations that he was attempting to ape Eminem's success and countered that the only reason people compared the two artists was because neither was African American and therefore both disrupted racial expectations. However, despite his claims otherwise, Jin and Eminem did share a similarity—both played *up* their racial difference as a way to disarm potential critics. On a song from his 2002 album, *The Eminem Show*, the rapper featured a song, "White America," that included the following lines.

> Look at these eyes
> baby blue, baby just like yourself
> If they were brown Shady lose
> Shady sits on the shelf[86]

By drawing attention to it and acknowledging that his race had helped him gain wider appeal, Eminem not only robbed his attackers of their main line of critique; he also earned broad acclaim in many critical circles. Eminem has been seen as more authentic because of his willingness to wear his race on his sleeve, so to speak. Compare this to the example of Vanilla Ice, the multi-platinum white rapper of the early 1990s who claimed to have grown up in the inner city when he was really from the middle-class suburbs. Vanilla Ice was rejected as inauthentic, not because he was white but because he lied about his background. In being up front about his whiteness, Eminem has been seen as more "real" by his audience.

Jin followed a similar strategy by tackling his racial difference head on. In doing so, he attempted to get his potential audience to look past his race and focus on his talent. It was a slightly more sophisticated version of a schoolyard taunt; "Yeah, I'm Asian. ... You want to fight about it?" Jin and Eminem prodded listeners to confront the specter of race, forcing skeptics to confront their own biases. The main difference was that Eminem, in "White America," could afford to rub critics' noses in his record-breaking album sales. It has cost him nothing to admit that his whiteness is a selling point, and he displays that awareness in the song's unmistakably mocking tone. Jin, on the other hand, could not use his ethnicity as a marketing tool, but his explicit discussion of race demonstrated a willingness to talk about the issue openly, gambling that audiences would respect him for that frankness.

Jin pursued this strategy in different ways on *The Rest Is History*. For "Love Song," he penned a narrative about a teenage interracial couple—a "Chinese dude" and his black girlfriend—and detailed the challenges they face.

> They found true love, living in a fantasy.
> Then reality attacks, his pops couldn't see past the fact
> His son was asian, but his girlfriend was black.
> Imagine having to choose between the one that you love or your fam[ily],
> That's like cutting off your right or left hand, damn.[87]

At the end of the song, Jin revealed that the "Chinese dude," was himself a few years back. "Love Story" was designed to appeal to people across racial lines, addressing the illogic of anti-miscegenation paranoia and prejudices. Jin deliberately drew attention to race again, strategically pushing his listeners to understand that people of different heritages can suffer the same forms of discrimination. Making this point within a personal story from his romantic past helped to humanize the issue further by creating a sympathetic set of star-crossed lovers with whom listeners could identify.

Elsewhere on *The Rest Is History*, Jin deployed a similar tactic of cross-racial identification in the song "Same Cry."

> Stuck between the rock and a hard place,
> Thinking about the refugees that went to see God's face.
> Sixteen thousand miles across the ocean tides,
> Some died, some got lucky and survived.

I wouldn't call it luck—they reached the destination;
Modern day slavery without the plantation.
Them sneakers on your feet cost a hundred a pop,
He's making fifty cent a day working in sweat shops.[88]

This was Jin's most politicized attempt to forge cross-cultural recognition between Asian and African Americans, appealing to a shared sense of struggle and oppression. Although comparing sweatshop labor with plantation slavery was a stretch, Jin suggested that Asian immigrants endured exploitation and suffering just as African Americans did. The chorus of the song repeats that same idea.

We may look different,
But we see the same sky.
We may see different,
But we cry the same cry.

The emphasis on *cry* proposed that both Asian and African Americans have endured their share of suffering and this mutual experience can lead the two communities to overcome their differences. Compared to "Learn Chinese," this is a different way of accentuating race as a way of defusing it. With "Same Cry," Jin drew attention to racial difference—we look different, we see different—but his point was that both communities suffered from similar histories and challenges, which ideally would help form points of commonality and coalition. In a sense, Jin brought Asian American hip hop full circle but with a twist. Like Fists of Fury, he discussed Asian American social issues—including sweatshop labor, refugee experiences, and oppressive conditions in Asia—but rather than broadcasting these issues just to Asian American audiences he sought to educate and entertain a broad, implicitly multiracial audience. Drawing attention to his racial difference was a way to push his listeners to look past it and instead find points of commonality.

Jin's emergence came at a time when there were other visible Asian American artists within hip hop, including the Neptunes' Chad Hugo (Filipino), Linkin Park's Mike Shinoda (Japanese), and the Black Eyed Peas' Allan Pineda, also known as Apl.de.ap (Filipino). Nonetheless, Jin recognized that he still had to convince people of his talents. In his own words, "I think all it comes down to is the quality of the music. ... I'm not going to say that the race thing isn't a big issue, but when the music comes out, if it's good music, it will be good, if it's bad, it will be bad."[89] This echoes similar comments by the Mountain Brothers and other rappers, positing that ultimately they believe that talent speaks the loudest. However, until an Asian American rapper enjoys the kind of mainstream success and sales that other rappers have attained, the importance of race versus talent will remain an open question.

As an epilogue, in May of 2005, Jin announced his "retirement," though his reasons for doing so were unclear.[90] He dispelled the notion that it was due to poor album sales—*The Rest Is History* sold a modest hundred thousand units—but failed to articulate a specific motivation for leaving his rap career behind. Jin's announcement was surprising for numerous reasons, not the least of which is that it is unusual for a young rapper to announce his or her retirement (most simply disappear from the charts quietly). Moreover, considering how much press Jin had enjoyed just half a year earlier, to see that kind of media bubble burst so quickly and suddenly surely took many observers by surprise.

Jin's retirement also means that as of the completion of this essay there once again is no Asian American rapper signed to a major label contract. As seen with Jin's meteoric rise (and fall), such circumstances can change suddenly, but the experience also shows how tenuous a hold Asian American rappers have within the music industry.

Leaders of the New School: Conclusions

Despite the diversifying audience that hip hop enjoys, race continues to play a central role in people's expectations of the music and culture. Although some hip hop audiences have historically been more accepting of rappers of all backgrounds, in the more commercial, mainstream world, racial authenticity is still an entrenched part of audience expectations. In reviewing the different strategies and identity politics that Asian American rappers have engaged in over the last fifteen years, I have demonstrated the ways in which Asian Americans tried to position themselves and their racial difference vis-à-vis hip hop audiences.

What emerges, however, is not just the different ways in which Asian American rappers perceive themselves in relation to hip hop but also their very perceptions of hip hop to begin with. Rappers from the early 1990s, influenced by the example of Public Enemy and other politicized artists, sought to make their race and ethnicity explicit as a means of inspiring their peers to listen and take notice. For them, hip hop was a mouthpiece for political awareness and education. Rappers from the mid-1990s such as the Mountain Brothers and Key Kool saw hip hop as an artistic outlet for personal expression that could include, but did not have to be beholden to, issues of race or ethnicity. They sought to connect with like-minded audiences that similarly believed in an identity centered around hip hop itself as a culture and art. New rappers such as Jin may think of hip hop as a culture worth their allegiance, but they are also savvy in recognizing the business realities that come with public performance.

The remaining question is whether or not Asian American rappers will face a more welcoming situation within the recording industry over the next few years. The conventional wisdom is that one Asian American rap superstar would help convince record labels to consider signing other Asian American acts. However, the success of the white rapper Eminem suggests another, less optimistic scenario. The overwhelming popularity that Eminem has enjoyed could be interpreted as a sign that racial authenticity no longer matters. However, while Eminem has been legitimated by hip hop's multiracial audience, his success has not represented—as of yet—a fundamental shift in the acceptance of white rappers writ large. It is telling that the white rappers who emerged after Eminem's rise, such as Haystack and Bubba Sparxxx, were inevitably compared to Eminem even when their styles and content had little in common with his. Despite Eminem's success, white rappers are still treated as a novelty within hip hop, suggesting that Eminem, far from breaking down racial barriers in hip hop, has instead been fixed into a niche as "*the* white rapper" against which all future aspirants will be judged, at least for the time being. In this sense, he is a privileged token, benefiting from his status as the lone white rapper able to garner support from the hip hop community but a token nonetheless given the paucity of other white rappers. Likewise, even if Jin's career had taken off, this would not necessarily have been an indication that rap audiences are willing to support other mainstream Asian American artists. I would argue that until the current authenticity paradigm moves away from its sole association with blackness nonblack artists are likely to face considerable challenges in finding mainstream support.

Moreover, it is not at all clear that such a paradigm shift is desirable, especially if it means that hip hop will be detached from Afro-diasporic traditions or the black community. As I have argued, the exclusion of nonblack rappers is less the product of conscious design and more an expected outcome given the deep ties that continue to connect hip hop with the black community. There is certainly a danger that the relationship will become overly essentialized, but the alternative risks treating cultural forms as strictly commodities with no sense of history or how culture moves within flows of power. As George Lipsitz warns, treating cultural forms as "infinitely open does violence to the historical and social constraints imposed on us by structures of exploitation and privilege."[91]

However, regardless of the current state of hip hop's racial authenticity paradigm, there is every indication that it will continue to play a major role in the cultural lives of Asian Americans.

For the past twenty years, hip hop has been a dominant cultural and musical force for Asian American youth. Even in other areas of Asian American cultural expression, from car racing to spoken-word poetry and filmmaking, the aesthetics of hip hop have become a common influence and theme. It also needs to be reiterated that, although the profession of rapping is still dominated by this racial authenticity, in most other sectors of the hip hop community Asian Americans are prevalent, even dominant, as in the case of Filipino American DJs.[92] The marginality that Asian American rappers contend with is largely the exception rather than the rule in terms of how Asian Americans have taken to hip hop and been accepted by like-minded peers.

As noted earlier, hip hop has its own power as a locus of cultural identity, one that may not trump ethnic or racial allegiances but at least provides an alternative. For generations of youths coming of age in America, and truly around the world, hip hop has become a powerful source of identity and culture. In hip hop's social matrix, race and ethnicity will not disappear permanently, but their enduring primacy may yet wane with the ever-diversifying audience the music attracts, compels, and inspires.

This is not to suggest that race has faded in importance within American society; there are myriad examples of how it continues to enforce abhorrent social divisions. However, it is worth noting how hip hop's massive, multiethnic popularity, which began in the 1980s, parallels the development of the rhetoric of multiculturalism in American society. Caution needs to be displayed here, for liberal multiculturalism has been rightly criticized for deflecting attention away from the damage done by continuing institutional racism.[93] However, as examples of two powerful social movements of the post-civil rights era, hip hop and multiculturalism have become entwined to the extent that there is a rhetoric of inclusion within hip hop—expounded through lyrics and personal testimonials—that embraces diversity as a key force within the culture. This in turn has impacted society at large as hip hop has saturated a mass media network with a global reach. Newcomers to hip hop are continually being inundated with the ideology of inclusion, no doubt partially espoused by the very beneficiaries of such a politics (i.e., nonblacks wishing to challenge black-oriented racial authenticity). Likewise, commercially savvy artists have no reason to refute this embrace of diversity since it aids their attempts to reach larger audiences.

The collision of all these forces has helped to make hip hop a leading, if not *the* leading, cultural force in American society today, one that pushes a politics of inclusion against the traditional divisions created by racial and ethnic difference. Hip hop is far from a utopia of course, with many divisive ideologies still rampant, especially around issues of gender. As well, it must be said that championing diversity has many economic benefits that have nothing to do with social altruism—such as building larger audiences. However, the experience of Asian American rappers over the last decade suggests that the currents of culture, race, and politics are never stagnant. Asian American rappers may not have reached a point where their racial difference is no longer a liability (let alone an asset), but their ongoing attempts to negotiate these issues reveal the continual transformations that hip hop itself undergoes. In the midst of those changes, the presence and perseverance of Asian American rappers can influence the directions in which hip hop will move, hinting at (though not promising) a more viable space of acceptance and success for themselves and their peers.

Study Questions

1. In what ways do Asian Americans share or not share the same experience of other performers within hip-hop?
2. How does the diversity that exists within the Asian American experience complicate the notion of a pan-Asian identity within hip-hop?
3. What is the relationship between talent, marketability and racial identity?

Notes

1. Heller, "Streetology."
2. Chung, "Hip Hop Asian America." The main difference is that rappers are the most visible of hip hop's various actors within the mass media. As will be explored shortly, racial characteristics are an instant signifier of authenticity for rappers. Other, less visible artists such as DJs and graffiti writers do not have to contend with this.
3. "Major labels" refers to the five multinational corporations that control the bulk of the record industry in the United States. Labels not affiliated with the majors are known as "independents."
4. Smith, "Ain't a Damn Thing Changed," 125–28.
5. McLeod, "Authenticity within Hip Hop and Other Cultures Threatened with Assimilation."
6. One of the most famous cases was that of the white rapper Vanilla Ice, who was found to have invented his hard-luck childhood in an effort to seem more credible "in the streets." Despite having one of the best-selling debut rap albums of all time, Vanilla Ice's authenticity problems plagued him and, along with other factors, led to a second album that sold dismally, after which the artist quickly faded from public view.
7. Perry, *Prophets of the Hood*, 10.
8. Ibid. Perry bases this claim on four primary characteristics of hip hop, including its use of African American vernacular, its origins in African American oral and musical cultures, and its political location within black society and traditions.
9. Rose, *Black Noise*; Forman, *The 'Hood Comes First*; Rivera, *New York Ricans from the Hip Hop Zone*.
10. Mitchell, *Global Noise*.
11. In using the term *myth*, I am not contesting the veracity of hip hop's origin narratives. I only mean to suggest that the story of hip hop's roots has been told and retold so many times—in songs, magazines, books, and so on—that its narrative wields a power analogous to mythology.
12. For an argument that favors erasure, see Flores, *From Bomba to Hip Hop*.
13. Kelly, "Hip Hop Chicano"; Del Barco, "Rap's Latino Sabor," 63–84; Flores, "Puerto Rocks," 85–116; Flores, *From Bomba to Hip Hop*; Rivera, *New York Ricans from the Hip Hop Zone*.
14. Mitchell, *Global Noise*.
15. It should be noted that most of these attempts to diversify hip hop's scope in academic discourse continue to marginalize Asian Americans. In Tony Mitchell's critique of American centrism in hip hop scholarship, he reviews works written on Latino and Native American rappers but ignores any mention of Asian Americans, instead jumping directly to rappers in Asia (ibid., 5). Likewise, William Eric Perkins is one of the only scholars to acknowledge the presence of Asian Americans in hip hop, but his anecdotal review of Bay Area hip hop is rife with errors that suggest a lack of research. For example, Perkins claims that Lani Luv was "the first Asian American female rapper" to begin rhyming in the Philippines, neither of which is correct. He also misspells DJ (disc jockey) Q-Bert as D-Bert and erroneously claims that he is Filipino-Hawaiian. See Perkins, "Youth's Global Village," 262.
16. I distinguish mainstream rap consumers as part of a more general public versus the so-called underground, which is a smaller, subcultural community. As will be explored later, underground audiences tend to be more open-minded with regard to their racial preferences in artists, and as a result many nonblack artists have found a welcome in the underground, Asian Americans included.
17. Smith, "Ain't a Damn Thing Changed," 126.
18. The success of the white rapper Eminem remains a complicated exception, and his impact on hip hop's racial politics will be briefly discussed in the conclusion.
19. One key element that I am leaving out of this analysis is the *music* of these artists. Other Asian American hip hop artists have used music as a form of signification, most notably South Asians and the Indian *bhangra* remix culture in New York and elsewhere (Maira, "Desis Reprazent"; "Identity Dub: The Paradoxes of an Indian American Subculture"; *Desis in the House*). There is also the example of Jamez, a Korean American rapper from New York who in the late 1990s incorporated traditional Korean musical aesthetics into his beats (Ling, "Jamez Chang"). For the artists I cover from this same period, however, music was not the primary location of any kind of ethnic or racial signification, even among those who explicitly rapped about identity politics in their rhymes. Those artists, wanting to firmly establish and identify themselves as Asian *Americans*, would have derived little benefit from music that incorporates traditional Asian elements since they would have ran the risk of painting themselves as alien or foreign. Therefore, their music tended to fall in line with dominant hip hop aesthetics in the 1990s that favored 1970s American soul and jazz influences. Ironically, by the early 2000s mainstream producers such as Timbaland and Dr. Dre were drawing inspiration" from Asian musical sources, most notably Indian movie soundtracks.

20. Rivera, *New York Ricans from the Hip Hop Zone*, 8. The title of this section, "The Afrocentric Asian," is taken from a song by the rap artist Nas, who on his 1994 single "It Ain't Hard Tell" rhymed, "Nas is like the Afrocentric Asian / Half Man/ Half Amazin." Nas's self-description of himself as Asian led some to erroneously report that he was actually half Asian, half African American, which is untrue. His use of the term *Asian* is equivalent to *Asiatic*, which is explained in note 32.
21. Ibid., 9.
22. Ibid., 187.
23. Ibid., 94.
24. Ibid., 96.
25. Espiritu, *Asian American Panethnicity.*
26. Hall, "New Ethnicities," 441–49.
27. Okihiro, *Margins and Mainstreams*, 33.
28. Aaron, "What the White Boy Means When He Says Yo"; Wimsatt, "We Use Words Like Mackadodious," 22–41.
29. Koshy, "Morphing Race into Ethnicity"; Chang, "Race, Class, Conflict, and Empowerment"; Zia, "To Market, to Market, New York Style"; Prashad, *Everybody Was Kung Fu Fighting.*
30. Mercer, "Black Masculinity and the Sexual Politics of Race"; Espiritu, *Asian American Women and Men*, 86–107. (Thanks to Shannon Steen for reminding me of this dichotomy).
31. Han, "Asian American Nation."
32. The use of the term *Asiatic* by Asian American rappers represents the term's unusual journey through hip hop culture. Traditionally, *Asiatic* has been deployed by African American artists (e.g., Big Daddy Kane's surname stands for "King Asiatic, Nobody's Equal") as a derivation drawn from the teachings of the Nation of Islam, an American offshoot of Islam. In Nation of Islam ideology, African Americans are referred to as Asiatic because their roots can be traced back to a mythical "black nation of Asia," the Tribe of Shabazz, which was the cradle of human civilization. Thus, calling oneself Asiatic, for African Americans, was a marker of pride for being descended from the original rulers of humanity. See Nathaniel Deutsch," "The Asiatic Black Man': An African American Orientalism?" Asian American rappers are not co-opting the term *Asiatic* so much as returning the term to its original scope, which was always meant to include people of "traditional" Asian descent such as Chinese, Japanese, and South Asians.
33. Han, "Asian American Nation"; Daphnie Anies, interview with the author, February 20, 2003; Eduardo Restauro, interview with the author, March 3, 2002. While there were Asian Americans rapping at the time, what is notable is that no official *recordings* were left behind by these artists. I am not privileging records over live performances, but it does reflect the extent to which Asian Americans did not exist within the urban music industry throughout the 1980s.
34. Han, "Asian American Nation."
35. Davis Yee, interview with the author, February 22, 1999.
36. The Seoul Brothers, Michael and Raphael Park, figure prominently in Renee Tajima-Peña's 1996 documentary, *My America ... or Honk if You Love Buddha.*
37. Rose, *Black Noise*. While many of Public Enemy's songs attracted the attention of conservative critics, it was accusations of anti-Semitism leveled against a side member of the group, Professor Griff, that gave it the most negative publicity.
38. Public Enemy's influence was felt throughout the larger hip hop community. In an article on Latino rappers, Mandalit Del Barco quotes respondents who admitted that Public Enemy had inspired them too ("Rap's Latino Sabor," 77).
39. Tseng, "Asian American Rap."
40. Fists of Fury, press material, 1993.
41. The reference to the "man from the caves" is an allusion to the teachings of the Nation of Islam, which holds that white Europeans were uncivilized, savage, and lived in caves until Moses came to liberate them from their ignorance. The idea of whites as cave dwellers appears elsewhere in hip hop, most notably in a song by the Los Angeles rapper Ice Cube, "Cave Bitch" (1993), a critique of white women. Pement, "Louis Farrakhan and the Nation of Islam," 32–36, 38.
42. Fists of Fury, "After School," unreleased demo, 1993.
43. Brand, "The New Whiz Kids," *Time*, August 31, 1987.
44. Wong, "Asian for the Man!"
45. Yellow Peril, "Asian for the Man," song from an unreleased demo, 1995.
46. Wong, "Asian for the Man!"; Wong, "The Invisible Man Syndrome"; Wong, "We Define Ourselves!"; Tseng, "Asian American Rap."
47. Darow Han, telephone interview with the author, San Francisco, 1992.

48. While none of these groups survived, individual members have gone on to pursue musical careers. Han-na Che, now Hana Choi, is an aspiring singer. Bert Wang now leads a rock-rap group called SuperChink in New York. Art Hirahara is a recorded jazz pianist now living in New York.

49. Yee, interview.

50. Tseng, "Asian American Rap."

51. Fists of Fury, press material.

52. Yee, interview.

53. Bertrand Wong, interview with the author, February 17, 1999.

54. Besides politically inspired artists, in the early 1990s there were other Asian American rappers, including Miami's Fresh Kid Ice (a Chinese Trinidadian), a member of a Live Crew, who recorded a solo album in 1992 entitled *The Chinaman*. There was also the Bay Area's Japanese American rapper, Rhythm X, also known as "the mental Oriental," who released his *Long Over Due* album in 1994. While both Ice and X drew attention to their ethnicity through titling (*The Chinaman*) and naming (the mental Oriental), none of their songs exhibited the same kind of political or issue-oriented fervor that groups such as Yellow Peril and the Asiatic Apostles invested in their music. Nor do they comfortably fit into the generation of artists I am about to discuss. Nonetheless, their presence is noteworthy.

55. When individuals are being interviewed or quoted from interviews, they are identified by their legal names. When rappers are being quoted from lyrics, their artist names will be used.

56. Mountain Brothers, "Invisible Man," song from an unreleased demo tape, 1996.

57. Eric B. and Rakim, "I Know You Got Soul," on *Paid In Full*, compact disc, 4th and Broadway, 1987.

58. Chris (Peril-L) Wang, interview with the author, December 5, 1996.

59. Scott (Chops) Jung, interview with the author, December 5, 1996.

60. Wong, "The Invisible Man Syndrome."

61. It is worth noting that Nishi included a song on *Kozmonautz* entitled "Reconcentrated" that both castigates the internment of his Japanese American grandfather during World War II and links it to current anti-Asian sentiment.

62. Jung, interview.

63. Ibid. Ironically, the group had to contend with racial stereotypes emanating not from audience members but from the recording industry. Jung recalls an occasion when a record executive approached the group about appearing onstage wearing Buddhist monks' robes, chanting, and hitting gongs.

64. The main exception to this was by so-called "AZN" rappers who began to emerge in the late 1990s. While more research is needed to fully flush out the cultural moment in which Asian American youths begin to identify themselves as AZN on Internet sites and in forums, this corruption in spelling bears similarities to other forms of linguistic alteration involved in black vernacular English, also commonly referred to as Ebonics. One particular musical product that emerged from these youths was rap songs with Asian themes using popular, preexisting instrumentals. For example, one widely circulated song, "Got Rice Bitch?" performed by a rapper only identified as AZN (and sometimes AZN Pride), features rhymes covering everything from Asian American import car culture to ethnic food but is set to the instrumental from Tupac's "Changes." Many of these songs feature groups with such names as the Khmer Boys, the Chink Boys, and Slant Eyed Descendents boasting about ethnic pride (i.e., Filipino pride, Vietnamese pride, Korean pride, etc.). In some ways, they bear similarities to the Asian American rappers of the early 1990s insofar as their raps are for, by, and about Asian Americans, but the various AZN rap songs lack the political context and intent that motivated such groups as the Asiatic Apostles and Fists of Fury. It is also important to note that these various AZN rap songs exist solely on the Internet rather than on CDs or cassettes. Such particular distribution suggests that these artists are community focused rather than aspiring to larger popularity in the music market.

65. Yokota, "Key Kool."

66. Lhamon, *Raising Cain*.

67. Futuredood, "Interview with Southstar," September 2, 2002, http://www.aznraps.com/public_site/artist/interviews/southstar_only/south_only.htm.

68. Even more complicated is the fact that, as someone of mixed ethnic heritage, Southstar is racially ambiguous. In the course of my research, I discovered comments that described him as "Caucasian"; others were not sure if he was of African American or Latino heritage. The point is that Southstar is able to "pass" in complex ways that have the potential to help (if he is read as black or Latino) or hinder him (if he is read as white or Asian). For example, besides the interview already noted, very few interviewers have asked Southstar or his partner, Smilez. About how audiences receive this pairing between an African American and a Chinese Filipino American. It is possible that because Smilez is black, audiences and critics do not perceive the duo as racially different in the same way as the Chinese American Mountain Brothers. In other words, because of their partnership Southstar attains another kind of "passing" privilege. This is similar to Taboo, a Filipino American member of the rap group Black

Eyed Peas. Because the other two members of the group are African American, the Black Eyed Peas rarely gets the same kind of questions about its ethnic makeup as would an all Asian American group or Asian American solo artist.

69. Yokota, "Key Kool."
70. Dan Emmiere, "Pacifics Interview 2001."
71. It is important to note that by the mid-1990s overtly *politicized* overtures to black identity had fallen out of favor with most fans and the recording industry. While blackness is still a vital part of contemporary hip hop discourse, it is now a blackness dominated by masculine ideals such as sexual prowess, criminal acumen, and violent temperaments rather than political affirmations of blackness that hark back to the 1970s Black Power movement. Regardless of what value judgments one makes over this change in attitude, it is worth noting that far from being a unitary, fixed ideal, blackness takes myriad forms.
72. Mountain Brothers, "Days of Being Dumb," on *Self Volume* 1, compact disc, Pimpstrut, 1998.
73. Mountain Brothers, "Galaxies," music video, dir. Richard Kim and Chris Chan Lee, 1999.
74. *Elephant Tracks*, compact disc, compilation by Asian Improv Records, 1999.
75. Fusco, *English Is Broken Here*, 32.
76. Parker, "Golden Child."
77. Coates, "Just Another Quick-Witted, Egg-Roll-Joke-Making, Insult-Hurling Chinese-American Rapper," 55; Kevin Kim, "Repping Chinatown."
78. Jin, 105 *and Park*, BET, week 2, 2002, http://www.holla-front.com/media.html (accessed August 2003).
79. Jin, 106 *and Park*, BET, week 3, 2002, http://www.holla-front.com/media.html (accessed August 2003).
80. Jin, 106 *and Park*, BET, week 7, 2002, http://www.holla front.com/media.html (accessed August 2003).
81. Jin, 106 *and Park*, BET, week 2, 2002, http://www.holla-front.com/media.html (accessed August 2003).
82. Jin, 106 *and Park*, BET, week 7, 2002, http://www.holla-front.com/media.html (accessed August 2003).
83. Jin, "Learn Chinese." On *The Rest Is History*, compact disc, Ruff Ryders, 2004.
84. Ironically, Jin was involved in a well-publicized Chinatown shout out with Chinese gangs in 2003. Christina Tam, "Jin and Juice."
85. Jin, "I Don't Know." (2003), http://www.ighetto.com/daveslyrics/JinThaMC/ IDont Know.html (accessed August 2002).
86. Eminem, "White America," on *The Eminem Show*, compact disc, Aftermath/Interscope, 2002.
87. Jin, "Love Story." On *The Rest Is History*, compact disc, Ruff Ryders, 2004.
88. Jin, "Same Cry." On *The Rest Is History*, compact disc, Ruff Ryders, 2004.
89. Jin, interview with the author, May 2002.
90. Strong, "Jin Says Rap Career Is Over, Records 'I Quit.'"
91. Lipsitz, *Dangerous Crossroads*, 62.
92. *Beats, Rhymes, Resistance: Pilipinos and Hip Hop in LA.*, video, Lakandiwa DeLeon, Dawn Mabalon, and Jonathan Ramos (USA, 1997, revised 1999).
93. Lowe, *Immigrant Acts*, 84–96.

References

Brand, David. "The New Whiz Kids: Why Asian Americans Are Doing So Well and What It Costs Them." *Time*, August 31, 1987.

Chung, Brian. "Hip Hop Asian America." *Evil Monito* 2, no II (summer 2002). http://www.evilmonito.com/011/hiphopasiaamerica/hiphopasia.htm (accessed October 4, 2006).

Coates, Ta-Nehisi. "Just Another Quick-Witted, Egg-Roll-Joke-Making, Insult-Hurling Chinese-American Rapper." *New York Times Magazine*, November 21, 2004.

Del Barco, Mandalit. "Rap's Latino Sabor." In *Droppin' Science: Critical Essays on Rap Music and Hip Hop Culture*, ed. William Eric Perkins. Philadelphia: Temple University Press, 1996. 63–84.

Deutsch, Nathaniel. " 'The Asiatic Black Man': An African American Orientalism?" *Journal of Asian American Studies* 4, no. 3 (October 2001): 193–208.

Emmiere, Dan. "Pacifics Interview 2001." *Asiatic Theory Online*, 2001. http://www.csu pomona.edu/dehad-inata/asiatic/music_pacifics.htm (accessed December 8, 2001).

Espiritu, Yen Le. *Asian American Panethnicity: Bridging Institutions and Identities*. Philadelphia: Temple University Press, 1992.

Flores, Juan. *From Bomba to Hip Hop*. New York: Columbia University Press, 2000.

Forman, Murray. *The 'Hood Comes First: Race, Space, and Place in Rap and Hip Hop*. Middletown, Conn.: Wesleyan University Press, 2002.

Fusco, Coco. "At Your Service: Latina Women in the Global Information Network." In *The Bodies That Were*

Not Ours and Other Writings. London and New York: Routledge with the Institute of International Visual Arts, 2001. 186–201.

———. *English Is Broken Here: Notes on Cultural Fusion in the Americas.* New York: New Press, 1995.

Hall, Stuart. "The Local and the Global: Globalization and Ethnicity." In *Dangerous Liaisons: Gender, Nation, and Postcolonial Perspectives,* ed. Anne McClintock, Aamir Mufti, and Ella Shohat. Minneapolis: University of Minnesota Press, 1997. 173–87.

———. "New Ethnicities." In *Stuart Hall: Dialogues in Cultural Studies,* ed. David Morley and Kuan-Hsing Chen. New York: Routledge, 1996. 441–49.

Han, Darow. "Asian American Nation." *SF Weekly,* June 24, 1992.

Heller, Skip. "Streetology: Joe Bataan's Rap on Latin Soul." *LA Weekly,* December 17, 1999.

Kelly, Raegan. "Hip Hop Chicano." In *It's Not about a Salary: Rap, Race, and Resistance in Los Angeles,* ed. Brian Cross. New York: Verso, 1993. 65–76.

Kim, Kevin. "Repping Chinatown." *Colorlines* 7, no. 4. (winter 2004–2005). http://www.colorlines.com/article.php?ID=48 (accessed October 4, 2006).

Koshy, Susan. "Morphing Race into Ethnicity: Asian American and Critical Transformations of Whiteness." *boundary 2* 28, no. 1. (2001): 153–94.

Lhamon, W. T. *Raising Cain: Blackface Performance from Jim Crow to Hip Hop.* Cambridge, Mass.: Harvard University Press, 1998.

Ling, Amy. "Jamez Chang." In *Yellow Light: The Flowering of Asian American Arts,* ed. Amy Ling. Philadelphia: Temple University Press, 1999. 355–61.

Lipsitz, George. *Dangerous Crossroads: Popular Music, Postmodernism, and the Poetics of Place.* New York: Verso, 1994.

Lowe, Lisa. "Epistemological Shifts: National Ontology and the New Asian Immigrant." In *Orientations: Mapping Studies in the Asian Diaspora,* ed. Kandice Chub and Karen Shimakawa. Duke University Press, 2001. 267–76.

———. *Immigrant Acts: On Asian American Cultural Productions.* Durham, N.C.: Duke University Press, 1996.

Maira; Sunaina. *Desis in the House: Indian American Youth Culture in New York City.* Philadelphia: Temple University Press, 2002.

———. "Desis Reprazent: Bhangra Remix and Hip Hop in New York City." *Postcolonial Studies* 1, no. 3 (1998): 357–70.

———. "Identity Dub: The Paradoxes of an Indian American Subculture." *Cultural Anthropology* 14, no. 1 (1999): 29–60.

McLeod, Kembrew. "Authenticity within Hip Hop and Other Cultures Threatened with Assimilation." *Journal of Communication* 49, no. 4 (autumn 1999): 134–50.

Mercer, Kobena. "Black Hair/Style Politics." In *Out There: Marginalization and Contemporary Cultures,* ed. Russell Ferguson, Martha Gever, Trinh T. Minh-Ha, and Cornell West. Cambridge, Mass.: MIT Press, 1990. 247–64.

———. "Black Masculinity and the Sexual Politics of Race." In *Welcome to the Jungle: New Positions in Black Cultural Studies.* New York and London: Routledge, 1994. 131–70.

Mitchell, Tony, ed. *Global Noise: Rap and Hip-hop Outside the USA.* Middletown, Conn.: Wesleyan University Press, 2002.

Okihiro, Gary. *Margins and Mainstreams: Asians in American History and Culture.* Seattle: University of Washington Press, 1994.

Parker, Eric. "Golden Child." *XXL,* September 2002, 158–62.

Perkins, William Eric. "Youth's Global Village: An Epilogue." In *Droppin' Science: Critical Essays in Rap and Hip Hop Culture,* ed. William Eric Perkins. Philadelphia: Temple University Press, 1995. 258–71.

Perry, Imani. *Prophets of the Hood: Politics and Poetics in Hip Hop.* Durham, N.C.: Duke University Press, 2004.

Prashad, Vijay. *Everybody Was Kung Fu Fighting: Afro-Asian Connections and the Myth of Cultural Purity.* New York: Beacon, 2001.

Rivera, Raquel Z. *New York Ricans from the Hip Hop Zone.* New York: Palgrave Macmillan, 2003.

Rose, Tricia. *Black Noise: Rap Music and Black Culture in Contemporary America.* Hanover, N.H.: University Press of New England, 1994.

Smith, Danyel "Ain't a Damn Thing Changed: Why Women Rappers Don't Sell." In *Rap on Rap: Straight-Up Talk on Hip Hop Culture,* ed. Adam Sexton, New York: Delta Trade, 1995. 125–28.

Strong, Nolan. "Jin Says Rap Career Is Over, Records 'I Quit.'" *Allhiphop.com,* http://www.allhiphop.com/hiphopnews/?ID=4412 (accessed May 20, 2005).

Tam, Christina. "Jin and Juice." *New York Post,* October 17, 2004.

Tseng, Judy. "Asian American Rap: Expression through Alternate Forms." Unpublished paper, Georgetown University Law Center, Washington, D.C., 1998.

Wimsatt, William Upski. "We Use Words Like Mackadocious." In *Bomb the Suburbs.* New York: Soft Skull Press, 1994. 22–41.

Wong, Sau-ling Cynthia. " 'Asian for the Man!' Stereotypes, Identity, and Self-Empowerment in Asian American Rap." Unpublished paper, 1996.

———. "The Invisible Man Syndrome: Politics of Representation in Asian American Rap." Unpublished paper, 1996.

———." 'We Define Ourselves!': The Negotiation of Power and Identity for Asian Americans in Hip Hop." Unpublished paper, 1996.

Zia, Helen. *Asian American Dreams: The Emergence of an American People.* New York: Farrar, Straus, and Giroux, 2000.

———. "To Market, To Market, New York Style." In *Asian American Dreams: The Emergence of an American People.* New York: Farrar, Straus, and Giroux, 2001. 82–108.

Part III

"Ain't No Love in the Heart of the City"
Hip-Hop, Space, and Place

Murray Forman

Themes of space and place are profoundly important in hip-hop. Virtually all of the early descriptions of hip-hop practices identify territory and the public sphere as significant factors, whether in the visible artistic expression and appropriation of public space via graffiti or B-boying, the sonic impact of a pounding bass line, or the discursive articulation of urban geography in rap lyrics. The dominant narrative of hip-hop's growth and development has traditionally described the formative stages in the streets, parks, community centers, and nightclubs of the Bronx and Harlem, documenting a gradual spread across New York's boroughs and throughout the northeast until it had penetrated virtually all regions and urban centers in the U.S. (Toop, 1984; Hebdige, 1987; Fernando, 1994; Ogg and Upshal, 1999). Most accounts tend to detail the localized struggles against adversity within urban ghetto environments as young black and Latino youths confronted authority and repression in their various forms. Through these narratives, a particular image of hip-hop has been constructed, one that binds locale, resistance, innovation, affirmation, and cultural identity within a complex web of spatialized meanings and practices.

Space and place are important factors influencing identity formation as it relates to localized practices of the self. For instance, graffiti has traditionally displayed spatial inflections, and the early tag "TAKI 183" that proliferated in New York in the early 1970s overtly emphasized locality, celebrating 183 Street as the young writer's home turf and amplifying him and his territory throughout the city. As the ink marker tags evolved into larger and more fully realized spray art pieces, the metal canvases of New York's Metropolitan Transportation Authority subways presented a mobile medium that privileged the expansive urban environment and extended young artists' reach while providing billboard-size surfaces for publicizing graffiti crews or the self-promotion of individuals. Although the city train yards are more stringently policed today than they once were, this mobile component has not disappeared; in the U.S., delivery vans or freight trains often carry the elaborate work of itinerant graffiti artists, while across Europe subway cars continue to feature some of the most exciting aerosol art.

Similarly, in rap lyrics the definition of one's home environment and surrounding urban spaces is a conventional aspect of the form. MC Rakim's flowing statement "Now if you're from Uptown, Brooklyn bound, the Bronx, Queens, or Long Island Sound, even the other states come right and exact, it ain't where you're from but where you're at" ("I Know You Got Soul," 1987) still reverberates within hip-hop even as the discourses and lyrical articulation of race, space, and place have advanced to a point where they begin to undermine Rakim's original concept. Although his line is widely referenced, it does, in fact, seem to matter a great deal "where you're from" *and* "where you're at." These are interconnected themes that are not easily segmented or compartmentalized. The tales of originary sites of significance that describe local places and place-based activities emerge as crucial indicators for the shaping of attitudes and identities among hip-hop's entrepreneurs, including Def Jam co-founder Russell Simmons, James Smith of Rap-a-Lot Records, or Bad Boy Entertainment creator Sean "Diddy" Combs, as well as among artists such as Eminem whose dysfunctional upbringing on Detroit's 8 Mile Road is now legendary. We might ask, can Jay-Z be realistically disconnected from Brooklyn or Nas from Queens? Can Snoop Dogg be fully comprehended without acknowledging his Long Beach, California roots, and can Outkast, the Goodie Mob or T.I. be isolated from Atlanta? Where these individuals are from is an essential element of who they are and what they project, whether in a broader regional sense of space or in the more finely nuanced and closely delineated scale of place.

Since rap music's inception, it has articulated the details of place with ever-greater specificity. In the process, MCs have transformed the abstract notion of space into a more closely circumscribed locus of experience, with the close-knit relations that cohere within neighborhoods and city blocks acquiring discursive primacy. If space is a broadly configured dimension, place, as framed within discourses of the 'hood, constitutes a micro-scale of experience that has, since roughly 1988, achieved greater significance within hip-hop; today, "the 'hood" prevails as hip-hop's dominant spatial trope. The emphasis on the geocultural character of "the 'hood" can be distinctly heard in Scarface's 2002 recording "On My Block" (released the same year as Tupac Shakur's posthumous single "My Block") when he proclaims, "on my block it ain't no different than the next block," stressing the continuity of a localized environment and the individuated places that are linked across urban space. Scarface and Shakur's hood-based thematics resonate globally as well, having provided a spatial model that was explicitly adopted by the German MC Sido on his 2004 track "Mein Block." With over a decade of experience in the rap music industry, Scarface's identification with his block and his 'hood is additionally infused with the expressive voice of a rap elder, someone who has been impacted and molded by his connection to the 'hood and who, approaching middle age, finds himself in a unique stance from which to analyze the allure and character of his immediate surroundings. For him, the local remains a touchstone linked to the foundations of personal character and fortitude.

By this stage hip-hop's inception within the geographic and cultural environments of uptown New York has been well documented, with scholars citing the nexus of cultural influences (especially those of the Caribbean, African-American, and Latino communities) and describing the rise of prominent innovators who merged artistry with commerce as they honed their hip-hop talents (Rose, 1994; Chang, 2005). New research has, however, intensely theorized the spatiality of hip-hop as well as casting the analysis more widely, resulting in two distinct shifts in the field. First, the careful exploration of hip-hop's development across the U.S. reveals distinct regional styles and patterns, outlining the myriad ways in which hip-hop converges with locally and regionally relevant social forces. This work connects the established narrative about hip-hop's nascent phase in New York with new origin tales that describe hip-hop's inception in other American locales and that define the characteristics of 'hoods in a variety of urban zones. These projects do not simply revise our understanding of how hip-hop expanded over the past 30 years but provide important knowledge about particular codes and localized practices that inform hip-hop's formation throughout the nation.

In the second instance, new research illuminates the emergence and vitality of hip-hop in far-flung places, encompassing global cultural phenomena and capturing the distinctive ways in which space and place are articulated in and through hip-hop's communicative apparatuses. This has the important effect of decentering the focus on U.S. hip-hop, diminishing the "Americocentrism" that has, in the past, often obscured the legitimate developments of hip-hop *and* hip-hop scholarship from other points on the global map. A growing body of academic research indicates that hip-hop is also part of the everyday practices and experience of youths around the world as they combine its expressive forms with their own national and local inflections. They display their affective alignment with their own 'hoods even as they acknowledge their role in an international culture that has its origins among African-American and Latino youths from the Bronx. DJs, MCs, B-boys, and graffiti artists in dispersed global contexts actively integrate hip-hop into their own everyday cultural experiences, creating new meanings and redefining their social environments as they do so. If at an earlier stage international hip-hop artists tended to replicate the dominant forms of U.S. innovators in the attempt to hone their skills and talents, that is certainly no longer the case.

As a dynamic cultural form and highly promoted set of cultural commodities, hip-hop has entered the consciousness of audiences and observers on a global scale. Yet how it is packaged and promoted and, correspondingly, how audiences have adopted *and* adapted it within their own daily conditions remain crucial issues for, as Marc Perry, Alex Perullo, and the panelists accompanying Cristina Verán note, hip-hop's international mobility is fraught with questions concerning local significance and authenticity in the face of the appropriation of African-American cultural practices. As the essays in this part indicate, the local and the global are inextricably imbricated through contemporary cultural circuits and media flows (what Robertson (1995) has termed "the glocal" or that Robins (1991) refers to as "the global–local nexus"). The urban sites under analysis here suggest the distinct ways that hip-hop is made meaningful according to local and national traditions, as well as identifying the different cultural stakes involved for the young hip-hop fans and artists across the continents.

REFERENCES

Chang, Jeff. (2005). *Can't Stop, Won't Stop: A History of the Hip-Hop Generation.* New York: St. Martin's Press.
Fernando, S.H. (1994). *The New Beats: Exploring the Music, Culture, and Attitudes of Hip-Hop.* New York: Anchor Books.
Hebdige, Dick. (1987). *Cut 'n' Mix: Culture, Identity and Caribbean Music.* London: Comedia.
Ogg, Alex and David Upshal. (1999). *The Hip Hop Years: A History of Rap.* New York: Fromm International.
Robertson, Roland. (1995). "Glocalization: Time–Space and Homogeneity–Heterogeneity," in *Global Modernities*, edited by Mike Featherstone, Scott Lash, and Roland Robertson. Thousand Oaks, CA: Sage.
Robins, Kevin. (1991). "Tradition and Translation: National Culture in Its Global Context," in *Enterprise and Heritage: Crosscurrents of National Culture*, edited by John Corner and Sylvia Harvey. New York: Routledge.
Rose, Tricia. (1994). *Black Noise: Rap Music and Black Culture in Contemporary America.* Hanover, NH: Wesleyan University Press.
Toop, David. (1984). *The Rap Attack: African Jive to New York Hip Hop.* Boston, MA: South End Press.

16

Black Empires, White Desires
The Spatial Politics of Identity in the Age of Hip-Hop

Davarian Baldwin offers a sophisticated reading of spatial practices and social power that are aligned across multiple dimensions and that are often intensely inflected by aspects of race, class, and gender. As Baldwin explains, space may refer to material, lived environments, but it is also politicized in myriad ways and the spatial character of any environment is often forged through the political alliances or antagonisms that unfold within social relations. Baldwin interrogates the often stated authority of the ghetto as the root of "real" hip-hop, challenging prevalent attitudes that assert the "truth" of compressed urban enclaves and nominate the 'hood as today's dominant locus of hip-hop identity.

Foregroundng the representational images and narratives of ghetto spaces that proliferate in the media, Baldwin offers an insightful critique of the manifold articulations of "the real" and the ways that they are interpreted and made meaningful among audiences and consumers, both white and black. The specific references to the infamous east–west animosities that prevailed throughout much of the 1990s are convincingly framed within a discursive conflict pertaining not simply to geographies of difference but to underlying ideological formations relating to distinctions across the geo-political landscape of U.S. blackness in which "ghettocentricity" emerges as "a counter move to the Afrocentricity and white supremacy of the day."

Black Empires, White Desires: The Spatial Politics of Identity in the Age of Hip-Hop

Davarian L. Baldwin

We have reached the point where our popular culture threatens to undermine our character as a nation.

Bob Dole

People are outraged, man, you get to the point where you're constantly hearing over and over talk about mugging people, killing women, beating women, sexual behavior. When young people see this—14, 15, 16 years of age—they think this is acceptable behavior.

Rev. Calvin O. Butts

I have seen a rise lately in the disrespect of black women.... Are we the ones influencing the world? If that was the case, what music was Bill Clinton listening to when he whirlpooled Lani Guinier?

Joseph Simmons (of Run DMC)

1997 was a pivotal year for black popular culture in general and hip hop in particular. Caught in the crossfire of the William Bennett/C. Delores Tucker censorship movement, the deaths of Tupac Shakur and the Notorious BIG (in a so-called East/West Coast battle), and an increase in its consumption (especially of "gangsta rap") among suburban white youth, hip hop has been placed under the "microscope and found ... to be the source of all that is wrong with American society" (Diawara, 1993, 2). From the right, hip hop is attacked as a practice that started in urban America but is infecting the morals and family values of suburban teens. At the same time, sectors of the left and the black middle-class distance themselves from hip hop because of its misogyny and homophobia. The critique of hip hop as a black popular culture form that exists as an outside threat or infection, ravaging "American" (and black middle-class) culture and values, must be understood within a history of identification located squarely in the ideological and material spaces of colonialism, racism, and national identity. The ability to fix hip hop as pure difference from the norm or as the source of wrongdoing must be interrogated. It suggests that there is an already-agreed-upon national character threatened by a deviant popular culture (Dole) and leaves unquestioned the border where national character ends and popular culture begins.[1]

Hip hop itself is not purely a U.S., let alone black, cultural form. However, it is not an understatement to say that the deviancy or threat in popular culture is racialized, particularly through old narratives of the dysfunction of the black family (Kelley, 1997). These stories are now being deployed to identify the source of the problem within hip hop culture. After the death of the Notorious BIG, *Village Voice* writer Touré suggests this vision: "I can see now that the murder and killings are coming from the same hands that make the beats and rhymes; how is living in hip hop any different than living in the dysfunctional black family writ large?" (1997, 30).

For many, it appears that the hip hop nation and the nation at large are no longer safe from the deviancy that the black family produces. Discourse on the black family with its female-headed home becomes shorthand to make sense of the supposedly unique violence and sexuality in certain genres of hip hop. The lazy connections made between mythologies of dysfunctional black families and hip hop ignore the performative aspects of black popular culture. These narratives understand the deviancy in hip hop to be an uncomplicated (re)presentation of black culture (Fanon, 1967). The performance of hip hop as a black cultural form, for better or worse, becomes a reference for "authentic" blackness. As an action and reaction against conservative and liberal backlash,[2] at times hip hop attempts to counter negative notions of blackness with its own "racial authenticity," where the position of absolute difference is self-induced. Racial authenticity is best articulated in these instances through the stance that the artistic production is pure and untouched by any means of dilution.[3]

Within black communities, this process of black authenticity has historically oscillated between the binaries of excess and austerity. As Greg Tate contends, "the controversies surrounding hip hop in the black community have revived an ongoing debate over who best tells black stories: our blues people or our bourgeoisie" (1997, 70). In order to combat the "negative" idealizations of blackness, middle-class moral purists (even draped in kente cloth) attack the sexual frankness of hip hop as "excessive" and tend to support what is understood as "positive rap" because of its Afrocentric rhetoric and/or political awareness,[4] where as some "Ghettocentric" advocates defend the explicit lyrics as reality-based and resent the possibilities of censorship as dilutions of the authentic "realness" of black experiences. This position in hip hop is exemplified by the characterization of the "keepin-it-real nigga."

It must be noted that these positions are not set in stone and often overlap and intersect. For example, a third position might be the one articulated by KRS-One, which contains a nationalist hip hop edge but is rooted in nostalgia, not for Africa's golden era, but for a hip hop golden age. In the midst of hip hop's international growth and change, this "reaching back" for better times attempts to figure out "what went wrong, and why did hip hop become the revolution that failed?" Instead of attempting to "keep it real," this position is set on correcting rap music's ills, so that, as a culture, the hip hop nation can "keep it right." In what way are the articulations of the "keepin'-it-real nigga" or the "African" complicit with a white patriarchal order by designating what behaviors, sexualities, and representations will be accepted into the space of black popular culture? In what way is the masking of these performances as "natural," "accurate," or "real" complicit with the traditional order, and in what way are they disruptive?

Ironically, both extreme critiques and defenses of hip hop as an authentic representation of black life converge upon a certain refashioning of the infamous Moynihan (1965) report. When black families and women are the point of focus, representations of black women stand in for authentic blackness. In turn, the visibility of black female purity or contamination signifies the success or failure of black culture; women's bodies become the terrain on which battles over black authenticity are waged. In this context, C. Delores Tucker is able to attend a Time Warner board meeting and exclaim that Lil' Kim's songs must be banned. As an example of what she calls "pornographic," Tucker quotes "No Time": "No money, money / No licky, licky / Fuck the dicky, dicky and the quickie" (1996). Kim's lyrics could be (and have been) read as part of a long musical history of black women taking a stance for sexual and economic self-satisfaction (Rose, 1994; Davis, 1998). However, alternative voices are now silenced as deviant, as false articulations of blackness, and therefore irrelevant. The primacy of familial and traditional values nearly overrides any focus on social/sexual inequalities. But the insistence on making an artist like Kim irrelevant also shows the centrality of her work. Despite the attempts to repress and regulate personal and interpersonal black conduct, artists like Kim have emerged as part of a hip hop-inspired black bourgeois aesthetic.

This aesthetic rejects both black petit-bourgeois respectability and ghetto authenticity. Its practitioners accept the black bourgeois notion of upward mobility without rejecting the desires and consumption habits of the black working class. This new black aesthetic offers a new identity outside the workplace by endorsing the consumption of luxury goods. As a form of "dressing up," it also offers a status for subordinate groups that blurs distinctions between themselves and their oppressors (Kelley, 1994, 167–69). They are changing what it means to be black and middle class in ways that make our proponents of traditional values cringe because they refuse to be disciplined into puritan characterizations of normative middle-class behavior. They have all the trappings of the middle and elite classes but wear Versace and Armani in a different way, drive their Bentleys to different places, and play out private inequalities in public arenas.

This black aesthetic potentially de-naturalizes the divides of black/white, male/female, authentic/commodified, and challenges normative notions of hip hop as a space that can purify the impure. It debunks the contention that if hip hop were practiced in its truest form, it could bring in the straying brothers and sisters who lack "knowledge of self" or who "ain't keepin it real," as if such pronouncements of identity were ever stable. The artists remind us that "in concept, hip hop was never anti-capitalist, pro-black or intentionally avant-garde. Up until Public Enemy, hip hop's intent was never to shock the world but to sell the market on its novelty and profitability" (Tate, 1997, 70). Hip hop as a musical form could never follow the traditional association of commodification with cooptation, because the revolution of hip hop was fought out within the circuits of the market. These artists have begun to discover that a black politics can also be organized within the processes of consumption.

In the same way as we consume these artists, they consume other American cultural icons. Through their performance of gangsters, rich women, and corporate culture icons, the new gangsta rappers like Biggie, Lil' Kim and Jay-Z are living the American dream of commodity obsession and appropriation. However, the appropriation of cultural icons is not a new formulation. Throughout the 20th century, Americans of all hues who have been marginalized as ethnic or "other" have utilized the "gangsta" as a site of socio-economic mobility. In this particular moment, the grammar of the gangsta's "hustle" or "game" has become the language of the culture industry. Hip hop artists and other culture workers have become "playas," and those who attempt to stop black progress in the game have become dubbed "playa haters." These workers have aesthetically, and begun to materially, appropriate the culture industry as a site for black institution-building and contestation.

Their music describes the American entrepreneur, for whom competitiveness is a way of life. While they don't like government restrictions any more than the Republicans and endorse rampant individualism within the markets, they also expose how the fervor for deregulation extends to everything except certain genres of the American music industry, genres which dominate the world market. In addition to money makers, these lyricists speak to the inequalities, restrictions, and uneven developments that have been aimed at African-Americans and women in their quest for the "American dream."

In the current backlash against gangsta rap, however, may be heard a decline-and-fall narrative that understands hip hop to be over-commodified and calls for a return to the roots of street parties and the "yes yes y'all" freestyle rhyme, which exemplifies a pre-commodified, undiluted era. This can be heard in KRS-One's 1997 hit, "Rapture," where the hook to the song says, "step into a world where hip hop is real." In the video, we see the re-invocation of a bygone era in the historic Boogie Down South Bronx, where breakdancers and graffiti artists don the early 80s fashions of warm-up suits and Puma sneakers while performing a corrective memory of the old-school concert as a utopic space.

But this utopic space has been (re)constructed in 1997, where people no longer perform or consume hip hop in the same ways. This video intentionally decontextualizes hip hop's transformations in the pursuit of a fictive realness. Such an excavation of a hip hop past doesn't question whether hip hop was ever purely outside the circuits of commodification or consistently and totally oppositional. Rather, it assumes the location of the South Bronx and the rhyming of KRS-One as correctives to contemporary hip hop. Through performances like the one above, hip hop becomes visually fixed through the designation of which images and behaviors will exemplify an "authentic" black cultural practice. However, the new gangsta/playa aesthetic is not a full embrace of marketplace ideology and commodified cultural production. The identities produced therein are important sites for a black politics at the end of the 20th century.

The general critiques circulating around gangsta rap highlight the patriarchal masculinity, drugs, sex, gunplay, and consumption habits without either remembering the Dapper Dan and Gucci days of hip hop's "golden age" or noting the earlier progressive move that gangsta rap was making against the evolution of nation-conscious hip hop in the early 90's. What many now term "positive" or conscious rap had begun to evoke a sense of gatekeeping that designated who was and was not authentically black.

"Moving on Up": Black Respectability in the Era of Nation-Conscious Hip Hop

The massive economic and cultural reorganization of life in the 1980s pulled black people in all directions. At the same time that a black middle-class was growing (in part due to affirmative action), a larger critical mass of African-Americans were left behind in the urban enclaves of all the major U.S. cities and rural locations. The Brooklyn Heights location of the *Cosby Show* and hip hop's "Boogie Down" South Bronx were talking to each other in previously unthinkable ways. The desire for upward class mobility through the market was confronting the black cultural form of hip hop, which in some ways was marketable because of its origins in urban poverty. The urban origins of hip hop and its artists' desire to become, as Eric B. and Rakim stated, "Paid in Full" (1987), were met by black audiences, who were grappling with what it meant to be paid and black. Up to this point, authentic blackness in hip hop was associated with the inner city. When African-Americans became more upwardly mobile in the 1980s, with (for example) many black youths entering the nation's elite universities, anxieties grew within the black middle class over its relationship to blackness. Black people's "moving on up" was accompanied by a sense of alienation from authentic spaces.

The icons of Afrocentricity and Africa itself served as bridges between upward mobility and historically black experiences. The notion that success and academic achievement were necessarily white experiences was met with a wave of Afrocentricity, where the study and consumption of Afrocentric goods and literature could justify a class distinction without raising issues of black authenticity. Designer wear and bourgeois habits were legitimized with, respectively, kente cloth and reconstructed Yoruba origins.

Concurrently, as hip hop became more mainstream, the nation-conscious Afrocentric genre grew. It does not seem a coincidence that in 1988, the formerly "criminally-minded" (1986) KRS-One took on the role of Malcolm X in "By All Means Necessary" (1988) and Long Island-based Public Enemy, who in 1986 were "rollin in their 98 Olds-mobile" began to state that "It

Takes a Nation of Millions to Hold [Them] Back" (1988). In part, nation-conscious rap became a cipher to understand blackness in arenas of upward mobility and hip hop's national growth. As well, this music shared its terrain with an African-American and white college-age audience who used African and Black Power fashions, hairstyles, and rhetoric to demonstrate political acts of rebellion and resistance. The academic Afrocentricity of Molefi Asante countered dominant academic politics by positioning "Africa" at the center of study and analysis (1987, 187).

Afrocentricity served as a powerful tool for African-American students as their professors and administrators questioned the validity of integrating multicultural education into the canon and strengthening African-American Studies programs. The aesthetic of the "African" became a stance where students could mount a counterattack against the academic claims that African-Americans had no culture worthy of the canon. Afrocentricity served as a safe space in threatening academic waters, a complement to nationhood rhetoric within the Reagan/Bush regime, and a language to maintain borders around the definition of hip hop during its national expansion.

The move toward empowering black populations outside urban spaces through a kind of Afrocentric/nation-conscious hip hop form was not entirely new. Its roots are visible in the collective known as the "Native Tongues," which was roughly comprised of the Jungle Brothers, A Tribe Called Quest, Queen Latifah, Monie Love, and De La Soul (Boyd, 1995, 299). Their origins point even further back toward the Universal Zulu Nation of the Bronx-based Afrika Bambaataa, who in the late 70s was hell-bent on not just transmitting his Kraftwerk-inspired "techno funk" to the nation, but on making the "Planet Rock."

Native Tongues followed in Bambaataa's footsteps by not letting their musical influences or artistic vision be impeded by fictive standards of how hip hop should sound. For example, De La Soul's first single "Me, Myself and I" ironized earlier rap posturings by counterpoising the popular b-boy stance to "being one's self." De La Soul is known for initiating hip hop's breakaway from the recycling of the same James Brown beats by introducing the samples of everything from Steely Dan to Disney. Introducing a class consciousness, De La Soul was also clear about being from a relatively affluent Long Island background, stating that this heavily influenced their sound and aesthetics, which ran contrary to the stereotypical urban style. Within this distinction, they rejected what had become the authentic style of sweatsuits, gold chains, and Kangol hats by presenting their bohemian style of flowered shirts, dreaded hair, and African medallions.

Released in 1988, "Me, Myself and I" attempted to open a space where blackness could be understood through parody and the interrogation of multiple identities within hip hop, while simultaneously making subtle political statements to the nation at large:

> Glory, glory hallelu
> glory for plug one and two
> But that glory's been denied by
> kudzids and gookie eyes
> people think they dis my person by
> stating I'm darkly packed
> I know this so I point at Q-Tip and he
> states "Black is Black"
> mirror, mirror on the wall
> shovel chestnuts in my path
> please keep all nuts with the nuts
> so I don't get an aftermath
> but if I do I'll calmly punch them in

the 4th day of July
cause they tried to mess with 3rd
degree
that's Me, Myself and I

In this song, De La Soul is exploring issues of cultural individualism within blackness through an ironic reference to American patriotism. They are asking that the rhetoric of cultural freedom be applied both inside and outside of "the race." But the political impetus of this Afrocentric style became statically and dangerously interpreted as the only option within blackness, a turn that may have prompted De La Soul to title their second album *De La Soul Is Dead.* The "Soul" in Afrocentric rap began to articulate an essentialist position that equated musical "soul" with a particular black nationalist, Afrocentric identity, instead of allowing for a multiplicity of black experiences to be heard. Afrocentric versions of nation-conscious rap deployed the sunny disposition of Egypt and a re-imagined Egyptian/African culture as sources of racial legitimacy in the face of racial oppression. But in its attempts to create a powerful picture of black life, Afrocentrism expected blacks to live up to an imagined identity based on a particular version of African-American history and painted over issues of gender with broad strokes. Black life was articulated primarily in the voice of black men, and if not from men, then from the position of patriarchy.[5]

The "fertile" soil of Egypt and "Mother Africa" were fetishized as female objects, primarily valuable for their production of melanin babies, otherwise known as the "original black man." Taking material from Asante, psychologist Frances Cress Welsing, and even 18th century white scholars (like the biologist Gregor Mendel), the melanin in black skin or the culture of African people is understood as making the black man naturally good, artistic, and superior.

As Jeffrey Decker has stated, work by the artist Isis was emblematic of this phenomena. In her music video "The Power of Myself Is Moving," she plays the part of a fertility goddess along the Nile: "I'm a self coming forth a creature bearing life / a renaissance, a rebirth" (1990). Even through a female voice, the message evokes the patriarchal order where women are revered solely for their inherent nurturing and reproductive skills. Because the black woman bears the seed of the black nation, she is viewed as an "object" that must be protected from both interracial and intraracial contamination.

As stated earlier, the absence of any discussion of intraracial class conflict is a crucial oversight in Afrocentric work. However, anxieties over class-based behaviors emerge through a rigid representation of regional differences and gendered behavior. One of the key groups to articulate this phenomenon was Arrested Development, which Todd Boyd rightly lauds for relocating hip hop outside urban spaces into the landscapes of the rural South, while also criticizing the group for its romanticization of this locale: "Arrested Development argues for a kind of cultural innocence or purity. This notion of purity is exemplified through a juxtaposition of the harsh urban realities of the street prominent in contemporary rap and their embrace of the premodern "country," the simplicity of a rural landscape" (1995, 300). Arrested Development promotes the romantic rural by defining and denigrating its other: the urban subject.

This rural-urban dichotomy creates a class hierarchy between the positive images of pastoral Afrocentric rap and the depressing dangers of urban experiences. A binary, expressed this time in terms of the "true black self," is established between the haves and have-nots: "Now I see the importance of history / why my people be in the mess that they be / many journeys to freedom made in vain / by brothers on the corner playing ghetto games" (1992). This trope of "knowledge to be acquired" through mastering designated Afrocentric texts and behaviors is understood as the entryway to authentic blackness. The revisionist Southern history of Arrested Development (AD) can easily be mapped onto the "return to family values" narrative, best depicted in idealization of rural New England communities by white conservatives like Newt Gingrich. In both narratives, place and family space became the loci for the creation of "proper values." As well, both rhetorics claim to speak from the position of the popular or "everyday people," while masking their privileged class positions.

Scholars like Boyd have prized AD for their positive and progressive gender politics. However, I am skeptical of such a position, because the voices of their women rappers are constrained by their role as a prize. In AD's work, the "black queen" serves as an object that must not be contaminated by "niggas." In the video "People Everyday," black men are performing the stance of the "urban nigga"—drinking 40's and grabbing their crotches—when an "African queen" approaches and one of the men grabs her butt. Simultaneously, Speech[6] can be heard in a voiceover criticizing their behavior: "My day was going great and my soul was at ease / until a group of brothers / started buggin out / drinking the 40 ounce / going the nigga route / disrespecting my black queen / holding their crotches and being obscene" (1992). The woman is given no agency and the nigga performs the stereotypical deviant role that gives the African the opportunity to do his duty and step in to protect his queen. An analogy is made between the ability of the African man to protect his woman and the intrinsic strength of the African identity: "That's the story y'all / of a black man / acting like a nigga / and get stomped by an African" (1992). Even in the midst of gender inclusion, masculine aggression rears its ugly head. The radical right's vision of the patriarchal family is upheld, but now in blackface and kente cloth. But what happens when the nigga speaks back?

"The Nigga You Love to Hate": Class Conflicts in the "G-Funk" Era

Rather than evading the nigga, gangsta rap actually engaged and mimicked the position of nigga as other, as performance. In the next section I, along with Robin Kelley and other scholars, postulate that the earliest manifestations of gangsta rap attempted to speak back to the middle-class-oriented position of nation-conscious rap. Kelley argues that, "L.A. gangsta rappers are frequent critics of black nationalists [as well]. They contend that the nationalist focus on Africa—both past and present—obscures the daily battles poor black folk have to wage in contemporary America" (1994, 212). In some regards, nation-conscious rap assumed that everyone agreed on the definition of "knowledge of self" and, in turn, blackness. Gangsta rap, however, provides another perspective on black life.

As well, gangsta rappers saw no inherent negativity in the term "nigga," defining themselves as niggas in defiance of the dominant society, both black and white. As hip hop was continuing to expand, more tensions arose around the definition of hip hop as a representation of blackness. Although hip hop originated and was most successful in urban New York and on the East Coast, the emergence of gangsta rap shifted the focus in hip hop to the lived experience of the post-industrial city on the West Coast, particularly Los Angeles.

The highly popular N.W.A. (Niggas With Attitude) album, *Straight Outta Compton* was released in 1988 at the same time that nation-conscious rap was becoming popular. However, it wasn't until the early 90s—when N.W.A.'s *efil4zaggiN* (Niggaz 4 life) reached number one on the *Billboard* charts before it was even released, Snoop Doggy Dogg was introduced on the *Deep Cover* soundtrack, and Dr. Dre's multi-platinum album *The Chronic* was heard on every street corner and video station—that everyone was forced to realize that gangsta rap was a force to be reckoned with. The West Coast began to dismantle New York's monopoly of hip hop and critiqued nation-conscious rap's politically correct disciplining of black bodies. Unlike the critiques of black nihilism that wax nostalgic for a bygone black community (West, 1993), gangsta rappers aren't anti-nationalist or apolitical, but they do oppose a political correctness which obscures the historical realities of class, gender, and locational difference within the representation of black communities.

On "Dre Day," Dr. Dre retorts: "no medallions / dreadlocks / or Black fist it's just that gangsta glare / with gangsta rap that gangsta shit, / brings a gang of snaps" (1992). Instead of seeing this position as exemplifying a movement of anti-politics, I see it as a shift in the way in which politics is articulated. In hindsight, it is an attempt to break the stranglehold of nation-conscious rap on hip hop expression. The political language of nation-conscious rap, in its most general sense, was traded in for the grammar of the hood and the particular day-to-day struggles of black people.

In gangsta rap, the nigga acquired a locational and economic specificity. Kelley argues that the experiences of young black men in the inner city were not universal to all black people, and furthermore, that "nigga does not mean black as much as it means being a product of the post-industrial ghetto" (1994, 210). This process exposes the limitations of politics based on skin color. Gangsta rap can be understood as resistance, where the nigga is seen as a performative identity that is not solely accessed by a black constituency.

Thus, we are encouraged to analyze the nigga within the American mainstream, especially since so much of the work in gangsta rap is inspired by popular action-adventure and gangster films and its biggest registered consumers are suburban white teens. Because of this phenomenon, we must think critically about white youth's influence over creating and maintaining the gangsta subject by purchasing the music. The gangsta subject would not continue to exist in commodified form if there were not buyers waiting for the product. Gangsta rap deals in fantasy and evil, constructing marketable stories that tell as much about its white teen listeners' desires as about its practitioners. In what ways do the consumption of and desire for a genre help to continue its existence?

The problematics that supposedly originate in the nigga subject are turned back onto America and its political/economic/racial regime. In Kelley's essay, a Chicano gang member makes visible his relation to the economic order in regard to his "deviant" behavior: "I act like they do in the big time, no different. There ain't no corporation that acts with morals and that ethics shit and I ain't about to either. As they say, if it's good for General Motors, it's good enough for me" (1994, 196). The desires of the "gangsta" are exposed equally as the desires of its consumers and creators, problematizing the belief in a pure pathological difference based on race. In other words, the behaviors of the nigga are found in all segments of American life.

Through the performance of the nigga, the gangsta rapper fights against fixity and attempts to make visible the multiple registers through which the hood, racial pathologies, and the nigga are actualized. In gangsta rap, individualism and criminality are continually tied to America culture. As Ice-T states: "America stole from the Indians sure and prove / what's that? / a straight up nigga move!" (1991). But in this position of rebelliousness, gangsta rap and the nigga became idealized as Ghettocentric, a counter move to the Afrocentricity and white supremacy of the day.

The nigga became the embodiment of black defiance against all comers through a highly masculinist imaginary, where the nigga was strong when he wasn't a "punk," "bitch," or "pussy." The project of uncovering the racially hybrid subjectivity of the nigga is halted when the nigga is flaunted as the only "real" black identity. The tropes of masculinity, promiscuity, and violence become naturalized as inherently black. However, this form of identification is no different from most young men in patriarchal societies who come to associate masculinity with aggression and violence. Blackness as hypermasculine becomes a romanticized position of strength and opposition that hopes to create "safe spaces" of uncontested male power. Furthermore, the belief that black family structures are deviant because of the instability of its women is a narrative that may also be found in gangsta rap.

The male rapper begins to call for the restoration of the patriarchal order, because for him, the female is fixed as a threat to the progress of his success or hustle. In the same way that gangsta rap performs the violence of an idealized America, it also calls upon traditional tales of black women as scapegoats for problems within the nation(hood). "African-American women are often portrayed as welfare queens making babies merely to stay on public assistance or 'gold-diggers' who use their sexuality to take black men's meager earnings" (Kelley, 1994, 217). This narrative can be found in Dr. Dre's song "Bitches Ain't Shit But Hoes and Tricks," or E-40's "Captain Save a Ho," in which men are chastised for taking care of a woman and her children, especially if they aren't his own. During this song's popularity, a man who listened to his girlfriend or spent too much time with a woman was accused of "having an S on his chest" because he was "savin' em" (his woman was in control). The woman is seen as putting the man's freedom in jeopardy by hustling him for his money and time.

At its most progressive, gangsta rap analyzes the contingent relationship between poverty and a racialized political economy but at the same time can explain women in poverty in terms of a behavioral problem, claiming that all a woman wants is to take you for your goods. Tricia Rose explains how black males fear the assertion of a strong woman's sexuality: within gangsta spaces, there is no guarantee that heterosexual male desires will be met because of women's capacity to reject or manipulate men's advances (1991). This is not a new narrative and indeed is based on longstanding fears of women's ability to trap men (e.g., through pregnancy), when sexual exchange is able to produce money and goods (Kelley, 1994, 219).

Just as the purified space of the black nationalist is insecure, so also is the stability of the gangsta. The terrain where black men attempt to assert their masculinity or evade the issues of class is always highly contested. Male gangsta rappers expose the vulnerability of heterosexual male desire in their exaggerated stories of dominance over female representations of black life.

The degree of anxiety expressed in these heavy-handed fantasies explains both an intense desire and distrust of women and the way in which their (in)subordination disrupts racial authenticity. However, gangsta rap is *not* vying for a sanitized vision of Africa, complete with corrective gender and class relationships. It forces us to deal with the everyday in a way that can't justify the harsh denigration of female and working-class desires, particularly in the marketplace. Gangsta rap seems suited for engaging the social contradictions and ambiguities of urban life.

In the context of racial distinctions, while gangsta rap's white consumers and critics are identifying the gangsta as something "other" than themselves or the white middle-class values they purport to inherit, these artists are parodying "normative" behavior. Peter Stallybrass and Allon White argue that:

> The "top" attempts to reject and eliminate the "bottom" for reasons of prestige and status, only to discover, not only that it is in some way frequently dependent upon the low-Other, but also that the top *includes* the low symbolically, as a primary eroticized constituent of its own fantasy life. The result is ... a psychological dependence upon precisely those others which are being rigorously opposed and excluded at the social level. It is for this reason that what is socially peripheral is so frequently *symbolically* central. (5, 1986)

Although gangsta rap has been constructed as deviant from middle-class normativity, examining the social texts of desire and consumption shows its relationship to those very norms. For example, the "vulgar" black female deviance performed or commented on in gangsta rap is not nor can be discretely separated from the sense of entitlement clothed in middle-class normative respectability. The gangsta performance forces those who embrace white middle-class patriarchy to stare the black gangsta in the face and see him- or herself. This shift to gangsta music has allowed black men and women trapped by oppressive systems to reinvent themselves through new performative acts, a reinvention defined by Manthia Diawara as the "defiant tradition in black culture that challenges every attempt to police the black body or mind" (1993, 4).

The Wretched of the Earth: Pleasure, Power, and the Hip Hop Bourgeoisie

Earlier conservative idealizations of black life evaded an engagement with the black body through policing it, whereas Diawara's notion of the "black good life society" "emphasizes the necessity for a productive space which is accompanied by consumption, leisure, and pleasure in black people's relation to modernity" (1993, 7). This engagement with pleasure and commodity consumption addresses realities that black middle-class and black church aesthetic forms often shun.

These traditional forms have historically functioned within ideologies that separate intellect and pleasure, mind and body, and have been articulated within the binary of a harsh middle class/working class divide. Historically, it has been black people's responsibility to link pleasure or freedom with the non-material. L.A.-based gangsta rap reopened a space where it is not sinful to link black pleasure with materialism. Rather than finding a politics through positive imaging, the "black good life" seeks a politics through performance and refashions identity through irony and play. If moral and cultural correctness is seen as denial, then open representations of sexuality and grotesque and carnivalesque characterizations/eroticizations of violence can be understood as potentially liberating.

The performance of so-called deviant acts and direct confrontations with black stereotypes create black industries, as well as make visible the social construction of what appear as natural black characteristics. These performances expose the interracial and intraracial formation of the nigga identity and "take ethical decisions away from the church, out of the moral and religious arena, and place them squarely at the feet of material well being and pleasure" (Diawara, 1993, 7). I argue that the backlash against the new cadre of male and female gangsta rappers, whether it be voiced by C. Delores Tucker, William Bennett, Rev. Calvin Butts, or hip hop purists, is mobilizing around an ethic that purports to speak "for the people" but in actuality does not. The gatekeepers of "authentic blackness" are anxiety-ridden over public displays of the black good life society, exemplified in the emergence of a new hip hop identity; a black middle-class aesthetic that will not be policed by traditional notions of morality and class status.

Confident in the freedom offered by the pleasures and profits of performing gangsta, New York-based Lil' Kim, Foxy Brown, Jay-Z, and The Notorious BIG are exemplars of this hip hop shift. Consequently, these artists are specifically attacked for their lines of commodity endorsements from Versace to Lexus and for their obsession with Italian-American mobsters. Yet, in the same way that white supremacy has created the nigga as a repository for its own not-so-laudable activities, "gangsta/playa" rappers have taken white American commodities as signs of achieving "the dream." By performing the roles of Italian-American mobsters and movie characters, they continue to question the idea that gangsta behaviors in hip hop are inherently an extension of deviant, let alone black, culture. At the same time, their gangsta performance critiques the notions of blackness expressed through ghetto authenticity or black bourgeois respectability. This version of gangsta rap questions the fictive boundaries placed around class status as a means of social exclusion.

One way in which upward mobility has historically been policed is by the coupling of class status with behavioral dictates. As working-class blacks advance financially through the entertainment arena, they are expected to change their behaviors in a way that "properly" suits their new economic status. However, the privacy traditionally afforded middle-class citizens is not given to these black cultural workers, who are placed under strict scrutiny as if their social advancement warranted a special kind of public attention. So many perceptions are shaped by the "you can take a nigga out of the hood, but you can't take the hood out of the nigga" narrative, that entertainment and sports pages begin to look like the Metro section. But I wonder if these entertainers are becoming more of an embarrassing spectacle, or whether there are larger anxieties about the changing composition of the American middle and upper class? This belief that particular behaviors can be linked to a specific class standing hardly ever makes visible that entrée into the normative middle-class space has historically been acquired and maintained through not-so-middle-class behaviors.

Instead of reacting to "culture of poverty" rhetorics by disassociating blackness from American culture, these gangsta collectives have crowned themselves Junior M.A.F.I.A., The Firm, and Roc-A-Fella (Rockefeller) Records. They problematize the lines drawn between legality and illegality, morality and immorality, by articulating not the culture of poverty but mainstream American culture. This American tale potentially tears the racial and economic structure of U.S. life away from the current trends in neo-Social Darwinist ideology (i.e., that there is something particular to black culture that is intrinsically deviant). Critics of gangsta rap hold to the claim that inherent to the middle-class identity are distinguishably different values. The lyrics of the new gangstas make it clear that the rhetoric of individualism pays homage to traditional mainstream values that are being used "to redistribute more income, wealth and power to classes that are already most affluent in those aspects" (Gans, 1995, 7).

Born amidst the same media that chain black identity to cultural pathology, this new black-entertainment middle class has viewed the slippery slope of ethical behavior in American life. They were children of the 1980s Yuppie and Buppie culture, when conspicuous consumption was a normative, elite class behavior. These artists have witnessed on television and movie screens the prominence of John Gotti, Manuel Noriega, and Saddam Hussein, all as a result of U.S. state intervention. For them, corporate culture *is* gangsta culture. Could witnessing and experiencing life within the American context have possibly encouraged and nurtured the violation of so-called family values within marginal communities? Jay-Z, owner of Roc-A-Fella Records, seems to think so:

> Your worst fear confirmed
> me and my fam'(ily) roll tight like the firm
> gettin' down for life, that's right, you betta learn
> why play with fire, burn
> we get together like a choir, to acquire what we desire
> we do dirt like worms, produce g's [thousands of dollars] like sperm
> Til legs spread like germs ...
> I sip fine wines and spit vintage flows—what y'all don't know?
> 'Cuz you can' knock the hustle
> Y'all niggas lunchin' punchin' a clock
> function is to make and lay back munchin'
> sippin' Remy on the rocks
> my crew, something to watch
> notin' to stop
> un-stoppable ...
> you ain't havin' it? Good me either
> Let's get together and make this whole world believe us, son
> at my arraignment screamin'
> All us blacks got is sports and entertainment—until we're even
> thievin' as long as I'm breathin'
> can't knock the way a nigga eatin' fuck you even
> (1996)

These lyrics might easily seem to promote illegality, self-indulgence, misogyny, and crudely hedonistic tendencies; however, they also provide a critique of the socio-economic structure that prevents many African-Americans access to decent wage labor. Jay-Z makes clear that large populations of African-Americans are still excluded from middle-class consumption except through sports and entertainment. On Jay-Z's latest album, he is inspired by the hook in the theme song from the musical *Annie*. While the song refers to a little white orphan, Jay-Z argues that "instead of treated we get tricked / instead of kisses we get kicked / it's a hard knock life" is an archetypal "ghetto anthem" (1998). Both sets of lyrics endorse a hustler's mentality, a strategic manipulation of the opportunities made available in light of socio-economic inequalities. This perspective suggests that consumption and pleasure could serve as working-class critiques of middle-class ideals and also utilizes the trope of the gangsta/playa to appropriate the terrain of the "free" market for black institution-building.

Another example of this manipulation of black identity is the platinum-selling artist, The Notorious BIG (aka Biggie Smalls). Before his untimely death, Biggie was one of the artists who freed hip hop from the tight grip of the "keepin it real" persona. After the Ghettocentric turn, rappers were forced to write their rhymes as if they reflected authentic lived experience. So as "keepin it real" in gangsta rap became prevalent, artists competed with one another to see who could depict the most devastatingly grim "personal" narratives. Biggie, however, was unabashed about his goal of upward mobility within the narratives of his ghetto background. He did not feel that he had to stay in the ghetto or necessarily back up his lyrics with authentic acts. In his first single, "Juicy," Biggie remarks, "fifty-inch screen / money green leather sofa / got two cars / a limousine / with a chauffeur / phone bill about two g's fat / no need to worry / my accountant handles that / and my whole crew is lounging / celebratin' everyday / no more public housing" (1994).

In his short career, Biggie took advantage of what was marketable and was never bound by the New York-centric formalism about how real hip hop should sound. In fact, he worked with Luke Skyywalker, Bone Thugs-n-Harmony, and even Michael Jackson, collaborations that would suffice to bar most from the "authentic" hip hop nation. He didn't totally leave the hood behind, but he was more self-conscious in his "performance" of the gangsta lifestyle.

On a number of occasions, Biggie stated that The Notorious BIG was nothing but a character or role that he performed; *he* was Christopher Wallace. In fact, the name "Biggie Smalls" comes from the 70s film *Let's Do It Again*, starring Sidney Poitier and Bill Cosby. Biggie even goes as far as to assume the role of a white movie figure, Frank White, from the film *King of New York*, and concluded his rhymes by exclaiming "MAFIOSO!"

This performance of Mafia culture begs the questions: whose culture is deviant? Isn't the acceptance of certain gangsta ethics in mainstream entertainment deviant? The rise of Roc-A-Fella, Death Row, and Bad Boy, with their commodification of illegality, cannot be divorced from the actual rise during Prohibition of the Irish-American Kennedy family or the Italian-American Gambino family. Likewise, these artists' conspicuous consumption habits cannot be seen as distinct from the mansion-and-yacht stories of Larry Ellison at Oracle, Jim Clark at Netscape, and Bill Gates at Microsoft, complete with feuds over who has the biggest "Cyber Boy Toy" (Kaplan, 1998), whose Horatio Alger narratives have served as models for this country's "formal" economy.

The posthumous indictment of Biggie at his 1997 memorial by Khallid Muhammad couldn't be more correct: "wearing the white man's clothes, showing up on TV dressed like you're Al Capone Baby Face Nelson, ugly as you are" (Marriott, 1997). Indeed, Biggie's is an ugly and messy performance that illuminates the muddled realities of racial and national identity and concurrently unfolds along the axis of gender. Even in his misogynist lyrics, Biggie wasn't shy about passing the mic. He gives props to "the honeys getting money, playing niggas like dummies" (1994). From this gangsta genre emerged a cadre of women artists headed by Lil' Kim of Junior M.A.F.I.A. and Foxy Brown of "The Firm."

These women questioned normative notions of male-female relations; in their stories, they acquire capital, express dissatisfaction with sexual partners, and reverse stereotypical gender roles. Foxy Brown declares:

> No more sex me all night
> thinking it's alright
> while I'm looking over your shoulder
> watching your whole life
> you hate when it's a ball right ladies this ain't hand ball
> nigga hit these walls right
> before I call Mike
> in the morning when it's all bright
> eggs over easy
> hope you have my shit tight
> when I open my eyes
> while I'm eating getting dressed up
> this ain't your pad
> I left money on the dresser
> find you a cab
> (1996)

In most scenarios, black males monopolize blackness through a relegation of the black female to the role of fetish, but here men have become the objects of desire. When patriarchal desires suddenly become articulated in a female voice, these desires are deemed "unnatural." Questions emerge as to what is ladylike and why a woman can't get hers like any man?[7]

Female identity in these musical texts becomes performance by coupling highly materialistic and aesthetically violent and excessive personas with infectious beats and rhymes.

The rhymes make it obvious that the relentless pursuit of status, power, and sexual satisfaction is not gender-specific, and thus reverse the objectification of women as sexual objects by viewing men as accesses to pleasure and capital accumulation, if necessary, through sexual exchange. Lil' Kim debunks the old myth that women only give sex for love and men only give love for sex; she makes it clear that the terms on which masculinity will be recognized will be her economic and sexual self-satisfaction:

> I knew a dude named Jimmy
> he used to run up in me
> night time pissy drunk
> off the Henne and Remy
> I didn't mind it
> when he fucked me from behind
> It felt fine
> especially when he used to grind it
> he was a trip
> when I sucked his dick
> he used to pass me bricks
> credit cards and shit
> I'd suck 'im to sleep
> I took the keys to the jeep
> tell him I'd be back
> go fool with some other cat ...
> it was something about this dude I couldn't stand

242 • DAVARIAN L. BALDWIN

something that coulda made his ass a real man
something I wanted
But I never was pushy
the motherfucker never ate my pussy
(1996)

In a *Vibe* interview, Lil' Kim describes this sexual commerce as the American way: "Sex ... Money is power to me. It's not power alone, but you wanna have money to get the girls. To me, men like what women like, or they learn to like it" (Good, 1997, 176). She and her fellow female artists have understood that "sex sells" and have indirectly initiated a transformation of the color-coded and gender-laden rules by which social relations are scrutinized. This is in no way a proto-feminist position; neither Kim nor Foxy increases the value of women's sexuality. Nonetheless, their performances in the cultural marketplace open up a dialogue about "natural" gender roles and explore issues of female pleasure.

However, the power in articulating bodily pleasure is not purely narcissistic; indeed, it is not just about individual freedom but also concerns the transformation of institutions. Transgressions of black/white, male/female binaries have led artists to challenge the "old-school" belief that "real" hip hop must reside only outside the market. We then begin to remember that hip hop nationalism or nation-conscious rap was created through commodification and market growth. Even the idea of a hip hop national consciousness was raised through the market and utilized market tools, including records, tapes, and stage shows. For example, the "Fresh Fests" of the mid-80s did more than make money; they became a medium to circulate and exchange dance steps, clothing styles, lyrics, and ideas. The commodification of hip hop fashions and aesthetics became a common point of reference for its fans nationwide. The concept of a national consciousness or hip hop nation was not diluted but was in many ways strengthened through the circuits of mass media.

Technological advances within the market such as the music video have revealed the regional and aesthetic diversity of hip hop. Music videos allowed regional artists the space to craft personal and social narratives and "represent" their home not only with visuals but by contextualizing the style and delivery of their rhymes to a national audience without fear of retribution. An example of the power of musical/visual context is the artist Tongue Twista from the group Do or Die. Before Do or Die's breakthrough single "Po Pimps" (Emotions), Tongue Twista had been considered a one-hit wonder in the late 80s, when he was performing Afrocentric styles, wearing African beads and Cross-Colors gear. His claim to fame was recognition by the *Guinness Book of World Records* as "the world's fastest rapper." But thanks to the space opened up by music videos and other alternative outlets, we may now learn that his rapid rhyme style can be located within a Midwest/Southern-influenced hip hop aesthetic identifiable by its staccato delivery blended with doo-wop harmonies and laid over rich Stax-style horns and bass lines. In addition, music video production has enabled the formation of black directors, camera operators, and production crews. Due to video training, these positions have bypassed the white male unions that control apprenticeship systems and employment networks. A perfect example of this breakthrough is F. Gary Gray, who started out directing hip hop/R&B videos and who in 1995 parlayed these skills into a highly successful feature film, *Friday*.

For the regional developments in gangsta/playa hip hop, technological innovations have made it easier and cheaper to own recording studios and gain access to other professional recording resources. Ironically, when conservatives like C. Delores Tucker led the backlash against "gangsta rap," its listeners were drawn closer together. The major labels that produced gangsta rap decided to stop manufacturing it at the same pace. However, while the production side submitted to "public opinion," consumers utilized music technologies to rework the genre based on regional tastes. The consumers of gangsta rap realized that they had more in common musically with the South, West, and Midwest than with the Northeast. For so long, New York had dictated what "real hip hop" is and how it should sound and look.[8] In the face of resistance from both conservative movements and "old school" purists, independent compilations were circulated locally that included artists from emerging Southern and Midwestern versions of California-based gangsta rap. Due to the regional desire for the music, car-trunk distribution turned into independent label empires.

This process has encouraged the formation of semi-independent hip hop labels nationwide, including Death Row and Ruthless Records in Los Angeles; Sick Wit It Records in Vallejo, California; Rap-A-Lot and Suave House Records in Houston; Fully Loaded Records in Decatur, Georgia; So So Def Records in Atlanta; Blackground Records in Virginia; and the Cash Money Clique in New Orleans. While these developments are laudable, it has not been easy for female artists to take advantage of this phenomenon. With the notable exceptions of Queen Latifah, Missy Elliott, and Lil' Kim, women artists/entrepreneurs have not been able to utilize this gangsta grammar to build independent labels. However, artists have been encouraged to look at the relationship between work and culture and to understand the business side of music. The No Limit Empire, headed by Master P, is something to take special note of. P inaugurated the two-pronged strategy of high production (between April 1996 and March 1997, his label released seven albums) and business autonomy that is more reminiscent of West Indian dancehall culture: "You have a product, a rap product. It belongs to you. And you're just going to give somebody 85% of what you make on the product? To do what? Organize your life, basically call you in the morning and tell you to be across town at such and such a time . . . shit, I can wake my own damn self up" (Green, 1997, 100). The only aspect of P's business that is not self-contained is a distribution deal with Priority Records.[9]

Probably the most important aspect of P's business is his engagement with multiple media. Unlike conventional black media entrepreneurs, he feels that nothing is beyond his grasp. Instead of trying to pitch a film deal to a movie conglomerate, P conceived, marketed, and created his own visual autobiography, I'm 'Bout It. He released it himself, taking it straight to video and distributing it through record stores and the Blockbuster Video chain. In 1997, the film had sold over 250,000 units and has surpassed video giants like Jurassic Park in weekly sales.

The strategic marketing of P's film projects used the subversive strategies of the new independent labels. Each No Limit CD is packaged with ads about upcoming work. His projects are a success because he eliminates intermediaries and up-front advances from other sources. P states: "Of course they gonna pop some money at you . . . but how much money can they pop at me that I ain't already seen? That's how white boys do ya. That's how they get our ideas, our inventions" (Jackson, 1998, 74). Master P's aim is to maintain ownership over the means of production by being clear about the consumption habits and tastes of his consumer base.

Whether an artistic flop or a stroke of marketing genius, I'm Bout It has been hailed as paving the way for a new wave of independent hip hop films from cities outside New York or L.A. While Master P was working on his second film, a comedy called I Got the Hookup, other black entrepreneurs and aspiring film-makers had been given an example of how to be "playas in the game." From Bruce Brown's D.C.-based 24–7 (1997), which is driven by a hip hop and go-go soundtrack, to Robert Hayes's urban crime drama Winner Takes All (1998), which depicts the post-industrial landscape of Louisville, Kentucky, a wide range of black filmic expressions abound. The strength of this new wave of filmmaking lies in its manipulation of technologies as a means of autonomy. The first wave of hood films in the early 90s (Boyz in the Hood, Menace II Society) were largely dependent on multimedia conglomerates for distribution and heavily targeted by the gatekeepers of "official" depictions of black life. But the new movie-makers no longer have to bow down to revenue sources or critics. They can go straight to TV or DVD or sell films in record stores. These filmmakers are breaking the rules of conventional budgets, subject matter, marketing, and distribution (Shaw, 1998, 102).

Conclusion

I don't want to suggest that these transgressions of the black/white, male/female authentic/commodified binaries contain any overtly political agenda, because, as we've seen, two artists have died over these attempts to build black empires. Biggie, who labeled himself the "Teflon Don" (aka Mafia boss John Gotti), was not invincible. Concurrently, young children are performing these identities to death, which only fuels the debate for hip hop's critics. Nonetheless, hip hop cannot be singled out without scrutinizing George Bush's endorsement of the violent and misogynist Arnold Schwarzenegger film *True Lies* as "friendly to families" (Pareles, 1995).

Moreover, hip hop can't be seen as all that is wrong with American life. The cultural oscillations of hip hop and the current gangsta trends bear witness to our national history. This music cannot be divorced from the numerous American-dream stories of this nation. Like early gangsta and Afrocentric rappers, the new rappers are not trying to hold black identity to some place of total opposition to consumption, commodification, or social mobility. They are claiming their U.S. citizenship by partaking of conspicuous consumption and performing the identities of a U.S. gangsta government and elite-class capitalists.

The gangsta/playa and the subject matter associated with this icon can now be understood as a strategy, a work in progress. This is a position of maneuverability, which in its present form doesn't endorse the cult of authenticity that must explicitly be a "pure" counter to the mainstream. Womanhood is not purely fetishized as the African Queen or the Streetcorner Ho. While one can still see black women being singled out as locations of deviance, so-called deviant tropes are seen as central to constructing not only successful black women but also, as Lil' Kim charges, "Miss Ivana ... Zsa Zsa Gabor, Demi Moore, Princess Diana and all them rich bitches" (1996). For so long, space had been the chief signifier of racial difference, and freedom and movement had become white prerogatives. Yet these artists are now turning static space into sites of creative play and parody. They are appropriating and rearticulating each and every identity like music samples, cutting and scratching the rigid binaries until they are no longer comprehensible. Democracy, nationhood, and struggles over identity are being theorized through the circuits of desire and spectacle and are best summed up by Jay-Z, who doesn't ask to "Rock the Vote" or "Just Say No," but "Can I live?"

Study Questions

1. How does hip-hop constitute a facet of black cultural empowerment?
2. What opportunities for the expression of female identities are facilitated within commercial hip-hop?
3. What is the "black aesthetic" and how is it articulated within hip-hop's various art forms?

Notes

1. Jon Pareles, "Rapping and Politicking: Showtime on the Stump," *New York Times*, June 11, 1995.
2. Michel Marriott, "Hard Core Rap Lyrics Stir Backlash," *New York Times*, August 15, 1995.
3. Marriott, "Hard Core Rap Lyrics Stir Backlash."

4. This class-based form of policing black bodies can be found in all aspects of black life. One important example was covered by *Village Voice* writer Lisa Jones in a review of a book entitled *Basic Black: Home Training for Modern Times* (ed., Elyse Hudson and Karen Grisby Bates; 1997). These women attempt to map "down-home training" onto the typical etiquette book: teaching black people how to receive first-class service in a first-class restaurant, telling black folk to avoid talking to characters on movie screens, etc. In music, this backlash can be found in the black media's embrace of the hip hop/soul artists Erykah Badu in 1997 and Lauryn Hill in 1998. Without minimizing these artists' talent, they were both praised for their mixture of Afrocentric/Rastafarian/Five-Percenter ideology and "old-school" credibility. Badu and Hill became exemplars of the "purist" revival against "negative" female artists like Lil' Kim, and have been particularly lauded for dressing and acting with self-respect and dignity.

5. Within the nation-conscious genre, not all groups or artists ignored issues of class or gender, e.g., Queen Latifah or the L.A.-based group The Coup. However, this essay is attempting to take note of a general "common sense" that located black authenticity within the simultaneous reverence for and restriction of the black woman. For example, see Decker's analysis of Public Enemy's song "She Watched Channel Zero." True, as Queen Latifah has commented, the women of the nation-conscious genre were not called bitches or hoes, but "queen" status also restricts the ways in which black femininity can be displayed. The weight of the queen's crown was sometimes too heavy a burden to bear.

6. Speech, the lead rapper of Arrested Development, belongs to a prominent black family in Milwaukee, Wisconsin, that runs a black-owned newspaper, *The Community Journal*, where his op-ed "racial uplift" pieces ran in his series, "20th-Century African." This series was known for its catchy and suggestive byline, "Here's the run-down, so you don't get gunned down." This phrase and column foreshadow the urban/African divide that becomes so prominent in his musical ideology.

7. While Foxy's disruption of gender roles within black communities is encouraging, it appears that her exploration of sexuality also reinforces the same patriarchal order. On her new album, *China Doll*, Foxy locates her sexual freedom within the stereotypical image of the exotic Asian woman.

8. In the 1980s, Miami Bass had been marginalized from hip hop as not "real" because it focused more on beats than lyrics. But as other regional versions of hip hop have gained economic and technological resources, this idea of "realness" was exposed as particular to the Northeast. Although conversation in this area is just beginning to emerge, New Yorkers have tended to see hip hop in other regions as "country," "bama," and unsophisticated. However, newer groups like Outkast and Goodie Mob from Atlanta and Timbaland and Missy Elliott from Portsmouth, Virginia, have gone on to parody and play with stereotypes aimed at the "Dirty South."

9. While it is encouraging that black artists/entrepreneurs are breaking into the production side of the music industry, they have yet to shatter the final frontier of the business: distribution. For example, two of gangsta/playa rap's powerhouse semi-independent labels, No Limit and Death Row, are both distributed by Priority Records. Until these labels develop distribution autonomy, they will be forever bound to the structural dictates of the music industry's multinationals.

Bibliography

Books

Asante, Molefi Kete. *The Afrocentric Idea*. Philadelphia: Temple UP, 1987.

Barnekov, Timothy, Robin Boyle, and Daniel Rich. *Privatism and Urban Policy in Britain and the U.S.* New York: Oxford UP, 1996.

Brown, Elaine. *A Taste of Power*. New York: Pantheon, 1992.

Davis, Angela. *Blues Legacies and Black Feminism: Gertrude "Ma" Rainey, Bessie Smith, and Billie Holiday*. New York: Pantheon Books, 1998.

Fanon, Frantz. *Black Skin. White Masks*. Trans. Charles Lam Markmann. New York: Grove, 1967.

Gans, Herbert J. *The War Against the Poor: The Underclass and Anti-Poverty Policy*. New York: Basic Books, 1995.

Kelley, Robin D. G. *Race Rebels*. New York: Free Press, 1994.

Moynihan, Daniel Patrick. *The Negro Family: The Case for National Action*. Washington, D.C.: Office of Policy Planning and Research, U.S. Department of Labor, 1965.

Rose, Tricia. *Black Noise: Rap Music and Black Culture in Contemporary America*. Hanover, NH: Wesleyan UP/UP of New England, 1994.

Stallybrass, Peter, and Allon White. *The Politics and Poetics of Trangression*. Ithaca: Cornell UP, 1986.

West, Cornel. *Race Matters*. Boston: Beacon, 1993.

Articles

Boyd, Todd. "Check Yo'Self. Before You Wreck Yo'Self: Variations on a Political Theme in Rap Music and Popular Culture." Black Public Sphere Collective (ed.). *The Black Public Sphere*. Chicago: U. of Chicago P., 1995.

Decker, Jeffrey Louis. "The State of Rap: Time and Place in Hip Hop Nationalism." Andrew Ross and Tricia Rose (eds.), *Microphone Fiends: Youth Music and Youth Culture*. New York: Routledge, 1994.

Diawara, Manthia. "A Symposium on Popular Culture and Political Correctness." *Social Text*, 1993.

Gilroy, Paul. "Revolutionary Conservatism and the Tyrannies of Unanimism." *New Formations* 28. Spring 1996.

———. "After the Love Has Gone: Bio-Politics and Etho-Poetics in the Black Public Sphere." Black Public Sphere Collective (ed.), *The Black Public Sphere*. Chicago: U. of Chicago P., 1995.

Good, Karen R. "More Than a Lil' Bit." *Vibe*. September 1997.

Green, Tony. "Stairway to Heaven." *Vibe*. June–July 1997.

Hall, Stuart. "The After-life of Frantz Fanon: Why Fanon? Why Now? Why "Black Skin, Where Masks?" Alan Read (ed.), *The Fact of Blackness*. Seattle: Bay Press, 1996.

———. "What Is This 'Black' in Black Popular Culture?" Gina Dent (ed.), *Black Popular Culture*. Seattle: Bay Press, 1992.

Jackson, Scoop. "Soldiers on the Set." *Vibe*. May 1998.

Jones, Lisa. "Home(girl) Training." *Village Voice*. March 19, 1997.

Kaplan, Tony. "Cyber Boy Toys." *Time*. July 1998.

Marriott, Michel. "At a Ceremony for Shakur. Appeals for Peace." *New York Times*. September 23, 1996.

———. "Hard Core Rap Lyrics Stir Backlash." *New York Times*. August 15, 1993.

Pareles, Jon. "Rapping and Politicking: Showtime on the Stump." *New York Times*. June 11, 1995.

Rose, Tricia. "A Symposium on Popular Culture and Political Correctness. *Social Text*. 1993.

———. "Never Trust a Big Butt and a Smile." *Camera Obscura*. #23, 1991.

Shaw, William. "Bustin' a Movie." *Details*. March 1998.

Smith, R. J. "Bigger Than Life." *Village Voice*. March 19, 1997.

Tate, Greg, "Funking Intellect." *Vibe*. June/July 1997.

Touré. "Bigger Than Life." *Village Voice*. March 19, 1997.

Weinraub, Bernard. "National Desk." *New York Times*. June 1, 1995.

Discography

Arrested Development. "People Everyday." *3 Years, 5 Months and 2 Days in the Life Of*. Chrysalis, 1992.

De La Soul. "Me, Myself and I." *3 Feet High and Rising*. Tommy Boy, 1988.

Dr. Dre. "Dre Day." *The Chronic*. Death Row Interscope, 1992.

Eric B. and Rakim. *Paid in Fall*. Island, 1987.

Foxy Brown. "Ill Nana." *ILL NANA*. Rush Recordings, 1996.

Ice Cube. "Species (Tales from the Darkside)." *AmeriKKKa Most Wanted*. Priority, 1990.

Ice T. "New Jack Hustler." *OG: Original Gangster*. Sire, 1991.

Isis. "The Power of Myself Is Moving." *Rebel Soul*. 4th and Broadway, 1990.

Jay-Z. "Can't Knock the Hustle." *Reasonable Doubt*. Roc-A-Fella/Priority, 1996.

———. "Hard Knock Life." *Hard Knock Life* Vol. II. Roc-A-Fella/Def Jam, 1998.

KRS-One. *Criminal Minded*. Sugar Hill, 1986, Reprint, 1991.

———. *By All Means Necessary*. Jive, 1988.

Lil' Kim. *Hard Core*. Big Beat, 1996.

The Notorious BIG *Ready to Die*. Arista, 1994.

N.W.A. *Straight Outta Compton*. Ruthless, 1988.

Public Enemy. "My 98 Oldsmobile." *Yo! Bum the Rush Show*. Def Jam, 1987.

———. "She Watched Channel Zero." *It Takes a Nation of Millions to Hold Us Back*. Def Jam, 1988.

———. "Welcome to the Terrordome." *Fear of a Black Planet*. Def Jam, 1990.

17

"Represent"
Race, Space, and Place in Rap Music

In this chapter, Murray Forman explains hip-hop's emergence and expansion in the context of localized labor and industrial capital. Hip-hop is not newly commercialized, having been integrated into highly localized marketing and promotional infrastructures since its inception, yet what is often overlooked in critical studies is how various enabling or restrictive factors operating at differing scales of influence have affected the growth and evolution of hip-hop at each stage of its development.

A fundamental issue in the study of space and place includes the role of the posse, crew, or clique and this chapter explores the ways in which the localized posse formation is integrated into the particular creative processes of rap music. Finally, Forman examines specific lyrical examples in order to chart some of the more prominent discursive shifts that have, over time, altered the spatial emphasis of rap music and hip-hop culture as the initial emphasis of the ghetto was subsumed by a pronounced articulation of themes and imagery from "the 'hood."

"Represent": Race, Space, and Place in Rap Music

Murray Forman

Say somethin' positive, well positive ain't where I live
I live around the corner from West Hell
Two blocks from South Shit and once in a jail cell
The sun never shined on my side of the street, see?

> Naughty By Nature, "Ghetto Bastard
> (Everything's Gonna Be Alright)," 1991, Isba/Tommy Boy Records

If you're from Compton you know it's the 'hood where it's good

> Compton's Most Wanted, "Raised in Compton," 1991, Epic/Sony

Introduction

Hip hop's[1] capacity to circumvent the constraints and limiting social conditions of young Afro-American and Latino youths has been examined and celebrated by cultural critics and scholars in various contexts since its inception in the mid-1970s. For instance, the 8 February 1999 issue of the U.S. magazine *Time* featured a cover photo of ex-Fugees and five-time Grammy award winner Lauryn Hill with the accompanying headline "Hip-Hop Nation: After 20 Years—how it's changed America." Over the years, however, there has been little attention granted to the implications of hip hop's spatial logics. *Time*'s coverage is relatively standard in perceiving the hip hop nation as a historical construct rather than a geo-cultural amalgamation of personages and practices that are spatially dispersed.

Tricia Rose (1994) arguably goes the furthest in introducing a spatial analysis when she details the ways that hip hop continually displays a clever transformative creativity that is endlessly capable of altering the uses of technologies and space. Her specific references to hip hop culture and space stress the importance of the "postindustrial city" as the central urban influence, "which provided the context for creative development among hip hop's earliest innovators, shaped their cultural terrain, access to space, materials, and education" (1994, p. 34). As this suggests, the particularities of urban space themselves are subjected to the deconstructive and reconstructive practices of rap artists. Thus, when, in another context, Iain Chambers refers to rap as "New York's 'sound system' ... sonorial graffiti" with "the black youth culture of Harlem and the Bronx twisting technology into new cultural shape" (1985, p. 190), he opens the conceptual door onto corresponding strategies that give rise to the radical transformation of the sites where these cultures cohere and converge or the spaces that are reimagined and, importantly, remapped. Rap artists therefore emerge not only as aberrant users of electronic and digital technologies but also as alternative cartographers for what the Samoan-American group Boo Yaa Tribe has referred to in an album title as "a new funky nation."

Indeed, there is very little about today's society that is not, at some point, imbued with a spatial character and this is no less true for the emergence and production of spatial categories and identities in rap music and the hip hop cultures of which it is a central component. Rap music presents a case worthy of examination and provides a unique set of contexts for the analyses of public discourses pertaining to youth, race, and space. Rap music is one of the main sources within popular culture of a sustained and in-depth examination and analysis of the spatial partitioning of race and the diverse experiences of being young and black in America. It can be observed that space and race figure prominently as organizing concepts implicated in the delineation of a vast range of fictional or actually existing social practices that are represented in narrative and lyrical form. In this chapter, I seek to illuminate the central importance of spatiality in the organizing principles of value, meaning, and practice within hip hop culture. My further intent is to explore the question of how the dynamics of space, place, and race get taken up by rap artists as themes and topics and how they are located within a wider range of circulating social discourses. The prioritization of spatial practices and spatial discourses that form a basis of hip hop culture offers a means through which to view both the *ways* that spaces and places are constructed and the *kinds* of spaces or places that are constructed.

The chapter traces the way in which hip hop's popularity spread from New York to other U.S. cities, most notably Philadelphia and Los Angeles but eventually more geographically marginal cities such as Seattle, and it discusses changes that have taken place in rap production, particularly the rise of artist-owned labels. Such developments encouraged the emergence of distinctive regional rap sounds and styles, as well as strong local allegiances and territorial rivalries, as the identities and careers of rap acts became more closely tied to the city and to its specific neighborhoods ('hoods) and communities. The chapter examines the effects of all this on the spatial discourse of rap. It points to a gradual shift within rap from a concern with broad, generalized spaces, to the representation of specific named cities and 'hoods (as illustrated by Gansta Rap from the Californian city of Compton which celebrates and glorifies Compton as well as the street warrior and gang rivalry) and the representation of smaller-scale, more narrowly defined and highly detailed places (as illustrated by rap from the North West city of Seattle which has a distinctively local flavor).

Locating Hip Hop

Describing the early stages of rap music's emergence within the hip hop culture for an MTV "Rap-umentary," Grandmaster Flash, one of the core DJs of the early scene, recalls the spatial distribution of sound systems and crews in metropolitan New York:

> We had territories. It was like, Kool Herc had the west side. Bam had Bronx River. DJ Breakout had way uptown past Gun Hill. Myself, my area was like 138th Street, Cypress Avenue, up to Gun Hill, so that we all had our territories and we all had to respect each other.

The documentary's images embellish Flash's commentary, displaying a computer generated map of the Bronx with colored sections demarcating each DJ's territory as it is mentioned, graphically separating the enclaves that comprise the main area of operations for the competing sound systems.

This emphasis on territoriality involves more than just a geographical arrangement of cultural workers and the regionalism of cultural practices. It illuminates a particular relationship to space or, more accurately, a relationship to particular places. As Flash conveys it, the sound systems that formed the backbone of the burgeoning hip hop scene were identified by their audiences and followers according to the overlapping influences of personae and turf. The territories were tentatively claimed through the ongoing cultural practices that occurred within their bounds and were reinforced by the circulation of those who recognized and accepted their perimeters. It is not at all insignificant that most of the dominant historical narratives pertaining to the emergence of hip hop (i.e., Hager 1984; Toop 1984) identify a transition from gang-oriented affiliations (formed around protection of turf) to music and break dance affiliations that maintained and, in some cases, intensified the important structuring systems of territoriality.

Flash's reference to the importance of "respect" is not primarily addressing a respect for the skills or character of his competitors (although, elsewhere [George 1993] he acknowledges this as well). Rather, his notion of respect is related to the geographies that he maps; it is based on the existence of circumscribed domains of authority and dominance that have been established among the various DJs. These geographies are inhabited and bestowed with value, they are understood as lived places and localized sites of significance, as well as being understood within the market logic that includes a product (the music in its various live or recorded forms) and a consumer base (various audience formations). The proprietary discourse also implies, therefore, that even in its infancy hip hop cartography was to some extent shaped by a refined capitalist logic and the existence of distinct market regions. Without sacrificing the basic geographic components of territory, possession and group identity that play such an important role among gang-oriented activities, the representation of New York's urban spaces was substantially revised as hip hop developed.

Clearly, however, the geographical boundaries that Flash describes and which are visually mapped in the documentary were never firm or immovable. They were cultural boundaries that were continually open to negotiation and renegotiation by those who inhabited their terrains and who circulated throughout the city's boroughs. As the main form of musical expression within the hip hop culture, the early DJ sound systems featured a series of practices that linked the music to other mobile practices, such as graffiti art and "tagging." Together, these overlapping practices and methods of constructing place-based identities, and of inscribing and enunciating individual and collective presence, created the bonds upon which affiliations were forged within specific social geographies. Hip hop's distinct practices introduced new forms of expression that were contextually linked to conditions in a city comprised of an amalgamation of neighborhoods and boroughs with their own highly particularized social norms and cultural nuances.

Hip Hop, Space, and Place

Rap music takes the city and its multiple spaces as the foundation of its cultural production. In the music and lyrics, the city is an audible presence, explicitly cited and digitally sampled in the reproduction of the aural textures of the urban environment. Since its inception in the mid- to late 1970s, hip hop culture has always maintained fiercely defended local ties and an in-built element of competition waged through hip hop's cultural forms of rap, breakdancing and graffiti. This competition has traditionally been staged within geographical boundaries that demarcate turf and territory among various crews, cliques, and posses, extending and altering the spatial alliances that had previously cohered under other organizational structures, including but not exclusive to gangs. Today, a more pronounced level of spatial awareness is one of the key factors distinguishing rap and hip hop culture from the many other cultural and subcultural youth formations currently vying for attention.

Throughout its historical evolution, it is evident that there has been a gradually escalating urgency with which minority youth use rap in the deployment of discourses of urban locality or "place," with the trend accelerating noticeably since 1987–1988. With the discursive shift from the spatial abstractions framed by the notion of "the ghetto" to the more localized and specific discursive construct of "the 'hood" occurring in 1987–1988 (roughly corresponding with the rise and impact of rappers on the U.S. West Coast), there has been an enhanced emphasis on the powerful ties to place that both anchor rap acts to their immediate environments and set them apart from other environments and other 'hoods as well as from other rap acts and their crews which inhabit similarly demarcated spaces.

Commenting in 1988 on rap's "nationwide" expansions beyond New York's boroughs, Nelson George writes, "Rap and its Hip Hop musical underpinning is now the national youth music of black America ... rap's gone national and is in the process of going regional" (George 1992, p. 80). George was right, as rap was rising out of the regions and acts were emerging from the South (Miami-based 2 Live Crew or Houston's The Geto Boys), the North-west (Seattle's Sir Mix-A-Lot and Kid Sensation), the San Francisco Bay area (Digital Underground, Tupac, Too Short), Los Angeles (Ice T, N.W.A.) and elsewhere. Indeed, the significance of the east–west split within U.S. rap cannot be overstated since it has led to several intense confrontations between artists representing each region and is arguably the single most divisive factor within U.S. hip hop to date. Until the mid-1990s, artists associated with cities in the Midwest or southern states often felt obligated to align themselves with either East or West, or else they attempted to sidestep the issue deftly without alienating audiences and deriding either coast. In the past several years, however, Houston, Atlanta, and New Orleans have risen as important rap production centers and have consequently emerged as powerful forces in their own right.

Today, the emphasis is on place, and groups explicitly advertise their home environments with names such as Compton's Most Wanted, Detroit's Most Wanted, the Fifth Ward Boyz, and South Central Cartel, or else they structure their home territory into titles and lyrics, constructing a new internally meaningful hip hop cartography. The explosion of localized production centers and regionally influential producers and artists has drastically altered the hip hop map and production crews have sprung up throughout North America. These producers have also demonstrated a growing tendency to incorporate themselves as localized businesses (often buying or starting companies unrelated to the music industry in their local neighborhoods, such as auto customizing and repair shops) and to employ friends, family members and members of their wider neighborhoods. Extending Nelson George's observation, it now seems possible to say that rap, having gone regional, is in the process of going local.

The Regional Proliferation of Artist-Owned Record Labels

Reflecting on the intensification of regional rap activity within the U.S. during what might be defined as the genre's "middle-school" historical period,[2] Nelson George writes that 1987 was "a harbinger of the increasing quality of non-New York hip hop," citing as evidence the fact that three of the four finalists in the New Music Seminar's DJ Competition were from "outside the Apple—Philadelphia's Cash Money, Los Angeles's Joe Cooley, and Mr. Mix of Miami's 2 Live Crew" (George 1992, p. 30). In the pages of *Billboard*, he observed that despite New York's indisputable designation as the "home" of rap, Philadelphia rappers in particular (most notably, DJ Jazzy Jeff and the Fresh Prince) were making inroads on the scene and on the charts, making it "rap's second city" (George, ibid.). This expansion was facilitated by the emergent trend in the development of artist-owned independent labels and management companies which entered into direct competition with non-artist-owned companies.

After years of bogus contracts, management conflicts, and poor representation, a growing number of artists began dividing their duties between recording or performing, locating and producing new talent, and managing their respective record companies. By forming self-owned labels and publishing companies and establishing themselves as autonomous corporate entities, forward-thinking rap artists were also able to maintain greater creative control over their production while ensuring increased returns on their sales. In a rather excessive discourse, artists spoke of throwing off the corporate shackles of the recording industry as well as invoking the quite separate issues of building something of which one can be proud or being remunerated in a more lucrative manner.

Once several key labels such as Luther Campbell's Skyywalker Records and Eazy-E's Ruthless Records had been established and had proven the viability of the venture, their initiatives were rapidly reproduced as numerous artists followed suit. For many recording artists, to gain wealth and material renumeration for their work suddenly meant learning the production and management side of the industry and exercising entrepreneurial skills as well. As the trend expanded, small artist-owned and operated labels burgeoned and another tier was added to the industry. With the rise of artist-owned labels there was also an increased emphasis on regional and local affiliations and an articulation of pride and loyalty in each label, its artist roster, and the central locale of operation.

Rap is characteristically produced within a system of extremely close-knit local affiliations, forged within particular cultural settings and urban minority youth practices. Yet the developments in the rap industry, whereby production houses or record labels might be identified on the basis of their regional and local zones of operation, are not unique to this current period. For instance, independent "race record" labels, which targeted blacks in the South and in larger northern urban centers throughout the 1920s and 1930s, flourished in part due to the enhanced mobility of black populations which maintained their affinities for the various regional blues styles. Nelson George's consistent attention to black musical tradition, the music industry's gradual permutations, and rap's growing national influence led him to note in *Billboard* that "regional music used to be the backbone of black music and—maybe—it will be again" (31 May 1986, p. 23). He recalls black American musical production in the immediate post–World War II period when independent labels were dispersed across the nation, recording locally and regionally based artists while servicing the needs of black music consumers within these regional markets.

Examining the history of black popular music in the 1960s and 1970s, the names Motown, Stax, or Philadelphia International Records (PIR) evoke images of composers, producers and musical talent working within very specific studio contexts in Detroit, Memphis, and Philadelphia. The dispersed independent labels and production sites that operated from the 1950s through the 1970s are therefore culturally meaningful and relevant to descriptions of black music of the period as they convey an idea of consistency and identifiable signature sounds or styles.[3] This trend has continued with rap, with more pronounced and explicit connection to specific locales and the articulations of geography, place and identity that sets the genre apart from many of its musical predecessors.

Of the smaller labels that had thrived in the 1950s, 1960s, and 1970s, most disappeared as musical tastes shifted, as economic transitions evolved, or as the industry majors swallowed them or bumped them out of the market by introducing their own specialty labels. Towards the end of the 1980s, the U.S. music industry was no longer even primarily American, with the major parent companies being massive transnational entities with corporate offices based in several countries. Yet, in both rock and rap there was a resurgence of regional production in the mid- to late 1980s and, with it, the resurgence of regionally distinct styles. In the black music sector these were exemplified by the Minneapolis funk that was a trademark of artists like Prince, The Time, Jimmy Jam and Terry Lewis, or Jesse Johnson; the Washington, D.C. go-go sound of Chuck Brown, Redd and the Boys, and especially Trouble Funk; and from Chicago, house music exemplified by DJ Frankie Knuckles. Rap production in New York, Los Angeles, and Miami also began to display regionally distinct "flavors" to a greater extent as individual producers emerged with their own trademark styles and influences. Individual studios such as Chung King in New York also became associated with specific production styles and sounds in rap.

As evidence of the arrival of artist-owned labels in the rap business, in December, 1989, *Billboard* featured advertisements in a special section on rap that illustrated the trend. Among these were ads for Eazy-E's Ruthless Records (Compton, CA), Luther Campbell's Skyywalker Records (Miami, FL), and Ice T's Rhyme Syndicate (South Central LA). Appearing alongside these were advertisements for the established independent rap labels Def Jam, Tommy Boy and Jive as well as ads for the newer "street" divisions of major labels including Atlantic ("The Strength of the Street"), MCA ("Wanna Rap? MCA Raps. Word!") and Epic ("Epic in Total Control. No Loungin', Just Lampin"). The phenomenon has since evolved to the extent that artist-owned operations have become relatively standard in the industry, existing as influential players alongside the major labels.

As a later entrant, Death Row Records (initiated in 1992 by principal investors Suge Knight and former member of the rap group Niggaz with Attitude [N.W.A.] Dr. Dre) flourished through a lucrative co-ownership and distribution alliance with upstart Interscope Records, which was itself half-owned by Time Warner's Atlantic Group. Although a series of misfortunes in 1996–97 decimated the label,[4] it rose to virtual dominance in the rap field between 1992 and 1997 with top-charting releases by Dr. Dre, Snoop Doggy Dogg, and Tupac Shakur as well as the soundtrack albums *Deep Cover* (1992) and *Murder Was the Case* (1994). One of the factors that characterized Death Row Records from its inception and which is common to the dozens of artist-owned and operated rap labels to emerge in the late 1980s and early 1990s, however, is an organized structure rooted in localized "posse" affiliations.

Homeboys and Production Posses

Greg Tate suggests that, "every successful rap group is a black fraternal organization, a posse" (1992, p. 134). On the same theme, Tricia Rose writes that "rappers' emphasis on posses and neighborhoods has brought the ghetto back into the public consciousness" (1994, p. 11). For Public Enemy's Chuck D, posse formations are a necessary response to the fragmentive effects of capitalism: "the only way that you exist within that mould is that you have to put together a 'posse', or a team to be able to penetrate that structure, that block, that strong as steel structure that no individual can break" (Eure and Spady 1991, p. 330). As each of these commentators suggests, the posse is the fundamental social unit binding a rap act and its production crew together, creating a collective identity that is rooted in place and within which the creative process unfolds. It is not rare for an entire label to be defined along posse lines with the musical talent, the producers and various peripheral associates bonding under the label's banner.

With collective identities being evident as a nascent reference throughout rap's history in group names like The Sugarhill Gang, Doug E. Fresh and the Get Fresh Crew, X-Clan, or the 2 Live Crew, the term "posse" was later unambiguously adopted by rap artists such as California's South Central Posse or Orlando's DJ Magic Mike, whose crew records under the name "the Royal Posse." In virtually all cases, recording acts align themselves within a relatively coherent posse structure, sharing labels and producers, appearing on each other's recordings and touring together.

The term posse is defined as a "strong force or company" (*Concise Oxford Dictionary*, 1985) and for many North Americans it summons notions of lawlessness and frontier justice that were standard thematic elements of Hollywood westerns in the 1940s and 1950s. This is, in fact, the basis of the term as it is applied within rap circles, although its current significance is related more precisely to the ways in which the Jamaican posse culture has over the years adapted the expressive terminology and gangster imagery of the cinema to its own cultural systems. In her illuminating research on the sinister complexities of the Jamaican posse under- world, Laurie Gunst (1995) explains how the posse system grew under the specific economic, political, and cultural conditions of mid-1970s Jamaica, evolving into a stratified and violent gang culture that gained strength through the marijuana, cocaine, and crack trade. As she explains, the Jamaican posse system has, since 1980, been transplanted to virtually every major North American city.

The Jamaican posse expansion is important in this context as it coincides almost precisely with the emergence of rap and hip hop in New York's devastated uptown ghetto environments. This connection is strengthened when rap's hybrid origins that were forged in the convergence of Jamaican sound systems and South Bronx funk are considered. The concept of the posse has, through various social mechanisms and discursive overlays, been traced upon many of rap's themes, images, and postures that take the forms of the pimp, hustler, gambler and gangster in the music's various sub-genres that evolved after 1987. Rap has also been influenced by the gangland models provided by the New York mafia and Asian Triad gangs.

Since roughly 1987 hip hop culture has also been influenced by alliances associated with West Coast gang systems. Numerous rap album covers and videos feature artists and their posses repre- senting their gang, their regional affiliations or their local 'hood with elaborate hand gestures. The practice escalated to such an extent that, in an effort to dilute the surging territorial aggression, Black Entertainment Television (BET) passed a rule forbidding explicitly gang- related hand signs on its popular video programs.

"The 'Hood Took Me Under": Home, Turf and Identity

It is necessary to recognize that the home territory of a rapper or rap group is a testing ground, a place to hone skills and to gain a local reputation. This is accurately portrayed in the 1992 Ernest Dickerson film *Juice* where the expression "local" is attributed to the young DJ Q, in one instance suggesting community ties and home alliances whereas, in another context, it is summoned as a pejorative term that reflects a lack of success and an inability to mobilize his career beyond the homefront. In interviews and on recordings most rappers refer to their early days, citing the time spent with their "home boys," writing raps, perfecting their turntable skills, and taking the stage at parties and local clubs or dances (Cross 1993). Their perspective emerges from within the highly localized conditions that they know and the places they inhabit.

As a site of affiliation and circulation, the 'hood provides a setting for particular group interactions which are influential in rap music's evolution. In rap, there is a widespread sense that an act cannot succeed without first gaining approval and support from the crew and the 'hood. Successful acts are expected to maintain connections to the 'hood and to "keep it real" thematically, rapping about situations, scenes and sites that comprise the lived experience of the 'hood. At issue is the complex question of authenticity as rap posses continually strive to reaffirm their connections to the 'hood in an attempt to mitigate the negative accusations that they have sold out in the event of commercial or crossover success. Charisse Jones has noted a dilemma confronting successful rap artists who suddenly have the economic means to "get over" and leave the 'hood. As she writes in the *New York Times* (24 September 1995, p. 43), contemporary artists such as Snoop Dogg or Ice T are often criticized for rapping about ghetto poverty and gang aggression while living in posh suburban mansions.

Those who stay in the 'hood generally do so to be closer to friends and family, closer to the posse. While a common rationale for staying in the 'hood is familiarity and family bonds, in numerous cases artists also justify their decisions to stay along a creative rationale, suggesting that the 'hood provides the social contexts and raw resources for their lyrics. Others leave with some regret, suggesting that the 'hood may constitute "home" but its various tensions and stresses make it an entirely undesirable place to live (this is even more frequent among rappers with children to support and nurture); there is no romanticizing real poverty or real danger.

The 'hood is, however, regularly constructed within the discursive frame of the "home," and the dual process of "turning the 'hood out" or "representing" (which involves creating a broader profile for the home territory and its inhabitants while showing respect for the nurture it provides) is now a required practice among hardcore rap acts. The posse is always explicitly acknowledged and individual members are greeted on disk and in live concerts with standard "shout outs" that frequently cite the streets and localities from which they hail. This continual reference to the important value of social relations based in the 'hood refutes the damning images of an oppressed and joyless underclass that are so prevalent in the media and contemporary social analyses. Rap may frequently portray the nation's gritty urban underside, but its creators also communicate the importance of places and the people that build community within them. In this interpretation, there is an insistent emphasis on support, nurture and community that coexists with the grim representations that generally cohere in the images and discourses of ghetto life.

As in all other popular music forms, "paying dues" is also part of the process of embarking on a rap music career, and the local networks of support and encouragement, from in-group affiliations to local club and music scenes, are exceedingly important factors in an act's professional development. One way that this is facilitated is through the posse alliances and local connections that form around studios and producers. For example, in describing the production house once headed by DJ Mark, The 45 King, the rap artist Fab 5 Freddy recalls that "he had this posse called the Flavor Unit out there in New Jersey. . . . He has like a Hip Hop training room out there, an incredible environment where even if you weren't good when you came in, you'd get good just being around there" (Nelson and Gonzales 1991, p. xiii).[5] This pattern is replicated in numerous instances and is also exemplified by the production/posse structure of Rap-A-Lot Records in Houston (home to acts such as the Geto Boys, Scarface, Big Mike, Caine, and The Fifth Ward Boyz) where the company was forced to relocate its offices because "artists were always kicking it there with their posses like it was a club" (*Rap Sheet*, October 1992, p. 18). By coming up through the crew, young promising artists learn the ropes, acquire lessons in craft and showmanship, attain stage or studio experience and exposure and, quite frequently, win record deals based on their apprenticeships and posse connections.

Few rap scholars (Tricia Rose and Brian Cross being notable exceptions) have paid attention to these formative stages and the slow processes of developing MC and DJ skills. There is, in fact, a trajectory to an artist's development that is seldom accounted for. In practice, artists' lyrics and rhythms must achieve success on the home front first, where the flow, subject matter, style and image must resonate meaningfully among those who share common bonds to place, to the posse and to the 'hood. In this sense, when rappers refer to the "local flavor," they are identifying the detailed inflections that respond to and reinforce the significance of the music's particular sites of origin and which might be recognized by others elsewhere as being unique, interesting and, ultimately, marketable.

The Spatialization of Production Styles

The posse structures that privilege place and the 'hood can be seen as influential elements in the evolution of new rap artists as well as relevant forces in the emergence of new, regionally definable sounds and discourses about space and place. For example, critics and rappers alike acknowledge the unique qualities of the West Coast G-funk sound which defined a production style that emerged with Dr. Dre's work on the *Deep Cover* soundtrack and the release of his 1992 classic *The Chronic* (Death Row/Interscope), and arguably reached its apex with the 1994 release of Warren G's *Regulate … G Funk Era* (Violator/Rush Associated Labels). Other local artists in this period, such as the Boo Yaa Tribe, Above the Law, Compton's Most Wanted, and DJ Quik, also prominently featured variations on the G-funk sound and reinforced its influence in the industry as an identifiable West Coast subgenre. G-funk makes ample use of standard funk grooves by artists including George Clinton, Bootsy Collins, Gap Band, or the late Roger Troutman, and is characterized as being "laid-back" and sparse, featuring slow beats and longer sample loops. While it was regarded as a regionally distinct sound, it was also often related specifically to Dr. Dre's production style and was comparatively categorized by its difference from the more cacophonous East Coast jams (recognizable in the early work of the Bomb Squad, the production crew of the rap act Public Enemy). As Brian Cross (1993) notes, however, the impact of the G-funk style among California rap acts is also related to the extended influence of late 1970s funk music in the Southwest that was a consequence of limited access to independently produced and distributed rap product in the early 1980s, delaying rap's geographic expansion from New York to the Los Angeles area.

Explaining the Bomb Squad's production processes following the release of Public Enemy's *Fear of a Black Planet* (1990, Def Jam), Chuck D describes his production posse's familiarity with various regional styles and tastes and their attempts to integrate the differences into the album's tracks. As he states:

> Rap has different feels and different vibes in different parts of the country. For example, people in New York City don't drive very often, so New York used to be about walking around with your radio. But that doesn't really exist anymore. It became unfashionable because some people were losing their *lives* over them, and also people don't want to carry them, so now it's more like "Hey, I've got my Walkman." For that reason, there's a treble type of thing going on; they're not getting much of the bass. So rap music in New York City is a headphone type of thing, whereas in Long Island or Philadelphia … it's more of a bass type thing. (Dery 1990, p. 90)

These regional distinctions between the "beats" are borne out in the example of the Miami production houses of Luther Campbell or Orlando's Magic Mike. In Florida (and to some extent, Georgia) the focus is on the bass—Florida "booty bass" or "booty boom" as it has been termed—which offers a deeper, "phatter," and almost subsonic vibration that stands out as a regionally distinct and authored style.[6] Within U.S. rap culture, artists and fans alike reflect an acute awareness that people in different parts of the country produce and enjoy regional variations on the genre; they experience rap differently, structuring it into their social patterns according to the norms that prevail in a given urban environment. Thus, the regional taste patterns in South Florida are partially influenced by the central phenomenon of car mobility and the practice of stacking multiple 10- or 15-inch bass speakers and powerful sub-woofers into car trunks and truck beds.

Add to these stylistic distinctions the discursive differences within rap from the various regions (i.e., the aforementioned Gangsta Rap from the West Coast crews, the chilling, cold-blooded imagery from Houston's "Bloody Nickle" crews on Rap-A-Lot Records, or the "pimp, playa and hustla" themes that are standard among Oakland and San Francisco cliques), the localized posse variations in vocal style and slang, or the site-specific references in rap lyrics to cities, 'hoods, and crews, and a general catalogue of differences in form and content becomes clearly audible. What these elements indicate is that, while the rap posse provides a structured identity for its members, it can also provide a referential value to the production qualities and the sound of the musical product with which it is associated.

Rap's Spatial Discourse

In his enquiry into the cultural resonance and meanings of the term "the 'hood," Paul Gilroy poses the question, "how is black life in one 'hood connected to life in others? Can there be a blackness that connects, articulates, synchronizes experiences and histories across the diaspora space?" (1992, p. 308). He criticizes the idea of "nation" that has emerged as an important structuring concept in American hip hop culture (mainly after 1987) and remains skeptical of the value invested in the discourses of "family" unity (communicated in the rhetoric of black brotherhood and sisterhood) when there is so much territorial antagonism evident in the strands of rap that privilege the spatialities of gang culture and turf affiliation. Gilroy expresses his perplexity with the closed contours that the 'hood represents, suggesting that its inward-turning spatial perspectives inhibit dialogue across divided social territories and cultural zones. He further argues that redemptive attempts to appeal to either the black "nation," or to the "family" of internationally dispersed blacks in the rap subgenre known as "message rap" are ill-conceived and based in a particularly North Americanist viewpoint that harbors its own exclusive and hierarchically stratified biases.

Perhaps more in line with Gilroy's expansive, trans-Atlantic visions of rap's diasporic potential is the track "Ludi" (1991, Island Records) by the Canadian act the Dream Warriors. Based in Toronto, the group is part of one of the world's largest expatriate Caribbean communities. Like Gilroy's London, Toronto could be seen as an

> important junction point or crossroads on the webbed pathways of black Atlantic political culture. It is revealed to be a place where, by virtue of factors like the informality of racial segregation, the configuration of class relations, the contingency of linguistic convergences, global phenomena such as anti-colonial and emancipationist political formations are still being sustained, reproduced, and amplified. (Gilroy 1992, p. 95)

In mapping a cultural "crossroads," the song "Ludi" utilizes an early reggae rhythm and a lightly swinging melody (based on a sample of the Jamaican classic "My Conversation," released in 1968 by The Uniques) that taps into a particularly rich moment in the evolution of the reggae style and revives a well-known Jamaican track while relocating it within the performative contexts of hip hop.

"Ludi" (which refers to a board game) begins with rapper King Lou stating that the song is for his mother—who wants something to dance to—and his extended family to whom he offers the musical sounds of their original home environment. The family to which he refers is not, in the immediate sense, the family of black-identified brothers and sisters that cohere within nationalistic and essentialist discourse but literally his siblings. He then expands his dedication to the wider "family" of blacks with a comprehensive roll-call of the English and Spanish-speaking Caribbean islands and Africa which inform (but by no means determine) his cultural identity. There is no attempt to privilege an originary African heritage nor is there a nostalgic appeal to the Caribbean heritage. This extensive list recognizes Toronto's hybrid Afro-Caribbean community and refers directly to a locally manifested culture of international black traditions (rather than a single tradition of essentialist blackness) within which the Dream Warriors developed as young artists. The song's bridge also reinforces the Caribbean connection by making several references to the turntable practices of Jamaican sound systems that are mainstays throughout internationally dispersed Caribbean communities.

Later in the track, King Lou's cohort, Capital Q, reminds him that "there are other places than the islands that play Ludi. Why don't you run it down for the people?" Herc, employing a distinctly Jamaican DJ "toaster" dialect, King Lou provides a wider expression of black diasporic identification as he expands his list to include Canada, the UK, and the United States, countries where the Afro-Caribbean presence is the largest and most influential. He concludes by mentioning his international record labels 4th and Broadway and Island Records and, finally, names the influential Toronto-based independent production house, Beat Factory, that first recorded the group. In this last reference to Beat Factory he effectively returns the scale to the local, closing the circle that positions the Dream Warriors within a global/local system of circulation.

There is no simple means of assessing the impact of this expansive global/local perspective but, within Gilroy's innovative theoretical *oeuvre*, the track can be celebrated for the ways in which its musical and lyrical forms reinforce the dispersed geographies of contemporary black cultures without falling victim to the conservative reductions of black essentialism. Without cleaving towards either the rhetorical rigidity of black nationalist Rap or the nihilistic vitriol of gangster rappers ("niggaz with (bad) attitude"), the Dream Warriors present an alternative path. As "Ludi" illustrates, the group unselfconsciously articulates an evolving hybrid identity informed by transnational migrations that are actively manifested on local grounds.

On the other end of the rap spectrum is the example of artists who mainly operate within a discursive field featuring spatialized themes of intense locality. Whereas the proponents of Message Rap evoke an expanded vision of black America, it is in contrast to the ghettocentric visions of urban black experience that also emerge in the genre, mainly within the lyrics of Gangsta Rap. Despite many shared perspectives on black oppression and systemic injustices, there exists a tension in the interstices between the expansive nationalisms of Message Rap and the more narrowly defined localisms of Gangsta Rap with its core emphasis on "the 'hood." This distance is widened in view of the unapologetic claim among numerous studio gangstas who, like the rap artist Ice Cube on the N.W.A. track "Gangsta, Gangsta" (1988, Ruthless/Priority), claim that "life ain't nothin' but bitches and money." The two subgenres are addressing generally common phenomena in their focus on black struggles for empowerment, yet they are deploying spatial discourses and programs of action that do not fit easily together.

The emergence of an intensified spatial terminology was not a sudden occurrence, but by 1987 when New York's Boogie Down Productions (also known as BDP), featuring rap acts such as KRS-1, Eazy-E, and Ice T broke onto the scene, the privileging of localized experience rapidly acquired an audible resonance. From New York, BDP released "South Bronx" (1987, B-Boy), a track that aggressively disputes the allegations of various rappers from Queens who, in the aftermath of Run-DMC's commercial successes, claimed that they were rap's true innovators. KRS-1's lyrics reaffirm his home turf in the South Bronx borough as the birthplace of hip hop, reinforcing the message in the now-classic chorus with its chant "South Bronx, the South, South Bronx."

Giving name to South Bronx locales and to the artists who inhabited them, anchors his testimony. He attempts to prove its dominance by recounting the genre's formative stages with close attention to locally specific and highly particularized details:

> Remember Bronx River, rolling thick
> With Cool DJ Red Alert and Chuck Chillout on the mix
> While Afrika Islam was rocking the jams
> And on the other side of town was a kid named Flash
> Patterson and Millbrook projects
> Casanova all over, ya couldn't stop it
> The Nine Lives crew, the Cypress Boys

> The Real Rock Steady taking out these toys
> As hard as it looked, as wild as it seemed
> I didn't hear a peep from Queen's ...
> South Bronx, the South South Bronx ...

The references to people and places provide a specificity that is comparatively absent in Eazy-E's important (but often overlooked) single release "Boyz-n-The Hood" (1988, Ruthless/Priority) from the same general period. Musically, "Boyz-n-The-Hood" is considered to have done little to advance the genre aesthetically. Yet, in its uncompromising linguistic turns and startling descriptions of homeboy leisure (involving beer, "bitches," and violence), it was riveting and offered a new hardcore funky model for masculine identification in hip hop:

> 'Cause the boyz in the hood are always hard
> Come talkin' that trash and we'll pull your card
> Knowin' nothin' in life but to be legit
> Don't quote me boy, 'cause I ain't sayin' shit

Describing the LP *Eazy-Duz-It* on which the single first appeared, Havelock Nelson and Michael Gonzales explain that it "overflows with debris from homophobia to misogyny to excessive violence. And yet, anyone who grew up in the project or any Black ghetto knows these extreme attitudes are right on target" (1991, p. 81). Despite such claims to authenticity, however, it is important to acknowledge that the rugged discourses and sensational imagery of violence and poverty are highly selective and are drawn from a range of mundane, less controversial and less marketable urban experiences.

Eazy-E's "Boyz-n-The Hood" reflects many of rap's earlier modes of spatial representation that conceive of the ghetto landscape as a generalized abstract construct, as *space*. The introduction of the terminology of the 'hood, however, also adds a localized nuance to the notion of space that conveys a certain proximity, effectively capturing a narrowed sense of *place* through which young thugs and their potential victims move in tandem. Claims to the representation of authentic street life or 'hood reality emerged with sudden frequency following the rise of Eazy-E and N.W.A., who were among the first to communicate detailed images of closely demarcated space in this manner. This suggests that "reality," authenticity and reduced spatial scales are conceptually linked among those who developed "Boyz-n-The Hood" is ultimately its influence on the popularization of a new spatial vocabulary that spread throughout hip hop from all regions as artists from the West Coast gained prominence in the field.

By most accounts, the spatial discourse that coheres around the concept of the 'hood emerges in rap by California-based artists with the greatest frequency and force. But in the popular media as well as in academic treatises, the focus on West Coast rap in this period tends to be on the expressions of "gangsta" violence and masculine aggression to the exclusion or minimization of prevalent spatial elements. For example, as David Toop writes, "the first release on Ruthless Records, launched by rapper Eazy-E and producer Dr. Dre in 1986, was like a tabloid report from the crime beat fed through a paper shredder" (1991, p. 180). The very term "gangsta rap" is more concretely concerned with the articulation of criminality than any other attributes that may emerge from its lyrical and visual texts. Having become sedimented in the popular lexicon as the key or trademark term for the subgenre, it is difficult to challenge critically the primacy of criminality and to replace it with a spatiality that precedes the "gangsta-ism" that saturates the lyrical texts. The criminal activities that are described in gangsta rap's intense lyrical forms are almost always subordinate to the definitions of space and place within which they are set. It is, therefore, the spatialities of the 'hood that constitute the ascendant concept and are ultimately deserving of discursive pre-eminence.

Since rap's invention, it has become somewhat of a convention for the rapper to be placed at the center of the world, as the subject around which events unfold and who translates topophilia (love of place) or topophobia (fear of place) into lyrics for wider dissemination. This is illustrated in Ice T's "Intro" track on his debut album *Rhyme Pays* (1987, Rhyme Syndicate/Sire). As an introduction, the track allows Ice T to present his hip hop curriculum vitae which is explicitly defined in spatial terms:

> A child was born in the East one day
> Moved to the West Coast after his parents passed away
> Never understood his fascination with rhymes or beats
> In poetry he was considered elite
> Became a young gangster in the streets of LA
> Lost connections with his true roots far away …

The description of a personal exodus embarked upon by the young rapper under conditions of extreme adversity is crucial to the construction of mystique and legend. Describing his entry into LA gang culture and the rap scene in the magazine *Rap Pages*, Ice T identifies cities, neighborhoods, high schools and housing projects that have meaning to him and to those familiar with these areas:

> I went to a white school in Culver City, and that was chill, but I was livin' in Windsor Hills near Monterey Triangle Park.... When I got to high school all the kids from my area were gettin' bussed to white schools and I didn't want to go to them schools. So me and a few kids from the hills went to Crenshaw. That's where the gangs were. (*Rap Pages*, October 1991, p. 55)

Here, place is a lens of sorts that mediates one's perspective on social relations. It offers familiarity and it provides the perspectival point from which one gazes upon and evaluates other places, places that are "other" or foreign to one's own distinctly personal sites of security and stability (no matter how limited these may be). Ice T may be from the East, but he is shaped by Los Angeles and it is the spaces and places of LA that provide the coordinates for his movement and activities.

Ice T (ibid.) goes on to make the distinction between East Coast rap and the emerging LA "gangsta" style, noting that the latter developed out of a desire to relate incidents and experiences with a more specific sense of place and, subsequently, greater significance to local youths who could recognize the sites and activities described in the lyrics. In this regard, rap offers a means of describing the view from a preferred "here," of explaining how things appear in the immediate foreground (the 'hood) and how things seem on the receding horizon (other places).

Adopting a boastful tone and attitude, Ice T also locates his origins in the New Jersey–New York nexus, essentially fixing his own "roots" in hip hop's cultural motherland. Ice T is in this mode clearly centering himself, building his own profile. In the process, he relates a history that invests supreme value in New York as the first home of hip hop, naturalizing his connections to the art form and validating his identity as a tough, adaptive and street-smart LA hustler, the self-proclaimed "West Coast M.C. king." Ice T's references to New York illuminate the spatial hierarchy that existed at the time; the Northeast was still virtually unchallenged as the dominant zone of hip hop cultural activity. Battles among rap's pioneers and upstarts were still being waged on the local, interborough scale in New York although, gradually, New York's monopoly on rap production and innovation was lost as various other sites of production emerged. The rise of the LA rap sound and the massive impact of the gangster themes after 1987 resulted in the first real incursion on New York's dominance. This development had the additional effect of polarizing the two regions as the aesthetic distinctions based on lyrical content and rhythmic styles became more defined and audiences began spending their consumer dollars on rap from the nation's "West side."

"The West Side Is the Best Side": Representing Compton

The West's arrival was heralded by a deluge of recordings that celebrated and glorified the street warrior scenarios of the California cities of South Central Los Angeles (with help from the 1988 Dennis Hopper film *Colors* and Ice T's galvanizing title song on the soundtrack), Oakland and, especially, Compton. Starting with NWA's "Straight Outta Compton" (1988, Ruthless/Priority), numerous recordings circulated the narrative imagery of vicious gang-oriented activities in Compton, including the tracks "Raised in Compton" (1991, Epic) and "Compton 4 Life" (1992, Epic) by the group Compton's Most Wanted, and DJ Quik's "Born and Raised in Compton" (1991, Profile) or "Just Lyke Compton" (1992, Profile). Appearing on the cover of his album *Way 2 Fonky* (1992, Profile), DJ Quik poses alongside a chain-link fence topped with razor wire, sporting a jacket emblazoned with the Compton logo, proudly advertising his home territory. Through these multiple means of signification the city of Compton rapidly gained a notoriety informed by the image of tough and well-armed homeboys and the ongoing deadly conflict between rival gangs operating with a near-total lack of ethics or moral conscience. This last point can be most clearly discerned in the ubiquitous refrain that "Compton niggaz just don't give a fuck."

Tricia Rose and Brian Cross situate the rise of Compton-based rap in two quite different frames of understanding. Rose writes that

> during the late 1980s Los Angeles rappers from Compton and Watts, two areas severely paralyzed by the postindustrial economic redistribution, developed a West coast style of rap that narrates experiences and fantasies specific to life as a poor young, black, male subject in Los Angeles. (1994, p. 59)

Her assessment situates the phenomenon of West Coast styles and lyrical forms in an internally based set of socio-economic conditions that are responsive to transitions within a complex convergence of global and local forces, or what Kevin Robins (1991) refers to as "the global/local nexus."

Brian Cross locates the rise of Compton's rap scene within a wider and more appropriate cartographic relation to New York and other California locales:

> Hiphop Compton, according to Eazy, was created as a reply to the construction of the South Bronx/Queensbridge nexus in New York. If locally it served notice in the community in which Eazy and Dre sold their Macola-pressed records (not to mention the potential play action on KDAY), nationally, or at least on the East Coast, it was an attempt to figure Los Angeles on the map of hiphop. After the album had gone double platinum Compton would be as well known a city in hiphop as either Queens or the Bronx. (Cross 1993, p. 37)

Refuting Rose's interpretation, the general narrative content of "Straight Outta Compton" sheds little light on the city or its social byways and does not demonstrate any particular concern with the locality's economics. Its basic function as a geographical backdrop actually follows the same standard constructions of abstract space heard in Grandmaster Flash and the Furious Five's "New York, New York," recorded five years earlier, or in Eazy-E's solo effort, "Boyz-n-The-Hood."

Without detailed spatial descriptions of landmarks and environment, Compton does not emerge as a clearly realized urban space on the N.W.A. track even though it is the group's home town. The California city is instead treated as a bounded civic space that provides both specificity and scale for the communication of a West Coast Rap presence. The group is "representing" their home territory and the song's release was their bold announcement that the "boyz" from the 'hoods of Compton were "stompin' " onto the scene and could not be avoided by anyone who paid attention to developments in the business. The Compton and South Central LA crews were not only serving notice to their neighboring communities that they were in charge, but they were also serving notice to New York and the entire hip hop nation that the new sound had arrived and the balance of power (forged in a mix of arrogance and inventiveness) had tipped towards the West. This was the beginning of a decade-long antagonism between East and West Coast rap that has too frequently proven that the gangster themes comprising the lyrical content are based in more than mere lip service or masculine posturing.

On the track "Raised in Compton" (1991, Epic/Sony), MC Eiht of the rap group Compton's Most Wanted explicitly racializes the urban spaces of the city, more fully addressing the specificities of its cultural character and providing a further sense of the place that he recognizes as his formative home. He reproduces several of the general elements that N.W.A. had already imposed on Compton's representational repertoire, but for him the city also has a personally meaningful history that is manifested in his identity as a gangster turned rapper:

> Compton is the place that I touched down
> I opened my eyes to realize that I was dark brown
> And right there in the ghetto that color costs
> Brothers smothered by the streets meaning we're lost
> I grew up in a place where it was go for your own
> Don't get caught after dark roaming the danger zone
> But it was hell at the age of twelve
> As my Compton black brothers were in and out of jail

The attempt to historicize his relations to the city and the 'hood makes this track slightly more complex than "Straight Outta Compton," as MC Eiht's bonds to the localized Compton environment are defined as the product of an evolving growth process, as a child becomes a man. Subjective history, conveyed here in an almost testimonial form, and the experiences of space, together offer relevant insights on the social construction of a gangster attitude or a gang member's *raison d'être*.

George Lipsitz isolates similar tendencies with his focus on the socio-political importance of merging musical and non-musical sources of inspiration and experience among California chicano rock musicians since the 1960s.

> As organic intellectuals chronicling the cultural life of their community, they draw upon street slang, car customizing, clothing styles, and wall murals for inspiration and ideas.... Their work is intertextual, constantly in dialogue with other forms of cultural expression, and most fully appreciated when located in context. (Lipsitz 1990, p. 153)

Like the California chicano music Lipsitz describes, "Raised in Compton" explicitly highlights a customized car culture, urban mobility and the sartorial codes of the Compton streets ("T-shirt and khakis"). In its inclusiveness of the minor details that are, in practice, part of the daily norm for many urban black youth in the cities surrounding Los Angeles, the song accesses the spatial and racial characteristics of the city of Compton that have influenced and shaped the man that MC Eiht has become. The closely detailed articulation of spatial specifics (place names and site references, etc.) is still lacking but there is also a rich description of some of the social formations that are spatially distributed and which reproduce the forces underlying the black teen gangster ethos with which MC Eiht, and many others, so clearly identify.

Maintaining the gang member's pledge to defend the gang (or the "set") and the 'hood forever is the theme of MC Eiht's "Compton 4 Life" (1992, Epic/Sony). This track also offers a personal profile that ties MC Eiht into the neighborhood environment and inextricably links him with the deeper gang structures that prevail. Mid-point in the track he challenges outsiders to "throw up your 'hood 'cause it's Compton we're yellin," in a calculated "turf" statement that is entirely consistent with the structures of spatial otherness that are fundamental to LA gang culture. Eiht and other gangsta rappers enter into the discourses of alienation and social disenfranchisement as a negative factor compelling them towards a criminal lifestyle. Yet they also expound their own versions of alienating power, drawing on the imagery and codes of the street and entering into a discourse of domination that subjugates women, opposing gang members or those who are perceived as being weaker and thus less than them. Framed in terms of gun violence and human decimation, these expressions are intended to diminish the presence of others who represent other cities and other 'hoods. This is the articulation of control through domination, ghetto style.

Spatial domination and geo-social containment are conceived in the threatening form of "one time" or "five-o" (the police) and other gang members, each of whom constitute unavoidable negatives of life in the 'hood. Defeating the enemy forces is the ultimate goal, but in establishing the competitive dynamic, MC Eiht acknowledges that, even in victory, the local streets and the 'hood impose their own kind of incarcerating authority:

> Compton 4 Life
> Compton 4 Life
> It's the city where everybody's in prison
> Niggers keep taking shit 'cause ain't nobody givin'
> So another punk fool I must be
> Learn the tricks of the trade from the street
> Exist to put the jack down, ready and willin'
> One more Compton driveby killin'

There is a brief pause in the rhythm that could be heard as hanging like doom, stilling the song's pace and flow and creating a discomforting gap in the track. When the chorus "Compton 4 Life" suddenly breaks in with the final echoing syllable, it becomes clear that the title is formed around a double entendre: it is an expression of spatial solidarity and loyalty to the 'hood, yet it also refers to the pronouncement of a life sentence and the apparent hopelessness of eternal imprisonment in the city's streets and alleys.

As "Straight Outta Compton," "Raised in Compton" and "Compton 4 Life" suggest, "our sensibilities are spatialized" (Keith and Pile, 1993 p. 26). This point is made resonant when considering Compton artist DJ Quik's mobile narrative on the track "Jus Lyke Compton" (1992, Priority), in which he witnesses and describes the nation-wide impact of the Compton mythology, and Bronx-based rapper Tim Dog's defensive articulation of Bronx pride in the lyrical assassinations of N.W.A. and all Compton artists on the track "Fuck Compton" (1991, Ruffhouse/Columbia). Compton's central significance is maintained through the lyrical representation of activities that are space-bound and which are then discursively traced onto the identities of the rappers who "claim" Compton as their own. The issue of whether or not the tracks refer back to a consistently verifiable reality is rendered moot by the possibilities they present as textual spaces of representation. Artists discursively locate themselves in an array of images and practices within the texts, constructing a relatively coherent identity out of the urban debris that is evidently a crucial aspect of the Compton they experience.

Despite claims by critics of gangsta rap, such as David Samuels (*New Republic*, 11 November, 1991), or folk musician Michelle Shocked, who suggests that "Los Angeles as a whole and South Central specifically bear little resemblance to the cartoon landscape—the Zip Coon Toon Town—of gangsta rap" (*Billboard*, 20 June, 1992, p. 6), the subgenre's narrative depictions of spaces and places are absolutely essential to an understanding of the ways that a great number of urban black youths imagine their environments and the ways that they relate those images to their own individual sense of self. The spaces of Compton and other similar black communities that emerge through their work are simultaneously real, imaginary, symbolic and mythical. With this in mind, the question that should be asked is not "is this real and true," but "why do so many young black men choose these dystopic images of spatial representation to orient their own places in the world?" By framing the question thus, the undeniable fascination with the grisly mayhem of the lyrical narratives is displaced and one can then embark on a more illuminating interrogation of the socio-spatial sensibilities at work.

Representing the Extreme Local: The Case of Seattle

By the end of the 1980s, Rap artists had provided an assortment of spatial representations of New York and Los Angeles that were both consistent with and divergent from the prevailing image-ideas of those urban centers. Rap artists worked within the dominant representational discourses of "the city" while agitating against a history of urban representations as they attempted to extend the expressive repertoire and to reconstruct the image-idea of the city as they understood it. This proved to be a formidable challenge since New York and LA exist as urban icons, resonant signs of the modern (New York) and postmodern (LA) city. They are already well defined, the products of a deluge of representational images, narrative constructions and social interactions.

Rap's emergence from city spaces that are comparatively unencumbered by a deep history of representational images, which carry less representational baggage, presents a unique opportunity for lyrical innovators to re-imagine and re-present their cities. As a traditional frontier city and a prominent contemporary regional center, Seattle might, in this light, be conceived as an *under*represented city that lacks the wealth of representational history common to the larger centers to the South and the East.

In the mid-1980s the Pacific Northwest was, for much of the U.S., a veritable hinterland known best for its mountains, rivers and forests and as the home of Boeing's corporate and manufacturing headquarters. In the music industry, Jimi Hendrix was perhaps Seattle's most renowned native son, but the city was otherwise not regarded as an important or influential center for musical production or innovation. The city's profile changed considerably with the rise of Bill Gates's Microsoft corporation in the outlying area and the emergence of the Starbuck's coffee empire and, by 1990, it was also garnering considerable attention as the source of the massively influential (and commercially successful) "Grunge/Alternative" music scene that spawned bands such as Hole, Nirvana, Pearl Jam, Soundgarden, and the SubPop label. Music has subsequently emerged as an essential element in the construction of Seattle's contemporary image although the industry's rock predilections have not been as favorable to the city's rap and R&B artists.[7]

In the spring of 1986, Seattle rapper Sir Mix-A-Lot's obscure track "Square Dance Rap" (NastyMix Records) made an entry onto *Billboard* magazine's Hot Black Singles chart. The release failed to advance any radical new aesthetic nor did it make a lasting contribution to the rap form. Its relevance, however, is in its capacity to reflect the diverse regional activity in rap production at that time as artists and labels attempted to establish themselves within the rapidly changing conditions fostering regional and local expansion. Mix-A-Lot's emergence illustrates the fact that rap was being produced in isolated regions and, as the track's chart status suggests, that it was selling in significant volume within regional "home" markets.

Despite this, an advertisement for Profile Records appearing six years later in *Billboard*'s "Rap '92 Spotlight on Rap" (28 November 1992), portrays the proliferation of industry activity with a cartographic cartoon entitled "Rap All Over the Map: The Profile States of America." New York, Chicago, Dallas, St Louis, Vallejo and Los Angeles are all represented with the names of acts and their respective regions and cities of origin. The Pacific Northwest is conspicuously labelled "uncharted territory," which refers to Profile's inactivity there but which also reproduces the dominant image of the region as a distant and unknown frontier in the view of those from the nation's larger or more centralized rap production sites.

Regardless of the advertisement's centrist biases, the fact that Seattle was at this stage on the charts (and, in hip hop parlance, "in the house") indicates that rap's consumer base had extended geographically and, moreover, that new and unforeseen sites of production such as Seattle were also being established. In an interesting spatial inversion, Bruce Pavitt, co-founder of the Alternative-oriented SubPop label, actually regarded Seattle's spatial marginality as a positive factor for local musicians, stating that, "one advantage Seattle has is our geographical isolation. It gave a group of artists a chance to create their own sound, instead of feeling pressured to copy others" (*Billboard*, 18 August 1990, p. 30). Sir Mix-A-Lot slowly solidified his Northwest regional base. His single "Baby Got Back" reached the number one position on the *Billboard* pop charts, eventually selling double platinum.

Displaying pride in his Northwestern roots, Sir-Mix-A-Lot provides an excellent example of the organization of spatial images and the deployment of a spatial discourse. In general terms, details that might be overlooked speak volumes about space and place, presenting additional information about the ways that an individual's daily life is influenced by their local environments and conditions. For instance, the standard group photo in the inner sleeve of *Mack Daddy* depicts Mix-A-Lot's Rhyme Cartel posse wearing wet-weather gear consisting of name-brand Gore Tex hats and jackets. This is a totally pragmatic sartorial statement from the moist climate of the Pacific Northwest that remains true to hip hop's style-conscious trends. It displays a geographically particular system of codes conveying regionally significant information that, once again, demonstrates hip hop's capacity to appropriate raw materials or images and to invest them with new values and meanings.

Of all the CD's tracks, "Seattle Ain't Bullshittin'" is exceptional for the manner in which it communicates a sense of space and place with clarity, sophistication and cartographic detail. Establishing himself on the track as a genuine Seattle "player," as the original Northwestern "Mack Daddy" (a term for a top level pimp), Mix-A-Lot bases his claim to local prestige in his persona as a former Seattle hustler who successfully shifted to legitimate enterprises as a musician and businessman. He adopts a purely capitalist discourse of monetary and material accumulation, reproducing the prevailing terms of success and prosperity that conform to both the dominant social values and the value system inherent within the rap industry.

As the title suggests, Seattle is the centerpiece to the track. This is clear from the beginning as Mix-A-Lot and posse member the Attitude Adjuster ad lib over a sparse guitar riff:

> Boy, this is S.E.A.T.O.W.N., clown (forever)
> Sea Town, Yeah, and that's from the motherfuckin' heart
> So if you ain't down with your hometown
> Step off, punk

Mix, tell these fakes what the deal is ...

As the bass and drums are dropped into the track, Mix-A-Lot lyrically locates himself as a product of Seattle's inner-city core known as the CD (or Central District):

I was raised in the S.E.A. double T.L.E.
Seattle, home of the CD, nigga
19th and, yes, Laborda,
pimpin' was hard ...
It wasn't easy trying to compete with my homies in the CD

Seattle's Central District is home to a sizeable concentration of black constituents who comprise roughly 10 per cent of Seattle's total population. Mix-A-Lot's portrayal of the CD neighborhood is not explicitly racialized yet the references to pimping and competition among "homies in the CD" easily fall into a common, even stereotypical definition of "the 'hood" that is pervasive throughout rap of the period.

The Attitude Adjuster states at one point that "it ain't nothing but the real up" that are evident in Seattle as well as the rest of the nation. Unlike most major American cities, Seattle's black presence does not have a huge defining influence on its urban character: black youths are a socially marginalized constituency within a geographically marginal city. The Attitude Adjuster's pronouncement may suggest a hint of defensiveness but it also gives voice to the region's black hip hop constituency that is, as the subtext implies, just as "hardcore" as that of other urban centers.

Having established his ghetto credentials, Mix-A-Lot expounds on several spatially oriented scenarios, shifting scale and perspective throughout the track with his descriptions of local, regional and national phenomena:

So even though a lot of niggas talk shit
I'm still down for the Northwest when I hit the stage
Anywhere U.S.A.
I give Seattle and Tacoma much play
So here's to the Criminal Nation
And the young brother Kid Sensation
I can't forget Maharaji and the Attitude Adjuster
And the hardcore brothers to the west of Seattle
Yeah, West Side, High Point dippin' four door rides ...

Mix-A-Lot adopts the role of Seattle's hip hop ambassador, acknowledging his own national celebrity profile while accepting the responsibilities of "representing" the Northwest, his record label and posse, and fellow rap artists from "Sea Town." Exploiting his access to the wider stage, he elevates the local scene, bringing it into focus and broadcasting the fact that hip hop is an important element of the Seattle lifestyle for young blacks living there as well.

The perspective shifts again as Mix-A-Lot adopts an intensely localized mode of description, recalling the days when he "used to cruise around Seward Park," moving out of the bounded territory of the city's Central District that is the posse's home base. Seattle is cartographically delineated here through the explicit naming of streets and civic landmarks that effectively identify the patterned mobility of the crew:

Let's take a trip to the South End,
We go west, hit Rainier Ave. and bust left,

... S.E.A. T.O.W.N., yo nigger is back again
... Gettin' back to the hood,
Me and my boys is up to no good,
A big line of cars rollin' deep through the South End,
Made a left on Henderson,
Clowns talkin' shit in the Southshore parking lot
Critical Mass is begging to box
But we keep on going because down the street
A bunch of freaks in front of Rainier Beach
Was lookin' at us, they missed that bus
And they figure they could trust us ...

With its references to the city's crosstown byways and meeting places, the track success-fully communicates an image of the common, "everyday" leisure practices of the Rhyme Cartel posse while also retaining a privileged local or place-based perspective that resonates with greater meaning for all Seattle or Tacoma audience members. This audience will undoubtedly recognize its own environment and the track will consequently have a different and arguably more intense affective impact among Seattle's listeners and fans. Unlike Compton, which was popularized through a relentless process of reiteration by numerous artists, Seattle is repre-sented much less frequently: "Seattle Ain't Bullshittin'" is a unique expression of Northwest identity. For example, there is no similar track on the Seattle-based Criminal Nation's *Trouble in the Hood* which was also released in 1992 (NastyMix/Ichiban), although references to the region are sprinkled throughout several tracks and on the liner sleeve one group member sports a Tacoma T-shirt identifying his home town.

In 1992, the trend towards such closely demarcated spatial parameters was not yet a common characteristic in rap, although it was increasingly becoming a factor in both lyrical and visual representations. Rather than an expression of a narrow social perspective cele-brating the local to the exclusion of other wider scales, "Seattle Ain't Bullshittin'" demon-strates a rather successful method of representing the hometown local "flavor" on an internationally distributed recording.

Conclusion

Rap music's shift towards a self-produced discourse introducing the 'hood as a new spatial concept delimiting an "arena of experience" can be weighed against larger trends currently restructuring global and national economies, transforming national and regional workforces, and, often, devastating urban localities. As numerous supporters have suggested, rap emerges as a voice for black and Latino youth which, as a large subset of North America's socially disen-franchised population, is at risk of being lost in the combined transformations of domestic and global economies that are altering North America's urban cultures today. The discourse of space encompassed by the term "'hood" may in this context also be interpreted as a response to conditions of change occurring at a meta-level, far beyond the scale of the local (and the influence of those who inhabit it).

The requirement of maintaining strong local allegiances is a standard practice in hip hop that continues to mystify many critics of the rap genre. It is, therefore, imperative to recognize and understand the processes that are at work and to acknowledge that there are different messages being communicated to listeners who occupy different spaces and places and who iden-tify with space or place according to different values of scale. It is precisely through these detailed image constructions that the abstract spaces of the ghetto are transformed into the more proximate sites of significance or places of the 'hood. Looking beyond the obvious, spatial discourse provides a communicative means through which numerous social systems are framed for consideration. Rap tracks, with their almost obsessive preoccupation with place and locality, are never *solely* about space and place on the local scale. Rather, they also identify and explore the ways in which these spaces and places are inhabited and made meaningful. Struggles and conflicts as well as the positive attachments to place are all represented in the spatial discourses of rap. This is not a display of parochial narrowness but a much more complex and interesting exploration of local practices and their discursive construction in the popular media.

Study Questions

1. What is the significance of "the 'hood" as a spatial zone in hip-hop?
2. How is "representing" related to the construction of one's subjective identity in hip-hop?
3. In what ways is the concept of "home" privileged and promoted in hip-hop and rap music?

Notes

1. As an indication of the distinctions between rap and the more encompassing hip hop culture, rap artist KRS-One has said "rap is something you do, hip-hop is something you live" (quoted in *The Source*, June 1995, p. 40). Rap is the music of hip hop and its central form of articulation and expression.
2. Hip hop's timeline can be roughly divided into three general eras: old school refers to the period from 1978–86; middle school covers the period between 1987–1992; and new school extends from 1993–1999. In some cases, the present is referred to as "now school."
3. See Reebee Garofalo (1997, pp. 257–264); see also, Brian Ward (1998).
4. The factors leading to the demise of Death Row include the murder of its marquee star Tupac Shakur, Suge Knight's nine-year sentence for probation violations, an FBI investigation of possible gang-related enterprises including money laundering, and the desertion of its key producer Dr. Dre. In 1998, the artist Snoop Doggy Dogg defected to Master P's New Orleans-based No Limit Records.
5. The Flavor Unit posse at the time included such Rap notables as Queen Latifah, Monie Love, Apache, Lakim Shabazz, and Naughty By Nature who, perhaps more than the rest, explicitly refer to their origins as New Jersey rappers hailing from 118th Street, "Illtown," in East Orange. After internal restructuring, the posse's most bankable star, Queen Latifah, emerged as the executive head of Flavor Unit Management.
6. For a detailed examination of the Florida "bass" phenomenon, see the special feature of *The Source*, March 1994.
7. Addressing the relatively minor industry consideration for Seattle's black artists, Sir Mix-A-Lot's Rhyme Cartel Records released the conspicuously titled *Seattle … The Dark Side* in 1993. The cover prominently proclaims that the release "flips the script. No Grunge … just Rap and R&B … Sea Town Style."

References

Chambers, Iain. 1985. *Urban Rhythms: Pop Music and Popular Culture* (London)
Cross, Brian. 1993. *It's Not About A Salary: Rap, Race, and Resistance in Los Angeles* (London)
Dery, Mark. 1990. "Public enemy: confrontation," *Keyboard*, September
Eure, Joseph and Spady, James (eds.). 1991. *Nation Conscious Rap* (New York)
Garofalo, Reebee. 1997. *Rockin' Out: Popular Music in the USA* (Boston)
George, Nelson. 1986. "The Rhythm and the Blues," in *Billboard*, May 31, p. 23
———. 1992. *Buppies, B-Boys, Baps and Bohos: Notes on Post-Soul Black Culture* (New York)
———. 1993. "Hip-hop's founding fathers speak the truth," *The Source*, November
Gilroy, Paul. 1992. "It's a Family Affair," in *Black Popular Culture*, (ed.) Gina Dent (Seattle)
Gunst, Laurie. 1995. *Born Fi Dead: A Journey Through the Jamaican Posse Underworld* (New York)
Hager, Steve. 1984. *Hip Hop: The Illustrated History of Break Dancing, Rap Music, and Graffiti* (New York)

Jones, Charisse. 1995. "Still hangin' in the 'hood: rappers who stay say their strength is from the streets," *The New York Times*, 24 September, pp. 43–46

Keith, Michael and Pile, Steve (eds.). 1993. *Place and the Politics of Identity* (New York)

Lipsitz, George. 1990. *Time Passages: Collective Memory and American Popular Culture* (Minneapolis)

Nelson, Havelock and Gonzales, Michael. 1991. *Bring the Noise: A Guide to Rap Music and Hip Hop Culture* (New York)

Pike, Jeff. 1990. "At long last, Seattle is suddenly hot," *Billboard*, 18 August, pp. 30–34

Rap Pages, 1991. "The world according to Ice-T," October, pp. 54–67

Rap Sheet, 1992. "The bloody 5: a day in the hood," October, pp. 18–26

Robins, Kevin. 1991. "Tradition and translation: national culture in its global context," in *Enterprise and Heritage Crosscurrents of National Culture*, (eds.) John Corner and Sylvia Harvey (New York)

Rose, Tricia. 1994. *Black Noise: Rap Music and Black Culture in Contemporary America* (Hanover)

Samuels, David. 1991. "The rap on rap," *The New Republic*, 11 November

Shocked, Michelle, and Bull, Bart. 1992. "LA riots: cartoons vs. reality," *Billboard*, 20 June, p. 6

The Source, 1994. Special Issue: Miami Bass, March

Tate, Greg. 1992. "Posses in effect: Ice-T," in *Flyboy in the Buttermilk: Essays on Contemporary America* (New York)

Toop, David. 1984. *The Rap Attack: African Jive to New York Hip Hop* (Boston)

———. 1991. *Rap Attack: African Rap to Global Hip-Hop* (New York)

Ward, Brian. 1998. *Just My Soul Responding: Rhythm and Blues, Black Consciousness, and Race Relations* (Berkeley)

18

Rap's Dirty South
From Subculture to Pop Culture

In a broad analysis encompassing regional history, cultural geography, and hip-hop aesthetics, Matt Miller's exploration of hip-hop in the U.S. "South Coast" offers a welcome respite from the frequent emphasis on east–west dynamics. According to Miller, the "Dirty South" is more than an offhanded spatial title but a discursive articulation of identity and difference that Southern artists invest with intense value and meaning. Southern hip-hop artists proudly celebrate their regional styles, accents, and attitudes even as they confront stereotypes and wider misperceptions from those who live elsewhere.

On display here are the circulating perceptions of urban–rural dichotomies as well as the distinctions between North and South that have, since the nation's inception, been informed by deeper issues including race, slavery, freedom and emancipation. Black southerners confront these regional characteristics directly with rap and hip-hop presenting new media apparatuses through which to challenge and subvert the dominant symbols of white repression that persist. We also see here how the "marginal" status of Southern rappers functions in a duel sense as a barrier to industrial access and as a bond of sorts; the symbolic values of "the Dirty South" produce shared affect and regional pride as well as distinguishing artists within larger nation-wide contexts.

Rap's Dirty South: From Subculture to Pop Culture

Matt Miller

"I'm from the dirty, filthy, nasty Dirty South."—Cee-Lo (Sanneh).

In the mid 1990s, a new phrase, "Dirty South," began to gain currency within the subculture of rap music. Introduced in a 1995 song by the Atlanta-based group Goodie Mob ("Dirty South"), the term became a standard way of referring to the American South among rap music listeners, commentators, and artists, both within and outside the South. Within five years, the idea of the Dirty South had passed from subcultural to broader usage, and had become a common way to refer to the South and its various rap music scenes within music journalism from all over the English-speaking world. Since that time, the concept has penetrated into popular culture to the degree that it has been appropriated or referenced by country and blues bands and has also appeared in such diverse and nonmusical contexts as high school sports teams, television ads for Pepsi, and the most recent collection of short stories by Elmore Leonard.

My investigation of the Dirty South idea began with the questions, why or how is this imagined space dirty, and how has the way it is imagined changed over time? I discovered that the meaning attached to the term is not fixed but fluid, shifting in accordance with the needs and preconceptions of those who employ it. Both aspects of this phrase—"dirty" and "South"—are problematic and wide-ranging in their meanings and associations. Dirt and dirtiness have negative connotations of uncleanliness, disorder (Douglas), corruption, unfairness, and sexuality, but dirt can also be a powerful symbol for place and land (Yaeger), and, in a biblical sense, for human life itself. At the same time, the idea of the South and its role in American political and cultural life—often bearing connotations of poverty, ignorance, rurality, and violence—has been a unique and volatile force in the culture of the U.S. The South exists less as an actual, coherent geographic region and more as a space which is imagined on collective and personal levels. This fluidity of meaning also applies to interpretations of southern history, which often break down along racial lines; the collective experience of African Americans in the South has produced a chain of negative associations that extends into the present day, while many whites subscribe to a more romanticized interpretation of the "Lost Cause" of the Confederacy. In many states, continuing tension between blacks and whites often takes the form of debates over Confederate symbolism in official contexts.

In the pages that follow, I offer a brief history of rap music in southern cities in order to situate Goodie Mob's song "Dirty South" within cultural, historical, and economic contexts. I subject the song's lyrics to close analysis in order to better understand the representation of the South as put forth by the rappers of Goodie Mob. I then examine the ways in which their articulation of this space was received first within the subcultural community of rap music listeners and subsequently by critics and journalists on a national and international level. I demonstrate that as more and more people began to employ (and thus define) the phrase "Dirty South," the understanding of its meanings, both overt and implicit, underwent significant shifts.

Several conclusions emerge after tracing the evolution of the Dirty South. First, the idea of what makes the Dirty South dirty underwent a significant shift as the term became accepted within a larger cultural context. The Dirty South envisioned by Goodie Mob ("Dirty South") and their artistic collaborators in 1995 and the Dirty South as understood by critics and journalists in 2000 share many of the same basic components but differ greatly in emphasis. Second, the creation of a distinct Dirty South identity has been shaped by forces both external and internal to the American South, with outsiders reacting through their preconceptions about the South and insiders reacting, sometimes out of their own economic self-interest, to their perception of those preconceptions. This extremely complex interplay of motives and influences result in a Dirty South which is far from a "natural" space within the larger context of American rap music. Rather, like country and western's cowboys and "hillbillies," it is a contrivance born out of the structures of artistic and economic dominance that have determined the development of rap music as a commercial art form. Finally, with regard to the Dirty South as a new aesthetic movement, while some general tendencies and trends emerge, it is impossible to narrow down the rap music produced in major Southern cities to one set of practices or conventions.

Rap Music in the South: A Brief History

Since rap music's initial development in New York City during the mid 1970s, it has been characterized by the production and consumption of place-based identities, to the extent that "representing" one's home town or neighborhood has become a defining element of the genre. The exact reasons why rap music seems to be keenly attuned to issues of place remain unclear, although they are likely related to the lack of adequate representation of marginalized communities in the mass media environment, a historically-rooted trend which continues to the present day. While rap music has become a powerful vehicle for the expression and transmission of place-based identities, these are not static in character or number—they are created and renegotiated in response to changes within the field of rap music production, as well as larger social forces.

The establishment of a particular place within the national geography of rap music depends upon a certain amount of production which is recognized by the wider listener base and critical community as representative of that place and therefore offering a unique perspective on the art form. The reputation or amount of prestige attached to particular places is also fluid, although a self-reinforcing tendency usually predominates once a certain amount of momentum has been achieved in terms of production and infrastructure. For this reason, the range of possible expressions of geographic identity has been expanding along with the infrastructure of the music itself. Initially limited to the various neighborhoods and boroughs of New York, the geographic repertoire of rap music has been steadily expanding and evolving in order to accommodate artists from other cities who began to express themselves using the new form.

From its point of origin, the production of rap music spread first to other large cities in the Northeast, then jumped the continent to colonize southern California. With the rise of greater Los Angeles as an up-and-coming center for rap music production, new forms of place-based identities were introduced. Although New Yorkers still dominated the rap music industry in the Northeast, they began to be grouped with artists and producers from nearby large cities such as Philadelphia to form a cultural bloc called "the East Coast." Meanwhile, the Los Angeles-based scene engendered another imagined region in the rap music universe, "the West Coast."

Economic and creative tensions between those who identified with one of these two imagined spaces were reflected in the development of distinct aesthetic and lyrical tendencies that were associated with each contingent. Although these differences were often more imagined than real, they did exist to some extent, as rap music from the "West Coast" during the mid-to-late '80s was often characterized by slower tempos and "gangsta"-themed lyrics. The perceived stylistic and thematic tensions between "East Coast" and "West Coast" artists were overlaid upon a pre-existing image of dangerous and violent black masculinity which constituted an important feature of rap music's discourse.

Until the late 1980s, major label investment in rap from southern cities was largely nonexistent. Independent record label owners initiated the development of the rap music infrastructure in the large cities of the South in the 1980s by producing records by local artists. What success these artists did enjoy was local, or, at best, regional. Building upon such local momentum in cities like Houston and Miami, artists and companies emerged that showed potential for wider audience appeal.

Luther "Luke Skyywalker" Campbell (born 1960), who grew up in the poverty-wracked Liberty City area of Miami, was able to create a new and lucrative market in the late 1980s for bass-heavy club music with simple, sex-oriented call-and-response lyrics such as those featured in the song "Me So Horny". Throughout the late 80s and early 90s Campbell achieved wide commercial successes despite, or perhaps because of, a highly publicized and antagonistic relationship with various state and county officials, as well as with self-appointed moral crusader Jack Thompson. Campbell entered into various distribution agreements with Atlantic and Island during these years but always maintained a significant amount of independence in his business dealings. Campbell, whose net worth was estimated at 11 million dollars in 1989, was forced into bankruptcy in 1995 after a series of lawsuits brought by former associates, prominent among them Atlanta-based rapper Peter "MC Shy-D" Jones (Smith). Campbell was the first southerner to grace the cover of rap music magazine *The Source*, appearing on the January 1991 issue as "Hip-Hop's Man of the Year."

In Houston, James Smith, an African American used-car salesman, and Cliff Blodget, a white software engineer with an interest in gangsta rap who had moved to the city from Seattle, founded the Rap-A-Lot label in 1987. The label was pushed into the national spotlight in 1990, when Rap-A-Lot teamed up with Rick Rubin's New York-based company Def American to release an album by the Houston group The Geto Boys. Citing the violent and misogynist content of many of the group's lyrics, manufacturer Digital Audio Disc Corp. refused to press the album. Subsequently, the agreement with Geffen, Def American's distributor, fell apart. Rubin was able to secure a last-minute distribution deal for the album with WEA, a subsidiary of Warner Bros., but this association would be short-lived; the company declined to distribute the group's next album, *We Can't Be Stopped*, which was eventually distributed through Priority Records in 1991. Rap-A-Lot continued its association with Priority until 1995, when Smith moved the label's distribution to the Virgin subsidiary Noo Trybe (Rosen). Although Rap-A-Lot has probably passed its peak in terms of sales and artistic relevance, its success and that of associated artists like The Geto Boys and Scarface (a member of the group who has had several successful solo releases) has paved the way for a flourishing rap music scene based in Houston. The Geto Boys were featured on the cover of *The Source* in February of 1992.

The history of rap music in Atlanta dates back to 1980, when Shurfine, a white-owned label that released records by soul artists like The Mighty Hannibal in the 1960s, released *Space Rap* by Danny Renee and the Charisma Crew. Throughout the 1980s, independent labels continued to play a significant role in the city's rap scene, but major labels invested significantly more in the development of Atlanta's rap music infrastructure in the late 80s and early 90s than they did in Houston or Miami. Labels such as So So Def and LaFace helped establish Atlanta as a center of production, and Atlanta-based groups like Arrested Development, Kriss Kross, OutKast, and Goodie Mob met with considerable success in national markets.

Antonio "L.A." Reid and Kenneth "Babyface" Edmonds (born 1956 in Cincinnati and 1959 in Indianapolis, respectively) started producing music together when they were both members of the R & B group The Deele in the late 1980s. In 1989, they moved to Atlanta and started the LaFace Records label as a joint venture with national label Arista—an event described as "a pivotal moment ... in Atlanta's role as a music center" (Paris). The features of the city that attracted them included its "unhurried pace, convenient airport, relatively cheap suburban office space and mostly untapped reserves of raw talent" (Dollar). LaFace initially focused on R & B acts like Jermaine Jackson, Damian Dame, and TLC but would soon become a major force in Atlanta's rap music scene in the mid 1990s with acts such as OutKast and Goodie Mob. A 1995 extension of their agreement with Arista was "reportedly worth $10 million" (Flick).

Jermaine Dupri (born 1973) grew up in the College Park area of Atlanta and achieved enormous commercial success with his So So Def label before the age of twenty. He benefited greatly in his endeavors from the experience and music industry connections of his father, Michael Mauldin, a former musician who managed rap and R & B artists. Mauldin was one of the coordinators for the New York City Fresh Fest, which in 1984 was the first rap music show to tour nationally, and in which Dupri performed as a breakdancer with the group Whodini, beginning when he was only twelve years old. He started producing music in his teenage years, and in 1991, at the age of eighteen, started the So So Def label. Dupri secured a distribution deal with Columbia, and, with his father acting as Chief Operating Officer, achieved breakthrough success for the new label with the 1991 debut album by teenage rappers Kriss Kross, *Totally Krossed Out*, which would eventually sell six million copies. Despite this and other achievements, he complained in 1993, "Being from Atlanta, it's hard to get respect from people in New York and L.A." (Murray "So So Successful").

The Atlanta-based group called Arrested Development, led by rapper Todd "Speech" Thomas, put forth an early expression of a selfconsciously southern identity within the realm of rap music. A native of Milwaukee, Thomas spent his summers with his grandmother in rural Tennessee and eventually moved south to attend the Art Institute of Atlanta. Partnering with Savannah, Georgia native Tim "DJ Headliner" Barnes, Thomas formed Arrested Development, a "southern-folk-ethnic-rap" group (White) which would eventually grow to include several other members. Hailed by music critics as an antidote to the self-destructive tendencies of gangsta rap, the group won two Grammys for their 1992 debut album on Chrysalis *3 Years, 5 Months and 2 Days in the Life of ...* (which sold over 1.5 million copies), before breaking up after a less successful follow-up album. The song "Tennessee"—the group's most prominent engagement with the South as a lyrical subject—tells of a narrator in search of an ancestral homeland, which he finds in the South, where he "climbed the trees [his] forefathers hung from." Through the use of such themes, as well as visual imagery in the form of stereotypically rural clothing such as overalls in contrast to the flashy gear preferred by many rappers, the group developed a critical reputation for their "distinctly southern style" (Dilday). Their music (sometimes characterized as "alternative rap") featured positive, spiritually uplifting lyrics and a "world music" aesthetic. The sense of southernness conveyed by the group was more closely linked to northern urban blacks' feelings of nostalgia and rootlessness than to the rap music of the South's major cities, which generally bore more resemblance to the bass-heavy, call-and-response lub music of 2 Live Crew.

In the 1980s and early 1990s, southern artists like The Geto Boys and 2 Live Crew engaged in the traditional rap music practice of "representing" their neighborhoods and cities in their lyrics, but they did not express an identity that encompassed the entire South. Similarly, southern producers and label owners like Jermaine Dupri who complained about marginalization within the rap music industry could only imagine the South in terms of what it lacked in comparison to the more established centers of production. These perceptions would begin to change in the mid 1990s, as artists, producers, label owners, and ordinary listeners from southern cities like Atlanta, New Orleans, Houston, Memphis, and Miami contributed to the construction of a new imagined space within the rap music universe, one which could operate on the same level as "East Coast" or "West Coast."

Several factors, including the growing investment in rap music in the large cities of the South and a certain degree of creative stagnation in the established centers of production, led to an opening in the market for music that expressed alternate regionally based identities. Artists and producers from the urban centers of the American South would fill this void, as listeners and corporations from both within and outside the South scrambled to stake their claim to this newly discovered territory. An increased interest on the part of critics and listeners in these local scenes from large southern cities—including but not limited to Atlanta, New Orleans, Miami, Houston, Memphis, and Richmond—brought to light many previously unknown artists and introduced the rest of the nation to new aesthetic and thematic interpretations of the art form. The developments in these southern cities also formed the basis for a new imagined space and an associated cultural identity, which grounded itself in the phrase "Dirty South."

The term entered the public discourse by way of a song, "Dirty South," which was featured on the Atlanta-based group Goodie Mob's 1995 debut album, *Soul Food*. While it is possible that the term was used in some circles of southern rap music listeners before it was codified in Goodie Mob's "Dirty South," the song seems to have served as the catalyst for its transformation to an imagined space claimed by many southerners and recognized by many from outside the South. At first, only rap insiders of various sorts picked up the term, which competed with such other contenders as "third coast" or "south coast," but by the year 2000, it was fully entrenched, and references to the Dirty South peppered the entertainment sections of major newspapers all over the country. As the phrase passed from Goodie Mob's song to the larger sphere of popular culture, the contours of this imagined region would undergo significant transformations.

The Goodie Mob's Dirty South

Along with the title track, "Dirty South" was one of the more commercially successful songs from Goodie Mob's 1995 debut album *Soul Food*. Although its authorship is often reduced to "Goodie Mob" among rap music listeners and in the popular press, the song features lyrics written and voiced by guest rappers (and fellow residents of the East Point suburb of Atlanta) Cool Breeze and Big Boi (of the rap duo OutKast). Big Gipp is the only member of Goodie Mob who actually raps on the song—the other members (Cee-Lo, Khujo, and T-Mo) perform back-up vocals. Nevertheless, the members of the group who did not rap on the song have made public commentary about its meaning and that of the term that it popularized. After the release of the song as a single, a Billboard reviewer described it as "another southern-bred tale from Atlanta's Goodie Mob [that] introduces listeners to the drug trade south of the Mason-Dixon line" and complains that "the insightful lyrics that Goodie Mob usually display are metaphorically lost in this yarn" ("Single Reviews"). While the lyrics could be said to fit this general description, to dismiss them as meaningless or trite ignores important features that differentiate "Dirty South" from similarly themed works.

In the first stanza of the song's chorus, the group makes reference to the Red Dogs, a paramilitary drug enforcement squad in Atlanta: "One to the two the three the four/Them dirty Red Dogs done hit the door/And they got everybody on they hands and knees/And they ain't gonna leave until they find them keys [i.e., kilos]." The remainder of the chorus describes the effects of several illicit drugs, then proceeds to make an epistemic challenge to the listeners, who are imagined as plural, male, and African American: "See powder gets you hyper, reefer makes you calm/Cigarettes give you cancer, woo-woos make you dumb/What you niggas know about the Dirty South?" [Note: For the purposes of my study, I have used the album version of "Dirty South"; in the radio version, the chorus is changed to "What you really know about the Dirty

South?"] The rappers use the local context of Atlanta as a framework around which they imagine a Dirty South characterized by repressive police tactics and a drug-dealing "gangsta" culture. The lyrics also convey an overarching theme of unfairness or injustice that draws upon imagery from previous visions of "the South."

These underlying themes of unfairness, injustice, and betrayal are explored in several ways within "Dirty South." On the CD release *of Soul Food*, "Dirty South" is preceded by a skit titled "Red Dog" which sets the tone for the song that follows. In a brief exchange, a man who identifies himself by the nickname "Straight Shooter" pounds on the door of a drug house or apartment and asks the respondent to "hit [him] three times" (sell him three bags of drugs). Immediately after the transaction is completed, members of the Red Dog counternarcotics squad break down the door, ordering all to the floor with guns drawn. It seems that the ironically named "Straight Shooter" was helping the Red Dogs in a drug sting. In the Dirty South, no one can be trusted.

Along these same lines, one of several narratives or narrative fragments within the song revolves around a scheme in which the narrator scams the nation's then chief executive in a drug deal: "Now if dirty Bill Clinton fronted me some weight/Told me keep two, bring him back eight/And I only brought him five and stuck his ass for three/Do you think that Clampett will sic his goons on me?" Used in this manner, the reference to Bill Clinton speaks to the complicity of (white) economic and political elites in the drug trade. The playful alteration of Bill Clinton's name to Jed Clampett (a reference to a character from the 1960s television series *The Beverly Hillbillies*) reveals a conflicted engagement with certain perceptions of the South, as well as with the political persona of Clinton himself. The Arkansas politician, whose rise to national power coincided with the institutional development of Atlanta's rap music scene, inspired both time-worn stereotypes of the backwards "good ole boys" of the Old South and a celebration of a capitalist, non-racist "New South." Clinton seemed to embody a racially inflected southern identity that included both white and African American elements—an intersection of "Bubba" and "our first black president." Still, one should not assume too much sympathy for Clinton on the part of the members of Goodie Mob. In "Goodie Bag," another song on the 1995 *Soul Food* album, the rapper first conflates Clinton and fellow southern politician Newt Gingrich, then complains that he "can't keep Billy and his uncle [Sam?] out [his] fuckin' goodie bag." New South politicians like Clinton and Gingrich are integrated into an imagined space where unfairness reigns, and where law enforcement is nothing but an extension of a corrupt and racist power structure—in other words, a space that looks a lot like the "Old South" from the perspective of many African Americans.

On the local level, the lyrics contain an engagement of sorts with the issue of police practices in Atlanta. Just what is "dirty" about the Red Dogs goes unsaid, but one possibility is that the adjective refers to the unnecessary violence and gang-like behavior that seem to plague police units of this type. The Red Dogs merged into the regular force after several of their number were dismissed or disciplined for reasons of corruption and excessive force. The unit was involved in several controversial shootings, including one which took the life of eight-year-old Xavier Bennett in November of 1991 at the East Lake Meadows housing complex (Scruggs). The young-ster's accidental death at the hands of police was mentioned in the song "Police Brutality," released by Atlanta-based rap group Success-N-Effect in 1992.

In addition to offering an (admittedly oblique) critique of power relations in the U.S. and the South in particular, the lyrics engage with the issues of slavery and its ramifications on the level of individual identity. Stating "See life's a bitch then you figure out/Why you really got dropped in the Dirty South/See in the third grade this is what you told/You was bought, you was sold," the rapper addresses the psychological effects upon African American identity formation that exist in the wake of the South's history of slavery and discrimination. Implied in this lyric is the suggestion that the educational system plays a role in the transmission of a racialized identity which de-emphasizes the agency of African Americans. The insinuation of these lines is that being born (black) in the South is a kind of curse, one that hinges upon black children being "told/You was bought, you was sold." Once a black person has been able to "figure out" why they were unlucky enough to be born into the American South, the song implies, the logical reaction is to suspend all rules of fairness in the pursuit of a criminal lifestyle and its material rewards.

Except for a brief reference to Atlanta's Piedmont Park, "Dirty South" unfolds against the backdrop of East Point (a small town within the sprawl of "metro Atlanta" which still maintains separate municipal government), as well as the proximate Southwest Atlanta area (referred to as "Southwest" or "the SWATs" in other songs on *Soul Food*). Within the political economy of the rap industry and listener base, the lyrics challenge those who would dismiss either the creative potential of the South or the determination of its inhabitants with its insistent question: "What you niggas know about the Dirty South[?]" The desire to "represent" is expressed through various references to Goodie Mob associates and their territories: "Perry Homes to Herndon Homes, to all the Homes/Adamsville to Pool Creek, shit just don't sleep in the Dirty South." Within the text of the song, the act of mapping and local knowledge are intimately tied to the ability of drug dealers to avoid police: "See East Point Atlanta threw this road block/Talkin'bout all this blow traffic got to stop/So the big time players off John Freeman Way/Had to find themselves another back street to take."

The verse rapped and written by Big Boi of OutKast presents another side of the Dirty South, one characterized by strip clubs, luxury cars, and objectified women. Whereas the Dirty South imagined by Cool Breeze and Big Gipp is a male space by virtue of its almost total absence of women, Big Boi—who built a simulacrum of a strip club stage in his home to act as "inspiration" for his rhyme writing (Murray, "The Poet and the Playa")—allows their presence only as sexual objects and receptacles. In his rap, he does not address the themes of drug dealing, local knowledge and representation, and unfairness that characterize the verses contributed by the other rappers. Still, his vision of the Dirty South as strip club *demimonde* introduces elements that have proved significant and enduring in the popular understanding of the concept. Also noteworthy among these is an identification with southern speech patterns—"Kickin' that same southern slang" (Goodie Mob, *Soul Food* LaFace Records, 1995)—that are perceived as distinctive.

In interviews following the release of "Dirty South," members of Goodie Mob generally characterized it as a politicized indictment of an unreconstructed New South and stressed their desire to illuminate "the political side, the real historical side of Atlanta that everyone doesn't really talk about" (Sarig 38). Many of their statements invoke the ongoing struggle, well engaged by 1996, over the presence of Confederate symbolism in the state flags of Georgia and South Carolina. A 1996 *St. Louis Dispatch* article (Hampel) cites group member T-Mo as "[saying] that the song portrays Atlanta as a racist stronghold where the confederate flag still waves for 'good ole boys and slavery.'" In 1998, Big Gipp, another group member, maintained that "the symbols of slavery still stand in the South, and it's evidence that the mentality still lives ... Ain't too much changed; they just learned how to make it look a little bit better" (Vognar).

Wills Felin's 2000 documentary film *The Dirty South: Raw and Uncut* features several interview portions in which the members of Goodie Mob expand on their notions of the South's dirtiness. Continuing racism and white domination is the most prominent of these themes. As Khujo explains,

> it's just dirty in the form of ... racism, ... it's still ... the old prune-face ass white folk who still run the ATL ... that's what's dirty about it, 'cause they still run it ... they run the ATL from the inside out. ... During the nighttime, the street is ours ... during the daytime they got white folk comin' from all over Roswell, I'm talkin' about Alpharetta, comin' in just to run ATL out of these big buildings that they done fuck around and built downtown. That's what dirty about it, you feel what I'm sayin'?

Big Gipp integrates themes of a rise in prominence of southern rap acts and the need for black economic empowerment to his comments about the meaning of "Dirty South," emphasizing the need to "start controlling this business and getting all the other folks up out of it so all of us can always eat, sleep, and go to the mailbox, just like everybody else."

Fellow group member Cee-Lo adds that the importance of the South lies in its civil rights legacy, portraying the region in metaphorical terms: "a great number of our black leaders ... come right from the South, so, the South is the heartland ... the South is ... a mother." Within the context of the film (but with larger correspondence to the entire Dirty South phenomenon), if the South is "a mother," then the strippers who make up the female interviewees in the film could be said to represent the flip side of a Madonna/whore binary. Big Gipp concludes that "at the end of the day, [the Dirty South is] all about family," as he mediates upon the material culture, spatial realities, and childrearing practices of southern black life: "Cadillacs, Lincolns, man ... I'm talking about bar-b-cue, back yards, big houses, man. ... Raised up by your Grandmama." Khujo's comments also touch upon themes of southern roots and family connections: "Now runaway slaves comin' back down to the South ... So it's like, before you down the South ... know what your roots are all about, 'cause without your roots you ain't gonna grow period, folk, and that what the dirty South is, dog."

Goodie Mob's assertions of anti-black racism and discrimination in the South and in "the ATL" in particular seem somewhat incongruous with recent data on the success of the black middle class in that city, often called a "black Mecca" for its combination of economic possibilities and historic civil rights legacy (Williams and Pearson). Their claims, however, should be considered in the context of the public discourse over official display of the Confederate "battle flag," which was featured prominently on Georgia's state flag from 1956 (when it was adopted as a statement against school desegregation) until 2001. The issue of confederate symbolism in the state flags of Georgia and Mississippi, as well as the presence of confederate flags atop the state capital buildings of Alabama and South Carolina, contribute to a racially charged debate that continues to the present day. Rappers from the South often use the potent symbol of the confederate flag to make the point that racism is still flourishing. In a skit featured on the debut album from Atlanta-based rappers OutKast, a pilot landing in Atlanta points out, "to the far left you can see the Georgia dome, which, by the way, still flies the confederate battle flag."

Complaints of black poverty and white economic domination contribute to another aspect of the South's (and Atlanta's) perceived dirtiness, one which is borne out by a recent investigation by Keating. In reference to the much-heralded Southern economic boom, he concluded in 2001 that in Atlanta, "the region's exceptional economic development did not ameliorate previous inequalities; it deepened them." Keating further argues that "business-driven public policy plays an integral role in augmenting the disadvantages of the economy" and reports that "49% of blacks looking for homes in the Atlanta area in 1989 reported that they had been discriminated against by real-estate agents" (1–2, 59). Despite these barriers, African Americans in Atlanta and other southern cities did make significant economic progress during the 1990s, but this was often unevenly distributed with regard to class, disproportionately benefiting middle- and upper-class blacks in suburban areas (Williams and Pearson). Framed in this context, Goodie Mob's perception of the prevalence of economic disparities and racial discrimination in "the ATL" would seem to be not so far off the mark. In addition to these economic woes, issues surrounding traffic gridlock and the use of public space during the annual African American college spring break event called Freaknik were a continuing source of racial friction in Atlanta during the mid-to-late 1990s. Whereas Khujo complained of white suburbanites flooding the city center to occupy "these big buildings that they done fuck around and built," a parallel side to this unofficial segregation of public space was the subject of comment by *The Source*'s Wilder, who observed in late 1994, "who's not chilling downtown is white people. Downtown Atlanta in the daytime is like thirty to one, blacks to whites."

Interviewed in 2001, New Orleans-based rap mogul Master P also referred to larger socioeconomic forces in his explanation of the term "Dirty South": "That's what we mean by the Dirty South—poverty, projects, congestion—all that. It's everything that's going on" (Wartofsky). Although he does not mention racism as an element of the "dirtiness," a review of recent economic data from the New Orleans area indicates similar inequalities to those seen in Atlanta. A 2002 article in the *Times-Picayune* used data from the 2000 Census to conclude "the median income for white households remains nearly twice that of black households in the New Orleans area." The article goes on to cite sociologist John Logan's observation that "the gap between white and black earnings in the New Orleans area remains striking," lagging behind a national trend toward a narrowing of that disparity. Logan points out that blacks often continue to live in "much worse neighborhoods" than whites with comparable incomes, a fact which he attributes to housing discrimination. As a result, blacks in New Orleans often face "a higher neighborhood crime rate and public schools of lesser quality," regardless of their income level (Warner and Scallan).

These perceptions about the South and its hostility to the interests of African Americans may be better understood in light of political and economic dynamics on the national level. While the New South ideology that developed in the wake of legal segregation contributed to the economic boosterism and reluctance to address issues related to racism and black poverty on the part of southern politicians like Bill Clinton and Newt Gingrich, their attitudes cannot be separated from the radical rejection of issues of racial and gender equity that began in the Reagan era. Carnoy describes the ideological undercurrents of the 1992 presidential election:

> Twelve years of conservative rule had a major impact on the ideology of racial inequality. Not only were race relations put on the back burner, but employers, teachers, social workers, and state and local governments all got the message that racial inequality was mainly blacks' problem, not one of government responsibility. The ultimate result was an ideological shift that forcefully and negatively affected minorities' ability to overcome entrenched discriminatory practices (219).

Although Bill Clinton's ideals about race and social justice were certainly more progressive than those of either of his two predecessors, many of his positions and policies reflected the rightward shift in American political discourse and policy that took place during the Reagan–Bush years. His failure to address the racial bias of the "war on drugs" and the resultant surge in incarcerated African Americans, as well as his support for radical welfare reform, represented a continuation of the most mean-spirited neoconservative policies of the 1980s. As the lyrics of "Dirty South" suggest, many working and middle-class African Americans were aware of their continuing status as outsiders within the southern and the national contexts in the decades following the civil rights movement.

While "Dirty South" and its subsequent explication featured largely negative perceptions, a related recording by Goodie Mob adds an element of balance to the group's portrayal of the South. "Dirty South Remix" was released as a single in 1996 and features an uncredited (most likely owing to contractual obligations) guest appearance by New Orleans-based rapper Mystikal. The standard definition of a rap music remix, in which elements from the original work are recombined or altered, does not apply to "Dirty South Remix," which would be more appropriately titled "Dirty South, Part 2." The lyrics voiced by Mystikal and the four members of Goodie Mob are completely new—the only elements that remain from the original "Dirty South" are a small portion of the backing track and a minor vocal sample.

In "Dirty South Remix," a new chorus (rapped by Cee-Lo) is introduced, one which links southern speech patterns, southern violence, and a defensiveness regarding stereotypes projected from outside: "Just 'cause we kind when we speak/Out-of-towners think we weak/But if you disrespect me/We can show you we dirty/Dirty South." In contrast to "Dirty South," in which the corrupt and lawless elements of the South are emphasized, the verses in "Dirty South Remix" feature references to distinctive features of the rappers' environment: "Born and became strong on this red clay soil/Pine cone fights and summer nights"; "Another scorcher—must be a day in ATL." The song does not appear on any of the group's albums, and, unlike "Dirty South," received virtually no media attention and never penetrated the Billboard charts. For this reason, the contribution of "Dirty South Remix" to the discourse around or understanding of the new conception of the South in rap music can be said to be much less than that of "Dirty South." Still, it gives us valuable insight into the ways that the South was imagined by these rappers.

Whatever Goodie Mob and their collaborators Cool Breeze, Big Boi, and Mystikal intended to express with the songs "Dirty South" and "Dirty South Remix," the Dirty South concept was quickly picked up by rap music aficionados, especially those located in the South. A post submitted to the Usenet forum rec.music.hip-hop on July 11, 1996 by a Texas-based contributor known as OverTime is one of the earliest instances of its use within this subculture of dedicated rap music listeners. OverTime's post, which appeared under the subject line "The DIRTY SOUTH!!!," not only employs the regionally based phrase and imagery introduced by Goodie Mob but also touches upon many of the issues and perceptions that they encapsulate.

According to OverTime, creative stagnation and excessive commercialization in the established centers of production make room for southern artists, who have not enjoyed the respect they are due: "everybody needs to recognize that the real underground shit in rap is coming out of the SOUTH COAST!!!! Both the east and the west are too commercialized." Like Goodie Mob's, OverTime's vision of the South is one riddled with contradictions. On one hand, the South is characterized by continuing white racism and discrimination: "Most Soutside [sic] rappers have their own record companies and labels because its no secret that white folks are racist and wont support you." On the other, the South is a cultural homeland for African Americans: "all yall follks NEED to come back home to the South Side [...] where yall roots are any way." OverTime cites the presence in the region of "most of the Historical Black Colleges & Universities" as evidence for this claim. Ultimately, he calls upon his peers to "cancel all the east *v* west beef" and "get wit the SOUTHSIDE and get on the Rise like them ELEVATORS," referring to a song "Elevators (Me & You)" by Atlanta-based rappers OutKast. In addition to putting forward some of the more abstract ideological issues invoked by the term "Dirty South," OverTime also provides an overview of the musical activity in the major creative centers of southern rap, which he breaks down along the lines of "Texas ... Louisiana ... Atlanta ... Florida ... plus a host of other artists from Tennessee, Arkansas, and all southern points between!!!"

OverTime's post also introduces the much contested idea of authenticity to the debate on the Dirty South. In addition to complaining about the commercialization of rap music from the established centers of production, he excoriates those who use the term "hip hop" to describe their music, prefacing his criticism with general praise for the diverse styles employed by southern artists:

The south coast has a huge diversity of artists, from gangsta to bass, and everything in between. Some even do 'hip hop' which to me is a code word for commercialization of the industry, just like the phrase 'keep it real' anyone who says this is a commercialized fake artist.

For OverTime, the Dirty South represented a space that had not yet been colonized by corporate forces interested in commercialization. If the Dirty South embodied some sort of underground authenticity, however, it would not do so for long.

Soon after the release of Goodie Mob's song, other rap artists began to appropriate the phrase "Dirty South." In 1996, the group Southern Playas released an uptempo dance song called "Dirty South Bass Track," while a compilation released in September of 1998 on the Memphis, Tennessee-based Dirty Harry Productions label featured a group calling themselves "The Dirty

South Boyz." These two examples are relatively obscure in terms of sales, but the term was gaining currency among big-name rappers as well. In November of 1998, New Orleans-based rapper Mystikal released his album *Ghetto Fabulous,* which debuted at number five on the *Billboard* pop chart and number one on the R & B chart and which featured a collaboration with New Jersey-based rappers Naughty By Nature called "Dirty South, Dirty Jerz." This use of the term especially highlights its potential to help locate southern artists within rap music's imaginary landscape of regionally based identities. By 1999, the phrase had spread beyond the purely musical realm and started to be attached to businesses associated with the rap music subculture such as record and clothing stores, tattoo parlors, and hair stylists; it was also employed as a nickname for a high school football team in Riverdale, Georgia.

Dirty South—From Subculture to Pop Culture

At the same time that the Dirty South was being absorbed by the popular imagination on a grass-roots level, the rap music industry in the South seemed to shift into high gear. Rappers and producers based in the urban centers of the South were making deals with national record companies and penetrating further and further into the *Billboard* charts and radio playlists all over the U.S. and beyond. The pent-up creativity of previously marginalized rappers and producers combined with the new economic possibilities introduced by the involvement of major labels and distributors like Universal, Atlantic, Loud, and BMG, among others, with the result that artists like OutKast and Mystikal were soon thrust into the forefront of commercial radio and retail sales. Meanwhile, the national press was beginning to take notice. Although Cooper had employed the term in its generic sense (i.e., not in specific reference to Goodie Mob's song) in July of 1998 in the *Village Voice,* more mainstream newspapers and magazines (including those located in the South) did not begin to follow suit until several years later. By the year 2000, articles in the national press had begun to portray the Dirty South as both a region and as a "new movement" within the rap genre. In that year, a *Billboard* writer observed that "radio has been embracing all the 'dirty South' it can get its hands on" ("Rap"). In 2002, a writer combined the aesthetic with the economic in the following statement about Atlanta rapper Ludacris, who parlayed his role as a local radio DJ into a successful career as a rapper: "[He] is part of the hip-hop movement bubbling up and boiling over from the Dirty South the last several years with an inescapable 'bounce' sound that's paying off for anyone involved" (Johnson).

For the majors who had established relationships with southern artists or labels early in the game (Arista/LaFace and Columbia/So So Def, both based in Atlanta), this trend paid dividends and drove their competitors to seek out new talent in the South. New Orleans was the next city to benefit from major label interest, with Priority teaming up with Master P's No Limit in 1993 and Universal striking a deal with Cash Money in 1998. The new economic opportunities posed by the "Dirty South" have led others, such as New York mogul P. Diddy, to forge artistic and economic relationships with the creative communities based in the large cities of the South. The investment in southern rap on the part of large entertainment corporations, which had previously been restricted to early centers of production such as Atlanta and New Orleans, was spreading to other cities like Houston, Richmond, and Memphis.

A March 5, 2001 article by Wartofsky in the *Washington Post* indicates a burgeoning national awareness among followers of rap music that something of economic and creative importance was going on in some of the South's major cities. Wartofsky sketches out the ownership and power centers of this new artistic region:

> The Dirty South belongs to the rappers who record for No Limit ... It belongs to another New Orleans powerhouse, Cash Money Records ... Atlanta rappers like OutKast and Goodie Mob are of the Dirty South, and so are Memphis-bred pioneers Eightball and

MJG and the rest of Houston's Suave House, as well as Rap-a-Lot and Atlanta's Organized Noise.

The article goes on to cite sales figures of these artists, most notably the quadruple-platinum status of rapper Juvenile's album, *400 Degreez*, on Cash Money Records. The years preceding the article were certainly groundbreaking in terms of the level of success that southern artists enjoyed. In the five years following the 1993 signing of a multi-million dollar manufacturing and distribution deal with New York-based Priority records, New Orleans' "visionary underground capitalist" Master P released 20 albums on his No Limit label, all of which went platinum (Cooper). At the height of its success in 1998, the company was valued at $230 million. Meanwhile, in 1998, No Limit's up-and-coming competitor Cash Money Records entered into a three-year distribution and manufacturing agreement with Universal Records worth $30 million (Forman 338). A 2001 article in *Billboard* notes that "Cash Money/Universal and No Limit/Priority represent the main success stories of independents joining forces with majors and their efforts skyrocketing. However, these joint ventures are not guaranteed to transform a regional success story into a national one" (Kenon 26).

In Atlanta, the mixture of major labels and southern talent was producing similar results to those in New Orleans, albeit with very different styles of rap music. The establishment of Atlanta as a center of music industry infrastructure, which began in the late 1980s, both aided this process and was itself accelerated by the growing market for southern rap music. LaFace Records, which had initially focused on R & B artists, brought several Atlanta-based rap acts into the national spotlight. The duo OutKast, who, according to David Mays of *The Source*, "began to change ideas about what southern rappers could do" (Murray, "The Poet and the Playa"), brought the label unprecedented success in the genre, selling over three million copies of its 2000 album *Stankonia*, which was named the "best album [in all genres] of 2000" in the *Village Voice*'s, annual "Pazz and Jop" poll of several hundred music critics ("Best Bets"). In 2001, they were named by *Spin* magazine as "the lead contenders for world's greatest living hip-hop act" (Lester). Meanwhile, in 2000, Jermaine Dupri's So So Def renewed its deal with Columbia Records, marking "the continuation of an eight-year relationship between the two labels" (Mitchell, "The Rhythm, The Rap and The Blues"). By 2002, it was estimated that "hip-hop music pumps an estimated half a billion dollars a year into Atlanta's economy" (Lovel).

Still, despite this success, Wartofsky's *Washington Post* article contains intimations that all was not well in the Dirty South. Some southern artists and producers expressed frustration that their colleagues from other parts of the country subscribed to stereotyped conceptions of the South as a culturally backward part of the country which had little commercial or creative potential within the context of rap music production. Cash Money's in-house producer Mannie Fresh observed, "We always did have tight songs coming from the South, but the West Coast and the East Coast never acknowledged them" (Wartofsky). This lack of acknowledgment was compounded by the structural and economic realities of the rap music industry. In a *Billboard* interview in late 1999 (just before his company abandoned Atlanta for Los Angeles in 2000), Antonio "L.A." Reid complains that the location of his company (LaFace) in Atlanta rather than in New York or Los Angeles

[is] still one of the biggest obstacles. And, while I love living and working in Atlanta—and we've certainly made some impact by being here—it's still not necessarily the choice of most people working in the recording industry. They would much rather live in New York, Los Angeles or Nashville.

Reid continues, "the distribution companies are not here. Of course, everybody has a branch office, whether it be in sales or A & R, but they're not based here" (Mitchell, "Antonio 'L.A.' Reid"

26). As Reid's comments illustrate, in terms of the industrial infrastructure of rap music production Southern cities continue to lag behind the power centers established early in the genre's history.

These structural realities are compounded by another area of friction between the Dirty South and the rest of the nation, which has its origin in the historically negative stereotypes and generalizations perpetuated about the South, its inhabitants, and their music. The conception of the South as an economic and cultural backwater is evident in a statement made by New Orleans-based rapper Juvenile in *Rolling Stone:* "RZA [a producer and rapper from New York and member of the group Wu-Tang-Clan] said that in the South, we was still livin' like it's 1985 … At first I was pissed off, but you know what? In a way, it's kinda true" (Reynolds). Again turning to Goodie Mob, some of their statements after the release of "Dirty South" indicate a similarly defensive posture towards "big-city visitor[s]" in response to their perceived attitudes about the South and its inhabitants:

> [Rapper Big] Gipp remembers many a big-city visitor looking down on the Mob's homeland, its accents, rural landscapes, and country ways. 'They used to come down here before the Georgia Dome and a lot of other things were built down here,' he says. 'It was a little bit more country than it is now, and people would always say, 'Man, you guys are so country. Why do y'all talk like that? (Vognar).

As the above comments suggest, historically rooted negative stereotypes about the South persisted within the culture of rap music. In his 1991 recording, "Straight Up Nigga," Los Angeles-based rapper Ice T compared himself to "a watermelon, chitlin-eatin' nigga down South," reinscribing the image of a shuffling, passive, and ultimately feminized southern black. This negative association of "southernness" with rurality is evident in a 2000 interview with Jacksonville, Florida-based director of urban programming for Clear Channel Radio Doc Wynter. In his description of the reaction among radio programmers to the rise of "Dirty South" rap artists, Wynter claimed, "a lot of stations in big markets wouldn't play'em. They felt like it was country bamified hip-hop. Yet it kept selling and selling and selling and by virtue of radio exposure, people started calling those radio stations saying 'Hey—play it!' " (Beecher).

These observations about the persistence of stereotypes and generalizations about the South and the resulting anti-southern bias within the rap music industry are echoed in Wartofsky's 2001 article. She frames the new music coming out of Atlanta and New Orleans as a departure from the past, when "the southern rap acts that sold nationally, like 2 Live Crew, performed 'booty music': sex-obsessed lyrics set to accelerated beats for jiggling rear ends, part of a genre dismissed by *The Source* magazine as being too much about 'country pork-chop-eatin'' individuals." Speaking from Florida in 2000, 2 Live Crew front man Luther Campbell imagined a South which was persecuted, disrespected or misunderstood by outsiders but united across racial boundaries by its cultural distinctiveness: " 'We in the South are a bunch of outcasts; nobody really respects us,' he points out. 'We speak a different language in the South, and it's not a black-white thing; it's South versus New York or California' " (Madera).

This brings us to another important aspect of the "dirtiness" of the South, that which relates to its perceived sexual culture. As illustrated by Big Boi's verse in "Dirty South," with its references to "pimpin'" and "fuckin' around wit hoes," rap from the South does seem to have a strong association with strip clubs and sexually explicit lyrics. In part, this association hearkens back to the phenomenal success of Miami's 2 Live Crew in the late 1980s and early 1990s. Significantly, the interpretation of the "dirty" in Dirty South as sexual has become increasingly prevalent in the press as rap music from the South has become more of a commercial force to be reckoned with. Writing in a Toronto newspaper in 2000, a reviewer of the soundtrack from the film *Big Momma's House* lamented the inclusion of "the wash-your-mouth-out up-and-comers of southern rap"

("Old Tricks Are the Best Tricks"). A 2002 article about child rapper Lil Bow Wow explains that he

> now considers himself part of the Dirty South sound epitomized by OutKast. That, too, is strange, because the Dirty South sound is so named because of its profanity, violence and sexual crudity. Meanwhile, Bow Wow's music remains innocent and clean. 'It makes sense to me, because I'm living in the South, and it's dirty,' said Bow Wow. 'There's a lot of dirt.'
>
> But 'Dirty' in Dirty South refers to the trashy music and lyrics, right?
>
> 'Nah,' he said. (Baca).

A few weeks later, Burr reviewed a performance by Atlanta-based rapper Ludacris in the *San Antonio Express-News* and praised "his fluency with Dirty South rap, which projects a laid-back vibe and incorporates humorous asides while retaining explicit sex-and-violence-themed lyrics."

Signifying Southernness

Within this framework, it is not surprising that rap artists who claim that the Dirty South seems to have a love/hate relationship with the South, both on a thematic and on a stylistic level, often bristle at what they perceive as unfair stereotypes and prejudices held by outsiders, while simultaneously rejecting the traditional symbolism of the white South. But they also walk a fine line between refutation and celebration, as the forces that have helped to marginalize them are the very same ones that can now make them distinctive (and marketable) within the context of the rap music industry.

To begin with, there is what Alona Wartofsky calls "the southern way with words: the drawl," a feature which evidently appeals to music critics from outside the South. Tate wrote admiringly in the *Village Voice* in 1998 that "Atlanta's long-drawling Goodie Mob sound about as Black and country as you can git [sic]," while in the same year Robert Christgau wrote of the Goodie Mob that their "drawls [are] as thick as their funk" ("Consumer Guide"). The idea that southern rappers should drawl, that they should sound distinct from rappers from other places, was not only projected from outside the South but also asserted by southern rappers themselves. Andre Benjamin from OutKast, cited in Wartofsky's 2001 article, illustrates this tendency when he claims that:

> I think it's harder for somebody from the South to rap ... You really have to work your mouth. We never say the whole word, so it's hard to understand sometimes, especially if you're rapping quickly ... Sometimes when you're really feeling it, and you just don't give a damn, that's when you really play it up. You just get a real draaaawwwwwl.

Wartofsky then turns to New Orleans' Juvenile, who adds a political dimension to the idea of a distinctive southern (black) way of talking while at the same time acknowledging its market value:

> The way I rap, my accent is a must ... People love my accent because it's so different. I'm from the South, and you from way up north, and you hear the way I talk, that flip you clean out. You like, 'Damn, he just rappin' like that, it's all ghetto and he don't say his words right, and I don't care.' Because black people was brought to this country, and the language our

ancestors had to learn wasn't our language. So we will never speak correctly … My style is ghetto, project, off-the-porch flowing, that's what I call it.

In addition to the value placed on "drawl" by critics and artists alike, there is a tendency on the part of both groups to employ traditional stereotypes about the South. Rap music journalists often display a weakness for timeworn stereotypes about the poverty and backwardness of southerners, as evidenced by the way they collectively received the Kentucky-based group Nappy Roots. Even though members of the group made statements explicitly denying association with the Dirty South, the fit was too good to pass up: more "black and country" than Goodie Mob, they presented an image which, in its familiarity, proved to be irresistible to many writers in national media outlets. Although they do not claim the Dirty South, the group still relies heavily upon images associated with southernness; the title of their 2002 release *Watermelon, Chicken & Gritz* (Doolittle) combines traditional southern foodways with stereotypes of both southerners and African Americans.

Whatever playfulness or irony is present in the "hillbilly hustla" image that they put forth seems to be lost on most reviewers, who are generally bowled over by the powerful combination of "wild hair, beans and pork chops, beat-up overalls, and … weed" (O'Connor). Doolittle, writing in the Allentown, Pennsylvania *Morning Call*, correctly observes that "Hip-hop's so-called 'Dirty South' has been primarily defined by an urban perspective" and lauds Nappy Roots for their ability to be "in the milieu without making them appear to be pawns of it," but he is no less susceptible than most reviewers to the pull of their "southern black take on Dukes Of Hazzard roguishness" (Gill). In March of 2002, Reines, writing in the *Los Angeles Times*, saw a new trend emerging: "with 9/11 (at least temporarily) stunting the rap world's urge toward materialism— to say nothing of the minor mudsplash made last year by über-hick Bubba Sparxxx's *Dark Days, Bright Nights*—well, it looks like Nappy Roots' time has come."

Reines refers to another recent artist to openly exploit the "hillbilly" Southern stereotype, Bubba Sparxxx, a white man who, according to Sinclair of the *Times* of London, "grew up on a cabbage patch 15 minutes north of the tiny rural town of LaGrange, Georgia," and who raps in a "hayseed voice that would seem to be the product of several generations of southern inbreeding." Although he seems to approve of Sparxxx's persona and music, Sinclair's prejudices about the South become evident when he claims that the artist "doesn't lack in either the Dirty or the South department," referring to "sexually regressive lyrics" as his justification for this statement. Artists like Nappy Roots and Bubba Sparxxx would seem to be manipulating traditional southern stereotypes in order to stand out in the crowded rap music market, profiting from preconceptions on the part of journalists about what southern rappers should look, act, and sound like.

These preconceptions are sometimes framed within the context of an imagined historical southern culture. An article in the *Dallas Morning News* by Vognar begins by invoking the names of "William Faulkner and Ray Charles, Robert Johnson and Flannery O'Connor," proceeding to make the profound observation that "the South has never been at a loss for grief, humor, soul, or artistic genius." To his credit, Vognar acknowledges that "southern hip-hop is hardly new," but, like many in the media, displays a fondness for southern stereotypes, describing the members of Goodie Mob (from urban-suburban East Point) as "more than a little bit country, and damn proud of it." Some writers seem to be aware of the ways in which this southernness is an artificial construction. Wartofsky observes that "images of the region have been defined by a range of cultural exports," citing as examples the fiction of William Faulkner and the music of Robert Johnson. Both Vognar and Wartofsky reduce the cultural contributions of the South to a handful of well-known Mississippians, while ignoring the degree to which outside influences have also shaped "southern" culture. Christgau, writing about OutKast in the *Village Voice*, was one of the few writers to fully grasp the way that "southernness" is not an innate identity, but rather something that is constructed in conversation with those outside of the South:

Their southernness signifies, evoking Booker T., endless Gregg Allman ballads, humid afternoons with horseflies droning over the hog wallow.

Catch is, I'm not sure I've ever seen a hog wallow, certainly not in the South, and I doubt many OutKast voters have either. For Northern whites, the Dirty South is exotic in an all too familiar way—whenever pop fans seek 'tradition' they flirt with exoticism, which often leads them south. (Christgau "La-Di-Da-Di-Di?")

The geographic meaning of the term "Dirty South" would initially seem to be the most straightforward one—if a person is from the region formerly known as "the South," they are now from "the Dirty South." Philadelphia resident Ollison writes in a letter to the *Village Voice* that he is "a 23-year-old black man and a son of the 'Dirty South.'" But it is imperative to bear in mind here Rogoff's claim that "geography [is] as much of an epistemic category as gender or race, and … all three are indelibly linked at every stage" (8). The geographic creation of the South/Dirty South is a highly contested process that involves deep-rooted patterns of thinking about geography and race. A statement by rapper Big V of the group Nappy Roots demonstrates the difficulty involved in matching the imaginative region of the "Dirty South" to an actual map of the U.S.:

We're not in the Dirty South, we're from the top of the South. Kentucky's the first state in the South, and we're too north to be southern and too southern to be north. So we're trapped right in the middle. It's a filter, you know? We connected with Tennessee, Virginia, Ohio, Indiana [not to mention West Virginia, Missouri and Illinois]. So Kentucky's a filter, and a lot of music runs through here (Reines).

The reluctance of Big V to see Kentucky (long viewed as a border state) lumped in with the Dirty South speaks to the obliteration of differences that occurs when "Dirty South" is used as a catch-all category for any artist or producer from the South. Nevertheless, their correspondence with older southern stereotypes of rurality and poverty seem to appeal to many critics as particularly representative of the Dirty South.

Despite the seeming dominance of Atlanta and New Orleans, the economic geography of the Dirty South is also conceived as flexible. In 2001, a reviewer observed that North Carolina-based rapper Petey Pablo's debut album "may signal a power shift in hip-hop's Dirty South … New Orleans … is no longer the commercial center of gravity … the pendulum may be swinging toward the Mason-Dixon line" (Chang). "Dirty South" often seems to refer specifically to commercially successful southern rap economies. A 1999 article in the St. Petersburg Times claimed that "when members of the hip-hop community use the phrase 'dirty South' to describe the phenomenon of popular artists from the southern U.S., they're talking about Georgia (Goodie Mob, OutKast) and Louisiana (The No Limits [sic] crew)," an understanding which underscores the fact that "Dirty South" can have a more specific meaning than just the geographic South. This is a fluid Dirty South, the composition of which can change over time. The same author, in an article about rapper Funkghost, writes, "Florida has yet to fly under hip-hop's 'dirty South' flag" (Welch).

For many critics and industry insiders, the Dirty South represented an economic and creative shot in the arm for an ailing art form. Writing in the *Times* of London, Sinclair claims, "the geographic and spiritual relocation of rap to the southern heartland breathes fresh life and not a little good humor into a genre that has become increasingly prone to self-parody." DJ Shadow, explaining in 2002 the sentiment behind the title of his track "Why Hip Hop Sucks In '96," claims that "since then, the barriers have been broken down with producers like the Neptunes [from Virginia] and those from the Dirty South, like OutKast" (Pearson). A *Los Angeles Times* writer combined this idea of "Dirty South" as creative renewal with the economic impact of the genre:

"The Dirty South is rising, and OutKast is leading the way. The Atlanta rap duo is at the fore of the Dirty South sound that has become a true force in hip-hop. It's not just the fans who are noticing" ("Best Bets").

While the importance of the Dirty South has often been situated in terms of the shifting geography of rap music production and the cultural impact of some of the rap music coming out of the South, it has also been imagined as a set of distinct aesthetic practices. Wartofsky correctly observes "because southern hip-hop developed organically out of various regional music scenes, there is no single sound of the South," but goes on to claim that "there is [still] something—something that's almost intangible—that links the various southern styles." This intangibility has proved frustrating to various attempts on the part of journalists to put their hands on the true aesthetic meaning of "Dirty South." Aesthetic claims have been made regarding tempo, timbre, and instrumentation ("the Dirty South's languid bass hits and flitting, double-time cymbals" (Keast)), as well as more abstract qualities like "attitude" ("the mean-spirited confrontation of Dirty South-style thug rap" (Moon)) and (as we have seen) "nastiness" in the sexual sense.

Some find a special rhythmic or syncopated quality in southern rap, citing "the groove-centric ethos of the Dirty South" ("Hip-Hop") or "tight Dirty South-style beat[s]" (Jones). Descriptions such as one referring to "bumptious, grimy Dirty South grooves" (Sterdan) seem to employ "dirt" as an updated signifier for "funk." A comparison of two descriptions of a Dirty South aesthetic illustrates the impossibility of reducing it to any one set of practices or qualities; while one author wrote in 2000 of OutKast "cement[ing] its position as standard-bearer for the new, soulful hip-hop sound of what's come to be called the Dirty South" (Guzman), another warned readers in the same year of "a southern form commonly known as the 'dirty south' style and exemplified by fast, bouncy beats and crass, trashy lyrics of acts like Juvenile and Master P" (Carter). The fact that many of Master P's songs are done over very slow tempos (reminiscent of the "g-funk" style associated with Los Angeles and environs) reveals the hazards of overgeneralizing, even within one city's musical culture.

Within the "Dirty South" construct, important variations among the styles of the cities of the South are often overlooked in pursuit of an aesthetic unity. Asked in 2001 to "explain the southern rap style to hip-hop fans who aren't already accustomed to it," Memphis-based rapper Project Pat responds,

> You know, the South has got different styles. I'm gonna break it down to you. Memphis doesn't sound like Atlanta, and Atlanta doesn't sound like Memphis, and Atlanta don't sound like Miami, and Memphis doesn't sound like Miami. The only thing that the South has that's a similarity is the up-tempo. But our sounds are totally different. A Memphis-type sound, it's more scary music or some real fancy bass and some wild-type, medium laid-back type. It's part of the club scene. That's mainly what's going on down in Memphis (Friedman).

The establishment of a definitive set of rules for the southern rap aesthetic has remained an elusive but alluring possibility for music journalists. For each proposed element, counterexamples abound. The use of more rapid tempos by southern producers has been associated with the South since the time when Miami bass was the only nationally recognized style from any city in the South. While southern rap, in general, tends toward faster beats-per-minute (bpm), to make this a defining characteristic would fail to account for the significant amount of slower rap that also comes out of the South, as well as the existence of high-bpm music in cities located outside the South (the Detroit-based style called Ghetto Tech, promulgated by artists such as DJ Assault, relies on speeds of 145–160 bpm). The use of a simplified rap style and call-and-response lyrics has been a prominent feature of New Orleans bounce rap and the more recent "crunk" style emanating from Atlanta, but this description does not fit many important southern rappers (for example, OutKast). Still, in very general terms, it can be asserted that southern rap music tends to be slightly faster than rap from other places, and that it is more likely than rap from other places to rely heavily upon call-and-response in its lyrics.

While OutKast is often cited as representative of the Dirty South, part of the success of the duo seems to be in their departure from regional preferences. In a 2003 interview, producer Rico Wade claimed that his interest in the duo was heightened by the fact that "they weren't no ghetto Atlanta niggas—no gold teeth. They were hip hop." (Sarig 37). This impression seems to be confirmed in the early history of the group; they were drawn together by "their admiration for New York rap groups A Tribe Called Quest and De La Soul, when other [local] kids were cranking local bass music acts" (Murray "OutKast 'Growing Up, Not Growing Apart'"). OutKast's success could thus be said to relate more to their lack of identifiable "southern" characteristics than to any regional representativeness that they might have displayed in their music. In fact, many critics feel that the latest developments in southern rap music—the "crunk" style of artists such as Lil Jon & the East Side Boyz and the Ying Yang Twins—represents a breakthough in acceptance of southern rap styles. A 2003 article claims that "Arista finally did embrace southern street rap this year [when] it broke Bone Crusher nationally" (Penrice). From these comments, it becomes apparent that the Dirty South aesthetic is still a work in progress, as artists like Lil Jon attempt to build careers upon a rap style that is more faithful to the club-based regional southern music that has been locally popular since the days of 2 Live Crew.

In its passage from subculture to the larger sphere of popular culture, the idea of the Dirty South lost much of its initial meaning as a critique of the racist legacy of the South. However, this view still persists among some southern artists. A compilation released in 2000 by Swirl Records (location unknown) in collaboration with the Atlanta-based 404 Music Group, LLC entitled *The South Will Rise Again—This Time It Won't Be the Same: A Dirty South Compilation*, could be said to represent the apotheosis of the Dirty South as originally envisioned by Cool Breeze, Big Boi, and Big Gipp in 1995. The cover of the CD features three men, two in ski masks and one wearing a gas mask, holding up the Confederate battle flag, which is depicted in flames. This ensemble is bordered by a collage of images of U.S. currency and platinum-encrusted watches and necklaces, creating a dissonant combination of political militancy and ostentatious materialism. The content of the CD includes artists from all of the Dirty South hot zones—Atlanta, New Orleans, Memphis, and Houston.

The CD begins with a spoken introduction by an unnamed African American man: "The Confederate flag—a symbol of heritage, or hate? The year is 2000, and the flag has come down. But now it is our turn. The South will rise again, but this time it won't be the same." The appropriation and qualification of the neo-Confederate slogan "the South will rise again" demonstrates an engagement with prior, white-defined incarnations of the South in the process of claiming a new African American southern identity. The statement is voiced over an aural backdrop of sirens, gunshots, and the chirping of birds and crickets. This seemingly absurd combination of sounds representing violence and social disorder with natural sounds that one might hear in a rural setting results in an expression of a violent, revolutionary cleansing giving way to a peaceful natural order.

An interlude halfway through the CD consists of collaged excerpts of interviews with black and white residents of South Carolina recorded during the summer of 2000, a period which saw the tension over the presence of the Confederate battle flag atop the Capitol building in that state come to a head—on July 1 of that year, a legislative compromise reached in May went into effect which resulted in the flag being moved to a less prominent location on the grounds. The interviews conducted by a man who identifies himself as "Brother Kashim" appear to have taken place both before and after this compromise was reached. In the interviews, he asks respondents "what [they] think about the Confederate flag." Several young white men who by their speech appear to be conversant with the conventions of rap music culture nevertheless defend the flag and its appeal with the clichéd "heritage, not hate" rationale. Black interview subjects contributed uniformly negative comments about the flag, which range from consummately rational arguments—"They wouldn't want me to hang a Black Panther flag on top of the Capitol building, right?"—to more tangential statements such as one made by a female respondent on the subject of interracial sex—"I do not put cream in my coffee." An interview subject identified only as a resident of "the hood" sums up the general sentiment of the African American respondents: "Bunch of bullshit, dog, that's all it is. They need to take the motherfucker down."

Regarding the musical content of the CD, few if any of the songs included could be said to engage in the same level of confrontational and explicit politics represented by the cover art, the introduction, or the interviews. Instead, these highly politicized engagements with the legacy of the racist South are juxtaposed with articulations of the most regressive and stereotypical dimensions of the Dirty South. The spoken introduction mentioned above is immediately followed by the track "Welcome to the South" by T Mac (associated with the Memphis-based Powermove Entertainment), which uses violence and misogyny in its signification of southernness: "Welcome to the South/where the bitches is stacked and haters get they brains blowed out." Other tracks, like Houston-based Boonie Loc's "Dime a Dozen," depict the player's lifestyle in the most demeaning terms possible to women. Some would argue that the presence of these more exploitative elements of the Dirty South neutralizes any political critique offered in other parts of the CD. However, this is not a burden unique to Dirty South rap or even to rap music in general; as Rose points out in *Black Noise*, "attempts to delegitimate powerful social discourses are often deeply contradictory, and rap music is no exception" (103).

A similar combination of anti-confederate imagery and generally apolitical music has been put forward by Atlanta-based group Lil Jon & the East Side Boyz. On the cover of their 2001 TVT Records release *Put Yo Hood Up*, Lil Jon is pictured with a confederate battle flag draped over his shoulders, with two similar flags in the background starting to burn from the top down. In September of 2003, Lil Jon was featured on one of two covers (the other cover featured OutKast) of a *Source* magazine issue devoted to the Dirty South scene—"the dirtiest dirty issue ever"— which shows Atlanta-based rapper Bone Crusher holding a burning confederate flag. Also featured on the cover is Mississippi-based rapper David Banner (who often burns confederate flags at his concerts). As debates over the presence of confederate symbolism in official contexts continue in various southern states, we can expect this to be a continuing issue of concern to rappers based in Southern cities.

Conclusions

What, then, is the ultimate significance of the Dirty South? For the rappers of Goodie Mob and those they could be said to speak for, the Dirty South is a space that young African Americans from the South inhabit and have helped create. Unlike the business-oriented boosters of the New South, the southern urbanites who imagined the Dirty South did not wish to sweep the legacies of slavery and racism under the carpet. Instead, they combined a frank critique of this legacy with a celebration of their own perceived cultural distinctiveness, investing the space with the dual legacies of African American cultural production and resistance to white racism. Through the medium of rap music, southern artists and listeners have attempted to collectively redefine the South in their own terms. Allegiances to housing projects, neighborhoods, cities, or states are subsumed into a fluid imagined community that is tied to the geographic South but also linked to a larger, trans-regional African American cultural identity. But as quickly as the rappers of Goodie Mob and likeminded others could imagine the symbolic destruction of the old plantation South, the national media was writing them back into it. In their treatment of southern rappers, journalists often seemed intent upon forcing these artists and producers into a constraining construction of stereotypes—which often originate in anti-black and anti-rural prejudices—about the South.

Like other imagined spaces or communities (e.g. "America"), the Dirty South defies simple attempts at definition. It is many things to many people, and these meanings often come into conflict, even within a particular individual's understanding. These threads of meaning are hopelessly tangled and co-dependent: the interpretation of Dirty South as meaning "strip club music" cannot be fully understood without considering the long-standing association, mainly on the part of Europeans and white Americans, of blacks with unbridled sexuality. The interpretation of the Dirty South as referring to a breeding-ground for drug-dealing gangstas is impossible to separate from the legacies, economic, judicial, and otherwise, of white supremacy within the region and in the larger national context.

However, such contradictory and complex meanings do not play well in a sound-bite media economy. Writers and critics from both within and outside the South have had trouble grasping the multiply-determined nature of the Dirty South. Whether by accident or design, many journalists—encouraged by major label marketing strategies, and, at times, the artists and producers themselves—have ignored the complexity of the term and reduced its meaning to a purely sexual one. This result owes as much to the commodification of both popular music and journalism as it does to the persistence of interwoven stereotypes about the sexual culture of the South and that of African Americans in general. The understanding of the Dirty South concept is clouded by a weakness for stereotype and a lack of tolerance for seemingly contradictory meanings, problems which seem to increase with distance—geographic, economic, and generational. Some artists have been able to turn this dynamic to their advantage; no doubt, others have suffered because of it.

With its complex and often contradictory identity, the Dirty South clearly represents an important stage in the evolution and development of rap music. Having originated in New York, the music established an association with that city that should be viewed as normative: there was no need to call it "New York rap," because, in the beginning, all rap music was by definition from New York. When rappers and producers from Los Angeles became a force to be reckoned with, the idea of "the West Coast" was born. The concentration of industry infrastructure in New York and Los Angeles combines with the cultural politics of rap music to make it extremely difficult for those outside those areas to establish a career, a state of affairs which speaks to "the persistent bi-coastal bias inherent in almost all cultural and intellectual production in this country" (Howard 38). This bi-coastal bias was strengthened by the fact that rap music is, in terms of its emergence and early development, one of the least southern of American musical genres. Additionally, rap music places a very high premium on issues of place and authenticity. Where an artist comes from, what place he or she can claim, becomes intensely important in this genre where lyrics often describe the immediate environment. The Dirty South, with all of its conceptual limitations, allowed southern artists to participate in the production of rap music outside of the East Coast/West Coast structure that had previously dominated the art form.

Like "the West Coast," the Dirty South extrapolates a larger region from the urban centers where the music is actually produced. As "West Coast" is little more than shorthand for "Los Angeles," so the musical production coming out of the Dirty South is really tied to two or three major cities, not evenly spread across the South. While rappers from the South still express their affiliations in terms of their neighborhood or city, the idea of a Dirty South gives them a larger regional identity to work with. Furthermore, specific political and economic realities informed the ways in which the Dirty South was imagined as a space, a community, and a subgenre of rap music. These realities included, but were not limited to, the spatial division of power within the rap music industry and its sub-cultural community, the debate over Confederate symbolism and the legacy of southern racism, and national shifts in attitudes toward issues of racism and discrimination. Ultimately, the meanings are personal—the ways that people define and describe the Dirty South tell us more about their ideas about the South than they do about any actual place or the people who live there.

The development, marketing, and consumption of the Dirty South came about as a result of the geography of the rap music industry, and built upon pre-existing ideas about the South and its inhabitants. What remains to be seen is whether the concept will continue to have currency, or whether it will fade into the background as rappers and producers from the South are drawn closer to the mainstream of rap music production. For many artists and record labels, the Dirty South has served its purpose, providing a backdrop against which they can develop their careers. Although the term is still used and is penetrating ever deeper into the world of advertising and marketing, it seems to be fading into the background in the context of rap music. As the Dirty South has become an accepted division within the rap music landscape, we can expect other imagined regions to follow in its footsteps.

Study Questions

1. What are the meanings and relevance of the designations "Third Coast" or "South Coast"?
2. In what ways does regional location benefit or constrain Southern hip-hop artists?
3. How do Southern rap artists acknowledge and resist the stereotypes associated with a Southern cultural identity?

Works Cited

Arrested Development. *3 Years, 5 Months and 2 Days in the Life of . . .* LP. Chrysalis Records, 1992.

Baca, Ricardo. "Rap's Boy WOW: At 15, Bow Can't Get Behind the Wheel, But His Career's on Overdrive." *Denver Post . . .* 1 Sep. 2002, Fl.

Beecher, Anna. "Spin Doctor Doc Wynter, Programmer for a Chain of Radio Stations and a DJ with a Soulful, Sexy Voice, Looks at the Influence of Urban Radio." *Florida Times-Union* 31 May 2000, Cl.

"Best Bets." *Los Angeles Times:* 9 Aug. 2001, Calendar section 5.

Burr, Ramiro. "Dirty South Rapper, Crew Get Set for Birthday Bash." *San Antonio Express-News* 27 Sep. 2002, H12.

Carnoy, Martin. *Faded Dreams: The Politics and Economics of Race in America.* New York: Cambridge UP, 1994.

Carter, Nick. "Okayplayer's Lyrical Rap Emphasizes the Positive." *Milwaukee Journal Sentinel* 28 Oct. 2000, B6.

Chang, Jeff. "Pablo's 'Diary': Not Exactly an Open Book." *Washington Post* 7 Nov. 2001, C5.

Christgau, Robert. "Consumer Guide." *Village Voice* 15 Nov. 1998, 128.

——. "La-Di-Da-Di-Di? Or La-Di-Da-Di-Da?" *Village Voice* 2 Mar. 2000, 77.

Cooper, Barry Michael. "Dope Tapes, No Limit." *Village Voice* 5 May 1998, 69.

Dilday, Kenya Alease. "Arrested Development Advanced Musically." *Essence* Dec. 1992, 38.

Dollar, Steve. "Who's Who on the Atlanta Music Scene: A List of the Leading Players in Local Rap, R & B, Rock, Country, Folk and Jazz Circles." *Atlanta Journal and Constitution* 21 Feb. 1993, N6.

Doolittle, James. "Nappy Roots, *Watermelon, Chicken & Gritz.*" *Morning Call* [Allentown, PA] 24 Aug. 2002, A57.

Douglas, Mary. *Purity and Danger: An Analysis of Concepts of Pollution and Taboo.* New York: Routledge, 2002.

Flick, Larry. "LaFace Chiefs Extend Deal with Arista." *Billboard* 8 Apr. 1995, 8, 117.

Forman, Murray. *The 'Hood Comes First: Race, Space and Place in Rap and Hip-Hop.* Middletown, CT: Wesleyan UP, 2002.

Friedman, David. "Interview with Project Pat." *Murder Dog* [2001?]. *Murder Dog Archives,* 24 Feb. 2004 <http://www.murderdog.com/archives/projectpat/projectpat.html>.

Gill, Andy. "This Week's Album Releases." *Independent* [London] 14 Jun. 2002, 19.

Goodie Mob. *Soul Food* LP. LaFace Records, 1995.

———. "Dirty South Remix." LEP. LaFace Records, 1996.

Guzman, Isaac. "Pop Music; Melody Makers of Hip-Hop." *Los Angeles Times,* 22 Oct. 2000, Calendar, p. 8.

Hampel, Paul. "Music Spotlight." *St. Louis Post-Dispatch* 3 Oct. 1996, 9.

"Hip-Hop." *Times-Picayune* 9 Mar. 2001, Lagniappe section: 15.

Howard, John. "Living Out Here." *Southern Changes* 15:3 (Fall 1993), 36–39.

Ice T. *O.G. Original Gangster* LP. Sire Records Company, 1991.

Johnson, Kevin C. "Ludacris' Southern-Style Raps Are Spread by 'Word of Mouf.'" *St. Louis Post-Dispatch* 21 Feb. 2002, 22.

Jones, Joseph. "Wainwright Balances Cabaret Style with Tuneful Pop Hip-Hop." *Virginian-Pilot* 6 Jul. 2001, E8.

Keast, Darrin. "Uncle Luke; Something Nasty." *Miami New Times,* 10 May 2001. *LexisNexis Academic.* Information Gateway. Emory University Libraries, Atlanta, Georgia. 24 Feb. 2004.

Keating, Larry. *Atlanta: Race, Class, and Urban Expansion.* Philadelphia: Temple UP, 2001.

Kenon, Marci. "To Keep It Real Or To Make a Deal? Many of Hip-Hop's Indie Label Owners and Their Artists Want a Piece of the Majors' Pie." *Billboard* 7 Apr. 2001, 26, 34.

Lester, Paul. "Friday Review: Partners in Rhyme." *Guardian* [London], 18 May 2001, Friday Pages section: 6.

Lil Jon & the East Side Boyz. *Put Yo Hood Up* LP. TVT Records, 2001.

Lovel, Jim. "Hip-Hop Incorporated: Atlanta Wins $11 Million from European Investors." *Atlanta Business Chronicle* 22–28 Feb. 2002, 1.

Madera, Tiffany. "Bastard Out of Miami: Dirty South Documents the Triumph of Down-Home Hip-Hop." *Miami New Times* 22 Feb. 2001. *LexisNexis Academic.* Information Gateway. Emory University Libraries, Atlanta, Georgia. 24 Feb. 2004.

Mitchell, Gail. "Antonio 'L.A.' Reid: The *Billboard* Interview." *Billboard* 11 Dec. 1999, 26, 28, 34, 36, 38, 40, 42.

———. "The Rhythm, the Rap and the Blues; Dupri's So So Def, Columbia Renew Deal; Thump Records Crosses Over to TV." *Billboard* 17 Feb. 2001, 23.

Moon, Tom. "Kast Party; Rap Duo's 'Stankonia' Moves Beyond 'Ba-Dum-Dum-Bap' and Into Legendary Soul." *Milwaukee Journal Sentinel* 13 Mar. 2001, El.

Murray, Sonia. "So So Successful: Jermaine Dupri Is 20, But Already He's the Mastermind Behind Kris Kross, Produces New Acts and Owns a Studio." *Atlanta Journal and Constitution* 3 Aug. 1993, Bl.

———. "The Poet and the Playa: OutKast Makes Sweet Music." *Atlanta Journal and Constitution* 30 Oct. 2000, Dl.

———. "OutKast 'Growing Up, Not Growing Apart.'" *Atlanta Journal-Constitution* 21 Sep. 2003, Ml.

O'Connor, Christopher. "Kentucky Dirty." *Village Voice* 2 Apr. 2002, 67.

"Old Tricks Are the Best Tricks; Pop Reviews." *Toronto Star* 24 Jun. 2000. *LexisNexis Academic.* Information Gateway. Emory University Libraries, Atlanta, Georgia. 24 Feb. 2004.

Ollison, Rashod D. Letter. *Village Voice* 29 Aug. 2000, 6.

OutKast. *Southernplayalisticadillacmuzik.* LP. LaFace Records, 1994.

OverTime. "THE DIRTY SOUTH!!!" *rec.music.hip-hop* 11 July 1996. *Google* 24 Feb. 2004 <http://groups.google.com/advanced_group_search>

Paris, Tony. "Hot 'Lanta Is Making Waves; Atlanta's Artists Attract a Southern Migration of the Music Biz." *Billboard* 21 Aug. 1993, Al.

Pearson, Beth. "Escaping Hip Hop's Long Shadow." *Herald* [Glasgow] 9 Aug. 2002, 25.

Penrice, Ronda Racha. "Avoiding the Trap: Rapper T.I. Sheds Light on the Real Atlanta." *Creative Loafing* [Atlanta] 21–27 Aug. 2003, 91.

"Rap." *Billboard* 19 Feb. 2000, 24.

Reines, Dan. "Kentucky Fried; Drinkin' Grand Marnier, Smokin' Pot; It's the Life God Chose for Nappy Roots." *New Times* [Los Angeles] 28 Mar. 2002. *LexisNexis Academic.* Information Gateway. Emory University Libraries, Atlanta, Georgia. 24 Feb. 2004.

Reynolds, Simon. "For the Love of Money." *Village Voice* 30 Nov. 1999, 123.

Rogoff, Irit. *Terra Infirma: Geography's Visual Culture.* New York: Routledge, 2000.

Rose, Tricia. *Black Noise: Rap Music and Black Culture in Contemporary America.* Hanover, NH: UP of New England, 1994.

Rosen, Craig. "Geto Boys Go Indie for Newest Hit; Rubin Says WEA Wouldn't Handle Act." *Billboard* 27 Jul. 1991, 5.

Sanneh, Kelefa. "So Stank, So Clean." *Village Voice* 8 Jan. 2002, 59.

Sarig, Roni. "Dungeon Family Tree." *Creative Loafing* [Atlanta] 18–24 Sep. 2003, 34–35, 37–39, 41–43.

Scruggs, Kathy. "Anatomy of a Shooting; 8-Year-Old Dies after Gun Battle During Drug Raid; Officer Thinks He May Have Killed Boy." *Atlanta Journal and Constitution* 14 Nov. 1991, A1.

Sinclair, David. "Sparxxx Fly Down South." *Times* [London] 23 Nov. 2001, Times2 section: 10.

"Single Reviews." *Billboard* 3 Aug. 1996, 90.

Smith, Eric L. "Hip-Hop Preneurs." *Black Enterprise* Dec. 1997, 66.

Sterdan, Darryl. "CD Reviews." *Toronto Sun* 23 Dec. 2001, S12.

Success-N-Effect. "Police Brutality." LP. WRAP Records, 1992.

Tate, Greg. "Mason-Dixon Rhymes." *Village Voice* 21 Apr. 1998, 85.

The Dirty South: Raw and Uncut: Tales of Sex, Music & Money. By JT Money et al. Dir. Wills Felin. Bottom Up Entertainment, 2000.

The South Will Rise Again—This Time It Won't Be the Same: A Dirty South Compilation. LP. Swirl Records/404 Music Group LLC, 2000.

Vognar, Chris. "Southern Spirit; Distinct Hip-Hop Voice Emerges." *Record* [Bergen County, NJ] 29 May 1998, Lifestyle, 3.

Warner, Coleman, and Matt Scallan. "Minority Income Gap Narrowing, Census Shows; But There's Still a Long Way to Go in N.O. Area to Reach White Levels." *Times-Picayune* 24 Sep. 2002, National, 1.

Wartofsky, Alona. "Hip-Hop's New Direction; Rap's Latest Wave Is Called the 'Dirty South,' and It's Already Starting to Clean Up at the Cash Register." *Washington Post* 5 Mar. 2001, G1.

Welch, Michael Patrick. "Getting Our Area Down and Dirty." *St. Petersburg Times* 24 Dec. 1999: T7.

White, Timothy. "Arrested Development's 'Revolution.' " *Billboard* 24 Oct. 1992, 5.

Wilder, Chris. "The World According to Darp." *The Source* Nov. 1994, 54.

Williams, Clint and Michael Pearson. "Leading the Way In Living Large: Black Middle Class Is Making Itself at Home In Metro Atlanta." *The Atlanta Journal-Constitution* 25 Sep.2002, A1.

Yaeger, Patricia. *Dirt and Desire: Reconstructing Southern Women's Writing, 1930–1990.* Chicago: U of Chicago P, 2000.

19

Global Black Self-Fashionings
Hip-Hop as Diasporic Space

The combined concepts of identity construction and social agency lie at the heart of Marc Perry's contribution. For Perry, hip-hop functions as a "conduit" of transnational black cultural identification and its various practices encompassing music, dance and art are among the primary circuits for the global communication of black political consciousness and counter-hegemonic resistance among disenfranchised youth. In this context, hip-hop is not merely a facet of the mass media but it constitutes a medium in its own right, amplifying the urgent issues of young people in diverse social environments.

Perry focuses on hip-hop's language, style, rhythm, and attitude, analyzing the manner in which they are harnessed in nationally and locally responsive contexts, facilitating the refashioning of youth sensibilities at street level. Demonstrating the global cohesiveness of hip-hop youth practices and the specificities and heterogeneity of global hip-hop practices, Perry embarks on a series of case studies (encompassing Cuba, Brazil, and South Africa) in order to carefully explore hip-hop culture in discreet locales and under distinct socio-political conditions. These examples illustrate different aspects of state intervention in the everyday lives and practices of hip-hop identified youth, showing that in some instances authorities attempt to co-opt and appropriate hip-hop while in others they provide supportive mechanisms and infrastructure to the respective scenes.

Global Black Self-Fashionings: Hip Hop as Diasporic Space

Marc D. Perry

¡Fundamentalmente hip hop quiere decir negro! Corto, pero penetrante. [Fundamentally hip hop means black! Concise, but penetrating].

"El Negro"—Los Paisanos

Since their emergence in New York City in the mid 1970s, rap music and the broader cultural phenomenon of hip hop have received bountiful scholarly attention.[1] This has increasingly been the case as a once-marginal youth culture encompassing expressive elements of music, verbal lyricism, dance, graffiti art, and fashion has evolved into a multi-billion dollar global industry. Although hip hop has undergone radical transformation during this movement from street to international marketplace, it has retained a critical capacity to convey a signifying blackness of aesthetic form and emotive force. To underscore this is by no means to flirt with essentialized notions, but rather a recognition of the significant (albeit highly mediated) ways hip hop continues to articulate a "black," largely masculine urban discourse of marginality. Indeed, hip hop today has emerged as the most visible and widely disseminated conduit of U.S. black popular imagery globally—commercially mediated not only through music, but increasingly through film, television, and corporate merchandising. While the majority of scholarship to date has tended to focus on the cultural politics of hip hop's domestic production and consumption within the United States, there have been more recent moves to examine the sociocultural dynamics involved in the trafficking and spread of rap music and hip hop culture globally.[2]

Here I address this second line of inquiry, mapping how the black racial significance of hip hop is received, interpreted, and redeployed transnationally. Rather than a broad survey, this exploration centers on the politics and poetics of hip hop as they find particular expression within the Afro-Atlantic world. Beyond simply posing questions of cultural consumption and reproduction, I argue that hip hop's expanding global reach has enabled the making of black diasporic subjects in and of themselves. In ways evocative of Benedict Anderson's insights into the instrumentality of print media in forging modern national imaginaries (Anderson 1991), hip hop today has assumed an increasingly significant role in shaping contemporary forms of black diasporic consciousness and subjectivity. Here, African-descendant youth in an array of locales are using the performative contours of hip hop to mobilize notions of black-self in ways that are at one time both contestive and transcendent of nationally bound, hegemonically prescriptive racial framings. Within these contexts understandings of diasporic belonging are often paramount, if not vitally constitutive of such black self-fashions. Thus, much like print media of a previous moment, hip hop has become a productive technology in the current global mapping and

295

moving of black political imaginaries via the social workings of diaspora. In pursuing this argument, this essay examines hip hop movements in Brazil, Cuba, and South Africa comparatively as compelling, yet varying examples of how transnationally attuned identities of blackness are marshaled in the making of diasporic subjects through the performative lens of hip hop.

When considering the international proliferation of hip hop one needs to be cognizant of the differing ways hip hop's black-signified cultural politics travel as they are engaged by communities beyond their initial sites of U.S. production. While such diffusion may move along similar global circuits as culturally and geographically divergent as Senegal and Japan, it is clear that hip hop's reception and recontextualization in the formation of local followings can often involve very different kinds of social meaning-making. While hip hop may indeed provide a cultural resource in the global shaping of local identities (Appadurai 1996), one must always remain attentive to questions of power and positionality. The query, then, becomes one of who is consuming whom, and to what ends.

It is, however, undeniable that globally hip hop has assumed a wide and particularly marked resonance among more socioeconomically marginal communities of youth. This is as much the case for working-class urban youth in Chile as it is for their ethnically subaltern Basque contemporaries in Spain. In both settings we find examples of how young people appropriate markers of blackness as a means of signifying their own subjective conditions of marginality. Chile's *Las Panteras Negras* (The Black Panthers), coupled with the Basque nationalist group Negu Gorriak's self-identification as "Afro-Basque," are exemplary of such discursive deployments (Urla 2001). Palestinian hip hop poet Suheir Hammad's evocations of Public Enemy, Amiri Baraka, and Malcolm X in her 1996 collection *Born Palestinian, Born Black* is further illustrative of blackness' global resonance as a hip hop-informed signifier of social marginality (Hartman 2002). Yet while a politics of subaltern identification may be at play in these above examples, such discursive practices do not in the end constitute these young people in any historical sense as "black" per se. Where lie then these practices of black self-making of which I speak?

Surveying the current literature on hip hop's transnational dimensions evidences a scarcity of scholarship examining the politics of race and racial identification in motion globally. In many treatments either African or African-descendant sites are absent from examination, or there is an analytical privileging of cultural or ethnic modes of differentiation vis-à-vis marginalized communities to the exclusion of the racialized processes that often shape the lived experience of these populations. While it is clear, as Tony Mitchell suggests, that hip hop in a global sense "cannot be viewed simply as an expression of African American culture; it has become a vehicle for global youth affiliations and a tool for reworking local identities all over the world" (Mitchell 2001: 2). This does not mean that race (or blackness for that matter) is necessarily erased from the equation.

When assessing hip hop's global racial significance one cannot deny the particular salience of the cultural form within the contemporary Afro-Atlantic world. Whether Haitian immigrants in Montreal, Afro-Colombians in Cali, Colombia, or Afro-Amerindian Garifuna in Honduras, African-descendant youth globally are using the performative space of hip hop as a vital site of critical self-expression. Yet beyond a simple claiming of voice, to what extent might hip hop's black signified cultural framings facilitate new, globally attuned identities of blackness themselves? When considering this question, one must be attentive to a notion of blackness rooted in the idea of diaspora. Rather than an essentializing trope, the Afrodiasporic condition is by definition one predicated on diversity and difference, yet at the same time one grounded in some shared, collective understanding of black historicity (Hall 1990). The marker "black" in this sense serves as a political signifier of a particular kind of racialized identity, one that binds African-descendant individuals and communities in lived historical terms of past and present. To borrow from Raymond Williams, blackness in this sense assumes its own shared "structure of feeling" (Williams 1977) among those of African descent; one neither limited by, nor beholden to U.S. racial prescriptions.

Regarding hip hop, a politics of diasporic affinity and articulation were part and parcel of the phenomenon's early development via the cultural exchange between African American, Puerto Rican, and West Indian youth in mid-1970s New York City (Chang 2005; Keyes 1996; Rose 1994). Cultural agencies of the like found creative expression through the melding of overlapping histories in diaspora coupled with shared conditions of social marginalization as youth of color in post-industrial urban America. It has been suggested that early period of hip hop's formation gave rise to new expressions of black urban subjectivity themselves (Rivera 2003).

At this present moment, however, hip hop can be seen globally as an increasingly important conduit for just those kinds of transnational black identifications and emergent subjectivities that have historically constituted the African diaspora as a lived social formation. The notion of diaspora referenced here is dynamic and ever-changing, one forged through historical plays of power and agency in the continual re-making of diaspora as a social reality through extra-national kinds of black identification and communicative interchange (Gilroy 1993; Gordon and Anderson 1999; Patterson and Kelley 2000). Such an understanding foregrounds Brent Hayes Edwards's notion of a "mobilized diaspora" in distinguishing between an historically *given*, "involuntary" sense of diaspora, versus an historically *responsive* recognition of the ways the African, or more appropriately "black" diaspora is actively used in the making of globally-conscious black subjects and social movements (Edwards 2001).[3]

This framing, in turn, not only foregrounds the political salience of what Paul Gilroy has termed the contemporary "routes" of diasporic identification (Gilroy 1993) but also opens up space for an appreciation of how transnational affinities of blackness can be fashioned among communities of African descent who may not necessarily share histories of displacement. Such expansiveness holds particular currency when considering the vibrant presence of hip hop movements across the African continent where young people can be seen as asserting their inclusion within a globalized space of "modern," post-colonial blackness through hip hop's diasporic spectrum. The suggestion, then, is that hip hop has become an increasingly consequential route of global black identity formation.

It is, however, precisely through rather than despite its hyper-commodification as a global cultural form that hip hop has managed to signify a blackness of emotive force that resonates with others in the diaspora. Here, Stuart Hall's work is informative in suggesting that "[h]owever deformed, incorporated, and inauthentic are the forms in which black people and black communities and traditions appear and are represented in popular culture, we continue to see, in the figures and the repertories on which popular culture draws, the experience that stand behind them" (Hall 1992: 27). Blackness, as such, becomes a transnational site of identification and self-making; one made most immediately tangible for many diasporic youth by way of hip hop. And while not necessarily beholden, self-constituting black identifications of the like are by no means disarticulated from U.S. historicity. The question rather concerns the dialogic manner of their re-articulations.

Brazil

The rise of Brazilian hip hop offers an insightful illustration of how black diasporic identities are currently mobilized through the performative spectrum of hip hop culture. Articulations of this kind carry added potential, given Brazil's location as the most populous concentration of peoples of African descendent outside of the African continent—an historical legacy courtesy of the largest and most enduring slave system in the Americas.[4] While hip hop's foundations in Brazil were first laid in the 1980s through the circulation of music and images emanating from the United States (Magaldi 1999), Brazilian hip hop's diasporic contours should be understood within a broader recent history of Afro-Brazilian engagement with U.S. black popular culture. Brazil's *Black Soul* movement of the 1970s represents a particularly notable example of such engagement.

Through music, dance, and fashion, *Black Soul's* ranks of young Afro-Brazilians drew upon the black cultural aesthetics and embodied self-awareness of 1970s U.S. soul music in the voicing of new, transnationally inspired expressions of Afro-Brazilian blackness. Parties were organized where young Afro-Brazilians sported bell bottoms, *dashikis*, and wore their hair in Afros while dancing to the likes of James Brown and Marvin Gay.

Transcending questions of simple cultural importation, Michael Hanchard has argued that *Black Soul* represented an effort to construct alternative forms of self-affirming black identity as oppositional responses to Brazil's historical privileging of whiteness and persistent forms of racial subjugation otherwise obfuscated by the nation's long-standing ideological claims as a "racial democracy" (cf. Freyre 1964). Emerging during the repressive era of Brazil's military dictatorship (1964–1985), *Black Soul* events became important venues for the dissemination of information pertaining to the nascent *Movimento negro*, a loose affiliation of Afro-Brazilian sociocultural and political organizations mobilized strategically around black identity claims. Endeavors of this kind, Hanchard suggests, were formative in the early framing of a black identity politics that continue today to be an instrumental facet of Afro-Brazilian sociopolitical organizing. Here, politicized assertions of blackness have been central in efforts to contest Brazil's hegemonic claims as a "racial democracy" where race and racism are alleged inconsequential, if not non-existent, within an ostensibly racially amalgamated national populace yet with one of the highest levels of social inequality in the world.[5]

The emergence of Brazilian hip hop needs therefore to be viewed within this continuum of transnationally engaged Afro-Brazilian identity politics. Young, largely male Afro-Brazilian *favelados*—residents of Brazil's urban shanty towns known as *favelas*—in and around São Paulo and Rio de Janeiro were the first to take up rap music in the voicing of their own racially informed experiences and concerns. The highly popular São Paulo-based Racionais MC's (Rational MC's) are a prime example of this early movement in Brazilian rap. Establishing their reputation in the late 1980s and early 1990s while performing primarily in *favelas* and the "darker" suburbs on the fringes of São Paulo, the group's aggressive lyrics focused on social themes most pressing in these marginalized communities such as racism, racially-targeted police violence, drug trafficking, and government corruption in the improvised *periferias* (peripheries). The duo's opening salvo of "Capítulo 4 Versículo 3" from their platinum-selling 1998 album *Sobrevivendo No Inferno* (*Surviving in Hell*) stands as a dramatic case in point,

> 60% *dos jovens de periferia sem antecedentes criminais já sofreram violência policial;*
> *A cada quatro pessoas mortas pela polícia, três são negras;*
> *Nas universidades brasileiras, apenas* 2% *dos alunos são negros;*
> *A cada quatro horas um jovem negro morre violentamente em São Paulo;*
> *Aqui quem fala é Prima Preto, mais um sobrevivente.*[6]
> 60% *of youth in the periphery without criminal records have already suffered police violence*
> *In every four people killed by the police, three are black*
> *In Brazilian Universities, only* 2% *of students are black*
> *Every four hours, a young black person dies violently in São Paulo*
> *Speaking here is "Prima Preto" (Black Cousin), another survivor.*[7]

As Primo Preto's introduction testifies, blackness and marginality are imbricated realities in many of Brazil's *favelas* and urban peripheral zones where systemic forms of racialized violence are quotidian. Indeed, Derek Pardue has suggested that São Paulo hip hop artists mediate marginality itself—both in social and geospatial terms—through discourses and practices of *negritude* (blackness) in ways that gesture toward diasporic belonging (Pardue 2004). His discussion of these dimensions and their articulations vis-à-vis questions of identity, however, remain largely implicit rather than explicitly explored. Alternatively, Jennifer Roth Gordon contends that Brazilian MCs constitute in effect "an alternative black consciousness movement" in Brazil largely through what she sees as their adoption of U.S. racial ideologies via the hip hop's transnational lens (Roth Gordon 2002). My argument is that diasporic rather than U.S. understandings of blackness are in the end instrumental in fashioning critical expressions of black Brazilian self. The emphasis here is on dialogic engagements rather than reductive appropriations of blackness. In developing this argument further I now shift to Rio de Janeiro.

Immediately following the infamous Candelaria murders of 1993 in which off-duty police systematically gunned down a group of black street children sleeping aside a Rio Janeiro church, a protest rally was coordinated in the city by a coalition of organizations within the *Movimento negro* to condemn the murders and the broader culture of racial violence from which these acts manifest. Among the rally's participants was the Rio-based rap duo Consciencia Urbana (Urban Consciousness). At the time of the event, member Big Richard described the political significance of his music this way.

> In the US blacks have a notion that racism exists. Not in Brazil. In Brazil racism is disguised. In Brazil we live in a racial democracy, believe it if you will. Here we have a small number of black youth who fight against racism, while the majority, even as they suffer racism everyday like being harassed on the bus by the police, prefer to believe what is shown to them on television and in the media. So what happens is that we present the counter-culture to this, and to fight as a counter-culture is not easy, especially in Brazil.[8]

In addition to using rap as a pedagogic device in an effort to inform Afro-Brazilian counter-hegemonic sensibilities vis-à-vis dominant Brazilian constructions of racial exceptionalism, Consciencia Urbana's songs evoke black diasporic imagery and identifications as a means of grounding the local within broader histories of black antiracist struggle. In referencing the significance of Malcolm X, for example, Big Richard explains,

> We decided to make a rap song about Malcolm X because he was not solely a black American. He lost his American-ness when he fought against racism, for any person who fights against racism anywhere in the world is fighting for blacks, for the survival of black people.[9]

Here, Malcolm X is resignified beyond his U.S. historical specificity in an effort to accommodate a more expansive diasporic reading. Similar moves are echoed in a song by Racionais MCs where baggy jeaned, baseball-cap-adorned member Mono Brown riffs, "We need a leader with popular credit like Malcolm X as in other times in America, who is black down to the bones—one of us—and reconstructs our pride from ruins" (McDaniels 1999: 7). These artists' adoption and rearticulation of U.S. black nationalist imagery within the context of Afro-Brazilian struggle is a cogent example of the ways African-descendant communities draw inspiration transnationally from experiences and cultures of black populations elsewhere. By mobilizing diasporic resources in this manner, to use Jacqueline Nassy Brown's term, Afro-Brazilian rap artists not only tie their struggles historically to others in the diaspora but in effect actively constitute the black diaspora itself as a *lived* social reality (Brown 1998). In the case of Malcolm X's imagery, such cultural appropriations were no doubt informed at the time by the revitalization of his legacy in the United States by rap artists such as Public Enemy who, along with Spike Lee, helped to feed the "X" fashion trend of the early 1990s. Although these commodified representations of Malcolm were not devoid of their commercially tied contradictions, they nonetheless retained a capacity to transnationally convey and generate meanings of a radical blackness for others.

Rather than simple appropriations, these examples illustrate how U.S. rap music and hip hop-attuned black popular culture serves as a mediated frame through which diasporically informed ideas, messages, and identifications can and are actively fashioned. Such black diasporic processes and understandings are clearly articulated by Big Richard who elaborates,

> By principle, we think that rap is not a [North] American music. Rap is a music of black people, and black people originated in Africa. In the case of those who are born outside of Africa, we are speaking of the Diaspora. Here in Brazil, it is a regional music, adapted to the Portuguese, to the Brazilian swing where we mix *timbalala* and *samba-reggae* with rap. We make a connection by joining American music with Brazilian music in creating our own style, but without ever losing the music's roots, because in fact these two roots are sisters—they originated in only one place, Africa.[10]

While emphasizing the African historical "roots" of rap music, Big Richard simultaneously evokes the contemporary routes of rap's black diasporic significance in referencing its aesthetically conveyed blackness as the basis for constructing transnational black "connections" between Brazil and the United States. He suggests that such identifications are made most real not simply through the consumption of hip hop but, rather, through the ways hip hop is pro-actively transformed in the making of a new culturally relevant, yet a signifyingly "black" Brazilian music form. Big Richard's reference to "creating our own style" through the fusion of Afro-Brazilian musical elements and the use of Portuguese to indigenize rap, further underscores the important interrelationality between style-making and identity. On both aesthetic and linguistic levels, then, the creative re-working of hip hop may give rise to not only a new Brazilian music genre but might in fact serve as an alternative modality for articulating blackness in Brazil altogether. The suggestion here is that hip hop may be facilitative of black social imaginaries that transcend nationally-prescriptive, historically-circumscribed fields of Brazilian blackness.

Within the broader space of Brazilian hip hop, style is also key to the ways blackness is performatively marked and bodily exhibited through popular fashion. Glossy hip hop magazines such as *Rap Brasil, Hip Hop en Movimiento,* and *Rap Rima* that have emerged over the past decade are filled with images of young black and brown, primarily male Brazilians dressed in U.S.-inspired hip hop attire. The exhibition of hip hop fashion is often accompanied by overt body posturing stylistically evocative of that used by young African American men. Many of Brazil's most established rap groups signify themselves in one form or another through such U.S.-inspired black urban style. As a mode of self-representational practice, style in this way must be understood as "performative" in its own right: performative in the productive sense in which Judith Butler (1990) speaks of how individual subjectivities and the social categories that define them are in the end constituted only in so much as they are enacted or *performed* in the quotidian. Indeed, if we consider Stuart Hall's suggestion that "it is only through the ways in which we represent and imagine ourselves that we come to know who we are" (Hall 1992:30), emphasizing the performative nature of black popular style in this way encourages considerations of the active self-representational force of style in its capacity to culturally articulate, more than simply reflect, identities of blackness and ways of being (cf. Hebdige 1981).

Afro-Brazilian rap duo Afro-X and Dexter further illustrate this performative mending of black urban style and the aesthetic production of black selfhood. The duo recorded their first album in 2000 while imprisoned in the infamous São Paulo Carandiru prison complex that first gained international attention in 1992 when 111 inmates were systematically massacred by military police following a prison uprising.[11] Referring to themselves as "509-E" after their prison cell number, Afro-X and Dexter's music assails a corrupt justice system while testifying to the violent realities of being black, male, and poor in contemporary Brazil. In addition to limited performances in prison, the duo recorded a video for MTV Brazil in which they can be seen sporting gold chains and designer sneakers (Darlington 2000). Their state-regulation beige pants are worn baggy off the hip, stylistically evoking U.S. hip hop-associated fashion practices first coined by young African American males that, ironically, arose out of U.S. prison culture.

As these Brazilian examples suggest, rap music and associated hip hop culture provide alternative cultural frameworks through which new meanings and identities of blackness can be strategically articulated and performatively mobilized. To the extent that these identifications are forged through transnationally-projected black imagery, they are not predicated on linguistic intelligibility. Rather, hip hop's black racial alterity is conveyed most tangibly through its signifying blackness of style. Such blackness, in turn, is transformed through both linguistic and stylistic innovations in the voicing and bodily performance of new kinds of critical black subjectivity that are both products of, and responsive to, the particular sociocultural imperatives of contemporary Brazil. Writing on Afro-Brazilian youth culture in Bahia, Brazil, Livio Sansone (1997: 461) observes that the fashioning of new black-signified youth styles as exemplified in hip hop "offers black people new opportunities for redefining black difference in Western societies by aestheticizing blackness, in the first place, through highly visible styles and pop music." Indeed, the adoption of these youth practices provides young Afro-Brazilians with means of not only marking their blackness more visibly but actively linking their struggles to a broader black diasporic experience and global frameworks of black antiracism.

Cuba

Much as in Brazil, race and blackness have long been at the center of Cuba's historical narrative dating back to the massive importation of enslaved Africans upon whose labor the island's sugar-based plantation economy grew to the largest in the colonial world by the mid-nineteenth century. Cuba's welding of race and nation was further deepened in the late nineteenth century during the island's anti-colonial wars of independence in which recently liberated Afro-Cubans comprised the vast majority of the independence movement's fighting force. Here the struggle to free the island from Spanish colonial control was inextricably tied to the struggle for black emancipation and corresponding visions for a racially just and equitable Cuban nation (Helg 1995). Such expectations remained largely elusive until after 1959 when the Cuban Revolution took up socialism and placed racial equality, at least initially, at the center of its declared program to build a socially egalitarian society. While the extent to which the Cuban Revolution was able to eliminate racism and hierarchical racial privilege remains debated,[12] it is unquestionable that many black Cubans did on the whole benefit significantly from the social reforms and programs undertaken during the early revolutionary period. This did not mean that the deep, historically rooted ideological structures of racism in Cuban society ceased to operate and reproduce themselves in the everyday. To speak publicly of racism's persistence, however, became taboo under revolutionary socialism, which by the mid-1960s declared racism and racial discrimination officially eradicated from the island. Assertions to the contrary were ultimately deemed divisive, counterrevolutionary if not counter-national declarations.

The collapse of the Soviet Union and Eastern Bloc ushered in yet another critical phase of Cuba's racial history. With the 1990 suspension of Soviet subsidies upon which Cuba's economy and the revolutionary project had been largely underwritten, the island fell into severe economic crisis known as the "Special Period." In a strategic move to revive the economy, the Cuban state initiated a series of economic reforms in the early 1990s that, in effect, represented a cautious opening of the heretofore-closed Cuban economy to global capital. Possibly the most dramatic consequence of this neoliberal shift has been the dollarization of Cuba's economy and its transformative impacts on the Cuban everyday.[13] In addition to engendering inequalities predicated upon differing levels of access to circulating dollars and other foreign currencies, race (re)emerged as a critical factor affecting who and how one gets such access within Cuba's new economy (Hammond 1999; de la Fuente 2001). Within these logics new levels of racialized modes of socioeconomic marginalization have surfaced in Cuba today. The ideological claims of a unified, "non-racial" Cuba under revolutionary socialism and the subsequent silencing of race were now laid bare by the lived social consequences of racial difference in the Cuban everyday. The critical question to be asked then concerns how black and darker-skinned Cubans are currently responding to these new racialized realities.

It is no coincidence that the emergence of hip hop in Cuba over the last decade or so has occurred precisely during this current period of rapid social transformation.[14] Though the early roots of rap music in Cuba can be traced back to the mid-1980s, it was not until amidst the economic crisis of the 1990s that hip hop as a cultural movement in Cuba began to take shape. It is neither insignificant that those who first and most ardently engaged in hip hop were overwhelmingly black and darker-skinned youth. This continued to be the case as interest in rap music spread throughout the greater Havana area as a cultural space—almost exclusively black and young—began to evolve around this transnationally introduced music form. Within a relatively short time, parties began springing up across Havana where young people gathered to listen, dance, and otherwise participate in the collective making of Cuba's nascent hip hop movement (Pacini Hernández and Garofalo 2000; Fernandez 2001). By the mid-1990s these new black spaces had a brief footing in a few state-run cultural centers before garnering the distrust of some Cuban officials who viewed these gatherings with suspicion, ostensibly associating them with capitalist culture and anti-social influences (Olavarria 2002).

Within today's vibrant Cuban hip hop movement black youth frequent dance clubs and additional venues throughout the island where the latest U.S. hip hop can be heard. Many of these youth, significantly, are often drawn from poorer, more socially marginal neighborhoods.[15] As many dance and sing along with the music—though most do not actually speak English themselves—scores of youth don baggy pants, foreign-made athletic shoes, and U.S. baseball caps and team jerseys. While these commodified expressions of U.S. black youth culture are tied to the recent opening of the island to transnational flows of people, capital, and cultural influences as well as a growing culture of consumerism in a once definitely anti-consumerist Cuba, much like their Brazilian peers these youth mobilize black-signified style as a self-constituting practice.

Yet, here lies a tension. While hip hop's global diffusion may in many ways be intimately tied to the international expansion of capital markets, it would be short-sighted to reduce the cultural form's transnational significance simply to that of a U.S. cultural export inactively and uncritically consumed by others. Such a reading recalls cultural imperialism arguments that view the spread of media and cultural commodities from economically more powerful nations (most notably the United States) as overpowering and / or displacent of local cultural practices in non-western locales and contributive, in turn, to a homogenization of global cultural diversity (cf. Tomlinson 1993). Arguments of the kind, however, largely obfuscate plays of agency. In the case of hip hop, it is important to recognize not only the ways it is actively consumed transnationally but also how its cultural framings—as commercially mediated as they may be—are rearticulated and redeployed in the formation of local rap artists and followings. Here, practices of cultural consumption can be generative of black self-making in ways that are largely dialogic (productive) rather than simply mimetic (reproductive) in nature (Slater 1997).

Indeed, the degree of cultural rearticulation within Cuban hip hop is most vividly pronounced in the way young Afro-Cubans are critically refashioning rap music and hip hop's black-signified aesthetics into their own idioms of self-expression. With an estimated 500 or more rap groups currently island-wide, there are sites throughout Cuba where local *raperos*, as Cuban MCs are termed, perform original material before packed audiences. While frequently using body posturing and gestures evocative of U.S. rap performances, their lyrics are sung in a distinctly Cuban Spanish vernacular over rhythms often incorporating Afro-Cuban musical elements. At the center of the music, however, is a thematic emphasis on social critique in which many *raperos* evoke their identities as *los negros* (black people) as the basis from which their perspectives are critically voiced. It is important to note that a significant number of *raperos* and their followers, who might not necessarily be categorized as "negro" (black) within Cuba's phenotypically graduated system of racial classification self-identify as such. In conversation with some of these individuals, many suggest that it was precisely through their involvement within the Cuban hip hop movement that they came to identify themselves as black. As Randy of the Havana-based duo Los Paisanos explains,

> Me? I'm black. Well here in Cuba I'm *jabao*. This is what they tell me here in Cuba, *jabao*. This light brown hair and eyes more or less light, all the same color, and with light brown skin.

When asked how long he identified as black (*negro*), Randy replied,

> Not very long. It has been a short time, since I began to take seriously the hip hop movement. Hip hop is a thing that frees the mentality, it is freedom. Many people don't understand but for us it is freedom. We have changed our way of thinking and we have completely opened our thinking. I don't know, it's a powerful weapon. Hip hop is a force, it's life, it's a way of life.[16]

As Randy's comments suggest, hip hop can indeed be instrumental in forging new understandings of black-selfhood. Though rather than simply a question of music, hip hop becomes for Randy a whole way of life, a transformative, liberating force associated with black self-actualization.

Yet such identities find their most active and politically demonstrative expression through their performance. In addition to everyday concerns, such as struggles for foreign-currency, the social impacts of tourism and the related sex trade, *raperos* frequently address manifestations of and struggles against anti-black racism both locally and internationally. In doing so, these youth are actively positioning themselves and their politics within a broader Afrodiasporic context of present-day black struggle. U.S. black radical figures, such as Malcolm X, the Panthers, and more recently Mumia Adu-Jamal have become important verbal references among many of Cuban MCs. The transnational sites of contact for such black radical iconography stem primarily from two related sources: the *raperos'* longstanding engagement with critically-oriented African American rap artists from the U.S. and a couple of influential African American political exiles, most notably Assata Shukur and Nahanda Abiodun. Abiodun has been particularly active in mentoring capacities within Havana's hip hop community, conferring on her something of a *la madrina*, or godmother, status within the movement.

Another key facilitator of these black radical connections has been the New York-based Black August Collective, which participated in a number of the early Cuban Hip Hop Festivals held annually in Havana. Black August's participation along these lines has been two-fold: organizing festival performances of more politically-identified African American artists such as Mos Def and Talib Kweli, Common, and Dead Prez, while strengthening bonds with African American political exiles on the island. Largely as a result of these varying engagements, *raperos'* transnationally envisioned notions of social justice are often advanced within overlapping discourses of "revolution"—one rooted in post-1959 Cuban revolutionary society and another informed by U.S. black radical / nationalist traditions and their contemporary struggles.

Yet on another level and resonant with similar examples in other Afro-Atlantic sites,[17] such diasporically attuned, self-consciously "modern" expressions of blackness overtly contest Cuba's dominant historical configuration of blackness within the nationally bounded trope of "folklore." Framings of this kind have tended to relegate Afro-Cubans to an ahistorical, unchanging "national" past, effectively freezing blacks within static representations of the "traditional" rather than recognizing the dynamic and ever-changing nature of Afro-Cuban culture, identity, and social agency. The self-affirming, nationally expansive black modernity asserted by Afro-Cuban *raperos* clearly stands in stark juxtaposition to, if not in implicit critique of such folklorized constraints.

Given the growing marginalization of darker-skinned Cubans from centers of economic activity in an increasingly socially stratified Cuba, *raperos* can be understood as using the black-identified cultural space of hip hop to articulate and mobilize their racial difference in response to the rise of racially lived social inequality. Hip hop's black-signified framings offer these youth a racially empowering, yet alternative, nationally transcendent source of black identification. Such globally aware blackness, in turn, serves as the basis upon which to act and move politically. Here, *raperos*' musical emphasis on social critique is often aimed at deconstructing the mounting contradictions between the claims of a socially just, racially egalitarian society under revolutionary socialism, and the growing realities of class and racial polarization within the island's new neoliberally impacted economy.

Most *raperos*, however, are far from counter-revolutionaries as some off the island might claim—quite the contrary. The majority of Cuban MCs see their music as critically engaged in one form or another in advancing key principles embodied in the ideals of the Cuban Revolution. As Kokino, a member of Havana's Anónimo Consejo (Anonymous Advice), put it,

> Our critique or our protest is constructive. The idea of Anónimo Consejo is not to throw the revolution to the floor. It is rather to make a revolution within the revolution. It is to criticize the things, or to protest the things that are not well within the Cuban revolution. But our objective is not to harass or be destructive, but it is to make a new Cuba for young people.[18]

Indeed, these youth represent a generation of socially engaged artists who remain shaped by the socialist-derived notions of egalitarianism embedded and still alive within Cuban society. Implicit critiques of capitalism and its debilitating effects on Cuban society are recurring themes within much of Cuban hip hop. Moreover, vocal challenges to U.S. imperialism—those articulating with both Cuban revolutionary discourse as well as more radical voices within U.S. hip hop—hold significant sway among many Cuban MCs. All this said, *raperos*' central object of critique remains Cuban society and its lived contradictions.

MCs Zoandris and Pelón, who comprise the Havana-based duo *Hermanos de Causa* (Brothers of Cause), are among the most respected and politically outspoken *raperos* on the island. One of their signature songs from 2003 is *Lágrimas Negras* (*Black Tears*). Taking the song's title from a classic Cuban *bolero-son* made famous in the 1930s by the celebrated Cuban composer Miguel Matamoros, Hermanos de Causa's *Lágrimas Negras* presents a lamentive though unabashed denunciation of the prevalence of racism in today's Cuba.

Lágrimas Negras
Hermanos de Causa

Yo de frente todo el tiempo realista	*I in front, all the time a realist*
No digas que no hay racismo	*Don't say that there isn't racism*
donde hay un racista	*where there is a racist*
siempre y cuando donde quiera que me encuentre	*Always, when and where ever I find myself*
el prejuicio de una forma o de otra	*prejudice in one form or another is always*
siempre esta presente	*present*

[...]

Siento odio profunda por tu racismo	*I feel profound hate for your racism*
Ya no me confundo con tu ironía	*I am no longer confused by your irony*
Y lloro sin que sepas que el llanto mío	*And I cry without you knowing that my cry*
Tiene lágrimas negras como mi vida	*has black tears like my life*

[...]

No me digas que no hay porque	*Don't tell me that there isn't any because I*
yo sé, lo he visto	*know, I have seen it*
No me digas que no existe porque	*Don't tell me that it doesn't exist because I*
lo he vivido	*have lived it*
No me niegues que hay oculto	*Don't deny that there is a hidden*
un prejuicio racial que nos condena y	*racial prejudice that condemns us and*
nos valora a todos por igual	*values us all the same*
No te dejes engañar	*Don't be fooled*
los ojos de par en par	*Eyes wide open*
No te dejes engañar ...	*Don't be deceived ...*

Hermanos de Causa in no uncertain terms seeks above to expose the stark incongruities between longstanding revolutionary discourses that deny the workings of racism versus the lived realities and social consequences of racialized existence in Cuba today. Rather than a marker of romantic sorrow as conveyed in the original rendition, in *Hermanos de Causa*'s version of "*Lágrimas Negras*" the song's title is resignified to foreground a racial positionality at the center of its testimonial critique—in short, a critical black subject, "no longer confused," who refuses to remain silent.

A particularly significant marker of hip hop's ascendance has been the Cuban state's response to its racially-signified cultural politics. In 1999 the Cuban Minister of Culture organized a meeting with representatives of Havana's hip hop community where he expressed the government's recognition of rap as a legitimate form of Cuban cultural expression. Prior to this moment, as suggested earlier, the Cuban state regarded rap music as an icon of U.S. capitalist culture with implied counter-revolutionary tendencies. Since this shift, however, the state became increasingly involved in the institutionalization of Cuban hip hop within the frame of revolutionary national culture.

The evolution of the annual Cuban Hip Hop Festival serves as a key indicator of the Cuban state's heightened interest in, and increased efforts to institutionalize the hip hop movement. Initiated in 1995, the Festival was founded by a small group of black cultural activists interested in creating a space to showcase Havana's emerging rap talent. With little support from the Cuban government, these individuals ran the Festival until 2000 when the cultural branch of the Union of Young Communists stepped in as the event's sole organizer. From this point on state institutions have played an increasingly active role in making resources and public venues available to rap artists.[19] At the same time the Cuban state has made consistent efforts to assume a position as a key arbiter and representational face of the movement. The establishment of the state-run La Agencia de Rap (Cuban Rap Agency) in 2002 represented the most dramatic expression of such incorporative moves. Yet in all its institutional expressions, the Cuban state has conspicuously—though not surprisingly—downplayed, if not completely ignored, the black racial significance of Cuban hip hop in its official dealings with the movement. To do so would open the Pandora's box of race and its contemporary dynamics to which the revolutionary leadership remains largely resistant to openly address itself.

Though initial reception on the part of many *raperos* to this new official attention was relatively positive, there was some ambivalence. On one level, the hip hop movement has long fought for recognition and the right to state resources within the context of a socialist society. Therefore, the recent access was much appreciated. Nonetheless, there remained at various levels caution, if not mistrust, on the part of many Cuban MCs regarding the extent to which the state sought to hold the reins. While the Cuban state's recognition of hip hop may have signaled a move toward authorizing it as a valid part of Cuban national culture and thus bestowing upon it just resources, it can also be read as an attempt to incorporate a previously marginalized youth culture and its racial underpinnings within institutional structures, thereby mitigating its oppositional potential.

While this may certainly be the case, I suggest that such incorporation has simultaneously enabled the development of an alternative space of racial articulation within an otherwise tightly controlled Cuban public landscape. I contend that Cuban hip hop has come to occupy an important site of racially positioned social critique and anti-racist advocacy within contemporary Cuba, and in doing so has helped push critical accounts of racial and class dynamics further into realms of public discourse. As such, hip hop can be understood as an increasingly important player in an evolving black public sphere predicated on the assertion of a contemporary black political difference within a previously configured "non-racial" Cuban national imaginary. Within this evolving black counter public (Dawson 1995),[20] Afro-Cuban intellectuals and artists are increasingly engaging *raperos* whose work is seen in vangardist terms vis-à-vis the island's current spectrum of racial politics. Moreover, courses at the University of Havana are now accessing Cuban rap lyrics as important sources of contemporary social commentary on Cuban society.

The future of Cuban hip hop, like the future of Cuba as a whole at this transformative moment, remains to be seen. Yet the efforts of Afro-Cuban *raperos* illuminate the dialect interplay between shifting regimes of racialized power and emergent forms of race-based social praxis as they are increasingly forged at the intersection of the local and the global. Here, the transnational, black-signified space of hip hop has been instrumental in enabling new forms of diasporically engaged strategies of self-making and self-action in the face of new globally-inflected imperatives of race.

South Africa

While traditional scholarship of the African diaspora has tended to concern itself with populations of African descent that share a common historical experience of dispersion—often involuntary—from an African "homeland," thus privileging the Atlantic as the primary locale of diasporic experience, others have underscored the necessity of recentering Africa as a contemporary site in the making and shaping of black diasporic identities and related political expression (Diawara 1998; Echeruo 1999). When considering the transnational contours of hip hop as a modern-day route of black racial identification, Africa itself has to be reckoned with. The widespread proliferation of rap artists and hip hop culture throughout Africa's urban centers represents an important manifestation of hip hop's global black reach. The rise of vibrant local hip hop movements in Senegal, Ghana, Benin, Kenya, and Cote d'Ivoire, to name just a few, suggest that African youth today are increasingly engaging in the black signified cultural space of hip hop as a medium of critical self-expression.[21]

The very real, structurally conditioned hardships that much of sub-Saharan Africa continues to live through have no doubt shaped the social commitments and political urgencies found in much of the hip hop produced on the continent. Before Kanye West's anti-"bling" single "Diamonds from Sierra Leone" (2005) helped draw U.S. attention to the economies of violence tied to Africa's diamond trade, Sierra Leonean youth in Freetown had long been active in using hip hop as a medium of social critique in the post-war nation.[22] In East Africa, Swahili language rap in cities like Dar es Salama, Tanzania, and Nairobi, Kenya have similarly become an important vehicle among urban youth for giving critical voice to present-day social concerns such as AIDS, joblessness, and state corruption (Perullo 2005).[23] For the purposes of this essay, however, the gaze is turned southward toward South Africa—one of the earliest sites of hip hop on the continent—as a poignant example of the ways critically positioned identities of blackness have been mobilized through the transnational lens of hip hop.

South African hip hop has undergone significant development since its emergence during the waning years of apartheid among Cape Town's colored or "mixed-race" youth in the late 1980s. Today, Johannesburg has joined Cape Town as one of South Africa's centers of locally produced hip hop, with each reflecting the particular cultural (and racial) dynamics of their regional settings. For one, Johannesburg-based hip hop has had to compete with the rise of *kwaito*—a frenetic, widely popular dance music out of Johannesburg's black townships that fuses older South African music genres such as *mbaqanga* with Western music styles including that of hip hop. Heavily incorporative of the township vernacular *isicamtho*,[24] *kwaito* artists have generally tended to gravitate more toward festive rather than explicit socio-political themes in their lyrics. Some have suggested such orientations reflect a celebratory post-Apartheid move among many black South African youth away from the more overt political imperatives of the apartheid era (Stephens 2000; Boloka 2004). Given the widespread popularity of *kwaito* among Johannesburg's black township youth—the same demographic fan-base from which the region's hip hop traditionally draws—it is not surprising that the music has had significant impact on local hip hop scene leading in some cases to a potential blurring of genres. There are those within Johannesburg's hip hop scene, however, who hold firm to what they see as a clear and necessary artistic distinction between the two genres.[25]

While South Africa's top selling, Soweto-born hip hop artist Pitch Black Afro may use blackness satirically as a performative trope (such as his ubiquitous oversized Afro wig), a differing and possibly more politically consequent mobilization of blackness can be found in the context of the genre's birth in Cape Town. Hip hop emerged in South Africa in the late 1980s primarily among colored youth of Cape Town's sprawling Cape Flats region.[26] Coloreds, as peoples of "mixed-race," were legally classified under apartheid's racialized caste system, literally occupied the racial middle-ground, historically positioned by the apartheid state as a buffer between the worlds of white and black. Residentially, educationally, and frequently professionally segregated from both black and white South Africans, colored communities often developed their own cultural identity drawing variously upon their African, Indo-Malaysian, and European cultural histories.[27] And unlike black South Africans, coloreds generally speak either Afrikaans or English as their primary language rather than local African vernaculars. Moreover, in accordance with apartheid's logic of divide-and-rule, coloreds were allotted limited class privilege over those of black South Africans. Such efforts contributed to the historical formation of a racialized class of South Africans who generally aspired to, and identified more with white South African status to the detriment of a non-white or "black" social identity—a development clearly attune with the grand designs of apartheid.

As with the rest of South Africa, however, the 1980s were a highly charged time in the Cape Town region with the rise of mass anti-apartheid political mobilization. During this period significant numbers of colored youth were politicized through varying forms of activism. The critical turning point in the anti-apartheid struggle culminated in 1990 with the release of Nelson Mandela and the unbanning of the African National Congress (ANC) and South African Communist Party (SACP). It was within this politically charged moment of social transformation that South Africa's self-defined Black Hip Hop Movement first found its footing among Cape Town's colored youth. Though the movement's followers eventually adopted "African" in place of "Black" as a self-identifying term, the initial choice was indicative of the movement's early deployment of blackness as an identity-based social marker.[28] And while the later shift may have in part been reflective of the broader move in post-apartheid South Africa toward non-racialism as a reconciliatory national project (Frederikse 1990), the use of "African" as a self-marker by colored youth clearly carried with it additional political significance.

Probably the most influential hip hop group to emerge during this early period was the Cape Flats-based Prophets of Da City (POC) who are often celebrated as key pioneers of South African hip hop. Formed in 1990 during that critical year of political openings, POC was headed by members Ready D, Shaheen, and Ramone who drew heavily upon Cape Town's preexisting b-boy (break-dancing) culture in their performances. From its initiation, the group's music embraced a strong sociopolitical focus often directed at addressing the everyday struggles of colored township life including those pertaining to poverty, unemployment, gang violence, and drug abuse (Faber 2004). At the center of these concerns, however, were explicit critiques of apartheid and its varying expressions of racialized oppression.

Yet a key and defining component of POC's early political voicings was their use of the term "black" as a self-referential marker. Through their music and other public engagements POC's members consistently positioned themselves as both black and African in oppositional stance to their historical classification as colored under apartheid. This move was particularly significant when considering that during this same period the colored population of the greater Cape Town region voted resoundingly for the white Afrikaner-lead Nationalist Party—the very architects of apartheid—over Nelson Mandela's ANC in South Africa's first multi-racial elections in 1994. POC's assertion of a black Africanness as colored youth, in turn, signified a political affront to a divisive racial paradigm designed to hinder political alliance between people of "mixed-race" and the larger "black" South African majority. Cognizant of the political stakes of such ideological trappings, POC's track "Black Thing" released one year after the national elections riffs,

> The term 'coloured' is a desperate case
> of how the devil's divided us by calling us a separate race.
> They call me 'coloured' said my blood isn't pure, but G,
> I'm not jakking my insecurity.
> So I respond to this and ventilate my mental state with Black
> Consciousness . . .[29]

Adam Haupt, who among others has chronicled the deployment of racial discourse within Cape Town's hip hop scene of the 1990s, draws attention to POC's above allusion to South Africa's Black Consciousness Movement of the 1960 and 1970s as a "unifying narrative" that "provides an alternative to the divisive discourse of apartheid" (Haupt 2003: 217).[30] Indeed, such appeals not only posit a broadened and racially inclusive notion of blackness but also seek to situate POC members' within an historical continuum of black political struggle and consciousness in South Africa.

While hip hop proves a performative frame through which such counter-hegemonic assertions of "black" subjectivity can be rooted nationally, it may also facilitate a forging of black-self through transnationally expansive understandings of blackness. Black Noise, another key pioneering Cape Town-based hip hop crew composed of colored youth, is illustrative of this kind of strategic melding of national and transnational frames of blackness. As their name attests, Black Noise placed a self-signifying "black" African identity and social message at the very center of their music and public image. The group's 1994 track "Who Taught You to Hate Yourself?" stands out as a particularly vivid expression of such black political fusions. The song's title is drawn from an oft-cited quote of Malcolm X in which he rhetorically chides his African American audience about internalized black self-hatred. The tract's chorus builds around a sequence of audio samples in which we hear Malcolm X forcibly prompting "Who taught you to hate yourself?, This blue-eyed man" followed by "Don't let the white man speak for you, And don't let the white man fight for you." Imbedded within the sequence we hear a South African voice intoning in Afrikaans

"*Kaffirs bly maar kaffirs*" ("Kaffirs [niggers] will remain kaffirs").[31] Through this intertextual montage a trans-Atlantic dialogue is forged between South African and U.S. historical realities of race. I suggest that it is precisely through such dialogic references that these artists facilitate a nationally transcendent understanding of black political struggle and subjectivity. The outlines of such positioned identity are given active voice by member Emile Jansen who follows in the song's second verse:

> *That's right the whites taught me to hate who I am*
> *They labeled us as coloured*
> *But now I know I'm a black man.*
> *Apartheid's divide and conquer, Made us believe we're a separate race*
> *And who wants to be a creation, of the supremacist pale face,*
> *And if you're not a perpetrator, of white supremacy,*
> *Then ask yourself*
> *Why you're now angry at me*
> *The word coloured implies*
> *That we're genetically 50 / 50*
> *But the black gene is dominant*
> *And therefore I'm black see*
> *You'll never say, Cause we know about our white past*
> *Making coloured s understand they're black, Is one hell of a task,*
> *Educated with self hatred*
> *Our black past was destroyed* ...[32]

Such lyrics not only provide poignant critique of the fragmentizing logics of apartheid's system of racial classification but give narrative form to the political agency of black self-constitution through the performative dimensions of hip hop.

The transnational routes of such black self-makings found further groundings through Black Noise's active participation in the local South African branch of Afrika Bambaataa's Bronx-based Universal Zulu Nation.[33] The extent of these commitments brought member Emile Jansen to New York in 1993 as South Africa's representative to the Zulu Nation's Twentieth Anniversary celebration.[34] Such affiliations, however, were not without their ambivalences. Jane Battersby has suggested that the African American-derived Afrocentric imagery upon which Bambaataa's Zulu Nation drew was woefully incongruent with the political realities of South Africa's ethno-racial landscape (Battersby 2004). The use of the expression Zulu Nation itself was particularly fraught because it evoked a complex set of politically charged meanings in South Africa given Zulu's pivotal role in the country's recent history of ethnically manipulated political violence. While such cultural translations clearly had their limitations, it would be wholly reductive to dismiss the social significance of those involvements altogether. The importance of such engagement lies rather in the transnational contours of Black Noise's articulations, if not identifications with the black-signified cultural symbolism of the Bronx-born Zulu Nation.

Political orientations of these kinds found active social expression through the numerous workshops and speaking engagements both POC and Black Noise have undertaken in South African schools, libraries, and prisons over the years. Such efforts illustrate the creative fusion of the pedagogic tendencies of rap music with social activism as these youth take their message and concerns to a generation of young people throughout the Cape Town region. One noteworthy example of such engagement was the headlining participation of POC and Black Noise in a youth AIDS awareness campaign in 2000 directed at mobilizing hip hop as a means to promote HIV education among secondary school students.[35] Black Noise member Emile Jansen has been particularly committed to community-based activism, embracing an acutely politicized position vis-à-vis questions of racial identity. Jansen initiated a series of local forums in the Cape Flats area dubbed the T.E.A.A.C.H. Project (The Educational Alternative Awakening Corrupted Heads) intended, as he explained, to "re-educate people to the proud past the black people have and to make them aware that respect for our people by themselves and others will only be attained if we know our past and supply our people with black role models that they can aspire to."[36] Jensen also founded a school-based touring project entitled "Heal the Hood" directed toward promoting what he described as "respect for being African and using these talents responsibly for the benefit of Africa."[37]

As these examples demonstrate, the politics of identity—in particular those embracing a recuperative notion of a black Africanness—stand central to the self-vision and social mission of groups like POC and Black Noise. From performative fashionings to political engagement, these South African youth can be understood as not only constituting new oppositionally positioned identities of blackness through the globally attune space of hip hop, but strategically deploying them in politically directed ways.

Reflecting on the political possibilities of global music circuits, George Lipsitz (1994: 6) has suggested that transnational music flows can provide resources for "the recognition of new networks and affiliations [while] they become crucibles for complex identities in formation that respond to the imperatives of place at the same time they transcend them." When considering the Afrodiasporic dimensions of present-day hip hop, such multivocal identity formations are decidedly at play. Here my attention has turned to local hip hop followings in Brazil, Cuba, and South Africa as testaments to how African and African-descendent youth use the space of hip hop to fashion and marshal globally conscious notions of black-selves toward liberatory ends.

Hip hop as Contemporary Ontology of Blackness

As I have argued, it is precisely through the political framings of diaspora that such contestive self-racializations find their most poignant expression. Nationally transcendent modes of black diasporic identification prove strategic in challenging local conditions of racial oppression, while at the same time remaining critically responsive to the ways global processes are increasingly reshaping such conditions. In the case of Brazil, hegemonic discourses tied to notions of "racial democracy" are increasingly unhinged as Afro-Brazilian youth use the diasporically configured black racial contours of hip hop to construct new identities as the basis to critically interrogate the racialized social realities of their everyday. Along analogous lines in Cuba, *raperos* are using hip hop to contest longstanding ideologies of Cuban national racelessness, while providing acute public critiques of the racialized workings of neoliberal transformations in a rapidly shifting Cuban social landscape. In South Africa a new generation of colored youth has attempted to position themselves amidst shifting racial paradigms of "old" and "new" where current claims to "non-racialism" run counter to the continued lived consequences of hierarchical racial privilege.

The cartography of maneuvers elucidates the social significance of hip hop not simply in terms of its international circulation and consumption but, rather, through the ways it is actively lived and politically used abroad as a site of racial mobilization and self-formation. Among these black-identified youth, the space of diaspora—through the performative lens of hip hop—operates as a key paradigm of both identity and politics, and as such has been instrumental in enabling transnationally engaged strategies of black self-fashioning and action in response to new, globally conditioned modes of racialization. In doing so, these young people not only marshal black selves but ultimately realize the Afro-Atlantic itself as a lived social formation. Hip hop in this way can be seen as an active site for the global (remapping of black political imaginaries via social dynamics of diaspora. Or, to return to Los Paisanos' more poetic rendering,

"*¡Fundamentalmente hip hop quiere decir negro! Corto, pero penetrante.*" ["Fundamentally hip hop means black! Concise, but penetrating"].

Study Questions

1. How does hip-hop communicate social ideals and cultural values?
2. What are the dialogic characteristics or potentials of global hip-hop?
3. In what ways does hip-hop facilitate or enable the reformulation of Black cultural identities?

Notes

1. In this essay I generally use the term "hip hop" to refer to the broad set of cultural practices, stylized aesthetics, and the larger cultural industry associated with, and inclusive of rap music. While the production and consumption of rap music may be central to many of these contexts, using hip hop's more expansive understandings underscores the contours of hip hop as a space of collective meaning making if not forms of subjectivity.
2. See, for instance, Mitchell 2001; Condry 2006; and Osumare 2007.
3. In developing this notion of mobilized diaspora, Edwards draws from the work of Harris 1996 and Edmondson 1986.
4. Consuming some 38.5 percent of all enslaved Africans brought to the Americas, Brazil's slave labor system operated from 1550 to 1888, making it the last nation in the Western hemisphere to officially abolish the institution (Behrendt 1999).
5. For critical discussions of Brazil's "myth of racial democracy" and its impact on black political mobilization, in addition to Hanchard 1994, see Winant 1994 and Lilly Caldwell 2006.
6. Original Portuguese lyrics accessed 18/9/2007 from http://www.coquim.hpg.ig.com.br/11.htm.
7. Translation drawn from Roth Gordon 2002.
8. Personal interview, 1993.
9. Personal interview, 1993.
10. Personal interview, 1993.
11. The prison complex was later closed in 2002. The massacre was more recently given cinematic form in the 2004 film *Carandiru* by Brazilian filmmaker Hector Babenco.
12. For a discussion of varying scholarly readings of and the relative effectiveness of Cuban Revolution's dealings with the historical problematics of race and racism, see Fernández 2001 and de la Fuente 2001.
13. This scenario remained intact until November 2004 when the Cuban state, in an effort to reduce the island's dependency on U.S. dollars, sought to discourage the flow of dollars by way of exchange tariffs in favor of other forms of hard foreign currency. While such moves may have contributed to a de-dollarization of the Cuban economy, the fundamental mechanisms of foreign currency dependency continued to function intact as Cubans remain largely dependent on some form of foreigner currency—Euros, Canadian Dollars, or British Pounds—to survive in Cuba's new neoliberalized economy.
14. My analysis of the Cuban hip hop movement is drawn primarily from two years of ethnographic field research conducted in Havana, Cuba, for my Ph.D. dissertation.
15. Frequently marked using the racially-signified term *barrios marginados* (marginal neighborhoods), these predominately poorer black neighborhoods are often associated with criminality and other related social "pathologies" in ways that resonate with Cuba's long-standing racialized association of blacks with notions of social pathology and "the primitive." For further discussions see Moore 1994; Palmie 2002.
16. Personal interview, 2002.
17. See Thomas 2004 and Godreau 2006.
18. Personal interview, 2001.
19. For a more detailed discussion of the Cuban state's efforts at institutionalizing Cuban hip hop see Baker 2005.
20. Drawing on the work of Nancy Fraser (1991), Dawson distinguishes an alternative, subalternly positioned black "counter public" from that of Habermas' bourgeois concept of the public sphere predicated on formal institutional civic structures such as the media, the academy, and other dominant organizational forms.

21. One only needs to glance at the website Africanhiphop.com to get a sense of the remarkable scope and depth to which hip hop has taken root in Africa. Although European administered, the vast majority of the site's inexhaustible collections of articles, news archives, interviews, web forums, and music and video clips are produced by contributors from the continent itself. And while possibly the most compressive, Africanhiphop. com. is only one of more than 200 websites dedicated to locally produced hip hop in Africa. Networks of these kinds, in turn, provide a once inconceivable space for communicative interchange among African practitioners and followers of hip hop, while testifying to the technological sawiness of those engaged in the production and promotion of hip hop in Africa, despite the continent's endemic levels of poverty and resource scarcity.

22. See, for instance, BBC Radio l's audio documentary "The Beautiful Struggle" (2005).

23. Regarding Kenya hip hop see the documentary "Hip-Hop Colony: The African Hip-Hop Explosion" (2005) produced / directed by Michael Wanguhu.

24. *Isicamtho* is derived from a fusion of regional African languages such as Zulu, Tswana, Sesotho, and dominant Afrikaans. In the shifting parlance of the townships, the term has come to replace the expression *tsotsitaal*, or "gangster-speak," previously used to refer to ever-evolving township vernacular.

25. Interview with Johannesburg-based Skwatta Kamp, one of South Africa's most commercially successful hip hop crews. Electronic document, http://www.musica.co.za/eMusica/news_article.asp?segmentID=99&-GenreID=99&ArticleID=1296. Accessed 10/4/2006.

26. A vast network of townships were erected in the 1960s along Cape Town's sandy floodplains to accommodate large numbers of coloreds forcibly displaced by Apart heid's social geography.

27. Significant numbers of enslaved and indentured laborers from what are today Malaysia and Indonesia were brought to the Cape Town region starting in the late 1600s by Dutch traders. These "Malays" later inter-mixed with European settlers and indigenous Africans resulting in the racial codification of "coloureds" as a population group under Apartheid. Large segments of Cape Town's colored community still practice the Islam first introduced via Malay / Indonesian influences, and the religion continues to be an important component of a distinct cultural identity for many coloreds. Within the broader colored population, both Afrikaans and English are spoken with a distinctive vernacular accent, cadence, and intonation.

28. This observation is drawn from my personal observations in Cape Town in 1991 during the early formation of the region's hip hop movement. At this juncture youth participating in the scene, the vast majority of who were colored, self-titled themselves as the Black Hip Hop Movement.

29. Cited in Haupt 2003.

30. Also see Watkins 2001 and Battersby 2004.

31. *Kaffir* is the Afrikaans term used derisively for black South Africans in ways historically resonant with the term "nigger" in the United States.

32. Cited from http://africasgateway.com/sections-viewarticle-105.html. Accessed 24/9/07.

33. The Zulu Nation was a social-cultural organization founded in the early 1970s in public housing projects of the South Bronx by Afrika Bambaataa and is credited as a key cradle of early hip hop culture in New York City. The now "Universal" Zulu Nation has its own website (www.zulunation.com) containing information ranging from the history of hip hop, to afrocentric teachings and readings of world events, to black-produced consumer products. The site even provides an on-line application service for membership, enabling the expansion of what is now the organization's global network of local branches.

34. See http://www.zulunation.nl/projects/southafrica/introducing_emile_yx.php. Accessed 12/4/2006.

35. http://www.africanhiphop.com/update/hivhop.htm. Accessed 4/4/2006.

36. Mario Pissarra, *Contemporary African Database*, http://people.africadatabase.org/en/profile/-11711.html. Accessed 24/9/2007.

37. Mario Pissarra, *Contemporary African Database*, http://people.africadatabase.org/en/profile/-11711.html. Accessed 24/9/2007.

References

Anderson, Benedict 1991. *Imagined Communities: Reflections on the Origin and Spread of Nationalism.* New York: Verso.

Appadurai, Arjun 1996. *Modernity at Large: Cultural Dimensions of Globalization.* Minneapolis, MN: University of Minnesota Press.

Baker, Geoffrey 2005. ¡Hip Hop Revolución! Nationalizing Rap in Cuba. *Ethnomusicology* 49(3): 368–402.

Battersby, Jane 2004. "Sometime it Feels Like I am Not Black Enough": Recast(e)ing Coloured through South African Hip Hop as a Postcolonial Text. In *Shifting Selves: Post-Apartheid Essays on Mass Media, Culture and Identity.* Hermans Wasserman and Sean Jacobs, eds. Cape Town, South Africa: Kwela.

Behrendt, Stephan 1999. Transatlantic Slave Trade. In *Africana: The Encyclopedia of the African and African American Experience*. Kwame Anthony Appiah and Henry Louis Gates, Jr., eds. Cambridge, MA: Harvard University Press.

Boloka, Gibson 2004. Cultural Studies and the Transformation of the Music Industry: Some Reflections on Kwaito. In *Shifting Selves: Post-Apartheid Essays on Mass Media, Culture and Identity*. Hermans Wasserman and Sean Jacobs, eds. Cape Town, South Africa: Kwela.

Brown, Jacqueline Nassy 1998. Black Liverpool, Black America, and the Gendering of Diasporic Space. *Cultural Anthropology* 13(3): 291–325.

Butler, Judith 1990. *Gender Trouble: Feminism and the Subversion of Identity*. New York: Routledge.

Chang, Jeff 2005. *Can't Stop Won't Stop: A History of the Hip-Hop Generation*. London: Macmillan.

Condry, Ian 2006. *Hip-Hop Japan: Rap and the Paths of Cultural Globalization*. Durham, NC: Duke University Press.

Darlington, Shasta 2000. Brazilian Rappers Speak to the Poor: Popular Duo Launch Recording Career From Notorious San Paulo Prison. *The Globe and Mail* (Toronto), 5 September.

Dawson, Michael C. 1995. A Black Counterpublic? Economic Earthquakes, Racial Aganda(s), and Black Politics. In *The Black Public Sphere*. Houston Baker Jr. and Michael C. Dawson, eds. Chicago: University of Chicago Press.

de la Fuente, Alejandro 2001. *A Nation for All: Race, Inequality, and Politics in Twentieth-Century Cuba*. Chapel Hill, NC: University of North Carolina Press.

Diawara, Manthia 1998. *In Search of Africa*. Cambridge, MA: Harvard University Press.

Echeruo, Michael 1999. An African Diaspora: The Ontological Project. In *The African Diaspora: African Origins and New World Identities*. Isidore Okpewho, Carole Boyce Davies, Ali Alamin Mazrui, eds. Bloomington, IN: Indiana University Press.

Edmondson, Locksley 1986. Black America As a Mobilizing Diaspora: Some International Implications. In *Modern Diasporas in International Politics*. Gabriel Sheffer, ed. London: Croon Helm.

Edwards, Brent Hayes 2001. The Use of Diaspora. *Social Text* 19(1): 45–73.

Faber, Jörg 2004. Cape Town's Hip Hop Scene. *Ntama: Journal of African Music and Popular Culture*, Mainz University, Friday, 23 January 2004. Electronic document, http://ntama.uni-mainz.de/hiphop/faber/. Accessed 24 September 2007.

Fernández, Ariel 2001. ¿Poesía urbana o la Nueva Trova de los noventa? *La Jiribilla*. Electronic document, http://www.lajiribilla.cu/2001/ul5_agosto/414_15.html. Accessed 4 May 2002.

Fernandez, Nadine 2001. The Changing Discourse on Race in Contemporary Cuba. *Qualitative Studies in Education* 14(2): 117–132.

Fraser, Nancy 1991. Rethinking the Public Sphere: A Contribution to the Critique of Actually Existing Democracy. In *Habermas and the Public Sphere*. Craig Calhoun, ed. Cambridge, MA: MIT Press.

Freyre, Gilberto 1964. *The Masters and the Slaves: A Study in the Development of Brazilian Civilization*. New York: Random House.

Frederikse, Julie 1990. *The Unbreakable Thread: Non-Racialism in South Africa*. Johannesburg, South Africa: Ravan Press.

Gilroy, Paul 1993. *The Black Atlantic: Modernity and Double Consciousness*. Cambridge, MA: Harvard University Press.

Godreau, Isar 2006. Folkloric "Others": Blanqueamiento and the Celebration of Blackness as an Exception in Puerto Rico. In *Globalization and Race: Transformations in the Cultural Production of Blackness*. Kamari Marine Clarke and Deborah A. Thomas, eds. Durham, NC: Duke University Press.

Gordon, Edmund T. and Mark Anderson 1999. The African Diaspora: Towards an Ethnography of Diasporic Identification. *Journal of America Folklore* 112(445): 282–296.

Hall, Stuart 1992. What Is This Black in Black Popular Culture? In *Black Popular Culture*. Gina Dent, ed. Seattle, WA: Bay Press.

Hall, Stuart 1996. Who Needs Identity? In *Questions of Cultural Identity*. Stuart Hall and Paul Du Gay, eds. London: Sage Publications.

Hammad, Suheir 1996 *Born Palestinian, Born Black*. New York: Writers & Readers Publishing.

Hammond, Jack 1999. The High Cost of Dollars. *NACLA Report on the Americas* 32(5): 24–25.

Harris, Joseph 1996. The Dynamics of the Global African Diaspora. In *The African Diaspora*. Alusine Jalloh and Stephen E. Maizlish, eds. College Station, TX: Texas A&M University Press.

Hartman, Michelle 2002. 'A *Debke* Beat Funky as P.E.'s Riff: Hip Hop Poetry and Politics in Suheir Hammad's *Born Palestinian, Born Black*. *Black Arts Quarterly* 7(1): 6–8.

Haupt, Adam 2003. Hip-hop in the Age of Empire: Cape Flats Style. In *Voices of Transition: The Politics, Poetics and Practices of Social Change in South Africa*. Edgar Pieterse and Frank Meintjies, eds. Johannesburg, South Africa: Heinemann.

Hebdige, Dick 1981. *Subculture: The Meaning of Style*. London: Routledge.

Helg, Aline 1995. *Our Rightful Share: The Afro-Cuban Struggle for Equality, 1886–1912.* Chapel Hill, NC: University of North Carolina Press.

Keyes, Cheryl 1996. At the Crossroads: Rap Music and Its African Nexus. *Ethnomusicology* 40 (Spring-Summer): 223–248.

Lilly Caldwell, Kia 2006. *Negras in Brazil: Re-envisioning Black Women, Subjectivity, and Citizenship.* New Brunswick, N J: Rutgers University Press.

Lipsitz, George 1994. *Dangerous Crossroads: Popular Music, Postmodernism, and the Politics of Space.* London: Verso.

Magaldi, Cristina 1999. Adopting Imports: New Images and Alliances in Brazilian Popular Music of the 1990s. *Popular Music* 18(3): 309–329.

McDaniels, Andrea 1999. Striking Cord with Youths, Brazil Rappers Nudge Reform. *The Christian Science Monitor,* 11 January.

Mitchell, Tony 2001. Introduction: Another Root: Hip Hop Outside the USA. In *Global Noise: Rap and Hip Hop Outside the USA.* Tony Mitchell, ed. Middletown, CT: Wesleyan University Press.

Moore, Robin 1994. Representations of Afro-Cuban Expressive Culture in the Writings of Fernando Ortiz. *Latin American Music Review* 15(2): 32–54.

Olavarria, Margot 2002. Rap and Revolution: Hip-Hop Comes To Cuba. *NACLA* 35(6): 28–30.

Osumare, Halifu 2007. *The Africanist Aesthetic in Global Hip-Hop: Power Moves.* New York: Palgrave Macmillan.

Pacini Hernández, Deborah and Reebee Garofalo 2000. Hip Hop in Havana: Rap, Race, and National Identity in Contemporary Cuba. *Journal of Popular Music Studies* 11/12: 18–47.

Palmie, Stephan 2002. *Wizards and Scientists: Explorations in Afro-Cuban Modernity and Tradition.* Durham, NC: Duke University Press.

Pardue, Derek 2004. Putting Mano to Music: The Mediation of Race in Brazilian Rap. *Ethnomusicology Forum* 13(2): 253–286

Patterson, Tiffany and Robin Kelley 2000. Unfinished Migrations: Reflections on the African Diaspora and the Making of the Modern World. *African Studies Review* 43(1): 11–45.

Perullo, Alex 2005. Hooligans and Heroes: Youth Identity and Hip-Hop in Dar es Salaam, Tanzania. *Africa Today* 51(4): 75–101.

Rivera, Raquel 2003. *New York Ricans from the Hip Hop Zone.* New York: Palgrave Macmillan.

Rose, Tricia 1994. *Black Noise.* Middletown, CT: Wesleyan University Press.

Roth Gordon, Jennifer 2002. Hip Hop Brasileiro: Brazilian Youth and Alternative Black Consciousness Movements. *Black Arts Quarterly* 7(1): 9–10.

Sansone, Livio 1997. New Blacks from Bahia: Local and Global Afro-Bahia. *Identities* 3(4): 457–494.

Slater, Don 1997. *Consumer Culture and Modernity.* Maiden, MA: Blackwell.

Stephens, Simon 2000. Kwaito. In *Senses of Culture.* S. Nuttall and C. Michael, eds. Cape Town, South Africa: Oxford University Press.

Thomas, Deborah 2004. *Modern Blackness: Nationalism, Globalization, and the Politics of Culture in Jamaica.* Durham, NC: Duke University Press.

Tomlinson, John 1993. *Cultural Imperialism: A Critical Introduction.* London: Pinter.

Urla, Jaqueline 2001. "We Are All Malcolm X!" Negu Gorriak, Hip-Hop, and the Basque Political Imaginary. In *Global Noise: Rap and Hip Hop Outside the USA.* Tony Mitchell, ed. Middletown, CT: Wesleyan University Press.

Watkins, Lee 2001. 'Simunye, We Are Not One': Ethnicity, Difference and the Hip-Hoppers of Cape Town. *Race & Class* 43(1): 29–44.

Winant, Howard 1994. *Racial Conditions.* Minneapolis, MN: University of Minnesota Press.

Williams, Raymond 1977. *Marxism and Literature.* Oxford: Oxford University Press.

20

Hooligans and Heroes
Youth Identity and Hip-Hop in Dar es Salaam, Tanzania

Alex Perullo confronts the issue of the vilification of youth in Dar es Salaam, Tanzania, responding to the widespread perceptions of youth in crisis that pervade official discourse and that taint conventional social attitudes. Perullo explains that hip-hop presents a crucial means of resisting the negative portrayal of youth and Tanzanian artists and activists adopt hip-hop's various apparatuses in an effort to re-present themselves and to articulate their priorities, their immediate needs, and their ideals for a better future.

Among the more progressive aspects of Tanzanian hip-hop is the emphasis placed on pro-social attitudes and the communication of initiatives pertaining to crime reduction, drug and alcohol cessation, safer sex practices, and the effects of chronic unemployment on young people. In this context, hip-hop is situated within a specific generational dynamic that is informed by cultural traditions and by national norms and standards. The commitment to self-improvement and to social responsibility that permeate hip-hop's "educational voice" is a sharp rebuttal to authorities that dismiss the role and importance of the youth constituency. By flipping between multiple languages and mobilizing multiple discourses, hip-hop youth in Tanzania display a wily strategy of empowerment and agency, navigating the socio-political terrain while delineating new avenues of action and opportunity.

Hooligans and Heroes: Youth Identity and Hip-Hop in Dar es Salaam, Tanzania

Alex Perullo

Introduction

In a letter to *The East African,* an anonymous author wrote about the "youth time bomb" that existed in Dar es Salaam. Lamenting the problems of youth in Tanzania and the difficulties they have leaving the country for more opportunities, he writes, "What, after all, is there to live for at home? Jobs have disappeared in the wake of economic liberalization. ... An army of petty hawkers has emerged, and drug dealing and crime have soared." He continues by stressing that places such as Dar es Salaam are social time bombs, where youth are on the verge of exploding with anger and disorder. The pressures of living in Tanzania have caused young people to use any means to survive (*The East African* 1999).

In examining the pressures that youth encounter daily, it may seem logical to assume that youth are on the verge of exploding through violence and disorder. In Dar es Salaam, a city of 3.5 million people, unemployment figures among the general population are estimated to be from 13 to 40 percent and potentially higher among young people, many of whom—even some who have an education—work menial jobs, sit on street corners waiting to be hired, or search the city for employment.[1] For those fortunate enough, families provide support until jobs materialize; for others, however, problems with hunger, corruption (being forced to pay bribes to police), and inadequate social institutions can make the city unbearable (Lugalla 1995; Moyer 2003; Tripp 1997).

Due to the ways young people are expected to react to these pressures—based on adults' preconceived notions of youth culture and media representations of young people's practices—youth are often associated with words such as *hostile, violent,* and *destructive* (Seekings 1993: xi). Particularly in regard to hip-hop culture in Tanzania, many rappers and rap fans are labeled *wahuni* (hooligans), and rap has been perceived as a music corrupting the minds of the country's young. Professor Jay, a Tanzanian rapper, explains that during the early years of rap music (late 1980s and early 1990s), youth were vilified for associating with rap music: "If you rapped during this time, you were immediately considered a hooligan. Even parents would not permit their children to rap, or even allow them to listen to someone else rap" (2001a). Many other artists pointed out similar trends, where parents and elders discouraged rap music fearing that it would encourage students to leave school, turn them into criminals, and make them forget their cultural traditions.

The views that social pressures cause youth to react violently and rap encourages hooliganism are certainly not limited to Tanzania. Several studies have examined youth who employ violence to cope with social pressures, political instability, or economic hardships (see Bucholtz 2002 and MacDonald 1997). In regard to hip-hop culture, some authors conclude that marginalized youth (those who experience the most dramatic social pressures) who listen to rap are likelier to be violent (Miranda and Claes 2004). While these conclusions may appear compelling, they create an unfortunate caricature of youth as a "lost generation" (O'Brien 1996) unable to deal with complex situations and find diplomatic solutions to adverse circumstances. Positioning youth in opposition to the rest of society ignores their contributions in language, dress, and popular culture, and negates the ways they cope with economic and social pressures. To say that they are going to "explode" is to fail to recognize their agency as social and political actors, and their ingenuity in creating opportunities for themselves and in moving public opinions beyond representations of youth as a marginal age group.

In this article, I explore the ways that youth in Dar es Salaam use rap music to deal with social pressures and project themselves as creative and empowered individuals in society.[2] In particular, I use rap lyrics and interviews with rap musicians to examine the voices that rap offers youth in urban Tanzanian society. Rap has become a central means for youth to teach others about joblessness, corruption, class differences, AIDS, and other problems. It has created a sense of community among young people in Dar es Salaam and other areas of Tanzania, and empowered youth by providing them with confidence and self-reliance, not anger and violence. It lets them know that others are facing pressures similar to the ones they incur daily.

Tanzanian rap is also a means through which youth are able to communicate their concerns: hip-hop "is about being a spokesperson and representative for those without power" (Whiteley 2004: 9). While it can also represent those with power, it has become an important means for marginalized Tanzanian youth to address mass audiences. By identifying their stance on important issues, they encourage others to consider the place of youth in society. For Tanzanian youth, this means altering popular conceptions of themselves as hooligans and allowing youth to become knowledge holders and educators within urban contexts. The process of representation and education through music allows youth to voice their concerns to the public and learn to cope with the hardships that they encounter on a daily basis. Other outlets are available to youth, including comics and youth-oriented magazines, but rap is a far more ubiquitous medium because of its dominance on the radio and the ease with which people can comprehend its message: literacy does not exclude one from listening to rap.

Tanzania has a long history of music that discusses social and political issues. Before Tanzania's independence from British colonial rule (in 1961), many *dansi* and *taarab* artists wrote songs that commented on problems of urban life. Mohamed Bwagajuga's song "Dar es Salaam Usiende" ("Don't Go to Dar es Salaam"), for instance, warned people about the dangers of the city (Graebner forthcoming). After independence, and particularly during the socialist period, many *dansi* and *taarab* artists altered the content of their lyrics. Although songs were still socially meaningful, artists often used their music to praise the government or promote socialist goals. A famous Tanzanian musician of the 1970s, Mbaraka Mwinshehe, composed songs titled "TANU Yajenga Nchi" ("TANU Builds the Nation"), "Kifo cha Pesa" ("Death by Money"), "Miaka 10 ya Uhuru" ("Ten Years after Independence"), and "Mwongozo wa TANU" ("The Guidance of TANU") (Perullo 2003: 84–85).[3]

Aside from strong feelings of nationalism after independence, one of the main reasons for prosocialist songs was the control that the government had on the country's radio station and recording studio. Before the emergence of independent radio stations and recording studios (in the early 1990s), artists typically went to Radio Tanzanian Dar es Salaam (RTD) to record their music.[4] To record at RTD, artists had to submit their lyrics to a censor, who often made changes to lyrics that did not support or fit with the socialist direction of the country. Most artists, including Mwinshehe, received a great deal of support from the government when they composed socially and politically appropriate lyrics; to avoid censors' comments, however, other composers wrote lyrics with double entendres and hidden meanings—a practice that has a long history in Swahili poetry (Knappert 1979) and *taarab* and *dansi* musical histories (Askew 2002; Fair 2001; Graebner 2000; Knappert 1983; Martin 1980).

By the late 1980s, when rap emerged, artists no longer needed to mask the meaning of their words. Artists avoided censors by using the independent radio stations and recording studios that emerged in the early 1990s. Independent radio stations had obligations to avoid offensive material, but rap artists were able to write, record, and air songs about any topic, as long as they did so in a "clean way" (Perullo forthcoming). Messages therefore became more direct than in pre-1990 *dansi* and *taarab* music. Currently, many contemporary *dansi* and *taarab* artists compose songs with more straightforward lyrics.

Liberalization was central in providing youth access to rap. During the mid-1980s, the government, under the presidency of Ali Hassan Mwinyi, began moving its economic policies away from socialism and toward capitalism.[5] Liberalization brought about easier access to foreign goods, including hip-hop clothing, music, and magazines, it allowed independent radio stations and newspapers to emerge, and it permitted many potential producers to import equipment needed to record local artists. Because of the emergence of new radio stations, newspapers, and recording studios, many youth were able to find jobs as deejays, announcers, journalists, and producers or engineers. Since many of these youth were also part of the local hip-hop scene, Tanzanian rap quickly attained a strong network of support. Liberalization gave many youth in Dar es Salaam the tools and the medium to promote their views.

In preparation for this article, I listened to several hundred rap songs recorded between 1994 and 2003. About half the songs had been commercially released on cassette tapes or compact discs, and the other half had been released to Tanzanian radio stations and recorded for me by radio deejays. Initially, I categorized the songs by the central message of their lyrics; if a song had several messages, I placed it in multiple categories. The broad thematic scope of hip-hop lyrics, from crime to drug use and alcoholism to AIDS, was impressive and daunting.

Because of the profusion of ideas in Tanzanian rap, I focus this chapter on two prevalent categories in rap lyrics: political issues, such as corruption and unfulfilled promises made by politicians, and social conditions, such as class, education, and the status of women. Specific songs that I discuss were chosen for their popularity (all the songs had been on various radio stations' top-ten lists) and social importance (in interviews with fans, deejays, producers, and performers, these songs were often mentioned for their popularity). Throughout the article, I place the songs within a social context and, wherever possible, allow the artists to discuss the importance of the songs. In the final section of this chapter, I examine the reasons why so many rap songs have lyrics that comment on life in Tanzania and do not follow foreign models for rap-music content.

Ujumbe Mkali—"Strong Messages"

A dominant theme in Tanzanian hip-hop lyrics is criticism of social and political conditions. Rappers write about problems they see in their communities, such as failing schools, limited employment and financial possibilities, lack of adequate healthcare, and corruption among local leaders. James Nindi, in a 2001 article on Tanzanian rap, writes, "When listening to one of this country's radio stations, it is common to hear rap songs by our artists with *ujumbe mkali* [strong messages]." These messages tend to recur in rap lyrics, as each artist sets out to present his or her viewpoint on important topics. The lyrics become a vehicle through which youth articulate their ideas without fear of repercussions.

One of the earliest artists to use rap for social commentary was Mr. II. His third album, *Niite Mr. II (Call Me Mr. II)* (1998), written when he was 25 years old, established a precedent for lyrics that spoke about injustices. As he explains: "I had my own ideas, and I saw the direction that we [Tanzanians] were heading. ... But who will listen to what I say? Can I climb up on stage and become a politician? It's not possible. I decided to use music, and to speak directly [to people] with rap" (2000a). The opening dialogue of *Niite Mr. II* displays the directness and the social message that Mr. II wanted to achieve. The "Intro" track is a conversation between a judge, speaking in a deep, menacing voice, and Mr. II, who sounds unmoved and indifferent.[6]

Mr. II "Intro"	
Hakimu:	**Judge:**
Kutokana na ushahidi wa upande wa mashtaka	Based on the evidence presented by the prosecution
Mshatikiwa unaonekana una hatia ya kosa la uzembe na uzururaji.	You are accused of negligence and loitering.
Hivi basi mahakama	Therefore, the court
Inakuhukumu miaka mitano jela na kazi ngumu au faini ya elfu ishirini.	Hereby sentences you to five years of hard labor or a fine of $20.
Una lolote la kujitetea?	Do you have anything to say for yourself?
Mr. II:	**Mr. II:**
Poa tu, Mheshimiwa Hakimu.	That's fine, Honorable Judge.
Mimi kosa langu ni uzembe na uzururaji kama nilivyoshtakiwa.	My crime is negligence and loitering, as I have been accused.
Sasa, kwa maana hio sina kazi, sio?	So, that means that I don't have a job. You see?
Sasa ukami nitazofanya?	How can I be told to pay the fine?
Kwa hiyo nitapoa tu kwenye jela,	So, I will just (go) rot in jail,
Yote [ni] maisha.	That's life.

While the dialogue between Mr. II and the judge may sound improbable—why would a judge sentence a youth to five years of hard labor for loitering?—loitering is a criminal offense in Tanzania. Since the late 1960s, the Tanzanian government has made efforts to remove youth who loiter from the streets of Dar es Salaam. In 1972, it launched Operation Kupe (Operation Parasite) to send jobless youth in Dar es Salaam to rural areas of the country (Burton 2005 and forthcoming). Four years later, the government initiated Operation Kila Mtu Afanya Kazi (Everyone Must Work). But in 1983, the government made its strongest attack on urban joblessness:

> The Human Resources Deployment Act (popularly known as *Nguvu Kazi*), passed by the Tanzanian government that year [1983], criminalised the urban presence of those without formal employment. As a result of "indiscriminate swoops" on people "loitering" on the streets between 10 A.M. and 2 P.M., 15,000 were arrested in the last three months of 1983. Those without employment were repatriated to their home regions or sent to work on sisal estates.
>
> (Burton 2000: 2)

Though Nguvu Kazi has since disappeared, the government still views loitering as a sign of laziness or criminality. This view, however, has done little to diminish the large number of unemployed, urban youth who gather in public areas—referred to as *kijiweni*, derived from the word *kijiwe* "pimple." Even with the local police (*askari*) occasionally arresting youth or forcing them to pay bribes (Andersson and Stavrou 2001), numerous young people continue to gather in downtown urban areas to discuss their situations and devise strategies for finding employment. Mr. II's introduction is therefore a reminder of the dilemmas youth face: they have no work, nor many opportunities for work, yet they are treated as criminals or vagabonds for sitting idle. By pointing out the hypocrisy of the situation, Mr. II gives a heavy-handed critique of government policies. At the same time, he is emboldening youth to understand their social plight. In the song that follows the "Intro," he speaks directly to these youth and offers a broader social critique.

Mr. II "Hali Halisi" ("The Real Situation")	
Tuna maisha magumu mpaka rais anafahamu	Our lives are hard, even the president knows
Na bado tunatabasamu kwa kila hali,	And we still have our smiles for every situation,
Ni hali halisi	Every real situation
Kila siku ni sisi na polisi na polisi na sisi.	Everyday it's us and the police, the police and us.
Pilato kizimbani anatungoja sisi	[Pontius] Pilate in the court is waiting for us.
Bwana jela gerezani anatungoja sisi.	The wardens and the jails are waiting for us.
Bongo mambo siyo mazuri,[7]	In Tanzania, things are not good,
Jua bado kali.	Things are still very hard.
Salamu kwa Papa John Paul wa pili	Greetings to John Paul II moto. Angry
Wananchi wenye hasira wachoma watu	citizens are burning people alive.
Tusio na kazi sasa tuko na matumbo joto	Those of us that do not have jobs, stay hungry.
Tutapochoka amani tutapigana na nani?	When we are tired of peace, who are we going to fight with?
Uzalendo unanishinda, miaka in avyokwenda.	As years go by, I become tired of patriotism. I see the same faces, the same leaders
Naona sura zile zile, viongozi wale wale	From primary school until the present.
Toka wakati nipo shule mpaka sasa.	Do not play with politics,
Usicheze na siasa,	Politics is a dirty game.
Siasa ni mchezo mchafu	They just want to be famous.
Wanataka umaarufu.	Lots of Tanzanian politicians are liars.
Wanasiasa wa Bongo wengi waongo.	

The laidback music of the song is punctuated with Mr. II's deep, angry voice. He directs the song at other youth, whom he tells of the obstacles that they continually encounter. He attacks Tanzanian politicians, calling them liars, and hints at the corruption that exists in the country when leaders can remain in power for decades uncontested. In the middle of the next verse, he raps, "I am saying that it is all right for youth to be mad. / This is the real situation. / Yeah! It is all right to be mad. / Who is going to put things right?" With these words, Mr. II tells other youth that they can be angry about social inequality and political incompetence. While not advocating violence, he is encouraging young people to stand up for themselves and voice their opinions. The answer to who is going to put things right is youth themselves. According to Mr. II, young people have the power and the need to make their voices heard.

When Mr. II released "Hali Halisi," it could be heard throughout the country, in rural and urban areas. Shopowners blasted it from their stores, bus drivers let it play repeatedly during their routes, and radio stations aired it several times a day. The cassette *Niite Mr. II* sold so quickly during the first few months after its release that vendors started inflating its cost to make more money, but it still sold out within days after every new shipment. The popularity of the song and the album reflected the way that Tanzanians, particularly youth in urban areas, identified with Mr. II's message. Though some people did criticize Mr. II for being too vocal and disrespectful of his elders, many others rejoiced in a rap anthem that reflected their concerns. The song was important for uniting disenfranchised youth who believed that the government was discriminating against them and not serving their interests.

After the release of Mr. II's album, many other artists incorporated similar political and social themes in their music. While I address social concerns below, it is worth looking at the development of politically based lyrics here to highlight the progression of one theme promulgated in rap lyrics. Before and after the 2000 presidential election, several songs that critiqued the local political situation appeared. Most of them attacked corruption, inefficient government spending, and the use of Western aid to line wealthy Tanzanians' pockets. Several artists used language to target specific audiences. In the song "Ngangari" ("Brave Person"), Magangwe Mob, also spelled Gangwe Mobb, employed slang from the Temeke section of Dar es Salaam to speak about political issues relevant to that part of the city. The select use of language created pride among members of the Temeke community, who often attended Magangwe Mob concerts with banners heralding their home district and neighborhoods. Despite the heavy use of Temeke-centric speech, "Ngangari" eventually garnered a large listening audience throughout Dar es Salaam (Perullo and Fenn 2003).

Other artists limited slang and used "standard" Kiswahili in their political raps. In "Mwananchi" ("Citizen," 2001), Balozi Dola warned Tanzanians about the difficulties involved in choosing a new president. He composed the rap to "awaken people and have them speak out about how they feel" (Dola 2004). In the opening verse, he states his position on the role that citizens need to play in contemporary politics.

Balozi Dola "Mwananchi" ("Citizen")	
Mwananchi mimi nina nini?	What do I have as a citizen?
Kwenye nchi yenye kila aina ya mali asili	In a country with abundant natural resources
Zaidi ya masakini uliokithiri	Other than the inherent poverty that keeps increasing
Na vipi tuwe na vitu vyote hivi na mfukoni tusiwena chochote?	How can we have all this and have nothing in our pockets?
Swala hila ndani iliulizwa kichwa	This situation keeps blowing my mind
Hasa ukizingitia kwamba Bongo tuna vichwa vingetatua matatizo yetu yote.	Considering we have smart people to solve our problem.
Wananchi wenzangu, tunapochagua kiongozi wetu hapa kwetu	My fellow citizens, when we choose our leaders
Tuemakini ili tuchague viongozi wenye busara,	Let's be very careful, so that we choose leaders with wisdom,
Viongozi wenye ishara ya maendeleo	Leaders with visions of progress
Tunataka mzalendo wala ushiba na kujaa maji ya bandera.	We want patriotic leaders.
Tusijatuchagua mtu wa kuuza yetu nchi na kubadalisha yetu bandera.	We don't want a leader that's going to sell our country off and change our flag.

Dola does not name politicians, but the song can be read as a critique of how CCM, the dominant political party, has governed. In one form or another, CCM has been in power in Tanzania since independence. To Dola, the policies of its government have exacerbated Tanzanians' problems:

I was really angry to see that CCM continued in their usual tradition of promising what they were not going to deliver. Sitting outside my home at Ilala [a district in Dar es Salaam], I started to look around me and see the improvised state that people live in—from muddy houses with thatched straws to brick houses with no lights, dirt all over the place. Most live off selling vegetables and fruits that cost a few cents, and they will be lucky to earn $3 a day, not enough to feed an extended family of five to ten people. The government preaches that gospel of democracy and the promise of a better tomorrow, but they don't fully understand what it means.

(2004)

Blaming the CCM government for its lack of effort in assisting ordinary people, Dola's song references the wealth of the country that never reaches the majority of the city. Calling for change and new leadership, Dola implores citizens to evaluate the candidates for whom they vote. The line "Considering we have smart people to solve our problems" entreats Tanzanians to look for an intelligent leader, not one who simply follows the practices of previous administrations.

"Mwananchi" made an impact among radio listeners. The 2000 presidential elections had just ended, with CCM retaining power. Many people believed that the elections would perpetuate the problems of the past. Dola describes the song's reception after it was broadcast on radio:

> DJ LP played the song on Africa FM.[8] He asked callers to call in and say what they felt about the song. It was like a town-hall-meeting type of atmosphere, with a lot of angry people calling in to say that the policies of CCM were not working, and accusing leaders of being corrupt and incompetent to lead. LP had to switch the topic because it started to get out of hand.
>
> (2004)

Although most rappers believe that they are free to state their opinions in rhythm, none directly mentions individuals or political parties in their lyrics. The same can be said of radio announcers. With the wave of angry callers, DJ LP most likely feared negative repercussions from airing so many criticisms of CCM. Since several radio stations in Dar es Salaam are owned by businessmen who support CCM or rely on CCM's support to advance their business concerns, DJ LP was unlikely to allow such explicit commentary to be heard on his show. Nonetheless, the effect of Dola's song was clear within the first few minutes of the broadcast: it formed a bond among those youth who blamed CCM for many of the country's problems; and it created an outlet for listeners to voice their views of the country's political leaders.

After the 2000 presidential election, drawing listeners' attention to a song by listing problems with government policies and practices became more difficult. Artists could still rap about corruption, political negligence, and misguided governance, but they needed to present these ideas in new ways. In the early 2000s, one of the best ways to critique politics, as well as social and economic situations, was through humor. Humor allowed artists to continue to make *ujumbe mkali*, while listeners could laugh at the absurdity of the country's political environment.

One popular Tanzanian rap that mixed politics with humor was "Ndio Mzee" ("Yes Elder"), by Professor Jay. In the song, Professor Jay acts as a knowledgeable elder proposing numerous ways to transform the country and rid it of its problems (Jay 2001b). Youth commonly call one another by the term *mzee*, which means "elder" in Kiswahili: in a subtle alteration of language, they appropriate the social power of being called *mzee*. In "Ndio Mzee," however, Jay becomes a real elder (someone senior in age) and a politician, to highlight what he sees as the inadequacies of the country's leaders. The song shows the falseness and absurdity of real elders' promises. In the transcription and translation below, the voice of the elder politician appears without quotes, while the answer of a group of supporters appears in quotes.

Professor Jay "Ndio Mzee" ("Yes, Elder")	
Nipe hiyo nafasi jamani Hamuoni hali ni mbaya? Nataka kuigeuza Tanzania kama Ulaya. Cha kwanza nitakachikifanya, nitafuta umasikini.	I would like to take this opportunity my friends Can't you see how bad things are? I would like to change Tanzania to be like Europe. The first thing that I will do is abolish poverty.

Wanafunzi mtafanyia practical mwezini.	Students will do their practical on the moon.
Kwenye mahospitali, nitamwaga dawa kama mchanga.	In the hospital, I will put as much medicine as there is sand.
Nitafungua account kwa kila mtoto mchanga.	I will open [bank] accounts for every young child.
Mabomba yatatoa maji na maziwa nchi nzima.	Pipes will deliver water and milk to the entire country.
	Villagers will forgot [problems] with wells. I will help witchdoctors build airplanes.
Watu wa-vijijini watasahau habari za visima.	
Nitafadhili wachawi waweze kutengeneza ndege.	Every person will get theirs, conductors and ticket takers
Kila mtu awe na yake, makonda na wapiga debe.	I will make Tanzanians happy, "Yes Mzee."
Si mtafurahi waTanzania jamani, "Ndiyo Mzee."	. I am accepted, am I not? "Yes Mzee."
Si ni kweli nakubalika jamani, "Ndiyo Mzee."	So, I am your Savior my friends, "Yes Mzee."
Basi mimi Mkombozi wenu, Jama, "Ndiyo Mzee."	And I will get rid of all your problems, "Yes Mzee."
Na nitafuta shida zenu zote, "Ndiyo Mzee."	These things, they are infuriating, "Yes Mzee."
Hivi nanii, ni vijimambo, "Ndiyo Mzee."	And they really annoy me, "Yes Mzee."
Na vinanikera kweli kweli mimi, "Ndiyo Mzee."	So, things will change, okay? "Yes Mzee."
Basi hali itabadilika, sawa? "Ndiyo Mzee."	And, I will take the reins [as a political official) okay? "Yes Mzee."
Na hatamu tutaishika, okay? "Ndiyo Mzee."	

"Ndiyo Mzee" was extremely popular in Dar es Salaam in 2001, when it was released. It dominated airplay on many local radio stations, and the lyrics were repeated and sung by Tanzanian youth—a practice that often occurs when a song reflects common concerns. Having attended political speeches or heard them on the radio, many urban Tanzanians understood that politicians made extravagant promises during their campaigns, but these promises were rarely fulfilled, and only acted as a means for garnering votes or political support. While broken promises by politicians are certainly not isolated to Tanzanian polities, many Tanzanians have become cynical of their leaders' extravagant claims for fixing the country's problems. Professor Jay seizes on this cynicism to present a politician rallying support during a speech. In the opening verse, the politician makes confident statements about his political abilities. After recognizing the problems that exist, he tells his audience that he will bring major changes if elected. Along with turning Tanzania into Europe, he will bring milk, water, bank accounts, and medicine. The absurdity of his claims, with Tanzanians' real desire for some of them to materialize, creates the humor of the song.

Hip-hop lyrics help legitimize youth ideologies to the broader public, adults and elders. Often, this process is difficult to notice, as changes in perception are subtle and based on individual relations to a song. Occasionally, however, responses to rap lyrics surface in public spaces. In a speech in Mtwara, the south of Tanzania, President Benjamin Mkapa reportedly said there is no room in his government for people who have a policy of "ndio mzee."[9] The comment, received with great laughter at the meeting, used Professor Jay's song to make the point that politicians should no longer be able to make bold claims and exaggerate their abilities. Mkapa's speech emphasized the potential for rap lyrics to reach even the highest levels of government, thereby empowering the voices of youth. This remark pleased Professor Jay, who relished the fact that his words could have such a significant impact.[10]

Mkapa's use of Professor Jay's lyric can be viewed as a political tactic: he humorously acknowledged criticisms of his administration while commenting that people who make false promises were no longer allowed in his government, diffusing the tension created by public interest in the song. But does this mean that Professor Jay's rap will effect actual changes in the Mkapa administration? Unlikely. While public interest in "Ndio Mzee" was enough for Mkapa to take notice, the lyrics are only part of a movement for changes to be made in government: Tanzanian journalists, radio announcers, television personalities, businessmen, academics, and others take part in the dialogue supporting or criticizing the administration. Nonetheless, rap, as exemplified by "Ndio Mzee," is powerful enough to reach mass audiences quickly, influence people's (particularly youths') outlook on issues, and place pressures on various areas of Tanzanian society. Since freedom of speech has increased during the postsocialist period and youth control many areas of the media, rappers' lyrics quickly move into broader public spaces, encouraging comment and reaction. The effects of these lyrics depend on individual listeners. In certain circumstances, a well-articulated rap can strengthen the presence of youth voices, opinions, and ideologies in contemporary society.

Social Conditions

Rap songs that discuss politics are often angry and resentful; even the humorous ones have a resentful undertone. Though they do not blame any particular individual, there is a sense, as Mr. II states, that politics is a dirty game, one that will never become clean. Some nonpolitical Tanzanian hip-hop songs, however, present an even direr message. Rap songs about social conditions are often far grimmer than political commentary, since they add personal narratives that explore the harsher realities of living in urban Africa.

A prominent theme of raps about social conditions is unemployment. Songs such as Uswahili Matola's "Ajira kwa Vijana" ("Employment for Youth") and Juma Nature and AY's "Biashara ya Utumwe" ("Slave Business") comment on the difficulties of living in a city where youth are more likely to be seen on streetcorners than in workplaces. Several rap artists comment on Tanzanians' standards of living. Songs such as Wachuja Nafaka's "Dhiki" ("Hardships"), the Daznundaz's "Maji ya Shingo" ("Up to One's Neck"), and Hardmad's "Picha Halisi" ("The Real Picture") present listeners with some of the "realities" of growing up poor and in impoverished conditions.

Since the emergence of rap in Tanzania, artists have commented on AIDS. One of the most popular AIDS-oriented raps of the past few years has been Mwanafalsafa's "Alikufa kwa Ngoma" ("He Died of AIDS," 2002). Mwanafalsafa narrates the story of a youth who tells his friends to protect themselves from AIDS by using condoms. At the end of the song, however, the youth himself dies of AIDS. Even though he had told his friends to use condoms, he himself never had. In the video for the song, Mwanafalsafa is shown in a coffin, dramatizing the results of dying for sex.

In many raps about social issues, the past is presented through an idyllic lens of positivism, nationalism, and hopefulness. Professor Jay raps: "The current situation in Bongo [Tanzania] is not like the past (*Bongo ya sasa siyo ya mwaka arobaini na saba*)."[11] He goes on to list the country's problems (older women becoming prostitutes, youth fighting one another for jobs, and the lack of humanity and respect in Dar es Salaam), implying that these problems did not occur in the past. Other artists look to the United States or Europe as the solution to Tanzania's difficulties. In "Ingeuwa Vipi?" ("What Would it be Like?"), Mwanafalsafa asks: "What would it be like if Bongo was like New York?" The message of these and similar songs is that things were better in the past, or they are better in other countries. For these artists, Tanzania is in a state of economic and social decay, where the conditions of daily life are worse than at any other time in the country's recent history.

Many Tanzanian rap artists also examine class issues in their lyrics. Magangwe Mob consists of two artists, Inspekta Haroun and Luteni Kalama, both from Temeke. Using local vernacular and discussing life in the "ghetto," they voice underprivileged urban Tanzanians' concerns. Even their name comments on their musical agenda. Inspekta Haroun explains, "Gangwe is a patient person who endures many problems. We decided to call ourselves Magangwe Mob because, with our music, we are able to endure living in a tough environment" (2001). Music became a way to cope with the problems of living in the "ghetto," a term Haroun uses to refer to his home area.

The song "Mtoto wa Gheti Kali" ("Upper Class Girl") is an example of Magangwe Mob's attempt to compare lifestyles between the rich and the poor in Dar es Salaam. Inspekta Haroun, who wrote the lyrics, discusses his interest with an upper-class girl. Through the song, he discusses how he wants to speak with her, but does not know what to say; how her family owns many cars, but he does not even have a bike; how she wears all sorts of makeup, but he remains *gozigozi* (a black African); and, how he does not even have enough money to buy Big G (a type of cheap bubblegum, similar to the American Bazooka Joe). In one verse, he describes what would happen if the wealthy girl visited his home.

Magangwe Mob "Mtoto wa Gheti Kali" ("Upper Class Girl")	
Tatizo ni pale atakapohitaji kutembelea nyumbani wakati kwetu	The problem is when she'll want to see my home
Jumba la udongo, choo cha makuti, passport size,	Mud buildings, toilet made of thatch, passport size,
Ni tonye,	Tell me,
Ni tumkaribishe wapi?	Where do we welcome her?
Kwao kashazoea kuketi sofani,	At her home she is used to sitting on a sofa
Sitting room, varandani,	In a sitting room on a veranda,
Jicho kideoni,	Eyes on a television,
Msosi wa draft, self service,	Food presented buffet style,
Mboga saba kujisevia	Served with seven types of vegetables
Kwetu ngangari, dona bamia,	In my poverty stricken home, we peck at *dona* and okra.
Aaah ananipagawisha.	She make me crazy.

The language Haroun uses to explain his home is a humorous exploration of class. The passport-sized toilet refers to outdoor latrines where the user's head appears over the top of the thatch walls when she or he stands. The food consists of *dona*, a bad-tasting porridge made of corn flour and okra, a cheap vegetable. The women's home is lavish in comparison. Through using phrases and ideas drawn from poverty, Haroun uses language to heighten the class tension that is the focus of his rap. Listeners connect with these linguistic cues and acknowledge their proximity to the world that Haroun explores in rhyme.

Many of my Tanzanian male friends laughed hysterically while listening to "Mtoto wa Gheti Kali." They enjoyed repeating the lyrics as they confronted their fears of finding a girlfriend who would be willing to endure their poverty (many Tanzanian males believe that you cannot marry a women until you have a sufficient and steady income). On one evening, a group of us sat together and each started a line of the song. Before each person finished, everyone else had joined in reciting the lyric. By the time we arrived at a humorous moment—as when Haroun stutters upon first meeting the wealthy woman—the group broke into ecstatic laughter. Almost no other words were spoken except the lyrics of "Mtoto wa Gheti Kali." Magangwe Mob's rap became a voice for the concerns of many male youth. It created solidarity among mostly male lower-class residents of the city, who find their poverty to be a heavy weight on their ability not only to make a living, but also to engage in honest relationships.

Education is an important concern for Tanzanian youth. With failing schools, limited resources in classrooms, and teachers who fail the same national examinations that they teach to their students, youth are aware of the problems that exist in their schools (*The East African* 2001; Galabawa et al. 2000). Some raps about education, such as Mash Y's "Kisa cha Mwanafunzi" ("The Student's Story") and Jay Moe's "Maisha ya Boarding" ("Life of Boarding School"), explore the experiences of life in Tanzanian schools. Many praise other students while helping them understand the difficulties that can occur in the classroom. Other artists put more energy into critiquing the failures of the country's educational system. Joni Woka's "Walimu" ("Teachers") comments on the reasons teachers are unable to educate their students. Woka takes on the persona of a drunken teacher complaining about issues that teachers encounter.

Joni Woka "Walimu" ("Teachers")	
Walimu tuna hali ngumu.	We teachers have a hard life.
Na sisi tuna umuhimu.	But we are important.
Tutazua kitimutimu,	We will march and cause trouble,
Hadi Wizara ya Elimu.	All the way to the Ministry of Education,
…	…
Haki mnatetea walimu sijasikia.	I have not heard you defending teachers.
Hivi vilio vya walimu mnavisikia?	So you hear the teachers' cries?
Au mnaamua tu kuvichunia?	Or have you decided to ignore them?
Maisha yao duni mnachekelea.	You are happy with their poor standard of life.
Wakifanya biashara ndogo mnawakemea.	If they engage in some petty business you reprimand them.
Mshahara mdogo ataishi vipi huyu	With the small salary how will this teacher live
Kama si kuuza pipi na ubuyu?	If not by selling candies and tamarind?
Watoto wenu wanatukana darasani	Your children use profanities in class
Wanapiga walimu hawana kitu kichwani.	They beat up their teachers, but they have empty heads.
Hivi matatizo haya yataisha lini?	When will these problems end?
OK let us go kijijini.	OK let us go to the village.
Na hii inanitia uchungu moyoni.	And this causes pain in my heart.
Walimu watatu tu wapo shuleni.	There are only three teachers in the school.
Wagawane masomo waingie darasani.	They divide the classes and go to teach.
Wakati mitaani walimu wamejazana	While there are many teachers on the streets
Wakitoka vyuoni ajira hakuna.	When they graduate from college, there is no employment.
Ngoja niweke lilizo langu bayana:	Let me lay out my complaint in the open:
Bila walimu viongozi wangetoka wapi?	Without teachers how would we have gotten leaders?
Nauliza sasa mbona mnanyamaza?	I asked a question, why aren't you answering?

On paper, these lyrics sound angry, cold, and full of contempt, yet Woka minimizes their directness by slurring and slowing his words, just as a drunk person might. When he asks, "I asked a question. Why aren't you answering?" the effect is less confrontational than humorous. He even belches after the question, diffusing the sort of tension he expects to be building in the song.

Despite the tactics of defusing the confrontation, the rap still questions the commitment listeners have to the country's teachers. Why are teachers struggling with such low salaries? Why are so few teachers in the classroom and so many on the street? Given the state of education in Tanzania, Woka's questions have a strong impact. There are few teachers in the classroom. Most do not teach during regular class hours, as they hope to force students to pay for "tuition," which is after-school training. Many teachers take on additional jobs, such as selling goods on the street, leaving minimal time for classroom preparation and instruction. As a result, many students drop out of schools to earn an income, rather than spend money on school fees (Tripp 1997: 129–130). Those who remain in schools may learn little, or be left with, in Woka's words, "empty heads."

Women and Urban Society

Of all of the material that I placed in the social-conditions category, songs about the plight of women in urban society are the most controversial. Most Tanzanians agree that unemployment, poverty, class struggles, education, and AIDS are problems in their country; therefore, songs that discuss these issues are typically well received. But songs that discuss gender inequalities are far more divisive among general listeners. The attitude of many urban males in Dar es Salaam is that women are inferior, second-class citizens, who need to rely on men for guidance and support (Che-Mponda 1991); they view women as sex symbols and objects of desire. As a result, women often become victims of domestic violence and public beatings (Moyer 2003: chapter 8); some become prostitutes to gain financial independence, and many are excluded from the best and most lucrative jobs.

Even though many people in Dar es Salaam view women as inferior to men, Tanzania has organizations, media programming, and cultural groups that promote gender equality. Radio shows carry programs about women's ability to divorce, own property, and protect themselves in sexual encounters. Television shows teach youth about the roles that men and women need to play in protecting themselves from HIV/AIDS. Organizations such as the Tanzania Gender Networking Programme (TGNP) hold meetings, training workshops, and lectures on gender issues. These forums tend to debate issues respectfully and use education as a means to empower men and women to make changes. Several rappers, however, choose more confrontational tactics to transform local cultural practices and attack specific social elements that they believe need to be changed.

The first rap artist to confront the treatment of women in Tanzanian society openly and directly was Mr. II, whose song "Chini ya Miaka Kumi na Nane" ("Under the Age of 18") became the most popular rap in Tanzania in late 2000. It discusses the distress of a girl who becomes involved in transactional sex, and her subsequent status.

Mr. II
"Chini ya Miaka Kumi na Nane" ("Under the Age of 18")

Ana miaka chini ya kumi na nane	She is under 18 years old
Wanamwita malaya	They call her a prostitute
Kilio nikimtazama, macho yanatazama chini	Every time I look at her, her eyes are looking down
Hawezi kunitazama usoni.	She can't look at me in the face.
Ana uzuli moyoni.	She has beauty in her heart.

Hana tena furaha maishani.	She no longer has happiness in her life.
Sitamwita kwa jina nitamwita binti fulani.	I can't call her by name, I call her the daughter of so-and-so.
...	...
Kila na anapopita watu wanamtazama kama cinema.	Whenever she passes, people look at her like a movie.
Hataweza kurudi kwa baba na mama	She can't return to her father or mother.
Anaishi maisha mabaya.	She lives a bad life.
Hawamwita tena kwa jina, wanamwita malaya	They will not call her by name again; they will call her a prostitute.

The personal narrative style that Mr. II uses adds to the overall affect of the song. Through using his encounters with one girl, he personalizes the struggles that women endure. It is an effective means of making listeners understand that the plight of women is something real, something visible, and something human. In this way, listeners sympathize with the girl, or, at least, learn about the problems of young, female Tanzanians. Toward the end of the song, Mr. II speaks directly to women: "I will not call you bad names / I will not call you a prostitute. ... / Us men are uncivilized." He then quietly repeats the word *pole* "sorry". The point of the song is to illustrate the problems that young girls encounter and recognize that men need to change how they view and interact with women.

Since Mr. II was an important figure in Tanzanian society at the time he wrote the song, his words influenced people's conceptions of women. Radio shows, such as "Deiwaka" on Radio Uhuru and "Dr. Beat" on Clouds FM, aired the rap and discussed its meaning. Listeners called in and debated the importance of the song. Newspapers and magazines carried stories about Mr. II and his music (Ngahyoma 2001; Osiah 2001). Even though many of these outlets typically shied away from directly discussing the hardships that women face, Mr. II's narrative made a sensitive topic more accessible. People could ask, "What do you think about the woman that Mr. II encountered?" They did not need to describe women's shame or "bad life," but could instead use the encounter as a basis for debate.

Though many public dialogues about "Chini ya Miaka Kumi na Nane" raised questions about women's status in Tanzanian society, several radio personalities and authors misinterpreted the lyrics of the song. In an album review in the glossy rap magazine *Rockers*, Seer writes, "The fifth track admonishes our loose and way [*sic*] ward sisters from becoming *playa fodder*. A mere stiletto step away from the lows of prostitution and finally the slammer, all before their 18th birthday" (2000). Seer places the blame for prostitution on sexually active women who stray from social norms, implying that all women can easily become prostitutes. His interpretation highlights the Tanzanian difficulty in discussing gender issues, even with regard to a song meant to question specific cultural practices.

After "Chini ya Miaka Kumi na Nane," only a few artists rapped as directly and clearly about Tanzanian women's struggles. King Crazy GK rapped about young women's plight in "Sisters," and many others, including Professor Jay and Balozi Dola, included in their songs verses that discussed women's life in Dar es Salaam. Several years after Mr. II's song, female rappers began to address the situation. Their delay reflects the difficulties they face in becoming performers. Many who perform as entertainers in public are quickly labeled prostitutes (Perullo 2003). Girls are at a disadvantage when learning to rap, since, according to several artists, they are expected to return home after school to help with chores, while boys can do other things, such as practice rapping. Many families do not let their daughters out at night, when most rap concerts occur, for fear that something bad will happen to them. Therefore, female voices are often neglected in public discourses on social injustices.

Since 2001, however, several female artists, such as Ray C, Sista P, and Zay B, have become popular in the Tanzanian rap scene. Zay B, whose real name is Zainab Lipangile, has made a name for herself with tough, socially conscious lyrics. Having performed in clubs in Dar es Salaam, released an album (*Mama Afrika*, 2002), and earned the respect of many fans, she has used her music as a voice to empower Tanzanian women. One of her more poignant songs, "Mama Afrika" ("Mother Africa"), speaks directly to young women—sometimes called children (*watoto*) in the lyrics—and comments on their need to take control of their lives.

Zay B "Mama Afrika"	
Watoto wa kike wanabakwa	Girls are raped
Kwa ajili ya pipipipi na offa za Aqwa.	When they are offered gifts at Aqwa.
Tunadhalilisha na kuonekana chombo cha starehe.	We are demeaned like an object of pleasure.
Tujaribu kujitunza.	
Watoto wadogo msiende kutembea na wazee.	We should take care of ourselves.
	Children, do not walk with male elders.
Fuatini wosia, hiyo tabia isiendelee	
	Follow these orders so that these traits do not continue
Tujithamini na tujiheshimu.	We value and respect ourselves.
Tusikae nyuma tuzingatie elimu	Let's not fall behind, let's focus on our education
Wazazi tuwape heshima zao.	Parents should respect us.
Watoto tusiwatie wazimu	Children, let us not push adults to insanity.
Kujirusha poa hakuna noma kama kawaida,	There is nothing wrong with having fun,
Lakini unakuwa take care.	But, you should take care.
Siyo unacheza kama makinda	Don't act immature
Hasa mnaochipukia hamjui wapi mnakimbilia	Especially since, as you grow, you don't know where you are running to
Mnaleta mapepe, angalia	You bring about silliness, look out
Mnacheza na dunia.	You are playing with the world.
Ishi kijanjajanja.	Life is cunning.
Mtego unaotega unajifanya unajua	The trap you set for yourself, you will know
Shauri lako utaishia kuuza vitumbua.	It is your problem if you live to sell rice fritters.

The opening verse of "Mama Afrika" is striking for two reasons. First, the lyrics are bold and aggressive. Zay B warns "children" not to "walk" with elders (*to walk* is slang for "to have sex"). She notes that men give gifts to women in return for sex. Well-off men (*buzi*) provide women with gifts, including candy, food, drinks, and clothes.[12] They often give these gifts at clubs, such as the Aqwa. Zay B suggests that the gifts are insignificant, not worth the problems that sex can cause. Importantly, she uses the word *rape* to refer to the sexual act of wealthy men buying the sexual favors of young "children." Second, the opening verse attempts to unify women to take control of their lives. In the chorus of the song, Zay B calls all women of the continent "Mother Africa," and tells them to not fall behind, but to get a good education. She directs them to be careful and to not "play" around, since life is filled with traps. She ends the verse by telling women that the choice of their futures is in their hands: if they want to end up hawking cheap goods ("rice fritters") on the streets, that is a choice that *they* make. Unlike Mr. II, who blames men for mistreating women, Zay B tells women that the problems they encounter are due to their decisions. The better choices women make, the better able they will be to make a prosperous living.

Zay B wrote "Mama Afrika" to strengthen women's position in Tanzania. She says, "Many Tanzanian women are reticent and have no confidence. ... This song encouraged a lot of women to be stronger. Even men told me that they agreed with the song's message" (2005). Although her song was popular, few subsequent rappers have tackled similar issues so directly. (Even she has not released any new material since 2002.) Typically, a theme that becomes popular is recycled in numerous raps. Because of the tension that rap about gender can cause, up-and-coming artists are unlikely to release a song about women's social roles. Established rappers may not agree that gender is the most important issue to present in socially conscious rap, or that it even needs to be discussed. Further, many female artists find more success rapping about love, romance, and personal strength. Rap about gender equality is therefore bound to stay on the periphery of the Tanzanian hip-hop scene.

Reasons for *Ujumbe Mkali*

In many countries, rap has political and socially conscious lyrics. In Brazil, Senegal, South Africa, Japan, and the United States, rappers have turned the basic form—rhyming over beats—into a powerful voice for youth ideologies (Mitchell 2001; Watkins 2004). Part of the reason for this style of lyrics reflects the origins of the genre. During the 1970s in New York City, rap emerged as part of hip-hop culture, which included graffiti, breakdancing, and deejaying; essentially, it functioned to get people to dance, and was not a kind of "urban streetgeist" (Samuels 2004:148). As its popularity grew and it was disseminated through albums and concerts, its verbal meanings changed, and it engaged larger audiences of people, rather than just those on a dance floor (Dimitriadis 2001). Groups such as Public Enemy and Boogie Down Productions brought elements of urban, African-American lifestyles into public consciousness (Rose 1994: 11). This process attracted young people from various sociocultural backgrounds, nationally and internationally (Bennett 2004: 179). It produced lyrics that were political and commented directly on social issues.

It was around this time, the mid-1980s, that many Tanzanian youth first heard rap. Initially, mostly affluent youth had access to it, since they could rely on relatives and friends in Europe or the United States to send them albums and cassettes. These youth, such as Conway Francis and Fresh X, either mimicked the American rap they heard, or wrote raps that reflected the ideas on the albums. By the late 1980s, youth from all over Tanzania had become interested in rap, particularly as the copying of albums and cassettes had become prevalent. Since many Tanzanians heard the music of rappers who spoke about daily life (performers such as Public Enemy, KRS-One, and NWA), they brought this element into their own musical compositions. Professor Jay explains:

I started to rap in O level, when I was in the seventh grade. In 1989, there were many different styles of rap music being heard in Tanzania. During this time, I listened to rap such as Public Enemy's "Fight the Power." This music really drew me straightaway to become a rapper because I saw the way that a black man was able to search for his own thing [identity]. Public Enemy had the power to stand somewhere and speak with people. Those people listened to what the group had to say, and followed their message, so it was this type of thing that drew me to rap—people such as Public Enemy, L. L. Cool J, KRS-One, and others like that.

(2001a)

A few years later, as lyrics started to be composed in Kiswahili rather than English, Tanzanians relied less on the lyrical content of American rap; instead, they localized rap with ideas and themes that exemplified their own struggles. The combination of linguistic changes and the localization of lyrics allowed Tanzanian rap to appeal to a broad audience throughout Tanzania.

Aside from the influence of American rap, the Dar es Salaam music scene plays an important role in shaping the content of rap lyrics. To receive airtime or a distribution contract, artists often have to listen to the advice of deejays, record producers, and, less commonly, record distributors. The leaders of this industry, many of whom are youth themselves, enforce strict guidelines for rap lyrics. Songs have to be about important social issues, make sense to local listeners, and avoid the topics of violence and sex. John Dilinga, a radio announcer on East Africa FM (a Tanzanian radio station), explains: "If I know you and your music is bad—that is, if it does not make any sense to society—I do not play it. If I think that it is leading society astray, I do not play it. If I think that it is educating society, I play it and promote it" (2002). Since deejays act as gatekeepers and thereby greatly influence the success and popularity of songs, rappers need to be sure that some of the content that they submit to radio shows is socially or culturally significant.

To avoid cursing is also an important part of the local rap scene, since most Tanzanians consider swearing unacceptable in public. Taji Liundi, manager and radio announcer at Times FM, explains why Tanzanian rappers do not swear, even though their American counterparts do:

> That is because from the very beginning I was the only one playing hip hop on radio and I decided that I am not going to put on the songs with the explicit content. If they [the artists] brought music in that had cursing, I would not play it. And at concerts, I would get them off the stage, make a lot of noise, and look disappointed.
>
> (2000)

Tanzanian rappers, fans, and radio announcers discourage the use of profanity or vulgar language in hip-hop songs. The rap community usually ignores artists who curse in English, and no one, to my knowledge, has rapped a song in Kiswahili with vulgar lyrics (although several groups have had their songs pulled from the radio because people thought the content too strong). As Liundi points out, the rap community is direct about discouraging vulgarity in rap because it distracts from the message in the song.

Tanzania's socialist past also affects contemporary rap music. Although socialism officially ended in the 1980s, it remains an important influence on local cultural and educational practices. Many musicians view their role in society as educators of the public—a conception that was greatly strengthened during the socialist period. Tanzanian rappers adopted this "educational voice" in an attempt to legitimize their music to a wider community and form an outlet for youth voices. An "educational voice" allows youth to disrupt conceptions that people have of youth as hooligans.

In commenting on the need for more educational music, Wilfred Edwin writes in the Tanzanian newspaper *Business Times*, "Musicians have failed to utilize the opportunity by informing and educate [sic] their audience, but have some [sic] how managed to dwindle and misinform them. Those old goldies taught us a great deal of lessons. Even if one would not know what is happening, he was likely to be told through the music" (2003: 10). Edwin comments that "old goldies," which generally means songs written after independence and during the socialist period, were far more educational than contemporary music; several rap groups, however, are an exception: "Thanks to some of the hip hop and rap musicians like Wagosi wa Kaya, Johnnie Walker and Mr. Ebbo for delivering to the mass [sic] current and vibrant messages which educate their audience. They should keep the spirits up" (Edwin 2003: 10).[13] Many other Tanzanians, particularly those of the generations that grew up under socialism, similarly conceive of music. It is this audience, as well as the country's young people, that youth hope to reach when incorporating educational issues in their music.

Conclusion

Rap has become popular all over Africa, and has availed youth on the continent opportunities to create their own identities as popular musicians. Almost anyone can participate in the genre, since it is both cheap (i.e., does not require instruments) and widely accessible (on radio, television, schools, and clubs). In Tanzania, it dominates the daily lives of many urban youth. Though many Tanzanians still see it as a music for hooligans, no other occupation has lifted youth so dramatically out of poverty into wealth and fame. Several Tanzanian rappers have become wealthy and bought new cars, homes, and fancy clothes; several groups have traveled to Europe, the United States, and other areas of East Africa. For people growing up in Tanzania, those who find success in rap are far from hooligans: they are role models and knowledge holders, who openly discuss the problems that Tanzanian youth encounter.

This conclusion does not imply that Tanzanian youth hold a unified vision for their country. As several authors have commented in other contexts, "It should be clear that 'youth' is not seen as a unified entity with a collective consciousness in pursuit of clearly defined objectives" (Van Zyl Slabbert et al. 1994: 15). Tanzanian youth are no exception. They frequently disagree on many issues, both in lyrics and in conversation. They often debate topics and, though rarely, have slandered one another in song. Tanzanian rap lyrics are not always about political or social issues: nearly the same number of artists currently release material about partying, dancing, and love as they do with *ujumbe mkali.*

For many Tanzanian youth, rap songs with *ujumbe mkali* exist to destroy stereotypical notions of youth culture, solidify and strengthen local communities, and correct problems that appear in everyday life. As an empowering form of legitimization, rap gives voice to many youth, often labeled as marginal, violent, or lost. And while these labels have meaning in certain contexts, the labels *creative, empowered,* and *socially conscious* are important to comprehend the state of contemporary youth in Africa. KR, a rapper from the groups G.W.M. and Wachuja Nafaka, states, "Rappers are modern poets because whatever they write is able to shake up the minds of even older people. That is why I can say that now, here in Bongo [Tanzania], rap music is more popular than any other genre" (2000).

Study Questions

1. How does rap function as a communicative medium?
2. How is humor in hip-hop important as a means of challenging authority and critiquing social norms in Tanzania?
3. In what ways is rap constituted as a legitimate voice among Tanzanian youth?

Notes

1. One author reported that unemployment in Tanzania is at 13 percent (Mihayo 2003). Not only is it unclear how Mihayo arrived at this statistic, but it seems improbably low. A significant percentage of employment in Tanzania is in the informal sector. Formal employment is limited—which would make unemployment figures much higher than 13 percent; unemployment in Tanzania is likelier nearer to Kenya's 40 percent.

2. In this chapter, I use the term *youth* to translate the Kiswahili word *kijana*. Generally, *kijana* refers to any young person between the ages of 15 and 30, but it can also refer to unmarried older individuals.

3. Tanzania African National Union (TANU) was the government's political party between 1961 and 1977. After merging with the Zanzibar Afro-Shirazi Party (ASP), it became the Chama cha Mapinduzi (CCM) or the Revolutionary Party.

4. Several artists traveled outside of Tanzania to record their music. Also, during the 1980s, the Tanzania Film Company (TFC) recorded music in Tanzania.

5. Culturally, many practices remained rooted in socialist ideology. The economic transition toward capitalism and the tendency to maintain socialist ideologies in cultural and political affairs is best termed postsocialism. The movement from socialism to postsocialism (rather than socialism to capitalism) has occurred in several formerly socialist countries in Eastern Europe (Verdery 1996). Elsewhere, I provide a more detailed discussion of postsocialism in Tanzania (Perullo 2003).

6. The Judge is played by Balozi Dola, a Tanzanian rapper, whose voice was modified to make it sound deeper and more threatening. The initial announcement of the court case is the voice of rapper Saigon.

7. *Bongo* literally means "wisdom", but is slang for "(1) the knowledge and skills needed to survive in difficult circumstances; (2) the city of Dar es Salaam; (3) Tanzania." in this example, Mr. II is referring to Tanzania, where people need wisdom to survive. Tanzanian rap is often called *bongo flava* "the flavor of *Bongo*."

8. The names of the deejay and the radio station have been changed for this article.

9. The reports of this speech come from several journalists in Tanzania, including Charles Mateso and James Nindi.

10. Several other rap groups have even been offered gifts by politicians who want to thank the artists for their work. The regional commissioner of Tanga, George Mkuchika, and the regional commissioner of Dar es Salaam, Yusuph Makamba, separately invited the group Wagosi wa Kaya to dinner events to thank them for their music.

11. The phrase *mwaka arobiana na saba* "the year 1947" is slang for the past, and does not refer specifically to the year 1947.

12. *Buzi* literally means "goat" but is slang for a male lover who provides financial support for a woman in exchange for sex. For a discussion of *buzi*, see Moyer 2003.

13. Joni Woka's name is occasionally written *Johnnie Walker*.

References

Andersson, C., and A. Stavrou. 2001. *Youth Delinquency and the Criminal Justice System in Tanzania.* Nairobi: UN Printshop.

Askew, Kelly. 2002. *Performing the Nation: Swahili Music and Cultural Politics in Tanzania.* Chicago: University of Chicago Press.

Bennett, Andy. 2004. Hip-Hop Am Main, Rappin' on the Tyne: Hip-Hop Culture as a Local Construct in Two European Cities. In *That's the Joint!: The Hip-Hop Studies Reader,* edited by Murray Forman and Mark Anthony Neal. New York: Routledge.

Bucholtz, Mary. 2002. Youth and Cultural Practice. *Annual Review of Anthropology* 31: 525–552.

Burton, Andrew. 2000. Wahuni (The Undesirables): African Urbanization, Crime, and Colonial Order in Dar es Salaam, 1919–1961. Ph.D. diss., University of London.

———. 2005. *African Underclass: Urbanisation, Crime, and Colonial Order in Dar es Salaam.* Athens: Ohio University Press.

———. Forthcoming. The Haven of Peace Purged: Tackling the Undesirable and Unproductive Poor in Dar es Salaam, c. 1950s–80s. In *The Emperor's New Clothes? Continuity and Change in Late Colonial and Early Postcolonial East Africa,* edited by Andrew Burton and Michael Jennings.

Che-Mponda, Chemi. 1991. Women in Africa, a Second-Class Life. *Seattle Times* (22 September).

Dilinga, John. 2002. Interview by author. Dar es Salaam, Tanzania, 4 July.

Dimitriadis, Greg. 2001. *Performing Identity/Performing Culture: Hip Hop as Text, Pedagogy, and Lived Practice.* New York: Peter Lang.

Dola, Balozi. 2001. *Ubalozini.* Audiocassette. Dar es Salaam,Tanzania: GMC.

———. 2004. Interview by author. New York City. 1 November.

The East African. 1999. Letter to the Editor. 5–12 July.

———. 2001. Teachers' Exam Shocker for Dar. 23–29 April.

Edwin, Wilfred. 2003. Arts as a Mirror of Society: Whither our Musicians? *Business Times.* 23 May.

Fair, Laira. 2001. *Pastimes and Politics: Culture, Community, and Identity in Post-Revolution Zanzibar, 1890–1945.* Athens: Ohio University Press.

Galabawa, J.C. J., F. E. M. K. Senkoro, and A. F. Lwaitama, eds. 2000. *Quality of Education in Tanzania*. Dar es Salaam, Tanzania: Faculty of Education, University of Dar es Salaam.

Graebner, Werner. 2000. *Ngoma ya Ukae*: Competitive Social Structure in Tanzanian Dance Music Songs. In *Mashindano! Competitive Music Performance in East Africa*, edited by Frank Gunderson and Gregory Barz. Dar es Salaam, Tanzania: Mkuki na Nyota.

———. Forthcoming. Club to Nightclub: Music Entertainment in Dar es Salaam. In *Dar es Salaam: The History of an Emerging East African Metropolis*, edited by Andrew Burton, James Brennan, and Yusuf Lawi.

Haroun, Inspekta. 2001. Interview by author. Dar es Salaam, Tanzania, 16 January.

Jay, Professor. 2001a. Interview by author. Tanga, Tanzania, 19 January.

———. 2001 b. *Machozi, Jasho, na Damu*. Audiocassette. Dar es Salaam, Tanzania: FKW.

Keyes, Cheryl. 2002. *Rap Music and Street Consciousness*. Urbana, Illinois: University of Illinois Press.

Knappert, Jan. 1979. *Four Centuries of Swahili Verse: A Literary History and Anthology*. London: Heinemann.

———. 1983. Swahili Songs with Double Entendre. *Afrika und Übersee* 66(1): 67–76.

KR (Rashidi Ziada). 2000. Interview by author. Dar es Salaam, Tanzania, 9 November.

Liundi, Taji. 2000. Interview by author, Dar es Salaam, Tanzania, 23 October.

Lugalla, Joe. 1995. *Crisis, Urbanization, and Urban Poverty in Tanzania: A Study of Urban Poverty in Tanzania*. Lanham: University Press of America.

MacDonald, Robert. 1997. Dangerous Youth and the Dangerous Class. In *Youth, the "Underclass" and Social Exclusion*, edited by Robert MacDonald. London and New York: Routledge.

Magangwe Mob. 2001. *Simulizi la Ufasaba*. Audiocassette. Dar es Salaam: GMC.

Mallan, Kerry, and Sharyn Pearce, eds. 2000. *Youth Cultures: Texts, Images, and Identities*. Westport: Praeger.

Martin, Stephen. 1980. "Music in Urban East Africa: A Study of the Development of Urban Jazz in Dar es Salaam." Ph.D. diss., University of Washington.

Mateso, Charles. 2000. Rap: Ukombozi, uhuni, fujo au laana kwa vijana. *Tanzania Leo*. 2 October.

Mihayo, Robert. 2003. Vexing questions about Tanzania's labor market remain unanswered. *Business Times*, 5 September.

Miranda, Dave, and Michel Claes. 2004. Rap Music Genres and Deviant Behaviors in French-Canadian Adolescents. *Journal of Youth and Adolescence* 33(2): 113–122.

Mr. II (Joseph Mbilinyi). 1998. *Niite Mr. II*. Audiocassette. Dar es Salaam: FM Music Bank.

———. 2000a. Interview by author. Dar es Salaam, Tanzania. 6 November.

———. 2000b. *Millenia* [sic]. MJ Production. Audiocassette. Dar es Salaam: GMC.

Mitchell, Tony, ed. 2001. *Global Noise: Rap and Hip-hop outside the USA*. Middletown: Wesleyan University Press.

Moyer, Eileen. 2003. In the Shadow of the Sheraton: Imagining Localities in Global Spaces in Dar es Salaam, Tanzania. Ph.D. diss., University of Amsterdam.

Mwanafalsafa. *2002. Mwanafalsafani*. Audiocassette. Dar es Salaam: GMC.

Ngahyoma, John. 2001. Muziki na Mister II. *Kitangoma* 1 (1): 16–19.

Nindi, James. 2001. Jay. *Mwananchi* (13 September).

O'Brien, Donal B. Cruise. 1996. A Lost Generation? Youth Identity and State Decay in West Africa. In *Postcolonial Identities in Africa*, edited by Richard Werbner and Terence Ranger. London: Zed Books.

Osiah, Angetile. 2001. Muziki na Maisha leo Uwe na kila Rapa. *Nipashe*. 30 March.

Perullo, Alex. 2003. "The Life that I Live": Popular Music, Urban Practices, and Agency in Dar es Salaam, Tanzania. Ph.D. diss., Indiana University.

———. Forthcoming. "Here's a Little Something Local": An Early History of Hip Hop in Dar es Salaam, Tanzania, 1984–1997. In *Dar es Salaam: The History of an Emerging East African Metropolis*, edited by Andrew Burton, James Brennan, and Yusuf Lawi.

Perullo, Alex, and John Fenn. 2003. Language Ideologies, Choices, and Practices in Eastern African Hip Hop. In *Global Popular Music: The Politics and Aesthetics of Language Choice*, edited by Harry M. Berger and Michael Thomas Carrol. Jackson: University Press of Mississippi.

Rose, Tricia. 1994. *Black Noise: Rap Music and Black Culture in Contemporary America*. Hanover, N.H.: University Press of New England.

Samuels, David. 2004. The Rap on Rap: The 'Black Music' That Isn't Either. In *That's the Joint!: The Hip-hop Studies Reader*, edited by Murray Forman and Mark Anthony Neal. New York: Routledge.

Seekings, Jeremy. 1993. *Heroes or Villains? Youth Politics in the 1980s*. Braamfontein, South Africa: Raven Press.

Seer. 2000. Review of *Millenia* [sic], by Mr II. *Rockers* 4: 10.

Tripp, Aili Mari. 1997. *Changing the Rules: The Politics of Liberalization and the Urban Informal Economy in Tanzania*. Berkeley: University of California Press.

Van Zyl Slabbert, F., Charles Malan, Hendrik Marais, Johan Olivier, and Rory Riordan, eds. 1994. *Youth in the New South Africa: Toward Policy Formulation.* Main Report of the Co-Operative Research Programme: South African Youth. Pretoria: HSRC.

Verdery, Katherine. 1996. *What Was Socialism, and What Comes Next?* Princeton: Princeton University Press.

Watkins, Lee. 2004. Rapp'in'the Cape: Style and Memory, Power in Community. In *Music, Space, and Place: Popular Music and Cultural Identity*, edited by Sheila Whiteley, Andy Bennett, and Stan Hawkins. Burlington, Vermont: Ashgate Publishing.

Whiteley, Sheila. 2004. Rap and Hip Hop: Community and Cultural Identity. In *Music, Space, and Place: Popular Music and Cultural Identity*, edited by Sheila Whiteley, Andy Bennett, and Stan Hawkins. Burlington, Vermont: Ashgate Publishing.

Zay B (Zainab Lipangile). 2002. *Mama Afrika.* Audiocassette. Dar es Salaam: GMC.

———. 2005. Telephone interview by author. 12 February.

21

Native Tongues
A Roundtable on Hip-Hop's Global Indigenous Movement

This fascinating roundtable discussion brings together indigenous hip-hop artists and community activists from four continents. They are influenced by their tribal legacies and draw inspiration and sustenance from their cultural traditions yet they remain resolutely committed to addressing contemporary themes and issues that most directly affect First Nations youth within their local contexts. Moreover, the discussion reflects a pronounced hybridity wherein hip-hop is merged with established tribal elements producing new narrative and aesthetic forms and alternative modes of articulation and movement that ingeniously link the present and the past; hip-hop crews and posses emerge as "a new kind of tribe." Each individual explains how tribal values and customs often collide with idiosyncratic social conventions in their home environment yet hip-hop's flexibility enables direct engagement within idiosyncratic systems of power and authority. Ultimately hip-hop is mobilized in a series of negotiations involving differences between tribal and non-tribal cultures, between rural and urban environments, and between youth and adult populations.

Native Tongues: A Roundtable on Hip-Hop's Global Indigenous Movement

A Roundtable Curated by Cristina Verán, with Darryl "DLT" Thompson, Litefoot, Grant Leigh Saunders, Mohammed Yunus Rafiq, and Jaas

New York City has long called out to a whole host of displaced "tribes," infusing the local culture with new ideas, social norms, and cultural practices. Once upon a rhyme, Bronx originals Soulsonic Force moved nations with the Zulu funk of *Planet Rock*, and Harlem's native sons Spoonie Gee & The Treacherous Three heralded *The New Rap Language*. Into this polyglot gumbo of aesthetics in performance, presentation, and expression today, Indigenous youth around the world are rocking the planet anew, fusing hip-hop's expressive elements of MCing, DJing, b-boying, and aerosol graffiti art with their own traditions of oratory, music, drumming, dance, and the visual arts. Make way for the new rap language(s) of this generation's most potent and expansive youth "tribe."

Rap lends itself as a motivational force and context in the promulgation of indigenous languages and group identity, for peoples as diverse as the Maluku of Indonesia to the Sami of Norway. Culturally significant sources too—think whale calls, as employed by Greenlandic Inuit DJs from the tundra-fied streets of Nuuk—provide rich soundscapes to remix infinitely. In Mexico City, meanwhile, hip-hop-style graffiti art (re)connects urban mestizo (the mixed-race, nontraditional-Indian mainstream) kids with their artistic patrimony and iconography from grand Aztec and Teotihuacán mural traditions. Even Diná (Navajo) b-boys on the rez have related the corporeal movements and rhythms of breaking and uprocking with their own styles of more traditional powwow dancing since the early 1980s.

Here are five Indigenous hip-hop artists and thinkers, from the United States, Chile, Australia, Tanzania, and New Zealand, representing both the pioneers and the latest vanguard of an urban Native aesthetic movement. Their work parallels the global rise of Indigenous Peoples' political and social activism and organizing, a ripe, fertile ground in which the seeds of hip-hop are thriving, strengthening its voice and spreading native pride to the beat of a proverbial new drum.

The Panelists

Darryl "DLT" Thompson is a pioneering DJ, b-boy, MC, and graffiti artist in Aotearoa/New Zealand and a founding member of Upper Hutt Posse. His staunch Maori-conscious vision and contributions *to* hip-hop culture in the Pacific set the bar high for Indigenous artists around the world. Of the Ngati Kahungunu tribe, he resides in the city of Auckland, where he continues to represent for the cause as a music producer, visual artist, and arts educator, as well as a hip-hop radio host.

Litefoot is the premier Native American rap artist promoting music-with-a-message, representing hip-hop and the Cherokee Nation of Oklahoma. As an actor, he starred in the feature film

The Indian in the Cupboard and has appeared in numerous big- and small-screen productions. Also an entrepreneur, he founded Red Vinyl Records as a home base for top hip-hop artists throughout Indian Country and today helms Native Style Entertainment and Clothing while visiting hundreds of reservations each year with his Reach the Rez tour.

Grant Leigh Saunders has been a devoted b-boy and MC since 1983, first catching the groove as a junior high student near Taree Township, New South Wales. He is Koori, from the Biripi tribal group; a Katang-language-speaking Aboriginal people of Australia. His documentary, *B.L.A.C.K.: An Aboriginal Song of Hip-Hop*, explores the history and impact of hip-hop among Indigenous Australians, as does the master's thesis he completed at Macquarie University: "D Hip-Hop Bakehouse: Indigenous Mob Hip-Hop & the Silenced Revolutionaries."

Mohammed Yunus Rafiq is a core member of Tanzania's Maasai Hip-Hop collective and the internationally renowned group X-Plastaz, promoting Indigenous pride that confronts neocolonial Black African mainstream societies and governments that have taken the place of the Great White Hunters of the past. A poet and music producer of Segeju origin (he is also of Punjabi/Kashmiri descent), he also cofounded Aang Serian, which provides culturally relevant educational opportunities for community development in the city of Arusha, as well as the Faza Neli Community Recording Studios, supporting the efforts of local hip-hop artists.

Jaas is a hip-hop artist in Santiago, Chile, proudly invoking her Mapuche roots in a country whose mainstream has long marginalized its Indigenous Peoples and their vibrant heritage. She raps in both Spanish and Mapudungun (the Mapuche language), with songs and videos that educate and serve as a call to young Mapuche to awaken and actively engage in the struggle to assert and maintain their land and cultural rights in Chile.

CRISTINA: I'd like to get a sense of what, in some of your communities, was the initial appeal of hip-hop? What kind of response did it receive?

DLT: Well, first of all, hip-hop offered a lot of reaffirmations for young Maori. Back in the early '80s, Afrika Bambaataa was talking "tribalism," and his whole Zulu Nation hip-hop thing turned all us Maori kids on to a *new* kind of tribe. It was like, hey, even scalawags like us could work together and build a new kind of village. That's what our early hip-hop crews became for us. Rap, specifically, was like this media created by other "have-nots," like us, and we could see that the averages of truths it spoke were higher than all that white, Western brainwash media out there.

LITEFOOT: Who I am as a human being in my culture, in my traditions as a Cherokee? That comes first, before anything else that I do, and through hip-hop I found another way of representing that to the fullest, every single day. When I first started doing shows for different tribes, someone there might get up to do a jingle dance. Another person might do a country music song, while someone else would play a traditional flute. Then I would go and do an hour or rap. In the beginning, the traditional drummers and singers would just look at me like, "Come on, man. This is a powwow." A lot of the elders complained, too, but I worked very hard to dispel some of the negative stereotypes about hip-hop that were held by many tribal leaders.

GRANT: In Australia, during the late '70s and early '80s, there was literally nothing on TV or radio representing Black *Australian* [that is, Aboriginal] aesthetics. Hip-hop, with its brown faces and voices, came and really filled a void, this lack of visibility and representation we felt in the media. It was very empowering, even politicizing, to see, and it gave us a framework in which to express pride in our Blackness—not as African Americans, of course, but as Aboriginal Australians and, in my case, as Koori. Early on, tracks like "The Message" really spoke to us, talking about the scenario of abject poverty in the States. It sounded a lot like what my extended family was living through, on the Aboriginal mission reserve outside Taree. At that time in particular, it was really all about identity politics for Aboriginal people.

YUNUS: When hip-hop arrived in Tanzania, it was like the sons and daughters of the land being welcomed back home, introduced back to the families, clans, and tribes. At the same time, it came to us like a needed rain when the earth is dry, bringing a new voice, new ideas. Its rain fell and transformed the land; those who resist the changing cosmic waters now face being swept away in its powerful torrents. If our cultures are going to survive, though, young people have to take it from this generation to the next—and hip-hop is making this possible. We can be tribal, and at the same time, we can also be global! It's opened more communication channels for us than if we only spoke through the traditional forms, because almost everyone listens to hip-hop. It's like a forest, this wild territory where we can go out and scream and scream, to talk about our dreams, vent our frustrations, and express who we are.

JAAS: I actually live in the community of San Joaquin, in metropolitan Santiago, and so my hip-hop awakening happened here—not in a Mapuche village. My mother's family comes from the pueblo of Los Angeles in the south of Chile, and my Mapuche roots are especially strong from this side. I'd always been encouraged to connect with our people there, and also to seek out those like us who are urbanized. Back in '95 or so, during this especially big hip-hop boom in Chile, I became very curious and would seek it out, going to all the places that hip-hop people would hang. Very quickly, I found myself moving in these circles of people who'd already been living hip-hop for years: the real b-boys, graffiti writers deep into the movement. With my own eyes, I saw how big this thing was … wow. I connected with it so much.

Around the same time, I also went to spend time in Temuco, in southern Chile, where I found myself as inspired to connect more to my Mapuche roots as I was connecting to hip-hop. I was curious about how the two worlds could possibly come together.

CRISTINA: What, if any, are some examples of your own Indigenous cultural practices that might themselves, perhaps, be evocative of hip-hop in some way, in terms of energy or form?

YUNUS: As with many East African oral performances, such as the Maasai *osongolios* and the *kuimbana* among the Swahili, the style of dialogue or talk in hip-hop is a similar convention. Our storytelling is done through an oral tradition, so songs—like raps—are like our books, used as media to criticize, to advocate, to relax, to entertain.

DLT: Maori youth are raised on *kapa haka*, a kind of performance battle which can also be like clowning, at times. In form, it's about moving your body; you gesture with your facial features, with your tongue protruding, making certain hand gestures and stomping your feet, all kinds of body language to make yourself, in a sense, bigger than you are. It says, "We are these proud people," while warning, "Fuck with me and I'll tear your throat out!" It's so like b-boying, really, and so we relate to it because we're into the challenge.

The *wero*, too, is a Maori ceremonial challenge presented in the first initial meeting on the *marae*—which is like a church, a spiritual safe ground—between a local tribe and a visiting group. Entering the *marae* during a ceremony is like engaging in a Shakespearean drama, and you have to be conscious and cautionary of ulterior motives and political maneuvers under the surface. When the *wero* begins, there's a thirty- to forty-foot gap between the visitors and the people of that *marae*. The fastest warrior of the tribe comes out carrying his weapon, while addressing the guests with a token gesture—usually a leaf of a tree or a branch. He must grab their attention in this ritual, this *wero*. In b-boy language, you could say he has to rock a routine. In doing so, he's representing many different forces of nature, changing his form, in essence. He may become like a *pukeko* [bird], while another might instead become a lizard—and enact that for the whole routine, giving it his all. A representative of the visitors then steps forward to pick up the gift to indicate an acceptance of the greeting, and then backs up to the group, which is led onto the *marae atia*, a kind of sacred space where both sides can come together under *kawa*—the law of the particular *marae*.

And so, for Maori kids, hip-hop's dancing, rhyming, piecing … these elements became a new way to go out there and do the *wero* to society, to confront this larger adversary and stare it down.

GRANT: The whole "cipher" concept in hip-hop in particular is, for us, a contemporary context for our traditional storytelling circles, where we as Aboriginal people would sit around a campfire and exchange stories—more egalitarian than a straight-up battle. You'd talk about who you are and where you're from, and about important or interesting things that have happened to you. There was an implicit contract between listener and speaker. The listener would verify what was being said at various points in the telling, like, "Oh, yeah, that's true. That part's true." Or else, it'll be more like, "Nah, you don't know what you're talking about. Go back to your place."

CRISTINA: How have Indigenous cultural practices and aesthetics directly influenced, perhaps even fused with, the kind of hip-hop being produced from and for your communities?

JAAS: For some hip-hop tracks, you might hear the sounds of some Mapuche instruments, like this certain kind of trumpet and the *chicluca*, into it. Graffiti artists, too, represent the *kultrung* symbol in their pieces, which indicates the heart of the people, the *tambor* of the street.

The idea to make a video for my song "Newen," in Mapudungun and Spanish, came about during a recent trip back to Temuco, in the south. The Mapuche community there was very enthusiastic about this, and they helped me with the ideas and whatever they could. We filmed half of it there, in the community, and then we went to Santiago to do the second part. We wanted to show the differences—and the links, too—between the country-side and the city experience of Mapuche, to give people a better understanding of how and why I represent as not only a hip-hopper but as Mapuche *in* hip-hop, how it's all linked together.

GRANT: In Australia, some of us adapted our own indigenous dances' movements to hip-hop—like the "shake-a-leg," for example—reappropriating them in a b-boy context to make it more Koori flavored. Many tribes here, especially on the east coast, are known for the shake-a-leg, which involves a sort of stomping on the ground, shaking your knees in and out while moving toward an audience or toward another dancer. Till today, this move's incorporated in our styles of breaking.

Musically speaking, hip-hop artists are using clapsticks, the traditional rhythm instruments among tribal groups throughout New South Wales. The didgeridoo has also been used to provide rhythm in Indigenous hip-hop music, because of its ability to emulate many different sounds through certain vocal and tongue acrobatics. A good didg performer can even reproduce the sounds of a turntablist scratching! The group Local Knowledge provides a segment in their live acts where there's a duel between rapper Abie on didg and the DJ on turntables. These sounds have also crept into tracks produced for other Aboriginal groups like MC Murris and the Barkendji Boys.

DLT: There's a quintessential Maori flavor, a Maori vibe to our hip-hop—especially in a battle-type situation. It's all in the attitude, this love of the hunt. Maori kids don't play all their cards; they'll always have something extra—mentally, spiritually, the whole nine.

In terms of my own art, one of my favorite pieces to this day is this huge 30-feet-high and 120-feet-long graffiti mural I did for the millennium with a gigantic Maui figure, representing our greatest ancestor: Tiki Tiki o Taranga Maui Potiki, who fished up this island we live on from the sea.

Our people were sailing all around the Pacific back when Europeans still thought the earth was flat. We're raised knowing our *whakapapa*, taking pride in our genealogies going all the way back to our ancestors who arrived here on those first *waka* (great canoes). My staunch old grandmother would tell us about Rongo Mai Wahine, who married Kahungunu—my tribe's name, Ngati Kahungunu, comes from him—and that his father was an *ariki* during the great migration from Hawaiki. From Ti Toku Waru, a great chief of Taranaki, to Rua Kenana and Te Kooti, these great ancestors represented this real, "word is bond" type of honor—they were hip-hop, eh! So by the time I discovered hip-hop, these people, these ancestors ... they were right there with me. That's who I represent in my graffiti stuff especially, incorporating elements of *maoritanga*, my knowledge of my culture and ancestral heritage in the design and presentation.

LITEFOOT: Around Indian Country, it's kind of sporadic, in terms of the crossover influences one way or the other. Mostly, you can see it in the style, in the clothing, bringing hip-hop into a Native context. Like at the powwows today, when you look at everyone sitting around in the drum circles, singing their songs: most of them are not dressed in traditional regalia. They're wearing some Roc-A-Wear or FUBU or Ecko gear. Also, if you just look at the back of the CDs for a lot of powwow music, beginning back around '95 till today, you'd swear you were looking at a rap album from the titles of songs they use. It's just more evidence that hip-hop style affects not just Detroit or Miami, or Dallas; it's hitting the reservations, too.

YUNUS: With X-Plastaz, for example, Faza Nelly and G-San come from the Haya tribe, and so they brought the traditional Haya sound and songs into the kind of hip-hop that the group would do, mixing rhymes and warrior chants. Haya music incorporates a lot of drums and a special type of guitar called a *zeze*, while Maasai music comprised mostly chants with very little, if any, instrumentation, and is noted for its "throat singing" elements. Putting Ki-Maasai to a hip-hop beat was a very big challenge, though, which our brother Yamat Ole Meiboko— also known as Merege ["Male Sheep"]—had to work out. When we all first met, Merege didn't know Ki-Swahili. We knew, however, that bridging these music styles and languages would also bridge together peoples.

CRISTINA: What about the incorporation of Native languages into your music—how does that work, and what are some challenges to doing this, if any?

YUNUS: The problem for our crew was how to fuse the music of the Haya members with the very different music of the group's Maasai members into the hip-hop mix—*and* do it all in Ki-Swahili, the national language of Tanzania, so everyone can understand it.

JAAS: Those of us living in the cities don't have the luxury of being surrounded by our Mapuche family members with whom we can speak it every day. The schools don't teach it. First is Spanish and then English, even though Mapudungun is an original language from here, the language of our roots. So I decided to actually rap and record my songs in Mapudungun— even though I am still learning the language.

A friend told me about some Mapuche guy who'd heard about me and was coming to the city one day, wanting to meet me to talk about the music I was doing. I was excited and really looking forward to meeting him. When we got together, I told him what I was feeling, as far as wanting to be more connected with Mapuche and to represent this in the songs I was writing. So he offered to translate them into Mapudungun for me. I thought, "What a great idea." I want for all the little kids to see and hear this, to grow up experiencing Mapudungun in their everyday life—even in a rap song. Hopefully then, they'll be inspired to study it and want to speak it themselves.

LITEFOOT: Unfortunately, I don't speak my own Cherokee language, so that's a real struggle for me. I know that if I rhymed in Cherokee, that would really help to get the point across, to encourage others to learn or maintain their languages, too. I need a platform through which

I can give the message to a lot of people, though, and so I've got to do it in the tongue everyone who plays my CD will understand: English. There's five hundred–something tribes out there, you know, so if I was to do my songs in Cherokee, I can just imagine the flack I'd get from all the others, like, "You didn't mention MY tribe!" Or, "How come you didn't mention OUR rez? Why you hatin'?"

CRISTINA: Has any slang crossed over, meanwhile, from your native language into the local hip-hop speak?

JAAS: Some of the Mapuche words that have woven into our slang are like, *nielay cullín*—which means "there's no money." Another is *kichiu*, which means "bracero." *Curiche*, in Mapudungun, signifies Blackness, Black people.

YUNUS: In terms of our slang, rappers will say *wa kuchana*—"we're ripping rhymes." Another interesting word is *kufoka*, which means "boiling" or "shouting at." That's how they will describe what they do—not "I'm rapping," but "I'm ripping, I'm boiling."

DLT: *Hori* has become like an equivalent to the *n* word for Maori, though not with the same heavy history. It's often used in hip-hop scenarios to refer to a brother, but it originates as the Maori version of "George." It became like a slur at some point; as slang used by white men to refer to *every* Maori as "hori." I say being *hori* means being barefoot, not being afraid to let my feet touch the earth—and that, to me, is hip-hop.

GRANT: A lot of MCs use the saying "young, Black, and deadly," and that's actually common speak around Australia now. The word *gammon*, which originates up in the Northern Territory, is also used a lot. It means "joking" or "fake."

CRISTINA: In terms of giving a voice to your communities over all, please share some examples of how this is happening and what's at stake, in terms of issues that need addressing toward the mainstream society and within your own peoples.

DLT: I'll just say that hip-hop really pushed us off the fence, to confront the system and be like, "Here's what I think, and I don't care if they don't like it." We became the first Maori kids to stand up and say, "Fuck the queen. We're not gonna be on no colonial, Union Jack bullshit."

GRANT: Hip-hop has proven itself a powerful voice and a powerful motivator in the way it's been utilized by Aboriginal Australians. It has, I believe, strengthened the longevity of our Aboriginal cultures. We're conscious that when our elders pass on, their knowledge will, too—unless we make it accessible to the young people, as hip-hop hop does indeed do.

YUNUS: During the 1960s' Pan-African movement era, there was more traditional music promoted and played on Radio Tanzania. Now, the radio stations are privately owned, and most all they play is Western or American music. This makes it especially hard for local artists to penetrate that barrier, no matter how passionate we may be about our cultures. To get that exposure, to get air-time, we must "modernize it." Mixing it with hip-hop in some way has helped it to be more accepted. It's so ingrained in the Tanzanian mainstream that one has to dress and act like Westerners to be successful, to really make it, so there is very little emphasis on or recognition of indigenous cultural values.

In Tanzania, maybe 95 percent of us are farmers and pastoralists, yet there aren't any real social programs to help the youth deal with the pressures that exist to "modernize." They run away from our villages to the big towns and cities, putting themselves at high risk for contracting HIV and falling prey to drug abuse and crime. Hip-hop is helping to educate them about these dangers, and in fact there's a Chagga rap group from the Kilimanjaro area, called Motomkali, doing this very well. Their name means "blazing fire," a term that's also a metaphor for AIDS. Most of their songs are geared to educating people about HIV and what should be the response of society.

JAAS: In Chile, you see nothing Mapuche in the mainstream media. There is exactly one TV program in Mapuche, and from time to time something on community radio, but you won't see an "Aboriginal" face on TV normally. The newscaster will be some skinny blonde lady. And the news here in Santiago will say nothing about what's going on in the south in Mapuche lands, where the government wants to take over one of the mountains to mine gold and where people have been protesting, for example.

I saw that I could use my rap to provoke this sleeping society of ours to wake up, to see how much injustice, how much discrimination, exists here against Mapuche and anything that's indigenous. The hip-hop community was a lot more open to and interested in these themes, to this *causa*, more conscious and seeking of truths. They really get it, I think. I feel good knowing that maybe my ideas will spread and people will be more conscious about and recognize the Indigenous side of Chile.

CRISTINA: What are some stereotypes or misinformation about Indigenous peoples in your country's prevailing mainstream attitudes which hip-hop has been vocally challenging?

JAAS: Well, the big, ugly stereotype in Chile is that Mapuches are just a bunch of drunks, people that only want to drink and drink. I mean yes, there are certain cultural ceremonies where wine is consumed, but in terms of drunkenness … that's in every community, eh? No more or less among Mapuche.

YUNUS: In Tanzania, there are different degrees in the social order of the country. Maasai or Hazabe, for example, are seen as *washamba*, which has this connotation as being "primitive" compared with other tribal groups. When Maasai come to town, they face a lot of prejudice from the Westernized Tanzanians. A Maasai friend of ours came to a hotel in Arusha for a meeting, wearing his traditional garb. When the hotel manager saw him, though, he told our friend to leave immediately. When he refused and tried to explain that he was meeting a hotel guest, the hotel security grabbed him and slapped handcuffs on him. They threatened to take him to jail and extorted a bribe to let him go.

CRISTINA: Have your Indigenous communities, hip-hop or otherwise, ever been exploited, stereotyped, or otherwise kept at a distance by the mainstream hip-hoppers you come across? If so, how do you feel about this?

LITEFOOT: In the States, definitely. As long as rap stars like Outkast are gonna show all Indians as living in teepees in 2004, insulting our sacred songs like they did on the Grammys, the show might as well show Black folks living in the jungle and white people living in caves! Would I ever dress up like a racist caricature of a Black person, some kind of Kunta Kinte slave, Al Jolson painted in blackface, sticking a bone in my nose or something? Hell no! Because I have respect and knowledge of my own culture, I wouldn't disrespect someone else's sacred traditions. I realize that African Americans are mostly disconnected from the tribal cultures of their ancestors back in Africa, but that's no excuse to come along and insult mine—or to tell me I don't have the right to feel insulted.

At the same time, I've definitely had my share of Native elders saying about me, "Why's this young man trying to be Black?" That's really funny, because if I was singing rock instead of rapping, I know these tribal folks wouldn't question me, saying I was trying to be "white."

I first started appearing at the Gathering of Nations Powwow, the biggest gathering in Indian Country for the year, back in 1993, and it has given me a platform to reach so many Native people. There in New Mexico, right in the middle of it all, you've got the largest tribe in the country just two hours away, in the Navajo Nation, all of those Pueblos, too, and still more tribes beyond that.

GRANT: Back in the '80s hip-hop was dominated here by brown kids, Aboriginal and migrants like the Greeks, Italians, Turkish, and Lebanese, who've all gone through similar things, as far as racism or marginalization in Australian society.

Ever since Eminem came out, however, hip-hop has actually been considered a *white* thing in Australia, affirming White Power. There's been a big, ongoing debate about this whole "accent" thing, in terms of Australian identity and hip-hop. White hip-hoppers are the gate-keepers, calling all the shots as far as hip-hop on a national level is concerned. They maintain that you gotta have that true "ocker" accent, the whole "Ay, g'day, mate" kind of talk. Anyone here who doesn't talk or rhyme like that gets classed as "inauthentic."

These white Australian groups like Hilltop Hoods or Buttafingaz ... what they talk about doesn't resonate with Aboriginal people; there's no connection there. We relate a lot more to Black American issues, so we align ourselves more with American styles.

CRISTINA: Are there any ways that hip-hop—maybe rap specifically—has influenced your communities in less positive, perhaps disturbing ways?

LITEFOOT: Look, I'll just put it out there that we have become in large part assimilated—to the good, the bad, and the ugly, as far as hip-hop in Indian Country.

DLT: Adverse effects that hip-hop may have had in Aotearoa come from the commercial side of things, really—like the growing obsession here with acquiring bling, this materialistic illusion/delusion stuff. Also, you shouldn't be surprised to find all these Maori kids following what American rappers show us by example on all their big hit records, in their movies, saying, "What up, my n#$*%s."

YUNUS: The thing that helps to "shield" us from what I understand to be some more negative kinds of rap music is that, for the most part, we don't understand the English words that they're saying! We just feel the power, the anger in their voices, though, and we connect with that. In a sense, through hip-hop, the Maori story becomes my story, the Lakota story is my story, and even the Zulu Nation story is my story, as I question the order of things and continue to discover these universal strands that connect us all as indigenous peoples.

Study Questions

1. How are traditional tribal cultures similar to hip-hop culture?
2. What aspects of hybridity emerge from the convergence of indigenous cultures and hip-hop?
3. In what significant ways does hip-hop communicate important lessons or values among indigenous youth?

Part IV

"I'll Be Nina Simone Defecating on Your Microphone"
Hip-Hop and Gender

Mark Anthony Neal

> I could do what you do, EASY! Believe me/Frontin' niggaz gives me heebee-geebees/So while you're imitatin' Al Capone/I'll be Nina Simone and defecating on your microphone.
> (Lauryn Hill, "Ready or Not")

Rap music and hip-hop culture have often been singularly cited for the transmission and reproduction of sexism and misogyny in American society. As sexism and misogyny are largely extensions of normative patriarchal privilege, their reproduction in the music of male hip-hop artists speaks more powerfully to the extent that these young men (particularly young black men) are invested in that privilege rather than providing any evidence that they are solely responsible for its reproduction. As journalist Kevin Powell eloquently cautions in the introduction to a collection of Ernie Paniccioli photographs of hip-hop artists,

> it is wrong to categorically dismiss hip-hop without taking into serious consideration the socioeconomic conditions (and the many record labels that eagerly exploit and benefit from the ignorance of many of these young artists) that have led to the current state of affairs. Or, to paraphrase the late Tupac Shakur, we were given this world, we did not make it.
> (Powell, 2002)

But there is also no denying that hip-hop's grip on American youth allows for the circulation of sexist and misogynistic narratives in a decidedly uncritical fashion. Questions of gender within hip-hop are multifaceted, including desires to cultivate more space for fully developed narratives about gender and sexuality and obvious concerns about the circulation of sexism, misogyny and homophobia.

The embrace of patriarchal privilege by some male hip-hop artists partly explains the marginalization of women in hip-hop, particularly when those women don't conform to the roles assigned to women within hip-hop (the chicken-head groupie, over-sexualized rhyme-spitter, and baggy-clothed, desexualized mic-fiend are prime examples). Thus many female rap artists are less concerned with challenging the circulation of sexism and misogyny (Sarah Jones's "Your Revolution" notwithstanding) than simply with being recognized as peers alongside male rappers. This is not simply a concern about being viewed as aesthetic or artistic peers; there are real economic realities within hip-hop, where the visibility of women rap artists, or lack of it, mirrors the very economic disparities that many women face in the workforce in relationship to their male peers. It is not lost on anyone that few women rappers have emerged in the last 15 years without the support of highly visible male benefactors, transforming many of these women into the proverbial "ride or die bitch(es)" as opposed to self-contained artists. "Stakes Is High," as De La Soul might say.

This is in part what Lauryn Hill asks us to consider in her verse (which serves as title for this section) from The Fugees' "Ready or Not" (*The Score*, 1996). Extolling the legacy of the legendary jazz vocalist and activist Nina Simone, Hill champions a notion of hard-core hip-hop not rooted in the Mafioso fantasy of the day, but that goes back to the risky aesthetic and political choices made by a woman (and women), who at the height of the civil rights movement in the 1960s spoke "truth to power" in songs like "Mississippi Goddam" and "Four Women." Hill's phrase represents a legitimate critique of the hyper-masculinity and phallocentrism that pervades hip-hop—a critique that is clearly gendered in its intent. What Hill and many other female rap artists like Salt-N-Pepa, Eve, MC Lyte, Queen Latifah, Jean Grae, Yo-Yo, Bahamadia, and Missy Elliott have been really asking for is a respect for women-centered narratives that exist alongside and not necessarily in competition with those of their male peers, though, as Hill attests, these women are more than willing and ready to battle.

In her essay "Empowering Self, Making Choices, Creating Spaces: Black Female Identity via Rap Music Performance," UCLA ethnomusicologist Cheryl Keyes charts the formation of "four distinct categories of women rappers" within the hip-hop performance tradition (Keyes, 2000: 256). Drawing on Jacqueline Bobo's concept of "interpretive community," Keyes examines the observations of female performers and audiences and identifies the "Queen Mother," "Fly Girl," "Sista with Attitude," and "Lesbian" as the dominant figures within female hip-hop performance. Keyes adds that "each category mirrors certain images, voices, and lifestyles" (ibid.: 256). The most provocative of these figures is the "Fly Girl." According to Keyes, "Rap's fly girl image ... highlights aspects of black women's bodies considered undesirable by American mainstream standards of beauty" (ibid.: 260). Citing the example of Salt-N-Pepa, hip-hop's quintessential "Fly Girls," Keyes also asserts that "they portray via performance the fly girl as a party-goer, and independent woman, but additionally, an erotic subject rather than an objectified one" (ibid.: 260).

Journalist Joan Morgan also finds value in the "Fly Girl" of hip-hop and the erotic power associated with her. In the opening pages of her book *When Chickenheads Come Home to Roost: My Life as a Hip-Hop Feminist* she relishes the opportunity to replicate the "proper Bronx Girl Switch" that she watched "project girls" employ when she was a young girl growing up in the Bronx (Morgan, 1999: 17). As she notes, these were woman-girls who could "transform into Black Moses capable of parting seas of otherwise idle Negroes" (ibid.: 17). Given the reverence held for the South Bronx in hip-hop lore, it is not a stretch to suggest that the prototype for the hip-hop "Fly Girl" may have been born on the streets of the South Bronx. It is in the context of black female sexuality that Morgan posits a hip-hop feminism that champions both a critical discourse around gender in hip-hop and the pleasures associated with flaunting the very female sexuality that some hip-hop artists regularly objectify. As Morgan queries in one passage,

> Is it foul to say that imagining a world where you could paint your big brown lips in the most decadent of shades, pile your phat ass into your fave micromini, slip your freshly manicured toes into four-inch fuck-me sandals and have not one single solitary man objectify—I mean roam his eyes longingly over all intended places—is, like, a total drag to you?
>
> (ibid.: 57)

Morgan in fact uses the power of female eroticism to flip hip-hop sexual politics on its head as she brazenly asks "how come no one ever admits that part of the reason women love hip-hop—as sexist as it is—is 'cuz all that in-yo-face testosterone makes our nipples hard?" (ibid.: 58).

In "Butta Pecan Mamis" the focus is again on the performance of hip-hop femininity on the streets of New York, but Raquel Rivera extends the gaze to consider the ways that black and brown women become part and parcel of the sexual fantasies performed in the music of rap artists. Highlighting Big Pun's chorus—"Boricua, Morena"—from "Still Not a Player," Rivera jests, "Boricuas and morenas may be distinct, but, as Pun constructs them, they are both sweet, thick, pretty, round and various shades of brown. And evidently, that is how he likes his 'hoes'" (Rivera, 2003: 129). More seriously, Rivera juxtaposes the relative silence of Latina women within hip-hop with their portrayal as a "tropical, exotic, and racially 'lighter' variation of ghetto blackness," noting that their image is why such women are highly coveted (ibid.: 148). Indeed it might be because of the images of women in hip-hop—as largely presented via the vehicle of music video—that the conversation about hip-hop and gender has reached such a fever pitch.

In the spring of 2004, for example, the young women students at Spelman College, a historically black, all-female college located in the Atlanta University Center, applied feminist praxis that they had learned in the classes of scholar Beverly Guy-Sheftall to challenge the misogyny and sexism that circulate within hip-hop culture. In an event that has become synonymous with activism within hip-hop, the women of Spelman challenged rap star Nelly, who was scheduled to visit the campus in the spring of 2004, over the content of his video for the song "Tip Drill." And yet the troubling imagery that circulates within hip-hop culture is not just about sexist and misogynist depictions of women, but also locks men—particularly black men—into media scripts that offer very little insight into their humanity or complexity.

Addressing the reality of mainstream hip-hop's penchant for hyper-masculinity and its relationship to American politics, Michael Eric Dyson tells filmmaker Byron Hurt in the essay "Cover Your Eyes as I Describe a Scene So Violent: Violence, Machismo, Sexism and Homophobia" that, "when we speak about hypermasculinity, we're speaking about the Frank Sinatratization of American political discourse: 'I did it my way.' Seeking compromise, looking for consensus, building a healthy coalition—this is not the natural inclination of hyperaggressive males" (Dyson, 2007: 96–97). The image of the hyper-masculine—and heterosexual—black male is one of the most consistent tropes of contemporary hip-hop, yet performances of masculinity are much more nuanced and complicated. Andreana Clay cautions in her essay "'I Used to Be Scared of the Dick': Queer Women of Color and Hip-Hop Masculinity" that it is

> important to examine how these masculinities are performative, and how queer women, in this case, perform them. Women exhibit the same sense of control or hardcoreness as the playa and the nigga to the windows to the walls with other women on the dancefloor ... the rigidity of Black male masculinity is flipped to fit the context.
>
> (Clay, 2007: 155)

In his essay "Scared Straight: Hip-Hop, Outing, and the Pedagogy of Queerness," Marc Lamont Hill discusses in detail the way in which masculinity and sexuality have been policed within hip-hop discourse. Citing the example of Big Daddy Kane, who was rumored to be HIV positive in the late 1980s, Hill examines "outing" practices within rap music, arguing that "the perception of fractured masculinity, which is an inevitable consequence of outing, serves as a professional death sentence from which there are few routes of redemption or recovery" (Hill, 2009: 31). Yet, despite attempts to police and contain masculinity in hip-hop, Ela Greenberg writes in her essay, "'The King of the Streets': Hip-Hop and the Reclaiming of Masculinity in Jerusalem's Shu'afat Refugee Camp," that young Arabic men in East Jerusalem find inspiration in those very images of black masculinity that circulate throughout hip-hop.

REFERENCES

Clay, Andreana. (2007). "'I Used to Be Scared of the Dick': Queer Women of Color and Hip-Hop Masculinity," in *Home Girls Make Some Noise: Hip-Hop Feminism Anthology*, edited by G.D. Pough, E. Richardson, A. Durham and R. Raimist. Mira Loma, CA: Parker Publishing.

Dyson, Michael Eric. (2007). *Know What I Mean?: Reflections on Hip-Hop*. New York: Basic Civitas.

Hill, Marc Lamont. (2009). "Scared Straight: Hip-Hop, Outing, and the Pedagogy of Queerness," *Review of Education, Pedagogy, and Cultural Studies*, 31.

Keyes, Cheryl. (2000). "Empowering Self, Making Choices, Creating Spaces: Black Female Identity via Rap Music Performance," *Journal of American Folklore*, 113.

Morgan, Joan. (1999). *When Chickenheads Come Home to Roost: My Life as a Hip-Hop Feminist*. New York: Simon & Schuster.

Powell, Kevin. (2002). "Notes of a Hiphop Head," in *Who Shot Ya?: Three Decades of Hip-Hop Photography*, by Ernie Paniccioli. New York: HarperCollins.

Rivera, Raquel. (2003). *New York Ricans from the Hip-Hop Zone*. New York: Palgrave Macmillan.

22

I Used to Be Scared of the Dick
Queer Women of Color and Hip-Hop Masculinity

Hip-hop culture has been as responsible as anything for the branding of black hypermasculinity in mainstream American culture—it is a cornerstone in the production and circulation of hip-hop culture. As such, the centrality of hypermasculinity makes hip-hop a relatively easy target in debates about hip-hop's role in reproducing sexist, misogynistic, and homophobic language and imagery.

As Andreana Clay argues in her essay, it is important to remember that gender—in this case masculinity—is also a performance and by definition a performance marked by nuance and context. In this vein, Clay examines how performances of hypermasculinity have been appropriated by queer women, offering comment on both hip-hop culture and the performances of gender in society.

I Used to Be Scared of the Dick: Queer Women of Color and Hip-Hop Masculinity

Andreana Clay

Walking around Lake Merritt on my way to teach my Gender class and I'm feeling on top of the world. I'm wearing my leather coat, my steel-toe boots, my natural is curled tight, and life in Oakland is pretty good. It's my second year of teaching at the university and one of my students just gave me a copy of *The Grey Album*, DJ Danger Mouse's mix of Jay Z's *The Black Album* with the Beatles' *White Album*. It's hard to believe that one of my favorite albums from my childhood has been remixed with a contemporary hip-hop CD. The music makes me feel confident as I walk, nodding to the dudes who sit and chat alongside their cars after a morning jog or walk around the lake. I hum along to Jay Z and catch myself agreeing with him, thinking, "Yeah, I might have some problems but a bitch ain't one of them: I don't have a girlfriend, have been out of a relationship and a nasty breakup for over a year, and things feel a new." Then I have to check myself, knowing that I've just called another woman—a potential girlfriend, no doubt—a bitch. What am I saying? Why is it that there is something about Jay-Z's tone and his discussion of race and gender that I enjoy singing along with and, at times, find myself identifying with as a Black, queer woman?[1]

It hasn't always been like this, until recently my beliefs as a feminist have not allowed for the number of times I had to hear bitch or ho in a three minute rap song. While I find the lyrics and flow of artists like Jay Z interesting, as a woman, I find it difficult to get down with having parts of my body or my demeanor referred to over and over again in the chorus of a random rap song. Or, having someone whisper how sexy they think my ass is and asking me if they can touch it. Well, I should say I don't have time for it when a man says it but when I'm listening to those lyrics and hearing other queer women of color say it, the lyrics and content changes for me. In fact, it wasn't until I came out as queer and started hanging out in all queer women's spaces that I started to appreciate and identify more with hip-hop music and culture.

In this paper, I examine how hip-hop, sexism and heterosexism intersect to complicate the discussion of hip-hop and feminism. In particular, I examine the relationship between hip-hop music and black masculinity among queer women of color on the dance floor. I look primarily at two images of masculinity, the "playa" and the "nigga," and ask why these images might appeal to women in all female, queer spaces? The same women who collectively still experience homophobia, racism and sexism at the same time that we play around with the bravado of hip-hop masculinity. Further, I ask what is the relationship between hip-hop masculinity and Black queer female identity in the contemporary context? By examining these texts and the club scene in the San Francisco Bay Area, I explore how queer women of color engage with and even celebrate hip-hop music in spite of sexist and homophobic lyrics.

My Hip-Hop Journey

Like other Black feminists of my generation, I grew up on hip-hop. As a teenager in the early to mid-1980s, I remember listening to LL Cool J's "I Need Love," Run DMC's "King of Rock," and NWA's "Straight Outta Compton" and being seduced by the lyrics and beats. Although I grew up in a small city in Missouri, NWA's lyrics felt like my experience. They were Black and articulating a sense of going nowhere, and my friends and I were Black and felt like we weren't going anywhere. That was enough. As a young woman, I looked to hip-hop for inspiration and role models of who I was supposed to be. After I came out, I never thought of hip-hop as a space for me as a queer woman, largely because queer people are not visible or out in mainstream hip-hop. While many of us have assumptions about which rappers might be lesbian or gay, no popular performer has come out and identified as queer.

This is not to suggest that queer hip-hop does not exist. A thriving queer music scene exists with artists like Deep Dick Collective (DDC) and Hanifah Walidah being some of the most visible and respected artists. One of the members of DDC, Juba Kalamka, also produces the Peace Out festival, which is an international gathering of Gay, Lesbian, Bisexual and Transgender hip-hop artists.[2] Recently I also acquired a "Gangsta Fag" CD from yet another one of my students. And then, of course, we have long had our independent, hip-hop artist and poster girl for bisexuals everywhere, Meshell Ndegeocello. So, independent "homo hop" is fully intact. But, whatever happened to Caushun, the much-hyped gay rapper signed to Baby Phat records? Gay and straight folks alike were waiting for this "hybrid child of homosexual and hip-hop cultures" to change the face of hip-hop forever.[3] Four years later and we're still waiting for his album to actually drop.

Perhaps one of the artists closest to the mainstream in recent years is Queen Pen, who made a name for herself with the single, "Girlfriend" which she performs with Ndegeocello. In this song, Pen begins to publicly play around with Black masculinity by flaunting her prowess with other women in clubs. Set to the tune of Ndeogello's "If That's Your Boyfriend," Pen goes into detail about women clockin' her at clubs and vice versa. However, she is the dominant one in the scene and wants men and women to know that. Although not a huge hit, it is one of the few explicitly queer rap songs. However, despite this outspoken pride, about same sex desire, as Gwendolyn Pough points out, Queen Pen relies on the misogyny in hip-hop to refer to her female "conquests."[4] But the DJs are not playing Walidah, DDC, or even Queen Pen in the clubs. And, according to the sales of albums by queer artists, homo-hop is not necessarily what we are spending our cash on either. So, who and why do queer women identify with this culture that is known for its homophobia and sexism? And, how do we continue to maintain queer feminist ideology and practice in this groove?

Other feminists have written about what it means to be a Black woman who embraces hip-hop, as both a consumer and producer.[5] For instance, in *When Chickenheads Come Home to Roost*, Joan Morgan discusses why a hip-hop feminist (read heterosexual) might defend her commitment to hip-hop (read male). In her chapter, "An Open Letter to Hip-Hop," she clarifies her decision to consume hip-hop in spite of the sexism that many rap artists espouse. As she states,

> My decision to expose myself to the sexism of Dr. Dre, Ice Cube, Snoop Dogg or the Notorious B.I.G is really my plea to my brothers to tell me who they are. I need to know why they are so angry at me … As a black woman and a feminist I listen to the music with a willingness to see past the machismo in order to be clear about what I'm really dealing with.[6]

Morgan's plea to hip-hop, in this instance, comes from her commitment to Black men as her brothers, friends and potential lovers. If Morgan's commitment to hip-hop is related to understanding who and what she is dealing with as a straight, Black woman, then what is in it for me as a queer Black feminist? While I am committed to my relationships with Black men, they are not my primary love interests.

As women who have sex with other women, Black lesbians have historically not been recognized as women in the Black community. Black feminists have been writing about this as both a women's and black issue for decades.[7] The expectations of womanhood for Black women revolve around our relationships with Black men. Jewelle Gomez discusses this in her essay "Homophobia in the Black community," co-authored with Barbara Smith. As she states,

> The stereotype ... mandates that you develop into the well-groomed Essence girl who pursues a profession and a husband. If you begin to espouse a proud lesbian growth, you find yourself going against the grain. That makes embracing your lesbianism doubly frightening, because you then have to discard the mythology that's been developed around what it means to be a young Black woman.[8]

Not much has changed in the fifteen years since these words were written. The expectations on Black womanhood are the same for the hip-hop generation. And, as Gomez suggests, identifying as lesbian or queer is interpreted as being a rejection of all things male. The 2003 murder of fifteen-year-old Sakia Gunn, who declared her lesbian identity to a group of men who were accosting her and her friends on a street in New Jersey, indicates that the rejection of all things male, can be a deadly endeavor for queer Black women.[9] This is true, in spite of the increasing visibility of gays and lesbians in mainstream culture.

All the Lesbians Are White, All the Blacks Are Men, but Some of Us ...[10]

In the current historical moment, Black gays and lesbians are experiencing a reversal of the celebration of queerness in popular culture. Same gender sex and desire is overshadowed in the Black community by discourses about Black men on the "down low." Often, the down low is characterized as being Black men's denial of their "true" sexual identity and subsequent rejection and (HIV) infection of Black women. For the last decade, magazine articles, television shows, and popular songs like R. Kelly's "In the Closet" vilify Black men for engaging in sex with other men. These discussions of the down low exploded when writer J. L. King who, according to Oprah, one of his biggest cheerleaders, did a "great service to African-American women" by appearing on her show to expose straight Black men's "dark secret."[11]

On the other end of the spectrum, the larger gay community has pushed a national debate about same-sex marriage into the public eye. Most of the poster children for the same-sex marriage debate are white: gay neighborhoods or scenes, like the Castro district in San Francisco, is predominantly white, male, and middle class. In both of these contexts, queer Black desire and identity has been erased, especially for women. Because we are absent from a discussion of Black same-sex sex on the one hand and one of gay and lesbian identity on the other, it's no surprise that young, queer women of color find reprieve anywhere we can—including the often sexist, homophobic and hyper-masculine genre of hip-hop.

Scholars agree that hip-hop culture is predominantly male and decidedly masculine.[12] In its current form, this genre is characterized by highly sexualized images: "video hoes" and sexually available women, pimps and playas, and economic capital in the form of an abundance of material goods. Essentially, this is a mythical world where men rule since Black men, who are often the protagonists in hip-hop music and videos, do not have the same economic, social or cultural capital outside of popular culture. This hip-hop fantasyland makes sense for a generation of disenfranchised Black men. Most of the images in hip-hop reflect and confirm larger, accepted understandings of Black masculinity: the thug, the hustler, the playa, the nigga and the inmate or ex-con. That's it. There is little variation in popular culture. Every once in a while, Black people are offered images of the "Cosbys," the "Obamas," and the [Jesse] "Jacksons" which suggest that other masculinities might be possible in popular discourse. However, Bill Cosby, in his ill-informed comments about Black youth, pointed to the reality that there is little room for any other type of black masculinity in mainstream American culture.[13]

The rigidity of Black male masculinity in popular culture is reflective of how we generally consume masculinity in popular culture, mostly based on white men. As Judith Halberstam explains,

> current representations of masculinity in white men unfailingly depend on a relatively stable notion of the realness and the naturalness of both the male body and its signifying effects. Advertisements, for example appeal constantly to the no-nonsense aspect of masculinity, to the idea that masculinity 'just is'. Indeed, there are very few places in American culture where male masculinity reveals itself to be stage or performative.[14]

I agree with Halberstam that white male masculinity is presented something that is unfailing, or real, because of white males' relationship to heteronormativity. However, I suggest that Black male masculinity is equally as rigid because of the ways that Black men and women consume and "decode" these representations.[15] In his new book, *Hung: A Meditation on the Measure of Black Men in America*, Scott Poulson-Bryant talks about how many of us, including Black men, internalize the notion that penis size is a measure of Black masculinity. After having sex with a white woman in college one told him "she thought he'd be bigger" because he's Black, Poulson-Bryant replied, "me too."[16] The candidness of both the woman's assumption and Poulson-Bryant's response indicate that there is a limited range of Black male masculinities in popular culture, including hip-hop.

Two of the hyper-masculine images associated with rap music are the "nigga" and the "playa." Each of these identities is male defined and expressed in mainstream rap music. Despite the debate surrounding both the history and contemporary use of the word "nigga," much of it centering on whether or not nigga is any different from the derogatory term, nigger, the hip-hop generation typically identifies a nigga as a man who is "hard," or hardcore, and able to withstand the toughest of times. Or, as R. A. T. Judy describes, "A nigga forgets feelings, recognizing, instead, that affects are communicable, particularly the hard-core ones of anger, rage, intense pleasure."[17] At the same time, he is also thought of someone that is "down" or loyal to others, as noted in the expression "That's my nigga." This image is reinforced over and over again in music videos and in lyrics of hip-hop artists like The Game, and 50 Cent.

Like the nigga, a playa is a person who forgets feelings, but instead of focusing on emotions like anger, rage, etc., the playa is all about getting what he can be it sex, money, or women. Sometimes used interchangeably with the term "pimp," a playa is most often characterized as a heterosexual male who sleeps with a lot of women, has more than one woman on his arm in public settings, and is in control of all of his interactions with women. He is the one who dominates. According to the *Urban Dictionary*, which has forty-two definitions of a playa, the most agreed upon definition is a "guy who is sustaining supposedly exclusive relationships with multiple girls simultaneously."[18] Both of these terms are firmly rooted in hetero-sexual culture, identity and lifestyle. They also, often, reflect our larger definitions of men of color and masculinity in popular culture.

This is especially true for Black men, who currently dominate popular culture and discussions more than any other "minority." Mark Anthony Neal, like Poulson-Bryant, has recently taken this limited view of black male masculinity to task in his work on Black men in America.[19] Neal articulates the need for "new black men" that are "pro-feminist, anti-homophobic and nurturing."[20] I agree with Neal's call for a range of representations of Black male masculinity in popular culture. However, before we can move entirely to the other spectrum of masculinity in popular culture, it is important to examine how these masculinities are performative, and how queer women, in this case, perform them. Women exhibit the same sense of control or hardcoreness as the playa and the nigga to the windows and to the walls with other women on the dance floor. In an instance, the rigidity of Black male masculinity is flipped to fit the context.

You Can Find Me in da Club

A variety of clubs cater to queer women of color in the San Francisco Bay area. Some are wall-to-wall women of color—Black, Latina, Asian and most play hip-hop music non-stop. In each club, there are all different kinds of women. For instance, there might be women over forty with long 'locks, Hawaiian shirts, shorts, and Teva sandals in one corner of the room and younger, Butch, women wearing crisp, indigo-colored Levi's with thick black belts, large belt buckles, and perfectly gelled hair in another. There are also femme women in tight jeans or skirts, heels, and short T-shirts, some cut around the collar so that they slide down around their shoulders. In every club that I've been to, there is always a clearly designated dance floor, which is usually packed tight with sweaty bodies. Some clubs have elevated dance floors or stages with one or two go-go dancers dressed in hot pants and knee-high boots. Below them are men lined up with dollars. In the background, hip-hop music fills the room with beats and voices, sometimes the only male presence the room. What type of male, and ultimately what type of masculinity, depends on the club.

On Gay Pride weekend this year, I went out to several of these clubs. Two in particular stuck out in my mind because of their similarities and differences in relationship to queer sexuality and black masculinity. For instance, at one of the clubs I went to, the deejay played songs that characterize more of the nigga, or thug image in hip-hop—2Pac, Biggie Smalls, the Game and 50 Cent. At the second club, the music had much more of a playa or sexualized tone—the Ying Yang Twins, David Banner and Khia. While there are two different types of masculinity being played at each club, in a room full of women of color, the lyrics fall to the background as the performances take center stage. For instance, nigga masculinity in the first club is reflected in a particular style, stance or code. It is more about an individual identity, one that each person can take on. Women throw up hand gestures as they dance, make eye contact with one another and mouth the words to the lyrics. Some women even had on T-shirts with the ultimate "nigga 4 life," 2Pac. The tone set at this club is also about community. The mood isn't so much about sex or domination sexually, but rather, a stance about who someone is or declares herself to be: being down, being able to take what comes in life, being loyal to this group, this identity and this community.

In the second club, the playa image was much more prevalent. If you wanted to find someone to help you get your groove on, this was the place to be. Women would grind their bodies into one another, and move one another's bodies around to the direction of the lyrics. Queer sexuality was much more on display, as a woman, you wanted to be looked at, have somebody notice you, and maybe take you home. For instance, at one point, I noticed two women on the stage, dancing with one another. One of the women, in baggy jeans and a baseball jersey picked up the woman she was dancing with who was wearing a short, silver skirt and tank top. She then lifted her up onto the bars surrounding the stage and then put her face into the woman's skirt under the musical direction of "work that clit, cum girl." I had to sit down.

Even though I was a little uncomfortable with this display, I didn't leave the bar, which is probably what I would have done had I been in a straight club. In a mixed setting, the lyrics and sexual display denote a different power struggle for me: with women more clearly marked as objects and men as subjects. That expression of sexual desire is one that all women see in music videos, movies, and hear it played out in the music we listen to. Similar to Laura Mulvey's definition of the male gaze in popular culture in which the female is the fetishized object and men are the spectators, mixed clubs are assumed to be spaces where women are expected to take on the passive quality of "to-be-looked-at-ness."[21] Over a hip-hop beat, men then possess the ability to look,

354 • ANDREANA CLAY

taking pleasure in looking at and dominating women. I am not suggesting that straight women have no power in these settings. Mulvey has been rightly critiqued for her failure to go beyond men as spectators and women as passive objects. She, and other feminists, forget that every once in a while a woman might like to "pile [he]r phat ass into [he]r fave micromini [and] slip [he]r freshly manicured toes into four inch fuck me sandals" for her pleasure as well as his when she goes out to a club.[22] However, I do suggest that these are the expected and most displayed roles in hip-hop music. What I am interested in is what women do with these roles.

Moreover, the expression of sexual desire between two queer women of color is rare, if at all existent, in popular culture. In these all female, queer club spaces, the decoding of black male masculinity is exciting, normalized and even "safe." First, these displays can demonstrate what queer women do and whom we do it with. Second, there isn't the fear of violence or being over-powered that may be associated with mixed, straight clubs. Popular discourse often warns women, gay or straight, about the dangers of going to clubs alone. We are all too familiar with the *Dateline* specials on GHB or "roofies" which capitalize on the horrible stories of women who go to bars sober and end up being sexually assaulted.[23] While these stories are used to make women fear and regulate our sexuality, I have never once been worried about these "dangers" when I have walked into queer clubs alone, freshly made-up in tight jeans and revealing blouse.

All queer women of color spaces have been one of the most liberating places for me as a Black queer woman, and consequently, as a feminist. I feel validated as a woman of color living in the current context of the *L-Word, Queer Eye for the Straight Guy*, and *Queer as Folk*, where the major-ity of the queer people are men and most of the lesbians are white. Scrambling to see images of myself and make connections with other women of color is an ongoing struggle in the twenty-first century. And it is always more than pleasurable, to tell your homegirls that you like to throw lips to the shit and have them know the queer context I am speaking of. In these moments we engage in what Stuart Hall calls an oppositional reading of rap lyrics and hip-hop music.[24] Queer women of color construct new meanings of the text and become active consumers who change the context of sexuality and masculinity.

In her research on drag kings of color, Halberstam points to this type of reading in her con-clusion that "when a drag king lip synchs to rap, she takes sampling to another level and restages the sexual politics of the song and the active components of black masculinity by channeling them through the drag act for a female audience and through the queer space of a lesbian club."[25] I argue that the same is true for lesbians and queer women in the clubs I have been to. For instance, some of the women in the clubs look and dress as hard as the men in rap videos. In these moments, black masculinity is changed in that these women are exploring their masculin-ity in relationship to the women that they love and have sex with.

In this sense, there is a clear link between a Black queer or lesbian identity and the nigga iden-tity. To clarify an earlier question, perhaps this is why Black queer women identify, at times, with the masculinity in hip-hop. In particular, the sense of outsider status in identities like the nigga. As Todd Boyd suggests in *Am I Black Enough For You*, "the nigga is not interested in anything having to do with the mainstream, though his cultural products are clearly an integral part of mainstream popular culture. The nigga rejects the mainstream even though he has already been absorbed by it."[26] Here, Black male masculinity occupies a space both in and outside of hetero-normativity through the rejection and absorption of it. Similarly, Black queer women reject het-eronormativity in both their identity and desire at the same time that we embrace mainstream cultures like hip-hop. This happens not only in relationship to sex and sexuality, but with racial and ethnic identity as well. For instance, even though Gwen Stefani has colonized the culture, language, fashion and stance of women of color from her use of Bindis, to dark eyeliner around her lips, her ska musical style (collaborations with Eve and Ladysaw) and, recently her "entourage" of Japanese girls, queer women of color run to the dance floor when her songs come on, singing louder than the music, perhaps reclaiming the identities that she has appropriated from us, cause "ooh, this *my* shit." The decoding of masculinity and race that happens in queer women's spaces indicates that each identity is indeed performative. And what I find important in these performances of masculinity on the dance floor is the sense of legitimacy and dare I say "pride" that comes from watching Black women gyrate with one another to a hip-hop beat, one wanting the other to know she's a hustler, baby. There is a celebration and declaration of same sex sex and sexuality in these moments that Black women and other women of color continue to be denied in popular discourse.

Conclusion: Queer Women, Masculinity and Black Men

Queer women of color flipping the script in dance clubs, does not eliminate the rigid representations of Black masculinity and femininity in popular culture or how we internalize these images as Black men and women. As I have demonstrated through the actions and spaces that I have described, queer engagement with hip-hop masculinity is mad full of complexity and contradiction. These complexities have a long history in the lesbian community long before girls told other girls they'd take to the candy shop and let you lick the lollipop. By examining this queer space, I am in no way suggesting that the objectification of women is thrown out completely. Bending your girl over to the front and telling her to touch her toes and having her do so in high heels and a thong may not be the path to liberation. I also make no claims that queer women don't engage in harmful acts upon one another. I was once at a party and heard a woman telling someone else that she and her friends pulled a train on "this bitch" that she picked up at a club one night. And, to my horror, one of her friends standing next to her asked her "why she didn't invite her to *that* party." The same objectification and violence towards women can happen regardless of the gender of the protagonist. And, queer communities are similar to the hip-hop community in that they reflect popular culture and discourse. This is not to exclude these actions, but to point out what this ideology, which some of us have internalized, suggests about the value of Black female bodies in this culture.[27] What does it mean to be in all female loving space and always question the sexist lyrics?

The contradictions in queer women's spaces are similar to the complexities that Mark Anthony Neal faces as a Black feminist man who enjoys songs that are derogatory against women. As he states, "My affection for Mos Def's 'Ms. Fat Booty' frames one of the contradictions of thinking oneself a black male feminist. For example, how does black male feminism deal with the reality of heterosexual desire?"[28] I must end this essay with a similar question: how do black queer feminists who love hip-hop deal with the reality that same sex desire and practice is sometimes played out over a sexist hip-hop beat? How do we recognize and value ourselves as part of the hip-hop generation, many of whom gay or straight don't identify as feminists? I don't have a clear answer to these questions, but I think it must begin with forcing a discussion of the current absence of a strong political voice among both queer and straight people of color that values women's bodies in the public sphere as as our identities resume that we do in the private. More importantly, I think it also begs for the continued development of critical analyses among this generation about the display of Black bodies in popular culture: gay, straight, female and male. I have provided a brief example of the ways in which queer women of color with and perform hip-hop masculinity in all female, queer spaces. However, I want to stress that it is the rigidity of Black male masculinity in popular cultures like hip-hop that indeed needs to be flipped. In doing so, it becomes more and more clear that these representations are inflexible and falsely perceived as natural. Men, women, queer, straight will have to build coalitions that continue to question and deconstruct these rigidities.

These collaborations are necessary for the post-civil rights generation. Political scientist Cathy Cohen outlines the importance of building alliances across identities in her discussion of transformational politics, particularly the need to include more folks under the term "queer." For instance the term "underclass," which is often used as a synonym for black men and women in popular and academic discourse, is an oppressed group in that it is placed outside of the hetero-normative standard. As she states, "sexuality and sexual deviance from a prescribed norm have been used to demonize and oppress various segments of the population, even some classified under the label 'heterosexual.'[29] I argue that popular discussions and representations of Black male masculinities solidify Black men's status outside of this norm, similar to the status of Black queer (and straight) women. One of the most important contributions of hip-hop feminism is to bridge these coalitions so that the small boxes Black sexuality (and women and men) has been forced into will longer keep us trapped. Holla back.

Study Questions

1. How has hip-hop culture benefited from the presence of hypermasculinity as a market-ing tool?
2. How do queer women challenge narratives of gender within hip-hop culture?
3. What does the embrace of hypermasculinity in hip-hop say about the performance of maleness in the broader society?

Notes

1. I use the term queer because that is how I identify, sometimes politically, but also in terms of my sex-ual preference. I also use this term interchangeably with lesbian and dyke, which also appear in the text.
2. See peaceoutfestival.com for more information. Also, see sugartruckrecordings.com for information on Deep Dick Collective, DDC member Tim'm West, and Katastrophe.
3. See Chris Nutter, "The Gay Rapper," *Vibe* (July 2001).
4. See Gwendolyn Pough, *Check It While I Wreck It: Black Womanhood, Hip-Hop Culture, and the Public Sphere* (Boston: Northeastern University Press, 2004).
5. See Joan Morgan, *When Chickenheads Come Home to Roost: A Hip-Hop Feminist Breaks It Down* (New York: Penguin Books, 1999); Pough 2004; and Tricia Rose, *Black Noise: Rap Music and Black Culture in America* (Wesleyan, CT: Wesleyan University Press, 1994).
6. Morgan, 1999, p. 42.
7. Combahee River Collective, "A Black Feminist Statement." Ed. G. Anzaldúa and C. Moraga, *This Bridge Called My Back* (New York: Kitchen Table Press, 1981 [1977]); Cheryl Clarke, *Living as a Lesbian* (Ann Arbor, MI: Firebrand Books, 1986); Jewelle Gomez and Barbara Smith, "Talking about It: Homophobia in the Black Community" *Feminist Review: Perverse Politics: Lesbian Issues* (Spring 1990); Audre Lorde, *Zami: A New Spelling of My Name* (Freedom, CA: Crossing Press, 1983).
8. Gomez and Smith 1990, p. 49.
9. See Jacquie Bishop, "In Memory of Sakia Gunn," www.keithboykin.com (May 16, 2003).
10. See Gloria T. Hull, Patricia Bell Scott, and Barbara Smith, eds, *All the Women are White, All the Blacks are Men, But Some of Us Are Brave: Black Women's Studies* (New York: The Feminist Press at CUNY, 1982).
11. Transcript Oprah Winfrey Show (April 16, 2004).
12. See Todd Boyd, *Am I Black Enough for You* (Bloomington, IN: Indian University Press, 1997); Rana A. Emerson "Where My Girls At: Negotiating Black Womanhood in Music Videos," pp. 115–135 in *Gender and Society*, vol. 16, no. 1. (February 2002) Neal 2004; Rose 1994.
13. In May 2004, comedian Bill Cosby gave a talk to the NAACP in which he criticized young, poor Black for, among other things, their style of dress and language. For an interesting critique see Michael Eric Dyson, *Is Bill Cosby Right Or Has the Black Middle Class Lost it's Mind?* (New York: Basic Civitas Books, 2005).
14. Judith Halberstam, *Female Masculinity* (Durham, NC: Duke University Press, 1998), p. 234.
15. See Stuart Hall, "Encoding/Decoding," pp. 163–173 in *Media and Cultural Studies: Key Works*, edited by M. G. Durham and D. Kellner (New York: Blackwell Publishers).
16. Scott Poulson-Bryant, *Hung: A Meditation on the Measure of Black Men in America* (New York: Doubleday, 2005), p. 10.

17. See R. A. T. Judy, "On the Question of Nigga Authenticity," in *That's the Joint!: Hip Hop Studies Reader*, edited by M. Forman and M. A. Neal (New York: Routledge 2004) p. 114.
18. www.urbandictionary.com
19. See Mark Anthony Neal, *New Black Man* (Durham, NC: Duke University Press, 2005).
20. Neal, *New Black Man*, p. 151.
21. See Laura Mulvey, "Visual Pleasure and Narrative Cinema," in *Screen* (1975), pp. 6–18.
22. Morgan 1999, pp. 57–58.
23. Sometimes referred to as the "date rape" drugs, Gamma Hydroxybutyric Acid is a powdered depressant that can easily be dissolved in liquid. It has been associated with sexual assault among young women. In response to the use of drug in sexual assaults, Congress passed the Drug-Induced Rape Prevention and Punishment Act in 1996.
24. See Hall 2001. Stuart Hall defines oppositional readings as "counter-hegemonic" readings, which change the meaning of the original text.
25. Judith Halberstam. "Mackdaddy, Superfly, Rapper: Gender, Race, and Masculinity in the Drag King Scene," In *Social Text: Queer Transexions on Race, Nation, and Gender* (Autumn–Spring), p. 123.
26. Boyd 1997, p. 33.
27. Among others, see Patricia Hill Collins, *Black Sexual Politics* (New York: Taylor and Francis) 2004 and bell hooks, "Selling Hot Pussy," in *Black Looks: Race and Representation* (Boston: South End Press, 1992).
28. Neal 2005, p. 127.
29. See Cathy Cohen, "Punks, Bulldaggers, and Welfare Queens: The Radical Potential of Queer Politics," pp. 200–229 in *Sexual Identities, Queer Politics*, edited by M. Blasius (Princeton, New Jersey: Princeton University Press, 2001).

References

"Men Living on the D.L." *Oprah Winfrey Show*. CBS Television. Transcript. April 16, 2004.

Boyd, Todd. *Am I Black Enough For You?* Bloomington, IN: Indiana University Press, 1997.

Combahee River Collective. "A Black Feminist Statement." Ed. G. Anzaldúa and C. Moraga, *This Bridge Called My Back*. New York: Kitchen Table Press, 1981 [1977].

Clarke, Cheryl. *Living as a Lesbian*. Ann Arbor, MI: Firebrand Books, 1986.

Cohen, Cathy J. "Punks, Bulldaggers, and Welfare Queens: The Radical Potential of Queer Politics," pp. 200–229 in *Sexual Identities, Queer Politics*, edited by M. Blasius. New Haven, CT: Princeton University Press, 2001 [1996].

Collins, Patricia Hill. *Black Sexual Politics*. New York: Taylor and Francis, 2004.

Emerson, Rana A. "Where My Girls At: Negotiating Black Womanhood in Music Videos," pp. 115–135 in *Gender and Society*, vol. 16, no. 1. February, 2002.

Gomez, Jewelle and Barbara Smith. "Talking about It: Homophobia in the Black Community," pp. 47–55 in *Feminist Review: Perverse Politics: Lesbian Issues*. No. 34. Spring, 1990.

hooks, bell. *Black Looks: Race and Representation*. Boston: South End, Press, 1992.

Halberstam, Judith. "Mackdaddy, Superfly, Rapper: Gender, Race, and Masculinity in the Drag King Scene," pp. 104–131 in *Social Text: Queer Transexions on Race, Nation, and Gender*. Autumn-Winter. No. 52/53. 1997.

———, *Female Masculinity*. Durham, NC: Duke University Press, 1998.

Hull, Gloria T., Scott, Patricia Bell and Barbara Smith, eds. *All the Women are White, All the Blacks are Men, But Some of Us Are Brave: Black Women's Studies*. New York: The Feminist Press at CUNY, 1982.

Judy, R.A. T. "On the Question of Nigga Authenticity," pp. 105–117 in *That's the Joint! The Hip hop Studies Reader*, edited by M. Forman and M. A. Neal. New York: Routledge, 2004.

Lorde, Audre. *Zami: A New Spelling of My Name*. Freedom, CA: Crossing Press, 1983

Morgan, Joan. *When Chickenheads come home to Roost: A Hip-Hop Feminist Breaks it Down*. New York: Simon and Schuster, 1999.

Neal, Mark Anthony. *New Black Man*. Durham, NC: Duke University Press, 2005.

Nutter, Chris. "The Gay Rapper." *Vibe Magazine*. July, 2001.

Pough, Gwendolyn. *Check It, While I Wreck It*. Boston: Northeastern University Press, 2004.

Poulson-Bryant, Scott. *Hung: Meditations on the Measure of Black Men in America*. New York: Doubleday, 2005.

Rose, Tricia. *Black Noise*. Middletown, CT: Wesleyan University Press, 1994.

Watkins, S. Craig. *Representing: Hip Hop Culture and the Production of Black Cinema*. Chicago: University of Chicago Press, 1998.

23

"Cover Your Eyes as I Describe a Scene so Violent"
Violence, Machismo, Sexism, and Homophobia

Michael Eric Dyson has written eloquently about black masculinity via the figures of Malcolm X, Marvin Gaye, Martin Luther King, Jr., and perhaps most famously Tupac Shakur. Film-maker Byron Hurt has used black masculinity to examine issues of gender and sexuality within hip-hop and the broader society. Here the two talk about the relationship between black masculinity and violence as it is reproduced and circulated within hip-hop.

According to Dyson there is a relationship between the embrace of hypermasculinity by young black men and the institutionalization of hypermasculinity within American political discourse. In this context, hypermasculinity emerges as a primary vehicle to disempowered black men to envision themselves as possessing power and influence.

"Cover Your Eyes as I Describe a Scene so Violent": Violence, Machismo, Sexism, and Homophobia

Michael Eric Dyson and Byron Hurt

Byron Hurt: Hip hop is suffused with violence. One of the recurrent themes that I hear in rap artists' freestyles and in their emcee battles is talk about guns, including GATs, AK-11s, and other weapons. Can you explain that?

Michael Eric Dyson: There's a preoccupation with the gun because the gun is a central part of the iconography of the ghetto. Too many young black and brown men view their sense of strength, and industry, and machismo, and manhood through the lens—and sometimes literally through the scope—of a gun. And what you hear a lot in the lyrics of gangster and hard-core rappers are descriptions of the physical effects of gun violence on the larger community—from the viewpoint of the perpetrators and the victims. The gun is at once the merchandise of manhood and the means of its destruction. The gun is the most lethal means of undermining the masculine stability that many rappers desperately seek.

The gun is a staple of the postindustrial urban setting where young black and brown men contest one another over smaller and smaller living and recreational spaces. The forces of gentrification and decreased availability of affordable housing in the inner city spur rising tensions because of shrunken physical and domestic space. So the gun becomes the violent means by which space is divided and status is assigned. The ghetto teems with arguments made through the barrel of a gun. This homeboy's getting shot at for dancing with the wrong girl at a party; that homeboy's trying to shoot somebody because he feels disrespected on the school playground; another homeboy's shooting back at somebody shooting at him. So the gun becomes the outlet for the aggression and the rage that young black and brown men feel.

We live in a culture where the obsession with the gun is painfully conspicuous, from its ubiquity in Hollywood action films to the ad campaigns for the National Rifle Association (NRA). No other industrialized nation is so consumed by the gun as the symbol of freedom, which, as it turns out, is the very thing that can lead to bondage to death and destruction. The gun can be the implement of the barbarity of our so-called civilized society. It is the very instrument that's taken up in the fight over the Second Amendment by the NRA and other citizens who believe that their right to own weapons and to possess arms is *the* extension of American freedom.

Hurt: How can you tie notions of black male violence to violent masculinity in American culture more broadly? Please also talk about how hypermasculinity can be seen in other cultural institutions in America—sports culture, military culture, and even presidential politics.

Dyson: Well, simply said, violent masculinity is at the heart of the American identity. The preoccupation with Jesse James, the outlaw, the rebel, the social outcast—much of that is associated in the collective imagination of the nation with the expansion of the frontier in the modern West. Violent masculinity is also tied up with the ability to defend American property from "illegitimate" stakeholders—above all Native Americans, although they were here first and we ripped off their land through a process of genocide that is utterly underappreciated to this day. Violent masculinity is central to notions of American democracy and cultural self-expression.

In fact national self-expression and violent masculinity are virtually concomitant; they came about at the same time, and they often mean the same thing. In the history of the American social imagination the violent male, using the gun to defend his kith and kin, becomes a symbol of virtuous and redemptive manhood. Some young hip hop artists zero in on the use of the gun as the paraphernalia of *American* masculinity, as the symbol of real manhood. Hip hop's hypermasculine pose reflects a broader American trait.

There are so many segments of American society where violence is linked to manhood, from video games to sports like football, hockey, and boxing. Take football, for instance. The guy who delivers the hardest hit while tackling an opponent is most widely celebrated. (Those of us old enough to remember can hardly forget how in a 1978 preseason game, Oakland Raiders football player Jack Tatum, a safety, delivered a vicious blow and broke the neck of New England Patriots wide receiver Darryl Stingley—rendering him a quadriplegic—with no apology, contending at the time that an apology would be an untruthful admission that the hit was dirty.) Sure, there's a cerebral side to sports as well. But it can hardly be denied that sports provide vicarious outlets for millions of fans with a visceral and aggressive payoff.

The stakes of hypermasculinity—or the exaggeration of the posture of manhood and the aggression associated with male identity—are dug deep in our collective psyches. Even in sacred circles aggressive forms of militarism are masked in religious metaphors: God seeks to punish those who disagree with America, and God seeks to put down nations that refuse to obey God. Of course, obeying God and agreeing with America are often conflated in the basest version of our civil theology. This can be clearly seen in religious figures like staunch fundamentalist Jerry Falwell and sophisticated conservative evangelical Ralph Reed.

The American military, of course, makes heroes of those with a command personality and a gung-ho mentality. War is the tragic symbol of the contagious chaos of hypermasculinity, and the leaders of war are the military men we most admire, whether we're speaking of Dwight Eisenhower, Colin Powell, or Norman Schwarzkopf. One of the most potent expressions of hypermasculinity in recent times is the so-called Powell doctrine, epitomized when Colin Powell, in responding to a question about his strategy in combating the Iraqi army in the Persian Gulf War of 1991, said, "First we're going to cut it off, then we're going to kill it." Damn, it just don't get no more violently masculine than that! That kind of testosterone politics brims in masculine quarters of the culture.

And when it comes to politics, especially during a time of national crisis, it's the guy who's willing to deny the need for dissent and debate in order to defend American exploits at all costs who's deemed a "real patriot" and "real man." And make no mistake: the two are joined at the ideological hip. The Republican party often conflates being a hawk with being able to handle national security. War detractors are painted as insufferably weak. Even in colleges and universities, this hyperaggressive masculine image of the professor who refuses to tote the politically correct line prevails in conservative academic quarters, where it's a badge of pride not to embrace multiculturalism in the curriculum. Clearly, hypermasculine images are influential in sports, in the military, in religion, and even in the academy.

Hurt: But isn't that a narrow view of masculinity, especially if we want to remove destructive images of manhood and embrace healthy alternatives?

Dyson: It is a very limiting perspective to see manhood as the ability to impose harm or do violence against another human being, even in retribution against some perceived or real offense. That view of masculinity is truncated and, I would argue, inauthentic. Authentic masculinity is about wisely defining strength and accepting vulnerability. Moreover, American conceptions of masculinity typically fail to acknowledge the virtue in consensus, cooperation, negotiation, and compromise—except in negative enterprises and problematic functions like corporate malfeasance.

When we speak about hypermasculinity, we're speaking about the Frank Sinatratization of American political discourse: "I did it my way." Seeking compromise, looking for consensus, building a healthy coalition—this is not the natural inclination of hyperaggressive males. Such a view of manhood prevents us from reaching out to other nations and seeking agreement and peaceful resolution. Instead we drop bombs on Iraq, warring with a nation that we falsely argued had weapons of mass destruction, and which, contrary to initial claims by some conservatives, had nothing to do with the terrorist attacks of 9/11. We refuse to see how we've precipitated violent responses to our wantonly destructive ways as a nation. We refuse to say to ourselves, "Perhaps our perverted and distorted conception of strength and masculinity has led to some devastating results and has limited the political options we're able to pursue."

Even when we pull back from foreign affairs to focus on domestic issues, our hyperaggressive vision of masculinity is problematic. For instance, patriarchy is the belief that heterosexual white men's lives are normal and any identity that falls outside of such a view is abnormal. Perhaps if we got rid of narrow, rigid quests for manhood in favor of more nuanced conceptions of masculinity, men wouldn't die as much from heart attacks and strokes. We might express ourselves in nonviolent ways and transmit to our boys a more noble and humane vision of manhood. This stuff in the men's movement—about thumping one's chest, going into the woods and beating on drums and giving voice to one's primal scream of masculinity—sometimes works against successful social negotiation in a civil space. That's especially true in the urban situation where testosterone-fueled conflicts often lead to harmful consequences for young men.

Hurt: Could you talk more about what the negative consequences are for black and Latino men, especially in the hip hop generation?

Dyson: Society is teaching many young men and women to believe that the only way to be an authentic man is to dominate a woman. To make matters worse, many young men see women almost exclusively in sexual terms. Violence is also highly glossed and eroticized in hip hop videos and rap lyrics where the appeal of aggression is intensified by the promise of sexualized release. I think real-life relations between young men and women are often trapped in fictional narratives of masculine dominance that hamper the growth of alternative models of healthy male-female relationships.

The moral outrage and feminist ire sparked by Nelly's "Tip Drill" video uncovered a powerful example of such a narrative. I suppose "tip drill" suggests either a female with a nice body but an unattractive face, or a male with a lot of money but an unattractive face. (It also refers to a basketball drill where each player tips the ball off the backboard.) The term also suggests an orgy, or a "train," where several men have sex with a single female. In the video, a young man swipes a credit card through a young woman's gluteus maximus.

Well, I'm hard-pressed to tell the difference between Nelly's video and the time two hundred years ago when black women and men were looked at for their gluteus maximus, for their latissimus dorsi, for their pectoralis major, for their testicles, to see if they were durable enough to procreate in order to extend slavery. Isolating body parts like that represents a sexualized fetish tied to the racial subjugation of black bodies by white supremacists. Such a state of affairs reinforces the vulgar status of black humanity, even when it has comic overtones like the troubling image struck in the Nelly video.

You'd think black folk would appreciate the fact that since black bodies were once sold on the auction block, you don't want to perpetuate the sort of visual injustice against women that occurs in the Nelly video. But there's a huge disconnection between older and younger black people that fuels the amnesia that such visual injustice feeds on. Of course, cultural amnesia isn't peculiar to black youth culture; it's really at the heart of American society. We barely remember stuff thirty years ago; God knows we don't remember events from fifty and sixty years ago; and forget history from 150 years ago. So it's very difficult to transmit these values in such cultural and historical circumstances.

In the aftermath of the controversy, the sisters at Spelman College rightfully opposed Nelly's coming to their campus, even to raise awareness about bone marrow donation in black communities, unless he was also willing to sit down and discuss the demeaning messages of his "Tip Drill" video. Nelly's insulting video was the last straw for the Spelman women. They had had enough of the sexist sentiments and patriarchal posturing of young men who sanctify their bigotry by suggesting it's a natural male reflex. In the end, Nelly canceled his campus visit rather than have an open conversation about sexism and misogyny in hip hop.

I applaud the women of Spelman for their courage. But the challenge to the sisters of Spelman is to apply this same moral standard to the clergymen and other civic and business leaders who are invited to their campus, who hold equally heinous views about women, if not as obviously virulent as those expressed in hip hop. But the problematic views of clergy who preach the biblical basis for female subordination to men, and the harmful gender views of civic and business leaders, are less likely to be scrutinized as sexist rap lyrics are. The women of Spelman must ask themselves if they are willing to be equally vigilant about decrying the sexism of an upstanding minister or educator as they are a well-known rapper.

Hurt: How do you respond to people who say that the women at Spelman were being contradictory and hypocritical?

Dyson: When the Spelman women took their stand against Nelly, some folk thought it was arbitrary because Nelly is hardly the most sexist or misogynistic rapper one might go after. But one can never predict what controversy will become socially opportunistic and what event will spark outrage or galvanize a community. Nelly's "Tip Drill" visually conjured all the ugly signifiers of black sexism that can be traced back to slavery's crude conception of the black female body. "Tip Drill" created a powerful groundswell of critique and debate. In fact the Spelman sisters' intervention should be applauded and repeated. I don't find them hypocrites at all. I think they acted on what they believed in a given period of time in response to a specific event that inspired their protest. They finally got to the point where the weight of insult on their collective psyches was so crushing that it demanded an immediate response.

In a sense, the Nelly video flap was like the O.J. Simpson case. There were all sorts of arguments about race and the criminal justice system long before O.J. was accused of murder, but O.J.'s criminal case got that idea across like few other events in our nation's history. His case also underscored just how radically different are black and white views on the subject. We couldn't predict that there would be an O.J. Simpson case, or that it would provoke such bitter debate over race in America. Nelly's "Tip Drill" functioned in similar fashion for the debate about sexism in hip hop, although it sparked nothing near the broad cultural conversation that O.J.'s case generated.

There were even some women who criticized the Spelman sisters' decision to make a big deal of the Nelly video and his potential visit to their campus. It just reminds us that we've got to grapple with instances of internalized sexism in women where the ventriloquist magic of patriarchy is occurring—women's lips are moving, but men's voices and beliefs are speaking. I'm not suggesting that *any* female critique of the Spelman sisters was necessarily a patriarchal gesture, but I am saying that a lot of the female criticism of the Spelman sisters suggests how pervasive and irresistible the logic of male supremacy is. Just as some blacks offer the most depressing defense of white supremacy, some women offer tortured defenses of sexism and male supremacy.

Hurt: A lot of people have asked why it took so long for the women of the hip hop generation to take a stand.

Dyson: Well, that's an incredibly shortsighted view of black feminist struggle. Think about the black women associated with African American Women in Defense of Ourselves, the ad hoc collection of women who stood with Anita Hill in her charge that Supreme Court nominee Clarence Thomas had sexually harassed her years before when she worked for him. Thomas had the white male establishment, and a significant portion of the black establishment, on his side. A lot of folk claimed that Hill was self-serving, that her claims were unbelievable because they came so long after the alleged offense, and that she was bringing a black man down and being disloyal to the race.

Some of those same arguments are at work against the Spelman sisters. Some critics claim that it took their generation too long to speak out, and that they were attacking a "good" black man like Nelly who was far from the worst sexist in hip hop. It's clear that some of the same intraracial fault lines that existed with the Thomas/Hill affair are present in the Spelman/Nelly dispute. And it's equally evident that another generation of black women acting in defense of themselves causes problems for patriarchal authority.

The black women who spoke out in defense of Anita Hill were largely established professional black women. They had social savvy and far greater access to media than did the Spelman women. The Spelman women were brilliant, articulate college students confronting huge media forces and the bulwark of black American sexism. The Nelly incident politicized many young black women in the way that the Hill/Thomas affair had done for an earlier generation of black women. We can't forget that black feminist activity has been hampered by black female devotion and loyalty to black men, often at the expense of their own interests and identities.

The Spelman sisters had to grapple with an unfair and absurd question put to activist black women through the ages: "Are you female first or are you black first?" The reality is that black women are black and female simultaneously—and in many cases, poor too. Identity isn't something one can parcel out. As feminist theorist Elizabeth Spellman memorably put it, we must not have an additive vision of identity, where you keep adding elements to increase your minority status—black, female, poor, lesbian, and so on. Still, you can't deny that black women have a lot of complex realities to confront in their bodies. Black women have displayed such extraordinary fidelity to the race that when they finally decide to speak up for themselves, they are viewed as traitors. Black men have often told black women that feminist concerns should only be addressed when the racial question is settled, but we all know that if black women wait that long, justice will never come.

Finally, the question is not what took the Spelman sisters so long to speak up; the question is what took black men so long to realize that we should have spoken out on this issue decades ago. The burden of response shouldn't rest exclusively on black women; the burden of opposing sexism should be shared by our entire community.

And popular culture ain't helping much. I mean, if all you're thinking about as a hormonally driven young male for twenty-four hours a day is the bouncing bosoms and belligerent behinds you see paraded endlessly on music videos, and you're almost exclusively focused on how women can serve your libido, you're not going to have a healthy understanding of women or yourself. If such images are not met with opposing interpretations of black female sexual identity, they can negatively affect the self-understanding and self-image of young black men. They can also have a destructive effect on the erotic and interpersonal relations between young folk.

Another factor that hampers healthy relations is the fact that males are not encouraged to be self-reflective or to take individual and collective self-inventory. To face ourselves is to face the world that men made, and that world doesn't often view women with great respect or appreciation. Young guys don't get a sense that their testosterone plague is somehow related to bigger social and political issues. You can imagine a cat like Nelly saying, "It's just me in the video. I'm just having fun. I'm just blowing off steam. I'm just doing what all guys do."

In this case, the behavior of young black males is isolated from its broader network of social meanings. They don't necessarily get the academic concept of the "social construction of masculinity," which is just a fancy term to say that you ain't born with a sense of what it means to be a man; you're socialized into that. Gender roles are not innate; they're assigned based on what society tells us is good and bad. "You're a woman; you stay home and clean the house and have babies. You're a man; you go out and get a job and support your family." When we begin to challenge those predetermined, heterosexist roles with feminist narratives of gender justice and social equality, we upset the patriarchal applecart. When you've got all that stuff going on around you, it's very difficult for young men to understand that their sexual identities and desires are shaped by the politics and the social struggles of a larger society.

Hurt: How difficult is it for black men to understand that, even though they're the victims of racism, they often perpetuate sexism toward black women?

Dyson: Historically, it has been difficult for black men to understand that although we're victims, we also victimize; that although we're assaulted, we also assault; and that while we're objects of scorn, we also scorn black women as well. As with all groups of oppressed people, it's never a matter of either/or; it's both/and. You can be victimized by white supremacy and patriarchy and at the same time extend black male supremacy. Just because "the white man's foot is on your neck" doesn't mean that your foot can't in turn be on a black female's neck.

We've also got to reckon with how certain forms of male privilege exist precisely because we don't acknowledge them. Male privilege is strongest (so strong that it was one of the first things white men permitted black men to share with them) when we are not forced to interrogate it, when we don't have to ask questions of it. We insulate ourselves from knowledge of its very existence, and sometimes we do that by seeking refuge in *our* victimization, as if that could prevent us from dealing with how we victimize more vulnerable folk.

In order to understand this, we should think about how race and racism operate for white brothers and sisters. When most of our white brothers and sisters hear the word "race," they think "black" or "brown" or "yellow" or "Native American." They don't think "white," as if white is not one among many other racial and ethnic identities. Men are the same way. When black men hear male supremacy, we often think, "white guys who control the world." We don't think, "Black guys who control our part of the world." You can be oppressed and still be dog-gin' somebody else who's lower on the totem pole.

In a society dominated by men, women are assigned a lower niche on the societal totem pole. Men often step on the faces of women to climb higher up on the perch of masculine privilege. Our boosted sense of masculinity comes at the expense of women's lives, identities, and bodies.

What's even more telling, but often overlooked, is that black men are also victims of black male supremacy and patriarchy and sexism and misogyny. Those horrible traits actually make *us* worse men. The profound investment in a violent masculinity costs many black men their lives, especially on the streets where codes of respect are maniacally observed and brutally enforced. And closer to home, many black men turn on their loved ones, striking them instead of hitting out at a punishing social order for whom their wives, or girlfriends, or babymamas, or children are the unfortunate proxy. Black men who can't get good jobs often blame their women who are employed. Some brothers blame black women for their success in a zero-sum calculation that suggests women are conspiring against them with white society's approval.

What such brothers fail to understand is how they and their women are victims of white male supremacy. Too many brothers fall into the trap of male supremacy by using its logic to explain their absence of payoffs, or rewards, in the patriarchal system. Instead of thinking through the complex dynamics of our vulnerable situation (black women are just as put upon by patriarchy and white supremacy as black men are, even if in different fashion), we become outraged at the women whose love has helped sustain us as men, as a family, and as a race.

Hurt: What about women's complicity in how they are portrayed in rap, especially in videos?

Dyson: Not only are women blamed for the harm that befalls men, but they are blamed for the limitation that male society imposes on them. This is best exemplified by the self-serving justifications commonly offered for the exploitative placement of women in rap videos: "Nobody is making these women appear in the videos; therefore, they must like it and want to do it." But that's like making early black actors the heavies when their only choice in movies was between stereotypical roles. It's not fair to blame them for the white supremacist practices that limited their roles in the first place.

Instead of men saying, "We have limited the roles that black women can play in videos to dime piece, hoochie mama, video vixen, eye candy, arm pleasure, sexy dancer, and more variations of the same," we blame women for accepting the crumbs from our sexist table and trying to eat off of our patriarchal leftovers, as self-destructive and spiritually undernourishing as that may be. We rarely probe the interior of a male-dominated world that forces women into such demeaning choices and roles.

Men just find it easier to blame women for the limited choices *we* leave them with while ignoring the economic and social constraints on young black women who seek a toehold in the world of hip hop culture and rap videos. It's a classic case of blaming the victim, but then there's little difference between what men in hip hop do, and what males in mainstream religion have always done through their theologies and holy texts.

Think back to Genesis 3:12, in the Garden of Eden, where Adam and Eve have disobeyed God and eaten from the forbidden tree only to realize that they're naked. They hide from God when they hear God's voice walking through Eden—I love that metaphor of God's voice walking, quite appropriate for a discussion of the walking voice of hip hop. God calls out to Adam in the Garden of Eden, asking where he is, and Adam finally speaks up, confessing that he's hiding because he's naked. God wonders how he knows he's naked, asking Adam if he's tasted fruit from the tree he wasn't supposed to eat from in the middle of the Garden of Eden. And then Adam blames it all on Eve: "And the man said, the woman whom thou gavest [to be] with me, she gave me of the tree, and I did eat." And of course, Eve blamed the slick serpent for "be-guil[ing]" her.

If hip hop has a theology, it's pretty consistent with the biblical justification of male misbehavior by blaming the seducing female. Now that's not to deny that there's female complicity. We have to ask the hard question of why certain women conform to the vicious images of female sexual identity promoted in misogynistic masculinity. Of course, that's not simply a problem that shows up in hip hop; it's a culture-wide phenomenon. When women go to religious institutions where they hear clergy justify their second-class citizenship, they are conforming to the dominant images of a religious culture that aims to subordinate them. But it's easier to jump on hip hop videos than it is to target the sermons of ministers, bishops, imams, and rabbis who reinforce a culture of male privilege and strident patriarchy.

Hurt: Why aren't more men confronting the sexism in hip hop?

Dyson: First, to put it crudely, it's not in their immediate interest to do so. The hip hop industry is built in large measure on the dominant masculine voice, a voice that rarely expresses respect for women as peers—only as mothers. Rappers love their mamas but hate their baby-mamas. Second, it's not as erotically engaging for the men in hip hop to adopt feminist stances, or at the very least, to concede the legitimacy of feminist perspectives. Third, the moment men begin to challenge the retrograde and crude crotch politics of hip hop culture, they feel that they're going to be ostracized.

Well, what hip hop males (and to tell the truth, a lot of older brothers too) don't understand is that one can have really liberating erotic experiences with women as equals. It just never strikes them that they could have beautiful, rapturous, loving, powerful relationships with beautiful, rapturous, loving, powerful, and independent women who don't feel pressure to have sex with men out of a dreadful lack of self-confidence that is encouraged in a brutally sexist culture.

Hurt: A lot of men in hip hop say they want a "good sister" and not a "ho." Of course, that distinction is problematic. What are the limitations of that perspective?

Dyson: Part of the perverse genius of patriarchy is that there's always elbow room for such distinctions and oppositions, like the one between the "good sister" and the "ho." But it's a tricky, loaded juxtaposition indeed. In the parlance, a "good sister" is someone who stays away from "bad boys," who doesn't give sex easily, who keeps herself clear of the troubled circles that men in hip hop frequent. A "ho" is a loose woman who gives sex easily, who drinks and smokes and is found in the company of males in hip hop.

What's interesting about such an ethical division between women is that the men in hip hop have much more experience with the ho than they do the good sister. The good sister they claim to adore—well, they don't spend that much time with her. In part, that's because the good sister, in their minds, is not the one most likely to concede to their erotic advances or otherwise behave as the men do. The ho, ironically enough, even as she is castigated, is granted a strange equality of ends with the males in hip hop: they both want the same thing, at least when it comes to sex, drugs, and music, even if they seek it for different ends—the men to flex their muscles of manhood, the women to enhance their access to male circles of power, privilege, and pleasure.

But isn't it interesting that males in hip hop have much more ethnographical data on the ho than on the good sister? They spend more time pursuing, pleasing, and "playing" the ho than the good sister, even though they often put the latter on a social pedestal. But the notion of placing women on a pedestal of respect is a severely limiting gesture. Respect can reinforce the "proper" role of women, which often means denying them the sexual pleasures, social standing, cultural perks, and erotic freedom that men routinely enjoy. Respect can be an iron fist in a velvet glove. Patriarchal notions of respect—such as keeping women at home away from the fray of professional spheres—often mock true independence of thought and behavior for women.

This understanding of respect means that a good sister must do more than not act like a ho to win male approval. For instance, a woman who shows no ho tendencies but challenges male conceptions of power and authority, or makes more money than her man and doesn't pretend that she doesn't, is a problem to her man as well. In many cases, her independent, challenging behavior is read as disrespectful. Upon closer inspection, the good sister/ho opposition doesn't hold up in defining the critical difference between the desirable/undesirable woman, because other elements intrude.

Too often, putting a woman on a pedestal of respect is the attempt to control her by softer, more subtle means. And the moment a woman steps off that pedestal—even if she's otherwise viewed as respectable—she's a problem. In the crude language of patriarchal disdain, she's a "bitch," the equally derided, often more powerful ideological twin of the "ho." Women who confront and vacate the pedestals of patriarchal respectability are viewed as bitches or hoes.

Hurt: You hear male rap artists constantly use "bitch" or "ho" to feminize other men. What does that reveal about black masculinity?

Dyson: The greatest insult from one man to another in hip hop (and beyond) is to imply that he's less than a man by calling him a derogatory term usually reserved for women or gay men: "bitch," "ho," "punk," "fag." It's an act of enhanced degradation because injury is added to insult with the double negative of being dissed to begin with and then being assigned a gender or sexual orientation epithet to boot. These epithets place a male lower on the totem pole of masculine identity by classifying him with the already degraded female or gay male.

In regard to women, look how deadly such an identification is, being made the ultimate equivalent of a despised male. This underscores another harmful use of "bitch" by men: it is what philosophers might call a "multievidential" term. It fits a lot of circumstances and can be used in multiple ways to either affirm or negate a specific identity or instance. It can be used to suggest good and bad, sometimes at the same time, and in the case of hip hop, sometimes in the same lyric. When the late Notorious B.I.G. created the song "Me and My Bitch," he didn't mean anything negative by the use of the term. He was celebrating his female companion. Others use the term regularly to suggest both meanings—problematic female or loving female companion—or women in general. In fact, for many in hip hop, saying "bitch" is natural, like saying "woman."

Of course, in hip hop as in the larger society you pick on the most vulnerable when you want to insult somebody. In our society, that's women, gays, and lesbians. Children are vulnerable too, but they're not usually attacked in hip hop circles.

More specifically, the accepted and misguided notions of maleness in society dictate which types of homosexuality are more tolerable. What's quite interesting, perhaps even paradoxical, is that hip hop in this regard reflects the values of mainstream conservative culture when it comes to the victimization of women, gays, lesbians, bisexuals, and transgender folk. And not just among white folk either. We're having a huge debate right now in American society about gay and lesbian marriage, and one thing we can depend on is black and brown communities offering extraordinary support to a conservative president and his allies in their assault on the liberties and civil rights of these gay and lesbian people. The president appeals to conservative evangelical beliefs about sexuality and gender, and a narrow, literal reading of the Bible that appeals to a lot of blacks and Latinos. That always trips me out because I wonder how people who were illiterate less than 150 years ago could be biblical literalists!

After all, the same religious folk who historically subscribed to a biblical literalism that castigated black folk and justified our oppression and enslavement now use the same principles of interpretation to justify resistance to gays and lesbians. And many black folk are in league with them. That's just crazy, and I say this as an ordained Baptist preacher rooted deeply in progressive evangelical territory. There is huge support for biblical texts that justify assault on gay and lesbian identity—or, for that matter, on women as first-class citizens. Ironically enough, hip hop, which is equally reviled in conservative circles and in many quarters of established black America, for its allegedly decadent morality, is in full agreement with these regressive viewpoints.

Of course, the sin of hip hop to many who abhor hip hoppers' virulent expression of sexism and misogyny is that they are explicit and vulgar in articulating their beliefs. What is required are the more subtle, sophisticated expressions of misogyny and patriarchy that are not nearly as outwardly venomous as the female antipathy found in hip hop. Hip hop captures the bigotry toward women and gays and lesbians found in the larger society—but on steroids, so to speak. It's the ugly exaggeration of viewpoints that are taken for granted in many conservative circles across the nation.

Of course, all of us have to confront the sexism, misogyny, patriarchy, and homophobia that are so deeply rooted in our culture. I try to embrace and live feminist principles, but I'm constantly at war with the deeply ingrained sexism of the culture that seeps into my brain. The same is true for homophobia. That's the challenge I face: to confront and reject male supremacy and heterosexist bigotry even as we together confront and reject them in the broader society.

Hurt: I'm against homophobia, but if I see a gay person kissin' somebody of the same sex on TV, I'm like, "Oh!"

Dyson: But if we, as heterosexual men, see two lesbians kissing each other, not only are we not necessarily turned off, we may even be turned on. Lesbian sexuality can in some cases be tolerated, even encouraged, because it can be subordinated to the heterosexual male erotic economy: two for the price of one. We can swing the women our way to allow us to participate in a ménage à trois! You can imagine a brother saying, "Oh, I don't mind if you get into bed with me with your other girl because she might please us both." So there's room in the heterosexual world for situational lesbianism that services the straight male crotch.

Hurt: Talk about the weird tension between homophobia and homoeroticism in hip hop.

Dyson: What's intriguing to me about the tensions and therefore the connections between homophobic and homoerotic men is that they both have a stake in the same body. Straight and gay men are equally invested in the same testosterone-soaked athletic contest where men are slapping each other's behinds on the football field or patting each other's booties after making a touchdown. The same straight and gay males go to church and leap to their feet and vigorously ejaculate, "I love him! I love him," speaking about another man—Jesus.

One of the reasons there's so much tension between men who can be virulently homophobic and those who can be vibrantly homoerotic (and make no mistake, they are often the same guys, except one group isn't aware of it) is because they both have investments in the same body. The same actions can count as grandly heterosexual or gleefully homoerotic. Slapping behinds, patting booties, hugging, and hollering about Jesus—all that is multievidential. Those actions count for heterosexuals and homosexuals at the same time, depending on how you interpret them.

To the horror of straight men, they're engaging in a lot of actions that could easily be interpreted as gay. I mean, I often joke with my son, "If you're so interested in protecting yourself from gay men, you're giving somebody an easy shot at your butt with your pants sagging so low and your drawers showing." So even in the most hallowed heterosexual circles, homoerotic bonding occurs on the regular. That's bound to cause a lot of straight guys to worry about their own sexuality, or to ask if what they're doing is pure or is contaminated with homoerotic sentiment. You can see how easily that might lead these straight men to question themselves and then direct enormous fury at gay males and gay culture. It's precisely because the meanings are shared, and the significations slide easily between straight and gay male culture, that there is such huge hatred for homosexuals among heterosexual men.

What's more, the gay male upsets the social order for the straight male. The straight male wants at the male body of his friends and comrades without the attribution of homoerotic union or homosexual desire. Straight males want to celebrate the athletic body, the cultural body, and the religious body without fear of being charged with an erotic or sexual attraction to it. The presence of a gay male throws things off, and therefore the straight male argues for erotic segregation, so that rigid lines can be drawn between the kind of desire the gay male has and the kinds of social and personal interests that animate the heterosexual male. You can understand that there'd be a lot of self-questioning, self-doubting, and questioning and doubting of others as a result of homoerotic desire invading the precincts of straight male desire.

It even invades the religious realm and the church sanctuary, where the tension between heterosexual and homosexual elements is especially pronounced—from the pulpit to the choir stand—and therefore vehemently resisted. You've got "straight" men proclaiming their love for

Jesus, even more than their love for parents, partners, or progeny. And even though they consider him God, he's still embodied on earth as a man. So their love for another man supersedes their love for anything or anybody else. In some readings, that's awfully homoerotic, maybe even a supernaturally supported homoeroticism.

Homoerotic moments show up in hip hop in at least a couple of ways. First, when hip hop artists speak about M.O.B. (money over bitches), they are emphasizing the crass relation between commerce and misogyny. But there's another element to M.O.B. as well: placing "homies" above women, because men make money with men—or take money from them. In any case, the male relation becomes a fetish in hip hop circles: hanging with "my boys," kicking it with "my crew," hustling with "my mens and them," and dying for "my niggas." There is an unapologetic intensity of devotion that surely evokes at some level homoerotic union.

Second, there is great exaggeration or even mythology about sexual conquests performed in the presence of one or more participating men. "I hit it, then my boy hit it," some young men brag, while others boast of multiple men having consensual sex with a woman. One assumes that males expose their sexual organs in such conquests, especially as they mimic the sexual gestures adapted from the pornographic tapes that are increasingly popular in certain hip hop circles. This is surely a heated and heady moment of homoerotic bonding.

Hurt: Finally, how do you respond to someone like Beverly Guy-Sheftall who says that often the issues that are prioritized, even in conscious hip hop, are issues that impact black men: racial profiling, the prison-industrial complex, police brutality, and so on. She argues that hip hop rarely deals with gender issues—sexism and misogyny—and never addresses homophobia.

Dyson: Well, there's no question that we've got to teach these young black men to be concerned about issues beyond their own body and bailiwick. But let's be honest: that makes them no different than most men in America. Dr. Guy-Sheftall, whom I admire greatly, is absolutely right. But as I'm sure she'd agree, that point can also be made about most civil rights leaders as well, or most black captains of industry. That point can be made about male television executives in charge of featuring women baring their bosoms and bopping their behinds on music videos all day. So the critique is right on, even though it can't be made exclusively about young black men.

But we've all got to learn as black men—whether in hip hop or business, academe or acting—that sexism and misogyny *are* our issues and *do* affect us as black men, because a world that makes women less than they ought to be, makes us as men less than we ought to be. We are not real men when we deny women their rightful place in our society or attack the networks of formal and informal support they have generated out of necessity. When men in hip hop finally learn that, they will be far ahead of men in other quarters of the culture who may appear to be more enlightened but hold tenaciously to antiquated beliefs that prove they are moral dinosaurs. Or better yet, gendersaurs.

Study Questions

1. How has the embrace of hypermasculinity by young black men contributed to the rise in violence in black communities?
2. To what extent is the hypermasculinity found in hip-hop related to normative issues of sexism and homophobia in American society?
3. Does hypermasculinity easily translate into sexist and homophobic attitudes?

24

"The King of the Streets"
Hip-Hop and the Reclaiming of Masculinity in Jerusalem's Shu'afat Refugee Camp

For young Arabs surviving in refugee camps in East Jerusalem, hip-hop music has become one of their coping mechanisms, as much for the political potential seemingly inherent in hip-hop culture as for hip-hop's capacity to offer a way to think through the performance of masculinity within the settlements.

Ela Greenberg's essay presents a compelling view of the myriad effects that globalization has had on black popular culture, in this case, examining the ways that black masculinity has become a critical component of what America exports to the world.

"The King of the Streets": Hip Hop and the Reclaiming of Masculinity in Jerusalem's Shu'afat Refugee Camp

Ela Greenberg

Introduction

On February 17, 2007, after several weeks during which Palestinian youths burned tires and threw stones at Israeli soldiers in protest against Israeli archaeological excavations at the Mughrabi gate,[1] a hip hop crew called G-Town—from Jerusalem's Shu'afat Refugee Camp—staged a very different protest. They drove a borrowed Hummer car into the busy and crowded Salah al-Din Street in East Jerusalem, stopped the car, climbed on its roof and began rapping until the police broke up the impromptu concert 40 minutes later (B-Boy, interview, August 6, 2007). For the members of G-Town, rap was more powerful and more provocative than throwing stones or burning tires as it enabled their voices to be heard.

Rap music is 'a musical form that makes use of rhyme, rhythmic speech, and street vernacular, which is recited or loosely changed over a musical soundtrack' (Keyes 2002: 1). Although rap music first originated among African-Americans in the 1970s as a voice of protest and resistance to their ghettoized, powerless status, by the 1990s, African-American rap music had lost much of its oppositional appeal in the United States as it became increasingly mainstream and lucrative (Chang 2005). Outside of the United States, however, marginalized minority youths have adapted rap to their own local socio-political contexts, using it to express their opposition or rage (Mitchell 2002), with rap's 'connective marginalities' linking them together (Osumare 2001).

Palestinian youth began experimenting with rap music in the late 1990s, with the creation of DAM (Da Arabian MCs) from Lod, and MWR (an acronym for the first names of the members of the group: Mahmoud, Waseem, and Richy) from Acre. Both groups rap about their experiences of discrimination and racism as Palestinians in the state of Israel, reflecting the parallels that they see between their own predicament and that of African Americans (Massad 2005: 194). DAM's song '*Meen irhabi*' (Who's a terrorist) released in 2001 was downloaded more than a million times from the now defunct Arabic rap site www.arabrap.net (Kahf 2007: 360). Since then, rap has gained popularity among Palestinian youth in the West Bank, Gaza, Lebanon, Egypt, and North America, fuelled in part by internet sites where groups can upload songs, and chat in forums devoted to Palestinian and Arabic rap. Almost all of die media coverage of Palestinian hip hop has focused on DAM, with little attention given to burgeoning Palestinian hip hop scenes elsewhere.

This chapter examines G-Town, an up-and-coming Palestinian rap group from Shu'afat refugee camp in Jerusalem. The members of G-Town are inspired by African-American rappers, and their first and only CD to date incorporates borrowed rap beats from well-known US hip hop songs (their most popular song '*al-Sharq al-awsat al-jadid*' ['the New Middle East'] is inspired by

Ice Cube's 'Why We Thugs'). Despite American inspiration, G-Town raps in Arabic to mostly local and almost entirely Palestinian audiences (unlike DAM, for example, who has a very large international following). The group's "hood' of Shu'afat Refugee Camp is central to their music, as it provides them with the authenticity needed to secure their position within the increasingly competitive Palestinian hip hop scene. While G-Town admittedly uses rap music as a vehicle to express political opposition to the Israeli occupation and anger at the apathy of Arab states vis-à-vis Palestinian refugees, I argue that G-Town has adopted rap music for survival purposes, similar to the way that youths in Dar el Salaam, Tanzania rap in order to 'deal with social pressures and project themselves as creative and empowered individuals' (Perullo 2005: 76). More specifically, I contend that G-Town and their followers use rap as a means of reclaiming their masculinity, by reconstructing it through rap, and thus empowering themselves as men, particularly at a time when Palestinian masculinity is being challenged and significantly weakened.

This chapter is based on field research conducted from late 2007 through the end of 2008, as part of a larger project on Palestinian youth culture in East Jerusalem. Having been impressed with G-Town's performance at an Israeli-Palestinian peace festival in June 2007, I easily found the group on MySpace and arranged a meeting with the leader. Later I met the rest of the group and conducted group interviews in their homes in Shu'afat Refugee Camp. Both through my initiative and theirs, I met with G-Town recurringly on a more casual basis in their homes, in local parks and café-bars in both East and West Jerusalem, and sometimes by chatting on the Internet. I also had both formal and informal meetings with some of G-Town's fans and those who were 'junior members,' that is, a select group of fans who were being trained by G-Town to rap with them.

The group also invited me to attend their concerts, providing me opportunities to interact both before and after the concerts. I made several trips with G-Town, including to the Oktoberfest in the West Bank city of Taybeh, and to Bethlehem, both in which they performed, as well as to Ramleh where we visited a fellow Palestinian rapper. In addition, they invited me to join them in painting graffiti on the wall around Shu'afat camp, and to observe a week-long hip hop summer camp for aspiring rappers in the camp. American student interns and two graduate students also joined me in many of these interactions. My contact with the members of G-Town gradually ended between October 2008 and January 2009 for inexplicable reasons.

Creating G-Town in Jerusalem's Shu'afat Refugee Camp

The three main members of G-Town all hail from Shu'afat Refugee Camp. United Nations Relief and Works Agency (UNRWA) established the camp during 1965 and 1966 in order to house some 1,500 Palestinians displaced during the 1948 war. Originally established on 203 dunams belonging to Shu'afat village, today the camp is spread across 347 dunams and is home to around 22,000 people, of whom 50 to 60 percent are registered refugees (International Peace and Cooperation Center, 2007: 91). Under Israeli occupation since 1967, Shu'afat camp, along with the rest of East Jerusalem, was declared part of Israeli-controlled Jerusalem. As a result, most of the camp's inhabitants acquired Jerusalem residency status (symbolized by the blue ID card), enabling them the right to work in Jerusalem (or in Israel), to benefit from Israeli health funds, national insurance, and child allowances, and to travel between Jerusalem, Israel, and the Palestinian Authority. While they do not have the right to vote in Israeli national elections, they can vote in Jerusalem municipal elections; very few Palestinian residents exercise this right, however, as it is tantamount to recognizing Israeli sovereignty over East Jerusalem.

Shu'afat Refugee Camp is perhaps unlike any other place in Jerusalem in that it has acquired a de facto 'extraterritorial' status (Ir Amin 2006: 3); the camp's history of defiance, like other refugee camps in the West Bank, has meant that Israeli control there is practically non-existent. Although the camp is within Jerusalem's municipal borders, the municipality refuses to service the camp, on the grounds that UNRWA provides educational, social, and health services to the camp's refugee population. While the camp's autonomous status could be celebrated, at the same time, the absence of any kind of security in the camp (Israeli police refuse to enter it and the Palestinian Authority police are prevented from operating within Jerusalem) has led to high rates of family violence, robbery, use of firearms in dealing with disputes, drug abuse, and public drug dealing (International Peace and Cooperation Center 2007: 94). As a result, Palestinians both inside and outside of Shu'afat camp refer to it as 'Chicago Camp,'[2] and accuse the Israelis of purposely allowing the camp, and especially the youth, to degenerate (Hilal and Johnson 2003: 63–4).

The defiance of Shu'afat Refugee Camp and its dangerous reputation may have had a high price, as Israel has placed it on the West Bank side of the Separation Wall. Currently built only on one side of the camp, upon completion, the Wall will completely sever the camp from East Jerusalem. The Wall has significantly weakened the quality of life within the camp, as it has become increasingly difficult for residents and non-residents to freely move in and out of the camp. In order to get to Jerusalem, camp residents must pass through a single operating checkpoint, manned twenty-four hours a day by Israeli military police who carefully scrutinize passers' ID cards. The completion of the Wall is expected to cause an exodus of families with means (Nasrallah 2006: 379), with some families having already moved, some into adjacent Jewish neighborhoods (Ir Amim 2006: 2).

Fifty-seven percent of residents of Shu'afat camp are under the age of 24 (UNRWA 2008: 1). The members of G-Town are representative of much of the camp's population specifically and East Jerusalem generally. For example, 'Error' had trained to become a computer technician, briefly owning an internet café within the camp, but was working in a supermarket in West Jerusalem at the time of my research. Seventy percent of the camp residents worked in the Israeli private sector, as employment opportunities within the camp, as in other parts of East Jerusalem, are very limited (UNRWA 2008: 5). 'Giant M' quit school in the tenth grade in order to support his parents and twelve siblings, and was employed in cleaning and construction jobs in West Jerusalem. Fifty percent of Palestinian males in East Jerusalem drop out of high school because of economic necessity, compounded by the impoverishment of the East Jerusalem educational system (Hever 2007: 59). 'B-Boy,' the leader of the group, was a rarity among his peers, as he had graduated from a municipal high school (outside the camp), and was pursuing a university degree in the West Bank settlement of Ariel. Although B-Boy joked about being the only refugee studying in a settlement (B-Boy, interview, August 6, 2007), it has become increasingly common for Palestinian Jerusalemites to attend Israeli universities and colleges as the Wall has made daily travel to Palestinian institutions in the West Bank time-consuming and difficult (interview with Khaled, director of a university preparatory institution, August 20, 2007). For a while, a young woman nicknamed '*Filastin*' (Palestine) from one of the upper class neighborhoods of Jerusalem was also part of the group. According to B-Boy, the few girls who have been interested in singing with G-Town have been reluctant to do so as they are afraid to enter the camp (interview, August 6, 2007). Although I was told that Filastin left in order to pursue her studies, it is conceivable that gender issues may have been the primary reason why she stopped rapping with G-Town.

B-Boy had formed G-Town during the Second Intifada in response to feelings of hopelessness and 'being lost.' Although the growing elusiveness of the two-state solution has contributed to these sentiments, the situation of Palestinians in Jerusalem is especially complex. Many Palestinian youths from East Jerusalem express a janus-faced identity: they suffer from the policies of the occupation and simultaneously derive some benefits from the occupier. For the members of G-Town, rapping is a chance to address some of these issues and to reaffirm East Jerusalem's Palestinian identity (B-Boy, interview, June 20, 2008). Forming a rap group has given these youths a purpose. As one young man who grew up in the camp said, the young men in the camp have 'nothing to do but sit … in the street looking for fights,' deal or use drugs (with the

374 • ELA GREENBERG

drug dealers working openly within the camp), or engage in trading weapons (Ahmad, conversation, August 22, 2008). In contrast to the idleness and the corruptive temptations commonly associated with the young men of the camp, the members of G-Town have 'learned how to record, how to make, how to use everything' (B-Boy, interview, June 20, 2008). Engaging in rap music also has given G-Town the 'license' to pursue other traditional elements of hip hop, such as painting G-Town-related graffiti (including an ambitious project to paint the entire wall around the camp); learning how to DJ; and practicing and teaching break dancing to camp youths, often taking the form of capoeira, which B-Boy had studied with Israelis in West Jerusalem.

Even though Shu'afat Refugee Camp offers these youths few options, G-Town uses their upbringing in the camp to assert their 'realness' and 'street cred' as Palestinian rappers. The camp features prominently in their overall image, their recorded music, and their performances, reflecting what Stokes (1994) and Forman (2000) have argued as the centrality of 'place,' the physical setting of a social activity, in making and performing music. Their connection to Shu'afat camp is reflected in their name, with G-Town standing for 'Ghetto Town.' Having listened to African-American hip hop, they perceive the camp as analogous to the African-American urban ghetto beset with poverty, lack of infrastructure, drugs, and guns. On their self-released CD, photographs show the group walking along a dirty street of the camp passing by ugly homes built haphazardly out of cement or composing a song with a view of the camp in the background. At first they performed in black and white t-shirts bearing the imprint of Handhala, who has become the ubiquitous symbol of Palestinian youth, representing hopes for the return of the refugees to their original homes (Najjar 2007). These t-shirts were later replaced with ones of their own design, reading 'G-Town, Refugees of Jerusalem' and adorned with images of Damascus Gate, the main gate of the Muslim Quarter in Jerusalem's Old City; a map of pre-1948 Palestine; and elements of hip hop, including a microphone, a bottle of spray paint, and sneakers for break dancing, emphasizing the links between hip hop, Jerusalem, and Palestinian refugees.

While the t-shirts are a reminder of G-Town's association with Jerusalem, it is specifically the *hummus* and *foul* (fava beans) that distinguishes them from other youths. The members of G-Town regularly told me that they ate hummus and foul for breakfast, while youths from other parts of East Jerusalem ate cornflakes. Eating hummus and foul suggests that they, as refugees, are the 'real homeboys' who maintain the traditions of Palestinian society, as opposed to other aspiring rappers who were 'posers' eating imported, Western goods. Ironically, this comparison does not question the adoption of rap music by Palestinian society; for these boys from the refugee camp ghetto, rap is both Palestinian and 'real,' and does not need validation. More importantly, hummus and foul constitutes a hardy meal, reflecting the notion that they, as refugee rappers, are tough and outwardly masculine, while those from outside the camp, particularly the middle and upper class neighborhoods of Beit Hanina and Shu'afat (distinct from Shu'afat refugee camp) are weak 'mama's boys' because cornflakes easily break (conversation, Ahmad, Malek, and 'Imad, October 12, 2008).

Rapping and Masculinity

There was a reason that the members of G-Town regularly brought up the hummus-foul and cornflakes analogy. Masculinity is an important construction among Palestinian youth, shaped and tarnished by the context of the Israeli occupation. Peteet (1994), in her groundbreaking work on Palestinian masculinity during the first Intifada, argued that beatings or interrogations by the Israelis empowered young Palestinian men, serving as a kind of 'rite of passage' that was crucial to the construction of their masculinity. During the Second Intifada, however, Johnson and Kuttab (2001) observed a 'crisis in masculinity,' created both by the growing difficulties faced by young men in becoming future providers and breadwinners, as well as by the reluctance of young men to confront Israeli soldiers, given the high rate of injury and death. As a result, the role of young Palestinian males 'as heroes and agents of national resistance' was considerably weakened (33).

More recently, this crisis in masculinity has been interpreted more severely as 'emasculation' or the total loss of male power. In the post Second Intifada period, Naaman claims that Palestinian men 'interpret the humiliation [at the checkpoints] as feminization. They are questioned, searched, ordered around, and in general have little control over their agency. Since they associate lack or power with the feminine position, they feel doubly humiliated' (2006: 175). Sharif Waked's 2005 video piece 'Chic Point' addresses the emasculating and humiliating experience of Palestinian men who have been forced to lift their shirts and drop their pants as they attempt to move between checkpoints (Waked 2006). Whereas during the First Intifada confrontations with soldiers and beatings endured were construed as empowering, today, it is just the opposite; the occupation humiliates and robs Palestinian men of their most precious characteristic, their *rujula*. Young men whose masculinity has been challenged or questioned may suffer serious consequences. Hart has shown in his work on masculinity in a Palestinian refugee camp in Jordan that young men who strayed from the camp's construction of masculinity were rendered as '*tant*,' or as 'homosexual,' and subjected to abuse (2008: 8–12). Among Palestinians in Jerusalem and the West Bank, the weakening of masculinity parallels reports of increased domestic violence and my own observations of aggressive behavior (such as owning attack dogs and guns or driving recklessly), corroborating the findings of Sa'ar and Yahia-Younis (2008) who argue for a similar crisis of masculinity among Palestinian Israelis caused by ongoing political and cultural marginalization.

In the very emasculating context of the current practices of the occupation, rap has made the members of G-Town feel increasingly masculine in ways that other typical male activities apparently have not. In particular, rapping has enabled G-Town to express their anger against the occupation, something that they are prevented from easily doing in their everyday lives. In a query that I posted on http://www.palrap.net, an Internet forum owned and operated by G-Town for promoting and discussing Palestinian rap music, mainly male members from Jerusalem as well as other parts of the West Bank agreed that rap is the best means of 'expressing anger against injustice' ('important question,' #10, March 12, 2008). Moreover, rap music is full of 'resistive transcripts,' which serve 'the dual purpose of using symbolism to critique power holders,' while at the same time, 'providing a dialogic arena in which rappers shape the terms of entry' (Stapleton 1998: 222). Although I did come across young men who engaged in individual acts of everyday resistance to the occupation, such as questioning why their identity cards had to be checked, or engaging in car-chases with the police, these acts carried a price. Instead of taking risks or appearing passive, G-Town uses rap to openly criticize and confront Israel's hegemonic practices while at the same time displaying a tough, resistant, masculine image.

African-American rappers, especially the late Tupac Shakur who came to codify the 'gangsta' rap genre, have influenced G-Town's understanding of rap and the ways in which it is used to reclaim masculinity. The members of G-Town identify with Tupac because he also originated from the 'ghetto' and wrote about the institutionalized discrimination against African-Americans in the US, which they relate to as Palestinians under Israeli occupation. I further argue that Tupac, in addition to other African-American rappers, offers an alternative construction of masculinity, especially as the local notion of masculinity has failed youths in resisting the occupation. Tupac's lyrics, his 'thug life' image, and his 'cool pose'—his physical postures, clothing styles, social roles, behaviors, styles of walk, speech, hand shaking, and so forth—all emit a hyper, almost threatening, masculinity that serves as a kind of coping mechanism against oppression and racism (Iwamoto 2003). Mimicking this hyper-masculinity through hand signals and the 'gangsta' style of dress (baggy pants, ostentatious gold jewelry ['bling'] and hooded sweatshirts, but adding the Palestinian *keffiya* as representative of the local context), the members of G-Town have constructed a new resistant and tougher masculinity that is rooted in the camp 'ghetto,' and with which Israeli authorities are unfamiliar. This hyper-masculinity was well illustrated by comments made on Facebook by Malek, a junior member of G-Town. During the Israeli war on Gaza, he declared that he was the 'king of the street,' emphasizing his masculinity and perceived sense of power, while suggesting that he led the youth of his neighborhood in their protests against the war, which the Israeli military police found difficult to subdue.

The members of G-Town have also become empowered through their music. Through music, they have become self-appointed youth leaders in the camp, a role that otherwise would be denied to them by both the Israeli occupation and elite segments of Palestinian society because of their refugee status. B-Boy stated that:

Rap artists are the voice of people who can't speak for themselves ... We are voicing the feelings of the oppressed ... People like what we say because these are things we feel from day to day. When I stop at a roadblock, when I leave the house, just by opening the window, I could write a whole book of rap songs.

(*G-Town*, 2007)

By representing the collective voice of Palestinians in Jerusalem, and not just rapping about their personal lives, G-Town has amassed a small following of youths from inside and outside the camp. They have taken some of these youths under their wings and taught them to rap. They also act as protective 'uncles,' scolding these youths when they engage in activities that might give G-Town and Palestinian rap music a negative image, such as drinking alcohol or smoking hashish (conversation, Ahmad, Malek, and 'Imad, October 12, 2008). According to B-Boy, the fans listen to everything he says and will do whatever he tells them (interview, August 6, 2007), suggesting a set of power relations similar to that of urban gangs in the US. While this relationship has enabled G-Town to emerge as local youth leaders, and to reclaim their masculinity in the process, it does not encourage those youths under G-Town's patronage to express their individuality as rappers or otherwise since the members of G-Town carefully watch them (Ahmad, conversation August 20, 2008; conversation, Daud, May 28, 2009).

G-Town's affinity for hip hop has led to a rejection of other musical genres popular among Palestinian youth, presumably because these genres do not provide youths with strong notions of masculinity. Although some youths that I spoke to liked the more traditional 'sad and romantic' Arabic (and often Hebrew) songs because, as one young man said, they could relate to the subjects of love, loss, and failed relationships ('Ammar, conversation, March 21, 2009), the members of G-Town and many of their fans have dismissed this genre as not able to 'speak' for or to young people. As B-Boy reasoned, such singers are only 'good for singing at weddings' (conversation, June 14, 2008), suggesting that these singers and the subjects they address do not help young males express their masculinity in the context of the Israeli occupation. G-Town also expressed their dislike for the mainstream Rotana-style, Lebanese Arabic pop stars such as Haifa Wehbe and Nancy Ajram, agreeing with the prevailing attitude of Middle Eastern youth that their overtly sexualized music fails to challenge the current political reality (Abdel-Nabi et al. 2004). The belief that rap can change the status quo may be one reason for its growing fervor among Arab youth across the Middle East, as indicated by the Arabic rap show ('Hiphopna') on MTV Arabia and the flourishing of Internet sites devoted to the subject. Yet the popularity of rap music might also be a reaction to the challenges that female pop stars are posing to traditional notions of gender by becoming public personas whose assertive sexuality is a significant component of their image (Smolenski 2007/2008). In contrast, the Arabic rap of G-Town, in its appeal largely to young males, reasserts the traditional male role of publicly defending the nation, while ignoring the role of young women. Although beyond the scope of this paper, Palestinian rap and other aspects of Palestinian hip hop culture have been almost entirely dominated by young males, paralleling the hip hop scene in the US (Chang 2005: 445), with young Palestinian women rappers finding it difficult to perform publicly, a point emphasized in the film *Slingshot Hip Hop.*

Although G-Town uses rap music to empower themselves as men, their lyrics do not explicitly address issues of gender, but rather are solidly nationalist, calling for the necessity of and adherence to *sumud* (steadfastness). *Sumud* refers to the all-consuming coping and resistance mechanisms that Palestinians living under Israeli occupation have developed—'to stay put, to cling to our homes and land by all means available' (Shehadeh 1982: vii). G-Town urges their listeners to engage in *sumud* against the 'quiet deportation' or 'silent transfer' policies of the Israeli government, designed to cause Palestinians to permanently leave Jerusalem: building the wall; routinely denying Palestinians the rights to building permits; demolishing houses built without permits; abrogating the Jerusalem residency status of Palestinians who no longer reside in Jerusalem; and rejecting residency rights for family members, including spouses, from the West Bank and Gaza (B'tselem and the Moked 1997). Their emphasis on *sumud* is illustrated well in the song '*al-Quds lana*' ('Jerusalem is ours'):

> As long as we're here/ Jerusalem is ours, and not for the Jews,[3] we'll never leave it/ and you animals will never triumph or prevail/ you won't fatigue us/ this is our land and our homes, here is our original blood/ Our Jerusalem and our holy land/ since thousand of years is for us/ it's true that you destroyed houses/ you've changed the world you've made borders/... we'll not permit you/ It's not possible to allow you/we are angry with you/ we will have a chance to destroy you.

G-Town's song '*Darrdakeh*' ('It's fucked up'), the opening song on the CD of the same name, is critical of Palestinian youth who believe that typical masculine behavior will free them from the Israeli occupation. They rap that 'from 2002 to 2007 it was fucked up/ Palestinian self-defense/ From the first push we went to the sky/ Afterwards we saw blindness,'[4] equating the attempts of defending Palestine through violence as being ineffectual to the point of blindness. Instead; the members of G-Town see rap as the best means of defending Palestine and self-empowerment: 'and the rap in front of our eyes has been thrown/ We are raising it with our country/ I am standing, looking, and knowing/ I am not afraid of the Rap/ I am not ignored, I am not blamed/ When I say everything is possible.' With rap empowering G-Town, they criticize their peers who do nothing but engage in typical male activities, rapping that fighting the occupation is 'not just eating hummus and foul/ and I am stoned like the fool.'

Being critical of those who remain passive to the Israeli occupation and whose masculinity thus becomes questionable is a common theme in G-Town's rap. In their song '*al-Hilm al-rama-di*' ('The Gray Dream)', a song about losing hope, B-Boy sings:

> we are not going to forget the daily killing and destroying of homes/ they are increasing and growing when we are dying/ they take up arms against us and think they are whales/ without a weapon I can hide in a coffin/ and our leaders are useless as a stand/ and your mate has become a spy/I sing, I sing, I sing/ no one hears what I keep saying.

The song suggests that Palestinians are 'digging their own graves,' by not resisting (or not being able to resist) Israeli policies or by becoming a 'spy,' that is, a collaborator with the occupation, making their masculinity dubious (Kanaaneh 2005: 262). The criticism of the 'spy' is directed particularly at those in the camps, where, despite being reputable sites of resistance, the socio-economic organization of the camps has been more conducive to collaboration, with Israel creating networks of collaborators through threats, drugs, bribery, and blackmail (Yahya 1991: 94).

The connection between rap and masculinity has influenced the kinds of subjects that the members of G-Town are willing to address in their songs. B-Boy told me that violence against women, women's rights, or gay rights were 'not the issue; the issue is Palestine' (conversation, July 29, 2008). Even though these subjects could assume a nationalist tone, the implication is that G-Town does not want to address any subject that could be interpreted as 'weak' and therefore detract from their masculine tough-guy image. At the time of writing this paper, however, G-Town had recorded a song condemning violence against women, after they had begun collaborating with a local Palestinian NGO. Although there is no room to expand upon this here, G-Town's lyrics, sound, and attitude have changed immensely since they began to work with the NGO. Although these changes could stem from personal growth, they also may reflect the interests of international supporters and upper class Palestinians rather than those of refugee camp youths (Hammami 2000).

G-Town also uses live performances as a means of encouraging the practice of *sumud* and of imbuing the primarily male audiences with a renewed sense of masculinity. This was particularly noticeable with their performance at a musical *hafla* (party) at the al-Hakawati Palestinian National Theater. Organized by residents of Shu'afat camp, the management of the theater had expressed concern that the (male) camp residents in attendance would live up to their reputations of being 'dangerous' (B-Boy, personal communication, June 14, 2008). This perceived sense of danger may have been one reason that the management of the theater insisted that the majority of the audience, almost entirely *shabab* (young men) between the ages of 12 to 23, sit up in the balcony, far from the stage, segregated from the small number of women, families and foreigners who were seated close to the stage. When asked about the segregation, one of the ushers said that the young men had to sit upstairs so that they would not 'disturb the girls.' As the theater did not usually impose segregation on its audience, it may have also been an attempt to accommodate the camp population, who were considered to be more 'traditional,' and who did abide by gender segregation within the camp, while putting the young males up in the balcony was clearly an attempt to rein them in and subdue their 'dangerous' masculinity for the evening. This gender segregation was maintained through all the performances until G-Town came on stage.

G-Town's concert at the al-Hakawati revealed the group's ability to connect with young men from the refugee camp (*mukhayyamjin*). G-Town was greeted on stage to thunderous applause, introduced by the emcee as being from Shu'afat Camp, living with injustice (*thulm*) and singing songs of the nation (*watan*). As soon as G-Town started to rap, the young men in the balcony ran down to the front of the theater; some of them found seats next to young women and families, while others went and stood close to the stage, completely disregarding the gender segregation that had been imposed upon them. The ushers, however, forced the young men to return to their seats in the balcony despite their protests, with B-Boy stating aloud that it was a shame that the women were downstairs and the young men forced to remain upstairs. The desire of the young men to move to the front of the stage to interact with G-Town and participate in their performance underlined the degree to which they saw G-Town as representatives of themselves. It also suggested that today's generation of Palestinian youth in Jerusalem, even those from the more conservative refugee camps, did not care too much about the cultural and gender barriers imposed upon them as long as they could reclaim their masculinity at least for one evening.

The Emasculating and Corruptive Sounds of Rap

Despite the potential that rap music has to empower Palestinian males, not all are supportive of the hip hop culture that G-Town and other youths have embraced. Some of their peers, both inside and outside the camp, ironically consider rap music as being rather effeminate. According to one young man who worked closely with G-Town, some of their peers perceive G-Town as having gone 'soft' or weak in that they no longer have time to pick fights (Ahmad, personal communication, August 20, 2008). Another friend of theirs criticized the hip hop style of clothing that G-Town wears as being 'homosexual' (Tareq, personal communication, November 14, 2008).

Others criticize rap as corruptive and inappropriate for Palestinian society. This idea was expressed strongly in a short documentary film about G-Town and two female fans (*G-Town*, 2007) made by a group of Israeli and Palestinian youth. In the film, an older man tells the two girls that they should listen to Umm Kulthum, Farid al-Attrash and 'Abd al-Halim instead of rap groups like G-Town. One young woman retorts that 'they sing about love. We're not interested in love,' reiterating the idea that traditional Arabic popular culture has not maintained its appeal among the younger generations. Another older man states that Palestinians 'should spread love, not hatred and enmity,' and encourages the two girls to listen to Palestinian folk songs, stating that 'they teach me love of the land, of the spade, the scythe, the crops, the grains, the Earth. They make an impression on me. Not rap and corrupt songs . . .' Whether or not this scene was staged or not is hard to tell, but it suggests that the older generation of Palestinians fears that rap music can ultimately raise issues that Palestinian society is not yet ready to address. The scene also suggests that members of the older generation are unaware of or refuse to acknowledge the crisis of masculinity that young Palestinian men have experienced, and therefore are unable to relate to the feelings of empowerment that rap has given to G-Town and their fans.

While G-Town may feel empowered through rapping, their masculine toughness is not necessarily well received in the upper and middle class Palestinian circles of Jerusalem. This was the case at a G-Town concert that I attended at the French Cultural Center, marking the opening of the now international 'Fête de la Musique,' created by Jack Lang, the former French Minister of Culture. Introduced in French by Jack Lang himself, G-Town performed on an outdoor stage in the Center's garden. Despite a shared nationalist identity, the East Jerusalem Palestinian crowd in attendance was rather unmoved by what they were watching. Their clothing styles and the uncovered, coiffed hair of the many young women in the audience suggested that they were from the upper class neighborhoods of Jerusalem. Later B-Boy told me that he believed that the audience was passive because they had never been to a rap concert before, based on their lack of hip hop style (personal communication, June 20, 2008). Indeed, the location of the French Cultural Center on the busy Salah al-Din Street and the afterschool hour of the concert may have brought in many curious bystanders who may have never heard rap music before. The audience's passivity and lack of emotion, however, also may have indicated that they could not relate to G-Town's hyper masculinity. G-Town's message, very much directed at young males, did not exactly correspond to the gender ideals of the mixed male and female crowd, reflecting Hart's observation that the masculinity of refugee camp youth is very much bounded as well as reinforced by the camp, but does not extend beyond the camp itself (2008: 12–13).

Conclusion

When G-Town climbed on top of the Hummer and began to rap in protest of the Mughrabi gate excavations, their rap voiced not only their anger at having come of age under Israeli occupation, but also empowered them as Palestinian men in the very emasculating context of the ongoing Israeli occupation of East Jerusalem. G-Town's appropriation of rap has given them a kind of elevated stature within Shu'afat Refugee Camp.

At the time of this writing, the future of G-Town undoubtedly stands to change as their subsequent involvement with a Palestinian NGO has cultivated a following among the youth in West Bank cities and refugee camps, and has provided them with increasing international exposure. Their new songs deal with new topics and include original Middle Eastern sounding beats that deviate from the borrowed beats with which their fans are familiar. Will G-Town continue to relate to young Palestinian males in Jerusalem who seek ways of reclaiming their masculinity so

388 • ELA GREENBERG

that they can challenge the emasculating practices of the Israeli occupation? With the intensifying of Israeli control in Jerusalem, Palestinian youths find themselves in a very precarious and volatile predicament. In Shu'afat Refugee Camp, the connection to Jerusalem has become even more tenuous, and in this context, G-Town's message of *sumud* plays an important empowering role for young Palestinian men from the camp. Yet as G-Town begins to rap across the West Bank and before international audiences, changing their sound and their focus, they risk losing their appeal among mainly local young males, desperate for means of hypermasculine expression that helps them survive the realities of Jerusalem's Palestinian ghettos under occupation.

Study Questions

1. What makes black masculinity such a valuable commodity in the global export of American culture?
2. What intrinsic value does black masculinity hold for young men in the Middle East?
3. What is lost or gained in the translation of black masculinity beyond the borders of the United States?

Notes

1. One of several gates leading to *al-Haram al-Sharif,* the Noble Compound that contains the Dome of the Rock and al-Aqsa Mosque, the third most holy site in Islam. The gate is adjacent to the Western Wall, the most holy site in Judaism, with the excavations intended to further strengthen Jewish claims to the area.
2. Suggesting that the camp is similar to urban city ghettos such as those found in Chicago.
3. 'Al-Quds' (Jerusalem) refers to East Jerusalem and not West Jerusalem, while the term 'Yahud' (Jews) refers to Israelis.
4. These lines are all in reference to the Second Intifada.

References

Books and Articles:

Abdel-Nabi, Shereen, Jehan Agha, Julia Choucair, and Maya Mikdashi (2004). Pop Goes the Arab World: Popular Music, Gender, Politics, and Transnationalism in the Arab World. *Hawwa*, 2(2): 231–254.

B'tselem and the Moked: Center for the Defense of the Individual (1997). *The Quiet Deportation: Revocation of Residency Rights of East Jerusalem Palestinians.* Jerusalem.

Chang, Jeff (2005). *Can't Stop Won't Stop: A History of the Hip Hop Generation.* New York: St. Martin's Press.

Forman, Murray (2000). 'Represent': race, space and place in rap music. *Popular Music,* 19(1): 65–90.

Hammami, Rema (2000). Palestinian NGOs since Oslo: From NGO Politics to Social Movements. *Middle East Report,* no. 214(30): 16–19.

Hart, Jason (2008). Dislocated Masculinity. Adolescence and the Palestinian Nation-in-exile. *Journal of Refugee Studies,* 21(1): 64–81.

Hever, Shir (2007). Education in East Jerusalem: Report on the Educational System in East Jerusalem. *The Economy of the Occupation, A Socioeconomic Bulletin* 13–15.

Hilal, Jamil and Penny Johnson (2003). Poverty in Jerusalem. *Jerusalem Quarterly File,* 17: 59–66.

International Peace and Cooperation Center (2007). *The Wall: Fragmenting the Palestinian Fabric in Jerusalem.* Jerusalem.

Ir Amim (2006). Jerusalem Neighborhood Profile: Shu'afat Refugee Camp. http://www.ir-amim.org.il/Eng/?CategoryID=212. Accessed December 20, 2008.

Iwamoto, Derek (2003). Tupac Shakur: Understanding the Identity Formation of Hyper-Masculinity of a Popular Hip-Hop Artist. *The Black Scholar,* 33(2): 44–49.

Johnson, Penny and Eileen Kuttab (2001). Where Have All the Women (and Men) Gone? Reflections on Gender and the Second Palestinian Intifada. *Feminist Review*, 69: 21–43.

Kahf, Usama (2007). Arabic Hip Hop: Claims of Authenticity and Identity of a New Genre. *Journal of Popular Music Studies*, 19(4): 359–385.

Kanaaneh, Rhoda (2005). Boys or men? Duped or 'made'? Palestinian Soldiers in the Israeli Military. *American Ethnologist*, 32(2): 260–275.

Keyes, Cheryl L. (2002). *Rap Music and Street Consciousness*. Chicago: Universiry of Illinois Press.

Massad, Joseph (2005). Liberating Songs: Palestine Put to Music. In Stein, Rebecca and Swedenburg, Ted (eds.), *Palestine, Israel and the Politics of Popular Culture*, pp. 175–201. Durham: Duke University Press.

Mitchell, Tony (2002). Another Root—Hip-Hop outside the USA. In Mitchell, Tony (ed.), *Global Noise: Rap and Hip Hop Outside the USA*, pp. 1–38. Middletown CT: Wesleyan University Press.

Naaman, Dorit (2006). The Silenced Outcry: A Feminist Perspective from the Israeli Checkpoints in Palestine. *NWSA Journal*, 18(3): 168–180.

Najjar, Orayb Aref (2007). Cartoons as a Site for the Construction of Palestinian Refugee Identity. *Journal of Communication Inquiry*, 31(3): 255–285.

Nasrallah, Rami (2006). To the Suburbs and Back: The Growth and Decay of Palestinian Suburbs around Jerusalem. In Misselwitz, Philipp et al. (eds.), *City of Collision Jerusalem and the Principles of Conflict Urbanism*, pp. 376–381. Basel: Birkhaüser.

Osumare, Halifu (2001). Beat Streets in the Global Hood. Beat Streets in the Global Hood: Connective Marginalities of the Hip Hop Globe. *Journal of American & Comparative Cultures*, 24 (1–2): 171–181.

Perullo, Alex (2005). Hooligans and Heroes: Youth Identity and Hip-Hop in Dar es Salaam, Tanzania. *Africa Today*, 54(4): 75–101.

Peteet, Julie (1994). Male Gender and Rituals of Resistance in the Palestinian *Intifada:* A Cultural Politics of Violence. *American Ethnologist*, 21(1): 31–49.

Sa'ar, Amalia and Yahia-Younis, Taghreed (2008). Masculinity in Crisis: The Case of Palestinians in Israel. *British Journal of Middle Eastern Studies*, 35(3): 305–323.

Shehadeh, Raja (1982). *The Third Way: A Journal of Life in the West Bank*. London: Quartet Books, 1982.

Smolenski, Natalie (2007/2008). Modes of Self-Representation among Female Arab Singers and Dancers. *McGill Journal of Middle East Studies*, 9: 49–80.

Stapleton, Katina R. (1998). From the Margins to Mainstream: The Political Power of Hip-Hop. *Media, Culture & Society*, 20(2): 219–234.

Stokes, Martin (1994). Introduction: Ethnicity, Identity and Music. In Stokes, Martin (ed.), *Ethnicity Identity and Music: The Musical Construction of Place*, pp. 1–27. Oxford and Providence: Berg Publishers.

UNRWA (2008). Shufat [sic] Refuge Camp Profile. http://www.ochaopt.org/infopool/opt_campprof_unrwa_shufat_oct_2008%20.pdf. Accessed April 25, 2009.

Waked, Sharif (2006). Chic Point: Fashion for Israeli Checkpoints. In Stein, Rebecca L. and Beinin, Joel (eds.) *The Struggle for Sovereignty: Palestine and Israel 1993–2005*, p. 213. Stanford: Stanford University Press.

Yahya, Adil (1991). The Role of the Refugee Camps. In Nassar, Jamal R. and Heacock, Roger (eds.) *Intifada: Palestine at the Crossroads*, pp. 91–106. Bir Zeit: Bir Zeit University and New York: Praeger.

Multimedia:

G-Town (2007). *Darrdakeh*. Self-produced CD.

G-*Town* (2007). Film directed by Rasha Jaber, Shaked Kahana, Abed Fuad, Miri Beckman, Abed Alkarim Darwish, and Alina Gansirovsky. Part of 'I am, You Are: Films and Identity,' Joint Arab-Jewish film workshop, produced by the Jerusalem Cinematheque and the Jerusalem Foundation.

Slingshot Hip Hop (2008). Directed by Jackie Salloum. Screened at the al-Hakawati Theater, Jerusalem, July 16, 2008.

25

Scared Straight
Hip-Hop, Outing, and the Pedagogy of Queerness

In 1989, rumors circulated within black media that rapper Big Daddy Kane was HIV positive. Occurring a few years before basketball player Magic Johnson would be diagnosed and before tennis great Arthur Ashe and seminal gangster rapper Eazy E would die of the disease, Big Daddy Kane's career, which was arguably at its peak, never really recovered. As Marc Lamont Hill argues, because HIV was thought to be a "gay" disease, the rumors, even after they were refuted, essentially were a death knell of Kane's commercial viability.

In his essay, Hill examines the politics of rumor and "outing" within the context of hip-hop and the culture's proclivity to police identity, and masculinity in particular. The attempts at outing figures in hip-hop are meant to damage a particular artist's hold on authenticity and, by extension, damage their status as competitors in the marketplace.

Scared Straight: Hip-Hop, Outing, and the Pedagogy of Queerness

Marc Lamont Hill

In 1989, a rumor swept through the streets of New York City with remarkable speed and lethal intensity. Various radio outlets, underground magazines, and unnamed sources were reporting that Big Daddy Kane, one of hip-hop culture's most respected and popular artists, was dying of AIDS. According to the rumors, Kane had confessed on *The Oprah Winfrey Show* that he contracted HIV through sexual intercourse. Although the rumor proved to be entirely fabricated, it nonetheless marked a critical moment in hip-hop history. In addition to creating undue concern about the health and life of one of hip-hop's towering figures, the incident marked the first public "outing" in hip-hop history.

Given the dominant belief that HIV/AIDS was a gay disease, public attention quickly shifted from Kane's health to his sexuality: Did hip-hop have its first gay MC? Was he gay or bisexual? Did he catch the disease from another rapper? These and other questions chased the rumor throughout the city's boroughs and into urban spaces throughout the country. Further enhancing and complicating the rumor was its apparent irony. In addition to being a lyrical giant, Big Daddy Kane was hip-hop's playboy extraordinaire. With good looks, braggadocious lyrics, a flashy persona, and even a pimp-like name, Kane's very identity signified a carefully crafted and extravagantly performed masculinity. After the rumors began to circulate, however, Kane's image was placed in serious peril. Hip-hop's Goliath of masculinity had been slain by a disease presumably preserved for "punks," "fags," and "queens."

In an effort to salvage his image and protect his career, Kane responded to the rumors by vigorously denying their accuracy and reiterating his heterosexuality. Perhaps the best example of this came on his 1993 track "Give It To Me," where he raps

> Like with that HIV rumor they tried to toss
> But I'm so good with the women that if I ever caught AIDS
> A woman doctor'd find a cure just so she could get laid
> So never fear my dear, just come on over here
> I practice safe sex, with girls I lay next
> In other words, the J-hat's on the head
> Cause I'm too sexy for AIDS like Right Said Fred[1]

Before the release of the song, Kane also appeared in various public venues, such as a 1990 Harlem voter registration drive, declaring his status as an HIV-negative heterosexual.[2] In June 1991, Kane posed partially nude for *Playgirl* magazine and appeared in Madonna's controversial

1992 photo book, *Sex*. Although the rumors eventually subsided, Kane's career never fully recovered from the ordeal.

Despite the untruthfulness of the Big Daddy Kane rumor, its construction, dissemination, and response in many ways foreshadowed several key aspects of contemporary hip-hop culture's relationship with sexual identity. Specifically, the rumor provided explicit proof that queer identities did not fit comfortably within the cultural logic of the hip-hop world. Also, it prefigured more recent public conversations about the sexual identities of hip-hop culture's most prominent citizens. Lastly, in addition to intensifying the already vicious antigay climate within mainstream hip-hop culture, the ordeal demonstrated how hip-hop polices its sexual boundaries through sophisticated practices of surveillance. Through these practices, the hip-hop community is able to sustain the myth of universal heterosexuality through its constant attempts to locate, isolate, and, most importantly, "out" the gay citizen. The threat of outing, or publicly exposing a person's non-heterosexual identity, has facilitated the development of a "don't ask, don't tell" climate within hip-hop culture. Within this atmosphere, the queer hip-hopper is forced to remain in the closet out of fear that his "sexual business"—sexual orientation, partners, proclivities, etc.—will be publicly exposed.

While the threat of outing is considerable for both male and female artists, the stakes are particularly high for male rappers. Whereas female artists like Queen Latifah and MC Lyte are able to achieve professional success despite perennial questions about their sexual orientation, no such possibility exists for the male MC. This is not to suggest, however, that women occupy a privileged position within hip-hop culture. On the contrary, women are merely beholden to different controlling images, such as the temptress, the mammy, the whore, or the baby momma, all of which delimit possibilities for identity development and performance within the rap world.[3] In addition to constraining artistic performance, these discursive strictures inform and reflect a broader public pedagogy that calls into question the very notion of a fully human Black female subject.

Still, as the case of Big Daddy Kane demonstrates, the perception of fractured masculinity, which is an inevitable consequence of outing, serves as a professional death sentence from which there are few routes of redemption or recovery. Unlike the aforementioned female MCs who are able to craft a functional and profitable professional identity within mainstream hip-hop culture, male MCs whose sexual identity is questioned are subjected to forms of marginalization and abuse that alienate them from the mainstream hip-hop community.[4]

In this article, I examine the politics of outing within hip-hop's public sphere. In particular, I explore how contemporary American hip-hop culture sustains hegemonic conceptions of masculinity through a variety of outing practices. Through these practices, which include but extend beyond traditional notions of outing, we are able to preserve falsely obvious notions of uniform heterosexuality while denying the legitimacy and viability of queer subjectivities within mainstream hip-hop culture.

Homophobia in Hip-Hop

In order to understand the significance and power of hip-hop's outing practices, it is important to examine the context in which they are situated. Like the larger social world, much of mainstream hip-hop culture reflects a collective fear, disdain, and outright hatred of gay and lesbian bodies. Moreover, these homophobic sensibilities translate into concrete forms of oppression, violence, and discrimination for those who openly identify as gay, lesbian, bisexual, transgender, or questioning. It is this homophobic sensibility that often protrudes from the work of some of hip-hop culture's most celebrated figures.

Ironically, given its extraordinary discomfort with queer identities, the hip-hop community has made considerable use of gay and lesbian contributions since the early stages of its development. Like other sites of Black cultural production, queer bodies have always been indispensable but typically silent partners in hip-hop's cultural infrastructure. Within mainstream hip-hop culture, openly gay men and women literally work behind the scenes as choreographers, song writers, make-up artists, hairstylists, set designers, fashion experts, and other such roles stereotypically attributed to gay and lesbian culture. Like the Black church, however, the division of labor that enables such participation is predicated upon a tacit (and sometimes explicit) code of silence in response to various homophobic and heterosexist discourses.[5] It is this exploitative arrangement that enables hip-hop to sustain its hypermasculine veneer while benefiting from the talents of those who compromise its legitimacy.

Rap lyrics operate as one of the most prominent and accessible sites for transmitting antigay beliefs and values within hip-hop culture. While it can be argued that all forms of popular music are pervasively heteronormative—that is, they presume, reinforce, and ultimately demand unquestioned heterosexuality—explicitly homophobic discourses are lyrically overrepresented within hip-hop culture. Consider, for example, the bodies of work for hip-hop's most commercially successful artists in the twenty-first century. With few exceptions, such as Outkast's Andre 3000, who also challenges hip-hop's cultural and aesthetic logic through his often-androgynous appearance and unconventional music, hip-hop's most popular artists over the past five years have consistently deployed antigay rhetoric within their music. For example, top-selling rappers like Nas, Jay Z, Nelly, 50 Cent, Eminem, Ja Rule, and DMX have all used terms like "faggot" and "homo" to disparage gay and lesbian people, as well as emasculate real and imagined enemies.[6] More recently, rap artists have even deployed homophobic slang like "pause" and "no homo" after uttering words that could be (mis)construed as homoerotic in order to preemptively defend themselves against allegations of homosexuality.[7]

Explicitly homophobic messages are not, however, limited to mainstream rap music and artists. Even hip-hop's ostensibly "conscious" sector, often considered the last refuge for progressive thought and activism within hip-hop culture, is replete with explicit antigay messages.[8] At the height of the political rap era during the late 1980s and early 1990s, the progressive agendas of political rap artists such as Public Enemy, X-Clan, Paris, and Sista Souljah were strongly informed by radical Afrocentric, Black Islamic, and crude Black Nationalist ideologies that were openly hostile to queer identities. As a result of these positions, homosexuality was viewed as a consequence of spiritual malevolence, political conspiracy, or European hegemony.[9]

Current leaders of hip-hop's progressive wing have also challenged the legitimacy of gay identity within their corpuses. Rappers like Common and Mos Def have consistently included antigay signifiers such as "faggot" within their songs, although Common has become increasingly open to the viability of gay identity beginning with his *Electric Circus* album.[10] Lauryn Hill, hip-hop's queen lyricist and self-appointed moral stewardess, suggests in her 2002 single "Adam Lives in Theory" that bisexuality is a consequence of American decadence and moral decline rather than a legitimate and functional identity.[11]

Perhaps the most significant and apparent indicator of hip-hop's pervasive homophobia and heterosexism is the virtual absence of openly gay and lesbian people within mainstream rap circles. While hip-hop's underground is occupied by avant-garde groups like Deep Dickollective (which received national coverage in the *New York Times*), Disposable Heroes of HipHoprisy, and Rainbow Flava, openly gay rap groups have received scant attention from major radio stations and record labels. With the exception of New York rapper Caushun, who signed a recording deal with Def Jam subsidiary Baby Phat Records in 2004 but has yet to release an album, no openly gay rapper has been signed by a major commercial hip-hop recording label.[12]

The Politics of Outing

The homophobic context in which hip-hop artists and fans are situated facilitates the development of its various outing practices. The term outing emerged in the latter part of the twentieth century to describe the act of exposing people who were "in the closet," or secretly engaging in gay, lesbian, bisexual, or otherwise non-heterosexual lifestyles.[13,14] Despite the relative youth of the term, the act of pulling people out of the closet is as old as the Western world itself. It is important to note that this section is not intended to provide an exhaustive genealogy of outing in the West, as such a move would exceed the intellectual aims of this article.[15] Rather, this brief overview is intended to provide an historical backdrop with which to contextualize and interrogate current outing practices.

As far back as ancient Greece and Rome, outing was a practice used to expose individuals who violated society's codes of sexual conduct. Despite relatively liberal sexual codes (even by today's standards), homosexual congress was permissible only under certain conditions.[16] Male citizens who operated outside of these sanctioned sites of sodomy were publicly identified and dismissed as "vulgar" and subjected to an array of social stigmas attached to perceived unmanliness. Additionally, those who engaged in what was considered sexual misconduct such as "homosexual prostitution, adult male passivity, effeminacy in dress, gait, and speech, and orgiastic excesses" were subject to public censure, gossip, and innuendo.[17]

In the modern era, several public sex trials led to the outing of several high profile public figures. In 1895, Oscar Wilde stood trial and was subsequently convicted and imprisoned for "gross indecency" after it became known that he had sexual relations with Lord Alfred Douglass. In 1907, the Harden-Eulenburg affair and its accompanying courts-martial and trials, marked the first major public outing of the twentieth century. The scandal was based on accusations by journalist Maximilian Harden of homosexual conduct between Prince Philipp zu Eulenburg-Hertefeld (the Kaiser's closest friend) and General Kuno Graf von Moltke. The affair, which was designed to undermine Eulenburg's considerable political influence, became the biggest domestic scandal of the German Second Empire.[18] Furthermore, the scandal led to one of the first public discussions of homosexuality in Germany.

In America, outing reached its maturity in the midst of the post-World War II homosexual rights movement. At the same time that real and suspected communists were the targets of witch hunts, gay and lesbian citizens in the late 1940s and 1950s were also subjected to intense speculation and harassment. In many cases, these two identities were collapsed into what gay scholar Larry Gross calls the "commie-queer bogeyman."[19] By labeling gays and lesbians as both sex perverts and threats to national security, the American government, under the influence of Senator Joseph McCarthy, was able to justify the firing of hundreds of government employees for suspicion of homosexuality. In 1949 alone, ninety-six people were fired from the State Department for sexual perversion.[20] Additionally, numerous closeted gays and lesbians quietly resigned from their positions in order to avoid being outed. Through real and imagined technologies of sexual surveillance, as well as highly punitive sanctions for outed individuals, the United States government reinforced the heteronormative boundaries of the public sphere.

The deaths of several prominent men such as Rock Hudson to HIV/AIDS in the latter part of the twentieth century prompted a new, postmodern form of outing. Hudson, whose status as a Hollywood matinee idol and sex symbol during the 1950s and 1960s was virtually unparalleled, maintained a heterosexual public persona complete with an arranged marriage to secretary Phyllis Gates. After his death in 1985, however, Hudson's life and sexual identity came into serious question after it became known that he died of a "gay disease."[21] This revelation prompted further investigation, which revealed that Hudson, along with his manager Henry Willson, meticulously fashioned Hudson into the prototype of all-American masculinity in spite of his "true" identity.[22]

The late twentieth century marked a critical change with regard to the politics of outing. No longer was outing a practice reserved for heterosexuals attempting to leverage information for deleterious purposes. Suddenly, outing became a political strategy deployed by gays and lesbians themselves. Larry Gross notes

The exposure of closeted homosexuals was long a favored tactic of social control threatened and employed by [LGBT] enemies. The adoption of outing as a political tactic has challenged their ability to determine the meaning of gay identity and the consequences of its visibility.[23]

As Gross states, the practice of outing enabled gay and lesbian individuals to sustain greater control over the ways in which queer identities are publicly discussed.

By exercising a degree of control over who is outed, the Lesbian, Gay, Bisexual, Transgender (LGBT) community has been able to spotlight the hypocrisy of many antigay public figures that secretly engage in the very acts that they condemn. For example, Ted Haggard, a staunchly antigay minister, Bush advisor, and leader of the religious Right, was outed right before the 2006 midterm elections by Mike Jones, a gay prostitute and drug dealer with whom Haggard reportedly had a three-year sexual relationship. When asked why he outed the preacher, Jones claimed

People may look at me and think what I've done is immoral, but I think I had to do the moral thing in my mind, and that is expose someone who is preaching one thing and doing the opposite behind everybody's back.[24]

In a separate interview, he further explained his decision to come forward:

I made myself cry and I made myself sick. I felt I owed this to the community. What he is saying is we are not worthy, but he is.[25]

In a less opportunistic outing effort, gay activists Keith Boykin and Jasmyne Cannick mounted a 2005 campaign to publicly out prominent Black ministers as a means of exposing the hypocritical nature of their antigay rhetoric. On his website, Boykin explains his request for outing information:

From New York to Los Angeles, black LGBT people have been the backbone of the black church. Through this network, we've discovered that many homophobic black pastors lead secret lives outside the church. We're not naming any names, yet, but if you know something to help us confirm the information from our sources, we'd like to know.[26]

In an interview with the *Washington Blade*, Cannick further explains the reason for their controversial decision by articulating the contradictions between Black preachers' homophobic eschatology and their lived practices:

If you chose to speak to thousands of people and tell them that I'm going to hell, then I have a right to challenge you. It's time we really did something to push the envelope and get a conversation started.[27]

Although their outing campaign yielded thousands of responses, both positive and negative, neither Boykin nor Cannick has publicly outed anyone to date. Nevertheless, the controversy surrounding their threats indexes the level of contention surrounding the ethics of outing within the Black community.

Within Black public life, the practice of outing has taken a vastly different historical form. Not only have few closeted Black men and women been outed, openly gay figures such as civil rights leader Bayard Rustin have been shielded from public scrutiny regarding their sexual identities by having their roles obscured by straight leadership.[28] Others, such as Luther Vandross, have had little public attention paid to their sexual identities until after their death.[29] As Mark Anthony Neal argues, these forms of protection are designed to promote racial solidarity, as well as promulgate the image of the "StrongBlackMan," which is predicated upon hypermasculinity, misogyny, and compulsory heterosexuality.[30]

In recent years, however, outing has played a greater role within the Black public sphere. In addition to the gay rapper rumors, gossip journalists like Wendy Williams devote considerable airtime to discussing the sexual identities and practices of numerous Black celebrities. Superstars like Usher, Henry Simmons, Eddie Murphy, Johnny Gill, and Tyson Beckford have all been accused of living secret sexual lives. In fact, such rumors are a nearly inevitable part of Black male superstardom, as nearly every major Black superstar must respond to gossip, lies, innuendo, and, of course, true stories about their sexual lives.

This brief account demonstrates that outing within hip-hop culture is not historically unprecedented. Rather, as in other historical moments, outing and the threat of outing have served to sustain particular forms of sexual surveillance that discipline, control, and punish individual bodies. Nevertheless, the particular form and fashion that the outing practices assume are linked to hip-hop culture's unique historical circumstances and cultural rituals.

Lyrical Outing

In addition to rhetorically attacking and ridiculing openly gay and lesbian people, hip-hop artists also police the sexual boundaries of the culture by "lyrically outing" ostensibly straight MCs. Lyrical outing refers to the practice of calling an individual's sexual identity into question through a variety of rhetorical maneuvers. Lyrical outing has been a central part of nearly all of hip-hop's most celebrated feuds. Legendary rap battles such as KRS-One vs. MC Shan/Marley Marl, Jay-Z vs. Nas, and DMX/50 Cent vs. Ja Rule have all been pervaded by allegations of homosexuality. By having the threat of lyrical outing as a legitimate and likely possibility, queer MCs are not only silenced during potential rap battles but also coerced to remain in the closet out of fear that they will be outed.

In many instances, lyrical outings are performed merely in order to gain the upper hand in a rap battle, rather than to create genuine speculation about another person's sexual identity. Under such circumstances, the artist's outing rhetoric is relatively superficial, playful, and largely unpersuasive. For example, in his battle with Jay-Z, Nas repeatedly attacked his opponent through lyrical assaults on his sexual identity. In his wildly popular battle rap, "Ether," Nas referred to his opponent as "Gay-Z" and his record label, Roc-a-Fella Records, as "Cock-a-Fella Records."[31] He went on to suggest that the company's name surreptitiously signified Jay-Z's preference for having sex with men:

> Put it togetha
> I rock hoes, y'all rock fellas[32]

Nas then, perhaps unwittingly, invokes the memory of the Big Daddy Kane affair when he adds

> Rockefeller died of AIDS that was the end of his chapter
> And that's the dude you chose to name your company after?[33]

In actuality, Jay-Z's Roc-A-Fella Records label was named after the nation's first billionaire, John D. Rockefeller, who died in 1937 at the age of ninety-eight, nearly forty-five years before the first reported case of AIDS.[34] Nevertheless, Nas was able to implicitly substantiate Jay-Z's ostensible queerness by linking him to AIDS. On "Super Ugly," Jay-Z's venomously ad hominem reply to "Ether," Jay-Z replied in kind by suggesting that Nas had unwittingly participated in vicarious fellatio:

> And since you infatuated with sayin' that gay shit
> I guess you was kissin' my dick when you was kissin' that bitch[35]

This practice of name-calling and dissing is directly linked to the African American rhetorical practice of signifying or "playin' the dozens," where verbal jousting is engaged in order to humiliate an opponent and generate laughter.[36] In cases like the Nas/Jay-Z battle, each rapper attempted to embarrass the other and amuse listeners by sonically outing the other through clever lyricism.

In the case of Nas and Jay-Z, it is important to note that neither rapper likely believed the other to be gay. In fact, in a pair of conciliatory postbattle interviews on BET and MTV, the duo dismissed their venomous exchanges as nothing more than a necessary consequence of rap war. Also, there is little evidence to suggest that the general public gave real consideration to the artists' lyrical allegations. Despite the seemingly endless string of public debates and analyses about the winner of the battle, no commentary was given about the sexual identities of Nas or Jay-Z. Instead, the entire exchange was viewed and dismissed as a harmless rhetorical exercise with little or no grounding in reality.

Despite the playful nature of their practices, Nas' and Jay-Z's use of lyrical outing as a battle strategy reiterated the inherently pejorative meaning of gay as a signifier within the hip-hop world. Each rapper's ability to deploy their rhetorical resources in order to "playfully" attack the other's sexual identity and consequent manhood served as a powerful ally to hip-hop's homophobic ethos. Similar to many Americans' everyday use of gay as an all-purpose negative signifier (e.g., "That movie was so gay!"), playful acts of lyrical outing are far from innocuous. Instead, they serve as a tacit reminder that gay and lesbian identities are highly problematic and ultimately unwelcome within hip-hop culture.

There are other instances within hip-hop culture where lyrical outing is not merely intended to provide entertainment but also to create genuine speculation about an artists' sexual identity. For example, following the messy breakup of gangster rap group NWA, founder Eazy E began to circulate rumors about Dr. Dre's sexuality. On "Real Muthaphuckkin Gs," the battle response to Dr. Dre and Snoop Dogg's "Dre Day," Eazy E made several references to Dre's predilection for wearing lipstick during his time working with the World Class Wrecking Crew, a 1980s R&B group:

> All of a sudden Dr. Dre is a G thang,
> But on his old album covers, *he* was a *she* thang[37]

In the accompanying video, Eazy E flashed several pictures of Dre wearing makeup and form-fitting, sequined outfits that stood in stark contrast to the hardcore image that he portrayed as a member of NWA. This visual juxtaposition was deployed to expose Dre as a fraud whose gangsta (and masculine) bona fides were challenged by his effeminized attire.

Unlike the Jay-Z/Nas battle, Eazy E's expressed intention was not only to win the battle but also to expose Dr. Dre's "hidden" sexuality. To be certain, it is possible that Eazy E did not truly believe his own claims, as his lyrical evidence was far from convincing. After all, Dr. Dre's Wrecking Crew attire, like much popular fashion in the 1980s, was appropriately tight despite its sharp divergence from post-1990s hip-hop style. By encouraging a presentist reading of Dre's sartorial choices, Eazy E blurred, perhaps deliberately, the lines between playful and serious outing. Regardless of his intentions, however, Eazy E's actions created strong speculation about Dr. Dre's sexual orientation, which extended beyond the sonic boundaries of the battle record.

Rumors about Dr. Dre's sexual identity never subsided after his lyrical outing at the hands of Eazy E. In fact, they later became fodder for future rivals Tupac Shakur and Marion "Suge" Knight following Dre's stormy departure from Death Row Records. At the conclusion of "To Live and Die in LA," Tupac punctuated the otherwise upbeat song with a subtle but noteworthy disclaimer:

> California Love part motherfuckin' 2
> Without gay ass Dre[38]

On his often sampled battle rap "Realest Shit," Tupac took another lyrical jab at Dr. Dre's sexuality:

> We shook Dre punk ass
> Now he out of the closet[39]

Ja Rule, who began to feud with Dr. Dre in 2003, echoed Tupac's claims in his single, "Blood in My Eye":

> Who the fuck you callin' gay nigga
> Must a been talkin to Em and Dre, nigga
> Pour out a little liquor and rest in peace to Tupac Shakur
> Cause you let us know that Dre was a queer before[40]

To be sure, Tupac's lyrical allusions were also buttressed by Death Row Records owner Suge Knight's extra-lyrical allegations about Dre. In a series of interviews, Knight implied that he had personal knowledge of Dre's same-sex affairs. In the November 2000 issue of *Gear Magazine*, he was even more explicit:

I can't stand [Dre]. People say I was cruel to call him a faggot but what's pissing me off the most is that he was dishonest about it. I don't have anything against gay people–to each his own. Back in the day, we would have parties and he'd pretend to be with all these women. Don't lie to somebody who is supposed to be your friend. That's why Eminem is trying to distance himself from Dre by rapping all this anti-gay shit. He doesn't want to be thought of as Dre's little white bitch.[41]

In an interview on *Thug Immortal*, a posthumous documentary about Tupac Shakur, Knight claimed that Tupac did not want Dre to stay with Death Row Records because of his alleged sexual relationship with a young man during his marriage to former Wrecking Crew singer Michel'le. Adding credence to the rumor was the fact that Michel'le later became Suge Knight's third wife, thereby suggesting that Knight had reliable inside information about Dre's personal life.

Ironically, many of the very same sexual rumors would soon follow Dre's biggest antagonists. Shortly after dying of AIDS-related illnesses on March 26, 1995, rumors about Eazy E's alleged closet homosexuality began to swirl. Although Eazy E publicly denied these claims prior to his death, insisting that he obtained the virus from one the numerous women with whom he'd had sex and fathered children, rumors about the source of his illness persisted and intensified after his passing.[42] Even Tupac, the poster boy for hip-hop's thug masculinity fetish, has never completely escaped sexual speculation due to his effeminate childhood mannerisms, as well as rumors that he was raped during his last stay in prison.[43]

One of the more extreme and vindictive cases of lyrical outing occurred during Ja Rule's feud with rival rapper DMX. The two artists, who were once friends, became embroiled in a bitter beef in 2000 after DMX accused Ja Rule of copying his gravelly vocal style and shirtless appearance, a claim that many fans, rappers, and critics echoed. As the intensity of their feud grew, each rapper began to publicly expose potentially embarrassing aspects of the other's personal life. While Ja Rule focused on DMX's well-documented substance abuse problems, referring to him as "crack man," DMX upped the stakes and began to publicly question Ja Rule's sexuality.

At first, DMX's lyrical outings were of the playful, Nas/Jay-Z variety. Like other artists, he poked fun at Rule's penchant for singing the choruses on his records, referring to him as a "diva" in several interviews.[44] Given their ostensibly ludic nature, DMX's early allegations generated little concern among fans and insiders. Soon, however, DMX's verbal taunts appeared less fictive and more geared toward exposing a genuine "truth" about Ja Rule. During a radio interview with San Francisco's KMEL, DMX claimed that Rule had sex with men while high on "X," or the party drug popularly known as ecstasy:

> Some nigga that was stylin' his clothes for one of them shows got him ecstasy'd up and fucked him. Ja-Rule is fuckin' niggas. I'm telling you dog! On my momma! The [stylist] told me that himself. You talkin bout me, you can't be serious! For all them homo niggas out there that want some dick, give ya man Ja-Rule some X and he'll fuck you.[45]

On his diss record "Where the Hood At?," DMX echoed his claim with a vicious lyrical outing:

> Fuckin with a nigga like me, D-to-the-M-to-the-X
> Last I heard, y'all niggaz was havin sex, with the same sex
> I show no love, to homo thugs
> Empty out, reloaded and throw more slugs
> How you gonna explain fuckin' a man?
> Even if we squashed the beef, I ain't touchin ya hand[46]

Unlike the Nas/Jay-Z and Dr. Dre/Eazy E/Tupac battles, DMX attempted to marshal legitimate evidence against Ja Rule in full public view in order to both out and humiliate him.

Soon after, DMX's claims were corroborated by 50 Cent, Ja Rule's other nemesis, who at one point promised to put the aforementioned hair dresser on his commercial debut album, *Get Rich or Die Trying*. Eventually, 50 Cent elected to use comedian Alex Thomas to portray Ja Rule's alleged gay lover on the album skit. There are several possible explanations for this decision; perhaps the story was untrue, the hairdresser did not want to appear, or 50 and his handlers were scared of legal and/or personal repercussions. Regardless of the reason, his extravagant endorsement of DMX's claims further alienated Ja Rule from his fan base and helped to sustain a public conversation about Rule's sexuality.

Like Big Daddy Kane, Ja Rule's career never recovered from his public outing. Prior to his feud with 50 Cent and DMX, Rule had sold nearly 17 million copies of his first four albums, each of which reached certified platinum (more than one million records sold) status. Since his vicious lyrical outing, he has yet to exceed gold (500,000 records sold) status. Even worse, Ja Rule has become a virtual punch line for many industry insiders due to his rapid loss of popularity and respect among the fans. While this devastating decline can be attributed to multiple factors, there is little doubt that the consistent and convincing conversations about his sexuality contributed to his professional demise.

The Search for the Gay Rapper

In 1997, *One Nut* magazine, the now-defunct Connecticut based hip-hop magazine, released a series of interviews with a famous rap artist who acknowledged that he was gay but insisted upon remaining anonymous. In the interviews, the rapper talked about the difficulties of hiding his sexuality from his homophobic rap peers. For example, he noted that his lover traveled on the road with him but had to pretend to be a member of the rapper's entourage. Most surprising to the hip-hop community and the general public was the rapper's claim that he was not alone in his secret life. On the contrary, he claimed that a large number of rappers currently in the industry were also closeted bisexuals or homosexuals.

That same year, gossip journalist Wendy Williams also announced that one of hip-hop's most famous artists was gay. Responding to the *One Nut* article, as well as other unidentified information about "a famous gay rapper with a lot of hits," Williams invited public speculation about the identity of the man she mockingly identified as "MC Ben Dover." Not to be outdone by the *One Nut* article, Williams read her own gay rapper missive, "Confessions of a Gay Rapper by Jamal X," over the airwaves. Like his anonymous peer, the pseudonymous Jamal X recounted stories of same-sex love, faux-friendships, and trusting girlfriends. X also emphasized the importance of drugs and alcohol as a means of justifying and forgetting their same-sex encounters. Although Williams admittedly created the segment to create a buzz among her listeners, the article created a bigger impact than even she imagined:

> I read the article on the radio and the audience went wild—they ate it up! People wanted to know who the gay rapper was. My life has not been the same since. I get stopped in the mall, on the street, and going to the bathroom while I'm about town has taken on a new meaning. For instance, girls follow me [until] their [sic] alone to ask 'Wendy girl, Who da gay rapper?'[47]

In addition to bolstering the rumor mill, these two moments marked another critical moment in the hip-hop's history of sexual politics.

After these two incidents, numerous major print and television media outlets began to speculate about the identity of "the gay rapper." Suddenly, rap lyrics were analyzed for furtive homoerotic messages and rap entourages were carefully inspected for potential "passers." Numerous fans, journalists, and industry insiders began to circulate information that implicated various stars within the rap world. The many casualties of this sexual witch hunt included Russell Simmons, Mase, Jay-Z, Keith Murray, Erick Sermon, Method Man, and Redman. While many artists, like Sermon and Redman, vociferously denied allegations that they were the gay MC, others elected to respond with silence. Unfortunately, neither approach proved effective in curbing the hip-hop community's obsession with the gay rapper.

One of the most consistent targets of the gay rapper search was Sean "Diddy" Combs. Unlike many of his hypermasculine cohorts, Combs has long been known for his attention to style, willingness to mingle with openly gay fashionistas, and lack of antigay song lyrics. In addition to his "metrosexual" image—a term coined in the mid-1990s and normalized in the early 2000s to describe a new generation of fashion conscious, self-pampering men—persistent rumors during the 1990s about Combs' private life kept him near the center of the gay rapper conversation. The intense public focus on Combs' romantic and sexual relationships was largely due to Wendy Williams, who allegedly posted pictures of Combs and sidekick Mase in compromising positions on the Internet. Later, Williams announced that she had a videotape of Combs having sex with fellow Bad Boy Records rapper Loon. Although she never produced any evidence to support either of these claims, Williams' firing from Hot 97—which Williams' and other insiders attributed to Combs' intervention—added credence to the rumor among the general public.

Since 1997, the notion of a singular gay rapper has been exploited not only by mainstream media outlets but by the artists themselves. No one has benefited more from this ideology than hairdresser-turned-rapper Caushun. Since his first appearance in 2001 on New York radio station Hot 97's Star 'n Buckwild Show, when he called the station and identified himself as "The Gay

Rapper," Caushun has been the mainstream poster boy for the gay MC. Although he clearly was not the "real" gay rapper—at that point Caushun had not even secured a record deal much less achieved the level of success attributed to the alleged gay rapper—his ability to impress the shock jocks with his lyrical skills created sufficient buzz on which to capitalize. Since his Hot 97 debut, Caushun has been promoted in various media outlets, including *Vibe*, *New York Times*, *Newsweek*, MTV, and the *Village Voice* as "the first gay rapper."

Although he has emphasized in several interviews that he is simply "the first *openly* gay rapper," Caushun's failure to acknowledge the pre-existence of a queer hip-hop community and his willingness to self-identify and literally trademark himself as "*the* gay rapper" are nonetheless problematic. By outing himself, Caushun plays into hip-hop's exploitative politics in order to satisfy his own pecuniary interests. Further, by prominently positioning Caushun within the public sphere, hip-hop culture is able to allay its masculine anxieties surrounding gay identity. By fetishizing the individual gay rapper, hip-hop culture is able to sustain the falsely obvious notion that the queer MC is an outlier within an otherwise heterosexual milieu.

The search for the gay rapper represents another, less apparent form of outing within hip-hop culture. While lyrical outings place a spotlight on particular individuals, the perennial search for the gay rapper creates an environment in which everyone's sexual identity is called into question. By allowing the identity of the gay rapper to go unidentified—to date, the search for the gay rapper has produced no confirmed outings—the hip-hop community is able to engage in an endless witch hunt that forces everyone into a defensive posture.

Homo Thuggin' It

At the same time that the search for the gay rapper has failed to yield any successful outings, the public birth of the "homothug" has exposed an entire community of queer hip-hoppers. Unlike lyrical outings or gay rapper witch hunts, which focus on famous individuals, the public conversation about the homothug addresses neither celebrities nor individuals. On the contrary, the bulk of the homothug conversation has focused on outing ordinary queer men who simultaneously negotiate multiple and ostensibly competing identities. Since the beginning of the twenty-first century, publications such as the *Village Voice* and *New York Times* have placed a spotlight on the once secret lives of the homothug community.

In many ways, the term "homothug" is misleading, since a person need not exhibit thuggish (i.e., illegal or violent) behavior in order to satisfy the conditions of a homothug identity. Rather, homothug refers to a gay or bisexual male who identifies with the hypermasculine accouterments of mainstream hip-hop. Like other hip-hop generation males, the prototypical homothug wears baggy jeans, doo-rags, throwback basketball jerseys, gaudy jewelry, and other such indices of hip-hop authenticity. In fact, the only difference between the homothug and the "normal" hip-hopper is the former's same-sex desires. The term homothug, which was coined by antigay former Hot 97 shock jock DJ Star, was initially intended to connote a humorous irony. The comedic value of this irony rested upon the falsely obvious assumption that "homo" (queer) and "thug" (hip-hop) were competing identities that could never be fully reconciled. As such, the homothug often represents a human punch line, a walking contradiction that could be looked to for easy insults and quick laughter.

The notion of the homothug is grounded in the sexual politics of the "down-low," also known as the DL. The term, which was initially popularized by R&B singer R. Kelly's top selling 1996 single "Down Low," came into its current popular usage within the African American public sphere near the beginning of the twenty-first century. While being "on the DL" (like its earlier manifestation, the "QT" or "quiet tip") initially signified participation in any secret activity, it now refers almost exclusively to the practice of participating in male same-sex acts while representing oneself (and often self-identifying) as a heterosexual. This shift in meaning and increase in discussion about the DL has been precipitated by a growing public conversation within the mainstream media, as well as the African American counter-public sphere.

Animated by the publication of J. L. King's sensationalist tome, *On The Down Low,* public discourse surrounding the down-low has largely been informed by a politics of terror that represents the Black penis as a "weapon of mass destruction."[48] At the same time that King's best-selling book garnered media attention, numerous network television shows (e.g., *Soul Food* and *E.R.*), daytime talk shows (e.g., *Jerry Springer* and *The Oprah Winfrey Show*), and major periodicals (e.g., *New York Times, Washington Post, Essence, Ebony*) also devoted considerable space to "warning" African American women of the dangers of the down-low man as the primary transmitter of HIV and a threat to the mythically sacrosanct nuclear African American family. It is within this context that the homothug has been outed and constructed as a down-low man deeply ensconced within hip-hop culture.

As part of its outing practices, the popular media has defined the homothug in two equally problematic ways: *the trickster* and *the psychopath.* The trickster is viewed as a predator that uses the homothug identity as a mendacious articulation of bisexuality or homosexuality. By shrouding himself in hip-hop's hypermasculine aesthetic, the trickster is able to manipulate unsuspecting women and satiate the full range of his sexual desires. While the trickster is preoccupied with hiding his sexuality from others, the psychopath becomes a homothug in order to hide his sexuality from himself. In order to resist the acceptance of a gay or bisexual identity, the psychopathic homothug performs a hip-hop identity as a maladaptive coping strategy that ultimately places his partners in emotional and physical peril.

By publicly discussing the homothug in this fashion, two separate but interrelated ideas are promoted: (1) the homothug/down-low identity is an inauthentic cover for a more authentic gay/bisexual identity and (2) hip-hop culture is fundamentally incompatible with queer identity. The representation of the homothug as trickster and psychopath reflects the beliefs of many experts and everyday people who argue that the down-low, and by extension the homothug, is merely a front for a more authentic gay or bisexual identity. For example, Keith Boykin argues

> The down low is popularly used to refer to men who have sex with men but do not identify as gay or homosexual. Maybe you've heard that concept before. Long ago, we called it "the closet." The term "down low" is just a new way of describing a very old thing ... The phrase itself may be new, but the practice is as old as history.[49]

While Boykin is correct to point out that the down-low does not signify a new set of practices or beliefs, he hastily dismisses the possibility that the down-low (and by extension the homothug) expands our critical vocabularies in order to accommodate a more complex and nuanced understanding of sexual identity. As *Village Voice* writer Jason King argues

> For some DL men, there is no "gay" essence to reveal, or a bisexual or straight one, for that matter. They may oscillate between male and female partners, but it would be a mistake to call such a brother a closeted bisexual, since it would imply that underneath the veil he's settled on a stable gender identity. DL is not an identity but a performance. It may even be working toward that elusive phenomenon hip-hop heads call "flow." Flow is when the MC locks his rapping into a groove, bringing the performance to a rhythmic, surging sense of balance.[50]

Although King runs the risk of overstating the level of voluntarism involved in identity performance, he nonetheless offers a more fluid conception of male sexuality that is unavailable in the dominant belief that the homothug is nothing more than a closeted gay man.

Through the representation of the homothug as a gay man in denial, the mainstream hip-hop community is able to distance itself from the homothug based on his lack of perceived authenticity. This distancing can be linked to hip-hop culture's obsession with "realness," or the belief in a one-to-one relationship between what one says and what one does. This framework not only demands congruence between artistic expression and lived experience but also privileges a particular set of experiences that are deemed appropriate within the culture. For example, despite his artistic honesty, few hip-hop observers would say that Will Smith was a "real" MC. On the contrary, Tupac's performances of reckless hypermasculinity are often deemed "real" by fellow rappers, critics, and fans despite their considerable contradictions. Through the rubric of realness, this perspective 'of'/worry the homothug is positioned as a poser whose "true" self not only violates hip-hop culture's code of compulsory heterosexuality, but also contradicts its shibboleth of "keeping it real."

More fundamentally, the rejection of the homothug hinges upon the belief that hip-hop and gay are two irreconcilable identities. This notion is informed by the traditional hegemonic conception of gay men as soft, weak, and effeminate. Further complicating the issue is the essentialist belief in a singular "gay culture" that subsumes all queer men irrespective of race and class. Such an idea allows White men, tight pants, and house music to serve as universal symbols of gay culture despite their frequent incompatibility with the cultural orientations of many Black gay men. These stereotypical cultural artifacts stand in sharp relief to the tough, strong, and masculine characteristics ascribed to the hip-hop thug. Although this idea is being challenged by more recent media representations of Black gay identity and culture such as *Noah's Ark, The Wire*, and *Real World Philadelphia*, which provide a wider range of possibilities for Black gay men within the public sphere, many Black men are still alienated by dominant conceptions of gay identity that do not cohere with the imperatives of their racialized identity. In addition to providing a more comfortable space for racial identity work, hip-hop culture provides a rich site for cultural expression. Like their heterosexual peers, many gay Black men have organic connections to hip-hop culture that are maintained through the homothug club scene. Through these clubs, homothugs are able to reconcile rather than choose between their racial and sexual identities.

The Wages of Outing

Hip-hop's politics of outing is a necessary consequence of the culture's contradictory disposition toward queer identity. As discussed earlier, this disposition is a signpost of hip-hop's simultaneous need for, rejection of, and obsession with sexual identities that do not cohere with its homophobic and hypermasculine cultural ethos. Despite its overt and pervasive homophobia, hip-hop practitioners frequently practice forms of masculinity that diverge from perceived norms. For example, all-male rap crews, numerous odes to lost friends, "homeboy hugs" (half-handshake/half-hug), and "niggas over bitches" mantras all index hip-hop's obsession with all-male relationships. Hip-hop's homosocial preoccupations often spill into the zone of the homoerotic, as in the case of men who "run trains," or participate in simultaneous and/or successive group sex acts with multiple men and one woman. Although the practice of running trains retains its heterosexual veneer by placing the female body as the exclusive point of erotic attention, its social value within the culture is directly linked to the level and quantity of participation and interaction among the men.

Through its outing practices, the hip-hop community is able to continuously ignore its own complex sexual ethic by keeping the focus on individual, anonymous, and, in the case of the homothug, aggregate queer bodies. By keeping the focus outward, the broader hip-hop community is able to ignore the fact that, like other cultural spaces, queer bodies and homoerotic practices are not only on the margins but also at the center of cultural production.

Study Questions

1. What would be the consequences of having a high profile and popular rapper outed in the contemporary moment?
2. How are threats of outing utilized by rival rappers against each other?
3. Does the set of circumstances associated with outing male rappers also apply to women rappers who might be rumored to be lesbian or bi-sexual?

Notes

1. Big Daddy Kane, "Give It To Me," *Looks Like A Job For ...* (Warner Brothers/Wea, 1993).
2. *POZ Magazine*, October 1996, www.poz.com/articles/254_1816.shtml. (accessed March 1, 2007).
3. For a discussion of these controlling images see Patricia Hill Collins, *Black Feminist Thought* (New York: Routledge, 2000) and *Black Sexual Politics* (New York: Routledge, 2005). For an examination of womanhood in hip-hop, see Gwendolyn Pough, *Check It While I Wreck It: Black Womanhood, Hip-Hop Culture, and the Public Sphere* (New York: Columbia, 2004).
4. At the risk of being redundant, I find it necessary to reiterate my assertion that hip-hop culture places equally, if not more, strict and dehumanizing limitations on female sexual identities. Nevertheless, various incarnations of the butch/femme subjectivity have a level of commercial viability and social acceptance within the hip-hop community that is completely unthinkable for queer male artists.
5. For a discussion of queerness within the Black church, see Kelly Brown Douglas, Homophobia and Heterosexism in the Black Church and Community, In Cornel West and Eddie Glaude (Eds.), *African American Religious Thought: An Anthology* (Louisville, KY: Westminster John Knox Press, 2003, 996–1017); bell hooks and Cornel West, *Breaking Bread: Insurgent Black Intellectual Life* (Cambridge, MA: South End Press, 1991); Cornel West, Christian Love and Heterosexism, In *The Cornel West Reader* (New York: Basic Civitas, 1999) 401–414; and Michael Eric Dyson, Homotextualities: The Bible, Sexual Ethics, and the Theology of Homoeroticism, In *Open Mike* (New York: Basic Civitas, 2002). hooks and West are particularly articulate about the moral contradictions inherent in using queer labor within the church (e.g., the gay piano player) while subjecting them to antigay discourses. Of course, this notion of contradiction hinges upon the assumption of a particular hermeneutical posture that enables one to question the belief that queer identity is antithetical to orthodox Christianity. As Douglas, West, and Dyson argue, such a reading is part and parcel of an appropriately historicized interpretation of antigay Biblical narratives, as well as a belief that Christianity's "love ethic," as espoused by Jesus in the New Testament, is superordinate to individual prohibitions or mandates.
6. My use of the term "emasculate" is not meant to suggest agreement with traditional heteronormative conceptions of masculinity that equate masculinity with heterosexuality. Rather, I intend to highlight the particular ways that narrow conceptions of masculinity inform much of hip-hop's, and indeed the broader community's, internal discourse.
7. For example, a fairly innocuous statement like "I need you to stand behind me on this project" or "These nuts are a bit too salty" would be punctuated with "no homo" in order to prevent misunderstanding or deliberate distortion for the purpose of playful or serious ridicule. While the origins of "pause" are uncertain, "no homo" originated with rapper Cam'ron and his Dipset crew. In all likelihood, Cam'ron's use of the term was at least a partial reaction to frequent speculation and taunts from rival rappers and fans who found Cam's predilection for adorning himself in pink and purple clothing and cars to be sexually dubious.
8. In line with my neo-Gramscian approach to popular culture, I strongly dispute the notion that "conscious" hip-hop provides a transcendent sphere within an otherwise hegemonic culture industry. Such a notion hinges upon the invocation of a faulty (and elitist) modernist dichotomy between high and low culture—in this case mainstream vs. conscious rap music—that obscures the complex interplay between reproduction and resistance in all sites of hip-hop cultural production.
9. I use the term "radical" Afrocentric in referencing the extremist wing of the Afrocentric tradition. In particular, I am referring to the work of scholars like Leonard Jeffries and Francis Cress Welsing, whose work occupies the fringes of African centered thought and practice. Heterosexist ideologies are not exclusive, however, to Afrocentricity's margins. In his early work, such as the first edition of *Afrocentricity* (Temple University Press), Afrocentric pioneer Molefi Asante argued that homosexuality was a byproduct of European decadence rather than biological determination. Although many mainstream Afrocentrists have departed from this position—including Asante, who removed the claim from

later editions of the book—the extremist wing of the Afrocentric school continues to shape the lyrics of artists like Public Enemy, Ras Kass, Nas, and Paris.

With regard to Black Islamic organizations, Minister Louis Farrakhan's Nation of Islam, Silis Muhammad's Lost-Found Nation of Islam, and Imam Isa's Ansaaru Allah community all deployed fundamentalist readings of the Bible and Quran, particularly the book of Leviticus, in order to substantiate an antigay theology. Like the Afrocentrists, these groups argued that Black homosexuality was an extension of White "devilishment" (evil and unnatural behavior) that had been taught to Blacks through "tricknology," or knowledge that would undermine prosperity, peace, and full realization of Black humanity.

10. On his *Electric Circus* album, Common included the song "Between Me, You, and Liberation," where he suggests that his friend was liberated by coming out of the closet. Although his subsequent album, *Be*, did not discuss homosexuality, it nonetheless marked a critical departure from previous albums, where he routinely attacked gays and lesbians.

11. Lauryn Hill, "Adam Lives in Theory," *Unplugged* (Columbia, 2002). In the song, Hill sings, "Eve was so naive, blinded by the pride and greed/Wanting to be intellectual/Drifting from the way she got turned down one day/And now she thinks that she's bisexual."

12. At the time of this writing, reports have confirmed that Caushun was dropped from Baby Phat and has yet to sign with another label. In 1998, public speculation arose about the sexual identity of female rapper Queen Pen, whose single "Girlfriend" explicitly addressed the issue of lesbianism. Although most fans and critics assumed that Queen Pen was a lesbian, she refused to identify as such, telling the *New York Times* "I'm black, I'm a female rapper. I couldn't even go out of my way to pick up a new form of discrimination. People are waiting for this hip-hop Ellen to come out of the closet. I'd rather be a mystery for a minute." See *Greatest Taboo: Homosexuality in Black Communities* (Los Angeles: Alyson Books, 2000).

13. The earliest public usage of the term "outing" can be found in the 1990 *Time* magazine article, "Forcing Gays Out of the Closet," by William A. Henry III (*Time, 29*, January 1996, 67).

14. Although "the closer" is typically used as a metaphor to signify a surreptitious negotiation of queer sexual practices or desires, it also reflects the complex formations of knowledge and power that have historically constituted the closet. As Michael P. Brown argues, "The closet is a term used to describe the denial, concealment, erasure, or ignorance of lesbians and gay men. It describes their absence—and alludes to their ironic presence nonetheless—in a society that, in countless interlocking ways, subtly and blatantly dictates that heterosexuality is the only way to be." For a deeper examination of the closet as an ideological and spatial metaphor, see Eve Sedgwick, *Epistemology of the Closet* (Berkeley: University of California Press, 1990) and Michael P. Brown, *Closet Space: Geographies of Metaphor from the Body to the Globe* (New York: Routledge, 2000).

15. For an exhaustive treatment of outing in the West, see Warren Johansson and William A. Percy, *Outing: Shattering the Conspiracy of Silence* (Binghamton, NY: Haworth Press, 1994); Martin Duberman, *Hidden From History: Reclaiming the Gay and Lesbian Past* (New York: Duberman, 1989); Lillian Faderman, *Odd Girls and Twilight Lovers: A History of Lesbian Life in Twentieth Century America* (New York: Penguin, 1992).

16. Within ancient Greek society, sexual relationships between adult men were deemed socially unacceptable. However, pederasty, or same-sex bonds between adolescent boys and adult men, were not only socially permissible but considered integral parts of moral, social, and educational development. Although, as Foucault and others argue, sexual practices were not constitutive of social identity until the latter part of the nineteenth century, pederastic relationships were nonetheless governed by a heteronormative sexual calculus that forbade sexual attraction or enjoyment on the part of the *eromenos*, or adolescent boy. Also, the *erastes*, or adult male, was allowed to participate in sexual congress with an adolescent boy only if he were the insertive (i.e., penetrating) partner. Although scholars have argued that it is too reductive to ascribe the terms "dominant" and "passive" to the *erastes and eromenos* roles, there was an indisputable correlation between masculinity and penetration that helped to arbitrate the social and moral acceptability of sexual practices. For more about homosexuality in Ancient Greece, see Kenneth J. Dover, *Greek Homosexuality* (New York: Vintage Books, 1978) and William A. Percy III, *Pederasty and Pedagogy in Archaic Greece* (Champaign, IL: University of Illinois Press, 1996).

17. Warren Johansson and William A. Percy, *Outing: Shattering the Conspiracy of Silence* (Binghamton, NY: Haworth Press, 1994) 31.

18. Larry Gross, *Contested Closets: The Politics and Ethics of Outing* (Minneapolis, MN: University of Minnesota Press, 1993).

19. Ibid., 13.

20. Ibid.

21. The idea that AIDS was a gay disease was not restricted to everyday discourse. Until 1982, AIDS was officially known as GRID, gay related immunodeficiency disease.

22. In addition to concealing Hudson's sexual identity, Henry Willson was largely responsible for the "beefcake" craze of the 1950s. See Robert Hofler, *The Man Who Invented Rock Hudson: The Pretty Boys and Dirty Deals of Henry Willson* (New York: Carroll & Graf, 2005).

23. Larry Gross, *Contested Closets: The Politics and Ethics of Outing* (Minneapolis, MN: University of Minneapolis Press, 1993) 6.

24. Interview with Denver Post quoted in http://www.smh.com.au/news/world/bush-ally-quits-evangelical-post-in-gay-scandal/2006/11/03/1162340050165.html. Accessed on November 13, 2008.

25. www.keithboykin.com/arch/2005/09/26/is/_td_jakes_gay. (accessed March 1, 2007).

26. www.washblade.com/2005/9–30/news/national/pastors.cfm. (accessed March 1, 2007).

27. Of course, the anxiety around Bayard Rustin's sexuality by civil rights leadership was not merely self-induced nor unwarranted. Although Rustin served as an early mentor to Martin Luther King, his role as an organizer and strategist for the Southern Christian Leadership Conference was minimized after Adam Clayton Powell threatened to spread a rumor that Rustin and King were lovers. For a fascinating examination of the relationship between Rustin's sexuality and political life, read John D'emilio, *Lost Prophet: The Life and Times of Bayard Rustin* (New York: Free Press, 2003).

28. For examples of posthumous discussion of Luther Vandross's queer identity, see Jason King's *Village Voice* essay, "Why Luther Vandross's Legacy Matters," www.villagevoice.com/music/0527,king,65563,22.htrnl (accessed March 1, 2007) and Craig Seymour, *Luther: The Life and Longing of Luther Vandross* (New York: Harper Paperbacks, 2005).

29. Mark Anthony Neal, *NewBlackMan* (New York: Routledge, 2005).

30. Nas, "Ether," *Stillmatic* (Sony, 2001).

31. Ibid.

32. Ibid.

33. It is likely that Nas was confusing, either deliberately or unintentionally, John D. Rockefeller with Rock Hudson, who died of AIDS in 1985. Another less likely explanation is that Nas was referring to a local street hustler by the same name who died of AIDS.

34. Although it was a popular song in New York for nearly a month, "Super Ugly" never made it to an official album.

35. For discussions of the relationship between hip-hop and the signifyin(g) tradition, see Russell Potter, *Spectular Vernaculars: Hip-Hop and the Politics of Postmodernism* (New York: SUNY Press, 1995).

36. Eazy E. "Real Muthaphuckkin G's" (Ruthless, 1998).

37. Tupac Shakur, "To Live and Die in L.A," *Makaveli* (Interscope, 1996).

38. Tupac Shakur, "Realest Shit," *Makaveli* (Interscope, 1996).

39. Ja Rule "Blood in My Eye," *Blood in my Eye* (Def Jam, 2003).

40. http://www.geocities.com/ambwww/enema.htm. (accessed March 1, 2007).

41. As Phillip Brian Harper points out in his book *Are We Not Men?* (New York: Oxford Press, 1996), the issue of being HIV positive is largely subordinate to the question of *how* the virus is contracted. In the case of Magic Johnson, Harper points out that the support he received from the African American community was directly connected to his consistent declarations of heterosexuality and public performances of homophobic and patriarchal masculinity. It was this sensibility that informed Eazy E's emphatic and repeated declarations of hypersexuality.

42. Like many hip-hop rumors, the primary source for the story on Tupac was gossip journalist Wendy Williams. Of course, Tupac vehemently denied the rumors in multiple post-jail interviews, such as the one with Chuck Phillips that famously appeared in the *Los Angeles Times* ("I Am Not A Gangster" by Chuck Phillips, October 25, 1995). Pac later created the unreleased song, "Why U Turn On Me," where he raps: "Said I got raped in jail, picture that/Revenge is a payback bitch, get your gat/Fuck Wendy Williams and I pray you choke/on the next dick down your throat, for turnin' on me."

43. http://www.allhiphop.com/hiphopnews/?ID=1164. (accessed March 1, 2007).

44. http://www.allhiphop.com/hiphopnews/?ID=1164. (accessed March 1, 2007).

45. DMX, "Where the Hood At?," *Grand Champ* (Def Jam, 2003).

46. http://www.io.com/~larrybob/gayrap2.html. (accessed March 1, 2007).

47. For a thorough examination of the factual inaccuracies, logical fallacies, and questionable motivations behind J. L. King's books, see Keith Boykin, *Beyond the Down Low: Sex, Lies, and Denial in Black America* (New York: Carroll & Graff, 2005).

48. http://www.thumperscorner.com/discus/messages/7242/2354.html?1107482549. (accessed March 1, 2007).

49. http://www.villagevoice.com/news/0326,king,45063,l.html. (accessed March 1, 2007).

50. For a fascinating examination of Tupac's complexities and contradictions, see Michael Eric Dyson, *Holler If You Hear Me: Searching For Tupac Shakur* (New York: Basic Civitas, 2002).

26

Empowering Self, Making Choices, Creating Spaces
Black Female Identity via Rap Music Performance

Though much has been made about gender issues within hip-hop and the genre's relationship to women in general, not nearly enough work has been devoted to how women function as artists within hip-hop. To this end, ethnomusicologist Cheryl Keyes has identified four distinct categories of women rappers and, accordingly, the audiences that are drawn to them.

Keyes's work offers an interpretive model that highlights the agency of women rappers, outside of the need to respond to their marginalization within hip-hop culture and the sexism and misogyny expressed by their male peers and practiced in the recording industry.

Empowering Self, Making Choices, Creating Spaces: Black Female Identity via Rap Music Performance

Cheryl L. Keyes

Critics and scholars have often associated rap music with urban male culture. However, females have been involved in the history of this music since its early years. This article explores Black women's contribution to and role in shaping rap music. In examining female rappers, this study engages an interdisciplinary model that employs cultural studies, feminist theory, and mass mediation theory of popular culture, and it employs an ethnographic concept, the "interpretive community," in its analysis.

Observers of rap music began to notice the proliferation of successful female rap acts during the 1990s. Though rap has often been presented as a male-dominated form by the media, women have been a part of the rap scene since its early commercial years. In general, "females were always into rap, had their little crews and were known for rocking parties, schoolyards, whatever it was; and females rocked just as hard as males [but] the male was just first to be put on wax [record]" (Pearlman 1988: 26). Rap music journalist Havelock Nelson notes, "While women have always been involved artistically with rap throughout the '80s, artists like [MC] Lyte, [Queen] Latifah, Roxanne Shanté, and [Monie] Love have had to struggle to reach a level of success close to that of male rappers" (1993: 77). Challenging male rappers' predominance, female rap artists have not only proven that they have lyrical skills; in their struggle to survive and thrive within this tradition, they have created spaces from which to deliver powerful messages from Black female and Black feminist perspectives.

Data utilized in this study derive from interviews (1993–1996) with "cultural readers" (Bobo 1995)—African American female performers, audience members, and music critics— referred to in this essay as an "interpretive community." In *Black Women as Cultural Readers*, film critic–scholar Jacqueline Bobo explores the concept of "interpretive community" as a movement comprising Black female cultural producers, critics and scholars, and cultural consumers (1995: 22). She writes,

> As a group, the women make up what I have termed an interpretive community, which is strategically placed in relation to cultural works that either are created by black women or feature them in significant ways. Working together the women utilize representations of black women that they deem valuable in productive and politically useful ways. (1995: 22)

Because much of the criticism of Black female independent film makers' works stems from male or white perspectives, Bobo finds it necessary to distinguish the interpretive community—Black women involved in making or consuming these films—in order to accurately determine the actual intent and effect of these films. Bobo's thesis of the interpretive community is appropriate to this examination of women in rap because rap music is a form transmitted by recorded and video performances. More importantly, the classifications of women rappers are based on the constructions of an interpretive community, as observed via recorded performance and personal interviews. When rapper MC Lyte was asked, for example, if she felt that there is a distinct female rap category, she separated women rappers into three groups, referred to as "crews," reigning in three periods—the early 1980s, the mid-1980s through the early 1990s, and the late 1990s: "Sha-Rock, Sequence, to me, that's the first crew. Then you got a second crew, which is Salt-N-Pepa, Roxanne Shanté, The Real Roxanne, me, Latifah, Monie [Love], and Yo-Yo.... Then after that you got Da Brat, Foxy Brown, Lil' Kim, Heather B" (1996).[1]

Queried about specific categories, both rap music performers and female audience members frequently used the buzzwords *fly* and *attitude* (as in "girlfriend got attitude"), leading me to more clearly discern the parameters of categories. My initial category of "Black Diva" in early interviews for the grand posture of these women was later revised to "Queen Mother" after one female observer convincingly said *diva* denotes a posture of arrogance and pretentiousness as opposed to that of a regal and self-assured woman, qualities that she identified with the Queen Latifah types (see Penrice 1995).

In the female rap tradition, four distinct categories of women rappers emerge in rap music performance: "Queen Mother," "Fly Girl," "Sista with Attitude," and "Lesbian." Black female rappers can, however, shift between these categories or belong to more than one simultaneously. More importantly, each category mirrors certain images, voices, and lifestyles of African American women in contemporary urban society. Let us now examine the four categories or images of Black women introduced to rap by specific female rappers or emcees (MCs) and considered by the interpretive community in general as representative of and specific to African American female identity in contemporary urban culture.

Queen Mother

The "Queen Mother" category comprises female rappers who view themselves as African-centered icons, an image often suggested by their dress. In their lyrics, they refer to themselves as "Asiatic Black women," "Nubian queens," "intelligent Black women," or "sistas droppin' science to the people," suggestive of their self-constructed identity and intellectual prowess. The "queen mother" is, however, associated with African traditional court culture. For instance, in the 16th-century Benin Kingdom of southeastern Nigeria, she was the mother of a reigning king. Because of her maternal connection to the king, she garnered certain rights and privileges, including control over districts and a voice in the national affairs of the state. During his reign, a commemorative head made of brass was sculpted in her honor adorned with a beaded choker, headdress, and crown, along with a facial expression capturing her reposed manner.[2]

It is certainly possible that female rap artists may know of the historical significance of African queens; women in this category adorn their bodies with royal or Kente cloth strips, African headdresses, goddess braid styles, and ankh-stylized jewelry. Their rhymes embrace Black female empowerment and spirituality, making clear their self-identification as African, woman, warrior, priestess, and queen. Queen mothers demand respect not only for their people but for Black women, who are "to be accorded respect by ... men," observes Angela Y. Davis (1998: 122). Among those women distinguished by the interpretive community as Queen Mother types are Queen Kenya, Queen Latifah, Sister Souljah, Nefertiti, Queen Mother Rage, Isis, and Yo-Yo.

Queen Kenya, a member of hip-hop's Zulu Nation, was the first female MC to use *Queen* as a stage name.[3] But the woman of rap who became the first solo female MC to commercially record under the name "Queen" is Dana "Queen Latifah" Owens. Queen Latifah's initial singles "Princess of the Posse" and "Wrath of My Madness" (1988), followed by her debut album *All Hail the Queen* (1989), established her regal identity. They include such lyrics as, "You try to be down, you can't take my crown from me," and, "I'm on the scene, I'm the Queen of Royal Badness." Latifah, whose Arabic name means "feminine, delicate, and kind," explains the origin of her stage name:

> My cousin, who's Muslim, gave me that name [Latifah] when I was eight. Well [in rap], I didn't want to be MC Latifah. It didn't sound right. I didn't want to come out like old models. So *queen* just popped into my head one day, and I was like, "Me, Queen Latifah." It felt good saying it, and I felt like a queen. And you know, I am a queen. And every Black woman is a queen. (1993)

Latifah's maternal demeanor, posture, and full figure contribute to the perception of her as a queen mother. Although Queen Latifah acknowledges that others perceived her as motherly even at age 21, she tries to distance herself from the label: "I wish I wasn't seen as a mother, though. I don't really care for that. Just because I take a mature stance on certain things, it gives me a motherly feel ... maybe because I am full-figured. I am mature, but I'm twenty-one" (quoted in Green 1991: 33). The ambiguity of Latifah's motherly image follows what feminist scholars Joan Radner and Susan Lanser identify as a form of coding in women's folk culture called *distraction*: a device used to "drown out or draw attention away from the subversive power of a feminist message" (1993: 15). Queen Latifah finds that her stature and grounded perspective cause fans to view her as a maternal figure or as a person to revere or, at times, fear. However, Latifah attempts to mute her motherly image offstage, as evidenced in the above interview, indicating to fans that she remains, nonetheless, a modest, down-to-earth, and ordinary person in spite of her onstage "Queen of Royal Badness" persona.

Despite the ambiguity, Queen Latifah represents a particular type of mother figure to her audience. In *Black Feminist Thought*, sociologist Patricia Hill Collins recognizes that, in the African American community, some women are viewed as "othermothers." Collins explains.

> Black women's involvement in fostering African-American community development forms the basis for community-based power. This is the type of "strong Black woman" they see around them in traditional African-American communities. Community othermothers work on behalf of the Black community by expressing ethics of caring and personal accountability which embrace conceptions of transformative and mutuality ... community othermothers become identified as power figures through furthering the community's well-being. (1990: 132)

Queen Latifah's othermother posture is no doubt reflected most vividly through her lyrics, which, at times, address political-economic issues facing Black women and the Black community as a whole. In Latifah's song "The Evil that Men Do" (1989) from *All Hail the Queen*, "she isolates several of the difficulties commonly experienced by young black women [on welfare]" (Forman 1994: 44) and shows how the powers that be are apathetic to Black women who are trying to beat the odds:

> Here is a message from my sisters and brothers, here are some things I wanna cover.
> A woman strives for a better life
> but who the hell cares because she's living on welfare.
> The government can't come up with a decent housing plan
> so she's in no man's land

it's a sucker who tells you you're equal ...
Someone's livin' the good life tax-free
'cause some poor girl can't be livin' crack free
and that's just part of the message
I thought I should send you about the evil that men do. (quoted in Forman 1994: 44)

Another example of Queen Latifah's role as queen mother of rap resonates in her platinum single "Ladies First" (1989), ranked in the annals of rap music history as the first political commentary rap song by a female artist. The lyrics of "Ladies First" respond primarily to males who believe that females cannot create rhymes:

Some think that we [women] can't flow
Stereotypes they got to go.
I gonna mess around and flip the scene into reverse
With a little touch of ladies first.

The video version is far more political, containing live footage of South Africa's apartheid riots overlaid with photographic stills of Black heroines—Winnie Mandela, Rosa Parks, Angela Davis, Harriet Tubman, and Madame C.J. Walker.[4] Pan-Africanism is tacitly evoked with these images—South Africa's political struggle against segregation and a salute to Winnie Mandela, the mother of this struggle, who is presented among U.S. Black women—reminders of Black liberation. Additionally, the bond between Black women in the United States and the United Kingdom is alluded to through the appearance of Monie Love of England, whom Queen Latifah refers to as "my European partner." These images locate Latifah as a queen mother and equal partner among those Black queens who struggled for the freedom of Black people.

Perceived by the interpretive community as a queen mother of rap, Queen Latifah opened the doors for other Afrocentric female MCs, such as Sister Souljah. Souljah, a former associate of the Black nationalist rap group Public Enemy, launched her first LP in 1992. The LP, *360 Degrees of Power*, features the rap single "The Final Solution: Slavery's Back in Effect," in which "Souljah imagines a police state where blacks fight the reinstitution of slavery" (Leland 1992: 48). With her candid and somewhat quasipreachy style of delivery, she earned the title "raptivist" from her followers. Souljah's fame grew after her speech at the Reverend Jesse Jackson's Rainbow Coalition Leadership Summit in 1992, where she chided African Americans who murder one another for no apparent reason by figuratively suggesting, "Why not take a week and kill white people[?]" (Leland 1992: 48). As a consequence, Souljah was ridiculed as a propagator of hate by presidential candidate Bill Clinton. In the wake of the controversy, her record sales plummeted dramatically while her "raptivist" messages skyrocketed with television appearances on talk shows like *The Phil Donahue Show* and speeches on the university lecture circuit. While Sister Souljah advocates racial, social, and economic parity in her rap messages, she also looks within the community to relationship issues between Black men and women in her lyrics and her semiautobiographical book *No Disrespect* (1994: xiv).

Although Nefertiti, Isis, and Queen Mother Rage are categorized as queen mothers via their names, lyrics, or attire, female rapper Yo-Yo is also regarded by the interpretive community as a queen mother.[5] Her lyrics illustrate her political ideology of Black feminism and female respectability, as advanced by her organization, the Intelligent Black Women Coalition (I.B.W.C.), which she discusses on her debut LP *Make Way for the Motherlode* (1991). But Yo-Yo's image—long auburn braids and very short tight-fitting *pum-pum* shorts (worn by Jamaican dance hall women performers)—and her gyrating hip dancing also position her in the next category, "Fly Girl."

Fly Girl

Fly describes someone in chic clothing and fashionable hairstyles, jewelry, and cosmetics, a style that grew out of the blaxploitation films of the late 1960s through the mid-1970s. These films include *Shaft* (1971), *Superfly* (1972), *The Mack* (1973), and *Foxy Brown* (1974), a film that inspired one MC to adopt the movie's title as her moniker. The fly persona in these films influenced a wave of Black contemporary youth who, in turn, resurrected flyness and its continuum in hip-hop culture. During the early 1980s, women rappers, including Sha Rock of Funky Four Plus One, the trio Sequence, and soloist Lady B, dressed in what was then considered by their audiences as fly.

They wore short skirts, sequined fabric, high-heeled shoes, and prominent makeup. By 1985, the hip-hop community further embraced the fly image via the commercial recording of "A Fly Girl," by the male rap group Boogie Boys, and an answer rap during the same year, "A Fly Guy," by female rapper Pebblee-Poo. The Boogie Boys describe a fly girl as a woman "who wants you to see her name, her game and her ability"; to do so, "she sports a lot of gold, wears tight jeans, leather mini skirts, a made-up face, has voluptuous curves, but speaks her mind" (1987).

By the mid-1980s, many female MCs began contesting the "fly girl" image because they wanted their audiences to focus more on their rapping skills than on their dress styles. Despite this changing trend, the female rap trio Salt-N-Pepa—Salt, Pepa, and Spinderella—nevertheless canonized the ultimate fly girl posture of rap by donning short, tight-fitting outfits, leather clothing, ripped jeans or punk clothing, glittering gold jewelry (i.e., earrings and necklaces), long sculpted nails, prominent makeup, and hairstyles ranging from braids and wraps to waves, in ever-changing hair coloring.

Rap's fly girl image is, however, far more than a whim, for it highlights aspects of Black women's bodies considered undesirable by American mainstream standards of beauty (Roberts 1998). Through performance, Salt-N-Pepa are "flippin da script" (deconstructing dominant ideology) by wearing clothes that accent their full breasts and rounded buttocks and thighs, considered beauty markers of Black women by Black culture (Roberts 1998). Moreover, they portray via performance the fly girl as a party-goer, an independent woman, but, additionally, an erotic subject rather than an objectified one.

Female rappers' reclamation of the *fly* resonates with the late Audre Lorde's theory of the erotic as power (Davis 1998: 172). In Lorde's influential essay, "Uses of the Erotic," she reveals the transformative power of the erotic in Black women's culture: "Our erotic knowledge empowers us, becomes a lens through which we scrutinize all aspects of our existence, forcing us to evaluate those aspects honestly in terms of their meaning within our lives" (1984: 57). Cultural critic and scholar bell hooks further articulates that Black women's erotic consciousness is textualized around issues of body esteem: "Erotic pleasure requires of us engagement with the realm of the senses ... the capacity to be in touch with sensual reality; to accept and love our bodies; [to work] toward self-recovery issues around body esteem; [and] to be empowered by a healing eroticism" (1993: 116, 121–122, 124).

Black fly girls express a growing awareness of their erotic selves by sculpting their own personas and, as folklorist Elaine Lawless (1998) puts it, "writing their own bodies." For example, Salt-N-Pepa describe themselves as "women [who have] worked hard to keep our bodies in shape; we're proud to show them off": moreover, "we're not ashamed of our sexuality; for we're Salt-N-Pepa—sexier and more in control" (quoted in Rogers 1994: 31).

Another aspect of the fly girl persona is independence. Salt notes that "the image we project reflects the real independent woman of the '90s" (quoted in Chyll 1994: 20). But for many women of rap, achieving a sense of independence from an entrepreneurial perspective has not been easy. For instance, it is common knowledge in the rap community that during Salt-N-Pepa's early years, their lyrics and hit songs ("I'll Take Your Man," "Push It," "Tramp," and "Shake Your Thang") were mainly written by their manager/producer Hurby "Luvbug" Azor, until the *Black's Magic* (1990) LP, on which Salt (Cheryl James) ventured into writing and producing the single "Expression," which went platinum. *Black's Magic* also contains Salt-N-Pepa's "Let's Talk about Sex" (written by Azor), which Salt later rewrote for a public service announcement song and video "Let's Talk about AIDS" in 1992.

On Salt-N-Pepa's fourth LP, *Very Necessary* (1993), the group wrote and produced most of the selections. The songs "Shoop" and "Whatta Man" from that album stand out as celebratory songs that deserve note.[6] In the video versions of both songs, the three women scrutinize desirable men, ranging from business types to "ruffnecks" (a fly guy associated with urban street culture). The "Shoop" video turns the tables on the male rappers; in it "ladies see a bunch of bare-chested, tight-bunned brothers acting like sex *objects*, servicing it up to us in our videos," said Salt (quoted in Rogers 1994: 31, emphasis added). In "Whatta Man," on the other hand, Salt-N-Pepa praise their significant others in the areas of friendship, romance, and parenting as the female rhythm and blues group En Vogue joins them in singing the chorus, "Whatta man, whatta man, whatta man, whatta mighty good man."

Other women whom the interpretive community categorizes as *fly* are Left-Eye and Yo-Yo. Left Eye is the rapper of the hip-hop/rhythm and blues hybrid group TLC (*T*-Boz, *Left* Eye, and Chili). When TLC first appeared on the music scene with the debut LP *Ooooooooohhh ... On the TLC Tip* (1992), their baggy style of dress ran counter to the revealing apparel of hip-hop's typical fly girl and invited their full-figured audience to do the same. TLC's T-Boz said, "We like to wear a lot of baggy stuff because for one, it's comfortable, and two, many of our fans don't have the so-called perfect figure; we don't want them to feel like they can't wear what we're wearing" (quoted in Horner 1993: 16). Throughout the 1990s, TLC remained steadfast with the message to women of all sizes regarding mental and physical wellness and body esteem, as underscored in both music and video performances of the single "Unpretty" (1999).

Like Salt-N-Pepa, TLC has made delivering "safe sex" messages *a priority*. While both groups do so through lyrics, TLC underscores the messages visually through wearing certain accoutrements. Left Eye of the trio wears a condom in place of an eyeglass lens, while other members of the group attach colored condom packages to their clothes. TLC's warning about unprotected sex, emphasized by the condoms they wear, is conveyed powerfully in their award-winning "Waterfalls" from their second LP, *CrazySexyCool* (1994). The message is amplified in the video: A man decides to follow his partner's wish not to use a condom. Following this encounter, he notices a lesion on his face, which suggests that he has contracted the virus that causes AIDS. TLC's espousal of being fly and sexually independent undoubtedly comes hand in hand with sexual responsibility via their lyrics and image.

Like TLC, Yo-Yo also delivers a serious message, which earns her a place among the queen mothers. But her gyrating hips, stylish auburn braids, short, tight-fitting outfits, and pronounced facial makeup also categorize her as fly. Yo-Yo writes about independent, empowered Black women, championing African American sisterhood in "The I.B.W.C. National Anthem" and "Sisterland" from *Make Way for the Motherlode* (1991). She takes on sexuality in "You Can't Play with My Yo-Yo" and "Put a Lid on It," which, as their titles suggest, explore being sexually in control and being sexually irresponsible.

In 1996, Yo-Yo moved beyond the shadow of her mentor Ice Cube with her fourth LP, *Total Control*, for which she served as executive producer. Following this success, Yo-Yo began a column entitled "Yo, Yo-Yo" in the hip-hop magazine *Vibe*, in which she addresses questions about male-female relationships and interpersonal growth in the name of I.B.W.C.

Since the late 1990s, female MC, songwriter, and producer Missy "Misdemeanor" Elliott has joined the fly girl ranks. Mesmerized by her debut LP *Supa Dupa Fly* (1997) and her single "The Rain," female fans also admire her finger-wave hairstyle, known to some as "Missy [finger] waves," and her ability to carry off the latest hip-hop fashions on her full-figured frame. Elliott has occasionally appeared in television advertisements for the youth fashion store Gap. She no doubt succeeds as a full-figured *fly* woman, breaking new ground in an area too often seen as off-limits to all but the most slender and "correctly" proportioned. In staking her claim to rap music's fly girl category, Elliott further reclaims sexuality and eros as healing power for all Black women, regardless of size. However, with her single "She's a Bitch" from her sophomore LP *Da Real World* (1999), Missy "Misdemeanor" Elliott appends another image to her fly girl posture. Her usage of *bitch* makes a self-statement about being a mover and shaker, on- and offstage, in rap's male-dominated arena, and thus she shares much in common with the next category, "Sista with Attitude."

Sista with Attitude

According to Black English scholar Geneva Smitherman, "'tude, a diminutive form of attitude, can be defined as an aggressive, arrogant, defiant, I-know-I'm-BAD pose or air about oneself; or an oppositional or negative outlook or disposition" (1994: 228). Prototypes of this category are grouped according to "'tude": Roxanne Shanté, Bytches with Problems (BWP), and Da Brat are known for their frankness; MC Lyte exudes a hardcore/no-nonsense approach; Boss is recognized for her gangsta bitch posture; and Mia X advances a militaristic stance, all in the name of her predominantly male posse No Limit Soldiers.[7]

In general, "Sista with Attitude" comprises female MCs who value attitude as a means of empowerment and present themselves accordingly. Many of these "sistas" (sisters) have reclaimed the word *bitch*, viewing it as positive rather than negative and using the term to entertain or provide cathartic release. Other sistas in the interpretive community are troubled by that view. These women, such as Lauryn Hill, have "refused to be labeled a 'bitch' because such appellations merely mar the images of young African American females" (1994; see also Harmony, quoted in Donahue 1991). The reclaimers counter this argument with the opinion that "it's not what you're called but what you answer to" (MC Lyte 1993). Some women of rap take a middle road, concurring that *bitch* can be problematic depending on who uses the term, how it is employed, and to whom one refers. As Queen Latifah explains.

> I don't really mind the term.... I play around with it I use it with my home girls like, "Bitch are you crazy?" Bitch is a fierce girl. [Or.] "That bitch is so crazy, girl." You know, that's not harmful [But.] "This stupid bitch just came down here talking ... ," now that's meant in a harmful way. So it's the meaning behind the word that to me decides whether I should turn it off or listen to it. (1993)

Female MCs revise the standard definition of *bitch*, from an "aggressive woman who challenges male authority" (Penrice 1995) to an aggressive or assertive female who subverts patriarchal rule. Lyndah of the duo BWP explained, "We use 'Bytches' [to mean] a strong, positive, aggressive woman who goes after what she wants. We take that on today ... and use it in a positive sense" (quoted in Donahue 1991).[8]

By the mid- to late 1990s, the "Sista with Attitude" category was augmented with rappers Lil' Kim and Foxy Brown, who conflate fly and hardcore attitudes in erotic lyrics and video performances, bordering both "Fly Girl" and "Sista with Attitude" categories. In doing so, they are designated by some as the "mack divas," "Thelma and Louise of rap" (Gonzales 1997: 62), or "bad girls of hip-hop" (Morgan 1997). Foxy Brown, whose name is derived from Pam Grier's 1974 screen character, emulates the powerful, desirable, yet dangerous woman: "I think it's every girl's dream to be fly" (Gonzales 1997: 63). Although Lil' Kim's debut album *Hard Core* (1996) and Foxy Brown's *Ill Na Na* (1997) have garnered platinum status, some members of the interpretive community criticize them for being "highly materialistic, violent, lewd" (Morgan 1997: 77), an impression exacerbated by their affiliation with male gangsta rap–style crews: Lil' Kim is associated with Junior M.A.F.I.A., and Foxy Brown is connected with The Firm.

The bad girl image also parallels the "badman" character (such as John Hardy, Dolemite, and Stackolee) peculiar to the African American oral narrative. African American oral narratives commonly exploit the "badman" or "bad nigguh" types in the toast, a long poetic narrative form that predates rap.[9] In these narratives, Black badmen boast about their sexual exploits with women, wild drinking binges, and narrow brushes with the law, symbolic of "white power" (Roberts 1989: 196). The feminist rendering of "the badman" includes those sistas who brag about partying and smoking "blunts" (marijuana) with their men; seducing, repressing, and sexually emasculating male characters;[10] or "dissin'" (verbally downplaying) their would-be female or male competitors—all through figurative speech.[11]

Some female observers I queried felt that sistas with attitude merely exist on the periphery of rap and are seen as just "shootin' off at the mouth." These artists are not highly respected for their creative skills; rather, they are viewed as misusing sex and feminism and devaluing Black men. In an *Essence* magazine article, hip-hop feminist Joan Morgan states that the new "bad girls of hip-hop" may not have career longevity because "feminism is not simply about being able to do what the boys do—get high, talk endlessly about their wee-wees and what have you. At the end of the day, it's the power women attain by making choices that increase their range of possibilities" (1997: 132). Morgan further argues that Black women's power—on- and offstage—is sustained by "those sisters who selectively ration their erotic power" (1997: 133).

Despite the controversies, sistas with attitude have acquired respect from their peers for their mastery of figurative language and rhyme. They simply refuse to be second best.

Lesbian

While representatives of the "Queen Mother," "Fly Girl," and "Sista with Attitude" categories came into prominence during the mid- to late 1980s, the "Lesbian" category emerged from the closet during the late 1990s. Not only does the female audience term this category "Lesbian," but the artist who has given recognition to this division is among the first to rap about and address the lesbian lifestyle from a Black woman's perspective. Though other Black rap artists rumored to be gay/lesbian have chosen to remain closeted in a scene described as "notoriously homophobic" (Dyson, quoted in Jamison 1998: AR34), Queen Pen's "Girlfriend," from her debut LP *My Melody* (1997), represents a "breakthrough for queer culture" (Walters 1998: 60).[12] "Girlfriend" signifies on or indirectly plays on Black lesbian love interest with a parody of the refrain section of Me'Shell Ndegeocello's "If That's Your Boyfriend (He Wasn't Last Night)." Ndegeocello, who is openly lesbian, appears on "Girlfriend," performing vocals and bass guitar. In "Girlfriend," Queen Pen positions herself as the suitor in a lesbian relationship. While this song may be a "breakthrough for queer culture," other issues still complicate Black female artists' willingness to openly address gay and lesbian culture in their performances.

Black lesbian culture and identity have been concerned with issues of race and role-play, note Lisa M. Walker (1993) and Ekua Omosupe (1991). Drawing on the critical works of Audre Lorde (1982, 1984), Omosupe notes that lesbian identity, similar to feminism, represents white lesbian culture or white women to the exclusion of women of color. In this regard, Black lesbians are at times forced to live and struggle against white male patriarchal culture on the one side and white lesbian culture, racism, and general homophobia on the other (Omosupe 1991: 105). Corroborating issues of race privilege raised by the Black lesbian community, Queen Pen contends that certain licenses are afforded to white openly lesbian performers like

Ellen DeGeneres and k.d. lang, who do not have to pay as high a price for their candidness as lesbians of color: "But you know, Ellen [DeGeneres] can talk about any ol' thing and it's all right. With everybody, it's all right. With 'Girlfriend,' I'm getting all kinds of questions" (quoted in Duvernay 1998: 88).[13] She continues, "This song is buggin' everyone out right now. [If] you got Ellen, you got k.d., why shouldn't urban lesbians go to a girl club and hear their own thing?" (quoted in Jamison 1998: AR34).

Queen Pen further stresses in performance her play on image, which suggests "role-play," another crucial issue to Black lesbian culture. Walker asserts, "Role-play among black lesbians involves a resistance to the homophobic stereotype … lesbian as "bulldagger," a pejorative term within (and outside) the black community used to signal the lesbian as a woman who wants to be a man" (1993: 886). On her album cover, Queen Pen exudes a "femme" image through wearing lipstick, a chic hairstyle, and stylish dress. However, in performance, as observed in Blackstreet's "No Dignity" (1996), one notices how Queen Pen "drowns out" her femme album cover image by appropriating "B-Boy" gestures (cool pose and bopped gait) commonly associated with male hip-hop culture. Regardless of issues concerning race privilege and role-play, Queen Pen concludes that in "two or three years from now, people will say I was the first female to bring the lesbian life to light [in an open way] on wax. It's reality. What's the problem?" (quoted in Jamison 1998: AR34).

Conclusion

Women are achieving major strides in rap music by continuing to chisel away at stereotypes about females as artists in a male-dominated tradition and by (re)defining women's culture and identity from a Black feminist perspective. Although rap continues to be predominantly male, female MCs move beyond the shadows of male rappers in diverse ways. Some have become exclusively known for their lyrical "skillz," while others have used a unique blend of musical styles or a combination of singer-rapper acts, as is apparent with Grammy awardees Left Eye of TLC and Lauryn Hill.

Women of rap still face, nevertheless, overt sexism regarding their creative capabilities. Female rapper Princesa recalls, "Only when I led them [male producers] to believe that a man had written or produced my stuff did they show interest" (quoted in Cooper 1989: 80). Mass-mediation scholar Lisa Lewis notes that, in the popular music arena, "the ideological division between composition and performance serves to devalue women's role in music making and cast doubt on female creativity in general" (1990: 57). However, female MCs of the 1990s have defied the sexist repression by writing their own songs, producing records, and even starting their own record companies, as with Salt-N-Pepa's *Very Necessary* (1993), Lauryn Hill's 1999 Grammy Award-winning LP *The Miseducation of Lauryn Hill* (1998), and Queen Latifah's record company, Flavor Unit. Additionally, Queen Latifah's Grammy Award-winning single "U.N.I.T.Y." (1993) challenges those males who use *bitch/ho* appellations in their lyrics.

While the majority of scholarly studies on female rappers locate Black women's voices in rap, they present only a partial rendering of female representation.[14] These works tend to focus on females' attitudes and responses to sexual objectification, ignoring the many roles and issues of women and female rappers. Rap music scholar Tricia Rose says female MCs should be evaluated not only with regard to male rappers and misogynist lyrics "but also in response to a variety of related issues, including dominant notions of femininity, feminism, and black female sexuality. At the very least, black women rappers are in dialogue with one another, black men, black women, and dominant American culture as they struggle to define themselves" (1994: 147–148). In rap music performance, a "black female-self emerges as a variation [on] several unique themes" (Etter-Lewis 1991: 43).

More importantly, female rappers, most of whom are Black, convey their views on a variety of issues concerning identity, sociohistory, and esoteric beliefs shared by young African American women. Female rappers have attained a sense of distinction through revising and reclaiming Black women's history and perceived destiny. They use their performances as platforms to refute, deconstruct, and reconstruct alternative visions of their identity. With this platform, rap music becomes a vehicle by which Black female rappers seek empowerment, make choices, and create spaces for themselves and other sistas.

Study Questions

1. How would Keyes's model of the four distinct categories of women rappers be updated to apply to the presence of women in hip-hop contemporarily?
2. What are the primary impediments to women rappers achieving the level of popularity and artistic respect of their male peers?
3. How does sexuality complicate Keyes's categories of women rappers?

Notes

Earlier drafts of this article were presented on the panel "Women Performers as Traditionalists and Innovators" at Resounding Women in World Music: A Symposium sponsored by the World Music Institute and Hunter College/City University of New York Graduate Program in Ethnomusicology, New York, 10–12 November 1995; and as a paper. "'Ain't Nuthin' but a She-Thing' Women. Race and Representation in Rap," at the 42nd Annual Meetings of the Society for Ethnomusicology with the International Association for the Study of Popular Music (USA Chapter), Pittsburgh, 22–26 October 1997. I wish to thank Lou Ann Crouther, Phyllis May-Machunda, the late Gerald L. Davis, and the anonymous reviewers of the *Journal of American Folklore* for their suggestions on earlier drafts, as well as Corinne Lightweaver, whose invaluable comments contributed to the article's refinement.

1. The following is a list of other artists who make up a roster of female MCs: Antoinette (Next Plateau), Bahamadia (EMI), Conscious Daughters (Priority), Eve (Ruff Ryders), Finesse and Synquis (MCA), Gangsta Boo (Relativity), Heather B (MCA), Lady of Rage (Death Row), Ladybug (Pendulum), MC Smooth (Crush Music), MC Trouble (Motown), Mercedes (No Limit), Nikki D (Def Jam), Nonchalant (MCA), Oaktown's 3–5–7 (Capital), Rah Digga (Flipmode), Solé (Dream Works), and 350 (Rap-a-Lot).
2. Accordingly, sculpting the queen mother's head was established in Benin by King Oba Esigies during the 16th century. Sieber and Walker (1987: 93) note that, during Esigies's reign, he commissioned a sculpted head made of bronze of his mother, Idia, and placed it in his palace to commemorate her role in the Benn-Idah war, thereby including, for the first time, queen mothers in the cult of royal ancestors. In addition to Sieber and Walker's work, refer to Ben-Amos 1995 and Ben-Amos and Rubin 1983 for photographs and a brief discussion of queen mother heads of Benin.
3. The Zulu Nation is an organization that was founded in the Bronx during the mid-1970s by DJ Afrika Bambaataa. He contends that the Zulu Nation is a youth organization that incorporates a philosophy of nonviolence and in which inner-city youths compete artistically as break-dancers, rhyming emcees (rappers), disc jockeys, and graffiti artists rather than physically with knives and guns. Bambaataa's Zulu Nation laid the foundation for hip-hop, a youth arts movement comprising the above arts, and an "attitude" rendered in the form of a distinct dress, language, and gesture—all of which is articulated via performance by rap music artists (see Keyes 1996).
4. For a more detailed analysis of this video, see Roberts 1994.
5. Isis once performed with the Black nationalist group X-Clan. After leaving this group, she also adopted a new stage name, Lin Que.
6. "Whatta Man" is adapted from Linda Lyndell's 1968 hit "What a Man."
7. For a more in-depth discussion of this category, refer to the section on female rappers in my book, *Rap Music and Street Consciousness* (Champaign: University of Illinois Press, 2002).
8. Another aspect of speech play is the manner in which sistas with attitude refer to men in their rap songs affectionately or insultingly as "motherfuckas" or "my niggas."
9. For further information about the toast, see Roger Abrahams (1970) and Darryl Dance (1978).

10. This emasculation can occur when sistas with attitude refer to their male competitors or suitors as "motherfuckas" or "niggas." Because the element of signifying is aesthetically appealing in this style of rap, these terms may have both negative and positive meanings depending on context.

11. Examples of selected rap songs that portray the distinct characteristics of sistas with attitude include the following: Boss, "I Don't Give a Fuck" and "Mai Sista Izza Bitch," *Bom Gangstaz* (1993), Bytches with Problems, "Two Minute Brother" and "Shit Popper," *The Bytches* (1991); Da Brat, "Da Shit Ya Can't Fuc Wit" and "Fire It Up," *Funkdafied* (1994); Foxy Brown. "Ill Na Na" and "Letter to the Firm," *Ill Na Na* (1997); Lil' Kim, "Big Momma Thang" and "Spend a Little Doe," *Hard Core* (1996); MC Lyte, "Paper Thin," *Lyte as a Rock* (1988), and "Steady F . . . king," *Ain't No Other* (1993); Roxanne Shanté, "Big Mama," *The Bitch Is Back* (1992).

12. While "Queen Pen" is a play on "King Pin," Queen Pen uses this moniker to indicate that she "pens" (or writes) her own lyrics. A skill that some believe female MCs lack in comparison with male rappers. Although "Girlfriend" and other selections on Queen Pen's LP were cowritten and produced by Teddy Riley, inventor of new jack swing style (a rap rhythm and blues hybrid). Queen Pen's real name (Lynise Walters) appears on all songs. In the music industry, it is not unusual for producers to take cowriting credit on their mentees' debut works. The discussion of Riley's input on "Girlfriend" is discussed by Laura Jamison (1998).

13. When asked about "Girlfriend" in her interview in *Rap Pages* with Duvernay (1998), Queen Pen asserts that there are other nonlesbian songs on her debut album *My Melody*, including "Get Away," which discusses domestic violence.

14. For more on this topic, see Berry 1994, Forman 1994, Goodall 1994, Guevara 1987, and Rose 1994.

References Cited

Abrahams, Roger. 1970. *Deep Down in the Jungle. Negro Narrative Folklore from the Streets of Philadelphia.* Chicago: Aldine Publishing.
Ben-Amos, Paula Girshick. 1995. *The Art of Benin.* Rev. edition. Washington, D.C.: Smithsonian Institution Press.
Ben-Amos, Paula Girshick, and Arnold Rubin, eds. 1983. *The Art of Power, the Power of Art: Studies in Benin Iconography.* Los Angeles: Museum of Cultural History.
Berry, Venise T. 1994. Feminine or Masculine: The Conflicting Nature of Female Images in Rap Music. In *Cecilia Reclaimed: Feminist Perspectives on Gender and Music,* ed. Susan C. Cook and Judy S. Tsou, pp. 183–201. Urbana: University of Illinois Press.
Bobo, Jacqueline. 1995. *Black Women as Cultural Readers.* New York: Columbia University Press.
Chyll, Chuck. 1994. Musical Reactions: Sexy Rap or Credibility Gap? *Rap Masters* 7(7): 19–20.
Collins, Patricia Hill. 1990. *Black Feminist Thought: Knowledge, Consciousness, and the Politics of Empowerment.* London: Harper Collins Academic.
Cooper, Carol. 1989. Girls Ain't Nothin' but Trouble. *Essence* (April): 80, 119.
Dance, Daryl. 1978. *Shuckin' and Jivin': Folklore from Contemporary Black Americans.* Bloomington: Indiana University Press.
Davis, Angela Y. 1998. *Blues Legacies and Black Feminism: Gertrude "Ma" Rainey, Bessie Smith, and Billie Holiday.* New York: Pantheon Books.
Donahue, Phil. 1991. Female Rappers Invade the Male Rap Industry. The Phil Donahue Show Transcript #3216, 29 May.
Duvernay, Ava. 1998. Queen Pen: Keep "EM Guessin." *Rap Pages* (May): 86–88.
Etter-Lewis, Gwendolyn. 1991. Black Women's Life Stories: Reclaiming Self in Narrative Texts. In *Women's Words: The Feminist Practice of Oral History,* ed. Sherna Berger Gluck and Daphne Patai, pp. 43–59. New York: Routledge.
Forman, Murray. 1994. Movin' Closer to an Independent Funk: Black Feminist Theory, Standpoint, and Women in Rap. *Women's Studies* 23: 35–55.
Gonzales, A. Michael. 1997. Mack Divas. *The Source* (February): 62–64.
Goodall, Nataki. 1994. Depend on Myself: T.L.C. and the Evolution of Black Female Rap. *Journal of Negro History* 79(1): 85–93.
Green, Kim. 1991. The Naked Truth. *The Source* (November): 32–34, 36.
Guevara, Nancy. 1987. Women Writin' Rappin' Breakin'. In *The Year Left,* 2nd ed. Mike Davis, Manning Marable, Fred Pfeil, and Michael Sprinker, pp. 160–175. New York: Verso Press.
Hill, Lauryn. 1994. Panelist. Hip-Hop Summit for New Music, Seminar 15, New York, 20 July.
hooks, bell. 1993. *Sisters of the Yam: Black Women and Self-Recovery.* Boston: South End Press.
Horner, Cynthia. 1993. TLC: The Homegirls with Style! *Right On!* (February): 16–17.

Jamison, Laura. 1998. A Feisty Female Rapper Breaks a Hip-Hop Taboo. *Sunday New York Times*, 18 January: AR34.

Keyes, Cheryl L. 1996. At the Crossroads: Rap Music and Its African Nexus. Ethnomusicology 40(2): 223–248. In *Rap Music and Street Consciousness*. 2002. Champaign: University of Illinois Press.

Lawless, Elaine J. 1998. Claiming Inversion: Lesbian Constructions of Female Identity as Claims for Authority. *Journal of American Folklore* 11 (439): 3–22.

Leland, John. 1992. Souljah on Ice. *Newsweek*, 29 June: 46–52.

Lewis, Lisa. 1990. *Gender Politics and MTV: Voicing the Difference*. Philadelphia: Temple University Press.

Lorde, Audre. 1982. *Zimi: A New Spelling of My Name*. Trumansburg. N.Y.: Crossing Press.

———. 1984. *Sister Outsider*. Freedom, Calif.: Crossing Press.

MC Lyte. 1993. Musical guest. Arsenio Hall Show, 8 October.

———. 1996. Interview by the author. Irvine, Calif., 11 August.

Morgan, Joan. 1997. The Bad Girls of Hip-Hop. *Essence* (March): 76–77, 132–134.

Nelson, Havelock. 1993. New Female Rappers Play for Keeps. *Billboard*, 10 July 1, 77.

Omosupe, Ekua. 1991. Black/Lesbian/Bulldagger. *differences* 3(2): 101–111.

Pearlman, Jill. 1988. Girls Rappin' Round Table. *The Paper* (summer): 25–27.

Penrice, Ronda. 1995. Interview by the author. *Manhattan*, 11 November.

Queen Latifah. 1993. Interview by the author. Jersey City. 8 July.

Radner, Joan Newlon, and Susan S. Lanser. 1993. Strategies of Coding in Women's Culture. In *Feminist Messages: Coding in Women's Folk Culture*, ed. Joan Newlon Radner, pp. 1–29. Urbana: University of Illinois Press.

Roberts, Deborah. 1998. Beautiful Women. 20/20, ABC Transcript #1796, 30 March.

Roberts, John W. 1989. *From Trickster to Badman: The Black Folk Hero in Slavery and Freedom*. Philadelphia: University of Pennsylvania.

Roberts, Robin. 1994. "Ladies First": Queen Latifah's Afrocentric Feminist Music Video. *African American Review* 28(2): 245–257.

Rogers, E. Charles. 1994. The Salt-N-Pepa Interview. *Rap Masters* 7(7) July: 30–31.

Rose, Tricia. 1994. *Black Noise: Rap Music and Black Culture in Contemporary America*. Hanover, N.H.: Wesleyan University Press.

Sieber, Roy, and Roslyn Adele Walker. 1987. *African Art in the Cycle of Life*. Washington, D.C.: Smithsonian Institution Press.

Sister Souljah. 1994. *No Disrespect*. New York: Random House.

Smitherman, Geneva. 1994. *Black Talk: Words and Phrases from the Hood to the Amen Corner*. New York: Houghton Mifflin Co.

Walker, Lisa M. 1993. How to Recognize a Lesbian: The Cultural Politics of Looking Like What You Are. *Signs: Journal of Women in Culture and Society* 18(4): 866–889.

Walters, Barry. 1998. My Melody (sound recording review). *Advocate* 755 (17 March): 59–60.

Discography

Boogie Boys. 1987[1985]. A Fly Girl. *Rap vs. Rap: The Answer Album*. Priority 4XL-9506.

Boss. 1993. *Born Gangstaz*. Def Jam/Columbia OT 52903.

Bytches with Problems. 1991. *The Bytches*. No Face/RAL CT 47068.

Da Brat. 1994. *Funkdafied*. Chaos/Columbia OT 66164.

Foxy Brown. 1997. *Ill Na Na*. Def Jam 547028.

Funky Four Plus One. Rapping and Rocking the House. *Great Rap Hits*. Sugar Hill SH 246.

Lauryn Hill. 1998. *The Miseducation of Lauryn Hill*. Ruffhouse/Columbia CT69035.

Lil' Kim. 1996. *Hard Core*. Big Beat Records/Atlantic 92733–2.

MC Lyte. 1988. *Lyte as a Rock*. First Priority Music/Atlantic 7 90905–1.

———. 1993. *Ain't No Other*. First Priority Music/Atlantic 7 92230–4.

Missy "Misdemeanor" Elliott. 1997. *Supa Dupa Fly*. The Gold Mind, Inc./EastWest 62062–2.

———. 1999. *Da Real World*. The Gold Mine, Inc./East West 62244–4.

Queen Latifah. 1989. *All Hail the Queen*. Tommy Boy TBC 1022.

———. 1991. *Nature of a Sista'*. Tommy Boy TBC 9007.

———. 1993. U.N.I.T.Y. *Black Reign*. Motown 37463–6370–4.

Queen Pen. 1997. *My Melody*. Lil' Man/Interscope INTC-90151.

Roxanne Shanté. 1992. *The Bitch Is Back*. Livin' Large 3001.

———. 1995. Roxanne's Revenge. *Roxanne Shanté's Greatest Hits*. Cold Chillin'/Warner Brothers 5007.

Salt-N-Pepa. 1986. *Hot, Cool and Vicious*. Next Plateau/London 422–828362–2.

———. 1990. *Black's Magic*. Next Plateau/London 422–828362–2.

————. 1993. *Very Necessary* Next Plateau/London P2–28392.

Sister Souljah. 1992. *360 Degrees of Power*. Epic EK-48713.

TLC. 1992. *Ooooooohhh … On the TLC Tip*. LaFace/Arista 26003–2.

————. 1994. *CrazySexyCool*. LaFace/Arista AC 26009–2.

————. 1999. Unpretty. *FanMail*. LaFace/Arista 26055–4.

Yo-Yo. 1991. *Make Way for the Motherlode*. EastWest/Atlantic 791605–2.

————. 1996. *Total Control*. EastWest/Atlantic 61898.

27
Hip-Hop Feminist

Joan Morgan's 1999 book *When Chickenheads Come Home to Roost: My Life as a Hip-Hop Feminist* remains a crucial text in discussions of gender in hip-hop and the black community at large. Morgan is generally credited with coining the term "hip-hop feminism." Less concerned with the impact of sexism and misogyny, Morgan's essay describes the ways that young women parlay sexuality in hip-hop as a vehicle towards agency.

Specifically, Morgan examines how women in hip-hop use the erotic as dynamic to challenge normative discourses of gender and sexuality as they exist in hip-hop and the larger society. In the end, for Morgan, a hip hop feminism is a feminism that places women firmly in control of their bodies and imagery.

Hip-Hop Feminist

Joan Morgan

Much had changed in my life by the time a million black men marched in Washington. I no longer live in Harlem. The decision had less to do with gunshot lullabies, dead bodies 'round the corner, or the pre-adolescents safe-sexing it in my stairwells—running consensual trains on a twelve-year-old girl whose titties and ass grew faster than her self-esteem—and more to do with my growing desensitization to it all. As evidenced by the zombie-like stare in my neighbors' eyes, the ghetto's dues for emotional immunity are high. And I knew better than to test its capacity for contagion.

So I broke out. Did a Bronx girl's unthinkable and moved to Brooklyn—where people had kids and dogs and gardens and shit. And a park called Prospect contained ol' West Indian men who reminded me of yet another home and everything good about my father.

It is the Bronx that haunts me, though. There a self, long deaded, roams the Concourse, dressed in big bamboo earrings and flare-legged Lees, guarding whatever is left of her memories. I murdered her. Slowly. By sipping miasmic cocktails of non-ghetto dreams laced with raw ambition. I had to. She would have clung so tightly to recollections of monkey bars, sour pickles, and BBQ Bontons, slow dances to "Always and Forever," and tongue kisses *coquito* sweet—love that existed despite the insanities and rising body counts—that escape would have been impossible.

It is the Bronx, not Harlem that calls me back. Sometimes she is the singsong cadences of my family's West Indian voices. Or the childhood memories of girls I once called friends. Sistas who refused the cocktail and had too many babies way too young. Sistas who saw welfare, bloodshed, dust, then crack steal away any traces of youth from their smiles.

Theirs are the spirits I see darting between the traffic and the La Marqueta vibes of Fordham Road. Their visitations dog my equanimity, demanding I explain why this "feminism thing" is relevant to any of their lives. There are days I cannot. I'm too busy wondering what relevance it has in my own.

... And then came October 16, the day Louis Farrakhan declared that black men would finally stand up and seize their rightful place as leaders of their communities.... It wasn't banishment from the march that was so offensive—after all, black women have certainly convened at our share of closed-door assemblies. It was being told to stay home and prepare food for our warrior kings. What infuriated progressive black women was that the rhetoric of protection and atonement was just a seductive mask for good old-fashioned sexism....

Kristal Brent-Zook, "A Manifesto of Sorts for a New Black Feminist Movement," *The New York Times Magazine.*[1]

The "feminist" reaction to the Million Man March floored me. Like a lot of folks, I stayed home to watch the event. My phone rang off the hook—sista friends as close as round the corner and as far away as Jamaica moved by the awesome sight of so many black men of different hues, classes, and sexual orientations gathered together *peacefully* for the sole purpose of bettering themselves. The significance of the one group in this country most likely to murder each other—literally take each other out over things as trifling as colors or stepping on somebody's sneakers—was not lost on us. In fact, it left us all in tears.

Still, as a feminist, I could hardly ignore that my reaction differed drastically from many of my feminist counterparts. I was not mad. Not mad at all. Perhaps it was because growing up sandwiched between two brothers blessed me with an intrinsic understanding of the sanctity of male and female space. (Maintaining any semblance of harmony in our too-small apartment meant figuring out the times my brothers and I could share space—and the times we could not—with a quickness.)

Perhaps it was because I've learned that loving brothers is a little like parenting—sometimes you gotta get all up in that ass. Sometimes you gotta let them figure it out *on their own terms*—even if it means they screw up a little. So while the utter idiocy inherent in a nineties black leader suggesting women stay home and make sandwiches for their men didn't escape me, it did not nullify the march's positivity either. It's called being able to see the forest *and* the trees.

Besides, I was desperately trying to picture us trying to gather a million or so sistas to march for the development of a new black feminist movement. Highly, highly unlikely. Not that there aren't black women out there actively seeking agendas of empowerment—be it personal or otherwise—but let's face it, sistas ain't exactly checkin' for the f-word.

When I told older heads that I was writing a book that explored, among other things, my generation of black women's precarious relationship with feminism, they looked at me like I was trying to re-invent the wheel. I got lectured ad nauseam about "the racism of the White Feminist Movement," "the sixties and the seventies," and "feminism's historic irrelevance to black folks." I was reminded of how feminism's ivory tower elitism excludes the masses. And I was told that black women simply "didn't have time for all that shit."

While there is undeniable truth in all of the above except the latter—*the shit* black women don't have time for is dying and suffering from exorbitant rates of solo parenting, domestic violence, drug abuse, incarceration, AIDS, and cancer—none of them really explain why we have no black feminist *movement*. Lack of college education explains why 'round-the-way girls aren't reading bell hooks. It does not explain why even the gainfully degreed (self included) would rather trick away our last twenty-five dollars on that new nineties black girl fiction (trife as some of it may be) than some of those good, but let's face it, laboriously academic black feminist texts.

White women's racism and the Feminist Movement may explain the justifiable bad taste the f-word leaves in the mouths of women who are over thirty-five, but for my generation they are abstractions drawn from someone else's history. And without the power of memories, these phrases mean little to nothing.

Despite our differences about the March, Brent-Zook's article offered some interesting insights.

> ... Still, for all our double jeopardy about being black and female, progressive black women have yet to galvanize a mass following or to spark a concrete movement for social change....
> Instead of picking up where Ida B. Wells left off, black women too often allow our efforts to be reduced to the anti-lynching campaigns of the Tupac Shakurs, the Mike Tysons, the O.J.

Simpsons and the Clarence Thomases of the world. Instead of struggling with, and against, those who sanction injustice, too often we stoop beneath them, our backs becoming their bridges....

Why do we remain stuck in the past? The answer has something to do with not just white racism but also our own fear of the possible, our own inability to imagine the divinity within ourselves.... [2]

I agree. At the heart of our generation's ambivalence about the f-word is black women's historic tendency to blindly defend any black man who seems to be under attack from white folks (men, women, media, criminal justice system, etc.). The fact that the brothers may very well be in the wrong and, in some cases, deserve to be buried *under* the jail is irrelevant even if the victim is one of us. Centuries of being rendered helpless while racism, crime, drugs, poverty, depression, and violence robbed us of our men has left us misguidedly over-protective, hopelessly male-identified, and all too often self-sacrificing.

And yes, fear is part of the equation too, but I don't think it's a fear of the possible. Rather, it is the justifiable fear of what lies ahead for any black woman boldly proclaiming her commitment to empowerment—her sistas' or her own. Acknowledging the rampant sexism in our community, for example, means relinquishing the comforting illusion that black men and women are a unified front. Accepting that black men do not always reciprocate our need to love and protect is a terrifying thing, because it means that we are truly out there, *assed out* in a world rife with sexism and racism. And who the hell wants to deal with that?

Marc Christian was right. *Cojónes* became a necessary part of my feminist armature—but not for the reasons I would have suspected back then. I used to fear the constant accusations—career opportunism, race treason, collusion with "The Man," lesbianism—a lifetime of explaining what I am not. I dreaded the long, tedious conversations spent exorcising others of the stereotypes that tend to haunt the collective consciousness when we think of black women and the f-word male basher, radical literary/academic black women in their forties and fifties who are pathetically separated from real life, burly dreadlocked/crew cut dykes, sexually adventurous lipstick-wearing bisexuals, victims. Even more frightening were the frequent solo conversations I spent exorcising them from my own head.

In time, however, all of that would roll off my back like water.

Cojónes became necessary once I discovered that mine was not a feminism that existed comfortably in the black and white of things. The precarious nature of my career's origins was the first indication. I got my start as a writer because I captured the sexual attention of a man who could make me one. It was not the first time my externals would bestow me with such favors. It certainly would not be the last.

My growing fatigue with talking about "the men" was the second. Just once, I didn't want to have to talk about "the brothers," "male domination," or "the patriarchy." I wanted a feminism that would allow me to explore who we are as women—not victims. One that claimed the powerful richness and delicious complexities inherent in being black girls now—sistas of the post–Civil Rights, post-feminist, post-soul, hip-hop generation.

I was also looking for permission to ask some decidedly un-P.C. but very real questions:

Can you be a good feminist and admit out loud that there are things you kinda dig about patriarchy?

Would I be forced to turn in my "feminist membership card" if I confessed that suddenly waking up in a world free of gender inequities or expectations just might bug me out a little?

Suppose you don't want to pay for your own dinner, hold the door open, fix things, move furniture, or get intimate with whatever's under the hood of a car?

Is it foul to say that imagining a world where you could paint your big brown lips in the most decadent of shades, pile your phat ass into your fave micromini, slip your freshly manicured toes into four-inch fuck-me sandals and have not one single solitary man objectify—I mean roam his eyes longingly over all the intended places—is, like, a total drag for you?

Am I no longer down for the cause if I admit that while total gender equality is an interesting intellectual lectual concept, it doesn't do a damn thing for me erotically? That, truth be told, men with too many "feminist" sensibilities have never made my panties wet, at least not like that reformed thug nigga who can make even the most chauvinistic of "wassup, baby" feel like a sweet, wet tongue darting in and out of your ear.

And how come no one ever admits that part of the reason women love hip-hop—as sexist as it is—is 'cuz all that in-yo-face testosterone makes our nipples hard?

Are we no longer good feminists, not to mention nineties supersistas, if the A.M.'s wee hours sometimes leave us tearful and frightened that achieving all our mothers wanted us to—great educations, careers, financial and emotional independence—has made us wholly undesirable to the men who are supposed to be our counterparts? Men whose fascination with chickenheads leave us convinced they have no interest in dating, let alone marrying, their equals?

And when one accuses you of being completely indecipherable there's really nothing to say 'cuz even you're not sure how you can be a feminist and insist he "respect you as a woman, treat you like a lady, and make you feel safe—like a li'l girl."

In short, I needed a feminism brave enough to fuck with the grays. And this was not my foremothers' feminism.

Ironically, reaping the benefits of our foremothers' struggle is precisely what makes their brand of feminism so hard to embrace. The "victim" (read women) "oppressor" (read men) model that seems to dominate so much of contemporary discourse (both black and white), denies the very essence of who we are.

We are the daughters of feminist privilege. The gains of the Feminist Movement (the efforts of black, white, Latin, Asian, and Native American women) had a tremendous impact on our lives—so much we often take it for granted. We walk through the world with a sense of entitlement that women of our mothers' generation could not begin to fathom. Most of us can't imagine our lives without access to birth control, legalized abortions, the right to vote, or many of the same educational and job opportunities available to men. Sexism may be a very real part of my life but so is the unwavering belief that there is no dream I can't pursue *and achieve* simply because "I'm a woman."

Rejecting the wildly popular notion that embracing the f-word entails nothing more than articulating victimization, for me, is a matter of personal and spiritual survival. Surviving the combined impact of racism and sexism on the daily means never allowing my writing to suggest that black women aren't more than a bunch of bad memories. We *are* more than the rapes survived by the slave masters, the illicit familial touches accompanied by whiskey-soured breath, or the acts of violence endured by the fists, knives, and guns of strangers. We are more than the black eyes and heart bruises from those we believed were friends.

Black women can no more be defined by the cumulative sum of our pain than blackness can be defined solely by the transgenerational atrocities delivered at the hands of American racism. Because black folks are more than the stench of the slave ship, the bite of the dogs, or the smoldering of freshly lynched flesh. In both cases, defining ourselves solely by our oppression denies us the very magic of who we are. My feminism simply refuses to give sexism or racism that much power.

Holding on to that protective mantle of victimization requires a hypocrisy and self-censorship I'm no longer willing to give. Calling rappers out for their sexism without mentioning the complicity of the 100 or so video-hos that turned up—G-string in hand—for the shoot; or defending women's reproductive rights without examining the very complicated issue of *male choice*—specifically the inherent unfairness in denying men the right to choose whether or not *they want* to parent; or discussing the physical and emotional damage of sexism without examining the utterly foul and unloving ways black women treat each other ultimately means fronting like the shit brothers have with them is any less complex, difficult, or painful than the shit we have with ourselves. I am down, however, for a feminism that demands we assume responsibility for our lives.

In my quest to find a functional feminism for myself and my sistas—one that seeks empowerment on spiritual, material, physical, and emotional levels—I draw heavily on the cultural movement that defines my generation. As post–Civil Rights, post-feminist, post-soul children of hip-hop we have a dire need for the truth.

We have little faith in inherited illusions and idealism. We are the first generation to grow up with all the benefits of Civil Rights (i.e., Affirmative Action, government-subsidized educational and social programs) and the first to lose them. The first to have the devastation of AIDS, crack, and black-on-black violence makes it feel like a blessing to reach twenty-five. Love no longer presents itself wrapped in the romance of basement blue lights, lifetime commitments, or the sweet harmonies of The Stylistics and The Chi-Lites. Love for us is raw like sushi, served up on sex platters from R. Kelly and Jodeci. Even our existences can't be defined in the past's simple terms: house nigga vs. field nigga, ghetto vs. bourgie, BAP vs. boho because our lives are usually some complicated combination of all of the above.

More than any other generation before us, we need a feminism committed to "keeping it real." We need a voice like our music—one that samples and layers many voices, injects its sensibilities into the old and flips it into something new, provocative, and powerful. And one whose occasional hypocrisy, contradictions, and trifeness guarantee us at least a few trips to the terrordome, forcing us to finally confront what we'd all rather hide from.

We need a feminism that possesses the same fundamental understanding held by any true student of hip-hop. Truth can't be found in the voice of any one rapper but in the juxtaposition of many. The keys that unlock the riches of contemporary black female identity lie not in choosing Latifah over Lil' Kim, or even Foxy Brown over Salt-N-Pepa. They lie at the magical intersection where those contrary voices meet—the juncture where "truth" is no longer black and white but subtle, intriguing shades of gray.

Study Questions

1. How does hip-hop feminism differ from the idea of feminism in general?
2. How does hip-hop feminism challenge the performance of hypermasculinity in hip-hop?
3. What is the relationship of hip-hop feminism to women performers in hip-hop?

Notes

1. Kristal Brent-Zook, "A Manifesto of Sorts for a New Black Feminist Movement," *New York Times Magazine* (Nov. 12, 1995). 86.
2. Ibid. 88–89.

28

Butta Pecan Mamis
Tropicalized *Mamis*: 'Chocolaté Calienté'

African-American gender politics have been the primary space where issues of gender and sexuality have been taken up in hip-hop culture, much the way black identity has dominated various discourses of identity in hip-hop. Raquel Rivera's work, following that of Juan Flores, has been primarily concerned with examining the Puerto Rican and Latino/a influence in hip-hop. To this end, her essay documents how gender discussions are complicated by the issues of language, skin color and region for Puerto Rican artists and audiences.

Rivera argues that Puerto Rican women exist as a tropical exotic other in comparison to black women in hip-hop, but that their relative visibility is also accompanied by a profound silence as Puerto Rican women rappers are few and far between. Additionally, Rivera highlights how the discussions of gender in hip-hop are largely premised on the centrality of visual culture.

Butta Pecan Mamis: Tropicalized *Mamis*: "Chocolaté Calienté"

Raquel Z. Rivera

An advertisement for the 1998 album *The Rude Awakening* by the Cocoa Brovas, a rap duo of African American MCs, features a cardboard cup—the kind with the blue-and-white "Greek" motifs, common in New York delis and *bodegas*—full of steaming cocoa.[1] Six chocolate-drenched young women are partially immersed in the liquid. On the right-hand side of the cup appear the erroneously accented words "Chocolaté Calienté."

The Spanish words seem to indicate that these women, or at least some of them, swirling in hot chocolate and sexily awaiting ingestion are Latinas. They are all various shades of caramel, unquestionably black by this country's standards but still light-skinned. Their relative lightness, and the fact that all but one have straight or slightly wavy hair, goes along with the butta pecan myth[2]—in other words, the stereotype of Puerto Ricans and other Latinas as golden-skinned (hence the association with butter pecan ice cream) and "good-haired" [*sic!*].[3] But butta pecan is somehow still imagined to be a variation on chocolate. Butta pecans are, after all, a crucial ingredient in the Cocoa Brovas' recipe for chocolaté calienté. The bottom line is that these hot cocoa girls' *latinidad* does not take away from their blackness. What their *latinidad* does do is add an element of exoticism—signified through the ad's use of Spanish—to their blackness.

The accentuation of words that, according to Spanish orthographic rules, should not be accented serves to further intensify a sense of exoticism. Accents are deemed exotic characteristics of an exotic language. Whether this accentuation was a mistake or was done on purpose does not change the fact that the accents in "chocolaté" and "calienté" serve as tropicalizing markers of difference that distinguish *mamis* from other black women.

Let us move on to another example of how Puerto Rican women are portrayed as ghetto-tropical, lighter-skinned variations on black femininity. "Set Trippin," a review of ten popular rap videos in *Blaze* magazine's premier issue, includes Big Punisher's hit song "Still Not a Player." The reviews by Rubin Keyser Carasco consist of short blurbs under specific headings, such as "Plot," "Ghetto Fabulous," "Estimated Budget" and "Black Erotica." Under "Black Erotica," the text reads, regarding "Still Not a Player": "Dozens of scantily clad, lighter-than-a-paper-bag sistas and mamis end up dancing outside. Sounds like a red-light district."

It is significant that the "Black Erotica" category includes mention of both "sistas" and "mamis." While these may be two ethnically distinct female populations, Carasco includes them both in the realm of eroticized blackness. The fact that their light skin tone makes the set seem like "a red-light district" is a commentary on gendered "color-caste hierarchies"[4] that equate "lightness" with sexual desirability as well as an acknowledgment of the prostitute as the embodiment of male sexual fantasy. Considering the common coding of Puerto Ricanness as butta pecanness, it is evident that their attributed phenotypic "lightness" plays a part in the collective erotization of Puerto Rican females.[5]

The text of the song itself poses Puerto Rican and African American women as two distinct groups. Its singsong chorus, which consists of multiple repetitions of "Boricua, Morena," differentiates these two groups of women through the use of New York Puerto Rican ethno-racializing terminology. The video adds a visual dimension to the distinction as the camera alternates between a group of lighter-skinned women when the word "Boricua" is being uttered and a group of comparatively darker-skinned women when the chorus mentions "Morena." The tiny chihuahua that one of the Boricuas is holding serves as yet another mark of difference. In New York City lore, chihuahuas are a dog breed considered to be popular among Puerto Ricans, and they also invoke the tropicalized *pan-latinidad* of Dinky, the famous chihuahua of the late 1990s' Taco Bell commercial campaign. However, although distinct, these two groups come together by virtue of Pun's sexual desire.

In this song, Pun boasts of not discriminating since he sexually engages "every shade of that ass." But the span of the "shades" that he "regulates" goes from blackberry molasses to butta pecan. Using the language of "gastronomic sexuality"[6] that also informs the Cocoa Brovas ad, Pun focuses his desire on African American and Puerto Rican "ghetto brunette[s]." *Boricuas* and *morenas* may be distinct, but, as Pun constructs them, they are both sweet, thick, pretty, round and various shades of brown. And, evidently, that is how he likes his "hoes."

African American rapper Jay Z., in "Who You Witt II?" defines the ethno-racial span of his sexual desire in a closely related manner when he claims to sexually engage "around the way" women as well as "*miras.*" "Mira" is used as a reference to Puerto Ricans—and perhaps, by extension, other Caribbean Latino women. It comes from Puerto Ricans' frequent use of the word "*mira*" ("look") at the beginning of sentences or as a way to get someone's attention.

While not focusing on Puerto Rican women specifically but on Latinas in general, West Coast Puerto Rican artist Son Doobie expresses similar preferences in Funkdoobiest's 1995 "XXX Funk." He boasts that both "black" women and "brown" women "know my name." Whereas Big Punisher makes use of the dichotomy *boricua/morena*, Son relies on a brown/black distinction. Both MCs, however, aim to distinguish Latinas from African Americans and, at the same time, chromatically identify both groups as objects of desire. Son goes one step further than Punisher because he not only celebrates the "black" and "brown" women he likes but explicitly poses thin, "pale bitches" with breast implants—as their opposite.

The Cocoa Brovas ad, Big Pun's "Still Not a Player" video and Son Doobie's and Jay Z's pronouncements are all part of rap's commercially dominant ghetto "nigga" discourse, where African American and Caribbean Latino men construct a landscape of desire in which *sistas* and *mamis* take center stage as "their" women.

Actress Jennifer López's ass is a good example of how Puerto Rican *mamis* have been eroticized within the hip hop zone as tropical Butta Pecan Ricans part of a ghetto black "us." As Frances Negron-Muntaner has noted, "for any Caribbean interlocutor, references to this part of the human anatomy are often a way to speak of Africa in(side) America."[7] López's status as a turn-of-the-century mainstream sex symbol and the totemization of her buttocks have shaped as well as been informed by popular perceptions of Caribbean Latina womanhood and their racial underpinnings, including those within the hip hop zone.

Tropicalized *Mamis*: Jennifer's Butt

> *Unlike hair and skin, the butt is stubborn, immutable—it can't be hotcombed or straightened or bleached into submission. ... And the butt's blatantly sexual nature makes it seem that much more belligerent in its refusal to go away, to lie down and play dead.*
>
> —Erin Aubry, "The Butt: Its Profanity, Its Politics, Its Power"

Welcome to the Realm of the Big Butt Cult. African American rappers Sir Mix-a-Lot and LL Cool J have celebrated strategically placed fatty tissue in their songs "Baby Got Back" and "Big Ol' Butt." Panamanian reggae artist El General has exalted voluminous backsides in "Tu Pum Pum." Island Puerto Rican rapper Vico C has given props to big butts in "Bomba para afincar," and so has Bronx Puerto Rican Fat Joe in "Shorty Gotta Fat Ass."

So central are female *nalgas* (butts) and *caderas* (hips) in the discourse of Afro-diasporic male desire that Frances Aparicio dedicated a chapter entitled "Patriarchal Synecdoques: Of Women's Butts and Feminist Rebuttals" to exploring Latino Caribbean music's (lower) body politics.[8] Negrón-Muntaner also identifies "the butt" as a compelling dimension of Afro-diasporic cultural discourses and practices that deal with sexuality, pleasure, power and the body.[9]

Iris Chacón, a Puerto Rican dancer and singer whose most celebrated asset was most often clad in a g-string, went beyond stardom to acquire mythical status through her immensely popular prime-time Spanish-language TV show of the 1970s and 1980s: *El Show de Iris Chacón*. Negrón-Muntaner identifies Bronx Puerto Rican actress Jennifer López as a symbolic heiress of Iris Chacón, describing her historical role as that of "the next big bottom in the Puerto Rican cultural imaginary and our great avenger of Anglo analphobia."[10]

López's butt, although initially eyed with worry and deemed in need of camouflage by Hollywood costume designers, has ended up being embraced by the mainstream media. Teresa Wiltz declared in the *Daily News* that López's posterior has "become something of a national obsession." *Entertainment Weekly* pronounced it "an erotic totem up there with Uma Thurman's lips and Pamela Anderson Lee's bust."[11] It has also been written about in *Time* magazine, *Playboy* and *Elle*, among numerous other print media.

A few perceptive observers have noticed how this actress's mainstream acceptance is related to her "embodying ideal 'Latin' beauty … neither too dark, nor too light."[12] However, these racial underpinnings of her acceptance have only rarely been discussed.

Jennifer López and her ass also have loomed large in the hip hop collective conscious as the embodiment of Latina desirability. In a *Vibe* article by dream hampton, she was pronounced "the biggest explosion outta the Bronx since the birth of hip hop."[13] Yeah, yeah … pretty eyes, flawless (light) skin, flowing (straight) hair, sharp "ghetto" wit. … But López might not be the sex icon she has become were it not for her voluminous ass cheeks. As Goldie wrote in the aptly entitled article "Ass Rules Everything Around Us" for hip hop music magazine *XXL:* "*ButtaPecanRican*. What makes Lopez lovely is not her sexy looks, her unbelievably flawless face or her nut-wrenching aura. It's her ass. It's not a special ass, because most Black women are born with ass like this, but JL makes it work. The half-circle. The sphere."[14]

According to Goldie, López's is a "Black" ass—mystifying to white men and revered by Black and Puerto Rican males. Puerto Ricans thus stand together with African Americans as admirers and/or bearers of voluminous black asses. Implicit in his argument is that Puerto Rican men know how to appreciate this feature of blackness because Puerto Ricans are part of it. Likewise, hampton describes López's butt as a feature of her blackness: "Women like her—namely black women—haven't exactly had issues of shame when it comes to that particular body part. In most sectors of our community, the bigger the better."[15]

Cristina Verán celebrates in *Ego Trip*—another hip hop music-oriented publication—"this pear-shaped Puerto Riqueña" for "single-handedly spearheading a big booty backlash against the supermodel types who espouse Schindler's List chic." Now not only can "los brothas on both sides of the border" feast their eyes on a gluteus after their own heart, but "women of color" can rejoice in a feminine icon that does not conform to "the blonder beauty barometer of Los Blancos." Verán, like Goldie, posits an "us" that includes Puerto Ricans (and other Latinos) and Blacks, and according to which Jennifer López, the Hottentot Venus and Iris Chacón are upheld as "our" images. "From the 19th Century's South African spectacle—unique-physiqued Venus Hottentot's humongous hindquarters—to the Risqué Rican TV variety vixen Iris Chacón and her bombastic Boricua booty, we've got a lengthy legacy of well-endowed icons of our own to look up to."[16]

After a few years of butt-related hype, references to J-Lo's anatomy have even crept into her own repertoire. Her song "Ain't It Funny," featuring African American rapper Ja-Rule and included in her 2002 album *J To Tha L-O!*, has him declaring that it is her fat ass that has made him crazy over her.

López's butt has been celebrated within the commercial hip hop realm as a vindication of "our" Afro-diasporic standards of beauty. In contrast, her ass has been celebrated in the mainstream media as a mark of the dark Other's racial/sexual difference. Dark Others with big asses may come a dime a dozen, but López's "racially nebulous features" or relatively "more Caucasian features" make her a palatable embodiment of racialized/sexualized difference.[17] For the mainstream, she has been the tropical, dark-enough—but not too dark—and big-assed exception to the Eurocentric rule.

While the mainstream celebrates the Other's big ass, "our" ass gets celebrated by African Americans and Latinos within the rap music realm. Both realms coincide in ignoring how approximation to whiteness is privileged even when the object of appreciation is nonwhite. *XXL* columnist Goldie allows that most black women have a butt like López's. The reason why her bottom is famous and other big black bottoms are not is, according to him, that "JL makes it work." Perhaps López does have a certain something that makes her ass seem extra special. But doesn't it seem too much in accordance with Eurocentric aesthetic hierarchies that a very light-skinned, straight-haired—white, by Latin American standards—woman is the icon celebrated for her so-called black ass?

Eurocentric aesthetic standards have historically informed Afro-diasporic standards of beauty. This is visible in what bell hooks has termed color-caste hierarchies, which, as she explains, are related not only to skin color but also to hair texture and other physical features. These hierarchies are also very gender-specific.

> The exploitative and oppressive nature of color-caste systems in white supremacist society has always had a gendered component. A mixture of racist and sexist thinking informs the way color-caste hierarchies detrimentally affect the lives of black females differently from black males. Light skin and long, straight hair continue to be traits that define female as beautiful and desirable in the racist white imagination and in the colonized black mind set. ... To this day, the images of black female bitchiness, evil temper and treachery continue to be marked by darker skin. ... Dark skin is stereotypically coded in the racist, sexist or colonized imagination as masculine. Hence, a male's power is enhanced by dark looks while a female's dark looks diminish her femininity.[18]

Among Afro-diasporic populations, lighter-skinned black women have been thought of as prettier, sexier and more feminine than darker women. Good hair/bad hair (*pelo bueno/pelo malo*) distinctions have been routinely made and are also gender-coded.[19] It is significant, for example, that the *mulata* has been the figure posed in the musical and literary traditions of the Spanish-speaking Caribbean "as the embodiment of rhythm, movement, and erotic pleasure."[20] The lighter beauty of the *mulata* has been privileged over darker female beauty.

Color-caste hierarchies also have been very much a part of hip hop music. On one hand, rap videos present a wider range of Afro-diasporic female beauty than many other contemporary entertainment mediums. According to rap and R&B video actress Anansa Sims: "To me, you'll find the most beautiful Black women in videos because it's where we're allowed to show our natural shapes—the big butts, breasts, and thick thighs."[21]

Slightly fuller female figures are the norm in rap and R&B videos, although they still are ruled by a cult of thinness. Sims's pronouncement does have a ring of truth to it with regard to body shape; however, the issue of color and other phenotypic characteristics is a whole other story. Rap videos and magazine spreads usually feature light-brown young females with long hair—be it naturally nonnappy, straightened or "weaved"—who are upheld as the epitome of female black beauty but run counter to the blackest, nappiest philosophy championed elsewhere. It seems that while naps and dark skin in men are a proud symbol of blackness, the same physical traits in women are perceived as questionable because they are deemed unattractive, unkempt, unfeminine, menacing, butch.

The Source's Second Annual Swimsuit Issue, published in June 1997, presents an illustration of color-caste hierarchies at work. The problematic character of this pictorial representation was noted by a *Source* reader by the name of Shannon who wrote in a letter to the editors: "Why oh why would you choose six slim, sexy, nearly white models? Are you dissing Black hip-hop culture? Can't you see that your representation of the 'hip-hop woman' is very misguided? A much more balanced and healthy view of hip-hop women is in order."[22]

Jennifer López's quintessential butta pecanness places her high in hip hop color-caste hierarchies. Her lightness combined with her being Puerto Rican, however, may have been a hindrance during rap's Afrocentric stage—before Latinos(as) were reclaimed as bona fide members of a ghettocentric hip hop "us." But as rap has shifted in emphasis from Afrocentricity to ghettocentricity, Puerto Ricanness and blackness have more often come to be seen as overlapping—though not always smoothly, as shown by the controversy among rap enthusiasts over López's use of the word "nigga" in her song "I'm Real." The phenotypic range of black female beauty has been expanded somewhat to accommodate light-skinned Caribbean Latinas. This expansion tends to be celebrated as an acknowledgment of the ethno-racial diversity and complexity of the black experience in the Americas.

But what about the problem of color-caste hierarchies? They are still in effect, of course, perhaps now being even more vicious and still most often going unacknowledged. Within this celebration of a multihued blackness, proximity to whiteness can be given even more privilege, but cloaked under the guise of Afro-diasporic inclusiveness.

Sadly, this all sounds eerily reminiscent of the Puerto Rican—and more generally, Latin American—tactic of deflecting accusations of racism by raising the banner of miscegenation.[23] *Us? Racists? Gringos are racists, but not us. We can't be racists, because we are all racially mixed here.* Ramón Grosfogel and Frances Negrón-Muntaner explain: "According to this ideology, all Puerto Ricans regardless of 'race' are the mixture of the same ethnic ingredients—Spanish, African, Indian—and therefore equal. This superficially more benign form of racist ideology is often as, *if not more*, effective than more overt racist discourses in preventing racism from being socially and politically challenged in public discourse."[24]

If historian Carl Degler was right in affirming that racial identity and categories in the United States have, since the 1960s, begun converging more with those of Latin America,[25] then hip hop may be a pertinent example. And if that is the case, we are up against some thorny challenges indeed. *Us? Privileging whiteness? Never! We are all black here and just celebrating all dimensions of blackness.*

And thus, Jennifer López, a tropicalized *mami* who practically dangles from the lightest end in the spectrum of blackness, gets celebrated as the totemic bearer of the big black butt.

Enchilada Rhymes and the "Mark of the Plural"

In a room dimly lit by candles, a Tunisian princess—played by Jennifer López—displays fiery Eddie Torres-type salsa moves as the hip hop beat in Puff Daddy and Mase's video "Been Around the World" switches to sounds more appropriately "Latin." Ras Kass, a West Coast-based African American MC, passionately describes in his 1998 song "Lapdance" a Guyanese stripper as a "tropical Latin American *mami*" with a "fat derriere" who put her crotch in his face and "worked it with a Latin thing."

Both images are constructed on the basis of a patriarchal desire that eroticizes and exoticizes. The heat and mystery that the images convey is all that matters. Tunisian princesses are deemed exotic, so they are spliced with exotic lustful *mamis* from the other side of the Atlantic. The tropicalized enchantment of Spanish-speaking *mamis* is extended to other women, thus stretching the *mami* category into oblivion. Who cares if Guyanese are not Spanish-speaking Latin Americans? After all, accuracy and specificity never did much for exoticism.[26]

Rap images, in this sense, are influenced by a larger culture that tends to splice together aspects of interchangeable "exotic" cultures, stamping them with what Albert Memmi terms the "mark of the plural." What is important is not these cultures' specificities but the feeling of desire, mystery, adventure, danger, revulsion and/or pleasure that they evoke. Ella Shohat offers as examples the silent-era films that "included eroticized dances, featuring a rather improbable mélange of Spanish and Indian dances, plus a touch of belly dancing [and the] superimposition in Orientalist paintings of the visual traces of civilizations as diverse as Arab, Persian, Chinese and Indian into a single feature of the exotic Orient."[27]

Ana M. López offers a few examples from 1940s' Hollywood films to illustrate the way in which, from the hegemonic U.S. perspective, inter–Latin American differences are masked behind the sign of *latinidad:* "all Latins and Latin Americans were from South of the Border and *that* border was the only one that mattered as far as Hollywood was concerned. Thus Carmen Miranda is incongruously 'Brazilian' in a studio-produced Argentina (*Down Argentine Way* ... 1940) and Cuba (*Weekend in Havana* ... 1941) ...."[28] Other examples include *Too Many Girls* (1940) with Desi Arnaz as an Argentinian student in a New Mexico college who plays conga drums; *Fiesta* (1947), where Ricardo Montalbán plays a Mexican classical composer who dances Spanish flamenco; and *Anchors Aweigh* (1945), which features Gene Kelly as an Anglo sailor who dances a "Mexican Hat Dance" to the sounds of the Argentinian tango "La cumparsita."[29]

The tropicalized *mamis* of rap's imaginary, as well as the filmic examples of "the mark of the plural," are informed by centuries-old colonialist imaginaries.[30] The classic cinematic "rescue" fantasy where the Western man is both civilizer and savior is present, for example, in Puffy's "Been Around the World" video. In this case, the U.S. Black male subject is the inheritor of Western (white) imperial discourses where the colonized territory and its inhabitants are constructed through gendered metaphors. The female Other (the "Latin"-dancing Tunisian princess) is the coveted object of desire, while the male Other (in the form of the stereotypical "Arab assassin") is the evil native from whom the Western hero must rescue the exotic damsel in distress. Jennifer López, as the video's Tunisian princess, bears "the mark of the plural" and is portrayed as an exotic blend of Arab royalty and tropicalized *mami* heat.

The ubiquitousness of the eroticized *mami* in rap videos and rhymes has been accompanied by a canned, stale and tropicalized injection of Spanish words and phrases into mostly English rhymes. Mase and Total's hit "Tell Me What You Want" provides what is perhaps the best (and corniest) example. In the song, Mase beckons a certain "mama" to come to "papa"; he gives her the phone number to his "casa" and asks her to call him "*mañana.*"

One of the most pleasurable aspects of the art of MCing is its mastery, manipulations and innovations based on urban vernacular language—particularly the so-called nonstandard or broken kinds.[31] Behold the simplicity and evocativeness of Guru passing the *bodega* and saying "*suave,*" Hurricane Gee dissing the "*pollos* in snakeskin stilettos," Jeru referring to cocaine as "*perico,*" Tony Touch rhyming "*títeres*" with "freakin' it," and Cam'ron's line about "Jimmy Jones frontin' in the *chancletas.*" Now compare their witty references and wordplay to Mase insipidly rhyming "mama" with "papa," "fatha" with "*casa,*" and "*mañana*" with "*enchilada.*" The clincher is his use of the quintessential cliché "the whole enchilada," particularly given its stereotypical evocation of Mexican food as if it had anything to do with the *mami* he courts. This is not an argument for Mase's language "inauthenticity." But it is important to distinguish rhymes that make skilled use of urban street vernacular(s) from those that pretend to but do not.

Ethnicity is certainly not the factor that determines whether an artist's infusion of Spanish into his or her lyrics is creative or clichéd. Of the MCs whose rhymes I praised before, two are Puerto Rican—Hurricane Gee and Tony Touch—and the other three are African American. By the same token, Mase may be African American, but Puerto Rican rappers often resort to similarly stereotypical language practices.

This tropicalized and trite use of Spanish is addressed in Danny Hoch's theater piece *Jails, Hospitals & Hip-Hop*. His character Emcee Enuff offers the audience a rhyme from his new album:

> Mister Big Poppa, flashin' a hun'ed dolla
> Poppin' Cristal at the club, doin' the *cha-cha*
> Actin' drunk, talkin' to *mama*, sayin' *la la*
> Where is the joy? That shit is *caca, da-da*[32]

Hoch parodies here not only the simplistic and contrived use of Spanish or Spanish-sounding words, but also commercial rap's fascination with the high life and all its trappings, which includes money, champagne—Cristal—and a surplus of *mamis*.

The Atlanta-based African American rap duo Outkast likewise pokes fun at rap's gimmicky use of Spanish words and *mami* fetishism.[33] In a song entitled "Mamacita," references to rice and beans are intertwined with a description of a woman lusting after her girlfriend as a "pit mixed with a chihuahua"—rice, beans and chihuahuas being markings of *latinidad*. The next verse has guest artist Witchdoctor rhyming about a "Miss Bilingual" whom he's trying to get horny by serving her Moët champagne. The irony in this song is subtle. One can almost miss its tongue-in-cheek reproduction of rap's clichéd references to the *mamis*. But clues like Witchdoctor saying that the *mami*'s speaking Spanish "got me feeling mannish" reveal that Outkast is making fun of rappers who brandish *mamis* as exotic trophies of their manliness.

The Source magazine editor-in-chief Carlito Rodríguez[34] lamented in an interview that the *mami* gimmick was still going strong in 2001: "Everyone wants a Spanish mami in their video. I think you need balance. Don't get me wrong, I'm full-blooded Latino; I love that too but sometimes, coño, alright, I've seen cuter girls before. You get tired of it. There's more to Latinas than that."[35] Despite these internal rumbles of discontent regarding the *mami*-related clichés, rap's obsessing over Latinas may not have yet reached saturation levels as a commercial trend. So brace yourself: We may yet be in for quite a few more *mami*-focused "enchilada rhymes."

The "mark of the plural" poses diverse "exotic" cultural signifiers as equivalent; thus, enchiladas, mangos, rice and beans, tango, salsa and flamenco can all be tropicalizing symbols pan-*latinidad*. Furthermore, according to the logic of the "mark of the plural," women of diverse cultural backgrounds are interchangeable. *Puerto Rican, Dominican, Chicana, Argentinian, Guyanese ... What's the difference? Who cares? They are all hot Latin* mamis, *aren't they?*

The "mark of the plural," as a trope of Eurocentric colonialist thought, though affecting the males differently from females, still encompasses both genders. But there is another such "mark" that is made to apply to women specifically—all women, not just those defined as subaltern in the colonialist discourse. Frances Aparicio writes of a "pluralizing of Woman (Woman as multiplicity)" that "not only maps the geography of a Latin male gaze and desire, but most centrally, it delineates a Don Juan subjectivity whose desire and libidinal economy are never static nor totally satisfied."[36] Although concentrating her discussion on representations of women in Latin American music, Aparicio acknowledges the transcultural character of this phenomenon. Unsurprisingly, rap is also ruled by an I-want-them-all mentality, where women—whether *sistas* or *mamis*—are not real subjects, complex and distinct, but interchangeable sources of masculine pleasure or pain. Funkdoobiest expresses this sentiment in particularly raw terms in their 1995 song "Pussy Ain't Shit," where they say "fuck the pussy" and then discard if, though "bitches" act like that part of their bodies is precious, to them, one pussy is the same as the next. Or as Noreaga says in 1998's "N.O.R.E.": He "fucks" the same woman twice only if she kneels and begs.

Mamis Speak

Yo estoy cansá de la mielda que yo oigo en el radio y que veo en MTV, porque cuando yo veo a esas mujeres bellas, lindas, en little bikinis shaking their ass like that's all they're good for, eso me dice a mi, coño, they don't have no kind of hope. No tienen esa fé de que podemos cambiar este mundo, que algo viene, algo bueno nos espera. Eso me rompe el alma.[37]

—La Bruja

African American female rap artists, although radically fewer in number than their male counterparts, and although severely constrained by patriarchal notions of appropriate/desirable/profitable female images and creativity, have managed to make inroads in this male-dominated realm. Lauryn Hill, Missy "Misdemeanor" Elliott, Foxy Brown, Lil' Kim, Mia X, Eve, Da Brat, MC Lyte, Heather B, Bahamadia and Queen Latifah are some of the better-known African American female rap artists. Without their diverse creative voices, Black female subjectivity within rap would be limited to male representations of female subjectivity and would be overwhelmingly one-dimensional.

The case of Latinas, however, is another story. The only Latinas to have garnered considerable media visibility as solo artists in the "core" hip hop music markets—as opposed to the *rap en español* niche—have been two New York Puerto Ricans. First, there was the Real Roxanne (Joanne Martínez) who appeared in the rap scene in 1984, right in the middle of the flurry of "Roxanne" response records spurred by UTFO's hit single "Roxanne, Roxanne." Since the Real Roxanne's heyday, there was no other Latina of comparable visibility until New York radio jock Angie Martínez began making inroads in the rap scene during the late 1990s through brief guest appearances on other artists' recordings. Within a few years, she landed a deal with Elektra and released her debut album *Up Close and Personal* in the spring of 2001.

The only other Latina MC to have garnered some media recognition is Hurricane G (Gloria Rodríguez), a seasoned artist who has collaborated with Redman, Eric Sermon, Keith Murray, Busta Rhymes, Xzibit, Cocoa Brovas, Puff Daddy and Funkdoobiest. G, also a New York Puerto Rican, released her first and only solo album in 1997, titled *All Woman*. It is significant that although *mamis* have been high on many a rapper's sexual agenda, Hurricane G has not reaped commercial rewards from rap's *mami* fetish. All this obsessing over *mamis* and the better-known Latina MC with solid lyrical skills and underground credentials—although not large-scale commercial success—hardly gets any play?

Angie Martínez's media visibility, contrary to Hurricane G's, seems to have benefited considerably from hip hop's newfound appreciation for the *mamis*. Though G is the stronger and more seasoned MC of the two, it is Martínez who has gotten the most commercially visible rhyming gigs. Could it be that Martínez's image is deemed more marketable than Hurricane G's? Could it have to do with the fact that, while Martínez's looks are quintessential "butta pecan," G is straight-up black?

Hurricane G's complex and strong subjectivity indisputably clashes with the hot-and-compliant mythical *mami* subjectivities being celebrated. When I asked a young Puerto Rican MC/producer what he thought of Hurricane G as an artist, his lack of enthusiasm for her work centered on her not being "ladylike." As he said, "women rappers have to be ladies to get treated as ladies." Such notions regarding appropriate female images are not *mami*-specific. Both

428 • RAQUEL Z. RIVERA

African American and Latina MCs are affected by these types of gender-based limitations and expectations.

According to Jeff Fenster, then vice president of A&R at the record label Jive, "males just don't want to hear hard things from women." That, combined with comparatively less label support for women, is the reason Fenster gives as to why African American female rap artists Boss, Yo-Yo and Queen Latifah did not fare well in terms of sales.[38] Un Rivera, rap producer, video director and president of the labels Undeas Records and Untertainment, gives credence to Fenster's pronouncements in his account of shaping Lil' Kim's image: "I used to buy Kim her clothes ... Me and Big used to go back and forth with ideas trying to figure what is it that niggas wanted to see. *Maybe*, they want to hear about Kim fuckin'. So, we started makin' records like that."[39]

Hurricane G is neither focused on exploiting her sexual appeal, as Kim is, nor is she a quintessential butta pecan *mami* like Martínez. She is a powerful and skilled Puerto Rican black woman MC who projects herself multidimensionally as loving, faithful, dedicated, horny, aggressive, demanding, vulnerable and spiteful, depending on the situation. The wounded lover who struggles to maintain her self-respect in "Somebody Else" gives way to the hard-rock MC from "Underground Lockdown." She goes from thankful and dutiful daughter in "Mamá" to lustful and eager to please lover in "Boricua Mami." She is also the mother who bitterly pokes fun at her lying and irresponsible baby's father as she kicks him out of her life. Whereas Hurricane G is, as her 1997 album title proclaims, *All Woman*, complex and ever-evolving, the mythical *mamis* of rap songs are simple and cartoonish. When their voices are heard, they are almost invariably sensuous creatures whose only interests are material goods and sexual pleasure.

We hear Puff Daddy's "Spanish girl" in the interlude right before the song "Señorita" slurping as she performs oral sex, moaning and teaching him a couple of phrases for hot pillow talk. All the while, as if to create a properly tropical ambiance, Cachao's "Descarga cubana" is playing in the background. During "Señorita" itself, two female voices are heard. One, presumably the song's subject, vows that she will be his forever. The second comes from a sample of a song by salsa singer La India where she accuses her lover of lying to her.

The "mamacita" of Cam'ron's "Horse and Carriage" video speaks once, exclaiming delightedly: "Oh, you're going to buy me diamonds!" Like Cam'ron's gold-digging *mami*, Puffy raps in "Señorita" about a woman who, presumably, shares his luxury-obsessed mentality. He attempts to charm her by promising to keep her laden with jewelry and thousand-dollar shoes, and detailing all the other material goods he is able to offer her.

In a notorious interlude, entitled "Taster's Choice," in Big Punisher's debut album, two Puerto Rican *mamis* get it on with the rapper. Their exchange takes place mostly in English but is peppered by words and phrases like "*ay, que grande,*" "*mámame la chocha*" and "*castígame*" ("oh, how big," "lick my pussy" and "punish me"). Amid slurping sounds, moans and a creaking bed, a fight breaks out between "Joanne" and "Lissette" as they both compete to be penetrated by Pun's "dick."

The Puerto Rican *mami* of R&B crooners Dru Hill's "How Deep Is Your Love?" (featuring rapper Redman) coos how much she misses her "*papi morenito*" and begs him to "*dámelo dura*" ("give it to me hard"). DJ Enuff, a Puerto Rican DJ who is part of radio station Hot 97's "Morning Show," has occasionally slipped in between songs a sample of a woman moaning: "*Ay, papi.*"

Black Star, an African American duo from New York, offers one of the welcome exceptions to this legion of sexually explicit caricatures of Latinas. In a beautifully crafted 1998 song entitled "Respiration" that plays with the notion of the city as a breathing organism, a woman's voice opens the track: "*Escúchala, la ciudad respirando*" ("Listen to the city breathing"). Her words are immediately followed by the guitar chords that establish from the beginning the reflexive, bordering on melancholic, mood of the song. The chorus offers a good example of how Mos Def, Talib Kweli and guest artist Common skillfully weave together images and feelings based on their home cities—New York for Black Star, Chicago for Common. Right after the chorus, the same soulful female voice comes in again asking the listeners in Spanish to notice the way in which the city, fearful and sorrowful, breathes like her.

The city is both feminized and Latinized through its association with the words and experience of this female subject. In contrast to most Latina voices heard in contemporary rap recordings, Black Star and Common incorporate a Latina voice into their music to weave a poetic narrative whose last concern is the usual Don Juan economics of sex. Lamentably, this trio of artists is an exception to the rule.

Foxy Brown's 1996 debut platinum-selling album, *Ill Nana*, incorporated a woman's voice with a distinct Puerto Rican accent as a marginal commentator in the opening track "Intro ... Chicken Coop." The "Intro" is partly a commercial for upcoming artists—some of them Latino—the Cru and Cormega. The latter was then the most recent member of The Firm, a crew made up of popular rap artists Foxy Brown, Nas and AZ. In an aggressive and exasperated tone, an unidentified female voice inquires in Spanish: Who is this "*maricón*" ("faggot") and "*mamao*" ("cocksucker")[40] Cormega? Although this woman's interjection is a marginal aside to add flavor and humor to the "Intro," it is also one of the few examples of Latina female voices in rap recordings that do something different than moan in ecstasy.

The problem with the prevalent representations of Latinas does not reside in the sexually explicit images. Explicit sex should not be confused with sexism. An image does not get more sexist as it gets more "hard core." Big Punisher's "Taster's Choice" interlude would be just as sexist if its protagonists were kissing instead of having sex. The problem with these representations is that the *mamis* are thought of only in terms of sexual desire. *Mamis* are not sisters, friends or mothers. Their only conceivable role is that of lovers. To compound the matter, the terms of these sexual representations are tragically misogynist and operate under a patriarchal logic. The *mamis* are frivolous, gold-digging and infinitely substitutable beings.

Big Pun's "Taster's Choice" again provides a telling example. Lissette and Joanne are portrayed as petty and egotistical, quick to jump at each other's throats in their competition for Punisher's "dick." They are, of course, desperate for the ultimate phallocentric prize. Pun, on the contrary, is way above their silliness. He demeans them by muttering under his breath "stupid bitches" and proceeds to mediate their spat. Of course, their being "stupid bitches" does not make them any less desirable for him. Dealing with female frivolity is just the heterosexual man's burden. Poor guys, that is what they have to put up with if they want to get laid.

Furthermore, lesbian pleasure is celebrated in "Taster's Choice," but only because it is for male consumption. Lesbian desire is redeemed only by male participation. Had Pun not been there, or had these women not conformed to stereotypically "feminine" standards of beauty, then Lissette and Joanne's desire for each other would be repulsive and a threat.

Lesbianism is acceptable only given a phallocentric logic, according to which, without a penis, there is no "real" sex. By the same phallocentric token, gay male desire is perceived as way too real, and thus under no circumstances is it deemed hot, cute or even remotely acceptable.[41]

"Lesbian chic" surfaces not only in rap but in popular culture in general, being a common male erotic fantasy. When asked about the commercial viability of an openly lesbian rapper, Lenny Santiago, an A&R at Roc-A-Fella Records, responded: "It's such a turn-on for guys, I think it would be marketable. It's every man's fantasy to sleep with two women. If she were *ghetto-sexy* and had skills, I could see that."[42] A clueless male reader asks Lana Sands, *XXL*'s sex columnist: "How do I get with a lesbian?" She responds: "I think you might be looking for a girl who is bisexual or maybe bi-curious as opposed to a full blown lesbian, 'cause you might not find what you're looking for by *Chasing Amy*."[43] The assumption that a lesbian woman would necessarily want to engage males sexually reveals an extremely heterocentric perspective and a lack of imagination. Lesbian fetishism is evidently not about actual female-to-female desire but about a cute show for male consumption.

In a conversation I had with two Puerto Rican teenage rap artists who expressed great admiration for Big Punisher, the "Taster's Choice" interlude came up. I asked what they thought about it. One of them dutifully informed me that "it was degrading to women." The following exchange ensued:

> *Raquel:* Why do you say it's degrading to women?
> *Jay:* Because it makes them seem like two freaks.
> *Raquel:* But isn't he a freak too, then?
> *Jay:* Yeah, he's a freak too. See, it's that double standard. If guys do it, it's all right, but if girls do it they're hoes or freaks.
> *Tony:* They probably got some hoodrats to do that! [laughter]

The assumption that the women who played Lissette and Joanne's roles were "hoodrats" struck me, particularly since Tony's statement followed Jay's acknowledgment that branding this kind of raw female sexual behavior as "freakish" is a sexist double standard. So not only does raw sexual behavior in real life make a woman a freak, but it also makes freakish (dirty, worthless "hoodrats") the actresses or models who enact such behavior. Reality and fantasy collide at a fascinating angle when playing a role in a staged sexual encounter, for commercial consumption, has bearing on the assumptions—coded as negative—about the real lives of this encounter's female participants.

The sexualized actresses and models of rap songs and videos, although indispensable in rap's landscape of male pleasure, are routinely debased. *Blaze* magazine's rap video reviewer Rubin Keyser Carasco quips that the estimated budget for Punisher's "Still Not a Player" consisted of "a three-piece meal at KFC for each girl," referring to the low compensation for their services the women most likely settled for.[44] If women selling sex for high prices is viewed as morally reprehensible,[45] selling sex cheap is viewed as even worse. And that is why the actresses who played Joanne and Lissette are assumed to be "hoodrats."

Seeking to challenge the dismissal of these actresses and models as "video hoes," Mimi Valdés reminds her *Source* readers that the success of a rap song is directly related to the beauty of the women in the video: "Ironically, no one knows much about these females; yet, *everyone* has something to say about them. Now don't go there and dismiss these ladies as 'video hoes.' Do you call actresses who star in dozens of movies 'movie hoes'? Don't hate these women because they're beautiful."[46]

Valdés makes a good point by highlighting the hypocrisy of singling out video actresses for negative judgments, while movie actresses are not judged as harshly. But to validate these women as respectable professionals, Valdés draws a clear separation between the "freaky" roles they portray and their real lives. She stresses that their video images are "just an act" and do not reflect their "morals and goals."

And what if it wasn't an act? What if these women were sexually aggressive and/or promiscuous in real life? Would that invalidate their also being respectable professionals? Unfortunately, the answer is yes. Female "freaks" are assumed to be ditzy, sleazy and unprofessional. The same judgment is not applied to males, due of course to the patriarchal sexual double standard.

Valdés also relies on denying the central role of sex as a commodity in these actresses' careers in order to validate them. She claims they are not selling sex but interpreting a character. There is no contradiction in selling sex through role-playing as a professional occupation, yet Valdés poses it as such. The so-called video hoes she aims to vindicate as "video queens" have to navigate between economic necessity (earning a living, building a career) and notions of female dignity (according to which selling sex is dishonorable).

Women within the rap music industry are overwhelmingly relegated to secondary roles. They are most highly visible as the models and actresses in magazines and videos. Indispensable as members of the collective at the core of male pleasure—females, honeys, hotties, bitches, hoes, freaks, chickenheads, pigeons, chicks—they are branded by the "mark of the plural" that makes them expendable and easily substitutable as individuals. Women are coveted and necessary but also debased and disrespected.

The ubiquitous tropicalized representations of Caribbean Latinas in rap music since the late 1990s present a striking and ethno-racially specific example of how women bear the "mark of the plural" that hypersexualizes and demeans them. These representations also illustrate, in a gender-specific fashion, the way in which Puerto Ricanness is constructed through navigations between a tropicalized *latinidad* and a ghettocentric blackness. Puerto Rican *mamis* are portrayed most commonly within the hip hop music realm as a tropical, exotic and racially "lighter" variation on ghetto blackness, and that is precisely why they are so coveted.

"Tropical" Blackness

Rap music's turn-of-the-millennium commercial ghettocentricity, old-school nostalgia and butta pecan *mami* fetish have all helped legitimize and even trendify Puerto Ricans—and by extension, Latinos as a whole. This renewed embracing of Puerto Ricans as entitled hip hop participants invested with cultural "authenticity" is also connected to the wider social context of the United States, where the rising population numbers, political clout and media visibility of Latinos highlight their desirability as consumers and/or objects of mass-mediated exotization.

Hip hop's "Latino Renaissance"—as Rigo Morales's 1996 article dubs it—of the latter half of the 1990s, on one hand signaled an era of greater legitimacy and visibility for Puerto Rican (and other Latino) participants and expanded their opportunities for participation and expression. At the same time, the constraints placed on artists through flavor-of-the-month commercial packaging has inhibited the potential for a wider range of creative expression. The market shuns those who dare to deviate from the profitable ghetto-tropical formula.

This redrawing of hip hop's realm of creative expression is reminiscent of freestyle music in the late 1980s, which pushed the bounds of New York Puerto Rican creativity through the inclusion of second- and third-generation perspectives but reproduced certain myths and stereotypes regarding Latino cultural production. One of freestyle's central myths was the construction of a Latino aesthetic that was imagined as disengaged from the Afro-diasporic history and context of Caribbean Latino cultural expression in New York.

Despite the similarities—in terms of perpetuating a stereotypical *latinidad*—between freestyle and "Latin rap" in the late 1980s/early 1990s and Latino hip hop participation at the turn of the century, a crucial distinction must be made, While freestyle and "Latin rap" were defined as Latino expressions, "core" hip hop is perceived to be an Afro-diasporic cultural sphere shared by African American and Latino youth. Caribbean Latinos may tropicalize themselves and be tropicalized by others, thus being readily distinguishable from African Americans. However, their participation in hip hop is still grounded in and celebrated as part of an Afro-diasporic cultural realm.

Study Questions

1. How do the bodies and images of black women and Latinas circulate differently within hip-hop?
2. What is the relationship of "brown" women in hip-hop to whiteness?
3. How would the presence of more Latina rappers impact perceptions of contemporary hip-hop?

Notes

1. See *The Source* (February 1998): 36.
2. New York's Hot 97 (WQHT) radio host/rap artist Angie Martínez and actress/singer Jennifer López are the Butta Pecan Ricans of greatest exposure—and loudly celebrated as such.
3. On the aesthetic and representational marginalization of black Puerto Ricans, see Javier Cardona, "Un testimonio para la muestra: revolviendo un oscuro asunto en la escena teatral puertorriqueña," *Diálogo* (April 1998): 11; Angela Jorge, "The Black Puerto Rican Woman in Contemporary Society," in *The Puerto Rican Woman: Perspectives on Culture, History and Society*, ed. Edna Acosta-Belén (New York: Praeger, 1986), pp. 180–187; Deborah Gregory, "Lauren Velez," *Vibe* 3, no. 10 (December/January 1995–96): 129; Celia Marina Romano, "Yo no soy negra," *Piso* 13 1, no. 4 (August 1992): 3; Piri Thomas, *Down These Mean Streets* (New York: Vintage Books, 1967). On perceived phenotypic distinctions between African Americans and Puerto Ricans, see "Satchmo" Jenkins and "Belafonte" Wilson, "Shades of Mandingo: Watermelon Men of Different Hues Exchange Views," *Ego Trip* 4, no. 1 (1998): 24–26. See also Samara, "Samara," in *Sex Work: Writings by Women in the Sex Industry*, ed. Frédérique Delacoste and Priscilla Alexander (Pittsburgh: Cleis Press, 1987).
4. bell hooks, *Outlaw Culture: Resisting Representations* (Boston: South End Press, 1994).
5. Samara, a dark-skinned African American twenty-six-year-old "veteran of live sex shows," says of her experience looking for work in strip clubs around New York City: "Some clubs did not want to hire me because I was black. ... Some like black girls, but black girls who have either big tits or light skin, *who tend to look more like Puerto Ricans.*" See Samara in *Sex Work*, p. 37.
6. Frances R. Aparicio, *Listening to Salsa: Gender, Latin Popular Music, and Puerto Rican Cultures* (Hanover, NH: Wesleyan University Press), p. 147.
7. Frances Negrón-Muntaner, "Jennifer's Butt," *Aztlán: A Journal of Chicano Studies* 22, no. 2 (Fall 1997): 185.
8. Aparicio, *Listening to Salsa.*
9. Negrón-Muntaner, "Jennifer's Butt."
10. Ibid.
11. See Teresa Wiltz, "Bottoms Up: Jennifer López's Big Derriere Takes Fanny Fawning to a Higher Level," *Daily News,* October 29, 1998, p. 67.
12. Negrón-Muntaner, "Jennifer's Butt." See also Erin Aubry, "The Butt: It's Politics, It's Profanity, It's Power," in *Adiós Barbie: Young Women Write About Body Image and Identity,* ed. Ophira Edut (Seattle: Seale Press, 1999), pp. 22–31; Theo Perry, "I, Latina," *Vibe* 5, no. 6 (September 1997): 58; Wiltz, "Bottoms Up."
13. dream hampton, "Boomin' System: Bombshell Supreme Jennifer Lopez Is the Biggest Explosion Outta the Bronx Since the Birth of Hip Hop," *Vibe* 7, no. 6 (August 1999): 98–104.
14. Goldie, "Ass Rules Everything Around Us: Some Late Night Thoughts on Jennifer Lopez," *XXL* 2, no. 3, issue 5 (1998): 80.
15. hampton, "Boomin' System," p. 102.
16. Cristina Verán, "Backyard Boogie: An Honest Assessment of Jennifer Lopez's Mo' Cheeks," *Ego Trip* 4, no. 1 (1998): 133.
17. See Perry, "I, Latina"; Wiltz, "Bottoms Up."
18. hooks, *Outlaw Culture,* p. 179.
19. See Paulette Caldwell, "A Hair Piece: Perspectives on the Intersection of Race and Gender," in *Critical Race Theory: The Cutting Edge,* ed. Richard Delgado (Philadelphia: Temple University Press, 1995), pp. 267–277; Lisa Jones, *Bulletproof Diva: Tales of Race, Sex and Hair* (New York: Doubleday, 1994); Jorge, "The Black Puerto Rican Woman in Contemporary Society"; Mayra Santos, "Hebra Rota," in *Pez de Vidrio* (Coral Gables, FL: North-South Center, University of Miami, Iberian Studies Institute, 1995).
20. Aparicio, *Listening to Salsa,* p. 143.
21. Mimi Valdés, "Malibu Dreamin': Who Are Those Video Queens Anyway?" *The Source,* no. 93 (June 1997): 72–79.
22. Shannon, "Bikini Beauties," *The Source,* no. 95 (August 1997): 20.
23. See Arcadio Díaz Quiñones, "Tomás Blanco: Racismo, historia y esclavitud," in *El prejuicio racial en Puerto Rico,* Tomás Blanco (Rio Piedras: Ediciones Huracán, 1985), pp. 15–91; Juan Giusti Cordero, "AfroPuerto Rican Cultural Studies: Beyond *cultura negroide* and *antillanismo,*" *Centro* 8, nos. 1 and 2 (1996): 57–77.
24. Ramón Grosfoguel and Frances Negrón-Muntaner, *Puerto Rican Jam: Essays on Culture and Politics* (Minneapolis: University of Minnesota Press, 1997), p. 14. Emphasis added.
25. See Carl N. Degler, *Neither Black Nor White: Slavery and Race Relations in Brazil and the United States* (Madison: University of Wisconsin Press, 1971).

26. See Ana M. López, "Of Rhythms and Borders," in *Everynight Life,* ed. Celeste Fraser Delgado and José Esteban Muñoz (Durham, NC: Duke University Press, 1997), pp. 310–344; Ella Shohat, "Gender and Culture of Empire: Toward a Feminist Ethnography of the Cinema," in *Visions of the East: Orientalism in Film,* ed. Matthew Bernstein and Gaylyn Studlar (New Brunswick, NJ: Rutgers University Press, 1997), pp. 19–66.

27. Shohat, "Gender and Culture of Empire," p. 47.

28. See López, "Of Rhythms and Borders," p. 317.

29. Ibid.

30. See Shohat, "Gender and Culture of Empire."

31. Jee proudly remarks regarding language use in hip hop culture: "The slang spitters/ standard English quitters/ Ebonics slingers/ Break Language, talk shit, and flip word thinkers. Speaking non-standard English is nothing new to those who are 'non-standard' americans. 'Non-standard' niggas twist words listed in dictionaries, we flip words from movies, we re-create, we innovate." See Jee, "Broken Language," *Stress,* issue 15 (1998): 22.

32. Danny Hoch, *Jails, Hospitals & Hip Hop and Some People* (New York: Villard Books, 1998), p. 73.

33. At least, I hope this song was intended to be tongue-in-cheek. If it wasn't, then it's a prime example of corny Spanish use and *mami*-philia. But I doubt it.

34. It is another sign of Latino relegitimation within rap that Rodríguez is currently editor-in-chief of one of the most popular hip hop music magazines on the market.

35. Antoinette Marrero, "Tribal Council," *Urban Latino Magazine* (June/July 2001): 26–29.

36. Aparicio, *Listening to Salsa,* p. 142.

37. "I'm tired of that shit I hear on the radio and see on MTV, because when I see those beautiful, gorgeous women in little bikinis shaking their ass like that's all they're good for, that tells me, damn, they don't have no kind of hope. They don't have faith that we can change this world, that something is coming, that something good is waiting for us. That breaks my heart."

38. Danyel Smyth, "Ain't a Damned Thing Changed: Why Women Rappers Don't Sell," in *Rap on Rap: Straight-up Talk on Hip Hop Culture,* ed. Adam Sexton (New York Delta Books, 1995), p. 126.

39. Rob Marriott, "R(Un)ning Things, *XXL* 1, no. 2, issue 2 (1997): 56–58.

40. "Cocksucker" is a rough equivalent of *"mamao,"* although the Spanish term literally means a man who still sucks his mother's breast.

41. In one of the few published articles that explores male homosexuality in hip hop, R. K. Byers states: "hip hop, which is quite unfairly [and perhaps problematically] seen as the last frontier of real *nigga-ness,* might suffer as an icon of Black masculinity if one of its more hard-core artists revealed himself to be gay." See R. K. Byers, "The Other Side of the Game: A B-Boy Adventure into Hip Hop's Gay Underworld," *The Source,* no. 99 (December 1997): 108.

42. See Thembisa S. Mshaka, "Lesbian Life in Hip Hop Culture," *Blaze,* issue 2 (December/January 1999): 84.

43. Lana Sands, "Whipping Girl," *XXL* 2, no. 3, issue 5 (1998): 31.

44. Rubin Keyser Carasco, "Set Trippin'," *Blaze* (Fall 1998): 206–207.

45. Anne McClintock, "Sex Workers and Sex Work," *Social Text* 37 (Winter 1993): 1–10; Gail Pheterson, "The Whore Stigma: Female Dishonor and Male Unworthiness," *Social Text* 37 (Winter 1993): 39–64.

46. Valdés, "Malibu Dreamin'," p. 73.

Part V
"The Message"
Rap, Politics, and Resistance
Mark Anthony Neal

"My president is black/My Lambo blue ..." could be heard in virtually every ghetto-hood in America during the autumn of 2008, as the election of Barack Obama as the first black American president seemed imminent. The lyric was recorded by Island Def Jam artist Young Jeezy and included on his album *The Recession*, which was released months before the presidential election. In an interview with NPR days after the election, Jeezy recalled his excitement at driving through various neighborhoods on the night of the election (presumably in his blue Lamborghini) and hearing "My president is black" blasting out of other car stereos. Jeezy also explained that Obama's campaign pulled him into the political process for the first time, joking to *Weekend Edition*'s host that registering to vote was as exciting as buying his first car with his own credit. As a purveyor of what some critics would refer to as "crack rap," Young Jeezy would never be mistaken for a so-called "conscious" rapper like Talib Kweli, Jean Grae, or Immortal Technique, but he recorded arguably the most significant political anthem in hip-hop since Jadakiss's "Why" (another rapper who would never be mistaken for a political activist) was released in 2005. That a rapper of Jeezy's reputation resonated as he did in 2008 speaks to how the terrains of political rap and hip-hop's role in broad notions of "politics" have shifted since the so-called heyday of political rap in the late 1980s and early 1990s.

In was during the early 1990s that Chuck D, lead vocalist of the political hip-hop group Public Enemy, famously described rap music as the "black CNN." Driven by almost a decade of neglect in the face of Reagan-era domestic policy and the inability of black elected officials to respond adequately to the worst aspects of those policies, a generation of black youth came of age full of rage. Unlike hip-hop's core audience at the time, Chuck D—a half-generation older than this audience—had been exposed to the late stages of the civil rights and Black Power era. In Public Enemy, Chuck D and cohorts DJ Terminator X, sidekick Flava-Flav, "Minister of Information" Professor Griff, and the S1Ws (security of the first world) aimed to re-fashion the "revolution" to the sounds of hip-hop. In his essay "Postindustrial Soul: Black Popular Music at the Crossroads," Mark Anthony Neal remarks,

> Chuck D's call for truth, justice and a black nationalist way of life was perhaps the most potent of any political narratives that had appeared on a black popular recording. Public Enemy very consciously attempted to have hip-hop serve the revolutionary vanguard, the way soul did in the 1960s.
>
> (Neal, 1998: 142)

In reality, Public Enemy's 1988 release *It Takes a Nation of Millions to Hold Us Back* might have been the apex of political hip-hop. The initial popularity of recordings like *It Takes a Nation of Millions* ... and Boogie Down Productions' (KRS-One) *By Any Means Necessary* (1988), but sub-sequent inability of those artists and recordings to inspire a sustained political or social movement, is at the heart of debates over the significance of hip-hop culture as a vehicle for political change. Ironically, the impact of these records was not limited to black listeners or the possibility of some grassroots movement, as a generation of young college-aged whites were politicized and sensitized about black urban issues via hip-hop. As thirty- and forty-something adults and parents two decades later, these whites did not find the possibility of electing a black president all that daunting.

Indeed, a comparison of the politics that shaped the hip generation of Public Enemy's era and the post-hip generation that consumes Young Jeezy suggests a generational split that is not unlike that experienced between the hip-hop generation and the civil rights generation. In the official/non-official narrative, hip-hop is often blamed for blinding post-civil rights era youth to the importance of the political gains made by civil rights era activists and for eroding the value of grassroots communal civic engagement, in lieu of a focus on individual survival and the attain-ment of material wealth. In his conversation with Yusef Nuruddin in the essay "Intergenerational Culture Wars: Civil Rights vs. Hip Hop," Todd Boyd frankly asserts, "I think the Civil Rights generation does a lot of playa-hating," adding more substantively:

> to me, hip-hop is about the community. People talk about my hood, my projects, my niggaz, my crew, my fam, my peeps. You get these communal references throughout hip hop ... maybe it functions differently than it did in the '60s and '70s, but that's to be expected because we're dealing with a new generation of individuals.
>
> (Boyd, 2004: 61)

In her essay "Rise Up Hip-Hop Nation: From Deconstructing Racial Politics to Building Positive Solutions," Kristine Wright challenges, to some extent, Boyd's points, by suggesting that "Hip-hop's power is realized in truth and self-determination, through community activism. Community activism in inner cities across the country is taking hip-hop sensibility and offering real alternatives for youth at community levels" (Wright, 2004: 19). Wright makes a nuanced distinction between the politics of art and the politics that art emboldens; she clearly sees hip-hop's most pronounced political impact in the latter. Imani Perry cautions, though, that politics takes multiple forms, in terms of both how rappers themselves construct political narratives and the ways that black youth, in particular, act on those politics. Perry reads hip-hop's politics in its investment in "otherness." In the essay "My Mic Sound Nice: Art, Community and Consciousness," Perry writes that other-ness "signals a crisis in black youth politics. It is impossible to isolate, in any coherent fashion, a clear system of political critique with a traceable eschatology or teleology in hip-hop." Using the example of hip-hop's relationship to the criminal justice system, Perry observes that "we find simultaneous movement of social critique and a celebration of the status quo" (Perry, 2004: 47).

Perry admits concern over hip-hop's "voyeuristic fantasies of black sociopathy and otherness," which are problematic for mainstream audiences as well as marginal communities who might find value in "fantasies of masculine power" (ibid.: 42). Jennifer Lena takes on the issue of cultural voyeurism head on in her essay "Voyeurism and Resistance in Rap Music Videos." Lena writes that the "voyeuristic gaze is a learned mode of apperception that draws upon stereotypic notions of the 'other.' ... Voyeurs mobilize preconceptions of experience, landscape, and people to see 'exotic' others." Specifically taking aim at the proverbial white rap fan, Lena argues that the "voyeurism of white rap fans is premised on the exoticism of the lyrical and visual content of those rhymes" (Lena, 2008: 266). Using the example of the political rap group Dead Prez, Lena discusses how some artists subvert the voyeuristic gaze by "rework(ing) hegemonic images of urban space, oper-ating within dominant representational discourses of the city, but simultaneously relating, fram-ing, or transforming these images in accordance with how those places are made meaningful through lived experience" (ibid.: 267).

Even with examples like Dead Prez and numerous others, Bakari Kitwana is careful not to view politicized hip-hop artists as some sort of revolutionary vanguard, warning that:

> as activist minded as their lyrics may be, as tuned in as they are to activist concerns, and as much as hip-hop generationers admire their politicized messages and activities, few are in the trenches day to day working to bring about change like those at the forefront of activism in our generation.
>
> (Kitwana, 2002: 155)

Instead Kitwana finds that vanguard in the cadre of young activists including Ras Baraka (son of the well-known poet and activist Amiri Baraka), AIDs activist Tamara Jones, and Van Jones, former executive director of the Ella Baker Center and internationally known green jobs guru. According to Kitwana this generation of hip-hop activists "have demonstrated that they are in this for the long haul, not just engaged in a passing fling" (Kitwana, 2002: 155), but he laments that "too often voices like these are missing from efforts to create the institutional structure needed to move the hip-hop generation into political power" (ibid.: 174). Ultimately Kitwana admits that, "until hip-hop is recognized as a broad cultural movement, rather than simply an influential moneymaker, those who seek to tap into hip-hop's potential to impact social change should not expect substantive progress" (ibid.: 206).

REFERENCES

Boyd, Todd. (2004). "Intergenerational Culture Wars: Civil Rights vs. Hip Hop (Interview with Yusuf Nuruddin)," *Socialism and Democracy*, 18:2, July–December.

Kitwana, Bakari. (2002). *The Hip-Hop Generation: Young Blacks and the Crisis of African American Culture*. New York: Basic Civitas.

Lena, Jennifer C. (2008). "Voyeurism and Resistance in Rap Music Videos," *Communication and Critical/Cultural Studies*, 5:3, September.

Neal, Mark Anthony. (1998). "Postindustrial Soul: Black Popular Music at the Crossroads," in *What the Music Said: Black Popular Music and Black Public Culture*. New York: Routledge.

Perry, Imani. (2004). *Prophets of the Hood: Politics and Poetics in Hip-Hop*. Durham, NC: Duke University Press.

Wright, Kristine. (2004). "Rise Up Hip-Hop Nation: From Deconstructing Racial Politics to Building Positive Solutions," *Socialism and Democracy*, 18:2, July–December.

29

Intergenerational Culture Wars
Civil Rights vs. Hip-Hop

The intense popularity of hip-hop and its centrality to post-Civil Rights era political movement has often served to pit the hip-hop generation against the Civil Rights generation. As such, hip-hop has often been referred to as Black America's Vietnam War. As the hip-hop generation began to look past Civil Rights leaders and to hip-hop artists and hip-hop generation activists for leadership, some affiliated with the Civil Rights establishment took offense.

In his conversation with Yusuf Nuruddin, Todd Boyd accuses the Civil Rights generation of "playa hating." At the crux of Boyd's discussion of the generational riff within hip-hop is the suggestion that political engagement and community involvement are fundamentally different for the hip-hop generation than for previous generations of African Americans.

Intergenerational Culture Wars: Civil Rights vs. Hip Hop

Todd Boyd and Yusuf Nuruddin

Interviewed by Yusuf Nuruddin

Yusuf Nuruddin: *I spent some time yesterday reading your book* The New H.N.I.C.[1]: The Death of Civil Rights and the Reign of Hip Hop, *and I have a couple of questions about it. First of all, could you give me the kernel or nutshell of your thesis!*

Todd Boyd: The title of the book sums up what the book is about: the death of civil rights and the reign of hip hop. In my mind, the Civil Rights generation, those African-Americans who came of age during the Civil Rights era—who were part of the Civil Rights era—have had a strong influence on African-American culture for quite some time now. And I think if we look at the way that things have changed—that society overall has changed and grown and evolved—a lot of the issues that defined that generation have been changed in nuance somewhat. I guess I find now a situation where that generation and their ideas are somewhat outdated and passé. It's not to say that the pursuit of one's civil rights is accomplished because I think that's an ongoing struggle. But it is to say that the sort of ideas that defined and motivated the Civil Rights era come across somewhat differently in the present.

So when I look out and see what's going on, I see hip hop as something that has connected a generation of people. Here's something that started as just music, but from that music it has grown to encompass a whole culture, a lifestyle, an ideology, a point of view, points of view, if you will. And so for that reason, when I look at the present, I see that hip hop has much more influence now than does civil rights, even though many of these old Civil Rights figures still want to maintain a lock on what happens in the community. But I think times have changed and hip hop is this new formation, which is why I refer to it as the new head niggaz in charge—H.N.I.C. In terms of the controversy, that's what it's all about. I think the time has come for somebody to step up and say what needs to be said. I think there's a lot of censorship that goes on in the Black community. There's a lot of things that people can't say, sacred cows that people can't challenge, and I don't think that's progressive, and so I think it was time for somebody to step up and be real, and that's where I see myself and my book fitting in.

Okay, now you said in your book that there was a transitional generation that talked about the New Black Aesthetic, for example Mark Anthony Neal, and that that was a bridge between what you call the Race Men of the Civil Rights generation and, I guess, niggaz of the hip hop generation. And I think you said you located yourself in that transitional generation although you tend to look to the hip hop generation because you think that the New Black Aesthetic generation was just transitional and really had no influence. Is that correct?

Somewhat. In my first book, *Am I Black Enough For You?*, I talked about what I saw as, not so much generations, but the three sort of transitional phases around identity. And I talked about the Race Man, I talked about the New Black Aesthetic, and then I talked about the emergence of the nigga. To me, the nigga is inherently part of hip hop culture. Of course, niggaz have been around for a long time, they didn't just start with hip hop but hip hop gives it, I think, a different twist. I'm 39. When I was in tenth grade, *Rapper's Delight* came out. I'm from Detroit, I'm not from New York, so I wasn't fortunate enough to be in the South Bronx or Brooklyn or Harlem when hip hop was first coming out in the mid-'70s. But by the late '70s, I was right there, when hip hop moved outside of New York and into other parts of the country. And still, by '79, very, very few people are listening to hip hop. So, for me, it's been a part of my life for quite a long time.

I think it's hard to really define when a generation starts and when it ends precisely. But I guess I would say that, to me, the idea of a nigga, N-I-G-G-A, is an individual who fits comfortably in hip hop and who is not interested in necessarily appeasing the masses or fitting into anybody's category, but instead is interested in doing things their own way in spite of the consequences. And this is one of the things about hip hop I've always found empowering. But I guess if I were talking about myself, I would say that I am a nigga, and I'm very much part of the hip hop generation and I don't make any bones about it.

Some people are offended by that, others are confused and others don't quite know what to do with it but to me this is who I am, so when I say that, it's not to me a negative thing, it's very much a sort of acknowledgement of the way I see myself and the way I relate to the world. The first time I went to Europe—and this is an experience that I think a lot of Black people who've been to Europe or other places have had—I think for the first time somebody called me an American. And I never thought of myself before that time as an American because to me American was another way of saying white. And I certainly wasn't white so I didn't think I was an American—What am I? Well, I'm a nigga. And I don't have no problems with that. But I think something clicked in me. Well, I was born in America, I was raised in America, so to that extent I guess I am technically an American. But you can be in something but not be of it. And to me that's what this whole thing is about. You're in this culture and to some extent you're a part of it but not fully, and hip hop, in the sense of being, gives you another option.

What option is that, and what is its vision? You said that there's a whole new ideology, but what 1 found in your book—if I may be slightly critical—is that you talk a lot about the death of the Civil Rights movement and you do mention the Black Power movement, but only in passing, and you do say that hip hop is an outgrowth of the Black Power movement. I'm 53. I am someone who was nurtured in the Black Power movement, and I know that you said that there is a dichotomy in hip hop between people who see Black Power or Black Nationalism as the way to go and those who see Underworld Entrepreneurialism—or basically the idea that you have to go after capital—as the main thrust. That's a big divide as far as I'm concerned and I don't know if there's any real unified vision in the hip hop community. For example, in the Black Power community, one of the things we wanted to do was to build alternative institutions. Is that part of the vision of hip hop?

Well, I think hip hop *is* an alternative institution. To me, the reason I made that point in the book—and I think you would feel me on this—is that a lot of people use civil rights to define the entirety of that era, but in my mind there's a big difference between the Civil Rights movement and the Black Power movement, of Black nationalism. This is what Malcolm was talking about. And I think it's important to separate those things. A lot of people would say we shouldn't separate them—Dr. King and Malcolm were going for the same thing. I disagree with that, because I think one of the problems we still face as African-Americans is that people want to sim-plify us and sort of pigeonhole us. And I think it's important to recognize that there are differ-ences in thought, differences in philosophy and ideology between Malcolm and Martin Luther King, differences in ideology between Civil Rights and Black Power. That's where I start—let's recognize Black Power as distinct, and not a subset of Civil Rights, because it was something that came from a completely different place.

Now, I think that the sense of self-determination, the sense of independence and freedom, all this grows out of Black Nationalism, Black Power, and sort of seeps its way into subsequent gen-erations. And to me, this is where hip hop came from, as opposed to coming out of Civil Rights. Now, I'm not somebody who looks at this as "there's a right way and a wrong way," because I think that ends the debate as opposed to expanding it. I think it's up to the individual to choose what's right and what's wrong for them. In my mind, though, hip hop is an alternative institu-tion. When hip hop started, these people were making beats and writing rhymes, and they were doing this for love, because they wanted to do it. It wasn't necessarily about getting a record deal. Well, at a certain point, that became possible. So I come from the standpoint that the more cap-ital one has, the more leverage they have, because as Barzini says in *The Godfather*, "After all, we are not Communists."

So you recognize that there was never any intention whatsoever that a Black person in this society, especially a Black man, was supposed to make any money, and yet you see that here with this culture of hip hop you have a number of individuals who have been able to become quite viable financially. I think that financial viability is a good thing. I think it is progress because my knowledge of Black Nationalism, my knowledge of Black Power, had to do not just with creating alternative institutions but also with having something you could call your own. And it's really impossible to have that in this society without having money because you don't have any real leverage. That's where I come from on that issue.

I agree with you there but I wonder about the emphasis on the individual as opposed to the collective or the communal sense of institutions.

Well, again, I think if you listen to hip hop, the communal is a very strong part of it. And I think one of the problems that we've have—one of the issues I keep coming up against since I've been talking about this book—is people still see politics in a very traditional way and I'm trying to get people to rethink how they see politics.

You're talking about cultural politics, right?

To me, hip hop is very much about the community. People talk about my hood, my projects, my niggaz, my crew, my fam, my peeps. You get these communal references throughout hip hop. So in that way you look at one hip hop artist who might be successful. They're artists, they're on a record label, the record label's trying to sell records. Yeah, they're going to try to market the individual and that one individual is going to be the face that you see. But I think that each of these individuals—and I don't know each and every case but that's not really the point—is very much into a sense of the community. It may be their community, as opposed to the entirety of the Black race, but I think that sense of communalism is very strong. Maybe it functions differently than it did in the '60s and '70s, but that's to be expected because we're dealing with a new generation of individuals.

Is it a sense of the community or is it the sense of the gang or posse (I guess that posse is an outmod-ed word)? In the foreword to your book, you said that the "competitive spirit has always defined Black culture." And you talked about wanting to go against Michael Eric Dyson or, in a more confronta-tional way, up against Spike Lee. You were saying that you were ready to take it to the streets. And I know that that's a metaphor that a lot of people use in their dealing with other Black people and it seems to be confrontational and so I don't know if it's communal so much as a gang spirit—this crew of niggaz against that crew of niggaz.

I guess that's one way to look at it. When I was growing up, we played at dozens. Dozens was very competitive. It didn't have anything to do with you having animosity towards the person you were going against; it was part of the culture. When we played basketball, it was very competitive. And when the game was over, you walked off the court, shook hands and went your separate ways. There were times when people crossed the line, yeah. But I don't think competition has to be violent. I think that sense of competition is what has, up to this point, made a basketball player like Michael Jordan great. So it doesn't have to be negative.

But at another point in your book you said that Martin Luther King's ethos was to be judged by the content of our character and not by the color of our skin but the ethos of this hip hop generation is to rather be judged by twelve than carried out by six—which seems to me to be confrontational.

Well, I think that's real. I don't think there's any stretch when you talk about the way in which violence sometimes unfortunately has a prominent place in our culture and society at large. That's very unfortunate. I guess what I'm saying is I don't think competition is inherently negative, that there are ways in which competition can be positive and progressive. To me, when two emcees battle, they're fighting for stylistic superiority. That doesn't have to be violent. When two great basketball players face off, when two boxers face off, it doesn't have to be negative. It is competitive. I'm trying to find a way to take what's positive out of that sense of competition and apply it to this game, as a matter of fact, writing and debating issues. So when I say I want to take on Dyson, it's like, okay let's argue it out.

And maybe let's bring in some of the elements of the street. We don't have to bring in every element of the street. We're not in the street. But my point is that so many times people dis the streets or dismiss it, they think everything about it is negative. I don't think so. I think there's some elements of that that are good and I want to bring that into this environment that I'm in because a lot of what I learned I learned there, arguing with brothers about a range of topics. And they weren't violent arguments that meant if you lost the argument you were going to die. It was people expressing their point of view with a passion. It's like if you've ever been in a barber shop. That's why I thought that whole controversy about the film ["Barbershop"] last year was ridiculous because any Black man that's ever been in a barber shop, if you've been there long enough, you heard people argue and say some of the most off-the-wall things in the world. But that doesn't have to be negative. I want people to maybe try and see that in a different way.

That brings up two points from your book. You talked about your father getting together with other men on Saturdays or Sundays for breakfast and how that was one of the arenas where they could feel free to express their feelings, express how they feel about white people, express how they feel about politics without having to worry about what the white man thinks. You said how those conversations used to be private in your father's generation but now hip hop makes those conversations public. But then there's also this concept in the book about playaz and playa-haters and so I know that a lot of hip hop is about one rapper dissing another rapper; do you see that just as healthy competition?

I do. I don't think it's any different than . . .

And the deaths that have happened in the hip hop community, how do you contextualize those, the deaths of Tupac and Biggie?

Here's the thing. There are people who cross the line. And I think that if you're not careful, things can be taken out of context; things can be misinterpreted. Again, I go back to that example of the Dozens. There was a point when it could be fair competition and there's another point when somebody might cross the line, when they might say the wrong thing. And that could be potential for drama. I don't think you can blame the death of Tupac and Biggie on hip hop, any more than you can blame the death of any other young Black man on hip hop. We live in a society that's still very racist and has been that way for some time and unfortunately, one of the ways that that racism has visited itself upon young African-American men is either they end up in the penitentiary or they end up dead. And that's very unfortunate and something that's constantly in need of address. It didn't start with hip hop. Biggie and Tupac are not the first two Black men to have words between each other and somebody dies. It doesn't make it right or wrong but I think it's part of the process, it's part of the culture. The Nation killed Malcolm X. We have to look at the fact that these issues are present and this was simply another manifestation of it.

How much of the culture of hip hop do you think emanates from the penitentiary? I didn't see much of that in the book.

I think a lot of it emanates from the penitentiary. I talk about that in the book, for instance, in terms of style; that's one obvious way, the way people wear their pants, cornrows and the whole bit. But I think the penitentiary is a reality for a lot of young black men unfortunately, and the penitentiary has had a very big hand in shaping ghetto communities for a long time but especially the last twenty years. So, just as the penitentiary has had a profound impact on lower-class African-Americans, it's had an extremely profound impact on hip hop. And again some people use that as a way of exposing and revealing the prison-industrial complex, which I think is a discussion that almost started in hip hop. So I think the penitentiary has had a profound influence. In some ways, that influence has been positive; in other ways, it's been negative.

Are you aware at all of the work of Dr. Maulana Karenga who's out on the West Coast with you? In one of his earlier books, Kawaida Theory: An Introductory Outline, *he talks about the difference between what he calls a national culture and a popular culture. He defines this popular culture as having what he calls lumpen values, which I suppose would be the same street/ghetto values, penitentiary values, etc. And he says that the main crisis in the Black community is a crisis of culture. Now you're talking about cultural politics. Here's a Black Nationalist ethos that would be opposed to what they call a lumpen ideology which I guess you would call a hip hop ideology. Your defense?*

Well, again, I talk about the profound impact of the lumpen-proletariat on contemporary Black culture and hip hop in my first book, *Am I Black Enough For You?* To me there has always been something that emerged from the Lumpen that a lot of more middle-class or bourgeois-minded African-Americans don't really want to deal with. I think there's value that comes out of the streets. Not everything that comes out of the streets is of value; of course not. For instance, I listen to somebody like Jay-Z who—in spite of the fact that a lot of people criticize him as being too pop—says some very real things. (You should listen to his albums—not the radio songs, the singles, but the albums.) So I'm listening to his last record, *The Gift and the Curse*, and Jay-Z says, "Bin Laden been happenin' in Manhattan/Crack was Anthrax back then/Back when, Police was Al'Qaeda to Black men." To me, that's real. It didn't come out of the mouth of a Black Nationalist, it came out of the mouth of a rapper. Am I to dismiss it because it came out of the mouth of a rapper? Or am I to look at the fact that here's someone speaking from a particular perspective and in my mind said some of the realest things that have been said about 9/11 and its pertinence to Black people; things that a lot of other people were, for whatever reason, unwilling to or didn't say. So if it comes from hip hop, I shouldn't just dismiss it because that's where it comes from. It's real.

So to me, there's a perspective that the Lumpen provides that a lot of times gets overlooked. And again, I think it's like anything else, you take what's useful to you and discard the rest. But I think that a lot of middle-class, sort of bourgeois-minded Black people, have spent all their life trying to be accepted by white people, they've spent all their life trying to be accepted in white institutions, and here come these niggaz straight off the street talking shit and not only are they making money, but they're influencing the culture at large. And so naturally, these gatekeepers of the community are upset because they wanted to be the ones in that position and they're not, because they were trying so hard to appease white people and appease the system that they lost their identity and their effect in the process. What I love about hip hop is that it says, look, this is who we are, take it or leave it. We didn't cross over. As Jay-Z says again, "we brought the suburbs to the hood." So, to me, there's something that can be learned from the Lumpen and a lot of times in the Black community, we ignore that but there's something to learn from it. There are other things that are not useful, so I think' you have to be vigilant in discerning what's useful and embrace it, and what's not and discard it.

Some people would say that the brothers from the hood really are not influencing the culture, that it's really the record companies—the multi-billionaire record industry—that decides what kind of hip hop is going to be played and, in that sense, that the hip hop artists themselves are pawns in the game.

Well, if they're pawns in the game, so were James Brown and Curtis Mayfield and Stevie Wonder and Marvin Gaye and Aretha Franklin and Donnie Hathaway. Do you know what I'm saying? Do I need to go on? The record industry didn't just come up with hip hop. Yeah, the record industry sells records. They're interested in making money and selling products. That allows people the opportunity to be heard by large numbers of people, and that's the agreement you make when you want to produce culture and you want people to hear it.

Well, let me just finish. I guess you've heard this a thousand times already, but of course from the Civil Rights generation's perspective, I suppose that they would see this as some kind of conspiracy by the White record companies to perpetuate some kind of culture that's basically self-destructive, dysfunctional.

Well, it's funny because I do hear this a lot. As somebody who's studied the record industry and who knows it intimately, the record industry is interested in one thing, making money. They have no other interest beyond that. So, again, if you go back to Public Enemy, everybody loves Public Enemy. The same record company that sold Public Enemy is still in existence and they're still selling hip hop. You know what I'm saying? Yeah, so were they perpetrating a negative image of Black people when they were selling Brand Nubian and KRS1 and Public Enemy? No. People didn't say that then. They said it when it changed. So, you've got to look at that issue and be honest about it. I mean, the record companies are interested in making money and they will sell whatever people will buy to make that money. They will even sell something that calls for their destruction if it will make them money. They don't care. They're not in the business of civil rights. They're not in the business of Black nationalism. They're in the business of making money.

But are they in the business of oppression?

I don't think they're in the business of oppression any more than any other institution or entity in American society is. If they are, then so is the American Government and people could make that argument. But if Jay-Z's wrong for being on a major record label, then Maxine Waters is wrong for being in the U.S. Congress. Where are we going to draw the line? You know what I'm saying? They're all part of the same larger American system of institutions—if we want to get specific about it—I think the record companies are in the business of making money. Now, does that mean that the record companies are without guilt? No, but they're going to sell whatever makes money, and if it's Public Enemy with *Black Steel in the Hour* or *Chaos*, they'll sell it. If it's Nellie, they'll sell it. They don't care; they want to make money. And I think people who understood the record industry better would know that there's not a bunch of people sitting in a room, smoking cigars, saying "we want to destroy these Black people." That's counter to making money. That might have been the case at one point but I don't think it's the case now at all.

Some people would argue that the Black Power movement threatened internal security in the United States at some point—

That's true.

—and COINTELPRO and other government agencies and police actions—agents provacateurs and so forth—came in and destroyed that movement, and part of the destruction of that movement is to create a decadent culture where you have this friction among different posses of Black people rather than a unity. I'm sure you heard this thinking before. But I wanted to go to another question, and that's the issue of generational playa-hating. You talked about the whole issue about Rosa Parks, and you said she was—her people were—very arrogant for wanting to have control over her name when it was used by OutKast. Was that right?

Right.

Do you want to elaborate on that? Is the Civil Rights generation the generation that are the playa-haters, basically. Is that what you're saying? Playa-haters against

I think the Civil Rights generation does a lot of playa-hating. I don't know if I'd call each and every individual in the generation a playa-hater, but I think that that generation has certainly done a lot of playa-hating, and Rosa Parks is just one example. I just don't believe Rosa Parks sat down and listened to OutKast. And if she did, I can't see how she'd be offended because the song—of all songs to be critical of—is about as innocuous as possible. You know what I'm saying? If she sat down and listened to that song, I can't imagine anybody being offended because it doesn't say anything about her. It really just uses her name as a metaphor. I think that's arrogant, myself. I think it's arrogant when somebody would dare stand up and say a movie studio should re-edit this movie and delete the scene that criticizes Martin Luther King and Rosa Parks. To me, that's censorship. And when Time-Warner stood up and said they were no longer going to distribute Ice-T's *Cop Killer*, that was censorship. It is the same thing when African-Americans say you should re-edit a movie so it doesn't include this commentary about Dr. King and Rosa Parks. To me, what point does that serve? That's censorship. It doesn't make any difference if it's coming from somebody White or somebody Black. It's still the same thing.

Well, you say that this generation should not be held hostage to the Civil Rights movement—

Right.

—but we haven't yet talked at all about Afrocentricity. How does Afrocentricity permeate this context now when we talk about respect for the elders and respect for tradition and respect for a history that has come before?

I would never be one to advocate not respecting your history. First of all, you need to be knowledgeable of your history before you can move forward. That's your base; that's your foundation. I would never suggest that anybody disrespect history, but, at the same time, you can't be a prisoner of history; you can't be a hostage to it. You can't be so bound to Civil Rights that you can never move forward. That was the point I was trying to make there. We can't—every time something goes a different way—jump up and impose some sort of Civil Rights idea on it. Things change. And I understand, the Civil Rights generation really were the first African-Americans to experience social mobility and have some sense of power in larger numbers. They've gotten used to being on top and they don't want to relinquish it. That makes sense to me but be honest about it. That's what I was saying in terms of that issue.

But do you see the Civil Rights generation as being unique or do you see the Civil Rights generation as being linked to, say, Garvey's generation or generations before it which were also fighting the battle against racial oppression?

Of course, things connect through history. Sure.

Then how, specifically, does the hip hop generation connect to that long stream of history (not just to the Civil Rights generation)?

You can connect through history, but I think Marcus Garvey's times were different than Martin Luther King's. I think the '20s in America were different than the '60s. Now, maybe they were still fighting for the same issue, but they had to do it in a different way because times were different and we can't deny the fact that things change, things evolve and some things stay the same. The '60s is not the '20s, the '90s is not the '60s. So, I think hip hop is connected to Civil Rights; Civil Rights is connected to the New Negro, that earlier era, the Harlem Renaissance, however you want to define it, that post-World War II generation and pre-World War II generation. They're all connected, but at the same time, they're all different because they came about at different times so maybe they represent themselves in different ways. I would never say that Civil Rights has no connection to hip hop. I'm just saying that that era is past and people need to accept that and act accordingly.

What do you think about the struggle for reparations, and does hip hop have anything to do with that?

One of the first groups of people I heard talk about reparations were hip hop artists back in the '80s. I look at it this way, again I quote Barzini, "After all, we're not Communists." America recognizes the dollar bill; they recognize cash; they recognize money. To pay a debt financially is significant within the way America does things. There are a million and one people who talk about what are they going to do and how are they going to do it. That's irrelevant. Deal with that after the fact. But the point is, hip hop has been dealing with that issue like it's been dealing with police brutality and the prison industrial complex and other issues for a long time. Again I quote Jay-Z who says, "we're overcharging niggaz for what you did to the Cold Crush/Pay us like you owe us for all them years that you hold us/we can talk but money talks so talk mo' bucks." That's reparations to me. The Cold Crush brothers got beat. They didn't make any money in hip hop, but Jay-Z does. So he's like hey "pay us like you owe us for all them years you hold us, we can talk but money talks so talk mo' bucks." So to me, yeah, that sense is alive and well and has always been alive and well in hip hop.

Now, you say over again that we're not Communists. I am a socialist so, but anyway—

No disrespect, brother.

—but what I want to ask is, what is your vision of how hip hop ultimately will transform this society. I know it's in transformation now and I'm not saying that you're a prophet with a crystal ball or anything like that, but what direction are we going in with this hip hop transformation? How, ideally, do you see things shifting in terms of these cultural politics?

Well one of the ways that I talk about in the book—that we've seen now and that as time passes will be more and more obvious—is that, going back to the Black Power movement, Civil Rights movement, these people, in my mind, wanted access—access that had been denied. Particularly, I was listening recently to Malcolm's speech *The Message to the Grass Roots.* Malcolm, in this speech, talks about nationalism and he says nationalism is based on land. How do you get it? Bloodshed. I think about land. Land is the basis of independence. Land can be metaphorical. It can be symbolic and it can also be quite real. What do you want that land for? So you can build something on it. You want to build your own institutions; you want to control your own capital; you want self-determination. To me, when I look at hip hop, I see a version of that.

Now, where it will go in the future, who knows? All I know, as someone who encounters a lot of young people (not all of whom are African-Americans, most of whom are not), is that with this generation of people outside the Black community there is a different sort of understanding than among the previous generation of White people or others, and the reason I think this present generation of young people has a different sense about race has to do with hip hop. They've grown up with hip hop as very much a part of their life and it's not been off limits to them, it's not been foreign or alien or exotic to them. It's been very much a part of their life. And I think as time passes, you're going to have a generation of people who have a better sense of Black people and African-American culture because—they're going to be at least open to it because—hip hop has had such a profound impact on their life. And I think this is the piece that a lot of people are missing because they're looking at it in a very '60s- or '70s-style way. They're looking at it in a sort of old-school way. But to me, before anything ever changes, people's minds have to be changed. And culture has always been one of the ways that people's minds have been changed. You look at somebody like Muhammad Ali, who in the '60s and early '70s was one of the most hated people in America, and now I think he's probably the greatest American living hero, embraced by some of the same people who twenty, thirty, forty years ago, dissed him. So things do change.

To elaborate on that, you talked about Eminem, Slim Shady, and his acceptance as a brother or whatever—as a part of the hip hop community—and you also talked about how you were almost embarrassed because some of the old guard Civil Rights Negroes did not want to support a Mexican-American, a Chicano, who was running for political office in California . . .

Mayor of L.A.

. . . so how do you see these coalition politics—to elaborate on what you were starting to talk about?

In the mayoral election of 2001 in L.A., you had a white candidate, James Hahn, who eventually won the election, whose father had been one of these white politicians back in the '60s who was elected in a Black district, and he was well loved by the people in that district at a time when it was impossible for a Black person to run for that sort of office. I think his father was commissioner or something. And so now his son comes along and he's sort of running on his father's legacy. A lot of prominent L.A. niggaz were supporting him, very visible, and very much saying "yeah we know his father, his father was cool with us, so we'll vote for him too." They wouldn't even consider Antonio Villaraigosa who I think represents the fact that we live in a city whose majority population is Latino.

As demographics change, Black people become more of a minority than they've ever been. Latinos become a larger group of people, and in the process they become more viable. I think for a long time, Black people had the minority card locked up. But a lot of people are freaking out because they don't know what to do now that a lot of Black people have become middle class and, in addition, the numbers of Black people have sort of stayed the same whereas the Latino population has grown in leaps and bounds to the point that California is supposedly going to be majority non-white in seven or eight years.

My point was this: when I ride down the streets of L.A., if I'm in what used to be a Black community, I don't see no signs in Ebonics, but I see a lot of signs in Spanish. And that tells me something. It tells me that demographics are changing and Black people are going to have to redefine the way they think about themselves and they're going to need to build coalitions with other people who are sympathetic because Black people alone are not going to be able to do things the way that they've done in the past because the world is just a very different place. I had a conversation with someone who was telling me about how James Hahn came to speak at this big Black church in L.A., and I said, "what about Villaraigosa?" And he goes, "Oh well I have not heard any of the prominent elected Black officials mention Villaraigosa so he must not be that important." And I thought, well, first of all, why are you waiting on some Black official to tell you who you should or shouldn't embrace, and secondly you know nothing about him but you're going to embrace this other character because he came to your church and spoke. What kind of shit is that?

It reminded me of Bill Clinton throughout his presidency who would go and sit in the Black church and sing hymns and clap his hands and Black people loved him. To me, that's not going to get it. It's about more than that. But I do think that Black people have to recognize that they won't be able to function in the same way that they did in the '60s. Black people in the '60s were able to appeal to the conscience of America in a way that they won't continue to be able to do, because population demographics have changed. So we have to look at what is our relationship to the Latino community, the Asian-American community, the progressive White community, the Gay and Lesbian community, the Muslim community. There are all sorts of constituencies of people who I think agree in principle on a lot of issues, but a lot of times I find African-Americans have these boundaries built up and they're not going to even entertain the possibility that a link can be made with another group because it's so much about being Black, which I understand, but you've got to look at that in light of what's happening now.

Two more questions. One is about how you said how hip hop has become global—so that any other ethnic group can and does adopt hip hop—and what that means.

Well, I was in Tokyo once and I was in this club where they were playing Biggie Smalls. And I look out and I see a lot of Japanese people who are really into this music, dancing and getting into the groove, so to speak. And I notice one particular young lady who knows every word of a particular Biggie Smalls song. This is kind of fascinating to me. So afterwards, I go up to her and as I try to talk to her, it's immediately obvious that she doesn't speak English; she says, "I'm sorry I can't speak English." And I thought, this is fascinating. She knows every word to Biggie Smalls but she doesn't speak English. So I started to think about how, as American culture gets transmitted throughout the globe, what does it mean for someone in Japan or Turkey or Croatia or Brazil or Sweden to hear hip hop and *that* be their introduction to the English language, *that* be their introduction to America? It gives you a different spin than if you're reading textbooks from an American high school.

To me, what has happened is you now have hip hop, this culture which is about free expression that can be shaped and molded to fit any community and any experience. So hip hop gives people the opportunity to represent themselves in their own way. I have a number of students who have, over the years, given me CDs of Croatian hip hop or hip hop from Thailand, all over the world. People trying to express themselves. And hip hop is the venue that gives them that opportunity. And so, in that way, I think the global possibilities are already something that's very important and will continue to be so.

My other question is about the role of women in hip hop (you spoke about Mary J. Blige and the Coca-Cola commercial); and that's one of the most controversial areas too because of calling them bitches and hos—the whole misogyny that exists.

It's funny again, people ask that a lot. And it's almost like the word bitch and the word ho were invented by hip hop, and that's not true. And then I remember that famous Huey Newton quote about a place for Black women in the movement was prone.

That actually was Stokely Carmichael.

It was Stokely Carmichael. I'm sorry, I said Huey, it was Stokely.[2] Hip hop didn't invent sexism or misogyny. It doesn't mean that there aren't many instances: in many cases hip hop is sexist and misogynist; that's not something to treat lightly or dismiss. But hip hop is real and I think it exposes that people have those attitudes. It's also interesting to me—and this is something that really gets me in trouble because people don't want to deal with this, but I'm going to try to keep it real—that when I look out, I see a lot of African-American women who are very, very, very successful, financially speaking; they're visible in the culture; they're quite prominent. Terry McMillan, as an author, has made a lot of money dissing Black men. Oprah Winfrey has one of the most popular shows on television and you can count the Black men who are on that show. And when they're on that show, with a few exceptions, they are of a particular type. To me, that's cool. When you look at Black literature, for instance, it's dominated by Black women. You look at other areas of the culture—dominated by Black women. Hip hop is different in that it's dominated by Black men, so what's the deal? Why is that a problem?

The other thing is, when I listen to hip hop, I often hear people talk about how much love they have for their mother. Whereas, they also talk in hip hop, in many cases, about how much hatred they have for their father. So you've got to look at this issue for what it is. Hip hop did not start sexism or misogyny. People have been saying bitches and hos for a long time. I heard those words well before I heard a hip hop record. And again, you sort of have to look at that for what it is. What I do is, instead of saying hip hop is incomplete in this way, I look at the culture as a whole and I think you've always found that Black women have found places in the culture where they've expressed themselves and Black men have found places in the culture where they are able to express themselves. They're often not the same place. I don't see that as a problem. I see it just as a result of the fact that people express themselves in different ways based on the context. In that way hip hop is not off the hook, because it certainly is at times sexist and quite misogynist and that's, I think, very unfortunate. But I think it's also reflective of some larger issues that people sometimes don't want to talk about.

Let me ask you one final question. I'd like to pursue that some more but I know we're down to the last few minutes. Your own background: you say in your book that you flunked out of the University of Florida when you were 22; by 32 you were a tenured professor. Reflections on your transition and how that connects to this whole hip hop vision?

I went to college and my friends in college were the guys on the football team and the basketball team. These were my friends, this was my crew. One of the places on a college campus where you can find a direct connection to the street is in the athletic department because we know the role that these athletes serve in these major universities. But this was my experience. I got a real good street education. I didn't get a very good formal education because I didn't spend much time studying and applying myself. I was studying and applying myself to different things. And that information was quite valuable to me. I woke up one day and I was 21 and I was a young Black man in Detroit who didn't have a college degree and didn't have much of a direction in life and, I think, realized for the first time that I could end up on the street, I could end up in the joint, I could end up dead, I could end up like a lot of other Black men had ended up. And I didn't want to do that.

Around that same time, my father turned me on to *The Autobiography of Malcolm X* and again, like a lot of young brothers, I read *The Autobiography of Malcolm X* and it changed my life. I saw how Malcolm had come from the street but he was not going to let that hold him back. He taught himself to read while he was in the penitentiary by reading the dictionary from cover to cover. He read all these texts from all over the world; he didn't just read texts on Black issues. Malcolm was so serious and so intelligent but at the same time, he could relate to a cat on the street just as well as he could relate to the most educated individual in the world. And I really, in my mind, saw that as something I wanted to be able to do but I had to raise my game. At this point I got serious and finished college, went to graduate school and got a Ph.D. by the time I was 27. I was on a mission. I wanted to make up for lost time and I wanted to prove to all those people who doubted me that they had made a big mistake and I have been on that mission ever since. I've got five books, a hit movie, tenured professor at the number one film school in the world, I've been quoted in every major media outlet in this country—newspaper, magazine, television, radio. And there's a whole lot more to do.

I mention all that only to say that that sense of competition we were talking about earlier has inspired me and motivated me to do big things because I want to have an impact on people's minds. But it all goes back for me to that turning point in my life when I was just really just down on my ass and I encountered Malcolm. It really transformed my thinking. And I've often found some of the same experiences in hip hop. To me, a lot of hip hop is about social mobility, about moving up, about raising your game, about pulling yourself up, about doing it, doing the damn thing because otherwise you can just be another number. And so I find the expression of all those things in hip hop and it sort of parallels my life. That's my story; everybody's story is different. Its like Biggie said, "Birthdays was the worst days/Now we sip champagne when we thirsty/Damn right I like the life I live/'Cause I went from negative to positive/And it's all good." So when I hear that, and when I hear Jay-Z say, "I ran errands for the bosses/'til I became one/now I got linen in the closet"—that inspired me. It continues to inspire me because in my own life I found similarities and I take again what's useful and discard that which is not.

Thank you very much, Dr. Boyd. It's been a pleasure.

Study Questions

1. Are political engagement and material wealth mutually exclusive endeavors?
2. How has the political terrain for Black Americans changed since the Civil Rights era of the 1960s?
3. How does the presence of a major social movement impact the political possibilities of popular music?

Notes

1. [*Ed.* H.N.I.C: "head niggaz in charge."]
2. Actually, there were sexist "pronouncements" by both "SNCC and Panther leaders that the role of women was best exercised in bed" (Michael Dawson, Black Visions, p. 117).—Y. N.

30

The Challenge of Rap Music from Cultural Movement to Political Power

Though there are numerous examples of politically engaged rap performers such as Chuck D, Dead Prez, KRS-One and many others, hip-hop's political impact is perhaps best evidenced in the emerging political bloc that hip-hop audiences comprise. It was that desire to create a political bloc that led to the first National Hip-Hop Political Convention during the summer of 2004.

Bakari Kitwana was one of the founders of the Hip-Hop Political Convention and his essay examines the role that the hip-hop generation can play in elevating the issues critical, such as depressed wages, a racially biased judicial system and environmental justice, to hip-hop's core constituencies to a national level.

The Challenge of Rap Music from Cultural Movement to Political Power

Bakari Kitwana

Mr. Mayor, imagine this was your backyard
Mr. Governor, imagine it's your kids that starve imagine your kids gotta sling
crack to survive, swing a Mac to be live ...

Nas, "I Want to Talk to You"

In June 2001, Rush Communications CEO Russell Simmons convened a hip-hop summit in New York City. With the theme "Taking Back Responsibility," the summit focused its agenda on ways to strengthen rap music's growing influence. The 300 participants included major rap artists and industry executives as well as politicians, religious and community leaders, activists, and scholars. Few forces other than rap music, now one of the most powerful forces in American popular culture, could bring together such a diverse gathering of today's African American leaders. In many ways, the summit signaled hip-hop as the definitive cultural movement of our generation.

As the major cultural movement of our time, hip-hop (its music, fashion, attitude, style, and language) is undoubtedly one of the core influences for young African Americans born between 1965 and 1984. To fully appreciate the extent to which this is true, think back for a moment about the period between the mid-1970s and the early 1980s, before rap became a mainstream phenomenon. Before MTV. Before BET's *Rap City*. Before *The Fresh Prince of Bel Air*. Before *House Party* I or II. It is difficult now to imagine Black youth as a nearly invisible entity in American popular culture. But in those days, that was the case. When young Blacks were visible, it was mostly during the six o'clock evening news reports of crime in urban America.

In contrast, today it is impossible not to see young Blacks in the twenty-first century's public square—the public space of television, film, and the Internet. Our images now extend far beyond crime reports. For most of our contemporaries, it's difficult to recall when this was not the case. Because of rap, the voices, images, style, attitude, and language of young Blacks have become central in American culture, transcending geographic, social, and economic boundaries.

To be sure, professional athletes, especially basketball players, have for decades been young, Black, highly visible, and extremely popular. Yet, their success just didn't translate into visibility for young Blacks overall. For one thing, the conservative culture of professional sports, central to their identity, was often at odds with the rebellious vein inherent in the new Black youth culture. While household-name ball players towed the generic "don't do drugs and stay in school" party line, rappers, the emissaries of the new Black youth culture, advocated more anti-establishment slogans like "fuck the police." Such slogans were vastly more in synch with the hard realities facing young Blacks—so much so that as time marched on and hip-hop culture further solidified its place in American popular culture, basketball culture would also come to feel its influence.

Largely because of rap music, one can tune in to the voices and find the faces of America's Black youth at any point in the day. Having proven themselves as marketable entertainers with successful music careers, rappers star in television sit-coms and film and regularly endorse corporate products (such as Lil' Kim—Candies, Missy Elliott—the Gap, and Common, Fat Joe, and the Goodie Mob—Sprite). In the mid-1980s, a handful of corporations began incorporating hip-hop into their advertisement spots. Most were limited to run-of-the-mill product endorsements. By the late 1990s, however, ads incorporating hip-hop—even those promoting traditionally conservative companies—became increasingly steeped in the subtleties of hip-hop culture. Setting the standard with their extremely hip-hop savvy 1994 Voltron campaign, Sprite broke away from the straight-up celebrity endorsement format. Says Coca-Cola global marketing manager Darryl Cobbin, who was on the cutting edge of this advertising strategy: "I wanted to usher in a real authenticity in terms of hip-hop in advertising. We wanted to pay respect to the music *and* the culture. What's important is the value of hip-hop culture, not only as an image, but as a method of communication."

By the late 1990s, advertisers like the Gap, Nike, AT&T, and Sony soon followed suit and incorporated hip-hop's nuances into their advertising campaigns. As a result, the new Black youth culture resonates throughout today's media, regardless of what companies are selling (from soft drinks and footwear to electronics and telecommunications).

Of course, none of this happened overnight. In fact, more important than the commercialization of rap was the less visible cultural movement on the ground in anyhood USA. In rap's early days, before it became a thriving commercial entity, DJ party culture provided the backdrop for this off-the-radar cultural movement. What in the New York City metropolitan area took the form of DJ battles and MC chants emerged in Chicago as the house party scene, and in D.C. it was go-go. In other regions of the country, the local movement owed its genesis to rap acts like Run DMC, who broke through to a national audience in the early 1980s. In any case, by the mid-1980s, this local or underground movement began to emerge in the form of cliques, crews, collectives, or simply kids getting together primarily to party, but in the process rhyming, DJ-ing, dancing, and tagging. Some, by the early 1990s, even moved into activism. In large cities like Chicago, San Francisco, Houston, Memphis, New Orleans, Indianapolis, and Cleveland and even in smaller cities and suburban areas like Battle Creek, Michigan, and Champaign, Illinois, as the '80s turned to the '90s, more and more young Blacks were coming together in the name of hip-hop.

In the early 1980s, the "in" hip-hop fashion for New York City Black youth included Gazelles (glasses), sheepskins and leather bombers (coats), Clarks (shoes), nameplates, and name belts. In terms of language, Five Percenter expressions like "word is bond" were commonplace. These hip-hop cultural expressions in those days were considered bizarre by Black kids from other regions of the country. A student at the University of Pennsylvania at the time, Conrad Muhammad, the hip-hop minister, speaks to this in reminiscing on the National Black Students Unity Conference he organized in 1987:

> Jokers were getting off buses with shower caps on, perms and curls. MTV and BET had not yet played a role in standardizing Black youth culture the way they do today. Young people from different cities weren't all dressing the same way. Brothers and sisters were stepping off buses saying "we're from the University of Nebraska, Omaha." "We're from University of Minnesota." "We're from Cal Long Beach."

But by the early to mid-1990s, hip-hop's commercialized element had Black kids on the same page, regardless of geographic region. In this hip-hop friendly national environment, hip-hop designers like Enyce, Mecca, and FUBU were thriving, multi-platinum sales for rap artists were routine (and dwarfed the 1980s mark of success: gold sales), and hip-hop expressions like "blowin' up," "representin'," and "keepin' it real" worked their way into the conversational language of Black youth around the country. Contrast this to the mid-1980s when even those deep into hip-hop didn't see the extent to which a national cultural movement was unfolding.

"Before the Fresh Fest Tour of 1984, few folks were defining hip-hop culture as hip-hop culture," says Hashim Shomari, author of *From the Underground: Hip-Hop as an Agent of Social Change.* "That was a relatively 1990s phenomenon." Practitioners like Africa Bambaataa, Grandmaster Flash, Fab-Five Freddy, Chuck D, and KRS-One were on the frontlines of those who saw the need to flesh out the definitions. Also, it wasn't until the early 1990s that breakthrough books like Joseph Eure and James Spady's *Nation-Conscious Rap* (1991), Michael Gonzales and Havelock Nelson's *Bring the Noise: A Guide to Rap Music and Hip-Hop Culture* (1991), and Tricia Rose's *Black Noise: Rap Music and Black Culture in Contemporary America* (1994) began to discuss hip-hop as an influential culture that went beyond the commercial.

Without question, rap's national exposure played a key role in the uniform way in which the local cultural manifestations evolved. More recently, given rap's commercial success, alongside limited employment options beyond minimum-wage jobs for young Blacks, hip-hop's cultural movement at the local level is increasingly marked by an entrepreneurial element. On the West Coast, East Coast, in southern and northern cities, and in rural and suburban areas in between, young Blacks are pressing their own CDs and selling them "out the trunk" regionally.[1] Many of them are hoping to eventually put their city on the hip-hop map. What all this around the way activity has in common is that kids are tuned in to the same wavelength via hip-hop, some aspiring to be the next Air Jordan of hip-hop, others engaging in what is to them a way of life without commercial popular culture aspirations, and still others tuning in as a basic engagement with the youth culture of our time.

The commercialized element of this cultural movement and the off-the-radar one fuel each other. The underground element provides a steady stream of emerging talent that in turn gets absorbed into commercialization. That new voice and talent again inspires more discussion (about the art form, new styles, trends, language, and larger issues and themes) and more talent at the local level, which later infuses the commercial manifestation of the cultural movement. Case in point: the more recent wave of talent (say, Master P out of New Orleans, Eve from Philly, and Nelly from St. Louis) is similar to the much earlier waves like the Geto Boys out of Houston and Compton's NWA. Those earlier waves of talent (the Geto Boys, NWA, Too Short, E-40, and others) most certainly provided inspiration for the No Limit Soldiers and Ruff Ryders, who came later. Like the earliest waves of artists, each group represents its distinct region, while tapping into the national movement. In turn, Master P, Eve, and Nelly will influence the next wave of talent breaking from the margins into the mainstream.

It's not exactly a chicken-or-egg question, however. Hip-hop as a culture indisputably emerged in the South Bronx in the late 1970s, and in other parts of the northeast shortly thereafter, before branching out around the country in the early 1980s. What's arguable is the extent to which hip-hop would have become the national cultural movement that it is today without commercialization.

In 1988, rapper Chuck D of the rap group Public Enemy described rap music as "the Black CNN." This was certainly true at the grassroots level at the time. However, the decade of the 1990s proved even more profound as rap music became thoroughly accepted and promoted in mainstream American popular culture. As such, rap provided the foundation for a resounding young Black mainstream presence that went far beyond rap music itself.

Understanding the degree to which the local and commercial are deeply entrenched and interdependent, one can began to grasp the far-reaching effects of hip-hop on young Blacks. As the primary vehicle through which young Blacks have achieved a national voice and presence, rap music transmits the new Black youth culture to a national audience. And in the same way as the mainstream media establishes the parameters for national discussion for the nation at large, rap music sets the tone for Black youth. As the national forum for Black youth concerns and often as the impetus for discussion around those issues, rap music has done more than any one entity to help our generation forge a distinct identity.

Another important aspect of what makes rap so substantive in the lives of young Blacks is its multilingual nature. In addition to beaming out hip-hop culture, rap also conveys elements of street culture, prison culture, and the new Black youth culture. Often all of these elements overlap within rap's lyrics and visual images. In the process, images and ideas that define youth culture for this generation—such as designer clothes, like Sean Jean, Phat Farm, and Tommy Hilfiger, ever-changing styles of dress, and local colloquialisms—are beamed out to a captive national audience. Also transmitted are cues of personal style, from cornrows and baby dreads to body piercing and tattoos.

And finally, even more important than fashion, style, and language, the new Black culture is encoded within the images and lyrics of rap and thus help define what it means to be young and Black at the dawn of the millennium. In the process, rap music has become the primary vehicle for transmitting culture and values to this generation, relegating Black families, community centers, churches, and schools to the back burner.

To be sure, rap marked a turning point, a shift from practically no public voice for young Blacks—or at best an extremely marginalized one—to Black youth culture as the rage in mainstream popular culture. And more than just increasing Black youth visibility, rap articulated publicly and on a mass scale many of this generation's beliefs, relatively unfiltered by the corporate structures that carried it. Even when censored with bleeps or radio-friendly "clean" versions, the messages were consistent with the new Black youth culture and more often than not struck a chord with young Blacks, given our generation's unique collective experiences. At the same time, the burgeoning grassroots arts movement was under way. All was essential to rap's movement into the mainstream and its emergence as the paramount cultural movement of our time.

Although hip-hop has secured its place as a cultural movement, its biggest challenge lies ahead. In the late 1980s when gangsta rap first emerged, community activists and mainstream politicians of the civil rights generation began to challenge rap's content. This criticism forced a dialogue that revealed one of the Black community's best kept secrets, the bitter generational divide between hip-hop generationers and our civil rights/Black power parents.

The key concern was Black cultural integrity: how have the very public images of young Blacks in hip-hop music and culture affected the larger Black community? Central to this discussion was the pervasive use of offensive epithets in rap lyrics, such as "nigga," "bitch," and "ho," all of which reinforce negative stereotypes about Blacks. What was the price of this remarkable breakthrough in the visibility of young Blacks in the mainstream culture? Had young rappers simply transferred images of young Black men as criminals from news reports to entertainment? And finally, had the growing visibility of young Black entertainers further marginalized young Black intellectuals and writers, who have remained nearly invisible?

A handful of responses emerged. The response from the rap industry was unanimous: free speech is a constitutional right. The predominant response from rap artists themselves was a proverbial head in the sand. Most reasoned that the older generation was out of touch with the concerns of hip-hop generationers. Just as our parents' generation was unfamiliar with the music, the thinking went, when it came to other matters of our generation, particularly issues involving hip-hop, they, likewise, didn't know what they were talking about. By and large, the question of rap's attack on Black cultural integrity went unaddressed. In fact, the use of incendiary words like "nigga" and "bitch" has become so commonplace in rap's lyrics that today even those in rap's growing white audience routinely use them when referring to each other and often their Black peers (a matter Spike Lee vaguely touched on in the film *Bamboozled*).

Lately, as the theme of the Simmons summit "Taking Back Responsibility" suggests, hip-hop is again undertaking the critical task of questioning its relationship to the community. David Mays, publisher of the hip-hop magazine *The Source*, and Reverend Al Sharpton held a series of summits eight months prior to the Simmons summit, which called for a code of conduct in light of arrests of numerous rappers and the growing association of rappers with criminality. Minister Conrad Muhammad, dubbed the hip-hop minister for the moral voice he's long brought to the hip-hop community, felt the Mays–Sharpton gathering didn't go far enough. Muhammad called for a summit of Black rap artists, rap industry executives, and activists to discuss ways of holding the hip-hop industry accountable to the Black community. Appalled by Muhammad's moral challenge to the rap industry, Simmons countered Muhammad with a call for his own summit to be held within a few weeks of the Muhammad one.

Simmons, a major player in the rap industry who earlier began flexing his political muscle by reaching out to Democratic Party insiders like Hillary Clinton in her bid for the U.S. Senate, brought together the largest and most media-celebrated summit to date. Joining rap industry insiders were African American notables like minister Louis Farrakhan, NAACP head Kweisi Mfume, U.S. Representative Cynthia McKinney, and scholars Cornel West and Michael Eric Dyson.

The Simmons event was impressive in terms of sheer numbers and diverse backgrounds. But where it most seriously came up short was in its failure to incorporate the grassroots segment of hip-hop's cultural movement, especially hip-hop generation activists. When hip-hop's true influence as a cultural movement is finally understood, events like these will recognize that the very same synergy at the heart of hip-hop's commercial success has also informed our generation's activists and political theorists. Just as some record executives can give us a blueprint for blowin' up rap acts, the ideas that our generation's activists hold about maximizing rap's potential for social change have been seasoned in their day-to-day work and experience. If our generation's cultural movement is to evolve to have a meaningful political impact, the local segments of hip-hop's cultural movement—from hip-hop generation activists to local entrepreneurs to the everyday hip-hop kids on the block—must not only be brought to the table, but must have a major voice.

Furthermore, rather than centering the discussion within our own generation—*and*, yes, including the expertise and insight of our parents' generation—the invitation-only Simmons summit turned to the mostly liberal–integrationist civil rights leadership and music industry executives. The result was predictable: a combination of the traditional music industry call for free speech, which allows for continued blockbuster sales without disrupting the minstrel-esque proven formula for success, and the traditional civil rights activist call for young voters to support Democratic candidates for public office. Neither of these same-game-with-another-name reforms challenge civil righters or industry insiders to do anything different than what they are already doing. Moreover, pushing activists of the civil rights generation to the forefront of this effort is tantamount to casting older-generation R&B singers like Dionne Warwick and Lionel Richie as leads in a 'hood film or featuring them at a concert alongside ODB or Lil' Kim.

Until hip-hop is recognized as a broad cultural movement, rather than simply an influential moneymaker, those who seek to tap into hip-hop's potential to impact social change should not expect substantive progress. A unified front between hip-hop's commercial and grassroots sectors on the issue of sociopolitical action would change the nature of the dialogue. For example, in the same way that the hip-hop community as a cultural movement inherently answered the question, "what is hip-hop culture?" a new inclusive framework inevitably would answer the question, "what do we mean by politicizing the hip-hop genera-tion?" Is our goal to run hip-hop generationers for office, to turn out votes for Democrats and Republicans, to form a third party, or to provide our generation with a more concrete polit-ical education?

Indications of the endless possibilities of this unified front approach are evident in the following examples of rap's demonstrated success in extending its influence beyond popular culture.

The Haitian Refugee Crisis

In April 1997, the Fugees held a concert in Port-au-Prince, Haiti, to raise money for local char-ities and to bring international media attention to the economic and political plight of Haiti's people. Financed mostly by Wyclef Jean, the event was also supported by local companies. Unfortunately, the effort got caught between U.S. foreign policy and the type of corruption that has come to plague new governments on the heels of dictators. As a result, the funds raised never reached the intended charities. Shortly before the event, the Haitian government took control of the fundraiser, including handling all receipts. Afterward they issued a report declaring that the event only broke even. The event did succeed in gaining media attention, however. Beyond that, it demonstrated one way that successful American entertainers can support larger international causes.

Rappers and Mumia Abu-Jamal

One of the major issues of our time has been the disproportionate representation of African Amer-icans in both the penal system and on death row. This issue is critical to a generation that during its lifetime has seen the Black prison population increase from fewer than 250,000 to nearly 1 million. Mumia Abu-Jamal's fight for justice brought the issue to the fore. Abu-Jamal was convicted in 1982 for the murder of Daniel Faulkner, a white Philadelphia cop. He and Faulkner were shot while Abu-Jamal was attempting to break up a confrontation between his brother and the officer. Abu-Jamal was later sentenced to death. Supporters say the former Black Panther was railroaded by a racist police department and received an unfair trial. Abu-Jamal insists that he did not commit the crime and says that he is being punished for his politics. The rap community's participation in Abu-Jamal's fight for justice persists in rap lyrics, in support at rallies, and at anti-death penalty benefits. KRS-One, Channel Live, and other rappers have been among Abu-Jamal's supporters. As a result of these efforts, few hip-hop generation kids are unfamiliar with Abu-Jamal's fight for justice. Most have an opinion on the death penalty and are aware of the inconsistencies in American justice for Blacks and whites.

The Million Man March

The Million Man March was the largest mass gathering in the history of the country. Young Blacks turned out in huge numbers partly because rappers have made it fashionable for Blacks of this generation to support Black causes. Furthermore, rappers like Ice Cube, Ice T, Puff Daddy, Das EFX, Common Sense, and others strongly supported the event. This certainly helped to heighten the importance of the march in the minds of young Blacks.

The Million Youth March

At the eleventh hour, the Million Youth March languished under various obstacles that seemed destined to sabotage the event. Responding to some of the needs to pull the event off, Master

P made a major donation to the event that helped the show to go on. As contributions from hip-hop generation athletes and entertainers to larger causes remain few and far between, the gesture was a much-needed breath of fresh air. In 1998, Danny Glover made a $1 million contribution to TransAfrica, the Washington, D.C.-based organization that lobbies on behalf of U.S. foreign policy toward Africa and the Caribbean Basin. Financial support from the hip-hop community for serious political efforts remains rare. Master P's support for the Million Youth March is an example of how rap artists can make the difference to such efforts.

East Coast/West Coast Conflict

Probably no other event in rap's history has received as much coverage in the mainstream media as the so-called East Coast/West Coast beef—imagined and real antagonism between rappers and fans on the East Coast (mostly New York City) and the West Coast (mostly rappers and fans in Los Angeles). The conflict, which in print often centered on rap labels Death Row and Bad Boy, climaxed with the gangland-style murders of Tupac Shakur in 1996 and Biggie Smalls in 1997. In the wake of their deaths, many rappers participated in efforts to end the seemingly out-of-control antagonisms. From a rapper summit called by Louis Farrakhan's Nation of Islam to rap lyrics denouncing the East–West feud, rappers like Nas, Jay-Z, Common, Snoop, and others succeeded in reducing East–West antagonism.

Social Programs and Foundations

Several rappers have founded social programs and foundations to give back to the communities that produced them; among them are the Wu Charitable Foundation, Camp Cool J, the Refugee Project, Christopher Wallace Foundation, and the Tupac Amaru Shakur Memorial Foundation. All of these organizations focus their efforts on urban youth who lack opportunities and access. Few venture far beyond the typical feel-good effort that boosts the celebrity's publicity. However, some of these programs have features that encourage community responsibility and participation. For example, Daddy's House Social Programs, Sean "P-Diddy" Combs' seven-year-old program for children aged 6–16, sponsors a Saturday school that teaches regular academic courses as well as manhood/womanhood training for teens. Daddy's House also sends a group of children to Ghana and South Africa as part of an Urban Youth Tour. In return, each student makes a presentation to their respective communities when they return home. Lauryn Hill's Refugee Project conducts a mentorship program where each child is assigned two mentors (a college student and a professional). In addition, Camp Hill, the Refugee Project's summer camp, has a required family day component built into the two-week camp, which parents of campers must attend. The Tupac Amaru Shakur Memorial Foundation helps former inmates who are single-parent mothers make the transition back to society. These are examples of community efforts that rappers have supported with their recently acquired wealth. These efforts can serve as a cornerstone for even greater, more cooperative efforts.

Most of the activities concerned with social change have taken place outside of the limelight of rap's growing popularity. In some cases, the activity may seem superficial, but careful examination reveals that some rappers individually and collectively have consistently responded to issues important to this generation. The response may not have always been effective, or even politically correct, but these are the types of activities that have galvanized community-building efforts. The extent of the impact seems to be directly proportionate to the degree that such efforts work themselves deeper into the fabric of hip-hop's cultural movement.

Rap music's ability to influence social change should not be taken lightly. The U.S. Department of Health and Human Services reported that rates of teen pregnancy fell by 4 percent in

1997 and that rates decreased by 17 percent in the 1990s overall. Social policy has had very little impact on this and related issues in the lives of America's poor. In many cases, social policy has only exacerbated the problems. Experts have offered numerous explanations for the decline, but none have considered rap music a factor. Perhaps rap music's influence as a transmitter of ideas should be more carefully considered.

At least one team of researchers at Emory University's Rollins School of Public Health agrees. In a recent study, they found that after Black boys and girls 11–14 years old listened to rappers like Big Pun, the Goodie Mob, and Lil' Kim, they were more knowledgeable about AIDS and were better prepared to discuss safe sex, condom use, and abstinence. "The knowledge they gain about themselves and the disease helps kids make informed decisions about sexual behavior and makes them less likely to engage in risky sexual practices," said Torrence Stephens, lead author of the study. This study adds to the growing body of evidence that hip-hop is much more than entertainment.

In each of these efforts, there is an *informal* exchange between hip-hop's commercial and grassroots sectors. A *formal* unified front could effect even greater change. Here are a few other ways that a unified front could begin to expand rap's influence into social and political arenas.

First, a unified front of rap artists, industry insiders, hip-hop generation activists, and everyday kids on the block could begin to challenge rap's ever-growing listening audience of white youth. How can that relationship build on America's unkept promise of inclusion? If this engagement with Black youth culture is more than simply a fleeting fascination, what will it take to motivate white youth to make the transition from simply enjoying and interacting with hip-hop to using their own power and influence to enhance the quality of American race relations?

In an April 5, 2001, *New York Times* article titled "Pressed Against a 'Race Ceiling,'" Black elected officials lamented the difficulty they have getting elected to statewide office where majority-white populations won't vote for them, a sentiment expressed by New Orleans Mayor Marc Morial in his comments to the *Times*: "People have asked, 'Wouldn't you like to run for the Senate, for governor or attorney general?' And I say, 'Certainly, I'd be interested in that at some point. But in Louisiana they haven't elected a statewide African-American official since the 1880s.'"

Since the passage of the Voting Rights Act of 1965, only one African American has been elected governor and only two have been elected to the U.S. Senate. If rap's white listening audience translated its familiarity and interest in Black youth culture to their voting habits and challenged their parents to deal with the continuing racial contradictions as well, this glass ceiling would be obliterated, and race relations as we know them would never be the same.

Second, young white movers and shakers within the rap industry could be challenged by a unified front to use their knowledge and insight to further narrow the racial divide not only inside the industry but outside of it. Insisting on multi-ethnic hires and diversified staffing in the industry, rather than hiding behind the old excuse "we can't find any qualified ones," and insisting on equal and fair pay across the board would be a good start. Likewise, challenging stereotypical and degrading practices, images, and lyrics in the rap industry is a must.

Third, a unified front could challenge successful rap artists to explore ways of pooling their resources and influence to lead and assist community rebuilding and economic revitalization efforts in poor communities. Activists from the civil rights generation challenged large corporations that do a significant amount of business with African Americans to support development within those communities; a unified front between commercial and around the way hip-hop could do the same. The seemingly endless list of companies marketing products to young Blacks through hip-hop's influence (from those whose ads lace rap music magazines and those who sponsor awards shows to rap labels themselves) should be challenged to reciprocate by supporting community development projects. Such efforts would contribute to and strengthen Black community development and further endear artists to fans. Local community activists will support these efforts to the degree that they improve the day-to-day lives of community residents.

Recently, the Church of God in Christ in West Los Angeles finished building a new $60 million sanctuary with the help of members, who include several major Black entertainers; with their support, a vision became a reality. In another effort, the 2000 Watts Foundation created by MTV VJ and R&B singer Tyrese is bringing together corporate sponsors to build a community center in Watts, Tyrese's hometown. Efforts like these provide models for future projects.

Fourth, a united front could challenge the rap industry to finally resolve the issue of hip-hop's responsibility to Black cultural integrity. Rappers like Chuck D, Queen Latifah, Lauryn Hill, Will Smith, and Common have long tried to raise the bar on lyrical content. Community activists like C. Delores Tucker and Calvin Butts and more recently Conrad Muhammad have challenged rap artists and the industry to do more to make socially responsible lyrics as pervasive in hip-hop as those that advance stereotypes. Along with the mainstreaming of rap throughout the 1990s, elements of street culture and prison culture have become more and more dominant in rap lyrics, compounding the now decade-old problem of stereotypical images in hip-hop.

Just as problematic is hip-hop's growing tendency to cross over into the adult entertainment industry—from the soft porn images of rap music videos and the XXX hip-hop video *Doggystyle* (a Snoop Dogg/Larry Flynt joint venture) to emerging magazines that blur the lines between pornography and hip-hop. Not only is hip-hop a major force in the lives of hip-hop generationers at the older end of the age group, but it also heavily impacts those at the younger end of the spectrum, some of whom are just approaching their teenage years. The commercial rap industry must begin to more seriously weigh the impact of exposing children to age-inappropriate (adult) situations. A unified front could develop workable approaches for addressing these issues. As Muhammad and Simmons squared off, Bill Stepheney, political activist and CEO of Stepson Media, put it succinctly in his comments to the *New York Post* (May 8, 2001): "What is the line that we [artists and industry executives] are unwilling to cross for profits? Is there a line? Or is it completely laissez-faire?"

Finally, the "Taking Back Responsibility" summit should be applauded for advocating artist development. Much more can and should be done in this area. An ongoing alliance between those in the commercial industry and those at the grassroots level would inevitably build on the Black community's traditional call for self-determination through greater Black ownership, control, and influence within the industry beyond being "the show." The current generation of rap industry insiders needs to develop a new generation of songwriters, performers, and music industry executives with real power and ownership within the industry. Kalamu Ya Salaam, activist-poet and former executive director of the New Orleans Jazz and Heritage Foundation, identified this need as part of the solution to America's long-standing race problem. In his *What Is Life: Reclaiming the Black Blues Self* (Third World Press, 1994), he proposes the music industry as an important sector for Black economic development:

> A current possible solution is what I call horizontal economic development at a mass level in a specific economic sector. The traditional vertical mode of economic development is simply individual wealth generated by climbing the earnings ladder in a given field. The miscellaneous array of athletes and entertainers celebrated in *Ebony* and *Black Enterprise* are a prime example of this in our community.... African Americans must make a concerted effort to carve out a significant niche in the ... music business.... It offers the broadest

array of opportunities for a diversity of skill areas while remaining focused in a particular economic sector. . . . The music business is one of the few segments of the modern American economy in which [African Americans] have any significant leverage. . . .

The real challenge of integration is to capture control of economic development. We are the creative labor of a significant portion of the music industry. Now is the time to become the controllers of the fruit of our labor. African Americans desperately need economic development and a move on the music industry is a feasible route. We make the music. Now, let's make the money.

A working unified front would greatly enhance rap's potential to contribute to needed sociopolitical transformations. The real question is this: why should hip-hop generationers continue to participate in and support a multibillion dollar industry if it fails to in any way address the critical problems facing our generation? What good is rap music if it does nothing more than give young Blacks the opportunity to "dance to our own degradation" (as Black studies scholar Maulana Karenga has noted) and if it enriches only a few at the expense of the many? If rap is to stand as not only the most significant cultural movement of our time but one of history's most salient, and I believe it will, hip-hop generationers both inside and outside of the rap music industry must rise to the challenge. All the components for a mass political movement in our lifetime are in place and functioning—but separate. Do we dare join them together?

Study Questions

1. Can popular culture and music inspire and sustain political movement?
2. Does the hip-hop political bloc have a role in policing or reflecting the lyrical content of hip-hop artists?
3. Are Hip-Hop Generation voters viewed as a legitimate voting bloc?

Note

1. My emphasis here is on Black youth—no disrespect to the countless folks of other racial and ethnic groups down with hip-hop. This is not to say that Latino and to a lesser extent Asian and Native American youth have not been influential in and touched by hip-hop culture. Neither is it meant to ignore the distinctiveness of Caribbean Americans. More recently white kids, a large segment of hip-hop's listening audience, are jumping into the fray. Nevertheless, rap music indisputably remains dominated by Black youth in both its commercial and local manifestations.

31

Voyeurism and Resistance in Rap Music Videos

For politically engaged artists whose lyrics and imagery are an extension of their political views, the marketplace presents a fertile, though complicated location. On the one hand, the marketplace offers the widest audience possible for many of these artists, but it also increases the heavy scrutiny of their lyrics. For those political artists who engage in anti-racist rhetoric, particularly that which challenges anti-black racism, there is the possibility of alienating one of the largest segments of hip-hop consumers. Additionally, given the focus on issues of authenticity or "street cred" in contemporary hip-hop, political artists often have to balance audience desire for "realness" with their political sensibilities.

Dead Prez is an example of artists who have to negotiate their celebrity with their political opinions. In her essay, sociologist Jennifer Lena examines how the group manages the white voyeuristic gaze while also remaining real and politically engaged. Specifically, Lena highlights how groups like Dead Prez subvert the voyeuristic gaze in order to shed light on the structural conditions that inform their politics.

Voyeurism and Resistance in Rap Music Videos

Jennifer C. Lena

The cultural hegemony promulgated by media corporations is often blamed for emptying political content from commodity culture. I argue that the meanings of popular culture are not fixed or guaranteed in advance by the operations of an economic base, but rather that these meanings are the site of struggle between classes. This theory of articulation draws from the work of Antonio Gramsci and Stuart Hall, and presumes that cultural forms and practices have relative autonomy from socioeconomic structures of power, and so meaning and cultural change can be effected through negotiation. Popular culture is thus a critical site for struggles between dominant and subordinate groups.[1] Subordinate groups resist not through the rejection of dominant ideology but through its adaptation. Thus, dominant discourse depicts "pimps" as a scourge, while, for a time, subordinate discourse frames them as anti-heroes, achieving the success and independence that would be denied to them. In this essay I am interested in how objects and practices are *disarticulated* from their dominant racialized and classed meanings and *rearticulated* in new contexts.

In a deep reading of a single set of rap images, dead prez's 2004 music video for their single "Hell Yeah!," I illustrate the rearticulation of race and class identities and of minority group members' relationship to conspicuous consumption.[2] dead prez, a Brooklyn-based rap duo comprising MCs M-1 and stic.man, is often cited as a commercially successful group performing "socially conscious," even transgressive, songs. The video documents the carjacking of white tourists lost in an inner city ghetto. The family's hand-held camcorder is stolen by the carjackers (members of the group dead prez), who then visually document vignettes from their life, in a *cinema verité* style. In so doing, they appropriate racist stereotypes of the ghetto to articulate a "nigga" identity that is both "revolutionary" and "gangsta." I demonstrate, contra Hall that the rearticulation of stereotypes reveals intra-group differences that dominant representations have concealed; thus, the relationships between representation and power are unveiled and contested.[3] In illustrating one case of the oppositional or resistant use of the gaze, I seek to engage the politics of possibility, particularly around race and class, offered by hip-hop as a product in and of commodity culture.

Voyeurism

Scholars celebrate rappers as "organic intellectuals" who constitute African Americans as subjects of knowledge, converting their particular histories and experiences into knowledge, giving significance to that experience, and then liberating significance from experience.[4] However, their claims are countered by those who argue that the predominant representations of race and class

463

in rap music affirm stereotypic depictions of spaces and people.[5] According to this critique, black inner-city communities are defined as the origin of social dysfunctions and threats to civil society.[6] The racial markers of people in these neighborhoods resonate with traditional discourse on blackness—that these Americans are angry, violent, unintelligent, criminally minded, and hyper-sexualized. The gendered discourse of rap lyrics and images reinforces male dominance and patriarchy through stereotyping women as sexual objects. Consequently, "terms like *nihilistic, dysfunctional,* and *pathological* have become the most common adjectives to describe contemporary black culture."[7] Furthermore, because dominant ideologies interpolate the consumer, making us feel as if we freely choose our consumptive practices while choosing on our behalf, the legions of white fans of rap have their racist and classist impulses confirmed with the "evidence" that comes, seemingly in an un-mediated fashion, from subordinate peoples themselves. The effectiveness of this mechanism is augmented by the discourse about rap insisting that it is "authentic street journalism." Thus, the white listener/viewer is depicted as a voyeur, observing a "highly charged theater of race in which white listeners become guilty eavesdroppers on the putative private conversation of the inner city."[8]

The noun "voyeur" links sexual titillation to the (secret) observation of a naked body or sexual acts by others. For Freud, scopophilia produces sexual stimulation or satisfaction "principally from looking," even if the gaze is not directed at others' naked bodies or sexual acts.[9] Thus, voyeurism has come to connote one who makes a practice of observing sensational, sordid, or otherwise private actions. This connotation frames the analyses of scholars who have used the concept of voyeurism as a lens for understanding the motives of white audiences for blackface minstrels, jazz and blues, and television and film, among others.[10]

The voyeuristic gaze is a learned mode of apperception that draws upon stereotypic notions of the "other." This conception of "the gaze" draws upon Foucault's conception of the power of surveillance to produce an explanation of how ideological hegemony is encoded over the objects of its view.[11] Voyeurs mobilize preconceptions of experience, landscape, and people to see "exotic" others. They draw upon expectations of what "typical black behavior" or "the inner city" will look like, when encountered. The presumption is that members of the dominant group utilize the voyeuristic gaze to consume, understand, or authenticate images.

In the case considered here, a group of rap artists visually highlights the significance of the white gaze and its role in the perpetuation of racial narratives. All too often, scholarship on rap focuses on the music, *to the exclusion* of its centrality to other media, despite the growing awareness that the rap community has led a revolution in merchandizing and marketing, and that images of rap saturate our visual space.[12] In this essay, I focus on visual images while relating these to ideas that are also and simultaneously developed in music lyrics and discourse.

Urban Spaces

The voyeurism of white rap fans is premised on the exoticism of the lyrical and visual content of those rhymes.[13] To wit, Samuels argues that "white fascination with rap sprang from a particular kind of racial tourism."[14] Rap lyrics and images most often locate protagonists within urban American spaces populated by lower- and working-class African Americans. The "ghetto" or "hood" is the dominant metaphor for the African American lower class.[15] The rap ghetto is exotic: Even to those rappers who claim it as home, the ghetto is an unnatural or hyper-real place, constructed from both stock images and hyperbolic renditions of lived experience. Thus, rap "attracts listeners for whom the 'ghetto' is a place of adventure, unbridled violence, erotic fantasy, and/or an imaginary alternative to suburban boredom."[16] Inner-city communities are defined as the origin of social dysfunctions and threats to civil society, effectively producing a problem and rendering it intelligible to the public.[17] It defines the ghetto as the origin of social dysfunctions (including teenage pregnancy, sexual violence, and violent crime) and articulates these dysfunctions as threats to social order.[18] Thus, the racial voyeuristic gaze draws upon the most pernicious *ethnic* stereotypes. This representation of the ghetto as dangerous has more than symbolic importance; it provides an impetus and rationale for the mobilization of coercive technologies of the state specifically against black, urban, poor Americans.[19]

In "Hell Yeah!" dead prez affirms stereotypic conceptions of the ghetto in several ways: by depicting only residents of color and defending the space against incursions by whites, through particularly resonant illustrations of violence, eroticism, and crime, and by celebrating these spaces' sources of meaning—to them as men, as African Americans, as members of the working poor, and as a rap group.

In the first scenes of "Hell Yeah!," we see a family of stereotypical middle-American tourists through the lens of their hand-held camcorder, mugging in front of a copula marked with the words "Miami Beach." Thus, the (literal and metaphorical) touristic gaze is referenced in the camcorder's images of a family on vacation. Next, we see the family inside their rental car, and the son holding the camera pans to show his father unfolding a map on the dashboard while the mother states matter-of-factly, "We are lost." The camera scans outside the window, showing a prostitute trolling a street corner in front of an abandoned lot. The scarred landscape and lurid gaze of the prostitute emphasize the radical disorientation and displacement of the tourists from comfortable and familiar white spaces. A collection of black men block the car's progress and crouch menacingly in front of the car, and the father wonders aloud: "Maybe we should get directions from these guys?" Seconds later, both children erupt in piercing screams: "*Mom!*" The car comes to a full stop, and one young man blocking the car's progress walks around to the driver's side door. To the sound of the daughter's scream we hear, and then see, an explosion of shattered glass from the driver's side window. There are more screams, and the camera swings wildly across the interior of the car, resolving in a shot of the rear driver's side door, the son being pulled out of the backseat, and the black men taking his place. The camera swings again, and we see that all the family members have been pulled out of the car, and the carjackers have taken their seats. "Let's do this shit, man," one says; the carjackers congratulate each other; and the front passenger says, "Hellll. Yeah. Hell Yeah, my nigga. Let's get the fuck outta here."

Viewers understand that the remainder of the video is shot within the carjackers' neighborhood—in an apartment squat, a welfare office, a run-down pizza shop, a clothing store featuring "urban wear," and in dark alleys. The group of carjackers, now depicted as rappers, defend these spaces against incursions by whites—in both the initial interaction with the tourist family and soon thereafter against a pizza delivery man who is described in the lyrics as a "white boy in the wrong place at the right time," even though the attackers presumably placed the delivery order.

However, dead prez also rework hegemonic images of urban spaces, operating within dominant representational discourses of the city, but simultaneously relating, framing, or transforming these images in accordance with how those places are made meaningful through lived existence.[20] Rap images like these shift between global and local significances—highlighting the transnational attachment of blacks to their communities (and urban black youth's attachments to the 'hood or ghetto), and specific attachments of rappers to particular neighborhoods. For example, after the carjacking depicted in the dead prez video, the white voyeuristic gaze is immediately used to document mundane domestic, if markedly male, activities: a man shaving his friend's head, another bench pressing weights, and a third banging the top of an old television while the narrator raps: "We been livin' in the dark since April." Instead of depicting the carjackers continuing a crime spree, we witness their peaceful and cooperative, if Spartan, living quarters.

The specificity of these locales is evident in the lyrics of the opening verse: "Holton Street/Dean Street/President/Orange Al/Tee Town/Brooklyn." The attachment of rappers to specific neighborhoods should be seen not as a parochial narrowness, but as an exploration of identity construction and autobiography whose effect is to shift commodity culture's link between generic urban dysfunction and authenticity to individual narratives of social mobility, to "privilege the local and private within the postindustrial city," and to question the "death of community" attributed to black urban spaces.[21] In exploring the particularity of ghettos, rappers document their negotiation of these spaces as occupational testing grounds—places in which they acquired and honed skills and built reputations.[22] This local reputation is critical to later success and to the maintenance of authenticity, in the eyes of rappers.

The global features of ghetto life depicted in "Hell Yeah!" are betrayed in the generic locations (pizza shop, house not shown from the exterior) and the emplacement of the video in Miami Beach (indicated on a clock tower in the first frame of the video) and not dead prez's community in Brooklyn, New York.[23] But the most powerful re-imagining of space is located in the concluding sequence of the video. In this dialogue, spoken in an unnamed and unrecognizable language, and transcribed at the bottom of the screen, a re-appropriated gaze is suggested. The purest indicator of dominant sight—a "clear and precise" picture—is used to reverse dream and reality. The voyeuristic gaze of the camcorder is replaced by an omniscient view, but one that reflects a reality presumptively unfiltered by hegemons. Beautiful women in brightly colored robes, sitting on a gorgeous beach, surround the two MCs; the transcribed discourse is as follows:

stic.man: Oh My Goodness!
Woman 1: What's wrong with my husband?
stic.man: I was having a very, very bad dream. We were in another country. In a foreign land and we had nothing. I mean nothing.
Woman 1: Look around my love, we are right here. Are you okay now?
stic.man: (looks at the camera, speaks in English without transcription) Hell Yeah.

This vignette posits the possibility or actuality of black freedom, under the guise of a 'return' to the African continent. However, more than its oblique reference to Marcus Garvey's plan for black renewal, the episode suggests a social inversion, wherein Africa is the new America, and blacks the new elite class. Thus, it reflects the substitution of reality with a dream, or of heaven with hell, as referenced in the lyric.

In linking new global constructions of the ghetto with local significances of a particular 'hood, rappers use mass media to forge new alliances across the African diaspora and other boundary lines maintained in the service of hegemonic control.[24] Rappers harness the global market for rap music to facilitate discourse across fractured national and international communities; a global conversation about the ghetto has emerged.[25] In this sense, then, communications media have enabled new forms of access and community. Ironically, "the transnational structures which brought the black Atlantic world into being ... now articulate its myriad forms in to a system of global communications" and this global conversation has allowed rap fans to "communicate, interact, and create new collective identities" and mobilize "competing discourses about the varied social, economic, and political currents that continue to alter their lives."[26] Thus, black culture becomes global culture, and globalizing culture multiplies interpretative possibilities as material culture and ideas are rearticulated in disparate localities.[27]

For many viewers, these images resonate with stereotypes of urban spaces, and with the people that live in them. However, for others, dead prez's "ghettocentricity" privileges black working class desires and culture, and engages in a partial critique of consumption and commodification, a topic discussed in more detail later.

Images of Race and Class: Gangsta but Revolutionary

While white rap voyeurs seek authentic experience, they are bound to find only "staged authenticity" because they are constrained to view commodified images.[28] In particular, voyeurs of black culture often seek "reconstructed" or staged ethnicity inscribed on the body in clothing and hair styles, in skin color and body art, and in dance and behavior. While the object of white voyeurism in black culture has changed over time, a process Boyd explores in detail, white rap voyeurs are frequently seeking interaction with a character called "the nigga."[29] The "nigga" is an unemployed, young black man who lives in a densely settled inner city, and who holds in derision dominant value systems.[30] Niggas are often the protagonists of rap songs; Judy argues that rap lyrics assert: "'this nigga is deadly dangerous.' It is this nigga who gang-bangs, this nigga who is destroying the fabric of society, who has spread across the country like an infestation, bringing an epidemic of death and despair to black America."[31] Judy's description of the nigga bears a closer correspondence to the "gangsta," and scholars have noted that by 1988, the rap nigga evolved into the "gangsta."[32] The gangsta is young, black, poor, and male, but also a criminal or psychopath.[33] Rap gangstas often participate in the underground economy as pimps, hustlers, drug dealers, or killers.[34]

White teens seek the gangsta world as an exotic port of call and easily find it in the subgenre style called "gangsta rap": "Gangsta rap's white consumers and critics are identifying the gangsta as something 'other' than themselves or the white middle-class values they purport to inherit."[35] Consequently, Samuels argues, "the more rappers were packaged as violent black criminals, the bigger the white audiences became," and the same is true of exaggerated depictions of sexuality.[36]

The lyrics of "Hell Yeah!" identify group members and their audiences as both "niggas" and "gangstas." These nigga/gangstas "stick up" a pizza deliveryman, engage in credit card fraud, return stolen merchandize for cash, appeal for expedited welfare assistance, take money from a cash register, steal merchandize, and destroy property. The identity of dead prez's as "gangsta" signals an alliance to working-class, black, urban values (or stereotypes of the same). When black is equated with "nigga," hegemonic constructions of blackness as monolithic are redeployed, and therefore little is done to illustrate how blackness (or "nigga") collapses different histories (from within and outside the African diaspora). Boyd argues that "as far as mainstream culture is concerned, it is as though the representation of African American culture operates monolithically, and that only one form of popular representation may be available at any given time."[37]

In keeping with the hegemonic order, the nigga/gangsta draws attention and censure from the state. In the dead prez video, the video extends the visual narrative after the lyrics are completed, filming the invasion of the group's flophouse by a rather large police contingent. The officers arrest the young men, and the scene points to the inevitability of white discipline and the validity of the mass incarceration of a generation of niggas; such discipline is understood by many as the most coercive racial function of the state apparatus.[38]

However, when the camera pans up to the police officer hovering over one arrestee, his face materializes as a grotesque papier-mâché pig head.[39] Moreover, the criminal acts described in the song's lyrics are rationalized as a matter of life and death, *not* consistently as a form of pleasure or irrational in the least; in one lyric, dead prez raps: "It's a deadly struggle/We all gotta hustle/This is the way we survive." The final verse summarizes the actions and justifications of the protagonists:

> If you coming gangsta,
> Then bring on the system,
> And show that you ready to ride.
> 'Till we get our freedom
> We got to get over
> Please, stay steady on the grind.

These lyrics ask "gangstas" to take on "the system," to prove their mettle, and to continue ("stay steady on the grind") to resist ("get over") until "we get our freedom." Lyrics like these cause viewers to "question the idea that gangsta behaviors in hip-hop are inherently an extension of deviant, let alone black culture."[40] They are not deviant insofar as they are necessary actions in the face of brutal poverty and dispossession, and they are not simply "black" as long as they link to *classed* narratives. The "gangsta" character itself is in fact a rearticulation of a white ethnic stereotype, as demonstrated in rappers' frequent references to "mob movies" like Coppola's *The Godfather* or De Palma's *Scarface*, and adaptation of nomenclature, as with rap group Junior M.A.F.I.A., and the Wu-Tang Clan anthem "Wu Gambino."

Both Junior M.A.F.I.A. and the Wu-Tang Clan invoke white ethnic gangsters in songs that emphasize the pleasures of conspicuous consumption. Unapologetic conspicuous consumption also appears prominently in the video for dead prez's song "Hell Yeah!." One episode begins when M-1 raps while a member of his crew releases a ceiling panel, out of which he pulls a wallet with a string of IDs. He shows a card to the camera and we realize it is a fake ID ("the name says you but the face is me")—one that he has used to fill out credit card applications. In the next shot, the crew buys name-brand clothing from a store bragging that they are now "rocking brand names" and the "Po Po [police] never know who to blame." Two women look approvingly at the rappers while the lyrics explain that two weeks later they report the cards stolen so that they can repeat the trick because "like a glitch in the system it's hard to catch." The lyrics also describe returning the merchandize in order to "get the cash," because "that's how we pay the rent." The chorus rationalizes this criminal action as an adaptive necessity: "It's a deadly struggle/We all gotta hustle/This is the way we survive." While other episodes more narrowly depict criminality in the service of providing for basic necessities, this vignette subverts brand-consciousness and the social prestige of commodity consumption into a means of subsistence.

Within rap discourse, there is a critique of monolithic depictions of both race and class; dead prez's depiction of criminality in the service of conspicuous consumption serves as evidence that the duo is participating in such a critique by their use of racial epithets (nigga) and crime. In fact, this critique resonates with the lyrics of rappers like Tupac Shakur and Notorious B.I.G., among others. Moreover, it echoes the longstanding challenge that baaadman and trickster characters in black art have always posed: "[They] embody a challenge to virtually *all* authority which makes sense to people for whom justice is a rare thing, creates an imaginary upside-down world where the oppressed are powerful."[41]

The clearest articulation of this reversal is demonstrated in the final vignette of the video, where the beach dreamworld promises redemption or absolution for the criminal, and justice for the subject of white supremacy. This sequence suggests a place outside the system of hegemonic control—an alternative space where oppressive systems of social stratification are removed or reversed. This is a bourgeois vision of redemption, echoing both the dreams of social reformer Marcus Garvey and the Utopian vision of racial harmony present in some other rap lyrics.

The "revolutionary" identity of dead prez is thus partially premised on the commensurability of consumerism and critique, a controversial (and again, deeply bourgeois) position for rap artists.[42] This position is unacceptable for scholars like Cornell West, who view the pursuit of status through commodity consumption as a detrimental form of compensation for black humiliation, exploitation, and degradation.[43] It is unacceptable to rappers like Tupac, who argues in "Rebel of the Underground" that authenticity and profit are incommensurable values for most rappers.[44] But these arguments are reductive, historically inaccurate (or at least partial), and naive of power.[45] They ignore the deep interconnections of hip-hop and commodity culture throughout the genre's existence.[46] They encourage scholars, fans, and artists to lament the commodification of hip-hop in service of the romanticization and sanctification of an impossible space in the underground, completely independent from market imperatives. They assert a unique space for hip-hop, while other scholars have demonstrated the same dynamic in other black arts: Porter writes of jazz that "the artistic ethos of Romanticism, including the ideal of not 'selling out,' existed side by side with the desire to gain remuneration and respectability through popularity."[47] Finally, these arguments perform the terrible violence of disassociating success and authentic black identities.

Instead, rap groups like dead prez (Master P, the Wu-Tang Clan, Raekwon, Ma$e, Jay-Z, and the Firm [Foxy Brown, Nas, and AZ]) do not view "their own participation in the marketplace as undermining their own authenticity as bearers of black culture."[48] In their partial reflection of bourgeois values, the images in dead prez's video offer "a status for subordinate groups that blurs distinctions between themselves and their oppressors."[49] These constructions of blackness betray the fact that rappers can never completely equate commodification with co-optation because they have always fought their battles in the marketplace. Rap music's coded and explicit political commentaries are broadcast to the widest possible audience, thanks to commodification and global technology and distribution systems, causing Public Enemy producer Bill Stephney to argue that "the revolution will be marketed."[50] Scholars note that black consumption can be part of a struggle to exploit the transformative potential of commodities.[51] For example, Tricia Rose argues that camouflage fatigues and half-face masks worn by members of the hip-hop community give them a "survivalist" look that criticizes urban ghettos as the site of daily guerrilla war.[52] Rappers like dead prez rearticulate what it means to be black and middle-class, in refusing to be disciplined into what Baldwin has called "puritan characterizations of middle-class behavior."[53]

Now we can see why dead prez self-identifies as "gangsta but revolutionary," according to the title of the album from which this single and video were released. They define themselves in defiance of middle-class morality—both black and white—rejecting these terms as inherently or necessarily pejorative.[54] Both the rearticulation of the word "nigga" from slur to proud self-appellation and the celebration of criminality defy black middle-class morality. Their brand-consciousness and facility with narratives of racial uplift and "revolution" echo black bourgeois values. Finally, the threat of moral disorder and criminality disturb white supremacy, while the impulse to self-sabotage and submission to market imperatives reinforce the hegemonic order.

The simultaneous play with racial and class narratives is not novel in the black arts. Neal argues that late nineteenth-century musicals like "The Octoroons" and "A Trip to Coon Town" "are no different from the 'gangsta rap' narratives that emerge in the late twentieth century in part because of popular culture's presence in black working-class mobility narratives."[55] These narratives invoke a nostalgia for a system of clear demarcations between race and class strata, before the threat of a homogenous citizenry dissembled simple divisions. "The commodification of black dysfunction, both real and imagined, is a centerpiece in this nostalgia. ... Because of precarious economic conditions, African Americans are often forced to be complicit in their own demonization by producing commercially viable caricatures of themselves."[56] What seems new here is that contemporary African American performers, including rappers, have the opportunity to make relatively large sums of money and so live a bourgeois lifestyle while profiting from an image that references, authenticates, and rejoices in stereotypes of the lower-class "nigga mentality." The use of "gangsta" and "nigga" in combination with the celebration of conspicuous consumption, the objectification of women, and Utopian visions of a new "back to Africa" campaign combine into a scathing criticism of black bourgeois values.

dead prez's rap aesthetic questions the fictive boundaries of social class and the social constructions that have linked class and race. Baldwin concludes that rappers employ a "position of maneuverability, which in its present form doesn't endorse the cult of authenticity that must explicitly be a 'pure' counter to the mainstream."[57] This appropriation of both black bourgeois and ghettocentric ideologies offers a new conversation, one that potentially denaturalizes a set of binary identity constructions (e.g., black/white, poor/rich, authentic/commodified) and "challenges normative notions of hip hop as a space that can purify the impure," such that a black politics can be discovered within the consumption process.[58] Thus, while the use of stereotypes reinforces or authenticates them, new alliances between old ideas unveil the social construction of "natural" characteristics. In exposing the social constructions of "niggadom" and "ghettocentricity" and reworking them, rappers like dead prez question conceptions of black urban culture as discrete or identifiable.[59]

Gender

I would be remiss not to note the gendered stereotypes implicit in constructions of both "niggas" and "gangstas." While some women have adopted the terms as self-descriptions, they are clearly monikers for *male* identities. So in keeping with Mulvey's analysis of the filmic medium, we can see rap videos as a mechanism for producing the "male gaze," building into the spectacle itself the way in which women (and men) are to be looked at.[60] Many rap images depict black women as "skeezers," "bitches," and "hos," or hyper-materialistic, hypersexual women intent on trapping men using pregnancy, money, manipulation, or even violence.[61] This depiction "only reinforces the perverted expression of male dominance and patriarchy, and reasserts the stereotyping of women as sexual objects intended exclusively for male pleasure."[62] This masculinist ethos resonates with the traditional associations of black musicians with pimps and hustlers; for example, Ferdinand "Jelly Roll" Morton claimed to have worked as a pimp in the 1910s and 1920s before he became a leading jazz practitioner, and rap artists like Snoop Dogg and Ice T play with the same identities today.[63]

The dead prez video employs extremely stereotypic depictions of women. While black men play "stick up kids," welfare recipients, and hustlers; engage in identity theft and credit card fraud; and steal from minimum wage employers, women are depicted as sexual partners for the rap group members. "Skeezers" and "hos" appear in two vignettes: In the first, two women shadow the rappers as they use fraudulent credit cards to buy name-brand clothes. The women follow the rappers, standing behind and to their side, caressing them with both fingers and eyes. They look longingly at the clothes and money the rappers have acquired through criminal activity. The moral vacuousness and voracious sexuality of black women is affirmed in the second vignette, where a scantily dressed woman leads a man into a bedroom, seducing him on camera. While she cloyingly eyes him, he looks directly at the camera, acknowledging her value as a conquest. In the final scene of the video, the two MC's are surrounded by beautiful black women dressed in "traditional" African clothing. In this, the only dialogue spoken by women, one asks, "What's wrong with my husband?" and after his summary of the video's content as a "very, very bad dream" reassures him: "Look around my love, we are right here." The dialogue is spoken in an unnamed language, and transcribed at the bottom of the screen. The woman is denied expression in English and objectified, depicted as a benefit the rappers obtain in this surreal beach world.

Conclusion

The gaze of the rap voyeur is passive, like that of other virtual travelers.[64] Interaction between the subject and object of the gaze is mediated by a screen (or a CD, etc.). It requires relatively little (financial, emotional, or physical) effort for the rap voyeur to be transported to the exotic locations and lifestyles they seek, and the mediation of this encounter by images on the screen ensures viewers will experience them in comfort and security. This is specifically an expression of white privilege and a combination of curiosity and fear; Public Enemy producer Hank Shocklee explains:

> If you're a suburban white kid and you want to find out what life is like for a black city teenager, you buy a record from N.W.A. It's like going to an amusement park and getting on a roller coaster ride—records are safe, they're controlled fear, and you always have the choice of turning it off. That's why nobody ever takes a train up to 125th Street and gets out and starts walking around. Because then you're not in control anymore: it's a whole other ball game.[65]

The same curiosity and fear lured jazz age whites and Beat poets to other inner-city locations, and Norman Mailer links these processes to voyeurism, fueled by white privilege and the commodification of blackness.[66]

However, media images are available for multiple, simultaneous, and even contradictory interpretations. In examining these images as polysemic, we attend to the "turning points, when relations are. ... restructured and transformed."[67] For example, in contrast to the explanation of white pleasure as voyeurism, some argue whites are attracted to rap's narrative of resistance to hegemony, just as the white avant-garde had been attracted to punk music.[68] Particularly for youths, rap can function as "rebel music"; Neal also notes that the antisocial behavior of "fictional" blacks in hip-hop music and videos is embraced as resistant, even though "this influence was manifested in stylistic acumen and not political mobilization."[69] Many hardcore rappers "see no contradiction between advocating a black Nationalist agenda and forging cultural/political alliances with sympathetic whites, and so they actively work to build crossover audiences."[70] Thus, and somewhat ironically, the most marked racial discourse can provide the greatest opportunity for combating dominant *racist* discourse.[71] Rap music has the potential to foment new collective identities, re-shuffle identities, and produce new "others" and alliances.[72]

Unfortunately, popular music discourses generally offer a choice between opposing interpretations of the social and political functions of culture—music as either entertainment or resistance. As I hope to have shown in my examination of "Hell Yeah!" the dichotomy between entertainment and resistance is unnecessary and fails to capture the complexity of how meaning is articulated. In "Hell Yeah!," the camera once used by white hands to discipline black bodies later becomes an instrument of critique. The instrument of critique authenticates racial/ethnic prejudice but then illustrates intra-ethnic stereotypes. The utopia or place of liberation is a surreal reimagining of a failed social project.

While I will resist the impulse to impute motives to the members of dead prez, it is fair to claim that *some* cultural producers consciously promote the value of both entertainment and resistance. In doing so, they, like consumers of media, extract multiple, simultaneous, and sometimes contradictory meanings from cultural products. These multiple meaning systems promote the political potentialities of media, allowing audience members to play with their own identities, and construct and dissemble their differences from other consumers. In this sense, white listeners of rap music are only sometimes voyeurs. In the moments they experience difference (from blacks, inner-city dwellers, poor Americans, etc.), whites may be stimulated and sated by the exoticism of other lifestyles, but they may also mobilize structural explanations for difference, thereby moving to deconstruct the inevitability of the exotic other. In moments of similitude (with relatively powerless young male others), whites may elide the processes of racial stratification that produce their enhanced life chances but also participate in a communicative process that undermines boundaries that support hegemonic control. Moreover, in rap music, both white and black listeners/viewers are subjected to (*made* subjects to) dominant images of the ghetto. In the reappropriation of the monikers "nigga," "gangsta," and "revolutionary," dead prez moves toward more than ritual resistance, revealing the relationship between representation and power by deconstructing monolithic constructions of blackness. In the cultural politics of identity found in dead prez's work, specifically their attempt to deconstruct a singular black identity, the instrument of critique authenticates racial/ethnic prejudice but then illustrates intra-ethnic class stereotypes.

Similarly, we might be served by a more complex account of the political potential of artists producing mass culture. Rappers also shuttle between what are typically regarded as mutually exclusive positions—both essentialist and constructivist, using stereotypes while trying to deconstruct them, building coalitions while authenticating difference. This vision is compatible with a theory of mobile, oppositional practices—Stuart Hall's notion that the "struggle for [ideological dominance] is never about pure victory or pure domination[;] it is always about shifting the balance of power in relations of culture."[73]

Finally, the plastic object—the album or video—loses its preordained authority in the processes of consumption. As listeners or viewers consume the object, they attach their local or political significances, transforming or adapting the "original meanings" of the object, leading Paul Gilroy to theorize that "the original performance trapped in plastic is supplemented by new contributions at every stage. Performer and audience alike strive to create pleasures that can evade capture and sale as cultural commodities."[74]

The images in "Hell Yeah!" represent the complexities of critique within contemporary mass media and suggest that both popular music producers and consumers are not automatic, uncritical prosthetics of hegemony or pleasure. Popular music discourse requires a space in which the intelligence of producers and consumers is prized, while we acknowledge the limited control they have over the structures of mass media production. Scholars must recognize that radical political discourse is not necessarily antagonistic with the logic of the marketplace. The history of rap music provides ample evidence that political discourse can be financially remunerative for media corporations. For these reasons, we must theorize a mass media, artistic community, and body of consumers that can be simultaneously entertained and critical of the status quo, rather than voyeuristic.

Study Questions

1. Can the voyeuristic gaze be used to provide insight into the experiences of the so-called 'hood?
2. Are political engagement and selling the most units mutually exclusive endeavors?
3. How does class and ethnicity complicate the voyeuristic gaze that Lena identifies?

Notes

1. Stuart Hall, "Notes on Deconstructing 'The Popular,'" in *People's History and Socialist History*, ed. R. Samuel (London: Routledge, 1981).
2. dead prez, *RBG: Revolutionary But Gangsta*, compact disc, Sony, 2004.
3. Stuart Hall, "New Ethnicities," in *Stuart Hall: Critical Dialogues in Cultural Studies*, ed. D. Morley and K. Chen (London: Routledge, 1988).
4. Angela Ards, "Organizing the Hip-Hop Generation," *Nation*, July 26, 1999: 11–20; Michael Eric Dyson, "The Culture of Hip–Hop," in *Reflecting Black: African–American Cultural Criticism* (Minneapolis: University of Minnesota Press, 1993), 3–15; R. A. T. Judy, "On the Question of Nigga Authenticity," *boundary* 21 (1994): 211–30; John Michael Spencer, "The Emergency of Black and the Emergence of Rap," *Black Sacred Music: A Journal of Theomusicology* 5 (1991): 1–94; Tricia Rose, *Black Noise: Black Music and Black Culture in Contemporary America* (Hanover, NH: Wesleyan University Press, 1994); Mark Anthony Neal, *What the Music Said: Black Popular Music and Black Popular Culture* (New York: Routledge, 1999); Ted Swedenburg, "Homies in the 'Hood: Rap's Commodification of Insubordination," *New Formations* 18 (1992): 53–66; Cornell West, "The New Politics of Difference," in *Out There: Marginalization and Contemporary Cultures*, ed. Russell Ferguson, Martha Gever, Trinh T. Minh-ha, and Cornell West (New York: The New Museum of Contemporary Art and MIT Press, 1990).
5. Dyson, "Culture of Hip-Hop"; Nelson George, *Hip Hop America* (New York: Viking Penguin, 1998); Bakari Kitwana, *The Hip Hop Generation: Young Blacks and the Crisis in African American Culture* (New York: Basic Civitas Books, 2002).
6. Rose, *Black Noise*.
7. Robin D. G. Kelley, "Looking for the 'Real' Nigga: Social Scientists Construct the Ghetto," in *That's the Joint!: The Hip-Hop Studies Reader*, ed. Murray Forman and Mark Anthony Neal (New York: Routledge, 2005), 119. Although images of dysfunction in white communities do appear in the media, it is often the case both that a diversity of images of white ethnic communities are produced and that only dysfunctional images of black communities emerge. See Mark Anthony Neal, *Soul Babies: Black Popular Culture and the Post-Soul Aesthetic* (New York: Routledge, 2002).
8. David Samuels, "The Rap on Rap: The 'Black Music' that Isn't Either," *New Republic*, 11 November

1991: 27. Although African Americans are proportionally more likely to purchase rap music than other ethno-racial groups, the largest consumer base for sales of the genre is white and suburban men. See Clarence Lusane, "Rap, Race, and Politics," *Race & Class* 34 (1993): 41–56; Norman Kelley, "Rhythm Nation: The Political Economy of Black Music," *Black Renaissance/Renaissance Noire* 2 (1999): 1.

9. Sigmund Freud, *Three Essays on the Theory of Sexuality* (New York: Basic, 2000), 142.

10. On blackface minstrels, see Dale Cockrell, *Demons of Disorder: Early Blackface Minstrels and Their World* (New York: Cambridge University Press, 1997); Ronald L. Jackson II, *Scripting the Black Masculine Body: Identity, Discourse, and Racial Politics in Popular Media* (Albany, NY: State University of New York Press, 2006); and Eric Lott, *Love and Theft: Blackface Minstrelsy and the American Working Class* (New York: Oxford University Press, 1993). On jazz and blues, see Neal, *What the Music Said*; Laurence Levine, "Jazz in American Culture," in The Jazz Cadence of American Culture, ed. Robert G. O'Meally (New York: Columbia University Press, 1998); and Eric Porter, *What is this Thing Called Jazz?: African American Musicians as Artists, Critics, and Activists* (Los Angeles: University of California Press, 2002). On television and film, see Todd Boyd, *Am I Black Enough for You?: Popular Culture from the 'Hood and Beyond* (Bloomington: Indiana University Press, 1997); and Neal, Soul Babies.

11. Michel Foucault, "Two Lectures, in *Power/Knowledge: Selected Interviews & Other Writings, 1972–1977*, ed. Colin Gordon (New York: Pantheon Books, 1980).

12. Rappers now own clothing lines, star in television shows, carry lead roles in big-budget feature films, produce video games, and play professional sports in addition to appearing on music television, in magazines, and endorsing consumer products.

13. This voyeuristic appeal fuels rap sales just as Kelley argued ethnographies of black ghettos translated "white America's fascination with the pathological urban poor" into "massive book sales." Kelley, "Looking for the 'Real' Nigga," 121. Samuels argues for a longer cultural heritage of white voyeurism: "White fascination with rap sprang from a particular kind of cultural tourism pioneered by the Jazz Age novelist Carl Van Vechten, whose 1926 best-selling book *Nigger Heaven* imaged a masculine and friendly black ghetto that served as an escape from white, middle-class boredom." Samuels, "Rap on Rap," 29.

14. Samuels, "Rap on Rap, 28.

15. Boyd, *Am I Black Enough for You*, 41. Despite the real spatial origins of any particular rap group, Dyson argues rappers are constrained to represent the ghetto life by "rap's self-defined and continuing challenge ... to maintain its aesthetic, cultural and political proximity to its site of original expression: the ghetto poor." Dyson, "Culture of Hip-Hop," 11.

16. Kelley, "Looking for the 'Real' Nigga," 130.

17. See Rose, *Black Noise*; and S. Craig Watkins, "Black Youth and the Ironies of Capitalism," in Forman and Neal, ed., *That's the Joint*, 564.

18. See Rose, *Black Noise*, Watkins, "Black Youth"; and Neal, *What the Music Said*.

19. Watkins, "Black Youth," 564.

20. Murray Forman, "'Represent': Race, Space, and Place in Rap Music," *Popular Music* 19 (2000): 65–90.

21. Neal, *What the Music Said*, 136.

22. Dipannita Basu and Pnina Werbner, "Bootstrap Capitalism and the Culture Industries: A Critique of Invidious Comparisons in the Study of Ethnic Entrepreneurship," *Ethnic and Racial Studies* 23 (2001): 236–62.

23. The members of dead prez first met in Florida, but are best known for their current location within the New York City, specifically Brooklyn, hip-hop community.

24. See Andy Bennett, "Hip-Hop am Main, Rappin' on the Tyne: Hip-Hop Culture as a Local Construct in Two European Cities," *Popular Music and Youth Culture* (2000): 133–65; and J. L. Decker, "The State of Rap: Time and Place in Hip Hop Nationalism," in *Microphone Fiends: Youth Music and Youth Culture*, ed. Andrew Ross and Tricia Rose (London: Routledge, 1994), 111.

25. See Neal, *What the Music Said*; Paul Gilroy, *Small Acts* (New York: Serpent's Tail, 1993), 80; and Watkins, "Black Youth."

26. Gilroy, *Small Acts*, 80; Watkins, "Black Youth," 568–9.

27. Gilroy, *Small Acts*, 80.

28. Dean MacCannell, *The Tourist: A New Theory of the Leisure Class* (New York: Schocken, 1976). Peterson argues that all claims to authenticity are staged, in that they are the result of ideological work or social constructions. In keeping with his conception, my references to authenticity are meant to indicate only discursive constructions of authenticity, not any presumption on my part of intrinsic realities. See Richard A. Peterson, "In Search of Authenticity," *Journal of Management Studies* 42 (2005): 1083.

29. Boyd, *Am I Black Enough for You*.

30. For a cultural etymology of the word, see Randall Kennedy, *Nigger: The Strange Career of a Troublesome Word* (New York: Pantheon Books, 2002).

31. Judy, "On the Question of Nigga Authenticity," 106.
32. Jennifer C. Lena, "Social Context and Musical Content: Rap Music, 1979–1995," *Social Forces*, 85 (2006): 479–95.
33. The underlying influences on gangsta rap range from the fiction of Iceberg Slim, the music of Parliament-Funkadelic, and the Brian De Palma 1983 remake of the film "Scarface." See Neal, *What the Music Said*, 145.
34. Davarian L. Baldwin, "Black Empires, White Desires: The Spatial Politics of Identity in the Age of Hip-Hop," *Black Renaissance/Renaissance Noire 2* (1999): 138–59.
35. Baldwin, "Black Empires, White Desires," 148.
36. Samuels, "Rap on Rap," 24.
37. Boyd, *Am I Black Enough for You*, 23.
38. See Rose, *Black Noise*; and George, *Hip Hop America*.
39. The author first retrieved the video from the band's website (http://www.deadprez.com) on or about 20 October 2004. This version of the video includes the pig-headed policeman. However, the version purchased from iTunes on 18 October 2005 depicted a regular face and head on the policeman in question. The iTunes version of the video has been edited in other ways; for example, it contains an abbreviated version of the carjacking and the bedroom seduction, and omits all curse words and uses of the word "nigga," or variants.
40. Baldwin, "Black Empires, White Desires," 148.
41. Robin D. G. Kelley, *Race Rebels: Culture, Politics and the Black Working Class* (New York: Free Press, 1994), 187.
42. There is some debate about whether commodification has always impacted rap music (and thus it was never free of hegemonic ideology) or if there was some period of development (in the mid-1970s, although some argue it lasted until the early 1990s) when rap was largely free of its influence. Whether or not rap was ever free of commodification, most scholars do note a commodification of rap's early critique of post-industrial, urban despair, such that radical critique through education, diagnosis, even anger, is transmuted into affect and thus denuded of its political potentiality. For example, Neal argues that "in less than a decade, hip-hop culture has been transformed from a subculture primarily influenced by the responses of black urban youth to post-industrialization into a billion-dollar industry in which such responses were exploited by corporate capitalists and the petit bourgeois desires of the black middle class." Neal, *Soul Babies*, 381. Additionally, he argues that "Increasingly, as programs like MTV's *Yo! MTV Raps* and major recording labels like SONY and Warner Brothers became the primary outlets to access hip-hop discourse, the discourse itself was subject to social controls rooted in corporate attempts to mainstream hip-hop for mass consumption." Neal, *Soul Babies*, 379.
43. Cornell West, *Race Matters* (Boston, MA: Beacon Press, 1993).
44. Tupac Shakur's, *2Pacalypse Now*, compact disc, Jive, 1991. We find the following lyrics: "They talkin' street slang, but the punks still can't hang./They makin' records 'bout violence/But when it comes to the real, some brothers go silent./It kinda make you wanna think about/ That ya gotta do some sellin' out, just to get your record out./But 2Pacalpyse is straight down/So feel the wrath of the revel—the rebel of the underground."
45. Thank you to an anonymous reviewer for this succinct summary.
46. To wit, as Basu and Werbner argue, "the notion that authentic culture is somehow outside the media and commerce ... ignores the way subcultures themselves are mediated in their construction by the media." Basu and Werbner, "Bootstrap Capitalism and the Culture Industries," 254.
47. Porter, *What Is This Thing Called Jazz*, 31.
48. Kelley, "Looking for the 'Real' Nigga," 124.
49. Kelley, *Race Rebels*, 167–8.
50. Quoted in Swedenburg, "Homies in the 'Hood," 57.
51. See Houston A. Baker Jr., "Hybridity, the Rap Race, and Pedagogy for the 1990s," in *Technoculture*, ed. Constance Penley and Andrew Ross (Minneapolis: University of Minnesota Press, 1991); and Dyson, "The Culture of Hip-Hop."
52. Rose, *Black Noise*.
53. Baldwin, "Black Empires, White Desires," 140.
54. Baldwin, "Black Empires, White Desires," 145.
55. Neal, *What the Music Said*, 10.
56. Neal, *What the Music Said*, 10.
57. Baldwin, "Black Empires, White Desires," 157.
58. Baldwin, "Black Empires, White Desires," 140.
59. Kelley, "Looking for the 'Real' Nigga," 120.

60. Laura Mulvey, "Visual Pleasure and Narrative Cinema," in *Visual and Other Pleasures* (Bloomington: Indiana University Press, 1989).
61. Charise L. Cheney, *Brothers Gonna Work It Out: Sexual Politics in the Golden Age of Rap Nationalism* (New York: New York University Press, 2005).
62. Dyson, "Culture of Hip-Hop," 9.
63. See Burton Peretti, *The Creation of Jazz: Music, Race, and Culture in Urban America* (Chicago: Ivan R. Dee, 1992), 35, on Jelly Roll Morton.
64. Lisa Nakamura, "'Where Do You Want to Go Today?': Cybernetic Tourism, the Internet, and Transnationality," in *Race in Cyberspace*, ed. Beth E. Kolko, Lisa Nakamura, and Gilbert B. Rodman (New York: Routledge, 2000).
65. Shocklee quoted in Samuels, "Rap on Rap," 29.
66. Norman Mailer, "The White Negro: Superficial Reflections on the Hipster," *Dissents* (1957).
67. Stuart Hall, "Popular Culture and the State," in *Popular Culture and Social Relations*, ed. T. Bennett, C. Mercer, and J. Woollacott (Milton Keynes: Open University Press, 1986), 23.
68. Samuels, "Rap on Rap"; Neal, *What the Music Said*; Swedenburg, "Homies in the 'Hood"; and Baldwin, "Black Empires, White Desires."
69. Neal, *What the Music Said*, 150.
70. Swedenburg, "Homies in the 'Hood," 59.
71. Naturally, this critique is limited to the extent that images refuse to adopt an ethical remove from the socially dysfunctional behaviors or communities they depict; Dyson criticizes rap groups like N.W.A. whose celebration of a "lethal mix of civil terrorism and personal cynicism" fails because they engage in the "luxury of moral neutrality." Dyson, "Culture of Hip-Hop," 10.
72. Watkins, "Black Youth and the Ironies of Capitalism," 558–9.
73. Stuart Hall, "What is This 'Black' in Black Popular Culture?," in *Black Popular Culture*, ed. Gina Dent (Seattle, WA: Bay Press, 1992), 24.
74. Gilroy, *Small Acts*, 39–40.

32

Postindustrial Soul
Black Popular Music at the Crossroads

Hip-hop is largely the product of a generation of diasporic youth who responded to the conditions of immigration, urban renewal, post-industrialization, and poverty. Hip-hop's rise also coincides with the marketplace's recognition of black buying power and a distinct youth culture within Black America. The pop culture landscape of the 1970s offers confirmation of this new reality.

In his essay, Mark Anthony Neal argues that, in the aftermath of Civil Rights gains, and as attention on the black inner-city waned, black and Latino/a youth utilized mass culture as a mechanism to articulate their concerns. Political rapper Chuck D's definition of hip-hop as the "Black CNN" is further evidence of how hip-hop artists and their audiences viewed their use of the mainstream marketplace.

Postindustrial Soul: Black Popular Music at the Crossroads

Mark Anthony Neal

Life on the margins of postindustrial urban America is inscribed in hip hop style, sound, lyric and thematics. Situated at the "crossroads of lack and desire," hip hope emerges from the deindustrialized meltdown where social alienation, prophetic imagination, and yearning intersect. Hip hope is a cultural form that attempts to negotiate the experiences of marginalization, brutally truncated opportunity, and oppression within the cultural imperatives of African-American and Caribbean history, identity, and community. It is the tension between the cultural fractures produced by postindustrial oppression and the binding ties of black cultural expressivity that sets the critical frame for the development of hip hop.

Tricia Rose, *Black Noise*, 1994

The emergence of the postindustrial city radically altered black communal sensibilities in the late 1970s and 1980s. Intense poverty, economic, collapse, and the erosion of viable public space were part and parcel of the new urban terrain that African-Americans confronted. Culled from the discourse of the postindustrial city, hip-hop reflected the growing visibility of a young, urban, and often angry so-called "underclass." Aesthetically the genre drew on diverse musical sensibilities like James Brown and the Parliament/Funkadelic collection and on black oral traditions like the prison toasts, "The Dozens," and the Black Arts poets of the 1960s. As the genre represented a counternarrative to black middle-class mobility, it also represented a counternarrative to the emergence of a corporate-driven music industry and the mass commodification of black expression. Relying largely on word of mouth and live performance as a means of promotion, hip-hop may represent the last black popular form to be wholly derived from the experiences and texts of the black urban landscape.

The emergence of hip-hop in the postindustrial city was far removed from the daily realities of an expanding black middle class. Inspired in part by Smokey Robinson's *A Quiet Storm* and the lusher recordings of Gamble and Huff, black popular recordings began to reflect the sensibilities of the black middle class. The subsequent Quiet Storm format, popularized on many radio stations with large black audiences, allowed the black middle class the cultural grounding that suburban life could not afford them, while maintaining a distinct musical subculture that affirmed their middle-class status and distanced them from the sonic rumblings of an urban underclass.

By the mid-1980s, both an urban-based working class/underclass and suburban middle class exhibited symptoms of "postindustrial nostalgia." Loosely defined as a nostalgia that has its basis in the postindustrial transformations of black urban life during the 1970s, many contemporary cultural workers began to appropriate the narratives and styles of black life in black urban spaces prior to the structural and economic changes of postindustrial transformations. While most visible in the burgeoning new black cinema of the late 1980s and 1990s, postindustrial nostalgia is also reflected in the popular music industry. The prevalence of nostalgia-based narratives in black popular culture would have particular effects on the maintenance of intradiasporic relations, at once providing the aural and visual bridge to reaffirm diverse communal relations, particularly those across the generational divide, while underscoring the black middle class' general refusal to adequately engage the realities of the Black Public Sphere in the postindustrial era.

Quiet Storms: Soul and Survival in the Suburbs

Excepting the trio of Holland, Dozier, and Holland, William "Smokey" Robinson has been the most influential black singer/songwriter/producer of his generation. After a long and productive collaboration with the Miracles, Robinson embarked upon a solo career in the early 1970s. Possessing one of the most gifted and distinct falsettos in the history of popular music, Robinson's songwriting skills, best exemplified by songs like "My Girl," "Ooh Baby, Baby," and "Shop Around," were no longer on the critical edge in the early 1970s. Momentarily regaining his creative energies, Robinson release his first "concept" recording with the 1975 classic *A Quiet Storm*. *A Quiet Storm* reflected the changing dynamics of popular music in the 1970s.

Some twenty years plus after the emergence of the 33-rpm long-playing format, artists began experimenting with longer recordings that often features self-contained themes examined over the course of the entire album. This was a concept that Album Oriented Rock (AOR) exploited to its fullest commercial potential with groups like Led Zeppelin and The Eagles. Marvin Gaye was the first black artist to embrace this concept with large commercial success with his 1971 recording *What's Going On,* though Isaac Hayes's groundbreaking *Hot Buttered Soul* charted this territory with some success among black audiences before Gaye's crossover success. These changes in popular music represented the first opportunities for black artists to experiment with improvisation and arrangement outside of the gene of jazz and partially ended the reign of the 45-rpm recording as the only viable commercial format for popular music. Hayes's eighteen-minute reworking of Jimmy Webb's "By the Time I Get to Phoenix," and Donny Hathaway's gospel-tinged recording of Bobby Scott's "He Ain't Heavy, He's My Brother," from *Donny Hathaway* (1970) are two of the best examples of this new creative terrain for black artists. Though neither attracted mainstream appeal—Hayes commercial breakthrough occurred with the soundtrack to *Shaft* and Hathaway's only mainstream success occurs with pop-soul duets with Roberta Flack—these recordings laid the foundation for the later artistic achievements of Flack, Earth, Wind and Fire, and Barry White. It was in this context that Robinson made his own self-contained suite of romance recordings in 1975.

Robinson's seven-minute title track to *A Quiet Storm* surprised him by becoming the aesthetic cornerstone of a more upscale and sophisticated soul sound that would captivate an older, mature, and largely black middle-class audience that relished its distance from a deteriorating urban landscape. The cover art to *A Quiet Storm* finds a pensive Robinson examining woodland terrain with a black Shetland pony, an image that was unthinkable as cover art for a black recording artist a generation earlier, though Robinson's cover photo appealed to the sensibilities and desires of a newly emerging black middle class. Covering traditional soul themes like love lost, love found, and love betrayed, the entire first side of the album, recorded as a suite, is held together by the sounds of whispering winds, hence the recording's title.

As important as the recording was to Robinson's then-fading career, it proved more important to black radio programmers searching for programming that would appeal to a growing
black middle class with disposable income, as a Howard University communications student
appropriated Robinson's title and introduced the Quiet Storm format to black radio programmers. The generally late-night format basically consisted of soul ballads interspersed with
some jazz and possibly a little contemporary blues. By the early 1980s, the format was a fixture
in virtually every major radio market that programmed black or, as it came to be known by the
late 1980s, urban contemporary music.[1] For Quiet Storm audiences, this format offered a
welcome reprieve from disco and funk, both of which were arguably driven by working-class
youth audiences. While the Quiet Storm format was in part shaped by middle-class sensibilities, particularly given its Howard University roots, it cut across class lines because it appealed
to adult sensibilities. Most notably, these recordings were in most cases devoid of any significant political commentary and maintained a strict aesthetic and narrative distance from
issues relating to black urban life.

Artists like PIR stalwarts Harold Melvin and the Blue Notes and the O'Jays were all at home
in this format. The solo careers of Patti Labelle and Teddy Pendergrass were in part shaped by
their appeal to Quiet Storm audiences. Tracks like Labelle's "If Only You Knew" and Pendergrass's "Turn Out the Lights" are still Quiet Storm staples. Vocal groups like Atlantic Starr,
The Whispers, Frankie Beverly and Maze, as well as solo acts like Denice Williams, Peabo
Bryson, Stephanie Mills, Roberta Flack, and Jeffrey Osborne offered Quiet Storm audiences an
aesthetic connection to the traditions of black popular music, particularly as postindustrial transformations further eroded public spaces in black communities and disco dance clubs migrated
from black locales into more mainstream provinces. Furthermore, as time passed, some
elements of the black middle class were decreasingly responsible for familial relations in black
urban centers and began to successfully develop institutions within their own provinces, like
churches and other social groups predicated on a common middle-class experience.

Gamble and Huff perhaps exploited this phenomenon best by always carefully packaging
their recordings with potential pop Top-40 singles and Quiet Storm type album cuts. The
O'Jays 1978 release *So Much Love,* is a case in point. Though the infectious pop-soul ditty "Use
Ta Be My Girl" is still their highest charting single, the album's "Cry Together" has gone on to
become a Quiet Storm classic. More importantly, much of this was occurring with little or no
corporate interference, in that this market, dominated by black middle-class consumers who
often equated consumption with acceptance in "integrated" America, was virtually ignored
by the major corporate labels. Veteran soul singer Tyrone Davis's 1979 release "In the Mood"
is such an example. Signed to the Columbia/CBS label, promotion of Davis's album *In the
Mood* was lost in the shuffle of releases by younger black artists like Earth, Wind and Fire and
Michael Jackson. Despite this the title track found a market niche among black audiences who
were attracted to Davis's old-styled soul balladry.

By the mid-1980s, Luther Vandross and Anita Baker were perhaps the two artists who most
benefited from the development of Quiet Storm radio. A veteran of stage musicals and
commercials, Vandross achieved some success with his guest appearance with the disco group
Change on its 1980 release *The Glow of Love,* in which Vandross sang lead vocals on the title
track and the exquisite "Searching." While "Never Too Much," the lead single of his first
Epic/CBS recording, garnered considerable support from black and white audiences alike, it
was Vandross's own seven-minute arrangement of the Hal David and Burt Bacharach song "A
House Is Not a Home," that gave him his reputation as a definitive soul balladeer. On subsequent releases like *Forever, For Always, For Love* (1982), *Busy Body* (1984) which included a
startling remake of the Carpenter's "Superstar," and *The Night I Fell in Love* (1985), Vandross
established himself as an innovative singer/arranger and producer, particularly within the
context of Quiet Storm radio.

With stellar sales among black listeners, Vandross's crossover success began with the release of his fifth recording, *Give Me the Reason,* in 1986. This success occurs at precisely the same moment crossover audiences were embracing Anita Baker's 1986 release *Rapture.* Possessing limited vocal range but a highly distinctive vocal quality, Baker attracted attention among black audiences as lead singer of the group Chapter 8 during the late 1970s and with her debut solo release, *The Songstress,* on the independent Beverly Glen label in 1983. Baker's jazz-flavored major label debut on the Elektra/Warner label found support among black radio and contemporary jazz stations that were embracing the pop-jazz of artists like David Sanborn, Grover Washington, Jr., and a still relatively unknown Kenny G. What is notable here is that the commercial successes of Vandross and Baker were overshadowed by the commercial appeal of another form of black music that developed largely in the shadows of black middle-class mobility and in the ruins of an eroding urban landscape. While mature black audiences supported the music and performances of what Nelson George has called "retro-nuevo" soul, corporate labels focused their attention on the crossover appeal of three young black men from Hollis, Queens, Run-DMC, who along with their white protégés, The Beastie Boys, sold more than six million records of a "new" genre of music known as hip-hop or rap.[2]

Postindustrial Context(s): Hip-Hop, Postindustrialism, and the Commodification of the Black Underclass

Despite national rhetoric that suggested the contrary, the Black Public Sphere of the postindustrial city represented a de facto state of racial segregation that was, arguably, much more insidious than segregated black spaces prior to the Civil Rights movement. Lacking an indigenous economic base, these new social constructs developed largely as bureaucratic props of the federal government, as the postindustrial economy institutionalized a veritable nation of displaced workers, as integral cogs in the federal government's economy and industry of misery.[3] Meanwhile public institutions, already taxed by black middle-class flight and the inability of the black working class to negotiate the economic burdens of community maintenance, were literally destroyed as part of the spatial logic of the postindustrial city. As Tricia Rose relates in her seminal text on hip-hop music:

> The city's poorest residents paid the highest price for deindustrialization and economic restructuring.... In the case of the South Bronx, which has frequently been dubbed the "home of hip-hop culture," these larger postindustrial conditions were exacerbated by disruptions considered an "unexpected side effect" of the larger politically motivated policies of "urban renewal." In the early 1970s, the renewal [*sic*] project involved massive relocations of economically fragile people of color from different areas of New York City into parts of the South Bronx. Subsequent ethnic and racial transition in the South Bronx was not a gradual process that might have allowed already taxed social and cultural institutions to respond self-protectively; instead, it was a brutal process of community destruction and relocation executed by municipal officials.[4]

Thus black urban populations were affected by economic and social transformations both internal and external to the traditional Black Public Sphere. In the quest to create a functional postindustrial environment, the masses of multiracial working-class and working-poor people were some of the most expendable urban resources human resources that, a half-century earlier were enticed to migrate to urban spaces in support of industrial development. As urban development changed in response to technological "advancement" and economic restructuring, so did social and economic investment in working-class communities. As John Mollenkopf suggests in his texts on the emergence of postindustrial cities like New York, "The magnificence of the Manhattan central business and shopping district and the resurgence of luxury residential areas may be juxtaposed to the massive decay of the city's public facilities and poor neighborhoods."[5] Many working-class communities and their inhabitants were deemed as peripheral to the mechanisms of the postindustrial city as high finance and the consumerist desires of a growing managerial class influenced municipal development, including well-publicized tax breaks to corporate entities that remained within certain municipalities without any specific commitment to their lower-tier workers. This phenomenon further challenged working-class communities as a diminishing tax base led to cuts in municipal and later federal aid, thus instigating a further spiral into poverty and community erosion for many working-class communities. Under the banner of "urban renewal," the black working class and working poor were marginalized and isolated from the engines of the postindustrial city—the privatization of public space in downtown areas being emblematic—and instead exposed to intense poverty and rampant unemployment, which subsequently challenged traditional desires to maintain community.

Poverty within the postindustrial city featured spatial dimensions that also altered African-American efforts to build and maintain urban communities. As David Theo Goldberg states, "The segregated space of formalized racism is over-determined. Not only is private space restricted by the constraints of poverty, so too is public institutional space."[6] By the mid-1970s, Goldberg's thesis found its logical icon in the sprawling federal housing projects that largely replaced the kitchenette tenements of black urban spaces in the North and Midwest.[7] Goldberg's "living space of poverty" acknowledges an urban landscape that privileges the private and the local—the manifestation of fractured communal relations and the pervasive aura of social isolation. Though many federal housing projects represented a marked improvement over the quality of urban housing prior to the Civil Rights movement, the very logic of federally subsidized "low-income" housing meant that the poorest blacks would be socially and economically isolated from the mechanisms of the postindustrial city in neighborhoods that were acutely overcrowded and lacked the necessary public and institutional space to build and maintain communal sensibilities. This social isolation has been defined by sociologist William Julius Wilson as "lack of contact or of sustained interaction with individuals and institutions that represent mainstream society."[8] Though isolation from mainstream culture remains a substantial barrier to survival in the postindustrial city, the fracturing of communal relations within the African-American diaspora has had a more profound effect on the black poor as communal exchange, critique, and other communal relations that were integral to black survival in the industrial era were severed by regional and spatial dislocations within the Black Public Sphere and economic and political transformations beyond it.

Given the paucity of private and public space, it was no surprise that the private and the public began to conflate, as the familial, communal, and social "dysfunction" of the African-American experience entered into mainstream public discourse. While dysfunction exists in many communal settings, regardless of race, class, and social location, African-American dysfunction was mass mediated and commodified for mass consumption via network news programs, Hollywood films like *Fort Apache,* and television programs like *Starsky and Hutch* and *Baretta.* By the late 1970s, the commodification of the black poor or underclass as human spectacle became a standard trope of mass culture, parlaying a clear sense of social difference from "blackness" for many mainstream consumers, including an emerging black middle class. My point is not to suggest that "dysfunction" among white communities was not present in mass culture, but that the mass-mediated images of the black underclass often served as the only images available to mainstream consumers, whereas a diversity of images for the white ethnic experience was often presented for consumption, albeit rife with its own internal markers of class and social difference. Many of the experiences of the "ghettocentric" poor were essentialized as a representative sample of the broader black community, to the obvious detriment of many segments of the African-American diaspora including the black poor. For instance, mass-mediated misrepresentations of the black poor often validated the rhetoric of conservative politicians like Ronald Reagan who opposed increased federal spending for social programs, by deemphasizing the roles of racism, poor education, inadequate health care, and the collapse of industrial-based economies and by instead projecting drug addiction, laziness, and the inferiority of African-American culture as the primary culprits of black misery.

The rather vivid imagery of black urban spaces within mass culture was further enhanced by the layout of communal spaces in many urban communities. For example, many of the federally subsidized housing projects of the Northeast and Midwest—Chicago's Cabrini-Greene comes to mind—represented the inverted logic of Jeremy Bentham's Panopticon, by providing surveillance from the bottom. Though I am not suggesting that the federal housing projects were part of some conspiracy to manage the black masses, the high visibility of such housing, with its distinct architecture that privileged more efficient use of urban space over livability and the concentration of the black poor within such spaces, increased notions that such communities were socially isolated from mainstream life and thus to be feared and neglected. Of course, in many locales like the Compton and Watts districts in Los Angeles, technological advancements in policing have allowed many police departments the ability to "patrol" black urban spaces via helicopters or "ghetto-birds."[9] Such developments countered historical examples where black isolation was often accompanied and defined by invisibility. To the contrary, in the postindustrial era, the black masses continued to be marginalized but remained highly visible within varying social constructs.

In response to poverty and unemployment, an illicit economy emerged as a primary conduit for economic survival among some segments of the postindustrial city. Illicit activities like petty thievery, numbers running, prostitution, and even drug dealing had been a small part of the informal economy of segregated black spaces throughout the twentieth century. For example, one of the few black patrons of the "Harlem Renaissance" was West Indian numbers runner Casper Holstein, who helped finance the Urban League's literary awards in 1926 from his profits.[10] What radically changed the nature of the informal economy of the Black Public Sphere in the post–Civil Rights era is the intensity of the economic collapse, accompanied by massive unemployment within those spaces and the emergence of an illegal drug that is perhaps the most destructive element to emerge within the contemporary Black Public Sphere.

Crack cocaine was a unique drug; its emergence exemplified the paradox of consumptionist desire in the midst of intense poverty. In his exhaustive examination of postindustrial Los Angeles, Mike Davis writes of the cocaine trade:

> Like any "ordinary business" in an initial sales boom, the cocaine trade had to contend with changing relations of supply and demand.... Despite the monopsonistic position of the cartels vis-à-vis the producers, the wholesale price of cocaine fell by half. This, in turn, dictated a transformation in sales strategy and market structure. The result was a switch from *haute cuisine* to fast food, as the Medellin Cartel, starting in 1981 or 83 (accounts differ), designated Los Angeles as a proving ground for the mass sales of rock cocaine or crack.[11]

To counter the flattening of demand for cocaine, a less expensive form of cocaine was introduced into poor communities within postindustrial cities like Los Angeles, New York, and Detroit in an effort to expand markets. Not only did crack cocaine increase demand for cocaine nationally, crack cocaine created its own thriving market. It featured a short, intense high that was highly addictive and thus offered "more bang for the buck." As Cornel West has suggested, the intensity of crack cocaine addiction mirrored the intensity of consumptionist desire in America.[12] The craving for the type of stimulant that crack cocaine provided made it popular among those who desired transcendence from the everyday misery of postindustrial life. In this regard, crack cocaine addiction resembled the historical examples of religion, recreational sex, and dancing as temporal releases from the realities of African-American life in the twentieth century. Crack cocaine differed from these aforementioned examples in that it also helped destroy communal relations within the Black Public Sphere as crack cocaine addiction led to increased black-on-black crime and the emergence of illicit sex acts "performed" within distinctly public forums where sex acts were exchanged often for drug money or drugs themselves.

More compellingly, the crack cocaine trade was attractive as a counter to poverty within the postindustrial city. As Davis maintains in *City of Quartz*, the crack cocaine industry was introduced to postindustrial Los Angeles after large numbers of blue collar workers were displaced from the industrial plant economy that was largely responsible for black migration from the South into Los Angeles immediately after World War II. The postindustrial transformation of Los Angeles, including the emergence of Japanese imports, effectively mitigated many of the economic and social gains made by the black working class in the post–World War II era. Furthermore, many African-Americans, particularly young black men, were excluded from both the service and the high-tech industries that were developing in the region, leading to unemployment rates well over 40 percent among black youth.[13] The significant demand for crack cocaine and the relative ease with which in could be produced on-site made the crack cocaine trade an attractive alternative to the abject poverty that defined the postindustrial experience for many blacks.

What was unique about the crack cocaine industry for many African-Americans is that it attempted to counter a poverty that was itself constructed against commodified images of wealth and consumption. Unlike previous periods of widespread poverty that existed somewhat in isolation of mainstream wealth, the impoverished masses within America generally faced a barrage of commodified images of wealth and consumption via television, film, and other organs of mass culture, as self-worth increasingly came to be defined by the ability to consume. African-American youth were particularly subject to this barrage of wealth and consumption as part of the first real generation of American youth socialized by television.[14] As mentioned previously, African-American youth investment in television was intensified as a corollary to corporate annexation of black popular expression, marking the post–Civil Rights generation(s) of African-American youth as the first who could readily consume the iconography of "blackness." As street-level sellers and producers of crack cocaine, African-American youth found a way to escape poverty and to consume as a measurement of self-worth. Thus unlike other ethnic groups who used the drug trade as a foundation to build upon "legitimate wealth"—Mario Puzo's examples in the *Godfather* chronicles immediately come to mind—African-American youth involved in the crack cocaine industry simply invested in material icons of wealth like cars, cellular phones, jewelry, and au couture fashions instead of transforming such wealth into familial or communal efforts to rebuild community. Furthermore, African-American youth interest in the crack cocaine industry was particularly profound because of the "juvenization of poverty" among many urban groups. In Los Angeles County, for instance, more than 40 percent of children lived below or just above the official poverty line. This mirrored a doubling of children in poverty across the state of California in just a generation.[15] These trends were further realized in many postindustrial urban environments across the nation.

What emerged in the shadows of many of these developments was a distinct African-American youth culture whose basic sentiments were often incompatible with mainstream African-American leadership and mainstream culture in general. In its worst case, it was a culture personified by gang turf wars over the control of the crack cocaine industry, a culture described by Michael Eric Dyson as a "ghettocentric juvenocracy" where economic rule and illegal tyranny is exercised by a cadre of young African-American males over a significant portion of the black urban landscape.[16] It is at this end of the spectrum that the postindustrial realities of black life continue to challenge the very idea of community as drive-by shootings and subsequent police occupation continue to rip communities apart by militarizing public spaces. At the more positive end of the spectrum a distinct discourse of African-American youth, with obvious regional variations, emerged to narrate, critique, challenge, and deconstruct the realities of postindustrial life. Hip-hop music and culture represented such a discourse.

The Discourse(s) of Hip-Hop: Resistance, Consumption, and African-American Youth Culture

While many African-American youth were not privy to the everyday realities of the black urban experience, a distinct urban-based African-American youth culture emerged in the mid- to late 1970s. Prior to World War II African-American youth culture was largely hidden from mainstream culture, subsumed within the parameters of segregated black spaces. The zoot suit riots and explosion of bebop music represented the first real glimpse into African-American youth culture for those beyond the confines of segregated urban spaces. Though bebop was essentially an aesthetic movement driven by the sensibilities of black male musicians, some well into their thirties who were reacting to racism in the North, the movement was given its energy and stylistic acumen by African-American youth who embraced the movement as a form of transcendence/resistance from the everyday drudgery of their existence. Zoot suits, the lindy-hop, and jive were all the nuances that African-American youth brought to the subculture of bebop music.

Historically African-American youth culture has rarely been driven by ideological concerns, but instead has embraced, appropriated, and reanimated existing structures, organizations, and institutions that African-American youth perceived as empowering them within various social, cultural, and economic constructs. Many of the stylistic excesses associated with African-American youth culture were conscious efforts to deconstruct and critique mass-mediated images of African-American youth. The impact of African-American youth culture on existing political and social movements was perhaps most profound when black youth embraced the Civil Rights movement of the early 1960s. The lunch-counter sit-ins, marches, and Freedom Summer bus rides were all emblematic of the impact of black youth culture on the movement. The development of the Student Nonviolent Coordinating Committee (SNCC), often referred to as the youth wing of the traditional Civil Rights movement, was a recognition on the part of the traditional leadership of the importance of black youth to mass social movement.

That importance was further realized when African-American youth began to reject the strategies of the traditional Civil Rights leadership and embraced the nationalist leanings of the Nation of Islam and later the Black Panther Party. The Black Panther Party, whose members were often culled from youth street gangs like the Slausons in south-central Los Angeles and the Blackstone Rangers in Chicago, personified African-American youth culture's ability to impact upon mainstream culture both within and beyond the Black Public Sphere.[17] Not surprisingly, such overtly political organizations gave way to less-inspiring constructs as a direct response to the collapse of the Civil Rights/Black Power movements and the increased commodification of wealth and consumption within mass culture. Thus the return to street-level gangs like the Crips and Bloods in Los Angeles or the Black Spades in New York City where emblematic of the belief within African-American youth culture that mass consumption and the accumulation of wealth for mass consumption were the most viable means of social transcendence afforded them in the post–Civil Rights era. The introduction of the crack cocaine industry into black urban spaces further enhanced such notions well into the 1990s.

Hip-hop music and culture emerged as a narrative and stylistic distillation of African-

American youth sensibilities in the late 1970s. Hip-hop differed from previous structures influenced by African-American youth in that it was largely predicated and driven by black youth culture itself. The fact that hip-hop emerged as a culture organic to African-American youth in urban spaces reflects the aforementioned social isolation afforded black youth and the conscious effort by many corporate capitalists to develop a popular music industry largely anchored by the sensibilities of American youth. Given this context, it was perfectly natural that the most profound aesthetic movement in black popular music in the post–Civil Rights era would be profoundly influenced by black youth culture. In reality, African-American youth appropriated many diverse examples of black expressive culture, including the Jamaican Toast tradition, and created an aesthetic movement that was uniquely tailored to their historic moment and their own existential desires.

I maintain that the emergence of hip-hop, which appeared in a rudimentary state in the mid-1970s, was representative of a concerted effort by youth urban blacks to use mass-culture to facilitate communal discourse across a fractured and dislocated national community. As Rose states, "Rappers' emphasis on posses and neighborhoods has brought the ghetto back into the public consciousness. It satisfies poor youth black people's profound need to have their territories acknowledged, recognized and celebrated."[18] While much of this activity was driven by the need to give voice to issues that privilege the local and the private within the postindustrial city—thus the overdetermined constructions of masculinity, sexuality, criminality, and even an urban patriarchy—hip-hop's best attempts at social commentary and critique represented traditions normalized and privileged historically in the Black Public Sphere of the urban North. Arguably the most significant form of counterhegemonic art in the black community over the last twenty years, the genre's project questions power and influence politically in the contexts of American culture and capitalism, the dominance of black middle-class discourse, but most notably the "death of community" witnessed by African-American youth in the postindustrial era.

Despite its intense commodification, hip-hop has managed to continuously subvert mass-market limitations by investing in its own philosophical groundings. Like bebop before it, hip-hop's politics was initially a politics of style that created an aural and stylistic community in response to the erosion of community with the postindustrial city. Perhaps more that any other previous popular form, hip-hop thrived on its own creative and aesthetic volatility by embracing such volatility as part of its stylistic traditions. This has allowed the form to maintain an aesthetic and narrative distance from mass-market limitations, though I must acknowledge that it is often a transient moment. As Tricia Rose suggests, "Developing a style nobody can deal with—a style that cannot be easily understood or erased, a style that has the reflexivity to create counter-dominant narratives against a mobile and shifting enemy—may be one of the most effective ways to fortify communities of resistance and *simultaneously* reserve the right to communal pleasure."[19]

Commercial disinterest in the form during its developing years allowed for its relatively autonomous development. Relying largely on word of mouth and live performance as a means of promotion, hip-hop represents the last black popular form to be wholly derived from the experiences and texts of the black urban landscape. In the aftermath of disco and corporate America's considerable retreat from its commitment to producing and distributing black popular music, hip-hop was allowed to flourish in public spaces and on several independent recording labels. Hip-hop's live performances were largely predicated on the recovery of commodified black musical texts, for the purpose of reintegrating these texts into the organic terrain of black urban communities. According to critic Paul Gilroy:

Music recorded on disk loses its preordained authority as it is transformed and adapted.... A range of de/reconstructive procedures—scratch mixing, dubbing, toasting, rapping, and beatboxing—contribute to new layers of local meaning. The original performance trapped in plastic is supplemented by new contributions at every stage. Performer and audience alike strive to create pleasures that can evade capture and sale as cultural commodities.[20]

Like bebop, hip-hop appropriated popular texts, often refiguring them to serve hip-hop sensibilities. This phenomenon contextually questions and ultimately undermines the notion of corporate ownership of popular music and would have legal ramifications well into the decade of the 1990s.[21] Gilroy's comments are instructive in that even as hip-hop became a thoroughly commodified form in the late 1980s, its ability to mine the rich musical traditions of the African-American diaspora through the process of sampling allowed the form to privilege local and specific meanings historically aligned with organic sites of resistance and recovery.

For African-American youth, hip-hop music also allowed them to counter the iconography of fear, menace, and spectacle that dominated mass-mediated perceptions of contemporary black life by giving voice to the everyday human realities of black life in ways that could not be easily reduced to commodifiable stereotypes. The release of Grandmaster Flash and the Furious Five's "The Message" was a prime example of these sensibilities in the early stages of hip-hop. Recorded and released in 1982 to mainstream critical acclaim, it is the first hip-hop recording to be accorded such praise. Part of the recording's obvious appeal to mainstream critics was its unmitigated and "authentic" portrayal of contemporary black urban life. "The Message" was the first significant political recording produced in the postsoul era, representing an astute critique of the rise and impact of the Reagan right on working-class and urban locales.

Melle Mel's narrative portrays the transformation of the individual spirit within a context that offers little or no choice or freedom for those contained within it. Within Melle Mel's text, the fate of the individual spirit living within the parameters of the postindustrial urban landscape has been consigned at birth to live a short and miserable life. Representative of the genre, hip-hop was perhaps the first popular form of black music that offered little or no hope to its audience. The fatalistic experience has become a standard trope of urban-based hip-hop—"The Message" is but one clarion example of this. Juxtaposing diminishing hope and the rampant materialism of the underground economy of the urban landscape, Melle Mel identifies a ghetto hierarchy that ghetto youth have little choice but to invest in. Here, Melle Mel is cognizant of the "role model" void produced by middle-class flight and the lack of quality institutions to offset the influence of the illicit underground economy. In this context, Melle Mel identifies the failure of inner-city schools to provide a necessary buffer against urban malaise.

Seven years after the release of "The Message," more than 600,000 black men ages twenty to twenty-nine were either incarcerated, paroled, or on probation. The American prison population doubled over the twelve-year period from 1977 to 1989.[22] What Stevie Wonder had emphatically prophesied in "Living for the City" had become a stark and inescapable reality for the urban constituency that Melle Mel represented in "The Message." Using dated tropes of black masculinity and political resistance, Melle Mel considers a penal system that is incapable of producing rehabilitated individuals and has become a site of sexual violence between men. If the ideological imagination of the Black Power movement was partially related to the reintroduction of a hypermasculine patriarchy within the black community, Melle Mel's imagery of black male rape is an assertion that the Civil Rights/Black Power eras were far removed historically and intellectually from the landscape of the postindustrial city. In the end, Melle Mel transforms his ghetto narrative into a contemporary slave narrative, in which the protagonist chooses death at his own hands as opposed to incarceration and enslavement.[23]

The closing moments of "The Message" find members of Grandmaster Flash and the Furious Five engaged in casual banter on a street corner in New York. The group is shortly confronted by members of the NYPD who immediately accuse them of and arrest them for some unnamed crime. In a comic moment, one of the group members asserts, "But we're Grandmaster Flash and the Furious Five," to which a cop responds, "What is that, a gang?" and proceeds with his arrest. While the scene on one level acknowledges the lack of status afforded hip-hop artists within mainstream culture, a recurring theme in hip-hop, it also is a thinly veiled appropriation of a similar moment during Stevie Wonder's "Living for the City." I suggest that a comparison of the two recordings adequately details the changes within the postindustrial urban landscape over a period of nine years.

The most significant difference in the two texts is the fact that Wonder's protagonist migrates from the American South, during what is the very last stages of the black migration from the South in the twentieth century. Melle Mel's protagonist was born in the urban North, and thus could never invest in the type of promise that was articulated in the oppositional meanings of the mass migration. It is this lack of hope that remains a constant marker of the differences detailed in both narratives. While Wonder's protagonist is unwittingly introduced to the economic subculture of the urban North, Melle Mel's protagonist makes a conscious choice to invest in the economic subculture of the postindustrial city, precisely because of the lack of educational and economic opportunities that Wonder's protagonist envisioned in the urban North in the first place. Both artists are critical of the lack of rehabilitation that takes place in the American penal system, though the world that Wonder's protagonist returns to after prison is more closely aligned to the world that Melle Mel's character is born into.

The death of Melle Mel's protagonist suggests that the continuing transformation of the urban landscape will produce an environment that is as unlivable as it is unbearable and perhaps unnameable, within Melle Mel's narrative imagination. For example, neither Wonder nor Grandmaster Flash could foretell the coming threat of crack addiction within the black community, though Melle Mel would document its presence on his solo recording "King of the Streets" in 1984, almost two years before mainstream culture would acknowledge the presence of what is defined as a "smokable, efficient, and inexpensive" drug, that produces "hyperactive, paranoid, psychotic, and extremely violent" addicts.[24] The introduction of crack cocaine into the black urban landscape would arguably have as much effect on the quality of life within the postindustrial city as black middle-class flights and the postindustrial economy. Hip-hop music and the burgeoning "ghetto" cinema that emerges from within its traditions were both uniquely poised to represent the realities of contemporary black urban life within mainstream culture. In their best moments, these cultural narratives create critical exchange within the vast constituencies of the African-American diaspora. In their worse moments, these narratives were too often interpreted by a dislocated black middle-class as the products of individuals who lack the civility and determination that befit their middle class sensibilities. Almost a full century after the first articulation of the "New Negro," the old Negro had been transformed from southern migrant to urban ghetto dweller, and the black middle class was equally disdainful of both.

Despite recordings like "The Message," early hip-hop recordings rarely ventured beyond themes associated with the everyday experiences of urban-based African-American youth. Because of hip-hop's intimate connection to African-American youth culture, its narratives usually mirrored whatever concerns were deemed crucial to black youth. Like the music that echoed throughout black dance halls in the 1930s and 1940s, the "party and bullshit" themes of most early hip-hop represented efforts to transcend the dull realities of urban life, including body-numbing experiences within low-wage service industries and inferior and condescending urban school systems. Though hip-hop represented an art form that countered mainstream sensibilities and clearly could be construed as a mode of social resistance, in and of itself, it was not invested with political dimensions, at least not any more so than African-American youth culture contained within itself. At best hip-hop represented a distinct mode of youthful expression primed to serve as a conduit for political discourse as it coincided with the sensibilities of black youth. Jesse Jackson's first presidential campaign in 1984 and the reemergence of Louis Farrakhan and the Nation of Islam represented two distinct though related phenomena that would politicize black youth and thus politicize some aspects of hip-hop music in the early to mid-1980s.

On the surface Jesse Jackson's presidential campaign in 1984 was largely rooted in the discourse of the traditional Civil Rights movement and thus was not initially attractive to hip-hop's primary constituency. The Civil Rights movement and electoral politics, for that matter, were often interpreted as being marginal to the primary concerns of the black urban poor. The failure of the increased numbers of black elected officials in various municipalities to adequately empower the black poor in those municipalities is one of many issues responsible for such interpretations. But Jackson's campaign, which was publicly parlayed as the first serious attempt at the presidency by an African-American—Shirley Chisholm's efforts in 1972 largely removed the black political landscape—attracted tacit support throughout the African-American diaspora because of its historic meaning.

Louis Farrakhan's public support of Jackson's efforts offered the Nation of Islam leader the mainstream visibility, if not credibility, that the Nation of Islam had not been afforded since the death of Malcolm X. Though Farrakhan's black nationalist politics and critiques of white supremacy were often oppositional to the broad mainstream appeal that Jackson craved and needed to be seriously considered for the presidency, his momentary alliance with Jackson gave him access to the black masses, particularly the urban masses who had long rejected the style of political activism that Jackson personified. Particularly appealing to black urban youth was Farrakhan's willingness, like his late mentor Malcolm X, to speak forcefully about the nature of American race relations and the evils of white supremacy. Farrakhan's penchant for rhetoric, which often bordered on anti-Semitism, effectively demonized him among mainstream pundits, and his subsequent outlaw status further attracted black youths who felt themselves demonized in mainstream culture. Farrakhan's inability to project lasting solutions to the problems that face the urban poor did not deter support from black youth, in that his channeling of black rage in a national context validated the black rage that black youth often expressed within their own personal and local contexts. Farrakhan's rage, within the context of the increasing misery of urban life, provided the impetus for segments of the hip-hop community channel their own critiques of white supremacy and expressions of black rage into their music.

The group Public Enemy was perhaps the most accomplished at projecting black rage as a political discourse that would prove attractive to the youth audiences that hip-hop garnered. Born and raised on the fringes of the Black Panther Party, Public Enemy leader Chuck D intuitively understood the attractiveness of black nationalism to urban youth in the 1960s and attempted to reintroduce many of those themes to black youth within a contemporary social and aesthetic context. Chuck D's political rhetoric for the Reagan era was initially and cautiously presented on Public Enemy's first recording, *Yo! Bum Rush the Show,* in 1987. It failed to attract black youth audiences, mostly because much of the music was undanceable, heresy for those who are serious about making music popular among black youth. Moreover, given black radio's initial rejection of hip-hop and the subtle transformation of the music from a live/public form of expression to one increasingly produced in a studio for mass consumption, it was imperative for its survival that hip-hop be conducive to the types of public spaces where black youth were most likely to convene. Dance halls or clubs continued to be the most accessible spaces for black youth to congregate, so the challenge for those who were interested in presenting hip-hop as political discourse was to make sure the music was danceable. Public Enemy later recorded a succession of twelve-inch releases that were not necessarily any more danceable than those found on *Yo! Bum Rush the Show,* but instead challenged and dared black youth to dance to them, much the way bebop artists dared black youth to lindy-hop to their self-styled musical tomes.

The sonic cacophony of "Rebel Without a Pause" and "Bring the Noise" represented the vanguard of hip-hop production styles. Chuck D's driving baritone was the perfect foil for the "organized confusion" that was a staple of Public Enemy's producers, The Bomb Squad. These innovations proved enticing to both a mainstream public and black youth, who were perhaps tired of the unimaginative drum machine programming that had come to dominate the genre. *It Takes a Nation to Hold Us Back,* released in the late spring of 1988, represented Public Enemy's vision for hip-hop's role in galvanizing a political vanguard in the post–Civil Rights era. As Greg Tate wrote at the time of the recording's release:

> Nation of Millions is a declaration of war on the federal government, and that unholy trinity—black radio programmers, crack dealers, and rock critics.... For sheer audacity and specificity Chuck D's enemies list rivals anything produced by the Black Liberation Army or punk—rallying for retribution against the Feds for the Panthers' fall ("Party for your Right to Fight"), slapping murder charges on the FBI and CIA for the assassinations of MLK and Malcolm X ("Black Steel in the Hour of Chaos"), assailing copyright law and the court system ("Caught, Can I Get a Witness").[25]

Chuck D's call for truth, justice, and a black nationalist way of life was perhaps the most potent of any political narratives that had appeared on a black popular recording. Public Enemy very consciously attempted to have hip-hop serve the revolutionary vanguard, the way soul did during the 1960s. Despite Public Enemy's vast popularity among black and white youth audiences, their 1960s-style rhetoric raised old antagonisms from those further on the political right as well as mainstream African-American leaders concerned about both the group's militancy and its obvious connections to Farrakhan and the Nation of Islam.

Chuck D clearly saw hip-hop as an alternative medium for black youth and their fellow travelers to access political and social reality as constructed by Public Enemy. Nowhere was this more evident than on the song "Don't Believe the Hype," where Chuck D offers a compelling argument for media education. Chuck D characterizes mainstream media as misinformed and malicious in their distribution of misinformation. Chuck D's narrative constitutes a counternarrative to mainstream attacks on the social and political commentary reflected in the work of the group. In an effort to democratize the mainstream critical establishment, the Public Enemy front man links his experiences to John Coltrane. Coltrane's jazz explorations in the 1960s were also criticized by a biased and misinformed critical establishment. Chuck D embraces a nationalist argument that suggests that critiques of black popular culture are best performed by those immersed in the organic culture that produces it. Within Chuck D's worldview, hip-hop represents the most natural environment in which to critique the social and political experiences of an urban-based African-American constituency. Black radio's early rejection of hip-hop, excepting the few late-night programming slots given to well-known hip-hop DJs in the major markets, reflected the sentiments of the black middle class regarding hip-hop and in part reflected a historical trend among the black middle class regarding popular art forms that emerge from the black working-class experience.

But Public Enemy's resuscitation of 1960s-style black political rhetoric was often problematic, particularly when considering that the group's primary constituents were not likely to provide the type of critique that was necessary to realize Chuck D's lofty goals. Chuck D's politics were particularly problematic in the area of gender, where tracks like "She Watch Channel Zero" could have been used as a chorus for Reagan's attacks on "welfare queens," as the track suggested that black women who watch soap operas are partially to blame for the precarious predicament of black children. Public Enemy's failure to adequately critique the ideals they espoused was of course logical in the type of vacuum that their rhetoric was reproduced in. The erosion of communal exchange that marked the post–Civil Rights period, also denied the movement the ability to critique itself in ways that would allow it to be self-sustaining and progressive. Thus a younger generation of activists emerged, many of whom were not privy to the type of communal processes that were crucial to black political discourse prior to the Civil Rights movement, and they appropriated the ideological themes of the era without the benefit of critiquing these themes to make them more applicable to a contemporary context. The fact that groups like Public Enemy were unable to critique the sexism inherent to much of black political thought in the 1960s is particularly disheartening in that black women have been the most outspoken critics of the movement's shortcomings, particularly in regard to gender issues.[26] Unfortunately, Public Enemy's political shortcomings were easy to ignore, as Greg Tate relates: "Were it not for the fact that Nation is the most hellacious and hilarious dance record of the decade, nobody but the converted would give two hoots about PE's millenary desires."[27]

The release of *It Takes a Nation of Millions to Hold Us Back* coincided with several industry initiatives that offered hip-hop much more accessibility and visibility. Two years after the release of Run-DMC's landmark *Raisin' Hell* recording, many independent recording labels that featured hip-hop entered into distribution deals with corporate conglomerates. The Def Jam label's sale to conglomerate CBS/Columbia was strikingly reminiscent of the conglomerate's relationship with Gamble and Huff more than a decade earlier. With distribution outlets increased and cooperate labels having more money to spend on artist development, hip-hop began its growth as one of the more popular music genres, this despite all of the negative connotations associated with it within mainstream society. Never radio-friendly, hip-hop got a necessary promotional boost with the debut of *Yo MTV Raps* on MTV in the fall of 1988. Music video opened hip-hop to an audience of mid-Americans youths, who relished in the subversive "otherness" that the music and its purveyors represented. By the time Gangsta rap (an often cartoonish portrayal of black masculinity, ghetto realism, and gangster sensibilities) became one of the most popular genres of hip-hop, a significant portion of the music was largely supported by young white Americans.

Despite such successful recordings as *Fear of a Black Planet* (1990) and *Apocalypse '91 . . . The Enemy Strikes Black* (1991), *It Takes a Nation . . .*, would be the apex of politically infused hip-hop and Public Enemy's popularity among black youth. The failure of explicit political discourse to remain an integral part of hip-hop was influenced by various dynamics. Placing a premium on lyrical content, artists like Public Enemy, Boogie Down Productions featuring KRS-One, Paris, X-Clan, former Public Enemy member Professor Griff, and Michael Franti and the Disposable Heroes of Hiphoprisy all failed to grasp the significance of producing music that would be considered danceable by the black masses they aimed to attract. As Tate surmised about Public Enemy's first recording, many of these artists produced music that consistently "moved the crowd off the floor."[28] The simultaneous emergence of NWA (Niggas with Attitude), whose production by Dr. Dre effectively altered the hop-hop landscape by removing the industry focus away from the East Coast and New York specifically, should have been instructive to artists with explicit political designs. Lacking a cohesive ideology but possessing an accessible critique of poverty, economic exploitation, and police brutality in postindustrial Los Angeles, NWA recordings like "Fuck the Police," from *Straight Out of Compton* (1988), ingratiated them to those who shared their experience and craved a funky beat. Ironically it was NWA's antipolice anthem that drew the most attention from federal agencies like the FBI and not the more ideologically sound rhetoric of groups like Public Enemy or Boogie Down Productions.

Ultimately, political hip-hop was undermined by hip-hop's own internal logic that often privileged constant stylistic innovation, both in narrative and musical content, as a response to intense commodification. Thus as Todd Boyd suggests, political hip-hop "seems to have functioned as a genre whose popularity had passed, instead of a sustained movement which connected both cultural artifacts and 'real' political events."[29] But political hip-hop was also challenged by efforts of segments of mainstream culture to control or "police" hip-hop, efforts that would ultimately transfer control of the genre away from its organic purveyors and limit access to the form in communal settings where alternative interpretations could be derived which countered mass-mediated presentations of the genre. These threats to hip-hop's ability to function as conduit for communal exchange came from those already entrusted to police black youth, the insurance industry and corporate America, the latter of which slowly began to continue their aborted effort to fully annex the black popular recording industry.

Fear of a Black Commodity: The Policing, Criminalization, and Commodification of Hip-Hop Culture

In November 1992, Spike Lee produced and directed the cinematic epic *Malcolm X*. The fact that the most visible icon of black political resistance over the past thirty years was the focus of a Hollywood film would suggest that the efforts of groups like Public Enemy and X-Clan had successfully altered the landscape of mainstream American culture. Only three years earlier another Spike Lee film, *Do the Right Thing,* which featured Public Enemy's now-classic recording "Fight the Power," was criticized for potentially stirring the black masses to violence in response to the film's vivid portrayal of race relations in a fictional Brooklyn neighborhood.[30] Several months before the release of Lee's *Malcolm X,* the city of Los Angeles exploded in violence in response to the acquittal of the police officers involved in the videotaped beating of black motorist Rodney King. On the surface the communal response to the highly controversial court decision further suggested that hip-hop had succeeded in producing a visible and influential political vanguard. But *Malcolm X* was instead released to much mainstream acclaim for the film, its director, and its star, Denzel Washington, who earned an Academy Award nomination for his portrayal of the black nationalist icon. The revolutionary vanguard that Lee, Public Enemy, Louis Farrakhan, and Malcolm X's memory supposedly inspired were instead to found "Rolling wit Dre." While such a reality clearly suggests that the political expediency that some hip-hop artists tried to instill in black expressive culture had been subsumed by the economic interests of a cadre of middle-class black artists driven by the demands of corporate capitalism, it also reflected the limits placed on political expression in an era where public expressions of identity and self-determination are so readily commodified and mediated for mass consumption, particularly when such consumption could in fact distribute values contrary to those valued in mainstream culture.

Following the highly influential solo efforts of former NWA comrade Ice Cube, whose recordings *AmeriKKKa's Most Wanted* (1990), *Death Certificate* (1991), and *The Predator* (1992) captured hip-hop's creative imagination, Dr. Dre released his first solo recording, *The Chronic,* in the autumn of 1992. Dr. Dre's musical ode to "good weed" and the self-styled lifestyles of postindustrial gangsters had all but solidified the Los Angeles area as the dominant creative and commercial force in hip-hop and the "G-Funk" of Dr. Dre and his protégés Snoop Doggy Dog and Warren G as the dominant production style. The underlying influences of G-Funk, or as it came to be known among mainstreams pundits, "gangsta rap," included narratives as diverse as the fiction of Iceberg Slim, the music of Parliament-Funkadelic, and Brian De Palma's 1983 remake of the film *Scarface.* Within contemporary black male culture, particularly that located within poverty-stricken urban spaces, the film had long been embraced as a contemporary example of a postimmigration attempt at pursuing the American Dream. Like the cocaine industry that framed the film's core themes, crack cocaine served a similar purpose in the real-life narratives of the young black men that the film appeals to. The culture and industry of crack's intimate relationship to the culture and industry of hip-hop would be realized with *The Chronic* and Dr. Dre's stirring production style.

The introduction of the G-Funk was largely framed by efforts of various social forces to curtail and control the popularity of hip-hop and its potential use as a conduit for oppositional discourse(s). Though Public Enemy's efforts to create a political insurgency for the 1980s were destined to fail because they existed beyond an actual political movement rooted in legitimate political concerns, and the efforts of NWA, while more closely aligned to sensibilities of black urban youth, ultimately lacked the political sophistication to be a legitimate threat to mainstream society, both efforts held the potential to galvanize popular resistance to some of mainstream culture's core sensibilities. Nowhere was this more evident than the response from law enforcement agencies in the aftermath of NWA's "Fuck tha Police." The circulation of the recording, which critiques police violence against black youth, instigated an unprecedented response from the assistant director of the FBI, who charged the group with advocating violence against law enforcement officers. The notoriety of the song was used against the group as law enforcement officers in several cities openly challenged the group to perform the song in concert with threats of detaining them or shutting down their shows.[31]

The policing of NWA reflected an increasingly common trend to criminalize hip-hop artists, their audiences, and the music itself. Thus seemingly random, incidental acts of violence and criminal activity occurring at hip-hop concerts were characterized as social intolerable communal acts capable of destroying the civility of mainstream society. Very often these random exchanges were instigated by the treatment that young concertgoers received from arena security, as many venues forced ticket holders to be searched for drugs, weapons, or any other paraphernalia that could be defined as counter to mainstream sensibilities. As Tricia Rose relates:

> The public school system, the police, and the popular media perceive and construct young African Americans as a dangerous internal element in urban America; an element that, if allowed to roam freely, will threaten the social order; an element that must be policed. Since rap music is understood as the predominate symbolic voice of black urban males, it heightens this sense of threat and reinforces dominant white middle class objections to urban black youths who do not aspire to (but are haunted by) white middle class standards.[32]

Mainstream reaction to hip-hop concerts, particularly the reactions of law enforcement agencies, was rooted in deeply held historical concerns about the congregation of African-Americans in public spaces. These concerns were heightened and legitimized within mainstream society in the post–World War II period as African-American youth began to assert themselves socially, culturally, and politically and in the process publicly question various forms of social authority that countered their own desires. Thus the criminalization of African-American youth in mass media contributed to the type of social paranoia already existent in American society, particularly since most major concert venues were in locations most suitable for access by white middle-class suburbanites. Thus in the eyes of many suburban whites, hip-hop concerts in places like Long Island's Nassau Coliseum represented a temporary threat to the day-to-day stability of white suburban life. The historic policing of public spaces where blacks often congregated often had a profound impact on the ability of African-Americans to build and maintain community, and such was the case when young African-Americans congregated at the local clubs and concert venues where the core values of the "hip-hop" generation were distributed and critiqued.

Despite such efforts to curtail community building within the hip-hop "community," hip-hop concerts remained a thriving industry for various promoters, performers, and venue operators, though increased collusion on the part of venue operators, the insurance industry, and law enforcement agencies began to erode acceptable public spaces for an art form, itself predicated on the lack of viable public space in black communities. The insurance industry had a particularly compelling impact by raising venue insurance rates for hip-hop concerts in relations to the public paranoia associated with hip-hop performances, in effect making the promotion of such events a distinct financial risk. Common strategies included the denial of insurance for any promoter who promoted a show where "significant" violence erupted or even a tenfold increase in the minimum insurance allowed to cover a hip-hop event. What was insidious about this practice is that the criminalization of hip-hop in mainstream society effectively helped mask racist efforts to deny black expression, as venue operators and insurance companies regularly facilitated concerts by white acts whose concerts also featured random and incidental acts of criminality, without the constraints placed on hip-hop artists. As Tricia Rose suggests, such efforts mirrored previous efforts to control the influence of jazz music via cabaret laws.[33]

As the number of venues willing to present hip-hop concerts evaporated, mass media increasingly dominated the presentation of not only mainstream critiques of hip-hop, but hip-hop itself. The social and public policing of hip-hop and its audiences coincided with the corporate annexation of the hip-hop industry and a subsequent period of intense commodification. Increasingly as programs like MTV's *Yo! MTV Raps* and major recording labels like SONY and Warner Brothers became the primary outlets to access hip-hop discourse, the discourse itself was subject to social controls rooted in corporate attempts to mainstream hip-hop for mass consumption. So successful were these efforts initially that Oakland-based rapper MC Hammer could legitimately claim Michael Jackson's "King of Pop" title, as he attempted to do upon the release of his 1991 recording *Too Legit to Quit*.[34] Part and parcel of Hammer's success was the mainstreaming of the iconography of black youth culture—Hammer's clothes and hairstyles were as appealing to young white as his music—and the distribution of narratives that were palatable to mainstream sensibilities even if they were often nonsensical.

But hip-hop's notoriety was also a stimulus for its own commercialization as recording labels carefully distributed recordings and videos to be accessed via alternative video outlets like the Black Entertainment Channel's (BET) *Rap City* or viewer request channels like *The Box*, who were more willing to present videos from artists who rejected mainstream impositions. This was particularly effective in the marketing of "gangsta rap" as the subgenre's notoriety and the notoriety of its artists correlated directly to recording sales. Like the jazz performers that Norman Mailer so eloquently describes in his essay "The White Negro," the apolitical "G," who stood at the center of the G-funk universe, proved attractive to young whites who viewed hip-hop as a conduit for oppositional expression and the "G" as a model for oppositional behavior. Via hip-hop music and videos, the antisocial behavior of "fictional" black drug dealers was embraced by many young whites as a mode of social resistance, though this influence was manifested in stylistic acumen and not political mobilization.

Hip-hop artists became the spokespersons for stylistic developments within black youth culture and hip-hop the vehicle for which these styles would be commodified for mass consumption both within and beyond mainstream culture. Clothing designers and companies as diverse as Timberland, Starter, Tommy Hilfiger, and even haute couture designers like Versace benefited from the visibility of hip-hop artists who willingly used their bodies, music, and videos—often without remuneration—to market these products. Of course the attraction of black youth to these products is the manifestation of complex identity issues where black youth equate social status with mass consumerism. Much of what is today a multibillion-dollar industry was stabilized when the black middle-class entrepreneurial spirit collided with corporate capitalist desire as hip-hop artists and fellow travelers begin to exploit hip-hop's mainstream influence for financial gain beyond recording contracts. Thus black entrepreneurs like Karl Kani and hip-hop artists like the WU-Tang Clan, who started a line of clothing called WU Wear, became petit bourgeois exploiters of hip-hop's popularity. These developments mirrored changes from within the recording industry itself that would have tremendous impact on hip-hop culture.

Reflecting the furious consolidation that has taken place in the entertainment industry, more than 80 percent of all music recorded in the United States was controlled by six major corporate entities. Black popular forms accounted for approximately 25 percent of the total sales of recorded music. Exploiting the black nationalist/capitalist rhetoric among the black working class and middle-class elite, still marginalized even after two decades of Civil Rights legislation, many corporate entities would turn "ghetto pop" producers into contemporary ghetto merchants. Arista/BMG for example, run by Clive Davis, was once home to three distinct boutique labels run by Antonio Reid and Kenneth Edmonds (LaFace), Sean "Puffy" Combs (Bad Boy) and until recently, Dallas Austin (Rowdy). While Quincy Jones and Gamble and Huff were seasoned songwriters, producers, and businesspersons, many of the ghetto pop vanguard were only a few years removed from high school and lacked any definitive critical perspectives beyond the marketing of their respective boutique labels. Many of these artist/producers remain distanced from the real seats of power within their respective corporate homes—power that could be defined along the lines of point or sole ownership of recording masters, control over production and promotional costs, and the authority to hire and replace internal staff members.[35] In many regards, many of these ghetto merchants are little more than glorified managers or overseers, involved in what was little more than a twenty-first century plantation operation.

Stephen Haymes's work on urban pedagogy and resistance constructs a broader paradigm to interpret the connection between contemporary hip-hop and mass consumer culture. In his work Haymes suggests that the intense commodification of African-American culture and the changes in the consumption habits of the black masses is rooted in structural changes linked to the process of American Fordism.[36] Historically linked to efforts to raise workers' wages as a vehicle to increase consumption, Fordism is the concept around which much of the industrial labor force has been structured throughout the twentieth century, as higher wages and concepts of leisure helped promote the burgeoning advertising industry, which emerged to help stimulate and institutionalize consumptionist desire in industrial workers. The consumptionist ethic became as valuable as the work ethnic in the construction of Americanness. But as Haymes further suggests, the failure of the Fordist model to counter market saturation in the post–Civil Rights era led to the emergence of a subsequent model, which he refers to as neo-Fordism, designed to both integrate the black populace into mainstream markets and increase consumption. As he states, "Unlike the strategy of Fordism, which sought to fuel demand by integrating the industrial working class via higher wages, neo-Fordism aimed, through an expanded welfare state, to fuel demand and economic growth by also integrating poor and working-class blacks into the American Dream."[37]

Of course much of this state-sanctioned expansion collapsed with the emergence of the Reagan right in the early 1980s, though the logic of neo-Fordism continued as the advertising industry increasingly became the vehicle by which not only goods and services were promoted but lifestyles and identities were constructed and consumed. This was partially achieved through the process of niche marketing, where specific products were aimed at various populations based on income, social status, race, gender, and ethnicity. What is important here is that individuals no longer consumed products, but also the social status and lifestyle that particular products represented. Accordingly, the high visibility of au couture fashions and other emblems of conspicuous wealth within hip-hop served to stimulate desire and consumption that transcended the structural realities of many black urban youth; processes that were often construed as forms of resistance against the invisibility and misery associated with black urban life. Not surprisingly, such marketing trends occur during an era when much of black popular expression has in fact been annexed by the engines of corporate capitalism and thus black popular expression is placed in the service of stimulating consumption among the very masses for whom the American Dream was inaccessible throughout much of the twentieth century.

In less than a decade, hip-hop culture had been transformed from a subculture primarily influenced by the responses of black urban youth to postindustrialization into a billion-dollar industry in which such responses were exploited by corporate capitalist and the petit bourgeois desires of the black middle class. The latter developments offered little relief to the realities of black urban youth who remained hip-hop's core constituents, though the economic successes of hip-hop artists and the black entrepreneurs associated with contemporary black popular music were often used to counter public discussions about the negative realities of black urban life. Economic issues aside, corporate control of black popular expression, often heightened the contradictions inherent in music produced across an economically deprived and racially delimited urban landscape. As Rose relates:

> In the case of rap music, which takes place under intense public surveillance … contradictions regarding class, gender, and race are highlighted, decontextualized, and manipulated so as to destabilize rap's resistive elements. Rap's resistive, yet contradictory, positions were waged in the face of a powerful, media-supported construction of black urban America as a source of urban social ills that threaten social order. Rappers' speech acts are heavily shaped by music industry demands, sanctions, and prerogatives. These discursive wars are waged in the face of sexist and patriarchal assumptions that support and promote verbal abuse of black women.[38]

Within this context, discourse(s) of resistance were undermined by narratives with privileged patriarchal, sexist, and even misogynistic ideals, that were themselves taken out of their organic contexts. In the past, socially problematic narratives were critiqued and distributed according to communal sensibilities in a process that maintained the contextual integrity in which the narratives were produced. Ironically the most visible critiques of hip-hop and ghetto pop emit from black middle-class groups who are in part responsible for the fractured quality of social and political narratives produced by black urban youths in the postindustrial city.

Postindustrial Nostalgia: Mass Media, Memory, and Community

In the spring of 1994, talk show host Arsenio Hall ended his successful run as host of *The Arsenio Hall Show,* a nighttime talk and variety show. Only a year earlier, Hall had celebrated the fifth anniversary of his show with a rousing rendition of Sly Stone's "Thank You (Falettinme Be Mice Elf Agin)" led by soul singer Bobby Womack and soul recluse Sly Stone himself. The song's performance was a metaphor for the show itself, as the show served as a vehicle for the presentation of black popular culture on black popular culture's own terms. Though Hall's own hyperblack antics often broached the worst stereotypes associated with black men, including his insatiable desire to fawn over white women guests, Hall and his audiences reveled in the insiderisms that mainstream America was not privy, but was so willing to consume. For a six-year period, *The Arsenio Hall Show* remained a fixture in African-American households, precisely because it represented a link to community and black expressive culture, as Hall used his own memories of black Cleveland as a springboard to personify contemporary black anxieties and concerns through humor. *The Arsenio Hall Show* was crucial to the hip-hop community because Hall allowed his show to be a forum for their concerns, not just as performers, but as public spokespersons and critics for their communities. Thus it was not unusual for Hall to interview the likes of KRS-One or female hip-hop artist YO-YO about the complexities of hip-hop and black urban life. Like *Soul Train* a generation earlier, Hall's show was an audiovisual remnant to seminal black public spaces that promoted communal exchange and critique. Though Hall's interviews often lacked depth, he covered an astounding diversity of issues and personalities.

Hall's late-night television show ended as Spike Lee premiered his seventh film, his first since *Malcolm X* appeared in late 1992. Personified by cultural workers like filmmaker Lee, the black middle class responded to the proliferation of ghetto imagery and "ghetto pop" that appeared in commodified form on television, film, and black radio stations with a nostalgic return to the 1970s. Lee's 1994 film *Crooklyn* is an example of what I call postindustrial nostalgia, loosely described as a nostalgia that has its basis in the postindustrial transformations of black urban life during the 1970s. While the pop-cultural texts of the 1970s have proved to be huge commodities for this generation of black cultural producers, I maintain that these nostalgic turns yearn more for the historic period they consume as opposed to the profit motives that inspire their appropriation and reanimation, as the decade of the 1970s marked the increasing tensions of a burgeoning postindustrial economy and the continued erosion of the Black Public Sphere. It is the realization of these tensions that frame the major concerns of the largely autobiographical *Crooklyn*.

Perhaps the opening sequence of *Crooklyn* best suggests Lee's foci for the film. Minus Lee's usual bravado and self-indulged wit, the film opens with the sounds of Russell Thompkins Jr.'s stirring falsetto from the recording, "People Make the World Go 'Round." Very clearly a film more about people than ideas, community than ideology, *Crooklyn* places the black family and community at the center of the film. Notions of people and community resonate throughout the film from the imagery of the opening sequence to continuous musical reminders like the Stylistics's "People Make the World Go 'Round" and Sly Stone's "Everyday People." Indeed as the closing credits begin to roll and we are treated to a "Soul Train line" circa 1975, one is reminded of the centrality of music and dance to black life and of the communal purposes such cultural activities have historically played for people within the African-American diaspora. Films like Lee's *Crooklyn* or Robert Townsend's nostalgic *The Five Heartbeats*, were clearly intended to counter the influence of ghettocentric filmmaking as represented by *New Jack City, Boyz N the Hood,* and *Menace II Society*.

Crooklyn introduces us to the Carmichael family as they attempt to negotiate the schisms of the postindustrial urban North and an eroding public sphere, as such schisms begin to threaten their multiethnic Brooklyn community. The Carmichael family members represent animate metaphors for the realities of postindustrial Black America. Both mother and father figures represent complex issues regarding the location of black women and men in the workforce, the potential effects of integration, and the challenges faced by organic cultural producers, who can no longer be sustained by the community they live in and have little or no value in the marketplace. Meanwhile, the unbridled fascination of the Carmichael children when confronting black images on the television in the form of *Soul Train* and Afro-sheen commercials portends the uncritical consumption of black images and sounds that stifle contemporary black youth sensibilities. The family patriarch, Woody Carmichael, is in many ways a living embodiment of the marginalization of high African-American art in the black community as well as a useful example of the lack of public spaces provided specifically for jazz music and jazz musicians. Woody confronts a world where the valued practice of African-American musicianship has given way to the demands of a recording industry that values less experimental and more formulaic approaches to popular music as well as an eroding public sphere that can no longer economically sustain jazz musicians.

The changes in the recording industry during that era are reflected in the two-volume soundtrack of classic soul from the late 1960s and 1970s, a period marked by corporate efforts to annex the black popular music industry. The two-decades-old catalogs of artists like Marvin Gaye, Teddy Pendergrass, and the O'Jays sold more than one hundred thousand units apiece in early 1995 to a largely black middle class consumer base weary of contemporary black popular music. Black radio would in turn respond to this commercial shift by radically changing programming formats to acquiesce to the taste and buying power of their middle-class audiences. Under the banner of "Classic Soul and Progressive R&B," many urban contemporary stations would begin programming classic soul recordings with upscale and less offensive (read: more adult) contemporary R&B. RKO Broadcasting, in a fairly interesting and innovative move, would purchase a rival station that exclusively featured "ghetto pop," transfer many of their younger DJs to the newly acquired station, and change the initial station's format to the "Classic Soul and Progressive R&B" format. This of course gave the parent company the opportunity to nurture two distinctly different audiences bases.[39]

Within the context of the black popular music tradition, this trend toward "nostalgia programming" provided invaluable access to a digitized aural Chitlin' Circuit for younger generations of artists and audiences. Part of this curiosity was peaked initially by the use of classic soul and soul jazz samples by innovative hip-hop producers who may have been introduced to the musical texts as kids. Within the context of a middle class critique of contemporary black popular culture, the emergence of "postindustrial" narratives offers few lasting solutions to the continued erosion of African-American diasporic relations. By embracing the soul narratives of twenty years ago, the black middle class yearns for a social and cultural landscape that they were, in part, responsible for transforming. In addition, while there should be some balance in the marketing and production of black popular music forms, ghetto pop, and hip-hop, particularly that which is derived from the real-life tension of young urban life, deserve to be supported. The production of many of these ghettocentric narratives partially reflects the black middle class' refusal to address these issues within the context of African-American diasporic relations.

Postindustrial nostalgia was not limited to the social imagination of the black middle class, however. It was also a construct of contemporary black youth, who attempted to reconstruct community, history, and memory by embracing communal models from previous historical eras. The erosion of the Black Public Sphere provided the chasm in which the hip-hop generation was denied access to the bevy of communally derived social, aesthetic, cultural, and political sensibilities that undergirded much of black communal struggle throughout the twentieth century, fracturing the hip-hop generation and the generations that will follow from the real communal history of the African-American diaspora. It is within this context that mass culture fills the void of both community and history for contemporary black youth, as it becomes the terrain in which contemporary hip-hop artists conflate history and memory in an effort to reconstruct community. The recording "Things Done Changed" from the debut release of the late Notorious B.I.G. (aka Biggie Smalls) is such an example.[40] Within his narrative, the Notorious B.I.G. reconstructs a community where young children engaged in games in various public spaces and where a communal ethic existed to support activities like cookouts and block parties. Though the artist was raised in the postindustrial era in a black urban community that was not immune to poverty, crime, or random violence, he chose to highlight the type of communal exchanges that dominated his childhood experiences. Even in his memories of hanging on street corners and drinking beer, he chose to forget the high unemployment and school dropout rates that black urban youth have faced for the past twenty-five years, effectively affording many black youths of Notorious B.I.G.'s generation the time to hang out on the street corners.

The point here is not to question the accuracy of the narrative but to note that it contains a sense of community that the author clearly finds missing within black urban life in the

1990s. Even more telling is his reading of how these changing dynamics have altered familial relations as a segment of black youth prey on their parents and other adults within the community. This aspect of communal erosion is so significant that many black adults have chosen to ignore decades of police brutality and have subjected their communities to an intensified police presence in order to control black youth. While Notorious B.I.G.'s narrative fails to convey some of the complexities of this reality, he clearly articulates a sense of community collapse and suggests that this collapse is partially connected to a generational divide within the African-American diaspora. While "Things Done Changed" adequately documents the impact of community erosion, other hip-hop artists used other modes of nostalgia to advance solutions to the plight of contemporary blacks.

The release of Arrested Development's *3 Years 5 Months and 2 Days in the Life of* ... in 1992 represented a challenge to the status quo in hip-hop as its Afrocentric "grunge" style distanced them from both gangsta rap and the political narratives of Public Enemy and KRS-One. As Todd Boyd suggests, Arrested Development shared its context with the emergence of a generation of black collegiates who used African garb and hairstyles to articulate their connection to the African continent.[41] As the group's name suggests, many of the recording's tracks were critical of the impact of migration and urbanization on the black community. Throughout the recording, but especially on tracks like "People Everyday" and "Tennessee," the group's lead vocalist articulated a notion of difference within the African-American diaspora that has its basis in class difference but is articulated as a difference between black rural and urban culture. The recording represented a clear revision of historic class sensibilities that posited southern migrants as the primary threat to black middle-class development in the urban North and Midwest. Within Arrested Development's framework, urbanization had clearly destroyed traditional black communal and familial sensibilities.

The track "Tennessee" perhaps best exemplified Arrested Development's use of nostalgia to counter the impact of urbanization on the black community. The track, which shares its postmigration theme with songs like the Gladys Knight and the Pips classic "Midnight Train to Georgia," represents an open rejection of black urban life. As many black creative artists and intellectuals ponder a vision of communal empowerment on par with the role "Promised Land" migration narratives played in the early to mid-twentieth century and emancipation narratives played in the antebellum period, Arrested Development lead vocalist Speech asserts that the American South will be the focus of the next stage of communal movement.[42] Using Tennessee as a symbol for this movement, Speech articulates his concern for his peers and his desire to reconnect with an African-American spiritual past. Speech's use of the American South as a metaphor for black homespaces is of course nothing new. As Farah Jasmine Griffin and Ralph Ellison both suggested, many migrants attempted to re-create southern homespaces within industrialized urban spaces, but the migrants were also clear about their memories of the Deep South's racial oppression, violence, and segregation.

As a postmigration narrative, "Tennessee" differs from traditional migration narratives in its suggestion that traditional black communal and familial values had been lost precisely because the most malicious aspects of the American South are no longer present to galvanize the black community as witnessed in the charcoal drawing of a lynching that serves as a subtext for the song's music video. But to read "Tennessee" as a rejection of the hard-fought political and social gains won as a corollary to mass migration and urbanization is to misread the song's text.[43] Given the proliferation of Afrocentric iconography that was present in the group's music videos and publicity photos, "Tennessee" clearly represents a contemporary metaphor for the African continent, as is suggested in the song's chorus, which states, "Take me to another place / Take me to another land...."[44] While a mass-migration movement to the African continent is perhaps more politically credible in the late twentieth century than it was in Marcus Garvey's era, Speech is not suggesting a return to Africa but instead posits the

American South and its physical terrain as the connection to forms of African spiritually that have been lost to migration and urbanization. The point here is not whether a return to the South would stimulate economic development in the black community, decrease homelessness, or affect public policy in any way, but rather how African spirituality could be one of the vehicles by which community could be reconstructed.

Several artists would embrace various modes of nostalgia to reconstruct a seminal relationship within the African-American diaspora. For instance, bisexual artist Me'Shell Ndegeocello uses the iconography of black plantation life to affirm same-sex love in a period of heightened homophobia. On the track "Mary Magdalene" from her recording *Peace Beyond Passion,* she states, "I imagine us jumpin' the broom."[45] The phrase "jumpin' the broom" was initially used by enslaved blacks in the antebellum period to signify marriage between slaves, when the legality of such was severely challenged. Here the phrase is appropriated to signify lesbian marriage in an era when the idea of homosexual and lesbian marriages is being sharply criticized and attacked in mainstream culture. Ndegeocello's use of the symbolic imagery of black marriage at once reaffirms her status in the African-American diaspora, even as black homosexuals and lesbians are being marginalized within that community, while linking the struggles of contemporary homosexuals and lesbians to the African-American tradition of social protest and resistance.

In another example, hip-hop artist Method Man appropriated the melody of the Marvin Gaye and Tammi Terrell's classic "You're All I Need to Get By" for his recording "I'll Be There for You/You're All I Need to Get By." The recording, which featured contemporary soul vocalist Mary J. Blige, used the Ashford and Simpson composition to reaffirm heterosexual relationships in the postindustrial era. The recording, which represented one of the more popular affirmations of the continuity of African-American expressive culture, highlights the role of popular music as a primary conduit to express various continuities within the African-American diaspora. Such continuities were perhaps undermined when the Coca-Cola Co. used both the original Gaye/Terrell recording and Method Man/Blige update in a commercial to signify a generation gap within the black community, a generation gap that was bridged according to the company, because of the continuity of Coca-Cola in the lives of black families. The commercial again highlights the increasingly intimate relationship between memory, history, and the marketplace.

Driven by his own realization of the commercial value of ghetto narratives and his own middle class and nationalistic sensibilities, Spike Lee has been one of the few contemporary black cultural workers to successfully integrate the often oppositional taste within both urban working-class/underclass locales and segments of the black middle class. The first volume of the *Crooklyn* soundtrack contains a hip-hop recording from a trio of solo artists, Buckshot, Special Ed, and Masta Ace, who combine their efforts under the banner of the Crooklyn Dodgers. The recording entitled "Crooklyn" is a stunning acknowledgment of postindustrial transformation within black urban spaces as mediated through the increased presence of mass culture. Within the context of the "Crooklyn Dodger" narrative, the erosion of black public life is represented by television sitcoms, in an interesting conflation of contemporary communal crises, 1970s television icons, and designer fashions.[46] The memories of the traditional Black Public Sphere of the early 1970s are contained, specifically in the narrative of a black sitcom like *What's Happening.* In one regard, this narrative serves to deconstruct romantic recollections of black public life, while also identifying the pervasive impact of mass culture on the lives of African-Americans. Consistent with hip-hop's own project, the artists use mass-market-produced imagery and meanings to parlay their narrative concerns.

The recording, which is sandwiched between broadcast accounts of the 1955 World Series, including Jackie Robinson at bat, highlights a phenomenon perhaps organic to post–Civil Rights generations of African-American youth. While memories of national and international events have been mass-mediated in the twentieth century through print organs, radio, and later television—how many people remember World War II via *Life* magazine's coverage?—*Crooklyn* highlights how some of the seminal memories of community life are mass-mediated via television for the generation of black youth that emerged immediately after the Civil Rights era. My point here is not to delegitimize these memories, particularly given the role television has played in socializing African-American youth since the early 1970s, but to suggest that contemporary efforts to reconstruct community would most likely also be mediated through mass culture, though not necessarily via television.

Study Questions

1. What are the concerns that arise when progressive political ideas become widely accessible in mainstream culture?
2. How has hip-hop's relationship with the marketplace changed in the Web 2.0 era?
3. What impact did the emergence of the video era in the 1980s have on the development of hip-hop?

Notes

1. George discusses the birth of Quiet Storm radio in *The Death of Rhythm and Blues,* 131–35, 172–73.
2. George defines "retronuevo" as black music that embraces the past to "create passionate, fresh expressions, and institutions." *The Death of Rhythm and Blues,* 186–88.
3. My commentary here is not of an effort to engage in debates about welfare reform, but to acknowledge the bureaucratic realities associated with many federal programs, particularly in their ineffectiveness in countering the general misery associated with black urban life.
4. Rose, *Black Noise: Rap Music and Black Culture in Contemporary America,* 30.
5. Mollenkopf, *Dual City,* 8.
6. Goldberg, "Polluting the Body Politic," *Racism, the City and the State,* 52.
7. Ibid., 51–52.
8. Wilson, *The Truly Disadvantaged,* 60.
9. Davis, *City of Quartz,* 250–53.
10. Lewis, *When Harlem was in Vogue,* 129–30.
11. Davis, *City of Quartz,* 311.
12. West, *Prophetic Thought in Postmodern Times,* 122.
13. Davis, *City of Quartz,* 304–305.
14. Jerry Mander addresses the relationship between American youth and television in his text *Four Arguments for the Elimination of Television.*
15. Davis, *City of Quartz,* 306.
16. Dyson, *Race Rules,* 140–45.
17. Davis, *City of Quartz,* 293–300.
18. Rose, *Black Noise,* 11.
19. Ibid., 61.
20. Gilroy, "One Nation Under a Groove," *Small Acts,* 39–40.
21. The litigation between Chic and Sugar Hill records over the use of "Good Times" was just the first of many celebrated sampling cases, of which the 1991 legal battle between artists Biz Markie and singer/songwriter Gilbert O'Sullivan is the most notorious. Many artists have dealt with this problem by simply giving sampled artists songwriting credit, though given the history of pop music, these credits simply enhanced the financial coffers of corporate entities who controlled the publishing rights.
22. Marable, *Race, Reform and Rebellion,* 194–96.
23. Manning Marable offers a credible argument in his text *How Capitalism Underdeveloped Black America,* that the increased rates of black male incarceration is related to the use of prison inmates in the maintenance of municipal works and services. Marable believes that the use of prison inmates in such a way is representative of a modern form of enslavement.

24. Marable, *Race, Reform and Rebellion,* 1972.

25. Tate, *Flyboy in the Buttermilk,* 125.

26. The works of black women like Angela Davis, Kathleen Cleaver, and Elaine Brown exemplify the type of necessary critique and reflection that needs to take place to more adequately consider the success and failures of the Civil Rights/Black Power era.

27. Tate, *Flyboy in the Buttermilk,* 126.

28. Ibid.

29. Boyd, *Am I Black Enough for You,* 39.

30. I am referring here to Joe Kleine's review of the film for *New Yorker* magazine in June 1989.

31. Rose, *Black Noise,* 128–30.

32. Ibid., 126.

33. Ibid., 130–35.

34. Despite a recording career that has been inconsistent at best and well-publicized financial problems, MC Hammer remains the best-selling hip-hop artist of all time.

35. During the summer of 1996 Combs renegotiated his deal with Arista/BMG, giving him ownership of his label's recording masters over a period of time. At the time of Comb's deal Reid and Edmonds were rumored to renegotiate along the same terms, issues of autonomy and product ownership were at the core of Andre Harrell's severed relationship with Uptown/MCA, the label he founded in the autumn of 1995. Harrell was subsequently chosen to lead Motown into the twenty-first century with considerably more autonomy and prestige than was offered at the boutique he founded in 1986, though his failure to produce new acts led to his forced resignation in August 1997.

36. Haymes, *Race Culture and the City,* 36–39.

37. Ibid., 37.

38. Rose, *Black Noise,* 104.

39. RKO owns both Hot 97 and KISS-FM in New York City. Hot 97, which is dedicated to a twenty-four-hour ghetto pop and hip-hop format, has also brought in popular artists, including former *Yo MTV Raps* hosts Dr. Dre and Ed Lover, to host segments of their programming. Ed and Dre, as they are affectionately known, are the station's morning drive-time hosts. WBLS-FM, the only-black owned station in the market, responded to these shifts only after RKO's experiment proved successful.

40. Notorious B.I.G., "Things Done Changed," *Ready to Die* (Arista/Bad Boy, 78612–73000–2).

41. Boyd, *Am I Black Enough for You?,* 43–50.

42. I am thinking here of works like Samm Art-William's *Home,* Cornel West's *Prophetic Fragments,* Farah Jasmine Griffin's *Who Set You Flowin'?,* and Spike Lee's film *Crooklyn* and *Clockers,* which all consider the lack of communal vision in the aftermath of the migratory movement.

43. Arrested Development, "Tennessee," *3 Years, 5 Months and 2 Days in the Life of* … (Chrysalis 1992).

44. Ibid.

45. Michelle Ndegeocello, "Mary Magdelene," *Peace Beyond Passion* (Maverick/Reprise 1996).

46. The Crooklyn Dodgers, "Crooklyn," *Music From the Motion Picture Crooklyn* (MCA 1994).

References

Boyd, Todd. *Am I Black Enough for You?* South Bend: Indiana University Press, 1997.

Davis, Mike. *City of Quartz: Excavating the Future in Los Angeles.* New York: Verso, 1990.

Dyson, Michael Eric. *Race Rules: Navigating the Color Line.* New York: Addison Wesley, 1996.

George, Nelson. *The Death of Rhythm and Blues.* New York: Pantheon, 1988.

Gilroy, Paul. *Small Acts.* New York: Serpent's Tail, 1993.

Goldberg, David Theo. "Polluting the Body Politic:" Racist Discourse and Urban Location. *Racism, the City and the State,* Malcolm Cross and Michael Keith, eds. New York: Routledge, 1993.

Griffin, Farah Jasmine. *"Who Set You Flowin?":* The African-American Migration Narrative. New York: Oxford University Press, 1995.

Haymes, Stephen. *Race, Culture and the City: A Pedagogy for Black Urban Struggle.* Albany: State University of New York Press, 1995.

Lewis, David Levering. *When Harlem was in Vogue.* New York: Oxford University Press, 1989.

Mander, Jerry. *Four Arguments for the Elimination of Television.* New York: William Morrow, 1978.

Marable, Manning. *How Capitalism Underdeveloped Black America.* Boston: South End Press, 1983.

———. *Race Reform and Rebellion: The Second Reconstruction in Black America, 1945–1992.* Jackson: University Press of Mississippi, 1993.

Mollenkopf, John, and Manuel Castells, eds. *Dual City: Restructuring New York.* New York: Russell Sage Foundation, 1991.

Rose, Tricia. *Black Noise: Rap Music and Black Culture in Contemporary America*. Hanover: Wesleyan University Press, 1994.

Tate, Greg. *Flyboy in the Buttermilk: Essays on Contemporary America*. New York: Simon & Schuster, 1992.

West, Cornel. *Prophetic Fragments*. Trenton. Africa World Press, 1988.

———. *Prophetic Thought in Postmodern Times*. Monroe, Maine: Common Courage Press, 1993.

Wilson, William Julius. *The Truly Disadvantaged: The Inner City, the Underclass, and Public Policy*. Chicago: University of Chicago Press, 1987.

33

My Mic Sound Nice
Art, Community, and Consciousness

Whereas the narratives of politically engaged hip-hop artists are easy enough to discern, much more difficult is indexing the impact that such narratives have on hip-hop audiences and the extent to which those audiences engage those lyrics in their own political engagement. This dynamic highlights the general problem of trying to assign political meaning and intent to youth culture, where youth are motivated by a range of social stimuli.

In her essay Imani Perry notes the difficulty of isolating a coherent political agenda within youth culture, arguing that black youth, for example, often simultaneously celebrate the status quo while challenging its meaning in their lives.

My Mic Sound Nice: Art, Community, and Consciousness

Imani Perry

Hip hop is half black and half Japanese
Digital chips on the shoulders of African
Lips
Hip hop is black Prozac
Hip hop is if you can't beat 'em blunt 'em
Hip hop is black sadomasochism
Where the hurting ends and the feeling begins.
　　　　　　　　—Greg Tate, "What Is Hip Hop?"

Rap music is a mixed medium. As an art form, it combines poetry, prose, song, music, and theater. It may come in the form of narrative, autobiography, science fiction, or debate. The diversity of media poses a challenge for the critic because she or he is called to evaluate the artistic production from a variety of disciplinary perspectives. Moreover, the embodied nature of the art, the slippage that exists between the art and the artist, makes for another set of challenges when it comes to assessment and interpretation on both aesthetic and political levels.

In this chapter, I will put forward a set of arguments about hip hop music as art. I will begin by exposing the central tension between ideology and art that hip hop presents. I will furthermore consider the inter-textualites in hip hop, represented musically by the call-response trope, through the lenses of ideology, culture, and art. The rapper or MC is both subject and artist in much hip hop composition; who he or she is, constitutes a direct part of our experience of the music, and often the artist is imagined in the popular realm as doing nothing more than verbally expressing his or her experiences, self, and ideas. The MC usually occupies a self-proclaimed location as representative of his or her community or group—the everyman or everywoman of his or her hood. As a representative, he or she encourages a kind of sociological interpretation of the music, best expressed by the concept of "the real." "This is the documentary story of my world," we are told. There exists in rap music an identity-based teleological stance. The work of the artist is not intended to be apparent so much as the lyricism is supposed to testify to organic brilliance. Often this stance becomes articulated via theological imagery, further obscuring ideas of labor by imagining the subject as divine and divinely inspired. This is not work that makes its seams visible. This stance, while clearly one that is supposed to conjure up the image of a kind of virtuosity and confluence of art and identity, makes it more difficult to understand definitively the location of artistry separate from social scientific claims.

While the music bursts with sociopolitical themes, it is quite dangerous for the critic or listener to interpret it purely as a reflection of social and political conditions, without thought to the presence of artistic choice in every narrative and composition. Purely social scientific interpretations limit analyses and tend toward reductionism, bell hooks writes that "thinking about the history of African-American engagement with performance-as-art, it is useful to distinguish between performance that is used to manipulate in the interests of survival (the notion of wearing a mask), and performance as ritual play (as art). Collapsing the two categories tends to imply that the performative arts in black expressive culture emerge as a response to circumstances of oppression and exploitation."[1] If we heed hooks's warnings and consider hip hop as an art with substantial sociopolitical ramifications and issues attendant to it yet not reducible to them, we avoid reducing the music, or the population it "represents," to a socioeconomic location. We also allow ourselves greater space to critically evaluate the content choices made by the artist. Clarence Lusane argues that "to their legions of fans, the legitimacy of gangsta rappers is conditioned on the real troubles that they find themselves in."[2] Part of the theater of hip hop becomes life and a representation of how life is conducted. As Michael Eric Dyson writes, "The genius of hip-hop is that its adherents convince each other—and judging by the attacks it receives, those outside its ranks—that its devices are meant immediately to disclose the truth of life through reportage. In truth, hip-hoppers construct narrative conventions and develop artistic norms through repeated practice and citation."[3]

Those wishing to support hip hop often feel an impulse toward social scientific explanations in order to defend or justify disturbing messages or practices. Many artists themselves encourage such a stance. Emcees often tell us that they are simply transmitting the "truth" or reality of living in poor urban communities. But realist movements in art of any sort are always decisive periods in which choices of how to represent truth or reality are made. Hip hop realism is filled with metaphors and metonyms of existence that trouble listeners or commentators from a wide range of political, social, and intellectual perspectives.

Let us take an abstract example that is not uncommon. Say there is a song that contains beautiful poetry, delivered in an interesting and compelling way, and backed with well-composed music. Yet it is also a narrative of destruction in which the narrator kills several people, refers to women as whores, and celebrates the excessive use of alcohol and marijuana. That which is artistically excellent in this case also proves politically and morally troubling. The reverse may hold true as well, that music embracing excellent moral values might turn out to be boring. Many people who are supportive of rap, with good intentions, make the mistake, in response to attacks on the music, of arguing that there is good and bad rap, thereby categorizing quality according to politics, such that the positive political message becomes construed as "good" music. However, the correlation of artistic quality and politics does not hold within hip hop any more than it would in another art form. As scholar and jazz musician Saleem Washington stated at the disChord Conference on Popular Music at the University of California, Los Angeles, in the summer of 1997, oftentimes that which is musically interesting or good within hip hop is not that which would be deemed "positive."[4] Or, as Robin Kelley has written, "In my book, the most politically correct rappers will never get my hard-earned ducats if they ain't kickin' some boomin' drum tracks, a fat bass line, a few well-placed JB-style guitar riffs, and some stupid, nasty turntable action. If it claims to be hip hop it has to have, as Pete Rock says, 'the breaks … the funky breaks … the funky breaks.'"[5]

The political Left often cites Public Enemy as one of the greatest rap groups, praising its members for their incisive social critiques. What often gets forgotten is that what made them great artistically was that these incisive critiques and sophisticated arguments came recited in infectious rhythmic style and in front of funky and soulful beats produced by their DJ Terminator X. Their artistry mattered. Lauryn Hill, the first woman to win four Grammy awards in one night, too is a beautiful lyricist as well as an artist who delivers an uplifting, explicitly religious sociopolitical message; she succeeds in her philosophical mission because her artistic strength holds listeners. But there is no inherent correlation between good music and respectability or good music and good politics. Because of the reunion space, discussed in the introduction, the blending of the high and low, the sacred and the profan, and the open discourse encouraged in rap, there is, moreover, no mandate on the artist to be politically uplifting all the time, or even at all. The tension so created for the listener is a tension between ideology and art.

Not only does hip hop manifest a tension between art and ideology but the ideology present in the art frequently responds to the complicated politics of race in America. Observations made by literary figure Charles Johnson about black literature ring true of hip hop as well:

> Black literature abounds with faintly Hegelian variations on the phenomenon of the black body as stained. Once you are so one-sidedly seen by the white Other, you have the option of (A) accepting this being seen from the outside and craftily using the "invisibility" of your interior to deceive and thus to win survival as the folk hero Trickster … does. … In this case, stain is like the heavy makeup of a clown; it conceals you completely. … Or you may (B) seize this situation at its roots by reversing the negative meaning of the black body. "It is beautiful," you might say, "I am a child of the Sun." … You applaud your athletic, amorous, and dancing abilities, your street wisdom and savoir faire, your "soul."[6]

The "cultural nationalist" period of hip hop on the one side, and the "gangsta" period on the other perfectly embody Johnson's two responses to white supremacist America. The West Coast gangsta mimicked a stereotype, thus becoming a survivalist hero, whereas the East Coast Afrocentrists with their natural hair and decked out in medallions declared essentialist black beauty and excellence.

As black American music, hip hop, with this tension between ideology and art, presents a serious challenge. Should we indulge our appreciation of the art when its messages prove disturbing? Particularly given the youth of much of hip hop's audience we have to wonder whether this democratic space simply provides a window through which negative values can be transmitted to our children. Some people, from prominent politicians to kitchen critics, have clearly decided that the United States cannot afford the luxury of a music with frequently problematic messages, and have responded by advocating the censorship of certain artists or by proselytizing to convert MCs away from the nastiness or violence in their work.

On the other hand, beyond the tension, there is the possibility, that the disturbing images themselves might in part account for the music's appeal. For a mainstream audience, rap may indulge voyeuristic fantasies of black sociopathy and otherness, while for an oppressed community, these images might engage fantasies of masculine power in people who feel powerless. Hence there are a variety of reasons why a listener might enjoy a song littered with violence and viciousness. While there are many MCs with lyrics that do not express destructive values, we cannot dismiss those that do as illegitimate subjects of artistic analysis, and we cannot dismiss their popularity as media-fueled glamorization of destructiveness.

While fostering progressive political consciousness in young people is of the utmost importance, the ideological reunion of the clean and dirty, of the sacred and profane, is a watershed of the post-civil rights era, one that itself constitutes a kind of black liberation, although one also beleaguered by difficulties. To refuse to concern oneself with proving decency in the face of stereotypes, racism, and white supremacy at least in part provides a psychic liberation. Still, we must develop a cognizance within multiple layers of the black community, and the external community of listeners, both child and adult, of the distinctions between and tensions within art and ideology. That kind of awareness should bring about enlightened decisions about the sort of music one wishes to consume. Recall that we have not expunged all white supremacist or misogynistic texts from English curricula in American high schools and universities, although the most astute of educators attempt to balance an understanding of artistic excellence with ideological critiques that promote contemplation rather than silence. Further, we find in many of those texts sex alongside spirituality, depravity alongside beauty. We should extend the open discourse already extant within hip hop to our conversation about hip hop.

The particular performative space of rap is located at the crossroads of several significant moments. Here one stands at the new grounds of Du Boisian double consciousness, the meeting and conflict of Americanness and blackness, where MCs and DJs are commodified, make commodities, and are both objects and subjects of capitalism as they produce improvisational and oppositional music. In the following two lyrics, the first from De La Soul, the second from A Tribe Called Quest, the MCs express a critical consciousness of that location: "I am Posdonus / I be the new generation of slaves / here to make tapes that my record exec rapes";[7] and "Industry rule number four thousand and eighty / record company people are shady / so kids watch your back / 'cause they're full of crap / don't doubt it / look at how they act."[8] Jadakiss adds this succinct statement: "Industry is like jail, nigga, double R's runnin' the yard"[9]

This tension-filled dynamic of double consciousness always inflects hip hop discourse. Because it is a spoken art form that cherishes open discourse, we find in hip hop a dialogic space in which artists' voices articulate ideas about existence on a number of registers. The space of hip hop is public and yet interior. It is the music of radios blasting through neighborhoods, parties, and hit lists. Houston Baker has argued that when boom boxes also known as ghetto blasters were popular, the controversy over their use was "more than generational ... the contest was urbanely propietorial: Who owns the public spaces?"[10] Rap is disseminated through record companies and radio stations far more than it is through local ventures, and yet it maintains a space of intellectual communication existing beyond the institutions of production and transmission. Within that space, the artist and the listener become creatively engaged with a world of ideas and experience. Albert Murray gives the following definition of art:

> Art is the ultimate extension, elaboration, and refinement of the rituals that reenact the primary survival techniques (and hence reinforce the basic orientation toward experience) of a given people in a given time, place and circumstance much the same as holiday commemorations are meant to do. It is the process of extension, elaboration, and refinement that creates the work of art. It is the playful process of extension, elaboration and refinement that gives rise to the options out of which comes the elegance that is the essence of artistic statement. Such playfulness can give an aesthetic dimension to the most pragmatic of actions.[11]

Applying Murray's observation to hip hop, we are asked to assess that extension of ritual and survival, and the kinds of ways in which that extension takes place.

It is thus unsurprising that hip hop figures in many lyrics as a nourishment essential for survival. It feeds the community of listeners, KRS-One announced, "I got the hip hop juice with the hip hop food."[12] Digable Planets rhymed, "Brewin' funk inside my soul kitchen, pull up a chair, here's a bit, have a listen."[13] All the nourishment needed is provided aurally and orally. Butterfly of Digable Planets also rhymed, "It's the children of the concrete / "Livin' off the fruits and the functions of the phat beats / hip hop's all around the members is growin' / Please dig off the sounds 'cause the good vibes they showin'."[14] Lines such as these construct hip hop as life-sustaining, and they also establish a contrast between the coldness of the city, metonymically represented by concrete, and the natural growth of artistic hip hop creation. Butterfly's words also anticipated the mid-1990s flowering of new styles and more sophisticated production in hip hop.

Hip hop nourishes by offering community membership that entails a body of cultural knowledge, yet it also nourishes by offering a counter-hegemonic authority and subjectivity to the force of white supremacy in American culture in the form of the MC. The centrality of the latter's experience and voice often also presents a transcendent or powerful model of survival. As A. L. rhymes in "Lyrics":

My streets are evil
minds are feeble
runnin' illegal
I'm savage like evil eye
trainin' my people to a needle
my mind cerebral
blesses the mic like a cathedral
thoughts'll lead you
verbals feed you
decede you
I breed you
to heed you
like psychics I came to read you
hip hop I love you and I need you.[15]

The mind and its creative capacity have transcendent powers in the face of dire streets. A love affair with thought and language offers salvation.

Alternately, some lyrics conflate hip hop with the general chaos of life, rather than a removal from it. And there is an abundance of lyrics describing young rich black folks engaged in consumerist excess. Even those, in their own strange way, do what a survivalist hip hop does better: they open up spaces to challenge the hegemonic structures of understanding and meaning propagated by the dominant culture of white supremacy. As a critic has noted, "The difference between [Wynton] Marsalis (and the tradition of black middle-class respectability he represents) and hip hop is really about who truly deserves to speak for the condition of black souls. Is it our institutionally approved elite, our bohemian bourgeois iconoclasts, or the folk who live on public assistance in the projects and their neighbors, the black working class?"[16]

The enunciative dynamic in hip hop allows for ideological struggle while simultaneously acknowledging identification with Americanism and articulating a Creole black American identity. Hence when Foxy Brown or Lil' Kim rhyme about countless highbrow designers and diamonds, they not only express vapid materialistic values but in fact also show their awareness of how, on some level, they transgress notions of racialized space and racialized gender when they—as young, dialect-speaking, ghetto-fabulous black women—enter the Henri Bendel or Bergdorf Goodman department stores. Lil' Kim rhymes in "Get Money": "So you wanna buy me diamonds and Armani suits / Adrienne Vittadini and Chanel Nine boots / Things to make up for all the games and the lies / Oh my God, sayin' I apologize."[17] And Foxy Brown, in "Ain't No Nigga," says: "From Dolce Gabbana to H. Bendel I'm ringing bells / So who the player? I keep you chillin' in the illest gators."[18] Both examples are taken from songs in which the exchange of material goods constitutes a required element of the male-female sexual relationship.

Soon after the two artists came onto the hip hop scene with their rich and vulgar black pinup girl styles, they faced charges of stereotypical pornographic hypersexuality, as well as accusations that they lacked autonomy and self-definition. The furor over the two women's disruptive presence reminded us that no one had quite done what they did before, nor was their image—that of the desiring black sexpot adorned with haute couture and jewels—part of the broad cultural imagination. We might consider the relatively clean-cut Eartha Kitt as the closest forerunner to Lil' Kim and Foxy Brown. Their transgression of class and racial spaces shifted notions about consumerism and gender. Although their work did not explicitly critique class and race politics, their mere presence signaled a shifting concept of how black women were imagined as black wealth and black celebrity multiplied. In addition, the attacks on their presence the two women faced effectively called attention to the fact that transgression does not necessarily entail liberation—the constant operation of white supremacy and sexism almost seamlessly neutralizes many potentially transgressive spaces.

In the song "Slam," Onyx subverts hegemonic discourses by relocating power and goodness in that which is impure and black. Here, Sticky Fingers rhymes:

> I'm a b-boy, standin' in my b-boy stance
> Hurry up and give me a microphone before I bust in my pants
> The mad author of anguish, my language polluted
> Onyx is a heavyweight (and still undisputed)
> So take the words right out my mouth or walk a mile in my shoes
> I paid so many dues also used and abused and um
> So confused, excuse me, for example, I'm an inspiration for a whole generation
> And unless you got ten sticky fingers it's an imitation, a figment
> Of your imagination, but but but but wait it gets worse
> I'm not watered down so I'm dyin' of thirst
> Comin' through with the scam
> foolproof plan
> B-boys make some noise and just, just slam.[19]

This rhyme celebrates "polluted" language as superior and inspirational, a construction that stands in direct opposition to the ways in which things are valued in an imperialist and capitalist society, in which value is accorded in direct proportion to perceived purity in everything from animals to aesthetics. And yet he subverts the Western ideal of purity through the concept of originality by saying, "unless you got ten sticky fingers," that is, are he who uses polluted language, you are an imitation, not as good, false. His impurity is original. He spurns the economy of purity and relocates the economy of originality from high culture and wealth to a young urban black man. Just as the reproduction of the Mona Lisa will never reach the quality of the original, neither will the reproduction of Sticky Fingers and what he stands for. But what proves even more subversive is that he makes this construction with allusions to Pepsi and Coke. "The inspiration of a generation, the Pepsi generation," was a slogan popular at the time this song came out, as was Coke's motto, "The Real Thing," an accusation of imitation lodged against rival colas. Here, commodity culture and the reproduction that takes place in recorded music are together used to assert originality. The listener witnesses a dance back and forth between the oneness suggested by originality and the multiplicity suggested by commodity. In this song, the abused and disenfranchised are called on to celebrate using the historically white working-class practice of slam dancing. And the critical subjective space is that of the young man and other young men like him. The listener is told to walk in his shoes. He is one of many low-level consumers in a consumer culture, and yet his authority serves to subvert hierarchies of value.

Hip hop music also manifests a commitment to otherness. It centralizes a realm of black existence and yet commits to the otherness of that location with respect to the larger society. On some level, it signals a crisis in black youth politics. It is impossible to isolate, in any coherent fashion, a clear system of political critique with a traceable eschatology or teleology in hip hop. Rather, we find a simultaneous movement of social critique and a celebration of the status quo. For example, while rappers do not espouse racism and imprisonment in the system of criminal law enforcement as positive there is a kind of revelry present in the lyrical treatment of the prisons as a fundamental element to the identity construction of male black youth. What some critics have termed nihilism in hip hop, I would instead describe as a radical commitment to otherness, which confounds those of us whose political standing comes out of either a civil rights or black power tradition.

The historic construction of blackness in opposition to whiteness, in which blackness is demonized, has become part of the art form's consciousness. Whereas previous generations of black Americans utilized various means to establish a self-definition that negated the construction of blackness as demonic or depraved, many members of the hip hop generation have chosen instead to appropriate and exploit those constructions as metaphoric tools for expressing power. Because this gesture is ultimately aggressive (in that it primarily claims power through the voice of black males, and thus, given the dichotomized racial structure in the United States, takes power away from white America, even if only by operating through white American fear), the black community generally does not perceive these acts as those of self-hating traitors, in the way it might the acts of black people adopting other stereotypical postures. Rather, these young men may even be seen as champions of a particular kind of black empowerment.

Of course, such empowerment depends on a larger level of power-lessness. And certainly that larger powerlessness in society is reflected in the economic politics of the music industry. Hip hop and its products have become a several-billion-dollar industry, but on a number of levels it maintains an anticapitalist aesthetic, even as it exists as a form of capitalist production, and even though a number of MCs who lyrically seem to wholeheartedly embrace conspicuous consumption. The anti-capitalist vein remains partly because the MCs often accurately understand themselves as exploited workers. In "God Lives Through," Q-Tip of A Tribe Called Quest rhymes, "Intellect is major / since heads like to wager / the skills on the hill overlooking dollar bills / Man you're crazy, thinkin' you can faze / the Ab doesn't study mere nonsense money."[20] One can, of course, find countless deeply capitalistic lyrics to match Q-Tip's words decommodifying hip hop. Blackstar, a duo comprised of Mos Def and Talib Kweli, respond to this dynamic in their CD jacket. Describing the song "Hater Players," Talib Kweli writes, "We started to see cats shouting 'player hater' to anyone who had nerve to critique they wack shit. A lot of rich players are making wack ass music, that's the bottom line! I remember when the worst thing you could be was a sell out. Then the sell-outs started running things. We call this song 'Hater Players' because there are many players who hate the fact that we do this for love."[21]

The term *player hater,* thrown at those imagined to be envious of one's wealth or abundant suitors, became a rallying cry for the consumerist explosion in late 1990s' hip hop, morphing from its original Southern and Midwestern neo-blaxploitation roots into an unseemly mess. The critiques of the stance celebrated are necessary and important. But it is also relevant to understand the way in which hip hop's capitalism is asserted as a black populist capitalism that exists as a desire for the acquisition of wealth, but also a desire to "stick it" to American economic and social inequities. And ultimately, hip hop artists, even at their most wealthy more often than not are at the mercy of and exploited by big-business capitalism for their continued economic success. At any rate, despite a number of notable exceptions, the overwhelming majority of professional hip hop artists are not wealthy, and many find themselves in unfair recording contracts or paid in luxury items and so seduced into debt to the record company. Only a small number of record companies actually owned by artists are not subsidiaries of larger labels that exercise ultimate control. Therefore even the odes to the almighty dollar negotiate an alternative and hybridized (by race and class) notion of capitalism into the popular sphere. The reality is that, by and large, these artists do not experience the black populist wealth they celebrate.

In the record jacket of Meshell Ndegeocello's *Plantation Lullabies,* an album that masterfully combines hip hop, funk, and folk, the artist writes, "Hip Hop is the inverse of capitalism / Hip Hop is the reverse of colonialism / Hip Hop is the world the slaveholder made sent into niggafide future shock."[22] Not *bona fide,* but *niggafide,* a context defined by a legacy of slavery and white supremacy, as well as black subjectivity, language, and culture. The quest for liberation coexists in this art with the desire to be the "baddest Negro" on the plantation, and often the latter aspiration seems more plausible, is pursued most vigorously, and finds expression through cash.

But as Richard Delgado and Jean Stefancic have argued when speaking of the potentials of liberatory speech for colored peoples in a First Amendment context, there is the danger that larger and longer narratives of race might dwarf hip hop speech's potential subversion. They write, "We interpret new stories in light of the old. Ones that deviate too markedly from our pre-existing stock are dismissed as extreme, coercive, political, and wrong. The only stories about race we are prepared to condemn, then, are the old ones giving voice to the racism of an earlier age, ones that society has already begun to reject."[23] I would add stories of past racism which were not explicitly rejected by the civil rights revolution, to the group of stories we fail to understand and address. They go on to say, "We subscribe to a stock of explanatory scripts, plots, narratives and understandings that enable us to make sense of—to construct—our social world. ... These observations imply that our ability to escape the confines of our own preconceptions is quite limited. The contrary belief—that through speech and remonstrance alone we can endlessly reform ourselves and each other—we call the empathic fallacy."[24] Even the most progressive lyricists are destabilized by what these authors term the empathic fallacy, and certainly the thug narrators, or the player celebrators, are especially vulnerable to being understood in terms of prescribed racial narratives, regardless of the more nuanced levels on which they communicate or aspire to communicate.

Incomprehensibility

One of the communication elements that resists white supremacy and co-optation has been the self-conscious incomprehensibility of hip hop lyricism. Rappers are misunderstood, both intentionally and unintentionally, not only as a side effect of the fact that we rely on figurative pidgins in the United States to cross borders in popular culture; but incomprehensibility is also a protective strategy. The general population often refers to hip hop as music in which "you can't understand what they are saying." By this, they usually mean the words, but even when the words are accessible to a white mainstream or global audience, there remains a frequently inaccessible cultural space—descended from black American history, culture, and language, expanded by the English- and Spanish-speaking Caribbean, which are far more complex than a few slang words and baggy pants. Difficulty is a strategy in hip hop, both in terms of words, which are fast and hard to understand if you are not privy to the hip hop community, and of demands for an authentic personal connection to hip hop and its geography, the hood. Difficulty is a cultural and political strategy, as well as an ideological one. In another context, cultural critic Trinh Minh-ha has rejected calls to clarity in a way apropos for a discussion of hip hop, "To write clearly one must incessantly prune, eliminate, forbid, purge, purify; in other words practice what may be called an ablution of language."[25] The lack of clarity is the structural correlate to the reunion ideal. It represents struggle against the repressiveness of traditional literariness in terms of content censorship, and, more important, in terms of the limitations tradition imposes on structural innovation. It allows for the expansion of black English within the spheres of intellectual exploration. Critical to this activity is the call to engage in the decoding of the messages that hip hop artists make for members of the hip hop nation. One works to understand the cleverness, the allusions, the suggestiveness. And even as hip hop is innovative, such obfuscation is part of black oral tradition. Mel Watkins discusses the lack of clarity as an indicator of cultural exclusivity, and as an intracultural practice, in his book on the history of black comedy, *On the Real Side*, citing Richard Pryor, who once said, "Niggers just have a way of telling you stuff and not telling you stuff, Martians would have a tough time with Niggers. They be translating words, saying a whole lot of things underneath you. All around you. That's our comedy."[26] It is also, more broadly, our language. And hip hop is an iteration of black vernacular, at a nexus or crossroads with our rhythms in—like black folks themselves—the middle of America.

Funk and Soul

> Feelin' somethin' all in your bones. Magically moved by the microphone.
> —Three Times Dope, "Greatest Man Alive"

As James Brown demanded of his grooves, hip hop, too, has to be funky to be good. A funky cut makes you want to move and sweat, or perhaps it sends a chill down your spine. It is earthy and erotic, even if not overtly sexy: "Drippin' with the fluid that wets you when you do it, know it like Otis 'cause your style is bogus."[27]

Funkiness might refer to an enticing beat or the smell of sweat-releasing pheromones. Funkiness is of the people, ordinary in an excellent way. It causes hips to sway and backs to curve. It is sensual, stimulating the auditory, visual, tactile, and gustatory senses. It is, as Method Man describes in his lyrics, "Poetry in motion, coast to coastin', rub it in your skin like lotion."[28] Funky sounds inspire both body and mind. The core of funkiness in hip hop is found in the bass: repetitive beats filled with bass that can be felt underneath the feet and inside the chest, bass that makes cars rumble and the floor shake. The percussion engages the listener in a historically learned pattern of response. But it is not just those clear thumping sounds that matter. Syncopation does as well. The senses must be engaged on multiple levels. For a song to "rock" it has to swing, listeners have to be able to move to it on several different rhythms, to feel the different textures of sound. In order for it to "bounce," it cannot be too heavy: even if the song is deep and strong, some lightness must be added to the rhythm in order to keep it coming at the audience, to create a sound arc that will make bodies move slowly up to the apex, which they hit suddenly and distinctly, and then curve down again. Although James Brown, Parliament Funkadelic, and other classic funk and R & B musicians provide much of the foundational musical text for hip hop songs, the funkiness does not simply reflect the use of funk or funky soul music. It is what the MCs, DJs, and producers do to make the song work, the particular combination of rhyming and mixing, along with the musical texts drawn on, that create the funky configuration. As Fife of A Tribe Called Quest rhymed in "Can I Kick It?"

> When it comes to rhythm Quest is your savior
> Follow us for the funky behavior
> Make a note on the rhythm we gave ya
> Feel free, drop your pants jack your hair
> Do you like the garments that we wear?
> I instruct you to be the obeyer
> A rhythm recipe that you'll savor
> Doesn't matter if you're minor or major
> Yes the tribe of the game rhythm player
> and you inhale like a breath of fresh air.[29]

The group's references to a rhythmic sensuality and spirituality that compel motion and self-emancipatory action capture what I said about funkiness in the world of hip hop.

Soul is important to hip hop also. By soul I mean that which has some spiritual depth and deep cultural and historical resonances to be felt through the kind of music and sounds made by the vocalists. Goodie Mob., a group from Atlanta, used their album and song entitled "Soul Food" as a culinary metaphor for the sustenance provided by black cultural traditions rooted in the South. Soulful music is music of joy and pain, unself-consciously wedding melody and moaning, the sound of the dual terror and exultation of being black in America. In 1988, Eric B. and Rakim released *Paid in Full*, which included the cut "I Know You Got Soul." They called on the soulfulness of the listeners with James Brown samples, digitized cymbal crashes, breathing sounds, and a bumping bass line. Rakim told the listeners to use their soulfulness to grasp his words as he ventured back and forth between a discussion of his self-conscious role as an MC in relationship with an audience and metaphysical metaphors about his excellence.

> I got soul
> That's why I came
> To teach those
> Who can't say my name.
> First of all I'm the soloist
> The soul controller
> Rakim gets stronger as I get bolder.[30]

The linguistic references to funkiness or soulfulness sometimes come through the metaphor of addiction in hip hop music. On the one hand, it is used as a reference to the high, that intoxicating pleasure, the music can give the listener. "I don't gang bang / or shoot out bang bang / the relentless lyrics the only dope I slang,"[31] comes from the tongue of Jeru the Damaja. The MC reminds listeners of how good the lyrics can make them feel. He seduces. On the other hand, he also reminds his audience about the yearning for the beats when they are not playing, the longing for renewed stimulation by the poetry. He tempts. On another album, Rakim rhymed about being a "microphone fiend," turning the addiction metaphor on himself. In this song, he talks about jonesing for the satisfaction found only in the high of rhyming.

> I get a craving like a fiend for nicotine
> But I don't need a cigarette, know what I mean?
> I'm ragin', rippin' up the cage 'n don't it sound amazin'
> 'Cause every rhyme is made and thought up
> 'Cause it's sort of an addiction
> Magnetized by the mixin' . . .
> The prescription is a hyper tone that's thorough 'n
> I fiend for a microphone like heroin
> Soon as the bass kicks, I need a fix
> Give me a stage and a mic and a mix.[32]

The addiction reference is most dramatically an invocation of the escape provided by art, particularly from the pains of daily life.

The Ancestors

One of the areas in hip hop that offers a very interesting ideological move is attention to the ancestors, to the history behind the music, despite rap's postmodern luster. Hip hop is incredibly nostalgic music. As KRS-One once humorously pointed out, before hip hop was even twenty years old, people were paying homage to the "old school."[33] While the block parties and humble beginnings of the 1970s gave way to late 1980s and early 1990s proclamations about black history and consciousness, which themselves gave way to less political and more decadent trends, the music remained a historical celebration. Popular songs from the 1960s, 1970s, and 1980s have continually surfaced as samples and hooks for hip hop music. Both in the composition of sounds and text, hip hop artists reference each other, in addition to soul, R & B, and funk musicians. In 1986 Rakim rhymed: "I don't bug out or chill / Don't be actin' ill / No tricks in '86 it's time to bill / Eric B. easy on the cut, no mistakes allowed / 'Cause to me MC means move the crowd."[34] Ten years later, Mos Def, rhymed on a De La Soul CD:

> I don't bug out or chill
> Don't be actin' ill
> No tricks in '96
> Not a doggone bill
> But you be easy on the cut no mistakes allowed
> 'Cause to me MC means, Make it cream ...
> I'm smooth like gabardine.[35]

While Mos Def riffs on Rakim's language, he also riffs on his tempo, adding pauses and fluc-
tuating intonation, yet loosely maintaining the meter. Heltah Skeltah reference MC Lyte's song
"Cappuccino" by rhyming, "Why oh why did I need cappuccino, scar on my face but I'm not Al
Pacino." Likewise, Lil' Kim plays on MC Lyte's "10% Dis," the Lyte version being: "Hot damn hot
damn ho here we go again / suckers stole a beat but you know they can't win / You stole a beat
are you havin' fun / Now me and the Aud' s gonna show you how it's done."[36] Lil' Kim self-
consciously cites Lyte's words and name: "Hot damn ho here we go again / Lyte as a Rock bitch /
hard as a cock bitch."[37]

Even covers have become part of hip hop with Snoop's remake of the Doug E. Fresh classic
"Ladidadi" (with intermittent word changes to suit West Coast slang and styles), and Puffy's
remake of Public Enemy's "Public Enemy #1," with word changes reflecting his materialistic
"rebellion" and envy-inciting wealth. These references to other artists constitute a signature feature
of the hip hop version of the call-response trope's intertextuality. The old school is consistently
celebrated in hip hop, even as the music becomes exponentially more sophisticated—particularly
among independent artists—more polished, and of a higher sound quality. As the commodification and commercialization that comes along with mainstream appeal threatens notions of community and authenticity in hip hop, nostalgia becomes an authenticating device. Good MCs and
DJs not only make the history present but they also enmesh it in the new entity created by the
given song, to be enjoyed in a distinct way. Substandard hip hop songs, which have inundated the
market, simply consist of rhymes over the music of other artists, but excellent ones take the flavor
of an earlier song and add it to the stew, creating something new and special with the old. Hip hop
fondly recalls itself as having been, at is origins, something that young blacks and Latinos did for
the love of the art form. And the sign of its decline to many hip hop heads is the exploitation of
already-cultivated appreciations for a given song or style matched with simplistic rhymes, without
any effort to bring the listener somewhere new, to captivate with one's own "flavor."

The nostalgia does not only emerge in response to commercialism, however. It also takes root
in the general nostalgia of the post-civil rights and black power movement generation, trying to
find symbolisms from those eras that can translate to more elusive contemporary struggles by
romanticizing an epoch of political movement and social defiance. The chorus of OutKast's
"Southernplayalisticadillacmuzik" goes: "All the players came from far and wide / wearin' Afros
and braids kickin' them gangsta rides / now I'm here to tell you there's a better day / when the
player's ball is happenin' all day e'ery day."[38]

The nostalgic motif consists of black power and blaxploitation era symbols brought back
into the contemporary urban South. Lauryn Hill's music video for "That Thing" features a
split screen, one side with Lauryn dreadlocked in late 1990s fashion, the other with Lauryn in
a Motown-inspired wig and a 1960s-style minidress. The doo-wop harmonizing at the
beginning of the song draws these two eras together in a hip hop composition. This song's theme,
which preaches a more conservative sexual morality than most contemporary music does also
hearken back to the doo-wop era when mainstream black popular music was clean-cut and
wholesome.

The romantic past as it exists in hip hop is not limited to the civil rights movement or the
black power era; it might also refer to an Afrocentric pre-enslavement vision of a healthy and

essentialized blackness posed in contrast to present dynamics, as in Killah Priest's song "From Then to Now":

> I can't take it
> Beauty that was once sacred is now gettin' face lifts,
> fake tits and fake lips
> Cold embraces, memory erases from the slave ships my princess
> I used to spot her from a distance holding my infant, burning incense
> The moment intent for her to step into my white tents
> Now we step in precincts.[39]

The sensual description makes tangible an existence romanticized yet quite emotional and symbolically meaningful. It encourages reengagement with a black holistic sensibility, indicating a kind of celebratory membership in the black community. The concept of membership is important to maintaining the racial and cultural identity of hip hop. And much of the nostalgic reference constitutes a challenge, as if to say, "If you were down, back in the day, you will remember this, or this statement or melody will have some meaning to you." Method Man begins his song "Bring the Pain" with his version of "Ding Dong," a black childhood rhyme. He says, "Yo' mama don't wear no drawers / I saw when she took 'em off/ standin' in a welfare line, eatin' swine, tryin' to look fine, with her stank behind."[40] In the same cadence, black children in Chicago in the 1980s sang:

> Leader: Yo' mama don't wear no drawers
> Response: Ding Dong
> Leader: I saw when she took 'em off
> Response: Ding Dong
> Leader: She threw them on the table
> Response: Ding Dong
> Leader: That table was disabled
> Response: Ding Dong Dong Dong Dong
> DING DONG!

The final couplet changes with each child who takes his or her turn to be the leader. This is an example of the kind of folk speech that predates hip hop, but which is part of the fabric of life and language that shapes and enters the music. Clap games, children's calls, recordings of the voices of great black leaders, mythic Africa, and music of the past all form part of hip hop's nostalgia.

Hip hop constantly references previous black music forms. This stands as testimony to the yearning for grounding in the post-civil rights era, to the nostalgia for the music of youth, but also to the definitive blackness of parents or grandparents generation. Nelson George writes that hip hop is a "postmodern art in that it shamelessly raids older forms of pop culture—kung fu movies, chitlin' circuit comedy, '70s funk, and other equally disparate sources—and reshapes the material to fit the personality of an individual artist and the taste of the times."[41] And he continues, "Some say this is the first generation of black Americans to experience nostalgia."[42] This nostalgia carries through nowhere more publicly than in hip hop. The musical memory for the listener forms part of the new musical experience. But of course listeners who are not members of the black community will not often possess such collective memory and will be less likely to intuitively understand the intertextuality of hip hop.

Another critical question raised by this nostalgia is, how does it coincide with the reunion? Why does the hip hop audience believe that it is OK to embrace the past, to converse with it, without adhering to its ideological divides or rules? It is the speed of late-capitalist production with the theater of freedom in the post-civil rights era that facilitates nostalgic sensibilities without tradition.

Study Questions

1. How can youth culture be simultaneously read as capitulating to the mainstream and challenging it?
2. Is there a clear link between popular music and the behavior of audiences, particularly as related to political engagement?
3. How do the sensibilities of youth add to the pathological view of urban life?

Notes

1. bell hooks, "Performance as a Site of Opposition," in *Let's Get It On: The Politics of Black Performance*, ed. Catherine Ugwu (London: Institute of Contemporary Arts, 1995), 210.
2. Clarence Lusane, *Race in the Global Era: African Americans at the Millennium* (Boston: South End, 1997), 86.
3. Michael Eric Dyson, *Holler If You Hear Me: Searching For Tupac Shakur* (New York: Basic Civitas Books, 2001), 158.
4. disChord: A Conference on Contemporary Popular Music, May 9–11, 1997. University of California, Los Angeles.
5. Robin D. G. Kelley, "Kickin' Reality, Kickin' Ballistics: Gangsta Rap and Post-industrial Los Angeles," in *Droppin' Science: Critical Essays on Rap Music and Hip Hop Culture*, ed. William Eric Perkins (Philadelphia: Temple University Press, 1996), 148.
6. Charles Johnson, *Being and Race: Black Writing since 1970* (Bloomington: Indiana University Press, 1988), 28.
7. De La Soul, "I Am, I Be," *Bulhoone Mindstate* (Tommy Boy, 1994).
8. A Tribe Called Quest, "Check the Rhime," *The Low End Theory* (BMG/Jive, 1991).
9. Jadakiss, "It's Time I See You," *Kiss the Game Goodbye* (Ruffryders/Def Jam, 2001).
10. Houston A. Baker Jr., *Black Studies, Rap, and the Academy* (Chicago: University of Chicago Press, 1993), 43.
11. Albert Murray, *The Blue Devils of Nada: A Contemporary American Approach to Aesthetic Statement* (New York: Pantheon, 1996), 13.
12. KRS-One, "Return of the Boom Bap," *Return of the Boom Bap* (BMG/Jive, 1993).
13. Digable Planets, "It's Good to Be Here," *A New Refutation of Time and Space* (EMI, 1991).
14. Digable Planets, "Pacifies (NY Is Red Hot)," *A New Refutation of Time and Space* (EMI, 1991).
15. A. L., "Lyrics," *The Lyricist Lounge Vol. 1* (Priority/Rawkus, 1999).
16. Greg Tate, "Fifteen Arguments in Favor of the Future of Hip Hop," in *The Vibe History of Hip Hop*, ed. Alan Light (New York: Three Rivers Press, 1999).
17. Junior M.A.F.I.A., "Get Money," *Conspiracy* (WEA/Atlantic, 1995).
18. Jay-Z, "Ain't No Nigga," *Reasonable Doubt* (Priority, 1999).
19. Onyx, "Slam," *Bacdafucup* (Uni/Def Jam, 1993).
20. A Tribe Called Quest, "God Lives Through," *Midnight Marauders* (BMG/Jive. 1993). Here *Ab* is an abbreviation for Abstract, one of Q-Tip's monikers.
21. Black Star, "Hater Players," *Black Star* (Priority/Rawkus Entertainment, 1999).
22. Meshell Ndegeocello, *Plantation Lullabies* (WEA/Warner Brothers, 1993).
23. Richard Delgado and Jean Stefancic, "Images of the Outsider in American Law and Culture: Can Free Expression Remedy Systemic Social Ills?" in *Critical Race Theory: The Cutting Edge*, ed. Delgado (Philadelphia: Temple University Press, 1995), 220.
24. Ibid., 221.
25. Trinh T. Minh-ha *Woman, Native Other: Writing Postcoloniality and Feminism* (Bloomington: Indiana University Press, 1989), 17.
26. Mel Watkins, *On the Real Side: Laughing, Lying, and Signifying; The Underground Tradition of African-American Humor That Transformed American Culture, From Slavery to Richard Pryor* (New York: Simon and Schuster, 1994), 544–45.

27. Three Times Dope, "Greatest Man Alive," *Original Stylin'* (Arista Records, 1988).

28. Method Man, "M.E.T.H.O.D. Man," *Tical* (Uni/Def Jam, 1994).

29. A Tribe Called Quest, "Can I Kick It?" *People's Instinctive Travels in the Paths of Rhythm* (BMG/Jive, 1990).

30. Eric B. and Rakim, "I Know You Got Soul," *Paid in Full* (Uni/Island, 1987).

31. Jeru the Damaja, "Come Clean," *The Sun Rises in the East* (Uni/Full Frequency Range Records, 1994).

32. Eric B. and Rakim, "Microphone Fiend," *Follow the Leader* (Uni/Universal Records, 1988).

33. Boogie Down Productions, "I'm Still #1" *By Any Means Necessary* (Jive Records, 1988).

34. Eric B. and Rakim, "Eric B. is President," *Paid in Full.*

35. De La Soul, "Big Brother Beat," *Stakes Is High* (Tommy Boy, 1996).

36. MC Lyte, "10% Dis," *Lyte as a Rock* (Atlantic Recording, 1988).

37. The Infamous Mobb Deep, "Quiet Storm," *Murda Muzik* (Loud Records, 1999).

38. OutKast, "Southernplayalisticadillacmuzik," *Southernplayalisticadillacmuzik* (LaFace Records, 1994).

39. Killah Priest, "From Then to Now," *Heavy Mental* (Geffen Records, 1998).

40. Method Man, "Biscuits," *Tical.*

41. Nelson George, *Hip Hop America* (New York: Viking, 1998), viii.

42. Ibid., xi.

34

Rise Up Hip-Hop Nation
From Deconstructing Racial Politics to Building Positive Solutions

Discussions about hip-hop and politics highlight the distinctions between the ways politically engaged individuals utilize hip-hop to their political ends and the contrasting ways that hip-hop might be thought to organically create the context for political engagement.

In her essay, Kristine Wright argues that hip-hop's power, not simply as an artistic form, is best realized within the context of structured political activity. As such, Wright argues that political activists must utilize hip-hop in order to reach youth.

Rise Up Hip Hop Nation: From Deconstructing Racial Politics to Building Positive Solutions

Kristine Wright

> *Life is your right, so we can't give up the fight.*
> —*Bob Marley*

Defining Hip Hop

From society's periphery, a generation created a cultural medium, *hip hop*, that served as both an expression of and an alternative to urban woes plaguing their lives, namely underemployment, poverty, and racial discrimination. Rap music and the associated fashion, language, and dance styles became hip hop's modes of expression. For many African American youth, hip hop has been a part of their cultural identity since the 1970s (Rose 1994; George 1998). Today, hip hop's influence on popular culture is undeniable. From its inception three decades ago, hip hop has grown from an urban, predominantly black and Latino youth culture into an international youth phenomenon transcending racial and ethnic lines.

The term hip hop describes urban youth culture in America (Smitherman 1997). Hazzard-Donald (1996) defines hip hop as an expressive cultural genre originating among marginalized African American youth. Forms of hip hop expression include rapping and rap music, graffiti writing, dance styles (originating with break-dancing), specific attire, and a specialized language and vocabulary. According to Smitherman, hip hop grew out of African oral tradition and other forms of black culture, as well as a long history of interaction between Black and Latino urban culture, originating in the Bronx, New York (Guevara 1996). George (1998) offers this succinct description:

> At its most elemental level hip hop is a product of post-civil rights era America, a set of cultural forms originally nurtured by African American, Caribbean-American, and Latin American youth in and around New York in the '70s. Its most popular vehicle of expression has been music, though dance, painting, fashion, video, crime, and commerce are also its playing fields (viii).

Hip hop culture transcends the commercialized product sold to mainstream America through commercials and music videos. It is more than the music, fashion, and style that is now so popular among youth everywhere. Although these are its modes of expression, hip hop as a culture is rooted in the day-to-day experiences of millions of inner city teens. As Spiegler (1996) describes it, hip hop is based on real life experiences, giving it more permanence than earlier teen trends.

In the beginning, the expression of hip hop culture known as rap was the voice of the urban youth underclass. According to Smitherman, rap music was a response to conditions of poverty, joblessness, and disempowerment, which still deeply affect the lives of the majority of African American urban youth today. Not only was rap music a black expressive cultural phenomenon, it was also a discourse of resistance, a set of communicative practices that constitute a text of resistance against white America's racism, and its Euro-centric cultural dominance. "This music has become a—or, perhaps the—principal medium for Black youth to express their views of the world and to create a sense of order out of the turbulence and chaos of their own, and our, lives" (Smitherman 1997: 6). In other words, rap was the political voice of this sector of society.

Old barriers faced by previous generations were knocked down during the Civil Rights movement, leading to a significant growth in the black middle class. At the same time, handships associated with postindustrial society like unemployment, poverty, crime, and drugs dramatically increased in the predominatly African American urban centers around the country, creating an even larger black lower class. Rap thus began as a cultural response by black and Latino youth to the "miseries of postindustrial urban America" (Baker 1995: 671). Rose (1994) writes:

> In the postindustrial urban context of dwindling low-income housing, a trickle of meaningless jobs for young people, mounting police brutality, and increasingly draconian depictions of young inner city resident, hip hop is black urban renewal (61).

Over the last twenty years, aspects of hip hop culture have been commodified, creating a multi-billion dollar culture industry (Holsendolph 1999). The most commodified aspect of hip hop culture is its music, rap. While African Americans constitute the majority of hip hop artists (rappers, DJs, dancers), and a significant proportion of its producers, white-dominated corporate America is now its primary distributor, with white-dominated mainstream media outlets its primary marketer (Neal, 1999).

Beginning as a cultural expression created to provide an outlet for youth from destitute urban living, hip hop is now also the extremely profitable packaging, marketing, and distributing (commodification) of "black rage" for mainstream consumption and enjoyment. Lusane (1993) offers a succinct description of rap music's duality:

> On the one hand, rap is the voice of alienated, frustrated, and rebellious black youth who recognize their vulnerability and marginality in post-industrial America. On the other hand, rap is the packaging and marketing of social discontent by some of the most skilled ad agencies and largest record producers in the world. It's this duality that has made rap and rappers an explosive issue in the politics of power (381).

By participating in hip hop's commodification, young African Americans receive jobs, financial stability, and a medium to express themselves to an ever-growing audience. However, corporate America's control of hip hop's production, marketing and distribution, subsequently translates into control of its image and voice.

With its commodification, the social structure that produced black rage, namely the "white supremacist capitalist patriarchy" (hooks 1994: 115), became its chief controller and profiteer. Once seen as a threat to the status quo, black rage is now—ironically—appropriated and controlled by the very power structure that produced it. In an industry in which African Americans are well represented, racial inequality exists because of society's (and congruently the music industry's) racially defined infrastructure. So also, perceptions of race persist through media-manipulated imagery. In this social climate, even a "black" cultural expression can reinforce the racialized power structure.

Gray (1995) argues that cultural matters are matters of power and politics. Cultural practices are significant only in relation to "the political power, economic positions, social conditions, and lived experiences of people" (6). He adds that culture is "deeply contradictory" (7), possessing both hegemonic and counter-hegemonic potentials. I contend that black culture in mainstream white America suffers the same paradoxical fate. This chapter hopes to provide necessary support for this argument as well as offer possible mechanisms to overcome this paradox.

Commodification Effects: The Macro-Level

Although the appropriation and commodification of black music is nothing new, the nature of rap music creates a unique result. As Shocklee asserts (Samuels 1991), rap songs can create, through words, complete characters that R&B formulas can't support. Through rap lyrics, images of black rap artists come alive. As rap has become more commodified, distinct shifts in themes can be observed. Although rap crossovers to mainstream audiences existed already, the introduction of the gangsta genre in late 1980s and early 1990s transformed rap into a mainstream staple, with the "gangsta" image representing the "real" black urban experience. Some rap artists highlight the music industry's role in socializing rap artists into profitable "gangsta" or "Mafia" images. Chuck D of Public Enemy (1997) offers this insight:

> Many in the world of hip hop believe that the only way to blow up and become mega-stars is by representing themselves in a negative light. The two recently slain hip hop artists Tupac and Notorious B.I.G. as well as other rap artists who have come under some criticism like Dr. Dre, Snoop Dogg, Ice Cube, or whoever you want to name, talk positivity in some of their records, but those records have to be picked by the industry executives and program directors to be magnified.
>
> That's what I feel happened with Tupac. Tupac had a loyalty to black people without a doubt. His early albums sound like a combination of Public Enemy and NWA. He was raw. Tupac found that when he said things that were pro-black and militant, people were not paying any attention to what he was saying so he decided to go more and more into the side of darkness, like Bishop the character he played in *Juice*. … The more he played the bad boy or rude boy image, the bigger and bigger he got.

A number of underground artists address the issue of rap's commodification in their lyrics (Ogbar 1999). In an interview, Franti, a member of the underground group, the Disposable Heroes of Hiphoprisy, addresses the image that young black rappers adopt to become commercially successful. He states:

> Through the commercialization of today's music, there is a lot of pressure for young black men to conform to very specific roles, and I try to just through my music let people know that those roles are not the only roles you have to play. … In order to be "real," we don't all have to be the same, and that there are as many black experiences as there are black people.

I gained insight into working in the industry from my interview with a radio personality who hosts an internationally syndicated hip hop program. Discussing the impact the music industry has on artists and others who work in it, he states:

> You kind of like have to be a certain way to keep your job. You kind of got to act, walk, talk, and like the guys that hired you, and you kind of adapt their mentality. It's a shame. I don't blame them, but they feel they kind of have to do that; otherwise they might not be able to maintain this position that they established.

He sums up rap's dilemma this way:

> The rap game man is good and bad, it's good and bad. It's created a lot of jobs for a lot of people that otherwise probably wouldn't have jobs, but at the same time, man, it's like mo' money, mo' problems [referring to rap song by the late Notorious B.I.G.].

Rap's commodification promotes some of its forms, while making other forms, which are often more "positive," unprofitable. So although artists have a choice, if they want to experience commercial success, they must stick to industry-endorsed formulas.

The themes in rap songs are homogeneous because certain formulas have proven to be profitable, and are therefore imitated exhaustively. While rap images of black rage were controversial at one time, after twenty years, they are now normalized, validating mainstream stereotypes of young African Americans. In truth, hip-hop culture's transition into mainstream America offers important insights on popular culture as mass culture, and popular culture as site of ideology construction and negotiation. Because they are socially constructed, popular culture and media representations are not independent of the power dynamics that inform popular culture's production. We must not only examine the content of popular culture and media representations, we must also examine the media industry's role in the creation process to better understand its influence.

The commodification of hip hop culture leaves the revolutionary aspect of the culture to be witnessed by only its most ardent supporters, once again, creating a "preaching to the choir" situation. As Gray asserts, cultural matters are, in fact, matters of power and politics. Through its commodification, hip hop culture's political representative becomes the corporate controlled, almighty dollar.

While mainstream media and record companies promote hip hop that's violent, misogynistic, materialistic, and individualistic, this depiction is really more of hip hop as commodity, a product of corporate America, and a reflection of mainstream America's appetite for reified black images. Black rage is now entertainment. Unfortunately, the cost is more than the $17.99 price tag on a CD. The real cost is an innovative and multi-dimensional culture that becomes essentialized, a revolutionary culture that's too often under-valued within its own community, and a collective identity that's too easily prejudged and misrepresented ... while the *whole world* watches.[1]

Commodification Effects: The Micro-Level

My analysis of micro-level commodification effects stems from experiences teaching in two *very* different environments: 1) a lower-income neighborhood in Compton, California that (dis)serves *only* African American and Latino students and 2) a university in an upper middle class suburb of Orange County, California, whose student population, although multicultural, includes almost *no* black and brown people. African Americans constitute less than 4% of the undergraduate population. One stark difference is that in the former setting, hip hop becomes an identity of necessity, whereas in the latter, it becomes an identity of choice.[2]

At this university, I teach a class that uses hip hop culture as a lens to view society, specifically social inequality. The course focuses on the racialized power structure of society, and the power of media framing and hegemony that in many ways shape our reality. We examine the institutional structures and racial politics that keep people of color in this country (and around the world) oppressed. We highlight how the structure of the hip hop industry parallels that of society in general. The game is the same as since the dawn of colonialism. Exploit people of color, their labor, and their culture while benefiting financially and gaining more power over them through hegemonic ideologies. As importantly, however, the course highlights how hip hop is also about resistance, protest, and perseverance—in many ways the political voice of inner city youth.

Over the years, I have taught more than 700 students of various backgrounds (the majority of Asian descent), many of whom embrace a hip hop identity. This experience has highlighted some micro-level repercussions of hip hop's commodification and the racial politics behind it. In many ways, the micro-level effects of commodification are most difficult to recognize and, possibly, most dangerous to racial progress. It shows in a number of ways, from non-African Americans embracing the n-word as a part of their vernacular, to the latest racialized perspectives on ghettopoly.[3]

I find most students only identify black in terms of skin color, and not culture, and for that reason, take offense to my labeling hip hop *black*. We need to be re-taught what race in this country actually stands for, and that is *power* and *privilege*. Instead of race, many social theorists choose to discuss the idea of *racialization* and a *racialized* system to show how "race" has been used to determine one's position in society. This understanding brings in the class aspect of racialization, showing it is no accident that the majority of black and brown citizens are socially and economically disadvantaged (Omi & Winant 1994).

When we look at the hip hop nation and the multiculturalism we find, we get a false understanding of racial solidarity. Hip Hop transcends racial barriers, if we define these in terms of ethnicity and skin tones. But that we are all dancing to the same beat does *little* to change the real social and economic conditions of those oppressed. The last twenty years offers substantial evidence for this. You need only do some research and look at the statistics, or better yet, visit your local hood. When a college student in my class claims to be hip hop and takes offense to hip hop as *black*, but does not recognize his/her privilege by looking around the class and seeing *few to no* African Americans or Latinos, racial inequality solidifies. Although my students in Compton were as bright as many I find at this high ranked public university, it is a fact that most will have fewer opportunities than their middle class hip hop counterparts. This is why I cannot join the club of *hip hop started as a voice of oppressed black and brown youth but now it's worldwide ...* because for these oppressed black and brown youth, little has changed and hip hop is still *their* voice. Hip hop should be defined as black when we define it in terms of culture, oppression, racialization, victimization and, of course, resistance.

Most of my college students recognize the macro-level effects of commodification, whether it be the black stereotypes highlighted in music videos, or the corporate control of hip hop culture homogenizing its image. What many students do not recognize, however, is their roles in the process, constructing their hip hop identity via mass mediated imagery. Using the example of the n-word, many will defend their use of it by either claiming to be "hip hop" or indicting rappers for normalizing the word, thus claiming a "*double standard*" by African Americans. They ignore context in their analysis, where the word's 400-year place in black vernacular becomes synonymous with the 10-year use by some that listen to rap records. They also ignore the consequences of hip hop that are often racialized. While non-blacks may embrace the n-word, their African American counterparts face the consequences of its use, within and outside of the community. For some, the word is just a word, but for others, it is a legacy of racism and, possibly, internalized oppression.

Another micro-level effect of hip hop's commodification can be seen in the varying reactions to ghettopoly. The fact that there is a market for ghettopoly underlies the racial politics in hip hop. Reactions to the controversy over ghettopoly were highly racialized in my class, with the line drawn between African American students and the majority of non-black students in the class. African Americans students took great offense to their culture being equated to "gangster, criminal, and drugs." They also took offense to seeing ghetto living and its structurally based miseries exploited in satire for profit (from game: "you get your whole neighborhood addicted to crack, collect $100"). For those that have lived ghetto experiences, crack is nothing to joke about.

Many of the non-black students found the game funny and "just entertainment." And those that were non-black but saw the game as offensive, were quick to defend its creator because "black rap artists do the same every day in song and video." A recurring claim was an indictment of the African American community for "protesting David Chang (the game's creator), but hot black rappers as vehemently." The problem with this argument is that many who indict African Americans are not in tune with the black community, black media and black activism—for many of the same reasons that residential segregation did not end with civil rights legislation. Those who are in tune, know that black media and thinkers often criticize African Americans' roles in the racial degradation process, while highlighting the larger social context that limits options.[4]

A final micro-level effect that becomes racialized is the growing divide between mainstream rap and its counterparts (read *black and lower class*) and the underground scene and its followers (read *white and middle class*). The hip hop underground movement must be applauded for its preservation of hip hop's original elements and its revolutionary spirit. Unfortunately in this movement, the debate over what is "real" hip hop has become racialized. Hip hop literature often highlights hip hop's appropriation by corporate America, but is only beginning to examine how middle class hip hop followers appropriate hip hop, and possible repercussions in the racial politics debate. To say that mainstream music, especially from African Americans, is not "real" hip hop is a lie and elitist, and it misrepresents hip hop, which they often indict mainstream media outlets for doing. At its essence, hip hop is making a way from no way, and in the case of mainstream hip hop, it has been a legal hustle for many youth from ghettos who would not have had many other opportunities.

Underground "conscious" hip hop is not any more real if only privileged persons hear it. Having access to underground websites and buying every CD that drops implies some level of middle class. Those on a college campus are better off than 90% of the world's population; this needs to be recognized in order to justly analyze one's context in hip hop. The underground scene often romanticizes revolution, but rarely reaches out to those most oppressed. Revolutions may start in lyrics but they must end in action. *It's bigger than hip hop*,[5] and it should be. Although I've noticed more hip hop activism, I'm fearful that the growing division in hip hop will undermine progress. It is like the activists are underground but those that need it are the mainstream masses. No progress can come from this equation; so *systemically*, little has changed. Without the masses, there can be no movement.[6] People of color are still victims of oppressive social systems that lock us up and out of self-determination, the only *real* solution. To achieve self-determination, we need a catalyst. The Civil Rights movement had the church as its catalyst. We now have hip hop.

Realizing Our Power

Given these micro and macro-level processes, we face deep institutional warfare to overcome, and our understanding of these processes offers a starting point for building solutions. When imperialist ideas and individualistic philosophies oppress the world as they do today, we often lose sight of the power *we* possess; we lose sight of where real power comes from. Real power comes from *us* ... the people. As a collective, we are power.

It is easy to doubt our power when *white supremacist, patriarchal, capitalist* ideologies (bell hooks) seem to have a stranglehold on the world. We see it in the peaking statistics of African Americans living in extreme poverty. We see it in famine and AIDS epidemics in Africa. We see it in the invasion of Iraq and the hawkish warmongers in the white house and department of defense who would like to export war to a long list of other countries. We see it in the education and social program cuts in states across the country. We see it in the incarceration of our youth of color courtesy of our so-called judicial system. We see it in the Patriot Act. We see it in the blacklisting of anti-war, peace proponents. We see it in water cooler French-bashing. We see it in the ever-increasing polarization of global resources. We see it in corporate greed. We see it in a patriotism that never questions but proudly displays the U.S. flag in cars as a symbol of superiority. We see it in the popularity of Bill O'Reilly. We see it in racial profiling of people of color, including now Arab Americans. We see it in the framing and minstrelsy of media and its increasing corporate concentration thanks now to the FCC. And yes, we see it in hip hop.

In many ways, hip hop may try to *keep it real*, but that voice is often silenced because oppressors control hip hop's *image*. Those in power get to reap the larger benefits of artists' labor, while simultaneously controlling their image and teaching the youth values that reinforce the same old nihilism. They get to make money, villainize the black man, and prostitute the black woman all at the same time. For them, it's a win-win situation. For the hip hop community, it becomes a trap we fall into because we believe money gets us power. Right now what money gets us is bought.

Hip hop today seems to be searching for meaning, while simultaneously spinning its wheels in battles and beefs; formulas and stereotypes. In a system that gives us so few options, we have made choices that have benefited us while hurting us simultaneously. For example, artists find they can sell more records by degrading life, others, and themselves. And for that realization, they have achieved unparalleled monetary gains. But these gains have come with a high cost. One cost has been progress. The very things helping some are hurting many others. Our youth learn that the gangsta, pimp, and drug dealer lifestyles will help them make the money they so desperately need to survive this cold system, but it is these same elements that kill our youth before they have even lived. Our seeds have learned from society that they are not valued. Then through choices we've made as a culture, we reinforce the lie by becoming a part of the problem through flip lyrics and risky behavior.

The power of hip hop is not in record deals or celebrity. It is not in money or world hype, and it is definitely not in its hypocrisy. Hip hop must decide *now* whether it wants to make the same mistakes others before it have made—by gaining the world (at least as its audience), but losing its soul. So where does hip hop's power come from, if not the world stage and bottomless money pits?

Hip hop's power is realized in truth and self-determination through community activism. Community activism in inner cities across the country is taking on a hip hop sensibility and offering real alternatives for youth at community levels. This activism has recently experienced national level successes, with Russell Simmons's *Hip Hop Action Network* (HHAN). It has been responsible for organizing hip hop summits bringing artists, activists, spiritual leaders, and politicians to the same table for change. Most recently, the HHAN joined forces with New York educators and students to protest budget cuts in education, and, due in part to these efforts, achieved retribution. The HHAN is also organizing a major voter drive targeting voters of the hip hop generation. Hip Hop's power is realized simply in its ability to *move the crowd*[7] as a collective, challenging hegemonic power and building solutions as a community. Power to the People!

Study Questions

1. Can contemporary youth movements exist without an engagement with hip-hop?
2. Is contemporary hip-hop culture capable of sustaining the attention of American youth?
3. What is the evidence of hip-hop's impact in the political realm?

Notes

1. Outkast, from their CD *Big Boi & Dre Present ...*
2. See Mary Waters, *Ethnic Options: Choosing Identities in America* (1990), for theoretical background.

3. Ghettopoly, created by Taiwanese-American David Chang. The following sources provide more detail on the game: http://story.news.yahoo.com/news?tmpl=story&u=/ap/20031009/ap_on_re_us/ghet-topoly; http://www.blackcommentator.com/59/59_guest_ghettopoly.html
4. Spike Lee's *Bamboozled* provides a critical analysis of the macro and micro processes in media.
5. dead prez, from CD *Let's Get Free.*
6. See the insightful piece by Adamma Ince, *No Masses, No Movement: Black Boomers Shout Reparations in the Court—But Go Silent in the 'Hood,* http://www.villagevoice.com/issues/0221/ince.php
7. Eric B. and Rakim, from their CD *Paid in Full.*

References

Chuck D. 1997. *Fight the Power: Rap, Race, and Reality.* New York: Delacorte Press.

George, N. 1998. *Hip Hop America.* New York: Viking Penguin.

Gray, H. 1995. *Watching Race.* Minneapolis: University of Minnesota Press.

Guevara, N. 1996. "Women Writin' Rappin' Breakin'." In *Dropping Science: Critical Essays on Rap Music and Hip Hop Culture.* E. Perkins, ed. Philadelphia: Temple University Press.

Hazzard-Donald, K. 1996. "Dance in Hip Hop Culture." In *Dropping Science: Critical Essays on Rap Music and Hip Hop Culture.* E. Perkins, ed. Philadelphia: Temple University Press.

Holsendolph, E. 1999. "Out of the Streets and into the Boardroom, Hip Hop has Become Big Business." *Emerge Magazine.*

hooks, b. 1994. *Outlaw Culture: Resisting Representations.* New York: Routledge.

Lusane, C. 1993. "Rap, Race, and Politics." In *Race, Class, and Gender: An Anthology.* 2nd edition. Andersen & Collins, eds. Belmont: Wadsworth.

Neal, M. 1999. *What the Music Said: Black Popular Music and Black Public Culture.* New York: Routledge.

Ogbar, J. 1999. "The Culture Wars and Self-Criticism in Hip Hop Music." *Journal of Black Studies.*

Omi, Michael, & Howard Winant. 1994. *Racial Formations in the United States.* New York: Routledge.

Rose, T. 1994. *Black Noise: Rap Music and Black Culture in Contemporary America.* Hanover: University Press of New England.

Samuels, D. 1995. "The Rap on Rap: The Black Music that Isn't Either." In *Rap on Rap: Straight up Talk on Hip Hop Culture.* A. Sexton, ed. New York: Delta, 1995.

Smitherman, G. 1997. "'The Chain Remain the Same': Communicative Practices in the Hip Hop Nation." *Journal of Black Studies* 29.

Spiegler, M. 1996. "Marketing Street Culture: Bringing Hip Hop Style to the Mainstream." *American Demographics* 18.

Stapleton, K. 1998. "From the Margins to Mainstream: The Political Power of Hip Hop." *Media, Culture, and Society* 20.

Part VI

"Looking for the Perfect Beat"

Hip-Hop, Technology, and Rap's Lyrical Arts

Murray Forman

It is obvious that technology figures prominently in hip-hop's creative process and has done so since hip-hop's emergence. This is especially true of rap music, although, once the media production and diffusion of hip-hop are factored into the equation, technology's deep influence in virtually all of hip-hop's constituent forms is evident. In some contexts it might be argued that hip-hop is, in fact, at the forefront of new technological applications. Beat-obsessed DJs and rap producers are necessarily attuned to new technical products. They search for equipment and (more recently) software that allow them to explore radically new possibilities, testing and tweaking the technology and pushing the range of standard uses in order to discover alternative sonic realms.

Despite a central impact, however, it is essential not to adopt a technological determinist position that identifies technology as the motivating force in the change and evolution of cultural practices; technology has never been the sole driver of hip-hop's development. Rather, the technologies of hip-hop are culturally influential at diverse scales of effect, woven into prevailing social contexts and enfolded within systems of production and exchange that are prone to transition in the face of historically specific stimuli. The modern human subject exists within a stratified environment, buffeted by high-tech and low-tech options, and under certain conditions one or the other may be most sensible or most promising. As Langdon Winner notes, "what matters is not technology itself, but the social and economic systems in which it is embedded" (1986: 20).

This is not to suggest, however, that technology is benign, since virtually every technology has the potential to extend power in ways that are both scripted and unscripted. For example, in the late 1970s Bronx the illegal hijacking of electricity from city sources rechanneled the "juice" to drive mighty sound systems at impromptu block parties. Through the amplification of disco, funk, and the first break beats, a new means of imposing a radical presence in the public spaces of the city parks and streets was discovered, producing cultural events that were accessible, meaningful, and *cool* for those close enough to palpably experience the powerful bass reverberations as the DJ worked "the wheels of steel." As numerous interviews and casual anecdotes affirm, more than a few of these original hip-hop jams were broken up with the arrival of the New York constabulary, who, reasserting hegemonic power and authority, summarily unplugged and dismantled the sound systems. To suspend the assembly of fun-loving hip-hop heads, the authorities deliberately attacked the technology.

Rap music traditionally relies on methods of *bricolage* involving the appropriation and reassignment of music technologies, especially the turntable, mixer, and vinyl records. In the hands of trailblazers such as Afrika Bambaataa, DJ Kool Herc, Grandmaster Flash, or Grand Wizard Theodore, these materials were employed in ways unforeseen by corporate manufacturers; the turntable was, for example, transformed from a playback unit mainly associated with domestic forms of musical reception to an instrument of creative production that facilitated the performance of new musical styles in alternative public contexts. Moreover, these hip-hop innovators redefined aspects of the black musical aesthetic, simultaneously paying respect to their predecessors even as they disrupted the musical continuum and upended the sonic sensibilities of a generation. Describing the merging of electronic technologies with emergent aesthetics, Iain Chambers writes:

> Rap is New York's "sound system"; the black youth culture of Harlem and the Bronx successfully twisting technology into new cultural shape. Rap is sonorial graffiti, a musical spray that marries black rhythms and the verbal gymnastics of hip street talk to a hot DJ patter over an ingenious manipulation of the turntable.
>
> (Chambers, 1985: 190)

The practice of rocking a beat between two turntables aided by electronic mixers rebuilt with efficient crossfade switches and, at times, small rudimentary rhythm boxes gradually developed into a full-fledged DJ art form through the late 1970s and into the 1980s.

Hip-hop historians such as David Toop (1984), Steve Hager (1984), Dick Hebdige (1987), and many others have recounted the historical roots of the DJ from Jamaican dance halls to the streets and parks in the Bronx and Harlem, charting the gradual ascendance of a new hybrid urban aesthetic as the Caribbean DJ practices, including the musical influences of Jamaican reggae and Puerto Rican or Cuban salsa, were blended with U.S. soul, R&B, rock and funk music. With the advent of studio recording in 1979 when the Sugarhill Gang released "Rapper's Delight" on Sugar Hill Records, rap DJs and producers increasingly combined their turntable skills with the technical possibilities of the studio, further enhancing the character of hip-hop's urban soundtrack.

Many of the prominent DJs from this period lamented the shift to studio production and the implementation of sophisticated production technologies within more controlled spaces, suggesting that the industrial structures of the recording business displaced the primacy and spontaneity of live performances—a point elucidated here by Greg Dimitriadis—and eroded the caliber of rap talent that was up to this point measured by the ability to "rock a party." By the mid-1980s, digital sound sampling had become a standard technological component of music production, again modifying the standards and skills involved in rap music production. Sampling was rapidly integrated into rap's studio arsenal, introducing radical capabilities that transformed the way music was conceived and constructed while simultaneously challenging the music industry's legal authority inscribed in copyright law. Most early applications of sound sampling technology involved the digital excision of brief rhythm "breaks" or song passages from previously recorded material including familiar choruses, catchy lyrical phrases, or distinct vocal exhortations.

Apart from constructing a bridge between musical antecedents and the present, digital sampling can imbue an element of authenticity on newer tracks as the patina of the past seeps into the new mix. The hiss or pop of old vinyl records provides a sonic link to the original recording by referencing its age and wear through what are, in most conventional recording contexts, deemed as imperfections. DJ or producer's tastes and cultural capital are also on display with their selection of classic recordings from the past, especially as they seek more compelling or obscure material to distinguish their musical creations.

After more than 30 years of rap recording, rap and hip-hop tracks are themselves constant sources in a repository of sound available to producers who might employ a snippet of an established rap track or include a beat from a time-proven funk masterpiece. While James Brown, George Clinton, or the Gap Band are today regarded as classic, if obvious, sources for rap's sonic appropriation, as Joseph Schloss points out it requires considerable knowledge and real labor to seek out exotic, unfamiliar, or forgotten tracks for an interesting horn progression, bass rhythm, or melodic signature. Moreover, the labor and effort of "digging in the crates" and the modes of employing sampled material are loosely guided by a set of ethical concerns that are widely understood by DJs and producers everywhere. The ethical principles for sample use cohere with the fundamental criteria of originality and creative innovation, providing the basis for judgments of excellence or of wackness.

Mass production and miniaturization of electronic and digital technologies allow a much wider degree of access, and today the "bedroom" recordings of thousands of budding DJs and producers, as well as the work emitting from a growing number of students enrolled in turntablist courses (such as those at Berklee College of Music, the Interactive Media and Performance Labs at the University of Regina, or Scratch DJ Academy as well as similar "labs" throughout the world), show impressive complexity and musical savvy. The so-called hip-hop underground is to a considerable extent fuelled by artists with talent and technical abilities, exploiting the resources available to them within the logic of a remix culture.

New research also emphasizes an intensified analysis of hip-hop's linguistic characteristics, including the discursive patterns of rap lyrics within what H. Samy Alim terms "hip-hop nation language." More than merely citing lyrics for their literal content, linguists and discourse analysts critically engage the use of language in hip-hop as a method of understanding the unique construction of meaning, as well as exploring language as a system of representation that is linked to the circulation of social ideals and ideological values. Electronic and digital technologies of communication (including new media and the myriad social networking websites) amplify and disseminate the words, sounds, ideas, and social critique that are forged within a hip-hop sensibility.

Through today's digital networks, contemporary hip-hop circulates globally and instantaneously, bypassing the traditional authority of corporate entities in the culture industries. With enhanced autonomy and viral media diffusion, hip-hop artists—not just music producers but also dancers, graphic aerosol artists, and others whose work subscribes to a hip-hop aesthetic—readily upload their work, sustaining the connective possibilities of African-American innovation within black diasporic relations that was initiated over three decades ago in New York City.

REFERENCES

Chambers, Iain. (1985). *Urban Rhythms: Pop Music and Popular Culture*. London: Macmillan.
Hager, Steven. (1984). *Hip Hop: The Illustrated History of Break Dancing, Rap Music, and Graffiti*. New York: St. Martin's Press.
Hebdige, Dick. (1987). *Cut 'n' Mix: Culture, Identity and Caribbean Music*. London: Comedia.
Toop, David. (1984). *The Rap Attack: African Jive to New York Hip-Hop*. Boston, MA: South End Press.
Winner, Langdon. (1986). *The Whale and the Reactor: A Search for Limits in an Age of High Technology*. Chicago: University of Chicago Press.

35

"Bring It to the Cypher"
Hip-Hop Nation Language

Language constitutes a crucial facet of hip-hop expression, not just in rap music but also in the broader contexts of everyday life. H. Samy Alim identifies what he calls "Hip Hop Nation Language" that reflects a shared attitudinal aspect of language while encompassing linguistic forms and systems of meaning that are unique to hip-hop. Alim is himself a dexterous wordsmith and he demonstrates the flexibility of hip-hop language within his essay, flipping between the formal definitions of the academy and the sophisticated free form style of the cipher. The similarities between hip-hop linguistics and graffiti are on full display as Alim defines "flow" and style, suggesting that an artist's rhymes simultaneously enunciate one's identity and talent while articulating regional aesthetics and other cultural affiliations.

Alim explains here that words have power but some of that power comes from the flexibility of language and meanings and a wily capacity to mobilize discourses that expose and critique various sociopolitical conditions. Included in this analysis are extensive discussions with some of hip-hop's most notable "verbal architects"—Kurupt, Pharoahe Monch, and Raekwon, among others—about hip-hop poetics and lyrical strategies for critiquing social issues, decimating the opposition, or uniting the audience.

"Bring It to the Cypher": Hip Hop Nation Language

H. Samy Alim

Four hundred years ago, when black slaves were brought to America, Africans who spoke the same language were separated from each other. What we're seeing today, with this insane campaign to intimidate rappers and rap music, is just another form of separating people that speak a common language.

(Ice Cube, June 25, 1990; cited in Sexton 1995)

The centrality of language to the HHN is evident in such song and album titles as "New Rap Language" (Treacherous Three, 1980), "Wordplay" (Bahamadia, 1996), "Gangsta Vocabulary" (DJ Pooh, 1997), "Project Talk" (Bobby Digital, 1998), "Slang Editorial" (Cappadonna, 1998), *Real Talk 2000* (Three-X-Krazy, 2000), "Ebonics" (Big L, 2000), *Country Grammar* (Nelly, 2000), *Project English* (Juvenile, 2001), "Dangerous Language" (Afu-Ra, 2002), and many more. In numerous ethnographic interviews, I have found that language is a favorite topic of discussion in the HHN, and its members are willing to discuss it with great fervor—and to defend its use.

In this chapter, we enter a Black Language Space as we take a journey through Hip Hop's linguistic landscape and explore the anatomy of language and language use within the HHN, providing a thorough description of Hip Hop Nation Language (HHNL). My research on the language and linguistic practices of the Hip Hop Nation Speech Community examines how HHNL both builds upon and expands the Black American Oral Tradition. Here I outline several Hip Hop discursive practices and cultural modes of discourse—*call and response, multilayered totalizing expression, signifyin* and *bustin* (*bussin*), *tonal semantics* and *poetics, narrative sequencing and flow, battlin* and *entering the cipher.*

In exploring the development of nation language in Anglophone Caribbean poetry, Caribbean historian, poet, and literary and music critic Kamau Brathwaite (1984: 13) writes: "Nation language is the language which is influenced very strongly by the African model, the African aspect of our New World/Caribbean heritage. English it may be in terms of some of its lexical features. But in its contours, its rhythm and timbre, its sound explosions, it is not English." Concerned with the literature of the Caribbean and the sociopolitical matrix within which it is created, Brathwaite used the term "nation language" in contrast to "dialect." Familiar with the pejorative meanings of the term "dialect" in the folk linguistics of the people, he writes that while nation language can be considered both English and African at the same time, it is an English which is like a "howl, or a shout, or a machine-gun or the wind or a wave." Then he likened it to the blues. Surely, nation language is like Hip Hop (as rapper Raekwon spits his "machine-gun-rap" (on *Wu-Tang Forever*, 1997)). HHNL is, like Brathwaite's description, new in one sense and ancient in another. It comprises elements of orality, total expression, and conversational modes (Brathwaite 1984).

Rapper Mystikal, known for having a unique, highly energetic rhyming style highlighted with lyrical sound explosions, provides a perfect example of nation language when he raps: "You know what time it is, nigga, and you know who the fuck this is/ DAANNN-JAH!!! [Danger] DAANNN-JAH!!! [Danger]/ Get on the FLO' [floor]!/ The nigga right, yeaaahhHHH!" (2000). Mystikal starts out speaking to his listener in a low, threatening growl, asserting his individuality ("you know who the fuck this is"), and then explodes as if sounding an alarm, letting everyone know that they have entered a dangerous verbal zone! "Get on the FLO'!" has a dual function—simultaneously warning listeners to lie down before the upcoming lyrical "DAANNN-JAH!" and directing them to get on the dance floor. When rapper Ludacris (2001) commands his listeners to "ROOOLLLL OUT!" and raps: "Oink, Oink, PIG! PIG! Do away with the POORRK-uh/ Only silverwuurrr [silverware] I need's a steak knife and FOORRK-uh!", he stresses his words emphatically, compelling one to do as he says. In that brief example, he is in conversation with Black American Muslim and Christian communities currently dialoguing about the eating of swine flesh (which Muslims consider unholy).

When we speak of "language," we are defining the term in a sense that is congruent with the HHN's "linguistic culture" (Schiffman 1996). Wideman (1976: 34) situates HHNL in the broader context of Black American speech:

> There is no single register of African American speech. And it's not words and intonations, it's a whole attitude about speech that has historical rooting. It's not a phenomenon that you can isolate and reduce to linguistic characteristics. It has to do with the way a culture conceives of the people inside of that culture. It has to do with a whole complicated protocol of silences and speech, and how you use speech in ways other than directly to communicate information. And it has to do with, certainly, the experiences that the people in the speech situation bring into the encounter. What's fascinating to me about African American speech is its spontaneity, the requirement that you not only have a repertoire of vocabulary or syntactic devices/constructions, but you come prepared to do something in an attempt to meet the person on a level that both uses the language, mocks the language, and recreates the language.

On her single recording "Spontaneity" (1996), Philadelphia rapper Bahamadia validates Wideman's assertion. She raps about her "verbal expansion" in a stream of consciousness style: "Everybody's on it cause eternal verbal expansion keeps enhancin brain child's ability to like surpass a swarm of booty-ass-no-grass-roots-havin-ass MC's." The verbal architect constructs her rhymes by consciously stretching the limitations of the "standard" language. In describing her lyrical influences, she cites Rappers Kool Keith of the Ultramagnetic MCs, De La Soul, and Organized Konfusion as "masters at what they do in that they explore the English language and they try to push the boundaries and go against the grains of it, you know what I mean?" (Spady and Alim 1999: xviii).

Wideman continues: "It's a very active exchange. But at the same time as I say that, the silences and the refusal to speak is just as much a part, in another way, of African American speech." Rapper Fearless of the group Nemesis exemplifies the point: Envisioning rappers, including himself, among the great orators and leaders in the Black community, he says:

> I always looked up to great orators like Martin Luther King, Malcolm X. Anybody who could ever stand up and persuade a group of young men or a nation ... Just the way they were able to articulate. The way they emphasized their words. And the way they would use pauses. They would actually use *silence* powerfully ... Just the way they made words cause feelings in you, you know what I'm saying? Just perpetuate thought within people, you know.
>
> (Spady and Alim 1999: xviii)

So, "language" in HHNL obviously refers not only to the syntactic constructions of the language but also to the many discursive and communicative practices, the attitudes toward language, understanding the role of language in both binding/bonding community and seizing/smothering linguistic opponents, and language as concept (meaning clothes, facial expressions, body movements, grafitti, and overall communication—"cuz as Beanie Sigel knows, '85% of communication is non-verbal'").

In addition to the preceding, HHNL can be characterized by ten tenets.

1. HHNL is rooted in Black Language (BL) and communicative practices (Spady and Eure 1991; Smitherman 1997; Yasin 1999). Linguistically, it is "the newest chapter in the African American book of folklore" (Rickford and Rickford 2000). It is a vehicle driven by the culture creators of Hip Hop, themselves organic members of the broader Black American community. Thus HHNL both reflects and expands the Black American Oral Tradition.

2. HHNL is just one of the many language varieties used by Black Americans.

3. HHNL is widely spoken across the country, and used/borrowed and adapted/transformed by various ethnic groups inside and outside the US.

4. HHNL is a language with its own grammar, lexicon, and phonology as well as unique communicative style and discursive modes. When an early Hip Hop group, The Treacherous Three, rhymed about a "New Rap Language" in 1980, they were well aware of the uniqueness of the language they were rappin in.

5. HHNL is best viewed as the synergistic combination of speech, music, and literature. Yancy (1991) speaks of Rap as "*musical literature* (or rhythmic-praxis discourse)." Henderson (1973) asserts that the Black poetry of the 1960s and 1970s is most distinctly Black when it derives its form from Black speech and Black music. HHNL is simultaneously the spoken, poetic, lyrical, and musical expression of the HHN.

6. HHNL includes ideologies of language and language use (see Pharcyde dialogue later).

7. HHNL is central to the identity and the act of envisioning an entity known as the HHN.

8. HHNL exhibits regional variation (Morgan 2001). For example, most members of the HHN recognize Master P's signature phrase, "Ya heeeaaard may?" (for "You heard me?") as characteristic of a southern variety of HHNL. Even within regions, HHNL exhibits individual variation based on life experiences. For example, because California Rapper Xzibit grew up in the Hip Hop-saturated streets of Detroit, New Mexico, and California, his HHNL is a syncretization of all these Hip Hop Nation Language varieties.

9. The fundamental aspect of HHNL—and perhaps the most astonishing to some—is that it is central to the lifeworlds of the members of the HHN and suitable and functional for all of their communicative needs.

10. HHNL is inextricably linked with the sociopolitical circumstances that engulf the HHN. How does excessive police presence and brutality shift the discourse of the HHN? How do disproportionate incarceration rates and urban gentrification impact this community's language? As Spady (1993) writes: "Hip Hop culture [and language] mediates the corrosive discourse of the dominating society while at the same time it functions as a subterranean subversion ... Volume is turned up to tune out the decadence of the dominant culture."

Rappers are insightful examiners of the sociopolitical matrix within which HHNL operates. Discussing the role of HHNL in Hip Hop lyrics, Houston's Scarface concludes that HHNL functions as a communal "code of communication" for the HHN:

It's a code of communication, too ... Because we can understand each other when we're rappin. You know, if I'm saying, [in a nasal, mocking voice] "Well, my friend, I saw this guy who shot this other guy and ..." I break that shit down for you and you say, "Goddamn, man!

Them muthafuckas is going crazy out where this dude's from." You know what I'm saying? It's just totally different. It's just a code of communication to me. I'm letting my partner know what's going on. And anything White America can't control they call "gangsters." *Shit*! I get real. Politicians is gangsters, goddamn. The presidents is the gangsters because they have the power to change everything. That's a gangster to me. That's my definition of gangster.

(Spady *et al.* 1999: xix)

Members of Tha Pharcyde actively debated the concept of HHNL:

Booty Brown: There's more than just one definition for words! We talk in slang. We always talk basically in slang. We don't use the English dictionary for every sentence and every phrase that we talk!

Pharcyde: No, there's a lot of words out of the words that you just said which all …

Booty Brown: Yeah, but the way I'm talking is not the English language … We're not using that definition … We're making our own … Just like they use any other word as a slang, *my brotha!* Anything. I'm not really your brother. Me and your blood aren't the same, but I'm your brother because we're brothas. That's slang … We make up our *own* words. I mean, it depends whose definition you glorify, okay? That's what I'm saying. Whose definition are you glorifying? Because if you go by my definition of "Black", then I can say "a Black person." But if you go by the *Webster Dictionary's* … You have your own definition. It's your definition.

(Spady, *et al.* 1999: xix)

Sociolinguistically, so much is happening in the exchange above. The HHN continues to "flip the script" (reverse the power of the dominant culture). Scarface is reacting to the media's labeling of reality-based rap lyrics as "gangster." By redefining gangster, he effectively turns the tables on what he believes is an oppressive state. If the presidents have the power to change everything, why ain't a damn thing changed?

In Tha Pharcyde conversation, when the *brotha* says the way he is talking is not the English language, he is talking about much more than slang. He asks pointedly, "Whose definition are you glorifying?" By making up your own words, he attests, you are freeing yourself of linguistic colonization (Wa Thiongo 1992). In an effort to combat the capitalistic commodification of Hip Hop culture, and to "unite and establish the common identity of the HHN," KRS-One refined the definition of Hip Hop terms and produced a document known as "The Refinitions" (2000)—putting the power of redefinition to action. KRS defines the language of Hip Hop Culture as "street language," and proposes that "Hiphoppas" speak an Advanced Street Language, which includes "the correct pronunciation of one's native and national language as it pertains to life in the inner-city." KRS is reversing "standard" notions of correctness and appropriateness, realizing that the HHN has distinct values and aesthetics that differ from the majority culture. Clearly, members of the HHN would agree that the use of BL stems "from a somewhat disseminated rejection of the life-styles, social patterns, and thinking in general of the Euro-American sensibility," as the writer of the first BL dictionary outside of the Gullah area put it (Major 1970:10).

The Relationship Between HHNL and BL: Lexicon, Syntax, and Phonology

"Dangerous dialect/Dangerous dialect/I elect … to impress America." That's it, that's what it was about … Dangerous dialect, dangerous wording, you know what I mean? "I elect," that I pick, you know. "To impress America." That's what I pick to impress America, that dangerous dialect, you know.

(San Quinn, 2000, Alim and Spady, unpublished interview)

The relationship between HHNL and BL is a familial one. Since Hip Hop's culture creators are members of the broader Black American community, the language that they use most often when communicating with each other is BL. HHNL can be seen as the *submerged area* (Brathwaite 1984: 13) of BL that is used within the HHN, particularly during Hip Hop-centered cultural activities, but also during other playful, creative, artistic, and intimate settings. This conception of HHNL is broad enough to include the language of Rap lyrics, album interludes, Hip Hop stage performances, and Hip Hop conversational discourse. Black Americans are on the cutting edge of the sociolinguistic situation in the US (as evidenced by the preponderance of recent sociolinguistic research). HHNL, thus, is the cutting edge of the cutting edge.

A revised edition of the lexicon of "Black Talk" (Smitherman 1994 (2000)) begins with a chapter entitled, "From Dead Presidents to the Benjamins." The term "dead presidents" (meaning "money" and referring to American notes with images of dead presidents) has been in use in the Black American community since the 1930s. In the late 1990s, Hip Hop group dead prez both shortened the term and made explicit its multivariate meanings (within the revolutionary context of their rhymes and philosophy, they are surely hinting at assassination—a form of verbal subversion). The "benjamins", referring to Benjamin Franklin's image on one hundred dollar bills, is a term from the late 1990s popularized by Rapper Sean "Puffy" Combs (P. Diddy).

While several scholars and writers have produced work on the lexicon of BL (Turner 1949; Major 1970; Smitherman 1994; Dillard 1977; Anderson 1994; Stavsky, Mozeson and Mozeson 1995; Holloway and Vass 1997), it is important to note that Hip Hop artists, as street linguists and lexicographers, have published several dictionaries of their own. Old School legend Fab Five Freddy (Braithwaite 1992, 1995) documented the "fresh fly flavor" of the words and phrases of the Hip Hop generation (in English and German). Atlanta's Goodie Mob and several other artists have published glossaries on the inside flaps of their album covers. Of course, as lexicographers Hip Hop artists are only continuing the tradition of Black musicians, for many jazz and bebop artists compiled their own glossaries, most notable among them Cab Calloway (1944), Babs Gonzales, and Dan Burley.

Vallejo Rapper E-40 discusses the genesis of *E-40's Dictionary Book of Slang, Vol. 1* (forthcoming):

> I feel that I *am* the ghetto. The majority of street slang ... "It's all good." "Feel me." "Fo' shi-iiiiziiie," all that shit come from 40. "What's up, folks?" As a matter of fact, I'm writing my own dictionary book of slang right now ... It's a street demand [for it]. Everywhere I go people be like, "Dude, you need to put out a dictionary. Let them know where all that shit come from," you know what I mean?
>
> (Spady *et al.* 1999: 290)

E-40 is credited with developing a highly individualized repertoire of slang words and phrases. If he were to say something like, "What's crackulatin, pimpin? I was choppin it up wit my playa-potna last night on my communicator—then we got to marinatin, you underdig—and I come to find out that the homie had so much fedi that he was tycoonin, I mean, pimpin on some real boss-status, you smell me?", not too many people would understand him. ("Crackulatin" = happening, an extended form of "crackin"; "pimpin" is sometimes used as a noun to refer to a person, like "homie"; "choppin it up" = making conversation; "playa-potna" = partner, friend; "communicator" = cell phone; "marinatin" = a conversation where participants are reasoning on a subject; "underdig" = understand; "fedi" = money; "tycoonin" = being a successful entrepreneur; "pimpin" = being financially wealthy; "boss-status" = managing things like a CEO; "you smell me?" = you feel me? Or you understand me?)

In HHNL, "pimp" refers not only to one who solicits clients for a prostitute, but also has several other meanings. One could be suffering from "record company pimpin" (the means by which

record companies take advantage of young Black artists lacking knowledge of the music industry), engaging in "parking lot pimpin" (hanging around the parking lot after large gatherings),
"pimpin a Lex" (driving a Lexus while looking flashy), or "pimpin somebody's ride" (custom
designing a car; see Xzibit in MTV's *Pimp My Ride*). As we also saw earlier, "pimpin" can also refer
generally to an individual, or specifically to one who sports a flashy lifestyle. The word "poli-
tickin" can refer to the act of speaking about political subjects relevant to the Black community,
simply holding a conversation, or trying to develop a relationship with a female. One might catch
"frostbite" or get "goose-bumps" from all of the "ice" they got on ["ice" = diamonds]. In the
HHN, "rocks" can be a girl's best friend (diamonds) or a community's silent killer (crack
cocaine), while "to rock" can mean to liven up a party, to wear a fashionable article of clothing,
or to have sexual intercourse. If you really wanna liven up a party, you would "lean widdit, rock
widdit" (like Dem Franchize Boyz) or get "crunk" (like Lil Jon 'nem boys down Souf be doin), or
get "hyphy" (like how E-40, Keak da Sneak and dem Bay Boys be gettin down).

Given the fluidity of HHNL, speakers take a lot of pride in being the originators and innovators of terms that are consumed by large numbers of speakers. Rappers, as members of distinct
communities, also take pride in regional lexicon. For instance, the term "jawn" emerged in the
Philadelphia Hip Hop community. "Jawn" is what can be called a *context-dependent substitute
noun*—a noun that substitutes for any other noun, with its definition so fluid that its meaning
depends entirely upon context. For instance, one can say, "Oh, that's da jawn!" for, "da bomb!" if
they think something is superb; "Did you see that jawn?" for "female" when an attractive female
walks by; "I like that new Beanie jawn"; for "song," when the song is played on the radio, and so
on. Recently, Philadelphia's Roots have handed out T-shirts with "JAWN" written on the front,
advocating the use of the distinctive Philly Hip Hop term. Placed in a broader context, the meaning of the distinct lexicon of HHNL can be nicely summed up: "Slick lexicon is hip-hop's Magna
Carta, establishing the rights of its disciples to speak loudly but privately, to tell America about
herself in a language that leaves her puzzled" (Rickford and Rickford 2000: 86).

Several scholars have written that the syntax of HHNL is essentially the same as that of BL
(Remes 1991; Smitherman 1997, 2000; A. Morgan 1999; Spady and Alim 1999; Yasin 1999;
Rickford and Rickford 2000; M. Morgan 2001). This is true. We must also examine the syntax of
HHNL closely enough to elucidate how the language users are behaving both within and beyond
the boundaries of BL syntax. What is happening syntactically when Method Man gets on the air
and proclaims, "Broadcasting live from the Apocalypse, it be I, John Blazzzazzziiinnnyyyyy!"
(KMEL 2001)? What is happening when Jubwa of Soul Plantation writes in his autobiography:
"Jubwa be the dope mc, freestylin' to the beat deep cover" (cited in Alim 2001)? An important
question is, How does HHNL confirm our knowledge of BL syntax—and how does it challenge
that knowledge?

Probably the most oft-studied feature of BL is *habitual* or *invariant be* (see Green 2004). Early
studies of BL syntax (Labov *et al.* 1968; Wolfram 1969; Fasold 1972) noted the uniqueness of this
feature and were in agreement that it was used for recurring actions (*We be clubbin on Saturdays*)
and could not be used in finite contexts (*She be the teacher*). Building upon this research, we
see that HHNL provides numerous examples of what I have called be3 or the "equative copula"
in BL (Alim 2001b, 2004a). Some examples of this construction (Noun Phrase *be* Noun Phrase)
follow:

> "I be the truth."—Philadelphia's Beanie Sigel
> "Dr. Dre be the name."—Compton's Dr. Dre
> "This beat be the beat for the street."—New York's Busta Rhymes
> "Brooklyn be the place where I served them thangs."—New York's Jay-Z
> "I be that insane nigga from the psycho ward."—Staten Island's Method Man

These are but a few of countless examples in the corpus of Hip Hop lyrics, but this equative copula construction can also be found in everyday conversation, as in these examples:

"We be them Bay boys." (Bay Area's Mac Mall in a conversation with James G. Spady)
"It [marijuana] be that good stuff." (Caller on the local Bay Area radio station)
"You know we be some baaad brothas." (Philadelphia speaker in conversation)

It is possible that speakers of BL have begun using this form only recently, and that it represents a recent change in the system. Alternatively, the form may always have been present in the language but escaped the notice of investigators. Certainly it is present in the writings of Black Arts Movement poets of the 1960s and 1970s, most notably in Sonia Sanchez's *We Be Word Sorcerers*. We also find the form being cited in one linguistic study of Black street speech ("They be the real troublemakers"; "Leo be the one to tell it like it is") (Baugh 1983). It is possible that members of the HHN, with their extraordinary linguistic consciousness and their emphasis on stretching the limits of language, have made this form much more acceptable by using it frequently.

The HHN's linguistic consciousness refers to HHNL speakers' conscious use of language to construct identity. Addressing the divergence of BL from "standard English," Baugh and Smitherman (in press: 20) write:

Graffiti writers of Hip Hop Culture were probably the coiners of the term "phat" (meaning excellent, great, superb) ... although "phat" is spelled in obvious contrast to "fat," the former confirms that those who use it know that "ph" is pronounced like "f." In other words, those who first wrote "phat" diverged from standard English as a direct result of their awareness of standard English: the divergence was not by chance linguistic error. There is no singular explanation to account for linguistic divergence, but Hip Hop Culture suggests that matters of personal identity play a significant role.

This conscious linguistic behavior deals with matters of spelling and phonemic awareness. (See Morgan 2001 and Olivo 2001 on "spelling ideology.") One case—one of the more controversial uses of language in Hip Hop culture—is the term "nigga." The HHN realized that this word had various positive in-group meanings and pejorative out-group meanings, and thus felt the need to reflect the culturally specific meanings with a new spelling ("nigger" becomes "nigga"). A "nigga" is your main man, or one of your close companions, your homie. Recently the term has been generalized to refer to any male (one may even hear something like, "No, I was talkin about Johnny, you know, the white nigga with the hair") though it usually refers to a Black male. And even more recently, one might hear the term being used by females of all ethnicities in the San Francisco Bay Area to refer to each other in much the same way that males do, as this example from a conversational exchange between White and Black female teenagers shows:

Black female: Call me, nigga!
White female: Yeah, nigga, you know wassup. I'ma call you.

Tupac Shakur, showing Hip Hop's affinity for acronyms, transformed the racial slur into the ultimate positive ideal for young Black males—Never Ignorant Getting Goals Accomplished.

As with the highlighting of regional vocabulary, HHNL speakers intentionally highlight regional differences in pronunciation by processes such as vowel lengthening and syllabic stress (Morgan 2001). When Bay Area Rappers JT the Bigga Figga and Mac Mall announced the resurgence of the Bay Area to the national Hip Hop scene with "Game Recognize Game" (1993), they did so using a distinctive feature of Bay Area pronunciation. The Bay Area anthem's chorus repeated this line three times: "Game recognize game in the Bay, man (mane)." "Man" was pronounced "mane" to accentuate this Bay Area pronunciation feature. Also, as fellow Bay Area Rapper B-Legit rhymes about slang, he does so using the same feature to stress his Bay Area linguistic origins: "You can tell from my slang I'm from the Bay, mane" (2000).

When Nelly and the St. Lunatics "busted" onto the Hip Hop scene, they were among the first Rappers to represent St. Louis, Missouri on a national scale. Language was an essential part of establishing their identity in the fiercely competitive world of Hip Hop Culture. For example, in a single by the St. Lunatics featuring Nelly they emphasize every word that rhymes with "urrrr" to highlight a well-known (and sometimes stigmatized) aspect of southern/midwest pronunciation (here → *hurrrr*, care → *currrr*, there → *thurrrr*, air → *urrrr*, and so on). By intentionally highlighting linguistic features associated with their city (and other southern cities), they established their tenacity through language, as if to say, "We have arrived." Since then, many other rappers, even some not from that region, have played and experimented with this phonological aspect of BL.

Nelly and the St. Lunatics are conscious not only of their pronunciation, but also of their syntax. On his platinum single "Country Grammar" (2000), Nelly proclaims, "My gramma bees Ebonics." Clearly, HHNL speakers vary their grammar consciously. An analysis of copula variation in the speech and the lyrics of Hip Hop artists concluded that higher levels of copula absence in the artists' lyrics represented the construction of a street-conscious identity—where the speaker makes a linguistic-cultural connection to the streets, the locus of the Hip Hop world. John Rickford has suggested (in a conference comment made in 2001) that the use of creole syntactic and phonological features by many rappers supports the ability of HHNL speakers to manipulate their grammar consciously (see Eve's reported use of Creole in Spady *et al.* 1999 and Lil Kim's 2005 street anthem, "Lighters Up"). Like San Quinn (see opening quotation in this section) HHNL speakers elect dialects to demonstrate their high degree of linguistic consciousness and in order to construct a street-conscious identity.

Hip Hop Cultural Modes of Discourse and Discursive Practices

Keyes (1984: 145) applied Smitherman's (1977) Black modes of discourse to HHNL. Working in Hip Hop's gestation period, she wrote that "Smitherman schematized four broad categories of black discourse: narrative sequencing, call-response, signification/dozens, and tonal semantics. All of these categories are strategically used in rap music." We know that rappin in and of itself is not entirely new—rather, it is the most modern/postmodern instantiation of the linguistic-cultural practices of Africans in America. Rappers are, after all, "postmodern African griots" (a class of musicians-entertainers who preserved African history through oral narratives) (Smitherman 1997). This section will demonstrate how the strategic use of the Black modes of discourse is manifested in HHNL and how the new ways in which these modes are practiced generate correspondingly new modes of discourse. This section is based on various forms of HHNL data–rap lyrics, Hip Hop performances, and Hip Hop conversational discourse.

Call and Response

Here is perhaps the most lucid definition of call and response:

> As a communicative strategy this call and response is the manifestation of the cultural dynamic which finds audience and listener or leader and background to be a unified whole. Shot through with action and interaction, Black communicative performance is concentric in quality—the "audience" becoming both observers and participants in the speech event. As Black American culture stresses commonality and group experientiality, the audience's

linguistic and paralinguistic responses are necessary to co-sign the power of the speaker's rap or call.

(Daniel and Smitherman 1976, cited in Spady 2000a: 59)

The quintessential example of the HHN's use of call and response grows out of funk performances and is still heard at nearly every Hip Hop performance today: "[Rapper] Say 'Hoooo!' [Audience] 'Hooooooooo!' [Rapper] Say 'Ho! Ho!' [Audience] 'Ho! Ho!' [Rapper] Somebody screeeaaaaammm! [Audience] 'AAHHHHHHHHHHHHHHHH!!!'" Anyone who has ever attended a Hip Hop performance can bear witness to this foundational call and response mechanism.

A description of a Hip Hop performance by Philadelphia's Roots paints a picture of a scene where lead MC Black Thought senses that there is a communicative schism developing between him and his Swiss audience (Jackson *et al.* 2001: 25). The rapper says, "Hold it, hold it, hold it!" and stops the music abruptly. What follows is "impromptu instruction" in the call and response mode of Black discourse:

> Y'all can't get the second part no matter what the fuck I say, right ... I wonder if it's what I'm saying ... A-yo! We gonna try this shit one more time because I like this part of the show.

Providing more explicit instruction, Thought slows it down a bit:

> Aight, Aight this is how I'm gonna break it down. I'm gonna be like "ahh," then everybody gonna be like "ahhh." Then—I don't know what I'm gonna say second but y'all gotta listen close cause then y'all gotta repeat that shit—that's the fun of the game!

Thought is not only providing instruction but he is also administering a challenge to his European audience: either *git sicwiddit* [get sick with it] *or git hitwiddit* [get hit with it]! (in this context meaning, "Become active participants in this activity or get caught off guard looking culturally ignorant!").

Call and response mechanisms are so pervasive in HHNL that talented MC's (Rappers, Masters of Ceremonies) have taken this mode to new heights. Mos Def describes one of the elements that made Slick Rick a legendary rapper:

> Slick Rick is one of the greatest MC's ever born because he has so many different facilities that he would use. Style. Vocal texture. The way he would even record. Like, he was doing call and response with himself! He would leave four bars open, and then do another character, you understand what I'm saying?

(Alim 2000, unpublished interview)

The individualized uses of call and response in the Hip Hop cultural mode of discourse deserve more attention. Also, as is evident from Mos Def's comments, HHNL speakers can be cognizant of the fact that they are operating within and expanding upon the Black American Oral Tradition. The linguistic and communicative consciousness of the HHN also needs further exploration.

Multilayered Totalizing Expression

Beyond the explicit instruction, one can witness the multilayered nature of the call and response mode at Hip Hop performances where both performer and audience are fully conversant with Hip Hop cultural modes of discourse. At the first Spitkicker Tour (2000) in San Francisco's

Maritime Hall, I observed this multilayered, multitextual mode. Here's an excerpt from my fieldnotes:

> Maaan, all performers are on stage at once—[DJ] Hi-Tek, Talib [Kweli], Common, Biz [Markie], De La [Soul], Pharoahe [Monch]—and they just kickin it in a fun-loving communal-type Hip Hop atmosphere! Common and Biz are exchanging lines from his classic hit ... The DJ from De La starts cuttin up the music and before you know it, Common is center stage freestylin. The DJ switches the pace of the music, forcing Common to switch up the pace of his freestyle [improvisational rap], and the crowd's lovin it! "Oooooooohhhhh!" ... Hi-Tek and Maseo are circling each other on stage giving a series of hi-fives timed to the beat, smilin and laughin all along, as the crowd laughs on with them. Common, seizing the energy of the moment, says, "This is Hip Hop music, y'all!" Then he shouts, "It ain't nuthin like Hip Hop music!" and holds the microphone out to the crowd. "It ain't nuthin like Hip Hop music!" they roar back, and the hall is transformed into a old school house party frenzy ... Gotta love this Hip Hop music.

What is striking about this description is that there are multiple levels of call and multiple levels of response, occurring simultaneously and synergistically, to create something even beyond "total expression" (Brathwaite 1984: 18). This is a *multilayered totalizing expression* that completes the cipher (the process of constantly making things whole). We witness a call and response on the oral/aural, physical (body), and spiritual/metaphysical level. My final note ("Gotta love this Hip Hop music") captures a moment of realization that meaning resides in what I've just witnessed—in the creation of a continuum beyond audience and performer. We hear varied calls made by the DJ and responded to by a freestylin MC; by the two MC's exchanging lines and by their impromptu leading of the audience in celebration of Hip Hop; by the physical reaction of performers to each other and the audience (who were also slappin hands with the performers); and by the spirited and spiritual response created during the climax of the performance. Like Common say, "Find heaven in this music and God/ Find heaven in this music and God/ Find heaven in this music and God" (cited in Jackson *et al.* 2001).

Signifyin and Bustin (Bussin)

Scholars have studied signification or signifyin—or, in more contemporary, semantically similar Black terms, *bustin, crackin,* and *dissin* (Abrahams 1964; Kochman 1969; Mitchell-Kernan 1971; 1972; Smitherman 1973, 1977). Signifyin has been described as a means to encode messages or meanings in natural conversations, usually involving an element of indirection (Mitchell-Kernan 1972). Ironically noting the difficulty in pinpointing a dictionary definition for the speech act, Rickford and Rickford (2000: 82) cite Mitchell-Kernan's (1972: 82) attempt:

> The black concept of *signifying* incorporates essentially a folk notion that dictionary entries for words are not always sufficient for interpreting meanings or messages, or that meaning goes beyond such interpretations. Complimentary remarks may be delivered in a left-handed fashion. A particular utterance may be an insult in one context and not in another. What pretends to be informative may intend to be persuasive. Superficially, self-abasing remarks are frequently self-praise.

In Scarface's comments and Tha Pharcyde dialogue given earlier, we see evidence of this folk notion that "standard" dictionaries are insufficient to interpret Black language and life. But looking more closely at Tha Pharcyde dialogue, we witness an extremely sly (skillful and indirect) signification in Hip Hop conversational discourse. In the dialogue, Booty Brown is advocating the Black folk notion described by Mitchell-Kernan earlier. He implies that his partner is glorifying a Eurocentric meaning-making system over a meaning-making system that is African-derived. This does not become clear until Brown chooses his examples—carefully and cleverly. "Just like they use any other word as a slang, *my brotha!*" He emphasizes the "slang phrase" *my brotha*, as it is usually used as a sign of cultural unity and familial bond between Black American males (females will use *my sista* in a similar way).

Then he proceeds to ask the direct question, "Whose definition are you glorifying?" which is, in fact, a statement. Finally, as if to *really* lay it on thick (add insult to injury), he chooses to use the word "Black" to show that *Webster's Dictionary* is inadequate. The heat is diffused when "P" says, "I'm sayin, I'm sayin, that's what I'M sayin!" and they—and others around them—break into laughter. This dialogue is an example of how language is used to remind, scold, shame, or otherwise bring the other into a commonly shared ethic through signification.

We see an example of signifyin in Rapper Bushwick Bill's (of Houston's Geto Boys) description of the ever-changing, fluid, and flexible nature of "street slang" and the dangers of not "keepin your ear to the street" (being aware of what's happening around you at all times). In this case, Bushwick is referring to the rapidly evolving street terminology for law enforcement officials. He takes us deep into the locus of Hip Hop linguistic-cultural activity:

> You lose flavor. You lose the slang. You lose the basic everyday kickin it, you know, knowing what's going on at all times, you know what I'm saying? Knowing the new names for "5-0s". They ain't even 5-0s no more. They call them "po-pos". That means everything changes. And they call them "one-time", you know what I'm saying? But you got to be in there to know that the police might know these words already. So they got to change up their dialect so that way it sounds like Pig Latin to the police.
>
> (Spady *et al.* 1999: 308)

Bushwick's comment refers us directly to tenet 10 above. He is describing the changing nature of the various terms for "police" in the streets—from "5-0s" to "po-pos" to "one-time." At one time, bloods referred to the "one-time" as "black and whites" (Folb 1980), while currently Young Jeezy refers to federal agents as "dem alphabet boys" (referencing the various acronyms of these agencies, such as the FBI, CIA, DEA, ATF, etc.). As I write this, brothas up in Harlem and Washington Heights got a new name for the po-po—squalie. Juelz Santana, operating like a street journalist, captures the multiple uses of the term, including its use as a general lookout call that's shouted when them cops is comin—squal-ayyyyyyyyyy! As New York-based Hip Hop historian Meghelli (personal communication 2005) notes, it is the sociopolitical context of many depressed and oppressed Black neighborhoods that necessitates these speedy lexical transformations.

Even though the police are not present in the dialogue above, Bushwick signifies on them with a clever one-liner that *also* serves to buttress his point. After runnin down all of the various terms (which have gone out of style as quickly as the police have comprehended them), he concludes, "So they got to change up their dialect so that way it sounds like Pig Latin to the police." "Pig Latin" is chosen here, rather than Greek, Chinese, Swahili, or other unfamiliar languages, to echo the fact that at one time police officers were called "pigs." Bushwick is not only signifyin on the police, but he is also demonstrating yet another term for police that has gone out of fashion! In addition, he is referencing an old form of Afroamericanized Pig Latin that employs innuendo, wordplay, letter and syllabic shifting, rhyming, and coded language designed to communicate with those in the know.

Like call and response, signifyin is ubiquitous in Hip Hop lyrics. In an example of male–female urban verbal play, in "Minute Man" (2001) with Missy Elliott and Ludacris, Jay-Z signifies on female R&B group Destiny's Child. Some insider knowledge is required to fully understand this speech act. Earlier that year, Destiny's Child had released "Independent Women," in which they asked a series of questions of men who dogged ("treated poorly") females. For example, they introduced each question with the word "Question" and then proceeded, "How you like them diamonds that I bought?" (to demonstrate to such men that they had their own income). Being that one of Jay-Z's many personas is the "playa-pimp"-type (one who uses women for sex and money), he rhymes to the listeners (including Destiny's Child): "I'm not tryin to give you love and affection/ I'm tryin to give you 60 seconds of affection/ I'm tryin to give you cash, fare and directions/ Get your independent-ass outta here, Question!" The signification doesn't become clear until the last line, or really, the last word, when Jay-Z borrows the word "Question" from their song (saying it in such a way as to completely match their prosody, rhythm, and tone). The only thing left to do is say, "Oooohhhhhh!"

We also witnessed signification in the call and response section of the Black Thought performance described above. As Jackson *et al.* (2001) note, Thought appears to be signifyin on the audience by highlighting their lack of familiarity with Black cultural modes of discourse: "I wonder if it's what I'm saying ... A-yo!" The Roots have been known to signify on audiences that are not as culturally responsive as they would like them to be. During a recent concert at Stanford University, they stopped the music and began singing theme songs from 1980s television shows like "Diff'rent Strokes" and "Facts of Life," snapping their fingers and singing in a corny (not cool) way. The largely White, middle-class audience of college students sang along and snapped their fingers—apparently oblivious to the insult. After the show, the band's drummer and official spokesman, Ahmir, said: "Like if the crowd ain't responding, we've done shows where we've stopped the show, turned the equipment around, and played for the wall, you know" (Alim 1999). In this sense, the Roots remove any hint of indirection and blatantly *bust on* the unresponsive audience. The examples above make clear that HHNL speakers readily incorporate *signifyin* and *bustin* into their repertoire. Whether Hip Hop heads are performing, writing rhymes, or just "conversatin," these strategies are skillfully employed.

Tonal Semantics and Poetics

Black American tonal semantics can be thought of as the creative force that drives Hip Hop lyrics. As such, I've added the category *poetics* to the discussion. Smitherman (1977: 134) describes tonal semantics as the "use of voice rhythm and vocal inflection to convey meaning in black communication," and depicts the voice as instrument. Black American tonal semantics consists of talk-singing, repetition and alliterative word play, intonational contouring and rhyme. In their lyrical production, Hip Hop artists have capitalized on all of these categories and have taken them to "da next level" ("to a higher level of creativity").

Like the preachers in Smitherman (1977), rappers also believe that word-sound (which places emphasis on *how* words are said, in addition to *what* words are said) can move people. Rappers call upon the use of repetition at will and use it to perform a variety of functions, such as: to tell cautionary tales, to drive important points/themes home, to elicit laughter, and to display their lyrical skillz. Several examples of repetition in Hip Hop lyrics demonstrate the effective use of this semantic category (see Table 4.1).

Alliterative wordplay also appears in various forms. For instance, Pharoahe Monch uses alliteration in this verse to flex his phat phonetic skillz ("impressive phonetic skills"):

F-f-f-f-f-f-f-f-f-follow me for now/ for no formidable fights I've been formed to forget/ For **Ph**aroahe fucks familiar foes first/ Befo fondling female MC's fiercely/ Focus on the fact that facts can be fabricated to form lies/ My **ph**onetics alone forces feeble MC's into defense on the fly/ Feel me, forreal-a

Table 4.1 Effective use of repetition

(A)

Never take a man's life cuz you hate yours
Never become so involved with something that it blinds you
Never forget where you from someone will remind you
Never take for granted what's been given as a gift
And **never** sleep on a nigga, less that nigga stiff . . .
Never say **never**, cuz I **never** thought this *clever* thought **never**

In "It's On," DMX begins 15 lines in this verse (most aren't shown) with the word "never." In the last line, he uses the word four times while interspersing clever rhymes like "never thought" and "clever thought" and punctuating the verse with a period in the form of "never." DMX is offering a tale of caution to young bloods in the streets. His repetition of the word "never" captivates his listener, making sure that his fans do not miss his point. He also makes sure to let them know that his repetition is "clever."

(B)

Nigga the **truth**, every time I step in the booth/ I speak the **truth**, y'all know what I'm bringin to you/ I bring the **truth**, muthafuckas know who I be/ I be the **truth**, what I speak *shall set you free*/ Nigga the **truth**!

In "The Truth," Beanie Sigel wants to be sure he is well understood. In an effort to convince others of his street credibility (authenticity) he wants to make sure listeners know that he speaks the truth, brings the truth and bees the truth! He also capitalizes on an oft-repeated Biblical phrase in the Black community, "The truth shall set you free."

(C)

I been around this block, **too** many times
Rocked, **too** many rhymes, clocked, **too** many nines, **too**
To all my brothas, it ain't **too** late **to** come **together**
Cause **too** much black and **too** much love equal forever
I don't follow any guidelines cause **too** many niggaz ride mines
So I change styles every **two** rhymes . . .

In "22 Two's," Jay-Z exploits the homonymy of "to/too/two" and also the letters "to" (together) to place "22 Two's" in a sequence. Jigga's main mission is to demonstrate that he's one of the most gifted rhymers in the game. In his undeterred confidence, he adds, "That's 22 two's for y'all muthafuckas out there, ya nahmean? Shall I continue?" Jigga is also driving the point home that he's learned lessons from the streets and "it ain't too late for brothas to come together."

(D)

That's what I ain't gon do
See the 5-0 and swing a tight donut
Uh-uh, **that's what I ain't gon do**
Be the nigga at the bar talkin shit but outside throwin up
Uh-uh, **that's what I ain't gon do**
Let baby tell me what I'm doin with my weekly check
Uh-uh, **that's what I ain't gon do**
Try hard to be the man and hit the club with a fake Rolex

In "Ain't Gon Do," Richie Rich is clearly using repetition for the purpose of humor. He is able to punctuate the listeners' laughter each time, lettin them know that's what he "ain't gon do."

As a street linguist, Pharoahe knows that his phonetics alone will "force feeble MC's into defense on the fly." His linguistic sophistication ("skillz" in HHNL) is evident in this verse.

The effective use of repetition and alliteration are often found in combination with complex rhymes. Rhyme is such an essential aspect of HHNL that one almost need not mention it, but we need a deeper exploration of Hip Hop poetics. Hip Hop Heads ("aficionados") are constantly evaluating rhymes, and what makes a perfect rhyme. Rapper Kurupt describes what makes a *dope* ("excellent") rhyme:

Perfection of the rhymes. Like Perfection. Selection, interjection. Election. Dedication. Creation. Domination. Devastation. World domination. Totally, with no Hesitation, you know what I mean? These are perfect rhymes ... Really. Silly. Philly, you know. These are perfected rhymes. Where you could take a word like *we will* and you connect that with a full word like *rebuild*, you know what I mean? You got two words in *we will*. One word in *rebuild*. But perfect rhyme connection is the key to writing when you write your rhyme. And meaning too. When you're saying something that makes sense. Them are the keys to writing a rhyme. Perfect rhyme connection. And *style*.

(Spady *et al.* 1999: 550)

A close examination of one verse from Talib Kweli on "The Truth" (1999) reveals multiple layers of complexity and creativity:

1. Check it, on my neck I still got marks from **the nooses**
2. The truth it **produces** fear that got niggaz on the run like Ca-**arl Lewis.**
3. **The truth is my crew is the smoothest** spittas of saliva **juices** like **the roots is**
4. More organic than **acoustics**
5. Heavenly ... set you free and kill you in the same breath
6. That shit you gotta get off your chest before your death and rest
7. The way you speak is lighter than a pamphlet
8. Cuz the truth give the words the weight of a planet goddammit
9. I ran wit what God planted in my heart and I understand it
10. To be to ***bring the light to the dark, breathe some life in this art***
11. This must be the truth ("why?") cuz we keep marchin on ("true")
12. The truth lay the foundation of what we rockin on ("true")
13. You can't see it if you blind but we will always prevail ("true")
14. Life is like the open sea, the truth is the wind in our sail
15. *And in the end,* our names is on the lips of *dying men*
16. If ever crushed in the earth, we always *rise again*
17. When the words of *lying men* sound lush like the sound of a *violin*
18. The truth is there, it's just the heart you gotta *find it in*

In examining Talib's *multirhyming* skillz (the ability to produce multilayered rhymes by employing multiple rhyme techniques synergistically), we'll begin with Line 1 where we see the beginning of a recurring assonance with the short /e/ vowel. This short /e/ is repeated several times in Lines 1, 5, and 6. Line 1 is also the starting point for a series of triple rhymes that follow the pattern: /a–oo–is/. In Line 3, we have a series of five triple rhymes, three of which are *back-to-back chain rhymes* (see Alim 2003). **Tha truth is** rhymes with **ma crew is, tha smoothest,** and **tha roots is.** These rhymes also match perfectly with two unexpected rhyme matches: (1) the last syllable in "saliva" and the word "juices,"–**a juices**, and (2) Talib splits the name "Carl" into two syllables, "Ca-arl" and uses the last syllable to continue the triple rhyme pattern with Ca-**arl Lewis.**

Talib continues with a series of feminine rhymes pairing up some unlikely suspects with: planet, goddammit, ran wit, planted, understand it. If you notice, all of these rhymes follow the pattern: a–nasal (either n or m)–it. In Line 10, Talib blesses us with a rare sextuple rhyme as he describes his Hip Hop mission to be to: "bring the light to the dark, breathe some life in this art." This sextuple rhyme is accomplished by the use of parallel phrasing in which the poet matches up like categories across the parts of speech. For instance, the parts of speech in this rhyme flow like this: verb–modifier–noun–prep–modifier–noun. The sound pattern of the rhyme is near perfect: /br–reduced vowel–long-i–reduced vowel–th–ar/.

Lines 15 through 18 contain another set of triple rhymes that follow the pattern of: /long i–reduced vowel-in/. What makes this verse even more complex, as far as tonal semantics are concerned, is that Talib begins Line 15 with "And in the end," which serves multiple functions. Not only does this phrase refer to a final moment in history, "the end," but it is also cleverly signifies the beginning of the end of the verse. In addition to this, Talib says "in the end" in such a way as to almost prepare us for the triple rhymes that are to follow. The intonation is what glues this phrase to the triple rhyme series.

Talib also exhibits wordplay in Lines 4 and 5. "The truth is my crew is the smoothest spittas of saliva juices like the roots is more organic than acoustics." The Roots is a Hip Hop group from Philly who released an independent LP entitled *Organix* (1993). So, not only are roots considered organic in the dictionary definition of the word, but the phrase here is complimenting The Roots for their strong musical production. The word "organic" is also used here in a play on "organ" and "acoustics."

In Line 16, Talib references a famous line from *Battlefield*, a poem by William Cullen Bryant (1794–1878), which reads: "Truth crushed to earth shall rise again/ The eternal years of God are hers/ But Error, wounded, writhes with pain, And dies among his worshippers." The first line of this stanza has been utilized by many Black American religious leaders, including Minister Louis Farrakhan and Reverend Jesse Jackson, although the phrase is most associated with Rev. Dr. Martin Luther King. Talib has taken this line, and through semantic extension, refers to him and his crew (and by extension, his people). "If ever crushed in the earth, *we always rise again.*" The collusion of "truth" with "we" brings the truth that much closer to heart.

Given all of this intricacy and poetic complexity, it is remarkable that the meaning of the verse is retained. Talib is giving us his understanding of "the truth," which, of course, means different things to different people. "The truth" to Talib is the pure unbridled power of Hip Hop. The beats, the rhymes, the content, the vibe. "The truth lay the foundation of what we rockin on." The truth will always remind one of one's own history (in this case, the days when Black Americans were lynched for the enjoyment of Whites—see *100 Years of Lynching* by Ralph Ginzburg, 1962), as well as protect one's own history (truth must be protected from the "words of lying men"). Talib uses the phrase "the truth" several times, invoking new meanings each time. And in classic Hip Hop call and response fashion, we see that the theme of "the truth" is reaffirmed by the clever and also classically Hip Hop affirmation—"True" (as sung by Talib's crew in Lines 11, 12, and 13).

Talib, by exploiting the use of tonal semantics and poetics, demonstrates the multilayered and multitextual complexity of HHNL. By employing talk-singing, repetition and alliterative wordplay, intonational contouring and extremely complex multirhyming, HHNL users have truly taken this Language Thang to newer heights and deeper depths of discursive activity.

While scholars usually turn to Rap lyrics, or perhaps music videos, to analyze the discourse of the Hip Hop community, few have turned to the Hip Hop conversational discourse of the very agents who create and recreate Hip Hop Culture—particularly those who display superior skill and staying power in a record industry that has always been *shady* ("ruthless and not trustworthy"). Spady (2001), writing on the link between Black American expressive culture and the dynamics of HHNL, provides an excellent analysis and theoretical frame for us to begin closely examining Hip Hop conversational discourse:

> A close examination of Kurupt's lyrical and musical *ouevre*, as well as his conversational narratives and overall communication practices reveal a highly sophisticated playa in the Hip Hop Nation Speech community. Kurupt's speech acts, witty, sardonic and satirical verbal exchanges, wordplay and play on words, ritualized speech and an assortment of distinct African American discourse markers single him out as a skilled member of this speech community. Contrary to the popular myth perpetrated and perpetuated by critics of mass

based black core culture, the Hip Hop Nation is not outside of the Black tradition. Kurupt and his confreres both maintain and expand that tradition in meaningful ways.

(Spady 2001: 18)

Contrary to the belief that Hip Hop artists lack the awareness and knowledge of the art form's cultural and linguistic foundations, Kurupt demonstrates his cognizance of Hip Hop's historical background in a memorable remark:

I think Black Language is an essential part of Hip Hop—period. Hip Hop is a Black culture influenced art form of music . . . "EEEEEEEEEEE Tidleee Wop/ This is the Jock and I'm back on the scene/ With the record machine/ Sayin Ooh Bop Da Boo/ How do you do?" That's rap. Ahhh, man! My stepfather been hit me upside my head, "Boyyy, rap ain't new. People *been* rappin, *years ago*, son. Years ago!!! Jocko, he's one of the first rappers, son."

(Kurupt in Spady 2001: 18)

An extraordinary repertoire of speech devices and constructions (both verbal and nonverbal) is found in Kurupt's extensive conversational narrative in *Street Conscious Rap* (Spady *et al.* 1999). In our analysis of Kurupt's Hip Hop conversational discourse, we offer an evidential treatment of Spady's comments just quoted. His use of hyperbole, metaphor and simile, narrative style, and dialoguing others (doublevoicing or inserting other voices into the dialogue), the many features of tonal semantics and poetics—talk-singing, repetition, wordplay, freestylin (free rhyming), word creations, and word pictures—offer us deep insight into the complexity of Hip Hop conversational discourse. Kurupt's narratives also serve as metacommentary on several relatively unexplored Hip Hop discursive practices, such as *battlin* and *entering the cipher* (to be discussed later).

Kurupt masterfully uses metaphor, simile, and hyperbolic language to paint word pictures and animated verbal images that allow us to visualize what is being said. The more outrageous the description, the clearer the image. Kurupt's narrative strategies—dialoguing other voices, imitating referential voices, talk-singing, word explosions, kinesics, and strategic use of key summarizing statements that highlight main points—can be seen in this discursive passage. The passage (annotated for this discussion) begins with Kurupt responding to a question about whether he ever asked Tupac for advice on writing lyrics:

I wasn't askin anything. I just sat around him, you know. Game [metaphor for knowledge of the music industry; also used for knowledge of other things such as women, business, sports, etc.] is learned from viewing rather than questioning. Questioning, you take the person off their focus, meaning they don't go naturally, because they go and try to show something and that's not natural. But when you just let them go natural and you peep [observe], and you got to just *learn*. It's certain things to look at, man. You can tell when you see it. He's in there. He writes a song. He gets behind the booth. His energy splits the room in half! [metaphoric word picture; hyperbole] You feel like jumpin off the top of the roof [hyperbole] . . . You ain't feel it?! You know, when he's speakin, I mean, just, "RAAAH!" [word explosion] . . . You could have the greatest words in the world, but you must have the emotion and feeling that people can just walk down the street and feel that sound wave [motioning with his hands as if to make a tidal wave]. They're walkin and just—booosh! [word explosion; kinesics—tossing his body to the side, signaling the impact of the wave word explosion]. You're like, "What's that?" [dialoguing other voices] Next thing you know, you hear the song as they rollin by, "AAAH-AH-AAAH!" [word explosion] It's that energy—bam! [kinesics—slapping his hands together; word explosion] You're like, "Yo! What's goin on?!" [dialoguing other voices] "I'm gonna run it down/ Runnin clown!" [imitating referential voices–any member of the HHNSC would recognize DMX's lines by the vocal texture and timing Kurupt employs] The feeling strikes you and at that second is when you decide on whether it's a good song to you or whether it's not. [key summarizing statement] ... But just like Master P, P is not the most poetical, the most lyrical, but he has *feeling* with music that smashes the board [hyperbole]. And so when the music is kickin–bam! [word explosion] "Oh, my goodness!" [dialoguing other voices] "I'm a No Limit Soldier/ That's what I told ya!" [imitating referential voices—using Master P's characteristic vowel lengthening and New Orleans phonology; kinesics—waving hands up and down]–boom, boom, boom, pshhh! [word explosions as referents to musical sounds in Master P's song]. Then you like, "Wow!" Then you hear his lyrics and it's, "Aww, he's alright." [dialoguing other voices] But then the delivery pulls you back in. You be like, "Woah! Okay!" Because you're startin to listen to things that he's sayin. Music is the first thing they catch. Then it is lyrics and delivery and the emotion for the situation. Then there's subject matter. Musical keys of making a hit: the music, the delivery and the lyrics that you spittin, and what you're talkin about, the subject matter. [key summarizing statement]

(Spady *et al.* 1999: 542–543)

Kurupt's use of metaphor and hyperbolic language in this passage is representative of the vast body of his Hip Hop conversational discourse. He does not merely describe Tupac as being energetic—rather, "his energy splits the room in half!" and makes one "feel like jumping off the top of the roof." In responding to a question about the changing demands made of him as an artist, he responds with a unique, witty series of metaphors and similes rooted in the oral tradition of Black American folklore:

You got to be hungry [eager, ambitious]. It's like seventy thousand other people, man, that's hungry as fifty five slaves with no food for seven years! [simile, hyperbole] ... So, while you lolly-gaggin. See a penny, pick it up, "I don't need a penny." He'll sneak up right behind you, pickin up all the pennies, "I'll take it." Hungry! [word explosion]. And then come the next thing you know, he just zippin right by you! You're like the tortoise, "Do-dum-do-do." And this boy is like the hare, "Trrrrrrrrrrrrrr!" Gone! [word explosions; similes; word pictures] You know, you can't lapse. You have to treat everyday like it's the first day. [key summarizing statement]

(Spady *et al.* 1999: 543)

He continues to describe the industry as a "race" where one has to "*stay* hungry, *stay* wantin to smash the game" (aspectual *stay* in BL is an emphatic habitual that expresses the frequency or intensity of events and states, see Spears 2000), because if you don't, "it's seventy thousand people right behind you, man, that's on they way!" (Spady *et al.* 1999: 543).

Besides key summarizing statements, Kurupt, much like Black religious leaders, also uses repetition of key words to drive important points home. These next two passages are illustrative:

I have kids. I have things I have to take care of, *man*. That's what I'm talking about, about "out here" [California], teaching you how to be a **man**. To let you know that you're a **man** before anything, *man*. A **man**! A hardworking **man**, before anything. You see what I'm saying? And you can't do it sittin around, *man*." [notice the strategic and oft-repeated use of both **man** as a noun, and **man** as a discourse marker]

(Spady *et al.* 1999: 539)

We're all under the same situation that we been under from day one, even though it looked like we was havin a ball. **Pressure** comes in all forms. **Pressure.** Huge forms of **pressure**, small forms of **pressure**, you know. But it's all **pressure**, you know. Basically, **pressure** can push you to do things you don't want to do, say things you don't mean to say. **Pressure** can make you act out of character. **Pressure** can make you crumble, you know what I mean?

(Spady *et al.* 1999: 545)

As in the previous discussion of the use of repetition in Hip Hop lyrics, Kurupt often combines repetition with other forms of figurative language. In the conversation, he describes himself using metaphor: "I'm a arsonist on the mic. I make it burn!" In this next passage, Kurupt narrates how he connected with other rappers (Ras Kass, Canibus, and Killah Priest) to form a group called the Four Horsemen. Notice his use of figurative language as he depicts each member of the crew:

Well, me and Canibus and Ras, we've always been folks. And I told them, man, we're gonna make a group called the Four Horsemen. The Horsemen was one of the most dangerous, deadliest, out of the wrestling people. They didn't play no games. The Four Horsemen wreak havoc, you understand what I'm saying? So, that was a great thing to label ourselves after. We're the Horsemen in this Rap game. We're here to chop everybody heads off! You don't have no groups that's strictly for choppin heads off. Me and Canibus, we're strictly MC's that love to battle. We love to rhyme. Ras Kass is our connection with the West. That's my boy and Canibus' boy. And he's the assassin with the mic when it comes to the pen. We look at it like when a person want to freestyle, we got me. And I'm choppin every last one of their heads. Everyone! When it comes to the written, we got Canibus and we got Ras. They're written experts. And Killah Priest plays no games when it comes to assassinations on the mic. And he has a camp of assassins behind him and that's Killah Priest's situation in there. And that's Canibus' main nigga, you feel me? And Ras and Canny is my main niggas. So, Canibus felt like we need to bring Killah Priest into this to detonate all the rest of the fools, you know what I mean? Canibus and Ras and Killah Priest will decide which one of them is gon chop they heads off. Anybody freestyling, that's when I come into the picture. I'm the Headless Horseman, you know. We all got aliases.

(Spady *et al.* 1999: 551)

In this passage, Kurupt turns to his *freestylin* abilities. His explanation of a perfect rhyme (earlier in this section) demonstrated *freestylin* ("improvisational rhyming") or what Henderson (1973) called *virtuoso free-rhyming*. Henderson identifies several features found in Black Arts Movement poetry of the 1960s and 1970s that have correspondences in Rap lyrics. What Henderson described as *virtuoso free-rhyming* was usually in the context of a rhyme couplet, or where a rhyme served as a witty punch line. In HHNL, this witty free rhyming is expanded and exploited to create a new form called *freestylin*. In *freestylin*, one is expected to *sustain* witty and clever improvisational rhymes for extended periods of time (skilled freestylers can rhyme until they literally run out of breath). Kurupt, in describing his lyrical writing process, explains:

I think in freestyle, I'll kick a rhyme right now, you see what I'm saying? That's like my whole thing. That's where I get my rhymes from. I might freestyle and say something that I just think is so catty [cool]. So, then I just sit down and write the freestyle rhyme I said, but then I calculate it more, you see what I'm saying? I put more brain power to it when I just sit and write it because I can think more about how I can word it, you see what I'm saying?

(Spady *et al.* 1999: 538)

Kurupt claims that he not only freestyles, but he *thinks* in freestyle (Jay-Z and other Rappers claim to have never written a rhyme on paper in their lives). Adding support to his claim to a freestyle mode of thinking, he *busts* ("Raps") a spontaneous freestyle in the middle of conversation. The passage begins with him speaking: "That's where Philly and Darby Township kick in, you know. Rhyming against others and outlasting, and lasting through the wars, you know. That's the key to building up that confidence ..." Then the freestyle begins dramatically: "Yo, check this out! I expose 575 flows, in the inkling of a second/ expecting to disassemble these in less than two verses/ I'm able to disengage mics and chew emcees up like Mike and Ikes when I recite/ Daylight's eclipsed/ I sink MC's like ships" (Spady *et al.* 1999: 550).

Clearly, Kurupt is a skilled user of language by any standard. Still unexplored are his word creations ("multimusical," describing someone who has a wide range of taste in music, a wide range of musical abilities, and the tendency to incorporate various musical forms into one), his unique phrasing (in describing his album, "I see it as being the East, West, North, and South. Upper East, upper West, upper North, upper South, downer East ... [Laughter]"), and his varied and diverse discourse markers ("woo-woo-woo"—used to provide structure in Black American oral narratives, common in the West Coast, along with, "woompty-woomp-woomp" and "woopty-woo-woo"). It is important to note that while Kurupt is a highly skilled user of language, his Hip Hop conversational discourse shares many elements with that of JT the Bigga Figga, Schoolly D, Beanie Sigel, Eve, Busta Rhymes, Mos Def, and other members of the HHN.

Narrative Sequencing and Flow

Narrative sequencing includes both ritualized story-telling and narrative speech as a frequently occurring genre in Black American discourse (Smitherman 1977). Storytelling is highly valued in the HHN. In the 1980s and 1990s, Slick Rick dazzled Hip Hop Heads with humorous narratives (*The Great Adventures of Slick Rick*) that quite often concluded with a lesson for the listener. Skilled storytellers, such as Slick Rick, have influenced the next wave of Hip Hop artists, and they in turn influence the next wave–and the narrative torch is passed on. In a prime example of the HHN's love for the art of storytelling, and the passing of the narrative torch, Outkast (coming onto the scene waves after Slick Rick) produced "The Art of Storytelling (Part 1 and 2)" (1998). Recognizing Slick Rick as the baaadest ("best") storyteller, they joined him on his album *The Art of Storytelling* (1999) on the single, "Street Talkin." The last four lines of the song capture the point:

> Slick Rick and Outkast is on this jam
> Tryin to help raise all youth to men
> Slick the Ruler Rick his space to slam
> The reputation of this man.

Slick Rick's innovative, pioneering story raps have influenced many rappers. In a conversation with Raekwon, a member of the Wu-Tang Clan, he explains Rick's (and other rappers) influence on him, as well as how the narrative torch is passed down:

R: I'm from the 21st Century Rhymers ... I grew up listening to Old School shit such as, you know, '89 and '90 with Kane and Slick Rick, Rakim. All of them niggas was doin it, you know. So, I'm like a replica of them, you know what I mean? And I'm a combination of them, as well as bein around my way in the projects, the [Wu-Tang] Clan ... It's like, Rick is a storyteller to me. He know how to put words together to perfection. Kane was a hardcore lyricist, which Kane would keep it street, too. You got G Rap ...
A: You said Slick Rick bein a storyteller. Do you see yourself that way, in that tradition?
R: Definitely, you know what I mean? Definitely. I know how to make vivid pictures come up from just experience and bein through a lot of shit. And like I said, bein able to watch

some of the best do it, such as brothas like Slick Rick, Rakim and them, you know what I mean? I'm just them niggas in a younger generation, you know what I mean?

(Alim 2000, unpublished interview)

Smitherman (1977) states that narrative sequencing may be found in these forms: preaching and testifying; folk stories, tall tales, and Toasts. While all of these forms are present in today's Hip Hop lyrics, Rickford and Rickford (2000) point to Toasts as a way to understand the "wicked self-aggrandizement" found in Hip Hop. In Toasts, much like many Hip Hop lyrics, the hero is "fearless, defiant, openly rebellious, and full of braggadocio about his masculinity, sexuality, fighting ability, and general badness" (Smitherman 1977: 157). Rickford and Rickford (2000: 85) make the link: "Remember, no creation in the Spoken Soul universe emerges from a vacuum. LL Cool J ... is as much a son of Rudy Ray Moore as he is of Muddy Waters."

On "How Many Licks" (2000), Lil Kim proves that she is also their daughter, puttin a sexual twist on the famous Tootsie Roll commercial. In one verse, she is all of what Smitherman describes in the previous paragraph and then some (but from a female perspective):

> If you drivin in the street, hold on to your seat
> Niggaz, grab your meat while I ride the beat
> And if you see a shiny black Lamborghini fly by ya
> Zoooooooooom! ... that's me the Night Ridaaa
> Dressed in all black with the gat in the lap
> Lunatics in the street—gotta keep the heat
> Sixty on the bezel, a hundred on the rings
> Sittin pretty, baby, with a Cash Money bling
> 12 A.M., I'm on my way to the club
> After three bottles I'll be ready to fuck
> Some niggaz even put me on their grocery lists
> Right next to the whip cream and box of chocolates
> Designer pussy, my shit come in flavors
> High class taste, niggaz got to spend paper
> Lick it right the first time or you gotta do it over
> Like it's rehearsal for a Tootsie commercial.

When Lil Kim says "while I ride the beat," she is talking about what is known as *flow* in HHNL. *Flow* relates directly to narrative sequencing because it impacts the telling of the story to a great degree. Flow can be defined generally as the relationship between the beats and the rhymes in time. In discussing the concept of flow with Raekwon, I asked him directly what he meant by flow, in orderto develop an understanding from the artist's perspective. His definition provides useful insight:

Flow is like, *how* you say it. Flow is like poetry goin to the beat, but you makin it connect like a bridge, you know what I mean? It's like buildin a bridge with your rhymes [see *bridge rhymes* in Chapter 6]. You want to be able to let everybody know that, "Yo, I could rhyme like this, but off of this type a beat. But when it comes to another beat, I could switch it up," you know what I mean? And make it still flow, but just a different way of usin it, you know what I mean?

(Alim 2000, unpublished interview)

In discussing the relationship between Rap and poetry, Pharoahe Monch provides additional insight with his definition:

P: I mean, poetry is a awesome art form in itself. I dabble in it before I write some of the songs that I do. I try to be poetic with some of the songs. Hip Hop is based upon a mixture of that, but more writing musically. Points and timing, you know. So is poetry. But on a level where it's based upon the music, you have to be more rhythmatically connected with your listener and crowd, in terms of rhythm, you know. And *how* are you ridin that beat. You know, you could do the same thing with poetry without any music at all, you know what I'm saying? Get a response rhythmatically. So, I'm not disrespecting that. I'm just saying, Hip Hop, it's about where you are on that fourth bar, where you are on that first bar ... You got to have flow, and I think that's something that just comes natural.

A: What exactly do you mean by that, by flow?

P: I mean, how the person rides the beat, you know. Some MC's ride the beat soulfully 100% like Slum Village, and they're funky with it. Some MC's go against the grain of the beat, but they're so on point and you understand what they're doing, you know.

(Alim, 2000, unpublished interview)

Keyes (1984: 145) provided an interesting analysis, which needs updating (due to the pioneering nature of her work, rather than any shortcoming on her part): "In Rap music, the bass line functions as a time line. The rhythmic structure and the rhymed couplets weave around a two-bar melodic bass line ... [The Rap is] superimposed on a four-beat bass melodic structure." The real challenge, as Keyes notes, is "synchronizing the rhyme couplets in a narrative form with the rhythmic pulse of the music" (p. 146).

The preceding accounts by Pharoahe and Raekwon indicate that a rapper need not always stay on the beat to have a good flow. The key is that there must be something recognizable in the pattern of one's timing, and it must be fresh and innovative to capture people's attention. Missy Elliott is skilled in rhyming off-beat, or "against the grain of the beat," and she sometimes describes her style as a "crazy flow." Superfast rhymers like Mystikal, E-40, Twista, Gift of Gab, and Pharoahe Monch are masters at alternating sequences where they are directly on beat, with stretches of rhymes where they may appear oblivious to the bass line. The remarkable thing is that they somehow land right back on the beat! A Hip Hop Head once described Method Man's rhyming talent as his ability to "dance all around the beat and decorate the beat with his rhymes."

Chuck D, in describing the relationship between Rap and poetry, touches on something very relevant to this discussion:

C: Poetry makes the beat come to *it*, and Rap pretty much is subservient to the beat.

A: What do you mean by that?

C: Well, you know, if you have a beat, you have to pretty much follow that beat in some kind of way. I think where you have the beginning of the meshing of the two (Rap and poetry) began with KRS-One, where they actually slowed the beat down to themselves. A poet would actually come around and do his or her particular thing and the beat had to ride to them.

(Alim 1999, unpublished interview)

Chuck's comments allow us to deduce that if rhythm is one's ability to stay on beat, then flow is one's ability to exploit the rhythm, rhyme around the rhythm, and yet be able to faithfully return to the rhythm on time.

Although it is extremely difficult to reproduce rhythm in print, Wood (1999) provides perhaps the most intricate analysis of the issue. While the analysis is preliminary, he bridges musicology and poetics in a way that is both refreshing and revealing. He states that "the primary rhythmic force of rap is to negotiate the varieties of possibilities set up by the sixteenth-note backbeat"

(Wood 1999: 9). He explains: "The simplest place to start a phrase when rapping is on the ONE of a four-beat measure, and the easiest place to drop the rhymes is on the TWO and the FOUR" (1999: 8). In this insightful piece, Wood goes on to demonstrate the differences between Chuck D, Snoop Dogg, and various other rhymers in the way they exploit the relationship between the rhymes and the beat—the *flow*.

Entering the Cipha and Battlin

You think you all that, son?
BRING IT TO THE CYPHER!
You holdin down platinum?
BRING IT TO THE CYPHER!
You think you got props, son?
BRING IT TO THE CYPHER!
You livin Hip Hop, son?
BRING IT TO THE CYPHER!

(Truck Turner and KRS-One 1999)

The Hip Hop cultural modes of discourse are at their peak in the communal and competitive *cipha* (sometimes spelled "cypher/cipha/cypha"). HHNL is both a communal and competitive discourse, with the cipher being the height of community and competition within the HHN. The cipher is where all (or some combination) of the Hip Hop cultural modes of discourse and discursive practices—call and response, multilayered totalizing expression, signifyin, bustin, tonal semantics, poetics, narrative sequencing, flow, metaphoric and hyperbolic language use, image-making, freestylin, battling, word-explosions, word-creations, word-pictures, dialoguing other voices, talk-singing, kinesics—converge into a fluid matrix of linguistic-cultural activity. The cipher is the height of linguistic creativity and is not for the faint of heart. Lyrical battling, which often occurs in the cipher, is a highly animated engagement where the Rap lyricist's skillz are sharpened and presented to a critical circle of Hip Hop conscious beings. When Truck Turner and KRS-One order their opponents to "bring it to the cypher," they are issuing the ultimate challenge.

Despite the centrality of the cipher to Hip Hop linguistic-cultural activity, this discursive speech event remains almost entirely unexplored by scholars. Rickford and Rickford (2000: 87) refer to the cipher as "the supercharged circuit of rap knowledge and creativity (something not dissimilar—in the vein of highly communal responsive rituals—to the ring shout)." Battlin in the cipher is also comparable to the competition among choirs in gospel music, "exchanges" in doo wop music, jam sessions in jazz music, and streetdancing (breakdancing) battles. The criteria in each one of these artistic endeavors are very high.

Addressing an audience at the University of Pennsylvania's conference on "Islam and the Globalization of Hip Hop," Peterson (2001) offers some insight:

The use of the term cipher in the Hip Hop vernacular is important. Ciphers are marvelous speech events. They are inviting and also very challenging. They have become a litmus test for modern day griots. Ciphers are the innovative formats for battles (the ritual of rhyming is informed by the physical arrangement of Hip Hop) ... The concept of the cipher is essential to Hip Hop Culture and to its vernacular. It indicates an epistemology that is non-linear.

California's Ras Kass supports Peterson's definition of the competitive nature of the cipher and offers some further insight:

It's kinda like a training field, you know what I'm saying? It teaches you delivery, you know what I'm saying? You got to react under pressure, because it ain't even really fans in the cipher. I mean, everybody's a Hip Hop fan, but they ain't YO fan. They a fan of themselves. So, you spittin! It's gladiators! It's jousting. I call it jousting. Joust from the mouth. So, you know what I'm saying, it's a necessity.

(Alim 2000, unpublished interview)

The cipha is seen as a linguistic training field for MC's. Several skillz are developed in the cipha—Rap delivery, reacting under pressure, verbal battling, or "jousting from the mouth." The cipha is like Hip Hop's classroom, where one studies to learn the tricks of the trade, so to speak. Raekwon alludes to the pedagogical nature of this discursive speech event and highlights the communal aspect:

You know, it's everybody enlightenin they skills with the next person, and you know, you learn off of the best, you know what I mean? It's like training. It's like basic training. It's like, sparrin, you know what I mean? So, you know, that makes a better MC, bein able to know that he can express hisself amongst people that can teach him as well as he teach them. Everybody's teachin each other, you know, because they say experience the best teacher. So, when people listen to famous artists . . . they acquire what they learn from them and what they got, and they put it together, and that makes them a better person. It's like, it's like how you got Reverends out there right now that's a replica of Martin Luther King, you know what I mean? They got the same goals, the same ways of thinkin as that man. And, you know, that's all a part of being able to be a great man, is to be able to learn from the best, you know.

(Alim 2000, unpublished interview)

Whereas Raekwon highlights the communal and pedagogical nature of the cipha (see Newman 2001), others speak about the intensely competitive nature of some Hip Hop ciphas. Kurupt discusses the importance of the cipha as a pivotal stage of development for an MC. His experience is one of fierce competition and verbal battling, where each MC is at war with the members of the cipha. The MC's are required to *spit* freestyle rhymes that will lead them directly to their next opponent, and the MC who outlasts everyone in the cipha, emerges victorious. Kurupt's story is especially interesting due to the fact that he battled Snoop Dogg in the early stages of his career. Due to his impressive performance in the battle cipher, they became recording industry partners. Kurupt explains how he and Snoop formed their relationship on the West Coast:

We both bust freestyles . . . At this club called the Roxy. We was just bustin with each other and all that and we was against each other at first. It's like our freestyles was so tight, you know what I mean, that he was bustin in his rhyme. He was like, you know, "We ain't gettin paid for this. If you tight, then I'm tight. Why don't we just bust together, you know what I'm saying? Let's kick some rhymes."

(Spady *et al.* 1999: 536)

Kurupt explains that he learned his battlin and freestyle skills as a youngster in the East Coast ciphas of Philly. He begins his narrative about his early days in the cipha with the classic Hip Hop frame, "back in the day":

Back in the day, I was like thirteen. A circle of ten or twelve people, ages of like thirteen and below, one might have been twenty, twenty one. And when it came down to the last two [rhymers], I was always there. And I've always been number one. Always. I never lost them type battles. You bust and it's like you don't say the next person's name, and you're out of there. I've always been in there. I just sit back and bust rhymes and I used to spell things on people's shirts. Like he'd have a shirt that says "Walk" on it. I'd break it down like the "W" is for this, the "A" is for that, the "L" is for this, and the "K" is for that. And they be like, "What?!" That's my style. Nobody else was doing that. That's something I created ... Like, he could have a soda can, "Pepsi." Once, I spelled Pepsi for this nigga. The "P" is for punctuating rhymes and woo-woo-woo. "E" is for executing. And they're like, "God!" And I'm like what—thirteen, fourteen. C'mon now. They called me "The Kid." That was my rappin name because I was the youngest nigga that would always make it into the cipher.

(Spady *et al.* 1999: 539)

What stands out so strongly in this reflective narrative on the cipha experience is the fierce intensity and the desire to be number one. HHNL is an extremely competitive discourse space. As John Wideman (1976: 34) noted:

What's fascinating to me about African American speech is its spontaneity, the requirement that you not only have a repertoire of vocabulary or syntactic devices/constructions, but you come prepared to do something in an attempt to meet the person on a level that both uses the language, mocks the language, and recreates the language.

The Rapper must come prepared to *do something* with this language. Kurupt describes the rules and rituals of this practice in Philly (as they varied in different cities). In his experience, the rhymer had to name the next person entering the cipher, which required the participants to always be on alert. Even those who are not called on are interacting with the rhymers by providing critical feedback, approval or rejection (see Jooyoung Lee's (2005) study of freestyle battlin in Los Angeles and Woods (2005)). Kurupt's language game of picking apart the words on other rhymers' articles of clothing demonstrates his creativity and inventiveness—"That's something I created." A deep sense of pride is communicated with regard to one's witty, inventive use of language and ability to outlast others in this linguistic competition.

As Rickford and Rickford (2000) suggested, the cipher has roots deep in the Black American and African Oral Tradition. Smitherman (1977: 82) cites H. Rap Brown's (Black leader in the 1960s and Muslim Imam today) experience with the dozens, which is remarkably similar to Kurupt's description above:

what you try to do is totally destroy somebody else with words. It's the whole competition thing again, fighting each other. There'd be some 40 or 50 dudes standing around and the winner was determined by the way they responded to what was said. If you fell all over each other laughing, then you knew you'd scored.

Recently, Sonia Sanchez, Black Arts Movement poet—professor of the 1960s and 1970s (and still rappin strong today), was a participant in a Hip Hop cipher on June 23, 1999 in Philadelphia to celebrate Hip Hop Week. The cipher was led by Xzulu, formerly the prime time DJ of Philly's major Hip Hop station and producer of a nightly freestyle competition called "The Ultimate Cipher Challenge." About 50 or 60 people were involved in the cipha, along with two DJ's and various graffiti artists. The competition was fierce. MC's would take the mic and bust a freestyle rhyme while others evaluated their performance with shouts, hand clapping, and other affirmations. Some MC's stood back with their heads cocked to one side and one eyebrow raised as if to say, "That's all you got?" Others walked right up to the rhymer and faced directly in the opposite direction with the coolest, most disinterested look on their face—only to snatch the mic and rip their own freestyle! These facial expressions and acts of indirection are common in the cipher.

You want to evaluate the other rhymer while maintaining a cool, calm, and confident exterior that lets the present rhymer know, "You got competition!"

In the heat of the moment, Sonia Sanchez entered the cipher and dropped a lyrical bomb on all those in attendance. With many Hip Hop artists on the scene like Parry P, Lady B, Da Fat Cat Clique, Legacy, Ehsan Jackson, and Supreem Da Regulata, Sonia stepped up and roc'd the mic right (*yeahhh*)! She described what moved her to do so:

> Well, I heard everyone before I got up in that circle. And, initially, I stood and watched it. And I watched not only the energy, but I watched the respect that people had for each other. And then I watched the young Brothas and Sistas, you know, rappin … And it reminded me a great deal of when we also got up on the stages … You could not go up and go [making a weak attempt] … you had to hold your own. And so when I see those young Sistas holdin their own, you know, I smiiile … It was not an alien circle. It was like, as I said, I belong there … We used to go out a lot in California. We used to go with Ed Bullins and Baraka and Marvin X and Sarah Fabio. We used to go out and do our poetry and our plays in the streets of Oakland.
>
> (Alim 2000: 21)

As Sonia Sanchez makes clear, the cipha is not alien to Black communicative and discursive practices. It is important to note, however, that while the cipher and other Hip Hop discursive practices are most certainly tradition-linked, they are not tradition-bound. What I mean by that is, HHNL is rooted in the Black American Oral Tradition, but also extends and expands that tradition in multiple ways to include new forms and styles of discourse. HHNL will continue to evolve and take it to "da next level."

Black Language Space, the Power of the Word, and the Hip Hop Nation Speech Community

HHNL exists within a Black Language Space (BLS)—a discursive space where Black Language is the culturally dominant language variety, and the power of the word is the overriding force of attraction. The Hip Hop Nation Speech Community (HHNSC) is driven culturally and linguistically by young Black males and females who are adept at language use in the Hip Hop-saturated streets of America. But who comprises the HHNSC? Hymes (1974) informs us that:

> Membership in a speech community consists of sharing one or more of its ways of speaking—that is, not in knowledge of a speech style (or any other purely linguistic entity, such as language) alone, but in terms of knowledge as well as appropriate use. There are rules of use without which rules of syntax are useless.

Membership in the HHNSC, then, hinges on having knowledge of HHNL and Hip Hop cultural modes of discourse.

This definition is suitable for defining the HHNSC because it is as catholic as the HHN's philosophy of race, ethnicity, and culture. Norfleet (1997), Cutler (1999) and Newman (2001) have demonstrated the HHN's strong anti-racist ideology—this ideology has led to the development of a multiracial, multiethnic, and multicultural speech community. Due to Hip Hop Culture's overwhelming influence on popular culture in America and the world, HHNL is influencing the far corners of the globe, creating what is perhaps the *illest* global speech community. Certainly there are differences in speech communities from city to city (and sometimes block to block), but the unifying elements of the HHNSC deserve attention. Spady (1994: 26) touches on this topic: "The Philly Hip Hop Language of Schooly D is preeminently modern [spreading beyond localized boundaries]. It shares common elements with Ice Cube, Snoop Doggy Dogg, Kool Keith, Ice T, Chuck D and Scarface," Rappers from various regions in the US.

Black Language Space (BLS)

Members of the HHN often refer to themselves as speakers of a common language. Ice Cube considers this notion, and roots this common language in the historical plight of Africans in America:

> Four hundred years ago, when black slaves were brought to America, Africans who spoke the same language were separated from each other. What we're seeing today, with this insane campaign to intimidate rappers and rap music, is just another form of separating people that speak a common language.
>
> (Ice Cube June 25, 1990; cited in Sexton 1995)

The common elements that unite people who "speak a common language" have been described earlier. But given the high value placed on individuality and originality in HHNL, the HHN, speakers of the many regional HHNLV (HHNL Varieties), are constantly shaping and reshaping existing language norms. These language norms exist and evolve in what we have termed a Black Language Space (BLS). It is the existence of a BLS that enables HHNL to come to life in full effect. By BLS, we mean a discursive space where Black Language is the prestige variety, where Black linguistic and communicative norms are the standard, where one cannot engage in meaningful conversation unless they are fully equipped to handle linguistic combat and competition. One has to come prepared to do battle, to hold their own, to enable the free flow of conversation. This is a space where language is the central focus, and the key element to maintaining and sustaining dialogue, as well as the primary site of authentication (Bucholtz 2003).

Spady's hiphopographic (1991) studies in the Umum Hip Hop Trilogy (*Nation Conscious Rap* (1991), *Twisted Tales in the Hip Hop Streets of Philly* (1995), and *Street Conscious Rap* (1999)) offer a key source of primary data in considering the concept of a Black Language Space. Several recent unpublished interviews will demonstrate how Spady, as an interlocutor who is fully conversant with HHNL, creates a BLS with a central focus on enabling the narrative. First, we hear from South Philly's Beanie Sigel, as he recounts the story of how he and Black Thought (from The Roots) used to be in the same grade school class:

S: Who was that 4th grade teacher who used to be tellin you and Tariq [Black Thought] to stop talkin in the back of the class?

B: Hah. Hah. Hah. [Beanie just laughin, as a challenge]

S: Who was that, man? Were you talkin or were you rhymin?

B: Tariq, he used to be in ah ...

S: What elementary school was that?

B: Ah man!

S: You don't remember it. You've forgotten it. [Returning the challenge]

B: Wow! What was her name?

S: You remember her don't you? [Pushing the interlocutor to remember]

B: Wow. McDaniel School. Me and Tariq was in that school.

S: Were y'all writin rhymes in her class or what?

B: Yeah actually.

S: She said y'all were disturbing her class. [He-said, she-said talk, reporting what others have said]

B: All the time. Actually. See, what it was, Tariq ...

S: On the real now. [Again, challenging, and enabling the truth]

B: On the real. Tariq was in a higher grade than me. He was one grade in front of me. [Recognizing the challenge to the truth]

S: He wasn't even called Black Thought at that time?

B: Nah. He was just Tariq. He was in my sista's class. They was in the 4th grade and I was in the 3rd grade.

S: You used to go to their room all the time.

B: I used to go to they fourth grade reading.

S: Oh. Reading?

B: I used to go fourth grade to read cause I was in a higher level than the kids in the third grade.

S: They were too slow for you? [Affirming and commenting on the narrative]

B: Ah. Ah. Well yeah. And that was all through elementary. When I was in kindergarten I used to go first grade and read. When I was in the first grade I used to go in the 2nd grade reading class. So that's how I was always in class with Tariq. And we used to be in the back just rappin, repeatin old Sugar Hill Gang Records and all that ...

(Spady 2001, unpublished interview)

What one does not see from the printed page is the rapid spit-fire rate of some of these exchanges. The story unfolds in a fluid interactive space where the interlocutors fully expect what some might view as "interruptions." Spady is constantly commenting on the narrative and challenging the speaker. He is also freely using terms and phrases rooted in HHNL, and Black Language in general, such as "on the real now," which highlights the listener's desire for *real talk* ("talk that is both factual and sincere"). The result is a previously unheard narrative about how Beanie Sigel and Black Thought used to rhyme and rap together in grade school.

The following sequence between Spady and Oakland's Saafir exhibits how both interlocutors are highly competitive. Throughout the conversation, they have been discussing Saafir's days as a young buck ("adolescent") growin up in "the town":

S: Lookin back on school, man, are there any particular teachers that you can recall ...

SA: Hell, naw! Hell, naw!

S: C'mon, man! I didn't finish the question yet ...

SA: Hell, naw! Hell, naw!

S: Get outta here, man?!

SA: Hell, naw! No teachers. None.

S: Why was school a turn off for you, man?

SA: School wasn't a turn off. I love to learn, but the teachers is assholes. A lot of the teachers bring a lot of their personal attributes to the fuckin classroom, you know what I mean?

S: What do you mean by bringing their personal attributes?

SA: As far as their emotional problems and the ills they're havin at their house, you know what I mean? They take the shit out on the kids and fuck the kids on a certain level, psychologically fuck them up, you know what I mean? Depending on the caliber of teacher. I have experienced some fucked up ones, but I ain't mad at them, you know what I'm saying? In actuality, it made me understand them and the people around them a lot more.

(Spady 2000, unpublished interview)

We can see that Saafir anticipates Spady's question and immediately cuts him off with, "Hell naw! Hell naw!" Spady, also fiercely competitive, responds, "C'mon, man! I didn't finish the question yet ..." Again Saafir cuts him off, "Hell naw! Hell naw!" Spady replies with "Get outta here, man?!" [said in a manner to mean something like, "Are you serious, man?"] These exchanges occur so quickly that they are difficult to separate line-by-line, as the speakers are speaking over and under each other. This creates a BLS where Saafir is then freed up to testify about his school experiences, which obviously still hold a lot of painful memories for him.

Spady's knowledge of HHNL and Black communication in general allows him to gain great insight from his interlocutors. In the following interaction, Spady's knowledge of the Black Oral Tradition (specifically Black DJ's and Jocko Henderson, who produced *The Rocketship* six months before Sugar Hill Gang's release is key). Kurupt, who grew up in Philadelphia, is the interlocutor:

K: I think Black Language is an essential part of Hip Hop—period. Hip Hop is a Black culture influenced art form of music.

S: So the discussion about Ebonics and other Black Language expressions was not new to you when it became a hot issue in 1997–98? I guess you'd always known Ebonics.

K: Since the 70's. The 40's. The 30's and the 20's. Jock! [Referring to famous Black DJ of the 1960s and 1970s, Jocko Henderson, and even further back in history]

S: Jocko, Jocko? [Recognition of the reference to Jocko by repeating the introduction to one of his raps, "Jocko, Jocko"]

K: "EEEEEEEEEEE Tidleee Wop/ This is the Jock and I'm back on the scene ..." [Spontaneous break into Jocko's rap]

S: With the record machine. [Finishing Kurupt's Jocko rendition]

K: Saying Ooh Bop Da Boo. [Continuing the Rap]

S and K: How do you do? [Said at the same time, completing the Rap]

S: How do you know that shit man? [Said in Black American falsetto, characteristic of Black male speech (Alim 2004a)]

K: Heyyyyyyyyyyyyy!!! [Elongated "hey," to confidently express his knowledge of the rap] No, please believe it, man. [Common phrase heard particularly in the Bay Area, California] I'm from Philadelphia. [Cementing himself in the place where Jocko's raps are best known, establishing authenticity] Listen to that: "E Tiddlee Wop. This is the Jock and I'm back on the scene with the record machine. Saying Ooh Bop Do Boo. How do you do?" That's rap. Ahhh, man! My stepfather been hit me upside my head, "Boyyy, rap ain't new. People *been* rappin, *years ago*, son. Years ago!!! Jocko, he's one of the first rappers, son." Ah Hah Hah! [Kurupt laughs]

S: So you knew rap was within the Black tradition?

K: Oh, Fo Sho. (Said slowly for emphasis in that hip, urbane North Philly way).

S: From the Get-Go, right? ["Get-Go", Black term meaning from the very beginning]

K: Oh, Fo Sho. [Meaning, "for sure," "certainly." Associated largely with California, though used elsewhere. Similar to the phrase associated with the East Coast, "No doubt."]

(Spady 2001, unpublished interview)

Needless to say, the narrative would have taken a completely different turn (or maybe would not have even been expressed at all) if Spady did not recognize what Kurupt meant by "Jock!" The spontaneous break into Rap opens up the discursive BLS and allows the interlocutor to know that he is speaking to someone who is conversant with these language practices. Too often, members of the HHNSC are depicted as being unable to communicate. For example, many hold the belief that members of the HHNSC cannot express their thoughts through language (which should be clearly seen as erroneous by now). Sentiments I have often heard, in reference to this speech community, are, "They can't put two sentences together when they are talking," or, "They can't say two words without cursing" (see Spears 1998, for a discussion of *uncensored mode*). As Spady (2001: 18) writes: "Many people who interview Kurupt and/or comment upon his work in or out of the Dogg Pound, are simply not prepared as worthy interlocutors. Black American expressive and competitive behavior is very complex." Kurupt expresses his views on the challenge of rappin in Philadelphia:

> It's just so much talent around that you really have to concentrate on your skills. We're a perfectionist city ... It's the word-connection. It's the type of words that either artist choose to use. It's the way you put those words together.
>
> (Spady 2001, unpublished interview)

In a Black Language Space, the word is the overriding force of attraction. HHNL is rooted, philosophically and ideologically, in the power of the word, or *Nommo*. As Smitherman (1994: 7–8) writes:

> The African American oral tradition is rooted in a belief in the power of the Word. The African concept of *Nommo*, the Word, is believed to be the force of life itself. To speak is to make something come into being. Once something is given the force of speech, it is binding—hence the familiar saying "Yo word is yo bond," which in today's Hip Hop Culture has become WORD IS BORN. The Hip Hop expressions WORD, WORD UP, WORD TO THE MOTHER, and similar phrases all stem from the value placed on speech. Creative, highly verbal talkers are valued.

The force of speech is expressed poetically by Mos Def in "Hip Hop" (1999), as if co-signing and bearing witness to the truth in Smitherman's statement. In one of the most oft-quoted opening lines of Hip Hop, he begins: "Speech is my hammer bang the world into shape now let it fall—HUH!" When asked directly about the genesis of this line, Mos explains:

> *A*: You say in "Hip Hop," "Speech is my hammer bang the world into shape."
> *M*: That's just something that came to me. It's my relationship to the way I'm using language in Hip Hop. You do build your world with language to a large degree. You build your world with what you say. Affirmations. "I'm gonna do this." "Things are gonna change." Then you start to act out those things. If you tell your children that you love them and that they're special to you, then they start to feel that way about themselves and they start to treat themselves that way. If you tell your children the opposite of that, then they start to live that out.
>
> (Alim 2001, unpublished interview)

Speech here is an agent of change. What does it mean to build your world with language? Linguistic anthropologists, much like Hip Hop artists have theorized, understand that we construct our realities, identities, and social worlds through language (Duranti 1997, 2004). The power of the word, of speech, is mos def ("most definitely") a driving force in HHNL. Many artists believe that their words have the power to change not only their lives, but the lives of members of their community as well. When Tupac joined Scarface on the memorable collaboration "Smile for Me Now" (2001), in which they lovingly expressed and assuaged the struggle of Black people in America–realizing that "through all the pain" you *got* to smile to remain sane in an insane world. Near the end of the song, Tupac speaks on the power of the word with a brief one-liner, "Embrace my words, make the world change."

Raekwon, in describing the power of the Rap, provides an added perspective on the phrase "word is life" (or "word life"):

R: We talk about things that involve life. Meaning that, we got joints that attack emotional spirits, you know what I mean? Meaning that, if we talk about—how could I say it?—if we talk about the streets or whatever showin you how shit be goin down in the streets, that's only one side of it, you know what I mean? Then we talk about emotional shit that make you want to cry, that make you flash back to your family, that make you go check out your moms and be like, you know, "We probably goin through some rough shit, mom, but you know how I feel about you." It's like, we make songs to be able to make you think about what's goin on in your life.

A: That's powerful shit right there.

R: Yeah, and that's what makes a great MC.

(Alim 2001, unpublished interview)

In Raekwon's moving testimony, we also see a spiritual dimension to the word, and to the power of the Rap. As more and more Black Americans continue to accept Islam, *Nommo* is being expressed through that spiritual experience. Mos Def has made a link between the power of the word/rhyme and the way that the *Holy Qur'an* was written. Rapper JT the Bigga Figga also made links between the way Rappers use metaphoric language and rhyme to "the way Allah be teachin us in the *Qur'an*."

Black religious leaders have long understood the power of the word. In this example, Nation of Islam leader, Minister Louis Farrakhan (perceived by many as the HHN's primary teacher, and he would add, student), placed the power of the word in a uniquely spiritual context as he addressed the Hip Hop Summit in New York City on June 13, 2001 (see also Spady, Alim and Meghelli, forthcoming):

I am a spiritual man so I have to speak to you from the Books (Bible and Qur'an). You may not think that I am too hip, but, when you hear from the Books who you are, why you are called, and, what your mission is that you have just begun to see, then, you will know that the Prophets of Allah (God) who saw all the way to the judgement and to the end of the present world, had to have seen hip-hop. You will not find the words "hip-hop" necessarily in the Bible or in the Qur'an, but, you are there in a very big way ... In the countries where governments do not like western music or western civilization, people are sneaking around listening to the word and moving to the beat of the hip-hop generation. If in the beginning was the Word and the Word was with God and the Word was God, then, God here means Force and Power. The Word has Force. The Word has Power; Force and Power to move men to think new thoughts and to do new things.

(Minister Louis Farrakhan 2001)

What I have attempted to do in this chapter is to demonstrate the creativity and complexity of language use in contemporary Black American expressive culture, particularly HHNL, language use in the HHNSC, and the Hip Hop cultural modes of discourse.

Study Questions

1. What are the similarities and differences between "hip-hop language" and poetry?
2. How is the concept of "technique" relevant to a discussion of hip-hop language and aesthetics?
3. Why is hip-hop language significant in the conversation of earlier Black artistic forms or cultural practices?

References

Abrahams, Roger. 1964. *Deep Down in the Jungle: Negro Narrative Folklore from the Streets of Philadelphia*. Chicago: Aldine Publishing Co.

Alim, H. Samy. 1999. The Roots Rock Memorial Auditorium. *Intermission*. Stanford University.

Alim, H. Samy. 2000. 360 Degreez of Black Art comin at you: Sista Sonia Sanchez and the dimensions of a Black Arts continuum. In James G. Spady (ed.), *360 Degreez of Sonia Sanchez: Hip Hop, Narrativity, Iquawe and Public Spaces of Being*. Special issue of *Bma: The Sonia Sanchez Literary Review*, 6(1), Fall.

Alim, H. Samy. 2001a. THREE-X-BLACK: Mos Def, Mr. Nigga (Nigga, Nigga) and Big Black Africa X-amine Hip Hop's cultural consciousness. In H. Samy Alim (ed.), *Hip Hop Culture: Language, Literature, Literacy and the Lives of Black Youth*. Special issue of the *Black Arts Quarterly*. Stanford, CA: Committee on Black Performing Arts, Stanford University, 4–8.

Alim, H. Samy (ed.). 2001b. *Hip Hop Culture: Language, Literature, Literacy and the Lives of Black Youth*. Special issue of the *Black Arts Quarterly*. Stanford, CA: Committee on Black Performing Arts, Stanford University.

Alim, H. Samy. 2003. On some serious next millennium rap ishhh: Pharoahe Monch, Hip Hop poetics, and the internal rhymes of Internal Affairs. *Journal of English Linguistics* 31(1), 60–84.

Alim, H. Samy. 2004a. *You know my steez: An ethnographic and sociolinguistic study of a Black American speech community*. Durham, NC: Duke University Press.

Anderson, Monica. 1994. *Black English Vernacular (From "Ain't" to "Yo Mama": the Words Politically Correct Americans Should Know)*. Highland City, Florida: Rainbow Books.

Baugh, John. 1983. *Black Street Speech: Its History, Structure, and Survival*. Austin, Texas: University of Texas Press.

Baugh, John and Geneva Smitherman. In press. Linguistic emancipation in global perspective. In H. Samy Alim and John Baugh (eds), *Black Language, Education, and Social Change*. New York: Teachers College Press.

Braithwaite, Fred (Fab Five Freddy). 1992. *Fresh Fly Flavor: Words and Phrases of the Hip-Hop Generation*. Stamford, CT: Longmeadow Press.

Braithwaite, Fred. 1995. *Hip Hop Slang: English–Deutsch*. Frankfurt am Main: Eichborn.

Brathwaite, Kamau. 1984. *History of the Voice: The Development of Nation Language in Anglophone Caribbean Poetry*. London: New Beacon Books.

Bucholtz, Mary. 2003. Language and gender. In Ed Finegan and John Rickford (eds), *Language in the USA*. Cambridge: Cambridge University Press.

Cutler, Cecelia. 1999. Yorkville Crossing: White teens, Hip Hop and African American English. *Journal of Sociolinguistics* 3/4: 428–442.

Daniel, Jack and Geneva Smitherman. 1976. How I got over: Communication dynamics in the Black community. *Quarterly Journal of Speech* 62, February.

Dillard, J. L. 1977. *Lexicon of Black English*. New York: Seabury.

Duranti, Alessandro. 1997. *Linguistic Anthropology*. New York: Cambridge University Press.

Farrakhan, Louis. 2001. Hip Hop Summit: Accept the responsibility of leadership. *Final Call*, June 26.

Fasoid, Ralph W. 1972. *Tense Marking in Black English: A Linguistic and Social Analysis*. Washington, DC: Center for Applied Linguistics.

Folb, Edith. 1980. *Runnin' Down Some Lines: the Language and Culture of Black Teenagers*. Cambridge, MA: Harvard University Press.

Green, Lisa. 2004. African American English. In Edward Finegan and John Rickford (eds), *Language in the USA: Perspectives for the 21st Century*, Cambridge: Cambridge University Press.

Henderson, Stephen. 1973. *Understanding the New Black Poetry: Black Speech and Black Music as Poetic References*. New York: William Morrow.

Holloway, Joseph and W. Vass. 1997. *The African Heritage of American English*. Bloomington: University of Indiana Press.

Hymes, Dell. 1974. *Foundations in Sociolinguistics: an Ethnographic Approach*. Philadelphia: University of Pennsylvania Press.

Jackson, Austin, Tony Michel, David Sheridan, and Bryan Stumpf. 2001. Making connections in the contact zones: towards a critical praxis of Rap Music and Hip Hop Culture. In H. Samy Alim (ed.) *Hip Hop Culture: Language, Literature, Literacy and the Lives of Black Youth*. Special issue of the *Black Arts Quarterly*. Stanford, CA: Committee on Black Performing Arts, Stanford University.

Keyes, Cheryl. 1984. Verbal art performance in Rap Music: The conversation of the 80's. *Folklore Forum* 17(2), Fall: 143–152.

Kochman, Thomas. 1969. "Rapping" in the Black Ghetto. *Trans-Action*, February, 26–34.

Labov, William, Paul Cohen, Clarence Robins, and John Lewis. 1968. *A Study of the Non-standard English of*

Negro and Puerto Rican Speakers in New York City. Report on Co-operative Research Project 3288. New York: Columbia University.

Lee, Jooyoung. 2005. "You wanna battle?": Negotiating respect and local rules in the emcee cipher. Paper presented at The Lehman Conference on Hip-Hop: From Local to Global Practice, New York.

Major, Clarence. 1970 (1994). *Juba to Jive: A Dictionary of African-American Slang.* New York and London: Penguin.

Mitchell-Kernan, Claudia. 1971. *Language Behavior in a Black Urban Community.* Monograph No. 2. Language Behavior Laboratory. University of California, Berkeley.

Mitchell-Kernan, Claudia. 1972. Signifying and marking: Two Afro-American speech acts. In John J. Gumperz and Dell Hymes (eds), *Directions in Sociolinguistics.* New York: Holt, Rinehart & Winston.

Morgan, Aswan. 1999. *Why They Say What Dey Be Sayin': an Examination of Hip-Hop Content and Language.* Paper submitted for LING 073, *Introduction to African American Vernacular English.* Stanford University.

Morgan, Marcyliena. 2001. "Nuthin' but a G thang": Grammar and language ideology in Hip Hop identity. In Sonja Lanehart (ed.) *Sociocultural and Historical Contexts of African American Vernacular English.* Athens: University of Georgia Press.

Newman, Michael. 2001. "Not dogmatically/ It's all about me": Contested values in a high school Rap crew. *Taboo: A Journal of Culture and Education* 5(2): 51–68.

Norfleet, Dawn. 1997. Hip-hop culture in New York City: The role of verbal music performance in defining a community. PhD dissertation, Columbia University.

Olivo, Warren. 2001. Phat lines: Spelling conventions in Rap Music. *Written Language and Literacy* 4(1): 67–85.

Peterson, James. 2001. Paper Presented at the University of Pennsylvania's conference on Islam and the Globalization of Hip Hop.

Remes, Pieter. 1991. Rapping: a sociolinguistic study of oral tradition in Black urban communities in the United States. *Journal of the Anthropological Society of Oxford* 22(2): 129–149.

Rickford, John and Russell Rickford. 2000. *Spoken Soul: The Story of Black English,* New York: John Wiley.

Schiffman, Harold. 1996. *Linguistic Culture and Language Policy.* London and New York: Routledge.

Sexton, Adam. 1995. *Rap on Rap: Straight-Up Talk on Hip-Hop Culture.* New York: Dell Publishing.

Smitherman, Geneva. 1973. The power of the Rap: The Black idiom and the New Black Poetry. *Twentieth Century Literature: A Scholarly and Critical Journal* 19: 259–274.

Smitherman, Geneva. 1977 (1986). *Talkin and Testifyin: The Language of Black America.* Houghton Mifflin; reissued, with revisions, Detroit: Wayne State University Press.

Smitherman, Geneva. 1994 (2000). *Black Talk: Words and Phrases from the Hood to the Amen Corner.* Boston and New York: Houghton Mifflin.

Smitherman, Geneva. 1997. "The chain remain the same": Communicative practices in the Hip-Hop Nation. *Journal of Black Studies,* September.

Smitherman, Geneva. 2000. *Talkin That Talk: Language, Culture and Education in African America.* London and New York: Routledge.

Spady, James. 1993. "IMA PUT MY THING DOWN": Afro-American expressive culture and the Hip Hop community. *TYANABA: Revue de la Societe d'Anthropologie.* December.

Spady, James. 1994. Living in America where the brother got to get esoterica: The Philly Hip Hop Language and philosophy of Schooly D. *Fourth Dimension* 4(1): 26–27.

Spady, James G. 2000a. The centrality of Black Language in the discourse of Sonia Sanchez and Rap artists. In James Spady (ed.), *360 Degreez of Sonia Sanchez: Hip Hop, Narrativity, Iquawe and Public Spaces of Being.* Special issue of *Bma: The Sonia Sanchez Literary Review* 6.1, Fall.

Spady, James G. 2001. Kurupt's journey from Pickett Middle School to a space boogie universe. *Philadelphia New Observer,* July 25, 18–19.

Spady, James G. and H. Samy Alim. 1999. Street conscious Rap: Modes of being. In *Street Conscious Rap.* Philadelphia: Black History Museum/Umum Loh Publishers.

Spady, James G. and Joseph Eure. 1991. *Nation Conscious Rap: The Hip Hop Vision.* New York/Philadelphia: PC International Press/Black History Museum.

Spady, James G., H. Samy Alim, and Charles Lee (Art Director). 1999. *Street Conscious Rap.* Philadelphia: Black History Museum/Umum Loh Publishers.

Spady, James G., H. Samy Alim, and Samir Meghelli. Forthcoming. *The Global Cipha: Hip Hop culture and consciousness.* Philadelphia: Black History Museum.

Spears, Arthur K. 2000. Stressed *stay:* A new African-American English aspect marker. Paper presented at the Linguistic Society of America Convention, Washington DC, January.

Stavsky, Lois, Isaac Mozeson and Dani Reyes Mozeson. 1995. *A 2 Z: The Book of Rap and Hip-Hop Slang.* New York: Boulevard Books.

Turner, Lorenzo. 1949. *Africanisms in the Gullah Dialect*. Chicago: University of Chicago Press.

Wa Thiongo, Ngugi. 1992. *Moving the Center: The Struggle for Cultural Freedom*. London: Heinemann.

Wideman, John. 1976. Frame and dialect: The evolution of the Black voice in American literature. *American Poetry Review* 5.5 (September–October): 34–37.

Wolfram, Walter. 1969. *A Sociolinguistic Description of Detroit Negro Speech*. Washington, DC: Center for Applied Linguistics.

Wood, Brent. 1999. Understanding Rap as rhetorical folk poetry. *Mosaic: A Journal for the Interdisciplinary Study of Literature* 32(4).

Woods, Emilee. 2005. Language socialization and cultural ideologies in underground Hip Hop. Senior honors thesis, Department of Linguistics, University of California, Santa Barbara.

Yancy, George. 1991. Rapese. Cited in James G. Spady and Joseph Eure, *Nation Conscious Rap: The Hip Hop Vision*. Philadelphia: Black History Museum Press.

Yasin, Jon. 1999. Rap in the African-American music tradition: Cultural assertion and continuity. In Arthur Spears (ed.), *Race and Ideology: Language, Symbolism, and Popular Culture*. Detroit: Wayne State University Press.

36

Airshafts, Loudspeakers, and the Hip-Hop Sample

Technological innovation and the history of creative production and interpretive strategies lie at the core of Andrew Bartlett's chapter. Citing often irreverent or contestatory practices of black cultural production, Bartlett establishes a viable link between antebellum spirituals or post-emancipation work songs and contemporary hip-hop and rap music. Of crucial concern here is the value of communality, being the shared contexts and conditions within which music is produced *and* the particular means through which music itself helps to weave connective webs that both align individuals with their cultural histories as well as linking them to one another.

With an emphasis on strategic production practices involving "selective adaptation" and radical—even resistant—cultural performance techniques, Bartlett contributes a valuable perspective on the cultural politics within which black youths forge their art. As in past contexts of African-American cultural production, youth of the hip-hop generation turn existing musical forms toward sonic communication, envisioning today's electronic and digital mechanisms as objects that facilitate the dissemination of African-American cultural values, ideals and aesthetics.

Airshafts, Loudspeakers, and the Hip-Hop Sample

Andrew Bartlett

The art of digital sampling in (primarily) African American hip hop is intricately connected to an African American/African diasporic aesthetic which carefully selects available media, texts, and contexts for performative use. Thomas Porcello explains that digital sampling allows one

> to encode a fragment of sound, from one to several seconds in duration, in a digitised binary form which can then be stored in computer memory. This stored sound may be played back through a keyboard, with its pitch and tonal qualities accurately reproduced or, as is often the case, manipulated through electronic editing. (69)

Porcello concludes, perhaps rightly, but in any case reductively, that "rap musicians have come to use the sampler in an oppositional manner which contests capitalist notions of public and private property by employing previously tabooed modes of citation" (82).

When *popular* discussions of rap or hip hop come around to digital sampling, they often do so by way of telling metaphors. Public Enemy's Hank Shocklee asserts that "rap culture" is "becoming more of a scavenger culture" when "mixing all the colors together" (Kemp 20); Mark Costello and David Foster Wallace liken sampling to "holding music at gunpoint" (57); and a March 1991 *Keyboard* magazine article refers to sampling as "audio junkyard collisions" (Dery, "Tommy" 64).

The oral pedagogical techniques hip hop artists utilize have maintained what Porcello calls "three capabilities of the sampler—the mimetic/reproductive, the manipulative[,] and the extractive" (69), and these capabilities reveal, among other things, what W.E.B. Du Bois in 1903 called "second sight" (5)—that process by which the "minority" knows the majority not only better than the obverse, but often better than the "majority" knows itself. Du Boisian second sight is not reserved for quietly ideological activity, but has historically been exercised in a thoroughly public and thoroughly popular forum—and thus a forum in need of contextualization—the African American musical performance.

In his study of African American musical aesthetics *Black Talk: How the Music of Black America Created a Radical Alternative to the Values of Western Literary Tradition,* Ben Sidran relies heavily on a distinction between literate and oral "*approaches* to perception and the organization of information" (3). This distinction, Sidran notes, is not concrete: Whereas "literacy freezes concept, as it were, through the use of print" (xxiv), the so-called oral mode relies on "basic actionality" (5), a functional elaboration, often through performance, that allows communication and perception a massive spectrum of referents. Whether Sidran's distinctions are accepted in full or not, there is a clear continuum in which African American artists have put things learned by listening into action by way of *performance*. Greg Tate argues that one of the most extraordinary transformations in African American aesthetic history—Miles Davis's late 1960s and 1970s electric band—was the result of an act of listening: "What Miles heard in the music of P-Funk progenitors James Brown, Jimi Hendrix, and Sly Stone was the blues impulse transferred, masked, and retooled for the space age through the lowdown act of *possession*" (73). The closeness of listening and performative possession becomes all the more clear as hip hop artists appropriate bits and pieces of numerous musics and nonmusical sounds into their performative matrices. And this appropriative process is hardly novel, despite digital technology, in the 1980s or 1990s.

References to Harlem in early Duke Ellington compositions—"Harlem Speaks" (1935), "Echoes of Harlem" (1936), and "Harlem Air Shaft" (1940)—often concern what Ellington heard in the community. Indeed, Ellington explained "Harlem Air Shaft" as a composition explicitly heard before it was written and arranged:

> You get the full essence of Harlem in an air shaft. You hear fights, you smell dinner, you hear people making love. You hear intimate gossip floating down. You hear the radio. An air shaft is one great big loudspeaker. You see your neighbor's laundry. You hear the janitor's dogs. The man upstairs' aerial falls down and breaks your window. You smell coffee.... An air shaft has got every contrast.... You hear people praying, fighting, snoring.... I tried to put all that in my *Harlem Air Shaft*. (Shapiro & Hentoff 224–25)

While "literate" Western culture is a stereotype at a certain point, it is so because Western culture(s) have largely fetishized reading as a function solely of print and the sole mode of learning and subsequent "actionality," whether musical or not. Ellington's exegesis for "Harlem Air Shaft" points to a musical actionality that *reads* context for potential material. The resultant composition is an evocative interchange. The *text* Ellington reads in order to offer the listener his performed reading is an evocative prompt which conjures up the possibility of composition and performance, and the narrative Ellington offers as discussion of his compositional technique shows that the evocative prompt goes to the listener as well. We are supposed to experience the "great big loudspeaker" where "every contrast" is possible at once.

This expansive idea of musical composition and performance is the center around which contemporary hip hop constellates. Possibilities for simultaneous contrast are enhanced—if not revolutionized—by the art of digital sampling so prevalent in hip hop and yet so seldom elaborated within the hip hop texts themselves. Within the musical performance is the kernel of the theoretical conviction that "the great big loudspeaker," a multi-sensory extravaganza, can be actualized performatively.

In her essay "The Race for Theory," African American feminist critic Barbara Christian points out that

> people of color have always theorized—but in forms quite different from the Western form of abstract logic. And I am inclined to say that our theorizing (and I intentionally use the verb rather than the noun) is often in narrative forms, in the stories we create, in riddles and proverbs, in the play with language, since *dynamic rather than fixed ideas seem more to our liking*. (336; italics added)

The textual "theorizing" Christian discusses has virtually always been present in African American musical aesthetics, as John Miller Chernoff's exploration of African and African diasporic traditions through his experiences as a drumming student in Ghana make clear.

Chernoff says early in his *African Rhythms and African Sensibility* that "the variations from formal and familiar structures in an actual performance are what count most in distinguishing and appreciating artistic quality in a certain type of music" (30). While Chernoff apparently sees them as separable—*variation* as a process and *structure* as a quasi-static model—"formal and familiar structures" are, in the African American tradition, intimately related, de facto, to controlled and cultivated variation.

Using Ghanian drumming and other "folk traditions" (an admittedly dubious designation which suggests an age-old dichotomy between folklore and art) in the context of hip hop sampling has to take into account the question of musical technology and the contexts for exercising that technology historically in the U.S. Obviously, sound recordings are not and have not always been widely available. Perhaps the best history of the *technology* (my term) of early African American music is John Lovell, Jr.'s *Black Song: The Forge and the Flame—The Story of How the Afro-American Spiritual Was Hammered Out*, a book rarely mentioned in bibliographies of African American historical material.[1] Using *technology* as a rubric for discussing the spirituals may seem out of place, but the components of musical performance—whether instruments or not—are technological by virtue of their presence in the performance. In *Black Song*, Lovell notes the slave's "special attitude toward the Bible, his selectivity with respect toward its contents, and his special way of turning Biblical materials to imaginative purpose" (255). Although this "turning" is complex and never altogether clear, the power of the oral pedagogical tradition has its origins here. While Eugene D. Genovese points out that "the estimate by W.E.B. Du Bois that, despite prohibition and negative public opinion, about five percent of the slaves had learned to read by 1860 is entirely plausible *and may even be too low*" (563; italics added), widespread selective adaptation of Biblical material had to have occurred by way of listening, rather than reading. Lovell writes,

> The Biblical item is selected most often for ... symbolization of the deliverer or overcoming the oppressors; inspiration from notable accomplishments under impossible circumstances (the slave considered himself a potential accomplisher in a universe where he had little or no hope but great expectation); and exemplification of the workings of faith and power. (257)

Rather than the *literal* learning of the Biblical text, there was, Lovell observes, a "thin Bible" (262) spread throughout Southern plantations as the highest textual technology that afforded singing opportunity (masters were placated by religious texts being sung) and momentary empowerment. "Nearly all of the Biblical personages the slave poet dealt with," writes Lovell, "were involved in upheaval and revolution (Moses, Daniel, David, the Hebrew children, Samson, Elijah, Gideon, Jesus, Paul)" (228).

The dissemination of Biblical knowledge does not perplex historians of slavery or the spirituals, but the *functionality* (Sidran's "actionality") of Biblical material relied on another disseminative presence:

> How a group without newspapers or any mass media, and mostly without the ability to read or write, kept informed on ... the news of the day, inventions and discoveries, the approach of underground agents, the details about David Walker and Nat Turner, the ebb and flow of wars ... can hardly be explained. The incontrovertible fact is that all this happened by a regular system.... From this kind of communication, and the resultant close interrelationships, the songs acquired impetus, ideas for poetic development, and power for dissemination. (Lovell 121)

A "regular system" of dissemination made performative space available for the carefully cultivated Biblical references, paired up with potent ideological commentary. The spiritual text is as much a chronicle of slave culture, a "massive archiving," as it is a religious document. Here I intend the term *culture* as John Miller Chernoff has defined it: "A culture may perhaps best be considered ... a dynamic style with which people organize and orient themselves to act through various mediators" (36). The dynamic style of organization through "various mediators" is, for Chernoff, and here, overtly musical.

David Coplan makes the important observation that "ultimately it is not any systemic logic of music as organised sound but rather *the nature of metaphoric enactment* that prevents the analytic reduction of music performance to other levels of action" (123; italics added). While Coplan is concerned with the metaphoric bridges musical performance builds between performers and the society around them in South Africa, metaphoric enactment is important in the African American context as well. Coplan says,

> In musical performances, metaphors fuse several realms of experience into single, encapsulating images linked to the formation of personal identity.... The images of performance embody values and characteristics that people identify, at some level, with themselves. (123)

Lovell, for example, discusses the centrality of *motion* to the spirituals: "In his mind, the slave was constantly on the move, partly because of his desire for a new life and partly because of his fascination with moving vehicles" (247). From the use of "arks and chariots," obvious Biblical references, Lovell charts the metaphorical usage of the railroad train in the spirituals (which is replete in jazz traditions as well):

> Songs about trains are a minor miracle. The railroad train did not come into America until the late 1820s; it did not reach the slave country to any great extent until the 1830s and 1840s. Even then, the opportunities of the slave to examine trains closely were limited. Yet, before 1860, many spiritual poems exploited the train: its seductive sounds, speed and power, its recurring schedules, its ability to carry a large number of passengers at cheap rates, its implicit democracy. (249)

Performatively, the train's potency was tonal, ideational, and not altogether explainable as a literally *technological* presence; this is further indication of a "regular system" of dissemination. The technology ran from the machine implications into the implications of the notion of *mass* transit itself. Inevitably, the "seductive sounds, speed and power" found their way into a rhythmic matrix that virtually every chronicler of African American and African diasporic performative aesthetics discusses.

Besides being frequent in hip hop discourse, associations of the African American rhythmic matrix with labor are common when dealing with early music like the spirituals. This is not to say that singing was confined to the fields or the "yard," but Harold Courlander's comment about prison gang songs in the early twentieth century is germane here: "A song starting out as a description of the prisoners' work shifts into a narration of the Noah story. The thread that binds the two parts together is *the pounding of the hammers*" (99; italics added). The rhythm of labor is expropriated carefully. Lawrence Levine observes that "the work song ... allow[s] the workers to blend their physical movements and psychic needs with other workers" (215) and quotes Bruce Jackson to underscore an earlier, harsher evocative prompt: "'By incorporating the work with theirs, by, in effect, co-opting something they are forced to do anyway, they make it *theirs* in a way it otherwise is not'" (215). Prompting an actional method of taking possession, the work became *frame*work for song.

The expropriation of work rhythms as a method for taking possession of one's physical labor is situated at an aesthetic/economic crossroads that long antedates the recording of work songs. In *Singing the Master: The Evolution of African American Culture in the Plantation South*, Roger D. Abrahams explores how "constantly ... within each other's gaze" (37) slaves (unwillingly) and the white-planter class participated in the evolution of not only *African* American culture but American popular culture in general. Abrahams focuses attention on an end-of-harvest celebration at which slaves were called upon to shuck enormous amounts of corn:

> Corn ... was not a demanding crop, since it might be cut away at any time and left in the field. The corn needing shucking would accumulate until all the other crops had been harvested.... Thus, the communal shucking of the corn was not crisis work, but rather the final act in the harvesting of the grain which provided the basic food resource for slaves and domestic animals. (74–75)

That the institution of corn shucking, from the "white" side of the gaze, was a "display event" (23) can be explained by the fact that corn shucking was not "crisis work" and that, as Abrahams further notes, Southern planters tended to cling "to many of the more aristocratic features which had characterized the Cavalier perspective in England" (65), particularly "ever more theatrical opportunities by which their public postures of power might better be appreciated" (40).

Briefly, an overseer or master elected two "captains" who picked "teams" which raced against each other to finish shucking their assigned pile of the corn harvest first. With the recognition of "the most powerful voice" came the selection of a leader from the slave community "to stand on top of the corn pile and lead the singing" (325). Abrahams points out more generally about "slave life" and singing that

> few observers ... failed to notice the importance of call-and-response singing. All [accounts] focus on the sense of power produced by the *overlapping* of the leader's voice with the voices of the chorus as they engaged with each other antiphonally. (91; italics added)

It is the centrality of "overlapping" that echoes throughout the African American musical tradition. From the vocalized overlap to the individualized instrumental meandering of much jazz, a constant is Thompsonian (as in Robert Farris Thompson) "apart playing," in which "a central performer interacts in counterpoint or some other contrasting mode with the rest of the performing group."[2] Of equal importance in the work/play matrix Abrahams discusses is the *overlap* of English quasi-aristocratic display and the actional engagement of the display opportunity, which slave singers found well (enough)-suited for their own performances.

The corn-shucking event—complete with the festivities that followed the shucking labor—is an oft-ignored aesthetic event which, Abrahams notes,

> has received scant attention from historians. Doubtless this is because it represents such an apparent capitulation to the image of the happy slave purveyed by the planter-apologists for slavery. (21)

But Abrahams locates the corn-shucking event as a pivotal occasion for white onlookers to learn "slave style." The "slave" qualification here is vital, as recognition of an *African* style would counteract the white dominant practice of inculcating the slave into the person at every turn. From this onlooker learning comes the institutionalization of the white "vernacular artist," who appears variously throughout the nineteenth century, "on the minstrel stage, the lecturer's platform, or the written page" (145). Vernacular artistry, for white performers, was a function of "an ardent effort to bring to the stage *studied imitations* of slave styles of singing and dancing and celebrating" (133).

570 • ANDREW BARTLETT

What we find here is the central presence of *imitation* in an emergent Anglo-American popular culture. While the corn-shucking event sits at the economic and aesthetic crossroads, every opportunity afforded slaves at that crossroads is transformatively worked into a multi-level aesthetic performance which whites tried to duplicate *exactly*, even to the point of using specific "tales of random encounters" to give their nineteenth-century stage acts authenticity. Regarding blackface entertainment and white minstrelsy, Abrahams notes that

> the authenticity of the material itself became an important feature of presentation for these singers and dancers wearing blackface. . . . By the end of the nineteenth century such authenticating stories had become almost conventional, so often had the theme been embellished upon by the most successful writers of the time: Joel Chandler Harris, Lafcadio Hearn, Mark Twain, and George Washington Cable. (142)[3]

While Anglo-American popular culture became saturated with the problematics of authenticity and the establishment of a standard for "vernacular artistry," singularity again was fetishized. That is, a one-to-one, unmediated knowledge of slave life offered "an abundance of stylized ways of acting, singing, and dancing" (142) in American popular culture. White minstrelsy in blackface did not rest once the performance was authenticated; instead, it reinforced a singular expression of what Joel Williamson describes as an organic society in which African Americans were considered and treated as innately incapable of operating beyond a social sphere of servitude and, ironically, the aping of the master class.

In opposition to this is the multiplicity of performatively engaged, metaphorically enacted *texts* worked into the slaves' performances during corn-shucking events (and elsewhere). When we read William Cullen Bryant's reminiscence of a post-corn-shucking celebration in which the "commander," called on to speak after dinner, confesses "his incapacity for public speaking," and in turn asks "a huge black man named Toby to address the company in his stead," we see a non-musical but nonetheless performative actionality that draws on numerous discourses. Toby, Bryant writes,

> came forward, demanded a piece of paper to hold in his hand, and harangued the soldiery. It was evident that Toby had listened to stump-speeches in his day. He spoke of "de majority of Sous Carolina," "de interests of de state," "de honor of ole Ba'nwell district," and these phrases he connected by various expletives and sounds of which we could make nothing. (qtd. in Abrahams 225)

From the "piece of paper" Toby "demanded," to his "political" discourse, Bryant can see nothing *coherent*, perhaps because of the "various expletives," etc. In any case, Toby appears not to have tried exact replication of any *specific* stump speech; rather, he used the tone and the pose and the props. In other words, this metaphoric enactment makes Thomas Porcello's map of the digital sampler's functions, "the mimetic/reproductive, the manipulative[,] and the extractive" (69), begin to look like an ahistorical overview of African American aesthetics rather than a comment on postmodern technology. I would add to Porcello's analysis the constant element of simultaneity. Distinguishing between mimesis and the actional uses of that process—that is, manipulation and extraction of one's stylized signature—is difficult, if not impossible.

Following the corn-shucking competition, slaves and guests—those who *worked* and those who *watched*, respectively—were treated by the plantation master to a large feast at which the captain of the winning team would make a speech, and following the feast the slaves, again, would become the spectacle. With the setting up of a platform dance floor, the entertainment began. Wood below the slaves' feet kept up the "multimetrical effects" (93) that were, Abrahams suggests, a pervasive presence throughout the dancing and music making, from "patting" to the ring shout. While patting (clapping) "created a field of rhythm in which each performer respond[ed] to a basic beat," it did so in an asymmetrically harmonious fashion: "By doubling or tripling the time, breaking each beat into doublets or triplets, a performer produced a rolling effect that played against the master pulse without necessitating an actual change in the basic meter" (95).

Abrahams further locates the "apart playing" of the dances which white planters watched from the distance of the owner's gaze. With the dancer's hips as the "center of gravity," there was division and cohesion, paradoxically engaged at once: "Thus the flexibility and fluidity of black dancing arises from the division of the body at the pelvis, with the upper body playing against the lower much as individual dancers or singers playfully oppose themselves to the rest of the performing community" (98–99). This bodily intertextuality, under the gaze of the planter class, presented a much more communally fluid aesthetic, contrary to "European social dancing," in which "the body is maintained as a single unit of behavior" (98).[4] The overlapping is multi-directional, with the body functioning similarly to the grouped voices.

The body in hip hop is again foregrounded, with the solid thumping of the backbeat speaking directly to the flexibility necessary to negotiate what Tricia Rose calls "the complex web of institutional policing to which all rappers are subject" (276). The contestation over "public space" Rose discusses was initiated in the early eighties with break dancing and the renegotiation of urban space to include the bodily appropriation of prerecorded music. Subsequent escalation of musics tailored specifically for breaking widened hip hop's appeal, as did the appropriative use of recognizable pop fragments which "hooked" listeners. Rose argues that the very musical signifiers, both samples and raps, that evoke comparisons to animalism in white mainstream journalism carry "the power of Black collective memory," which initiates the automaticity of the body's appropriation of the digital sounds. These " ... cultural markers, and responses to them are," Rose asserts, "in a sense 'automatic' because they immediately conjure Black collective experience" (286). From the outlandish space costumes Sun Ra and his various Arkestras sported over the decades from the 1950s to the 1990s, to the space age rhetoric and massive stage shows of George Clinton's Parliament in the 1970s, to the current streamlined (and newly mass-marketed) hip hop style, the body has been vital as a locus within and around which theorizing performance occurs.

Commonly working in tandem with the "cultural markers" of sampling in hip hop is the thump of the sampled bass/rhythm line, that beat which signals the automaticity of the body's appropriation of digital sound. Repetition supplies a groove within which the rap can be executed and to which the audience can dance. Balanced against deep bass repetitions are the variations which other sampled material (and the rap) supplies. This complex sonic arrangement has an important analog in Chernoff's drumming experiences: "In essence, if rhythmic complexity is the African alternative to harmonic complexity, then the repetition of *responsive* rhythms is the African alternative to the development of a melodic line" (55).

It may be a tired story at this point,[5] but it is important to explicate briefly the re-emergence of a cross-roads aesthetics—where performance merges, balances, and elaborates rhythmic complexity and "the repetition of responsive rhythms" with renewed fluidity in what would become hip hop. Houston Baker quotes Jazzy Jay from a June 19, 1988, *Village Voice* article:

> "We'd find these beats, these heavy percussive beats, that would drive the hip hop people on the dance floor to breakdance. A lot of times it would be a two-second spot, a drum beat, a drum break, and we'd mix that back and forth, extend it, make it twenty minutes long." ("Hybridity" 199)

Baker's genealogy of hip hop ("the Rap Race," as he calls it) reaches back to DeeJay Kool Herc, a Jamaican national who came to New York in 1967 and brought with him the Jamaican dance hall/recording techniques of "dub" and "talk over," formative aesthetic techniques that have explosively invigorated popular culture in the United States.

In a 1991 essay on hip hop, Elizabeth Wheeler argues that "fragmentation and reassembly describe both black music and black history" (199). In light of this "fragmentation" Dick Hebdige's vague, early 1960s, "One day" reassembly-genealogy-scenario of dub and talk-over offers this portrait of then-producer King Tubby "working in his studio mixing a few 'specials' (i.e. exclusive recordings)":

> He began fading out the instrumental track, to make sure that the vocals sounded right. And he was excited by the effect produced when he brought the music back in. So ... he cut back and forth between the vocal and instrumental tracks and played with the bass and treble ... until he changed the original tapes into something else entirely. (83)

From the studio, with the knobs and controls close by, it is but a transference of technology to the live dance hall and eventually the New York "disco," where performative reassembly happens live. In a 1973 article "The Impact of Technology on Rhythm and Blues," April Reilly points out with some trepidation that

> authorities of the music industry have observed that modern music has become more and more "the creature of the control room and less the documentation of a musical event." As a result, we have for the first time in history the phenomenon of "a musical entity being created that has its first existence on tape." *The tape is, indeed, the performance.* (140)

Indeed Reilly's comment that, in the late '50s and early '60s, " ... the live-performance concert was the occasion that offered the audience the opportunity to appreciate the music, skills, and talents of the R&B artist" (140) specifies an historical era at the tail end of two decades which Ronald L. Morris points out had seen a 40 percent decline in "night club and dance hall dates" (192).[6] While Reilly says that the "live concert of yesteryear was a total theatrical experience, as distinguished from the primarily listening experience that it is today" (141), the work of King Tubby, et al. turned a static product into fluid process.

Rather than succumb to an industry specification for a product that would relegate live performances to promotional support for a recent release, DJs and performers picked up the variation-prompt. Houston Baker says,

> Why listen—the early hip hop DJs asked—to an entire commercial disc if the disc contained only twenty (or two) seconds of worthwhile sound? Why not work that sound by having two copies of the same disc on separate turntables, moving the sound on the two tables in DJ-orchestrated patterns, creating thereby a worthwhile sound? The result was an indefinitely extendable, varied, reflexively signifying hip hop sonics. ("Hybridity" 200)[7]

Greg Tate illustrates the transformation thus: "The advent of hip hop can be said to have contributed ... radical acts of counterinsurgency, turning a community of passive pop consumers into one of creative ... producers" (154).

Production, in the sense Tate uses the term, also refers literally to an economic process which has allowed numerous African American performing artists and aesthetic improvisationalists to earn a living, to work profitably, successfully, and critically, often by utilizing Porcello's "previously tabooed modes of citation" (82).

Working the turntables, Public Enemy's Chuck D insists, is not far removed from the lofty plateau of *musicianship*, from which sampling is often looked down upon as unoriginal:

... when Terminator X rocks the beat back and forth, it gives the music a real feel, almost like playing real drums.... You gotta understand that when the deejay cuts the record in and out, it's almost like a live drummer's kick.... Deejays like Jeff or X are able to play the turntables like somebody else might play the guitar.... If you strum a guitar or play the keys, the real creativity lies in your ability to make those strings or those keys do something original. (Dery, "Public Enemy" 85–86)

The turntable places the record at the center of the hip hop performance, turning the notion of musical virtuosity on its head by using prerecorded material not only as rhythm but also as melody and harmony. The questions of authorship, musicianship, "creativity," and "originality" are, thus, problematized. Like the purveyors of African American improvisational jazz, whether bebop or the so-called "new thing" of the 1960s and onward, hip hop artists have to negotiate the charge of being labeled musically unfit. They do so with the aid of the growing complexities of sampling.

It is this re-cognition of the multiform possibilities for records that makes hip hop, ultimately, what Houston Baker calls a "massive archiving" ("Hybridity" 200). The hip hop archive serves as a miniaturized repository for vast interactive historical material—interactive because all archival material is handled by the archivist, who listens carefully (with Du Boisian "second sight") for the beats and snippets which will accompany and be accompanied by vocalized narrative. The pro-active artistic process which utilizes and makes *functional* what is heard backdrops hip hop from start to finish.[8] Indeed, the fascination with sounds of myriad shapes, pitches, and durations that characterizes the Chicago avant-garde continuum (including Henry Threadgill, the Art Ensemble of Chicago, Anthony Braxton, et al.) ups the aesthetic ante considerably for African American musical aesthetics overall, serving to "archive" an immeasurable range of sonics.[9]

The "massive archiving" Baker alludes to is also the backdrop to the various military/robber metaphors rampant throughout hip hop criticism and commentary. Like Tricia Rose, who excellently explores "the exercise of institutional and ideological control over Hip Hop and the manner in which the Hip Hop community (e.g., fans and artists) relate and respond to this context" (277), my focus here is on popular depictions of sampling, mostly in music periodicals. Ethnomusicologist Louise Meintjes argues in a 1990 essay that Paul Simon's album *Graceland* "operates as a sign which is principally interpreted by means of the notion of collaboration" (37). Listeners, Meintjes continues, go through a series of "interpretive moves" which link "formal stylistic components" to the listener's "unique set of accumulated musical and social experiences," and the preponderance of "social experiences" (49) lead to judgments based on the *social* collaboration at hand as much as, if not more than, the musical collaboration.

Sampling in hip hop is not collaboration in any familiar sense of that term. It is a high-tech and highly selective archiving, bringing into dialogue by virtue of even the most slight representation—"a short horn blast, a James Brown scream, a kick or snare drum" (Kemp 20)—any range of "voices." The transformation enacted in hip hop's "radical acts of counterinsurgency" hinge on the recording, which turns, as Tate notes, the "community of passive pop consumers into one of creative ... producers" (154). This transformation addresses Rose's tripartite summary of her concerns with the politics of hip hop: "It is not just what one says, it is where one can say it, how others react to what one says, and whether one has the means with which to command public space" (276–77). De La Soul's Posdnuos says,

We don't exclude anything from playing a part in our music. I think it's crazy how a lot of rappers are just doing the same thing over and over—Parliament/Funkadelic/James Brown—and all that. I bought Steely Dan's *Aja* when it first came out, and "Peg" was a song

I always loved, so when it came down to making my own music, that was definitely a song I wanted to use.... It doesn't make any difference whether a sample is from James Brown, Cheech and Chong, Lee Dorsey, or a TV theme; if there's something that catches my ear, I'll use it. (Dery, "Tommy" 70)

High-tech selection allows this form of archiving/orchestration to act similarly, albeit in a different context of virtuosity, to the various jazz "archivings" often read and re-read by critics and historians. So we have the ever-pivotal bebop evoked by Q-Tip, on A Tribe Called Quest's *The Low End Theory*:

> Back in the days when I was a teenager
> before I had status and before I had a pager
> you could find the abstract by listenin' to hip hop.
> My pops used to say it reminded him of bebop.
> I said well Daddy don't you know that things go in cycles.

The mention of bebop is fitting, because the conscious and often referred to selectivity of pop tunes and chord structures which took flight in the 1940s and '50s does, indeed, look like hip hop—of course in proportion to the technology available. Indeed jazz lexicographer Robert S. Gold locates one of the earliest uses of the term *lick* in popular music criticism in a 1932 *Melody Maker* article: "They manage to steal a 'lick' from an American record" (188–89). References to African American musical aesthetics and their relationships to "American" products have consistently relied on theft to dismiss or explain these aesthetics.

Musicologist James Patrick's 1975 essay "Charlie Parker and Harmonic Sources of Bebop Composition: Thoughts on the Repertory of New Jazz in the 1940s" brought briefly to jazz discourse, "by analogy to text substitution in medieval music," the term *melodic contrafact* (3). The contrafact is an expropriated piece of another tune, brought in as the basis for the composition/performance at hand. It is not always localizable as its own entity, however:

> ... many contrafact compositions derive at least in part from solo improvisations on well-known tunes and the blues. In general there are two possibilities. The original solo line (or a close variant) may appear as part of a composition either in its original (or similar) harmonic context or in a completely different harmonic context. The original material may often be nothing more than a pet phrase which becomes formalized as an incipit of a contrafact composition. (7)[10]

The bebop use of contrafact harmonies cannot really be isolated except insofar as players of the era perfected their playing in small ensembles outside regular gigs but always within earshot of the emerging ubiquity of recognizable popular music.

Dizzy Gillespie points out that "when we borrowed from a standard we added and substituted so many chords that most people didn't know what song we really were playing" (Gillespie and Fraser, 209). Many players, though, put a more ideological spin on their doings. With the move "downtown" in the New York jazz crucible of the 1940s, players had to accommodate requests and the (white) desire to be entertained in a familiar fashion. Max Roach says,

> When we got downtown, people wanted to hear something they were familiar with, like "How High the Moon," "What Is This Thing Called Love?" Can you play that? So in playing these things, the black musicians recognized that the royalties were going back to these people, like ASCAP, the Jerome Kerns, the Gershwins. So one revolutionary thing that happened, they began to write parodies on the harmonic structures.... If I have to play it,

I will put my own particular melody on that progression.... If you made a record, you could say, "This is an original." (Gillespie and Fraser 209)

The statement *This is an original* points handily and dually to the issue of technological dissemination and the treatment generally afforded what became, by virtue of dissemination, communal knowledge.

Roach's enthusiasm for his appropriation of previously copyrighted music is, of course, shortsighted on the level of legal ownership. However, communal knowledge has perhaps always been the basis for selectivity and appropriative utility in African American aesthetics. Lawrence Levine quotes Newman White from his 1928 *American Negro Folksongs*:

> The notes of the songs in my whole collection, show nothing so clearly as the tendency of Negro folk-song to pick up material from any source and, by changing it or using it in all sorts of combinations, to make it definitely its own. (196)

I quote this passage not to equate bop or hip hop with White's version of "Negro folk-song," but rather to illustrate further and historicize the question of originality and ownership vis-à-vis communal knowledge.[11]

Communal knowledge in the 1990s initiates a discussion of issues like intellectual property rights. Currently, hip hop artists like EPMD credit those works they have digitally sampled in this fashion: "This recording *embodies* portions of the recording and composition 'The Message' by Grand Master Flash and the Furious Five; appears courtesy of Sugar Hill Records."[12] Embodiment and its physical implications intensify Newman White's confounded observations of performative appropriations of communal knowledge. While exactitude is mandatory contemporaneously, James Patrick, when faced with a specific Dizzy Gillespie solo figure reminiscent of Louis Armstrong, could assert that "it is ... likely that these phrases and thousands of others were simply 'in the air' and had become associated with familiar harmonic contexts" (10).

This "in the air" ubiquity of phrases and progressions is not simply an historical product of the phonograph or other technology, just as sampling is not simply an historical product of the digital technology now widely available. The propensity for selective expropriation, for the dually directed evocative prompt, gains more and more exposure as time goes on. This propensity in the African American musical text is akin to the blues singer whose power is in the "anonymous (nameless) voice issuing from the black (w)hole" which "comprises the 'already said' of Afro-America" (Baker, *Blues* 5, 206). Traces of the "original" are lost in translation, whether digitally sampled or instrumentally improvised. Technology serves and has served well the dissemination of important aesthetic elements. Levine points out that "Negroes living far apart could now share not only styles, but experiences, attitudes, folk wisdom, expressions, in a way ... simply not possible before the advent of the phonograph" (231). Contrary to April Reilly's fear of the rise of industrial technology in music production, Levine contends that " ... records can be seen as bearers and preservers of folk traditions" (231).[13]

The evolution of American popular culture happens with African American culture at its hub. The popularity of *authentic* entertainment in African American idioms would become highly prevalent in the early twentieth century.[14] What needs to be looked at and looked for in the future is the *theorizing* Barbara Christian discusses. From slavery days to emancipation to the early-to-mid twentieth century, the musico-social collaborations between African American aesthetics and available texts become variously more obvious and more oblique. With digital sampling, expropriated material is (often minutely and momentarily) recognizable, yet placed so that it often sounds radically anomalous, especially when the sampled material is overlapped or layered.

Porcello quotes a 1988 *Billboard* magazine article from which he draws on record producers who "have often claimed that rap records using [sampling] techniques are simply pioneering a new phase in popular music's already extensive history of recycling source material" (72). This recycling stands historically situated at an aesthetic/economic crossroads still of great importance today. Hip hop sampling has a disseminative function which tends to be ignored, especially if we refer to the sample as *recycling* and be done with it. Public Enemy's Chuck D. says,

> "Our music is filled with bites, bits of information from the real world, a world that's rarely exposed. Our songs are almost like headline news. We bring things to the table of discussion that are not usually discussed, or at least not from that perspective." (Dery, "Public Enemy" 93)

In no way do I want to *equate* any two aesthetic expressions, but historically such cultivations of discursive space have been constant and constantly a function of available resources. The contingencies of historical situations resist, I think, any dismissals which often attend associations with general pop culture.

Nearly 175 years ago these cultivations of discursive space were the central focus of a growing (white) authenticating impulse that spawned an *imitative* popular culture. African American musical aesthetics are historically little concerned with the exactitude of *imitation*. The "massive archiving" Houston Baker insists on is centrally present as a highly selective aesthetic/economic/historical catalog. Regarding his drumming in Ghana John Miller Chernoff says,

> In more than one sense, music carries the mark of tradition to an occasion, and at a rudimentary level it thus signifies the traditional solidarity of a community; but aesthetically, the music involves people with their community in a more dynamic way, thus recreating the tradition, and ... the nature of this involvement is the key to understanding the integrative power of the music. (125)

So the massive archiving stands to signify and theorize communality. With sampling technology, this solidarity may be the aim, but issues of authenticity, ownership, and property seem part and parcel of high-tech aesthetic exercises. And as the disjuncture seen by some in hip hop sampling indicates to them the fragmentation of post-modernity, there is a simultaneous inability to see the *act's* vibrant connectedness in historical relation to African American aesthetics.

Study Questions

1. How does hip-hop embody and extend African-American rhythmic tendencies?
2. In what ways is the concept of the musical archive relevant to hip-hop?
3. How are hip-hop's technologies of production rendered audible in rap music?

Notes

1. Ishmael Reed makes this observation in a review of Harold Courlander's *Treasury of Afro-American Folklore* (152). In my own work, I rarely see any mention of Lovell's *Black Song*.

2. Abrahams (91–92) alludes to Robert Farris Thompson's term *apart playing*, first coined in 1966.

3. Note especially that Abrahams uses *success* here rather than a valuative term like *best*, or even *noted*, to describe these writers. *Success* obviously means monetary support, and this points further to the institution of the black body/encounter as an authenticating force in whose presence either redemption or profit occurs.

4. Zora Neale Hurston points out that adornment, asymmetry, and angularity are key polyphonic features of African American art and that African American dance not only incorporates these elements but acts as a "realistic suggestion" in light of the fact that "no art can ever express all the variations conceivable" (56).

5. Several good histories of hip hop and rap exist, the best of which, *Rap Attack*, is authored by David Toop and comes in two volumes. The examples that follow are more useful for their hemeneutics than is Toop's study—thus its absence.

6. Morris quotes a *Time* magazine story on the American Federation of Musicians from May 7, 1956, that used 1930 as a "base year" with "99,000 live dates open to musicians. . . . by 1954 only 59,000 night club and dance hall dates were available, a decline of 40% in two decades" (192).

7. The importance here of a "reflexively signifying" aesthetic is at the heart of hip hop and its aesthetic continuum. Baker's juxtaposition of this concept with the phrase indefinitely extendable needs clarification, perhaps, precisely because the "commercial disc" relies so much on indefinito extendability as a marketing device.

8. As an indication of the "massiveness" of the hip hop archive, Mark Dery says Public Enemy DJ/producer Hank Shocklee estimates his record collection at "nearly 19,000 records" ("Hank" 83).

9. For more on this, see Lock, Radano, and Wilmer.

10. The presence of "pet phrases" is central to the modes of collaboration, both social and musical, present throughout jazz history. Leonard and, later, Ogren discuss these interactions and collaborations in jazz's formative years, with soloists who would themselves become icons for later generations of players.

11. Royalties and credits have always ridden alongside the controversies over the explicitness of rap, but in a more muted "high legal" discourse which seeks to curtail hip hop artists' use of the sampler.

12. Liner notes to EPMD's "Nobody's Safe Chump," *Business Never Personal*.

13. For more on expropriation in jazz, see Gabbard.

14. See Ogren for further discussion here, especially of the growing nostalgia evident in club settings (The Plantation Club, Club Alabam, etc.).

Works Cited

Abrahams, Roger D. *Singing the Master: The Evolution of African American Culture in the Plantation South.* New York: Pantheon, 1992.

Baker, Houston A. Jr. *Blues, Ideology, and Afro-American Literature: A Vernacular Theory.* Chicago: U of Chicago P, 1987.

———. "Hybridity, the Rap Race, and Pedagogy for the 1990s." *Technoculture.* Ed. Constance Penley and Andrew Ross. Minneapolis: U of Minnesota P, 1991. 197–209.

Chernoff, John Miller. *African Rhythm and African Sensibility: Aesthetics and Social Action in African Musical Idioms.* Chicago: U of Chicago P, 1979.

Christian, Barbara. "The Race for Theory." *Making Face, Making Soul (Haciendo Caras): Creative and Critical Writings by Feminists of Color.* Ed. Gloria Anzaldua. San Francisco: Aunt Lute, 1990. 335–45.

Coplan, David. "The Urbanization of African Music." *Popular Music 2: Theory and Method.* Cambridge: Cambridge UP, 1982. 113–29.

Costello, Mark, and David Foster Wallace. *Signifying Rappers: Rap and Race in the Urban Present.* New York: Ecco, 1990.

Courlander, Harold. *Negro Folk Music U.S.A.* New York: Columbia UP, 1963.

Dery, Mark. "Hank Shocklee: Bomb Squad Declares War on Music." *Keyboard* Sept. 1990. 82–96.

———. "Public Enemy: Confrontation." *Keyboard* Sept. 1990. 81–96.

———. "Tommy Boy X 3: Digital Underground, Coldcut, and De La Soul Jam the Beat with Audio Junkyard Collisions." *Keyboard* Mar. 1991. 64–78.

Du Bois, W. E. B. *The Souls of Black Folk.* 1903. New York: Penguin, 1989.

Ellington, Duke. *Music Is My Mistress.* New York: Doubleday, 1973.

Gabbard, Krin. "The Quoter and His Culture." *Jazz in Mind: Essays on the History and Meanings of Jazz.* Ed. R. T. Buckner and Steven Weiland. Detroit: Wayne State UP, 1991, 92–111.

Genovese, Eugene D. *Roll, Jordan, Roll: The World the Slaves Made.* New York: Pantheon, 1974.

Gillespie, Dizzy, and Al Fraser. *To BE, or not to . . . BOP.* New York: Doubleday, 1979.

Gold, Robert S. *A Jazz Lexicon.* New York: Knopf, 1964.

Hebdige, Dick. *Cut 'N' Mix: Culture, Identity, and Caribbean Music.* London: Comedia, 1987.

Hurston, Zora Neale. "Characteristics of Negro Expression." 1935. *The Sanctified Church.* Berkeley: Turtle Island, 1983. 49–68.

Kemp, Mark. "Issue by Issue: The Death of Sampling." *Option Magazine* Mar.–Apr. 1992. 20.

Leonard, Neil. *Jazz and the White Americans.* Chicago: U of Chicago P, 1962.

Levine, Lawrence. *Black Culture and Black Consciousness: Afro-American Folk Thought from Slavery to Freedom.* Oxford: Oxford UP, 1977.

Lock, Graham. Forces in Motion: Anthony Braxton and the Meta-Reality of Creative Music, Interviews and Tour Notes, England 1985. London: Quartet, 1988.

Lovell, John, Jr. *Black Song: The Forge and the Flame—The Story of How the Afro-American Spiritual Was Hammered Out.* 1972. New York: Paragon House, 1986.

Meintjes, Louise. "Paul Simon's Graceland and the Mediation of Musical Meaning." *Ethnomusicology* 34.1 (1990): 37–73.

Morris, Ronald L. *Wait Until Dark: Jazz and the Underworld, 1880–1940.* Bowling Green: Bowling Green U Popular P, 1980.

Ogren, Kathy J. *The Jazz Revolution: Twenties America and the Meaning of Jazz.* New York: Oxford UP, 1989.

Patrick, James. "Charlie Parker and Harmonic Sources of Bebop Composition: Thoughts on the Repertory of New Jazz in the 1940s." *Journal of Jazz Studies* 2.2 (1975): 3–23.

Porcello, Thomas. "The Ethics of Digital Audio Sampling: Engineers' Discourse." *Popular Music* 10.1 (1991): 69–84.

Radano, Ronald. *New Musical Figurations: Anthony Braxton's Cultural Critique.* Chicago: U of Chicago P, 1993.

Reed, Ishmael. *Shrovetide in Old New Orleans.* 1978. New York: Avon, 1979.

Reilly, April. "The Impact of Technology on Rhythm and Blues." *Black Perspective in Music* 1.2 (Fall 1973): 136–46.

Rose, Tricia. "'Fear of a Black Planet': Rap Music and Black Cultural Politics in the 1990s." *Journal of Negro Education* 60.3 (1991): 276–90.

Shapiro, Nat, and Nat Hentoff. *Hear Me Talkin' to Ya: The Story of Jazz as Told by the Men Who Made It.* 1955. New York: Dover, 1966.

Sidran, Ben. *Black Talk: How the Music of Black America Created a Radical Alternative to the Values of Western Literary Tradition.* 1971. New York: Da Capo, 1981.

Tate, Greg. *Flyboy in the Buttermilk: Essays on Contemporary Music.* New York: Simon, 1992.

Thompson, Robert Farris. "An Aesthetic of the Cool: West African Dance." *African Forum* 2.2 (1966): 85–102.

Toop, David. *Rap Attack: African Jive to New York Hip Hop.* Boston: South End P, 1984.

———. *Rap Attack, Number 2: African Rap to Global Hip Hop.* London: Serpent's Tail, 1992.

Wheeler, Elizabeth. "'Most of My Heroes Don't Appear on No Stamps': The Dialogics of Rap." *Black Music Research Journal* 11.2 (1991): 193–216.

Williamson, Joel. "The Genesis of the Organic Society." *The Crucible of Race: Black-White Relations in the American South since Emancipation.* New York: Oxford UP, 1984. 11–43.

Wilmer, Valerie. *As Serious As Your Life: The Story of the New Jazz.* London: Allison & Busby, 1977.

Discography

EPMD. *Business Never Personal.* Chaos/Sony, 1992.

A Tribe Called Quest. "Excursions." *The Low End Theory.* Zomba, 1418-2-J, 1991.

37

Hip-Hop

From Live Performance to Mediated Narrative

Greg Dimitriadis identifies a process of transformation, suggesting that with the gradual changes in hip-hop culture and rap music production there have been both gains and losses. He describes the shifting aesthetic properties of rap in the mid-1980s as new forms of production and reception emerged that attenuated the primacy of live hip-hop, placing primary significance on recorded rap and its musical and lyrical forms of expression. Yet in this phase a new narrative style also emerged, bringing with it more elaborate forms of expression.

Dimitriadis assesses the impact of the emergent emphasis on "verbal discourse" in rap and the concurrent positioning of hip-hop within the mass media flows of national and global dissemination as well as locating it more directly within a commercial logic of production. As he explains, these shifts have generally constrained hip-hop's live component and limited audience congregation in public performance contexts.

Hip-Hop: From Live Performance to Mediated Narrative

Greg Dimitriadis

Hip hop culture originated during the mid-1970s as an integrated series of live community-based practices.[1] It remained a function of live practice and congregation for a number of years, exclusive to those who gathered together along NYC blocks, in parks, and in select clubs such as the now famous Harlem World or T-Connection. Early MCs (or "rappers") and DJs, graffiti artists and breakdancers, forged a "scene" entirely dependent upon face-to-face social contact and interaction. Indeed, the event itself, as an amalgam of dance, dress, art and music, was intrinsic to hip hop culture during these years. As one might expect, the art's earliest years went largely unrecorded and undocumented. However, in 1979, Sugarhill Records, a small label in New Jersey, released a single entitled "Rapper's Delight." It was an unexpected event for many of hip hop's original proponents, those pioneers immersed in the art's early live scene. Grandmaster Flash comments:

> I was approached in '77. A gentleman walked up to me and said, "We can put what you're doing on record." I would have to admit that I was blind. I didn't think that somebody else would want to hear a record re-recorded onto another record with talking on it. I didn't think it would reach the masses like that. I didn't see it. I knew of all the crews that had any sort of juice and power, or that was drawing crowds. So here it is two years later, and I hear "To the hip-hop, to the bang to the boogie," and it's not Bam, Herc, Breakout, AJ. Who is this? (quoted in George 1993, p. 49)

Many of those who were a part of early hip hop were also puzzled and asked similar questions. This all-but-unknown group, The Sugarhill Gang, was not a part of the early hip hop scene in any real sense, as Grandmaster Flash makes clear. "Rapper's Delight" clearly ruptured the art form's sense of continuity as a live practice known to all its "in group" members. This rupture was a defining one for hip hop as it marked the art's entrance into the public sphere of worldwide cultural discourse, where it has remained ever since. The decentralized face-to-face social dynamic which marked early hip hop has thus given way to a different dynamic, one mediated by way of commodity forms such as vinyl, video and CD. These configurations have separated hip hop's vocal discourse (i.e., "rap") from its early contexts of communal production, encouraging closed narrative forms over flexible word-play and promoting individualized listening over community dance. This shift towards in-studio production has affected the art in a number of crucial ways, most especially by redefining hip hop culture by and through the relatively more narrow and more easily appropriated idiom of "rap music."

Hip hop emerged from the experiences and practices of economically disadvantaged Afro-American, Latin, and Afro-Caribbean youths. These youths—early hip hop practitioners and participants—formed a culture distinct from that of the dominant order. This culture was marked by a whole series of integrated practices, including dance, music and visual art. It is important to note that this aesthetic integration was nurtured by the availability of spaces for face-to-face interaction and communication. The availability of such autonomous space is crucial for "marginalized" groups, a point Katrina Hazzard-Gordon makes well throughout her book *Jookin': The Rise of Social Dance Formations in African-American Culture* (1990).

In her study, Gordon explores how community dance and social interaction have been linked to the availability of different kinds of "dance arenas," including "jooks, honky-tonks, and after-hours joints" (Hazzard-Gordon 1990, p. 76). Gordon defines "dance arena" as "any institution of social interaction in African-American life in which secular social dancing plays an integral part" (1990, p. ix). Such spaces, she notes, have allowed "esthetic and technical commonalities" to be retained throughout the histories of African and African-American dance (1990, p. 18). These commonalities are, of course, not biologically determined, but rather are the product of body-to-body socialization processes made possible through the availability of dance spaces.

The particular form of dancing most associated with hip hop's formative years is "break-dancing." This art's seminal role in hip hop's history is noted by early dancer Crazy Legs: "See, the whole thing when hip-hop first started was the music was played in the parks and in the jams for the dancers, and those dancers were B-Boys" (quoted in Fernando, Jr. 1994, p. 17). Pioneering DJ Afrika Bambaataa elaborates upon the role of dance in hip hop's origins, pointing out that his influential Zulu Nation began as a breakdance crew:

> When I seen that hip-hop started rising with myself and Kool Herc, I decided to switch the Organization [a Zulu Nation prototype], after a two-year run, into the Zulu Nation. Then, once the Zulu Nation came out, it was basically just a break-dance crew—the Zulu Kings and Queens and later the Shaka Kings and Shaka Queens. And then as it progressed, years after, it became more than that. (quoted in Fernando, 1994, p. 7)

The connection between dance and music is intrinsic to understanding African and African-inspired musics. Music is not a reified discourse in these cultures, an attitude brought by Africans to the Americas, where maintaining flexible contexts for social interaction became a method for survival. Chris Small writes, "Music itself . . . hardly exists as a separate art from dance, and in many African languages there is no separate word for it, although there are rich vocabularies for forms, styles and techniques" (1987, p. 24).

The role of dance in hip hop history, however, is often understated or ignored, especially by critics with logocentric biases. The constant search for meaning through rap's vocal content alone has led to much cross-cultural misunderstanding, especially concerning the role of social dance. The link between protest lyrics and social resistance, for example, is often assumed, while the body itself is often ignored or dismissed. However, as Susan McClary notes:

> The musical power of the disenfranchised—whether youth, the underclass, ethnic minorities, women or gay people—more often resides in their ability to articulate different ways of construing the body, ways that bring along in their wake the potential for different experiential worlds. (1994, p. 34)

New ways of being in the world, "new forms of subjectivity" (Foucault 1982, p. 216) if you will, can thus be located and nurtured in and through the body itself, a point Stuart Hall echoes in his article "What Is This 'Black' in Black Popular Culture?" (Hall 1992, p. 27).

By engaging in a myriad of experiential and representational practices, the body can connect with "experiential worlds" different from those articulated by dominant orders. Community dance is pivotal here as it allows the self to experience these "new forms of subjectivity," while placing the self within a group context. Individuals exploring different ways of being in collective contexts is the prelude and precursor to all important social or political action. Hip hop club activity in the late 1970s thus offered sites of resistance as potent as the social realism or protest discourses of the late 1980s and early 1990s. However, most critics still fetishize these discourses alone and ignore the ways in which community space has been contested and bodies have been constrained, controlled, and liberated.

The integration of dance with music is, again, crucial to understanding African and African-inspired musics, such as blues or jazz. Unlike composed "classical" European forms (arts which are represented by some sort of written score), such musics are brought to life through live production and concurrent improvisation. Such arts often reflect a more flexible lyrical or musical aesthetic than do Western arts such as classical European music. Peter Manuel notes this distinction in his *Popular Musics of the Non-Western World*:

> Since the Renaissance on, there has been a strong tendency for Western musical pieces to be sectionally structured, goal-oriented, discrete units with a clear sense of dramatic climax and closure; genres as diverse as sonatas, pop ballads, Tin Pan Alley tunes, and Beatles songs all exhibit this "song" format. Such an organized format contrasts with open-ended, expandable or compressible approaches used in narrative epics, *juju* music, *ch'in* variations, and, indeed, most musical genres outside of Western bourgeois traditions, which often operate more through repetition and variation of short motifs. (1988, p. 23)

Many Western musics rely, in short, on closed narrative, while "most musical genres outside of Western bourgeois traditions" do not. For example, Afro-American blues, when performed live, is a flexible art form, one which relies on a fluid interchange between floating verses, rhymed couplets, and other vocal tools. The performers need to maintain a kind of flexibility as they engage different kinds of crowds in different kinds of social settings. Christopher Small notes:

> The verses sung by the blues performer consist of a succession of rhyming couplets, with the first line repeated, making three lines to a stanza. Each of these stanzas stands independently, not as part of a narrative sequence as in a ballad; indeed, it is rare for a blues performance to tell a story.... The form in which the blues performance is cast relates to the orality and the improvised nature of the art; the repeated first line can give the singer time to think of a punch-line, while the absence of narrative thread gives a freedom to the improvising artist, allowing him or her not only to insert lines and even whole stanzas from any number of sources but also to shape the performance, in the time-honoured African and Afro-American way, as the social situation develops between singer and listeners. (1987, pp. 199–200)

The absence of a strict narrative thus allows for a kind of spontaneity appropriate to live production and performance. Neither performers nor audiences are aware of any particular story's outcome, allowing for an open-ended and engaging social experience. Small notes further:

> The musician regards himself as responsible, not just for the sounds that he makes, but for the whole social progress of the event, for its success as a human encounter. The musician

as he improvises responds not only to the inner necessities of the sound world he is creating but also to the dynamics of the human situation as it develops around him. It is his task to create not just a single set of sound perspectives which are to be contemplated and enjoyed by listeners, but a multiplicity of opportunities for participation along a number of different perspectives. (1987, p. 295)

By creating a text open to different interpretations or perspectives, performers allow for various points of intersection between themselves and the audience.

By contrast, post-Renaissance classical musics have come to claim a kind of autonomy from social contexts, allowing more room for single-perspective narrative or narrative progression *per se*. Composer Aaron Copeland betrays how intrinsic narrative is to the ideals of Western music-making in his bestselling book, *What to Listen for in Music*:

It is insufficient merely to hear music in terms of the separate moments at which it exists. You must be able to relate what you hear at any given moment to what has just happened before and what is about to come afterward. In other words, music is an art that exists in point of time. In that sense it is like a novel, except that the events of a novel are easier to keep in mind, partly because real happenings are narrated and partly because one can turn back and refresh one's memory of them. (1988, p. 6)

Copeland's metaphor for the extended composition as a novel is both apt and telling. The novel, like the composed classical European piece, demands attention to a larger continually unfolding structure. This larger structure often demands "delayed gratification" as an ideal of music appreciation.[2] One listens with an ear towards what has happened and what will happen. Physical engagement is, accordingly, downplayed in favor of polite listening.

Composed pieces, in broad contrast to dance musics, have a kind of autonomy across time and space. They can be worked with and thought about in a context entirely separate from their point of production. The written or sound recording introduces and eventually facilitates this autonomy from socially specific contexts, reducing musical experiences or performances to "music-object[s]," thus placing the entirety of the piece at the fingertips of the listener and potential composer (Small 1987, p. 43). Such composers are less apt to privilege "repetition and variation of short motifs" and more apt to take a linear approach to their art, constructing pieces which place phrases in narrative order, implying beginnings, middles, and ends, suggesting progression. The recording thus allows for a manipulation (often a splitting up and ordering) of sound bytes, in a manner similar to the way movable type allows for a manipulation of language. Both technologies encourage the construction of longer narrative paradigms separate from their immediate contexts of production (e.g., dance spaces).

These contexts of production often embrace much more than music itself. Early hip hop, again, was comprised of a number of interlocking and integrated practices, including graffiti writing and (as noted) breakdancing, arts which reflected hip hop's rough and abrupt "cut and mix" aesthetic in visual art and physical movement, respectively (Hebdige 1987, pp. 136–48). Tricia Rose notes hip hop's "cross-fertilization" of practices in her book *Black Noise*:

Stylistic continuities were sustained by internal cross-fertilization between rapping, break-dancing, and graffiti writing. Some graffiti writers, such as black American Phase 2, Haitian Jean-Michel Basquiat, Futura, and black American Fab Five Freddy produced rap records. Other writers drew murals that celebrated favorite rap songs (e.g., Futura's mural "The Breaks" was a whole car mural that paid homage to Kurtis Blow's rap of the same name). Breakdancers, DJs, and rappers wore graffiti-painted jackets and tee-shirts. DJ Kool Herc was a graffiti writer and dancer first before he began playing records. Hip hop events featured breakdancers, rappers, and DJs as triple-bill entertainment. Graffiti writers drew murals for DJ's stage platforms and designed posters and flyers to advertise hip hop events. (Rose 1994, p. 35)

This hip hop aesthetic, broadly speaking, allows for sharp and abrupt discontinuities or "cuts" as it encourages continuity by way of the all-important "mix." Breakdancing, one case in point, relies on a sharp "segmentation and delineation of various body parts" as arms and legs are manipulated to juxtapose the smooth and the circular with the abrupt and the linear. Part of the art's visual appeal lies in its ability to engage—and resolve—such apparent dichotomies. The sharp fragmentation of individual body parts gives the art a feeling of indeterminacy, evoking a postmodern aesthetic. However, fluid execution gives the dance an overriding sense of cohesion, a feeling of "asymmetry as balance" (Hazzard-Gordon 1990, p. 18). Hip hop's instrumentals resolve many of these same dichotomies as the DJ juxtaposes a steady and continuous beat with rough and abrupt "breaks" between turntables. This "cut and mix" duality is crucial for understanding why hip hop has had such a lasting appeal for so many for so long. Hip hop engages the postmodern present in its stress on the discontinuous and the contingent while it nurtures a community building musical tradition rooted in the oral.

The earliest books on the subject of hip hop did not see fit to separate hip hop's musical discourse from dance and aerosol art. Steven Hager's *Hip Hop: The Illustrated History of Break Dancing, Rap Music, and Graffiti* (1984) illustrates this cohesion of practice in its very title. Yet, Tricia Rose notes "Unlike breakdancing and graffiti, rap music had and continues to have a much more expansive institutional context within which to operate. Music is more easily commodified than graffiti, and music can be consumed away from the performance context" (Rose 1994, p. 58). Because music is most easily "consumed away from the performance context," it has emerged as hip hop's most visible signifier. The majority of peoples now exposed to rap (including most artists) are receiving this exposure by way of an "institutional context" which has only commodified hip hop's musical discourse. Note that the full title of Tricia Rose's 1994 book on hip hop is *Black Noise: Rap Music and Black Culture in Contemporary America*. Her title places "rap music" at the forefront, while Hagar's work (written a decade before Rose's) highlights "hip hop" and "breakdancing."

Hip hop's musical discourse was at one point integrated in the context of live social interaction and dance. This integration accounts for early hip hop's unorchestrated sound (relative to later endeavours). Early rappers, for example, often had a number of floating chants such as "shock the house" or "throw your hands in the air"—chants which framed freestyle rhymed couplets, calls to members of the audience, or short non-semantic vocable routines. Rhymed tales or stories were a part of the music, but such stories were usually not related to some longer thematic song-structure. "Rapper's Delight," for example, was just that— 14-plus minutes of sprawling enjoyment rather than a coherent narrative with a beginning, a middle and an end. The following is a brief excerpt from the 1979 release:

> I got a little face and a pair of brown eyes
> All I'm here to do, ladies, is hypnotize
> Singin' on 'n on on 'n on
> The beat don't stop until the break of dawn
> And singin' on 'n on on 'n on
> Like a hot butter pop the pop the pop
> Di bi di bi, pop the pop pop you don't dare stop
> Come alive y'all, and give me what you got

Note the use of rhymed couplets ("I got a little face and a pair of brown eyes / All I'm here to do, ladies, is hypnotize"), artist-audience chants ("Come alive y' all, and give me what you got"), and vocable routines ("Di bi di bi, pop the pop pop you don't dare stop"). Clearly, like much early rap, "Rapper's Delight" is in the rich and varied Afro-American rhetorical tradition, a tradition explored and explicated by critics such as Roger Abrahams and Henry Louis Gates, Jr.

Many early "crews" or groups, like The Sugarhill Gang, had three or more members. Most often these groups were loosely structured, members delivering and trading verses, rhymes and chants in a flexible and non-thematic manner. The Treacherous Three, The Cold Crush Brothers, The Fantastic Five, and The Furious Five (Grandmaster Flash's crew) are all key examples of such early collectives. These artists, again, did not have a strictly orchestrated or linearly composed approach to the art. Engaging crowds—both individually and as a group— was more important than delivering clearly composed narrative "messages."

A 1979 performance (captured on tape) featuring Grandmaster Flash and the Furious Five at T-Connection clearly evinces this flexible approach to live performance. The Furious Five trade boasts, brags and chants throughout the night, as members enter and exit the verbal flow often and seemingly at will. There is absolutely no evidence of a clearly organized and delineated song structure here. Rather, loose boasts and brags (about themselves, each other, and Grandmaster Flash) and loose chants (such as "wanna hit the top" and "to the beat y' all") are most important. These boasts and chants are often repeated with slight variations, further evincing the absence of a narrative song-structure. Indeed, "repetition and variation of short motifs" is of primary import, both in The Furious Five's vocals and in Flash's instrumental track (Manuel 1988, p. 23). As Peter Manuel notes, such patterns mark musics outside of the dominant Western tradition, musics that often depend on small-scale interaction between artists and audiences.

Grandmaster Flash's opening quote gives voice to the more context-specific nature of the early live performance. Flash speaks of knowing all the "crews" at the time, all those drawing crowds. Hip hop, once again, was dependent upon face-to-face interaction and small-scale mediation during the late 1970s. The event itself was more important than any particular separable discourse to its earliest devotees. Flash's question—who would want to hear a record of a record with someone talking over it?—attests to this sense of aesthetic integration. Hip hop, as a concrete experience all about the particulars of a complex multi-tiered social event, is privileged here (however implicitly) for Flash. Early hip hop reflected this sense of live practice in its sound, in its spacious dance grooves, in its stress on the particularities of time and place, in its flexible word play. It took time for more accessible choruses, themes, and longer narratives to be introduced as a vital part of the art.

Run-DMC was the first group to work successfully with the recorded medium and its temporal and sonic constraints. The group made the most out of the three- to four-minute song structure, composing pieces such as the popular 1983 single "It's Like That." This single, like many that would follow, employs the traditional popular song structure, including the use of a chorus ("It's like that and that's the way it is") and theme (the trials of poverty). In addition, collective delivery—often used as a loose, non-thematic framing devise by early collectives such as the Cold Crush Brothers—is employed here in an organized and thematic manner. Run-DMC exposed rap to much wider audiences, ultimately bringing it into the mainstream of American popular culture. Yet, it should be noted that the media form which Run-DMC consolidated and commodified was the easily duplicatable aural form. And along with opening up this medium they effectively diminished the importance of two other dimensions of hip hop culture born along with rap music—graffiti and breakdancing.

The emergence of rap music in commodity form resulted, thus, in a very basic redefinition of hip hop culture. A key example of how language-use shifted to prioritize rap music over and above integrated communal participation will prove helpful here. Run-DMC gave wide currency to the term "b-boy" during the mid-1980s, employing it freely in songs such as "Sucker M.C.'s." Lines such as "cold chill at a party in a b-boy stance," for example, imply the laid back street-corner aesthetic which would become the group's trademark. However, the term meant more than stance and attitude early on. In a rather symbolic and telling moment, Mr. Wiggles, a member of the early breakdance crew the Rock Steady Crew, comments on seeing Run-DMC live in concert:

> The first rappers to get on a mike and call themselves B-boys, who did know how to B-boy, was Run-DMC. And that group did impress 'em. Everybody thought *this* was a B-boy: anybody who posed like that like with an attitude. So when I went to see my first Run-DMC jam, I was saying these brothers are gonna get on the mike and they gonna break, because they call themselves B-boys. I got there; they didn't B-boy. I was upset, so I said what the phukk is this? That was the first time I ever seen a rapper call himself a B-boy just 'cause he could jam. (quoted in Allah 1993, p. 55)

Thus, what it means to be a part of the culture shifted at this time, as attention focused on hip hop's vocal discourse alone. In group face-to-face interaction in a live setting took a back seat to a more codified notion of the art. Performers had only to "jam" now, giving consummate priority to the recorded or aural medium of transmission. Many Old School pioneers, those immersed in the art's early live scene, those *not* as accustomed to the confines of vinyl, were, as a result, made obsolete. Bill Adler notes:

> Few debuts in the history of rock have been as momentous as the assassination attempt called "It's Like That"/"Sucker M.C.'s." With this one record, Run-D.M.C. not only laid the foundation for the next five years of rap, they incidentally created what is now referred to as the Old School. Rappers who'd recorded before Run—as had such notable acts as Grandmaster Flash & The Furious Five, The Fearless Four, The Treacherous Three, The Cold Crush Brothers, and The Sugarhill Gang—were suddenly Old School. (1991, p. 5)

Attention thus shifted to rap's verbal discourse during these years, decreasing the importance of dance, live congregation, and those who could create a live scene. This shift allowed, however, a number of very creative and talented vocalists to emerge for a brief and thrilling period. An amazing group of singles and albums by artists such as Eric B. & Rakim, Big Daddy Kane, Boogie Down Productions (KRS-One), and Kool G Rap & D.J. Polo were released during the mid-to-late 1980s, making these years a "golden era" in rap for many. Rap music, as a self-conscious art form, flowered with these performers turned poets.

Rakim, for example, takes rap lyric to a new level on tracks such as "Follow the Leader," released in 1988. No longer are boasts and brags dependent upon face-to-face interaction and communication. Rakim claims a more consummate control over his listeners, employing "rhyme displays that engrave deep as X-rays." Rakim blurs the line between his words and their invisible and all-penetrating means of transmission here as throughout the single. The power to communicate, always intrinsic to orality, is thus intensified by an acknowledgement of the mass-disseminated media forms now so much a part of rap. "Follow the Leader," like other singles by Eric B. & Rakim, including "In the Ghetto" (1990) and "Let the Rhythm Hit 'Em" (1990), are among the most fondly remembered by many hip hop aficionados today.

However, the widening reach of rap music offered more than aesthetic possibilities. A kind of black nationalist identity politics became apparent in rap during the late 1980s as its community stretched irretrievably beyond local boundaries. A brief example of how the recorded medium engendered black nation building within the idiom will prove illuminating.

Public Enemy released a song in 1987 entitled "Raise the Roof" off of the album *Yo! Bum Rush the Show*. An aggressive boasting and bragging track, it contains the line, "It takes a nation of millions to hold me back." There are very definite political overtones here and throughout the track, as chaotic abandonment bordering on the riotous is evoked (reminiscent, perhaps, of Martha and the Vandella's "Dancing in the Street"). Yet, at best, the language here is coded, not explicit. The first-person "I" abounds throughout, reflecting the loose kinds of self-aggrandisement which were so much a part of early party rap. A radical social consciousness was emerging in rap, though it was tied to the local, to a party tradition.

Public Enemy's next album, *It Takes a Nation of Millions to Hold Us Back*, however, was quite different from *Yo! Bum Rush the Show*. Note that the more personal "me" from "Raise the Roof" has been replaced here by the more inclusive "us," reflecting the album's encompassing black nationalistic theme. Their political agenda became more pronounced on this second release as evinced by track titles such as "Rebel Without a Pause," "Prophets of Rage," and "Party for Your Right to Fight."

Indeed, Chuck D and Flavor Flav wed a pro-black stance with Nation of Islam ideology on "Party for Your Right to Fight" as well as on others, such as "Bring the Noise." Terms such as "devil" and "Asiatic" abound throughout, referencing the intricate genesis beliefs preached by Nation founders W.D. Fard and Elijah Muhammad. The Nation of Islam became a pronounced force in rap at this point in time, its blend of militancy and pro-black ideology finding enthusiastic support among many young Afro-Americans.

Public Enemy's radical new conception of the idiom as a nation building force was intrinsically a part of their new and innovative uses of mass-disseminated technology. Unlike most early rap albums, *It Takes a Nation of Millions to Hold Us Back* is not a collection of singles. Rather, *It Takes a Nation* is structured as a 58-minute self-contained radio broadcast, its individual songs linked together along conceptual lines. Tracks are interspersed with portions of a UK concert, static, the sound of a radio dial turning, and bits and pieces of radio shows. Communication itself became most important as Public Enemy envisioned an Afro-American community that could be linked together through postmodern media technology. Thus, their second release marked a shift in the rap aesthetic. Community performance and entertainment on a decentralized scale gave way to worldwide mediation by and through centralized recording media. Rap became, in short, an idiom that could create solidarities beyond the boundaries of face-to-face communication.

The relationship between technology and nation building is explored by Benedict Anderson in his book *Imagined Communities: Reflections on the Origin and Spread of Nationalism* (1991). He notes, early on, that nations are "imagined communities" which foster feelings of deep solidarity between peoples who do not know each other and might never meet each other:

> [A nation] is *imagined* because the members of even the smallest nation will never know most of their fellow-members, meet them, or even hear of them, yet in the minds of each lives the image of their communion.... It is imagined as a *community*, because, regardless of the actual inequality and exploitation that may prevail in each, the nation is always conceived as a deep, horizontal comradeship. (Anderson 1991, pp. 6–7)

As Anderson observes, mass-disseminated technology—most notably print-technology or "print-capitalism"—was essential to envisioning these large scale "imagined communities." This revolutionary technology "made it possible for rapidly growing numbers of people to think about themselves, and to relate to others, in profoundly new ways" throughout disparate areas in Western Europe beginning in the eighteenth century (Anderson 1991, pp. 11, 36). Similarly, recorded technology allowed artists such as Public Enemy to envision their audience as a wide and encompassing nation within a nation, one which transcended any and all local contexts of production. Indeed, unity was the cry of the moment late in the decade, as groups such as X-Clan and Boogie Down Productions stressed similar (though not identical) black nationalist aesthetics on albums such as *To the East, Blackwards* and *By All Means Necessary* (respectively).

It is an ironic and uncomfortable reality that so-called "gangsta rap" emerged at almost exactly the same point in time on the West Coast that Public Enemy and other nationalist rappers did on the East. While many have attempted to draw sharp distinctions between the lyric content of "positive pro-black" artists such as Public Enemy and "negative gangsta rap" artists such as NWA (Niggas With Attitude), these groups share at least one formal characteristic. Both groups encountered and engaged hip hop as a mass-mediated, primarily verbal, art form—one no longer continually negotiated and processed in live practice and performance. Public Enemy's shows, for example, seem less like small-scale community performances and more like major-label rock extravaganzas. Elaborate props and rigid codification all give their performances a kind of large scale grandiosity foreign to most early—clearly less formal—hip hop music. The group, for example, is often flanked on stage by the Security of the First World (or the S1Ws), a paramilitary "outfit" which carries fake Uzi submachine guns, dresses in camouflage, and does an elaborate stage show behind band leaders Chuck D and Flavor Flav. NWA, now disbanded, shared a similar aesthetic. The group made a similar use of elaborate stage-props, including "Do Not Cross—Police Line" tape, which was spread across the group's performance space on occasion. The message, again, was "Do Not Cross" the line between those on stage and those off stage. Like many popular rock stars, both artists replicated their album tracks on stage ("in concert") with maximum amounts of spectacle and pageantry, formalizing the line between artist and audience.

This stress on mass-mediation and large-scale dissemination, as opposed to small-scale community performance, helped to forge in rap a more "informational" narrative-based music. The now familiar "rap as ghetto reporter" equation entered West Coast parlance during this period as Chuck D's oft quoted "rap as black America's CNN" entered that of the East. Former NWA member Ice Cube notes:

> I give information to the people in Atlanta, that the people in Atlanta never even thought about. It's a form of unity, it does form a unity that we're startin' to put together.... [Rap is] a formal source to get our ideas out to a wider group of peers. (quoted in Cross 1993, p. 206)

Characters, plots and "messages" became most important for West Coast "gangsta rap" as the art's verbal discourse alone was severed from its context of live congregation and production. "Repetition and variation of short motifs" was replaced by narrative story telling within a closed song-structure.

An example from Ice Cube's work will prove helpful. "Dead Homiez" is from Ice Cube's *Kill at Will* EP, released a short time after his first album, *AmeriKKKa's Most Wanted*. Cube tells a vivid story on this track, narrating, in the first-person, his experiences at the funerals of friends who died early and violent deaths. The track, it is important to note, does not stress word play or metaphor and no sense of artist-audience interaction is acknowledged in this text. This is not a music created for the purpose of engaging live crowds. Rather, "Dead Homiez" communicates straightforward information, albeit with passion and emotional clarity. The video for this track is similarly poignant, and follows the action of the song faithfully. For example, the line "I still hear the screams from his mother," is accompanied by—appropriately enough—a grieving woman.

Indeed, the video became a much more prevalent part of rap during the late 1980s and early 1990s, primarily through the influence of MTV's *Yo! MTV Raps*. The video medium reinforced prevailing currents in hip hop music during this period, moving it towards a kind of literality that was exceedingly appropriate for all kinds of mass-mediation. The gun-carrying gangster was and is capable of signifying parallel messages in both sight and sound. For example, there was a clear link early in rap between the power to communicate orally and the power of a weapon. The microphone was often metaphorically referred to both as a gun and as a phallus. However, after about 1989, with the increasing importance of the video, there was a move to a kind of literality rooted in the visual. The gun came to signify (referentially) a gun and a gun alone. The power of this symbol stood on its own. Realism in the realm of the mass-mediated became more important than engaging live crowds or working with the language itself.

The "gangsta rap" narrative struck a chord in American popular culture, most especially with solvent, young, white teens. Artists such as Ice-T, NWA, Eazy-E, Dr. Dre, Ice Cube, MC Ren, and Snoop Doggy Dogg reached platinum-plus status, prompting artists and record companies alike to attempt to replicate their formula for success. Part of the wide cultural currency of the "gangsta" comes from the universally extractable nature of his narrative. The violent outlaw, living his life outside of dominant cultural constraints, solving his problems through brute power and domination, is a character-type with roots deep in American popular lore. Indeed, the gangster holds a very special place in the American popular imagination. He embodies such capitalist values as rugged individualism, rampant materialism, strength through physical force, and male domination, while he rejects the very legal structures which define that culture. He is both deeply inside and outside of mainstream American culture, his position not unlike that which Afro-Americans have occupied in the Americas for over 400 years. It is not surprising that the black gun-toting gangster has had such limitless appeal for so many young males, both black and white. The "gangsta" is a "romantic" figure, a ready-made tool for male teen rebellion. The following is from Ice-T's single "New Jack Hustler":

> Hustler, word, I pull the trigger long
> Grit my teeth
> Spray till every brother's gone
> Got my block sewn, armored dope spots
> Last thing I sweats, a sucka punk cop
> Move like a king when I roll, hops
> You try to flex, bang
> Another brother drops
> You gotta deal with this
> Cause there's no way out
> Why? Cash money ain't never gonna play out
> I got nothin to lose, much to gain
> In my brain, I gotta capitalist migraine
> Gotta get paid tonight
> To keep my hustle right
> Quick when I speak, check my freak
> Keep my game tight
> So many girls on my jock
> Think I'm a movie star
> Nineteen, I got a fifty thousand dollar car
> Go to school, I ain't goin' for it
> Kiss my butt, bust the cork on the Moet
> Cause I don't wanna hear that crap
> Why? I rather be a New Jack Hustler
> H-U-S-T-L-E-R Hustler[3]

Ice-T's "New Jack Hustler" embodies the super-gangster character-type. Sexist ("check my freak"), violent ("spray till every brother's gone"), utterly materialistic ("I gotta capitalist migraine"), and all but impenetrable ("keep my game tight"), Ice-T creates a larger than life bad guy along the big screen lines of Don Corleone or Al Pacino's *Scarface*. Indeed, many "gangsta rap" singles and albums have a strong visual feel to them and a number of popular artists working within the genre, including Ice Cube, Ice-T, and MC Eiht, have made a successful transition to film. "New Jack Hustler" was, in fact, originally contained on the *New Jack City* soundtrack, an action film which features Ice-T as an undercover cop. Ice-T blurs the line between "ghetto reporting" and cinematic fantasy in this film, as have many rap artists entering the realm of American popular culture.

The gangster narrative has become an intrinsic part of the art, engendering an entire musical genre. Its wild financial success has helped to shape the contours of rap's present landscape, the "language" through which rappers articulate their raps. Most artists today acknowledge the genre either implicitly or explicitly, as values such as "hardness" and "realness" now dominate across the board. "Hard-core" artists of the early-to-mid 1990s such as Nas, Redman, Lords of the Underground, Naughty by Nature, Casual, and Das EFX have all embraced the violently impenetrable outlaw stance on some level, though they have all proclaimed a love for rap as an art form as well. They have all also employed performance tools such as word play and freestyle-sounding delivery though they are all operating on a popularly determined landscape both in medium and message.

The following is "Time 4 Sum Aksion," from Redman's debut album, *Whut? Thee Album*. It offers a particularly apt example of rap's current state:

> Let's get ready to rumble!
> In this corner we have the funk bodysnatcher
> P Funkadelic and I gotcha
> Hard enough that I can chew a whole bag of rocks
> Chew an avenue, chew an off street, an off block
> Then turn around and do the same damn thing to a soloist
> 'Cause Reggie Noble's pissed
> I'll crush the whole brain frame
> 'Cause you couldn't maintain the funk
> That have your rap style for lunch, chump
> 'Cause '92, I take a whole crew
> Give 'em a punch of the funk
> Knock all of their gold tooth loose (pow!)
> To show you what type of stuff I'm on, you can't puff or sniff it
> Because I was born with it, the Funkadelic devil
> Hit you with a rap level of 10, then 1, 2, 3, you're pinned
> I get action
> So everybody jump with your rump
> If you like the way it sounds, punk pump it in your back trunk
> And let loose with the juice when I do rock
> I'm too hot
> Some say I got more juice than 2Pac[4]
> Straight outta Jersey, you heard me, my brother
> I'm laughing (he he he he)
> *Time, Time 4, Time 4 Sum Aksion*

Redman is clearly displaying a flexible control over language in this frenetic non-narrative piece. His delivery resonates with freestyle vocal improvisation, a practice intrinsic to rap's continuum as a live practice. Lines such as "And let loose with the juice when I do rock / I'm too hot / Some say I got more juice than 2Pac," seem to tumble out of his mouth freely and without effort. This control over language is crucial, for Redman frames "Time 4 Sum Aksion" as a vocal "battle" or competition. Such "battles" have been an intrinsic part of hip hop almost from its inception. Artists such as The Cold Crush Brothers and The Fantastic Five routinely engaged in verbal "cutting" contests during the late 1970s and early 1980s, as did jazz musicians and blues singers before them. "Time 4 Sum Aksion" has much of the sprawling energy of such battles, though it is very much contained within a kind of pop formalism.

The chorus "*Time, Time 4, Time 4 Sum Aksion*," for example, frames the song's three verses, one of which is printed above. Such devices became important as hip hop left the context of live dance-hall production and entered the realm of the recorded. Early face-to-face battles were, as one might imagine, more dialogic than were later popular recordings such as "Time 4 Sum Aksion." Early competitors both knew each other and had to react to each other's challenges. Boasts and brags and insults were often personalized during these early battles, an aesthetic clearly evinced during a famous match between Kool Moe Dee and Busy Bee Starski at Harlem World in 1981.

During the competition, Kool Moe Dee insults Busy Bee's trademark "bom ditti bom" routine ("Busy Bee I don't mean to be bold but put that 'Bom ditti bom' bullshit on hold") as well as his general lack of originality. Busy Bee, according to Kool Moe Dee, "bit" his name from Lovebug Starski and "hugs" other MC's "jocks." Note that these insults are both individualized and center upon the act of MCing itself. Redman's single is, in contrast, inscribed within a one-sided gangster narrative, a narrative that often blurs the line between rhetorical competition and violent threat. Lines such as "Give 'em a punch of the funk / Knock all of their gold tooth loose" are neither personalized nor contained clearly within the realm of the performance. Redman places himself explicitly within the "gangsta rap" genre when he raps, "straight outta Jersey," an allusion to NWA's seminal album, *Straight Outta Compton*. Tricia Rose notes that much of today's hardcore rap is directly indebted to "gangsta rap":

> During the later 1980s Los Angeles rappers from Compton and Watts, two areas severely paralyzed by the postindustrial economic redistribution, developed a West Coast style of rap that narrates experiences and fantasies specific to life as a poor young, black, male subject in Los Angeles. Ice Cube, Dr. Dre, Ice-T, Ezy-E, Compton's Most Wanted, W.C. and the MAAD Circle, Snoop Doggy Dog, South Central Cartel, and others have defined the gangsta rap style. The Los Angeles school of gangsta rap has spawned other regionally specific hardcore rappers, such as New Jersey's Naughty By Nature, Bronx-based Tim Dog, Onyx and Redman, and a new group of female gangsta rappers, such as Boss (two black women from Detroit), New York–based Puerto Rican rapper Hurricane Gloria, and Nikki D. (Rose 1994, p. 59)

Redman, thus, recoups much of rap's freestyle energy on "Time 4 Sum Aksion," though he is operating within a context made popular and prevalent by West Coast gangster narratives.

Rap is today driven by the closed song-structure. The closure of rap's narrative structure has come as a parallel phenomenon to the increasing lack of space for live production and congregation. The majority of rap is now produced in-studio and is received in solitary settings, such as in jeeps, home stereos and Walkmans. While many people are exposed to rap in such decentralized settings, the art itself is increasingly constituted through a centralized recording industry. This industry has reified hip hop's vocal content alone and has downplayed the significance of dance, graffiti, and other face-to-face community building practices. Brian Cross sums up much in his *It's Not About a Salary: Rap, Race and Resistance in Los Angeles*:

> Hiphop in LA today is a community of bedrooms, occasional open mikes and airwaves. In homes all over the city people gather around turntables, record collections, SP1200s and MPC60s and conjure worlds that intersect with and absorb reality. Connected by a network of tapes, hard to find samples, a nomadic and often underground club scene, and places like the open mike at the Good Life, different perspectives are shared, microphone techniques are invented and beatbrokers collage new soundtracks for urban survival. (Cross 1993, p. 64)

Cross notes that spaces for community production are limited in LA. "Occasional open mikes" seem the closest thing the city has to offer to a live scene. Rather, people gather together around turntables, record collections, SP1200s and MPC60 samplers in more private contexts, such as in bedrooms. The community is constituted vicariously, linked together by an available number of recordings. Cross notes that such mass-mediation of rap engenders flexible "soundtracks for urban survival," allowing great numbers of people to cope with a violent and hostile reality.

Yet, how strong are these support systems? The spaces which have traditionally nurtured Afro-American community interaction and congregation are now all-but gone. Such spaces, as noted throughout, are vital for people of colour dealing with life in often hostile and alienating territory. Indeed, while a sense of rebellion and resistance is certainly fostered by many of rap's contemporary mass-mediated narratives, one wonders how strong—or better, how resilient—are the bonds formed by their mass-dissemination. One wonders whether a vibrant and varied "hip hop culture" can exist by way of a popularly constituted "rap music" idiom.

Study Questions

1. What were the benefits of face-to-face interaction in early hip-hop?
2. How is the gangsta rap musical genre associated with the notion of "hardness" or "realness?"
3. What is the significance of the development of rap's narrative lyrical style?

Notes

1. Special thanks to Charles Keil, William Youngren, William Fischer, Rob Bowman, Bruce Jackson, Larry Chisolm, Michael Frisch and John Wright all of whom commented upon and critiqued this project in its various stages.
2. See Leonard Meyer's *Emotion and Meaning in Music* (1956) as well as Charles Keil's rebuttal piece, "Motion and feeling through music" (1966), republished in *Music Grooves* (1994).
3. The above was copied directly from the liner notes to Ice-T's *O.G. Original Gangster*. Certain differences exist between this text and the text as performed.
4. Rapper 2Pac starred in a film entitled *Juice*, hence Redman's reference.

References

Adler, B. 1991b. Album notes to *Run-DMC: Greatest Hits 1983–1991*. Profile Records.

Allah, B. 1993. "Can't Stop the Body Rock," *Rappages*, June, pp. 54–7.

Anderson, B. 1991. *Imagined Communities: Reflections on the Origin and Spread of Nationalism* (London).

Copeland, A. 1988. *What to Listen for in Music* (New York).

Cross, B. 1993. *It's Not About a Salary: Rap, Race and Resistance in Los Angeles* (London).

Fernando, Jr., S. H. 1994. *The New Beats: Exploring the Music, Culture, and Attitudes of Hip-Hop* (New York).

Foucault, M. 1982. "The Subject and Power," in *Michel Foucault: Beyond Structuralism and Hermeneutics*. H. Dreyfus and P. Rabinow (Chicago), pp. 208–26.

George, N. 1993. "Hip-Hop's Founding Fathers Speak the Truth," *The Source*, November, pp. 44–50.

Hager, S. 1984. *Hip Hop: The Illustrated History of Break Dancing, Rap Music, and Graffiti* (New York).

Hall, S. 1992. "What Is This 'Black' in Black Popular Culture?," in *Black Popular Culture*, ed. G. Dent (Seattle), pp. 21–33.

Hazzard-Gordon, K. 1990. *Jookin': The Rise of Social Dance Formations in African-American Culture* (Philadelphia).

Hebdige, D. 1987. *Cut 'n Mix: Culture, Identity and Caribbean Music* (London).

Keil, C., and Feld, S. 1994. *Music Grooves* (Chicago).

Manuel, P. 1988. *Popular Musics of the Non-Western World* (New York).

McClary, S. 1994. "Same as It Ever Was: Youth Culture and Music," in *Microphone Fiends: Youth Music & Youth Culture*, eds. A Ross and T. Rose (New York), pp. 29–40.

Meyer, L. 1956. *Emotion and Meaning in Music* (Chicago).

Rose, T. 1994. *Black Noise: Rap Music and Black Culture in Contemporary America* (New England).

Small, C. 1987. *Music of the Common Tongue* (London).

Additional Reading

Abrahams, R. 1970. *Deep Down in the Jungle: Negro Narrative Folklore From the Streets of Philadelphia* (Chicago).

Adler, B. 1991. *Rap: Portraits and Lyrics of a Generation of Black Rockers* (New York).

Baker, Jr., H. 1993. *Black Studies, Rap, and the Academy* (Chicago).

Bourdieu, P. 1977. *Outline of a Theory of Practice* (Cambridge).

Dent, G. (ed.) 1992. *Black Popular Culture* (Seattle).

During, S. (ed.) 1993. *The Cultural Studies Reader* (New York).

Evans, D. 1982. *Big Road Blues* (Berkeley).

Foucault, M. 1977. *Discipline and Punish: The Birth of the Prison* (New York).

Gates, Jr., H. L. 1988. *The Signifying Monkey: A Theory of African-American Literary Criticism* (New York).

Grossberg, L., Nelson, C., and Treichler, P. (eds) 1992. *Cultural Studies* (New York).

Hebdige, D. 1991. *Subculture: The Meaning of Style* (London).

Jackson, B. 1974. *Get Your Ass in the Water and Swim Like Me: Narrative Poetry from the Black Oral Tradition* (Cambridge).

Jones, L. 1963. *Blues People: Negro Music in White America* (New York).

Keil, C. 1991. *Urban Blues* (Chicago).

Murray, A. 1976. *Stomping the Blues* (New York).

Ogren, K. 1989. *The Jazz Revolution: Twenties America and the Meaning of Jazz* (New York).

Sidran, B. 1981. *Black Talk* (New York).

Southern, E. 1983. *The Music of Black Americans: A History* (New York).

Toop, D. 1991. *Rap Attack 2: African Rap to Global Hip Hop* (New York).

West, C. 1993. *Keeping Faith: Philosophy and Race in America* (New York).

Discography

Boogie Down Productions, *By All Means Necessary*, Jive. 1097–4-J. 1988.

Boogie Down Productions, *Criminal Minded*. Sugarhill. SHCD 5255. 1991.

EPMD, *Strictly Business*. Fresh. CDRE-82006. 1988.

Eric B. & Rakim, *Paid in Full*. 4th & Broadway. CCD 4005. 1987.

Eric B. & Rakim, *Follow the Leader*. Uni. UNIC-3. 1988.

Eric B. & Rakim, *Let the Rhythm Hit'Em*. MCA. MCAC-6416. 1990.

Ice Cube, *AmeriKKKa's Most Wanted*. Priority. 4XL57120. 1990.

Ice Cube, *Kill at Will*. Priority. E4V7230. 1990.

Ice-T, *O.G. Original Gangster*. Sire/Warner Brothers. 9 26492–2. 1991.

Keith Murray, *The Most Beautifullest Thing in This World*. Jive. 01241–41555–4. 1994.

Kool G Rap & D.J. Polo, *Road to the Riches*. Cold Chillin'/Warner Brothers. 9 25820–2. 1988.

Kool G Rap & D.J. Polo, *Wanted: Dead or Alive*. Cold Chillin'/Warner Brothers. 9 26165–2. 1990.

L.L. Cool J, *Radio*. Def Jam. FCT 40239. 1985.

Nas, *Illmatic*. Columbia. CK 57684. 1994.

N.W.A., *Straight Outta Compton*. Priority. 4XL57102. 1988.

Public Enemy, *Yo! Bum Rush the Show*. Def Jam. BCT 40658. 1987.

Public Enemy, *It Takes a Nation of Millions to Hold Us Back*. BWT 44303. Def Jam. 1988.

Redman, *Whut? Thee Album*. RAL/Chaos/Columbia. OK 52967. 1992.

Run-D.M.C., *Together Forever: Greatest Hits 1983–1991*. Profile. PCD-1419. 1991.

Sugarhill Gang, "Rapper's Delight." Sugarhill. VID-153RE-BW. 1979.

Various Artists, *Hip Hop Heritage Volume One*. Jive. 1291–4-J. 1989.

Yo Yo, *Make Way for the Motherlode*. East West. 7 91605–2. 1991.

38

"Dead Prezence"
Money and Mortal Themes in Hip-Hop Culture

James Peterson's emphasis on "dead presidents" explores the exegesis and discursive potency of one of hip-hop's more iconic concepts. Tracing the term from its early application in Eric B and Rakim's "Paid in Full," Peterson explores transitions in hip-hop's linguistic structures and meaning since 1987, noting the ways in which discursive patterns are established and then circulated or amplified through repetition. For Peterson, there are two constitutive elements that are embedded within the term and the essay embarks on a detailed interrogation of mortality and money as they emerge in a hip-hop sensibility. While the primary emphasis is on language and discourse, hip-hop's various media forms (cinema in particular) are also addressed, reinforcing the fact that lyrical representation is not the only facet of meaning-making within hip-hop's artistic community.

The term dead presidents is indeed pervasive, yet it does not always communicate precisely the same values in every context or moment. Peterson carefully analyzes the distinctions in its enunciation over the years, evaluating the lyrical contributions of MCs Rakim, Nas, Jay-Z and Dead Prez and addressing each artist's stamp on its meaning. As we see, dead presidents is an expression imbued with deeper ideological values pertaining to race, class, aspiration, authority, and identity.

"Dead Prezence": Money and Mortal Themes in Hip Hop Culture

James Peterson

This essay is based on research that investigates the vernacular phrase *Dead Presidents* as an underground sociolinguistic phenomenon emerging in a particularly multifaceted way through Hip Hop culture. In the simplest semantic sense, *Dead Presidents* refers to presidents who have passed. In the sociolinguistic context of the United States (who reveres her past presidents with mythological devotion) and in the pragmatic discourses of Hip Hop culture, *dead presidents* has come to mean money. In this sense, it is functioning as a synecdoche. The image/simulacra of the president on U.S. currency means or refers to *all* money. The phrase, as far as we can discern etymologically and sociolinguistically, (re)emerges into the public sphere(s) through Hip Hop Culture in the 1980s. There are, moreover, amazing linguistic, lyrical, and cultural manifestations as well as (morphological) metamorphoses of this phrase in Hip Hop Culture that reflect a complex discursive engagement with mortality and the sociopolitical conditions that create the staggering mortality rates for young black men. "[T]he most progressive elements of hip hop culture, represented by artists such as Dead Prez [...] articulate a language of protest. Yet their creative talents rarely yielded new modes of collective intervention that could forcefully challenge the existing structures of political power and corporate capitalism" (Marable 59). Dead Prezence is a patterned discourse that refers to one such collective intervention attempting to "forcefully challenge the existing structures of political power and corporate capitalism."[1] The intervention in question here is discursive, but its potential impact on the public spheres, especially black public spheres, warrants the critical analyses initiated in the following discussion. "[T]hrough discourse [...] the world of experience acquires meaning and it is likewise in and through *patterned discourses* that social subjects are located or positioned, suggesting important implications for human agency and identity formation [my italics]" (Forman 10). This chapter seeks to chart some of these patterned discourses that I am framing as Dead Prezence, but it is by no means a total account of the Dead Prezence in Hip Hop Culture, nor is it an exhaustive catalogue of all mortal or monetary themes circulating within the culture. It is, however, an introduction to how the phrase *dead presidents* enters into Hip Hop Cultural discourses and the various semantic and morphological trajectories that this phrase conceptually covers.

"Thinkin' of a master plan / this ain't nothin' but sweat inside my hand. / So I dig into my pocket all my money is spent / So I dig deeper. I'm still comin' up with lint / So I start my mission leave my residence / Thinking how I can get some dead presidents" (Eric B and Rakim).[2] Rakim's narrator in the now-classic title track from Eric B and Rakim's debut album, *Paid in Full*, is the prototypical rap figure at the crossroads of lack and desire.[3] As he contemplates ways to "get some dead presidents," he remembers when he was a "stick-up kid" and reaffirms a more righteous present for himself as a 9-to-5 job seeker. Of course, for Rakim and for his narrator, postindustrial urban unemployment rates suggest his penchant for rapping over beats might be the only logical employment option. The narrator's decision to transition away from robbery and sticking people up is telling: "I need money / I used to be a stick-up kid / So I think of all the devious things I did." Through simple lyrical verse, Rakim's narrator performs the thinking behind his decision to pursue dead presidents via his verbal skills and abilities. In fact, the album *Paid in Full* gestures to what was, at the time, the amazing possibility for inner-city African American men to make a decent living by recording their stories (over rudimentary musical production) on vinyl and selling them to the world. "These rappers are party to a long collective memory of fore-fathers [...] who did not get paid, who received neither the financial success nor the critical acclaim they deserved" (Swedenburg 583). Accordingly, the album cover art features Eric B and Rakim standing side by side in front of a dollar bill, collage-like background, in ghetto Gucci suits with cash in their hands.[4] Judging from the imagery here and the popularity of this first Eric B and Rakim record, the paid-in-full slogan was quite apropos. According to Rakim, himself: "When we got the deal with 4th and Broadway we got the check and it said paid in full; so we was lookin at it and Eric said [...] that's what we're gonna name the album. I wasn't sure about it at first but that idea definitely worked. It was a statement" (Coleman 67). Consider especially its prophetic announcement of the realizable cultural and traditional capital produced by and through Hip Hop culture and rap music. Hip Hop, as it were, *is* paid in full. It is a multi-billion dollar music industry with numerous African American millionaires, and its cultural impact on globalized late-capitalist society can be readily measured by its ubiquitous presence in the marketplace. Hip Hop culture, especially rap music, has paid folks in full since the early 1980s.[5]

Rakim's subtle reference to dead presidents is a point of entry into the Dead Prezence discourse that wrestles with the sociopolitical issues that underwrite the extraordinary transfer of currency from fans to artists, from the cultural constituents of Hip Hop into mainstream American, as well as the mortal conditions that swirl around, in and through, these transactions. It is not accidental that Rakim's narrator's humble desire to eat (fish in this case) connects his lack of financial resources to the particular vernacular phrasing of dead presidents. He, like his discursive counterparts featured in this essay, signifies on America's reverence for passed (past) presidents and the fact that these presidents reflect a legacy of American leadership that is classist and racist. Since Hip Hop culture's origins are utterly folk in form (i.e. it develops in economically challenged conditions and it is initially the music of working class and poor young people of color who are socially invisible) the signifying eloquence of a dead presidents reference here stands in bold relief. Presidents, dead or alive, tend to represent the middle and wealthy classes first and the lower and working classes second (if at all), and then only as a distant second.

Rakim, whose government name is William Griffin, cites the lyrical prowess of Melle Mel and Caz and the musical inclinations of James Brown as his most poignant influences. "Melle Mel was always using big words and ill rhythms, but he'd break it down and get a little political too, like 'White Lines' ... Kool Moe Dee and Caz (from Cold Crush) were conscious and lyrical with their skills" (Coleman 62). Rakim knew that the discourse of Hip Hop, at that moment (the early 1980s), was predisposed to a modicum of political reflection in the content of the music. Thus his dead presidents reference in the opening lines of "Paid in Full" engenders as much critical political meaning as listeners are able to invest in it. Once this particular reference in the song "Paid in Full" is juxtaposed with tracks on this record and the cover art imagery, the complexity of the Dead Prezence discursive sphere begins to take shape. Rakim posits the crossroads of lack and desire for a Hip Hop generation within the context of an exaggerated (e.g., dooky gold chains, fake Gucci suits, and cash money on display) capitalist twist on the desire component of this equation. This capitalist twist urges the socially invisible youth of Hip Hop Culture to get money at any cost and to demonstrate those dead presidents ostentatiously. Remember, also, that

Rakim is regularly referred to as the God or God MC, which is suggestive of the influence of his approach to socioeconomic issues within the rap music industry and Hip Hop Culture.

Hip Hop Culture's course here was forever altered. "The corporatization of hip hop is undeniable. Since its popularization in the early 1980s, the profits of hip hop-related products have increased exponentially. As a result the linkage of corporate strategies and marketing techniques with the expressive cultures of black youth undeniably alters the trajectory of hip hop" (Watkins 569). *Paid in Full* reaches its zenith of popularity from 1986 to 1987, functioning almost as the advance guard of what would come to be known as gangsta rap, a subgenre of rap music proper that has been studied comprehensively by scholars and journalists alike because of its ability to describe the postindustrial environments in which misogyny, gang warfare, and the crack epidemic thrive. In many ways Eric B and Rakim's desire to be paid in full gently forecasts the extent to which Hip Hop culture would become obsessed with the pursuit of dead presidents.

On Nas' critically acclaimed debut album *Illmatic*, "The World is Yours" is a striking addendum to Rakim's recorded introduction to the Dead Prezence discourse. In "The World is Yours," Nas (né Nasir Jones) and producer Pete Rock engage in a call-response exchange: "I'm out for presidents to represent me / say what? I'm out for presidents to represent me / say what? I'm out for dead presidents to represent me." Here, Nas and Pete Rock create a traditional call-and-response repartee; Nas posits a statement and Pete Rock asks for clarification. The form of these lines mimics prototypical blues lines of verse that repeat themselves in lines 1 and 2 and then ultimately resolve in the third line, which repeats words with a signifying difference. The signifying difference here (that distinction between presidents and *dead* presidents) captures the central tension between those artisans of Hip Hop who are continuously challenged by American Dream-like success with accompanying capitalistic pursuits (i.e., economic success translated as selling out the community), and an audience within Hip Hop culture that desires its own economic success, but only occasionally connects economic empowerment to political representation. The mere suggestion here that Nas is "out for" presidential representation vocalizes the political frustration of millions of black and brown urbanites struggling with the burden of the Civil Rights legacy in an era of confused electoral suffrage systems and political figures who exhibit open disdain for the young Hip Hop voting bloc.[6] The line is so politically potent that it demands both the question (say what?) and the repetition. A president that would represent Nas would be forced to redress the economic disparities of late capitalism (or globalism) and the wretched conditions of so many postindustrial urban neighborhoods, all of which are manifest in the residential conditions of project living, regularly detailed in the narratives of Hip Hop culture. "Black communities like the South Side and West Side of Chicago, North Side of Philadelphia, Harlem and other parts of New York City, and South Central Los Angeles have the appearance of cities recently at war: dilapidated housing, gutted buildings, pothole-filled streets, and little economic activity" (Kitwana 180). Without having lived through these conditions, no president can/could genuinely relate to them. In much of his work on *Illmatic*, Nas invites them (and us) to do so—to live through them and relate. "He's able to evoke the bleak reality of ghetto life without losing hope or forgetting the good times, which become all the more precious when any day could be your last. As a narrator, he doesn't get too caught up in the darker side of life—he's simply describing what he sees in the world around him" (Bogdanov, Woodstra, Erlewine, and Bush 346).

Just in case presidential representation of project residents seemed farfetched to the average Hip Hop listener in 1994 (as was most probably the case), *dead* presidential representation offers a signifying Hip Hop response to the material conditions that so readily (and violently) separate the haves from the have-nots in our beloved country. In this instance, "dead presidents" is a complex and deliberately complicated reference to American money—that stuff of which/from which most American Dreams are made. It is complex because while it functions as a synecdoche for cash money (i.e., it refers to money as the simulacra of the deceased presidents depicted on U.S. dollars), it also bears, in its vernacular meaning, an abstract delight in the death of American political leaders. The complicated suggestion being: if living presidents won't represent me, dead ones will. Do note here that Nas's aspiration to dead presidential wealth is typical of many of the existential pitfalls of the inner-city youth who decide to engage in illegal drug trafficking, thievery, and prostitution. However, the term "dead presidents," also (always/already) secures an inherent political question of presidential representation even as it gestures toward monetary gain.

As Nas's *Illmatic* was enjoying its critically acclaimed introduction to the Hip Hop world, Hip Hop generation filmmakers Allen and Albert Hughes were preparing to release their second feature film, *Dead Presidents*. The Hughes brothers' first film was a Hollywood dream—made for very little, making very much. That film, *Menace II Society*, was also about the pursuit of an economic American dream by the socially invisible. In *Menace II Society* these monetary pursuits had drastic outcomes for the main characters and the communities they terrorized in the process of securing their own collection of dead presidents. In *Dead Presidents*, the Hughes brothers provide an historical context (the Vietnam War) during and after which various characters struggle to deal with the physical and psychological battle scars in a "home" environment, which has a glaring lack of opportunities for African American Vietnam veterans.

> Even though *Dead Presidents* is more about the effects of poverty than those of racism, only the most naïve viewer could completely dissociate the two. Nevertheless, the Hughes Brothers don't overtly introduce race as an issue. Instead, this is about the failure of society, and how desperation, more than greed, can lead to radical and violent acts.
>
> (Berardinelli)

Larenz Tate plays the lead character, Anthony, who, after two tours of duty in Vietnam, finds it extraordinarily difficult to re-acclimate himself to the Bronx circa 1973, just a year or two before Hip Hop culture is born in the very same borough. Anthony's troubles begin before Vietnam: he has a child on the way before he leaves for military service. While he is at war, his platoon experiences the usual violence and mayhem. The members of his platoon also decide to keep souvenirs of the dead. At one point, one of these souvenirs is the decapitated head of a Viet Cong soldier. As the platoon continues its missions with this head in a knapsack, they are also occasionally peppered with Viet Cong propaganda pamphlets that challenge the "Black Man" to reconsider his position in the Vietnam conflict, especially in lieu of the racial oppression that exists in the United States. This pamphlet and the head are powerful symbols for the postwar realities of all of the characters in *Dead Presidents*. For Anthony, the pamphlet is prophecy for the challenges (including lack of opportunity) with which he must contend when he returns home. Anthony, like his real-life, historical counterparts, was unaware of or disconnected from the staggering mortality rates for African American men and what these statistics reveal about fundamental inequalities in U.S. society.

In a powerful study about the importance of mortality rates for comprehensive analysis of quality of life for populations across economic, regional, and racial barriers, Amartya Sen unveils a chilling portrait of the mortal plight plaguing African American men:

> The residents of Harlem combine the disadvantages of race with special problems of inner city deprivation. While it is still remarkable that their survival chances fall behind those of Bangladeshi men, it is perhaps more surprising that the U.S. black population, in general, have lower chances of reaching a mature age than do the immensely poorer people— women as well as men—in Kerala or China.
>
> (Sen 18)

The ironic twist of Anthony's nearly all black platoon fighting in Vietnam, where people are perceived to be more deprived (at least economically) than Americans, reveals itself poignantly upon his return. Members of a deprived race fight in an economically deprived country and then, wounded and scarred, they return to their own country to be deprived yet again. Home again, Anthony garners work as a butcher ever so briefly before he must go back to the underground economy as a numbers runner and general hustler with his friend and mentor, Kirby. Once he is back in league with Kirby, it is only a matter of time before the two conspire to organize the ultimate heist. They plan on stealing several hundred thousand dollars—money that the U.S. government was preparing to incinerate. These conspiracy scenes are almost the climax of the film. Audience members know, either from history or from the tragic tendencies of the Hughes brothers' narratives, this heist will not be successful. What we do not come to terms with is the fact that this money, even if secured, will not necessarily save the lives of the "endangered" black men and women who are planning to steal it. Here the Dead Prezence discourse gestures toward the complex and inextricable connection between mortality and money, or more accurately, the ironic fact that although inner-city Hip Hop generation African American men (in particular) seem to be ready to die for dead presidents, the economic resources that these simulacra represent do not actually exist in an absolute sense. This is why Dr. Sen's comparative study across nations is so telling.

> Comparisons of this kind, based on mortality rate, are important because of the light they throw on existing inequalities in life chances. They are also important for the questions they raise about policy issues. If the relative deprivation of blacks transcends income differentials so robustly, the remedying of this inequality has to involve policy matters that go well beyond income opportunities for the black population. It is necessary to address such matters as public health services, educational facilities, hazards of urban life, and other social and economic parameters that influence survival chances.
>
> (Sen 17)[7]

Mortality differentials expose aspects of the challenges of inequality in the United States, for which traditional economic analyses simply cannot account. And in *Dead Presidents*, this exposure is (for the characters in the film) a tragic fact of urban black reality. They do not get away with the caper. One is shot, one overdoses on heroin, one snitches on the rest, and ultimately Anthony and Kirby are caught and imprisoned. The Hughes brothers are deliberate in establishing an array of tragic outcomes for their characters that exactly reflect typical outcomes for these characters—with or without the illusory and elusive dead presidents they so desperately seek.

All of the Dead Prezence narratives that derive from Hip Hop culture or from Hip Hop generation artisans do not confront the mortality of African Americans so directly or with such tragic consequences. It is here, in 1996, that Jay-Z (aka Shawn Carter) emerges from Brooklyn's underground economy to release his debut album, *Reasonable Doubt*, which was later deemed a Hip Hop classic, but was critically acclaimed even during its debut. It functions as a blueprint for partying, dealing crack cocaine (hustling), and navigating the labyrinthine streets of Brooklyn. Jay's penchant for compelling braggadocio outstrips all of his contemporaries as well as his Hip Hop predecessors. Although Jay-Z does not enter the Dead Prezence discourse until the song entitled "Dead Presidents II," his status, stature, influence, and impact on Hip Hop culture and the current generation of American youth should not be underestimated.

After selling tens of millions of records for his imprint (Roc-A-Fella Records) on Def Jam Records, he graduated to President and CEO of Def Jam.[8] He refers to this moment as the Carter Administration, a savvy encapsulation of his personal accumulation of dead presidents and his current executive sway over the Hip Hop world through one of its most enduring brands, Def Jam. Recently (playing on Jay's reference to himself as El Presidente), El Presidente's executive prominence was challenged when a representative of the Cristal Champagne company distanced himself (and Cristal) from its aspirational Hip Hop audience. As absurd as this may sound, Jay promptly called for a boycott of the outrageously priced champagne for all of his loyal constituents. Indeed, Jay-Z had reason to be miffed, because he had been providing free advertising for Cristal as early as 1996 on *Reasonable Doubt*, with multiple references to the pricey bubbly in his lyrics.[9]

Champagne wars aside, "Dead Presidents II" is a unique selection from Jay-Z's oeuvre for several reasons. First of all, it is the second incarnation of these particular themes with new verses. "Dead Presidents," the first version, was released on 12-inch vinyl as a promotional tool for the album. In addition, "Dead Presidents" and "Dead Presidents II" both sample Nas's voice from "The World is Yours." Thus the refrain for both versions of the song features Nas's now-classic lines: "I'm out for (dead) presidents to represent me." In Nas's version, the call is answered with a nonplussed "say what?" In Jay-Z's versions, Nas's sampled line is finished with an emphatic "Get Money!" This distinction became a heated touchstone during the well-known lyrical battle between Jay-Z and Nas in 2002–2003. Both rappers traded sometimes playful—other times vicious—lyrical jousts on formally and informally released singles and album tracks. On one such turn, Jay-Z jabs: "Yea, I sampled your voice. You was usin' it wrong / You made it a hot line. I made it a hot song" (*The Takeover*). Jay and Nas have since resolved their beef and its accompanying tensions (more on this later). But the fact that Jay samples Nas's voice for two versions of a song entitled "Dead Presidents" again underscores the import of the phrase "dead presidents" and the far-reaching impact of the Dead Prezence discourse.

Jay-Z's "Dead Presidents" and "Dead Presidents II" both seek to establish him as one of the most illustrious hustlers ever to talk about his dealings on record. Based upon the title and a cursory hearing of the various lyrics from both songs, listeners might think that these songs are purely about dead presidents—in this case, illegal money. These listeners would not be inaccurate. But certain phrases invoke some of the more subtle aspects of the Dead Prezence discourse. On the third verse of "Dead Presidents," Jay-Z raps:

> Little monkey niggas turn gorillas / Stopped in the station; filled up on octane / And now they not sane and not playin' that goes without sayin'/ Slayin' day in and day out with money playin' and then they play you out / Tryin' to escape my own mind, lurkin' the enemy / Representin' infinite with presidencies / you know?
>
> ("Dead Presidents")

Jay reveals the twin evils of the dire pursuit for dead presidents and the lethal violence that must accompany these pursuits. The daily slaying does not deter Jay's narrator or any of his hustling-prone listeners; early, violent death has become commonplace in inner-city communities. Instead, Jay represents "infinite with presidencies," highlighting the enduring representational connection between dead presidents, dead hustlers and death-dealing dollars.

On "Dead Presidents II," Jay-Z continues his diatribe of violence, bling, and consumption fantasy. After briefly mourning the loss of one of his hustling partners to a violent death he rhymes the following lines:

> I'll do you one better and slay these niggaz faithfully / Murder is a tough thing to digest, it's a slow process / and I ain't got nothin but time / I had near brushes, not to mention three shots / close range, never touched me, divine intervention / Can't stop I, ... / I dabbled in crazy weight without rap, I was crazy straight / Partnah, I'm still spendin money from eighty-eight ... what?

Even as Jay acknowledges his fallen comrade, he knows that the only way to provide his compadre with a peaceful violent death is to promise him that he will slay the perpetrators of his murder. Here Jay-Z also acknowledges his real life brush with death, from which he emerged miraculously unscathed. But ultimately, he returns to the dead presidents in one of his most famous verse-ending punch lines: that he is (in 1996) still spending money illegally made (and saved) in 1988.

By all accounts, Jay-Z's influential contributions to the Dead Prezence discourse should be legendary. "Dead Presidents" and "Dead Presidents II" are two of dozens of songs that extol the pursuit of dead presidents while simultaneously detailing the horrifically violent realities, within which these deadly pursuits occur. In many ways, Jay-Z, as popular figure (i.e., crack dealer-turned-super-popular-rapper-turned-corporate-executive) elides the impossible conditions of violence and poverty that condemn so many of Jay's constituents and listeners to a violent end.

Jay-Z's Dead Prezence reflects one extreme (the relentless pursuit of money) within the discursive sphere outlined by the likes of Rakim and Nas on their early contributions. The rap duo Dead Prez reflect another extreme: socially and economically conscious politics. In 1997 Dead Prez released a promotional EP entitled *Food, Clothes, and Shelter*. Their debut album *Let's Get Free* was released on Loud Records several years later, in 2000. The titles of these first two releases directly reflect the ethos of Dead Prez's music.

> dead prez's economic perspective on black liberation is similar in many ways to those of Du Bois, sociologist Oliver Cox, and other social theorists who have written about the social and economic conditions for African peoples. Clearly influenced by a Marxist analysis of their economic condition, dead prez points to unbridled capitalism as the culprit in black poverty and advocates a cooperative, communal, and classless economic system as a viable solution. Their economic philosophy reflects views similar to those of Du Bois in the 1930s and 1940s and the Black Panther Party of the late 1960s and early 1970s.
>
> (Aldridge 231)

Stic.Man, who was born into poverty in Tallahassee, Florida, and M-1, who was born into poverty in Jamaica and migrated to Brooklyn during his formative years, are the duo better known as Dead Prez. Initially linking up at Florida A&M University (FAMU) in the mid-1990s, the two eventually decided to apply their budding political knowledge to the music of Hip Hop Culture. They have accomplished this feat with extraordinary results. Apart from recording music that radically challenges the status quo in both the music industry and the United States, Dead Prez have been engaged in various grassroots campaigns geared toward the uplift of African American and Latino peoples.

At the forefront of the Uhuru (Freedom) Movement, Dead Prez has organized food drives, physical fitness trainings, and political and nutritional training for university and inner-city communities around the country and abroad.[10] I had the privilege of working with undergraduate students at various institutions to bring them to college campuses from 2001–2002. These lecture/talks featured M-1 and Stic distilling their lyrical politics for a university audience; they were accompanied by political activists Rosa Clemente and Fred Hampton, Jr., who relayed riveting narratives of history, social protest, political education, and activism. Hampton described his father's murder. His father was executed by police officers in his home while Hampton was in his mother's womb. Dead Prez fleshed out aspects of their political ideology and some of their most politically in-depth lyrics. Statements such as "the plantation is the American system of exploitation. ... It's at McDonalds; it's at Sony" sparked intense discussions amongst undergraduates at the events themselves, as well as in the residence halls and class rooms.[11] This particular idea, that global corporate entities function racially and economically as plantations, is an important component in the political strain of the Dead Prezence discourse. It contextualizes Dead Prez's critique of capitalism and globalization—a critique that flows through the lyrics of their music—

directly within the history and economics of American slavery, even as it challenges students to consider their position in elite institutions that groom them for success on these very same corporate plantations. "Dead Prez often do a great job riding the line between the economic and racial politics of their socioeconomic revolution. At certain points, however, they seem unable to separate these aspects, and end up conflating the two" (Drake).

In "I'm a Afrikan," Dead Prez claim an artistic space "somewhere in between NWA [Niggaz With Attitude] and PE [Public Enemy]." This classic lyric generates Hip Hop history discussions from university campuses to the 'hood. Situating themselves "somewhere in between NWA and PE" is a masterstroke for Dead Prez. The content of their music, much of which thematically reflects the title of their second album, *Revolutionary But Gangsta*, is equal parts NWA gangsta and PE revolutionary. The juxtaposition of PE and NWA (especially with the interstitial placement of Dead Prez) gestures toward an extraordinary moment in the history and economics of Hip Hop culture. The shift in the music industry away from Hip Hop acts like Public Enemy toward Niggaz With Attitude and gangsta rap signaled the beginning of the end of what most Hip Hop scholars consider to be the Golden Era of Hip Hop.[12] This is not an internecine juxtaposition. The first NWA album, *Straight Outta Compton*, is deeply influenced by the work of Public Enemy and the politicism of Hip Hop culture and rap music at that time. Together, PE and NWA represent a powerful transition in the culture of Hip Hop; a transition from a New York City based subculture to an international, mass-mediated cultural movement. In the late 1980s, political content and Afrocentric musings (á la Boogie Down Productions, X-Clan, A Tribe Called Quest, Public Enemy, and others) were the most popular forms of rap music. And by the early 1990s, gangsta rap took center stage with groups like NWA, Ice T, Snoop Dogg, and even East Coast rappers such as the venerable Notorious B.I.G., who presented a gangster ethos through lyrical expression. Dead Prez demonstrate that gangsta and revolutionary content are not diametrically opposed to each other. In these panel discussions and lectures, students at Lincoln University, Princeton University, and Swarthmore College were personally invited to become a part of the discourse.

Notwithstanding their college successes, Dead Prez have been beset by challenges within the music industry. After Loud Records folded in 2002, they were left without a recording home and almost immediately turned to the thriving underground of mix-tape sales in Hip Hop culture. These days, the mix tape is actually not a tape at all; it is a CD. In the early years of Hip Hop, mix tapes were the lifeblood of rap music that was not professionally recorded or distributed. As mix-tape DJs became more prominent and the music industry realized the extraordinary promotional potential of the mix-tape industry, mix-tape sales became more commercialized. However, Dead Prez, went "underground" during the dissolution of their relationship with Loud and released two projects under the "dpz" moniker. These mix-tape projects often featured songs that employed popular rap tracks (originally recorded with lyrics about partying, misogyny, consumption, and/or violence) and superimposed their trademark politically conscious Dead Prez lyrics. "[D]ead prez—represents one of the most unflinchingly didactical acts ever to gain a widespread audience, and their [...] move into the mixtape arena can be understood as a unification of two central elements of Brecht's theory (and indeed elements indigenous to hip-hop itself): production and politics" (Maher 142). In his brilliant essay on Dead Prez, mix tapes, and Brechtian echoes in Hip Hop culture, Maher reifies the political potency of Dead Prez: their power is even greater when they produce / manufacture their own CDs. I argue, however, that the merging of production and politics happens whether the group pays for the physical production (i.e., manufacturing) of their own CDs (without label backing) or not, because they *produce* rap lyrics and music. Because their lyrics are political and their political messaging can and has been disseminated live, over the Internet, and in film, this important synthesis is complete whether a record label is present or not. This merging of production and politics is a telling example of the Dead Prezence discourse. Dead Prez champion economic empowerment through their music and their artistic careers even as they lay out lyrical critiques designed to challenge a capitalist system that oppresses the poor and people of color around the globe.

In many ways, Dead Prez creatively channel some of the most significant themes within the Dead Prezence discourse. On their most recognizable song to date, "It's Bigger than Hip Hop" (not to be confused with the concert / documentary film of the same name), one half of the duo critiques the limitations of popular rappers and rap music:

> MCs get a little bit of love and think they hot / Talkin' 'bout how much money they got; all y'all records sound the same / I'm sick of that fake-thug, R&B-rap scenario, all day on the radio / Same scenes in the video, monotonous material / Y'all don't hear me though.

Over a simple but compelling bass-heavy track produced by Kanye West, Dead Prez chant the chorus that Hip Hop heads need to hear in the era of bling. The chant / refrain on "Propaganda" summons a nuanced socioeconomic perspective and the verses provide specific details on how a political sensibility must emerge in the face of misrepresentation and apathy. "We don't fall for the regular shit, they try to feed us / All this half-ass leadership, flippin position / They turn politician and shut the hell up and follow tradition / For your TV screen, is telling lies to your vision." These lyrics are not empty ciphers. Dead Prez pour all of their career resources into organizing people around the principles of their music. For many young people, Hip Hop drives consumerism and sociopolitical apathy; Dead Prez offer perspective and spur political agency and activity amongst the Hip Hop generations.

The concert / documentary film *Dead Prez: It's Bigger Than Hip-Hop* focuses on the inadequacies of public education, the need for minority-owned business development, sociocultural uplift, and the powerful performances of these ideas at an intimate Dead Prez concert in San Francisco. In this award-winning concert / documentary film, an interviewer poses the fundamental question. "What does Dead Prez mean?" Stic.Man replies: "Dead Prez is short for dead presidents [....] it has two meanings: Dead Prez [means] dead presidents as in the money—be about the hustle—but also dead presidents because we recognize Bush, Clinton, and all these dudes—they ain't no life to our community. They're dead to us. Their policy, their system is dead."

Dead Prez represent potent political potential within Hip Hop culture. Their impact is not limited solely to those spheres of influence generated by their politically loaded, occasionally didactic lyrics. Their books, lectures, rallies, film appearances, documentaries, and other works must also be considered when critics look to Hip Hop culture for political energy. Ultimately, the musical production and lyrical creativity of Dead Prez function as kind of *aesthetic* violence in the midst of the traditional violence so often celebrated by the rap music industry. This aesthetic violence is political in nature. "Long linked to destructive street violence, rap also displays *aesthetic violence*. The swift, intense force of its beat, its very methods of sampling and scratching records, its aggressively loud, confrontational style give rap the aesthetic vigor that raises the energy and consciousness of its listeners" (Shusterman 59). Dead Prez have consistently raised the energy and consciousness of their listeners through a sturdy commitment to exploit rap music for all of its political and educational potential. The group's moniker has a direct nominative influence on the title of the discourse pattern discussed in this essay; their power to name suggests the import of their powerful work on / in the Dead Prezence discourse.

Even though these various contributions to the Dead Prezence discourse in Hip Hop culture began as early as 1986 and the pattern peaked in 1996–1997, the discourse still persists in the current milieu of rap music. On an unreleased track entitled "Death Anniversary," Nas reignites his fiery lyrical history with money and mortality. The hook or refrain goes:

I know all of ya'll hear me / None of ya'll scare me / Cause niggas die daily / Comin' out with my guns real early / laying in your stairway / Cause niggas die daily. / So I got niggas around you mad like they back for they man you killed just a year ago today / So call it a death anniversary / Rushing to emergency / Niggas die daily.

"Death Anniversary" signals a paradigmatic shift in the presence / treatment of death within the lyrics of rap music. This shift calls for artists and audiences to reflect on how death is expected, normalized, and commemorated within the lived experiences of the Hip Hop generations.[13] Since "Niggas die daily," Nas's listeners (not necessarily the same as his consumers) readily connect to his analogical reference to the cycle of retribution that continues to plague inner-city youth engaged in underground economies. The guns, the stairway (a subtle project reference), and the rush to the emergency room are all unfortunately familiar touchstones amongst inner-city youth. But he asks his listeners here to focus on the commemoration, the anniversary of death, in order to probe the mental and spiritual disconnections from our own realities.

In the first verse Nas poses a series of questions designed to deconstruct various aspects of his artistic career. His career has been rife with contestation (i.e., beef), underappreciation, and creative disappointment. He questions his personal and creative relationships with other artists including AZ, Jay-Z, and his wife, a popular vocalist known as Kelis. AZ, a longtime friend, fellow MC, and homie has been at odds with Nas (at least on record), recently. Nas does not directly disrespect AZ in usual Hip Hop battle-mode. Instead he questions AZ's existence and flows into the following quip: "cause niggas spit fake shit and y'all respect it / I spit that real shit and y'all won't buy the record." He also questions his well-publicized lyrical feud with Jay-Z. As mentioned earlier, this historic battle, which lasted over the course of approximately two years, ended amicably just before Nas signed with Def Jam early on in Jay-Z's (Carter Administration) tenure as president. Nas challenges his listeners to consider if his battle with Jay-Z had been a publicity stunt. He poses the same what-if question of his marriage to Kelis. He juxtaposes his life against his murdered childhood friend's as well as Tupac Shakur's. Some Nas fans will not appreciate Nas's flippant deconstruction of his authentic artistic presentation, but most will wrestle with the larger questions regarding media manipulation and the fact that Jay and Nas's battle produced violence only in words. For Hip Hop, that is progress.

In the last verse of "Death Anniversary," Nas begins with a gritty description of an interaction with an anonymous gun-toting hood who is dying:

Scream at the nigga; Breath! Don't breath your last breath / But you know a nigga dead when he pee on his self / Bladder givin' up on him / Face start to puff on him / Bloating up / Nigga cold as fuck tryin to hold on'em

And here in the grimy details of an anonymous gun-toting murder victim, the spectacle of the death anniversary implodes and the complexity of the Dead Prezence discourse re-emerges. Similar to the way in which Nas demands presidential representation in his inaugural turn in the Dead Prezence discourse, in "Death Anniversary" Nas demands that we reflect on our desensitized experience with death. By defamiliarizing the scene of an urban homicide, he invites listeners to wrestle with the visceral experiences of murder and death. In fact, the title of this song "Death Anniversary" contradicts the song's theme, which is to question the extent to which members of a community, plagued by this kind of internecine violence, actually remember, in meaningful ways, the horrors of violent homicide.

In a primary oral culture, to solve effectively the problem of retaining and retrieving carefully articulated thought, you have to do your thinking in mnemonic patterns, shaped

606 • JAMES PETERSON

for ready oral recurrence. Your thought must come into being in heavily rhythmic, balanced patterns, in repetitions or antitheses, in alliterations and assonances [...] and in standard thematic settings [....] Serious thought is intertwined with memory systems.

(Ong 34)[14]

"Death Anniversary," in this sense, coheres the various examples in the Dead Prezence discourse into a pattern that is mnemonic in its capability to refresh the minds and spirits of listeners who may have become just as jaded by their own socioeconomic circumstances as they are by a flimsy political process whose presidents are dead to them. This discursive trajectory, or what I am calling "Dead Prezence," is, finally, a complex code or shorthand for the politico-economic discourse that treats current economic challenges in chronologically and conceptually overlapping public spheres within Hip Hop culture. Dead Prezence is a signal part of a "mnemonic pattern" (including the aforementioned lyrical references—Rakim, Nas, Jay-Z, the artistic and activist careers of Dead Prez, and the Hughes brothers film *Dead Presidents*) that critically engages economic and political topics that are urgently pertinent to the constituents of Hip Hop culture.

Study Questions

1. Why is it important to establish a narrative point of view in rap lyrics?
2. In what way is memory significant in the context of a "dead presence" discourse?
3. How do the factors of money and mortality overlap in rap and hip-hop?

Notes

1. In the fall of 2005, I delivered a lecture in Michael Eric Dyson's Hip Hop Course at the University of Pennsylvania, entitled "Dead Prezence." Here I dissect this term thoroughly tracing its origins in hip hop from the Rakim quote (on the seminal track "Paid in Full") through Nas, Jay-Z, and finally to one of Hip Hop's most political duos, Dead Prez.
2. Eric B and Rakim. *Paid in Full*. (album title track, first verse) New York: 4th and Broadway Records, 1986.
3. The reference to the crossroads of lack and desire is originally connected to Hip Hop culture via Tricia Rose in *Black Noise*, but the concept itself is crystallized in Houston Baker's *Blues, Ideology, and Afro-American Literature: A Vernacular Theory*.
4. "Ghetto Gucci suits" refers to the fact that the athletic styled suits were designed with Gucci brands that were likely knockoffs.
5. Hip Hop culture consists of at least four elements: DJ-ing, MC-ing or rapping, graffiti art, and break dancing. Rap music has taken center stage, consistently overshadowing the other elements in popular culture. In the last thirty years, Hip Hop culture has developed from a relatively unknown and largely ignored inner-city culture into a global phenomenon. The foundational elements of Hip Hop culture (DJ-ing, MC-ing, break dance, and graffiti/graf) are manifest in youth culture across the globe, including Japan, France, Germany, South Africa, Cuba, and the UK.
6. Please remember that this is circa 1994 and even the venerable President Bill Clinton has singled out rapper/activist Sista Souljah for promoting violence and racial hatred. Of course that's not to mention the attacks of Bill Bennett, Tipper Gore, Bob Dole, and C. Delores Tucker.
7. Sen, Amartya. "Mortality as an Indicator of Economic Success and Failure." *The Economic Journal*, Vol. 108, No. 446. (January 1998), pp. 1–25 (17).
8. Roc-A-Fella records derives its moniker from a signifying transformation of the name of that famous Rockefeller family.
9. Jay-Z released a statement in June of 2006 that criticized Frederic Rouzaud, the managing director of Louis Roederer, the company that makes Cristal, for his racist comments in *The Economist*.
10. "The International People's Democratic Uhuru Movement (InPDUM) organizes around the question

of democratic rights for African people, and the understanding that self-determination is the highest expression of Democracy." *International People's Democratic Uhuru Movement,* 1 Aug. 2006 <http://www.inpdum.org>.

11. Stic.Man gives this analysis on the concert documentary film *Dead Prez: It's Bigger than Hip Hop,* Starz InBlack, 9 June 2006.

12. Hip-hop's development can appropriately be broken down into several eras:

1) Old School: From 1979 to 1987, hip hop culture cultivated itself in and through all of its elements usually remaining authentic to its counter cultural roots in the post-industrial challenges manifested in the urban landscape of the late-twentieth century artists associated with this era included Grandmaster Flash and the Furious Five, the Sugarhill Gang, Lady B, Big Daddy Kane, Run DMC, and Kurtis Blow.

2) The Golden Age: From 1987–1993, Rap and rappers begin to take center stage as the culture splashes onto the mainstream platform of American popular culture. The extraordinary musical production and lyrical content of rap songs artistically eclipse most of the other primary elements of the culture (breakdancing, graf art, and DJ-ing). Eventually the recording industry contemplates rap music as a potential billion-dollar opportunity directly as a result of the popularity of gangsta rap. Mass mediated rap music and Hip Hop videos displace the intimate, insulated urban development of the culture. Artists associated with this era include Run DMC, Boogie Down Productions, Eric B and Rakim, Salt N Pepa, Queen Latifah, De La Soul, A Tribe Called Quest, Public Enemy, and NWA.

3) The Platinum Present: From 1994 to the present, Hip Hop culture has enjoyed the best and worst of what mass-mediated popularity and cultural commodification has had to offer. The meteoric rise to popular fame of gangsta rap in the early 1990s set the stage for a marked content shift in the lyrical discourse of rap music toward more violent depictions of inner-city realities. Millions of magazines and records were sold, but two of Hip Hop's most promising artists, Biggie Smalls and Tupac Shakur, were literally gunned down in the crossfire of a media-fueled battle between the so-called East and West Coast constituents of Hip Hop culture. With the blueprint of popular success for rappers laid bare, several exceptional artists stepped into the gaping space left in the wake of Biggie and Tupac. This influx of new talent included Nas, Jay Z, Master P, DMX, Big Pun, Snoop Doggy Dogg, Eminem, and Outkast.

13. Bakari Kitwana defines the Hip Hop generation as those born between 1964–1985 with a similar set of watershed historical moments, relationships to media, interactions with the justice system, etc. My sense is there maybe more than one Hip Hop generation chronologically and/or conceptually.

14. Mnemonics are a technique or system of improving the memory by the use of certain formulas. In this case, I am suggesting that "Dead Presidents" symbolizes in various sociolinguistic formulas a "Dead Prezence" throughout hip hop culture, which is current and politically relevant even as it remains rooted in the economics of slavery.

Works cited

Alridge, Derrick P. "From Civil Rights to Hip Hop: Toward a Nexus of Ideas." *The Journal of African American History* 90.3 (Summer 2005): 226–252.

Baker, Houston. *Blues, Ideology, and Afro-American Literature: A Vernacular Theory.* Chicago: U of Chicago P, 1987.

Berardinelli, James. "*Dead Presidents*: A Film Review." Internet Movie Database. 1 Aug. 2006 <http://www.imdb.com/Reviews/41/4113>.

Bogdanov, Vladimir, Chris Woodstra, Stephen Erlewine, and John Bush, eds. *All Music Guide to Hip Hop: The Definitive Guide to Rap and Hip Hop.* San Francisco: Backbeat Books, 2003.

Coleman, Brian. *Rakim Told Me: Hip-Hop Wax Facts, Straight From the Original Artists.* Somerville, MA: Wax Facts Press, 2005.

Dead Prez. "It's Bigger Than Hip Hop." *Lets Get Free.* Loud Records, 2000.

———. "Propaganda." *Lets Get Free.* Loud Records, 2000.

Drake, David. Review of *RBG (Revolutionary But Gangsta),* by Dead Prez. 28 Apr. 2004. Stylus Magazine. 1 Aug. 2006 <http://www.stylusmagazine.com/ review.php?ID=1942>.

Eric B and Rakim. "Paid in Full." *Paid in Full.* 4th and Broadway Records, 1986.

Forman, Murray. *The 'Hood Comes First: Race, Space, and Place in Rap and Hip Hop.* Middleton, CT: Wesleyan UP, 2002.

Jay-Z. "Dead Presidents." *Dead Presidents.* Roc-A-Fella Records, 1996.

———. "The Takeover." *The Blueprint.* Roc-A-Fella Records/Def Jam, 2001.

Kitwana, Bakari. *The Hip Hop Generation: Young Blacks and the Crisis in African American Culture.* New York: Basic Civitas, 2002.

Maher, George Ciccariello. "Brechtian Hip-Hop: Didactics and Self-Production in Post-Gangsta Political Mixtapes." *Journal of Black Studies* 36:1 (Sep. 2005): 129–160.

Marable, Manning. *Living Black History: How Reimagining the African American Past Can Remake America's Racial Future.* New York: Basic Civitas, 2006.

Nas [Nasir Jones]. "Death Anniversary." Unreleased mix-tape single. 2006.

———. "The World Is Yours." *Illmatic.* Columbia Records, 1994.

Ong, Walter: *Orality and Literacy.* New York: Routledge, 2002.

Rose, Tricia. *Black Noise: Rap Music and Black Culture in Contemporary America.* Middleton, CT: Wesleyan UP, 1994.

Sen, Amartya. "Mortality as an Indicator of Economic Success and Failure." *The Economic Journal* 108 (Jan. 1998): 1–25.

Shusterman, Richard. "Rap Aesthetics: Violence and the Art of Keeping It Real." *Hip Hop & Philosophy: Rhyme 2 Reason.* Eds. Derrick Darby and Tommie Shelby. Chicago: Open Court, 2005.

Swedenburg, Ted. "Homies in the Hood: Rap's Commodification of Insubordination." *That's the Joint: The Hip Hop Studies Reader.* Eds. Mark A. Neal and Murray Forman. New York: Routledge, 2004. 579–591.

Watkins, S. Craig. "Black Youth and the Ironies of Capitalism." *That's the Joint: The Hip Hop Studies Reader.* Eds. Mark A. Neal and Murray Forman. New York: Routledge, 2004. 557–578.

39
Sampling Ethics

In a rare study of an "ethical system" of sampling in hip-hop production, Joseph Schloss identifies a loosely enforced series of rule-based practices that guide the labor of hip-hop's beat makers. The ethnographic approach allows hip-hop producers to describe the social norms of their "community" in their own terms, revealing the extent to which producers from different regions operate within an impressively consistent arrangement of shared values. Schloss's interviewees explain the evolution of a crucial "foundation" as producers honed their formal practices over the years, establishing the criteria of acceptable and unacceptable techniques and defining the characteristics of professional obligation.

Focusing on aesthetics and production methods, Schloss illustrates not only *how* certain beats are made but also *why* particular decisions are taken and what rationale guides the creative process. Producers address the essential requirements of "hard work" and "effort" that are embedded in such practices as "digging in the crates" to locate crucial recordings. Alternative approaches may be more time-efficient but they are also looked down upon by producers, resulting in admonition and disrespect from one's peers. The labor involved in locating beats is a means of paying one's dues in the hip-hop sector and the work ethic involved is, accordingly, related to respect among producers.

Sampling Ethics

Joseph Schloss

JOE: It's one of those things, that there seem to be. ... I don't know if "rules" is the right word. ...

VITAMIN D: Yeah.

JOE: But there are certain things. ...

VITAMIN D: They're rules! It's all following rules.

(Vitamin D 1998)

One major influence on the artistic practice of hip-hop producers is their general adherence to a defined set of professional ethics. In this chapter, I will explore the major themes of this ethical system, in order to set the stage for questions regarding the producers' philosophical outlook and aesthetic approach. I will argue that at base these ethics tend to equate creativity with moral value. From that axiom, a variety of rules have been derived, disseminated, and enforced within the producers' community.

It is important to note at the outset that what is at issue here is the validity of various *strategies* toward sampling; producers' ethics are not concerned with whether sampling *itself* is appropriate or not. Hip-hop producers, among themselves, feel no need to justify sampling; it is the foundation of the musical system. This may be why the so-called producers' ethics have largely been overlooked by the academic community—they simply do not bear on the questions that most scholars have been interested in. But they do shed light on many issues that are important to this study, including the way a community's social norms may be reflected in its specific musical choices, how an ethical system may be used to create and maintain social boundaries, and how music can mediate between the interests of individuals and their community.

Furthermore, it must be said that many of these rules hold little significance for the larger hip-hop community. If a producer violates them, it will often only be apparent to other producers. At the same time, high ethical standards are largely valued only within the production world. But, as will become clear in the following pages, concern for one's reputation among other producers is often enough to enforce a sense of ethical obligation. The community of hip-hop producers is small enough that the threat of ridicule among one's peers can be a substantial sanction. Similarly, a sense of ethical obligation serves to demonstrate producers' concern for their peers' opinions. In a spoken interlude on their 1998 album *Moment of Truth*, for instance, Gang Starr's DJ Premier berates other hip-hop artists for "lettin' the industry control the rules of the hip-hop world that *we* made." In doing so, he is implicitly arguing that this hip-hop world can be distinguished and protected from the "industry" by its control of a set of rules. In other words, pro-

610

ducers' ethics are one of the primary factors that allow hip-hop musicians to see their work as an endeavor that is separate from commerce: as art.

Section headings in this chapter reflect my own attempt to express each ethical principle in its most generally applicable form; the rules were not necessarily stated to me in these terms by any one consultant. Furthermore, I want to make it clear that by distilling the various ethical issues into a prescriptive form at the beginning of each section, it is not my intention to endorse that particular approach to the ethic in question. I have taken this step merely to delineate the ethics in their most generic terms before discussing the complexities that inevitably underlie them. Similarly, such an approach may appear to impose a systemicity on the rules that does not actually emerge from the community. While the following pages will clearly demonstrate that these ethics are highly contested, it is essential to their function that they not be seen as the construction of particular individuals. I would suggest, therefore, that regardless of how unsystematic the enforcement of the rules may be in practice, the systemicity of the rules *as a matter of principle* is of the utmost importance to producers.

Although the development of an individual producer's particular ethical sensibility is often based on his own participant-observation, its very existence in the first place is founded on the assumption that the ethics have an internal systemicity that exists independently of the observer: "I guess where the ethics came from, to me, is just because I figured out what other people were doin' and just kinda did what they did. And then found the system in it" (DJ Kool Akiem 1999).

Ethical debates tend toward the theological, which is to say that despite many disagreements, the rules themselves are seen as being timeless and unchanging. As deejay Strath Shepard comments: "I don't know how those things come about, exactly. And you just know 'em. I mean, I don't know who told me those rules. But everyone just kinda knows" (Shepard 1998). Though many specific rules probably date back to the earliest days of hip-hop, it is difficult to say with certainty when the idea of an overarching ethical system first developed. My sense, though, is that it developed in the late eighties or early nineties. One piece of evidence for this hypothesis is that many of what would now be considered to be fairly strict rules were routinely violated in the mid-eighties. For example, it is considered a violation to sample a recording that has already been used by another producer without substantially changing it. But the Rap Sample FAQ, an online compendium of sample sources, lists almost two hundred songs that sampled from James Brown's "Funky Drummer," virtually all from the middle to late eighties—and the actual number is probably closer to several thousand (http://www.members.accessus.net/~xombi/intro.html, accessed 23 August 2002). And when I raised this issue with Steinski, a producer who first came to prominence in the early 1980s, it resulted in the following exchange:

> JOE: A lot of people only sample from vinyl, as a matter of principle. A lot of people won't sample from a compilation, because they feel like the work has already been done, you should be digging for your own records, and things like that. ... Obviously, you don't feel strongly about those things. ...
> STEINSKI: Yeah. In the interview you can say "made face."
>
> (Steinski 2002)

Today, the rules exist in the background, and are rarely discussed unless violated:

> If I hear somebody do something that's unethical, I'll just make a note of it. It's not all that often that I do hear that. ... I've talked to people and heard tracks, and I'm like, "What are you doing? You sampled that offa Lord Finesse. You sampled that beat. That's wack [objectively bad]." I've gotten into arguments over stuff like that. ... [But] the cats that I talk to mostly are in my same school of ethics, really. We don't really talk about that all that much.
>
> (DJ Kool Akiem 1999)

Ethical arguments among producers usually make use of one of two strategies. They will either appeal to other rules that supersede the one in question or argue for specific exceptions to a rule without technically violating it. Such practices, in a backhanded way, serve to demonstrate the symbolic power of the rules; if the rules were not endowed with symbolic significance, individuals would simply ignore them, rather than develop elaborate philosophical rationalizations. Moreover, even producers who have no intention of actually using the exemptions they've created still enjoy developing these arguments on an abstract level.

For the purist, the ethics are one of the major tools for preserving the essence of hip-hop, even to the degree that producers in search of greater purity will actually create new rules for themselves. As producer Vitamin D put it, "I'm trying to keep it as close to the foundation as I can keep it. ... And this is just a philosophy that I came up with later on, 'cause before I was using drum machines, break records, and whatever—I didn't care—just 'cause it was new to me. But I feel that in order to have growth, your standards have to grow, so I'm kind of raising up my standards" (Vitamin D 1998). Note that Vitamin D's explicit goal in raising his standards is to "keep it ... close to the foundation." In his formulation, increasingly stringent practice, such as rejecting drum machines and break records (also known as "compilations"), brings him closer to the "foundation" of hip-hop. The new rules are seen as implicit in past hip-hop practice.

For those of a less purist bent, the rules are valued almost for their own sake; the more rules producers can take on without compromising the quality of the finished product, the greater their skill is considered to be. From this perspective, following the rules is seen as a challenge whose rewards come mainly in the social realm. As producer Samson S. describes it, "Some producers have ethics and some don't. So it's a ethical thing, basically. If you wanna feel like this is your creation, and you hooked it up, and you wanna be proud of your shit, have other producers like, 'Whoo!', you're not gonna get that respect without ethics" (Samson S. 1999). For those who hold this philosophy, then, the ethics serve to define the boundaries of originality.

None of these perspectives are in any way exclusive. In fact, more than one approach comes into play in most situations. The common thread that unites them is their sense that the rules themselves can define the essence of hip-hop. But following the rules—demonstrating one's dedication to the form on a philosophical level—does not necessarily mean that one will produce music that will be accepted by the production community; there are other aesthetic and social variables as well. Vitamin D, for example, is explicit about the distinction between music that he feels violates a "hip-hop principle," and music that he personally does not care for. "There's some things that are wack, and there's some stuff that I'm just not feelin'. But it's not wack. I'm just not feelin' it. There's a difference. A lot of stuff, I'm not feeling. [But] it doesn't go against any of the hip-hop principles that everybody else knows" (Vitamin D 1998). The ideal song, of course, will be both ethically correct *and* pleasing to listen to. Such judgments and the distinctions they entail are much easier to make in the abstract than in actual practice. In many—if not most—cases, ethics are intertwined with aesthetics or practical concerns.

"No Biting": One Can't Sample Material That Has Been Recently Used by Someone Else

The most basic ethic is to be original, often expressed in simple terms as "No biting." Discussion of this rule requires that I introduce four terms that frequently arise in production-oriented conversations: "biting," "flipping," "chopping," and "looping." My intention here is to present these meanings in their most skeletal forms in hopes that their various connotations will become apparent in the discussion to come.

"Biting" is a term that is used throughout the hip-hop world, and it refers pejoratively to the appropriation of intellectual material from other hip-hop artists. Generally speaking, it *does not* apply to the appropriation of material from outside the hip-hop community. Again, this supports the general idea of ethics as being responsive to community needs—the concerns of outsiders are not at issue. "Flipping" refers to creatively and substantially altering material in any way. This term tends to be limited to the producing community, although one can also "flip" lyrics, by, for instance, taking a common phrase and using it ironically. The idea is that one is adding value through the creativity of one's alterations. "Chopping" and "looping" are technical terms that are specific to the production arena. "Chopping," as its name suggests, refers to altering a sampled phrase by dividing it into smaller segments and reconfiguring them in a different order. "Looping," by contrast, refers to sampling a longer phrase (one or more measures) and repeating it with little or no alteration.

DJ Kool Akiem defines biting:

> To me it means, one, I'm not gonna just take a loop that somebody else did—if that's all they did, just loop it—I'm not gonna come and do the same thing without doing something to it to make it better. ... Also, I'm not gonna take two elements of something that somebody else took. Like, if somebody samples this James Brown piece and then they put the "Substitution" [drum break] on top of that? I won't do that. To me, that's biting.
>
> (DJ Kool Akiem 1999)

Samson S. explains the social repercussions for violating this rule: "You can't knowingly do that. I mean, you can if you want, but you ain't gonna get no credit. Everybody gonna be like, 'Oh, you bit such-and-such.' So why even put yourself through that?" (Samson S. 1999).

There are three generally recognized exceptions to the "No biting" rule: if one flips the sample, if one is specifically parodying the other known usage, or if the bite is unintentional.[1] Vitamin D is in the mainstream of producers when he states that he would not use the same sample as another hip-hop artist "unless I'm just one hundred percent flippin' it impossibly" (Vitamin D 1998).[2] Taken in conjunction with DJ Kool Akiem's and Samson S.'s earlier comments, it is clear that this is basically a matter of creativity deployed in a manner similar to its use in other forms of music. To do the same thing someone else does is not creative, but taking a new approach to familiar material is. Strath Shepard is emphatic about the boundaries of the exception: "Drums can get reused, but samples can't get reused. I don't think they should be reused. That's a rule. ... Unless you chop it up. But I'm saying: you have to chop it up really good. And do something totally different with it. ... Samples shouldn't be used more than once unless they are really flipped" (Shepard 1998).

As producer Negus I explains, the creativity may be valued either on its own terms or in relation to another use of the same sample, that is, as parody, which is the second exception:

> It would have to be an obvious thing that I was doing. Like, "I'm obviously using this sound that is already out right now, or it's just been out, but look how I'm doing it. Look, I'm changing it" So it wouldn't be like a underslide, like "Oh, I'm using a sound that I wonder if people are gonna notice that it's the same sound." No. I would make it obvious that, yeah, that is the same sound, but look what I did with it. Or commenting on the other song, almost.
>
> (Negus I 1998)

One frequently cited example of this practice is the track "Ya Playin' Ya-self," produced by DJ Premier in 1995 and featuring Jeru Tha Damaja: "There was one instance where I really noticed it was a response. The Junior M.A.F.I.A., the 'Player's Anthem.' Premier and Jeru came with a song called 'Ya Playin'Yaself.' They used the same bass sound, and he flipped it around, and they changed the title. I thought that was quite clever. And he made it into something totally different. But it was the same elements, two totally different songs" (Jake One 1998).

In Figure 39.1, I present the essential bass line from each song. I have numbered each note of "Player's Anthem" sequentially. For "Ya Playin' Yaself," each note has retained its corresponding

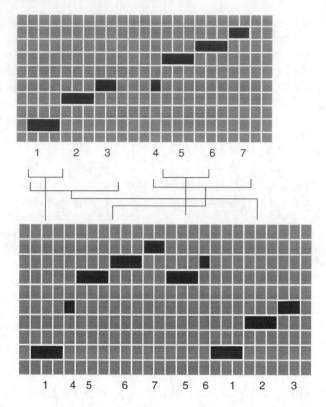

Figure 39.1 Chopping. Relationship between primary bass riff from "Player's Anthem" by Junior M.A.F.I.A. and primary bass riff from "Ya Playin' Yaself" by Jeru the Damaja.

number, so that the figure shows how DJ Premier chopped and rearranged the riff. DJ Premier's reorganization of the sample retains enough of the original bass line to be recognizable, yet changes its melodic contour and rhythmic emphasis. The lyrics of "Ya Playin' Yaself" support its interpretation as a response to "Players Anthem." The Junior M.A.F.I.A. song is a celebration of materialism, and the response is a criticism of such attitudes, deconstructing the original lyrics in a manner parallel to the way DJ Premier's beat recasts the original bass line. "You're a 'player,'" Jeru rhymes, "but only because you be playin' yourself."

Finally, the same song may be sampled coincidentally, as Seattle MC Wordsayer (who works with Negus I) notes:

> The thing that trips me out is how you can have producers in the same time, but in different places—like thousands of miles apart—taking those same elements from the same song. Using them in different ways, but using that same song, or that same album, around the same time, around the world. That's a trip, and that happens a lot. You hear somebody has a beat that's out, and you have the same elements that you're working on, or have worked on, at the same time.
>
> (Wordsayer 1998)

This raises the question of whether any given instance constitutes a coincidence or a bite, and more to the point, how such a determination would be made within the hip-hop community. To some degree, circumstantial evidence comes into play, such as which song was released first or how widely circulated each song was (i.e., whether producers are likely to have even heard the song that they are accused of biting). But in my experience, the decision is largely based on the reputation of the individual being accused. Producers of high repute are virtually never accused of biting, even in circumstances where others might be criticized. A producer who has demonstrated ethics in the past is more likely to be given the benefit of the doubt in a questionable case.

Essentially, then, the prohibition against biting reflects an approach to creativity that is similar to that employed in other forms of popular music, with one difference. Since the music is sampled, originality cannot be the ethical "default category." That is to say, in other forms of music, one is assumed to be creating original work, unless there is evidence to the contrary. In hip-hop, by contrast, one must always be prepared to defend one's creativity, and this requires standards. The producers' ethics in general and the "No biting" rule in particular help to promote those standards.

Records Are the Only Legitimate Source for Sampled Material

> I don't even have too many CDs. I don't like anything about CDs.
> I'm definitely a vinyl man.
>
> (Stroman 1999)

There is a sense among many producers that vinyl records are the only legitimate source for sampled material. This sensibility is, in many ways, a point of intersection for several otherwise unrelated concerns. On a philosophical level, the rule is closely tied to the practice of digging in the crates and represents an intellectual commitment to the deejaying tradition as the foundation of hip-hop. Aesthetic issues may also come into play, with the analog sound quality of records being preferred over the digital qualities of compact discs. Practical concerns also arise, insofar as records are more convenient to sample from, in certain ways, than other recording formats. Furthermore, the specific musical material that producers are interested in is often available only on vinyl. Finally, a practical connection between deejaying and producing is also a factor: producers who are also deejays tend to already have records available. Although, strictly speaking, these are not all ethical factors, each will be dealt with in this section because they all work to reinforce what is seen as ethical behavior.

Many aspects of hip-hop deejaying practice, such as digging in the crates, have become central to the ideology of hip-hop generally, even for those who are not deejays themselves. On some level, most hip-hoppers hold some deejay-oriented philosophical positions, not only because they love deejaying for its own sake, but also because deejaying positions itself as traditional, and they are committed, on a more abstract level, to the *idea* of tradition. Oliver Wang is particularly candid about this fact:

> I might critique the kind of overly purist perspective on "vinyl only," but I still agree with it. Like, I've never bought something on CD because it had breaks on it. And if I could do it, I'd always find it on vinyl. And the thing is, I've actually thought about it, and I don't know why I do it, except that it's just the tradition I learned. Because, I gotta say, CDs are more convenient. And if it is about the music, I'd rather listen to the music, instead of just isolating a break every time. In which case I'd rather have it on CD, because I can take it with me in the car, et cetera, et cetera. But when I dig, I only dig in vinyl.
>
> (Wang 1998)

Producer Specs sees digging for vinyl as a process of paying dues and expresses some distaste toward those who are spared that process by the increasing availability of CD reissues of classic records: "It just seems too easy. ... Because you don't have to go out shopping for CDs. You don't have to dig through CDs because they're remastering everything on 'em. You don't have to search. You have to search for records. ... So it cuts down the whole searching aspect. Like, most any good deejay or producer is gonna have to do some work. And now you don't" (Specs 1998).

Strath Shepard positions digging for vinyl as an expression of a philosophical commitment to hip-hop culture:

> It's like Zorro said in [the 1983 hip-hop film] *Wild Style*: it's like, "painting on canvas: that's not graffiti. You have to go out and rack up; you have to take the flak from everyone." You have to take the flak from the record dealers, you have to wake up in the morning and get your hands dirty. You have to be willing to go through some crazy shit to get your records. And with a CD, it's like you could just go to Blockbuster and buy that thing. Part of the culture is just digging.
>
> (Shepard 1998)

Another issue is the sound of the vinyl medium itself. While this was important in principle to many of my consultants, for many others, the value is purely situational; that is, they value the sound of records when they are looking for that particular sound. In this regard, the sound of vinyl becomes like any other aspect of a potential sample. Domino, for example, sees both the pros and cons in the use of vinyl, stating that "I like grittiness, but a lot of the pops and stuff, I'm not into" (Domino 1998). For Negus I, whether or not to use a record is a decision that must be made on a case-by-case basis: "An Al Green CD and Al Green record: it's no different to me. If I want some of that character from the vinyl, I'll use it. But if I don't need that, and I just want a clean sound I hear on that, I'll take the CD" (Negus .I.1998). DJ Kool Akiem characterizes this as an issue of aesthetics and practicality, with few ethical underpinnings:

> I don't really sample off of CDs. Unless I have a certain reason, like I wanted something really clear that I have on vinyl, that I found ... [but] it's too messed up, or something like that. Actually, I can't really remember sampling offa any CDs. If that's the only format that that comes in, that I could find, I might. But I don't see ... ethically, anything wrong with it. I mean, it's a format. [But] I don't sample offa tape, 'cause it sounds crappy.
>
> (DJ Kool Akiem 1999)[3]

Such aesthetic determinations, while they may be left to the tastes of individual producers, are rarely value free, and this one is no exception. The Angel, for instance, characterizes the exclusive emphasis on vinyl as "snobbery":

> I never had a particular snobbery about whether or not I got things from vinyl, because I could get something clean off of a CD and add vinyl noise to it. It's not about how you do it, it's about how you put it together. You know what I mean? It's how much ingenuity do you infuse into the process to get to where you want to be. There's so many different ways of achieving what you need in the process, that it's not really a problem. But I know some people [are] very, very, strict about that; I personally think it's ridiculous. ... There *is* a different sound to vinyl compression. [But] if you need it, you can do that these days. You can process things in that way and you can get it to sound that way.
>
> (The Angel 1998)

Aesthetic issues aside, records may simply be valued for their practicality. Producers are interested in "breaks"—segments of several seconds each that may be located anywhere on a recording. A producer can search a record in mere moments, simply by dropping the needle at various points. This cannot be done with a compact disc or cassette:

> I think it's just easier to do it with records. It's just easier to manipulate, you can listen to it a lot faster, go through stuff quicker. You know, you could listen to little niches in the song a lot quicker, as opposed to having to deal with a CD player. Or a tape player, even worse. To me, there's no connection to those two different things. It just seems hard to even conceive of me sampling from some CDs.
>
> (Domino 1998)

In addition to general convenience, Domino continues, there is a more specific benefit to sampling records: "I know for a lot of people that got samplers that don't have as much sampling time, they sample on 45 [rpm], which means you can get more out of your time. And you can't do that if you had a CD player" (Domino 1998). That is, many samplers have a limited amount of memory, or "sampling time." A producer can maximize this time by speeding up a 33 rpm record to 45 rpm (thus making the sample half as long), sampling it, and then slowing the sample back down to the original speed. The result may be of slightly lower quality, but it uses far less memory.

For Samson S., this—more than aesthetics or tradition—is the reason for using records: "I don't have anything against [sampling from CDs]. We haven't done it yet; it takes too much sampling time. See, on the vinyl, you can just speed it up and sample it. It's practical reasons. And plus most of the stuff you wanna sample is on vinyl anyway" (Samson S. 1999). Another reason for relying on vinyl, as Samson S. points out, is that it is the only format in which most of the valued music is available. As Domino puts it, "There's not too much on a CD that's appealing to me, the kind of stuff that I look for" (Domino 1998).

Finally, there are more general issues of practicality as well. Many producers may simply not have CDs available, as my conversation with producer King Otto confirms:

> KING OTTO: I probably wouldn't sample off a CD. But I've sampled off tape before, only a couple times, because I didn't have the record. But I would pretty much stick with records, as a rule. ...
>
> JOE: It's interesting, I noticed you said you "probably" wouldn't sample off a CD, as if it's just never come up before.
>
> KING OTTO: Well, I don't have any CDs. [But] I wouldn't sample off CDs, I don't think.
>
> JOE: And that's just for the sound?
>
> KING OTTO: The sound, and maybe the ethic thing of it.
>
> (King Otto 1998)

This is a particular issue for producers who are also deejays; they use records for their other pursuits. All other things being equal, it still is far more efficient to simply buy the record, which, in addition to being a source of samples, can be played in a club or on the radio in its original form (hip-hop deejays prefer vinyl over other media because many of hip-hop's foundational deejaying techniques, such as scratching, can only be performed with vinyl records, although the electronics industry is working hard to create CD players that can emulate the feel of a turntable).

> NEGUS I: That only makes sense. Because why would you spend your money on a CD, when you could spend that money to buy the same thing on a record? And as a deejay you could use it.
>
> JOE: Especially if it's your *job* to be a deejay.
>
> NEGUS I: Yeah, 'cause a lot of it come down to economics and finances.
>
> (Negus I 1998)

One Cannot Sample from Other Hip-Hop Records

As far as, like, for your music? Oh hell no! (Samson S. 1999)
Nah. Hell nah. That's like crazy wrong. And cats be doin' that! That's just ridiculous, man. Totally ridiculous.

(DJ Kool Akiem 1999)

The value of "digging in the crates" is again manifested in this rule. One shouldn't sample from another hip-hop record because one would be exploiting the effort of the original producer who dug for the sound. As King Otto puts it, "It doesn't take any work to sample from a rap record, basically. Because it's already there for you, it can be sampled" (King Otto 1998). The rationale behind this rule is so self-evident to producers that it only becomes an issue in three rather narrow areas: sampling individual drum hits, sampling vocal expressions as a tribute to the original MC, and briefly sampling the instrumental track for purposes of parody or homage.

In our conversation, Jake One describes how the first practice, sampling drums, works:

JAKE ONE: People ... sample drums off of hip-hop records. You know, somebody leaves the kick open or something. ...

JOE: When you say, "leaves the kick open," you mean there's just the drum sound with nothing on top of it. ...

JAKE ONE: Yeah. You can take it and put it in your beat, you know?

JOE: So do people purposely *not* do that [leave drums open], so that [other] people won"t ...

JAKE ONE: I don't know. ... Q-Tip used to always leave drums open. I remember the Mobb Deep single "Give Up the Goods," he had a kick and a snare on there. The snare is too recognizable, though. See, you wanna be able to take something that nobody knows. ... What was that other record? "The World is Yours" remix? He left kicks and snares open with that. ... "One Love," people take drums off of "One Love." Premier, I noticed, doesn't leave drums open. Like if you have an instrumental, he'll have a voice echoing through it. ...

JOE: Do you think he does that on purpose?

JAKE ONE: I think so. Cause if the only dropout in the song, he happens to throw an extra delay on it in an instrumental mix, it sounds kind of weird. ... It's crazy. ... I think about this stuff way too much. Way too much.

(Jake One 1998)

In noting that he thinks about these issues "way too much," Jake One is, at least in part, referring to the fact that he was immediately able to call to mind several examples of hip-hop songs which contained moments where a drum was played in isolation, including one on which there was only a single potentially usable drum hit in the entire song. This is typical of the way hip-hop producers listen to music. In fact, it is perhaps the most significant aspect of this particular prohibition: in order to invoke the rule in the first place, a listener must be able to identify the recorded origins of a *single strike of a drum.*[4]

Later in our conversation, Jake (now joined by Strath Shepard) makes reference to this fact and notes the sanctions that can be expected for a violation:

JAKE ONE: You'll get ridiculed! I'll ridicule someone if I hear 'em use the "One Love" drums, or something like that.

Strath: He probably did that [left it open] on purpose, actually, because that drum is so ...

JAKE ONE: Yeah, it's so distinct.

STRATH: And no one knows what it is.

JOE: So do you think he did that just as a challenge to people?
STRATH: Yeah. Like, "I'll know if you take my drum."

(Jake One 1998)

The use of ridicule as a viable sanction suggests a relatively unified and small community, regardless of the physical distance involved. The idea that producers in New York might be concerned that a producer in Seattle is laughing at them speaks volumes.

Mr. Supreme discusses sampling from hip-hop records in the plaintive tone of one who feels that his own work has been devalued by the lowering of ethical standards: "I don't think it's appropriate to take the instrumental of a rap record and use it. But I'm sure people would argue with me. They'll say, 'Well, what's the difference if we took that or Bobby Azzam from Switzerland?' Well, to me, there *is* a difference, you know? There's a difference" (Mr. Supreme 1998).

The producer Specs, though he admits committing this particular breach of etiquette in a certain case, has a similarly visceral reaction to this particular rule: "That's a weird one because I've actually done that before, because I don't have an 808 [a Roland TR-808 drum machine]. And there's a certain record, Brooklyn Alliance, that has this 808 kick that I always sampled. ... But not music, though. I would never sample something that was already sampled from somebody else. That just seems like some weird type of incest or something. Just kind of strange. I would definitely say that was a rule" (Specs 1998). Specs's reasons for not sampling from other hip-hop records suggest that, as with Mr. Supreme, the practice is actually emotionally uncomfortable: it's "kind of strange" and "like some weird type of incest." At the same time, though, he makes an exception for drum sounds, as does DJ Kool Akiem:[5] "Nah. Possibly if it's like a 808 boom maybe, or something like that. That's just no big deal, but I wouldn't sample something that somebody else sampled" (DJ Kool Akiem 1999).

Like Specs and DJ Kool Akiem, King Otto exempts drum sounds from the rule, but holds fast when it comes to nondrum sounds: "I'd say that's a rule. I think everyone has, once or twice. Like a kick [drum]. I've taken a kick off a record before. I took some drums off a Tribe Called Quest record once, when nothing was playing but the drums, so that you couldn't really tell that I got it off there. But, other than that, I wouldn't do it. I wouldn't condone it" (King Otto 1998). King Otto specifically states that not only would he not do this himself, but he would also not condone the practice for others. This supports the idea of it being a rule, rather than a personal preference.

The use of vocal samples from other hip-hop songs is more problematic. For some, the resistance to their use exists primarily in the realm of emotion. As Mr. Supreme says, "It just kinda makes me mad. ... I don't know why, it just does" (Mr. Supreme 1998a). For others, it's a matter of aesthetics more than ethics: "Yeah, I agree [that it's bad to sample vocals]. But I'm not totally against it. As long as it ain't like, 'Punks jump! Puh-Puh-Puh!' you know, like in them drum and bass records. ... That gets to be corny. But if you strategically place it in a song, it don't matter. To me, at least" (Samson S. 1999). Perhaps the most intriguing take on this rule came from Vitamin D. He argued that it was permissible to use vocals from other hip-hop records, but only if they were placed there in real time by a deejay playing the original record on a turntable—it was not permissible to insert the vocals with a sampler:

Let's say I wanted to take [a] Greg Nice [vocal] and put that in the chorus. ... I have to cut it in if it's gonna be in the song. I can't sample it in; a lotta people will just sample it in. ... I have to cut it with the turntables, I can't sample it in. ... [When people sample vocals], I be like, "Hey, what are you doing, man? You're taking away, man!"

(Vitamin D 1998)

DJ Topspin agrees, at least in principle:

Yeah. I mean, yeah, you should cut it in. He's a very hardcore deejay, and I believe that, too. I mean, I don't have a *problem* if it's sampled. I have more in my life than to have a problem with what somebody does on a record. ... [But] if you're doing nothin' but sampling a vocal and just hittin' it, then that says that you have no deejay skills or desire to showcase them. Really ... you should scratch them in if you can. Anybody can learn a machine and load 'em into a machine.

(DJ Topspin 1999)

When I asked Negus I about this restriction, he theorized that it was based on Vitamin D's dual identity as a producer and a deejay:

I think ... that's because ... He may think that using vocal samples is kind of cheesy, unless you actually do it as a deejay ... 'cause he's a producer *and* a deejay. And I think he may feel that sampling somebody's vocals and laying it on your track is kind of cheesy, as a producer. *So he does it as a deejay.* ... But I know D has a lot of those rules.

(Negus I 1998)

This supports the social nature of these rules; the appropriateness of using vocal samples from other hip-hop records depends upon the identity of the individual in question, and the tradition that individual claims to represent. The sampling of rap vocals, in Vitamin D's view, is a violation of the professional ethics of the producer, but not of the deejay. In addition, Negus I's comment that Vitamin D was a particularly rule-oriented producer (a contention supported both by Vitamin D himself and by other producers who know him) illustrates that it is not uncommon for producers to have rules that only apply to themselves.

DJ Kool Akiem, however, does not accept the distinction: "Nah. I don't agree with that. I mean, I could see why that rule would exist, but I don't agree with it. Because ... Well, put it like this: say you don't want the scratch on it, you just want the cut? How're you gon' know? What's the difference gon' be? If you cut it in, or you sample it in, you ain't gonna know [the difference]" (DJ Kool Akiem 1999). DJ Kool Akiem's approach is based on the sound that ultimately emerges rather than the method with which it was created. To "scratch" the vocal sample into the recording is to emphasize the sound of the vocal being moved back and forth on a turntable—something that cannot be done with a sampler. But to "cut" the vocal sample in is to use only the sound itself. This would sound the same whether it was done with a turntable or a sampler. And if you can't hear the difference in the final product, DJ Kool Akiem argues, then there's no basis for claiming an ethical violation. This approach to ethics has a practical value; in most cases, the only evidence of how something was created is how it sounds on the final record.

The final exception to the rule against sampling other hip-hop records is the use of brief sections for the purposes of parody or reference. When I asked him about sampling from other hip-hop records, DJ Kool Akiem was emphatically opposed to the practice, except in this case: "You have to have, like, a certain specific reason. And I can't hardly see nothin' except for when Ice Cube did 'Jackin' For Beats.'[6] That's like the only possible way I could see. ... You know what I'm sayin', it's like a novelty thing" (DJ Kool Akiem 1999). DJ Topspin agrees: "Me, personally, DJ Topspin in Seattle, I'm not gonna sample anybody else's record that came out a year ago for any other purpose instead of a quick reference" (DJ Topspin 1999).

Not everyone is opposed to sampling from hip-hop records. Domino, for example, feels that recent events may have conspired to make digging-related ethics obsolete. Note, however, that before he explains his philosophical acceptance of the practice, he is careful to state that he personally doesn't—*ever*—sample from hip-hop records:

I don't ever ... do that. [But] I don't think it's a big deal. ... I know a lotta people that you could tell they sampled a known sample from, like, a Tribe record, as opposed to getting it from the original. I think that, back a couple of years ago, I woulda been like, "Oh that's wack," 'cause I think to a lot of producers, part of the art was finding the record. But now, with the popularity of these breakbeat records. ... that put out all the hard to find records, anyway—in abundance ... it's the same thing [as sampling from hip-hop records].

(Domino 1998)

As this example illustrates, producers often construct legalistic exceptions to production ethics, even when they have no intention of actually using the exceptions they create. This was an attitude that I encountered regularly during my research, and it shows the abstract enjoyment that can be derived from working with the ethical system.

The rule against sampling from hip-hop records emphasizes the value of hard work and creativity. Sampling from a hip-hop record, producers argue, does not demonstrate either of these qualities because the record has already been discovered, presented, and optimized for a hip-hop aesthetic.

One Can't Sample Records One Respects

Another rule I have: I don't sample records that I respect. I don't know, but that's the only way I can really put it. The reason why I haven't sampled some of the records down here is just 'cause I got too much respect for it, man. The record still bugs me out, to the point where I don't know how I'd flip it, you know? I get that when I listen to Miles Davis . ... He just trips me out. I be like, "Man!" Can't really mess with that. That's a sacred type thing.

(Vitamin D 1998)

To a large degree it's like: unless you can add something, or flip it in a totally amazing way, leave it alone. Like, there's some artists, I just kind of feel like, "Don't mess with Stevie Wonder or Marvin Gaye stuff."

(Dere 1998)

There are records that are just there. They're fresh already. And you taking it isn't gonna make you a better producer. I mean, there's records I've used, I'm, "I can't sample this. This guy's tight! You just gotta sit back and listen to this." 'Cause you can mess up a good record. ... A nice song, until you loop it and say how fresh you are over it. It's like, there's some records that can be left alone . ... Something that you can't really mess with, just because it's so pure, it's like putting it into a hip-hop context can be difficult and almost detrimental to the record itself.

(DJ Topspin 1999)

This rule rests on three pillars: that sampling may be disrespectful to a great artist, that some music is so good that sampling does not improve it, and that sampling something that was already good is not sufficiently challenging. The first and second of these are telling in that sampling is not seen as being disrespectful to artists in general, only to particularly esteemed ones. The third pillar supports the idea that ego gratification and fun are a part of hip-hop in production; listeners are presumed to make an assessment of the degree of difficulty when they judge the accomplishments of other producers.

Not everyone agrees with this rule, however.

Nah. ... If I respect a record, I'm samplin' the hell out of it! Now, I mean, I ain't gonna force it. If there's a record I like a lot, but I can't find nothin' on it. ... But, nah, I don't have that rule.

(Samson S. 1999)

Nah. I don't agree with that. I mean there's some fantastic stuff that I have high praise for. But I'll still sample it. To me, it's the highest praise to sample it.

(DJ Kool Akiem 1999)

While Negus I agrees with Samson S. and DJ Kool Akiem, his take on this issue shows that the underlying concern of individuals on both sides of the issue is essentially the same—how one can best exercise one's creativity. "I would definitely use a part of a song that I loved, because it has that spirit in it. And I would like to get some of that spirit. But I would have to put as much of my spirit into changing that sound and doing something to it, to make it worthwhile. I wouldn't wanna just use the [melody] and put a beat over it" (Negus I 1998).

One Can't Sample from Reissues or Compilation Recordings of Songs with Good Beats

Midway through their 1998 album, *Moment of Truth*, Gang Starr's DJ Premier abruptly stops the music, in order to deliver the following rejoinder to unnamed individuals in the hip-hop community that he feels have violated ethical principles:

What's the deal with you break-record cats that's puttin' out all the original records that we sample from, and *snitchin'* by puttin' us on the back of it; sayin' that we use stuff? You *know* how that go! Stop doing that! Y'all are violatin', straight up and down! Word up, man; I'm sick of this shit. Y'all muhfuckas really don't know what this hip-hop's all about. So while y'all keep on fakin' the funk, we gonna keep on walkin' through the darkness, carryin' our torches. Underground will live forever, baby! We just like roaches: never dyin', always livin'. And on that note, let's get back to the program. ...

The general tone of DJ Premier's polemic is consistent with the conception of professional ethics that I am proposing. Both his use of the term "violating" and his argument that "you *know* how that go" (i.e., ignorance is no excuse) suggest a world in which all who participate are expected to abide by the professional ethics of the producer. In this case, DJ Premier is specifically referring to the use of so-called breakbeat compilations.

It was not long after sampling began in the mid-1980s that Lenny Roberts's *Ultimate Breaks and Beats* compilations popularized the practice of deejays and record collectors assembling rare jazz, funk, and soul singles into anthologies, thus reducing the need for producers and deejays to dig for original recordings. Since that time, hundreds of such anthologies have been released— usually unlicensed, often unlabeled, almost always on vinyl—and they have become something of a sore point for producers who do dig for beats: "[They] get scorned, 'cause you spent so much time looking for records and you got these fools samplin' off hip-hop records and compilations. ... Your time isn't well spent, you know? It's like they're just making a mockery of your searches. ... And it's obvious, you know, sometimes when somebody uses a certain drum sound, and you know they don't have that record" (Jake One 1998).

Other producers agree:

People are putting out breakbeat records and stuff and that's not really cool ... 'cause it makes it super-easy. All these kids in the suburbs can sound like they're just the greatest producer in the world.

They got all these breaks that everyone else has. So it's just weird. I don't think it should be that easy. It's not meant to be easy, you know?

(Specs 1998)

People can be a producer and don't have to really search and find the good records. Before, it was kinda like you were as good as the records that you found. ... The better records that you found, the better you would be.

(Domino 1998)

Simply stated, compilations are seen as a shortcut. They save the producer much of the effort that was previously necessary to make a beat. While the producers' statements demonstrate that this is resented for that reason alone, Beni B adds two other complaints: the first is that taking the easier path denies the producer the musical education that he could have gained from digging, and the second is that by not "putting in the work," one is taking unfair advantage of the knowledge developed by an earlier generation of producers and deejays and thereby exploiting hip-hop itself.

BENI B: The thing to understand about reissues is that reissues are just that: they're reissues. They're not an education, OK? They're not an education. Some people are of the belief that "OK, I can go out and I can buy all these reissues." But you know what? Let's face it: again, it's not an education.

JOE: So you mean you have to do more work than that.

BENI B: Yup. You gotta put in the work, baby. And a lot of times, you know, cats are not trying to put in. ... Some people put in the effort, other people don't. And you have to be willing to put in that work. And if you don't put it in, you always wind up short-changing it. You just can't do that. ... You have to respect it, man. And a lot of people, it's like they *claim* they respect it, but, let's face it, they really don't. Everything has a past. And everything has a beginning. And so you gotta ... have respect for that.

(Beni B 2002)

Many producers—while acknowledging the annoyance of seeing others have easy access to records that they had to invest a great deal of time, money, or effort to acquire—still do not feel that this rises to the level of an ethical violation:

I'm not against compilations, personally. Sometimes it really burns me up, though, when I see stuff that I spent a whole lotta money for, that people didn't really know about; now all of a sudden everybody on the block has it for, like, nine dollars. That kinda burns me up. But I've gotten a lot of stuff that I couldn't find elsewhere on compilations, too. So it's a double-edged sword. Take the good with the bad; that's all there is to it.

(Stroman 1999)

Samson S. sees digging for original records as a function of ethics, which are themselves a function of ego. One holds oneself to a higher ethical standard out of pride: "I understand [sampling from compilations], but my ethics won't allow me to do it ... only because, like I said, it's all ego and being proud of your shit. Being like 'Yeah, I found this'" (Samson S. 1999).

A similar approach may be at work for Domino:

In the end of the day, when it comes out, no one's gonna know the difference. I think that's kinda like a producer pet peeve. That's kind of like part of the fun. Like you can say, "Look, I got all these songs! I got the originals, I got this, I got that!" It's almost, in a sense, no different than pullin' out the John Coltrane *Blue Trane* original. And then a kid comes and pulls out the reissue, on vinyl. You know what I'm sayin'? If you put on the records, you'd hear the same shit. In fact, the new one would probably sound better! But ultimately, when you listen to it, it's the same thing. But … certain people, like collectors, would say, "No. The original's the one." So it all depends on what you're getting out of it, your outlook.

(Domino 1998)

This formulation likely accounts for the apparently paradoxical philosophy espoused by most producers when they explicitly grant legitimacy to compilations while simultaneously making an emphatic point of their own strict avoidance of them: "I don't have no rule against it. [But] I don't really do it. I could see where I would, if I just couldn't get something. That's, again, it's 'Who's gonna know?' It could be like a compilation, or it's a re-pressing, or them breakbeat records. What's the difference? Everybody sampled offa them *Ultimate Breakbeats* back in the eighties. I can't think of no artist that didn't" (DJ Kool Akiem 1999).

Prince Paul takes this argument one step further; he feels that his ethical sensibility actually works against his creativity.

You have these records now, especially the new ones—not like Super Disco Breaks and the other ones in the early days, the Ultimate Beat Breaks and stuff—but the ones now that they have everybody's sample—"They used this, they used that"—and it has it all on one record? That was a *crime* back in the days! It's more like, I came from the era when you found records that nobody had, or you got the original. To me that's cheating: "Oh, I got all these beats on one record." And, unfortunately, I kind of keep that with me to this very day. But I'm breaking out of that. It's something like … an internal fight inside me: like, "It's not right." 'Cause it's a moral sense. Sometimes what you're stating is not a technical sense, it's just a morality thing. It's like staying true to whatever you think is real. … I have, like I said, these old-school ethics, but then I'm not blocking myself from learning. That's the important thing.

(Prince Paul 2002)

Harkening back to Vitamin D's rule about not sampling vocals from other hip-hop records, some producers make a situational distinction for the use of compilations. DJ Topspin, for example, feels that compilations are acceptable for live deejaying purposes but should not be sampled on recordings: "If you're spinnin' 'em somewhere, that's cool. You know, you can't have every record. No matter how much searching you do, you can't have every piece of vinyl. So I appreciate compilations that have tight songs, to play 'em. But as far as me making a song from it? Nah. 'Cause someone else did the footwork to get it in your possession. And that's half the fun: coming out with something you either made or found or manipulated yourself" (DJ Topspin 1999). Even people who use compilations can still think it's wrong: "I used to buy 'em, back in the days. To have records with just drum loops on 'em. It would be popular loops, and it would just go for like three minutes, or whatever. And back then, I'd be known to sample some of that stuff. I always felt like I was cheating. And I still kinda feel like it's cheating if you sample from a reissued record, or one of those breakbeat records" (King Otto 1998).

It is important to remember that the ethical issue here has nothing to do with the fact that the record is unlicensed and the original artists are being deprived of royalties. The ethical problem for producers is that those who use compilations are not doing the work of digging for their own beats. This is significant because it is an example of how ethics can run parallel to a legal concept and yet be based on an entirely different set of concerns. Oliver Wang's perspective on this issue is an incisive one:

The interesting thing … is that artists don't get paid off of used records. So, for instance, let's use Bob James, a lot of people sample Bob James. If you find a copy of *Two*, which has "Mardi Gras," which is the break that everyone knows, right? Collectors will sell that [for] upwards of twenty dollars, which is actually woefully overpriced for that. But it's not like Bob James makes any profit off of that. Versus if someone puts "Mardi Gras" on a legitimate compilation, which are much more frequent nowadays. Most compilations these days, permission has been granted. In theory, the artist is actually getting paid off the compilation. Versus if you're digging in a used record store for stuff, the artist is never gonna see a penny of that. ... So then the question becomes who's more important: the artist you're sampling from, or the deejay that you're working with? I mean, that's kind of a side issue; you still shouldn't sample from compilations, 'cause it's lazy.[7]

(Wang 1998)

For most hip-hop producers the answer to Wang's question is simple: without question the deejay, the producer, is more important. But this is also an example of the kind of legalistic theorizing I mentioned earlier: after Wang lays out his argument, he declares it moot. The use of compilations is considered inappropriate regardless of whether or not the original artist is paid, for all the reasons my consultants cited.

The problematic relationship between producers' ethics and legality is also brought to light in yet another way with compilations. On some more recent compilations, the labels contain information not only about the original song, but also about hip-hop songs that have sampled it. This is viewed as an ethical violation for two reasons. The first is that it gives away privileged information that should rightfully be acquired through diligent digging or at least through word of mouth. The second is that it puts the cited hip-hop producer at legal risk: many of the samples have not been legally cleared, particularly if they were, for example, only one or two notes from a saxophone solo. Although such a sample would probably not require the producer to pay publishing rights to the original composer, it would still technically require a payment to the record company for use of the master recording. This is what DJ Premier refers to as "snitching."

As Domino explains, with regard to DJ Premier's statement on *Moment of Truth*, which began this section:

On Biggie's second album, he has a song called "Ten Crack Commandments" that Premier produced. And, basically, it's like a drum and then he's scratching in [a two-note pattern], and all he doin' is scratchin', and it's just he's scratching in a little sound. Well, not too long ago, I was looking at these break records. ... I played the record, and it was like—you hear it—but it was like, *wow*, you know what I mean? Someone who found that record *peeped* it. Even though it was such a little piece, they put it on the back of a record, and so now everyone knows. And probably the guy who made the [original] song probably wouldn't even have recognized that that was his record, unless he reads ... this breakbeat record that someone came out with. And so that's what they were talking about.

(Domino 1998)

I have heard three exceptions to the "no compilations" rule, all of which are in dispute: if one only samples drums, if one "does the work" to dig for the original record, and if one only samples from the original *Ultimate Breaks and Beats* compilation.

For Negus I, the use of drums from breakbeat records is an issue of creativity, analogous to the "No biting" rule:

I know that's a big no-no. I've taken drum sounds from breakbeat records, but not looped the break, as it is on the record. I've just chopped up the snare and the kick, or take a high-hat off it. And I usually do that when I'm getting frustrated, 'cause drum sounds are hard to find. And when I'm getting frustrated, I'll just take a couple drum sounds off of a breakbeat record, just so I don't get frustrated and turn my machine off and do something else, because I can't find any drum sounds. I'll just do that just to keep the process going. ... That's a whole thing too: even if you do use sounds, like drum sounds, from a break-beat record, if you can flip 'em up in a way that nobody's done it before? True, you're using the sounds ... but you are doing something that's creative ... so if you use it like that, I think you won't be in violation as much.

(Negus I 1998)

Strath Shepard agrees that sampling drums isn't a serious violation: "I'm kinda undecided about sampling off of bootlegs. I definitely don't think you should sample loops off bootlegs. Your music should not be from bootlegs. Because someone else essentially found it before you, and if they didn't use it, they could have used it. So I don't think you should sample the music part, but drums are a little different. You could sample drums off bootlegs" (Shepard 1998).

The second exception is sometimes made on the basis of the producer's level of effort in digging for records. This refers to the essence of the complaint about compilations in the first place: that one hasn't done the work. Theoretically, producers can posit situations in which the work *was* done, but for some practical reason, one is deprived of the original record. This may be acceptable. The following conversation with Mr. Supreme illustrates how such an argument may be constructed.

> MR. SUPREME: I'm kind of mad that the comps come out. It kinda ruins it. We've spent all these years trying to be fresh, and dig, and find all this shit. And then some asshole puts it out for the whole world to use. It kinda hurts you, you know? ... But at the same time, who cares? ... If it's good, it's good. Why not? If you can make a good record, why not?
> JOE: Yeah, but you're *saying* that, 'cause you're ... open minded. But you don't actually *do* that [sample from compilations], though. You know what I mean?
> MR. SUPREME: [laughs] No, you're right! I don't do that ... [but] we really created this hip-hop shit. Like Premier said, we did create this shit. So for some jackass to try to sell me a beat for fifty dollars that he wouldn't give a fuck about. ... If it wasn't for us it would be a one-dollar record! So how's he gonna try to sell it to us for fifty dollars? It's like "So forget you, I'll go buy the bootleg for eight bucks up the street!" But at the same time, [buying compilations is] kinda wrong, you know? Its gotten out of hand, that's what it's come down to, is that it's gotten out of hand. But, yeah, like you say ... I don't do it. There are rules; I try to be open minded, but there's just some things I don't do. (Mr. Supreme 1998a)

Mr. Supreme begins with a strong statement of general opposition to compilations before suggesting that the value of a good sample may, in some cases, outweigh the "No compilations" rule. At this point I call to his attention the fact that despite his theoretical acceptance of that exception, he still regards the rule as binding on himself personally. He responds by developing a different exception to the "No compilations" rule: why should producers be forced to pay inflated record prices, when they were the ones who created the demand in the first place? He presents himself, hypothetically, as someone who has a choice between the original record and a compilation; this implicitly requires that he have done the appropriate digging (otherwise he wouldn't have the option of choosing the original). Thus the exception is drawn: *Assuming one has done the work*, it would be acceptable to avoid paying the inflated price to a record collector by buying the compilation. (Notice, however, that although Mr. Supreme develops two different rationales for violating the compilations rule, he, like several other producers I interviewed, ends his statement by saying he still wouldn't do it.)

This approach—that compilations are justifiable if one does the work—is not unique to Mr. Supreme; Phill Stroman maintains a similar position:

> Maybe if I was a person who didn't have any records, maybe I'd have a little complex about it. But I *got* records. I don't have nothin' to prove to anybody. ... I got credentials, as far as diggin'; I'm not some kid who just picked something up from the store down the corner. I mean, I dig. I put in my work, you know? I paid the dues. So, yeah, I'll take something from a compilation, what the hell.
>
> (Stroman 1999)

Finally, Samson S. articulates an exception that is particularly interesting. He distinguishes between the original series—*Ultimate Breaks and Beats*—and other, more recent compilations. In his formulation, apparently, *Ultimate Breaks and Beats* has been around long enough that it has, in some sense, become an original recording.

> JOE: Sampling from compilations.
> SAMSON S.: Oh, like them breakbeat records? Man, we've *all* did it! And I don't care what nobody say! People can talk about rules and shit, [but] everybody done sampled offa them *Ultimate Break and Beat* records. I mean, that's why they made 'em back in the days—for that. But ... you don't wanna do no beat sampling goddamn *Q-Bert Marshmellow Breaks* [a more recent compilation] or nothin' like that. ... Just go get the old school *Ultimate Breaks and Beats.* ... You can use those, that's not really forbidden. But all these new breakbeat records coming out, it's not wise to do that. You should just go out and get your own shit.
>
> (Samson S. 1999)

DJ Kool Akiem's response to this assertion demonstrates the rhetorical complexity that invariably ensues when these discussions begin. He addresses Samson's exemption from the perspective of one who doesn't agree with the original rule to begin with. In essence, his intent is to demonstrate the hypothetical weakness of the exception (which he, in reality, agrees with) in order to show that the boundaries of the rule itself are untenable: "I can kinda understand. The reason is because everybody sampled off of them. So that's not a good enough reason, 'cause your rule should still stand fast. Just 'cause everybody else did it, that don't make it OK. Say you take another one of them compilation sets, everybody started sampling it, would it be OK then? When it wasn't before? So that's why I don't have no problems with compilations" (DJ Kool Akiem 1999).

One Can't Sample More Than One Part of a Given Record

> I have another rule: "Thou shall not sample two sounds from the same record." Unless it's a continuous loop, like if you're choppin' something ... But don't fuckin' jack a bass line from the record, horns from that same record, Fender Rhodes. ... We call that cheating.
>
> (Samson S. 1999)

The association of ethical righteousness with creativity is manifested in this rule. Essentially, the rule argues that it is not creative to combine things that already go together. This is a point of pride with many producers:

> I wouldn't do that either. One thing that's real wack to me is, in the same cut, using sam-

ples from two different cuts on the same [original] album. Or even the same artist, I would-n't do that. Unless it's maybe just a drum, you know. Something real small, maybe. But I wouldn't do that. I guess the reason why for that is because it ... feels like cheatin' a little bit. Or too easy, because you're blending two sounds that are almost the same. ... Part of the artistry is to combine elements that wouldn't be combined normally. You know, that's one aspect of the artistry. I wouldn't put two samples of the same artist on the same cut, at all. Ever. Won't do that at all. And I almost wouldn't sample—like for a album—I would-n't sample the same artist twice, either. You know, maybe something real small or some-thing, but definitely not two loops, 'cause then you might as well just be makin' *his* album.

(DJ Kool Akiem 1999)

DJ Topspin explicitly characterizes this as a matter of personal pride: "As far as the producers' ethic is concerned, it's all in what you want to do and what you feel *proud* of doing. I wouldn't feel proud taking more than one thing from the same record and putting it on the same beat" (DJ Topspin 1999).

It is significant that when producers are judged to be breaking a hip-hop rule, they are often accused of "taking away." The phrase is telling; it assumes hip-hop is a collective enterprise, and it suggests that when producers violate rules, they are not only failing to contribute to the collec-tive project, but actually undoing what has already been accomplished by others.

This, I submit, is due to the values that the producers' ethics encode: material effort or hard work, and intellectual effort or creativity. The value of material effort is manifested in the empha-sis on vinyl records over other media and the rejection of compilations and other hip-hop records as sample sources. Producers are expected to put in a certain amount of effort to obtain their samples. To circumvent this expectation is unethical.

The value of intellectual effort can be seen in producers' reluctance to indulge is such creative shortcuts as sampling records that are already great and sampling more than one part of a par-ticular record. This value is also the underlying rationale for the more general "No biting" rule: one is expected to inject a certain amount of creativity into the process.

When producers make unethical beats, they are implicitly suggesting that hard work and cre-ativity are not important. They are *taking these things away* from the practice of hip-hop pro-duction:

KRS-ONE once said to me that every wack record sets hip-hop back five years. He may have been speaking in a hyperbolic sense, but there he was expressing an idea based on the interconnectivity to which you allude. ... Maybe it has to do with the fact that musical ideas are so viral. They're so easily transferred and they're like colds. You can really pass them along easily. You can get them easily and pass them along easily. ... It's like if you had a rare gas and you were supposed to protect it. And then one day somebody just walked around and picked the bottle up and opened it. It's hard to get that gas back. It's hard to bring that rare thing back. And when you do something that's bad, these ideas have a way of spreading and becoming part of the body. And so people really look at that as very severe. It's not like building blocks where you can pick them up, they're all discrete. ... Ideas are hard to locate and hard to stop.

(Allen 2003)

In contrast, to express oneself *within* the traditional boundaries honors the form as a whole and elevates the individual producer. Deejay Strath Shepard, for instance, defends the producer DJ Shadow, essentially making the argument that regardless of how his music *sounds*, it is hip-hop if it follows the ethics of hip-hop: "A lot of people argue about whether DJ Shadow is hip-hop or not. Because he claims real hip-hop, to the fullest. But then, you get the album, you listen to it, and most people are like, 'Well, that's not hip-hop.' But I consider it hip-hop, because of the way it's made. It's made with records and sampling and a deejay. So ... to me, if he wants to call it hip-hop, he can call it hip-hop" (Shepard 1998). What Shepard is suggesting is that an artist may maintain an allegiance to the hip-hop producers' community through his adherence to ethical practice, and that such dedication may carry more weight than the actual sound of the music.

That said, the ethics are merely the price of admission; a producer must have ethics in order to be respected, but the mere adherence to traditional ethics alone does not guarantee the praise of other producers. The acceptance of one's musical peers requires a keen grasp of a more abstract and malleable set of standards, of what might be termed "aesthetic expectations"—collective ideas about what sounds good. Prince Paul is rather blunt about the distinction:

> There's a lot of underground records that people [are] like, "I'm so true to hip-hop," that's *crappy*. It doesn't matter how you make the record, or what style you use. It matters if it's good. That's the bottom line, man. 'Cause I can go to Fat Beats [a New York record store that sells underground hip-hop] now—not to name names—but a lot of kids like, "Yo, we're from the *true* school, we only perform in underground clubs and we make no money 'cause we keepin' it real. And we got X amount of people while we perform. We got a break-dancer and a graffiti artist and we wear only shell toes." And you listen to the record, and it's *garbage!* It's flat-out garbage. You know, it's like, "Yo, that has nothing to do with the quality of your music."
>
> (Prince Paul 2002)

The quality of a producer's music is therefore judged by standards that are far more subjective and abstract.

Study Questions

1. How are legitimacy and authority established within the ethical system of hip-hop music production?
2. What is the role of tradition among hip-hop DJs and record producers?
3. Through what means do DJs and producers demonstrate creativity and originality?

Notes

1. A fourth possibility, that a usage is a tribute or homage to an earlier hip-hop song, does not apply here; the "No biting" rule only applies to songs that are released at roughly the same time. Tributes must be created several years later to be acceptable.
2. Flipping is also valued for its own sake, aesthetically, as opposed to as an indicator of an ethical orientation. This is a somewhat arbitrary distinction that I'm making for the sake of clarity and does not necessarily reflect the views of the producers.
3. Note the telling phrase "that I have on vinyl, that I found." This suggests that, even if he were to sample from CDs, he would only sample material that he had also found on vinyl, thus fulfilling the ethical obligation to search out one's records.
4. Producers are proud of the combination of listening skills and background knowledge necessary to perform such tasks. Beni B (in the conversation to which I refer in the section of this chapter regarding compilations) berated a producer for sampling a song from a compilation rather than from the original release. He could tell, he explained, because he owned both the original and the compilation and could hear the difference: The compilation version was slightly distorted.
5. In fact, they make the same exception: the bass drum sound of the TR-808 drum machine. This is apparently based on a distinction between sampling the sound of a musician playing an instrument

and sampling the sound of a machine. Human performances are all different, so a producer must invest effort to find the proper performance to sample; if another producer then samples *that*, then the first producer's effort has been exploited. Drum machine sounds, by contrast, are all the same, so sampling one from a record is essentially the same as using the actual machine—no one is being exploited. See Theberge (1997: 196–198) and Rose (1994: 75–76) for extensive discussions of the TR-808.
6. This is a song in which Ice Cube rhymed over the instrumentals of various other songs that were popular at that time. The title locates it as self-referential parody—the song is about stealing beats.
7. Wang conflates the role of the deejay with that of the producer. This is common practice in the hip-hop world.

Bibliography

Rose, Tricia. 1994. *Black Noise.* Hanover, N.H..: Weslyan University Press.
Theberge, Paul. 1997. *Any Sound You Can Imagine: Making Music/Consuming Technology.* Hanover, N.H.: Weslyan University Press.

Part VII

"I Used to Love H.E.R."

Hip-Hop in/and the Culture Industries

Mark Anthony Neal

On his 1994 disc *Resurrection*, Chicago-based rapper Common recorded "I Used to Love H.E.R.," a song that on the surface was simply about a failed relationship. Instead, the song's title is really a metaphor for Common's own relationship with hip-hop and hip-hop's relationship to the culture industries. In the song, Common questions hip-hop's fixation with "gangsta" culture (taking a clear shot at Left Coast artists like Ice Cube and N.W.A., who responded in kind) and hypersexual imagery. The song becomes the basis of a decade-long narrative where artists such as The Roots ("Act Too (The Love of My Life)") and Erykah Badu (the Grammy Award-winning "Love of My Life") also question hip-hop's transition from an organic, grassroots art form to a transnational commodity. All are clear in their opinions that hip-hop's travels into the mainstream have fundamentally changed its production, distribution, reception, and functions as an art form. The essays collected in Part VII of *That's the Joint!* explore, from myriad vantages, the kind of crisis that Common alludes to in "I Used to Love H.E.R."

Though few outside of the music industry think of it as such, for the vast majority of people whose livelihoods are tethered to the production, distribution, selling, and consuming of music, hip-hop is little more than a job, recalling Bonz Malone's observation on De La Soul's *The Grind Date* that hip-hop provides jobs for people who don't like it. For all of the bantering about authenticity and street credibility in contemporary hip-hop, most artists, especially those signed to mainstream labels, are most concerned with maintaining and furthering their careers—their rap careers. As Mickey Hess writes in his book *Is Hip-Hop Dead?*,

> Hip-hop is big business, and these rappers are entrepreneurs who seek to maintain control of their product, both in financial and artistic terms, using street smarts to negotiate contracts that allow them more control than was granted to earlier black rock and roll and blues musicians.
>
> (Hess, 2007: 13)

In many ways the focus on crass materialism that marks much of mainstream hip-hop is an attempt to make more explicit the inner machinations of the music industry, if not capitalism itself. The gap between the believability of so many narratives of expensive cars, big houses, and disposable jewelry and the day-to-day operations of a music industry worker perhaps better indexes the reality of a "rap career."

In truth, many of the rank-and-file rappers who populate the music industry have desires to become hip-hop moguls, on par with figures like Russell Simmons, Sean Combs, Sean Carter, Curtis Jackson, and others. The hip-hop mogul becomes a visible symbol of possibility with a capitalist structure, for diverse and divergent audiences. In his essay "'I Don't Like to Dream about Getting Paid': Representations of Social Mobility and the Emergence of the Hip-Hop Mogul," Christopher Holmes Smith suggests that

> the hip-hop mogul becomes a charged figure precisely because of his ability to appeal to the varied sensibilities of apparently disparate public spheres ... they may "stand in for" the desires and values of those individuals who are not eligible to occupy similar positions of mass mediation and discursive credibility.
>
> (Smith, 2003: 69)

Yet Smith remains cautious of the political value of such figures, arguing that the

> emergence of the hip-hop mogul is symptomatic of an age wherein, despite a prevailing wish to the contrary, the crowd's volatile possibility for social change has become exhausted as a model of political mobilization, even as it has become a highly marketable simulacrum of exactly that sort of transgressive human potential.
>
> (ibid.: 85)

That doesn't mean that there isn't value in the mogul performance of social and political possibilities. As S. Craig Watkins observes in his essay "Black Youth and the Ironies of Capitalism" from his book *Representing: Hip-Hop Culture and the Production of Black Cinema*, "popular media culture is perhaps best understood as a perpetual theater of struggle in which the forces of containment and resistance remain in a constant state of negotiation, never completely negating each other's presence or vigor" (Watkins, 1998: 51). For some rappers, hip-hop's engagement with the mainstream has forced them to negotiate between long-standing narratives within the black community that have equated mainstream acceptance with "selling out" and basic desires to craft a lifestyle out of their skills and visibility as rap artists. In his essay "The Business of Rap: Between the Street and the Executive Suite," Keith Negus notes that, "in the struggle against racism and economic and cultural marginalization, and in an attempt to 'live the American dream,' rap has also been created as a self-conscious business activity as well as a cultural form and aesthetic practice" (Negus, 1999: 84). Moreover Watkins writes, "at the same moment that black youth have become especially vulnerable to shifts in the postindustrial economy and political landscape, they, too, have gained unprecedented access to the technologies of communications media," adding that "what has emerged in the process is the structuring of a historically distinct terrain upon which the varying repertoires of black youth cultural production dramatically reorganize the scope and possibilities of social and political struggle from the margins" (Watkins, 1998: 62).

Both Eric K. Watts and Keith Negus suggest there is a deeper relationship to be found between the "street" and the tenets of mass cultural production. In the case of gangsta rap group N.W.A. and their song "One Less Bitch," Watts observes in his essay "An Exploration of Spectacular Consumption: Gangsta Rap as Cultural Commodity" that

> Eazy E's (Eric Wright) misogynistic protestation can be profitably exploited by more than just a mass-marketed culture industry. If we listen carefully, we can discern how N.W.A. gleefully acknowledge participation in their self-promotion as "niggas" who condemn women by limiting their self-realization to the status of "bitches" and "hoes" in a perverse dramatization of street oriented relations.
>
> (Watts, 1997: 48)

In Watts's view, the N.W.A. song represents a "commercialized spectacle designed to thrust the street code through the doors of corporate boardrooms" (ibid.: 48). Perhaps obvious in this analysis is the shared investment that a group like N.W.A. and mass cultural producers have in exporting sexism and misogyny to those who have desires to consume such practices. Less obvious are the ways that "there exists a spectacularly symbiotic relationship between the dictates of the street code and an energetic American consumerism" (ibid.: 50).

Part of the explanation for this relationship, according to Watts, "resides in the fact that consumerism is in the midst of symbolically reproducing the street code, commodifying it in the form of an easy-to-open package of hip" (ibid.: 51). Watts adds that "this awesome replication and consumption of street-coded imagery is significant precisely because the processes of spectacular consumption are implicated ... in the validation of what becomes reasonable street protocol" (ibid.: 51). Additionally, Negus notes that

> street intelligence is about "knowing markets" and "knowing consumers" and, like street marketing, it involves employing conventional business activities that are elided through the discourse of the street, denying that this is similar to the other activities that are daily being conducted and initiated from the corporate suite.
>
> (Negus, 1999: 99–100)

REFERENCES

Hess, Mickey. (2007). *Is Hip-Hop Dead? The Past, Present and Future of America's Most Wanted Music*. Westport, CT: Praeger Publishers.

Negus, Keith. (1999). *Music Genres and Corporate Cultures*. New York: Routledge.

Smith, Christopher Holmes. (2003). "'I Don't Like to Dream About Getting Paid': Representations of Social Mobility and the Emergence of the Hip-Hop Mogul," *Social Text*, 77, 21:4, Winter.

Watkins, S. Craig. (1998). *Representing: Hip-Hop Culture and the Production of Black Cinema*. Chicago: University of Chicago Press.

Watts, Eric K. (1997). "An Exploration of Spectacular Consumption: Gangsta Rap as Cultural Commodity," *Communication Studies*, 48, Spring.

40
The Rap Career

When hip-hop emerged in the Bronx and elsewhere more than three decades ago, it was viewed as little more than a musical fad or simply a popular musical genre that would disappear when fickle youth audiences tired of it. Hip-hop is now a billion dollar business and artists no longer see themselves as rappers or lyricists or DJs, but as entrepreneurs.

In his chapter Mickey Hess charts the development of rap music from the underground economy of urban life into its role in creating so-called rap careers. These transitions highlight current concerns within the industry about marketability and longevity as well as the diversification of business interests. The focus on career-oriented goals in hip-hop may go hand-in-hand with the sudden focus on crass materialism.

The Rap Career

Mickey Hess

From Scarface's "Money and the Power" (1995) to 50 Cent's *Get Rich or Die Tryin'* (2003), making money is a legitimate goal for rappers, and one that is stated outright in lyrics. This motivation to make money separates hip hop music culture from other forms like punk or indie rock, where monetary success is equated with selling out. In hip hop, money equals power, and making money is celebrated as long as it happens on the artist's own terms. Mike Jones and Slim Thug brag about selling hundreds of thousands of records before they ever signed with a major label. Wu-Tang Clan and Jay-Z boast about maintaining control of their music even as they sign with corporate record companies. Hip hop is big business, and these rappers are entrepreneurs who seek to maintain control of their product, both in financial and artistic terms, using street smarts to negotiate contracts that allow them more control than was granted to earlier black rock and roll and blues musicians. Because of this emphasis on street smarts, hip hop is hostile to rappers who came from privileged backgrounds and didn't have to struggle for their success. Even the wealthiest hip hop artists have established credibility through rags-to-riches stories of the socioeconomic disadvantage they experienced during their rise to fame. In telling these rags-to-riches stories, rappers often juxtapose their childhood poverty with displays of the money they have made through rap music. Rap videos feature tenements and mansions, street corners and penthouse suites, bicycles and limousines. Images of wealth are contrasted with an earlier poverty that authenticates the artist's struggle for success.

This struggle is tied to overcoming a system of racial disadvantage that placed these rappers in ghettos and housing projects. The heroes of songs like RZA's "Grits" (2003) and Naughty by Nature's "Ghetto Bastard" (1991) are born into poverty and struggle to survive by traditional means before turning to crime. Naughty by Nature's Treach says that he started robbing people because, "I couldn't get a job, nappy hair was not allowed." Masta Killa, in a guest verse on RZA's "Grits," tells listeners "I'm too young, no jobs would hire me legit" before he robs a grocery store to get food. When presented with a lack of educational and occupational opportunities, these rappers forge their own paths by turning this disadvantage into entertainment. They write and sell songs about poverty, street life, and crime. Hip hop developed in some of the poorest sections of the United States, and its lyrics have long reflected the social conditions from which it came: Artists authenticate themselves through their experience of social struggle, and stories of disadvantage give MCs the credibility they need to appear "real" to their listeners. In lyrics, rappers assert that the very qualities of self-reliance and ingenuity they gained growing up poor have helped them forge careers in the music business without leaving behind the ghetto mentality and street smarts that were the impetus for their success. Because this negotiation of race, wealth, and social class is so important to establishing credibility, many MCs devote song lyrics to describing their own career paths.

Lyrics from artists like Jay-Z and The Notorious B.I.G. present achieving a career in rap music as a story of hard work and ingenuity. These artists justify their wealth, success, and celebrity by presenting their careers as a rise from poverty, while Kanye West, who comes from a more middle-class background, devotes "Last Call," the final track on his debut album, *College Dropout* (2004), to telling the story of how he struggled to get the album produced. Here and elsewhere on the album, West tells us he was initially dismissed by Roc-A-Fella Records because of his relatively middle-class background, saw a record deal fall through with Capitol, and nearly died in a car crash along his path to getting his record signed to Roc-A-Fella. Although the types of struggles may vary, each of these stories plays on an archetypal American story of perseverance in achieving one's goals. Rap music becomes a vehicle for self-advancement, but at the same time artists must prove their dedication to preserving hip hop's original culture, rather than selling it out to the mainstream. Through narratives of the hip hop career, artists assert their commitment to an ongoing body of musical work and link their work to agendas of survival, wealth, and philanthropy, which find roots within a larger body of African-American literature. Hip hop lyrics show a unique focus on the artist's role in production and circulation, areas from which popular musicians have traditionally distanced themselves. It is rare to hear a rock or pop star sing about how she secured her record deal. This lyrical attention is framed in response to the threat of appropriation by the music industry. In making their business roles visible, artists reclaim such work as creative and frame themselves as hip hop emissaries to the corporate world. They claim to have maintained the integrity of hip hop culture while at the same time producing a marketable product. Their songs tell the stories of how they came to their careers.

The term "rap career" has entered the hip hop vocabulary recently, but it is used interchangeably with "rap game," a term used in lyrics for more than a decade to describe the hip hop career. Hip hop artists since at least the mid-1980s have highlighted their music's commercial potential in lyrics, album titles, and names of artists and record labels. In rock music, the Mothers of Invention's *We're Only in It for the Money* (1968) and Supergrass's *In It for the Money* (1997) are ironic album titles, yet hip hop artists like EPMD (Erick and Parrish Makin' Dollars) and Too $hort more straightforwardly embrace a financial agenda, and 50 Cent's album *Get Rich or Die Tryin'* portrays making money as essential to survival. The emphasis on wealth and consumerism in commercial rap has overshadowed hip hop's existence as a creative form, and has sparked nostalgia in critics, who long for a purer moment in hip hop as though this focus on materialism were a new development. Scholarship on hip hop has shifted from reading the music and culture as an expressive community that resisted co-optation, to understanding it as a commercially dominant culture and industry.[1] Earlier scholars theorized hip hop as a resistant art form, yet the music's rise to become the biggest-selling form in the United States has caused more recent scholars to question if an industry as economically dominant as rap music still can be considered resistant.[2] This shift toward skepticism reflects a popular reaction to mainstream rap's heightened focus on materialism since the late 1990s. After all, Cash Money Records is one of the more visible labels of the era, and songs like Puff Daddy's "It's All About the Benjamins" (1997) and B.G.'s "Bling Bling" (1999) would appear to confirm that rap artists are in it only for the money.

Hip hop has drawn criticism from journalists for its artists' focus on wealth and excess. For example, in a 2004 *Atlanta Journal-Constitution* article, Phil Kloer wrote that "hip hop has gone from a vibrant music that embraced many aspects of life and challenged the world to a narrow, one-way street where popular rappers care only about having the pimpest car, the best intoxicants, the sexiest hotties and money to burn."[3] Yet when critics complain about hip hop's excess, they ignore the fact that many types of artists confront these same issues in their lyrics. Hip hop is unique among popular music forms in the extent to which its artists confront the commercial nature of their music. This critique often takes place within the music *itself*. This attention to the commercial is one of the most vital aspects of hip hop, and though artists cannot escape hip hop's commercial nature (and many in fact embrace it), they critique its position through their unprecedented artistic attention to the stories of their careers.[4]

Hip hop artists authenticate themselves to listeners by describing how they came to their careers, and how their lives intersect with their music. The question of hip hop authenticity relates to both musical style and performer identity. Proponents of "real" hip hop oppose integrating the music with pop styles to sell more records, and "real" MCs must speak as themselves and not take on affectations to enhance marketability. Obviously, though, MCs are in the business of selling records. This shared focus on business and autobiography positions the MC to narrate not only a life, but also a professional agenda that is accountable to the experiences of that life. Hip hop extends black rhetorical traditions that value self-knowledge and knowledge gained from lived experience, as well as traditions of resistance to what R.A.T. Judy calls a history of "dehumanizing commodification" that began with the American slave trade and extends to exploitive systems of wage labor that exist today.[5] Rappers claim that growing up in the streets taught them skills necessary for survival. Hip hop positions the MC as experienced knower, as in Ice Cube's claim "I'm from the street, so I know what's up" on the N.W.A. song "I Ain't Tha One" (1988). N.W.A.'s breakthrough album *Straight Outta Compton* (1988) begins with the spoken disclaimer, "You are now about to witness the strength of street knowledge."

This focus on street knowledge was complicated by the platinum sales of albums such as MC Hammer's *Please Hammer Don't Hurt 'Em* (1990), which spent twenty-one weeks as the number one album in the U.S. Other artists accused Hammer of selling out hip hop because the style of his music and performance were so geared toward pop success. White rapper MC Serch screamed, "Hammer, shut the fuck up!" on 3rd Bass's debut single, "The Gas Face" (1989). A Tribe Called Quest criticized Hammer on "Check the Rhime" (1991), where they call out Hammer by name and state, "Rap is not pop. If you call it that, then stop." Yet even such a pop-oriented album as Hammer's included the track "Crime Story," which served to authenticate him to listeners through stories of his experience in the ghetto.

After hip hop's backlash against MC Hammer and Vanilla Ice rap artists found it necessary to assert that their own stories of the ghetto were not far removed from their experience or their musical performance. Rap performance shifted from Hammer's colorful costumes, high-energy choreography, and videos set in mansions, to Dr. Dre's denim jackets, weapon-brandishing, and videos set in Compton neighborhood house parties with refrigerators full of forty-ounce bottles of malt liquor. In telling stories of their careers, gangsta rappers assert that they remain criminals even as stars, and maintain the streetwise qualities that make their music so compelling and marketable. When rap performance shifted back to an emphasis on mansions and choreography with the advent of Puff Daddy and Bad Boy Records, these new performances were framed within a distinct gangsta agenda of getting rich. Stars brandished nine-millimeter pistols while sitting in hot tubs, and the message was clear: Rap's street criminals had become its moguls.

This integration of street knowledge with record industry success was inevitable. As hip hop climbed toward its position in 2003 as the biggest selling music in the U.S., artists refused to cede control of the music to industry executives. Several hip hop artists used their songs to warn aspiring rappers of unfair industry practices. On "Check the Rhime," for example, A Tribe Called Quest invokes "Industry rule number 4080—record company people are shady." Tribe's song "Show Business" (1991) extends their critique of industry practices to specific labels. Wu-Tang's GZA, who found himself signed to an unfair contract early in his career, recorded "Labels" (1995), a song that opens with RZA's spoken introduction: "You gotta read the label. If you don't read the label you might get poisoned." This critique of the music business is a central feature of hip hop lyrics. Though rap artists want to make money, they don't want to achieve sales at the cost of culture and community, or at the cost of their artistic control over the music. GZA's group

Wu-Tang Clan, and other artists such as Master P, laid groundwork in the 1990s for unprecedented artist control in recording and distribution contracts with major record labels. Wu-Tang Clan's lyrics tell stories of the group's struggles to maintain artistic individualism in the face of industry conformity, and describe their work to achieve new levels of artist control. GZA's "Shadow Boxing" (1995) points out the ineffectiveness of the traditional process of new artists shopping their publicity headshots and demo tapes to record execs, and urges new artists to follow his example by taking charge of their careers: "You must break through, like the Wu, unexpectedly." Rather than market themselves to record companies with publicity photos and demo tapes, Wu-Tang built an audience through touring and selling independently-produced CDs "out the trunk" at their shows, and then used their established fan base to negotiate more artist control in their contract with a corporate record label. Wu-Tang members RZA and GZA, who had earlier record deals as solo artists Prince Rakeem and Genius, claim that those earlier experiences helped them study the industry's annexation of hip hop, and that now they understand ways to manipulate a pliable music industry, and to maintain more control of production. Selling records and selling out become two very different concepts as Wu-Tang celebrates entrepreneurship and the manipulation of industry business practices to the artist's advantage.

A more skeptical reading finds that the freedom Wu-Tang enjoys is an illusion, and that record companies allow rap artists a modicum of control, or the illusion of control, in order to keep them happy and ultimately make more money from their work.[6] This skepticism is not limited to critics from outside hip hop. In 2004, Mos Def parodied Jay-Z's "The Takeover" (2001) a song that claims that "we runnin' this rap shit." Jay lists himself and his Roc-A-Fella labelmates Freeway and Memphis Bleek, as those in charge of hip hop, but Mos Def's parody "The Rape Over" (2004) instead lists major corporations like Viacom (the parent company of MTV) and AOL/Time Warner as those who run rap. In Mos Def's view, rappers rush to sell themselves out to these corporations. Yet the true power of Mos Def's parody is that he, himself, is a major-label recording artist. In fact, his label, Geffen, was started with funding from Warner Brothers Records, which is now a part of AOL/Time Warner, one corporation he mentions by name in the song. Warner Brothers Records had a history of artists, who, unhappy with how the label treated their contracts, staged public battles with Warner (Frank Zappa in the 1970s, and Prince in the 1990s). Not to exclude his own career from scrutiny, Mos Def preserves the first-person plural "we" from Jay-Z's original song, and thereby includes himself in his criticism of rap stars who sell their souls to multinational media conglomerates, rather than take them over.

Stories of shady record executives have existed in hip hop since the late 1980s, with songs like 3rd Bass's "The Gas Face" (1989) and A Tribe Called Quest's "Check the Rhime" and "Show Business" (1991), which expose industry practices and warn rappers to watch their backs. Since the late 1990s, however, artists like Wu-Tang Clan, Slim Thug, MF DOOM, and Jay-Z have taken this critique further to claim to have beaten the record execs at their own games. On "I Ain't Heard of That," (2005) Slim Thug, who claims he sold a hundred thousand records recording for Houston's independent Swisha House label, describes demanding a bigger advance for his first major-label album. Slim says he secured more money for his advance than most rappers make from sales, and that he made Geffen and Interscope Records "pay for all the days I was livin' in hell." Masta Ace takes this concept of rappers strong-arming record executives to a physical level in his song "The Ways" (2004), where Ace claims to know rappers who got signed to record labels by threatening the staff with weapons. The song is a revenge fantasy in which rappers menace label executives, but Ace connects the fantasy to the real-life examples of Keith Murray, Diddy, and Suge Knight, members of the rap community who have been charged with assault and battery. In 1995, Murray was sentenced to a five-year prison term for his assault on show promoters at a Connecticut nightclub. In 1997, Diddy was arrested for assaulting Interscope Records executive Steve Stoute, after he refused to shelve a music video with which Diddy was unhappy. Suge Knight is rumored to have used violent threats to coerce Vanilla Ice into signing over his publishing rights to his hit "Ice, Ice Baby" (1990) and to coerce Eazy-E into releasing Dr. Dre from his contract with Ruthless Records. Ace contextualizes these violent acts within America's history of violence and intimidation: "Just ask the Indians or the African slaves," he says, and he urges rappers to use violence to counter the record industry's role in this history of exploiting minorities.

The power struggle between rap artists and record executives is a topic of several hip hop songs, and the question of whether rap is a "cake over" or a "rape over" remains. The different perspectives on who controls hip hop music speak to a larger issue of how theories of industry exploitation may ignore the work black artists and businesspeople have done to make hip hop the commercial force that it has become. This question is complicated by the fact that hip hop artists often present themselves as entrepreneurs who engage with a record industry that was built, at least in part, by white rock and roll covers of songs by black R&B groups in the 1950s (Mos Def's most revealing line in "The Rape Over," in fact, is "all white men are runnin this rap shit," which touches on a subject of white-black interaction). This history of white record executives annexing black sounds contextualizes hip hop's resistance to industry appropriation, and artist-entrepreneurs often use their lyrics to convince listeners that they have maintained their integrity while making money from their music. The reality of who controls rap is impossible to determine, but skeptical readings that see rappers as victims of exploitation rob hip hop of the credit it deserves for its lyrical critique of the individual's interaction with the music industry, and for the ways artists like Wu-Tang Clan have gone beyond critique, and negotiated contracts that offer greater levels of artist control over production and distribution. Whether an artist like Jay-Z believes he has taken control of his music, or an artist like Mos Def believes he is selling himself out to Warner Brothers, what these artists share is an interest in using their lyrics to critique the way the record industry works.

Hip hop critiques corporate entertainment, and presents hip hop artists both as outlaws and savvy participants in the business of producing commercial music. Hip hop artists want to change the record industry by taking it over. Several artists have become label CEOs: Dr. Dre with Aftermath Records, Jay-Z with Roc-A-Fella and Def Jam, Master P with No Limit Records, and Scarface with Def Jam South. These new roles are explored in lyrics. Dr. Dre rhymes about scouting and signing new talent on *Chronic 2001*. Jay-Z's *The Black Album* (2003) asserts his active role in selling his own music, and connects his business agenda to his creativity and to financial survival and philanthropy. Throughout *The Black Album*, Jay-Z reminds listeners that it was not just musical skill, but also his business savvy that helped him reach his position in the industry, and he critiques the industry's marketing practices in lines like "Rap mags try and use my black ass so advertisers can give 'em more cash for ads" ("99 Problems," 2003). Essentially, Jay-Z justifies his platinum sales through his own role in marketing and distribution, arguing that his control over the business side of his music confirms his extension of street knowledge to his position as label CEO.[7]

The opposing concepts of music industry success and fidelity to hip hop culture can create a doubleness for the performer who finds himself accountable to both realms. To maintain his credibility, Jay-Z must be careful in lyrics to narrate his industry position through its accountability to hip hop's origins *outside* the industry. Key dimensions of real hip hop center on remaining true to concepts of a culture that existed before 1979, when Sugarhill Gang's "Rapper's Delight" became a crossover pop hit and sold platinum worldwide.[8] This precommercial culture of hip hop is characterized as African-American, poor, and urban, and focused on musical skills in live performance rather than recordings. Hip hop realness is negotiated through connections to hip hop's origins, whether via geographic proximity to the New York boroughs where the culture originated, through connections to artists who were important players in the creation of the culture, or through emphasis on skills in performing live rather than selling records. Commercial artists, though, have to maintain sales in order to keep their record contracts, and at the same time connect their performance to this conception of hip hop culture.

A theory of hip hop's conflicting concerns of creativity and commerce, or skills and sales, reframes W. E. B. Du Bois's concept of double-consciousness in commercial terms, as artists work to produce marketable music for mainstream listeners, yet at the same time to maintain a necessary level of accountability to the music's cultural origins. While Du Bois described the self-perception versus societal perception of the American Negro at the turn of the century, hip hop double-consciousness finds the rap artist caught between the personal and the commercial: rappers are expected to present a sincere and verifiable self on commercial recordings. Speaking to this double-consciousness, Paul Gilroy situates rap music as one of a series of modern black cultural forms that draw special power from "a doubleness" through artists' understanding of their practice as "autonomous domain," and of "their own position relative to the racial group and of the role of art in mediating individual creativity with social dynamics."[9] Christopher Holmes Smith, illustrating a further doubleness for rap music, positions the ghetto as both crucial signifier of authenticity and a marketable aspect of self, arguing that the ghetto becomes "simultaneously commodity and safe-haven" as MCs market themselves through narratives of their place as other within mainstream culture.[10] I would extend these readings to argue that MCs also address their place within the music industry through career narratives that plot the individual's movement between the worlds of the ghetto and music industry. In lyrics, top-selling MCs often narrate their own struggles from two perspectives, pre- and post-stardom. They claim that socioeconomic hardships helped shape their creativity, but they also represent their interaction with the music industry as a different kind of social dynamic, one that Wu-Tang Clan and Jay-Z claim to understand so well that they can negotiate greater control over their artistic production.

The debate over hip hop's industry position takes place not only in scholarship, but in lyrics. Hip hop artists critique and revise the work of their contemporaries, and hold them accountable to hip hop's origins. Rap artists write lyrics that justify their relationship with the industry and criticize others for selling out. Both Basu and Mark Anthony Neal argue that hip hop functions as part of the black public sphere, and Neal claims that groups like De La Soul, Common, and Jeru the Damaja have served as "critical vanguards" against the same excesses critics attack: "Arguably, no popular genre of music has been as self-consciously critical of itself as hip hop."[11] Through this self-criticism, hip hop extends the black rhetorical tradition of "Signifying," or responding to a text through critique, imitation, or parody.[12] In revising rap's emphasis on wealth and excess, artists like De La Soul move to create or reclaim a space for their own work as they criticize the commercial spectacle of hip hop. From their first MTV video, "Me, Myself, and I" (1989), a song that "ironized earlier rap posturings by counterpoising the popular b-boy stance to 'being one's self,'"[13] De La Soul has challenged commercial representations of the MC, parodying rap's fashion, tough-guy posturing, and conformity to a standardized image of the rapper.

De La Soul's parody works to create a space for the different image they project in their music, and they assert that this different image speaks for their originality and integrity because they do not follow trends. De La Soul is not the lone voice of dissent among rap artists. MF DOOM criticizes the shirtless posturing (and emphasis of visuals over vocals) in recent videos from artists like Lil Wayne and 50 Cent: "Yuck, is they rhymers or stripper males?" ("Beef Rap," 2004). DOOM attacks the commercial spectacle of hip hop as untrue to the art form, and claims that he is concerned more with rhyme skills than publicity, while more commercially successful acts are known less for their vocal performance than for the theatrics that keep them in the public eye. Such criticisms of rap music's commercial spectacle separate hip hop into two camps: the fake and the real. The rhetoric of "real" hip hop developed in response to the threat of industry appropriation, and became prevalent in lyrics as hip hop on the radio and on MTV began to move away from the hip hop aesthetic that artists like DOOM and De La Soul claim to preserve. I use the term aesthetic because these groups do not seek to preserve a specific sound or image they label as hip hop. Instead, these artists promote themselves as musical innovators, who preserve hip hop music by keeping it vibrant and evolving. Real hip hop, then, does not have a certain sound, but instead is an aesthetic by which the artist interacts with the music and the industry. Hip hop's career narratives illustrate this aesthetic and justify this interaction through stories of how the artist became a star.

What Is Real Hip Hop?

The use of terms like "real," "fake," and "phony" in hip hop lyrics illustrate hip hop's ongoing concern with the real, which necessitates that artists stay true to the notions of hip hop as a culture by establishing autobiographical truth, personal sincerity, and integrity of their performance. The dialogue between "mainstream" and "underground" hip hop artists reveals an ongoing lyrical debate over industry structure, the rap career, and notions of "real hip hop" and "real MCs." There is even a commercial tension between the terms "hip hop" and "rap." Hip hop can refer to a culture that extends beyond music to include graffiti art and b-boying (breakdancing), and can even refer to a lifestyle (as in KRS-One's statement that rap is something you do, but hip hop is something you live), but MCs also use the term "hip hop music," or say "hip hop," instead of "rap," to refer specifically to music. In lyrics, "rap" can be used to mean commercial music, and "hip hop" can be used to mean authentic music, as when Defari warns his listener "Don't mistake this for no pop rap, Pop, but that raw deal feel, that real hip hop" ("Focused Daily," (1998)). Other vocalists make the distinction between calling themselves rappers versus MCs, or *real* MCs. Defari's fellow San Francisco Bay area group, The Lootpack, claims that before listeners can appreciate their CD, they "have to know the difference from a fake MC to a real MC" (*The Anthem*, 1999). Dead prez claim to perform *real* hip hop. Other artists use this phrase in lyrics and song titles, such as Das EFX's "The Real Hip Hop" (1995) or KRS-ONE's "Represent the Real Hip Hop" (1995). The term extends to performer identity. N.W.A., Nelly and The St. Lunatics, Jay-Z and Too $hort, The Diplomats, B.G., and Redman all have recorded songs titled "Real Niggaz." Nas claims to be "the last real nigga alive." Eminem reminds listeners that he's "the real Slim Shady."

Concepts of the real and the authentic have long and complex philosophical histories.[14] Scholars have theorized that popular music's concern with authenticity is a strategy to preserve an original culture. Philip Auslander views the 1990 Milli Vanilli lip-synching scandal as a reaction to increasing simulation of the live performance that had been central to rock authenticity. Kembrew McLeod reads hip hop's emphasis on the real as a strategy to preserve the culture as it had existed outside the mainstream. This attempt at preservation created a model of "real" hip hop based on performer identity as well as musical style. For hip hop music, realness centers on avoiding pop structures and the mixing of hip hop with dance, rock, or R&B to reach wider audiences. For the performer, realness centers on the proximity of his or her experience to a model of hip hop as black-created, urban music. Edward G. Armstrong identifies three "initially evident" forms of hip hop authenticity that are argued through being true to oneself, claiming "local allegiances and territorial identities," and establishing a connection to hip hop origins—to "an original source of rap"—through locale, style, or links to an established artist.[15] McLeod maps six semantic dimensions of claims to realness as they respond to the threat of assimilation. Through an extensive study of lyrics, hip hop media, and a series of interviews with artists, McLeod developed an outline of the different terms through which realness is argued. The "deeply intertwined" dimensions he defines are: social-psychological (staying true to yourself vs. following trends), racial, political-economic, gender-sexual, social locational, and cultural.[16] Both McLeod and Armstrong include the concept of being true to yourself as a central dimension of realness, and I argue that it is the dimension most called into question by the artist's interaction with the music industry.

Certain artists have parodied hip hop's representations of black identity, and argue that other rappers' performances of black masculinity are adopted to fit a model of hip hop blackness. In establishing their individuality as a key component of what makes them real, rap artists often use their lyrics to reject a more standardized rap image. In fact, artists often assert their individuality by the very fact that they don't fit in. The Atlanta-based group OutKast was booed by fans from New York and Los Angeles when they won "best new artist" at the 1996 Source Awards, because they made their music distinctly Southern. Their vocals emphasize a Southern drawl and they titled their albums *Southernplayalisticcadillacmusik,* and *ATLiens* (which combines "Atlanta" (the ATL) with "aliens" to comment on their initial lack of acceptance because of their Southern locale and style). Also, Eminem inverts a racial struggle narrative to show the trials he has faced as a white minority in hip hop. While Eminem emphasizes the poverty of his youth, his lyrics employ a strategy of anticipation as they address the ways that Eminem's identity does not meet traditional concepts of hip hop realness through blackness. Like Eminem's career narrative, the biographies of rural artists like Kentucky's Nappy Roots and white redneck rappers like Tennessee's Haystak and Georgia's Bubba Sparxxx are framed in response to notions of real hip hop as a black, urban form, and these artists emphasize their authentication through McLeod's social-psychological dimension, arguing that they stay true to their own lived experiences rather than following trends by imitating a black, urban identity that lies outside their experience. Through making their white or Southern identities visible, these artists assert that they are staying true to themselves.

The importance of staying true to oneself is evident in many rap narratives. While hip hop is a collaborative and dialogic form, artists cannot represent their geographical community, racial heritage, or the culture of hip hop unless they first establish themselves as unique individuals. The importance of basing lyrics in autobiography is supported by Krims's theory that the hip hop performer must symbolically be collapsed onto the artist, so that when O'Shea Jackson performs as Ice Cube, the experiences Ice Cube reports are accepted as Jackson "speaking from authentic experience."[17] In a broader study of popular music forms, Simon Frith explains the listener's judgment of authenticity as "a perceived quality of sincerity and commitment. It's as if people expect music to mean what it says."[18] Rappers' assertions of their personal sincerity in lyrics are tied to concepts of hip hop as a creative, expressive form that opposes the co-optation of its culture for record sales. KRS-ONE, for example, in "Represent the Real Hip Hop" (1995) claims that his career longevity and his role within hip hop's formative years establish his authority to judge the performance of another artist.

In "Represent the Real Hip Hop," KRS lists creativity, as well as skill in composing and performing, as markers of rap quality. To him, platinum sales prove nothing but marketability; the MC's skills must be proven in live performance. Jay-Z, on the other hand, claims that his marketability is an extension of his creativity as he describes building his label, Roc-A-Fella, into a rap dynasty using the street knowledge he developed growing up in New York City's Marcy housing projects. KRS-ONE focuses on the artistic innovation he considers crucial to hip hop, while Jay-Z includes his skill in *selling* music as part of his innovation as an artist and CEO. As hip hop innovation can take these two forms, Frith's idea of a "perceived quality of sincerity" may be lost, or alternatively enhanced, when an artist articulates his intent to make marketable music. Both KRS-ONE and Jay-Z emphasize their accountability to the communities and culture that created hip hop: KRS-ONE through fidelity to its expressive practices, and Jay-Z through an extension of street mentality to the industry. Both artists assert their realness through the lived experiences that demonstrate their connection to the cultures where hip hop developed. In negotiating their realness with listeners, they narrate careers in which they maintain control of their individual expression even while producing music for industry labels.

As rap artists narrate their interaction with the music industry, many artists currently identify their music as "underground" hip hop to indicate a musical aesthetic that differs from mainstream pop rap. The term "underground" can designate artists who record for independent—rather than corporate—labels, yet even those artists who do record for major labels can align themselves with underground styles, and these artists are able to speak within multiple genres. Redman, a commercially successful artist who maintains underground credibility, distinguishes his fashion style from that of other artists on the pop charts (specifically the metallic suits worn in videos by Bad Boy artists Puff Daddy and Ma$e) when he says "I'm too underground to dance with that shiny shit on" ("Can You Dig It?" 1998). De La Soul, on "Oooh" (2000) also target "shiny suit rappers." As usage of an earlier term, "hardcore," shifted from its original usage (hip hop that stayed true to its musical origins and was not integrated with pop music) to indicate a harder gangsta style, the term underground replaced it. As the hardness that had distinguished MCs from the pop styles of crossover rap had itself become a style that sold platinum for groups like N.W.A. in the early 1990s, "hardcore" came to represent a musical subgenre rather than an antimainstream aesthetic. Usage of "underground" was popularized in the mid-1990s, as a new wave of artist-run independent labels like Rawkus Records, Stones Throw, Definitive Jux, Quannum Projects, and Hieroglyphics Imperium began to release influential albums and define new sounds.

Black entrepreneurs played a key role in the development of the hip hop industry, yet early black-owned labels like Sugarhill Records and Def Jam were not artist-run, and by the 1990s, many of hip hop's first wave of independent labels were annexed by larger corporate labels. During the 1990s, the emergence of new independents like Hieroglyphics and Stones Throw proved an important moment for hip hop's self-identity, for its artistic innovation, and for more artist control of production and distribution. The independent labels in this second wave tend to operate not as smaller versions of the corporate model, but as artist collectives, with in-house production and hands-on distribution at live shows, and through mail-order and online sales. This aesthetic of the underground finds precedent in other music forms, like punk and indie, where small independents have fought for control of their own production and distribution. David Hesmondhalgh identifies the labeling of an "indie" genre of rock music as the first moment industry structure had dictated musical style, as independent record labels like Britain's Ten Little Indians created an indie sound in opposition to the pop charts. This sound has developed in different directions and into various subgenres, and "indie" today has come to describe a sound that corporate labels also produce. The term now can stand for either musical style *or* industry structure. This history is similar to 1990s alternative rock, where a genre that was named for its oppositionality to the mainstream came to so influence that same mainstream that "alternative" came to designate a subgenre of the mainstream. Yet although indie and underground styles of music—as well as many of the labels that create them—ultimately are bought up by the industry, it is inevitable that new independents rise up to take the place of the old, and to challenge the mainstream with new sounds that ultimately will influence and change the shape of that mainstream.

Underground hip hop has challenged and changed not only the sound of mainstream hip hop, but the role of the artist in producing the music. In his study of rock music, Jon Stratton argues that popular musicians historically have distanced themselves from the business side of their careers, leaving their repertoire and marketing to the record executives. Stratton sees the production of popular music flowing in one direction: From artist to A&R (artist and repertoire) man—whose job is to recruit and develop new talent—to company, and then out to press and radio, then to consumers. He cites a tension between creativity and commercialism that leads popular music artists to form oppositional personae even as they produce music for the industry:

> The artist, the innovator, tends to see him/herself in opposition to the industry as a commercial enterprise which appears to be continually pressuring the artist to produce new marketable ptoducts. In this situation the artist protects him/herself by mystifying the creative process which is experienced as being distinct from the commercial, capitalist side of the industry which would prefer rational, analysable standardisation.[19]

Stratton's article was published in 1982, before rap had reached its current commercial dominance. Throughout rap music's history of commercial success, artists have taken on active roles in marketing and distributing their music. In addressing these roles in their lyrics, rap artists narrate careers in which they work to recast these commercial roles as creative, and to claim the artist's control over the processes traditionally handled by corporate executives—production, distribution, and marketing. In asserting their active roles in these processes, rap artists reclaim an individual sincerity believed to be lost when record companies disconnect them from the steps between the artist's recording the music and listeners' hearing it. Rather than mystifying the creative process as distinct from the commercial, Jay-Z and other rappers synthesize these processes and make them visible in lyrics.

In his influential essay "The Work of Art in an Age of Mechanical Reproduction," Walter Benjamin theorizes the ways that the artist's role in production affects the audience's reaction to, and relationship with, a work of art. Benjamin argues that mechanical reproductions lack the artist's aura, which can be perceived only in a one-of-a-kind original. Benjamin wrote about the perceived loss of authenticity that comes as art objects are mass produced, and he links authenticity to the existence of the original work from which copies are made. Popular music listeners may be less concerned with the existence of a master recording than they are with their perceptions of the authenticity of the recording artist. As Stratton shows that artists often are removed from the processes of production and marketing, he indicates that popular musicians have lost their control of these processes to corporate executives, and the effects of mass production extend to the creation of the recording, not only to its reproduction. Hip hop's new business models challenge this loss of control as artists move between corporate and independent labels.

A hip hop artist's contract with a major or independent label can play an important role in the way listeners categorize his or her music as "mainstream" or "underground," or even as "rap" or "hip hop." Yet perhaps because of hip hop's emphasis on history and tradition, the hip hop career has proven to be a lengthy one, and an artist may shift between major label and independent. Although indie and alternative rock artists tend to follow a career trajectory that takes them from independent to major labels as their fan bases increase, MCs like MF DOOM, Del the Funky Homosapien, or Count Bass D all recorded their first albums on major labels, and then lost their contracts. Yet each remains active and popular recording for independent labels. As the hardcore or gangsta image became hip hop's best-selling subgenre in the 1990s, MCs performing in other subgenres began to lose their record deals. Count Bass D's live instrumentation and Del's bohemian image and non-violent lyrics no longer found a place in corporate labels' marketing of rap music.

When Del and Count Bass D moved outside corporate recording, they were put in a unique position to critique the business practices of that industry as they took control over the production and distribution of their own recordings. After Sony did not renew his contract for a second album, Count Bass D titled the first CD release from his own Count-bassd.com label, *Art for Sale* (1997). The title track's chorus repeats "My record company is jerking me." Since leaving Sony, Count Bass D has released six full-length albums. Though none of his independent albums has received the level of coverage the mainstream press gave his Sony release, he continues to tour internationally and to produce songs and record guest vocals for other underground artists such as MF DOOM and Jon Doe. He also recorded a remix of a Beastie Boys song for their 2003 *Criterion Collection* DVD. When asked in an interview if he'd consider a return to a major label, Count Bass D said "I would love to sign with a major and get dropped again just like the first time. That way, they pay to put my name out there and I just give them one album. I'm still living off of the reputation that experience gave me. Hell yeah I'd do it again!"[20]

Count Bass D offers a counterstory in which artists manipulate the marketing structures of the music industry to their own advantage. Count's career trajectory is similar in this way to Del the Funky Homosapien, who was publicized by his label as the bohemian cousin of gangsta rapper Ice Cube. As gangsta increased its grip on the charts, Del's bohemian style became more difficult to sell. After Elektra released Del's second album, *No Need for Alarm,* in 1993, the label dropped Del from their roster. When Del's fellow San Francisco Bay-area artists Casual and Souls of Mischief also lost their major label contracts around that same time, they worked together to form an artist-controlled independent company, Hieroglyphics Imperium. In lyrics, Del critiques corporate recording, stating "This is real hip hop, not your phoney phranchise" ("Phoney Phranchise," 2000), and criticizing rappers' "brown-nosing in the industry" ("Fake as Fuck," 2000). Del—who began his career writing lyrics for Ice Cube's gangsta protégés Da Lench Mob—uses his lyrics to criticize gangsta rap's aggression and pop rap's consumerism, which he argues hinder lyrical innovation. Within the rhetoric of underground hip hop, artist-owned labels achieve heightened levels of artist control. And in recording outside the influence of industry marketing strategies, artists claim to recover the individuality of their music, making it more real than the standardized corporate product. On "Jaw Gymnastics" (2000), Del rhymes, "This art form is truly in danger, so I change it, never doin' the same shit." It is through this integrity to his own aesthetic, even at times when that aesthetic wasn't selling in the mainstream, that Del maintains his personal commitment to making real hip hop music by continuing to reinvent the form.

Underground artists believe that making teal hip hop music does not always make money, and that the agenda of getting rich can stand in the way of making real hip hop music. While The Notorious B.I.G. tells us that his dream of becoming a hip hop star included "lunches, brunches, interviews by the pool" ("Juicy," 1994), Del describes "sleepin' in the lobby in the Day's Inn" ("Phoney Phranchise," 2000)." Another MC, Supastition, wears his poverty as a badge of his underground status, claiming "My last show I barely made enough to pay for gas" ("The Signature," 2003). The focus on money in these lyrics represents more than the underground's reaction to MTV images of champagne parties and Cadillac Escalades. Stories of the rap career are stories about how a music culture that developed in some of the U.S.A.'s poorest neighborhoods has become one of the world's biggest-selling forms of entertainment. As artists tell stories that situate them within this journey from ghetto to industry boardroom, making money has become not only an objective for the rap artist, but a topic of lyrics. Underground artists claim that this lyrical focus on getting rich detracts from the quality of hip hop lyrics.

Criticisms of hip hop excess respond to the displays of wealth that rap artists use to prove they are living like stars. The St. Lunatics' "Real Niggas" (2001) tells a story of driving in expensive vehicles, dressing in expensive clothing, and abusing drugs and alcohol. Each verse describes specific aspects of the group's excess. The chorus of the song positions the group as real niggas, in opposition to the haters—those jealous of their display of wealth. These images of excess have drawn criticism from journalists and scholars writing about hip hop, yet these readings tend to overlook vital criticisms from within hip hop itself. Redman's "I Don't Kare" (1998) makes fun of rappers who dedicate songs to listing their possessions. Count Bass D claims, "I want an IRA, not a woman's bracelet" ("Dwight Spitz," 2002). The Lootpack assert their own realness through artistic originality and skill rather than outward displays of excess; they criticize their mainstream contemporaries for confusing "representin' " with "smoking Phillies, acting ill, getting bent." The St. Lunatics embrace the same lifestyle of excess that the Lootpack rejects, yet their performances share a basis in personal sincerity as each group presents an aesthetic of being real, and describes a lifestyle by which the group adheres to its own aesthetic. The Lootpack frames rhyme skills in opposition to mainstream sales, while the St. Lunatics emphasize the wealth they have gained selling records. This dialogue of skills and sales fits into the larger debate of what constitutes real hip hop, real niggaz, and real MCs. The next section explores the ways the potential for selling records meets with nostalgia for hip hop's origins outside the record industry. The agenda of getting paid has existed since hip hop's formative years, yet critics and MCs both tend to remember these years as an era of creative expression untainted by commercial concerns.

Back in the Day: Hip Hop's Nostalgia

The concept of authenticity necessarily centers on the existence of an original. For something to be judged as authentic requires an original model with which we can make comparisons. For hip hop music, this model is the era before rap music made it big, the moment when hip hop existed in city parks and house parties instead of on MTV. This era is characterized as a pure moment of creative expression, untainted by concerns of getting rich from the music. In the beginning of this chapter, I referred to criticisms from both music journalists and scholars who understand rap artists' consumerism as a new development and a regression from the creative potential of hip hop's early years. These critics' nostalgia reflects the rejection of consumerism in lyrics from the underground artists I discussed in the previous section. Lyrics from Del and The Lootpack describe an aesthetic that they claim holds truer to hip hop's origins, and they fault "the industry" for corrupting the music. Such nostalgia forms in reaction to the threat of losing hip hop culture to the mainstream.

In telling the stories of their careers, many artists describe their interaction with hip hop culture from a young age, and narrate the changes they have watched the culture endure as it has grown into an industry. These "back in the day" narratives promote rap artists' desires to preserve real hip hop, even as they profit from its marketability in the mainstream. Several hip hop songs depict rap's formative years as less violent, more uplifting, less divisive, and most importantly, untainted by the record industry. Common Sense's "I Used to Love H.E.R" (1994) chronicles the artist's relationship with hip hop music, which he personifies as a romantic interest.[21] The song begins with a picture of Common at ten years old, first meeting a girl who was "old school" and "not about the money," but who soon shifts to a gangsta image she uses to argue her credibility through her connection to street life. Common criticizes, "Stressin' how hardcore and real she is. She was really the realest, before she got into showbiz," and blames the corporate entertainment industry for corrupting what was a pure love for him as a child. The song ends with the revelation that the woman in these lyrics is hip hop personified, and with Common's promise to "take her back" from the industry. Since the release of this song, though. Common has gone on to write hip hop songs for television commercials, most notably his collaboration with R&B singer Mya on "Real Compared To What," a commercial they recorded as part of a 2003 advertising campaign called "Coca-Cola … Real."[22]

My examples here illuminate two issues: First, the extent to which hip hop's discourse of realness has entered the mainstream, and second, the contradictions of this discourse's entrance by way of a TV advertisement. Common's "I Used to Love H.E.R." is one of rap music's central self-narratives, and his criticism of rap's commercialization is echoed in songs like C-Rayz Walz's "86" (2003) and Missy Elliott's "Back in the Day" (2003) that call for current artists to take their music back to the old school. The hip hop phrases "the old school" and "back in the day" can refer to a time before the music became commercial, as it does in Missy Elliott's song title. In one verse she asks "What happened to those good old days? When hip hop was so much fun?" Back in the day invariably refers to an era when hip hop was performed at house parties and block parties, such as those organized by DJ Kool Herc, the "father of hip hop." Yet Kool Herc himself admits a commercial agenda as he charged people to attend his parties and admits his goal to make money.[23] Kool Herc was an entrepreneur, and his version of hip hop history includes profit, community, and fun as legitimate coexisting intentions, while Common and Missy Elliott point us back in the day to a time when hip hop was fun, and was for the people, but not about making money. Yet in emphasizing the fact that he was both promoter and DJ, rather than a DJ for hire by promoters, Kool Herc asserts his control over his own operation. He justifies commercial intent through his entrepreneurship, and through his working outside the system, maintaining artistic control and at the same time making more money than DJs that sold their services to other business entities. Davey D, involved in hip hop since 1977, claims a desire for profit existed from the beginning:

"First, from day one people sought to get paid ... if the opportunities that exist now existed then ... the early 'hip hoppers' would've taken advantage. ..."[24]

If hip hop events began with a commercial intent, where did the culture experience the shift toward the anti-commercialism of some of today's lyrics? Missy acknowledges that rap has changed, but rap artist KRS-ONE points to one specific moment: "When 'Rapper's Delight' sold two million records in 1979, all the attention was placed on rap music as a selling tool, not on hip hop as a consciousness-raising tool, as a maturing of the community. When hip hop culture got discarded for the money to be made into rap product, we went wrong right there."[25] But for how long did rap exist as a music form unto itself before "Rapper's Delight" hit the radio in 1979? Kool Herc debuted as a DJ in 1973, which would limit "back in the day" to a six-year period during which both Missy Elliott and Common were too young to participate.

Social theorist Jean Baudrillard describes the urge to reclaim media-simulated culture through narratives of creation: "When the real is no longer what it used to be, nostalgia assumes its full meaning. There is a proliferation of myths of origin and signs of reality."[26] Auslander translates this concept to rock music as he argues that notions of rock authenticity often center on the rejection of another form perceived as inauthentic: "rock ideology is conservative: authenticity is often located in current music's relationship to an earlier, 'purer' moment in the mythic history of the music."[27] Baudrillard links such myths of origin to the escalation of the real to hyperreal, to commodified and mediatized images that have become more real than reality. Hip hop's nostalgia calls our attention to current, retrospective, constructions of the pure origins of the culture outside commercialism, and the "back in the day" narratives of top-selling artists like Missy Elliott and Common reflect Renato Rosaldo's notion of "imperialist nostalgia," by which individuals yearn for the culture they have commodified or transformed.[28] Hip hop's nostalgia yearns for a time in which the sincerity of its artistic expression could not be called into question by the marketability of the artistic product, and often emphasizes that era's focus on live performance, which has much more limited potential for circulation than a recording. In practice, nostalgic artists today turn to performance to demonstrate their connection to concepts of this earlier culture, and to assert that their vocal skills are not studio-simulated.

Hip Hop as a Performance Culture

Kool Herc and other 1970s DJs were the main attraction at early hip hop parties. They inverted the structure of musical celebrity as the audience paid not to see a performance from the group featured on the recording, but to see the neighborhood celebrities who manipulated those recordings, cutting and looping the best parts of the records into breakbeats, and eventually creating new sounds out of those recordings as DJs Grand Wizzard Theodore and Grandmaster Flash invented techniques of scratching. The DJ's presence was a central part of the performance, and initially the MC's job was to motivate the crowd, to incite them to respond to the DJ's work with the turntables. As MCs began to develop more complex rhymes, their own performance became more of a focus, and became the aspect of hip hop culture that proved most marketable. Today, more than thirty years after Kool Herc first organized his block parties, more rap listeners hear the MC's voice on recordings than in performance. Yet many MCs continue to describe the importance of performing live, and to emphasize that they began their careers performing at block parties rather than in the studio recording booth.

This emphasis on live performance connects with the nostalgia I discussed in the previous section. S.H. Fernando identifies tensions between rap performance and recording as early as Sugarhill Gang's "Rapper's Delight," the group was created by a record label, did not have a history of performing live, and did not write its own lyrics. Grandmaster Caz of the pioneering rap group Cold Crush Brothers claims that a Sugarhill MC stole the "Rapper's Delight" lyrics from him, and he argues that Sugarhill "didn't really represent what MC-ing was or what rap and hip hop was."[29] Because of this mistrust of groups created by record executives, rap vocalists must perform live to authenticate their skills as real MCs. This imperative is not unique to hip hop. In two studies of rock music, Auslander and Theodore Gracyk agree that rock culture today centers on recording rather than performance. Although Gracyk believes today's rock artists essentially are studio musicians rather than live performers,[30] Auslander argues that live performance still plays a pivotal role in "establishing the *authenticity* of the music for the rock fan."[31] Seeing a band play live can prove that the musicians can play their instruments, and that the singer's voice can exist outside the digitized version heard on a CD. Rock differs from hip hop, though, in that hip hop performance often requires the improvisation of new rhymes, while rock groups tend to play live versions of songs that they have recorded in the studio. Although rock performance does feature improvisation in the form of live jam sessions, rap performance goes further to emphasize freestyle (improvised rhyming) and the MC battle (a competition in which two freestyle rhymers go head to head) as necessary outlets for MCs to prove their rhyme skills outside the studio.

Hip hop radio shows often call on their guests, as commercial recording artists, to freestyle live on the air. Sway and King Tech's "Wake-Up Show" on San Francisco Bay-area KMEL 106, released a CD anthology of the best freestyles from their program, from such rap luminaries as Nas, Tha Alkaholiks, and Wu-Tang Clan. A freestyle performance demonstrates the artist's roots in hip hop as a performance culture, and proves his or her skills in constructing and delivering rhymes outside the studio. While Davey D acknowledges that MCs from the 1970s, such as Melle Mel, Grand Master Caz, and Kurtis Blow, all rehearsed and prewrote much of their freestyle content, he claims what was important in performance was "to present yourself" as if the rhymes were being composed spontaneously.[32] Hip hop culture finds these early performances of spontaneous freestyle rhyme at the heart of its vocal tradition, and many MCs have built careers on their ability to improvise, to adapt the prewritten to the moment of performance, and therefore to compose, in at least some sense, spontaneously. MC Supernatural, for example, has earned a reputation for performance more than for recording, through his use of freestyle in concert. At a July 15, 2000, show in Cincinnati, Ohio, I saw Supernatural invite the crowd to hand him random items that he would incorporate into his lyrical flow without breaking rhythm or rhyme.

An extension of freestyle, the MC battle is a competition in which MCs go head to head to improvise rhymes over music that is randomly chosen and constantly changing. To win points with the audience, MCs must prove the spontaneity of their rhymes. Battle rules often specify "no written." Performers need to reference their opponent's rhymes and to react to the immediate situation in their lyrics to establish skill. The battle is a common feature of hip hop cinema, from the documentary footage of *Style Wars* (1983) to the more recent scripted battle scenes of Eminem's partially autobiographical film *8 Mile* (2002). While Eminem's scenes in *8 Mile* were scripted, they represent the documented success he saw in MC battles like Scribble Jam prior to the release of his first commercial recordings. In the film, Eminem's character B. Rabbit freezes in response to the pressure of improvising rhymes in front of a hostile crowd. In formal competition, rhymers are awarded points judged by audience reaction, and it is crucial to show that these rhymes are at least in some part spontaneous. MCs often are expected to address their opponent directly, and rhyme topics often center on jabs at the opponent's fashion style, rhyme skill, and physical appearance. To further assert the spontaneity of their rhymes, MCs can make references to their immediate situation and surroundings, often creating rhymes that incorporate the name of their opponent and the name of the venue, and referring directly to the rhymes offered by the competitor. The immediacy of detail is central to establishing a performance as freestyle.

It is important to note that many mainstream MCs do not engage in battles, but rather use their career narratives to convince the listener of the success they saw as they performed in battles on their way to the top. Eminem does not participate in battles today, but *8 Mile* works to convince the viewer that Eminem paid his dues in performance on his way to becoming a platinum-selling recording artist. While the battle traditionally is how disputes between rappers have been settled, the practice has become less common among commercial artists, perhaps because they stand to lose credibility, and therefore sales. Yet battles do still occur in the underground, and MTV has organized two separate MC battles over the past two years that invited unsigned rappers to win a recording contract by out-battling their competitors. MTV's involvement proved problematic as Roc-A-Fella Records refused to honor the contract they had promised the winner of MTV's second battle. With the MTV battles, the corporate music industry attempted to simulate a competitive process that *8 Mile* and other hip hop career narratives had presented as a forum through which MCs had paid their dues in establishing their skills in vocal performance, and fought their way up the ladder to success in the mainstream. As MTV attempted to simulate this process and offer a Roc-A-Fella Records contract as first prize, winning the competition did not establish the MC's realness in the same way.

Though many listeners may have been first introduced to the battle in its MTV form, or in the scripted battle sequence from *8 Mile,* such mainstream representations of the battle do acknowledge the importance of live vocal performance to hip hop. Because rap's vocal origins are so rooted in live performance, a real rap artist must argue his or her ability to perform not only on recordings, but in concert, freestyle, or battle. A Tribe Called Quest's "Phony Rappers" (1996) defines its subject as those "who do not write," and "who do not excite," and the song tells the story of a rap career in which Tribe has achieved some level of success as mainstream recording artists, only to find themselves challenged to perform in the streets by rap listeners who believe that "an MC that they seen on TV can't hold it down in the NYC." By Tribe's definition, the real MC pens his or her own lyrics, can excite a crowd in live performance, and can improvise lyrics to respond to an opponent. "Phony Rappers" targets those wannabe rap vocalists who approach Tribe's Q-Tip and Phife Dawg in public settings and challenge them to battle. Phife and Q-Tip claim that they must consistently prove their skills in live performance, which validates their commercial success as it proves their skills in creativity, improvisation, and crowd interaction. The question remains, though, of how these skills translate to the music industry and its emphasis on selling records more than putting on a good live show.

Lil Wayne tells a similar story from a different perspective in the skit "On the Block #1" (*Tha Carter II*, 2005), where he's approached on Miami's South Beach by a fan who wants to videotape himself battling the rapper. While Tribe's Q-Tip and Phife accept the challenge on "Phony Rappers," Lil Wayne doesn't want to waste his time. He asks "Dawg, how much we gonna make for this?" Wayne argues that, with his status in hip hop, he doesn't need to battle to prove himself anymore, and reminds his listeners that just because he's from the South and doesn't brag about his rhyme flow doesn't mean he isn't at the top of the rap game. The "On the Block #1" skit leads into and serves an introduction to the next track, "Best Rapper Alive," where Wayne illustrates his skills. When Lil Wayne brings up money in response to being asked to battle, he reflects the aesthetic of his record label, Cash Money. Cash Money artists flaunt their money and jewelry as testament to their success, and as testament to their skills. For a battle to be worth his time, Lil Wayne says he needs to get paid.

Hip Hop Career Stories: The Skills to Pay the Bills

In the 1990s, the Beastie Boys titled a song "Skills to Pay the Bills" (1992), and Positive K titled his debut album *The Skills Dat Pay the Bills* (1992). More recent hip hop lyrics, however, separate rhyme skills from sales, dead prez for example, claim that they're tired of "monotonous material. All ya'll records sound the same" ("Hip Hop," 2000). *Billboard*'s pop charts tend to favor less complex topics and rhyme structures, and place more emphasis on marketability for dance clubs. Crossover hits like J-Kwon's "Tipsy" (2004) or 50 Cent's "In Da Club" (2003) take on the club atmosphere as their topics. These Top 40 songs feature basic rhyme structures over sparse beats, and are lyrically very repetitive, relying heavily on the verse-chorus-verse structure of pop music. This contradiction between skills and sales recalls hip hop's narratives of an earlier, purer, hip hop culture, unadulterated by concerns of profit. These narratives tell us that back in the day MCs were not held accountable to the musical styles that sell in the mainstream. Because these back-in-the-day narratives are so pervasive, top-selling mainstream artists must prove that they maintain connections to hip hop's original culture. Artists who abandon real hip hop skills to increase sales describe getting rich in terms of getting out of, and giving back to, the ghetto.

Jay-Z justifies getting rich in terms of giving back to the ghetto communities that invented hip hop, even when getting rich means abandoning hip hop's original aesthetic. On "Moment of Clarity" (2003), Jay-Z responds to hip hop purists with a message of survivalism, invoking the question of skills versus sales, and addressing those listeners who consider the music of artists Common or Talib Kweli more real than Jay-Z's platinum-selling singles. Jay claims to "dumb down" his music in order to sell more records, and criticizes these more lyrically complex MCs for focusing on skills instead of sales. Jay claims that he chooses to produce radio-friendly music in order to get rich and give back to the community. By linking his commercial agenda to the style of hip hop he records, Jay-Z claims to put his community above his own artistry, and to simplify his rhyme style to achieve mainstream success. Yet on the same song, Jay-Z also claims "I built a dynasty by being one of the realest niggas out." This line, in context of his claims to dumb down his music, would emphasize his personal sincerity and philanthropy over his accountability to the creative expression of hip hop culture. As he responds to criticisms, Jay-Z becomes "one of the realest" rappers as he makes visible his financial agenda and the ways that agenda conflicts with his artistic production.

While I can't argue whether Jay-Z has dumbed down his music, his actions do hold true to the philanthropic agenda he proposes. He has started programs like "Team Roc" to provide scholarship opportunities and after-school programs for inner-city kids, and his annual Christmas toy drive provides $10,000 in gifts to children in the Marcy Housing Projects where Jay-Z grew up. He also hosts a Christmas dinner each year at Marcy's Recreation Center. Jay-Z's "Moment of Clarity" lyrics speak to the conflict between aesthetics and politics in black artistic production. In 1937, Richard Wright's "Blueprint for Negro Writing" argued that black writing should have a political content because of the black writer's social responsibility, and because of his or her role in creating values for the community.[33] Wright's notion of social responsibility reflects a wider tradition that goes back to Marcus Garvey, and to Booker T. Washington's idea of African-American responsibility to be "a credit to the race." William M. Banks traces the tensions between aesthetics and politics from the Harlem Renaissance through the black radicals and intellectuals of the 1960s. Banks argues that imperatives of social responsibility and a necessary political content may stand in conflict with making money in the mainstream. These historical tensions are complicated by the unprecedented commercial potential of hip hop. The global visibility of hip hop again raises questions of how African-American celebrities can, or should, speak for the African-American community.

While the black traditions Banks identifies tend to understand political content and social responsibility in their *opposition* to commercialism, and to frame political content in opposition to producing a consumer-friendly product, Jay-Z frames making commercial music as a political act in itself: Getting rich and giving back to the community does more good than producing music that holds truer to hip hop's cultural origins. Hip hop outsells every other form of popular music in the U.S., whether invented by black or white Americans. Hip hop's unprecedented sales prompt reconsideration of commercialism's influence on aesthetics and politics in black artistic production. Several black artists who make money in the mainstream emphasize the fact that they circulate that wealth within the black community. An act of philanthropy, like Jay-Z's scholarship foundation, becomes itself a form of activism, as he shows his audience he hasn't forgotten where he came from, and that he remains accountable to that community. As Jay-Z frames his sales within accountability to his community, he rejects artistry for commercialism, as does Jadakiss in his line "Screw your awardz, my son can't eat those plaques" ("Scenario 2000," 2000). Such declarations tie commercialism to politics, rather than aesthetics, as artists like Jay-Z, Jadakiss, and 50 Cent embrace their Top 40 record sales and justify getting rich as a form of survival. These and others mainstream artists frame their commercial success within a rhetoric of financial common sense. A line from Master P and Ice Cube's "You Know I'm a Hoe" (1998), "If it don't make dollars then it don't make sense," suggests a model in which producing art that won't sell becomes a selfish and frivolous pursuit, and accountability to the community through one's aesthetics does less to support that community than do the social programs Jay-Z uses his platinum sales to fund.

Skills, Sales, and Career Longevity

Jay-Z's *Black Album* (2003) ends with the announcement of Jay's retirement from hip hop at the peak of his success. He claims the album will be his last release, and it celebrates his achievements in coming "from bricks to Billboards, grams to Grammys," and from his childhood in Marcy Projects to his sold-out concert at Madison Square Garden. In chronicling his rise to stardom, Jay-Z links his artistic achievements to a financial agenda, and as he looks back at his accomplishments, he uses the phrase "rap career." De La Soul, as well, uses "rap career" on their seventh album, *The Grind Date* (2004), which celebrates the group's longevity and perseverance even as their mainstream sales and celebrity have wavered. While written from different perspectives of success, *The Black Album* and *The Grind Date* confront the artists' interaction with the record industry, and describe a meeting of the personal and the professional in the rap career. Rap artists' experiences within the music industry become important subject, matter, and an important part of hip hop's dialogue about culture and commerce.

Earlier in this chapter I mentioned De La Soul's 1988 debut video "Me, Myself, and I," in which they introduced themselves to MTV viewers by parodying the nascent culture of rap videos. Essentially, De La Soul parodied the standardization of the rap image, and the formula followed by many rap acts of that era, as standing in opposition to rap's emphasis on individuality and creativity. The "Me, Myself, and I" video features Pos, Mase, and Trugoy as high school classmates taking a class to learn to become rappers. As the group cannot fit into the formulas of rap's fashion and posturing, they are ridiculed by their classmates and instructor. The parody used in this video works to create a space for the different image De La Soul projects in their own music. De La Soul's debut album *3 Feet High and Rising* (1989) reached platinum in ten years of sales, but they have not produced another album to match that success. After sixteen years of recording, they remain on the fringe of the mainstream, but still enjoy a cult following as one of hip hop's most influential groups. While De La Soul has by no means fallen into obscurity (they performed with Gorillaz at the 2006 Grammy Awards), their sales are no match for the multiplatinum Jay-Z, and their website, Spitkicker.com, enlisted fans during 2005 to sign a petition for MTV to play their latest video, "Rock Co Kane Flow" which extends and updates their critique of mainstream rap. Along with several other tracks from *The Grind Date*, "Rock Co Kane Flow" focuses on the group's career, chronicling the reality of their current position in hip hop, the labor that went into the making of the album, and the question of their longevity in the face of those newer, less innovative acts that are selling more records through conforming to proven pop-rap formulas ("yo, let's cookie-cut the shit and get the gingerbread, man"). The album's liner notes include a month-by-month calendar that outlines the work they did to produce the album.

The Grind Date ends with De La Soul's assessment of the group's current position in the rap game: "Too old to rhyme? Too bad." ("Rock Co Kane Flow," 2004) Through this continuing critique of the rap image, De La Soul claims to have found staying power in their personal commitment to a hip hop aesthetic that lies outside commercial trends. Throughout their career they have continued to critique hip hop's commercial image, and their own image as well. Following the chart success of their debut album, the group titled their 1991 sophomore release *De La Soul is Dead*, and opened that album with a skit in which a group of kids, calling Vanilla Ice "better than any rapper I ever seen," find a De La Soul tape in the garbage. Three gangstas looking for rap with pimps, guns, and curse words, steal the tape and critique De La Soul's music in spoken interludes, until at the end of the album they return the tape to the garbage. In extension of this self-effacement that stands in opposition to rap's emphasis on boasting, 1993's "Fallin" contains the line "Read the paper, the headline say 'Washed-up rapper got a song.'" In conjunction with such self-critique, De La Soul parodies the excess of popular hip hop videos in 1993's "Ego Trippin' (Part Two)," which displays the caption "It's a rental" as Trugoy cruises in an expensive car. On *The Grind Date*, De La Soul targets the much-publicized charity fundraising of Sean "P Diddy" Combs, as televised on the MTV special "Diddy Runs the City." On the track "Verbal Clap," (2004), they say, "We run mics, let Sean run the marathon." As narrated in their lyrics, their career trajectory speaks for the sacrifices they have made to continue to produce real hip hop, and from this position they critique those hip hop superstars who can afford to stage charity events.

As MCs focus on where they came from, they must work to tie this history to where they've gone in their music careers. Concepts of performer realness seek consistency between an artist's origins and his or her current position in the record industry. De La Soul narrates its trajectory as a group that refuses to follow rap trends. Jay-Z tells the rags-to-riches story of a rap superstar, and ties his celebrity to stories of his younger days as a drug dealer, thereby connecting his business agenda to a streetwise mentality. As artists narrate their own careers, they revise and reclaim narratives of the self-made man (or millionaire), and frame a story of the individual's interaction with the music industry. Concepts of real hip hop center the autobiographical basis of lyrics, and on the fidelity of the performance to hip hop's original culture. These central dimensions of realness are complicated by the reality that most rap music is recorded to be sold. The conflicts between creativity and commerce lead artists to write career narratives that reconcile their backgrounds with their work as recording artists. Hip hop career narratives present counterstories that challenge the accepted history of the exploitation of black music, like rock and roll, by white record companies. Hip hop counterstories complicate criticisms of materialism and excess in the music as they employ metaphors of music as a drug. Rap stars frame their rags-to-riches narratives within hip hop's criminal discourse, to present making and selling rap music as an extension of crime, and to reconcile this criminal aesthetic with their roles in the record industry. These narratives represent a social reality, one that is oversimplified by arguments that hip hop has been co-opted by the record industry, or has become too materialistic to still matter.

Study Questions

1. Can novice artists really envision hip-hop as a viable career option?
2. To what extent to hip-hop artists make explicit the business side of the industry to audiences?
3. What are the career opportunities in hip-hop beyond being the "talent"?

Notes

1. Scholars such as Tricia Rose and Russell A. Potter theorized hip hop's resistance, while more recent studies by Krims and Negus challenged earlier theories of hip hop's resistance, and focused on hip hop's growth as an industry.

2. Krims, *Rap Music and the Poetics of Identity*, 1.
3. For further examples of print journalists' criticisms of hip hop excess, see Wedge, E12, and Izrael, B13.
4. For examples in other forms of music, see Graham Parker's "Mercury Poisoning" (1979), The Sex Pistols' "EMI" (1977), and Aimee Mann's "Calling it Quits" (1999).
5. Judy, 216.
6. Negus, in "The Music Business and Rap: Between the Street and the Executive Suite," is skeptical, not recognizing the advances hip hop has made toward artists' control of their musical production. Negus argues that rap artists seek both autonomy and recognition from corporate labels, and he identifies a hip hop business model that "challenges tales of co-optation, exploitation, and forced compromise" (Negus 492). Yet in the end, he believes that "the making of rap is managed by the music industry," and that "major companies tend to *allow* rap" certain levels of independence because it furthers their own commercial agendas (Negus 503, 500, emphasis in original). Although Negus does acknowledge the efforts hip hop artists make to challenge corporate music, he finds their efforts ineffective, and believes the artists are duped by industry executives who co-opt their work. Dipa Basu, in "What is Real About 'Keeping it Real'," challenges such a reading in her study of black entrepreneurship within hip hop, where she identifies "entrepreneurial strides, in a context of systematic racism" and argues that, "On an unprecedented level African Americans are making business footholds in the music industry; rappers and black rap entrepreneurs are transgressing cultural boundaries, and the boundaries between business, pleasure and politics" (Basu 372).
7. Negus articulates hip hop's "deliberate attempts to maintain a distance between the corporate world and the genre culture of rap." (Negus 488.)
8. While the Fatback Band's King Tim III (Personality Jock) was released prior to "Rapper's Delight," in 1979, making it the first rap record ever released, its commercial success and cultural impact did not match that of Sugarhill Gang's "Rapper's Delight," which technically is rap's second commercial release.
9. Gilroy, 73.
10. Smith, 348.
11. Neal, 161.
12. Henry Louis Gates defines Signifyin(g) as "the figure of the double-voiced," a process by which texts speak to other texts (Gates xxv). Gates identifies the function of revision in Signifying (Gates 88–94), and argues that a motivated Signifying "functions to redress an imbalance in power, to clear a space, rhetorically" (Gates 124). Kopano, Potter, and Wheeler each connected hip hop rhetoric to the tradition of Signifying. Wheeler uses Gates' reading of Mikhail Bakhtin's dialogism in its connections to African-American rhetoric, yet her study came too early to fully engage the current dialogue over commercialism that I take on as my subject here.
13. Baldwin, 4.
14. See Trilling, *Sincerity and Authenticity: The Charles Eliot Norton Lectures, 1969-1970*, for a detailed history of these terms.
15. Armstrong, 7–8.
16. McLeod, 139.
17. Krims, 95.
18. Frith, 71.
19. Stratton, "Between Two Worlds: Art and Commercialism in the Record Industry," 12.
20. Ano, "Count Bass D: Down for the Count."
21. Because of a conflict with a West Coast reggae group using the same name, Common Sense changed his name to Common on 1997's *One Day It'll All Make Sense*. Many fans and other artists still refer to him by his original artist name, Common Sense, as Jay-Z does in the lyrics to which I refer in this chapter.
22. See Morrisey Brian. "Coke Adds Interactive Fizz to New Ad Campaign," *Internet News.Com* (January 10, 2003), http://boston.internet.com/news/article.php/1567731.
23. Fricke and Ahearn, 28: "I was giving parties to make money, to better my sound system. I was never a DJ for hire. I was the guy who rent the place. I was the guy who got flyers made. I was the guy who went out there in the streets and promote it. You know? I'm just like a person who bring people together, like an instrument, an agent who bring people together, and let 'em have fun. But I was never for hire. I was seeing money that the average DJ never see. They was for hire, I had my own sound system. I was just the guy who played straight-up music that the radio don't play, that they should be playin', and people was havin' fun."
24. Davey D. "March Letters."
25. Merwin, 33.
26. Baudrillard, 12–13.
27. Auslander, 71.

28. Rosaldo, 69.
29. Fernando, "Back in the Day," 21.
30. Gracyk, 75.
31. Auslander, 65 (emphasis in original).
32. Davey D. "An Historical Definition of the Term Rap."
33. Christian, Margena A. "Has Hip Hop Taken a Beating, Or Is It Just Growing Up?" *Jet* 111:14 (2007): 54–59.

Bibliography

ANO. "Count Bass D: Down for the Count." http://www.alphabeats.com/interviews/artists/bassd.htm (February 13, 2005).

Armstrong, Edward G. "Eminem's Construction of Authenticity." *Popular Music and Society* 27:3 (Fall 2004): 335–55.

Auslander, Philip. *Liveness: Performance in a Mediatized Culture.* New York: Routledge, 1999.

Baldwin, Davarian L. "Black Empires, White Desires: The Spatial Politics of Identity in the Age of Hip-Hop." *Black Renaissance* (July 31, 1999): 138–51.

Basu, Dipannita. "What is Real About 'Keeping it Real'" *Postcolonial Studies* 1:3 (1998): 371–87.

Baudrillard, Jean. *Simulacra and Simulation.* Translation by Sheila Faria Glaser. Ann Arbor: University of Michigan Press, 1994.

Davey D. "March Letters." November 10, 2004. http://www.daveyd.com/marchletters.html.

———. "An Historical Definition of the Term Rap." November 10, 2004. http://www.daveyd.com/whatis-rapdav.html.

Fernando, S.H., Jr. "Back in the Day: 1975–1979." *Vibe History of Hip-Hop,* edited by Alan Light. New York; Vibe, 1999: 13–21.

Fricke, Jim, and Charlie Ahearn, eds. *Yes Yes Y'all: The Experience Music Project Oral History of Hip-Hop's First Decade.* New York: Da Capo Press, 2002.

Frith, Simon. *Performing Rites: On the Value of Popular Music.* Cambridge: Harvard University Press, 1996.

Gates, Henry Louis, Jr. *The Signifying Monkey: A Theory of African-American Literary Criticism.* New York: Oxford University Press, 1988.

Gilroy, Paul. *The Black Atlantic: Modernity and Double-Consciousness.* Cambridge, Mass.: Harvard University Press, 1993.

Gracyk, Theodore. *Rhythm and Noise: An Aesthetics of Rock.* Durham, N.C.: Duke University Press, 1996.

Izrael, Jimi. "Hip-Hop Needs More Than a Good Beat to be a Political Force: Bling-Bling and Ching-Ching are No Substitutes for a Civic Education." *Los Angeles Times* (August 27, 2004): B13.

Judy, R.A.T. "On the Question of Nigga Authenticity." *boundary 2* (1994): 211–31.

Krims, Adam. *Rap Music and the Poetics of Identity.* Cambridge: Cambridge University Press, 2000.

McLeod, Kembrew. "Authenticity Within Hip-Hop and other Cultures Threatened with Assimilation." *Journal of Communications* 49 (1999): 134–50.

Merwin, Scott. "From Kool Herc to 50 Cent, the Story of Rap, So Far (Bustin' Rhymes/First in a Three Part Series)." *Pittsburgh Post-Gazette* (February 15, 2004). http://www.post-gazette.com/ae/20040215rap0215aepl.asp.

Morrisey, Brian. "Coke Adds Interactive Fizz to New Ad Campaign," *Internet News.com* (January 10, 2003), http://boston.internet.com/news/article.php/1567731.

Neal, Mark Anthony. "Sold Out on Soul: The Corporate Annexation of Black Popular Music." *Popular Music and Society* 21.3 (1997): 117–36.

Negus, Keith. "The Music Business and Rap: Between the Street and the Executive Suite." *Cultural Studies* 13:3, 1997: 488–508.

Potter, Russell A. *Spectacular Vernaculars: Hip-Hop and the Politics of Postmodernism.* Albany: SUNY Press, 1995.

Rosaldo, Renato. "Imperialist Nostalgia." In *Culture and Truth.* Boston: Beacon, 1989: 68–87.

Rose, Tricia. *Black Noise: Rap Music and Black Culture in Contemporary America.* Middletown, Conn.: Wesleyan University Press, 1994.

Smith, Christopher Holmes. "Method in the Madness: Exploring the Boundaries of Identity in Hip-Hop Performativity." *Social Identities* 3.3, 1997: 345–75.

Stratton, Jon. "Between Two Worlds: Art and Commercialism in the Record Industry." In *Popular Music: Critical Concepts in Media and Cultural Studies,* edited by Simon Frith. New York: Routledge, 2003.

Trilling, Lionel. *Sincerity and Authenticity: The Charles Eliot Norton Lectures, 1969–1970.* Cambridge, Mass.: Harvard University Press, 1972.

Wedge, Dave. "Gangsta Clichés Reign on 'R.U.L.E.'" *Boston Herald* (December 10, 2004): E12.

41

The Business of Rap
Between the Street and the Executive Suite

Many have linked the entrepreneurial spirit in hip-hop to a broader political activism that attempts to combat racism, particularly on an institutional level, and impoverishment, by acquiring economic resources. Considering that hip-hop exists as a billion dollar industry, its ability to provide jobs for myriad folk is often overlooked.

Keith Negus argues that hip-hop's business practices are an important corollary to its aesthetic values and artistic practices. Negus suggests that at the core of hip-hop's sensibilities is the pursuit of the American Dream, a pursuit invested in challenging the political realities of the past.

The Business of Rap: Between the Street and the Executive Suite

Keith Negus

Rap has usually been approached as an aesthetic form of African-American expression: a resistant, oppositional, countercultural style created via the appropriation of technology and existing musical signs and symbols (scratching, sampling, mixing), drawing on a long tradition of diasporic creativity (with varying inflections of both an essentialist and anti-essentialist argument that point both back to and away from the slave routes of the Atlantic). Although the music industry has been referred to and acknowledged by a few writers,[1] most of the writing has tended to concentrate on cultural criticism[2] and locate the "politics" of rap within the domain of a cultural struggle conducted across the broad terrain of "consumption" that is lived outside the world of the corporate entertainment industry.

This perspective has clearly demonstrated that rap has been made as a cultural practice that involves the quite explicit creative appropriation of existing sounds, images and technologies and their reconstitution as a new art form. The creation of rap has also highlighted the tangible connecting points that link the often inadequate concepts of "production" and "consumption," and has illustrated how consumption can *become* production. In the process, creative practice and aesthetic discourse have produced a particular type of cultural-political identity which can be understood in terms of a long tradition of black creative activity, not only within the United States (Fernando Jr, 1995; Vincent, 1996) but within the context of a diaspora of the black Atlantic (Gilroy, 1993).

This chapter is not a direct challenge to such an account but an attempt to add a further dimension to the arguments and knowledge through which rap is understood as both a musical genre and cultural practice. My argument is that to understand rap, both in the past and its potential in the future, then cultural explanations alone are not enough. Rap is also a very particular U.S. business. As Kevin Powell wrote in a magazine profile of the highly successful Death Row Records, prior to the death of Tupac Shakur and the imprisonment of Suge Knight:

> There is no way to truly comprehend the incredible success of Death Row Records—its estimated worth now tops $100 million—without first understanding the conditions that created the rap game in the first place: few legal economic paths in America's inner cities, stunted educational opportunities, a pervasive sense of alienation among young black males, black folk's age-old need to create music, and a typically American hunger for money and power. The Hip Hop Nation is no different than any other segment of this society in its desire to live the American dream. (Powell, 1996, p. 46)

In the struggle against racism and economic and cultural marginalization, and in an attempt to "live the American dream," rap has also been created as a self-conscious business activity as well as a cultural form and aesthetic practice. A skim through consumer magazines such as *The Source* or *Vibe*, publications that address both artists and fans (often at the point where the two merge), reveals frequent references to issues of "career planning" and business management, often presented as a form of educational intelligence. A typical article in *The Source* began in the following way:

> We all have dreams, aspirations and goals ... things that we dream of but for whatever reason don't follow through on. For many of us, that dream is getting into the recording industry. So before you just dive with reckless abandon into the murky waters of the biz, here are some steps that might make the going a bit easier.
>
> Knowledge: Go to the library and do your homework. This will give you a basic knowledge of the day-to-day operations of an independent label. It's also very important that you do an internship at an independent label (a minimum of 6 months). Make contacts, ask questions and take notes. It is important that you are able to experience, first-hand, the struggles you will inevitably face.
>
> Business plan: As in starting any business, you must have a plan. You need a 5-year business plan that includes a projected budget. Your business plan should reflect you. You're the one who has to live by it. (Payton, 1997, p. 96)

The article then goes on to cover other issues under the subheadings of cash, legal counsel, operating a business, communication, artist, production, manufacturing and distribution and promotion—throwing quite a different light on to the idea of rap spontaneously emerging from "the streets" (an issue I shall come back to shortly).

In a similar way, a reading of trade magazines such as *Billboard* will turn up a number of articles in which rap artists and entrepreneurs, whether Suge Knight or Chuck D, explicitly discuss their commercial strategies and business plans or where executives such as Angelo Ellerbee, President of Double XXposure, discusses his "charm school for rap artists" (Snyder, 1996). As Bahamadia commented during the promotion for her first album:

> You have to understand that this is a business. When you sign your name on the dotted line on your contract you are literally a walking human business as well as a human being. So you have to study this business, ask questions, educate yourself and have a plan B and a plan C. (Fitzgerald, 1996, pp. 22–23)

I hope that in some small way this chapter might educate and inform. I also wish to argue that, to understand what rap might mean and its potential as a form of cultural expression and communication, it's also necessary to understand it as a business that links—and perhaps more significantly separates—artist and audience in quite distinct ways. In very broad terms, this chapter follows the central theme set out earlier in this book by considering how the industry sets up structures of organization and working practices to produce culture and also by highlighting the way that broader culture processes and practices connect with the industry—the uneasy relationship between the genre culture of rap and the corporate cultures of the music industry.

In developing the theoretical focus I outlined earlier, I shall illustrate these dynamics by analyzing how the industry organizes the production of rap in a very specific way and bases working practices on a particular construction of knowledge about the social world. The approach to the relationship between rap music and the recorded entertainment industry that I am proposing here is more complex than the often narrated tales of co-optation, exploitation and forced compromise to a commercial agenda, although these pressures are certainly not absent. At the same time, it is an attempt to avoid the celebration of black entrepreneurialism or the endorsement of rap as a type of material success-oriented "fun capitalism."[3]

The title of this chapter, "Between the street and the executive suite," signals a further broad argument and general theme that weaves throughout. First, it signals the way in which rappers who have often been identified solely with "the street" are also executives. I consider this important, for while the portrayal of rap artists as creative iconoclasts from the margins certainly reclaims a value for activities that have been devalued, it fails to adequately acknowledge that rap is, potentially, not "outside" or bursting out from the periphery but central to the development of the practices and aesthetics of the contemporary music industry. However, this is not simply to replace rap artists and entrepreneurs at the center of a fun type of capitalism. Instead, my aim is to raise questions about *why* and *how* rap has remained "on the street"— materially and discursively. Here "the street" operates as a metonym for a particular type of knowledge which is deployed by executives throughout the music industry, a type of knowledge which legitimates the belief that rap *is* and *should be* outside the corporate suite. Hence, I use the theme of the street and executive suite to signal the way in which the discourse of the street (and the mythical "being in touch" with it) is integral to how the music industry deals with rap practices. One consequence is that this maintains a separation of experiences and contributes to the ongoing reproduction of the broader economic, cultural, and racialized divisions across which r 'n' b and rap have been and continue to be made.

In approaching rap in these terms, this chapter ... is a deliberate attempt to try and steer a course away from the dichotomy between modernist despair at the power and influence of corporate commodity production and postmodernist celebration of the possibilities provided by cultural consumption and appropriation. It is also an attempt to suggest that the politics of culture need not simply be waged on one side or the other, but during a significant series of connections and relational practices which connect production and consumption and the articulations through which the corporate organization and music industry occupations are linked to broader cultural formations.

Corporate Decisions and Cultural Divisions:
The Major Companies and the Black Music Department

To understand how the recording industry has come to deal with black music in general and rap in particular, it's necessary to recall ... how the industry, and specifically the U.S. music business, deals with different genres. As I discussed, the major record companies use a technique known as portfolio management in order to divide labels, genres and artists into strategic business units, making visible the performance, profile and financial contribution of each division. Well-established genres are often referred to as "cash cows." A genre such as rap, however, despite the revenues it has continued to generate, may be classified as a "wild cat" by industry analysts who are uncertain about its future aesthetic changes and nervous when trying to predict "potential market growth," and by business personnel who are uncomfortable with the politics of black representation foregrounded by the genre and anxious about confronting political pressure from the moral opponents of rap (these issues I shall elaborate over the following pages).

It is within the context of corporate strategies of portfolio management that the major companies and their labels have come to deal with black music in separate divisions. Historically, the contemporary management of rhythm and blues within separate formally defined corporate entities can be traced back to a reorganization of the music business that occurred during the late 1960s and early 1970s. The creation of "black divisions" during this period was a response to commercial opportunity, social and political pressure and cultural changes.

A number of factors contributed to this. One involved pressure from activists associated with the civil rights movement and the National Association for the Advancement of Colored People, who urged the major labels to give a more equitable remuneration to black artists and sought greater representation for industry personnel. Additional pressure came from the so-called Fairplay Committee. This was a group, associated with DJs and radio personnel, that managed to combine what many supported as "commendable aims" (a fair deal for African-American artists and music industry staff) with alleged acts of intimidation and violence and a desire to extort money through being "the prime collector of payola for all black disc jockeys" (Wade and Picardie, 1990, p. 175).[4]

A further influence came from within the major companies themselves, where senior executives were beginning to reassess how they dealt with different types of music. After commissioning research, the major companies selectively followed the key recommendations of a 1971 report for CBS by the Harvard Business School, that had advocated the formation of black music divisions.[5] This was for many executives a logical restructuring and response to promotional practices and radio broadcasting which had dealt separately with African-American recordings through a series of euphemisms which began with the term "race music" during the 1920s (Garofalo, 1994, 1997). Reebee Garofalo (1993) has also pointed out that when the "race music" labels of the 1920s (such as Black Swan, Merit and Black Patti) were hit by the Great Depression, they were bought up by major labels (such as OKeh and Paramount) and maintained as a distinct "race music" series, kept separate from other parts of the catalogue. Hence, although the major labels began setting up black music divisions and departments from the early 1970s, the practices upon which this built can be traced back throughout the twentieth century.

One benefit of such a practice is that these divisions have provided a space for black staff within a company, people who may not otherwise have gained employment in the music business. These separate divisions have also ensured that musicians are managed by personnel with knowledge, skills, and understanding of their music (not all of whom are black, obviously). However, staff within the black divisions have experienced an unstable and uncertain existence. One of the most significant disadvantages is that the department can easily be cut back, closed down or restructured by the corporation (whether this is due to an assessment that the genre has changed or simply because cuts have to be made). A similar fate can befall many departments when exposed as business units, from the cutting of the smallest Latin division in the 1980s to the reorganization of the largest hard rock division in the wake of the rise of post-Nirvana "alternative rock" in the early 1990s.

However, it is often the black music division that is subject to greater cutting than others. A notorious example of this occurred in February 1996 when Capitol Records closed its urban division, canceling the contracts of most artists and sacking eighteen members of staff (most of them black). This was yet another example of EMI's drastic restructurings. On this occasion the company publicly explained that they had closed this division so as to concentrate resources on their "stars" (such as Bonnie Raitt and Richard Marx) and their modern rock artists (Everclear and Radiohead). In the week that this occurred, I happened to have an interview arranged with Havelock Nelson, a *Billboard* writer who, over the years, has been involved in organizing various hip hop workshops and educational events. As he remarked: "This happens so much whenever there is a budget cut to be made; it's always the black department that suffers."[6]

For J.R. Reynolds (1996), another columnist working for *Billboard*, this event represented "the systematic extermination of black music at Capitol Records" and "cut the company's ties to the r 'n' b community." As such, this was far from simply an "economic" decision. Reynolds pointed out that it could not be justified in market terms: in 1995 r 'n' b and rap had sold 132 million albums and accounted for over 21 per cent of the music market in the U.S.[7]

Despite the corporate reasoning presented to the press, the "commercial" strategies of music corporations are not simply business decisions alone, but are informed by a number of value judgments and cultural beliefs. In this instance, whatever the dynamic within the company, to many outsiders this looked suspiciously like racism and a distinct lack of commitment (in terms of staff and investment) to sustain an involvement in black music and what Nelson George (1989) has called the "rhythm and blues world." George has used this phrase to refer to the "extramusical" significance of rhythm and blues as an "integral part" and "powerful symbol" for "a black community forged by common political, economic and geographic conditions" (1989, p. xii).

Hence, one issue here is that of occupational insecurity. The music industry is a notoriously insecure place to work, but black music divisions can be particularly unstable. For as long as they have been in existence the variously named r 'n' b/black/urban divisions have been chopped and changed. They have been closed down and reopened as a way of dealing with financial booms and slumps, and staffed and restaffed as senior management has continually changed its thinking about how to deal with r 'n' b. Recent shifts include the transition from appointing senior staff with backgrounds in promotion during the middle of the 1980s to heading the black divisions with attorneys, artists' managers and producers in the early 1990s, and then bringing in artists and producers in the middle of the 1990s.[8] This instability was rather ironically signaled by a panel organized for a music business convention by the coalition Sista Friends, entitled "You're Not Really in the Record Business Until You've Been Fired."[9]

This instability intersects with a broader issue of historical continuity. Although numerous African-American executives have contributed to the formation of the modern music industry and the history of recorded popular music, all have continued to occupy a "precarious position" (Sanjek, 1997). The black music divisions have not been allowed the space to establish their own agenda. One conspicuous point here is that there are very few senior black executives within the corporate hierarchy who are above the black division and hence involved in the decision about closing down business units or restaffing existing departments. This is frequently acknowledged within the industry and has been emphasized by Garofalo, who has noted that "black personnel have been systematically excluded from positions of power within the industry" (1994, p. 275). There is a strong sense, and a justifiable belief held by many in the industry, that the black divisions have not been allowed to develop a continuity and a sense of history that is consonant with the African-American contribution to U.S. musical culture.

This issue was publicly raised by Andre Harrell, whose music industry career has seen him move from performer (in the act *Dr Jekyll and Mr Hyde*), to head of Uptown Records (a joint venture with MCA which broke acts such as Mary J. Blige and Heavy D and The Boyz) to President and CEO of Motown for a few years in the middle of the 1990s. While at Motown he observed:

> Black music is becoming *the* music of the popular culture. Because of that, companies are repositioning their priorities and trying to get in the game. But as black music becomes more important, there should be more black presidents and black chairmen. As soon as the black executive's artist reaches platinum, suddenly the artist and manager have to deal with the president of the corporation, because *he* controls the priorities at pop radio. The black executive becomes obsolete. As his music gets bigger, his power diminishes. He's more or less told, "Go find the next act and establish it." ... That's why young black executives don't get to become the old chairmen—the wise men who've seen it and done it. They get to stay hot black executives so long as their instincts are hot ... the black executive is not given the opportunity to become the business *and* the music. Why not? Why shouldn't he be the one that everybody reports to? When you get an act that sells 5 million—at a major company— the black executive's out of the room. But when there's some sort of problem, the major

label looks at the black executive: "Why can't you handle this act?" When the artist hires a violent manager and the violent manager is coming up to the record company the label's like: "How did it get to this?" How? Because *they* [the white executives] couldn't see it coming. Because *they're* not sensitive to his issues. By then the relationship between the record company and the artist is dysfunctional. And the black executive gets blamed and fired. But *they* created the monster.

When I had the artist, I talked to his mother, his girlfriend, his babies' mother with the two children, dealt with his drug counsellor, and whatever other dysfunctional Generation X problems he has. He'd call me late at night.

But he feels like they're just business people. And they *don't* understand. And they *might* be racist. He's comin' with all that energy. Even if they like him as a person, he still has 400 years of issues he has to get over to accept them. And they have a lot of work to do to gain his trust and respect. (DeCurtis, 1995, p. 94, emphasis in original)

Harrell spoke these words with considerable experience, highlighting how racial identity, racism and the history of racial antagonism inform relationships that are often blandly referred to as "business decisions" within the corporate suite. Ironically, Harrell did not last long in his post at Motown, but his comments were publicly vindicated just under two years after the publication of this interview. It was then that PolyGram (the current owners of Motown and the corporation which had appointed Harrell) removed Eric Kronfeld, their domestic music president, from the board after he made "several racially insulting remarks" in relation to the company's R&B act Dru Hill. Alain Levy, PolyGram President, immediately appointed Clarence Avant who became the company's first African-American director (Johnson, 1997).

It is within the context of this history that the music industry began dealing with rap (or not dealing with rap) during the 1980s. At one point it seemed that the major companies had neither the inclination, the understanding, nor the skills to deal with rap. It was partly anxiety, partly lack of expertise and incomprehension on the part of the majors that allowed many small companies to carve out a considerable niche during the 1980s. It's often claimed that the small companies were in touch with "the streets." But it is not as straightforward as this— the large companies have also allowed small labels to carve out such a niche.

Independents on the Street: Keeping It outside the Corporation

If one way in which the major companies have attempted to manage African-American music has involved the continual cutting and restructuring of their R&B division, the other has been based on a series of changing relationships with minor companies. There is a familiar explanation offered for why so many successful rap recordings have come from independent labels: they are "closer to the street." It's a view held by many observers of the music industry. As Tricia Rose has written:

It became apparent that the independent labels had a much greater understanding of the cultural logic of hip hop and rap music, a logic that permeated decisions ranging from signing acts to promotional methods. Instead of competing with smaller, more street-savvy labels for new rap acts, the major labels developed a new strategy: buy the independent labels, allow them to function relatively autonomously, and provide them with production resources and access to major retail distribution. (1994a, p. 7)

This perspective draws on the long-running argument that changes in popular music are driven by the activities of independent companies. There is an element of truth in this claim;

it is often easier to identify a new sound and participate in its circulation from outside the gatekeeper-riddled systems of the major companies. It should also be acknowledged that many black independent companies are also attempting to assert their autonomy and self-sufficiency (George, 1989). However, this is a partial and rather too neat and tidy explanation of why rap has ended up *produced* on so many small labels, even if the artists do tend to be *marketed* and *distributed* by the major companies.

There are a number of ways in which this argument has been challenged. One counter-claim has proposed that rap has been somewhat closer to the middle-class suburb than the street. According to David Samuels:

> Since the early 1980s a tightly knit group of mostly young, middle-class, black New Yorkers, in close concert with white record producers, executives and publicists, has been making rap music for an audience that industry executives concede is composed primarily of white suburban males. (1995, p. 242)

There would seem much evidence to support such a claim. Many of those involved with the influential "street savvy" labels—such as Tom Silverman at Tommy Boy, and Russell Simmons and David Harleston at Def Jam, were from educated and middle-class backgrounds. The backgrounds and actions of various artists, such as De La Soul or Chuck D, for example, could also be cited to support this argument.[10]

Yet, this claim is equally partial. In terms of production, rap has, since it first began to appear on recordings, been produced from multiple points of origin with distinct inflections of geographical place (Houston, Atlanta, Los Angeles, Washington, Philadelphia, Georgia), class identity (De La Soul or NWA), ethnic representation (Fugees, Tres Delinquents, Cypress Hill), urban, rural differences (Arrested Development, Smoothe Da Hustler). Not only has rap been stylistically diverse, this diversity has been created across complex identity amalgams. Hence, it is misleading and partial to collapse these variances into any straightforward model of inspiration from the streets or collusion of the black middle class with white executives.

Equally, the idea that the integrity of rap is undermined because a large part of consumption can be located within the white suburb is also simplistic. A strong case against this claim has been argued by Rose (1994a), who has pointed out that purchasing statistics do not in any straightforward way equal "consumption." Sales figures—such as "75 per cent of rap records are owned by white teenagers" (Whalen, 1994, p. 12)—cannot account for the complex ways in which rap is *circulated* and how recordings are appreciated, used and re-used. Young males in the white suburbs may have the disposable income to purchase a recording that will sit on a shelf looking cool, while, in contrast, black urban youth may circulate recordings and listen to them repeatedly, record them, mix them—there may be a much higher "pass-along-rate" (Rose, 1994a).

What does seem clear is that, as rap has been and continues to be made, appreciated and circulated, it has intersected with and crossed numerous borders of class, neighborhood, gender, ethnic label and "national" belonging. Yet it has not been crossing many divisions *within* the music industry. There are two distinct, but interrelated, regimes of containment I want to identify here: first, organizational practices through which rap is confined to a specific "position" within the industry and not accorded as much investment (economic, staff, time) as other types of music; and second, those through which a particular type of knowledge finds expression in a discourse of "the street." These simultaneously deny the complexities I have just referred to, and in doing so construct a simplistic commercial cultural "reality" for rap production that is easily accommodated to the management practices adopted by the music industry.

Major Anxieties: Affiliations, Representations and Expectations

One of the characteristics of rap that initially confused the major companies was the way that rap proposed a series of working relationships across different musical entities: cliques, collectives, affiliations and group and label identities that connected together different "bands" and individual performers. This is signified in the continual appearance of performers on each other's recordings and the way that this establishes very specific networks of affiliation and alliances, e.g., the performers who have grouped around such entities as The Dogg Pound, Dr Dre's Aftermath and Puff Daddy and The Family.

The genre culture of rap posits a different notion of musical practice, not only in the well-documented use of existing musical elements and technologies but in terms of the idea of a "career" and sense of belonging to a musical entity. This is quite a contrast from that of the stable, bounded and predictable rock unit or pop band, the solo performer and self-sufficient singer-songwriter which the industry has become competent at producing and comfortable in dealing with. Rap posits a fluid series of affiliations and associations, alliances and rivalries—occasionally serious, and usually related to neighborhood and representation.[11] These affiliations are lived across various group and individual identities.

This is connected to another issue which the industry has also found uncomfortable, the representation of "the real" or what is often referred to as "being real" and the politics of identity which has accompanied this. This aspect has often received more superficial mass media coverage than serious debate about the issue that it raises and has frequently been reduced to simple arguments about profanity and the generic imagery of violence and misogyny that has characterized so-called gangsta rap. The "discussion" is often informed by a simple stimulus–response model of media effects and an aesthetic reductionism through which rap becomes merely lyrics. One consequence is that there have been overt political pressures put on record companies—from "community" organizations, government and state forces—and this has further encouraged the major companies to distance themselves from the genre culture of rap.[12]

Further judgments made by staff within business affairs and international departments have also had a decisive influence on the acquisition and drawing up of contracts for rap artists. There are two "business decisions" here which are far more than straightforward commercial judgments. First is an assessment of the ongoing revenue that can be generated from rap: what is referred to as "catalogue value." Rap tracks are routinely compared to conventional songs and it is asserted that they cannot be "covered"—re-recorded, re-sung, re-performed by other artists. Hence, rap tracks are judged to have a short catalogue shelf life, in terms of their ability to bring in ongoing copyright revenue from their re-use.[13] In addition, the revenue that rap can generate during any assumed "shelf life" is considered to be less than other types of music. In the words of one corporate attorney:

> Music publishing and rap is a nightmare because so much of it is parts of songs. You know, they have, like, one-eighth of this song and two-thirds of another song . . . because everything is owned by someone else that can make those deals less expensive, but also less lucrative for the publishers than otherwise. . . . The publisher looks at how much they can collect on a particular album, and sometimes because of the number of samples on the album the amount they can collect can be pretty low.[14]

As Thomas Schumacher has observed in his discussion of sampling and copyright law, rap "highlights the ways in which notions of authorship and originality do not necessarily apply across forms and cultural traditions" (1995, p. 265). Not only do they not apply, they pose problems for the "universals of legal discourse" (Schumacher, 1995, p. 265). Hence, the music industry copyright system, itself established upon culturally coded assumptions about the character of a composition and performance which can be traced back to the nineteenth century (Frith, ed., 1993), is inscribed into these business relationships and informs these apparently straightforward "commercial" decisions. One consequence is that rap is perceived to be less attractive in terms of the criteria through which long-term catalogue value is accorded. Hence, less will be paid to artists as advances and royalties, because less can be earned.[15]

A further pragmatic business judgment that affects the amount invested in rap is the assumption that it does not "travel well." Here a strand of racist anxiety that permeates the international music industry manages to combine with a narrow aesthetic evaluation. One senior executive in an international department remarked that he had sat in meetings and heard rap recordings being referred to as "too black" for international promotion,[16] a broad sweeping claim that is justified specifically with the assertion that lyrically rap is "parochial"— although the history of popular music is littered with parochial lyrics appearing in numerous places around the world. While rap does foreground poetic vocal performance, it is misleading to imply that this works simply as lyrics and not as an emotional performative sound event. This argument from within the industry, like Tony Mitchell's claim that U.S. rap has remained "resolutely local" (1996, p. 26), seems to reduce the genre's aesthetic complexity and rhythmic, harmonic and melodic cosmopolitanism to rap lyrics.

Hence, there are a number of ways in which the music industry seeks to contain rap within a narrow structure of expectations: through confinement within a black division; through arm's-length deals in an attempt to avoid dealing with various alliances and affiliations; through judgments about rap's long-term historical and geographical potential to endure. One consequence is a straightforward lack of investment, and the adoption of practices to keep investment down (it is easier to deal with production units than to invest in staff and office space within company). At the same time, rather than bringing the culture—the people, the practices—into the industry, the major companies have tended to maintain a sharp border. This can be contrasted with the treatment of rock in the late 1960s and early 1970s. During this period there was a noticeable and often commented upon movement from the rock subculture and so-called counter-culture into the music industry—a period when the "revolutionaries" were on CBS (as one marketing slogan proclaimed at time).[17] This has continued, with a new wave of young white males recruited into the U.S. music industry in the early 1990s following the success of Nirvana and the stabilization of grunge into modern or alternative rock. As Joe Levy, a music writer for a number of years, observed in 1996:

> I have not seen R&B and hip hop have the same impact that the big boom in alternative rock had on the industry. Certainly two years ago there was this influx of young people in their twenties going to labels as A and R people and vice presidents of this or that, and these were almost uniformly young white kids who were coming into work alternative rock in the wake of Nirvana.... There's a career path in the industry that has to do with alternative rock and I don't necessarily know that it's there for rap and R&B.[18]

Rap personnel have not been embraced or recruited in the same way. For example, when Capitol closed its black music division the company dropped most of its artists and moved only a few acts over to the EMI label. The company publicly announced that this was because EMI had the expertise to deal with them. Yet a few weeks later, when I interviewed Davitt Sigerson, President of EMI Records, and asked him to explain how he deals with rap, he said:

> I don't have anyone doing R&B A&R. What I've adopted as a model is to have a bunch of different production deals or first-look arrangements with entrepreneurs who bring me stuff ... it's a very affiliative sort of creative community and process and I don't need to be in a camp.[19]

Earlier I referred to George's use of the term "rhythm and blues world" to suggest that R&B is more than a genre of music. Likewise, George has characterized rap culture as a "post-civil rights, ultra-urban, unromantic, hyperrealistic, neonationalistic, anti-assimilationist, aggressive Afro-centric impulse" (George, 1992, p. 93). In the above discussion I have highlighted how these genre cultures relate to the organization of the major companies and inform major independent relationships within the music industry, suggesting that rap culture is kept at a distance from the main offices of the corporations. Despite the influence of rap and hip hop on the aesthetics of music, video, television, film, sport, fashion, dancing and advertising, the potential of this broader cultural formation to make a contribution to music industry business practices is not encouraged. Indeed, as I now want to argue, this distance is maintained by the discursive practices articulated through the myth of the street.

Rebels, Indies, and the Street

I have already suggested that the major companies tend to *allow* rap to be produced at independent companies and production units, using these producers as an often optional and usually elastic repertoire source. This is not to deny the struggles of artists and entrepreneurs for both autonomy from the recognition by the major music companies. However, I am stressing the above point because I think we need to be wary of the increasingly routine rhetoric and romanticization of rap musicians as oppositional rebels "outside" the corporate system, or as iconoclasts in revolt against "the mainstream"—a discourse that has often been imposed upon rap and not necessarily come from participants within hip hop culture itself. In addition, it is important to remember that small companies are not spontaneously or straightforwardly inclined to be more in tune with new musical developments. That certain independent labels (such as Atlantic, Stax, or Def Jam) have been so at specific historical moments is beyond dispute. But most rap labels have very soon entered into formalized and fairly standard commercial relationships characteristic of those between major and minor companies, a division of labor based on a production/distribution split. Despite such close ties, the making of rap is usually explained with numerous references to "the street."

In very general terms, rap is often associated with the street by senior executives when talking about different types of music. For example, Kevin Conroy, Senior VP of Marketing at BMG, remarked that, compared to other styles, rap and hip hop "is a business that really grows from the streets."[20] In a similar way, the corporate *Advertising Age* once informed its readers, "The streets where a rap album begins, of course, are very far from the suburban record stores where it ends up" (Whalen, 1994, p. 12). As Michael Rosenblatt, Senior VP of Artist and Repertoire at MCA, remarked, aware that he was using a somewhat clichéd idea: "A lot of the rap does happen on the small labels because rap is much more of a street thing, it happens on the street. I know it sounds trite, but it really does."[21]

Apart from these very general associations of rap with the street, there are two further and more formal ways in which "the street" is articulated. First, in terms of "taking it to the streets"—what is often referred to as street marketing. Second, in terms of "bringing it from the streets"—frequently referred to as "street intelligence." Both practices involve formalized management practices and systematic commercial procedures that are by no means peculiar to rap or R&B.

Taking It to the Streets

The promotion and marketing of rap, like other genres of music, involve the use of techniques that, elsewhere, I have characterized as "promotional war games" due to the way that they are referred to by staff within record companies through a number of "war-like metaphors"

(Negus, 1992). So, for example, when Capitol still had a presence in black music, the label's rap promotion unit was called "Capitol Punishment," and the head of the section was referred to as the "chief commander and warden" (Nelson, 1994, p. 26). The term "sniping" is routinely used to refer to fly-posting bills that make no reference to the record label involved, merely signaling the name of the act and tracks or album. The so-named "street teams" (largely made up of college or radio DJs) have been described as "right there in the trenches"[22] and as engaging in "reconnaissance missions into urban enterprise zones" (Rubin, 1997, p. 99). When I spoke to David Harleston, then Senior VP of the Black Music Collective at MCA, he referred to "the use of guerrilla marketing tactics and street promotion." When I rather naively asked what this might involve, he explained:

> Well, it's going to places where consumers are and hitting them where they live. So we no longer just rely on radio or rely on video, which are both very important. We also promote at barber shops and swap meets and things like that and ... playgrounds where folks are shooting basketball ... we have street teams who hit people with singles and flyers and stickers and stuff like that.... When you take a rap project to radio, radio wants to know that the street is behind it before they'll commit to it. You can't go to radio cold.[23]

The term "street marketing" is shorthand for building an interest in a track or artists through a long process that can involve circulating recordings to influential party-givers, using word-of-mouth networks, approaching local radio mix shows and college radio and promoting through stickers and flyers placed in public places where the targeted "demographic" will take notice. This was institutionalized by Loud Records, a label half-owned by BMG, in their promotion of a number of acts, particularly the Wu-Tang Clan. As Steve Rifkind, Chairman of Loud Records, has claimed:

> I can tell a record company in two days if they have a record or not.... We know that kid from the time he steps out of his house, every step he's making, where he's going to hang out, what's the scoop on where to eat lunch at, where he's getting his hair cut, what's the cool way to get it cut, what's the cool record store to go to. We know all these things, and before we attack we get all the information from the street first. (quoted in Rubin, 1997, p. 99)

Prior to forming Loud Records, Rifkind had established his reputation by promoting recordings by acts such as Boogie Down Productions and Brand Nubian. He followed this by promoting Nike sports gear, spending some time with Nike founder Phil Knight. This gave him the experience that he drew upon when formulating a strategy for selling the Wu-Tang Clan. In his own words: "a kid who's going to buy a pair of Nikes is the same kid who's going to buy a Wu-Tang record" (quoted in Rubin, 1997, p. 100).

The ultimate aim of street marketing is to build up such a "buzz" that the radio stations will feel that they have to programme a recording as they themselves will want to be heard to be "in touch with the streets." As Marcus Morton, VP of Rap Promotion for EMI, commented:

> You have to have the DJs and the people that are the trend-setters. They kind of herd the sheep around. They have to like it. And everybody else—y' know, if you look at the people that program the crossover stations, nine out of ten of them think that they are the hippest thing on the planet, but in reality they're not. They listen to somebody else. Which is either their DJ—that's why you have a mix show DJ because he's supposed to be really in tune with the streets and really in tune with what's going on. And he's supposed to play it on his show and then translate it back to the people who run the stations so that they can put it into regular rotation.[24]

In practice, the activity of "street marketing" relies upon a number of well-developed acts of persuasion that have been deployed within various industries for a number of years. This includes utilizing the "personal influence" of key opinion-formers, "selecting target markets," using concepts of "followers" and "niches," and "branding" and "positioning" products.[25] These practices are not peculiar to rap, but are used when selling a range of products throughout the entertainment and fashion industries. As Terri Rosi, VP of Black Music Marketing for BMG Distribution, commented when I remarked that "there's a lot of talk about 'the street' ": "I know and that's very annoying because the end result is that you talk about 'the street' but you really want it on radio and you want it on MTV."[26]

Bringing It from the Street

As implied in Rifkind's comments about following the movements of "the kids," street teams are also responsible for information gathering and feeding that data back to headquarters. This is sometimes described as an informal process of intuitively hanging out in colleges, neighborhood record stores, clubs, playgrounds and parties, an experiential process of "developing an instinct" by keeping an ear and eye on what is going on. However, the process is also far from spontaneous and is organized in comparable ways to other types of information gathering. To quote from Terri Rosi once more, this time at length:

> It is systematized. You have a guy out there called a street promotion person who is hanging out in stores and clubs and talking to people, and he may even actually go into a college campus. He may be wherever people gather that are those people. He has to learn his marketplace and know where he's supposed to go. They put up stickers in advance so when it comes two months, three months later, "well, yes, I know the ABC band," or whatever. So in that sense, it is a form of street intelligence and you get feedback and you learn after a while who can pick the hit, you figure that out, but it's very people-intense. You're out there, you're moving, talking and working and doing all that kinda stuff.... We've got twenty of them all across the country, and there will be one person in the record company who works with the street team. So they give their reports, where it's going to work, where it's not going to work and their reputation is on the line. I can't tell you that I'm the street person in Oakland and tell you, "Man, this is gonna jam," and then I ship these records in there and nobody likes it at all. Because, well, "Who did you talk to?" ... You don't want to lose your job because you didn't do the right thing. So, yes, in that way it is very systematized.[27]

Street intelligence is about "knowing markets" and "knowing consumers" and, like street marketing, it involves employing conventional business management techniques based on monitoring, data gathering and accumulation. Yet these conventional marketing practices and business activities are elided through the discourse of the street, denying that this is similar to the other activities that are daily being conducted and initiated from the corporate suite.

More Than Music: Rap, Fashion and Product Endorsement

I referred to Steve Rifkind's association with the Nike company and highlighted how this influenced the way Loud Records presented and promoted the Wu-Tang Clan. From the days when Run DMC made reference to Adidas in their songs to the appearance of Coolio and Method Man on the catwalk to present Tommy Hilfiger's new 1996 fashions, clothing has been central to the marketing and making of rap. This has been increasingly recognized by magazines such as *The Source* (which accrue a large part of their revenue from the clothing and sports shoe manufacturers who place advertisements in their pages), performers (who have been increasingly endorsing different products and creating their own lines of clothing), and record labels. As Jim Parham, Director of Sales at Tommy Boy, remarked when explaining how the music and merchandizing were being brought closer together:

> We are gradually tying the music into the clothing. Right now the clothing is sort of an entity unto itself, but the way it originally started was that we made clothing items as promotional items for the music or the label and they were really popular, so we developed it into an actual selling line and we will hopefully be expanding that in the next couple of years.[28]

Many rap musicians have recognized such connections and formed their own successful companies. Notable here is Wu-Wear, the clothing and accessory company established by the Wu-Tang Clan. This company has stores throughout the United States where you can purchase T-shirts, socks, baggy jeans, coffee mugs, and keychains, all featuring the distinctive Wu-Bat brand logo. Like other companies, Wu-Wear has recognized the importance of music video for promoting clothing as much as for selling music. As Mike Clark, CEO of Wu-Wear, observed: "Videos are hands down the best advertising you can have" (quoted in Edwards and Stein, 1998, p. 71). Not surprisingly, the Wu-Tang Clan themselves wear their own clothing in their videos. But, like other major clothing companies, they have sought other celebrity endorsements, and artists including Bjork and Rage Against The Machine have publicly worn Wu-Wear, as have various athletes. In 1997 the company made $10 million (Edwards and Stein, 1998) and also signed a deal with the Federated Department Store retail corporation, the owners of Macy's and Bloomingdale's (Parker, 1997). As Public Enemy's Chuck D proclaimed in an advertisement which appeared in *The Source* of September 1996 and in which he was launching his own Rap Style International: "So You Wanna Be in the Music Business ... Whatcha' Gonna Wear?"

The business of rap is about more than music and clothes and can embrace all manner of consumer products, visible and audible in the way that Queen Latifah has appeared in a box of cereal during an advertisement for Frosted Cheerios, as LL Cool J has been rapping in advertising for major league baseball, and as Method Man has appeared on billboards dressed in Reebok clothing while KRS-One was promoting Nike. "Business awareness" and the range of revenue sources that can be linked to the genre have been recognized by numerous rap performers. As Allen S. Gorden "Tha Ebony Cat" explained, discussing the range of endorsement opportunities being pursued by different artists and companies: "In an increasingly complex, often hostile, marketplace, many rappers are refining their portfolio by pursuing endorsement opportunities" (1997, p. 98). Whether or not rap culture might enter the corporate suites and boardrooms of the major record labels, the discourse of portfolio management has certainly entered the business of rap.

Culture, Industry, and Rap

This chapter has focused on how the making of rap is managed by the music industry, and it has been highlighted how various corporate strategies, which utilize the technique of portfolio management as a way of allocating staff, artists, and investment, directly intersect with the deployment of a particular type of knowledge used to understand the world and to produce a "reality" that informs the perceptions and activities of staff. It is not that there are organizational structures (such as the black music division and deals with small production companies): it is that these are operated according to a particular type of knowledge through which the world is imagined in a particular way, a knowledge that depends upon many systematic data-collecting techniques. At the same time, uncritically received cultural assumptions and common-sense ideas about the social location of rap are continually articulated to notions of the street. In many ways this situation is symptomatic of broader social relationships and beliefs about rap culture and the way in which these intersect with and become "part" of the industry—a process that requires much more empirical and theoretical work before it can be fully understood, but which I have tried to evoke through the idea of "culture producing an industry." Such broader cultural political tensions are structured into what are often taken to be straightforward economic, organizational and business practices, activities that are lived by those working within the industry as if they are merely responding to "the world out there." One significant consequence is that the rhythm and blues world and the genre culture of rap in particular are kept at a distance from the dominant interests and agendas within the main offices of the music corporations.

Yet rap produced in the United States has managed to move out from such regimes of containment—both at home and abroad. There is a final twist. The physical and discursive borders erected by the organizational arrangements and knowledge practices of the contemporary music industry have meant that rap music and musicians have not been "co-opted" or invited into the boardroom in quite the same way as have other types of music and their makers, most notably the way in which rock moved from the street to the executive suite.[29] Often denied direct access, offered licensing deals, lower budgets, poorer contracts, or simply cut from the roster when there is a financial crisis, rap has (partly out of necessity) been able to generate alternative resources, and through these the genre has continually reinvented and redefined itself in those spaces and places designated (for want of terminology rather than as a transparent description of a "reality") as "underground." That rap musicians have managed continually to redefine the style itself while crossing social and cultural barriers, both within the U.S. and beyond is a process which has occurred despite, rather than because of, the ways in which the recording industry has sought to organize the production of contemporary popular music.

Study Questions

1. Does hip-hop have something to offer as a model for entrepreneurial business practices?
2. Is economic power a legitimate way to challenge the political status quo?
3. To what extent does economic development in hip-hop funnel down to its core audiences?

Notes

1. Notable here is Tricia Rose (1994a) who notes the importance of independent labels and the significance of video in the distribution of rap. She is also careful to acknowledge that the commercial marketing of rap has produced a contradictory situation whereby the music is affirmative of black identity, yet can also be used by corporations such as McDonald's, Coke, and Nike in ways that are directly connected to anxieties about U.S. cultural imperialism. Rose (1994b) has also discussed rap in relation to the general contractual arrangements operating within the music industry, particularly in an interview with Carmen Ashurst-Watson. Also notable here is Reebee Garofalo's (1997) discussion of the music industry and rap in his history of popular music, and Nelson George's coverage of rap within the context of his critique of the music industry and its role in the "death of rhythm and blues" and formation of post-soul culture (1989, 1992).
2. A useful collection of essays is Adam Sexton (ed.) (1995).
3. An argument proposed by Ann Marlowe who has stated that: "For some time now the problem with capitalism hasn't been that it doesn't work but that it's no longer fun. Opposition culture has failed to make good on this.... The business of rap is just business, yet it looks like fun" (1995, p. 223).

4. Discussed at length in relation to Atlantic and Stax Records in Wade and Picardie (1990).
5. For a more detailed discussion of this report see George (1989).
6. Personal interview, New York City, 27 February 1996.
7. See Reynolds (1996) and Rosen (1996). See also Clark-Meads (1996) for a discussion of Capitol redefining their "core business."
8. These types of changes are discussed in Sandler (1995).
9. Referred to by J.R. Reynolds in "Confab Covers Urban Industry Issues" *Billboard*, 18 May 1996, p. 20.
10. Backgrounds of various producers, artists and entrepreneurs are discussed in Fernando Jr (1995).
11. Most notable here is the well-publicized East–West NYC–LA dispute which, in the early to mid-1990s, became focused in a series of highly public confrontations between those associated with Death Row Records and Bad Boy Records.
12. Most notably C. Delores Tucker, Chairwoman of the National Political Congress of Black Women, and William Bennett (previously Ronald Reagan's Secretary of Education) put pressure on Time-Warner shareholders. Likewise (then) Senator Bob Dole continually accused Warner Music and other labels of "putting profits ahead of common decency" and "glamorizing violence." For a perspective on this and its impact from within the industry see Nunziata (1995). One immediate consequence was that Michael Fuchs, Chairman CEO of Warner Music Group, announced that the company would form label groups made up of an A and R person, label head, someone from business affairs and legal personnel to judge the suitability of future releases, with particular attention paid to lyrics. On this point see Jeffrey (1995). In addition, when MCA purchased Interscope, the label that had been distributing recordings by Death Row Records, Doug Morris, CEO of MCA Music Entertainment, publicly announced that the company had an option "not to release any music it deems objectionable" (Morris, 1996).
13. This was most explicitly raised by a senior executive at a major corporate group when explaining how the company would strategically assess the value of different musical genres. It was an off-the-record interview.
14. Personal interview, Paul Robinson, Associate General Counsel, Warner Music Group, New York City, 13 February 1996.
15. This is acknowledged within the industry, but I was unable to obtain any verifiable figures.
16. This was again an off-the-record interview.
17. For discussion of recruitment from rock subculture into the industry, see Chapple and Garofalo (1977) and Frith (1983).
18. Personal interview, Joe Levy, *Details Magazine*, New York City, 22 March 1996.
19. Personal interview, New York City, 19 March 1996.
20. Personal interview, New York City, 5 April 1996.
21. Personal interview, New York City, 6 February 1996.
22. Greg Peck, a former VP of Black Music at Warner Music, quoted in Reynolds (1995, p. 26).
23. Personal interview, Universal City, Los Angeles, 6 May 1996.
24. Personal interview, EMI, Los Angeles, 24 April 1996.
25. All similar to many referred to in textbook guides to marketing; see, for example, Kotler (1994).
26. Personal interview, Terri Rosi, VP Black Music Marketing, BMG Distribution, New York City, 11 April 1996.
27. Personal interview, Terri Rosi, VP Black Music Marketing, BMG Distribution, New York City, 11 April 1996.
28. Telephone interview, 15 April 1996.
29. For an argument about the co-optation of rock, see Chapple and Garofalo (1977). For a discussion of the way in which rock has been central rather than peripheral, or oppositional, to the development of the modern recording industry, see Frith (1983).

References

Chapple, S. and Garofalo, R. (1977) *Rock 'n' Roll is Here to Pay*, Chicago: Nelson Hall.
DeCurtis, A. (1995) Dre Day, *Vibe*, December, pp. 92–94.
Edwards, T. and Stein, J. (1998) Getting Giggy With a Hoodie: Young Black Designers are Giving Urban Fashions Street Appeal, *Time*, Vol. 151, No. 1, pp. 71–72.
Fernando, Jr., S.H. (1995) *The New Beats: Exploring the Music Culture and Attitudes of Hip-Hop*, Edinburgh: Payback Press.
Fitzgerald, T. (1996) Uknowhowsheduit, *Beat Down*, Vol. 4, No. 2, pp. 22–23.
Frith, S. (1983) *Sound Effects, Youth, Leisure and the Politics of Rock 'n' Roll*, London: Constable.
——— (ed.) (1993) *Music and Copyright*, Edinburgh: Edinburgh University Press.

Garofalo, R. (1994) Culture Versus Commerce: The Marketing of Black Popular Music, *Public Culture*, Vol. 7, No. 1, pp. 275–288.

———— (1997) *Rockin' Out, Popular Music in the USA*, Needham Heights, Mass.: Allyn and Bacon.

George, N. (1989) *The Death of Rhythm and Blues*, London: Omnibus.

———— (1992) *Buppies, B-Boys, Baps and Bohos*, London: HarperCollins.

Gilroy, P. (1993) *The Black Atlantic, Modernity and Double Consciousness*, London: Verso.

Gorden, A. (1997) It All Adds Up, *The Source*, January, p. 98.

Jeffrey, D. (1995) Warner's Fuchs Pledges Scrutiny, *Billboard*, 14 October 1995, p. 1/91.

Johnson, R. (1997) PolyGram: The Hits Just Keep on Coming. Racial Tensions at Record Label, *Fortune*, Vol. 36, No. 12, p. 40.

Kotler, P. (1994) *Marketing Management; Analysis, Planning, Implementation and Control*, New Jersey: Prentice Hall.

Mitchell, T. (1996) *Popular Music and Local Identity: Rock, Pop and Rap in Europe and Oceania*, Leicester: Leicester University Press.

Morris, C. (1996) MCA Purchases 50% of Interscope: Gangsta Rap Issue Minimized by Execs, *Billboard*, 2 March 1996, p. 13/84.

Negus, K. (1992) *Producing Pop: Culture and Conflict in the Popular Music Industry*, London: Edward Arnold.

Nelson, H. (1994) Rap: In an Ever-Shifting Climate, Rap Holds Steady and Grows Strong, *Billboard*, 26 November 1994, p. 25/46.

Nunziata, S. (1995) The Year in Business, *Billboard*, 23 December 1995, p. YE–10.

Parker, A. (1997) Wu-Wear Urban Clothing Chain Opens Store in Norfolk Va, *Virginia Pilot*, 2 May 1997, p. 5.

Payton, T. (1997) Set It Off, *The Source*, January, p. 96.

Powell, K. (1996) Live From Death Row, *Vibe*, Vol. 4, No. 1, February, pp. 44–50.

Reynolds, J. (1995) Rap Confab Assembles Nation, *Billboard*, 11 November 1995, p. 26.

———— (1996) Capitol Records Setting a Bad Example, *Billboard*, 9 March 1996, p. 18.

Rose, T. (1994a) *Black Noise: Rap Music and Black Culture in Contemporary America*, Hanover, NH: Wesleyan University.

———— (1994b) Contracting Rap; An Interview with Carmen Ashurst-Watson in A. Ross and T. Rose (eds) *Microphone Fiends*, London: Routledge.

Rosen, C. (1996) Capitol Moves Urban Division to EMI: 18 Staffers Laid Off, *Billboard*, 9 March 1996, p. 3.

Rubin, M. (1997) Secrets of the Ch-Ching, *Spin*, October, pp. 95–102.

Samuels, D. (1995) The rap on rap: The "Black music" that isn't either, in A. Sexton (ed.) *Rap on Rap: Straight-Up Talk on Hip-Hop Culture*, New York: Delta, pp. 241–52.

Sandler, A. (1995) Big Labels Ride Black Music Bandwagon, *Variety*, 28 August 1995, Vol. 360, p. 13.

Sanjek, D. (1997) One Size Does Not Fit All: The Precarious Position of the African-American Entrepreneur in Post WW2 American Popular Music, *American Music*, Vol. 15, No. 4, pp. 535–62.

Schumacher, T. (1995) This is a Sampling Sport: Digital Sampling, Rap Music and the Law in Cultural Production, *Media, Cutlure and Society*, Vol. 17, pp. 253–73.

Sexton, A. (ed.) (1995) *Rap on Rap: Straight-Up Talk on Hip-Hop Culture*, New York: Delta.

Snyder, M. (1996) Artist Support Groups, *Billboard*, 8 June 1996, p. 30/44.

Vincent, R. (1996) *Funk, the Music, the People and the Rhythm of the One*, New York: St Martin's Press.

Wade, D. and Picardie, J. (1990) *Music Man, Ahmet Ertegun, Atlantic Records and the Triumph of Rock 'n' Roll*, New York: W.W. Norton.

Whalen, J. (1994) Rap Defies Traditional Marketing, *Advertising Age*, No. 65, 12 March 1994, p. 12.

42

"I Don't Like to Dream About Getting Paid"

Representations of Social Mobility and the Emergence of the Hip-Hop Mogul

As a corollary to hip-hop's business practices and the elevation of icons of hip-hop into the ranks of American celebrity, the so-called hip-hop mogul has attained a status that outshines that of the most popular rappers. Indeed, some of the most well-known moguls—Shawn Carter, Sean Combs and Curtis Jackson—initially established their reputations as artists and performers.

In his chapter, Christopher Holmes Smith says that the hip-hop mogul has become one of the most visible symbols of achievement in the post-Civil Rights era and of the value of diversity within corporate structures. Smith cautions, though, that the high visibility of the hip-hop mogul might dampen desires to undermine or reform the political and economic status quo.

"I Don't Like to Dream About Getting Paid": Representations of Social Mobility and the Emergence of the Hip-Hop Mogul

Christopher Holmes Smith

During the Clinton 1990s—a time not so long ago when the social consensus rendered "the ballot box and the box office [as] one"[1] the ensemble of aspirations and practices that constitute hip-hop culture became accepted as common-sense elements of the American experience. In this article, I describe this process of incorporation by paying attention to a figure who proved catalytic to this cultural movement, the "hip-hop mogul." On the one hand, the hip-hop mogul bears the stamp of American tradition, since the figure is typically male, entrepreneurial, and prestigious both in cultural influence and personal wealth. The hip-hop mogul is an icon, therefore, of mainstream power and consequently occupies a position of inclusion within many of the nation's elite social networks and cosmopolitan cultural formations. On the other hand, the hip-hop mogul symbolizes something new about traditional American corporate culture since he is also typically young (under the age of 50), typically African American, and typically tethered either literally or symbolically to America's disenfranchised inner cities. He is, therefore, worthy of further critical scrutiny because he crystallizes and makes visible a variety of social tensions that are otherwise so widely scattered across disparate social knowledge formations as to go either unnoticed or unmentioned. Young black and Latino entertainers and entrepreneurs like Sean "P-Diddy" Combs, Russell Simmons, Percy "Master P" Miller, Jennifer Lopez, and Damon Dash thus bring together, at a point of prominent visibility and maximum volatility, an expansive constellation of discursive formations and the requisite ideological tensions that inhere within them, whether they concern social identity politics or issues of equal opportunity and social mobility.

Politically, the hip-hop mogul becomes a charged figure precisely because of his ability to appeal to the varied sensibilities of apparently disassociated public spheres. In this respect, the emergence of the hip-hop mogul in contemporary American culture over roughly the past decade, and his ascension to the uppermost layers of the nation's celebrity classes during that span, also raises the issue of "representation" both in a semiotic sense—as may regard the codes and symbols through which these figures generate social recognition—and in terms of an ethical responsibility to serve as stewards for the thoughtful composition of these codes as they may "stand in for" the desires and values of those individuals who are not eligible to occupy similar positions of mass mediation and discursive credibility.

The axis around which this representational dilemma revolves is the mogul's glamorous lifestyle, which serves as a symbolic proxy for the more mundane strivings of those with whom the mogul shares an apparent racial or ethnic affiliation. The hip-hop mogul is not intelligible without credible accounts of the lavish manner in which he leads his life, nor is he intelligible unless his largesse connotes not only his personal agency but also a structural condition that squelches the potential agency of so many others. What makes the hip-hop mogul significant is the degree to which his celebrity alleviates the tension within this symbolic relationship by appealing to the power of socially competitive consumption as a viable mode of civic participation and personal fulfillment. Indeed, I will argue that the hip-hop mogul's rise to social and cultural prominence is symptomatic of a new paradigm in the nation's long-standing consumptive ethos,[2] one in which average people engage in a push for what commentators have dubbed the distinction of "mass prestige," a phenomenon whereby "America's middle-market consumers ... [trade] up to higher levels of quality and taste ... while feeding their aspirations for a better life."[3] In short, the mogul inspires his more downtrodden constituents to "buy in" to the emerging paradigm of accessible luxury and social status and in the process assumes an influential role as social mediator. Thus, the hip-hop mogul exemplifies the changing dimensions of African American political platforms for those generations born after the civil rights movement, particularly the changing regard for the residual modern social ideal of an aspiring "mass" social formation as a meaningful referent and basis for an activist-oriented black public sphere. Similarly, the emergence of the hip-hop mogul as a visual signifier for the "good life" identifies growth-mediated forms of social uplift as rapidly normalizing black political discourses, as opposed to the support-led communal development blueprints from the civil rights era. What remains unclear is the relationship between the hip-hop mogul's ability to represent opulence and aspiration and the mogul's ability to signify and enable enhanced modes of development and freedom for communities wherein such enhancements would mean quite a lot.[4]

Taking an ethical approach, I will identify and examine the primary discursive frameworks through which the hip-hop mogul achieves relative social intelligibility and will subsequently interrogate the extent to which, and with what effects, his upward mobility becomes emblematic of the aspirations of a largely disenfranchised constituency. To what extent do hip-hop's captains of industry capitalize upon those pent-up ambitions and how did this paradoxical form of social, cultural, and economic currency achieve such a profound level of liquidity during the 1990s bull market? Finally, and perhaps most importantly, what explains the longevity of the mogul's mainstream circulation as an index of prosperity long after other symbolic elements of the 1990s growth cycle have either dissolved or been discredited?

Theoretical and Historical Contexts for the Hip-Hop Mogul's Emergence and Incorporation

To the best of my knowledge, the hip-hop mogul reached a critical mass of public recognition and acclaim in 1999, at the peak of the record-breaking "long boom" in U.S. economic expansion. Curiously, while other prominent figures of the period—from the celebrity CEO, celebrity publicist, celebrity magazine publisher, celebrity financial news anchor, celebrity equity analyst, and even the celebrity president—have been brought low by impeachment, corporate scandal, bear market, technological change, and post–September 11 geopolitical uncertainty, the hip-hop mogul's efficacy as a symbol for a bygone golden age persists. Rather than utilize the hip-hop mogul as a point of departure for an empirical investigation of the likelihood of future capital investment and productivity gains, I would like to suggest that he is exemplary of a dominant cultural logic that seems more durable than any particular business or investment cycle, and symptomatic of a cultural propensity that strives for a synergistic balance between systemic efficiency and productively disruptive narratives of cultural irreverence. Indeed, in this era of late capitalism and American empire, novel conditions for social identity formation and knowledge production have evolved whereby the mutually exclusive polarities of individual and systemic truth claims merge at the level of commercial necessity, if not at the level of ideological intention.

Jean-François Lyotard has been one of the more prescient and lucid of the scholars who have focused on the links within postmodern times between narratives of liberation and narratives of productivity, and his thoughts on the "performative" aspect of the relationship deserve special mention at this stage of my discussion. In *The Postmodern Condition*, Lyotard notes that the dominant power apparatus's need for synergy between the networks of regulation and social agency complicates the exertion of its influence over the social body's widely scattered knowledge formations. Lyotard describes this crisis of knowledge as a residual analytical binary between scientific knowledge, which he calls "speculative," and narrative knowledge, which he refers to as "emancipatory." In the face of a profusion of different "language games," or local accounts of "the real," scientific knowledge offers a totalizing narrative that operates on the basis of selective assessment and exclusion, in a manner analogous to what Foucault has called a "regime of truth." Therefore, the narrative of speculation is generated by entities that Lyotard calls "decision makers," who have a pedagogical and somewhat magisterial relationship to the people. Since the various communities within the social field do not play the knowledge games of the broader culture according to any shared set of rules, interactions between these localities are not stable, or even necessarily tenable. Undaunted, the decision makers scan the dissensual field in order to grant the clamor a measure of utility.

Lyotard insists that this selection process is a hallmark of post-Enlightenment society's most pernicious form of hyperrationality and a subtle form of authoritarianism. Within this matrix of officialdom, the people go against the grain to generate narratives of liberation in a quest for self-legitimation. These narratives call for "inclusion," whereby local knowledge is employed by the people in the name of their full participation in the social order. Unfortunately, Lyotard says, these narratives reify rather than dismantle the elitist structure of which the people are so justifiably skeptical.

It is at this juncture, I contend, that Lyotard suggests how the body politic's irreverent narratives of freedom might be said to contribute to the dominant discourses that cohere into something called a "New Economy." Lyotard argues, for instance, that the people's narrative of neo-mastery and their rhetoric of emancipation eventually lead to the predominance of what he calls "performativity," or an "optimization of the global relationship between input and output." Eventually, in other words, the dominant hegemonic order learns how to absorb certain aspects of cultural resistance into its own mandate for self-preservation. With regard to social agency, Lyotard insists:

> One's mobility in relation to these language game effects ... is tolerable ... at least within certain limits (and the limits are vague); it is even solicited by regulatory mechanisms, and in particular by the self-adjustments that the system undertakes in order to improve its performance. It may even be said that the system can and must encourage such movement to the extent that it combats its own entropy; the novelty of an unprecedented "move," with its correlative displacement of a partner or group of partners, can supply the system with that increased performativity it forever consumes.[5]

Essentially, I want to argue that the American postmodern cultural logic of empire is one whereby (1) conditions arise that are ripe for the incorporation of the people's rhetoric of emancipation within the normalizing tenets of the capitalist world system[6] and (2) narratives of utopian impulse found within many forms of black expressive culture, and particularly hip-hop culture, have helped supply the specifically American discourse of empire with the necessary manna of "performativity" it needs to sustain itself as global Leviathan. Indeed, during the 1990s, hip-hop evolved from being the symbolic anathema of the dominant commercial apparatus to serving as one of its most strategically effective symbolic instruments. This evolution is a function of both black cultural producers' increased ability to reference the mainstream marketplace as a locus for identity formation,[7] and the ability of white youth to rearticulate black style back to official market logic via an increasingly seamless form of stylistic adoption. These newfangled cool poses, like those of an Eminem, can convey the sexual frisson of older social dispensations like Jim Crow while somehow managing to avoid the baldest forms of moral panic typical to boundary transgression.[8]

Such viral outbreaks of mass trend adoption, like that which occurred around the film *8 Mile*, form the unpredictable "tipping points"[9] that are every marketer's dream. At such moments of excitement, empirical figures on ratios of risk to reward are not nearly so persuasive as the blind willingness to believe in any particular form's ability to generate a profitable outcome. In speculative historical eras, as in individual acts of gambling, there is a moment, of variable duration, when anything goes, as the saying goes—moments when not even the magistrates of officialdom know how to bring historical precedent to bear on present and future outcomes and exert a moral claim on the recognition of value. At topsy-turvy moments like these, when the dowdy appear willing to cast aside their hallowed pretensions of dignity and the appropriate calculus for valuation is anyone's guess, power is somewhat up for grabs, and a semblance of freedom is more evident because the actual utility and value of precepts and goods are called into question. Thus, a reordering of hierarchies takes place, and depending on where one previously stood in the pecking order, that may not be such a bad situation within which to find oneself.[10] In fact, when entire societies or nations find themselves mired in an identity crisis or when their confidence in the ability to carry on or preserve past glories is flagging, they can often wish for such indeterminate periods of social and economic speculation since they offer the opportunities for repositioning and resurrection. The 1990s New Economy offered just such an opportunity for protean national redefinition.

Black cultural producers and their arbiters—chiefly the hip-hop moguls and their kin—benefited, to a certain degree, from this reversal of authority. Indeed, as they rose to more elevated positions along the social hierarchy, Generation X and Y's cultural tastes and consumption habits helped make quite a few black cultural producers wealthier and more influential. Thus, by the decade's close, hip-hop culture, for example, though still vilified on occasion, had nevertheless become more respected as a model for the new "horizontally structured" business world and therefore a more tolerable presence in the U.S. millennial celebration of prolonged economic growth. Indeed, black popular culture's symbolic-strength, fueled as it was by new money—something that all adults either envy or admire—inevitably enabled the black cultural producers who best embodied the new era of "Nobrow Culture"[11] to move toward the center of the nation's widely circulated, and enthusiastically emulated, celebrity class.[12]

Within such a virtual matrix of interaction, black cultural expressions emanating from the bottom of the social hierarchy and the standards of social and moral value that they enact and uphold have fashioned performative innovations that are best viewed in terms of what Clay Christensen once called "disruptive technologies."[13] On this count, the inner city's constructions of cultural value continually arise within media representation as managerial problems for the magistrates of official knowledge, including traditional black leadership. As the 1990s have lapsed into the twenty-first century, however, black cultural tastes have increasingly become—most notably through the commodification of hip-hop culture—extremely efficient devices for extracting profit from the consumption habits of America's youth. Ideas on how to identify and market black cultural knowledge and tastes have come to embody dynamic management solutions. Herein we find the hip-hop mogul's primary mandate, namely the effective identification, packaging, and symbolic management of the politically and socially volatile minority underclass's expressive culture.

In representational terms, these solutions are all about the packaging of possibility and not outright containment or foreclosure. In other words, the ongoing project for American industrial managers, particularly those—like the newly emergent hip-hop moguls—who govern the industries of culture and leisure, has been to harness the uniquely modern experiential opportunities afforded by America's oceanic multicultural flows in the name of commodity production, consumption, and further economic growth. In the United States, this endeavor has always insisted upon using art and performance to overcome social stratification, thereby enabling new modes of interracial, interethnic, and class-transcendent contact, no matter how circumscribed and degraded such contact may inevitably have been. Indeed, in American popular culture, the threatening, yet strangely reassuring, proximity of the other within the crowd must necessarily accompany the individual's auspicious quest toward modernity's Holy Grail of enlightenment, since that proximity exacts "the price for which the sensation of the modern age may be held: the disintegration of the aura in the experience of shock."[14]

Indeed, through the boundary-defying powers of the electronic and digital media, socially isolated territories of allegedly disreputable knowledge, such as American inner cities, have become essential to the new modes of personal identity—and social knowledge formation.[15] This unlikely symbolic reversal has been progressive to the extent that it has shattered the old high–low cultural hierarchy predicated upon "good breeding," "proper schooling," and "aesthetic appreciation" and has placed the market's "equal opportunity" brand of consumption at the center of the individual's protean capacity for self-development.

Many black cultural practitioners—especially those in the hip-hop entertainment sectors—certainly benefited from this phenomenon, and with the bottom-most layers of minority communities deemed more valuable for the sake of the global entertainment complex than had been previously thought possible, rap music unit sales escalated significantly. In 2000, for example, "the Recording Industry Association of America [estimated] that rap music generated more than $1.8 billion in sales, accounting for 12.9 percent of all music purchases" and "has surpassed country music as the nation's second most popular genre after rock and roll."[16] These figures have since softened, along with the music industry as a whole, but the fact remains that hip-hop culture has unquestionably solidified itself over the past half-decade as a key rampart of the national structure of feeling.[17]

Rap's explosive growth trends during the better part of the 1990s also led to unprecedented black economic clout for the hip-hop moguls, with two hip-hop entrepreneurs, Percy Miller (a.k.a. Master P) and Sean Combs (a.k.a. P-Diddy) recently listed squarely in the middle of *Fortune* magazine's roster of "America's Forty Richest under 40." Master P sat directly behind Vinny Smith, chairman and CEO of Quest Software, with a net worth of $293.8 million; P-Diddy, whose persona) fortune came in at a cool $293.7 million, ranked ahead of such luminaries as actress Julia Roberts, the golf wunderkind Tiger Woods, and a slew of technology and software tycoons.[18] As exemplary signifiers of the New Economy's ability to promote Dionysian categorical dissolution, select hip-hop glitterati became widely deemed as unlikely, but ultimately legitimate, representatives of the new American state of prosperity, privy as they now were to a magical Shangri-la of mushrooming capital gains and seemingly endless liquidity.[19] As the 1990s wound to a close, many forward-thinking taste-makers of the chattering classes were keen to feature hip-hop artists prominently at the most swank social galas of the day, whether real or imagined.

In a February 1999 issue of *New York* magazine, for example, one finds a retro-inspired, black-and-white photo spread heralded by a printed announcement that reads:

> You are invited to a feverish fin de siècle fling, Manhattan-style.
> What will you eat?
> Whom will you dine with?
> And what in the world will you wear?[20]

As a means of relieving this banal bout with premillennial tension, the next few pages convey ample information on how consumption can be articulated with the stylishly adorned body. In the montage of images that follows, the rap diva Foxy Brown is depicted at a table with the aging but spry Manhattan socialite Anne Slater. Foxy is seen sporting a garishly large diamond ring.

The photo caption tells us that the bauble belongs to Slater. The caption also points out that the rapper has a 57.7-carat diamond bracelet set in platinum, courtesy of Harry Winston jewelers, draped around her willowy wrist. In keeping with these glitzy accoutrements, both women are smiling brilliantly and appear to be having a grand time, reveling, it seems, in their ability to flow casually between oppositional categories such as "old" and "new," "high" and "low," and "rich" and "poor." During the 1990s, an entirely new repertoire of keywords emerged to refer to such moments of hierarchical deconstruction. Each of them, from "ghetto-fabulous," to "flossing," to "bling, bling"—now more commonly shortened to "bling"—all became normalized as mainstream catch-phrases that described the hyperconsumption of luxury goods by celebrities and average folk alike. As the millennial countdown accelerated, the New Economy's already overt promise of social inversion became more and more explicit and so too did the idea that hip-hop's garish sense of style and taste could signify fashionable abundance and set the millennial standard of even the most highly regarded fashion cognoscenti.[21]

It was not altogether surprising, therefore, to see the hip-hop impresario Sean Combs headlining the Metropolitan Museum of Art's annual Costume Institute gala merely weeks before the catastrophe-free arrival of Y2K. Imagine! Within a prime citadel of official Western culture—at an end-of-the-century celebration cochaired by *Vogue* editor Anna Wintour and attended by such disparate luminaries as comedian Jerry Seinfeld, billionaire Ronald Perelman, Miramax Films cochair Harvey Weinstein, former Secretary of State Henry Kissinger, actress Gwyneth Paltrow, and socialites Patricia Buckley, Nan Kempner, and Alexandra von Furstenberg—rap, the gruff baritone voice of the ghetto, was chosen as the most appropriate musical keynote with which to "ring out the old and ring in the new."[22]

With this notion of tenuous, almost criminal, social collusion apparently in mind, that same year *Time* posed a rhetorical question to its readership that would have been unthinkable when the decade began. "And how will we remember the last days of the '90s?" the magazine asked. "Most likely, to the rough-hewn beat of rap. Just as F. Scott Fitzgerald lived in the jazz age, just as Dylan and Jimi Hendrix were among the rulers of the age of rock, it could be argued that we are living in the age of hip-hop."[23] Similarly, the *New York Times* fashion columnist Amy Spindler wrote that when historians recalled the stylish excesses of the Internet gold rush, they would do so in terms of hip-hop's ascendance as a cultural pacesetter for the champagne and caviar set. "Silicon geeks and dot-comers may earn triple-digit billions," Spindler noted, "but the folks who *really* have the knack for spending—the true nouveau riche, our Carringtons of the new Millennium—are hip-hop impresarios like Puffy Combs."[24] And what kind of new age goodies did Spindler conflate with the Combs lifestyle? How about the following: a sable vest from Fendi ($18,500); silver stilettos from the red-hot designer Jimmy Choo ($650 a pair); an 18-karat gold Tiffany necklace and matching bracelet, both decked out in diamonds ($33,500 and $27,000, respectively); a bottle of Burgundy at Alain Ducasse's new restaurant at the Essex House on Central Park South ($800); a pound of Crème de la Mer facial lotion designed to spec for NASA ($1,000); and title to the 90th-floor penthouse at Trump World Tower at United Nations Plaza ($38 million).

Not surprisingly, rap's spendthrift ways were hardly marginal practices at that time. Indeed, every major symbolic figure of that halcyon age, from celebrity CEOs and upstart technology entrepreneurs to magazine publishers and publicity mavens, were known for spending lavishly to promote their goods, their services, and themselves. Consequently, rap's tactics of consumption became articulated rather quickly as a meaningful aspect of the New Economy's dominant social and cultural formation. Many everyday folk celebrated these figures because during the long boom of the 1990s, more Americans had a chance to have their personal fortunes lofted in the updraft of the speculative winning streak, and they rewarded themselves by spending relatively extravagantly in their own right. Now, however, in light of a jobless recovery, a volatile equities market, and widening federal and state budget deficits, the tide of this inexorable period of excess has turned, and everyday people feel less wealthy and more vulnerable. Some even seem prepared to begin sacrificing their whimsies and start spending less.[25] Along with this shift in fortune has come a backlash against the members of the New Economy's celebrity wealth class, particularly the CEOs, investment bankers, and equity research analysts who appeared to service their greed by bilking the masses with phony information. Amid this moral crusade, how and why does hip-hop continue to thrive as what one columnist in the *New York Times* calls the last "safe haven for ridiculous expenditure"?[26] Why aren't Americans bashing a big spender like rap/R&B diva Jennifer Lopez as vigorously as they are Kenneth Lay, former CEO of the now infamous Enron Corporation, or the free-spending Dennis Kozlowski, former CEO of Tyco, the giant industrial conglomerate?

In the current post-dot-com Zeitgeist, it seems that in order to escape the jeremiads against the "fabulous life" of greed and excess, one must view individual wealth and the consumptive practices that accompany it as a legitimate outcome of strenuous striving to succeed, and representative therefore of an unexpected (almost divinely ordained) social mobility that arose against the grain of conventional wisdom. Thus, in most rap devoted to the intractable virtues of "bling," artists regard having "clawed ... out of a brutal ... housing project to become a multi-platinum star" as a common theme: "Often it is not even articulated; it goes without saying that the squandering protagonist is a rags-to-riches figure who beat overwhelming odds and has every right to the fruits of that success."[27] Thus, the rapper's upwardly mobile ascent is not tethered to a sense of either individual propriety or communal accountability in the same manner as is the ascent of a CEO for a publicly traded company. As the *New York Times* recently quipped, "Sean Combs was once accused of hitting a record executive with a chair and a Champagne bottle, but at least he has never smacked your 401(k) around."[28]

The typical hip-hop mogul does not have the same degree of culpability for the New Economy's hegemonic meltdown as, say, Morgan Stanley's Internet stock maven Mary Meeker since, unlike the other symbolic figures of the age who have now hit the skids, he never had to sell his customers on anything other than his belief in his own fantasies. His trade is purely in the realm of socially mobile aspirations—the quintessential pixie dust of the postwar American dream.[29] Thus, magically, and quite tautologically, he always stands a good chance of convincing his target market of a satisfactory return on their psychic and material investments, and he can continue to be representative of mass expectation of the good life without being responsible for its fulfillment. In the end, neither the corporate CEO of the publicly traded institution nor the equity research analyst has had such luxury. As Americans continue to ponder the possible shape of populist movements to come in the wake of the dot-com implosion, it might be productive to consider the values, beliefs, and practices that could shape such popular sentiment if it does indeed begin to cohere. It might be fruitful, therefore, to consider the way in which the black youth publics that continue to serve as hip-hop culture's core constituencies imagine the shared utopia toward which they may be attempting to strive.

Hip-Hop Utopia and Mass Spectacle in the Black Public Sphere

There has always been a utopian creative impulse within hip-hop culture that defies the progressive political frameworks that prioritize civic, educational, and legal meritocracies over a politics of pleasure and chance that revels in often ill-begotten wealth, street-corner prestige, and explicit sexual titillation. Indeed, prototypical rap utopian fantasies blend ethereal instrumentation with wistful lyrics that offer alternating visions of ghetto upward mobility, intoxication devoid of either physical side effect or legal penalty, unlimited access to sexual pleasure, anti-apocalyptic perseverance, and the end of white world supremacy. In short, they typically represent historical materialist modes that take account of present, past, and future disenfranchised lifestyles in the distinctive linguistic accents of America's various ghetto communities. These typically adolescent renditions of the world are utopian in their frustration with the pauperized and hyperscrutinized status of black and Latino ghetto residents and politically familiar because of their frequent lyrical homage to twentieth-century black empowerment iconography and rhetoric. Yet despite their alternative activist readings of American progress, these songs and their music video corollaries exhibit the sort of generic fixation with commodity culture and upward social mobility that thwart their full recognition as typical grass-roots rallying cries. It is precisely the rap utopian imagination's insatiable hunger for the capitalist commodity that alienates so many members of the civil rights era political consensus from black youth culture generally, and prevents them from regarding these subaltern dreamscapes as the stuff of "real politics." Fancying themselves as moral crusaders against the evils of capitalism's "false consciousness," the members of political coalitions from the New Deal and Great Society heydays want the hip-hop generation upstart to reform his or her behavior relative to the contemporary commodity culture of "mass prestige" facilitated by aspiration-savvy marketers and their luxury knock-off merchandise.[30]

In this manner, a high-minded attitude of Puritan restraint of the civil rights era political establishment stands in contradistinction to the opportunistic demeanor of the hip-hop mogul, who recognizes that utopian aspirations can be bought and sold, and the higher the price the better.[31] As the labor-oriented activists of industrial-era utopias would like to suggest, the mogul's typical dreamscape is individualistic rather than communal, and its material bounty extends to a limited inner circle composed mostly of the mogul's mother, his crew of friends, his children, and from time to time a lover—just enough people to fit on a private yacht. In the mogul's world of like-minded insiders, gone is much of the "old school" utopian longing for the arrival of a monolithic blackness in a shared promised land. The mogul may lament the plight of the black masses, and he may simulate reference to these constituencies in the name of performative "authenticity," but he doesn't sacrifice his own quest for the American good life on their behalf. Rather, the mogul's vision of gilded glory is as competitive and exclusive as it is opulent. As the prototypical mogul anthem "Hate Me Now" attests, moguls and their talented minions flaunt their rise from among the ranks of the downtrodden by making public displays of their newly begotten wealth. For the mogul, jealousy, envy, and hatred from the crowd are merely rites of passage; to be the object of such "hatred" merely serves to crystallize his essential charisma and mark him as one of God's chosen few. As far as the mogul is concerned, once his surroundings reach a reasonable facsimile of what he desires, anyone who doesn't approve of his elevated social position can rot in hell.

Frequently, moguls, like their talent rosters, will depict themselves as "gangsters" or members of criminal "families" in the mafioso tradition of Al Capone, John Gotti, and the Gambino crime syndicate. A major aspect of the mogul's utopian sense of freedom is one of identity shifting, or at the least, identity "layering." In other words, while hip-hop moguls can never be said to deny their racial and ethnic heritage, they are encouraged to use the material aspects of gangster social formations, even those constructed by other ethnic groups, to expand the options for social performativity normally afforded blacks or Latinos. Moguls use "gangsterism," then, as a trope for escaping the limited "place" afforded minority men of color in American society.

Through the gangster motifs of fast cars, fast women, fancy clothing, strong liquor, and a "never say die" attitude, the mogul can gain social mobility and transcend what Manthia Diawara has called the imprisoning common sense of racial "immanence" that confines black people to the immutable realm of the stereotype.[32] Material goods present life-and-death stakes for the mogul's version of utopia precisely because they represent socioeconomic benchmarks of achievement that blacks have been told will forever elude their grasp. The mogul knows that the world of high-priced merchandise and elite social experiences was not meant for him—indeed, he has been barred by the mainstream "from all social roles not conventionally associated with blackness"[33]—however, he refuses to accept the stark terms of this disenfranchisement.

In a certain sense, the word *nigga* is the signifier for comradeship and rivalry that inner-city black men have given to those who make a whole way of life from the loud gestures that pre-emptively mock the very people who would mock their ghetto strivings for mobility and social significance. Niggas take the heat for their brazen social pageantry without flinching and are willing to pay the ultimate price to make their great escape from the anti-utopia to which they have been relegated. If the nigga lives long enough to realize recompense for his initiative and is savvy enough to leverage his gains within and against his immediate surroundings, then he can graduate from relative obscurity and move up to the more elevated plane occupied by the moguls and their handpicked superstars. While niggas are out to establish their self-worth and prove themselves in a hostile environment, moguls possess the sense of entitlement required to begin speculating on the value of the surrounding world. Given that black disenfranchisement has been predicated upon making black people the objects rather than the subjects of capitalist speculation, there is something to be said for the mogul's display of nerve. In fact, it is this gumption that makes him worthy of celebrity status and mass mediation.

However, in a not-so-progressive manner, the mogul achieves his version of utopia via social isolation from, and antagonism toward, less successful ghetto residents—even as he claims, paradoxically, to represent and inspire their aspirations for greater glory. Whether or not he portrays himself as a gangster, above all else, the mogul calibrates the distance between the lowly member of the hoi polloi that he once was and the elite persona to which he can now lay claim in terms of money, jewels, automobiles, VIP parties, exotic travel, and an abundance of willing sexual partners.[34] In short, the mogul "is a self-made aristocrat, a former member of the underclass who's raised himself up from its ranks and seized his chance to 'shine.'"[35] Because of his largesse, the mogul is an elect member of the ghetto community, the speculative confidence man extraordinaire, and he regards himself as an activist of sorts, an example to others of what they could make of their lives if they would simply seize the right opportunity when the time comes.[36] As self-made men, moguls are not inclined to wait around for social intervention; they spot available opportunities for material advancement and seize them as best they can. They simply want people to get out of their way and let them handle their business.

When those whom the mogul has left behind betray their envy for him and become "playa-haters,"[37] they simply let the mogul know that he has done the "right thing," further reinforcing his solipsistic moral code. This form of spiteful self-absorption that poses as neighborliness is typically at the root of all capitalist-derived notions of community and is one of the more regrettable elements of the postwar consumptive consensus that has infiltrated the ghetto's childhood dream of what it wants to be when it matures. Nevertheless, despite the relative tedium of the mogul's message, "rap fans continue to find vicarious enjoyment in the … fantasy, in which being hated is the inevitable price for being one of the few who makes it in a world that otherwise guarantees anonymity and poverty for most."[38]

Still, the mogul is not solely a figure of ideological alienation, for he can never be too discursively disconnected from the spectacle of the black masses because it is the volatile energy of the crowd that gives him a creative impulse to channel, to package, and to sell. In this respect, the mogul is a figure who attains celebrity through his mastery of what I call the "ghetto sublime," which means he can grant us thrilling proximity to a form of social danger of truly monumental proportions while simultaneously providing us safe remove from the object of our fascination. The mogul, therefore, is the figure capable of extracting the productive element from the yawning ghetto maw, for the benefit of broader society. This figure is a speculative prospector if ever there was one. The hip-hop mogul thus simultaneously symbolizes inclusion within and resistance toward mainstream capitalism and emerges as a potent blend of the "speculative con," the "disciplined self-made man," and an entrancing figurehead of racial double-consciousness with a capitalist twist.[39]

There is always a political dimension to the mogul's balancing act with respect to the symbolic multitudes of everyday folk. Even as postindustrial American society has almost ceased to imagine the oceanic crowd as a sublime wellspring for social possibility and political engagement, there is still a residual cultural recollection that the masses in the public square once symbolized almost unfathomable "heterogeneity and instability ... the result of the promiscuous intermingling and physical massing of social classes, age groups, races, nationalities, and genders along the great boulevards of the industrial metropolis ... atomic particles ... the result of multiple liquids combined in a single test tube always with an uncertain outcome: a new substance, an explosion, a surge of energy, accelerated decay, a fizzle, new fermentations."[40] Hip-hop culture, whether under the auspices of moguls or not, always needs periodically to resurrect this foundational thematic element from its own hallowed past. Indeed, if the mogul cannot claim to understand and be able to tap the volatile energies of the street, he will cease to exist as a viable figure of commercial and cultural enterprise. In this regard, the mogul is the epitome of utopian double-consciousness with respect to the masses, for he

is the man of the crowd: at once immanent and transcendent, at once an insider and an outsider, at once everyman and the exceptional individual who provides the masses with a singular identity, a singular face, a mirror image of a sovereign collectivity that is now always in motion. ... Fully swept up in the multicolored and polyphonic waves of modern revolution, he is able to channel their tidal fury towards higher and nobler ends: national sovereignty, liberty, empire, progress.[41]

Thus, for all of his upwardly mobile pretensions, the hip-hop mogul needs the spectacle of the more impoverished masses for they give him the raw material, the literal human canvas, for which, and upon which, his ascent can be made emblematic. Even as American ghetto cityscapes have formed a contemporary scene of "excess with respect to the imagination's ability to comprehend the whole [that] renders a plunge into the abyss inevitable," the hip-hop mogul has been a useful figure in the sedimentation of recent American hegemonic formations, for he enables "the plunge [to be] productive because it is controlled."[42]

The emergence of the hip-hop mogul is symptomatic of an age wherein, despite a prevailing wish to the contrary, the crowd's volatile possibility for social change has become exhausted as a model of political mobilization, even as it has become a highly marketable simulacrum of exactly that sort of transgressive human potential. In this respect, we might regard the rise of the hip-hop mogul as not so much the sign of the end of history on an unnecessarily grand scale—and given prevailing diplomatic conditions on the geopolitical stage such an extrapolation might not even be possible—but at least as a leading indicator that in the United States "modernization has run its full course" and the "model of politics based upon the physical massing of bodies in public spaces or the performance of symbolic marches in real time and space" is being "superseded by a politics of gestures that relies upon virtual, indirect, and asynchronous forms of presence, organization, and participation."[43] From this basis, mass gatherings like the Million Man March are less viable as templates for the mass expectation and mass action of the future and less significant than the proliferation of more diverting images of sensuous collectivity. These new forms of mediated mass utopia might include the carnivalesque revelry of Damon Dash and Jay-Z's celebrated "Big Pimpin" video, and the updated "Dr. Frankenstein and the monster" iconography of rapper 50 Cent's video for his hit single "In Da Club," wherein a black "gangsta" is created in a pristine secret laboratory and inserted into a writhing mass of dancing black, brown, and white bodies at a nightclub, under the panoptic scrutiny of his creators (Dr. Dre and Eminem), who observe the mass spectacle from behind a two-way mirror in the manner of some weird virtual-reality focus group. In varied dreamscapes such as these, hip-hop moguls represent new forms of iconographic leadership that emerge from within and at the same time from beyond the populist mob. Thus, the hip-hop mogul utilizes his marketing skills to become both the fuse that kindles the crowd into a riotous frenzy and simultaneously an effective mechanism for its discipline, regulation, and conversion into circumscribed simulacra.

Conclusion

Typically, the utopian imagination of progressive factions and coalitions in American political life responds to the disaffecting tendencies of the marketplace with a prophetic critique that refutes the prevailing capitalist obsession with unfettered speculation, commodity exchange, and social inequality.[44] The New Deal–Great Society consensus that held sway in the American political landscape between 1947 and 1970—and has been on the decline, along with American real-wage growth, ever since—generally rejected the fantasy world of the free market as the primary locus for utopian yearning because the market demeans the sanctity of the social contract and leads to the excessive self-interest at the root of many manifestations of evil. For adherents of this almost archaic sensibility, the commodity is the cutting edge wielded by a system of domination that sunders more egalitarian forms of communal bonding while it sows reactionary seedlings of resignation among the citizenry.[45] Nevertheless, despite the work of progressives to shift national civic objectives to something other than commerce and common stock dividends, and even after the 9/11 terrorist attacks and the war in Iraq, "millions of Americans are refocusing on the one thing that most defines their lives, the upward and downward ticks of interest rates, the gyrations of their mutual funds, the achingly palpable lure and temptations of wealth."[46] This is to be expected at a time when the majority of American households and an increasing portion of the electorate have some sort of ownership of common stock.

Indeed, by 2001, the Federal Reserve determined that 52 percent of the nation's citizens had some form of stock ownership, with the percentage of all stock-holding households moving upward from 31.6 percent in 1989, 36.7 percent in 1992, and 48.8 percent in 1998. Politically speaking, the growing ranks of small investors represent an emerging and potentially significant political bloc within which blacks are sorely under-represented.[47] Among registered voters, shareholders now outnumber those not in the market by a ratio of 53 percent to 43 percent.[48] The escalating visibility of this group signifies a new development in the story of America's postindustrial evolution in the age of globalization, one that redefines the very meaning of mass political constituencies. Indeed, if "every political and cultural struggle of the past century that called itself democratic was waged for a mass constituency, and in its name," then it seems that shareholders rather than citizen-workers may constitute the next significant electoral bloc of the twenty-first century.[49] This trend represents a challenge to progressives and hip-hop moguls alike who are seeking to overtly revitalize the support-led social movements of the past—as Russell Simmons is attempting to do through his Hip-hop Summit Action Network—because, for all of the democratic changes wrought by commercial entertainment, the fact of lagging asset-ownership within black communities relative to that of white ones continues to exert a structuring influence upon American social life. Quite simply, African Americans are generally not part of the rapidly growing "equity class." This means that many blacks do not share an important characteristic of contemporary American life with their fellow citizens. Recent statistics suggest, for example, that blacks "still account for just 5% of stock investors."[50]

Besides constructing an entirely new electoral category—one over-represented as white—the migration of average citizens to the asset-owning class has had tangible economic spillover effects. Indeed, the typical American's stock portfolio enjoyed healthy gains during the 1990s, rising in value from $10,800 in 1989 to $25,000 in 1998. Stock holdings across a broader base of American households helped send the net worth per family from $59,700 in 1989 to $71,600 in 1998.[51] These gains have been preserved largely through asset rotation into real estate ventures and holdings despite the past three years of bear market downturn in the equity markets. Again, according to the latest Federal Reserve statistics, "the median net worth for all families rose 10%

to $86,100 in 2001 from 1998 and was up 41% from 1992."[52] To some extent, these figures of aggregate gains in household wealth mask growing discrepancies between white and black households. Indeed, the most recent statistics indicate that while the median net worth for whites rose 17 percent in 2001 to $120,900, it fell 4.5 percent to $17,000 for minorities.[53] Part of the reason for the durability and recent increase in the wealth gap has been the underparticipation of African Americans in equity ownership. Perhaps this discrepancy enables minority celebrity figures like the hip-hop mogul to assume such grand representational proportions through the simulation of communal wealth in the guise of individual achievement.

Despite, or perhaps because of, these sobering circumstances, politicians who seek to galvanize and subsequently win over the slumbering hip-hop electoral base will have to go against the conventional wisdom of the civil rights establishment, who typically are slow to consider growth-mediated paths out of disenfranchisement. This reluctance clearly stems, in part, from a tendency to view the aspiring spending patterns of the minority working classes as pathological. Indeed, a wide range of potential progressive factions that could coalesce into productive political coalitions—from civil rights–era holdovers even to members of the hip-hop generation—do not have faith that underprivileged groups will know what to do with their capital gains when they monetize them and are convinced that these groups will go on detrimental spending binges in pursuit of unnecessary trinkets of the high life.[54] Indeed, popular comedians of color like the cable channel Comedy Central's David Chappelle consistently mock the hypothetical scenario of working-class black Americans feverishly hoarding cartons of menthol cigarettes and urban athletic apparel in the unlikely event that the U.S. government were to grant blacks monetary reparations for slavery. Following from this prevailing assumption regarding minority and working-class "false consciousness," many progressives also generally contend that to advocate even a small measure of the growth-mediated approach for social development, as Jesse Jackson has done with his Wall Street Project initiative,[55] is to capitulate to a consensus that does "not dream of a future qualitatively different from the present ... [and at] best ... envision[s] a modified society with bigger pieces of pie for more customers."[56]

It may be time, however, to give growth-mediated measures for social development more consideration and find ways to articulate this need persuasively to democratic constituencies. Bruce Robbins interrogates the reticence within progressive constituencies of the academy—especially those ensconced within the interdisciplinary bastions of cultural studies that have their own celebrity academic figures who enjoy a quasi-mogul status in their own right—to adopt this rhetorical stance. He asks:

> Does the critic's, anthropologist's, or sociologist's progress indeed *require* arrest and stasis in the characters or cultures under discussion? The one example of upward mobility that is not doubted, indeed seems only confirmed by all this complexity of argument and research, is the upward mobility, the "cumulative" advancement, of [cultural studies] itself. But it remains to be seen whether the contrast between an upward mobility blocked in society and permitted in scholarship is really a necessary one. Could the latter have perhaps worked just as well if the research had shown the opposite, in other words that there *is* significant upward mobility in society? Or could this alternative logic only emerge in some different disciplinary constellation?[57]

Given the unlikely prospect for politically viable alternatives, it would be wise for progressives to consider ways to encourage their respective constituencies to prepare for growth-mediated modes of communal development and upward mobility in various public spheres, even if such propositions undermine their typical interventionist methods and motivations.[58] Clearly, lack of financial aptitude is an unnecessary obstacle before the desire of minority populations to share in the nation's economic good fortune when capital investment cycles turn favorable. As Federal

Reserve Chairman Alan Greenspan himself advocates, "improving basic financial education ... is essential to help young people avoid poor financial decisions that can take years to overcome."[59] Efforts to utilize the allure of celebrity figures like the hip-hop moguls for such pedagogical imperatives need to be explored and pursued. Such efforts will prove effective, however, only if they do not come across to would-be progressive constituencies as "holier than thou" discourses that seek to convert and cure the mass pathology of "consuming prestige" but rather as empathetic discourses of fellowship that acknowledge that the pursuit of wealth, and the symbolic elements of the "good life" that wealth enables, are part of the very fabric of freedom in modern capitalist democracies. By so doing, we may find the kind of ideological flexibility necessary to make celebrity figures like the hip-hop moguls more ethically responsible for the widely held public aspirations that they already currently signify. And by so doing, perhaps we can gradually defuse the explosive charge that the moguls trigger in a tautological commodity culture with an insatiable appetite for the spectacular aura of racial and ethnic authenticity, and we can begin to pay more attention to how these folks are going to sustain their businesses amid unremitting technological and industrial change. If nothing else, the ascension of the hip-hop mogul has gone a long way toward opening up space in working-class and poor minority communities to view mainstream corporate enterprise with more than absolute suspicion and disdain. These openings may enable new progressive coalitions to proceed with building their proposed agendas without being hamstrung by the class-based friction that has typically plagued the hip-hop generation from within.[60]

To continue to dream of *only* non-market-driven, support-led engines for political mobilization represents a disabling blind spot that will only let figures like the mogul off the hook for other forms of representative capacity that they might embody if they were compelled to acknowledge the full complexity of their behind-the-scenes business and social lives. Too frequently, however, progressive intellectuals can think only within the realm of market-averse myopia. For example, in his critique of the New Economy and its virulent strain of market fundamentalism, Tom Frank writes that "the key to reigning in markets is to confront them from outside. ... What we must have are not more focus groups or a new space where people can express themselves or etiquette lessons for executives but some countervailing power, some force that resists the imperatives of profit in the name of economic democracy."[61] But how does one even begin to conceptualize "economic democracy" without at least considering the beneficial spillover effects of the profit motive, individual initiative, and entrepreneurship? How does one consider persuading marginalized folks who view themselves always already on the outside looking in not to pursue commercial routes to cash in on that outlaw status when the hip-hop moguls are succeeding by doing exactly that via increasingly hyperreal methodologies? Indeed, imagining where an "outside" might be in twenty-first-century public life looks increasingly difficult, especially as mainstream notions of human perfectibility and social improvement, indeed of "utopia" itself, have become tethered ever more closely to the processes of financial speculation and the prospect of these processes trickling down to the lower stratum of our society through the wonders of new developments in information technology. The digital economy, complete with the hip-hop mogul as a newfangled "knowledge worker" adept at the manipulation and management of urban culture's increasingly open-source code of stylistic innovation, is merely the newest version of the postindustrial society as American utopia.

Certainly, any enthusiasm for the benefits of various market mechanisms should not get in the way of preserving and refashioning what sociologist William Julius Wilson has called the "nation's equalizing institutions," such as public education, unions, government-sponsored safety nets, and certain forms of international trade protection.[62] Indeed, if the demise of the New Economy in the fires of corporate malfeasance proved anything, it is simply that the quest for wealth and the personal liberties that it facilitates require compassionate guidance and earnest cooperation. As pedagogues and scholars we can and must be available to confer with a range of constituents, within and beyond the academy, in this crucial enterprise. But, in order to do so, we must recognize that our efforts will be complementing, rather than replacing, the influence of celebrity figures like the hip-hop mogul. A multipronged intervention in this regard might not be such a bad thing to which to acquiesce. What better way, after all, to combat the "authoritarian irrationalism"[63] of our World? What other method but a multifaceted one can contend with the information inundation endemic to discursive formations like the rapidly ossifying New Economy and similar maelstroms of moral and economic ambivalence that will surely confront us again in the not-too-distant future?

Study Questions

1. What is the relationship between the hip-hop mogul and the "race man" of previous generations?
2. Are hip-hop moguls viable as political spokespersons?
3. To what extent does the hip-hop mogul displace attention from the political realities of everyday people?

Notes

1. Walter Kirn, "The End of the Affair," *New York Times Magazine*, 26 May 2002, 11.
2. Lizabeth Cohen, *A Consumers' Republic: The Politics of Mass Consumption in Postwar America* (New York: Knopf, 2003). Cohen argues that the quarter century following World War II forms an era of consensus on the United States as a "consumers' republic," namely "an economy, culture, and politics built around the promises of mass consumption, both in terms of material life and the more idealistic goals of greater freedom, democracy, and equality," 7.
3. Michael J. Silverstein and Neil Fiske, "Luxury for the Masses," *Harvard Business Review*, April 2003, 48.
4. In the words of the Nobel Prize-winning economist Amartya Sen, we can think of the social tension embodied in the hip-hop mogul as a "relationship between incomes and achievements, between commodities and capabilities, between our economic wealth and our ability to live as we would like." Amartya Sen, *Development as Freedom* (New York: Knopf, 1999), 13.
5. Jean-François Lyotard, *The Postmodern Condition* (Minneapolis: University of Minnesota Press, 1984), 15.
6. In a conversation that he conducted with VA Linux CEO and open-source software champion Larry Augustin, highbrow talk show host Charlie Rose summed up the New Economy's emancipatory populism with a pithy quip: "Everyone's innovation is everybody's opportunity." *The Charlie Rose Show*, PBS, 6 January 2000.
7. In a personal anecdote he offered during an interview, Ralph Ellison points out that, to some extent, black Americans have always activated their subjectivities against the grain of, yet from squarely within, mainstream popular culture. For instance, when asked how he overcame his childhood in racially intolerant Oklahoma, Ellison replied: "There were the accidents through which so much of that world beyond the Negro community became available to me. Ironically, I would have to start with some of the features of American life which it has become quite fashionable to criticize in a most unthinking way: the mass media. Like so many kids of the Twenties, I played around with radio—building crystal sets and circuits consisting of a few tubes, which I found published in radio magazines. At the time we were living in a white middle-class neighborhood, where my mother was a custodian for some apartments, and it was while searching the trash for cylindrical ice-cream cartons which were used by amateurs for winding tuning coils that I met a white boy who was looking for the same thing. I gave him some of those I'd found and we became friends. ... I moved back into the Negro community and ... was never to see him again, but knowing this white boy was a very meaningful experience. ... Knowing him led me to expect much more of myself and of the world." Ralph Ellison, "That Same Pain, That Same Pleasure," in *The Collected Essays of Ralph Ellison*, ed. J. F. Callahan (New York: Modern Library, 1995), 63–64.
8. Not only is this form of mimicry embodied at the grassroots level, it is also enacted through verbal

expression at the most rarefied heights of the financial services arena. For instance, if one had been watching CNBC "Business Center" on 19 January 2000, one could have borne witness to Bear Stearns technology and Internet analyst Scott Ehrens encapsulating his analysis of America Online's wellspring of liquidity in terms of a healthy backorder of advertising sales, a pleasant circumstance that Ehrens described via reference to the hip-hop-savvy euphemism "Baby Got Backlog," a remark made in an obvious attempt to piggyback on the enduring popularity of an immensely popular rap song from the mid-1990s called "Baby Got Back," by Sir-Mix-A-Lot. The key difference being, of course, that the rapper penned his lyric in musical tribute to the evergreen allure of the black woman's stereotypically callipygian backside, the denigration of which served as a formative salient of natural science in the West.

9. Malcolm Gladwell, *The Tipping Point: How Little Things Can Make a Big Difference* (Boston: Little, Brown, 2000).

10. For example, Matthew Grant writes that "in the sphere of the culture industry, the 'anarchy' inherent in capitalist relations of production expresses itself in the moment of indeterminacy, the unavoidable moment of autonomy granted the cultural producer. The music industry, like the movie industry, cannot produce a hit through formula and hype alone. It requires a moment of aesthetic autonomy to produce (at least) the appearance of diversity in the market, a diversity necessary to generate desire for the latest product. Although a calculated part of the system, this autonomy gap does allow for the insertion of something else into the cultural commodity. ... we can understand this gap as the site for intervention and resistance." Matthew T. Grant, "Appendix 2: Of Gangstas and Guerrillas," www.gsd.harvard.edu/~appendix/issue2/grant/index2.htm.

11. John Seabrook, "Nobrow Culture," *New Yorker*, 20 September 1999, 104–11.

12. Laura M. Holson, "Dot-Com to the Stars: The Intersection of the Internet and Celebrity," *New York Times*, 6 June 2000.

13. Clay Christensen defines technology as "the processes by which an organization transforms labor, capital, material, and information into products and services of greater value ... [a] concept of technology [that] extends beyond engineering and manufacturing to encompass a range of marketing, investment, and managerial processes." Christensen goes on to say that "*innovation* refers to a change in one of these technologies." Clayton Christensen, *The Innovator's Dilemma* (Boston: Harvard Business School Press, 1997), xiii. I am seeking to account for the ways in which black popular culture's potentially adverse, or "disruptive," technological effects have been managed by various agents within the global entertainment complex and converted into market-enhancing, or "sustaining," ones.

14. Walter Benjamin, "On Some Motifs in Baudelaire," in *Illuminations*, ed. Hannah Arendt, trans. Harry Zohn (New York: Schocken, 1969), 194.

15. Robin D. G. Kelley, "Playing for Keeps: African-American Youth in the Postindustrial City," in *The House That Race Built: Black Americans/U.S. Terrain*, ed. Wahneema Lubiano (New York: Random House, 1997), 195–231.

16. Kelefa Sanneh, "Gettin' Paid," *New Yorker*, 20 and 27 August 2001, 60.

17. Just days before the release of Eminem's hit film *8 Mile* in November 2002, the *New York Times* reported that "after more than two decades of growth, hip-hop album sales hit a wall in [2001], declining about 15 percent to 89 million ... from a peak of 105 million the previous year, according to the Nielsen SoundScan company, which tracks sales figures. Album sales for the music industry were down overall, but less—3 percent in 2001—reflecting both the recession and the growth of free Internet file-sharing services. For the first six months of 2002, sales of hip-hop albums were down almost 20 percent from the same period [in 2001], compared with a general industry drop of 13 percent." Lola Ogunnaike, Laura Holson, and John Leland, "Feuding for Profit," *New York Times*, 3 November 2002.

18. *Fortune*, 16 September 2002, www.fortune.com/fortune/40under40/.

19. Orlando Patterson, *Rituals of Blood* (Washington, D.C.: Civitas, 1998), 249.

20. Roxanne Lowit, "Ciao!" *New York*, 22 February 1999.

21. Constance C. R. White, "It's All about Ice," *Talk*, December 1999–January 2000, 186–89. Such marketing efforts probably influenced the spending habits and style predilections of aspiring consumers. As one recent *New York Times* article reported, overall, the diamond market was up 12 percent in 2000 over figures posted in 1998. Monique P. Yazigi, "Bigger Diamonds Are a Girl's Best Friend," *New York Times*, 13 February 2000.

22. Frank DiGiacomo, "It's the Last Party of the Century," *New York Observer,*13 December 1999, 3–8.

23. Christopher John Farley, "Hip-Hop Nation," *Time*, 8 February 1999, 54–57.

24. Amy M. Spindler, "Character Development," *New York Times Magazine*, 23 July 2000, 54.

25. Gretchen Morgenson, "Economy Can No Longer Count On the Consumer," *New York Times*, 9 March 2003.

26. Rob Walker, "When Diamonds and Escalades are O.K.," *New York Times*, 19 January 2003, 16.

27. Ibid., 17.
28. Ibid.
29. Stuart Elliott, "Advertising," *New York Times*, 19 November 1999.
30. Silverstein and Fiske, "Luxury for the Masses," 50.
31. In this respect, the rap Utopia exemplifies what columnist David Brooks has described as the "realm of abundance." He writes that "in the land of abundance, a person's lower-class status is always temporary. If the complete idiot next door has managed to pull himself up to the realm of Lexus driver, why shouldn't the same thing happen to you?" David Brooks, "The Triumph of Hope over Self-interest," *New York Times*, 12 January 2003.
32. Manthia Diawara, "Homeboy Cosmopolitanism," in *In Search of Africa* (Cambridge: Harvard University Press, 1998), 239.
33. Ibid.
34. A rap magazine profile of the New Orleans rap collective, the Cash Money Millionaires, describes their rap utopia in the following manner: "Welcome to a world where life is truly beautiful. A world where Cristal flows from bottles like water from fountains. Every expensive car sits on chrome. Rolexes decorate wrists like cuff links, and every foot is covered with the hide of some endangered species of reptile. Every citizen in this utopia is adorned with a minimum of $10,000 worth of jewelry at all times, women are treated like showpieces, ballers ditch their $100,000 cars for candy-painted helicopters, cell phones chime in unison like a well-orchestrated symphony, and players make paper airplanes out of $50 bills for fun. It's gross materialism, and you'll hear it on every Cash Money release." Eric Robinson, "It's a Wonderful World," *Rap Pages* February 1999, 96. For those who don't know, Cristal is made by the esteemed French winery Louis Roederer. A recent catalog from the premium Manhattan wine boutique Sherry-Lehmann describes the 1995 vintage of Cristal as "the ultimate in rare 'luxury cuvée' Champagnes ... one of the most sought after wines in the world." At Sherry-Lehmann, a case of 1995 Cristal will set you back $2,159:40 plus tax. A bottle will require a mere $179.95.
35. Simon Reynolds, "It Isn't Easy Being Superman," *New York Times*, 10 October 1999, 29.
36. Consider the right-wing-leaning call for ghetto self-sufficiency in DMX's hardcore track, "Do You": "Do you—Cuz what it boils down to it's true / Do you—Cuz you are held accountable for you / Do you—is that really what you want me to see? / Do you—Cuz I'mma do me, truly."
37. Memoirist and fiction writer Dave Eggers attributes the *ressentiment* of "the hater" to information overload: "The average one of us is absolutely overwhelmed—as he or she should be—by the sheer volume of artistic output in every conceivable medium given to the world every day—it is simply too much to begin to process or to comprehend—and so we are forced to try to sort, to reduce. We designate, we diminish, we create hierarchies and categories. ... But you know what is easiest of all? When we dismiss. Oh how gloriously comforting to be able to write someone off. ... It's exhausting. It's born of boredom, lassitude. Too cowardly to address problems of substance where such problems actually are, we claw at those close to us. We point to our neighbor, in the khakis and sweater, and cry foul. It's ridiculous. We find enemies among our peers because we know them better, and their proximity and familiarity mean we don't have to get off the couch to dismantle them." Dave Eggers, "Too Legit to Quit," *Harper's*, August 2000, 20–22.
38. Reynolds, "It Isn't Easy Being Superman," 38.
39. Jackson Lears, "Luck and Pluck in American Culture," *Chronicle of Higher Education*, 24 January 2003, B15.
40. Jeffrey T. Schnapp, "The Mass Panorama," *Modernism/Modernity* 9, no. 2 (April 2002): 244–46.
41. Ibid., 247.
42. Ibid., 248–49.
43. Ibid., 278.
44. "Over the years and against conventional wisdom, utopians sustained a vision of life beyond the market. ... The goal is not a new economic order, but freedom from an obsession with economics." Russell Jacoby, *The End of Utopia: Politics and Culture in an Age of Apathy* (New York: Basic Books, 1999), 27.
45. Susan Buck-Morss, *Dreamworld and Catastrophe: The Passing of Mass Utopia in East and West* (Cambridge: MIT Press, 2000), x.
46. Peter Applebome, "Where Money's a Mantra, Greed's a New Creed," *New York Times*, 28 February 1999.
47. Jeanne Cummings, "Small Investors Now a Big Bloc," *Wall Street Journal*, 27 September 2002.
48. Jacob Weisberg, "United Shareholders of America," *New York Times Magazine*, 25 January 1998, 29.
49. Buck-Morss, *Dreamworld and Catastrophe*, xiii.
50. Ianthe Jeanne Dugan, "Broken Trust," *Wall Street Journal*, 12 September 2000, 1.
51. Richard W. Stevenson, "Fed Reports Family Gains from Economy," *New York Times*, 19 January 2000.
52. Barbara Hagenbaugh, "Nation's Wealth Disparity Widens," *USA Today*, 23 January 2003.
53. Ibid.

54. Alex Kotlowitz, "False Connections," in *Consuming Desires: Consumption, Culture, and the Pursuit of Happiness*, ed. Roger Rosenblatt (Washington, D.C.: Island Press, 1999), 65–72.

55. George Packer writes in the *New York Times Magazine*, for instance, that, "if the Wall Street Project lacks the high moral tone of the civil rights movement, it echoes the noise of a bottom-line society moved more by power and access than by moral appeal. Jackson seems to have reached the shrewd conclusion that Bill Clinton's America is not swayed by a desire for economic justice, and that government is unlikely to attempt anything on the scale of the movement's gains. And who can blame him for facing those facts." George Packer, "Trickle-Down Civil Rights," *New York Times Magazine*, 12 December 1999, 76.

56. Jacoby, *The End of Utopia*, 10–11.

57. Bruce Robbins, "Double Time: Durkheim, Disciplines, and Progress," in *Disciplinarity and Dissent in Cultural Studies*, ed. Gary Nelson and Dilip Parameshwar Gaonkar (New York: Routledge, 1996), 188–89.

58. David Brooks asks, "Why don't more Americans want to redistribute more wealth down to people like themselves? People vote their aspirations. ... None of us is really poor; we're just pre-rich. ... Democratic politicians proposing to take from the rich are just bashing the dreams of our imminent selves. ... As the sociologist Jennifer Lopez observed, ... As long as rich people 'stay real' ... they are admired. ... All this adds up to a terrain incredibly inhospitable to class-based politics. ... You have to be more hopeful and growth-oriented than your opponent, and you cannot imply that we are a nation tragically and permanently divided by income. In the gospel of America, there are no permanent conflicts." David Brooks, "The Triumph of Hope over Self-Interest," *New York Times*, 12 January 2003.

59. "Greenspan Urges Better Money Sense," *New York Times*, 7 April 2001.

60. Henry Louis Gates, Jr., "Must Buppiehood Cost Homeboy His Soul?" *New York Times*, 1 March 1992.

61. Thomas Frank, *One Market under God: Extreme Capitalism, Market Populism, and the End of Economic Democracy* (New York: Doubleday, 2000), xvi.

62. William Julius Wilson, "All Boats Rise. Now What?" *New York Times*, 12 April 2000.

63. Paul Gilroy, "Black Fascism," *Transition*, nos. 81/82: 91.

43

Black Youth and the Ironies of Capitalism

As hip-hop artists increasingly provide details about both their illicit and legitimate business practices, artistic expression and capitalist desire have been wedded together, creating an aesthetic of consumption. Though many are wary of this development, it has been one of the ways that hip-hop has directly and indirectly addressed inequality.

S. Craig Watkins explains that popular culture has become one of the primary terrains for the struggle over political representation, access to economic and cultural resources, and control of media imagery. Even as black youth have been subjected to economic shifts that have eroded their quality of life, they have gained access to technologies to challenge those shifts.

Black Youth and the Ironies of Capitalism

S. Craig Watkins

[I]n the struggles of urban youths for survival and pleasure inside of capitalism, capitalism has become their greatest friend and greatest foe. It has the capacity to create spaces for their entrepreneurial imaginations and their "symbolic work," to turn something of a profit for some, for them to hone their skills and imagine getting paid. At the same time, it is also responsible for a shrinking labor market, the militarization of urban space, and the circulation of the very representations of race that generate terror in all of us at the sight of young black men and yet compels most of America to want to wear their shoes.

Robin D.G. Kelley[1]

Although African American filmmaking is the primary locus of inquiry, the scope of my analysis is considerably broader. It is difficult to understand the significance of filmmakers like Spike Lee and the Hughes brothers in American cinema without situating their arrival on the cultural stage in relation to the social transformations that reorganize the material and symbolic worlds inhabited by black youth. The creative labor of African American filmmakers takes place upon a complicated sphere from which the production of blackness, a historically situated racial signifier, proliferates across many sites.[2] But before discussing African American filmmaking practices specifically, it is important to consider the historical formations and decisive shifts that transform the social landscapes, everyday experiences, and cultural productions of black youth more generally.

According to sociologist David Brain, cultural production is the "collective production of skills and practices which enable social actors to make sense of their lives, articulate an identity, and resist with creative energy the apparent dictates of structural conditions they nonetheless reproduce."[3] The cultivation of skills that allow them to participate in a rapidly expanding and global communications media culture enables black youth to produce a broad range of cultural products. The most arresting features of black youth popular cultural productions represent distinct forms of agency, struggle, and social critique. But the vigorous commodification of African American cultural productions also develops complicated features.

The study of popular media culture generally oscillates between two opposing poles: containment or resistance. Whereas the former maintains that the ideas, values, and representations that shape popular media discourses are determined by the dominant classes, the latter argues, alternatively, that popular cultures have the capacity to subvert dominant ideologies and regimes of representation.[4] Yet popular media culture is remarkably more complex than the containment/resistance binary opposition implies. Similar to the social world from which it is produced, popular media cultures are marked by instability and change. It is, in fact, one of the main locations where the struggle for ideological hegemony is waged. But as Stuart Hall explains, this "struggle for [ideological dominance] is never about pure victory or pure domination[;] it is always about shifting the balance of power in relations of culture."[5] From this view, then, popular media culture is perhaps best understood as a perpetual theater of struggle in which the forces of containment and resistance remain in a constant state of negotiation, never completely negating each other's presence or vigor.

While the different spheres of commercial media culture—television, film, music, video, and the Internet—function as sources of pleasure and entertainment, they also perform a pivotal role in patterning the cultural and ideological landscape. The popular media productions created by black youth represent a distinct sphere of cultural production. Any serious consideration of black cultural productions must examine the relationship between several interlocking factors: the specific culture industries within which these productions are organized; the changing landscape of communications media technologies; emergent mood shifts and sensibilities that lead to the creation of new collective identities; and finally, the unsettled social world within which black youth cultural practices take shape. Sociologist Herman Gray argues that commercial media culture is an essential location to think and theorize about African American culture, representation, and politics. Gray reminds us that "commercial culture serves as both a *resource* and a *site* in which blackness as a cultural sign is produced, circulated, and enacted."[6]

Commercial forms of popular culture are a rapidly growing field of study. Scholars and social historians are beginning to understand it as a plentiful and remarkably revealing reservoir of practices and formations that are inextricably linked to the changing contours of American life: urbanization/suburbanization, technological innovation, and shifting conceptions of racial, gender, class, and sexual identities. Commercial forms of popular media culture, for example, are central to how we (re)produce and experience socially constructed formations like race.

More precisely, my aim is to more fully explain the increasingly complex ways in which young African Americans have mobilized around a changing racial and popular media landscape. Moreover, it is a story about how the pulsing gestures, performances, and representations practiced by black youth are structured, in large part, by the profound ways in which they experience the changing contours of American life. The focus on the production of black youth cultural styles and popular movements also recognizes that a notable feature of the late twentieth century, as Stuart Hall and Martin Jacques write, "is the proliferation of sites of antagonism and resistance, and the appearance of new [actors], new social movements, new collective identities—an enlarged sphere for the operation of politics, and new constituencies for change."[7]

My research pivots around a particular site of antagonism and resistance—the sphere of popular media culture—and more precisely, the ferment and creative energy that drive the cultural innovations of African American youth and their strategic participation on this terrain. The buoyant surge in black youth popular cultural production raises important questions about the evolving disposition of cultural and representational politics in a media-saturated universe. Early critics of "mass culture" demonstrated concern that popular media culture was controlled by and for the dominant classes. But this view fails to consider how popular media culture functions as a site of intense ideological struggle. Quite simply, can the commercial media, long regarded by many critical theorists as the modern-day "opium of the masses," function as a location of counterideological struggle? Similar to other institutional milieus, commercial media also develop specific antagonisms. So as new subjects gain access to the most prominent sites of media and representation, the possibilities for new collective identities, social movements, and distinct modes of struggle are also established.

To contend that cultural innovation and production among black youth have flourished and achieved a discernible niche in the arena of popular media culture is certainly a tenable position. This is not to imply that African American youth have only recently begun to cultivate spaces for producing cultural objects and expressing themselves but rather that the symbolic practices created by the post–civil rights generation have achieved greater visibility and resonance in the global popular culture economy. But before discussing some of the specific attributes of black youth agency, I would like to consider an initial question first: Why have cultural innovation and production among black youth exploded or, as they might boast, "blown up"? Even more to the point, how has the social, political, and historical terrain on which black youth cultural productions do their work enabled them to intervene in the remaking of society in ways that are more visible, invigorating, and problematic?

The New World Order: Black Youth and the Racialization of Crisis

> Oh you know what else they trying to do, make a curfew especially for me and you. The traces of the new world order, time is gettin' shorter if we don't get prepared people its gone be a slaughter. My mind won't allow me to not be curious. My folks don't understand, so they don't take it serious. But every now and then, I wonder if that gate was put up to keep crime out, or our ass in?
>
> Goodie Mob[8]

A cursory glance at the cultural landscape—music, video, film, television, advertising, and sports—reveals that the expressive cultures created by African Americans play a lively role in patterning the racial and gender identities of youth as well as the general popular culture scene. The precarious relationship between youth subcultures, media technology, and commercial culture has been the subject of numerous inquiries.[9] Still, despite the fact that we can speak broadly of youth cultural practices, it is essential to appreciate the historical specificities that enable distinct formations of youth culture to take shape. Historian Robin D. G. Kelley reminds us that, "unlike more mature adults, young people are in the process of discovering the world as they negotiate it. They are creating new cultures, strategies of resistance, identities, sexualities, and in the process generating a wider range of problems for authorities whose job it is to keep them in check."[10]

Admittedly, it is difficult to pinpoint with precision when and why a distinctive mood shift or transition in youth cultural production originates. However, it is possible to identify those factors that work, more or less, to establish the circumstances from which youth popular culture formations emerge. Certainly, any discussion of late twentieth-century black youth cultural practices that does not consider the social context that situates their agency would be severely impaired.

So why have cultural innovation and production among black youth exploded? One approach might look solely at the innovators of the new symbolic practices that lead to the creation of new popular culture products. This can be called the genius view of cultural innovation because it presupposes that certain periods of cultural production are the result of talented individuals.[11] However, a more discerning approach would seek to understand the historical particularities that produce the resources and opportunities that unleash and enable the creative energies of cultural producers. Moreover, this view understands that the creative

labor of cultural producers does not take place in a vacuum. Innovators of new symbolic practices and cultural products do their work in relation to other cultural producers and within
specific social historical contexts. Like all historical actors, then, black youth operate within
the context of structural and historical constraints not of their own making.

Consequently, any serious interrogation of the symbolic efficacy of black youth cultural
practices must understand their social, economic, and political milieu. Sociologist Ann
Swidler states that "unsettled times"—that is, periods of great disorder and transition: population shifts; wars; social, economic, or moral crisis—tend to create moments of fierce
struggle, instability, and social action.[12] New ideas, social movements, and ideological strategies are mobilized to make sense of societal flux and instability. In the process, the ideas, belief
systems, and symbolic terrain of a given period become more fragile and increasingly vulnerable to competing ideological worldviews. Similarly, dominant cultures produce "emergent"
social formations that cultivate alternative/oppositional practices and ideologies that modify
hegemonic practices and cultural discourses.[13]

To be sure, the presumed "dominant ideologies" of any given period do not always penetrate and shape the consciousness, ideas, and practices of aggrieved populations.[14] In fact,
dominant economic and political classes do not consistently fashion consensus in ways that legitimate their authority. This view of culture and society seems especially plausible when
thinking about the United States in the late twentieth century, a period of tremendous political agitation and social discord.

The ideological and political formations of the postindustrial United States are marked by
profound social, economic, and cultural transition. Moreover, this period of transition has
established the conditions for the construction of different crisis scenarios, both real and
imagined. In the process, crisis-tinted discourses are mobilized to make sense of and effectively manage the flux and uncertainty that abound. Even in cases where crises may in fact be
real, they are typically *made* intelligible and, as a result, are defined, shaped, interpreted, and
explained. For instance, a complex assemblage of crisis discourses revolves around the postindustrial ghetto. The ghetto has become an intensely charged symbol, particularly as it patterns
discourses about crime and personal safety, welfare, familial organization, and the disintegration of American society.

African American (and Latino) youths are prominently figured in the crisis scenarios that
stage some of the more contentious social and political episodes of the late twentieth century.
Some researchers contend that increases in violent crimes, teen pregnancy, female-headed
households, and welfare dependency can be *partially* explained by the sheer growth in the
number of young people, particularly black and Latino, residing in many cities across the
United States.[15] Moreover, the concentration of black and Latino youth in postindustrial cities
corresponds with structural changes in the postindustrial economy, especially the movement
of industry and meaningful employment opportunities away from the communities in which
they are most likely to live.[16]

One of the peculiar developments of postwar economic transformations is what economist
Juliet Schor describes as an increase in work hours for some segments of the population and the
overproduction of idleness for others.[17] Schor argues that, as the U.S. economy and the labor
market continue to undergo substantive reorganization, they are increasingly unable to provide
work for some segments of the population. One of the persistent tensions in the postindustrial
economy is the widespread erosion of meaningful employment opportunities for poor, inner-city
youth. As the labor-force participation of black youth hovers around chronically low levels, both
their real and perceived prospects for upward mobility become more grim. Indeed a tenacious set
of factors restricts the social and economic mobility of poor youth: inadequate schools, lower
levels of educational attainment, low self-esteem and personal confidence, discriminatory hiring
practices, and racially inflected tensions on the job site.[18]

As the face of urban poverty in the United States continues to evolve, one of the distinguishing features is the growing number of youth who now live in poverty-stricken households, a trend not replicated across other industrialized nations.[19] Cultural critic Mike Davis writes: "[C]orrelated to the economic peripheralization of working-class blacks has been the dramatic *juvenation of poverty* amongst all innercity ethnic groups."[20] By the end of the 1980s, roughly 20 percent of America's youth were poor. And while youth and single-parent mothers represent a disproportionate share of the poor, the probability of being a poor child is not equal across racial/ethnic groups. In fact, research consistently indicates that African American children are significantly more likely to grow up in impoverished households and neighborhoods than their white counterparts.[21] By the end of the eighties, an astonishing 44 percent of African American youth were living in poverty. In contrast, 38 percent of Latino and 11 percent of white youth lived in similar conditions.

The incorporation of African American youth into a broad complex of crisis scenarios develops specific social and political dimensions. Black youth tend to be concentrated in poor communities that have been the primary targets of the post-1960s conservative social and political backlash packaged in numerous movements: antigovernment, antitaxes, antiwelfare, and anticrime. The drive to correct the perceived excesses of "big government" has ignited a broad-based movement of disinvestment in inner-city job training, social, education, and crime-prevention programs. Ghetto youth are prominent icons in the seemingly indefatigable efforts of an emboldened conservatism committed to the enforcement of "traditional values," law and order, and personal responsibility. But the association of black youth with social instability is indelibly marked by the production and popular dissemination of the "underclass" label.

The making of the "underclass" label is congruous with the general rise of social-issue conservatism in post-1960s American political culture. Social-issue conservatism is the explicitly focused debate about values, morality, behavior, two-parent households, and respect for authority. While cultural issues have historically shaped American politics, they have been elevated from a peripheral to a central role.[22] One journalist goes so far as to argue that whereas politicians and political consultants operate from the assumption that economic issues drive electoral politics, "values matter most."[23] However, the author's focus on issues like crime, welfare, and affirmative action suggests that perhaps "race matters most." The "values matter most" contention is at best disingenuous, but it nevertheless illustrates how conservatives have attempted to elevate what are increasingly racialized themes above concerns about the inherent nature and instabilities of capitalism as the central dilemma in American social and political life.

Contemporary discourses about African Americans are increasingly patterned by sensational representations of the black "underclass." Sociologist Herbert Gans maps the evolution of the "underclass" label and its absorption into mainstream social and political discourse. Despite the newness of the label, it plays a definitive role in shaping popular discourses about race, poverty, and social change in general. According to Gans, the term has passed through three descriptive stages: economic, racial, and finally behavioral.[24] By the 1970s, he argues, descriptions of the term turned decisively behavioral as news journalists began to devote substantial time and coverage to the proliferation of social dislocations in poor ghetto communities.[25] The emphasis on the alleged deviance of the poor refashions "culture-of-poverty" explanations of poverty and strengthens the notion that misbehavior is the primary culprit in the reproduction of poor ghetto communities.[26]

The "underclass" is customarily portrayed as one of the most distressing social problems facing the United States. Stephen Hilgartner and Charles Bosk have proposed what they call the public arenas model for understanding the rise of social problems.[27] According to the model, social problems are collectively defined, selected, framed, and disseminated within a dynamic arena of public discourse. In this arena, a broad population of potential problems competes against each other for attention and notoriety. Given the vast number of potential social problems, only a few are able to capture the attention of the public and major institutions. As a result, social problems are necessarily stratified: problems considered the most urgent occupy the top of the "social problems ladder," while those achieving little or no public cognizance are typically positioned near the bottom.

Furthermore, Hilgartner and Bosk contend that the career of a social problem variegates over time and hinges on its ability to capture the attention of the institutions that have the power and resources to effectively define the problem for broad public consumption. These institutions, in effect, *make* the social problem and render it intelligible to the broader public. The carrying institutions include, for example, the cinema, made-for-television movies, news media organizations, book publishing, and political parties. These are the major institutions that select, define, and disseminate social problems to the public. Because of the vast population of potential problems, creators of social problems must package them in dramatic terms. Once a social problem achieves prominence in one arena, it may then begin to saturate other arenas. When multiple carrying institutions devote substantial attention to a particular problem, it develops a "celebrity" status. Moreover, the problem begins to dominate public, and especially media, discourse.

Visualizing the Underclass, Representing Danger

> Today's dangerous classes included segments of the diverse communities of racial and ethnic minorities; young people who exhibit some degree of independence from their elders' direction and values.... The likelihood that the identified group creates danger—crime, urban decay, challenge to authority—is an article of faith, as both the public and the policymakers point to high levels of urban disorder, family dissolution, and unwed motherhood.... What is needed to construct them as enemies is a bridge between group identity and an experience of social threat—a neighborhood mugging ... or the dramatic depiction of a murder on the nightly news—that is familiar to many people.
>
> Diana Gordon[28]

It only takes a quick glance at legislative and electoral politics, the news media, public opinion polls, or popular entertainment culture to recognize that the "underclass," and poor youth especially, has attained the dubious distinction of being a celebrity social problem. The absorption of the "underclass" label into mainstream vocabulary corresponds with the social and economic transformations that configure postindustrial life. And even though the label circulates as if it were ideologically neutral, representations of the "underclass" are sharply coded in both racial and gender terms. Moreover, historian Michael Katz maintains that the label implies that the problem of late twentieth-century urban poverty is profoundly novel in character and kind, and unprecedented in scope.[29]

Take, for example, the proliferation of news media discourses that play a leading role in framing public perceptions of postindustrial ghetto life. Perhaps even more than social scientists or politicians, the news media industry has played a crucial role in coloring the public discourses that render the "underclass" seemingly more intelligible. The television news industry is a distinct sphere of commercial media and discourse production. Unlike most of television entertainment, it is nonfictional—in other words, real. But the news media is a peculiar blend of fact and artifice. Thus, while news media journalists deal with real-world phenomena, they do so in a way that is always selective and interpretive.[30]

News discourse is one of the primary means by which a society comes to know itself. In their analysis of television news, Richard Campbell and Jimmie Reeves contend that it is "a spectacle of surveillance that displays a range of cultural performances—all of which articulate visions of order by representing legitimate authority, reproducing commonsense, and visualizing deviance."[31] The news media are also an important site of racial discourse. In fact, part of the evolving role of the news media industry has been to determine what is most newsworthy about race, construct images and definitions of race, and pattern the range of potential connotations the idea of race produces. For example, television news discourse typically constructs African Americans as conflict-generating and problematic.[32] And though it would be faulty to conclude that the news media are the primary agent in the racial fissures that percolate throughout the late twentieth century, the way in which television news frames race certainly occupies a crucial position on the embattled terrain of racial conflict.

The news media serve several functions at once.[33] A primary purpose is to provide their mass audience with information and descriptions of events that take place in the world. However, another less obvious function is the news media's role as a mechanism of social control. The news media, to be sure, can be viewed as a central component of the social control processes that define and produce meaning about what constitutes difference and deviance. In this particular role, as explained by Ericson, Baranek, and Chan, the news media are a kind of "deviance-defining elite" that play a key role in constituting visions of order, stability, and change and in influencing the control practices that accord with these visions.[34] News media organizations specialize in visualizing—and accordingly, defining—deviant behavior for their audience. In the process, the news media also reproduce commonsense notions of civility, social order, and community consensus. Moreover, the focus on deviance develops an entertainment angle that appeases the commercial interests of news media organizations. Cognizant of its role in commercial television entertainment and the competition for ratings, the television news industry relies heavily on dramatic, sensational, and titillating images in order to attract and hold a wide viewing audience.[35]

The preponderance of television news stories highlighting black youth, violence, and the arrival of crack cocaine in the middle 1980s stands out as a dramatic orchestration of a "moral panic" and demonstrates how news media organizations aid in shaping the way social problems are selected, defined, packaged, and disseminated to the public.[36] Campbell and Reeves maintain that the news media's construction of the cocaine crisis in the 1980s embodied the racial, gender, and class tensions that shaped the most celebrated crisis scenarios of the period.[37] The authors argue that, with the emergence of crack cocaine, the news media developed a "siege" narrative that replaced earlier news stories regarding cocaine use. This rewriting of the cocaine narrative shifted from *class*-coded themes focusing on recreational drug use and therapy to *race*-coded themes focusing on violence, criminality, and punishment. Using production techniques like clandestine footage, the news media began to serve as a surveillance device, built largely on visual clichés that portrayed the burgeoning crack cocaine economy in hyper-villainous terms.[38] The authors persuasively claim that this particular rewriting of the cocaine narrative fit the demonology of racial conservatism, stigmatized poor inner-city youth, and played a central role in legitimating, for example, the "hard" disciplinary ethos of social control initiatives like the war on drugs.[39]

A main set of organizing themes in the "underclass" discourse is the alleged social pathologies of ghetto youth. To be sure, the connection of black youth with illegal drugs, gangs, and violence performs a distinct role in shaping how many of the crisis scenarios of the period were understood. More crucially, inner-city youth arouse public anxiety and precipitate what Diana Gordon describes as "the return of the dangerous classes."[40] Members of the dangerous classes, she argues, are believed to pose a threat to the personal safety of law-abiding citizens and, if unchecked, to the social, economic, and moral order of the larger society. Accordingly, black and Latino youth are prominently figured in the widely shared notion that inner cities—and by association, their racially coded populations—constitute a fiscal and moral strain on national resources. Subsequently, some of the salient crisis scenarios coloring the postindustrial United States have been redefined. In the process, meanings about race, class, gender, and youth undergo substantial revisions.

In many ways, the "underclass" is as much a cultural construction as it is a sociological reality. At stake, of course, is how the widespread impoverishment of black youth is comprehended. To be sure, before any society can create new laws and mobilize punitive measures for the express purpose of controlling those portrayed as dangerous, it must conduct a sufficient amount of ideological work in order to legitimate the use of coercion. In essence, the general public must be made to feel vulnerable, to feel that the stability of the moral and social order is threatened, thus necessitating dramatic acts to preserve social order. Representing ghetto youth as dangerous is not simply a symbolic exercise; it has serious implications for social policy and also influences the social control mechanisms put in place to restore a sense of order. Indeed, initiatives like the war on drugs, school dress codes, and evening curfews achieve their popular status precisely because of the work that crisis discourses perform in the criminalization of black youth.[41] The perceived dangerousness of the urban poor legitimates the deployment of the coercive technologies of the state and the adoption of elaborate crime management operations.

It is within this social context that the cultural productions of black youth amass energy and ever-increasing ingenuity. The transformations of urban ghetto life situate different formations of racial discourse and enable them to take shape. One aim of black youth popular culture is to redefine the crisis scenarios that prominently figure young African Americans. The symbolic practices of black youth develop distinct styles, moods, and imaginative contours that engage a broad spectrum of cultural producers—journalists, politicians, scholars—about African American life. The explosive surge in popular cultural productions by black youth prompts a reconsideration of how unsettled times reinvigorate not only social control discourses but resistive discourses, too. This is not to suggest that social and economic dislocations are the determinate causes of black youth cultural productions. Instead, I am suggesting that the ways in which black youth experience a rapidly changing society and how they practice cultural politics to express these experiences correspond.

Paradoxically, the intensification of racial and economic polarization in the United States produces space for the emergence of cultural practices that derive much of their symbolic efficacy from locations of marginality. The popularization of black youth expressive cultures is an excellent case in point. Despite high rates of poverty, joblessness, and criminal arrests, black youth occupy a dynamic role in the shaping of the popular cultural landscape. Many of the major culture industries—sports, television, advertising, music, cinema—incorporate the innovative styles and expressive cultures of black youth in order to appeal to their respective markets and revitalize their own commercial viability. Ironically, social isolation and economic marginalization contribute to the energy and imaginative capacities that enable black youth to participate effectively in the ever-expanding universe of popular media culture. In the process, black youth have accumulated significant amounts of symbolic capital.[42]

So despite the currency of conservative discourses, black youth have mobilized their own discourses, critiques, and representations of the crisis-colored scenarios in which they are prominently figured. More important, young African Americans are acutely aware of the social world in which they live and the vast structural inequalities that impose severe restrictions on their economic mobility. All members of society exercise some measure of agency—that is, capacity to exert some degree of power over the social arrangements and institutions that situate their lives. Faced with the increasing trend toward structurally enforced idleness and state-sanctioned coercion, black youth have fought diligently to create spaces of leisure, pleasure, and opposition from the social structures and institutional arrangements that influence their life chances.

How do black youth maneuver to contest and destabilize the growing tide of racial conservatism? Ironically, at the same moment that black youth have become especially vulnerable to shifts in the postindustrial economy and the political landscape, they, too, have gained unprecedented access to the technologies of communications media. What has emerged in the process is the structuring of a historically distinct terrain upon which the varying repertoires of black youth cultural production dramatically reorganize the scope and possibilities of social and political struggle from the margins. Indeed, the popular cultures of black youth reveal that they experience, interpret, and make sense of the world in ways that are both historically specific and highly performative.

The Making of the Hip Hop Nation: The Social Transformation of Black Youth Culture

> It was not long before similarly marginalized black and Hispanic communities in other cities picked up on the tenor and energy in New York hip hop. Within a decade, Los Angeles County (especially Compton), Oakland, Detroit, Chicago, Houston, Atlanta, Miami, Newark, and Trenton, Roxbury, and Philadelphia, have developed local hip hop scenes that link various regional postindustrial urban experiences of alienation, unemployment, police harassment, social, and economic isolation to their local and specific experience via hip hop's language, style, and attitude.... In every region, hip hop articulates a sense of entitlement and takes pleasure in aggressive insubordination.
>
> Tricia Rose[43]

Despite the widespread popularity of black youth expressive culture and the vast amount of critical attention it currently receives, our understanding of the historical processes that situate its varied articulations remains underdeveloped. The relationship between African American youth and communications media technology is also underexamined. The histories of black youth and their relationship to commercial media culture, to be sure, remain largely unwritten. Black youth continue to create new cultural practices and products that penetrate and reconfigure the production and distribution strategies that govern the culture industry. Moreover, the collective mobilization around popular media technologies by black youth raises intriguing questions about their participation in a vast and rapidly expanding communications media and information economy.

Sociologist Claude Fischer explains that the study of technology and society is commonly informed by technological determinism.[44] According to Fischer, the determinism model views a technology as an autonomous or external "force" that "impacts" social life. The main assumption from this view is that technology dictates changes that are far-reaching and fundamental in scope. Further, it is assumed that a technology produces homogeneous consequences for the larger society. In other words, the impact of a technology on members of society is believed to be uniform.

Critics of technological determinism maintain that while technology can and often does lead to change, the process is socially rather than technologically determined. Moreover, Fischer argues, the determinism view fails to appreciate how specific technologies are adopted by particular members of society and used in ways that accommodate specific intentions and priorities. Fischer writes: "[O]nce we have understood the genesis of a technology, its development and promotion, we can begin looking at consequences. Here we should ask: Who adopted the device? With what intention? How did they use it? What role did it play in their lives? How did using it alter their lives?"[45] According to Fischer, the value of this position is that it emphasizes the agency and intentionality of those who use technology. Fischer adds, "[P]eople are neither 'impacted' by an external force, nor are they the unconscious pawns of a cultural Geist. Instead of being manipulated, they manipulate."[46]

Technological determinism typically informs how the relationship between black youth and popular media culture is comprehended. For example, it is commonly argued that communications media exercise unrelenting power in shaping the worldviews, behavior, and lived experiences of black youth.[47] There are at least two immediate problems with this position. First, it does not adequately specify how media technology has entered and altered the social lives of black youth. Second, and perhaps more important, it does not address how black youth manipulate media technology and, in the process, reshape the sphere of popular media culture.

Take as an example the study of black youth by historian Carl Nightingale.[48] Nightingale contends that analysts of the black urban poor fail to understand the way in which black youth are connected to the larger mainstream culture. Whereas theories about economic, spatial, and cultural alienation emphasize the exclusion of black youth from the mainstream, Nightingale seeks to understand the problematic ways in which mainstream culture penetrates the lived experiences of black youth.[49] Furthermore, he directs his critical gaze toward popular media culture and its "impact" on the racial, gender, and economic identities of black youth. The exploration of the relationship between black youth and the commercial media is certainly an important site of study. But the framing of his inquiry presumes technological determinance. It is taken for granted that the practices of black youth are rigidly conditioned by the media and corporate strategies of consumer socialization. However, it is equally important to consider how black youth influence the culture industry, the cultural marketplace, and consumer trends. In other words, it is important to understand that youth are not simply passive victims of commercial media culture but are actively involved in its making.

The emergence of hip hop culture illustrates black youth agency. In many ways, hip hop represents a particular species of social movement. The movement is made possible by new social and economic arrangements, technological innovations, and the global dissemination of U.S. popular media cultures. Sociologists broadly define social movements as collective efforts to produce social change.[50] Any attempt to discuss hip hop as a movement demands careful delineation because it is variously preoccupied with style, performance, opposition, leisure, consumption, representation, and entrepreneurship. First, this particular movement takes place on the field of popular culture, a site not immediately discerned as political, or capable of producing social change. Second, hip hop is invigorated by the creative labor of a constituency not ordinarily regarded as interested in effecting social change: youth. Third, like social movements in general, hip hop enables its participants to imagine themselves as part of a larger community; thus, it produces a sense of collective identity and agency. To be sure, this particular movement constitutes a distinct mode of intervention in the social world.

Communications media have become an especially important location for both individual and collective agency. Many black youth believe that the sphere of popular media culture is an especially important space in which to articulate many of their frustrations and grievances with their disproportionate membership in the growing ranks of the underemployed/unemployed, impoverished, and incarcerated. Ironically, and as Kelley points out, capitalism has been both a foe and a friend of black youth. Within the interstices of late twentieth-century capitalism, black youth have fought to create productive spaces to counter the dominant discourses deployed to both demonize and discipline them. The hip hop movement has developed into a fertile reservoir of youth cultural production. In fact, numerous expressive cultures have been created in the process: graffiti art, break dancing, and most notably, rap music. The origins of hip hop are difficult to record precisely.[51] And while my focus is on African American youth, hip hop has never been an exclusively "black thing." Many of the creative elements of hip hop developed in correspondence with the postwar migrations and subsequent shifting racial geography of New York City. The interaction between Latino, Afro-Caribbean, and African American expressive cultures established the conditions for the development of alternative modes of youth expression.[52]

The evolution and transformation of hip hop are patterned by class, generational, and gender cleavages. These three markers of differentiation within the African American community make crucial imprints on black popular culture. According to cultural critic Todd Boyd, the most recent generational shifts in black popular culture came into view with the passing of what he refers to as the ideology of the race man, animated best by Bill Cosby.[53] This particular period of black cultural production, Boyd contends, reflected the views and aspirations of a generation concerned with civil rights, assimilation, and the production of what are often alluded to as respectable or "positive" images of black Americans. Further, Boyd maintains that a new black popular culture sensibility—the new black aesthetic (NBA)—supplanted the race man ideology sometime during the middle to late 1980s. This particular generation of black cultural producers—he uses Spike Lee and Wynton Marsalis as illustrations—came of age after the protests of the 1960s and represented the first creative community of African Americans to benefit from the resources and networks made available because of greater access to higher education. This generation practiced a black American version of bourgeois nationalism that emphasized the infiltration of mainstream institutions. These two periods or regimes of cultural politics were informed by a middle-class sensibility that distinguishes them from the most recent generational shift in black popular culture—a shift that is related to the ascendancy of hip hop as a leading signifier of black culture.

Whereas the first two periods are shaped by middle-class priorities and notions of assimilation and respectability (the Cosby era) and new conceptions of black-style politics and upward mobility (the new black aesthetic), the succeeding shift identified by Boyd is governed by a hardcore ghetto sensibility that represents a radical break. This particular generation eschews both the comportment of social acceptability and the racial chic of neo-black nationalist politics. More specifically, Boyd argues that the emergence of hardcore ghetto iconography altered the orbit of black popular culture and is representative of working-class definitions of blackness that contest bourgeois-inflected definitions. While the transitions and breaks that distinguish one period from the other are never total, Boyd's analysis does help to further elucidate class differentiation within the African American community and its implications for a varied terrain of cultural politics and production.

The issue of gender is equally important. While it is true that hip hop is shaped by narratives that emphasize male hegemony, pleasure, and desire, it is important to emphasize that female cultural practices also inflect this particular movement. In her analysis of black youth culture, Tricia Rose maintains that most academic and popular discourses tend to marginalize the presence and contributions of women to hip hop. The presence of females has been integral if not always adequately recognized. Although the commercial media landscape is overwhelmingly dominated by men, women continue to forge new territories for their active involvement and pleasure. The hip hop scene is no different. Indeed, as many female authors point out, women have long struggled to gain access to and control over the resources and sites that animate the production of hip hop culture.[54]

If hip hop is preeminently a generational discourse, it is also a historically specific formation that articulates with the shifting contours of the late twentieth century. The dominant themes expressed in hip hop develop their creative shape in relation to a social world in which new forms and sites of political antagonism proliferate. Romanticized descriptions of hip hop portray its emergence as an explicit reaction against the racially conservative policies of the Reagan presidency. However, the seeds of this movement were planted much earlier. The elaboration of hip hop preceded the Reagan years; in fact, the movement began to blossom in the mid- to late 1970s.[55] The creators of hip hop devoted immense energy to carving out spaces of pleasure and recreation in the face of an eroding urban infrastructure devastated by a diminishing tax base, decaying public schools and parks, drugs, and political retreat from the redistributive policies born from the civil rights era.[56] Hip hop began in public parks, on street corners, in subway terminals, and in apartment basements. It soon moved to community centers, dance clubs, radio airwaves, and later the visual media—music video, television, and cinema—thus accentuating what analysts claim is one of the central themes in the movement: the struggle over public space, who occupies it, and how its resources are put to use.

Yet it is the subsequent role of technology and the commodification of hip hop, more than anything else, that continues to drive and animate provocative debates about the relationship between youth, cultural production, and commercial media culture. Does the intrusion of technology and commodification—most notably, the mass production, distribution, and merchandising of rap music—conspire to dull the oppositional edges of hip hop? Moreover, is the participation of black youth in the popular cultural economy a legitimate expression of opposition? These questions, of course, rekindle debates about the capacity of commercial culture to contain oppositional cultural practices. But rather than view technology and commercial culture as resources that prohibit creative action, I would like to invert this idea and consider an alternative proposition instead: How do technology and commercial culture enable new repertoires of black youth agency and cultural production?

The use of technology to produce media cultural products was viewed by the early critics of commercial culture as an indication that mass production would enforce standardization and stifle creativity.[57] But technological innovations in the production of popular music, for example, facilitate the opposite effect: creativity has flourished, and new musical styles and genres continue to thrive.[58] Yet technology only provides the possibility for new practices to take shape; individuals adopt a technology and use it in creative ways that lead to new cultural formations. In the case of rap music production, digital technology, sampling machines, multitrack recording devices, and video forge new creative frontiers for "fresh" innovations and formations of youth culture.[59] The innovation of rap music production suggests that technology does not manipulate individuals but rather that individuals adopt and manipulate technology to accommodate their intentions.

Furthermore, the intersection of hip hop and technology vividly illustrates what Michael Schudson calls the integrative effects of mass-mediated culture on modern societies.[60] The electronic dissemination of hip hop has proved to be powerfully integrative. By that, I mean it has established the conditions for mobilizing a youth culture that is rapidly becoming global in scope as it connects youth from disparate conditions and places. For example, it would be impossible to make reference to the "hip hop nation" without the broadcasting capabilities of media technology. One of the most impressive attributes of the electronic media is their capacity to connect people and organize collective identities despite physical distance.[61] The communications media enable new forms of access to and association among communities that transcend geographical boundaries. The growth and spread of hip hop culture are an illustrative example.

While its origins in the United States are typically traced back to the urban polyglot of postindustrial New York City, the hip hop movement has expanded far beyond the local youth cultures of its social and geographical base. The electronic dissemination of hip hop multiplies its constituency, complicates its articulations, and serves as the primary circuit through which youth have been able to produce an expanding sphere of influence within the rapidly evolving global media village. To be sure, the hip hop nation is an "imagined community."[62] But as Schudson points out, all communities are fictive in the sense that "personal identification with any grouping of people beyond those one encounters face to face in daily life depends on an imagined leap."[63] So while black youth in New York City, Mexican American youth in East Los Angeles, and black youth in Brixton, London, do not literally know each other, the various media technologies—music, video, film, print, and cyberspace—allow them to communicate, interact, and create new collective identities. In addition, it is the increasing prowess of media technology through which youth have been able to mobilize competing discourses about the varied social, economic, and political currents that continue to alter their lives. Hip hop, then, develops both local and global particularities that build a broad terrain for youth production and discourse.[64]

Whereas early critics of "mass" media culture viewed technology as stifling creativity and encouraging passivity, they were even less optimistic about the effects of commodification on culture. The diffusion of hip hop throughout the different spheres of commercial culture is commonly viewed as undermining the authenticity of this youth practice. For example, it is common to see the sartorial styles made popular in hip hop merchandised and packaged in suburban shopping malls. The contention, however, that commercial culture subverts the intentions and resistive qualities of hip hop is, at best, misguided. Tricia Rose insists that this critique obscures the fact that many of the original participants in hip hop (i.e., break dancers, rappers, disc jockeys) were in fact concerned with monetary compensation for their creative labor. Further, she makes the crucial point that "the contexts for creation in hip hop were never fully outside or in opposition to commodities, they involved struggles over public spaces and access to commodified materials, equipments, and products of economic viability."[65] Still, it must be acknowledged that, as the popularity and profits of hip hop soared, the rap industry has changed substantially. The major shift, according to Rose, is not that hip hop suddenly became commercial but rather that "control over the scope and direction of the profit making process"[66] has shifted from local black and Latino entrepreneurs to the major media and entertainment industries.

The corporatization of hip hop is undeniable. Since its popularization in the early 1980s, the profits of hip hop–related products have increased exponentially. As a result, the linkage of corporate strategies and marketing techniques with the expressive cultures of black youth undeniably alters the trajectory of hip hop. But the corporatization of hip hop reflects a more general trend toward the global spread of consumer culture made possible by new media technologies, marketing techniques, distribution patterns, and a wider conception of consumer markets as well as potential profits. It is indeed difficult to imagine any aspect of cultural life that has not been influenced by corporate culture.[67] In the case of hip hop, then, what has taken place is the joining of an urban street and youth aesthetic with the technological resources and distribution muscle of corporate organizations.

But the corporatization of hip hop seems only to enliven rather than to stifle the struggle to control its commercial vigor. Similar to other subcultural practices, hip hop creates its own symbolic universe and commodities. Furthermore, hip hop has made more explicit the political nature of popular culture. When emergent cultural practices disrupt the social equilibrium, they usually provoke the dominant culture to take some kind of action as a means of maintaining order.[68] Dick Hebdige argues that the process of recuperation typically comes in the form of co-optation and commodification or labeling. I would like to discuss the former.

The commodification of rap produces paradoxical results. For instance, recognition by the music industry—the Grammy and American Music Awards—validates its place as an "official" genre of popular music and therefore stimulates production. But commodification also domesticates and defuses rap of some of its subversive energy. Once distributed on a mass scale, rap is packaged and made more palatable, rendered at once a consumable good and profitable merchandise. But is commodification simply a form of containment? In other words, does the packaging of hip hop erode its oppositional possibilities? While it is true that the transformation of hip hop into a vast assortment of commodities alters its course, it is presumptuous to view commodification as the utter erasure of black youth agency and cultural politics. For as Hebdige points out:

[T]he relationship between the spectacular subculture and the various industries which service and exploit it is notoriously ambiguous. After all, such a subculture is concerned first and foremost with consumption. ... It communicates through commodities even if the meanings attached to those commodities are purposefully distorted or overthrown. It is therefore difficult in this case to maintain any absolute distinction between commercial exploitation on the one hand and creativity/originality on the other, even though these categories are emphatically opposed in the value systems of most subcultures.[69]

It would be a mistake to assume that black youth have been idle in, or even resistant to, efforts to merchandise hip hop. For as historian Robin D.G. Kelley reminds us, black youth meticulously hone their expressive cultures and forms of play and leisure into income-gener-ating practices.[70] Few today understand the exuberant and sometimes subtle ways in which black youth maneuver to exploit a cultural marketplace that generates a seemingly endless flow of commodities produced to satisfy changing consumer desires and tastes. One of the most striking ironies of late twentieth-century capitalism is the simultaneous structural and economic displacement of black youth along with the emergence of a voracious appetite for the cultural performances and products created by them. In the process, some black youth have been able to translate their creative labor into social and economic mobility as they carve out small entrepreneurial enclaves while still practicing, in their unique way, "small acts" of opposition.

Dipannita Basu sharply illuminates this point in her observation of Los Angeles's hip hop community.[71] Basu asserts that participation in commercial culture by black youth is *not* a sign of surrender to the recuperative powers of capitalism but is instead a crucial element in their attempt to counter some of its most crippling effects. In fact, many youth do not view association with the popular culture industry as a form of "selling out." In her discussion of the burgeoning rap industry in Los Angeles, Basu writes: "[R]ap music has given a substantial number of black youth a world view, a political philosophy, a language, and lifestyles that have in turn become the articulating principles for economic activity, from creativity to business, from music to films, magazines, clothing, and a whole host of auxiliary position."[72]

Admittedly, it is difficult to imagine that striving for and achieving economic success in a capi-talist society are oppositional. Such practices are typically viewed as complying with rather than subverting the dominant priorities of capital accumulation. But as Basu claims, black youth do not see a contradiction in their efforts to "get paid" and simultaneously contest the institutional prac-tices that severely limit their prospects for social and economic mobility. No action or gesture is inherently oppositional. Social context determines the extent to which practices develop opposi-tional characteristics. The potential economic benefits and prestige associated with rap music pro-duction are viewed as a direct challenge to a social and economic structure that is becoming increasingly impenetrable for a number of black youth. From the perspectives of black youth, then, the production of popular commodities and economic success belie the widespread belief that they are criminal-minded and lack industriousness, intelligence, and a commitment to work.[73] So even though black youth turn their symbolic practices and creative skills into work that reproduces the master ideal of capital accumulation (a principle that historically works to their disadvantage), it is work that enables some to escape the serial employment and menial labor widely regarded as humiliating, stigmatizing, and oppressive.[74]

Angela McRobbie has described youth subcultures as practices that are both productive and empowering. According to McRobbie, the styles and commodities created by youth do more than just publicize subcultures. These practices also provide opportunity for cultivating skills that can be utilized to provide access to substantive employment or even self-employment. She writes: "[T]his involvement can be an empowering experience, particularly for young people with no access to the skills and qualifications acquired as a matter of course by those other young people destined for university and for the professions. Subcultures are often ways of creating job opportunities as more traditional careers disappear. In this undocumented, unrecorded and largely 'hidden economy' sector, subcultures stand at one end of the culture industry spectrum and the glamorous world of the star system and the entertainment business at the other."[75] To the degree that hip hop has produced an alternative economy that provides the resources and opportunities for black youth to exert their own creative energies and also realize their entrepreneurial ambitions, it can be viewed as a formation that enlivens rather than subverts the ability of youth to more effectively negotiate social and economic deprivation.

Consequently, rather than challenge the legitimacy of capitalism, black youth confront a more immediate problem—how to turn the contradictory contours of capitalism to their advantage. The strategic movement of black youth into commercial culture does not intend to destroy a flourishing information and entertainment economy. On the contrary, their skillful interventions drive the production and commodification of cultural products. Still, while it is true that they do not seek to subvert the notion of capital accumulation, black youth do seek to play a more substantial role in the rapidly expanding frontier of communications media and information technology. Describing this distinctive generational ethos, journalist Kevin Powell writes: "[T]he hip hop nation is no different than any other segment of this society in its desire to live the American dream. Hip hop, for better or for worse, has been this generation's most prominent means for making good on the long promises of the civil rights movement."[76] Black youth maneuver to exploit those emergent spaces that are opening up in the new information economy. And in the process of struggling for that space, black youth continue to shape the popular cultural world in which we all live.

It should also be noted that while some hip hop purists claim that commodification erodes the subversive demeanor and style of hip hop, the youth culture did not develop explicitly political expressions until after the road to commercial success had been paved. In truth, the earliest rap recordings were mostly first-person narratives that boasted about the acquisition of status-conferring objects: jewelry, designer clothing, and women. And though narratives that portrayed women as sources of heterosexual male pleasure were certainly political, they did not embody the counterideological themes that would later be labeled "message rap."[77] The production of message rap developed as the rap genre was becoming commercial. Indeed, the arrival of rap groups like Public Enemy in the late 1980s signaled a decisive turn in the politicization of rap lyrics. Thus, it is quite possible to argue that by enlarging the creative terrain of rap production, commodification, ironically, forged open spaces that now include styles and performances that nourish rather than impoverish resistive discourses.

Yet we must also bear in mind that black youth are operating on historical terrain clearly not of their own making. Moreover, the sphere of popular media culture is only one of numerous sites where the struggle for hegemony is waged. Additionally, the transformative powers of each site differ. For example, the symbolic efficacy of holding a political office (Newt Gingrich) versus occupying a niche in the arena of popular music production (Ice Cube) differs in kind and extent. Therefore, it must be acknowledged that the potency of black youth intervention on the field of popular culture has serious limitations for effecting social change. Still, it must also be noted that oppositional practices come in different guises and are governed by different intentions. Black youth are acutely aware of the social world they inhabit and that current structural arrangements produce limited opportunities for their generation. This particular formation of black youth culture is, then, a strategic attempt to make use of the fissures produced by social, economic, and technological change.

So while it is true that hip hop did not originate as an explicit critique of the rising tide of racial conservatism, its growth, evolution, and multiple deployments illustrate how the cultural politics, moods, energies, and lived experiences of everyday life provide black youth with the resources and imaginative capacities to respond creatively to material and symbolic domination. The evolution of hip hop teaches us, as cultural critic Michael Dyson writes, "that history is made in unexpected ways, by unexpected people with unexpected results."[78] As youth continue to re-create hip hop, they also continue to penetrate and shape the popular media cultures, which are becoming global in scope. In fact, hip hop has generated a broad range of cultural products that enlarge its creative community and sphere of influence. The diffusion of hip hop throughout mainstream culture has led to the creation of new independent record labels, magazines, television programs, and advertising campaigns.[79] More important, the success and spread of hip hop culture have forged open productive spaces for young cultural producers beyond the field of popular music.

Like their contemporaries in the production of rap music, black filmmakers attempt to exercise similar modes of agency and intervention in the intensely mobile world of information technology. Whereas the producers of rap attempt to manipulate the new technologies and distribution systems that govern popular music production, filmmakers, in like fashion, attempt to manipulate the new technologies and distribution systems that govern popular film production. But because commercial film is a more expensive arena of production, breaking through industry barriers is a far more formidable task. Besides, the commercial film industry is extremely insular, and practices of nepotism and cronyism are customary. The producers of commercial film tend to constitute a closed inner circle whose members are constantly recycled within the industry. Commercial film is a profession that requires specialized training, large sums of capital, and expensive equipment. Discussing the costs involved in film production, Robert Withers writes:

> Perhaps only architecture can begin to rival it in the amount of capital required for production, and in the potential demand for laborers. The high cost of filmmaking has always placed limitations on the kind of work filmmakers could do, and the financial risk involved has consistently affected the relationship between producers and audiences.... Because of its high cost, film production is generally controlled or influenced by those powers in a society that command financial resources and determine how products are distributed.[80]

It is perhaps the high cost of film production that, historically, has limited the effective participation of African American filmmakers. However, for a select group of African American filmmakers, the transformation of the popular cultural landscape and the popularization of black youth expressive cultures changed the prospects for their own filmmaking careers.

Also, the production of black cinema is driven by the constant search for new consumer markets and expressive cultures to exploit. Historically conditioned opportunities in the production of popular film create productive spaces for the post–civil rights generation of African Americans that did not exist for previous generations. This is not to suggest that African Americans have never participated in the production of film but rather that the combination of a new film industry landscape, a changing cultural marketplace, and a more vibrant black culture industry establishes a creative environment in which the film narratives created by African American filmmakers attain greater commercial value. These particular arrangements work to give a small group of African American filmmakers a precarious niche along the production hierarchy of commercial film.[81]

The creation of popular cultural movements like hip hop suggests that black youth struggle to mobilize their own meanings about and representations of societal change. George Lipsitz argues that the emergence of new cultural producers and popular movements is made possible by the very economic shifts that also produce historically distinct forms of social and economic inequality: flexible accumulation.[82] It is crucial to point out, however, that the new formations in capitalism and the global spread of communications media do not intentionally produce new popular movements or expressive cultures. Rather, the new economic regimes, media technologies, and popular culture economy provide the resources and opportunities that make it possible for new symbolic practices to be created by historically situated cultural producers. The immediate challenge, then, is to further examine how the new media-scape enables black youth to creatively intervene in the making of the larger popular cultural universe.

Study Questions

1. How have black youth used digital technologies to combat inequality?
2. How have black youth utilized popular culture to critique the political establishment?
3. How has the value of digital technologies been lessened by the inaccessibility of such technologies to those most in need?

Notes

1. Kelley (1997, 224).
2. Herman Gray (1995) contends that commercial media culture is a primary site for producing discourses about and representations of blackness.
3. See Brain's (1994) theoretical discussion of the relationship between the production of symbolic artifacts and the reproduction of social relations and social-political hierarchies.
4. Hall (1981b) discusses the theoretical tension between these two positions.
5. Hall (1992, 24).
6. Gray (1995, 2).
7. Hall and Jacques (1990, 17).
8. This is a quote from a popular rap song by the Goodie Mob (1995).
9. For some good examples of this genre of scholarship, see Hebdige (1979). Willis (1977), Frith (1981), Lipsitz (1990), Gilroy (1993), Gray (1995), Rose (1994b), McRobbie (1991), and Boyd (1997).
10. Kelley (1994b, 11).
11. See Griswold (1994).
12. Swidler (1986).
13. For a more elaborate discussion of what Raymond Williams refers to as dominant, emergent, and residual forms of culture, see Williams (1977).
14. For a more elaborate critique of the dominant ideology thesis, see Abercrombie et al. (1980).
15. For an example of this view, see Wilson (1987).
16. For a succinct, yet informative, discussion of the transformation of urban life and the construction of postindustrial cities, see Katz (1989, 124–84).
17. Schor (1991, 39–41).
18. For engaging explorations on the schooling of black and poor Americans, see Kozol (1991). Kirschenman and Neckerman (1991) discuss the discriminatory hiring practices of employers against black youth. Anderson (1980) also addresses the racially inflected tensions black youth face on the job site. For a discussion of the self-esteem and confidence of poor black youth, see Nightingale (1993).
19. The Center for the Study of Social Policy (1992) reports that the United States has a greater percentage of its youth living in poverty than other advanced capitalist nations.
20. M. Davis (1992, 306).
21. Center for the Study of Social Policy (1992) and Lerner (1995).
22. Edsall and Edsall (1992).
23. Wattenberg (1995).
24. For a full discussion of the three phases, see Gans (1995).
25. A variety of symbol handlers and cultural producers have played a role in the making of the "underclass" label. While the work of social scientists and politicians has been important, the news-reporting conventions and visual strategies employed by the national news media played a crucial role in the broad circulation and use of the label. In 1977, *Time* magazine ran a cover-story feature on the "underclass." The photos accompanying the story focused primarily on black and Latino poor inner-city residents. Also, in 1978, ABC News produced a prime-time news-story feature that focused on dislocated youth and the escalation of juvenile delinquency. The feature was titled "Youth Terror: The View Behind the Gun." Moreover, what is interesting about this news piece is that it is unnarrated. The producers of the program

elected to create a documentary-style news report that certainly appealed to viewers as an authentic representation of black and Latino youth dislocation. In the late 1980s, CBS News produced the feature "The Vanishing Black Family," which also visualized the "underclass" for television viewers. To be sure, black and Latino youth have been central in the creation and visualization of the label. For analysis of the formation and politics of the label, see Katz (1991 and 1989), Gans (1995), and Lemann (1991).

26. The culture-of-poverty position essentially argues that the poor suffer not from structural and economic problems but rather from cultural deficiencies. The emphasis from this perspective is on family history, lifestyles, and the behavior of the poor. The term itself was born from the work of anthropologist Oscar Lewis (1968), who coined it to describe the rural poor in Mexico. The concepts behind the term, however, have been fashioned to discuss and explain the poor in the United States. Whereas Lewis developed the term to discuss how the poor adapt to impoverished conditions in ways that tend to facilitate the reproduction of poverty, the manner in which conservatives have claimed and defined the culture-of-poverty discourse seems to blame impoverished conditions on the culture and behavior of the poor. For a critique of the term, see, for example, Katz (1989 and 1991), Wilson (1987), and Steinberg (1981).

27. For a full discussion of the public arenas model, see Hilgartner and Bosk (1988).

28. Gordon (1994, 125–26).

29. Katz writes, "[T]he term underclass offers a convenient metaphor for use in commentaries on inner-city crises because it evokes three widely shared perceptions: novelty, complexity, and danger. Conditions within inner cities are unprecedented; they cannot be reduced to a single factor; and they menace the rest of us. The idea of the underclass is a metaphor for the social transformation embedded in these perceptions" (1991, 3).

30. To be sure, the specific manner in which the news media work to suppress their ideological dimensions in the selection, organization, packaging, and presentation of news is also crucial. For example, Campbell (1991) stresses that TV news stories operate as "narratives" that follow familiar boundaries of plot, character, setting, problem, resolution, and synthesis. Tuchman (1979) and the Glasgow University Media Group (1980) focus on how filmic conventions tend to legitimate news's claims of representational facticity. Hall (1981a) argues that television news conceals its ideological operations by offering itself as authentic visual transcriptions of the "real world."

31. Campbell and Reeves (1994, 38).

32. For studies of how the news media construct images and definitions of race, see, for example, Hartman and Husband (1981), Dijk (1987), Entman (1990 and 1994), and Jacobs (1996). The growing body of literature suggests that the news media typically address issues of racial conflict and protest rather than racism.

33. For a discussion of the function of the news media, see Gans (1979, 290–99).

34. Ericson, Baranek, and Chan (1987) examine how the news media produce images and definitions of deviance.

35. TV news can be viewed as a form of popular culture due, primarily, to its role in TV entertainment and the formulaic conventions that news workers employ. During the last few decades, many of the local news media affiliates have adopted a strategy referred to by some critics as "If it bleeds, it leads." This is a reference to the fact that producers of television news often shape the content and form of broadcast news in ways that can compete for higher ratings and higher revenue. In particular, television news stories are increasingly accompanied by graphic images and horrific descriptions of murders, acts of terrorism, and plane crashes.

36. In his discussion of the media's discovery of the mods and rockers, Cohen (1972) defines a moral panic as follows:

> Societies appear to be subject, every now and then, to periods of moral panic. A condition, episode, person, or group of persons emerges to become defined as a threat to societal values and interests; its nature is presented in a stylized and stereotypical fashion by the mass media . . . and other right-thinking people. . . . Socially accredited experts pronounce their diagnoses and solutions; ways of coping are evolved or (more often) resorted to; the condition . . . deteriorates and becomes more visible. Sometimes the object of the panic is quite novel and at other times it is something which has been in existence long enough, but suddenly appears in the limelight. Sometimes the panic is passed over and forgotten, except in folklore and collective memory; at other times it has more serious and long-lasting repercussions and might produce such changes as those in legal and social policy or even in the way society conceives itself. (p. 28)

37. For a more detailed analysis, see Campbell and Reeves (1994).

38. Clandestine footage usually involves a TV camera crew's following a drug bust, or drug raid, into someone's place of residence.

39. Reeves and Campbell (1994) argue that the (re)writing of the cocaine narrative follows a journalistic rite

of inclusion/exclusion. The authors write: "[R]ites of inclusion are not centrally about Us versus a marginal Them, but, instead, are devoted generally to the edification and internal discipline of those who are within the fold. Rites of inclusion are, in other words, stories about Us: about what it means to be Us; about what it means to stray away from Us ... about what it means to be welcomed back to Us" (p. 39). Alternatively, rites of exclusion "are preoccupied with sustaining the central tenets of the existing moral order against threats from the margins. News reports that operate in this domain emphasize the reporter's role of maintaining the horizons of common sense by distinguishing between the threatened realm of Us and the threatening realm of Them" (pp. 41–42).

40. See Gordon (1994).
41. Various local ordinances in cities like Los Angeles; Dallas and Austin, Texas; Minneapolis; and New Orleans have been established to exercise greater control over youth. The enforcement of dress codes is a direct attempt to discipline the body. For example, in Irving, Texas, a suburb of Dallas, a large mall recently prohibited the wearing of baseball caps backward, baggy pants, or other "gang" paraphernalia. Many cities have also turned to nightly curfews that generally target black and Latino youth. See M. Davis (1992) for a discussion of how curfews are arbitrarily enforced in Los Angeles.
42. I use the term *symbolic capital* in this instance similarly to Bourdieu (1990), who refers to the capacity of cultural creators to enforce meaning, label, and define our world. I should also note that the symbolic capital gained by a rapper like Ice Cube in the commercial culture arena works differently, for instance, than the symbolic capital gained by a political figure like Newt Gingrich in the arena of legislative politics. Both are cultural producers. Both also attempt to pattern discourses about urban ghetto life. However, their efforts to shape the symbolic landscape take place on different terrain. More important, there is a differential in the kind and extent of power each terrain provides.
43. Rose (1994, 60).
44. Fischer contends that the study of technology and society can be broadly divided into two areas: technological determinism and symptomatic approaches. For a complete discussion of these two approaches, see Fischer (1992, 8–21).
45. Ibid., 17.
46. Ibid.
47. Indeed, the persistent call for regulating control over media content is driven by the belief that youth are especially impressionable and therefore vulnerable to media messages. Thus, the introduction of the V-chip is a more recent illustration of how prevalent technological determinism is in the larger public imagination.
48. Nightingale's (1993) study examines the experiences of black youth in Philadelphia.
49. For a more detailed discussion of the various alienation theories on black urban poverty, see Nightingale (1993).
50. Social movements come in different forms. Immediate examples of social movements include the civil rights movement, New Right conservatism, and feminism. Some representative work on social movements and social theory can be found in Morris's (1984) analysis of the civil rights movement and its relationship to the black church and political networks or the classic theoretical statement on the contexts and content of movements by Piven and Cloward (1979).
51. While hip hop is commonly associated with black American youth, the imprint, for example, of Caribbean musical forms on hip hop is clearly evident. Elsewhere, U.S. cultural critic Tricia Rose (1994b) and British cultural critics Isaac Julien and Paul Gilroy map out the African diasporic elements embedded in rap. See, for example, Gilroy (1993) and Julien's independent film feature *The Darker Side of Black* (1994). Julien discusses, for example, the similarities between gangsta rap in the United States and dance hall reggae in Jamaica (Grundmann 1995).
52. See Toop (1984), Guevara (1987), and Rose (1994b) for discussions of the formation of hip hop culture.
53. See Boyd (1997) for a more elaborate analysis of the class and generational dimensions of black popular culture forms.
54. See Guevara (1987) and Rose (1994b) for examples of this genre of scholarship. Also, Carby (1986) discusses the sexual politics of black women and the production of blues music.
55. For an interesting journalistic history of hip hop culture, see Owen (1994–95).
56. For discussions of the relationship between the transformation of urban life and the formation of hip hop culture, see, for example, Rose (1994b), Kelley (1994b), Cross (1994), and Boyd (1997). For an excellent discussion of the social and political retreat from racial equality, see Steinberg (1995).
57. The pessimistic viewpoints regarding the influence of electronically produced popular media cultures over capitalist societies were vehemently expressed by members of the Frankfurt school. For an example of this view, see Adorno and Horkheimer (1989). Also, for a history of the theories, ideas, and significance of the Frankfurt school approach, see Wiggershaus (1994). For an example of how the Frankfurt school influenced media studies, see Rosenberg and White (1957).

58. See, for example, Gendron (1987) and Kealy (1982).
59. See Rose (1992) for an informative discussion of the relationship between new music-recording technologies and rap music production.
60. Schudson (1994) considers how communications media technology establishes a context for societal integration and nation building.
61. See Meyrowitz (1985) for an intriguing analysis of how electronic forms of media transform social behavior and relations.
62. Anderson (1983) examines some of the factors crucial to how members imagine themselves to be part of a national culture.
63. Schudson (1994, 24).
64. I do not want to suggest that hip hop is expressed in a uniform fashion. For instance, rap varies sharply across regions, styles, subgenres, and gender. Nor do I want to suggest that there is a monolithic constituency operating within the hip hop community. Indeed, different subjective positions, ideas, and experiences are communicated through hip hop, thus creating a vastly diverse body of discourses and cultural practices. See Cross (1994) for a discussion of how hip develops locally specific features.
65. Rose (1994b, 40).
66. Ibid.
67. For example, the Internet, the Olympic Games, collegiate athletics, and national political party conventions have all been uniquely transformed as a result of their relationship to the corporate sphere. For a more complete discussion of the corporatization of culture, see Schiller (1989).
68. Williams (1977) discusses the relationship between what he calls hegemonic, residual, and emergent cultures. Williams argues that dominant, or hegemonic, cultures must always contend with emergent cultures that are constantly struggling to destabilize the hegemonic center.
69. Hebdige (1979, 94–95).
70. Kelley (1994a).
71. Basu's analysis (1997) is based on observational studies of how the rap music recording industry has created niches of entrepreneurship for black youth in Los Angeles.
72. Basu (1997). Greg Tate, a longtime observer and analyst of hip hop, contends that rap music is arguably the first black American expressive culture that African Americans have commercially exploited as much as, if not more than, whites.
73. For a candid discussion of white (and black) employer perceptions of black youth, see, for example, Kirschenman and Neckerman (1991).
74. See Anderson (1980) for an analysis of the disdain black youth developed toward menial labor.
75. McRobbie (1994, 161–62).
76. Powell (1996, 46) discusses hip hop culture as an avenue of social mobility for some black youth in the context of Death Row Record label, a successful producer of gangsta rap in particular.
77. For a discussion of the rise, vitality, and contradictions of message rap, see Allen (1996).
78. Dyson (1996, 77).
79. Take, for example, the rap entrepreneur Russell Simmons. Simmons started out as a rap performer but soon realized that his talents were best put to use on the business side of the hip hop industry. Using rap music as his core product, Simmons has created a multimillion-dollar entertainment company that features television sitcoms, cable television specials, and clothing merchandise (Hicks 1992). Simmons talks openly about the commercial viability of rap and the drive by many African Americans to exploit its commercial success (Marriott 1992).
80. Withers (1983, 8).
81. African American filmmakers who have achieved a notable degree of commercial success tend to be male graduates from prestigious film programs and business schools. For example, Spike Lee attended New York University film school, and John Singleton received several awards for writing while attending the University of Southern California filmic writing program. Reginald and Warrington Hudlin received their training from Harvard and Yale Universities, respectively. George Jackson, a successful producer of black films, graduated from Harvard Business School.
82. Lipsitz (1994) considers how changes in technology and the globalization of popular media cultures generate the possibility for aggrieved populations to engage in new forms of cultural production and resistance.

References

Abercrombie, Nicholas, et al. 1980. *The Dominant Ideology Thesis.* London: G. Allen & Unwin.
Adorno, Theodor W., and Max Horkheimer. 1989. *Dialectic of Enlightenment.* New York: Continuum.
Allen, Ernest. 1996. Making the Strong Survive: The Contours and Contradictions of Message Rap. In *Drop-*

pin' Science: Critical Essays on Rap Music and Hip Hop Culture, edited by Eric Perkins. Philadelphia: Temple University Press.

Anderson, Benedict. 1983. *Imagined Communities: The Origins and Spread of Nationalism.* London: Verso.

Anderson, Elijah. 1980. Some Observations of Black Youth Employment. In *Youth Employment and Public Policy*, edited by Bernard E. Anderson and Isabel V. Sawhill, 64–87. Englewood Cliffs, N.J.: Prentice Hall.

Basu, Dipannita. 1997. The Economics of Rap Music: An Examination of the Opportunities and Resources of African Americans in the Business of Rap Music. Paper presented at the American Sociological Association Annual Meeting, Toronto, Ontario.

Boyd, Todd. 1997. *Am I Black Enough for You?: Popular Culture from the 'Hood and Beyond.* Bloomington: Indiana University Press.

Brain, D. 1994. Cultural Production as 'Society in the Making': Architecture as an Exemplar of the Social Construction of Cultural Artifacts. In *The Sociology of Culture: Emerging Theoretical Perspectives*, edited by Diana Crane. Cambridge, Mass.: Blackwell.

Campbell, Richard. 1991. *60 Minutes and the News: A Mythology for Middle America.* Urbana: University of Illinois Press.

Carby, Hazel. 1986. It Jus Be's Dat Way Sometime: The Sexual Politics of Women's Blues. *Radical America* 20, no 4: 9–22.

Center for the Study of Social Policy. 1992. *Kids Count: Data Book: State Profiles of Child Well-Being.* Washington, D.C.: Center for the Study of Social Policy.

Cohen, Stanley. 1972. *Folk Devils and Moral Panics: The Creation of the Mods and Rockers.* London: MacGibbon & Kee.

Cross, Brian. 1994. *It's Not about a Salary: Rap, Race, and Resistance in Los Angeles.* London: Verso.

Davis, Mike. 1992. *City of Quartz: Excavating the Future in Los Angeles.* New York: Vintage.

Dijk, Teun A. Van. 1987. *Communicating Racism.* Newbury Park, Calif.: Sage.

Dyson, Michael Eric. 1996. *Between God and Gangsta Rap: Bearing Witness to Black Culture.* New York: Oxford University Press.

Edsall, Thomas, with Mary Edsall. 1992. *Chain Reaction: The Impact of Race, Rights, and Taxes on American Politics.* New York: Norton.

Entman, Robert. 1990. Modern Racism and the Image of Blacks in Local Television News. *Critical Studies in Mass Communication* 7, no. 4 (December): 332 45.

———. 1994. Representation and Reality in the Portrayal of Blacks on Network Television News. *Journalism Quarterly* 71, no. 3 (autumn): 509–520.

Ericson, Richard V., Patricia M. Baranek, and Janet B.L. Chan. 1987. *Visualizing Deviance: A Study of News Organization.* Toronto: Toronto University Press.

Fischer, Claude. 1992. *America Calling: A Social History of the Telephone to 1940.* Berkley: University of California Press.

Frith, Simon. 1981. *Sound Effects: Youth, Leisure, and the Politics of Rock 'n' Roll.* New York: Pantheon Books.

Gans, Herbert J. 1979. *Deciding What's News: A Study of CBS Evening News, NBC Nightly News, Newsweek, and Time.* New York: Pantheon Books.

———. 1995. *The War against the Poor: The Underclass and Antipoverty Policy.* New York: Basic Books.

Gendron, B. 1987. Theodor Adorno Meets the Cadillacs. In *Studies in Entertainment*, edited by T. Modleski. Bloomington: University of Indiana Press.

Gilroy, Paul. 1993. *The Black Atlantic: Modernity and Double Consciousness.* Cambridge, Mass.: Harvard University Press.

Glasgow University Media Group. 1980. *More Bad News.* London: Routledge.

Gordon, Diana R. 1994. *The Return of the Dangerous Classes: Drug Prohibition and Policy Politics.* New York: Norton.

Gray, Herman. 1995. *Watching Race: Television and the Struggle for "Blackness."* Minneapolis: University of Minnesota Press.

Griswold, Wendy. 1994. *Cultures and Societies in a Changing World.* Thousand Oaks, Calif.: Pine Forge Press.

Grundmann, Roy. 1995. Black Nationhood and the Rest of the West: An Interview with Isaac Julien. *Cineaste* 21, no. 1–2 (winter-spring): 28–30.

Guevara, Nancy. 1987. Women Writin' Rappin' Breakin'. In *The Year Left 2: Essays on Race, Ethnicity, Class, and Gender*, edited by Mike Davis et al. New York: Verso.

Hall, Stuart. 1981a. The Determinations of News Photographs. In *The Manufacture of News: Social Problems, Deviance, and the Mass Media*, edited by Stanley Cohen and Jack Young. London: Constable.

———. 1981b. Notes on Deconstructing the Popular. In *People's History and Socialist Theory*, edited by Raphael Samuel. London: Routledge.

———. 1992. What Is This 'Black' in Black Popular Culture? In *Black Popular Culture*, edited by Gina Dent. Seattle: Bay Press.

Hall, Stuart, and Martin Jacques, eds. 1990. *New Times: The Changing Face of Politics in the 1990s*. London: Verso.

Hartman, Paul, and Charles Husband. 1981. The Mass Media and Racial Conflict. In *The Manufacture of News*, edited by Stanley Cohen and Jack Young. London: Constable.

Hebdige, Dick. 1979. *Subculture: The Meaning of Style*. London: Methuen.

Hicks, Jonathan. 1992. A Big Bet on the Godfather of Rap. *New York Times*, June 14, sec. 3, pp. 1, 6.

Hilgartner, Stephen, and Charles L. Bosk. 1988. The Rise and Fall of Social Problems: A Public Arenas Model. *American Journal of Sociology* 94, no. 1: 53–78.

Jacobs, Ronald N. 1996. Civil Society and Crisis: Culture, Discourse, and the Rodney King Beating. *American Journal of Sociology* 101, no. 5: 1238–1272.

Katz, Michael B. 1989. *The Undeserving Poor: From the War on Poverty to the War on Welfare*. New York: Pantheon Books.

———. 1991. *The "Underclass" Debate: Views from History*. Princeton, N.J.: Princeton University Press.

Kealy, Edward R. 1982. Conventions and the Production of the Popular Music Aesthetic. *Journal of Popular Culture* 16, no. 2 (fall): 100–115.

Kelley, Robin D.G. 1994. *Race Rebels: Culture, Politics, and the Black Working Class*. New York: Free Press.

———. 1997. Playing for Keeps: Pleasure and Profit on the Postindustrial Playground. In *The House That Race Built: Black Americans, U.S. Terrain*, edited by Wahneema Lubiano. New York: Pantheon.

Kirschenman, Joleen, and Kathryn M. Neckerman. 1991. "We'd Love to Hire Them, but . . . ": The Meaning of Race for Employers. In *The Urban Underclass*, edited by Christopher Jencks and Paul E. Peterson. Washington, D.C.: Brookings Institution.

Kozol, Jonathan. 1991. *Savage Inequalities: Children in America's Schools*. New York: Crown.

Lemann, Nicholas. 1991. *The Promised Land: The Great Black Migration and How It Changed America*. New York: Knopf.

Lewis, Oscar. 1968. The Culture of Poverty. In *On Understanding Poverty: Perspectives from the Social Sciences*, edited by D.P. Moynihan. New York: Basic Books.

Lipsitz, George. 1990. *Time Passages: Collective Memory and American Popular Culture*. Minneapolis: University of Minnesota Press.

———. 1994. *Dangerous Crossroads: Popular Music, Postmodernism, and the Poetics of Place*. London: Verso.

Marriott, Michael. 1992. Hip-Hop's Hostile Takeover: Rap Joins the Mainstream. *New York Times*, September 22, sec. 9, p. vi.

McRobbie, Angela. 1991. *Feminism and Youth Culture: From "Jackie" to "Just Seventeen."* Boston: Unwin Hyman.

———. 1994. *Postmodernism and Popular Culture*. New York: Routledge.

Meyrowitz, Joshua. 1985. *No Sense of Place: The Impact of Electronic Media on Social Behavior*. New York: Oxford University Press.

Morris, Aldon. 1984. *The Origins of the Civil Rights Movement: Black Communities Organizing for Change*. New York: Free Press.

Nightingale, Carl Husemoller. 1993. *On the Edge: A History of Poor Black Children and Their American Dreams*. New York: Basic Books.

Owen, Frank. 1994–95. Back in the Days. *Vibe* (December–January): 66–68.

Piven, Frances Fox, and Richard A. Cloward. 1979. *Poor People's Movements: Why They Succeed, How They Fail*. New York: Pantheon Books.

Powell, Kevin. 1996. Live from Death Row. *Vibe* (February): 44–50.

Reeves, Jimmie, and Richard Campbell. 1994. *Cracked Coverage: Television News, Reaganism, and the Journalistic Crusade against Cocaine Use*. Durham, N.C.: Duke University Press.

Rose, Tricia. 1992. Black Texts/Black Contexts. In *Black Popular Culture*, edited by Gina Dent. Seattle: Bay Press.

———. 1994a. Black Males and the Demonization of Rap Music. In *Black Male: Representations of Masculinity in Contemporary American Art*, edited by Thelma Golden. New York: Whitney Museum of American Art. Distributed by N.H. Abrams.

———. 1994b. *Black Noise: Rap Music and Black Culture in Contemporary America*. Hanover, N.H.: Wesleyan University Press.

Rosenberg, Bernard, and David Manning White, eds. 1957. *Mass Culture: The Popular Arts in America*. Glencoe, Ill.: Free Press.

Schiller, Herbert I. 1989. *Culture Inc.: The Corporate Takeover of Public Expression*. New York: Oxford University Press.

Schot, Juliet B. 1991. *The Overworked American: The Unexpected Decline of Leisure*. New York: Basic Books.

Schudson, Michael. 1994. Culture and the Integration of National Societies. In *The Sociology of Culture: Emergent Theoretical Perspectives*, edited by Diana Crane. Cambridge, Mass.: Blackwell.

Steinberg, Stephen. 1982. *The Ethnic Myth: Race, Ethnicity, and Class in America*. Boston: Beacon Press.

————. 1995. *Turning Back: The Retreat from Racial Justice in American Thought and Policy.* Boston: Beacon Press.

Swidler, Ann. 1986. Culture in Action: Symbols and Strategies. *American Sociological Review* 51: 273–286.

Toop, David. 1984. *The Rap Attack: African Hand Jive to New York Hip Hop.* Boston: South End Press.

Tuchman, Gaye. 1978. *Making News: A Study in the Construction of Reality.* New York: Free Press.

Wattenberg, Ben. 1995. *Values Matter Most: How Republicans or Democrats or a Third Party Can Win and Renew the American Way of Life.* New York: Free Press.

Wiggershaus, Rolf. 1994. *The Frankfurt School: Its History, Theories, and Political Significance,* translated by Michael Robertson. Cambridge, England: Polity Press.

Williams, Raymond. 1977. *Marxism and Literature.* New York: Oxford University Press.

Willis, Paul. 1977. *Learning to Labor: How Working Class Youth Get Working Class Jobs.* New York: Columbia University Press.

Wilson, William Julius. 1987. *The Truly Disadvantaged: The Inner City, the Underclass, and Social Policy.* Chicago: University of Chicago Press.

Withers, Robert S. 1983. *Introduction to Film.* New York: Barnes and Noble Books.

44

An Exploration of Spectacular Consumption

Gangsta Rap as Cultural Commodity

As useful as popular culture and digital technologies have been to those who wanted to challenge the status quo through music, both structures also offer access to those who would employ them to further circulate narratives of oppression, violence, sexual violence, and pathology.

In his essay, Eric K. Watts offers insight into the ways gangsta rap, a popular and profitable sub-genre of rap in the 1990s, exploited access to the mainstream marketplace and emergent technologies to reproduce narratives of sexism and misogyny. As such, gangsta rap helped to normalize such expression and behavior in popular culture and corporate boardrooms.

An Exploration of Spectacular Consumption: Gangsta Rap as Cultural Commodity

Eric K. Watts

Gangsta rap narratives are treated as testimonials that provoke conflicted strategies for constituting urban African American male identity and social intercourse. I argue that hard-core rap artistry participates in a complex and fluid set of economic exchange relations among the lived experiences of artists, the operations of a consumer culture, and the dictates of rap music industry. The concept of "spectacular consumption" is posited as a discursive template for understanding how rhetorical strategies of self-promotion in gangsta rap artistry alter and are altered by the sophisticated interdependence among private, public, and economic spheres.

> I'm a product of your sins / though you say I never heard of ya / a killer, a dope dealer, gangsta / murderer, merciless maniac / monarch of manipulation / primary focus of your local police station ... (C.P.O., 1992, p. 51)

> It's really sick / young brothers and sisters today have a lack of understanding about what it really means to be Black ... (Ice Cube, 1991)

> The Spectacle is the moment when the commodity has attained the total occupation of social life ... (Debord, 1983)

In 1991, *Rolling Stone* magazine, usually considered to be a liberally hip source of music criticism, seemed to be at a loss to explain the success of the latest album by Niggaz With Attitude (N.W.A.). "Hell has apparently frozen over," proclaimed the lead to the *Rolling Stone* story detailing the meteoric rise of N.W.A.'s last album as well as the phenomenal popularity of the so-called "gangsta rap" genre (Wilson, 1994, p. B25). The editors of the magazine seemed stupefied when they lamented that the "album was released without a single, a video, or even a track suitable for radio play. So how did it get to the top?" ("Beating up," 1991, p. 65). The answer to such an inquiry is both deceptively simple and surprisingly complex. It appears simple when we assume that market strategists can sell the average American consumer any kind of cultural expression, especially the racially provocative and perverse impulses of hard-core hip hop (Cocks, 1991; see also McAdams, 1991). Since it is both traditional and trendy for mainstream America to exploit and relish black cultural artifacts (hooks, 1990), the glimmering presence of gangsta rap merely stands as another example of a smart, expert market procedure. On the other hand, the answer becomes more complex if we shift from a perspective promoted by an overbearing consumer calculus and move toward a perspective that explores the ways in which consumerism is altered in correspondence with rap artistry's "political soul" of agitation and mobilization (Lusane, 1994b, p. 58). By shifting perspectives, we are encouraged to assess its "popularity" with a more meaningful discursive frame.

In an effort to explore the controversial and contradictory musical genre known as "gangsta rap," I develop a frame that recognizes the complex interactions among the material conditions of urban living, artistic production, and the culture industry, thus rectifying the problem of analytical isolation often experienced when taking a particular approach to cultural criticism. That is, many scholars have concerned themselves with the structure of hip hop discourse as a means of understanding its symbolic force (Dyson, 1996; see also Rose, 1994). Some critics have deconstructed the machinery of mass reproduction, treating the artifact as mere product of power (Crane, 1992; see also Jameson, 1991; Ewen, 1988). Still other analysts have viewed sociological data gathered in urban communities as the key to unlocking the secrets of hip hop discourse (Lusane, 1994a; see also Bell, 1992; Anderson, 1990). I offer an alternative frame based on the concept of "spectacular consumption" as an interpretive schema for defining and clarifying the relations among hip hop culture, gangsta rap narratives, and the interposition of an expanding rap industrial complex into the American culture industry.

In *Society of the Spectacle*, Guy Debord (1983) describes the spectacle as a general condition in a society oriented toward mass consumerism as a way of life. Moreover, the spectacle is constitutive of a separation of sign and signified wherein the market value of the detached image gets magnified—made spectacular—through the processes of mass production and distribution. Importantly, the spectacle is fully realized when the enhanced appearance of the image becomes more significant than the social world it previously represented. Jean Baudrillard (1993) argues that post-industrial societies have perfected modes of artistic replication so as to nearly eradicate the relationship between the sign and the signified, modifying the essence of both. Thus, spectacular consumption describes a process through which the lifeworld of the artist, the meaning of representation, and the operations of the culture industry get transformed based upon terms generated by public consumption of the art.

Elijah Anderson's (1994) conception of "street" and "decent" orientations can be used as a means of ordering and assessing the conflicted and brutal representations of urban living reproduced in the artistic performances of gangsta rap. I will demonstrate the way in which the social configurations of these orientations serve as rhetorical resources for the discursively captured and occupied sites of urban survival and conquest. Gangsta rap narratives are inscribed with compelling rationales concerning making a living in urban America. Artists attempt to offer good reasons supporting the strategies their narrative protagonists use to "make ends." And so, I hope not only to describe and evaluate rap strategies and the lifeworlds that promote them, but by understanding their service to spectacular consumption, critique the character of their relationship with the production of their mass appeal. I argue that the dialectical energies produced by the confrontation between the "street" and "decent" orientations to effecting better urban living provoke conflicting rhetorical strategies for civic life. These narrative strategies enter into a pact with American cultural outlets and are selectively enhanced so that urban (and suburban) youth can share in an artist's attempt to "live large" by replicating and consuming the imagery. I also contend that spectacular consumption can, in part, be seen as the cause and effect of a reproduction of the "street" orientation as the means for successful performance in both public and private sectors. Thus, spectacular consumption's tendency to commodify, over-value, and sell the "street" orientation must be recognized and critiqued. Lastly, I intend to show how this seller's market advertising gangsta rap artistry, in more than just a figurative way, also provides the "juice" for the invention of creative possibilities for reconstituting the terms of "making ends." But, in order to see more clearly the "public" and "private" self-performances of many urban youth and to hear the words of dissent and "dissing," let us begin our exploration on the streets.

The Street Orientation of the "Young and the Ruthless"

Playing on the name of a popular daytime soap opera, ABC's *World News Tonight*'s Peter Jennings labeled the teenage perpetrators of crime "the young and the ruthless" as he reported the grim statistics on the escalation in violent teenage crime. The criminal activity of today's youth, as well as the likelihood of their meeting with violent death had risen several hundred percentage points since 1988 (*World News Tonight*, 1994). But, as so often happens in these days of hit-and-run reporting, the story veered away from any substantive account of poverty, unemployment, drug abuse, broken dreams and shattered hearts to discuss President Clinton's crime bill. What frequently escapes public scrutiny is the fact that people living in these communities are pulled by contentious orientations toward self-empowerment and survival. However, for the University of Pennsylvania's Elijah Anderson, what the popular media overlooks in its search for tidy conclusions to its grim headlines becomes the special site of sociological inquiry.

Anderson (1994) identifies two conflicting worldviews ordering social interaction in urban America—"street" and "decent." According to Anderson, the "street" orientation is represented as a culture "whose norms are often consciously opposed to those of mainstream society" (Anderson, 1994, p. 82). On the streets, a different set of rules and guidelines structure interpersonal interaction, and one's ignorance of them can lead to unfortunate consequences. Thus, even though the majority of families in urban environments promote "decent" values, their children must be schooled in the ways of the street for self-defense. Conversely, a "decent" family is a loving, nurturing unit that has internalized traditional, mainstream American values—especially those associated with education and a strong work ethic. Children from these families tend to have a vital respect for themselves and others, constructing social and psychical living quarters out of the lessons passed on through meaningful interaction with community "old heads" (Anderson, 1990, p. 65). This issue is important for the present study for two reasons. First, many of the vital directions about the performance of "blackness" and "black manhood," as themes in a larger historical drama, get reproduced and passed on within these relationships.[1] Second, Anderson ascribes values associated with American morality to the "decent" orientation.

By contrast, since thoroughly street-oriented youth have little in the way of parental guidance and support in the home, they come of age in accordance with the outlaw code. And, "at the heart of the code is the issue of respect—loosely defined as being treated 'right,' or granted the deference one deserves" (Anderson, 1994, p. 83). Urban youth, whether oriented predominantly toward "street" or "decent," learn at an early age that aggression and toughness earn respect among peers. Being able to handle affronts, verbally and physically, is a valuable skill on the streets. As such, one's capacity to "dis" others while not being "dissed" enhances one's reputation and self-image. Given the fact that many of our youth come of age in urban centers blighted with poverty and an educational system overwhelmed and underfunded, it sometimes follows that our kids see themselves as damaged or deficient. Therefore the street environment poses a dangerously exciting game; a kind of "ghetto-rama" where players are eager to "campaign for respect" (Anderson, 1994, p. 86). The dictum is clear: the greater one's ability to decipher and execute the street code, the greater one's self-worth.

For inner-city young males in particular, the street code not only structures their daily interactions with others who are also "campaigning for respect," but provides them with precarious rites of passage into "manhood" (Anderson, 1990, p. 165). There is a complex relationship among the acquisition of material possessions, the maintenance of "juice" or respect, and the concept of manhood. A street-oriented young man has a particularly heightened sense of the importance of self-presentation because the respect others give him is disproportionately based on whether others see him as a potential threat. That is, his bearing and comportment in public are based on sending the undeniable message that he is not someone to be messed with.

To make matters more volatile, the assembly of expensive items for show enhances his juice. Jackets, sneakers, jewelry, cars, and women are treated as "trophies" (Anderson, 1994, p. 88) that demonstrate and create self-worth. As Ray Dog, of the Mighty RSO, says "[t]hat shit built up your self esteem" ("Reality check," 1994, p. 67). However, since to own it is to risk its loss, the flow of juice demands the defense of its wells. And therein lies the potentially deadly rub. For the more expensive the item, the more valuable the prize seems to another, the more likely he will be "stepped to" (confronted or challenged), the more frequent will be acts of physical violence and interpersonal crime. Since this brutal form of social intercourse is promoted and legitimized by the street code, his earnest participation in it already produces a certain amount of regard. In fact, his willingness to play the game signals his "readiness" for the street-coded manhood rituals. Meanwhile, those attempting to circumvent the code are judged as weak and are thus subject to attack precisely because they are viewed as easy prey.

Explicit in the dynamics of the street code is an award system for the unabashed use of aggression in lieu of diplomacy in social relations. Accordingly, a black male's "manhood" seems to rest on negotiating the combative terrain of the streets so as not to get "punked out," "beat down," or generally abused. Throw into this confrontational formula crack cocaine, gangs, and guns, and it is no wonder the black community is reeling from multiple blows delivered by its youthful citizenry and increasingly uncoupling from what some black and white leaders refer to as a "lost generation" (Vogel, 1994, p. 56). Paradoxically, Anderson and others adamantly argue that it is exactly the community "old heads" who must take a stand and initiate the young men into a more meaningful manhood, one steeped in the diverse and rich cultural history of family and black community ritual, rather than ruthless and rugged adventurism.

Given the unforgiving street orientation and its self-promoting norms, a generation of black youth left to find its own means of attaining selfhood has been accused of producing packs of "predators" who consume weaker or more "decent" youth to feed their voracious but delicate personae. Concomitantly, inner-city youth argue that running in gangs is an inevitable and necessary form of self-preservation. At a recent "gangsta rap summit," MC Eiht, formerly of Compton's Most Wanted, had this to say about the function and formation of gangs:

I couldn't see school. I couldn't see a job, I couldn't see moms, nobody. All I seen was the 'hood, the colors and I'm out there. I didn't give a fuck. Nigga put a strap [gun] in my hand. I had back [support] from about fifty niggas. So I didn't have to worry 'bout a nigga. All I had to do was throw on my khakis and my sweatshirt, put my rag in my back pocket and mothafuckas was intimidated by that shit.... ("Reality check," 1994, p. 67)

In any case, Anderson contends that the street-oriented black male is dissociated from the values corresponding to the traditional black family; he makes "the [street-coded] concept of manhood a part of his very identity, [but] he has difficulty manipulating it—it often controls him" (Anderson, 1994, p. 92). And it is precisely this sense of careening, intimidating public display that has alarmed civil authorities. "Ironically, this perceived dangerousness has become important to the public self-identity of many local black men." It is of special import that "[t]he public awareness is color-coded: white skin denotes civility, law-abidingness, and trustworthiness, while black skin is strongly associated with poverty, crime, incivility, and distrust" (Anderson, 1990, p. 168, p. 208).

With the mass production of gangsta rap and its massive array of detractors and supporters, with the public tribulation over violent street crime, the mounting concern over abuse against women and children, and racial tensions strangling important public debate, you may wonder aloud while reading the next section of this essay whether or not the '70s funk group, War, was on to something when it announced "The World Is a Ghetto."

Consumerism Meets Gangsta-ism: The Selling of a Street Code and Shock Appeal

Undeniably one of the most meaningful accomplishments of gangsta artistry has been to open a window on the daily, gritty grind of inner-city living. The social dynamics of the 'hood were largely obscure to mainstream America until the protestations of hard-core hip hop in the mid to late 1980s. Artists like Ice-T, Schooly-D, and N.W.A. emerged from the hip hop under-ground with shocking and touching portrayals of life and death. Other performers such as The Geto Boys, Tupac Shakur, Too Short, Warren G., D.J. Quik, and Snoop Doggy Dogg began to take us on tours of their blighted neighborhoods, forcing us to witness a devastating proces-sion of human roadkill. Gangsta artists relate to us stories about pimps, pushers, "niggas," "hoes," and "bitches," both real and imagined, who, like deer, are terrified and mesmerized by the dazzling headlights of oncoming perversion and mayhem.

In the 1980s, the West Coast quickly established itself as the center of foul-mouthed agita-tion, mainly through the music of N.W.A. On their first full-length album, *Straight Outta Compton*, the members of N.W.A., Easy-E, Dr. Dre, Ice Cube, MC Ren, and Yella, proudly announced that America was "now about to witness the power of street knowledge" (N.W.A., 1988). N.W.A. set the pace and the standard for gruesome and controversial passion on tracks like "Gangsta, Gangsta," where Ice Cube introduced himself as "a crazy mothafucka from around the way," and on "If It Ain't Ruff," where we came to know the troublesome and turbu-lent persona of MC Ren. Part of the significance of N.W.A. was that they realized that rebel-lious street norms could be exploited for economic gain and made to serve rhetorical ends. On "Parental Discretion Is Advized," N.W.A. warns us that there are necessarily some black issues and street-coded performances that will fall outside of mainstream America's comfortable understanding. Moreover, the promotion of the street code by America's political economy constitutes a conspiracy because it justifies the imposition of a form of marshal law in the ghetto. To punctuate this point, N.W.A. waves a defiant middle finger in the face of racist and oppressive social institutions on their infamous track, "Fuck Tha Police." In the song, a cop is dragged into "N.W.A. court," tried and "found guilty of bein' a red-neck, white-bred, chicken-shit mothafucker ... "[2] As Ice Cube explained in a later interview, "[i]t's like fuck Uncle Sam. We just narrowed it down to the police. Because the black kid out there don't give a fuck about who's mayor or who's governor or who's the president ... the police is the government in the ghetto" (Baraka, 1991, p. 33).

Having confirmed the financial viability of a hard-core street aesthetic (*Straight Outta Compton* sold 2 million copies), N.W.A., along with the self-proclaimed "Original Gangster," Ice-T, helped set in motion an impulse to describe and manipulate the horrors of the "United States Ghetto" ("Reality check," 1994, p. 70). Thus, artists began articulating a chaotic world where young urban males, locked in the grip of an unrelenting and unrepentant street code, are pressured to become what Compton's Most Wanted referred to as "trigger happy niggas" who are "ready for the apocalypse. ... " (Ice Cube, 1992). Ice Cube (1990, 1992) seems thor-oughly prepared for self-destruction when he speaks of "genocide" on "Endangered Species," and on "Now I Gotta Wet 'Cha" relishes the murders of those he views as doing him wrong: "Now wet mothafuckas all bloody 'cause a bullet will mold yo ass like silly putty ... comin' out yo back, Mr. Mack / now they got your guts in a sack. ... " Similarly, Ice-T (1991a) gives this account of where he's from: "I'm from South Central, fool, where anything goes / snatch you out of your car so fast you get whiplash ... gang-bangers don't carry no switch blades / every kid's got a tech-nine or hand grenade / 37 killed last week in a crack war / hostages tied up and shot in a liquor store / nobody gives a fuck … " Note the Geto Boys' classic trip into the deranged psychosis of a paranoid psychopath:

> Thinkin' I got to fuck somebody before the weekend / the sight of blood excites me / shoot you in the head, sit down and watch you bleed to death / I hear the sound of your last breath / shouldn't have been around, I went all the way left / you was in the right place with me at the wrong time I'm a psychopath in a minute, lose my fuckin' mind…. (Geto Boys, 1989)

Musical artists dramatizing the street code depict violent confrontation as a black ghetto norm, present misogyny as an organizing principle of sexual relations, and equate this mentality with mental illness. Underlying this characterization of the street code is the assumption that hip hop's so-called social pathologies are derived from America's ills. Despite the belief by legislators, politicians, and black community leaders that the civil rights movement secured human dignity for African Americans, gangsta rap artists maintain that those social institutions designed to promote human dignity and preserve civil order actually contributed to the reinforcement of the street code. Ice Cube (1990) strongly concurs with this assessment and offers a tremendous description of this process on the track, "The Product." In this song, Ice Cube highlights the role that prison plays in hardening an already rigid street code. Similarly, Snoop Doggy Dogg, premiering on Dr. Dre's (1992) first solo effort, laments in the song "Li'l Ghetto Boy," that "I spent four years in the county [jail] with nothin' but convicts around me / but now I'm back at the pound and we expose ways for the youth to survive / some think it's wrong, but we tend to think it's right. … " Also, Tupac Shakur (1993) alludes to the manufacture of an oppressive selfhood on "Keep Ya Head Up," when he remarks that "I was give [sic] this world, I didn't make it. … "

Interestingly, in this song ostensibly dedicated to bolstering the spirits of black urban women, Tupac Shakur also identifies what is arguably the production line for much of the misogynistic tendencies in hard-core hip hop. Recall that Anderson contends that the street etiquette validates the objectification of women in terms of their potential sexual and "juice" values, and in the process discredits the historical and cultural significance of black womanhood (Anderson, 1990). In song after song, black women are assumed to be "skeezers" or "hoodratz" (*Compton's Most Wanted*, 1992). And so, a street-oriented young man may view a woman as a pawn to be played in the larger chess game for respect. The "ownership" of an attractive young woman builds a young man's self-esteem in a way similar to the donning of a fresh, new pair of Air Jordans. But, since the development of genuine affection is discouraged by the street credo of acquisition, this social-exchange dynamic encourages female abuse. Therefore, it is ironic that as Tupac raps for the elevation of women, in tracks like "I Get Around" he relies on the very code that compels him to put them down. In gangsta artistry, women are routinely referred to as "hoes" and "bitches" who justify their degradation by scheming against men, using sex as a lure for financial gain. The population of artists who frequently represent women in this manner is too large to characterize fully here, but N.W.A.'s (1991) "One Less Bitch" serves as a prime example:

> In reality, a fool is one who believes that all women are ladies / A nigga is one who believes that all ladies are bitches / And all bitches are created equal / to me, all bitches are the same / money-hungry, scandalous groupie hoes! / that's always ridin' on a nigga's dick / always in a nigga's pocket / and when a nigga runs outta money, the bitch is gone in the wind / to me, all bitches ain't shit. …

Easy E's (Eric Wright) misogynistic protestations can be profitably exploited by more than just a mass-marketed culture industry. If we listen carefully, we can discern how N.W.A. gleefully acknowledge participation in their self-promotion as "niggas" who condemn women by limiting their self-realization to the status of "bitches" and "hoes" in a perverse dramatization of street-oriented relations. Not only is manhood mutated into "nigger-hood," and the black female mystique twisted into prostitution, but N.W.A. suggest that their caricatures should be taken as such. That is, they consistently hint that their "raging erections" (Reynolds, 1991, p. 27) display what Nelson George (1992, p. 156) calls "cartoon machismo," a commercialized spectacle designed to thrust the street code through the doors of corporate boardrooms.

As "maniacs" and "lunatics" stalk our city streets, as car-jackers murder tourists for the keys to rental cars, and as this mayhem is sampled and shipped to record stores so that the marketers of the shameless are "once again beatin' on your mothafuckin' eardrums" (N.W.A., 1991), we find ourselves doing an absurd kind of public dance, both retreating and advancing to the frenzied cadence of spectacular consumption. Long gone are the days of wine and roses and whimsical waltzes in New York City's Central Park. Now we participate in a media-orchestrated bump-and-grind—a wild "wilding" where our social sensibilities are gang raped (Baker, 1993). This spectacle makes for great TV because consumers love to talk about hating to eat it (Hughes, 1993), and since the intensity of the pleasure of perverse consumption is directly related to our gross diet, we want nastier stuff to digest. Indeed, Americans can't seem to get enough of this commercial indigestion because somehow we all sense that there is an essential void we need to fill.

As we peer down the dark and frequently dangerous streets of our urban communities, the sense of a psychical abyss can overwhelm us. Listen to Elijah Anderson's voice as it echoes softly into that openness:

> Simply living in such an environment places young people at special risk of falling victim to aggressive behavior. Although there are often forces in the community which can counteract the negative influences ... the despair is pervasive enough to have spawned an oppositional culture ... [t]his hard reality can be traced to the profound sense of alienation from mainstream society and its institutions felt by many poor inner-city black people, particularly the young. The code of the streets is actually a cultural adaptation to a profound lack of faith.... (Anderson, 1994, pp. 81–82)

And so perhaps the "young and the ruthless" show symptoms of social heresy because they suffer from a kind of dis-ease transmitted by "[l]iving in a post-industrial, Reagan-molded, increasingly-racist, anti-immigrant, less tolerant, more sexist, Jesse-dissing, King-beating, Quayle-spelling, Clarence Thomas-serving America. ... " (Lusane, 1992, p. 37). It is hardly surprising that, given the apparent loss of hope in urban America, hard-core rap would be center stage in the searing debate about how to save our children (Saunders, 1994).

As generational wisdom and black-folk beliefs fall into the gulf separating the "old heads" and the "young bloods," historical, cultural discontinuity is displayed through acts of mutual cynicism. Reporting on an interview with the President of the National Political Congress of Black Women, Kierna Dawsey makes this disturbing observation: "Although some of us will, it's a little scary that Dr. [Dolores] Tucker would assume that Snoop Doggy Dogg, or me for that matter, cares that she marched with King ... [a]t this very moment, the gap between the generations in Black America is as wide as the Sahara. 'Kids have it better today,' she tells me. Really?" (Dawsey, 1994, pp. 58–59). As lessons learned through a "street" orientation seemingly take the place of black-folk lifestyles inscribed within a "decent" orientation, and as "music in the combat zone" (Pareles, 1990) irritates the antagonism between the two worldviews, cultural critics of diverse ideological hues are looking toward the heavens for spiritual guidance regarding the "hole in our soul."

Using the "down-home" idiom that rebukes a philistine-like, anti-blues, dead aesthetic,

Martha Bayles (1994, pp. 3–4), in *Hole in Our Soul*, documents the tailspin that popular culture has endured since the rebellious, yet devoted '60s generation. Bayles traces the evolution of the black folk spiritual through the blues and jazz factions to what she perceives as the decadence of today's pop music scene. Of particular importance is the manner in which Bayles demonstrates the joint influences of a peculiarly American aesthetic and an overblown consumer economy on pop music and on black artistry.

This Harvard graduate provides a comprehensive account of African New World music and details its trials and tribulations as it participates in a conscious effort at cultural reclamation. She takes Theodor Adorno to task for not really understanding the psychical motivations of jazz and, after negotiating the diverse ideological terrain of modernity, she arrives at the threshold of "postmodernity," which is when she claims nearly all things go wrong for art. Instead of the triumph of postmodernity over modernity, the victory of popular culture over "high" culture, Bayles contends that at least some strains of postmodernism are fetid achievements of "perverse modernism" over modernism. Moreover, Bayles (1994, p. 387) believes that perverse modernism exhibits the ability of a Western "civilization" to champion an aesthetic that seeks, as its guiding principle, to destroy the idea of morality as such. By this she means that despite postmodernity's claims of a liberating aesthetic, one that blurs distinctions so as to undermine oppressive forms of elitism, Bayles argues that perverse modernism thrives by promoting the myth that there is no "good" (read "moral") art. Ensconced in this myth is the conception that the vulgar subverts elitism and that the masses can celebrate their common experiences through the cultural reproduction of the mundane. Since this move also eliminates the restrictions that morality used to place on art through the dictates of "fine taste," it follows that the baser, more "obscene" the artifact, the more palatable its form for mass consumption.

At this point, perverse modernism is prepared to pounce and capitalize on the seediest forms of cultural expression, with the skillful support of some culture industry brokers. For Bayles (1994, p. 345), gangsta rap answers the call for self-perversion because it caters to its own lowest common denominator. By obscuring the fact that some "popular" music can also be "good" in terms of decency and morality, perverse modernism provokes a jubilee wherein patrons feast on the vile and vicious, at the same time provoking the awkward question, what is *really* what?

I want to be careful here because this question cannot be answered simply by saying that art imitates life, or that the music is just entertainment (Jones, 1993), or that rappers talk "the real shit" (Shecter, 1991, p. 24). What we need to do at least is to delve into the interstices of popular cultural production. The battle lines in the debate over whether or not hard-core rap possesses insightful commentary or seeks to merely shock and incite are nearly as blurry as the lines between art and life itself in post-industrial American entertainment (Hughes, 1993). But we need to understand that this is only part of the scenario. By linking rap theatrics with punk and heavy metal imagery, Bayles paints a larger picture that includes the accusation that a European Anglocized aesthetic strategy fosters the perverted turn for youthful desire. The fact that black art has historically performed at the core of a white pleasure principle leads this critic to the poignant, yet overly determined conception that the insatiable hunger of predominantly white youth dictates the flow of "aggressive noise dominated [*sic*] sound; obscene violent lyrics; and emotions ranging from sadistic lust to nihilistic rage" (Bayles, 1994, p. 342). In sum, Bayles (1994) puts her point this way: "As we've seen, obscenity is the preferred weapon of those willing to do anything to get a rise out of the public. The faces are black, but the strategy is *European:* seek out a submerged anti-social custom that is considered marginal even by its participants, drag it kicking and screaming to the surface, and celebrate it as 'art'" (p. 352, my emphasis).

The fact that so-called gangsta rap narratives are complex collages of social proclamations booming out of previously muffled throats-angry, confused, frustrated voices speaking from what Robin D.G. Kelley (1992) calls the "social and spatial fringes" of our society—is a precious one. Lest we forget: the Geto Boys' Robert Shaw, a.k.a. Bushwick Bill, was actually shot in the head during a suicidal tirade (DeCurtis, 1991); 22-year-old Calvin Broadus did roll with the Long Beach Insane Crips before his album *Doggystyle* went multi-platinum and before he was charged with and tried for murder (Wilson, 1994; "Witnessess," 1995); the handsome and charismatic Tupac Shakur couldn't learn important lessons about becoming a man at home (Powell, 1994), and so he gleaned them from the street code pervasive in Marin City, California, and was charged with assaulting a limousine driver and shooting two off-duty Atlanta police officers, was convicted of sodomizing a fan in his hotel room and was recently murdered during a drive-by shooting ("Three rap sheets," 1995). Similarly, Chris Wallace, a.k.a. The Notorious B.I.G., was gunned down outside a Los Angeles night club (Kinnon, 1997); the 2-year-old son of the Wu-Tang Clan's, U-God, was critically injured in a Staten Island drive-by (Alexander, 1994); and the very real brilliance of Dr. Dre cannot excuse the fact that he man-handled the female host of a rap video show because he reportedly felt he was dissed on the air ("Microphone check," 1991).

My point is not simply that these artists exemplify a "street" orientation in their artistry and in their lives, but that there exists a spectacularly symbiotic relationship between the dictates of the street code and an energetic American consumerism. It looks somewhat like this: Taking Elijah Anderson at his word, we appreciate the manner in which the street code legitimates aggression in the pursuit of juice and manifests it in material possession. As rap artists graphically explore this reality, the processes of spectacular consumption become vivid. Gangsta rap artistry vivifies harsh imagery and its consumption establishes a set of exchange relations among public culture, rap music, and the rap industrial complex.[3] Moreover, these exchange relations legitimate themselves by pointing to increased market consumption and by increasing the status of some of its more talented spokespersons. For example, *Time* magazine asserted that N.W.A. climbed to No. 1 by "bearing down as hard as it always had," and by not selling out (Cocks, 1991, p. 78). Similarly, *The New York Times* suggested that "market research had shown demand for harsher lyrics," and so Rap-A-Lot records urged the Geto Boys to go insane (Parcles, 1990, p. 29). Therefore, as the street code gets explosively commodified and artists get juiced beyond their maddest dreams, they are compelled to maintain their celebrity status by "authenticating" their self-presentations in increasingly grittier street terms. And as rappers scramble to position themselves beyond the range of the kind of humiliating parody that 3rd Bass leveled at Vanilla Ice in their video, "Pop Goes the Weasel," their magnified rage and profiteering gets portrayed as the way it really is—everywhere. What this also means is that artists, encouraged to display the ferocity of street knowledge on and offstage, perform outrageous and seamless characters. The Harvard-trained former editor of *The Source* gives us this illuminating piece of reporting: "When N.W.A. hit No. 1, mainstream America was dumbfounded." " *People* magazine wanted to catch the group casually at home, sitting on their couch and smiling," a spokesperson from Priority told us. "I tried to explain to some 40-year-old white woman that they don't sit on their couch and smile. They're gangsters for God's sake' " (Shecter, 1991, p. 24). And so it would seem that Guy Debord (1983) was incisive when he argued that the "spectacle is not a collection of images, but a social relation mediated by images" (p. 4).

Undeniably there are those young men who have so thoroughly internalized the street code that, if they were not clever or talented artists, they would have a hard time putting the "street" orientation aside long enough to get through a standard job interview, but this issue only grazes the point. The hyper-reality and hyperbole of gangsta rap is constitutive of dynamic exchange relationships that make moot nearly all discussions of what is "real." If Snoop Doggy Dogg can appear on the Fox network with a harem of "trophies," boast about how he doesn't "love 'dem hoes" on the now-expired *Arsenio Hall Show*, roll through Long Beach and choose among many adoring fans while keeping a watchful eye out for Bloods or others who are just itching to "step to" the star (Hampton, 1993), what's the point of bickering about a distinction between fact and fiction?

Todd Shaw's argument that "Too Short" is a character and that he is a "businessman" who isn't "brainwashed by the shit I sing" (Dennis, 1992) has merit, but it doesn't resolve this dilemma. American popular culture is today constitutive of the vigorous exchange relations of spectacular consumption—an intensely overblown interactive consumer network where some black (and white) folk gladly sell their "souls" for a thrill ride toward ultimate juice and "manhood." Meanwhile, on the streets of the "United States Ghetto" rap artistry is celebrated as the profit-making industry that it most assuredly is and hailed for allowing brothers and sisters in the 'hood to share in the dissing of society's repressive institutions and leadership. In short, many hip hop enthusiasts are so because they get a chance to make something out of nothing, to participate in the transposition of poverty into profit by "punking out" America. And so, perhaps it's more meaningful to say that gangsta rap is neither fact, fiction nor some exotic combination, but part of an *overdose of commercialized reality*; that it constitutes some of the ugly and obscene excesses of pop culture and is constitutive of the mess we've gotten ourselves into; that it poses as death-on-a-stick, a low-fat, low-calorie poison that is sure to satisfy anyone's "appetite for destruction."

Part of the explanation resides in the fact that consumerism is in the midst of symbolically reproducing the street code, commodifying it in the form of an easy-to-open package of hip (Lacayo, 1994). This awesome replication and consumption of street-coded imagery is significant precisely because the processes of spectacular consumption are implicated not only in the validation of what becomes reasonable street protocol, but also in the promotion of strategies that can get anyone "jocked" by an entire MTV generation. And although I share Jonathan Alter's (1993) pained query, "How did we get to a point where 'art' became a code word for money?" (p. 67), there is a bit more at stake here than a requiem for a Platonic idealism in music.

For all the strengths of *Hole in Our Soul*, Bayles, in my opinion, not only overstates her case for perversion, but badly misreads the righteously imaginative funk of George Clinton and the political protestations of Chuck D. Part of the problem is that she treats rap discourse in precisely the same terms as holistic cultural movements. In truth, she doesn't engage rap as discourse at all, but understands it as the static feedback from the electrified colloquy of mass consumerism. And as piercing and insightful as she is when discussing our perverted "hole," she overlooks the fragments, traces, or momentary utterances of "soul" found in the ruptured speech of rappers like Ice-T and KRS-One. For example, Bayles (1994) derides KRS-One, of Boogie Down Productions, for his gangsta-style message on their debut album, *Criminal Minded*, and, therefore, backhandedly dismisses subsequent releases with the clipped retort, "[b]ut it was too late" (p. 353). Too late for what? In a single stroke, Bayles reveals a cultivated prejudice not only against hard-core rap, but against the recuperative energies of rhetoric. As a social production, the marketed articulations of the street code provoke idioms that speak synecdochically in our behalf. As such, they are vast and vital representations of our lost-and-found cultures and histories. Bayles exerts great energy describing gangsta rap's menacing "noise," but has very little sense of its evocative and provocative features; that is, the myriad ways in which rap performance invents life-affirming possibilities for "making ends." Perhaps, therefore, it is not surprising that this critic does not actively engage in the act of criticism.

With this said, the final section of this essay critiques the discursive competition between distinct rhetorical norms of black communal tradition, illuminating what counts as a reasonable lifestyle. Through a textual analysis of a selected rap text, I will demonstrate how the rhetorical resources of both the "decent" and "street" orientations constitute an important dialectical relationship in gangsta rap narrative. I will argue that this dialectic provides resistance against consuming impulses through inquiries into and assertions of strategic means for transfiguring urban livelihood.

The Street Hustler's Spectacular Paradox

Before both the "Cop Killer" controversy and the Warner Brothers split with Ice-T over "creative differences" (*USA Today*, 1993, p. D2), the motion picture *New Jack City* propelled the former gang member-turned-rapper into movie stardom. The successful soundtrack of the same name contained a virulent trek into the mind of gangsta. In "New Jack Hustler," Ice-T participates in a perverse spectacle in which the Hustler is consumed by a street-provoked obsession with materialism and consumes others with a voracious street-coded persona. By this I mean that the Hustler's identity is constituted through a near-seamless rapport with a street code composed of a consumer-dominated rationality. In the text, a commodified street code encourages the kind of behavior that translates into ghettoized profit and power.

> Hustler! / word, I pull the trigger long / grit my teeth, spray 'till every nigga's gone / got my block / sewn up my dope spot / last thing I sweat, some sucka punk cop / move like a king when I road hop / you try to flex, bang! / another nigga drop / you gotta deal with this 'cause ain't no way out / why? / cash money ain't never gonna play out / I got nothin' to lose, much to gain / in my brain I gotta capitalist migraine / I gotta get paid tonight, you mothafuckin' right / pickin' my grip, check my bitch, keep my game tight.... (Ice-T, 1991a)

From the outset the Hustler surveys his kingdom and metes out brutal forms of territorial control. When a dispute arises the challenger is violently dismissed. If we inspect the warrant supporting the Hustler's authority, we understand that it is defined in correspondence with a kind of virtual reality where aggressive norms are legitimized by a profit-oriented street code (ain't no way out ... cash money ain't never gonna play out). The fact that the Hustler feels as if he has "nothin' to lose" suggests the important point that he is apparently detached from a worldview that instills a sense of immanent self-worth based on communal forms of support and guidance. In this brief excerpt, we begin to understand how a Hustler views the conditions in which his selfhood is constituted.

> So many hoes on my jock, think I'm a movie star / nineteen, I gotta $50,000 car / go ta school? / I ain't goin' for it / kiss my ass / bust the cap on the Moet / 'cause I don't wanna hear that crap / Why? I'd rather be a new jack hustler. ...

The beginning of an enormous tension is revealed to us here. A traditionally stable form of initiation into social values and "manhood," the educational system, gets summarily dismissed in favor of a street-coded market consumption. Listen to this same rationale in an interview with MC Eiht: "If you gave a child an option, you can hang on the streets, sell dope, have the cars, the bitches or you can go to school eight hours a day, come home, can't go outside, go to church. You tell me which one you gonna pick? I'm going for the streets goddammit" ("Reality check," 1994, p. 74). Eiht's comment illustrates the notion that the "decency" orientation garners none of the precious commodity of juice for urban youth. Moreover, women are treated as "hoes" and "bitches" precisely because the Hustler views all community relations through a prism of street-jaded consumerism. These degrading labels signal women's status and value in a seemingly exigent materialistic hierarchy. But also notice that women are *jocking him* because of his enhanced status as trophy. The terms for this distorted social structure are, as Anderson points out, provided by a reckless "street" orientation that undermines traditional black folk sources of authority. In effect, then, the Hustler, in describing his justification for his way of life, clarifies the conditions for the development of his self-image.

This conception of nihilistic bravado, absurdly framed by an illusion of invincibility, begins to crack open, however, to reveal the inner chambers of the Hustler's psyche.

> What's up, you say you wanna be down? / ease back, a mothafucka get beat down / out my face, fool / I'm the illest / bullet proof / I die harder than Bruce Willis / got my crew in effect, I bought a new Jag / so much cash gotta keep it in Hefty bags / all I think about is t's and g's / imagine that, me workin' in Mickey D's / that's a joke 'cause I'm never gonna be broke / when I die it'll be bullets and gunsmoke / you don't like my lifestyle? / fuck you! / I'm rollin' with the new jack crew / and I'm a hustler. ...

With this latest turn we can see how the Hustler's social identity seems manufactured by Guy Debord's splendid machinery. The Hustler defines himself in terms brokered by an orientation that replicates humanity as commodity. Thus, it is easy to understand why to be broke is a fate worse than death ("never gonna be broke ... bullets and gunsmoke"). Since the Hustler's being is constituted through the pressures of a street code, and since it seems to be a foregone conclusion that one will meet with some kind of untimely death in the ghetto (Foster, 1994), poverty represents a kind of living nothingness. In a moving way, then, gangsta rap articulates an important perspective on the sad stasis of discharged personhood—the cultivated refusal by a cannibalistic consumer society to own up to its inability to meet its fabulous promises for livelihood. And so, the Hustler is a spectacular facade whose public performances both refute and sustain his status as a glamorous image. Debord (1983, p. 12) reminds us that this paradox is integral to the spectacle because one's brilliant *appearance* conceals the contradiction.

> Here I come, so you better break north / as I stride my gold chains glide back and forth / I care nothin' 'bout you, and that's evident / all I love is my dope and dead presidents / sound crazy? well it isn't / the ends justifies the means, that's the system / learned that in school, then I dropped out / hit the streets, checked the grip, and now I got clout / I had nothin' and I wanted it / you had everything and you flaunted it / turned the needy into the greedy / with cocaine my success came speedy. ...

The Hustler seems systematically trained for brutality. The ends-means rationale he references is not only influential in his production as a trophy, it binds him to the street orientation. The Hustler demonstrates an utter lack of consideration for the welfare of anyone. Not only does he allude to the prominence of degenerate consumption ("you had everything"), he internalizes the distorted lesson ("learned that in school") and executes its systems logic with cold efficiency ("with cocaine my success came speedy"). Importantly, notice how the glare of the spectacle ("you *flaunted* it") illuminates one potential set of strategies, while overshadowing alternative schemes constitutive of "decent" black communal processes. Materialism is presented here as everything that determines the Hustler's identity.

> Got me twisted, jammed into a paradox / every dollar I get another brother drop / Maybe that's the plan and I don't understand / Goddamn! / you got me sinkin' in quicksand / but since I don't know ain't never learned / I gotta get paid / I got money to earn / with my posse out on the ave, buck my sounds, crack a forty and laugh / cool out and watch my new Benz gleam / is this a nightmare or the American dream?

What we witness here is a kind of textual revelation (revolution?). Formerly, the Hustler only understood his social world in terms of a rigidly enforced mentality of street consumption. But here the Hustler briefly reconsiders his behavior from a different standpoint. The idea that his rampaging impulses may have been constituted through a devastating alliance between perverse materialism and a ruthless street ethic virtually flickers before his eyes. But, his overdetermined selfhood rationalizes the potential insight away.

By examining both the pragmatic and symbolic modes of production for the street code we find a social structure that emerges out of harsh economic despair. Also, by understanding that the code valorizes the campaign for respect and manhood in terms of the brutal acquisition of material goods, we can appreciate that in the absence of black folk values and cultural ritual, black personhood under these conditions can be constituted as "thug life" (Powell, 1994, p. 37). The Hustler's tale dramatizes the (near) triumph of street nihilism and individualism over the social responsibility traditionally embraced and celebrated by a vital black community. In other words, the Hustler is blinded by the glare of materialism, constitutes his social identity in accordance with the street code, and actualizes his self-worth as an objectified street agent by objectifying others; that is, by blinding others with the oppressive glare of his materialistic presence.[4] And, "maybe that's the plan. ... "

The rupture that the dialectic of the street/decent orientations creates in the text is fantastic. For an instant the Hustler re-orients his perception in terms of previously unrecognized values constitutive of black community (another *brother*—not nigga—drop) and vaguely apprehends the outlines of potential "genocidal catastrophe. ... " This dramatic shift in perspective is important in understanding that the competing rhetorical resources of the "street" and "decent" orientations destabilize the normativity of *both* orientations in the text. Jeffrey Louis Decker (1990) provides a valuable discussion of the symbolic process of dominance and subversion in *The Interpretation of American Dreams: The Political Unconscious in American Literature and Culture.* In brief, Decker argues that the meta-narrative of the American Dream denies harsh realities, while making poetic arguments on behalf of materialism. Put another way, the American Dream, as an endearing and enduring literary trope or ideograph, provides mythic justification for spectacular consumption. This is accomplished, says Decker (1990), because the American Dream demonstrates a mode of self-promotion fueled by a fictionalized "ideal of possibility" (p. 3) if you do the right thing. Gangsta rap disputes and sustains this warrant by drawing upon competing lifestyle codes as its chief rhetorical resources. And so, as Decker points out that there are other ways of dreaming, gangsta rap provides conflicted and contradictory testimony for the American Dream.

While "cooling out," the Hustler's insight into the absurd and unreasonable constitution of the American Dream is nearly blotted out by the gleam of a trophy of the Dream—the "new Benz." But the Hustler tacitly knows that the answer to his question, "Is this a nightmare or the American Dream?" must be *yes to both.* The Hustler's nightmare is exposed in a horrific collage of some of the sights and sounds of ghetto life:

> So think twice if you comin' down my block / you wanna journey through hell? / well shit gets hot / pregnant teens, children scream / life is weighed on the scales of a triple beam / you don't come here much and you better not / wrong move—bang—ambulance, cops / I gotta get more money than you got / so what if some mothafucka gets shot. ...
>
> That's how the game is played, another brother slain / the wound is deep but they givin' us a bandaid / my education's low, but I got long dough / I'm raised like a pitbull, my heart pumps nitro / sleep on silk, lie like a politician / my uzi's my best friend, cold as a mortician / lock me up, it's genocidal catastrophe / there'll be another one after me. ...

The psychical struggle the Hustler experiences here is remarkable. The dialectical perspective allows him to see the nightmare *despite* the brilliance of the Dream. This paradoxical image is produced by the conflicting rhetorical demands placed on the discourse by the "street" and "decent" orientations. Viewed in this way, the Hustler's tale is about how social economic processes bolstered by the American Dream and encoded in the materialistic aspect of street relations conceal nightmarish effects. Indeed, the "decent" orientation provokes the reference to a history of oppression as well as the speculation about forms of abuse ("with cocaine ... education's low ... raised like a pitbull"). However, this resistant space is always susceptible to the dictates of a street code that, through market impulses, becomes virtually consubstantial with realizing the American Dream. And so, in these final sections of this track, the Hustler partially recognizes the terms of his subjection, but continues to participate in it.

This precarious positioning is also evident if we emerge from the textual world of the "Hustler" and confront Tracy Marrow's (Ice-T) rap artistry. "New Jack Hustler" is a conflicted narrative because Ice-T uses a dialectical lens as a kind of refractory tool; he bends visions of reality so as to both blend and distinguish arguments justifying aggressive acquisition and the communal life it threatens. Ice-T (1991b) performs a similar maneuver in "Original Gangster," where he raps "for the brothers just like myself / dazed by the game and the quest for extreme wealth. ... " In this way, Ice-T constitutes an important confrontation of worldviews. Ice-T's comments on being imprisoned in the "jungle" reveal a source of destabilization for meaning: "The greatest tragedy in the ghetto is watching people become accustomed to the prospect of a bleak future.... I see the frustrations of this mind-set so clearly; I'm basically a product of it" (Marrow & Siegmund, 1994, p. 13). However, if this is so, then, gangsta rap's use of the "street" orientation allows for economic *possibility* while the "decent" orientation is constitutive of *impossibility*. Or, is it the other way around?

Conclusions

Yes, the Hustler is ultimately consumed by his own spectacle. However, the final line of the song, "there'll be another one after me," compels a fundamental question: What kind of social knowledge will emerge next? A hustler's? This question, in turn, maintains the destabilizing energy of the text. This is so because a critical audience is invited to further question and intervene in the commercial reproduction of social identity and knowledge (Rasmussen & Downey, 1991). We are shown a particular perspective on making a living in post-industrial America and on the flaws of strategies distinguished by individuation and profit.

Having made his name (not to mention his money) in hip hop, Ice-T represents some of the best and worst of perverse consumerism. His successes demonstrate the effectiveness of a rap discursive strategy that disrupts the strict polarity of the "street" and "decent" orientations. While his compelling brand of public discourse supports the mass appeal of the "street" orientation, his interrogation of *what it means to be successful* provides for moments of critical reflection. Indeed, these moments are crucial for it seems as though in order for gangsta rap to maintain its popularity, it increasingly has to submit to a form of tragic humiliation: The influence of market consumption on rap artistry is patently denied by the oft-repeated assertion of street authenticity. This refutation not only obscures corporate power, but it reifies a dangerous social equation. As rappers depict themselves as prowling "niggas," their popularity, as I mentioned before, relies on their "authenticating" these performances. And so black manhood is degraded within the dynamic intersticiality of "ghettonomics." This symbiosis among street dictates and market strategy is both revealed and strengthened by the gangsta artist's spectacular presence. However, for this dialectic to fulfill itself, it must do more than provoke talk about poverty and crime and how brothers are stuck in a market-induced dilemma. It must do more than mediate argumentative tensions through the imagery of despair and material deliverance. It must broker the articulation of the conditions under which an orientation can be rebuked, revised, or rejected.

To achieve this understanding, I contend that critics need to pay more attention to the terms of exchange and interaction among cultural performances, regulatory institutions, and the contours of our public culture. We must carefully assess the modes of transference and redefinition invented by and invested in speech performances. The areas, or "venues," occupied by these performances are, as Thomas Farrell (1993, pp. 284–285) elucidates, powerfully conflicted to the extent that the normative constraints exerted upon discourse can be called into question by interested others. It is this participatory stake that gives rise to the forms of rhetorical recuperation and transformation that Bayles dismisses. Surveying the ground of this stake allows critics to recognize, for example, how so-called gangsta rap narratives are colonized by strategic interests of culture industry, are constitutive of the unique and crucial interests of urban youth, and are re-inscribing the rules of a spectacular game (Roberts, 1995). In order to reflect upon, to question, the features and forms of spectacular consumption (the exhibition and exchange of bodies, assaults, sex, drugs, and treasures) critics need to become acquainted with the "performance conditions" of various realms (McKerrow, 1990, p. 24). To do so our epistemologies will need to resemble organic relations among diverse social practices. They could extend from within a kind of nexus where rhetoric benefits from anthropology, argument from aesthetics, and economics from semiotics. Framing the matter differently, my analysis clarifies the fact that it has become increasingly difficult to assess the character of conflicted, mediated cultural performances precisely because they cohabit in multiple social spheres at once. It is also increasingly pressing that we do so.

Study Questions

1. In what ways has popular culture made sexism and misogyny more accessible in contemporary times?
2. Has gangsta rap help desensitize youth to violence?
3. What is the relationship between gangsta rap and the logic of contemporary consumerism?

Notes

1. Anderson (1990, 1994) is not suggesting that institutions like the African American church and school systems have no important role in this process, only that they are, or ideally should be, secondary to traditional and non-traditional family structures.
2. This inflammatory track provoked an equally incendiary letter of protest by the FBI.
3. These exchange relations can be powerfully binding. Following the death of Tupac Shakur, the now jailed CEO of Death Row Records, Marion "Suge" Knight, told a reporter that he doesn't want "to give up gangsta rap, not at all. It is the real shit. It's not about us [record executives]. It's about the community; it's about our people, and we can't turn our backs on them." Not to mention the $100 million the record label earned in 1996 (Farley, 1996, p. 70).
4. This model was dramatized by Grand Master Flash and the Furious Five more than 15 years ago. As one of the first rap groups to explicitly discuss the root causes of living conditions in the ghetto, their song, "The Message," lamented that "a child is born with no state of mind / blind to the ways of mankind the places you'll stay and where you'll play looks like one big alleyway / you'll admire all the number book takers, thugs, pimps, and pushers, and big money makers / drivin' big cars, spendin' 20s and 10s / and you'll wanna grow up to be just like them!" (Grand Master Flash and the Furious Five, 1992, p. 152).

References

Alexander, D. (1994). Life is hectic. *The Source,* 56, 22.

Alter, J. (1993, November 29). Let's Stop Crying Wolf on Censorship. *Newsweek,* 81, 67.

Anderson, E. (1990). *Streetwise: Race, class, and change in an urban community.* Chicago: University of Chicago Press.

Anderson, E. (1994, June). The code of the streets. *Atlantic Monthly,* 24, 81–94.

Baker, H., Jr. (1993). *Rap and the academy.* Chicago: University of Chicago Press.

Baraka, R. (1991). Endangered species. *The Source,* 24, 33.

Baudrillard, J. (1993). *Symbolic exchange and death.* London: Sage Publications.

Bayles, M. (1994). *Hole in our soul: The loss of beauty and meaning in American popular music.* New York: The Free Press.

Beating up the pop charts. (1991, August 8). *Rolling Stone,* 66, p. 65.

Bell, D. A. (1992). *Faces at the bottom of the well: The permanence of racism.* New York: Basic Books.

Cocks, J. (1991, July 1). A nasty jolt for the pop charts. *Time,* 74, p. 78.

Compton's Most Wanted. (1992). *Music to driveby.* New York: Epic Records.

C.P.O. (1992). Ballad of a menace. In L. A. Stanley & J. Morley (Eds.), *Rap: The lyrics* (p. 51). New York: Penguin Books.

Crane, D. (1992). *The production of culture: Media and the urban arts.* London: Sage Publications.

Dawsey, K. M. (1994). Caught up in the (gangsta) rapture. *The Source,* 56, 58–59.

Debord, G. (1983). *Society of the spectacle.* Detroit: Black and Red Press.

Decker, J. L. (1990). *The interpretation of American dreams: The political unconscious in American literature and culture.* Unpublished doctoral dissertation, Brown University, Providence, RI.

DeCurtis, A. (1991, June 27). Geto Boy Bushwick Bill shot in head. *Rolling Stone,* 66, p. 17.

Dennis, R. (1992). Pimpin' ain't easy. *The Source,* 35, 35.

Dr. Dre. (1992). Li'l ghetto boy. On *The chronic.* |Compact disk|. Los Angeles: Interscope Records.

Dyson, M. E. (1996). *Between God and gangsta rap: Bearing witness to black culture.* New York: Oxford University Press.

Ewen, S. (1988). *All consuming images: Politics of style in contemporary culture.* New York: Basic Books.

Farley, C. J. (1996, September 30). From the driver's side: gangsta rap mogul "Suge" Knight finally breaks his silence on Tupac Shakur's murder. *Time,* 79, p. 70.

Farrell, T. B. (1993). *Norms of rhetorical culture.* New Haven, CT: Yale University Press.

Foster, D. (1994). The disease is adolescence. *Utne Reader,* 36, 50–56.

George, N. (1992). *Buppies, b-boys, baps, & bohos: Notes on post-soul black culture.* New York: Harper-Collins Publishers.

Geto Boys. (1989). Mind of a lunatic. In *Grip it! On that other level.* |Compact Disk|. Houston: Rap-A-Lot Records.

Grand Master Flash and the Furious Five. (1991). The message. In L.A. Stanley & J. Morley (Eds.), *Rap: The lyrics* (p. 152). New York: Penguin Books.

Hampton, D. (1993). G-down. *The Source,* 48, 64.

hooks, b. (1990). *Yearning: Race, gender, and cultural politics.* Boston: South End Press.

Hughes, R. (1993). *Culture of complaint: The fraying of America.* New York: Oxford University Press.

Ice Cube. (1990). Endangered species. In *Kill at will.* |Compact disk|. Hollywood: Priority Records.

Ice Cube. (1991). Us. In *Death certificate.* |Compact disk|. Los Angeles: Priority Records.

Ice Cube. (1992). Now I gotta wet'cha. In *The predator.* |Compact disk|. Los Angeles: Priority Records.

Ice-T. (1991a). New Jack hustler. In *New Jack city.* |Compact disk|. New York: Giant Records.

Ice-T. (1991b). Original gangster. In *Original gangster.* |Compact disk|. Los Angeles: Warner Bros. Records.

Jameson, F. (1991). *Postmodernism, or, the cultural logic of late capitalism.* Durham, NC: Duke University Press.

Jones, J. T., IV. (1993, November 3). Art or anarchy? Gunplay spurs rap debate. *USA Today,* p. D1.

Kelley, R. D. G. (1992, June 8). Straight from underground. *The Nation,* p. 794.

Kinnon, J. B. (1997, June). Does rap have a future? *Ebony,* p. 76.

Lacayo, R. (1994, August 8). If everyone is hip … is anyone hip? *Time,* 77, 48–55.

Lusane, C. (1992, September). Rap, race, and rebellion. *Z Magazine,* 28, p. 37.

Lusane, C. (1991a). *African Americans at the crossroads: The restructuring of black leadership and the 1992 elections.* Boston: South End Press.

Lusane, C. (1994b). Rap, race, and politics. *Alternative Press Review,* 1, 58.

Marrow, T., & Siegmund, H. (1994). *The ice opinion.* New York: St. Martin's Press.

McAdams, J. (1991, November 23). Credibility and commerciality. *Billboard,* p. R-4.

McKerrow, R. (1990). The centrality of justification: Principles of warranted assertability. In D. Williams & M.

Hazen (Eds.). *Argumentation theory and the rhetoric of assent* (pp. 17–32). Tuscaloosa, AL: University of Alabama Press.

Microphone check. (1991). *The Source*, 28, 18.

N.W.A. (1988). Straight outta Compton. In *Straight outta Compton.* |Compact disk|. Hollywood: Priority Records.

N.W.A. (1991). One less bitch. In *Niggaz4life.* |Compact disk|. Hollywood: Priority Records.

Pareles, J. (1990, October 7). Gangster rap: Life and music in the combat zone. *The New York Times*, p. 29.

Powell, K. (1994, February). This thug's life. *Vibe*, 2, p. 37.

Rasmussen, K., & Downey, S. D. (1991). Dialectical disorientation in Vietnam war films: Subversion of the mythology of war. *Quarterly Journal of Speech*, 77, 176–195.

Reality check. (1994). *The Source*, 56, 67–74.

Reynolds, S. (1991, November 2). Rap's reformation. *New Statesman Society*, p. 27.

Roberts, J. (1995, December 18). A piece of the action. *Newsweek*, 83, 48.

Rose, T. (1994). *Black noise: Rap music and black culture in contemporary America.* Hanover, MA: Wesleyan University Press.

Saunders, M. (1994, May 25). The oversimplification of "gangsta rap." *Boston Globe*, p. 30.

Shakur, T. (1993). Keep ya head up. In *Strictly 4 my N.I.G.G.A.Z ...* |Compact disk|. New York: Atlantic Records.

Shecter, J. (1991). Real niggaz don't die. *The Source*, 24, 24.

Three rap sheets, one R. I. P. (1995, April 10). *Newsweek*, 83, p. 74.

USA Today. (1993, January 20). p. D2.

Vogel, J. (1994). Throw away the key: Juvenile offenders are the Willie Hortons of the '90s. *Utne Reader*, 39, 56–60.

Wilson, Y. (1994, May 31). Back beat of pain and anger in music. *The San Francisco Chronicle,* p. B25.

Witnesses in rapper trial alter stories. (1995, December 5), *The Los Angeles Times*, p. B1.

World News Tonight with Peter Jennings. (1994, July). *ABC News.* New York.

Contributors

H. Samy Alim

H. Samy Alim is Associate Professor of Education and is affiliated with the Linguistic Center for Comparative Studies in Race and Ethnicity at Stanford University. He is author of *Roc the Mic Right: The Language of Hip Hop Culture* and *You Know My Steez: An Ethnographic and Sociolinguistic Study of Styleshifting in a Black American Speech Community*. He has also co-edited several books, including *Global Linguistic Flows: Hip Hop Cultures, Youth Identities, and the Politics of Language* (with Awad Ibrahim and Alastair Pennycook) and *Tha Global Cipha: Hip Hop Culture and Consciousness* (with James G. Spady and Samir Meghelli).

Davarian L. Baldwin

Davarian L. Baldwin is Associate Professor of History at Boston College. A historian, cultural critic, and social theorist of urban America, his work examines the landscape of global cities through the lens of the Afro-Diasporic experience. Baldwin's related interests include intellectual and mass culture, Black radical thought and transnational social movements, competing conceptions of modernity, the racial economy of heritage tourism, and universities and urban development. Baldwin is the author of *Chicago's New Negroes: Modernity, the Great Migration, and Black Urban Life*.

Andrew Bartlett

Andrew Bartlett holds a Ph.D. from the University of Washington, where his work focused on African American aesthetics after World War II. He is a freelance music critic and has worked at Amazon.com since the twilight of the 20th century, helping build the company's music business, the groundbreaking show, *Amazon Fishbowl* with Bill Maher, and, presently, a program for companies to advertise across Amazon sites. His writing has been published in *African American Review, Perspectives of New Music, The Encyclopedia of Northwest Music, The Da Capo Jazz and Blues Lover's Guide to the U.S., Musichound Jazz: The Essential Album Guide, Coda Magazine, Lingua Franca*, and elsewhere. He lives in Seattle with his wife and two kids.

Todd Boyd

Todd Boyd is The Katherine and Frank Price Endowed Chair for Study of Race and Popular Culture in the School of Cinematic Art at the University of Southern California. His books include *Young, Black, Rich, and Famous: The Rise of the NBA, the Hip Hop Invasion, and the Transformation of American Culture; The New H.N.I.C: The Death of Civil Rights and the Reign of Hip Hop.*; and *Am I Black Enough For You?: Popular Culture form the 'Hood and Beyond.* Boyd is also editor of *African Americans and Popular Culture*. His articles have appeared in the *New York Times, Los Angeles Times, Chicago Tribune,* and ESPN.com. Boyd has lectured to the NBA Players Association and the Nike Global Basketball Marketing department and in 1999, he produced and co-wrote Paramount Pictures' *The Wood.*

Craig Castleman

Craig Castleman's students at the High School of Art and Design on 56th Street first introduced him to New York City graffiti in the 1970s. Castleman was encouraged to extend his interest in the topic by one of his professors, noted anthropologist Margaret Mead. Castleman recalls, "I spent a year interviewing writers and cops and visiting yards and stations at all hours of the day and night and wrote *Getting Up* which got me my degree. I invited Lee, Bama, Tracy, Doc and a dozen more of my primary sources to attend my doctoral defense. The committee found their responses to questions more interesting than mine and ended up spending most of the time talking to them. When it was over, the writers and I stood around shaking hands and addressing each other as 'doctor'." After roughly three decades as a teacher of English as a Second Language in inner-city public schools Castleman relocated to Española, New Mexico where he is currently a professor of education at Northern New Mexico College.

Jeff Chang

Jeff Chang writes extensively on culture, politics, the arts, and music, having contributed to *The Nation, The New York Times, The San Francisco Chronicle, Foreign Policy,* and *Mother Jones,* among others; in 2007, he interviewed Barack Obama for *Vibe.* In 2008 he was both a USA Ford Fellow in Literature and winner of the North Star News Prize. His book *Can't Stop Won't Stop: A History of the Hip-Hop Generation* won the American Book Award and the Asian American Literary Award. Chang is also editor of *Total Chaos: The Art and Aesthetics of Hip-Hop.* Chang was a co-organizer of the first National Hip-Hop Political Convention in 2004.

Andreana Clay

Andreana Clay is Associate Professor of Sociology at San Francisco State University where she teaches courses on hip-hop culture and music, popular culture, queer studies, and contemporary theory. Her first book, *What Are We Fighting For?: Youth, Activism, and Post-Civil Rights Politics* is based on her research with youth of color activists in Oakland, CA. She has also published articles on Black youth and hip-hop culture; hip-hop feminism; and the use of hip-hop as a social justice tool for youth activists. Her current work focuses on race, gender, and sexuality in popular representations of Michael Jackson and the "queering" of Black male sexuality.

Greg Dimitriadis

Greg Dimitriadis is Professor of Educational Leadership and Policy at the University of Buffalo. He is author of *Performing Identity/Performing Culture: Hip Hop as Text, Pedagogy, and Lived Practice; Friendship, Cliques, and Gangs: Young Black Men Coming of Age in Urban America;* and *Studying Urban Youth Culture* as well as several collaborative publications. His work has appeared in numerous journals and Dimitriadis also edits the book series *Critical Youth Studies.*

Michael Eric Dyson

Michael Eric Dyson's critical acuity and insights about race, culture, and society make him one of America's most prominent public intellectuals and a powerful commentator on hip-hop culture. Among his many publications are *Between God and Gangsta Rap: Bearing Witness to Black Culture; Holler if You Hear Me: Searching for Tupac Shakur;* and *Know What I Mean?: Reflections on Hip Hop.* He is also co-editor (with Sohail Daulatzai) of *Born to Use Mics: Reading Nas's Illmatic.* Dyson is currently University Professor of Sociology at Georgetown University.

Juan Flores

Juan Flores is Professor of Social and Cultural Analysis at New York University. From 1994 to 1997 he served as Director of the Center for Puerto Rican Studies at Hunter College-CUNY. Flores is renowned for his theoretical analyses of diaspora and transnational communities, particularly concerning Puerto Rican studies and Latino and Afro-Latino culture. He is author of *Divided Borders: Essays on Puerto Rican Identity; From Bomba to Hip-Hop: Puerto Rican Culture and Latino Identity;* and *The Diaspora Strikes Back: Caribeño Tales of Learning and Turning.* Flores has served in an advisory role with the Latin Jazz Project of the Smithsonian Institution, the Afro-Latin@ Project, Recovering the Hispanic Literary Heritage, and Jazz at Lincoln Center. He is a recipient of a Ford Foundation grant and a National Endowment for the Humanities research fellowship.

Robert Ford, Jr.

Robert "Rocky" Ford, Jr. was among the first journalists to take hip-hop seriously. Ford covered the Disco, Soul and Black music sectors as a reporter at *Billboard* in the late 1970s. He was also a crucial player in the rise and success of Kurtis Blow, co-writing several of Blow's earliest hits and appearing on his recordings.

Murray Forman

Murray Forman is Associate Professor of Communication Studies at Northeastern University. He is the author of *The 'Hood Comes First: Race, Space, and Place in Rap and Hip-Hop* and *One Night on TV is Worth Weeks at the Paramount: Popular Music on Early Television,* for which he received a 2003–2004 National Endowment for the Humanities Fellowship. Dr. Forman serves on the Advisory Board of the Archives of African American Music and Culture as well as serving on editorial advisory boards of scholarly journals, including *The Journal of Popular Music Studies; Music, Sound, and the Moving Image; Souls: A Critical Journal of Black Politics, Culture, and Society;* and *Topia: Canadian Journal of Cultural Studies.*

Nelson George

A true renaissance man, Nelson George is an author, filmmaker, television producer, and cultural critic. Throughout the 1980s and 1990s George was a columnist for *Billboard* magazine and the *Village Voice* newspaper where he wrote about the emergent hip-hop culture. George's books on African-American music, culture, and politics include *Where Did Our Love Go: The Rise and Fall of the Motown Sound; The Death of Rhythm & Blues; Post-Soul Nation;* and *Hip Hop America* as well as co-writing *Life and Def* with hip-hop impresario Russell Simmons. He won a Grammy Award for his contribution to the liner notes on the James Brown *Star Time* 4 CD boxed set as well as co-editing (with Alan Leeds) *The James Brown Reader: 50 Years of Writing About the Godfather of Soul.*

Paul Gilroy

Paul Gilroy holds the Anthony Giddens Professorship in Social Theory at the London School of Economics. As a graduate student at the vaunted Centre for Contemporary Cultural Studies at Birmingham University he co-authored *The Empire Strikes Back,* one of the foundational texts of British Cultural Studies. A prolific writer, Gilroy's publications include *There Ain't No Black in the Union Jack; Small Acts: Thoughts on the Politics of Black Cultures; Between Camps: Nations, Cultures and the Allure of Race; Against Race: Imagining Political Culture beyond the Color Line;* and, most recently, *Darker Than Blue: On The Moral Economies of Black Atlantic Cultures.* His book *The Black Atlantic: Modernity and Double Consciousness* remains a benchmark in critical race studies.

Ela Greenberg

Ela Greenberg is currently an independent researcher working on Israeli-Palestinian issues at a non-profit organization in Jerusalem. Originally from Ann Arbor, Michigan she finished her Ph.D. in Islam and Middle East Studies at the Hebrew University of Jerusalem. Her research interests include Palestinian history, gender in the Middle East, education, and youth culture. She is the author of *Preparing the Mothers of Tomorrow: Education and Islam in Mandate Palestine*. From 2007 to 2009, she was a postdoctoral fellow at the Truman Institute for the Advancement of Peace where she conducted research on Palestinian youth culture in Jerusalem. She continues to listen to Palestinian hip-hop.

Mickey Hess

Mickey Hess is Associate Professor of English at Rider University where he specializes in creative writing, composition studies and popular culture. Hess is author of *Is Hip Hop Dead?: The Past, Present, and Future of America's Most Wanted Music*, and he edited the two-volume collection *Hip Hop in America: A Regional Guide* and two volumes of *Icons of Hip Hop: An Encyclopedia of the Movement, Music, and Culture*. His stories, essays, and critical articles have been published in journals and magazines ranging from *Punk Planet* and *McSweeney's* to *Popular Music and Society* and *Critical Studies in Media Communication*. He is also the author of the memoir *Big Wheel at the Cracker Factory*.

Marc Lamont Hill

Marc Lamont Hill is Associate Professor of Education at Columbia University. Trained as an anthropologist, his research focuses on the intersections between youth culture, identity, and educational processes, covering topics including hip-hop culture, politics, sexuality, education and religion. Hill is author of *Beats, Rhymes, and Classroom Life: Hip-Hop Pedagogy, and the Politics of Identity* and co-editor (with Lalitha Vasudevan) of *Media, Learning, and Sites of Possibility*. A regular commentator in the mainstream media, Hill is currently a political contributor for Fox News Channel. He is also engaged as a social justice activist and organizer working in several capacities including youth and adult literacy education.

Byron Hurt

Byron Hurt is an award-winning documentary filmmaker, a published writer, and an anti-sexist activist. His documentary, *Hip-Hop: Beyond Beats and Rhymes* premiered at the 2006 Sundance Film Festival. It was later broadcast nationally on the Emmy award-winning PBS series *Independent Lens*, drawing an audience of more than 1.3 million viewers. To date, *Hip-Hop: Beyond Beats and Rhymes* has been selected to appear in more than 50 film festivals worldwide and *The Chicago Tribune* named it "one of the best documentary films in 2007." In addition to being a filmmaker, Hurt is a nationally respected activist, challenging audiences to interrogate the damaging effects of patriarchy, racism, and sexism in American culture.

R. A. T. Judy

A Professor of English at Pittsburgh University, Ronald Judy's is the author of *(Dis)forming the American Canon: The Vernacular of African Arabic American Slave Narrative*. His research interests encompass literary theory, post-structuralist theory and post-colonial theory. His work involves exploring the ways in which particular "popular cultural movements" engage in thinking about the problems of authenticity and sovereignty in relation to an emerging global economy. This work includes an emphasis on the globalization of hip-hop. A co-editor of *boundary 2*, Judy's articles have also appeared in *Surfaces, Cultural Studies*, and *Noesis*.

Usama Kahf

Usama Kahf earned a Master's degree in Communication Studies from California State University, Long Beach where he focused on Arab-American feminism, cultural hybridity, ideological criticism and environmental activism. Kahf's interest in Arabic hip-hop stems from his early involvement with traditional Islamic and Arabic song ("nasheed") and he was co-founder of the West Coast percussion-based group NOOR. He is currently a Litigation Associate at the Los Angeles office of an international law firm.

Robin D. G. Kelley

Robin D. G. Kelley is one of America's top historians whose work focuses on social movements, labor, and race and class struggles. Professor of American Studies and Ethnicity at the University of Southern California, he is the author of numerous prize-winning books including *Hammer and Hoe: Alabama Communists During the Great Depression*; *Race Rebels: Culture Politics and the Black Working Class*; *Yo' Mama's DisFunktional!: Fighting the Culture Wars in Urban America*; and *Freedom Dreams: The Black Radical Imagination*, as well as co-authoring and editing several additional publications. His latest book is *Thelonious Monk: The Life and Times of an American Original*.

Raegan Kelly

Raegan Kelly is an interactive designer, programmer, cinematographer, and screen printer. Formerly the Co-Creative Director and site designer for *Vectors*, Kelly now works as an artist. She has a BA from University of California at Berkeley and an MFA in Film from California Institute of the Arts.

Cheryl L. Keyes

Cheryl Keyes is Associate Professor of Ethnomusicology in the Herb Alpert School of Music at the University of California, Los Angeles. She is the author of *Rap Music and Street Consciousness* and her research has been published in major journals such as *Black Music Research Journal*, *Ethnomusicology*, *Folklore Forum*, *Journal of American Folklore*, and the *Journal of Popular Music Studies*. Keyes became the first woman as well as the first African-American to serve as the president of the International Association for the Study of Popular Music, US Chapter (IASPM-US) from 2007 to 2009. Her 2008 debut CD, *Let Me Take You There* (Keycan Records), received an NAACP Image Award in the category of "Outstanding World Music Album."

Bakari Kitwana

Bakari Kitwana is a journalist, activist, political analyst, and university lecturer whose writing and lectures on hip-hop have helped establish the tone and content of discussion on the subject around the country. He is author of *The Rap on Gangsta Rap*; *The Hip-Hop Generation: Young Blacks and the Crisis in African American Culture*; and *Why White Kids Love Hip Hop: Wangstas, Wiggers, Wannabes, and the New Reality of Race in America*. Kitwana has also served as the Editorial Director of Third World Press, Executive Editor of *The Source* and he is co-founder of the first ever National Hip-Hop Political Convention. As a public intellectual, Kitwana is regularly featured in the mainstream media and he is also the CEO of Rap Sessions: Community Dialogues on Hip-Hop, which conducts town hall meetings around the country.

Jennifer C. Lena

Jennifer C. Lena is Assistant Professor of Sociology at Vanderbilt University. Her research focuses on cultural organizations and how they influence culture, with a particular focus on music. Her essays have appeared in the *American Sociological Review*, *Communication and Critical/Cultural Studies*, and *The Sociological Quarterly* and in several books. She has served on the Editorial Board of *Social Forces*, and is finishing terms as the COO of the American Sociological Association's Sociology of Culture Section, and Culture Network Chair of the Social Science History Association.

Kembrew McLeod

Kembrew McLeod is Associate Professor of Communication Studies at the University of Iowa. His work focuses on both popular music and the cultural impact of intellectual property law and he is author of *Owning Culture: Authorship, Ownership and Intellectual Property Law* and *Freedom of Expression®: Resistance and Repression in the Age of Intellectual Property*. His latest publication is *Creative License: The Law and Culture of Digital Sampling* (co-authored with by Peter DiCola). McLeod has also produced two documentary films, *Money For Nothing: Behind the Business of Pop Music* and *Copyright Criminals*. Apart from being an occasional music journalist whose pieces have appeared in *Rolling Stone*, *Mojo*, *Spin*, and *The Village Voice*, McLeod is also a renowned media prankster and famously attempted to sell his soul on E-Bay and on January 6, 1998 successfully registered "Freedom of Expression" as a legal U.S. trademark.

Matt Miller

Matt Miller is a practicing musician who earned his Ph.D. in American Studies at Emory University's Graduate Institute of the Liberal Arts. He has published articles on rap in the U.S. South and New Orleans in *The Journal of Popular Music Studies*, *Southern Spaces*, and *Poetics*, as well as contributing chapters on Atlanta and Miami in *Hip-Hop in America: A Regional Guide*. Miller is currently completing the manuscript *Bounce: Rap Music and Local Identity in New Orleans, 1980–2005* and he is the co-director of *Ya Heard Me?* (2008), a feature-length documentary on rap music in New Orleans.

Joan Morgan

Joan Morgan is an award-winning journalist, author and cultural critic who also taught at Vanderbilt University as Scholar-in-Residence in African American and Diaspora Studies. A pioneering hip-hop journalist, Morgan began her professional writing career freelancing for *The Village Voice* and she was one of the original staff writers at *Vibe* and a contributing editor and columnist for *Spin*. Morgan has written for numerous publications among them *MS.*, *More*, *Interview*, *Working Mother*, *GIANT*, and *Essence* magazines where she served as Executive Editor. Morgan coined the term "hip-hop feminism" in 1999 with her groundbreaking book, *When Chickenheads Come Home to Roost*.

Mark Anthony Neal

Mark Anthony Neal is Professor of Black Popular Culture in the Department of African & African-American Studies at Duke University. Neal is the author of *What the Music Said: Black Popular Music and Black Public Culture*; *Songs in the Key of Black Life: A Rhythm and Blues Nation*; *Soul Babies: Black Popular Culture and the Post-Soul Aesthetic* and *New Black Man*. A frequent contributor to National Public Radio and various on-line sites, Neal blogs at http://newblackman.blogspot.com/ and can be followed on Twitter at http://twitter.com/NewBlackMan. He resides in Durham, NC with his wife and two daughters.

Keith Negus

Keith Negus is Professor of Musicology at Goldsmith's University of London. A foremost scholar on the intersections of popular music, culture, and media industries, he is the author of *Music Genres and Corporate Cultures*; *Popular Music in Theory: An Introduction*; *Producing Pop: Culture and Conflict in the Popular Music Industry*; and *Bob Dylan*. Among other collaborative projects, he is co-author (with Paul du Gay, Stuart Hall, Hugh Mackay, and Linda Janes) of *Doing*

Cultural Studies, The Story of the Sony Walkman and co-editor (with David Hesmondhalgh) of *Popular Music Studies*. Negus is also a coordinating editor of *Popular Music*.

Yusuf Nuruddin

Yusuf Nuruddin teaches Africana Studies at the University of Massachusetts at Boston and, via distance learning, at the University of Toledo. He serves on the editorial boards of *Socialism and Democracy*; *The Black Activist*, an online journal; and the forthcoming *Timbuktu Review: Progressive Islamic Thought in the African Diaspora*. He is a contributor to these and other journals as well as to several anthologies and encyclopedias. He has a keen interest in independent/alternative broadcast media, and has hosted interview-format talk shows on community radio and public access TV. Believing in the necessary unity of theory and practice or study and struggle, he is both an omnivorous reader/bibliophile and a longtime political activist/community organizer.

Jorge "Popmaster Fabel" Pabon

Fabel was born and raised in New York's Spanish Harlem. At an early age, he developed his dance and choreography career, making moves at hip-hop jams and clubs throughout the city. His b-boy resume includes the title of President of the Hierophysics crew, Senior Vice-President of the Rock Steady Crew, member of Magnificent Force, and an honorary member of the Electric Boogaloos, featured in the classic 1984 hip-hop movie *Beat Street*. Fabel also toured internationally and he was the first U.S. hip-hop dancer to perform in Cuba, in 1986 and 1988, with the dance company Ballet D'Angelo. In 1999, he served as a consultant, moderator, panelist, and writer for The Rock and Roll Hall of Fame and Museum's exhibit and conference, "The Hip Hop Nation: Roots, Rhymes and Rage." Fabel regularly lectures on hip-hop history, offers b-boy demonstrations and master classes, and participates in outreach programs and conferences in the U.S. and around the world.

Imani Perry

Imani Perry is Professor in the Program in Law and Public Affairs and an interdisciplinary scholar in the Center for African American Studies at Princeton University. She is author of *Prophets of the Hood: Politics and Poetics in Hip Hop* and *More Beautiful and More Terrible: The Embrace and Transcendence of Racial Inequality in the United States* as well as publishing numerous articles in the areas of law and legal history, cultural studies, and African American studies.

Marc D. Perry

Marc D. Perry is Assistant Professor in Anthropology and African and African Diaspora Studies at Tulane University with research specializations in comparative racializations, neoliberal subject formations, and black music and expressive culture in the Caribbean, Latin America, and broader Afro-Atlantic world. He is currently completing a book manuscript examining race and social transformation in late socialist Cuba via the politics and poetics of the island's evolving hip-hop movement. He has also initiated research exploring the shifting social landscape of post-Katrina New Orleans with attention to questions of citizenship vis-à-vis neoliberal regimes of urban reconstruction and renewal. His publications include essays in *Identities* and *Transforming Anthropology*.

Alex Perullo

Alex Perullo is Associate Professor of Anthropology, Ethnomusicology and African studies at Bryant University. He has published articles in *Africa Today*, *Popular Music and Society*, *Ethnomusicology*, and several edited volumes. His forthcoming book, *Live from the Dar es Salaam: Popular Music and Tanzania's Music Economy*, explores the fastest growing music scene in contemporary Africa, examining the formation of radio stations, recording studios, copyright law, and performance venues after the incorporation of neo-liberal economic reforms. Perullo is the recipient of the Laura Boulton Fellowship to conduct archival research on the early recordings of East African music. He is also co-editor of the EVIA Digital Archive, an interdisciplinary repository of fieldwork videos, which are annotated and published online, and founder of Project Tanzania, a non-profit organization that collaborates with schools and universities in Tanzania on educational initiatives.

James Peterson
James Braxton Peterson is Assistant Professor of English at Bucknell University. His articles have been published in *Callaloo*, *Black Arts Quarterly* and several scholarly compendiums and he has also contributed to *Technitions Magazine*, *Vibe* and *XXL*. He is the founder of Hip Hop Scholars, LLC, an association of hip-hop generational scholars dedicated to researching and developing the cultural and educational potential of hip-hop, urban, and youth cultures. Peterson is a regular contributor to The Root.com and he has appeared on CNN, MSNBC, ESPN, and various national/local television networks.

Raquel Z. Rivera
Raquel Rivera holds a doctorate in Sociology and is Affiliated Researcher at the Center for Puerto Rican Studies, Hunter College, New York City. Her areas of scholarly interest are popular music and culture, race and ethnicity, nation and diaspora, and the intersections between Latino and Africana studies and she has taught at Columbia University, Hunter College and Tufts University. Rivera is author of *New York Ricans from the Hip Hop Zone* and co-editor (with Wayne Marshall and Deborah Pacini-Hernandez) of the anthology *Reggaeton*. As a freelance journalist, her articles have been published in numerous magazines and newspapers, including *Vibe*, *One World*, *Urban Latino*, *El Diario/La Prensa*, *Hoy*, *The San Juan Star*, *El Nuevo Día*, *Claridad* and *Diálogo* A singer-songwriter, Rivera is also a former member of the group Yerbabuena and a founding member of Boricua bomba group Alma Moyo. In 2010, Rivera released the CD *Las 7 Salves de la Magdalena* with the group Ojos de Sofia.

Gilbert B. Rodman
Gilbert Rodman is Associate Professor of Communication Studies at the University of Minnesota. He is the author of *Elvis After Elvis: The Posthumous Career of a Living Legend*, and co-editor (with Beth E. Kolko and Lisa Nakamura) of *Race in Cyberspace*. His research has appeared in journals including *Cultural Studies*, *Journal of Communication Inquiry*, and *Popular Communication*. Rodman is the founder and manager of the CULTSTUD-L listserv, the Book Review Editor for *Cultural Studies* and he also serves on the editorial boards of *Communication and Critical/Cultural Studies* and *Critical Studies in Media Communication*.

Joseph Schloss
Joseph Schloss is an ethnomusicologist who has taught at Tufts University, New York University and Baruch College-City University of New York. A past recipient of the Society for Ethnomusicology's Charles Seeger Prize, Schloss is author of *Making Beats: The Art of Sample-Based Hip-Hop* (which won the International Association for the Study of Popular Music's 2005 book award) and *Foundation: B-Boys, B-Girls and Hip-Hop Culture in New York*. His writing has also appeared in music and culture magazines including *The Flavor*, *The Seattle Weekly*, *URB*, and *Vibe*.

Christopher Holmes Smith
Christopher Holmes Smith is a Clinical Assistant Professor in Communication at University of

Southern California's Annenberg School for Communication where he also serves as Director of the Johnson Center for Communication Leadership. Smith's primary research and teaching interests concern the relationship between modern financial markets, news media, and everyday culture and he writes and teaches about hip-hop as a "money culture." His research has been published in several scholarly journals and he is a regular media commentator pertaining to contemporary cultural and political events. Smith's writing about entertainment and popular culture has also appeared in AOL.com, BlackEnterprise.com, *Elle*, *Interview*, *The Source*, *XXL*, and *Vibe*.

Greg Tate

Greg Tate is an author and literary iconoclast whose brilliant writing challenges the orthodoxies of American culture and African-American cultural production. Tate was a long-time critic and cultural commentator with *The Village Voice* as well as contributing to *The New York Times*, *The Washington Post*, *The Nation*, *Artforum*, *Essence*, *Rolling Stone*, *Spin*, *Vibe*, and *DownBeat*. His trenchant analysis of race, culture, and society has earned him a reputation as one of the nation's most unrelenting critics and he displays an unparalleled capacity to merge astute observation, high theory, and a wily sense of humor. Tate is author of *Fly Boy in the Buttermilk* and *Midnight Lightning: Jimi Hendrix and the Black Experience*; he is editor of *Everything But the Burden: What White People Are Taking From Black Culture*. Tate is also a playwright, filmmaker, and musician who, co-founded (in 1985) The Black Rock Coalition and currently provides "conduction" for the musical collective Burnt Sugar The Arkestra Chamber.

Cristina Verán

Born in Lima, Peru and raised in New York City, Cristina Verán is a journalist and historian whose writing has appeared in *ColorLines*, *Ms. Magazine*, *News From Indian Country*, *The* Source, *Vibe*, and *The Village Voice*. She is a United Nations news correspondent (appearing on the UN's news-roundtable television program *World Chronicle*) covering issues primarily pertaining to indigenous people from around the world. A long-time associate with hip-hop arts collectives TC5, the Rock Steady Crew and the mighty Universal Zulu Nation, Verán also contributed chapters to *The Vibe History of Hip Hop* and *Vibe Hip Hop Divas*. Verán also collaborates with cultural institutions, schools, and youth agencies, sharing her media experience and focus on first nations and indigenous people.

Oliver Wang

An Assistant Professor of Sociology at California State University-Long Beach, Oliver Wang is author of a forthcoming study of the Filipino American mobile DJ community in the San Francisco Bay Area. In 2003, he edited *Classic Material: The Hip-Hop Album Guide*. A prolific writer about pop music, culture, and politics, his articles have appeared in a variety of publications including, *LA Times*, *Oakland Tribune*, *Minneapolis City Pages*, *SF Bay Guardian*, *URB*, *Vibe*, *Village Voice*, *Wax Poetics*, amongst others. Oliver also hosts the audioblog Soul-Sides.com, producing the CD compilation *Soul Sides Vol. 1* in 2006 and *Soul Sides Vol. 2* in 2007.

S. Craig Watkins

S. Craig Watkins is Associate Professor in Radio-Television-Film at the University of Texas at Austin where he also teaches in the Sociology department and the Center for African and African American Studies. Watkins studies the intersections of youth, race, media, social networking, and popular culture and he is author of *The Young and the Digital: What the Migration to Social Network Sites, Games, and Anytime, Anywhere Media Means for Our Future*; *Hip Hop Matters: Politics, Pop Culture and the Struggle for the Soul of a Movement*; and *Representing: Hip Hop Culture and the Production of Black Cinema*. Watkins also works as a consultant and thought leader for research and educational organizations, publishers, and communication companies interested in gaining greater insight into the lively worlds young people create, both online and offline.

Eric K. Watts

Eric K. Watts is Associate Professor of Communication Studies at the University of North Carolina at Chapel Hill. Watts's scholarship explores the conditions in which the rhetorical voice can be invented, performed, consumed, mutated, and suppressed. In particular, he examines how the endowment of African American voices intervenes in the manner in which the public and the social materialize forms of social justice. He is finishing a book on the rhetoric, aesthetics, and ethics of the New Negro Renaissance. His work has appeared in such venues as *Quarterly Journal of Speech, Rhetoric & Public Affairs, Critical Studies in Media Communication,* and *New Media and Society.* Watts served as Editor (2008–2010) of *Critical Studies in Media Communication,* an international and inter-disciplinary journal.

Kristine Wright

Kristine Wright teaches at Los Angeles Southwest College, where she pursues her research interests in race, class and gender, and social stratification and the sociology of hip-hop. She is a regular contributor to several online web sites where she explores themes and issues pertaining to the hip-hop generation and national politics.

Permissions

Part I "Hip-Hop Ya Don't Stop": Hip-Hop History and Historiography

Castleman, Craig. 1982. "The Politics of Graffiti." In *Getting Up: Subway Graffiti in New York*. Cambridge, MA: M.I.T. Press, pp. 135–157. Reprinted by permission of the publisher.

Jeff Chang. 2005. "Zulus on a Time Bomb: Hip-Hop Meets the Rockers Downtown." In *Can't Stop, Won't Stop: A History of the Hip-Hop Generation*. New York: St. Martin's Press, pp. 141–165.

Ford, Robert Jr. 1979. "B-Beats Bombarding Bronx," *Billboard*. July 1, p. 65 (c) 1979 VNU Business Media, Inc. Used with permission from *Billboard* magazine.

Ford, Robert Jr. 1978. "Jive Talking N.Y. DJs Rapping Away in Black Discos," *Billboard*. May 5, p. 3 (c) 1978 VNU Business Media, Inc. Used with permission from *Billboard* magazine.

George, Nelson. 1993. "Hip-Hop's Founding Fathers Speak the Truth." *The Source*, no. 50. November 1993, pp. 44–50. Reprinted by permission of the author.

Jorge "Fabel" Pabon. 2006. "Physical Graffiti: The History of Hip-Hop Dance." In *Total Chaos: The Art and Aesthetics of Hip-Hop*. (ed.) Jeff Chang. New York: Basic Civitas Book, pp. 18–26.

Greg Tate. 2005. "Hip-Hop Turns 30: Watcha' Celebratin' For?" In *Village Voice*. January 4.

Part II "No Time for Fake Niggas": Hip-Hop Culture and the Authenticity Debates

Flores, Juan. 2000. "Puerto Rocks: Rap, Roots, Amnesia," in *From Bomba to Hip-Hop: Puerto Rican Culture and Latino Identity*. New York: Columbia University Press, pp. 115–139. Reprinted by permission.

Gilroy, Paul. 1992. "It's a Family Affair." In *Black Popular Culture*, edited by Gina Dent. Seattle: Bay Press, pp. 303–316. Reprinted by permission.

Judy, R.A.T. 1994. "On the Question of Nigga Authenticity," *boundary 2*, 21: 3, pp. 211–230. Copyright, 1994, Duke University Press. All rights reserved. Used by permission of the publisher.

Usama Kahf. 2007. "Arabic Hip Hop: Claims of Authenticity and Identity of a New Genre," I *Journal of Popular Music Studies*, 19: 4, pp. 359–385.

Kelley, Robin D.G. 1997. "Looking for the 'Real' Nigga: Social Scientists Construct the Ghetto," in *Yo' Mama's Disfunktional: Fighting the Culture Wars in Urban America*. Copyright © 1997 by Robin D.G. Kelley. Reprinted by permission of Beacon Press, Boston.

Kelly, Raegan. 1993. "Hip Hop Chicano: A Separate but Parallel Story." In *It's Not About a Salary: Rap, Race + Resistance in Los Angeles*, by Brian Cross. New York: Verso, pp. 65–76. Reprinted by permission of the publisher.

Kembrew McLeod. 1999. "Authenticity Within Hip-Hop and Other Cultures Threatened With Assimilation," *Journal of Communication*, vol. 49, pp. 134–150.

Gilbert Rodman. 2006. "Race . . . and Other Four Letter Words: Eminem and the Cultural Politics of Authenticity," *Popular Communication*, 4: 2, pp. 95–121.

Oliver Wang. 2007. "Rapping and Repping Asian: Race, Authenticity, and the Asian American MC." *Asian Encounters: Popular Culture in Asian America.* (ed.) Mimi Thi Nguyen and Thuy Linh Nguyen Tu. Durham: Duke University Press, pp. 35–68.

Part III "Ain't No Love in the Heart of the City": Hip-Hop, Space, and Place

Baldwin, Davarian L. 1999. "Black Empires, White Desires: The Spatial Politics of Identity in the Age of Hip-Hop," *Black Renaissance/Renaissance Noir*, no. 2, Summer, pp. 138–159. Reprinted by permission.

Forman, Murray. 2000. "Represent: Race, Space, and Place in Rap Music," *Popular Music*, 19: 1, January, pp. 65–90. © Cambridge University Press, reprinted with permission.

Matt Miller. 2004. "Rap's Dirty South: From Subculture to Pop Culture," *Journal of Popular Music Studies*, 16: 2, pp. 175–212.

Marc Perry. 2008. "Global Black Self-Fashionings: Hip Hop as Diasporic Space," *Identities*, 15: 6, pp. 635–664.

Alex Perullo. 2005. "Hooligans and Heroes: Youth Identity and Hip-Hop in Dar es Salaam, Tanzania," *Africa Today*, 51: 4, pp. 75–101.

Cristina Verán, with Darryl Thompson, Litefoot, Grant Leigh Saunders, Mohammed Yunus Rafiq, JAAS. 2006. "Native Tongues: Hip-Hop's Global Indigenous Movement." In *Total Chaos: The Art and Aesthetics of Hip-Hop*. (ed.) Jeff Chang. New York: Basic Civitas Books, pp. 278–290.

Part IV "I'll Be Nina Simone Defecating on Your Microphone": Hip-Hop and Gender

Andreana Clay. 2007. "I Used to be Scared of the Dick: Queer Women of Color and Hip-Hop Masculinity." In *Homegirls Make Some Noise: Hip Hop Feminism Anthology*. (eds.) Gwendolyn D. Pough, Elaine Richardson, Aisha Durham, and Rachel Raimist. Mira Loma, CA: Parker Publishing, pp. 148–165.

Michael Eric Dyson and Byron Hurt. 2007. "'Cover Your Eyes as I Describe a Scene So Violent': Violence, Machismo, Sexism, and Homophobia," Michael Eric Dyson. *Know What I Mean? Reflections on Hip Hop*. New York: Basic Civitas Books, pp. 91–122.

Ela Greenberg. 2009. "'The King of the Streets': Hip Hop and the Reclaiming of Masculinity in Jerusalem's Shu'afat Refugee Camp." *Middle East Journal of Culture and Communication*, vol. 3, pp. 231–250.

Keyes, Cheryl L. 2000. "Empowering Self, Making Choices, Creating Spaces: Black Female Identity via Rap Music Performance," *Journal of American Folklore*, vol. 113, pp. 255–269. Reprinted by permission.

Marc Lamont Hill. 2009. "Scared Straight: Hip-Hop, Outing, and the Pedagogy of Queerness," *Review of Education, Pedagogy, and Cultural Studies*, 31: 1, pp. 29–54.

Morgan, Joan. 2000. "Hip-Hop Feminist." Reprinted with permission of Simon & Schuster Adult Publishing Group from *When Chickenheads Come Home to Roost: A Hip-Hop Feminist Breaks it Down*. Copyright © 1999 by Joan Morgan.

Raquel Z. Rivera. 2003. "Butta Pecan Mamis." In *New York Ricans From the Hip Hop Zone*. New York: Palgrave Macmillan, pp. 127–149.

Part V   "The Message": Rap, Politics, and Resistance

Todd Boyd and Yusuf Nuruddin. 2004. "Intergenerational Culture Wars: Civil Rights vs. Hip Hop," *Socialism and Democracy*, 18: 2, pp. 51–69.

Kitwana, Bakari. 2002. "The Challenge of Rap Music," from *The Hip-Hop Generation: Young Blacks and the Crisis in African American Culture*. Copyright © 2002 by Bakari Kitwana. Reprinted by permission of Basic Books, a member of Perseus Books, L.L.C.

Jennifer C. Lena. 2008. "Voyeurism and Resistance in Rap Music Videos," *Communication and Critical/Cultural Studies*, 5: 3, pp. 264–279.

Neal, Mark Anthony. 1999. "Postindustrial Soul: Black Popular Music at the Crossroads." In *What the Music Said: Black Popular Music and Black Popular Culture*. New York: Routledge, pp. 125–157. Reproduced by permission of Routledge/Taylor & Francis Books, Inc.

Imani Perry. 2004. "My Mic Sound Nice: Art, Community and Consciousness." *Prophets of the Hood: Politics and Poetics in Hip Hop*. Durham: Duke University Press, pp. 38–57.

Kristine Wright. 2004. "Rise Up Hip-Hop Nation: From Deconstructing Racial Politics to Building Positive Solutions," *Socialism and Democracy*, 18: 2, pp. 9–20.

Part VI   "Looking for the Perfect Beat": Hip-Hop, Technology, and Rap's Lyrical Arts

H. Samy Alim. 2006. "Bring It to the Cypher: Hip Hop Nation Language." In *Roc the Mic Right: The Language of Hip Hop Culture*. New York: Routledge, pp. 69–108.

Bartlett, Andrew. 1994. "Airshafts, Loudspeakers, and the Hip-Hop Sample: Contexts and African-American Musical Aesthetics," *African American Review*, no. 28, pp. 639–652. Reprinted by permission.

Dimitriadis, Greg. 1996. "Hip-Hop From Live Performance to Mediated Narrative," *Popular Music*, 15: 2, May, pp. 179–195. © Cambridge University Press, reprinted by permission.

James Peterson. 2006. "Dead Prezence: Money and Mortal Themes in Hip Hop Culture," *Callaloo*, 29: 3, pp. 895–909.

Joe Schloss. 2004. "Sampling Ethics." In *Making Beats: The Art of Sample-Based Hip-Hop*. Middletown, CT: Wesleyan University Press, pp. 101–133.

Part VII   "I Used to Love H.E.R.": Hip-Hop in/and the Culture Industries

Mickey Hess. 2007. "The Rap Career." In *Is Hip Hop Dead? The Past, Present, and Future of America's Most Wanted Music*. Westport, CT: Praeger, pp. 13–41.

Negus, Keith. 1999. "The Business of Rap: Between the Street and the Executive Suite." In *Music Genres and Corporate Cultures*. New York: Routledge. Reprinted by permission of the publisher.

Christopher Holmes Smith. 2003. "'I Don't Like to Dream About Getting Paid': Representations of Social Mobility and the Emergence of the Hip-Hop Mogul," *Social Text*, 21: 4, pp. 69–97.

Watkins, S. Craig. 1998. "Black Youth and the Ironies of Capitalism." In *Representing: Hip-Hop Culture and the Production of Black Cinema*. Chicago: University of Chicago Press. Reprinted by permission of the publisher.

Watts, Eric K. 1997. "An Exploration of Spectacular Consumption: Gangsta Rap as Cultural Commodity," *Communication Studies*, vol. 48, Spring, pp. 42–58. Reprinted by permission.

Index